WORLD CULTURES
A GLOBAL MOSAIC

AREA SPECIALISTS

Africa
Marylee Susan Crofts, University of Wisconsin
Madison, Wisconsin

South Asia
Susan Wadley, Syracuse University
Syracuse, New York

Southeast Asia, Australia, and Oceania
Carol J. Compton, University of Wisconsin
Madison, Wisconsin

East Asia
Burton F. Beers, North Carolina State University
Raleigh, North Carolina

Latin America
Herbert Klein, Columbia University
New York, New York

Canada
Suzann Buckley, State University of New York
Plattsburgh, New York

Middle East
Donald Quataert, State University of New York
Binghamton, New York

Europe and the Former Soviet Union
Douglas Skopp, State University of New York
Plattsburgh, New York

MULTICULTURAL REVIEWERS

Guillermo Lawton Alfonso, New York, New York
Anne Beusch, University of Maryland, Catonsville, Maryland
Sylvia K. Eisen, Great Neck, New York
Charles Hancock, Ohio State University, Columbus, Ohio
Michiko Kaya, International Society for Educational Information, Tokyo, Japan
Rabbi David A. Kaye, Potomac, Maryland
Djun Kil Kim, Director, Korean Cultural Service, New York, New York
Marina Liapunov, Briarcliff Manor, New York
Sushama Sarin, Vienna, Virginia
Chi Wang, Chinese Section of the Library of Congress,
Washington, D. C.

TEACHER REVIEWERS

Ellen Bizoza, Kellenberg Memorial High School, Uniondale, New York
Sister Mary Joan Burke, Mission Church High School, Roxbury, Massachusetts
David Broadhurst, Gaithersburg Intermediate School,
Gaithersburg, Maryland
Dale Cable, Mount Lebanon High School, Pittsburgh, Pennsylvania
John Collins, Newfield High School, Selden, New York
Dominick De Cecco, Bethlehem Central High School, Delmar, New York
Catherine Fish-Petersen, East Islip High School, Islip Terrace, New York
Karen B. Leshin, Middle County School District, Centereach, New York
Barry Nelson, John Dewey High School, Brooklyn, New York

WORLD CULTURES
A GLOBAL MOSAIC

Iftikhar Ahmad
Herbert Brodsky
Marylee Susan Crofts
Elisabeth Gaynor Ellis

PRENTICE HALL

ABOUT THE AUTHORS

Iftikhar Ahmad is a researcher at the Fernand Braudel Center, State University of New York-Binghamton. Dr. Ahmad holds a BA from Forman Christian College, Lahore, Pakistan, an MA from Columbia University, and a PhD in sociology from SUNY-Binghamton. His publications include *Pakistan General Elections, 1970; South Asia: Selected Resource Materials;* and *Seminar Papers From the South Asian Institute.* He has taught at the South Asian Institute, Punjab University, and SUNY-Binghamton. He is currently teaching in the City University of New York.

Herbert Brodsky is an assistant principal in the New York City school system. He holds a BA from Queens College and an MS from Pace University. He has served as a consultant to the New York State Department of Education.

Marylee Susan Crofts has served as Outreach Director at the Center for Advanced Studies of International Development and the African Studies Center at Michigan State University. She was Outreach Director, African Studies Program, University of Wisconsin. Dr. Crofts holds a BA from Hanover College and an MA and a PhD from the University of Wisconsin. She has taught African history in Africa and has served as a consultant to several state education departments. Her publications include *Tanzania; The Third World: Africa;* and numerous articles.

Elisabeth Gaynor Ellis is a historian and writer. A former social studies teacher and school administrator, she has taught world cultures, Russian studies, and European history. She holds a BA from Smith College and an MA and MS from Columbia University.

About the Cover

The stamps on the cover come from nations around the world. They reflect elements of past and present cultures. A schematic to identify each stamp appears on page 828.

Staff Credits

Editorial: Anne L. Falzone, B'Ann Bowman, Frank Tangredi, Naomi Kisch, Marion Osterberg, Rick Hickox, Barbara Harrigan

Marketing: Lynda Cloud, Laura Asermily

Production: Suse Bell, Joan McCulley, Garret Schenck

Publishing Technology: Deborah Jones, Monduane Harris, Gregory Myers, Cleasta Wilburn

Pre-Press Production: Laura Sanderson, Kathryn Dix, Annette Simmons, Denise Herckenrath

Manufacturing: Rhett Conklin, Loretta Moe

Credits for World Literature and Other Excerpts

Every effort has been made to trace the copyright holders of the documents used in this book. Should there be any omission in this respect, we apologize, and shall be pleased to make the appropriate acknowledgment in any future printings. Acknowledgments appear immediately following each World Literature excerpt.

ISBN: 0-13-831801-8

8 9 10 11 12 04 03 02 01 00

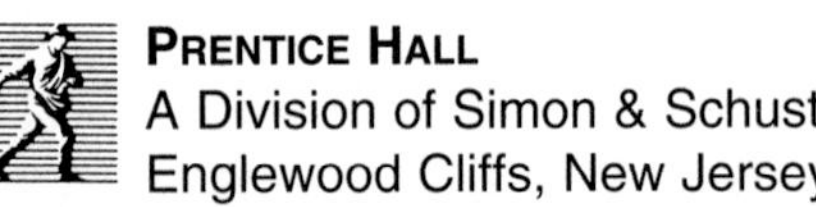
PRENTICE HALL
A Division of Simon & Schuster
Englewood Cliffs, New Jersey 07632

UNIT 1 INTRODUCTION

UNIT 2 AFRICA

UNIT 3 SOUTH ASIA: INDIA, PAKISTAN, BANGLADESH 158

UNIT 4 SOUTHEAST ASIA, AUSTRALIA, AND OCEANIA 246

UNIT 5 East Asia: China, Korea, Japan 320

UNIT 6 LATIN AMERICA AND CANADA 436

UNIT 7 THE MIDDLE EAST 548

UNIT 8 EUROPE AND THE FORMER SOVIET UNION 636

OF SPECIAL INTEREST

Up Close

GEOGRAPHIC CONNECTION

SCIENCE AND TECHNOLOGY

BUILDERS AND SHAPERS

TRADITION AND CHANGE

WORLD LITERATURE

GLOBAL CONNECTIONS

Skill Lessons

Writer's Workshops

Maps

China: Physical
RUSSIA
MONGOLIA
ALTAY SHAN
TIAN SHAN
TARIM BASIN
TAKLIMAKAN DESERT
ALTUN SHAN
KUNLUN SHAN
GOBI DESERT
GREATER HINGGAN RANGE
NORTH KOREA
SOUTH KOREA
SEA OF JAPAN
JAPAN
PACIFIC OCEAN
NORTH CHINA PLAIN
YELLOW SEA
HIMALAYAS
PLATEAU OF TIBET
CHINA
NEPAL
SICHUAN BASIN
EAST CHINA SEA
INDIA
BHUTAN
BANGLADESH
YUNNAN PLATEAU
TAIWAN
MYANMAR
BAY OF BENGAL
LAOS
VIETNAM
HAINAN
SOUTH CHINA SEA
THAILAND
0 300 600 Miles
0 300 600 Kilometers
Elevation
Meters Feet
4,000 14,000
2,000 7,000
500 1,500
200 700
0 0
Below sea level Below sea level
Present-day national boundaries are shown.

ATLAS

CHARTS, GRAPHS, AND TIME LINES

WORLD DATA BANK

ABOUT THIS BOOK

World Cultures: A Global Mosaic is organized in 8 units and 34 chapters. The Table of Contents lists the titles of the units and chapters. It also lists special features, skill lessons, maps, charts and graphs, and material in the Reference Section.

IN EACH UNIT

UNIT OPENER

Each unit opens with a color map and related pictures that illustrate the cultures included in the unit. Picture captions explain the connections between the map and the pictures. In addition, a time line presents major events and dates in the cultural, economic, and political history of the region covered in the unit. The unit outline lists the chapters in the unit.

SKILL LESSONS

Two step-by-step skill lessons in each unit help you to understand and practice important skills.

WORLD LITERATURE

Each unit includes an excerpt from literature that reveals something about the lives and culture of the people in the region being studied. The fine art that accompanies the literature adds another view of how people live and see themselves.

GLOBAL CONNECTIONS

An illustrated essay shows how the contributions of each area of the world have traveled beyond regional borders. The essay reveals how these contributions have affected your own life, either directly or indirectly. The essay also highlights cultural diversity, diffusion, and interaction.

UNIT REVIEW

Each Unit Review helps you to review and apply what you have learned. In addition, it contains these features:

Learning by Doing: These suggestions for creative projects include alternate ways of learning and presenting information.

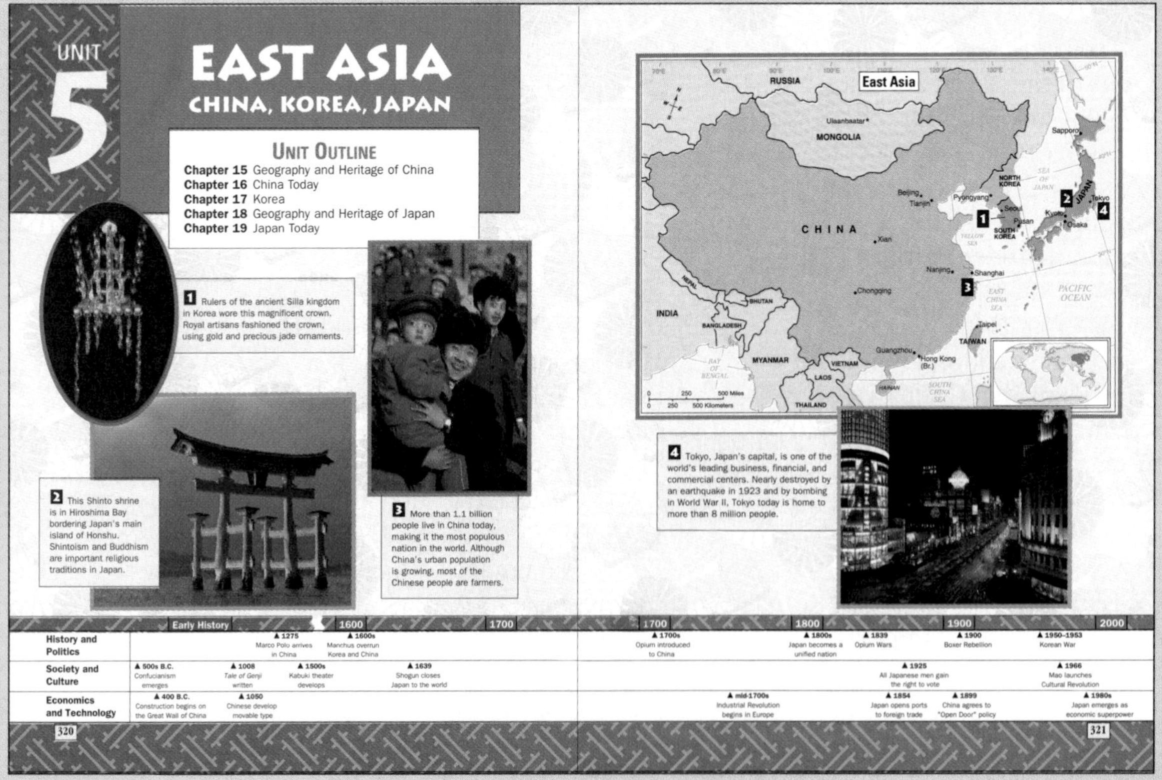

Writer's Workshop: This workshop helps you to develop the writing and research skills needed to write a one-paragraph answer.

In Each Chapter

Chapter Opener

Each chapter opens with an interesting story that illustrates a chapter theme. The Chapter Perspective provides an overview of the main topics and themes of the chapter. The Literature Connections identify the literature excerpts that appear in the chapter.

To Help You Learn

Several features help you to read and understand the chapter:

- **Find Out:** Questions at the beginning of each section guide your reading.
- **Vocabulary:** Vocabulary words are printed in blue type and clearly defined the first time they are used. These terms also appear in the Glossary at the back of the book.
- **Section Reviews:** Questions help you to test your understanding of what you have read and to sharpen your critical thinking skills.

Of Special Interest

Two special features appear in every chapter. There are several kinds of special features throughout the book.

- **Up Close** provides an in-depth look at an interesting person or event that reveals a particular aspect of a region's culture.
- **Geographic Connection** investigates the ways in which land and climate have influenced people's lives.
- **Builders and Shapers** is a short biography of an individual who is important to the region.
- **Tradition and Change** illustrates how a society changes while still holding on to elements of its earlier culture.
- **Science and Technology** presents an example of a scientific or technological achievement that a society has developed and transmitted to others or has adapted for its own use.

Illustrations

Hundreds of pictures and other graphics illustrate how people live, work, and play throughout the world:

Pictures: Many works of fine art, photographs, and cartoons help to bring the regions of the world to life. Picture captions include a question that encourages you to explore a theme that is important to understanding world cultures.

Maps, Charts, and Graphs: Maps, charts, and graphs help you to understand major economic, political, and social developments. Captions provide important background information and also include questions designed to sharpen your map, chart, and graph skills.

Chapter Review

The Chapter Review helps you to review vocabulary words and main ideas and to strengthen your critical thinking skills.

Reference Section

At the back of the book, you will find a Reference Section of materials for use throughout the course. It includes an atlas, charts with information about the regions of the world, a gazetteer of important places, a glossary, Connections With Literature, and an index.

UNIT 1

INTRODUCTION

UNIT OUTLINE

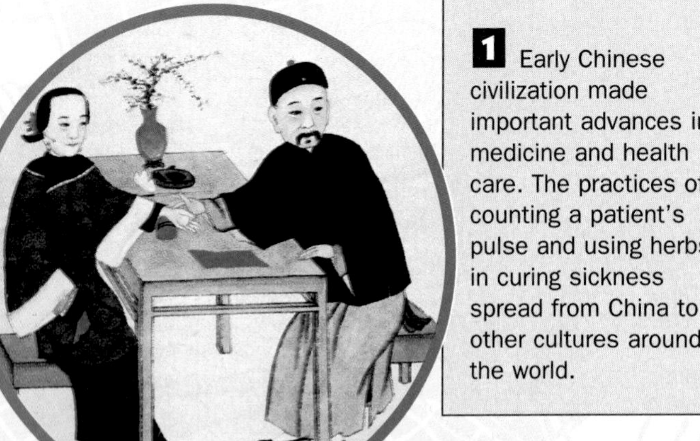

1 Early Chinese civilization made important advances in medicine and health care. The practices of counting a patient's pulse and using herbs in curing sickness spread from China to other cultures around the world.

2 Falashas, or Ethiopian Jews, are waiting for visas outside Israel's embassy in Addis Ababa. They are among the many people in recent years who have migrated to other lands seeking political and religious freedom.

3 Cotton is grown, woven into cloth, dyed, and spread to dry in Bangladesh. Technology, or the methods used to produce goods, has changed throughout history and varies greatly among nations today.

	Prehistory		1200	1400
History and Politics	▲ **2 million years ago** First people live in Africa			▲ **1300s** China develops a strong empire
Society and Culture		▲ **10,000 years ago** Stone Age people create cave paintings		▲ **1300s** Aztec and Inca civilizations emerge in the Americas
Economics and Technology		▲ **10,000 years ago** Stone Age people farm and domesticate animals	▲ **1200s** Roads link China with Middle East	▲ **1300s** Europe develops a money economy

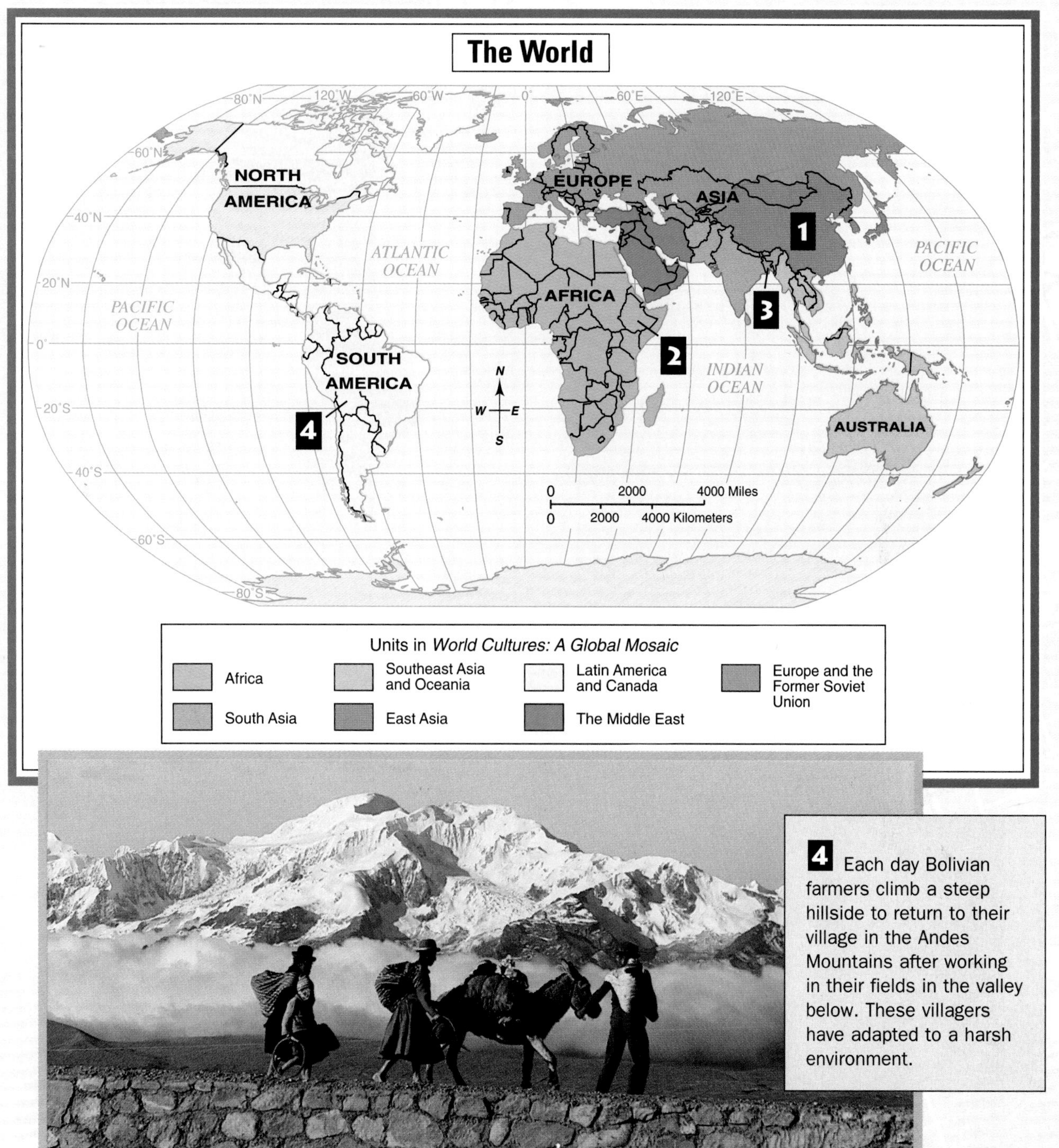

4 Each day Bolivian farmers climb a steep hillside to return to their village in the Andes Mountains after working in their fields in the valley below. These villagers have adapted to a harsh environment.

1400	1600	1800	2000

▲ **Late 1400s** Strong monarchs emerge in Europe and overseas expansion begins

▲ **1870s** Age of Imperialism begins

▲ **1945** United Nations formed

▲ **1400s–1500s** Timbuktu is center of Islamic learning

▲ **1975** Helsinki Agreement signed

▲ **1569** Mercator develops new map

▲ **1700s** Industrial Revolution begins in Europe

▲ **1957** Soviet Union launches first artificial satellite

Chapter 1

The Global Environment

A Temple at Angkor Angkor Wat is the largest religious complex in the world. It was built in the 1100s by the Khmers, a people who once ruled Cambodia and nearby areas of Southeast Asia. Angkor Wat has become a lasting monument to this early Khmer civilization.
Culture What evidence do you think Angkor Wat provides about early Khmer culture?

Chapter Outline

Creaking and swaying, the huge ship dropped anchor off the coast of what is today Cambodia. Aboard, an impatient and excited Chou Ta-kuan prepared to go ashore. The year was 1297, and Chou had sailed to this distant land on orders from the emperor of China. Chou's mission was to promote trade with the Khmer people who lived here.

Once ashore, Chou took careful notes about everything he saw. He admired the rich city of Angkor and the beautiful temple of Angkor Wat. He paid special attention to the crops the people grew and the goods they bought and sold. He commented on the mild climate. "Their whole year is like our summer months," Chou wrote, "for they have neither frost nor snow." He also noted that most Khmer merchants were women.

Like all travelers, Chou wanted to find out how the people lived in a land that was different from his own.

CHAPTER PERSPECTIVE

In this book, you will learn about people in many parts of the world. Their ways of life have developed over thousands of years. In some ways, their ideas, customs, and traditions differ from one another as well as from those familiar to us in the United States. Some differences can be traced to geography. As you begin to study world cultures, it is useful to look first at geography in order to discover how it affects the way people live.

As you read, look for these chapter themes:

- Geography affects the way people live in different regions of the world.
- Maps give us vital information about the world.
- Culture is the total way of life of a particular people.
- Many factors, including geography, influence the culture of a region.
- A number of forces influence how cultures change.

Literature Connections

In this chapter, you will encounter passages from the following works.

Land of the Spotted Eagle, Chief Luther Standing Bear

The Life of an Irish Travelling Woman, Sharon Gmalch

For other literature suggestions, see Connections With Literature, pages 804–808.

1

EXPLORING THE WORLD AROUND US

FIND OUT

What are the five themes of geography?

How does movement contribute to global interdependence?

What are some ways of defining regions?

Vocabulary geography, location, latitude, longitude, export, import, interdependence

One hundred years ago, Chief Standing Bear spoke of the vital connection between his people, the Lakota, and their environment:

> "[They] . . . loved the earth and all things of the earth. . . . To sit or lie upon the ground is to be able to think more deeply and to feel more keenly; . . . to see more clearly into the mysteries of life and come closer in kinship to . . . all creatures of the earth, sky, and water."

Wherever people live, they have shaped the environment to suit their needs. The human ability to change the environment, however, is limited. Often, people must adapt their agriculture, industry, arts, and daily habits to their surroundings. People who live in desert regions wear light, loose-fitting clothing. People who live in the northernmost and southernmost regions of the globe adjust to winters without daylight and summers without night. To understand world cultures, it is important to see the connections between people and their environment.

What Is Geography?

Geography is the study of people, their environments, and their resources. In ancient Egypt, priests studied the land. Through careful observation and mathematics, they calculated how much grain the land could produce. They then used that knowledge to collect the taxes that supported their temples. Later, Greek geographers built on these and other advances to create maps of Europe, Africa, and Asia.

Geography has many uses beyond creating maps and boundaries. Today, geographers have developed five basic themes to help us understand the links between people and the Earth. The five themes are location, place, interaction between people and their environment, movement, and region. Each theme offers a way of looking at the world and its people.

Location

Imagine that a friend told you she was flying to Goa next week. "Where is that?" you ask. You want to know Goa's location, its position on the Earth's surface.

Your friend tells you that Goa is a former Portuguese colony on the southwest coast of India. By describing the position of Goa in relation to another place, your friend is giving its relative location. Sometimes, people need to know the absolute, or exact, location of a place. To give absolute location, people use the grid of numbered lines of latitude and longitude seen on many maps or globes.

Lines of latitude measure distances north or south of the Equator. The Equator divides the Earth into two halves, called hemispheres. The Northern Hemisphere lies north of the Equator, and the Southern Hemisphere lies south of it. Lines of longitude measure distances east or west of the Prime Meridian. The Prime Meridian is an imaginary line that runs through Greenwich (GREHN ihch), England. The circle formed by the Prime Meridian divides the Earth into the Eastern and Western hemispheres.

Using lines of latitude and longitude, you can locate any place on Earth. Find Goa on the map on page 188. As you can see, Goa's exact location is 15 degrees (°) north latitude and 73 degrees (°) east longitude. This location is written as 15°N/73°E.

Place

Geographers describe places in terms of their physical and human characteristics. Physical characteristics include the landforms, climate, soil, and animal life of a place. Human characteristics include the people's way of life—their activities, means of transportation, religion, and languages.

Every place in the world has its own physical and human characteristics. Think of Albany, the capital of New York State. Albany's physical characteristics include its position on the Hudson River, its weather, its landforms, and its plant and animal life. Among Albany's human characteristics are state office buildings, stores, houses, and roads.

Albany's physical and human characteristics are connected. Albany's position on the Hudson River drew settlers there in the 1600s. Today, the city is still a busy river port. As you read about different places in this book, notice their physical and human characteristics.

Interaction Between People and Their Environment

Wherever people live, they change the world around them. They may clear forests, blast tunnels through mountains, or plow fields. Indeed, throughout history, much of what we call progress has involved people changing the environment.

Hidden costs. Today, we are learning that this kind of progress can have hidden costs. Some of our actions have polluted the air, water, and land. People have built highways to ease travel from place to place. Cars and trucks, however, are a major cause of air pollution. Farmers have used pesticides to kill insects that destroy crops, yet pesticides in our water and in food can harm us.

A key issue is how we interact with the environment. As you will read, people in all parts of the world face hard choices. They must decide how to develop their economies without destroying the environment.

People adapt. People's effort to change the environment is only one form of interaction. As you have read, sometimes people adapt to their environment instead. In the frozen lands of the Arctic north, for example, the Eskimos build homes out of ice. In parts of China where there are few trees, people chop vegetables, fish, and meat into bite-sized pieces. They "stir-fry" the food quickly, using little fuel. Many Americans enjoy stir-fried foods. However, probably few people realize that this style of cooking resulted from Chinese cooks adapting to their environment.

The Nile River Valley Ninety-six percent of Egypt is desert. The Nile River Valley is a strip of fertile land that contrasts sharply with the surrounding land. Most people in Egypt live in the Nile Valley or near the mouth of the Nile where it empties into the Mediterranean Sea. ***Geography*** How does the geography of Egypt affect where people live?

Brasília–A City Built From Scratch

GEOGRAPHIC CONNECTION

Early in the 1950s, Brazilian president Juscelino Kubitschek gave architect Oscar Niemeyer a challenge. "How would you like to be my Michelangelo?" Kubitschek asked, referring to the great Italian artist. Niemeyer's task was to design and build a new capital city deep in the heart of Brazil. Brasília was to be an ideal, ultramodern city—a new place created in the wilderness.

For years, Brazilians had debated moving the capital inland from Rio de Janeiro on the coast. A new capital, many argued, would bring people and trade into the interior region. In 1957, work finally began. The location chosen was the Planalto Central, a bare plateau 3,500 feet (1,067 m) high. Almost overnight, the Planalto became a 24-hour-a-day construction site for the city of Brasília. Machines, materials, and workers by the thousands were ferried in by raft.

The new city was designed roughly in the shape of an airplane. Government buildings are located where the pilot would sit, while the "tail" houses a railroad station. In between is a large downtown area, with hotels, shops, and recreational facilities. The "wings" are 60 residential superblocks with apartment buildings, gardens, schools, shops, and theaters.

After more than three years of nonstop work, Brasília was officially dedicated on April 21, 1960. Years later, Niemeyer said, "I'd have more gardens and a center where cars couldn't go, and perhaps I'd have given the buildings a few more stories." Still, he was proud that the city he designed was "disciplined and above the chaos of other cities."

1. Where was Brazil's old capital located?
2. Why was Brazil's interior chosen as the site for Brasília?
3. **Applying Information** How does the building of Brasília illustrate the theme of interaction?

Movement

Another theme of geography is the movement of people, goods, and ideas. These movements often occur together.

Migration. Even before recorded history, people traveled from one place to another. Early peoples often moved in order to find food. In more recent times, millions of people came to the United States to find freedom or a better life. Sometimes, people leave their homelands because of natural disasters or wars. Still others are moved against their will. Over a period of 400 years, slave traders took millions of Africans by force. From the 1500s to the 1800s, they shipped them across the Atlantic Ocean to plantations in the Americas.

Trade. Trade is the movement of goods between areas. It occurs because areas of the world have different resources and different levels of economic development. Trade involves exports, or goods sent to markets outside a country, and imports, or goods brought into a country. Some countries export natural resources such as copper, or farm products such as coffee beans. Other countries export manufactured goods such as computers, tanks, and cars.

Ideas spread. The movement of ideas occurs with the movement of people and goods. More than 2,000 years ago, missionaries and merchants from India spread the religious teachings of Buddhism to the peoples of China and Southeast Asia. Today, advanced communication and transportation help to spread ideas faster. Television viewers in Angola in Africa, for example, can watch the latest movies from Brazil in South America.

Interdependence. The rapid movement of people, goods, and ideas adds to global interdependence. Interdependence is the dependence of countries on goods, resources, and knowledge from other parts of the world. For example, Americans get their coffee from South America, tea from India, and oil from the Middle East. For our economy to prosper, we must sell American-made products to people around the globe. In this book, you will read about how interdependence is affecting our world.

Region

A region is an area with its own unifying characteristics. Geographers define regions in several ways. Regions can be identified by physical characteristics, such as landforms or climate. The world's continents are examples of physical regions. The Rocky Mountain area of the United States and the rain forests of Brazil are also physical regions.

A region can also be identified by cultural, political, or economic features. The Muslim world, for example, is the cultural region influenced by the religion of Islam. It includes parts of Africa and Asia, including the Middle East.* Nations are examples of political regions.

Because regions can be defined in different ways, a country can belong to several different regions. Pakistan, for example, is part of the physical region of South Asia. Because most Pakistanis are Muslims, Pakistan is also part of the Muslim world, a cultural region. Pakistan also belongs to the economic region known as the developing world, sometimes called the Third World. Nations in the developing world are working to build modern industrial economies.

In this book, you will read about many regions. They include Africa, South Asia, Southeast Asia, East Asia, Latin America, Canada, the Middle East, and Europe. The location, history, resources, and people of each region help it to create its own identity. As you will discover, each region also has great variety.

SECTION 1 REVIEW

1. **Locate:** (a) Africa, (b) South Asia, (c) Southeast Asia, (d) East Asia, (e) Latin America, (f) Middle East, (g) Europe.
2. **Define:** (a) geography, (b) location, (c) latitude, (d) longitude, (e) export, (f) import, (g) interdependence.
3. Briefly describe the five themes of geography.
4. (a) Give two examples of how people have reshaped their environment. (b) Give two examples of how they have adapted to their environment.
5. How have modern communication and transportation affected movement?
6. **Applying Information** Describe three different ways to identify the region in which you live.
7. **Writing Across Cultures** Write a paragraph describing how movement affects the way of life of people around the world.

---

* The Middle East lies in the physical region of southwestern Asia. North African nations such as Egypt and Algeria are part of the physical region of Africa. Through their history and culture, the nations of North Africa have strong ties to the Muslim world of the Middle East.

2

UNDERSTANDING THE PHYSICAL WORLD

FIND OUT

Why have mapmakers created different map projections?

What are the four major landforms?

What factors influence climate?

Vocabulary map projection, topography, vegetation, mountain, elevation, hill, plain, plateau, climate.

About 2,500 years ago, the leaders of Athens, a city-state in Greece, asked the rulers of nearby Sparta for aid in a war against Persia. To convince them to fight, the Athenians sent the Spartans a map of the world made out of bronze. The Athenians wanted the Spartans to see how close the two cities were. They hoped that Sparta would then join them in the fight against Persia.

The gift had an unexpected result, however. Studying the map, the Spartans noted that Persia lay across the Aegean Sea. They refused to fight, saying that Persia was too far away to be a threat. The Spartans were wrong. Within a year, Persian armies had crossed the Aegean, and Sparta had to fight.

Since ancient times, people have used maps to learn about the world. Knowing the location of continents and countries is important to understanding world cultures.

Tools of Geographers

Geographers use globes and maps to represent the Earth. A globe is more accurate than a map. Shaped like the Earth, a globe gives a true picture of the size and shape of landmasses and of distances across oceans. But globes are awkward to carry around, so most people use maps instead. Even so, maps have a major drawback. Because the Earth's surface is curved and maps are flat, all maps distort the Earth in some way.

Over the years, mapmakers have developed many map projections. Map projections are ways of showing the curved Earth on a flat surface. Each projection has advantages and disadvantages. Some show the shape of landmasses correctly but not their size. Others show accurate sizes but distort shapes.

Mercator projection. By the mid-1400s, sailors from Europe were exploring the oceans. They needed better maps than those that had been made in the past. In 1569, a European mapmaker, Gerardus Mercator, created a map that showed direction accurately. Sailors could then know if they were sailing north, south, east, or west.

Besides showing direction, a Mercator map gives an accurate view of land areas near the Equator. However, it distorts the size and shape of lands near the North and South poles. Greenland, for example, is only one eighth the size of South America. Yet in a Mercator projection, Greenland looks larger than South America.

Interrupted projection. In an interrupted projection, mapmakers show the correct sizes and shapes of landmasses by cutting out parts of oceans. The cuts, however, make it impossible to measure distances accurately or to plot a course across an ocean.

Peters projection. The Peters projection shows the correct areas of landmasses and oceans. Directions are also accurate, as they are on a Mercator map. Still, a Peters projection distorts the shapes of Africa and South America. They appear longer and thinner than they really are.

Robinson projection. Today, many maps use the Robinson projection. It shows the correct sizes and shapes of most landmasses. It also gives a fairly accurate view of the sizes of oceans and the distances across land areas. But even the Robinson projection has distortions, especially in regions shown along the edges.

Types of Map Projections

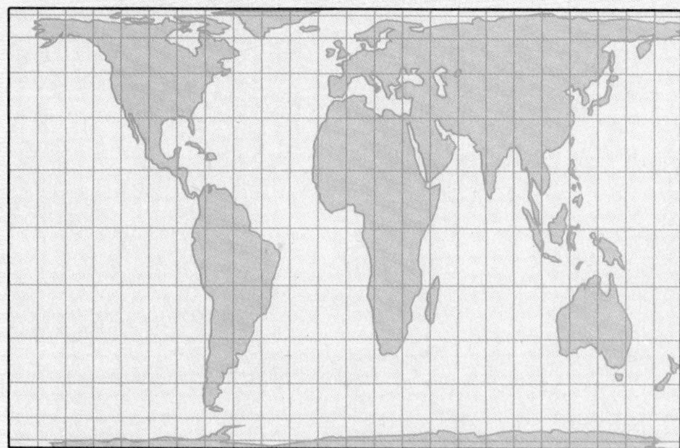

Peters Projection

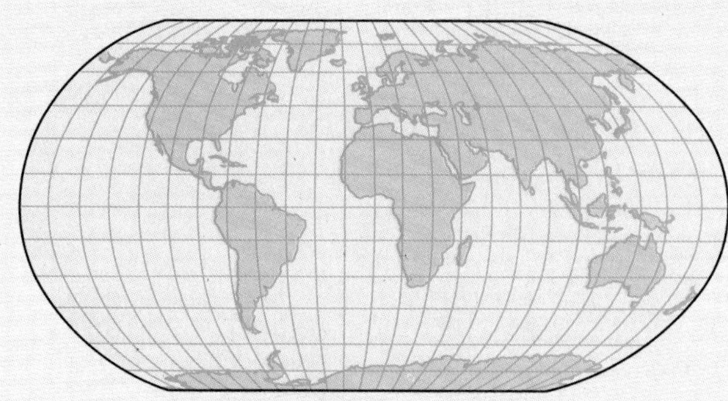

Robinson Projection

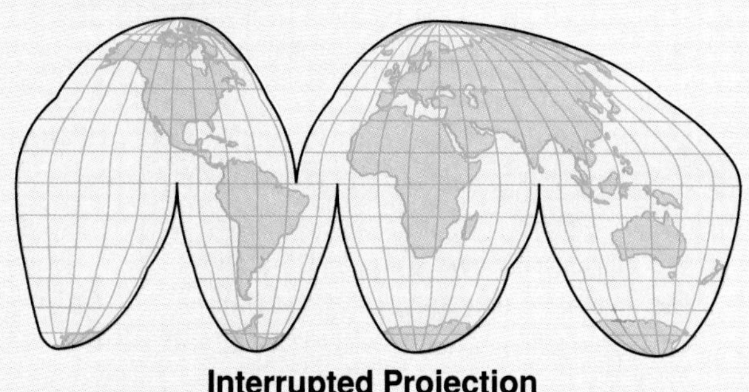

Interrupted Projection

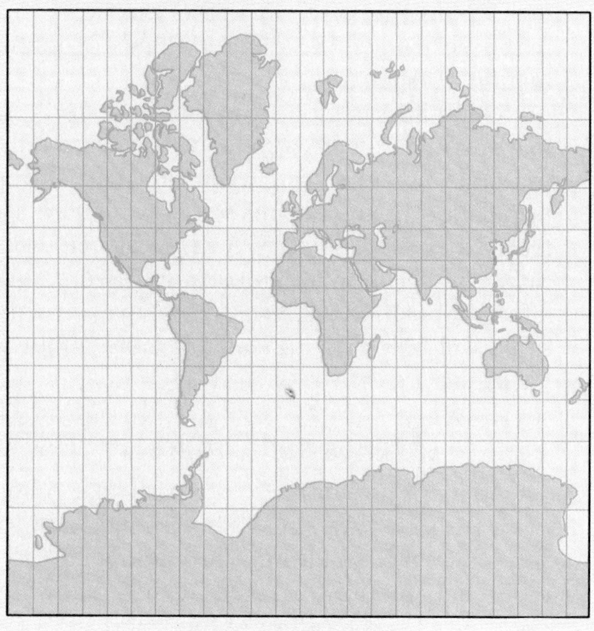

Mercator Projection

MAP STUDY

Each map projection shows a round world on a flat surface in a different way. None of the projections can show area, shape, distance, and direction accurately at the same time.

1. **Location** On which map projection are Africa and South America most distorted?
2. **Movement** Which map projection would give navigators trouble if they tried to trace a water route between two places?
3. **Comparing** On which two map projections do the landmasses look most similar?

Special-Purpose Maps

Geographers have developed many kinds of maps to show different information. Each has a special purpose. A political map shows the borders that divide nations from one another. A physical map shows features such as mountains, lakes, and rivers. The physical features of a place or region are called its topography

A population map shows how many people live in each area on the map. A natural resources map shows where coal, uranium, oil, and other important resources are found. Still other maps show climate and vegetation. Vegetation is the plant life of a place or region. Skim the maps in this book. Read the map titles to see the different kinds of information they include.

Using information from different kinds of maps, you can learn a lot about a region. For example, by comparing a climate map and a population map, you can see how climate affects where people live. A physical map will help you see how mountains and rivers also affect population patterns. Each map in this book will help you understand more about a particular region.

Maps and Culture

All maps are made from a particular point of view and usually stress what is important to the mapmaker's culture. Throughout history, different peoples created maps showing themselves at the center of the world.

During the early Middle Ages, Europeans drew maps expressing a religious view of the world. They placed their holiest city, Jerusalem, at the center. Ancient Chinese maps showed the world from the Chinese emperor's viewpoint, with his throne placed under the North Star. Modern Chinese world maps show China near the center, while American maps put North America there.

Major Landforms

People have adapted to different kinds of natural features, or landforms. The major landforms are mountains, hills, plains, and plateaus. (See the illustration on page 24.)

Mountains are high, steep, rugged land that rises above the surrounding land. Mountains vary in elevation, or height above sea level, but all mountains are at least 2,000 feet (610 m) high. The Himalaya Mountains in South Asia and the Andes Mountains in South America include some of the world's highest peaks.

Mountainous areas generally have small populations. Some people, however, have found ways to live on the steep slopes of high

Landforms of Mexico Most of Mexico occupies a plateau. Several mountains with elevations of more than 17,000 feet (5,182 m) rise above the plateau. Popocatepetl, shown in this photo, is a range of volcanic mountains near Mexico City. ***Geography*** Identify the two landforms that are shown in this photograph.

mountains. The ancient Inca city of Machu Picchu in Peru was built on a mountaintop 8,038 feet (2,450 m) above sea level. (See Connections With Literature, page 804, "In Suspect Terrain.")

Hills are also areas of raised land, but they are lower and less steep than mountains. Hilly areas have more settlers than mountains have because farming is easier there.

Every major region includes **plains,** large areas of fairly level or gently rolling land. Plains generally have low elevation. If plains have fertile soil and receive enough rainfall, they are good for raising crops. A vast plain that spreads across the center of North America has long been the "breadbasket" for the United States and Canada.

Coastal plains are lowland areas that border oceans. Many cities are found along coastal plains. Because of their location on the water, these coastal cities developed as trading ports.

Plateaus are large areas of high, flat or gently rolling land. Plateaus have elevations ranging from a few hundred to several thousand feet above sea level. Like plains, plateaus can provide good farmland depending on rainfall and soil quality.

In hot, tropical regions, plateaus offer relief from high temperatures. As a result, some plateaus are densely populated. Mexico City, the capital of Mexico, is located on a high plateau. With more than 22 million people, it is the world's largest city.

Graph Skills Climates vary in different regions of the world. Geographers classify world climates into twelve types, based on the weather and rainfall in a region. ▶According to this chart, which two climate types have the most rainfall? Which two have the least rainfall?

Climates of the World

Climate	Weather/ Yearly Rainfall
Tropical wet	hot, humid/ 100 in.
Tropical wet and dry	hot, wet summers; warm, dry winters/ 50 in.
Semiarid	hot summers; mild to cold winters/ 18 in.
Desert (arid)	hot and dry/ 5 in.
Mediterranean	hot, dry summers; cool, moist winters/ 23 in.
Humid subtropical	hot summers; cool winters/ 50 in.
Marine	warm summers; cool winters/ 45 in.
Humid continental	warm summers; cold winters/ 27 in.
Subarctic	cool summers; very cold winters/ 17 in.
Tundra	cold summers; very cold winters/ 16 in.
Polar	cold all year/ 8 in.
Highlands	climate depends on elevation/ 3 in. to 123 in.

Climate Zones

The physical characteristics of a region include climate as well as landforms. Climate is the average weather a place has over a period of 20 to 30 years. Turn to the world climate map on page 778. Note the different climate zones that are found around the world.

Climate can have a major effect on people's lives. Until the widespread use of air conditioning, businesses in regions with hot climates closed during the hottest part of the day. They reopened later when it was cooler. In Spanish-speaking countries, this time was called the *siesta*, a Spanish word that means both "the hottest part of the day" and "afternoon nap."

Location. One factor that affects climate is latitude. Lands close to the Equator have tropical climates. One tropical climate is the tropical rain forest. It has high temperatures and ample rainfall all year. Another tropical climate combines hot temperatures with a rainy season and a dry season.

Areas farther north or south of the Equator have temperate climates, with a warm and a cold season. Many areas in the United States have temperate climates, as do large areas of central Asia and Europe. Parts of South America and Africa also have temperate climates. Study the chart at the left to learn about the different kinds of temperate climates.

Located far from the Equator, lands near the North and South poles have arctic climates. They are cold all year.

Nearness to oceans also affects climate. Ocean currents carry warm or cool water in circular patterns around the world. These warm and cold currents influence the climate of nearby coastal areas.

Elevation. Elevation, or height above sea level, also influences climate. In general, highland areas are cooler than lowlands because air cools as it rises. Quito (KEE toh), the capital of Ecuador in South America, is located almost on the Equator. Because the city sits high in the Andes Mountains, daytime temperatures do not rise above 90°F (32°C). Nighttime temperatures can drop as low as 40°F (4°C).

SECTION 2 REVIEW

1. **Define:** (a) map projection, (b) topography, (c) vegetation, (d) mountain, (e) elevation, (f) hill, (g) plain, (h) plateau, (i) climate.
2. Describe one advantage and one disadvantage of each of the following map projections: (a) Mercator, (b) interrupted, (c) Peters, (d) Robinson.
3. List three kinds of information that a map might show.
4. **Applying Information** How does climate affect the way people live?
5. **Writing Across Cultures** Jot down five ways that the way of life in a warm climate might differ from that in a cold climate.

3 THE MEANING OF CULTURE

FIND OUT

What are the major elements of culture?

Why is the family the most important unit of social organization?

What kinds of governments and economies have societies developed?

Vocabulary culture, nuclear family, extended family, monotheism, polytheism, democracy, republic, dictatorship

"You don't have to be afraid. Look at me when you speak, Eleanor," the teacher urged.

Eleanor Wong looked up. She had arrived in New York from Hong Kong only a week earlier. Now, on her first day in an American school, her teacher seemed displeased.

Eleanor was confused. Didn't the teacher know that it was disrespectful to look directly at a person in authority? Even Eleanor's father did not look his boss in the eye. Only later did Eleanor find out that Americans think it is rude not to look them in the eye when speaking.

Many misunderstandings between people around the world occur because we do not know enough about each other. As Eleanor Wong and the teacher found out, even the way we look at another person depends on where we grew up. To understand other people, we must understand their culture, that is, all the things that make up a people's entire way of life. (See World Literature, "The All-American Slurp by Lensey Namioka," page 50.)

Elements of Culture

Everyone is born into a culture. We inherit our culture from parents and grandparents. In turn, we pass on our culture to our children. From birth, we are taught the ways of thinking, believing, and behaving that are accepted in our culture. Our culture shapes our lives.

Culture is made up of many different elements. It is reflected in what we eat, the clothes we wear, and the jokes we tell. Culture influences the buildings we live in, how we spend our free time, and the skills we learn. It also affects our ideas of what is beautiful or ugly, our beliefs about what is right and wrong, and our goals for the future.

In this book, you will read about cultures that have developed in different parts of the world. You will look at the many elements that make up those cultures. Among these are social organization, customs and traditions, language, arts and literature, and religion. Forms of government and economic systems are also key elements of culture.

Social Organization

Every culture creates a social structure by organizing its members into smaller units. This social organization is meant to help the people of a culture work together to meet their basic needs.

Family patterns. In all cultures, the family is the most important unit of social organization. Through the family, children learn how they are expected to behave and what they are expected to believe. Although all cultures are built around families, family patterns differ among cultures.

The nuclear family includes a wife, a husband, and their children. It has been the typical family pattern in industrial societies such as the United States. In these societies, a family usually does not need to be large to accomplish the tasks of living. Most Americans live in cities and work in business and industry. They buy what they need with money they earn. They have many machines, such as vacuum cleaners and washing machines, that make daily tasks easy.

Nuclear families, however, are not always small. Some nuclear families have many children.

The extended family has several generations living in one household. It may include grandparents, parents, children, and sometimes uncles, aunts, and cousins. This family pattern is common in many societies. In a farming culture, grandparents may look after the youngest children while older children and adults work the land. Although the family owns animals and tools and grows enough food to eat, it may not have much money. Family members may pool their savings to buy a tractor or send a child to school.

In cultures with extended families, respect for elders is strong. The elders pass on their wisdom to the young. Often, this family pattern is more common among those members of a community who have the wealth to keep the family together. In both nuclear and extended families, people place high value on family ties.

The person who exercises authority, or power, within a family also varies from one culture to another. For centuries, in most cultures, families were patriarchal. Men exercised more authority than women did. In traditional patriarchal families, the oldest man made the important decisions. In some African and Native American cultures, families are matriarchal. Women have greater authority than men and are the main decision makers.

Today, family patterns are changing around the world. Women in many cultures are taking jobs outside the home. As this occurs, men and women tend to share power more equally. The movement from farms to towns and cities is also affecting family patterns. The nuclear family is becoming more common in all cultures. However, traditional ties to the extended family remain strong.

Social classes. Most cultures have social classes that rank people in order of status. Social class may be based on money, occupation, education, ancestry, or any other factor that a culture values highly. In farming cultures, people who own much land or many animals have high status. In a culture where religion plays a key role in people's lives, religious leaders belong to the upper class.

In the past, a person was usually born into a class and stayed there for life. Today, people in most cultures enjoy at least some degree of social mobility. They have some chance of moving up the social ladder. Some ways of rising in society include obtaining a good education, earning more money, or marrying into a family from a higher class. Of course, people can also move down in society if they lose their money or other things their society values.

Customs and Traditions

Among the most important elements of a culture are its rules of behavior. Some rules, such as what to wear or how to be polite, affect everyday life. Children learn to eat with a fork or with chopsticks, to sleep on a bed or in a hammock, to greet friends with a handshake or with a bow.

Cultural rules vary in importance, and different rules are enforced in different ways. Often, social pressure is used to enforce minor rules of daily behavior. If you show up at a formal school dance dressed in jeans and a T-shirt, your classmates will probably make fun of you. You will feel embarrassed, and the next time you may dress differently.

People enforce their ideas about right and wrong more strictly than minor rules of be-

An Extended Family People live in extended families for many reasons. Members of this family in Mongolia, in Asia, live and work together as herders. Extended families provide a means of caring for older family members and passing traditions on to the young. ***Culture*** Why do you think that extended families are less common in industrialized societies?

havior. Often, these ideas are part of a culture's written laws. In most cultures, these include laws against stealing and murder.

Language

Language is the cornerstone of culture. Without it, people would not be able to communicate their thoughts, feelings, and knowledge. They could not pass on what they know or believe to new generations. All cultures have a language, although not all cultures have developed forms of writing.

Language reflects a culture's identity. People who speak the same language often share the same customs. The United States, for example, does not have an official language, but most Americans speak English.

Many societies, however, include large numbers of people who speak different languages. India, for example, has more than 700 languages. The Indian government has recognized 15 official languages. Canada has two official languages, French and English. The former Soviet Union, too, included speakers of many different languages.

Elements of Culture People's behavior reflects elements of their culture. Many American students express themselves as they wish and have a great deal of freedom to dress as they please. Students in some other cultures are more restricted. ***Diversity*** What differences can you point out between the school life of the American students and the students of Nepal shown here?

For many countries, language presents a thorny problem. National governments want to develop a unified culture. They choose one or two official languages for schools, government, and business. Many citizens feel loyal to their local languages, however. Giving up their language, they say, is the first step toward losing their culture.

Arts and Literature

Products of the human imagination, such as art, music, and literature, please and entertain us. They also teach us about our culture's values.

Children around the world listen to folk tales that are traditional to their culture. Folk tales are handed down from generation to generation. They help to pass on a culture's basic beliefs and values. American children hear the tale of "The Tortoise and the Hare." This story tells about how a slow but steady tortoise wins a race against a fast but lazy hare. It teaches the values of determination and hard work.

Art, music, and literature help to strengthen a culture's identity. They encourage people to feel proud of their customs and give them a sense of belonging. Today, many governments support the arts with public funds because the arts promote cultural pride and unity.

Religion

The arts are often closely linked to people's religious beliefs. People created beautiful temples, churches, paintings, and music to express their faith. Within a culture, people usually share religious beliefs. Religion helps people answer basic questions about the meaning and purpose of life. Like other elements of culture, it also supports the values that a group of people consider important.

Religious beliefs vary. The worship of one god is called monotheism. The worship of more than one god is called polytheism. Religious practices such as prayers and rituals also vary from one culture to another.

History has played a central role in shaping the religion of a society or region. Among the major world religions are Hinduism, Buddhism, Judaism, Christianity, and Islam. Christianity, for example, began among a small group of people in the Middle East. Missionaries and conquering armies helped spread the religion around the world. Christianity absorbed ideas from other cultures and also helped to shape those cultures.

Religious differences are a troubling problem in many regions. Struggles over religion are not new. Today, there is fighting between Protestants and Catholics in Northern Ireland and between Muslims and Christians in the Balkans. Religious differences are usually not the only cause of the fighting. Ethnic rivalries or the lack of political power or economic opportunity often fuel conflicts.

Forms of Government

People form governments to provide for their common needs. These needs include keeping order within a society and protecting the society from outside threats. The term government is used in two ways. It refers to the person or people who hold power in a society. It also refers to the society's laws and political institutions.

People organize governments. Different people organize their governments in different ways. For much of human history, people lived in small groups. Government was fairly simple. Usually, a chief or council of elders made important decisions. Leaders based decisions on the culture's beliefs and customs.

Monarchies Great Britain is a monarchy and a democracy. Queen Elizabeth II, shown here, is a figurehead, and her role is largely ceremonial. The Cabinet and the people's elected representatives in Parliament hold the real power to govern Britain. ***Political System*** How does the British system of government allow for a democracy headed by a monarch?

As societies expanded, more complex forms of government developed. Today, very large numbers of people live together in nations. Each nation has its own government based on a written code of law. National governments include thousands of officials who collect taxes, enforce laws, and administer justice.

Types of government today. Nations have different types of government. Today, we often classify governments as democracies or dictatorships. In a democracy, the people have supreme power. The government can act only by and with their consent. In the form of a democracy called a republic, the people choose the leaders who represent them. The United States is an example of a democracy with a republican form of government.

In a dictatorship, a ruler or group holds power by force. Dictators usually rely on military support to stay in power. In many cases, dictatorships claim to be republics although the people have little or no power. In the 1980s and 1990s, a number of nations that were once ruled by dictators became more democratic.

Economic Systems

Economics refers to how people use limited resources to satisfy their wants and needs. People as well as nations must answer three basic economic questions. What goods and services should we produce? How should we produce them? For whom should we produce them? Over the centuries, people have created various economic systems to answer these questions.

Traditional economy. In a traditional economy, people produce most of what they need to survive. Hunting and gathering, farming, and herding cattle are the bases of a traditional economy. People hunt for the food they eat or raise it themselves. Often they make their own clothing and tools. If they produce more food than they need, they trade the surplus, or extra food, for goods made by others. For thousands of years, most cultures had a traditional economy.

Market economy. In a market economy, individuals answer the basic economic questions by buying and selling goods and services. Businesses and industries produce and sell goods for money. People earn the money to buy what they need or want by working for others or running their own businesses. Business people decide what to produce based on what they believe consumers will buy.

Command economy. In a command economy, the government controls what goods are produced, how they are produced, and what they cost. Individuals may produce goods and sell them to one another on a small scale. Individuals, however, have little economic power. Until the early 1990s, the communist countries of Eastern Europe had command economies. The governments owned the factories, land, and stores. They made the major economic decisions.

Mixed economy. Today, most nations have mixed economies. In a mixed economy, individuals make some economic decisions and the government makes others. The United States has a mixed economy. It has features of a market economy and a command economy. For example, American car makers decide what to produce and sell. However, the government says cars must meet certain standards for safety and fuel use. As you will learn, the amount of government control over the economy varies from country to country.

SECTION 3 REVIEW

1. **Define:** (a) culture, (b) nuclear family, (c) extended family, (d) monotheism, (e) polytheism, (f) democracy, (g) republic, (h) dictatorship.
2. Describe three elements that help give a culture its identity.
3. How are family patterns related to culture?
4. How does religion strengthen a culture?
5. (a) What three basic economic questions must every society answer? (b) How do different societies answer those questions?
6. **Synthesizing Information** How do the arts in the United States help to unify the nation?
7. **Writing Across Cultures** Write a paragraph explaining how the arts and literature can help us learn about other cultures.

4

HOW CULTURES CHANGE

FIND OUT

What factors cause cultures to change?

Why has the rate of cultural change increased in this century?

Why do people often have trouble understanding one another's cultures?

Vocabulary technology, diffusion, subculture, ethnocentrism, racism

Warren Cromartie steps up to home plate. The pitcher winds up, then delivers a blistering fast ball. Cromartie drives the ball over the left field fence. As the fans cheer, he rounds the bases. This familiar scene takes place not in the United States but in Tokyo, Japan. Fans are eating grilled squid, not hot dogs.

Cromartie, an African American, played with the Tokyo Giants for six years. The game was the same, but the team was very different. Cromartie was used to the hot tempers and fierce individualism of American baseball players. In Japanese *besoboru*, or baseball, players stress harmony, group identity, and loyalty to the team owners.

Baseball began in the United States and spread to other countries. It became popular in Japan. Although the Japanese adopted

Baseball in Japan The Japanese have been playing baseball for more than 100 years. They have had professional teams since 1935. These teams are owned by large Japanese corporations. Today, Japan has two baseball leagues with six teams each. ***Culture*** In what ways is baseball in Japan like baseball in the United States? How is it different?

baseball, they adapted it to their own society. Borrowing and adapting new ideas and ways of doing things is one way in which cultures change.

Causes of Cultural Change

Many forces can cause cultural change. These forces include discoveries and inventions, changes in the natural environment, and new ideas.

Technology. Since earliest times, a major source of cultural change has been new technology. Technology refers to the skills and tools a people use. When people first learned to use tools made of stone and bone, they became more successful hunters and food gatherers. In Chapter 2, you will read about how early people developed a new technology—farming—and changed their whole way of life.

A more recent example of technology and cultural change is the invention of the automobile. To use cars, people need a network of roads. In the United States, the government paved roads and built interstate highways. People who could afford to buy cars moved out of the cities to live in suburbs. The sale of cars spurred the growth of other industries, such as steel, rubber, and paint.

Changing environment. Since ancient times, the natural environment has shaped human culture. People's ways of life have been influenced by where they lived.

For hundreds of years, the Native Americans of the Great Plains hunted buffalo. They ate buffalo meat and made clothes and homes out of buffalo hides. The Native Americans needed these animals in order to live as hunters on the plains. In the late 1800s, settlers from Europe wanted to farm the plains. As a result, they destroyed the huge buffalo herds. As buffalo vanished, the way of life of the Plains people disappeared also. The Native Americans had to adapt if they were to survive.

New ideas. Recently, people have become more aware that they have the power to destroy the environment. For example, concern for garbage disposal has led to recycling and conservation. People have begun to alter their actions to protect the Earth. This new behavior is an example of cultural change.

Diffusion

Among the most important causes of cultural change is diffusion, the movement of customs or ideas from one place to another. Much of human history concerns the migration, or movement, of people across different regions of the globe. Wherever people travel, they exchange goods, skills, ideas, and technology with the people they meet.

In the past, people moved on foot, on the backs of animals, by boat, or in wagons. No one knows who invented the wheel that rolled those wagons. Gradually, the knowledge of the wheel spread around the globe, changing cultures everywhere.

A recent example of cultural diffusion is rock music. In the 1950s, American musicians developed rock-and-roll. This new form of music soon became popular around the world. But rock-and-roll itself came out of the earlier musical traditions of blues and jazz. Those traditions had their roots in the work songs and spirituals of African Americans who had been forced to work as slaves. Slave songs in turn drew on the rich musical traditions of various African cultures.

Diffusion can occur either through peaceful means such as trade or through war. Many conquerors throughout history forced their ideas on the people they defeated. In some cases, the conquered people saw that their enemies were successful because they had more advanced technology. They adopted the new ways in order to strengthen their own culture.

Tradition and Change

For thousands of years, cultures changed slowly. Recent technology has quickened the pace of change. Airplanes, telephones, cars, movies, computers, fax machines, and space satellites have advanced transportation and communication. As a result, contacts among different cultures have increased.

The world has become what the writer Marshall McLuhan called a "global village."

News spreads almost instantly. In 1991, people on tiny islands in the Pacific Ocean watched the Gulf War on television. The images of war were bounced off space satellites into their homes.

Improved communication and transportation have brought many benefits. Better technology in medicine and other fields is improving people's lives. In Australia, doctors use two-way radios to give medical information to people living in remote areas. Increased trade makes more goods available to more people.

New technology can also bring negative effects. Rapid changes threaten the foundations of many cultures. In the rush toward progress, valuable traditions may be lost. A challenge for many cultures is how to take advantage of today's opportunities while preserving the best of the past.

Modern technology is changing cultures in many ways. Older generations recall "the good old days." Often, they are caught between two worlds, the traditional and the modern. One example is the Travelling People of Ireland.

A Way of Life Changes

Nan Donohoe was one of the Travelling People of Ireland. She was born in a tent by the side of a country road in 1919. Her family traveled around Ireland in a donkey cart. Her father swept chimneys in farmhouses. Her mother sold scrub brushes, needles, lace, and shoe polish at kitchen doors.

The Travelling People For many years, the Travelling People roamed through the Irish countryside selling goods and doing odd jobs. They carried their possessions in donkey carts from village to village. Today, most of them have moved to the cities and have given up their old way of life. ***Change*** How did advances in technology affect the life of the Travelling People?

An Irish subculture. The Travelling People are a subculture of Irish society. A subculture is a group of people within a society who share certain beliefs, values, and customs. The Travelling People share some traditions, such as the Roman Catholic faith, with other people in Ireland. But for hundreds of years they have had their own way of life.

Like Gypsies, extended families of Travelling People wandered the countryside on foot or in horse-drawn wagons. They made their living as tinsmiths, making tools out of metal. They did odd jobs, traded donkeys and horses, begged, and told fortunes. Nan Donohoe loved the traveling life, despite its hardships. She enjoyed the people she met and the constant movement.

> "I think it an awful thing to stay in a farm, just to walk around the one yard, do the same thing day after day, never to leave that farm, and to die and be buried there . . . .
>
> When I see a trailer or a wagon or a tent, I think freedom."

The impact of technology. By the 1950s, advances in technology were changing Ireland. People bought mass-produced metal goods from stores instead of from wandering tinsmiths. Tractors took the place of donkeys and horses. As a result, the lives of the Travelling People changed dramatically. Today, most of them live in cities. They collect scrap metal and car parts for resale. Many beg or live on welfare. Some crowd their trailers into vacant lots. Others move into government housing.

When social change brought hard times, Nan and her large extended family moved into a housing project in Dublin. As an old woman, Nan recalled her people's traditional values and customs. She did not think the changes were an improvement.

The Travelling People "used to be harmless and innocent," she explained. "They believed in nothing, only telling stories. But they've gone spiteful and jealous" under the pressures of modern life.

> "If I was travelling again, I wouldn't go into towns or near a city. They're not healthy; there's too much smoke. You think you're getting fresh air in a city—you're not. And cities are nothing but trouble for anyone rearing a young family. . . . In the country they [the children] won't go wrong on you. . . . A child always has something to do in the country. I'd rather be in a tent at the side of a woods than in a town." ■

Understanding Other Cultures

Traditional cultures everywhere are facing pressures similar to those of the Travelling People. The younger generations are adapting to the changes. As they do so, their cultures change to meet the new demands of surviving in a new situation.

Most people prefer their own culture because it is familiar and comfortable. Our customs feel so natural to us that we think they are the way things are supposed to be. People in other cultures feel the same about their customs. Around the world, most people have a tendency toward ethnocentrism. They judge other cultures by the standards of their own culture.

Some people say negative things about people they view as different from themselves. The ancient Greeks, for example, felt superior to anyone who did not speak Greek. They called such people barbarians, from the Greek word for "strange, foreign, or uncivilized." Today, people around the world often have similar reactions to other cultures.

Another form of ethnocentrism is racism. Racism is the belief that one racial group is naturally superior to another. It is largely a modern problem. The ancient Greeks were not racist. Although they believed they had a superior culture, they did not think they themselves were superior to the Africans or Asians with whom they traded.

Racism most often results when groups of people compete for food, land, money, and

Tolerance Versus Intolerance Worldwide protests, such as this rally in South Africa, led to dramatic changes in South African race laws. In 1994, black South Africans voted for the first time and helped elect Nelson Mandela, South Africa's first black president. ***Human Rights*** What actions might South Africans take to heal wounds caused by years of legal separation?

social power. The group that wins the struggle uses racist ideas as an excuse for dominating others. Years ago, Europeans used racism to justify enslaving people.

Today, most people recognize that racism is destructive. They realize that differences in culture are the result of many factors. Appreciation of cultural diversity can help to combat the destructive effects of racism.

SECTION 4 REVIEW

1. **Define:** (a) technology, (b) diffusion, (c) subculture, (d) ethnocentrism, (e) racism.
2. (a) Give an example of how technology can lead to cultural change. (b) What other factors can lead to cultural change?
3. Describe two ways in which cultural diffusion occurs.
4. Why has the pace of cultural change increased?
5. **Forecasting** Do you think increased awareness of other cultures will help to end racism? Explain your answer.
6. **Writing Across Cultures** Jot down five items from your everyday life that are examples of cultural diffusion. Write a sentence describing each item and telling what culture it comes from.

DICTIONARY OF GEOGRAPHIC TERMS

The list below includes important geographic terms and their definitions. All of these terms are illustrated on the diagram.

1. **bay** part of a body of water that is partly enclosed by land
2. **cape** narrow point of land that extends into a body of water
3. **coast** land that borders the sea or an ocean
4. **delta** area formed by soil deposited at the mouth of a river
5. **divide** ridge that separates rivers that flow in one direction from those that flow in the opposite direction
6. **hill** area of raised land that is lower and more rounded than a mountain
7. **isthmus** narrow strip of land joining two large land areas or joining a peninsula to a mainland
8. **lake** body of water surrounded by land
9. **mountain** high, steep, rugged land area that rises sharply above the surrounding land
10. **mouth of a river** place where a river empties into a larger body of water
11. **peninsula** piece of land that is surrounded by water on three sides
12. **plain** broad area of fairly level land that is usually close to sea level
13. **plateau** large area of high land that is flat or gently rolling
14. **river** large stream of water that empties into an ocean, a lake, or another river
15. **river valley** land drained or watered by a river
16. **source of a river** place where a river begins
17. **strait** narrow channel that connects two larger bodies of water
18. **tributary** stream or small river that flows into a larger stream or river

Chapter 1 Review

Understanding Vocabulary

Match each term at left with the correct definition at right.

1. geography	**a.** physical features of a place or region
2. topography	**b.** belief in many gods
3. culture	**c.** the entire way of life of a group or people
4. polytheism	**d.** study of people, their environment, and their resources
5. ethnocentrism	**e.** judging other cultures by the standards of one's own culture

Reviewing Main Ideas

1. How do location and place differ?

2. (a) How do geographers define movement? (b) How does movement contribute to interdependence among countries?

3. How is it possible for one country to belong to several regions?

4. Describe three special-purpose maps.

5. How does location affect the climate of a region?

6. What are the seven major features of any culture?

7. (a) How can technology lead to cultural change? (b) How does the natural environment help to shape human cultures?

8. Why do many people tend to judge other cultures by standards of their own culture?

Reviewing Chapter Themes

1. The physical characteristics of a region include landforms and climates. Choose two landforms and describe how they help shape human culture.

2. A climate map, physical map, natural resources map, vegetation map, and population map each provides key information about a region. Describe the relationship between information on any two of the maps.

3. Choose two of the following elements of culture. Tell how each helps shape a culture: (a) language, (b) religion, (c) government organization, (d) economic organization.

4. New technology, changes in the environment, and diffusion can lead to cultural change. Give an example of each and describe how it could lead to cultural change.

Thinking Critically

1. Making Global Connections (a) When people first settled your area, how do you think landforms and climate affected their lives? (b) Are those same features important to you today?

2. Forecasting Assume that cultural diffusion continues at its current rapid pace. What positive and negative results do you foresee?

3. Defending a Position Knowledge of other cultures can help to promote tolerance. What arguments can you offer to support this statement?

Applying Your Skills

1. Reading Maps Study the maps on page 9. (a) Which map distorts distance? (b) Which map distorts shapes? (c) Which maps are least accurate near the poles? (d) Why do the curved lines of longitude and latitude on the interrupted projection and Robinson projection more accurately illustrate the land areas? (See Skill Lesson 1 on page 48.)

2. Identifying the Main Idea Reread the subsection "Interaction Between People and Their Environment" in Section 1 on pages 4–5. Write a sentence that summarizes the main idea of the subsection.

Chapter 2

THE WORLD TODAY

Farming in Africa Throughout the world, farmers mix the old with the new. Some farming methods date back to earliest times. For centuries, farmers have planted trees between fields to protect and nourish their crops. Farmers also adopt modern scientific ways of growing crops. ***Choice*** What benefits do farmers gain from blending traditional and new ways of raising crops?

CHAPTER OUTLINE

Rattan Lal was eager to get started on his first job. Just out of college, he was going to set up a model farm in Ibadan, Nigeria. Using the latest methods, Lal plowed, fertilized, and planted. A few days later, he recalled, "a tropical storm washed away everything in my fields, including the topsoil and seeds." The disaster taught him that he had a lot to learn about soil erosion in Africa.

Lal was part of an international team of scientists. They hoped to develop ways to increase food production in Africa. But as Lal found out, new methods were not always the answer.

The scientists then studied how African farmers cleared land. Local farmers burned off the grass and bushes but left the palm trees standing. The trees protected the crops and added nutrients to the soil. With this knowledge, the researchers saw how they could combine old and new methods. They used modern science to develop new types of rice and corn that resisted tropical insects and diseases. But they used traditional ways of clearing the land.

Throughout history, people have invented and adapted a variety of technologies. Today, sharing technology is contributing to interdependence.

CHAPTER PERSPECTIVE

In this chapter, you will look at the large sweep of human development, from ancient times to today. This overview provides a framework for understanding how a wide variety of cultures have developed. Many of the topics here will be discussed in more depth in later chapters.

As you read, look for these chapter themes:

- The agricultural revolution led to the rise of civilization.
- The Industrial Revolution helped European nations to control much of the world.
- Developing countries face many challenges as they work to build modern political and economic systems.
- Interdependence is a key feature of today's world.

Literature Connections

In this chapter, you will encounter a passage from the following work.

The Cave of Lascaux, Mario Ruspoli

For other literature suggestions, see Connections With Literature, pages 804–808.

1 PATTERNS OF EARLY CIVILIZATIONS

FIND OUT

What technologies did early people develop?

What are the chief characteristics of a civilization?

How did cultural diffusion influence early civilizations?

What major civilizations thrived in the year 1300?

Vocabulary nomad, civilization, archaeologist, artisan

A lost dog led young Marcel Ravidat to the cave entrance. Excited, the boy and his friends brought lamps to explore the underground cave. Marcel was amazed by what they found. He wrote his teacher:

> “We raised the lamp . . . and saw in its flickering light several lines in various colors. Intrigued by these colored lines, we set about meticulously exploring the walls and, to our great surprise, discovered several fair-sized animal figures.”

News of the boys' discovery brought scientists to Lascaux, in southern France. They concluded that the animal figures had been painted more than 10,000 years before. The cave paintings at Lascaux, along with those discovered in other parts of the world, give us a glimpse of how early people lived.

Stone Age People

Scientists think that the first people lived more than 2 million years ago in eastern

Africa. Very little evidence about these ancient people has survived. They probably gathered fruits, seeds, nuts, and insects. They also may have hunted small animals.

Early achievements. Over thousands of years, people developed important skills. They learned to make stone tools and weapons during what is now called the Stone Age. Stone Age people chipped rocks to shape simple knives, spear tips, and arrowheads. They also learned to control fire. Perhaps most important, Stone Age people developed language. Language allowed Stone Age people to pass on important information. (See Connections With Literature, page 804, "Clan of the Cave Bear.")

With better tools and knowledge, Stone Age people were able to hunt larger animals such as mammoths and bison. These hunting peoples were nomads. They traveled from place to place to find food. As a result, people migrated across a wide area. They also learned to adapt to different climates and landforms.

About 90,000 years ago, the Earth's climate became colder. Huge sheets of ice covered parts of the Earth. During this Ice Age, bands of Stone Age hunters took shelter in caves like the one at Lascaux. Climate changes such as the Ice Age may have spurred people to develop new technologies. For example, people probably learned to make warm clothing from animal skins at this time.

The agricultural revolution. About 10,000 years ago, Stone Age people made two key advances. They learned to farm and to domesticate, or tame, animals. Because these new technologies had such important effects, scholars call these changes the agricultural revolution.*

Scholars used to think that farming first developed in the Tigris-Euphrates Valley of the Middle East in about 6000 B.C. Recent evidence suggests that people in Southeast Asia may have started to farm 2,000 years earlier. Farming developed independently in the Americas, probably in the area of present-day Guatemala and Mexico.

The agricultural revolution changed how people lived. Farming people no longer had to travel in search of food. Instead, they could settle in permanent communities. At first, people hunted and farmed. Slowly, farmers depended more and more on the crops they planted and the animals they raised.

In farming communities, people developed new ways of life. Hunting bands were small. Farming communities could support a greater number of people. To deal with the new conditions, people began to develop new forms of government. Religious beliefs also changed. The ceremonies and beliefs of hunting people centered on the animals they hunted. Farmers looked to gods of nature, such as sun and rain gods. They believed that those gods controlled the harvest. Farmers also developed new tools such as hoes. They wove baskets to store grain and learned to irrigate the land.

The First Civilizations

As farming methods improved, populations grew. Over time, some villages grew into towns and cities. City dwellers relied on the surplus, or extra, food that farmers raised. Cities were a key feature of the first civilizations. A civilization is a highly organized group of people with their own language and ways of living.

Many civilizations developed in river valleys where conditions favored farming. (See the map on page 29.) These included the Nile River Valley in northeastern Africa, the Indus Valley in South Asia, and the Huang He Valley of China. You will read more about these river valley civilizations in later chapters.

Although they were different from one another, civilizations everywhere had certain features in common. In addition to cities, these included well-organized governments, complex religions, specialized skills and jobs, social classes, and methods of keeping records.

Government and religion. What we know about the first civilizations comes from archaeologists. Archaeologists are scientists

---

* The agricultural revolution is also called the Neolithic revolution. Neolithic means New Stone Age.

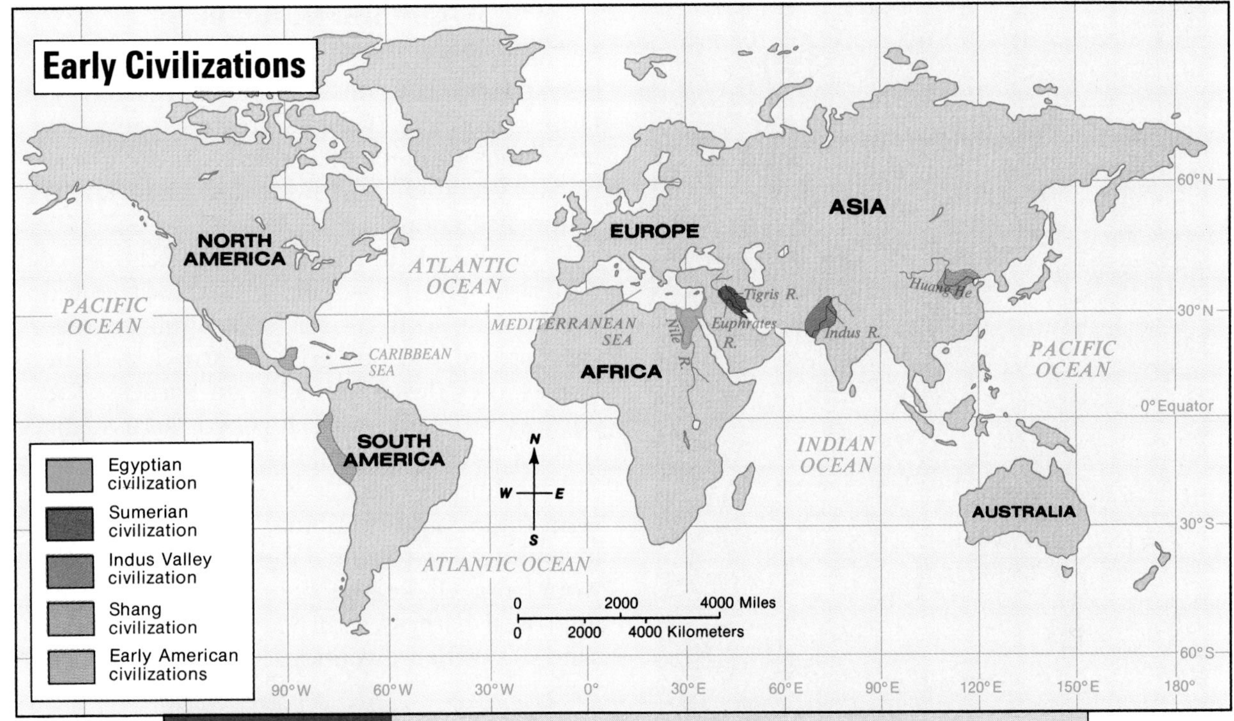

MAP STUDY

As early farming peoples prospered, their villages grew into cities. These cities became the centers of early world civilizations.

1. **Location** What early civilization developed in the Nile River Valley?
2. **Location** Name three early civilizations that developed in Asia.
3. **Comparing** (a) What was similar about the location of early civilizations in Asia? (b) What was similar about the location of early civilizations in the Americas?

who study the objects left by early people. They have uncovered ancient cities such as Sumer in the Middle East and Machu Picchu in Peru. In various locations, they have found the remains of huge palaces and temples as well as large irrigation systems. From this evidence, scientists have concluded that ancient civilizations had powerful governments. Only a strong government could have organized the large numbers of people needed to build such projects.

Temples and religious objects show that the people had well-developed religious beliefs. In fact, the rulers of the first civilizations may have been priest-kings. People believed that priests alone knew the special ceremonies and prayers that pleased the gods.

Specialized jobs. As early civilizations grew, people developed new technologies. They also acquired special skills. Some people became artisans, or skilled craftworkers. Weavers, for example, turned plant fibers into cloth. Metalworkers made tools and weapons out of bronze or iron. Other people became merchants and traders who made a living by exchanging goods.

Social classes. Early civilizations had similar social structures. At the head of society was the ruler, usually a king. Below him was a class made up of priests and nobles. Nobles had high status because they owned or controlled land. The next class included government officials and perhaps wealthy merchants. The majority of people were artisans

Early Civilization The Assyrians developed an early civilization in the Tigris River Valley. The work of art shown here, called a bas-relief, was used to decorate a building in Nineveh, the capital of ancient Assyria. ***Fine Art*** What does the existence of this bas-relief and its subject matter reveal about Assyrian civilization?

or farmers. At the bottom of society were slaves. Slaves included people captured in war as well as those who could not pay their debts.

Record keeping. Most early civilizations developed systems of writing. Writing allowed officials to keep tax records as well as to record religious ceremonies and prayers. The first forms of writing were pictographs, pictures that represented objects. Later, people invented ways to express ideas such as justice and independence.

Cultural Diffusion

As you have read, cultural diffusion has been taking place for thousands of years. Early farmers and city dwellers created many new inventions to meet their needs. These inventions were then borrowed and changed by other civilizations.

The use of the harness is an example of diffusion. The Sumerians probably invented the harness so that oxen could pull wagons. Later, when the Sumerians learned to tame horses, they developed a lighter harness. The harness, though, was attached across the horse's throat and could strangle the animal. This technology may have traveled along ancient trade routes to China. The Chinese then invented a way to attach the harness so that it would not choke the horse. Eventually, this improved harness returned to Sumer. Thousands of other inventions spread in similar ways.

Ideas also spread. In the ancient Middle East, most people worshipped many gods. One group, the Hebrews, developed Judaism, a religion based on worship of one God. Hebrew monotheism later influenced both Christianity and Islam. Today, millions of people around the world belong to these three religions, which had their roots in the ancient Middle East. (See Chapters 25 and 26.)

Changing World Powers

Over thousands of years, a variety of civilizations thrived in different parts of the world. In A.D. 100, two great powers ruled vast empires. Rome controlled the Mediterranean world from Spain to the Middle East. At the same time, China controlled much of East Asia.

The world in 1300. If you had lived in 1300, you would have found the centers of world power very different from those of A.D. 100. Rome was no longer a power. Islamic rulers prospered in much of the world from Spain to the borders of China. As you will learn in Chapter 26, Islamic civilization blended the learning of many earlier civilizations. Trade flourished throughout the Islamic world. Muslim traders carried goods from India and China to the Middle East and parts of Africa.

Several African kingdoms grew wealthy from trade. Muslim rulers in the wealthy West African kingdom of Mali sent ambassadors to cities in the Middle East. Later, Muslim scholars flocked to Timbuktu, an important center of Islamic learning.

At Delhi in northern India, Muslim rulers, called sultans, reigned over wealthy courts. India produced valuable silks, cotton, and spices. Loaded with rich cargoes, Indian merchant ships sailed to Mombasa in East Africa or to Guangzhou in China.

China was a major world power in 1300. The Mongols, nomads from central Asia, had conquered China in the 1200s. To control China, Mongol emperor Kublai Khan set up a great highway system. The Mongol network of roads encouraged trade between China and the Middle East. Caravans brought Arab, Italian, Russian, and other traders across the vast Mongol empire. They were impressed by a huge number of Chinese inventions, ranging from paper to gunpowder.

In 1300, two powerful empires were developing in the Americas. In Mexico, the Aztecs were setting out on a course of conquest. Before long, they would rule a large area. In the Andes Mountains of South America, the Incas were building on the achievements of earlier people to develop a highly advanced civilization.

Marks of Greatness A Chinese emperor in the third century B.C. had the Great Wall of China (left) completed as a defense against invaders. Muslim rulers of Spain built the Alhambra (right) in the A.D. 1200s as a center of government and Islamic religion in the Spanish city of Granada. ***Culture*** What can we learn about a civilization by studying its major public structures?

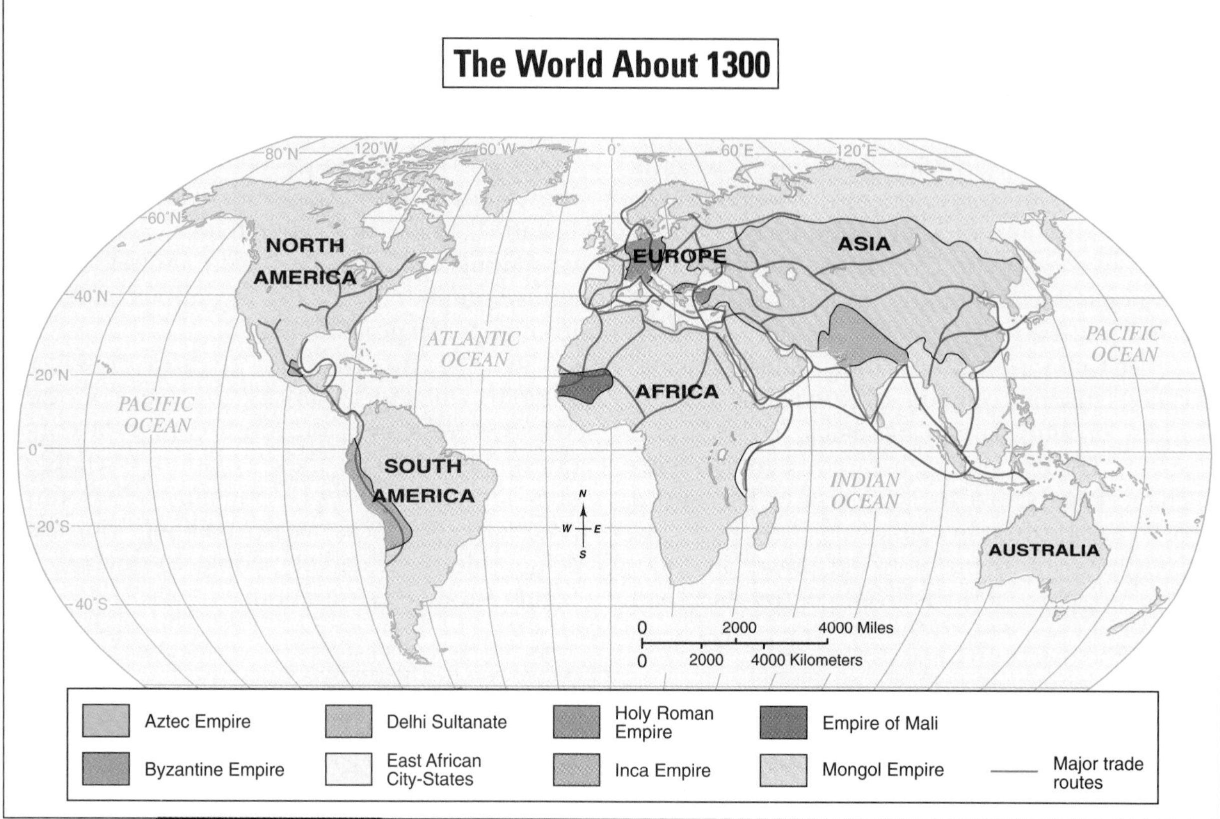

MAP STUDY

By 1300, major world civilizations had developed in Africa, Asia, the Middle East, Europe, and the Americas.

1. **Location** Which two civilizations developed in lands bordering the Indian Ocean?
2. **Movement** Which American empires were linked by major trade routes?
3. **Drawing Conclusions** Why were goods from Asia scarce and costly in Europe?

Europe on the fringes. In 1300, Europe was on the fringes of the trade routes that linked Africa and Asia. The region was less developed than the civilizations of China, India, and the Middle East. The rulers of small European kingdoms were fighting with one another and with powerful nobles who controlled much of the land. The relationship between Europe and the rest of the world, however, was beginning to change.

SECTION 1 REVIEW

1. **Identify:** (a) Stone Age, (b) agricultural revolution.
2. **Define:** (a) nomad, (b) civilization, (c) archaeologist, (d) artisan.
3. What technological advances did Stone Age people make?
4. What main features do most civilizations have in common?
5. How does cultural diffusion affect civilization?
6. What areas of the world were centers of power in 1300?
7. **Understanding Causes and Effects** How did the agricultural revolution lead to the development of civilizations?
8. **Writing Across Cultures** Write a brief article describing how the three major religions that originated in the ancient Middle East—Judaism, Christianity, and Islam—affect the lives of people in the United States today.

2

SHAPING THE INDUSTRIAL WORLD

FIND OUT

What changes contributed to the growing power of Europe?

How did the Industrial Revolution affect Europe?

What were the causes and effects of imperialism?

How did the Cold War shape the world after World War II?

Vocabulary capital, entrepreneur, urbanization, imperialism, westernization, nationalism

Vasco da Gama was enjoying his welcome home. Portugal's King Manuel I congratulated the bold sea captain on his successful voyage. Da Gama had made the king's dream come true. He had discovered a sea route around Africa to India. Portugal stood ready to grow rich from the spice trade.

During the celebrations, a Portuguese noble demanded to know what goods da Gama had brought from India and what the Indians wanted in exchange. The Indians traded pepper, cinnamon, and ginger, replied da Gama. In return, they wanted gold and silver from the Portuguese.

"In that case," replied the noble in disgust, "it seems to me that it is *they* who have discovered *us!*"

In 1499, when Europeans began to trade directly with Asia, they had few goods to interest the people of India or China. At first, Asian rulers dictated the terms of trade. In time, however, European nations grew stronger, and they seized control of many parts of the world.

Emergence of Europe

For 1,000 years before da Gama's voyage, Europe had been divided into many small kingdoms. By the late 1400s, ambitious rulers were building strong nation-states. In Portugal, Spain, England, and France, strong monarchs ruled over centralized governments. Over the next 300 years, these nations competed to expand their power both in Europe and overseas.

Advances in technology. New technologies helped European nations expand. During the Renaissance, from about 1350 to 1600, Europeans rediscovered the learning of ancient civilizations. Much of this knowledge had been preserved by Muslim scholars in Spain and the Middle East. Building on this ancient learning, European thinkers made important new scientific discoveries and developed practical inventions.

Europeans also adapted technologies from other lands. The magnetic compass, which was invented in China, reached Europe by way of the Middle East. Europeans improved the compass, allowing sailors to find their location at sea. Along with new kinds of ships and instruments, the compass helped Europeans to take long sea voyages.

Gunpowder also reached Europe from China by way of the Middle East. Europeans then invented new weapons such as muskets and cannons. With these weapons, some Europeans were able to conquer other lands.

A money economy. By the 1300s, Europe was moving away from a barter economy, in which people exchanged one set of goods for another. Instead, they used money. The new money economy allowed some people to store up capital, or money that can be invested in business ventures for the purpose of making a profit. Investors risked their capital on overseas trading voyages. They expected to make large profits by selling silks and spices from Asia.

Overseas expansion. Some rulers also invested capital in trading activities in the hope of getting richer. King Manuel I of Portugal paid for Vasco da Gama's voyage to India. Similarly, Queen Isabella of Spain paid for the voyage of Christopher Columbus. Columbus was looking for a sea route across the Atlantic Ocean to what Europeans called "the Spice Islands" of Southeast Asia. Instead, in 1492 he reached the West Indies in the Caribbean. His voyage opened up what was a "new world" to Europeans.

The voyages of Columbus and da Gama spurred Europeans to explore regions unknown to them in the past. Soldiers and settlers soon followed, claiming lands in the Americas and setting up trading outposts in Africa and elsewhere. Over the next 300 years, Spain, Portugal, England, and France built huge colonial empires.

The Industrial Revolution

By the mid-1700s, two changes had ushered in a new age in Europe. They included a revolution both in agriculture and in industry. Each was as important for the modern world as the ancient agricultural revolution had been 10,000 years earlier.

A second agricultural revolution. The new agricultural revolution had three main causes. New plants from the Americas, such as potatoes, corn, and squash, helped European farmers to produce a wider variety of crops. In addition, improved farming methods and new farm machines such as the seed drill allowed farmers to grow more food.

Increased food production led to rapid population growth. However, the new farming methods also meant that fewer people were needed to work the fields. Forced off the land, thousands of farmers moved into towns, where the need for workers was growing.

New systems of production. Between 1750 and 1914, an industrial revolution transformed Europe and the United States. The Industrial Revolution had two key features. Machines replaced hand tools. Steam and electricity took the place of human and animal power.

The Industrial Revolution began in Britain's cloth-making industry. Inventors developed new machines to speed up the process of making thread and weaving cloth.

The Industrial Revolution in Britain The Industrial Revolution had its first impact on the textile industry in Britain. Women and children operated the machinery in the new cloth-making mills that sprang up. Low wages and long hours marked their lives. ***Technology*** How did the Industrial Revolution change the way people lived and worked?

Entrepreneurs, people who risked their money to set up businesses in order to make a profit, financed these inventions. They built factories that brought machines and workers together under one roof. The factory system quickly spread to other industries.

Effects of industrialization. The Industrial Revolution led to urbanization, or the growth of cities. Millions of people crowded into cities to work in factories. The new industrial workers suffered hardship and poverty. They worked long hours in dangerous conditions for low wages. Reformers protested the terrible conditions. Slowly, workers won better wages and safer working conditions.

During the Industrial Revolution, reformers also urged their governments to become more democratic. Many European governments slowly extended the right to vote to all male citizens. Women fought an uphill battle for the same right.

In Europe and the United States, inventors developed better means of transportation, such as railroads and steamships, and devised new methods of mining. The development of the telegraph and the telephone improved communication. Many inventions made life easier and helped improve the standard of living. New medical discoveries led to better health care.

Imperialism

Industrialization helped set off a new wave of European expansion overseas. European factories needed raw materials from Africa, Asia, and Latin America. In the late 1800s, European nations competed to control the sources of raw materials. They also looked to lands overseas as markets where they could sell their manufactured products.

The period from 1870 to 1914 has been called the Age of Imperialism. Imperialism is

MAP STUDY

By 1914, European nations had gained large overseas empires and ruled peoples in many regions of the world.

1. **Movement** (a) Which European colonial empire was the largest? (b) On which continents did it control colonies?
2. **Location** Name the two non-European nations that controlled other lands in 1914.
3. **Comparing** (a) How did the location of United States territories differ from the location of European colonies? (b) How would you account for this difference?

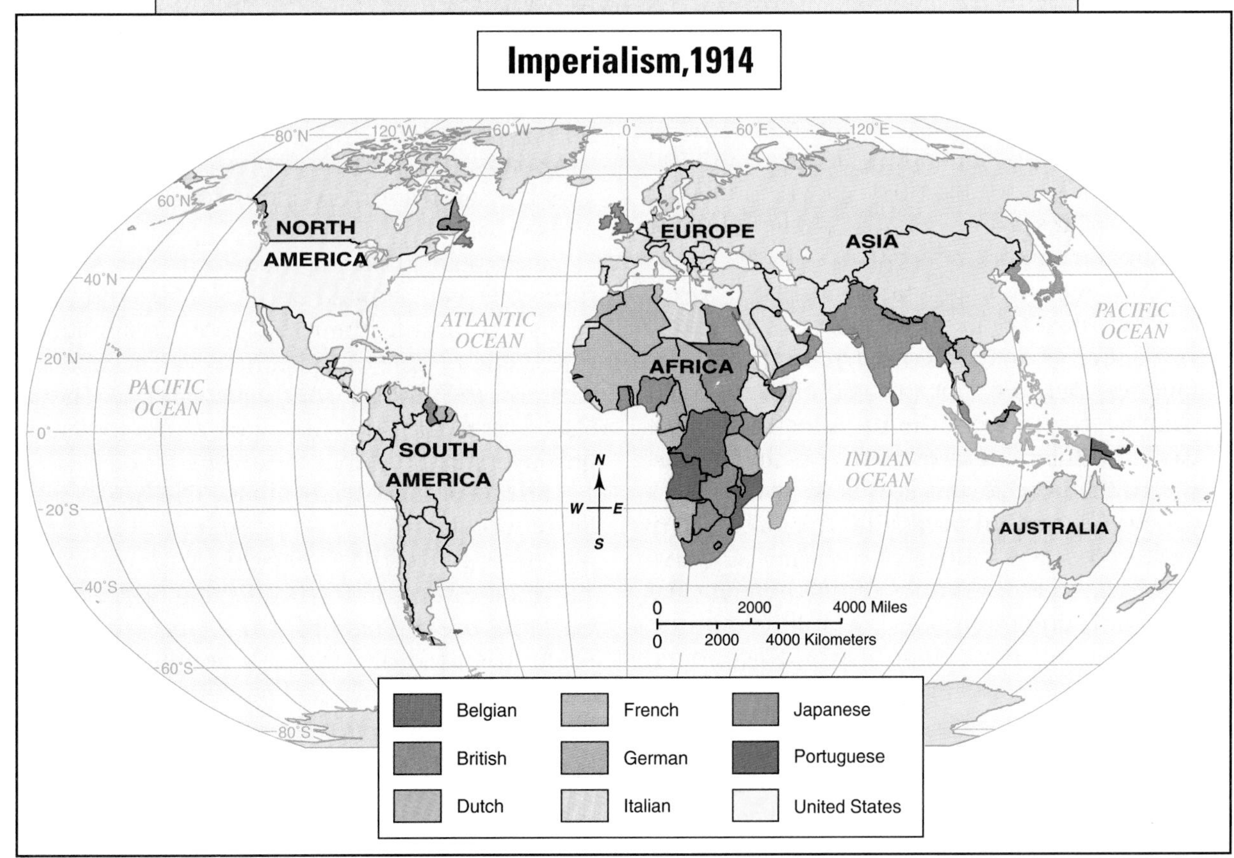

A Railroad in India The British directed the construction of the first railroad in India in 1853. The last car on this train is a "purdah car" used only by women and children. In Indian society, women and children often were separated from men in public places. ***Diversity*** Why did the people of India accept some parts of western culture while rejecting other parts?

the control by one country of the political, economic, or cultural life of another country or region. European imperialist powers included Great Britain, France, Germany, Portugal, Italy, Belgium, Russia, Spain, and the Netherlands. In addition, Japan and the United States also expanded their influence during the Age of Imperialism.

The Age of Imperialism changed power relationships around the globe. Before the 1800s, Europeans had conquered much of the Americas but were not strong enough to build colonial empires elsewhere. After the Industrial Revolution, however, European nations used their wealth and advanced weapons to extend their influence around the globe. They took colonies in Africa and Asia. They also controlled the economies of independent nations in Latin America. As you will read in the next section, they set up a world economic system that has lasted well beyond the Age of Imperialism.

Westernization. Many people in imperialist nations felt that western culture* was better than the cultures of other regions. They encouraged westernization, or adoption of western culture. Europeans tried to persuade or force people in other lands to become Christians, use western forms of government and law, and adopt western food, clothing, and customs.

European efforts to transform other cultures met with limited success. Most Indians remained loyal to their Hindu or Muslim cultures. The people of India, however, accepted western technology such as railroads. They also adopted the western idea of democratic government.

Nationalism

Another major force affecting the world was the rise of nationalism. Nationalism is pride in and loyalty to one's country. During the 1800s, nationalist feeling helped both the Italians and the Germans to form strong nations out of many small states.

Nationalism created rivalries among European powers and added to the spread of imperialism. Britain, for example, took control of parts of West Africa to prevent France from

* The term western culture generally refers to the culture of Western Europe and the United States.

expanding there. Nationalism also threatened a number of older European empires. Austria-Hungary ruled many ethnic groups such as Serbs, Croats, and Poles. Each of these groups sought to form its own independent nation. In 1914, nationalist feelings helped spark World War I.

Nationalism spread to other parts of the world. In Africa, Asia, and Latin America nationalist leaders fought to end foreign control. In the decades after World War II, nationalist movements forced European powers to give up their colonies. Many new nations celebrated their independence. You will read in the next section how these new nations also faced many problems.

The Cold War

After World War II, the Cold War shaped the international scene. The Cold War was a political and economic struggle between the democratic nations of the West, led by the United States, and the Communist bloc, led by the Soviet Union. (See Chapter 33.) The Cold War led to a dangerous arms race between the United States and the Soviet Union. The two superpowers stockpiled nuclear weapons capable of great destruction.

During the Cold War, the superpowers competed for influence in the developing world. Many leaders of developing nations received money, weapons, and advice from the Soviet Union or the United States. Some saw communism as a way to free themselves of western control. After Mao Zedong led a successful communist revolution in China, the United States began to oppose some nationalist movements. Sometimes, the United States stepped in directly to oppose Soviet influence. It fought a long, costly war to stop communist rebels in Vietnam.

Most developing nations wanted economic aid from the industrial world. They did not, however, want to become involved in the Cold War.

As you will read in Unit 8, the Cold War ended in the early 1990s with the collapse of the Soviet Union. That dramatic change led to new hopes of an end to the arms race between the superpowers.

SECTION 2 REVIEW

1. **Identify:** (a) Industrial Revolution, (b) Cold War.
2. **Define:** (a) capital, (b) entrepreneur, (c) urbanization, (d) imperialism, (e) westernization, (f) nationalism.
3. Why were European nations able to expand overseas in the 1500s and 1600s?
4. Explain two effects of (a) the second agricultural revolution, and (b) the Industrial Revolution.
5. Why were European nations able to gain colonies in the 1800s?
6. **Applying Information** How did the Cold War create tensions around the world?
7. **Writing Across Cultures** Imagine that you are an African in a European colony in Africa during the 1800s. Write a diary entry detailing your feelings about European efforts to westernize your land.

3 THE DEVELOPING WORLD

FIND OUT

What are the main goals of developing nations?

What economic problems do developing nations face?

How does underdevelopment contribute to widespread poverty?

Vocabulary cash crop, modernization, tariff, privatization, literacy, population density

"Man has become crazy," noted Davi Yanomami after spending a few hours observing people in New York City. "They look all the time at the ground and never see the sky. Why do they do that?"

Davi was a long way from the Brazilian rain forest where he was a leader of the Yanomami people. He had gone to New York to ask the United Nations for help. Gold miners were polluting rivers and destroying traditional hunting areas. They also carried diseases that were killing the Yanomami.

Today, mining and other kinds of development threaten traditional cultures around the world. Many developing nations like Brazil face difficult choices in their efforts to build modern industrial economies.

World Economic Patterns

As you have read, in 1300 a vast trading network stretched across the Islamic world from the Mediterranean Sea to Southeast Asia. European nations gained a share of this trade by finding their own routes to Asia. During the Age of Imperialism, western nations took control of this global trade. They also created a new trading pattern.

Imperialist nations encouraged people in Africa, Asia, and Latin America to grow cash crops that could be sold on the world market. These cash crops included cotton, rice, coffee, and sugar. Industrial nations also imported mineral resources such as iron, copper, and tin from less-developed areas. The developed countries, in turn, sold manufactured goods, such as clothing and weapons, to less-developed lands.

This trading pattern made less-developed areas dependent on Europe and the United States. Even after developing nations won independence in the years following World War II, they remained tied economically to their former rulers. This dependence created problems for the new nations. Many of them relied on the export of a single crop or commodity. If the world demand for a product

Plantation Workers In British colonies such as Ceylon (now Sri Lanka), Britons owned many of the plantations and companies, and the people of Ceylon provided the labor. In the 1920s, these workers packed tea and rubber for export.
Interdependence How did the imperialist powers gain from having colonies? How did the colonies suffer from this rule?

such as cotton or copper fell, prices dropped. Nations that depended on earnings from cotton or copper suffered. In addition, as people in developing nations depended increasingly on imported manufactured goods, local economies based on crafts declined.

Goals of Modernization

After winning independence, developing nations devised political and economic policies aimed at modernization. They wanted to set up stable governments and produce a high level of goods and services. Those goals have often proved hard to achieve. As you study each region, you will learn how different countries have tried to modernize.

Political stability. Newly independent nations have faced many challenges. Colonial powers drew artificial borders to create new nations. Often those borders put people with diverse cultures into a single nation. Without common traditions to unite them, these groups competed for power. In some countries, military leaders seized control. On occasion, former colonial rulers or one of the superpowers interfered in political affairs.

Economic diversity. For developing nations, modernization includes improving both agriculture and industry. A key goal of modernization is economic diversity. This means producing various kinds of crops and goods so that the nation is no longer dependent on a single export. Just as western nations did during the Industrial Revolution, developing nations are introducing modern farming methods and building factories to produce manufactured goods.

Developing nations have also tried to end dependence on foreign imports by imposing high tariffs. A tariff is a tax on imported goods. Tariffs make foreign goods more costly than those produced locally. This encourages people to buy from local manufacturers.

The policy has had mixed results. In many countries, the government owned major industries. These state-owned companies were often inefficient and produced low-quality goods. Many governments in developing nations have now moved toward privatization. They are selling state-owned industries to private investors. These governments hope that putting businesses in private hands will improve quality and efficiency.

Education and services. A major goal of developing nations is to increase literacy. Literacy is the ability to read and write. Governments have set up schools to train students in the skills needed in a modern industrial economy. New nations also have tried to improve other services such as medical care, housing, and water and sewage systems.

Mixed success. Some nations have had great success. South Korea and Singapore, for

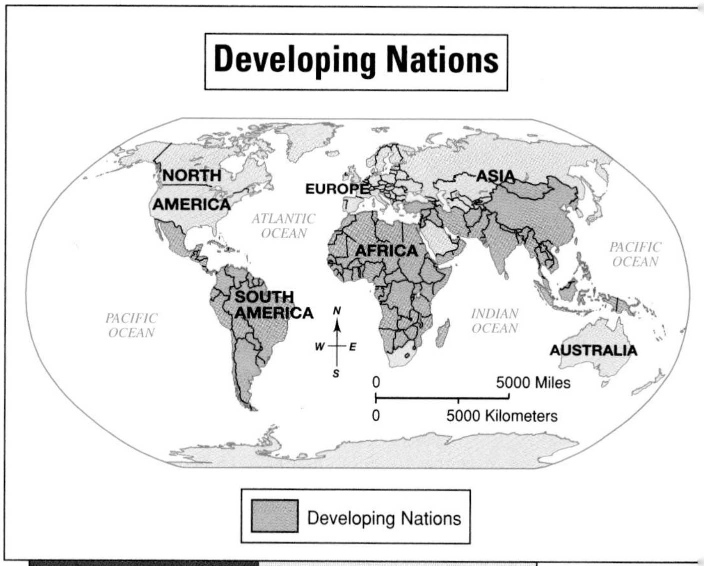

Developing Nations

MAP STUDY

Many developing nations tried to stay out of the Cold War struggle. During these years, developing countries were working to build their economies and to improve the lives of their people.

1. **Location** In which areas of the world are most developing nations located?
2. **Interaction** Which superpowers provided money, weapons, and military advisers to many developing nations during the Cold War?
3. **Making Global Connections** Compare this map with the map on page 35. (a) What experience did many developing nations share in 1914? (b) How might that experience have contributed to their present situation as developing nations?

example, have grown dramatically. Their success is based on technological skill and a decision to produce goods that will sell in the world market. Such nations are often called newly industrialized countries (NICs). Many other nations, however, remain economically dependent.

The Debt Crisis

To modernize, developing nations have had to build transportation and communication systems such as airports and satellite dishes. However, most did not have the money to invest in such projects. As a result, these nations borrowed from the western industrial world. (See the charts on page 786.)

In the 1970s, the price of oil soared. Oil-rich nations of the Middle East put their wealth in western banks. The banks, in turn, wanted to earn interest on the money. They therefore encouraged developing nations to borrow. Developing nations needed the money to pay higher fuel costs and for major projects.

When interest rates rose in the 1980s, many nations that owed money could not pay their debts. A worldwide economic slowdown made the debt crisis worse. Prices fell for the crops and goods that were sold by developing nations.

Lenders and borrowers then worked out ways to ease the crisis. Some lenders agreed to lower interest rates and to cancel parts of the debt. Even so, debt continues to be a problem for developing nations. Nations with debts have to spend much of their income to pay back loans. As a result, they cannot afford to provide many basic services such as schools. They have also had to cut spending on new development projects.

Problems of Development

In 1990, the world's population topped 5 billion. More than three quarters of the world's population lives in the developing world. Since birth rates are high in many developing nations, that percentage will rise in the future.

Population explosion. Traditionally, people in farming societies have had large families. Farm families needed children to help

Graph Skills In the next 20 years, the world's population will increase by more than one third. ▶According to these graphs, which regions will have a smaller percentage of the world's population in 2010 than they had in 1993? How will the population growth of the developing nations compare with that of the industrialized nations?

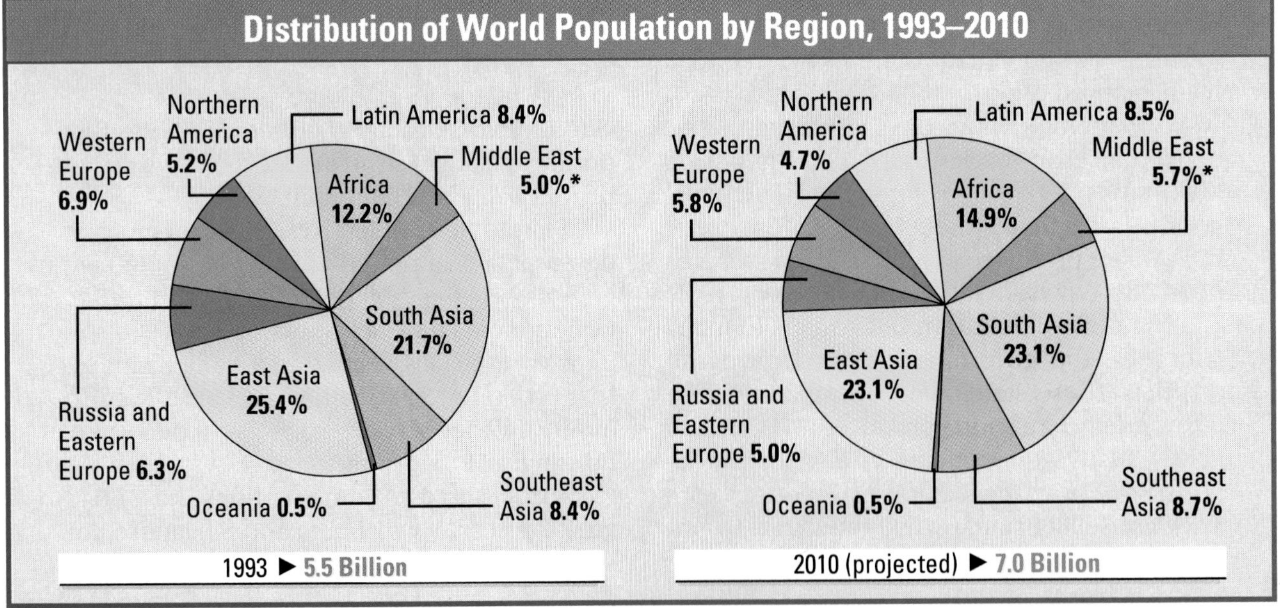

Source: *Encyclopaedia Britannica, 1994 Book of the Year.*

*Figures include some former Soviet republics.

Urban Crowding Population pressure today is creating a shortage of housing in cities throughout the world. In Rio de Janeiro, newcomers from rural areas of Brazil have settled in "favelas," or sprawling slums, that border modern apartment buildings. ***Choice*** Why are people from rural areas attracted to the cities despite poverty and overcrowding?

work the land. Also, because a large number of children died in infancy, a family had to have many children to ensure that some lived to adulthood.

Today, better health care has helped increase life expectancy. People live longer, and more children survive to have children themselves. The result is a population explosion, especially in developing nations.

Governments have taken steps to limit population growth. Some nations, such as China, have harsh laws that discourage parents from having more than one child. Others try to inform people about family planning. However, because of traditions and religious beliefs, many people choose to have large families. (See Connections With Literature, page 804, "If I Forget Thee, Oh Earth.")

Urbanization. The population explosion and the push to industrialize have led to rapid urbanization. Each year, millions of people leave farms for already crowded cities. The population of Mexico City, for example, doubled between 1980 and 1991 and is expected to double again between 1991 and 2000.

Some cities have very high population densities. Population density is the average number of people living in an area of a specific size. Parts of Bombay, India, have a population density of 939,000 people per square mile, compared to Chicago, with an average of 13,200 people per square mile.

Rapid population growth puts a great strain on poor nations. Cities cannot keep up with the need for housing, schools, or even basic health and sanitation services. In later chapters, you will learn why people choose to live in cities despite these problems.

Cultural change. Cities have contributed to changes in traditional ways of life. In cities, people may have fewer ties to family and community than people in farm villages.

Some leaders of developing nations note that western societies have paid a price for their wealth. They point to high crime rates, drug abuse, and the loss of traditional values in the industrial world. These leaders welcome western technology but warn against other parts of western culture. Their goal is to preserve the positive traditions of their own cultures.

A growing gap. Rapid population growth and the failure to modernize have widened the gap between developing and developed nations. In the poorest countries, crop failures brought on by drought or other natural disasters condemn millions to hunger. As you will read in the next section, rich nations support international efforts to aid developing countries.

SECTION 3 REVIEW

1. **Identify:** (a) economic diversity, (b) debt crisis, (c) population explosion.
2. **Define:** (a) cash crop, (b) modernization, (c) tariff, (d) privatization, (e) literacy, (f) population density.
3. Describe four goals of developing nations.
4. How has dependence on a single crop or commodity hurt many developing nations?
5. What effects has rapid population growth had on developing nations?
6. **Comparing** How are the changes taking place in developing nations today similar to those that occurred in Europe during the Industrial Revolution?
7. **Writing Across Cultures** Write a speech for a leader of a developing nation in which you welcome western technology but warn against other aspects of western culture.

4 GROWING INTERDEPENDENCE

FIND OUT

How is the world becoming more interdependent?

Why is concern for the environment increasing?

What efforts are underway to protect human rights?

How is technology shaping the future?

The doctors congratulated Ali Maow Maalin as he left the hospital in October 1977. Maalin, a health care worker, had just recovered from the deadly disease of smallpox. But Maalin's case was special. His was the last known case of smallpox in the world.

Maalin had been helping to vaccinate villagers in rural Somalia as part of a campaign to rid the world of smallpox. The World Health Organization, an agency of the United Nations, had begun the campaign in 1967. The campaign was so successful that today, only two frozen samples of the smallpox virus remain in the world.

The campaign against smallpox showed how international cooperation could solve a worldwide problem. Today, many problems, such as the illegal drug trade and air pollution, cross national boundaries. Governments have begun to realize that they must work together to find solutions to global problems.

International and Regional Organizations

In 1945, delegates from 51 nations signed the United Nations (UN) Charter. Member nations promised to preserve world peace and to cooperate in solving global social and economic problems. Today, the UN has grown to more than 160 member countries. By supporting UN programs, these nations recognize the interdependence of today's world.

Through its many agencies, the UN has helped developing nations. As you have just read, the World Health Organization supports programs to wipe out deadly diseases. Along with national and private groups, it is working to slow the spread of AIDS. Another UN agency, the Food and Agriculture Organization, provides experts to help farmers increase food production. The International Monetary Fund encourages the expansion of world trade. In times of crisis, the UN also sends emergency food and other aid.

The UN tries to solve threats to world peace. On occasion, it has sent troops to keep the peace in troubled areas. During the Cold War, however, the United States and the Soviet Union often used their power to limit UN action. With the easing of Cold War tensions, the UN hopes for increased cooperation in its peacekeeping efforts.

Both the UN and regional organizations support development projects to help people in poor nations. Groups that promote regional cooperation include the Organization of American States (OAS) and the Organization of African Unity (OAU). Member nations share common interests based on their location and work together to promote trade and economic growth.

Private groups also make a difference by helping people at the local level. For example, people in developing countries often find it hard to save enough money to set up businesses. With poor nutrition, little or no schooling or medical care, and few jobs, even the most energetic and talented people face a life of poverty. Private banks that give small loans offer a first step out of poverty. One of these banks is the Grameen Bank.

Bringing Hope to the Poor

Inside a tiny house in rural Bangladesh, five women sit cross-legged on a dirt floor. In hushed, serious voices, they negotiate a loan with an official of the Grameen Bank. The loan is small, just a few dollars. Yet it is enough to let one of the women open a pottery shop. At first, only one woman is eligible for a loan, but all five are responsible for seeing that the money is repaid. Once the first woman begins to

Banking in Bangladesh
Employees of the Grameen Bank in Bangladesh hold classes in sanitation, health care, and nutrition to enable people to better their conditions. The bank's goal is to aid the poor and landless by loaning money they can use to improve their lives.
Change How could a loan change a person's outlook on life?

repay her loan, plus interest, each of the other members of the group, in turn, will be allowed to borrow.

The Grameen Bank was founded in 1976 by Dr. Yunus, an economics professor in Bangladesh. He thought of the idea while trying to help a poor village woman get a loan worth about three dollars. He said, "I realized how difficult it was to convince the bank to make that loan without collateral." (Collateral is money or property that is pledged to guarantee a loan.) Dr. Yunus decided to open a bank that specialized in making small loans.

The development program set up by the Grameen Bank focuses on helping women. As in many other countries, women in Bangladesh seldom own property. With the loans, they can buy dairy cows or set up small businesses to make pottery or weave cloth.

The bank makes loans to groups of women. The women meet every week with a bank official. Those meetings give women a feeling of support. People from the bank also use the meetings to teach the women about health care, family planning, and nutrition. The women show that they take their responsibilities seriously when they recite this pledge:

> "Prosperity must we bring to our families,
> We shall have decent houses,
> We shall keep the family size small,
> We shall make sure that our children get an education . . .
> We shall always help each other."

The women feel pride in helping their families. "With the bank's assistance, I'm now able to provide food for my children every day and send them to school," said one woman who started a small business. In addition, as the women earn money, they feel that they are treated with more respect. ■

Issues of Global Concern

Through organizations like the Grameen Bank, some people in developing countries have taken the first steps away from poverty. Others, however, see little hope within their own nations. Every year, hundreds of thousands of people in developing nations move to industrial nations in the West. Today, millions of immigrants live in the United States. Many are refugees, seeking to escape poverty, war, or harsh governments. Floods of refugees have swept into other areas such as Australia, Hong Kong, France, and Germany. The problem of such refugees is one of many issues that concern both the rich and the poor nations.

Drug trade. Poverty and underdevelopment contribute to the illegal drug trade. Poor farmers in parts of Latin America and Asia have turned to growing crops that are made into illegal drugs. A farmer in Bolivia, for example, can make more money growing coca plants than raising food. Drug traffickers buy the coca from farmers and turn it into cocaine. The worldwide drug trade has grown into a huge business.

The drug trade has a direct effect on western industrial nations. Today, nations that produce illegal drugs and nations that buy them realize that they must work together. The United States and Bolivia, for example, have set up programs to convince farmers to grow other crops.

The environment. Two industrial disasters in the 1980s shocked the world into awareness of the hazards of development. In 1984, a chemical plant in Bhopal, India, accidentally released deadly gas into the air. The accident killed more than 2,100 people and permanently injured 86,000 others. Two years later, an explosion at the Chernobyl nuclear power plant in the Soviet Union released radioactive materials. The damage from the accident will be felt for years to come.

As you read in Chapter 1, we have begun to recognize how our actions add to pollution. Western nations, with their trucks, cars, and factories, have produced much of the world's pollution. As developing nations industrialize, they also become polluters. Many developing nations argue that they cannot afford expensive programs to end pollution. They must first develop their economies.

Mining in Brazil This open-pit mining operation in the interior of Brazil scars the land and endangers the environment. Many nations are faced with a dilemma: Should they protect the environment or earn money from the export of raw materials and cash crops? The answer to the question is not easy. ***Choice*** Give an argument to support each side of the debate.

Population pressures and the desire to earn income from raw materials have led to the destruction of tropical rain forests around the world. These forests provide much of the world's oxygen and support 90 percent of all plant and animal species. International efforts are underway to slow the destruction. These include debt-for-nature swaps, where lender nations forgive part of a borrower's debt. In return, the borrower must agree to protect its rain forests.

Human rights. Another global issue is human rights. In 1975, representatives from 35 nations signed the Helsinki Agreement. This agreement states that freedom of speech, religion, and the press are basic human rights. Nations agreed to protect the rights of their citizens to get a fair trial, to earn a living, and to live in safety from attack.

Private groups such as Amnesty International check human rights around the world. Through well-publicized campaigns, they expose abuses and pressure governments to respect the rights of their citizens.

During the 1980s, many nations imposed sanctions, or trade limits, on South Africa, because it practiced a harsh policy of racial segregation. This economic pressure helped convince South Africa to change its policy. (See pages 141–142.)

Technology and the future. People are turning to science to solve global problems. You will read in later chapters about the efforts of scientists to develop new food crops, combat diseases, and repair environmental damage. Some advances bring progress and make life easier for millions. They also promote cultural change.

Satellites Link the World

SCIENCE AND TECHNOLOGY

A farm family watched from their living room in Kansas. A group of college students watched from an apartment in Calcutta, India. Villagers in Zaire crowded into a local store to watch. At the same moment, all of them heard the command—"Let the Games begin!" The 1988 Summer Olympic Games were underway.

As the competition was broadcast from Seoul, South Korea, billions of viewers around the globe enjoyed a close-up view. Thanks to communications satellites, the world had become a smaller place.

In 1957, the Soviet Union launched the first artificial satellite. Since then, many other nations have put satellites into orbit. Today, about 1,000 artificial satellites are circling the Earth. They are used for weather forecasting, for scientific experiments, for spying, and for communication.

Communications satellites have had the greatest effect on everyday life. Two hundred years ago, it might have taken more than a month for a message to travel from the United States to Europe. Today, a message bounced off a satellite can reach anywhere on Earth in half a second. Most international telephone calls are now sent by satellite. In Indonesia, a satellite system allows communication among widely scattered islands. In Canada, satellites provide the only link to some remote areas of the Northwest Territory. One satellite expert has written:

> "Civilization is founded upon communication and the exchange of knowledge. Where communication is open and efficient, knowledge multiplies, countries prosper, and the likelihood of war is lessened. Better communication between the world's peoples can only lead to a better world. There is no finer tool for this task than the communications satellite."

1. How do satellites make the Earth seem smaller?
2. **Understanding Causes and Effects** (a) What are some benefits of satellites? (b) What might be some disadvantages?

SECTION 4 REVIEW

1. **Identify:** (a) United Nations, (b) Helsinki Agreement.
2. How do the United Nations and regional organizations promote international cooperation?
3. Explain why the drug trade and the environment are issues of global concern.
4. How have nations cooperated to promote human rights around the world?
5. **Defending a Position** Do you think technology can solve the world's problems? Give reasons to support your position.
6. **Writing Across Cultures** Imagine that you have moved from a developing country to the United States. Write a letter home describing differences in the cultures.

Chapter 2 Review

Understanding Vocabulary

Match each term at left with the correct definition at right.

1. nomad	**a.** person who sets up a business in order to make a profit
2. entrepreneur	**b.** pride in and devotion to one's country
3. westernization	**c.** selling state-owned industries to private investors
4. nationalism	**d.** person who travels from place to place
5. privatization	**e.** adopting western culture

Reviewing the Main Ideas

1. List the major achievements of Stone Age people.

2. What six features do all civilizations share?

3. Name one invention and one idea that spread among early civilizations as a result of cultural diffusion.

4. What three developments helped Europe emerge as a world power?

5. (a) How did nationalism increase the spread of imperialism? (b) How did the Cold War affect developing nations?

6. (a) How are developing nations attempting to achieve modernization? (b) How has the financial cost of modernization affected these nations?

7. How do international and regional organizations create interdependence?

8. Name four global concerns that affect both developing and industrial countries.

Reviewing Chapter Themes

1. The agricultural revolution changed the way people lived. (a) List three changes. (b) Explain how these changes led to the rise of the first civilizations.

2. The Industrial Revolution led to a new wave of European expansion overseas. (a) Give one reason nations wanted overseas colonies. (b) List two developments that made them possible.

3. The gap between rich and poor nations widened in recent years. (a) Give three causes. (b) Discuss how industrial nations help developing countries narrow this gap.

4. Improved technology has led to greater interdependence among nations. How is each of the following a global issue: (a) drug trade, (b) the environment?

Thinking Critically

1. Comparing Explain the difference between the first agricultural revolution and the second agricultural revolution.

2. Making Global Connections (a) List examples of objects that originated in the United States that are now available around the world. (b) List examples of objects from around the world that have been adopted by Americans.

3. Solving Problems Other than the debt-for-nature swap, how might the developed nations help slow or stop destruction of the rain forests?

Applying Your Skills

1. Reading Maps Study the map on page 29. (a) Name the rivers on which early civilizations began. (b) Where did the civilizations in the Americas develop? (See Skill Lesson 1 on page 48.)

2. Making a Generalization Use the photographs in the chapter to make a generalization about the developing world.

SKILL LESSON 1

Reading a Map: The Pacific Rim

Maps can be useful tools in learning about the world and its people. Some maps show physical features such as oceans, rivers, and mountains. Others provide information about people, such as how they use the land and where they live.

To read a map, it is important to look at all its parts. Most maps have a title, key, scale, directional arrow, and lines of latitude and longitude. Use the following steps to read the map below.

1. **Scan the map carefully to find out what information it contains.** The title tells you the subject of the map. The key explains what the symbols or colors on the map represent. **(a)** What is the title of this map? **(b)** List the countries labeled on the map. **(c)** Why do you think these nations are referred to as the Pacific Rim? **(d)** What do the stars on the map symbolize? **(e)** What is the capital of Malaysia?
2. **Practice reading distances on the map.** The scale tells you the actual distance in miles and kilometers between places on the map. **(a)** About how far in miles is it from Bangkok to Jakarta? **(b)** In kilometers?
3. **Study the map to read directions.** The directional arrow shows which way is north, south, east, and west. **(a)** Which Pacific Rim nations are west of Japan? **(b)** In which direction is Singapore from the Philippines?
4. **Locate places on the map using map coordinates.** The horizontal lines on the map are called lines of latitude. Each line of latitude is numbered in degrees north or south of the Equator. The vertical lines on the map are called lines of longitude. Each of these lines is numbered in degrees east or west of the Prime Meridian. Latitude and longitude are helpful in locating places on a map. **(a)** Which capital is located at 35° N/139° E? **(b)** Where is Phnom Penh located?

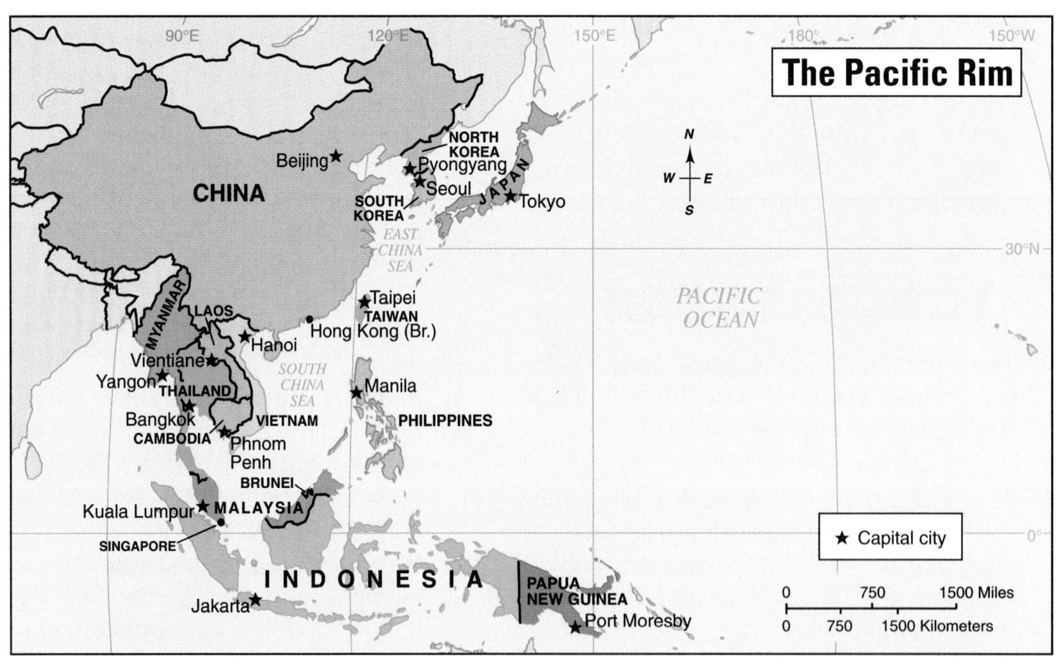

SKILL LESSON 2

Making Generalizations: The Quality of Life

A generalization is a broad statement that is based on data, or facts. It is a statement that links information or ideas together. To make a generalization based on data, look for relationships among the data. Does a rise in one statistic accompany a rise or fall in another statistic?

The chart below contains information about five countries. The male life expectancy refers to the number of years a male child born in a given year can be expected to live. Population doubling time, which is the number of years it takes for the population to double in size, provides a clue to how fast the population of a given place is growing. The lower the number given for population doubling time, the higher the rate of growth. Electricity consumed per person provides a clue to a country's level of industrialization, urbanization, and income.

Analyze the information below, using the numbered steps as a guide.

1. **Study the information on the chart.** (a) What information does the chart provide for each country? (b) Which country has the highest male life expectancy? (c) Which country has the fewest people per doctor? (d) Which country has the lowest male life expectancy? (e) How many people per doctor are there in that country?
2. **Look for relationships in the information.** (a) What is the apparent relationship between life expectancy and the number of people per doctor? (b) Does the availability of food seem to have a bearing on life expectancy? (c) Are the countries with the highest literacy rates the countries that are most industrialized or least industrialized? (d) Are the countries with the fastest-growing population more or less industrialized?
3. **Make a general statement based on the facts.** (a) What are the characteristics of highly industrialized societies? (b) What would you say are the characteristics of less-industrialized societies? (c) What two suggestions would you make to improve the quality of life in societies that are less industrialized?

Quality of Life

	Minimum food supply available	Male life expectancy in years	People per doctor	Literacy rate	Population doubling time in years	Kilowatt hours of electricity per person
United States	138%	73	416	95.5	99	12,281
Venezuela	99%	67	590	92.2	28	2,893
South Korea	120%	69	1,007	96.3	77	3,020
Bangladesh	88%	56	5,264	34.8	32	77
Nigeria	93%	51	4,946	42.4	22	88

Source: *Encyclopaedia Britannica, 1994 Book of the Year.*

WORLD

The All-American Slurp

Lensey Namioka

INTRODUCTION When she was a teenager, Lensey Namioka (1929–) moved with her family from China to the United States. Her family, like many Chinese, probably had some trouble adjusting to life and culture in the United States. The narrator in this excerpt from Namioka's short story, "The All-American Slurp," shows how easily misunderstandings can occur when two cultures meet.

Vocabulary Before you read the selection, find the meaning of these words in a dictionary: emigrated, mortified.

The first time our family was invited out to dinner in America, we disgraced ourselves while eating celery. We had emigrated to this country from China, and during our early days here we had a hard time with American table manners.

In China we never ate celery raw, or any other kind of vegetable raw. We always had to disinfect the vegetables in boiling water first. When we were presented with our first relish tray, the raw celery caught us unprepared.

We had been invited to dinner by our neighbors, the Gleasons. After arriving at the house, we shook hands with our hosts and packed ourselves into a sofa. As our family of four sat stiffly in a row, my younger brother and I stole glances at our parents for a clue as to what to do next.

Mrs. Gleason offered the relish tray to Mother. The tray looked pretty, with its tiny red radishes, curly sticks of carrots, and long, slender stalks of pale green celery. "Do try some of the celery, Mrs. Lin," she said. "It's from a local farmer, and it's sweet."

Mother picked up one of the green stalks, and Father followed suit. Then I picked up a stalk, and my brother did too. So there we sat, each with a stalk of celery in our right hand.

Mrs. Gleason kept smiling. "Would you like to try some of the dip, Mrs. Lin? It's my own recipe: sour cream and onion flakes, with a dash of Tabasco sauce."

Most Chinese don't care for dairy products, and in those days I wasn't even ready to drink fresh milk. Sour cream sounded perfectly revolting. Our family shook our heads in unison.

Mrs. Gleason went off with the relish tray to the other guests, and we carefully watched to see what they did. Everyone seemed to eat the raw vegetables quite happily.

Mother took a bite of her celery. *Crunch.* "It's not bad!" she whispered.

Father took a bite of his celery. *Crunch.* "Yes, it is good," he said, looking surprised.

I took a bite, and then my brother. *Crunch, crunch.* It was more than good; it was delicious. Raw celery has a slight sparkle, a zingy taste that you don't get in cooked celery. When Mrs. Gleason came around with the relish tray, we each took another stalk of celery, except my brother. He took two.

There was only one problem: long strings ran through the length of the stalk, and they got caught in my teeth. When I help my mother in the kitchen, I always pull the string out before slicing celery.

I pulled the strings out of my stalk. *Z-z-zip, z-z-zip.* My brother followed suit. *Z-z-zip, z-z-zip, z-z-zip.* To my left, my parents were taking care of their own stalks. *Z-z-zip, z-z-zip, z-z-zip.*

Suddenly I realized that there was dead silence except for our zipping. Looking up, I saw that the eyes of everyone in the room were on our family. Mr. and Mrs. Gleason, their daughter Meg, who was my friend, and their neighbors the Badels—they were all staring at us as we busily pulled the strings of our celery.

That wasn't the end of it. Mrs. Gleason announced that dinner was served and invited us to the dining table. It was lavishly covered with platters of food, but we couldn't see any chairs around the table. So we helpfully carried over some dining room chairs and sat down. All the other guests just stood there.

Mrs. Gleason bent down and whispered to us, "This is a buffet dinner. You help yourselves to some food and eat it in the living room."

Our family beat a retreat back to the sofa as if chased by enemy soldiers. For the rest of the evening, too mortified to go back to the dining table, I nursed a bit of potato salad on my plate.

Next day Meg and I got on the school bus together. I wasn't sure how she would feel about me after the spectacle our family made at the party. But she was just the same as usual, and the only reference she made to the party was, "Hope you and your folks got enough to eat last night. You certainly didn't take very much. Mom never tries to figure out how much food to prepare. She just puts everything on the table and hopes for the best."

I began to relax. The Gleasons' dinner party wasn't so different from a Chinese meal after all. My mother also puts everything on the table and hopes for the best. . . .

Dong Kingman, a Chinese American artist who lives in California, painted this watercolor, *San Francisco Festival.* Kingman is well known for his paintings of West Coast life. In this painting, Chinese Americans in San Francisco are celebrating the Chinese New Year. Why do people everywhere continue to practice customs that are part of their cultural heritage?

Source: "The All-American Slurp" by Lensey Namioka from *Visions*, edited by Donald R. Gallo.

THINKING ABOUT LITERATURE

1. What cultural differences are highlighted by the family's experience at the Gleasons' dinner party?
2. How does the narrator realize that her family might not be so different from American families after all?
3. **Recognizing Points of View** (a) Show how the "errors" made by the Lin family made sense from their point of view. (b) What mistakes might a family from the United States make at a Chinese dinner party?

A Culture of Cultures

Some Americans are not aware of how connected the cultures of the world have always been. They do not realize that many of the things they think of as American actually come from different places.

Some Americans, in fact, are like Mr. Smith.

The Annual Picnic

Every year, the Smith family and the Jones family get together to celebrate Independence Day. Everybody has a great time—until Mr. Smith and Mrs. Jones get into their yearly argument.

It always starts the same way. Mr. Smith begins to brag about America. Mrs. Jones, who comes from England, then interrupts to ask, "What do you mean by America?" (Mr. Jones says it is because his wife is still angry about the American Revolution.)

The first year, Mr. Smith answered simply, "America is America."

Mrs. Jones replied, "America includes South America as well as North America. Besides, the whole hemisphere was named after an Italian navigator, Amerigo Vespucci." Mr. Smith coughed but said nothing.

The next year Mr. Smith was better prepared. When Mrs. Jones interrupted him, he said, "America is its people. America is Americans."

"But everybody here came from someplace else," argued Mrs. Jones. "Look around! There are people from Costa Rica, Jordan, and Vietnam. Even the Native Americans migrated here from Asia." Mr. Smith murmured something under his breath and walked away.

At the following year's picnic, Mr. Smith said, "America is the land—our eastern woodlands, Great Lakes, midwestern prairies, and colorful deserts."

"Really?" Mrs. Jones asked. "Don't you share these woodlands, lakes, prairies, and deserts with your neighbors, Canada and Mexico?" Frustrated, Mr. Smith pounded his palm with his fist.

Diverse Roots

This year, Mr. Smith was sure he had the answer. He said, "America is its history and traditions—like the Fourth of July. You can't get more American than the Fourth of July!"

"What's so American about it? The number 4, like all the numbers we use, is of Arabic origin and July is named after a Roman emperor."

Mr. Smith was not going to give up so easily this time. "You English think you're so smart. What about the 'Star-Spangled Banner' we just finished singing?"

Mrs. Jones smiled. "Actually, the tune comes from an old English song."

"How about the Declaration of Independence?" demanded Mr. Smith.

"Most of the ideas in it come from Scottish and French philosophers. Even the author of the Declaration, your Thomas Jefferson, admitted that."

"Our flag? Old Glory?"

"The flag is a Chinese invention."

"Well, what about this delicious all-American picnic of—"

"Actually," Mrs. Jones was quick to explain, "the word 'picnic' comes from the French *piquenique,* and the lawn we're picnicking on grew from Bermudan grass seed."

"As I was just saying," Mr. Smith continued, turning red, "what about this delicious picnic of all-American foods?"

"Like the coleslaw?" asked Mrs. Jones. "A dish from Holland. The hot dogs are from cattle, first domesticated in East Asia—but they're kosher hot dogs, so they were made according to Hebrew dietary laws."

Mrs. Jones continued. "The potatoes in the potato salad were first grown in Peru. The watermelon is of West African origin. The lemonade is made from lemons, which originally came from Central Asia, and is sweetened with sugar from cane, a plant first raised in India thousands of years ago. Even the plates are made of paper—invented by the Chinese."

Rising Arguments

"Forget the food!" shouted Mr. Smith. "How about the activities? Don't tell me we haven't been doing some all-American things today!"

"Like the baseball game we were playing?" asked Mrs. Jones. "It's derived from our English game, cricket. In fact, people played ball in the ancient Maya civilization."

Mr. Smith was getting frustrated. "Oh, yeah? Well, what about tonight's concert? It's all-American rock-and-roll—"

"Sorry to disappoint you again," said Mrs. Jones. "But it's a musical form based on African rhythms and modified by English, Scottish, and Irish folk tunes. And I'll bet that tonight's band features some guitars, an invention of the Spanish, you know. The piano, of course, is from Italy. And drums are native to nearly every culture around the globe."

"I give up," said Mr. Smith wearily. "I guess we can't even claim the Fourth of July as our own."

"I wouldn't say that," replied Mrs. Jones. "After all, it's still the birthday of the United States of America."

Mr. Smith beamed. "That's right! We're the only country to celebrate our independence on the Fourth of July!" With that, Mr. Smith and Mrs. Jones agreed to stop arguing—at least, until next year.

1. According to Mrs. Jones, what cultures contributed to (a) the Declaration of Independence, (b) the food at the picnic, (c) rock-and-roll music?
2. **Applying Information** How does American culture illustrate the process of cultural diffusion?
3. **Writing Across Cultures** List 10 ways in which life in your home, school, and community reflects a variety of cultures.

UNIT 1 REVIEW

Reviewing the Main Ideas

1. Describe your town or city using the geography themes of location and place.
2. (a) List four types of special-purpose maps and tell what information is provided by each. (b) What kind of map is on page 62?
3. (a) What is culture? (b) What role does the family play in shaping a society's culture? (c) How does language contribute to culture?
4. (a) Why do people form governments? (b) What is the difference between a democracy and a dictatorship?
5. (a) What is cultural diffusion? (b) Give an example of how a custom or idea is passed on through cultural diffusion.
6. Describe the key features of the Industrial Revolution.
7. (a) How did industrialization contribute to imperialism? (b) How did imperialism affect the economies of Africa, Asia, and Latin America? (c) How are developing nations trying to improve their economies?
8. What are some of the problems facing developing nations?

Thinking Critically

1. **Evaluating Information** (a) List the major landforms. (b) On which landforms is life more difficult? On which is life easier? Explain.
2. **Making Global Connections** Cultures undergo change in many ways. (a) How does American culture influence other cultures around the world? (b) How is American culture influenced by other cultures? (c) Why are some cultures more influential than others?
3. **Understanding Causes and Effects** (a) What were three causes of the second agricultural revolution? (b) What three effects occurred as a result of the revolution? (See Skill Lesson, page 628.)

Applying Your Skills

1. **Analyzing a Quotation** Read the quotations on page 22. (a) Do you agree or disagree with Nan Donohoe's opinion of the differences between farm and city life? Explain. (b) Do you think Nan's opinions are ethnocentric? Why or why not?
2. **Reading a Graph** Study the pie graph below and answer the following questions. (a) What percentage of world population is Hindu? (b) Which religion has the greatest percentage of followers? (c) What two religions make up about 50 percent of the world's population? (d) Why do you think that in the twentieth century people in the Middle East, Eastern Europe, and the Soviet Union rarely changed their religion even when faced with revolution, invasion, or war? (See Skill Lesson, page 238.)

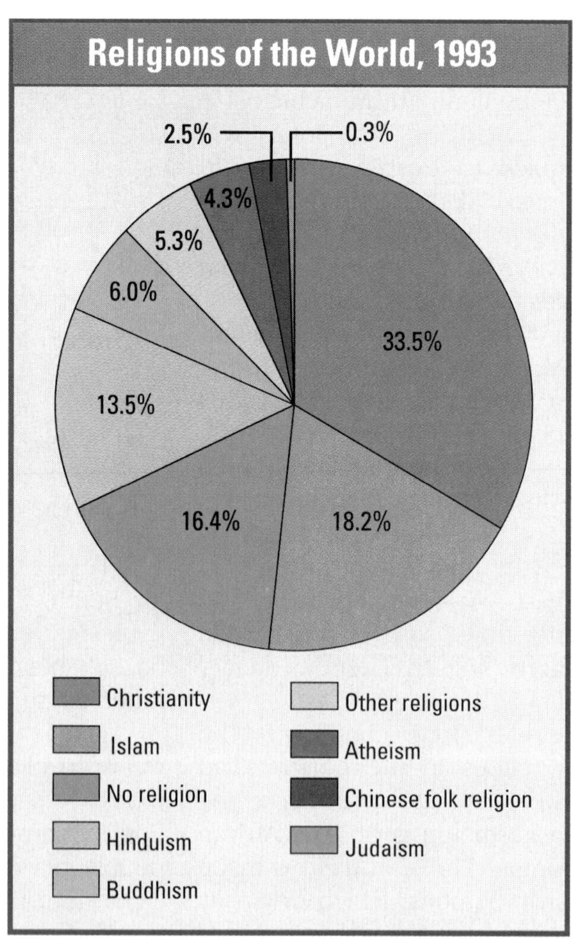

Source: *Encyclopaedia Britannica, 1994 Book of the Year.*

Learning by Doing

1. **Creating a Map** On an outline map of the world, label the continents, oceans, Mediterranean Sea, and the following rivers: Nile; Tigris and Euphrates; Indus; and Huang He. Draw and label the Equator and a directional arrow. In a color key, identify the five early civilizations. Key the colors to the map. Next, label the modern countries in which the earliest civilizations were located. See the map on page 29.
2. **Making Flash Cards** Make a set of flash cards based on all of the vocabulary words in Chapters 1 and 2. Write each vocabulary word on one side of an index card and its definition on the other side. You may want to share this assignment with a partner. Practice flashing the vocabulary words and recalling the definitions. Then, use the flash cards with a group or another student.
3. **Making a Chart** Make a comparison chart based on information in Chapter 2, titled *The First and Second Agricultural Revolutions.* Make three columns. In the first column, write *Facts*. Beneath it write: *Who, How, Where, When, Effects*. Title the remaining columns: *The First Revolution, The Second Revolution*. Fill in the chart, and compare entries with a classmate.

WRITER'S Workshop

Analyzing a Question Before Writing

Before you answer a question, look for key words. The key word is usually an instruction word. Some common instruction words are: *Explain* (make understandable by telling how or why); *Compare* (provide similarities or differences); *Describe* (provide a detailed account of); and *Summarize* (tell important ideas in as few words as possible).

Sometimes the key word is a question word. Some common question words and their meanings are: *Why* (give reasons), *How* (tell in what way or by what means), and *What* (give specific examples).

Some words or phrases in a question tell you how to limit your answer to a certain person, event, geographic area, or time period. Other words or phrases might tell you the number of examples or ideas you need to include.

Practice Analyze this question: *What are the five themes of geography?*

1. What does the key word tell you to do?
2. What clue tells you how many themes you need to include?
3. What does the clue of *geography* tell you?

Writing to Learn

1. Write a folktale that conveys a basic belief or value of your native culture. Before writing, decide on the value, such as honesty, wisdom, or patience, that your folktale will teach. Next, write a short plot outline. As you are writing the first draft, describe the characters and focus their dialogue on the topic. Check for word choice and for whether the lesson in your folktale is clear. Proofread your story. Check for spelling and grammar errors and make a final copy. Read your story to the class.

2. Write an essay about the clothes, food, films, or leisure activities of your native culture. Select a topic and brainstorm a list of points or examples you wish to make. Write a brief outline. As you write your essay, express and support your opinions with vivid descriptions and specific examples. Revise your first draft. Make sure the details support the topic sentences and your closing statement sums up your observations. Proofread your writing. Check for spelling and grammar errors and make a final copy. You might publish your essay in the school newspaper.

UNIT 2 AFRICA

UNIT OUTLINE

1 This painting on glass of an Islamic leader reflects both religious and artistic traditions of Senegal.

2 Children in South Africa are on their way to school. South Africa's new all-race government has vowed to improve education for blacks, whose schooling was neglected under white rule.

3 More than 1 million people live in Nairobi, the capital of Kenya. Nairobi is a busy city that serves as the nation's center of business, transportation, and communication.

Early History — 1400					
History and Politics		▲ **750 B.C.** Kushites conquer Nile Valley		▲ **1324** Mansa Musa travels to Egypt	▲ **1400s** Europeans reach Africa
Society and Culture		▲ **3000 B.C.** Egyptian civilization emerges		▲ **1300s** Rulers of Zimbabwe organize a kingdom	▲ **1400s–1700s** Benin artists create fine works in bronze, brass, and ivory
Economics and Technology	▲ **6000 B.C.** Egyptians live in farming villages				▲ **1300s–1500s** Trade thrives between East Africans and Arabs

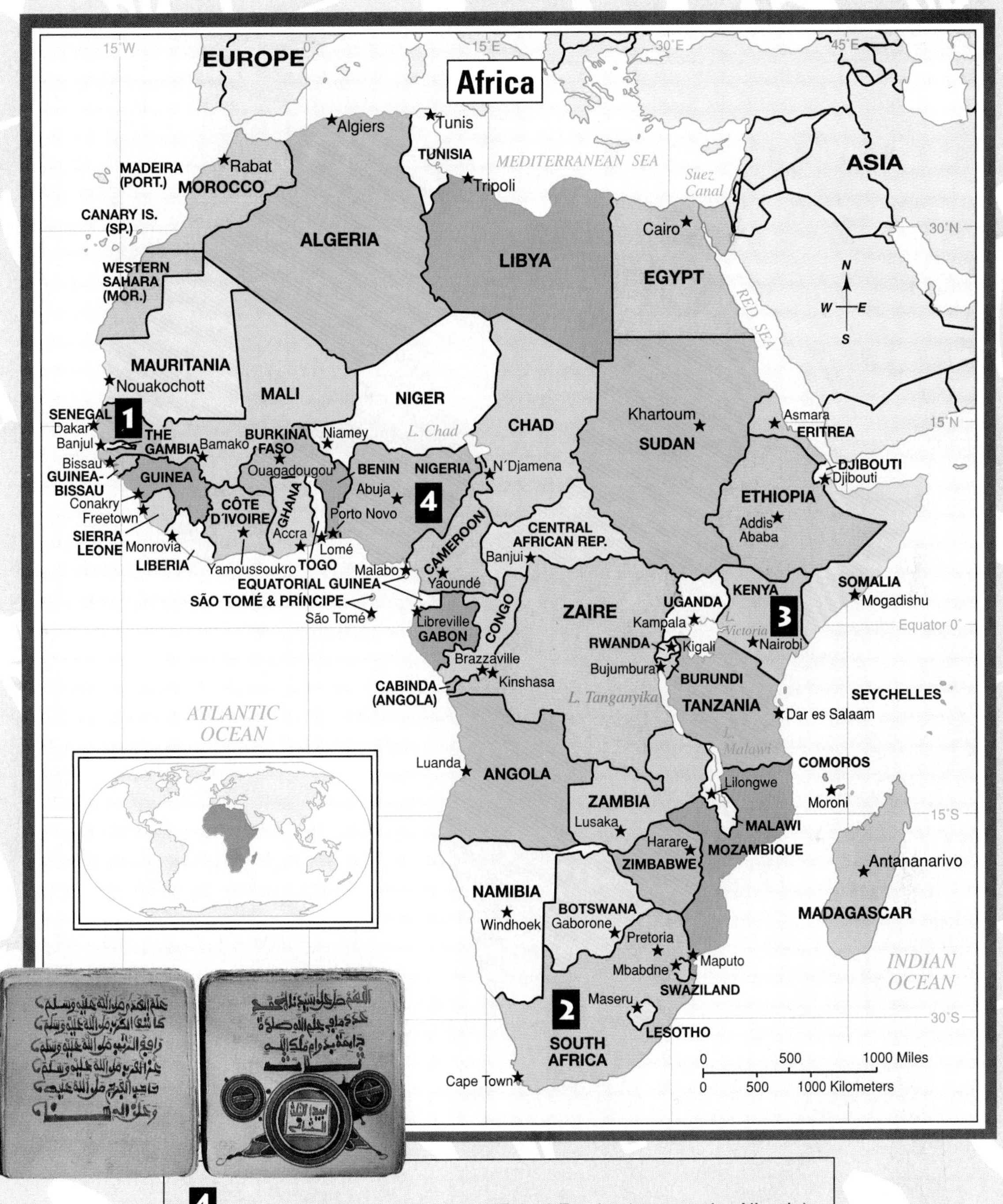

4 Muslim scholars in the Hausa-Fulani Empire (present-day Nigeria) copied these pages of the Koran in the late 1700s.

1600		1800		2000
▲ **1591** Songhai falls to Moroccan invaders		▲ **1800s** Europeans begin to colonize Africa	▲ **1900s** Pan-African movement begins	▲ **1994** All races vote in South Africa for the first time
		▲ **1787** Sierra Leone founded as settlement for freed slaves		▲ **1958** Chinua Achebe writes *Things Fall Apart*
▲ **1600** African slave trade established	▲ **1700s** African slave trade at its highest point		▲ **1869** Suez Canal completed	▲ **1980s** Economic sanctions imposed on South Africa

Chapter 3

Geography and Early History of Africa

Mount Kilimanjaro The vast continent of Africa includes a wide variety of landforms, including mountains. The snow-covered summit of Mount Kilimanjaro in Tanzania, seen here, provides a sharp contrast with the plains at the base of the mountain. ***Diversity*** How do varied landforms and climate contribute to cultural diversity?

Chapter Outline

"There was wind and rain. And there was also thunder and terrible lightning." So begins a story of creation as told by the Kikuyu people of Kenya. While the land was in darkness, the Creator put up a holy tree. At the foot of the tree, the Creator set the first people—the man Kikuyu and the woman Mumbi. Immediately, the sun rose.

The Creator then took Kikuyu and Mumbi from his holy mountain to the "country of ridges." There the Creator showed them all the land. He told them,

> "This land I hand over to you. O man and woman
> It's yours to rule and farm in peace, sacrificing
> Only to me, your God, under my sacred tree."

Through stories like this one, the peoples of Africa explain their roots. The stories differ across the continent because Africans belong to many distinct groups. In this unit on Africa, you will learn about the forces from within and from without that have shaped Africa's many cultures.

CHAPTER PERSPECTIVE

In Africa, as elsewhere in the world, people have adapted to many different environments. The story of Kikuyu and Mumbi, for example, describes mountains and ridges that are found in East Africa. In other parts of Africa, stories tell of mighty rivers, flat grasslands, and wide deserts. Such stories show how differences in climate and topography shape cultures.

As you read, look for these chapter themes:

- Geographic features have influenced where people live in Africa and contributed to the cultural diversity of the continent.
- Since earliest times, people, goods, and ideas have crossed the physical barriers that divide Africa and separate it from other regions.
- Recent evidence suggests that the first humans lived in Africa.
- The fertile Nile Valley supported one of the world's first great civilizations.

Literature Connections

In this chapter, you will encounter passages from the following works.

"Creation Story," Kikuyu tale

"A Hymn to the Nile," from the Papyrus Scrolls

For other literature suggestions, see Connections With Literature, pages 804–808.

1 THE SHAPE OF THE LAND

FIND OUT

What is Africa's relative location in the world?

How have landforms influenced movement across Africa?

What natural resources are important to African nations?

Vocabulary escarpment, cataract, hydroelectric power

Thousands of years ago, hot ash and melted rock spewed out of the earth, creating a giant mountain. Today, Mount Kilimanjaro towers 19,340 feet (5,895 m) over northeastern Tanzania. Kilimanjaro stands almost on the Equator. Yet, because of the mountain's great height, its summit is covered with snow all year round.

Mount Kilimanjaro is a spectacular sight. It is just one of the wide variety of landforms that make up the African continent.

A Vast Continent

Africa is the world's second-largest continent, the biggest after Asia. It is more than three times the size of the United States. It also contains more independent nations than any other continent on Earth—55 in all.

Location. Africa is centrally located on the Earth's surface. It straddles the Equator, extending for thousands of miles north and south of that line. The continent stands between two major oceans. To the west is the Atlantic Ocean and to the east lies the Indian Ocean. The Mediterranean Sea in the north and the Red Sea in the northeast also border Africa.

Although oceans set Africa apart from other regions, they also link it with the rest of the world. In ancient times, ships sailed along the Mediterranean and Red Sea coasts. These ships carried people, goods, and ideas between Africa and Europe and the Middle East. As you will read in Chapter 4, seasonal winds also allowed traders to sail from Africa across the Indian Ocean to South Asia. Today, Africa's location places it squarely in the center of world transportation routes.

Regions. Africa, like other continents, has many distinct regions. The main regions are North Africa, West Africa, East Africa, Central Africa, and Southern Africa. Geographic features give each region its own identity, although great variety also exists within each region. Regional differences contribute to the diversity of African peoples.

North Africa stretches from Morocco in the west to Egypt in the east. Because of its location, it has always had close contact with Europe and the Middle East. At the same time, North Africa is closely linked to the regions south of the Sahara. These regions are sometimes referred to as sub-Saharan Africa.

South of the Sahara, West Africa bulges into the Atlantic. It includes many nations, from Mauritania to Nigeria. Central Africa includes the large nation of Zaire, on the Equator. In East Africa, the largest nations are Kenya, Uganda, and Tanzania. The region of Southern Africa stretches from the Atlantic Ocean to the Indian Ocean and includes Zimbabwe, Zambia, and South Africa. (See the map on page 62.)

Landforms

Most of Africa is a vast plateau. Toward the edges of the continent are mountain ranges, such as the Atlas Mountains in the northwest and the Drakensberg Mountains in the southeast. Narrow plains fringe the coasts.

Plateaus. The plateaus of Africa lie at different elevations. The highest plateaus are in the east and south. The continent then tilts gradually downward toward the west and north. Large basins, swamps, and lakes are scattered across the plateaus.

As you move from the plateaus toward the coast, the land drops sharply. In places, escarpments, or steep cliffs, divide the plateau from the coastal plain. These changes in elevation affect the course of Africa's rivers. As rivers flow from the plateau to the coast, they tumble over a series of cataracts, or large waterfalls, and rapids.

Over thousands of years, Africans have migrated across the plateaus. Traders followed well-traveled routes through parts of the continent. The land, however, discouraged early Europeans who tried to explore the continent. When they tried to sail up rivers, they found the way blocked by cataracts.

Great Rift Valley. The Great Rift Valley slices through the eastern part of the continent. This giant fault, or break, in the Earth's crust runs from the Red Sea to the Zambezi River. The valley—actually a series of mountains and valleys—was formed millions of years ago. (See the feature at right.)

Flanking the Rift Valley are high, clifflike walls. Over centuries, rich soils from the highlands have washed down into the valley. As a result, the region contains some of Africa's most fertile farmland. The Rift Valley is rich in minerals and metals, but mining and transportation are difficult. The sheer cliffs, high mountains, and deep valleys make building roads and railroads costly and dangerous.

Rivers

The rivers of Africa provide fish, water for irrigation, and a means of transportation. They are also a source of hydroelectric power, energy produced by moving water. Today, African nations are constructing dams across rivers to supply cities and industries with electricity.

The Nile. Flowing for 4,160 miles (6,695 km) northward across Africa, the Nile River is the longest in the world. The Nile has played a key role in human development. As you will read, one of the earliest civilizations developed in the fertile Nile Valley of northeastern Africa.

Until recently, the Nile flooded each year. The flood waters deposited silt in the river valley, adding nutrients to the soil. The rich farmlands along the Nile supported a large population.

The Great Rift Valley

After sailing over the Great Rift Valley in a hot-air balloon, a visitor commented:

> "The view of the Rift made a tremendous impression on me, partly because I was terrified. . . . Mountains often have cliffs, but not, in general, a succession of steep descents. The ground fell away dramatically, as if giant steps had been carved in the rock."

The Rift is a split in the African continent. It extends 4,000 miles (6,437 km) from the Middle East southward along East Africa to Mozambique.

Several natural forces have formed the Great Rift Valley. According to scientists, the plates that make up the Earth's crust have moved apart over millions of years, creating the deep gap. (The island of Madagascar may have split off from Africa in the same way.) Erosion has deposited rich soil in the base of the valley. Volcanic activity has created mountains, such as Mount Kilimanjaro and Mount Kenya.

The rift zone supports a wide variety of economic activities. The volcanic soil provides fertile farmland. Two of the Earth's deepest lakes—Lake Tanganyika and Lake Malawi—cover the western branch of the rift along the borders of Zaire and Malawi. The lakes are a rich source of salt and soda ash. Steam and hot springs lie below the surface of the valley. Scientists hope to harness these sources of clean energy.

Other scientists are interested in the region for a totally different reason. The rich volcanic ash is a good agent for preserving bones. Archaeologists have dug up the world's oldest human fossils in the Great Rift Valley, leading to the theory that this may be the site of the origin of all humans.

1. What natural forces have helped create the Great Rift Valley?
2. **Forecasting** As shifting continues in the Great Rift Valley, how might the map of Africa look in 40 million years?

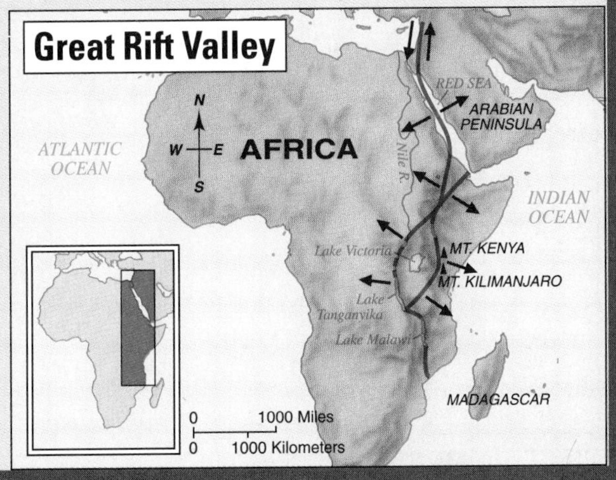

Technology has changed the yearly flooding of the Nile. In 1970, Egyptians completed the massive Aswan Dam, located on the upper Nile. The dam supplies hydroelectric power. It also created a vast lake that stores water for irrigation. The dam, however, has been a mixed blessing. It traps the rich silt that once renewed Egyptian soil, so farmers in the lower Nile Valley now must buy fertilizer.

In the 1800s, European explorers became fascinated with the idea of finding the source of the Nile. In daring expeditions, they competed to reach the headwaters of the great

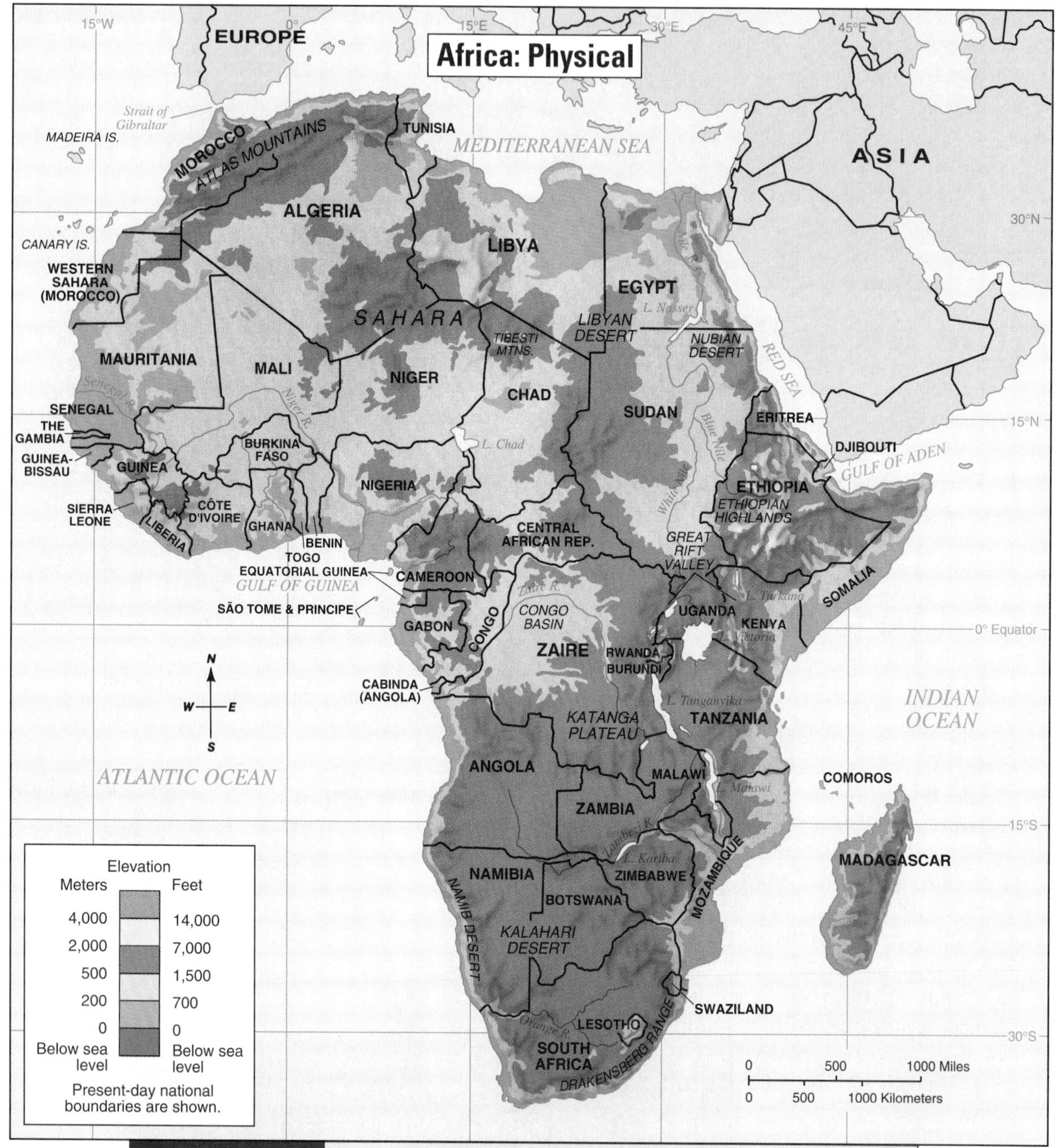

MAP STUDY

Africa is the second-largest continent in the world. Most of its land is a plateau.

1. **Location** What two rivers come together to form Africa's longest river?
2. **Region** (a) Which parts of Africa have the highest elevation? (b) Which parts have the lowest elevation?
3. **Drawing Conclusions** In what parts of Africa do you think most people live today? Check your answer by referring to the map on page 782.

river. In time, they traced the river's various sources in the highlands of East Africa.

Other key rivers. The Zaire (zah EER) River drains a huge area in Central Africa. The river is fed by many tributaries on both sides of the Equator before emptying into the Atlantic Ocean. The Zaire carries an enormous volume of water, and it provides hydroelectric power. Only part of the river, however, can be used for transportation. Waterfalls and rapids prevent boats from traveling all the way to the ocean.

The Niger River rises in the West African nations of Sierra Leone and Guinea. It first flows north toward the Sahara, where it forms a large inland swamp. Then it turns southeast and plunges from the plateau toward the sea. Along the Niger, farmers pump water to irrigate crops of rice and millet. Local residents pole long, pointed boats through the waters and use nets to catch fish. Large riverboats carry passengers and cargo along the deeper sections of the Niger.

The Zambezi River in Southern Africa is fed by sources in Angola and Zambia. As it descends to the sea, the Zambezi rushes over Victoria Falls. The Zambezi forms the border between Zimbabwe and Zambia, where Lake Kariba and the huge Kariba Dam are found. The dam provides hydroelectric power to both nations.

Natural Resources

Africa's rivers are a source of precious metals. For more than 2,000 years, people in Africa have sifted through riverbeds to uncover gold and diamonds. They have also mined gold from pits deep below the surface. For centuries, West Africa served as a major source of gold for Europe. The desire to discover gold was one cause of European interest in Africa.

Mineral exports. Today, African nations sell many other valuable resources to the industrial world. Zaire and Zambia have huge deposits of copper. South Africa, Zaire, and Botswana are among the world's leading suppliers of platinum and cobalt. Nigeria and Angola have built offshore oil platforms to

Mining Mineral Wealth Many African nations depend on the export of natural resources for income. Pictured here is a mining operation in Mauritania, a nation of West Africa. Mauritania earns three fourths of its national income from its export of iron ore. ***Interdependence*** How do Mauritania's natural resources link it to other nations?

pump oil from underwater sources. Libya, Algeria, and Gabon also have oil deposits.

Some African countries lack the money to develop their mineral resources. As you will read in Chapter 5, they have allowed foreign companies to invest in mining and other ventures. As a result, much of the profits from these resources flow out of Africa.

Uneven distribution. Although Africa is rich in natural resources, those resources are unevenly distributed. Only a few African nations, for example, have oil to export. The rest must rely on expensive imported oil.

Some countries, like Uganda, have relatively few mineral resources but have rich soils and abundant water. The fertile soils of the Great Rift Valley allow Ugandan farmers to produce a variety of crops. Much of Africa, however, is not very fertile. In addition, uncertain rainfall often makes farming difficult.

SECTION 1 REVIEW

1. **Locate:** (a) Atlas Mountains, (b) Great Rift Valley, (c) Nile River, (d) Zaire River, (e) Niger River, (f) Zambezi River.
2. **Identify:** (a) Aswan Dam, (b) Kariba Dam.
3. **Define:** (a) escarpment, (b) cataract, (c) hydroelectric power.
4. (a) Describe the relative location of Africa. (b) How has Africa's location both set it apart and linked it to the rest of the world?
5. (a) How have the landforms of Africa encouraged movement of people and goods? (b) How have they discouraged movement?
6. What resources do African nations export to the world?
7. **Defending a Position** Some people believe the Aswan Dam is a major achievement. Others consider it a sad mistake. What evidence would you give to support each argument?
8. **Writing Across Cultures** Look at physical maps of Africa and the United States. Make a list of all the African countries that have the same landforms as your state.

2 CLIMATE AND DIVERSITY

FIND OUT

How do climates differ across Africa?

What ways of life did Africans develop?

How do Africa's languages reflect its cultural diversity?

Vocabulary tropics, leaching, drought, desertification

If you visit Africa, you can probably leave your winter coat home. Africa is the most tropical of all the continents. Temperatures in most parts of Africa are generally warm or hot.

Rainfall, however, varies greatly from one part of Africa to another. To a large degree, it is rainfall—or lack of it—that determines climate on the continent. Indeed, the people of Botswana consider rainfall so important that they call their money *pula*, which means "rain."

The Roles of Latitude and Elevation

The Equator runs nearly through the middle of Africa. As a result, 80 percent of the continent is in the tropics, the area between the Tropic of Cancer and the Tropic of Capricorn. Because of this tropical location, African climates are generally warm throughout the year.

The coolest regions of Africa are found in the highlands. Because temperature drops as elevation increases, temperatures in the highlands are considerably lower than in low-lying regions. For example, Accra, Ghana, on the West African coast, has hot, humid weather. Temperatures reach the 80s F. On the other hand, Nairobi, Kenya, lies at about the same latitude as Accra but is 5,300 feet (1,615 m)

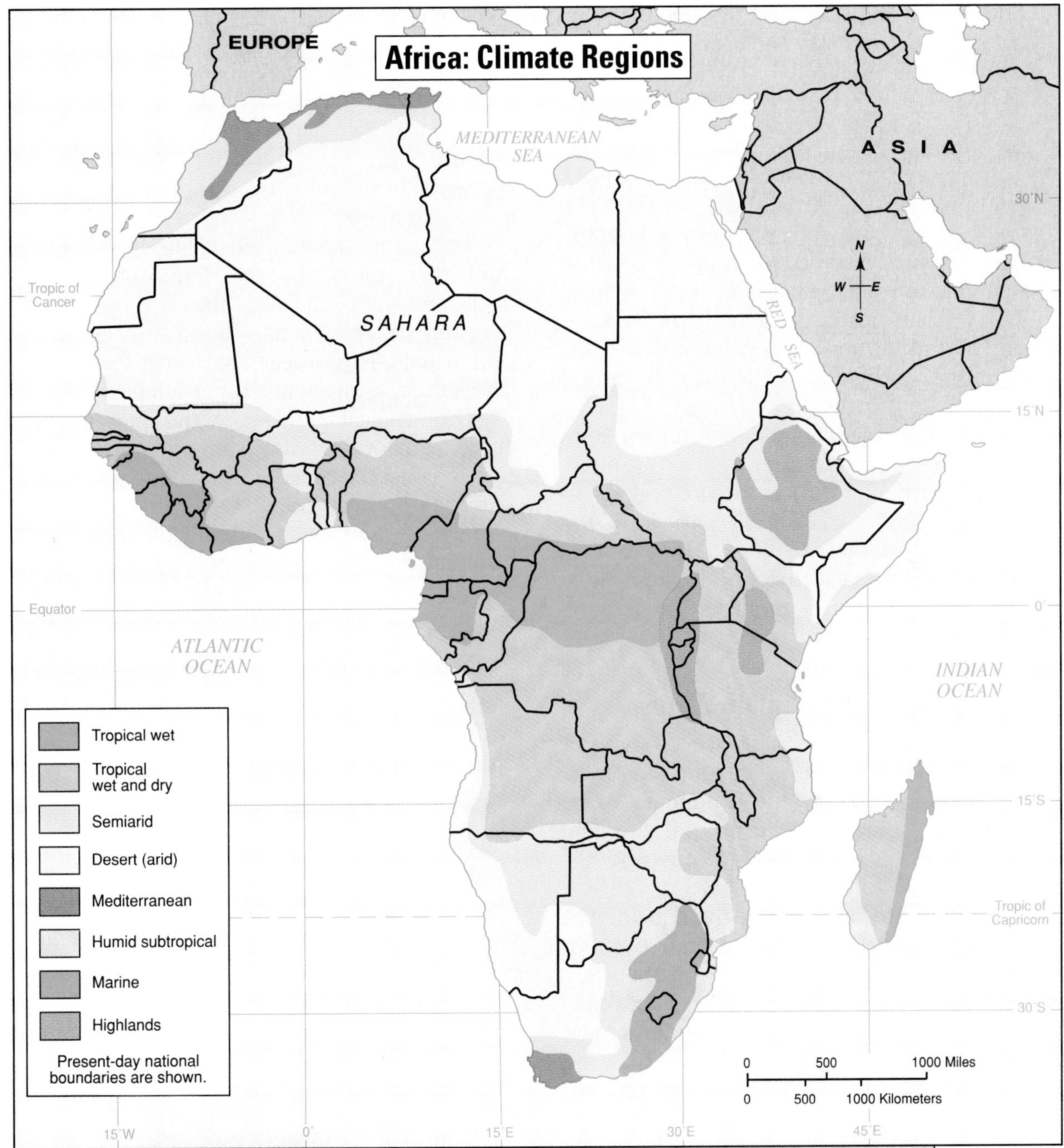

MAP STUDY

Africa is a vast continent with varied climates as this map shows. In most parts of Africa, however, the temperatures are warm all year round.

1. **Place** Why is the climate of most of Africa warm throughout the year?
2. **Region** (a) Which climate region extends across the largest part of Africa?
   (b) Which climate region covers the smallest area of Africa?
3. **Drawing Conclusions** Why does the amount of rainfall determine climate zones in Africa?

above sea level. Its pleasant daytime temperatures are in the 60s and 70s F. At night, Nairobi is quite chilly.

Rainfall

A major feature of African climates is a pattern of alternating wet and dry seasons. The seasons vary north and south of the Equator. When rains fall on areas south of the Equator, areas to the north experience a dry season. The pattern is reversed later in the year. In general, the farther north or south one gets from the Equator, the shorter the rainy period is and the longer the dry season is.

Rainfall is distributed very unevenly in Africa. Average annual rainfall varies from less than an inch (2.5 cm) in desert regions to more than 80 inches (203 cm) near the Equator. In addition, the rains may vary greatly from one year to the next. These variations in rainfall cause problems for farmers and herders, as you will read.

Four Major Climate Zones

Because of its size, almost every type of climate and vegetation can be found in Africa. For purposes of study, the continent can be divided into four major climate zones. In general, differences in the amount of rainfall distinguish these zones.

Because Africa sits astride the Equator, the climate zones of its northern and southern halves are mirror images of each other. Setting out from the Equator and moving north or south, a traveler would encounter similar bands of climate and vegetation. In turn, these are tropical wet, tropical wet and dry, desert, and moderate Mediterranean climates. (See the map on page 65.)

Tropical Wet Climate Region

Rain forests thrive in the wet tropical climate region. This climate zone occupies a narrow belt along the Equator, covering only 8 percent of Africa. It extends from Guinea on the west coast to the Great Rift Valley in the east.

The tropical rain forest is hot and humid all year round. Temperatures average around 80°F (27°C), and annual rainfall from 60 to 120 inches (152 to 304 cm) is common. The abundant rainfall and warm temperatures help to produce lush plant growth. Thousands of species of birds and animals make their home in the rain forest.

With all its plentiful plant life, you would think that soil of the rain forest would be deep and rich. In fact, the soil is poor. Constant heavy rains dissolve and wash away its nutrients. This process, known as leaching, leaves the soil unsuitable for farming.

The tropical climate of the rain forest poses many problems for settlement. Disease-carrying insects breed in standing pools of water left by heavy rains. Other insects, such as termites, attack wooden buildings and furniture. In addition, dampness causes even everyday items such as clothing to become moldy or rot. Today, builders can solve some of these problems by using concrete and steel in the rain forest, but these materials are costly.

Tropical Wet and Dry Climate Region

The largest climate zone in Africa is the tropical climate with a wet and dry season. The savanna, a grassland, occupies this region, which covers almost half the continent. It is home to most Africans.

Like the tropical rain forest, the tropical savanna region is warm all year. In the summer, or rainy season, the climate is hot and wet. But in the winter, or dry season, it is warm, with little or no rainfall.

Rainfall in the savanna varies from 20 to 80 inches (51 to 203 cm) a year, depending on distance from the Equator. Close to the Equator, the wetter parts of the savanna support many trees and grasses. On the outer edges of the savanna, the semiarid climate is very dry with only a short rainy season. Here, only scattered grasses and small trees grow.

Unpredictable rainfall. Each year, millions of people living on the savanna anxiously

The Savanna Kenya, in East Africa, lies in the wet and dry tropical climate zone. The grasses and shrubs that grow in the savanna support many species of wildlife. Herds of elephants and flocks of birds like those in this photograph live there. ***Environment*** Why is unpredictable rainfall a serious concern for all life in the savanna?

ask the same questions: When will the rains come? Will they bring enough moisture?

Rainfall on the savanna is unreliable and hard to predict. Rains may be heavy or light. The rainy season may come weeks early or weeks late. Some years, it may not come at all. **Drought,** or prolonged periods of little or no rainfall, is common.

Rainfall has great impact on the people's lives. Heavy downpours wash away the soil and cause flooding. If the rains fail to arrive or last for only a short time, few grasses grow. Herders must slaughter their livestock or let them starve. Farmers watch crops die from lack of moisture.

Desertification. Population growth has created serious problems in the drier parts of the savanna. During periods of plentiful rainfall, people seeking land move into these semiarid areas. They chop down trees to clear farmland and to use as fuel for cooking and heating. Herders graze their cattle on the shrubs and grasses.

Natural forces and human action put the land at risk. When droughts occur, crops wither. In addition, the grazing herds have destroyed the roots of the grasses, so the thin layer of topsoil turns to dust. The result is desertification, the turning of semidesert land into desert.

Desertification is especially widespread in the region known as the Sahel. It separates the savanna from the Sahara to the north. Because the Sahel receives so little rain, its growing population is causing serious destruction. Some nations in the Sahel are taking steps to control the problem by planting trees and limiting grazing.

Deserts

Deserts cover about 40 percent of Africa. They include the Sahara in the north and the Kalahari and Namib deserts in the south. In fact, the word *Sahara* means "desert" in Arabic.

The Sahara. The vast Sahara is larger than the continental United States. It extends across northern Africa from the Atlantic to the Red Sea. The Sahara is a region of windswept rock, gravel, and shifting sand dunes. Parts of the Sahara are very harsh. Temperatures can reach as high as 130°F (54°C). Ten years can pass without rainfall.

A few areas have grasses that can support grazing animals. Rainfall in the Sahara averages less than 10 inches a year. After a short rainstorm, grasses will sprout. Streams fill, and people can plant crops.

From ancient times, the Sahara has been as much a highway as a barrier. For thousands of years, traders traveled back and forth across the Sahara. They carried goods and ideas between the peoples of North Africa and the peoples of the savanna. This back-and-forth movement played a role in the

The Sahara The largest desert in the world is the Sahara in northern Africa. For hundreds of years, caravans of camels such as the one below in Niger carried salt and other goods across the Sahara. Today, airplanes and truck convoys are replacing camels. ***Environment*** How does technology change the ways people adapt to their environment?

further development of Africa's diverse societies and cultures.

The Kalahari and Namib. The Kalahari, in Southern Africa, is not quite as dry as the Sahara. Grasses and wild melons grow in a few places, and animals such as antelopes graze. The Namib Desert, however, is one of the driest places on Earth. Small trees get water largely from mists that drift in from the nearby Atlantic Ocean.

Mediterranean Climate Zones

At the southern tip and along the northern coast of Africa, small areas enjoy a mild Mediterranean climate. The climate is similar to that of Los Angeles, California. Summers are hot and dry. Winters are cooler and moist.

The mild climate and fertile soils of these areas support many kinds of crops as well as herding. The pleasant conditions also attracted European settlers. French, Italian, and Spanish colonists carved out farms along the North African fringe. Dutch and British settlers claimed lands in Southern Africa.

Climate and Health

Many disease-carrying insects breed in tropical climates. Throughout tropical Africa, the effect of this on the people's health is enormous. For example, malaria spread by mosquitoes kills up to 1 million children each year. Those who survive the disease suffer from its weakening effects all their lives.

Sleeping sickness is widespread in the savanna. The disease is carried by the tsetse fly, which infects both people and their livestock. Because the disease kills cattle, many Africans have little meat in their diet. Without this source of protein, they are more likely to develop other diseases.

In savanna nations from Senegal to Kenya, other flies transmit river blindness. Before a cure was found recently, this disease caused many people to lose their sight. Millions of Africans suffer from bilharzia (bihl HAHR zee uh). This disease is transmitted by snails that carry parasitic worms. People become infected when they wash or swim in streams where the snails live. As you will read in Chapter 6, scientists are working with some success to combat the diseases that affect large numbers of Africans.

Population Patterns

Today, the population of Africa is approaching 680 million and is growing rapidly. The continent, however, is not densely populated.

As elsewhere around the world, climate, water resources, and soil influence where people live in Africa. Many areas have few people because the land and climate discourage human settlement. Among the most heavily populated areas are the southern part of West Africa, the nations of Morocco and Algeria, the Nile Valley, the region around Lake Victoria, and the eastern part of Southern Africa.

Adapting to the Land

Africa is home to an immense variety of cultures. These cultures have different histories, religious beliefs, values, and traditions. The varied lands and climates of Africa have contributed to this diversity.

Thousands of years ago, people in Africa began migrating across the continent. Depending on where they settled, they developed one of five basic types of societies: farming, herding, fishing, hunting and food gathering, and urban. Most of these ways of life continue in Africa today.

Today, the majority of Africans live in the savanna. Most of them are farmers. Those parts of the savanna that are free from the tsetse fly also support cattle-herding societies.

As in ancient times, people living near lakes and rivers or along the coasts support themselves by fishing. Very few hunting and food-gathering societies remain in modern Africa.

Cities have long flourished along the Mediterranean coast of North Africa, in the savanna of West Africa, and on the coast of East

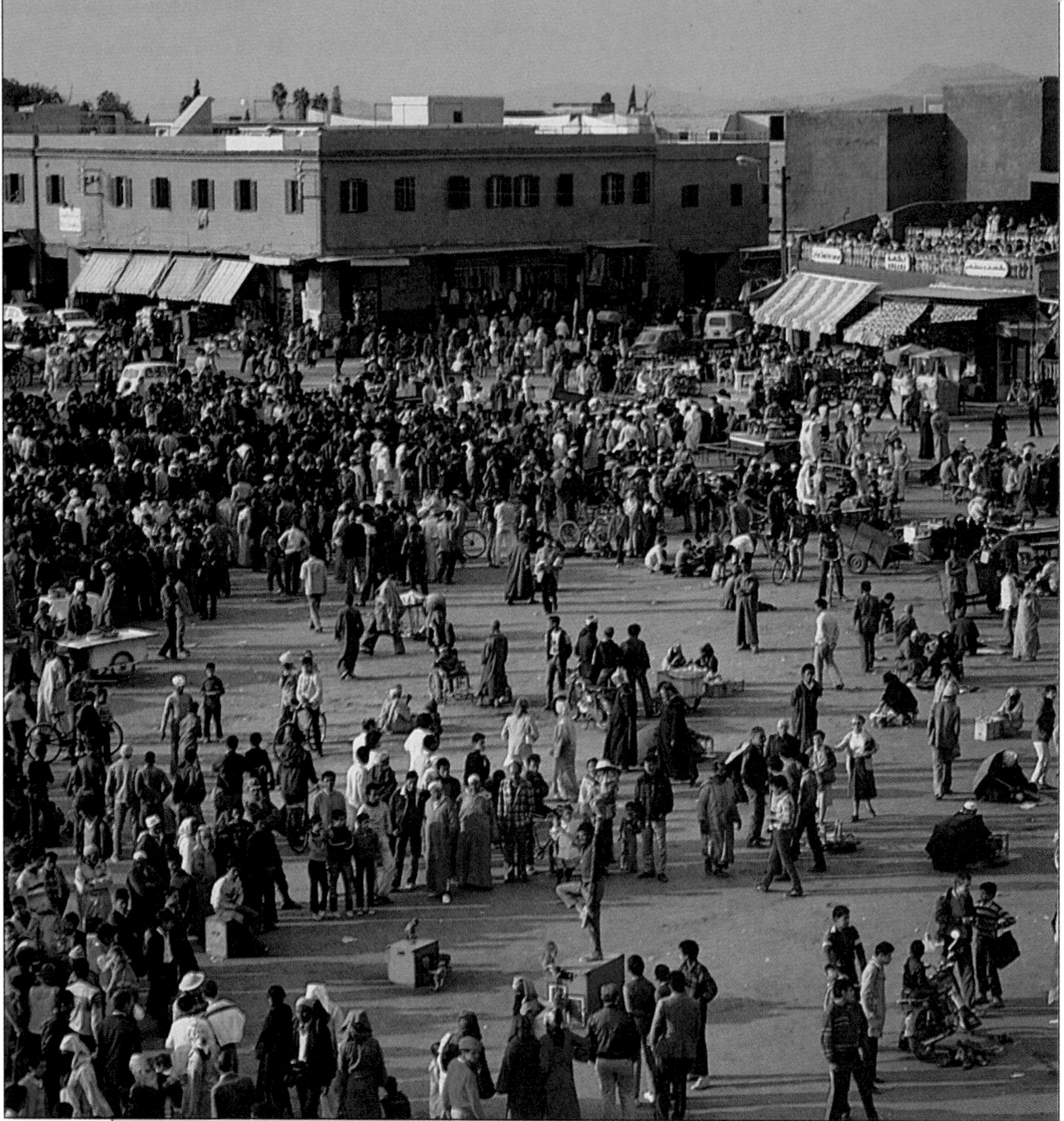

A Market in Marrakesh The mild Mediterranean climate in northern Africa encouraged the growth of cities. For centuries, Marrakesh was the capital of a vast North African empire. Today, people of different cultures still flock to this city in Morocco to trade in its busy marketplace. ***Culture*** How does trade promote cultural diffusion?

Africa. Today, African cities throughout the continent are growing rapidly.

Languages

Africa's cultural diversity is reflected in its many languages. Africans speak more than 1,000 different languages. Often, groups living within a few miles of one another speak different languages. Some areas also have common languages that are used for trading and business purposes.

Scholars divide the languages of Africa into several language families. All languages within the same family share a common root. For example, people living in a wide belt extending from West Africa across Central and

Southern Africa speak languages of the Niger-Congo family. But even though they are part of the same family, those languages may be as different from one another as English is from Swedish.

By studying language families, we can learn about the early movement of African peoples. For thousands of years, small groups of people migrated across the continent. When they came into prolonged contact with each other, their languages slowly changed. They added new words or pronounced words differently.

In East Africa, for example, Arabs from the Middle East traded with local African people. Over time, some Arabic words blended into the basic Bantu languages of East Africa. The result was a new language called Swahili (swah HEE lee). Swahili is still spoken by many people in East Africa today. In the last 150 years, European languages such as Portuguese, French, and English joined the list of languages spoken in Africa.

SECTION 2 REVIEW

1. **Locate:** (a) Tropic of Cancer, (b) Tropic of Capricorn, (c) Sahara, (d) Kalahari Desert.
2. **Identify:** (a) Sahel, (b) sleeping sickness, (c) Swahili.
3. **Define:** (a) tropics, (b) leaching, (c) drought, (d) desertification.
4. (a) What are four major climate zones of Africa? (b) Why is rainfall a key to Africa's climate?
5. (a) What were the five basic kinds of societies in Africa? (b) How has the land affected the location of these societies?
6. **Analyzing Information** How might the many languages of Africa be a problem in building unified nations?
7. **Writing Across Cultures** Choose one of Africa's four climate zones. Write a paragraph comparing it to the climate zone where you live.

3 EARLY CIVILIZATIONS OF AFRICA

FIND OUT

What kinds of evidence help us learn about the past?

How did climate changes affect ancient Africa?

What were some achievements of early African civilizations?

Vocabulary pharaoh, hieroglyphics

Egypt's ruler Hatshepsut wanted to be remembered. She had a record of her deeds carved on the walls of a great temple. One of Hatshepsut's greatest triumphs was a highly successful trade expedition to Punt,* a land to the south of Egypt. According to the temple carvings,

> "A command was heard from the great . . . god [Amon-Re], that the ways to Punt should be searched out. . . .[I Hatshepsut commanded] to send to [Punt] . . . according to the command of my father, Amon."

Thanks to the carvings on Hatshepsut's temple, we know about this early contact between the peoples of Africa. Often, however, early people did not leave such clear records. Scholars must piece together bits of evidence to learn about the past.

Tracking the Evidence

Olduvai Gorge is located on the edge of the Great Rift Valley in Tanzania. There, in the late 1950s, a team of scientists, headed by

* Scholars think that Punt was located at the southern end of the Red Sea in what is today Somalia.

Mary and Louis Leakey, uncovered exciting evidence. They found pieces of bone embedded in ancient rock. After careful study, they determined that the bone, which was almost 2 million years old, belonged to one of the ancestors of modern people. The discoveries at Olduvai have led some scientists to suggest that Africa was home to the first people.

Archaeologists study objects left by early people. From pieces of bone, a few seeds, or charcoal from an ancient fire, they try to create a picture of the past. Scientists in many fields help in the task. If ancient grain is found buried in rock, geologists study the rock to learn when it was formed. Botanists analyze the type of plant and the climate it would have needed to grow.

Despite scientific advances, we still know little about the earliest people. Archaeologists continue to hunt for evidence linking the earliest people in Africa to later cultures that emerged there. Africa's climate often works against our learning more. Heat and humidity, for example, destroy wood and bone, which often provide scientists with valuable information.

Records on Stone

Some records of early people have survived, especially pictures on stone. From Southern Africa to the Sahara, archaeologists have studied paintings on rock cliffs and cave walls. The paintings show the tools, weapons,

African Rock Art Early peoples in several regions painted scenes on the rock walls of cliffs or in caves. These paintings on a rock cliff in the Algerian desert are among the largest and best-preserved examples of such art. ***Fine Art*** Based on the painting, what conclusion can you draw about how early people lived in northern Africa?

and hunting and food-gathering methods of early African peoples.

Rock art. The rock art of the Sahara lets us look at the lives of people who once lived there. In one scene, a woman uses a digging stick to pry edible roots from the ground. In another, figures move in graceful patterns, perhaps as part of a religious ceremony. In yet another, a hunter stalks a giraffe.

These rock paintings reveal that herds of animals once roamed the Sahara. Based on this evidence, scientists now think that the Sahara was once much wetter than it is today. Thousands of years ago, the region had lakes, rivers, and green grasses. Arrowheads, fish hooks, and cattle bones show that people hunted, fished, and herded cattle there.

A changing environment. About 4,000 years ago, the climate of the Sahara was changing. Less rain fell. Lakes and rivers dried up. Without water, grasses no longer grew. Animal herds migrated to other parts of Africa to find food. The people who hunted those animals also moved. Some people probably migrated to the Nile Valley.

Nile Valley Civilization

Even before the Sahara dried up, people in various parts of the world had learned to raise crops. As you have read, the agricultural revolution had far-reaching effects. (See page 28.) Some people gave up the nomadic life of hunting and food gathering. They settled into farming communities. These communities became the basis for advanced civilizations.

The earliest civilization in Africa developed in the Nile Valley of Egypt about 7,000 years ago. Fertile soils and plentiful wildlife allowed people to farm and hunt. As the people perfected their farming skills, they produced more food, allowing the population to grow.

By about 3,000 B.C., powerful rulers had emerged and united the villages along the Nile. The rulers of ancient Egypt were called pharaohs (FAIR ohz). In time, pharaohs expanded their power and built a large empire. Through trade and conquest, Egyptians exchanged knowledge and ideas with distant cultures.

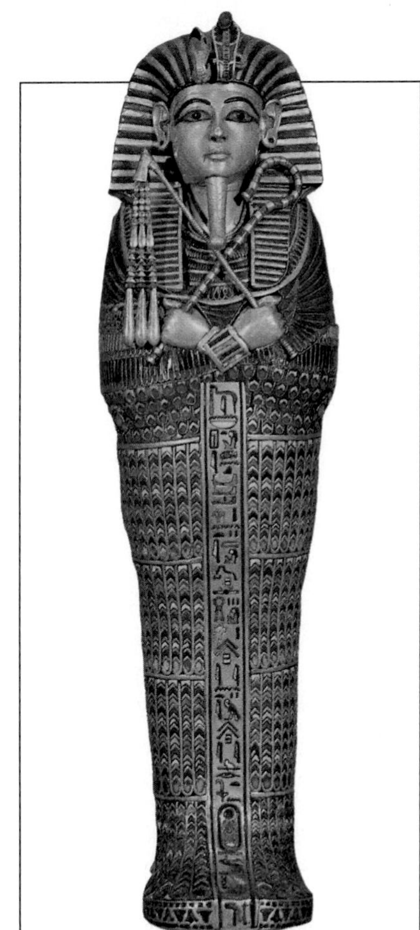

A Pharaoh's Coffin Richly decorated coffins showed the great wealth and power of Egypt's rulers. This coffin of the young pharaoh Tutankhamen, who ruled in the 1300s B.C., was found in 1922. Furniture, weapons, clothing, and a chariot, all trimmed with gold and jewels, filled the burial tomb. ***Fine Art*** What can you learn about Egypt's civilization from this work?

Religion and Government

The Egyptians were polytheistic. They believed that different gods controlled the forces of nature. The chief god was Amon-Re (AH muhn RAY), the sun god. Other important gods and goddesses included Osiris (oh sī rihs), god of the underworld and of the Nile, and his wife, Isis (ī sihs).

A belief in life after death was central to Egyptian religion. Pharaohs and rich nobles prepared carefully for the journey through the underworld to the "Happy Field of Food."

Ancient Egyptian Art Paintings on the walls of Egyptian tombs provide evidence about civilization in the Nile Valley. In this painting from about 1250 B.C., a worker uses a shaduf, or water hoist, to draw water from the Nile. Farmers still use this method of irrigation. ***Technology*** Why are some ancient methods of farming still in use today?

They built huge pyramids, or tombs, and filled them with food, clothing, and jewels that they would need in the afterlife.

To the Egyptians, the pharaoh was a god, descended from Amon-Re. The pharaoh had total power over the lives of the people. Priests and nobles helped the pharaoh run the government. Priests conducted the ceremonies needed to please the gods. Other officials collected taxes in the form of grain and other goods to pay the costs of government.

The Gift of the Nile

As far as the eye can see, flood waters cover the land. Here and there, villages stand on slight rises above the swirling river. In one such village—let us call it Perhaa—live a man called Heti and his wife, Senen, with their children. The family is an imaginary one. But from paintings on temple walls and other records of ancient Egypt, we know how ancient Egyptians lived.

Season of the Flood. An ancient historian called Egypt the "gift of the Nile." Each year, the river flooded and spread rich Nile mud over nearby farmlands. Farmers like Heti and Senen welcomed the Season of the Flood with hymns like this one:

> "Praise to thee, O Nile, that flows out of the Earth and comes to nourish the dwellers of Egypt. . . .
> If the Nile is sluggish, the nostrils are stopped up, and the people are brought low;
> The offerings of the gods are reduced, and millions die.
> When the Nile rises, the Earth is joyous and everyone is glad; every jaw laughs and every tooth is uncovered."

During the 100 days their fields are under water, Heti and other men from Perhaa must work for the pharaoh. They wrestle huge chunks of stone from the cliffs that line the river and load them onto wooden rafts. In cities far from Perhaa, other workers will use the stone to build a temple to Amon-Re. The pharaoh's overseer pays Heti and the others with grain from the royal storehouses. The food is welcome because the villagers have little left from last year's harvest. (See Connections With Literature, page 804, "The Story of the Flood.")

Season of Going Out. When the flood waters retreat, the Season of Going Out begins. Heti and Senen guide a pair of cows that pull a wooden plow through the muddy soil. Along with other villagers, they plant fields of wheat and barley. Near their mud-brick home, they tend a small garden, weeding rows of onions, beans, carrots, radishes, turnips, cucumbers, melons, and gourds.

When desert sun dries the fields, the people of Perhaa use a shaduf, a simple water hoist, to spread water from ditches and ponds onto their crops. As the crops ripen, the people perform the ceremonies that the priest of Osiris orders. New life will rise from the fields only if the god of the underworld gives his permission.

Season of the Harvest. Four months after planting, the crops are ready for harvesting. At sunrise, Heti and his sons go to the fields to cut the grain. Senen and her daughters gather the grain into baskets. Later, they put the harvest into large storage jars. They dry the vegetables from their garden and brew beer from barley or grapes.

The people of Perhaa keep only about half the harvest. The rest goes to the pharaoh's tax collectors. Before the grain is cut, the tax collector arrives to measure the village grain fields. Based on those measurements, he decides how much tax the village must pay. The grain feeds the pharaoh's court and officials. In years when the harvest is bad, however, the pharaoh might send grain to areas hit by famine. ■

Achievements of Egyptian Civilization

The Egyptians left remarkable monuments to their civilization. Only a wealthy and well-organized society could have built the huge temples and pyramid tombs that still stand along the Nile. The Egyptians also developed a form of writing, called hieroglyphics, that used pictures and symbols. Hieroglyphics and paintings on temple walls tell us about the knowledge, beliefs, and everyday lives of early Egyptians.

Egyptian priests used their knowledge of the stars and planets to produce a calendar with a 365-day year. Officials used their mathematical skills to survey the land each year after the Nile floods washed away boundary markers. Egyptian doctors studied the human body. They set fractured bones, treated spinal injuries, and successfully performed some types of surgery.

Egyptian civilization survived for thousands of years. Gradually, Egyptians passed on much of their knowledge to other peoples of Africa and to peoples of the Mediterranean region.

The Kingdom of Kush

Trade flowed along the Nile between Egypt and neighboring peoples in Nubia and Kush to the south. At times during Egypt's long history, powerful pharaohs sent armies to conquer these lands. Traders and conquering armies spread Egyptian culture southward.

By 750 B.C., Egyptian power had weakened. King Kastha of Kush led his forces north and conquered the Nile Valley. Kushite rule over Egypt was short-lived. It ended when the Assyrians, armed with iron weapons, invaded Egypt from the Middle East, forcing the Kushites to retreat.

Despite the defeat by the Assyrians, Kush continued to flourish. The rulers of Kush built a new capital at Meroë (MEHR uh wee), on the banks of the Nile. At first, Egyptian influences remained strong. The people worshipped the sun god Amon-Re. Kings and priests built temples and pyramids like those in Egypt. However, over time, the gods of Meroë replaced Egyptian gods. The Kushites adapted Egyptian hieroglyphics and in time developed their own alphabet.

Near Meroë were deposits of iron ore. After their contact with the Assyrians, the Kushites learned to make iron tools and weapons. Using wood from nearby forests, ironworkers heated their ovens and melted the iron ore. Despite their contact with Kushites, the Egyptians did not adopt this technology but continued to use bronze. Today, mounds of waste material from the Kushite iron industry can still be seen in the ruins of Meroë.

Kush also profited from trade. Kushite merchants exchanged goods with Egypt and the Mediterranean world. From ports on the Red Sea, they shipped cargoes to Arabia, East Africa, and India. Traders pushed southward and westward, perhaps as far as Lake Chad.

By A.D. 200, invasions and internal rivalries had weakened Kush. After 1,000 years, the once powerful kingdom of Kush collapsed.

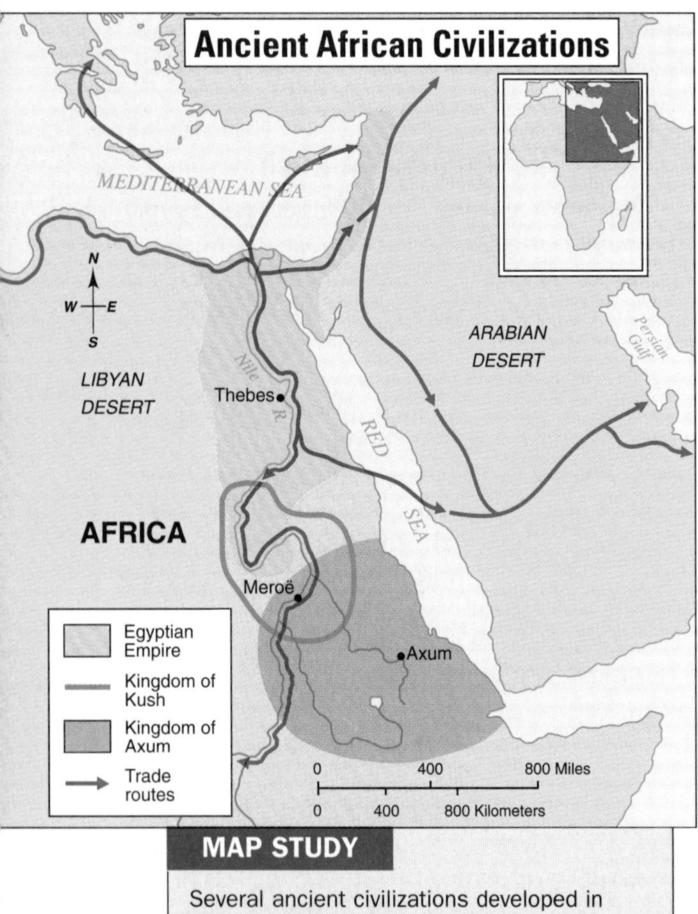

MAP STUDY

Several ancient civilizations developed in Africa, including Egypt, Kush, and Axum.

1. **Place** Which early African civilizations bordered the Red Sea?
2. **Location** Describe the relative location of the kingdom of Kush.
3. **Applying Information** How did trade routes help Egypt to become a powerful empire?

The Kingdom of Axum

Even before the last king of Kush died, another African kingdom was emerging farther to the south. The kingdom of Axum developed on the high plateaus of what is today Ethiopia. Like Kush, Axum was an important center of trade. Its merchants sent spices, gems, and ivory north into Egypt, across the Red Sea to Arabia, and across the Indian Ocean to South Asia.

In A.D. 330, King Ezana of Axum conquered Kush. He boasted of his success:

> “I burnt their towns, both those built of brick and those built of reeds, and my army . . . destroyed the statues in their temples, their granaries, and cotton trees and cast them into the Nile.”

Earlier, King Ezana had converted to Christianity. As you will read, Christianity began in the Middle East and spread across the Mediterranean world. (See pages 565–566.) Early Christians carried their beliefs across North Africa and up the Nile into Axum.

Christian beliefs took firm root in Axum. Later, the religion of Islam spread across North Africa. As a result, Christian communities in Axum were cut off from the rest of the Christian world. Yet the Ethiopian Christian Church survived. Today, it is among the oldest forms of Christianity. Ethiopians have their own sacred written language, called Geëz (gee EHZ), as well as strong traditions of religious art.

SECTION 3 REVIEW

1. **Locate:** (a) Egypt, (b) Kush, (c) Meroë, (d) Red Sea, (e) Axum.
2. **Identify:** (a) Olduvai Gorge, (b) Kastha, (c) Ezana.
3. **Define:** (a) pharaoh, (b) hieroglyphics.
4. (a) How do different scientists help us learn about the ancient past? (b) What do ancient rock paintings reveal about the Sahara?
5. Describe three achievements of Egyptian civilization.
6. How was the culture of Kush affected by trade and warfare?
7. **Analyzing Ideas** According to an archaeologist, “In this field, a person kicks over a stone in Africa, and we have to rewrite our textbooks.” What does the archaeologist mean?
8. **Writing Across Cultures** Write a paragraph comparing the importance of the Nile to ancient Egyptian civilization with the importance of rivers in the United States today.

Chapter 3 Review

Understanding Vocabulary

Match each term at left with the correct definition at right.

1. escarpment	**a.** steep cliffs
2. cataract	**b.** form of writing that used pictures and symbols
3. hydroelectric power	**c.** energy produced by moving water
4. leaching	**d.** large waterfall
5. hieroglyphics	**e.** dissolving nutrients and washing them away from the soil

Reviewing the Main Ideas

1. (a) Describe Africa's relative location in the world. (b) What bodies of water surround the continent?
2. (a) What are Africa's most important rivers? (b) What contribution does each make to the lives of the people?
3. Describe four factors that affect the climate of Africa.
4. How have natural forces and human actions increased the spread of desert land in Africa?
5. How have the climates of Africa affected population patterns?
6. How did changes in the climate of the Sahara about 4,000 years ago affect the people living there?
7. (a) Why did the kingdom of Kush flourish? (b) What were the results of interaction between the kingdom of Axum and other civilizations?

Reviewing Chapter Themes

1. The lands and climates of Africa are varied. Choose two regions of Africa and explain how the climate and landforms of each have influenced how people live.
2. The oceans surrounding Africa and the Sahara have been both barriers and highways. Describe two examples of how people have used them as highways.
3. Archaeologists and other scientists have concluded that Africa was home to the first people. What evidence has led them to that conclusion?
4. Civilizations differ but they share certain features. See pages 28–30. Describe three features of ancient Egypt that indicate that it was a highly developed civilization.

Thinking Critically

1. **Making Global Connections** Imagine you are visiting Africa. (a) Which features of its geography will remind you of the United States? (b) Which will not? Explain.
2. **Understanding Causes and Effects** How did the landforms of Africa and its climates affect the early pattern of interaction between the peoples of Africa and those of Europe and Asia?
3. **Forecasting** How might the development of a more extensive transportation network throughout Africa influence patterns of settlement and economic development?

Applying Your Skills

1. **Using Your Vocabulary** Use the Glossary on pages 794–803 to review the meaning of the following terms: *elevation, plateau, climate, culture*. Use each term in a separate sentence about African geography.
2. **Analyzing a Quotation** Reread the quotation by King Ezana of Axum on page 76. What does it reveal about life in the kingdom of Kush?

Chapter 4

HERITAGE OF AFRICA

Mansa Musa In the 1300s, the West African empire of Mali reached its height of power by controlling the gold trade between West Africa and North Africa. This map of Mali features its most powerful ruler, Mansa Musa. Here, Mansa Musa is seated on his throne, holding a gold orb in his hand. ***Fine Art*** What impression of Mali might this map have given to those who saw it? Why?

CHAPTER OUTLINE

1 Trading States and Kingdoms

2 Patterns of Life

3 The Slave Trade

4 Age of European Imperialism

5 Effects of European Rule

The people of Cairo, Egypt, gazed in awe at the procession. Before their eyes marched hundreds of servants, carrying golden staffs and wearing gold jewelry. Hundreds of camels plodded by loaded with gold. At the head of the caravan rode the owner of all this wealth—Mansa Musa of Mali.

Mali was a powerful empire in West Africa. In 1324, its emperor, or *mansa*, crossed the Sahara. He traveled almost 3,000 miles to Mecca, the holy city of Islam. As a Muslim, he was fulfilling his duty to make a pilgrimage to Mecca.

Mansa Musa's visit deeply impressed the people of Cairo. "This man," wrote an Egyptian, "spread upon Cairo the flood of his generosity. There was no person or holder of any office who did not receive a sum of gold from him. Musa was the most feared by his enemies and the most able to do good to those around him."

Mali was one of the rich trading states in West Africa. Trade was important in many African societies. However, the slave trade and later European conquest would bring vast changes to Africa.

CHAPTER PERSPECTIVE

Across Africa, people developed many different ways of organizing their lives. Sometimes, strong rulers organized villages into large, centralized states. Other self-sufficient villages stayed independent.

As you read, look for these chapter themes:

- In parts of Africa, trade helped to support large states and empires.
- The peoples of Africa developed many different societies.
- The slave trade disrupted traditional patterns of life in parts of Africa.
- European imperialism, helped by advanced technology and economic power, led to great changes in Africa.

Literature Connections

In this chapter, you will encounter passages from the following works.

Yoruba proverbs, *Wit and Wisdom from West Africa*, Richard F. Burton

Soweto, My Love!, Molapatene Collins Ramusi and Ruth S. Turner

The Interesting Narrative of Olaudah Equiano, or Gustavus Vasa, Written by Himself, Gustavus Vasa

"The nations, Shaka, have condemned you," B. W. Vilakazi

For other suggestions, see Connections With Literature, pages 804–808.

1 TRADING STATES AND KINGDOMS

FIND OUT

Why did powerful kingdoms emerge in West Africa?

How did trade affect the peoples of East Africa?

How did trade encourage cultural diffusion in Africa?

Vocabulary mosque, city-state

The streets of Timbuktu echoed with the sounds of arriving and departing caravans. Traders and their pack animals crowded the streets. Salt and gold were the chief objects of this lively trade. Ideas, too, traveled along the trade routes. As a result, Timbuktu flourished as a wealthy center of trade and learning. The university at Timbuktu was a great center for Muslim scholars. According to a traditional saying,

> "Salt comes from the north, gold from the south, and silver from the city of white men. But the word of God and the treasures of wisdom are only to be found in Timbuktu."

The Gold-Salt Trade

From early times, people in Africa traded across a long route that stretched from the Middle East and North Africa to the savanna lands of West Africa. This route crossed through the vast Sahara. Caravan leaders developed the skills and knowledge to survive this difficult journey. Travelers rested by day to escape the desert heat. Moving on at night, they used their knowledge of stars and the land to reach oases, where they could find water. Death from lack of water or blinding sandstorms was a real threat.

Why did people cross the desert? They stood to profit from the exchange of scarce goods. The savanna lands of West Africa lacked salt, which is essential to human survival. In parts of the Sahara, however, salt was plentiful. At Taghaza, people even used blocks of salt to build their houses.

The savanna had its own resources, especially gold. Traders journeyed to Taghaza, where they exchanged gold for salt. They then loaded camels with blocks of salt for the return trip south. In West Africa, salt was more valuable than gold or silver.

Trade contributed to the rise of strong kingdoms in West Africa. As trade grew, some towns along the trade routes expanded into cities. The ruler of a wealthy city would conquer neighboring areas to control the sources of gold. In time, the city would become the center of a large empire.

The Empire of Ghana

The first powerful West African kingdom developed in the open plains between the Senegal and Niger rivers. Its ruler was known as "king of the gold." He also bore the title *ghana,* meaning "war chief." In time, the land became known as Ghana.*

Government and trade. The founders of Ghana were probably the Soninke (soh NIHN kuh) people. By A.D. 500, the rulers of the Soninke had begun to extend their control over a large area. They governed their lands through princes and officials chosen by the emperor. For a time, the city of Kumbi Saleh was the capital of Ghana. As many as 15,000 people may have lived there.

The emperor's power rested on his control of the gold trade. He alone owned all gold mined in his empire. Wealth from gold allowed the emperor to build a large army. Carrying iron-tipped spears, his soldiers had an advantage over neighboring people who were less well armed.

As Ghana grew, its rulers created a lavish court. The Arab writer Al-Bakri (ahl bahk REE), who visited Ghana in about 1065, described its riches.

> "When the king gives audience to his people, to listen to their complaints and to set them to rights, he sits in a pavilion around which stand ten pages holding shields and gold-mounted swords."

People in the towns of Ghana welcomed trade, especially with the Berbers. These merchants from the northern edge of the desert brought salt, cloth, and horses to the savanna settlements. They carried gold, precious woods, and kola nuts back across the sands. Each caravan that entered or left Ghana had to pay a tax.

Invasions. In the eleventh century, conflicts far to the north began to affect Ghana. A group of Berbers, called Almoravids (ahl MOH rah vihdz), attacked the rich empire. In 1076, they seized the capital of Ghana. Almoravid control did not last long, but the empire of Ghana broke into a number of smaller states.

The Empire of Mali

After the breakup of Ghana, other peoples competed for power. One group was the Mandingos, farmers who had lived under Ghana's rule. A series of strong Mandingo leaders conquered neighboring lands. By seizing some gold-producing areas, they were able to set up the empire of Mali. (See the map on page 82.)

Mansa Musa. An outstanding ruler of Mali was Mansa Musa. (See page 78.) He ruled 30 years, from about 1307 until his death in 1337. Mansa Musa pushed out the borders of his empire in every direction. His armies captured Taghaza and its salt mines, increasing Musa's power.

The emperor used his power to ensure peace and order. "There is complete security in their country," wrote Ibn Battuta (IHB uhn bah TOO tah), a visitor from North Africa. He traveled through Mali just after Mansa Musa's death. "Neither traveler, nor inhabitant in it,

* Ancient Ghana lay far to the north and west of the present-day nation of Ghana.

has anything to fear from robbers or men of violence."

Influence of Islam. By the time of Mansa Musa, the religion of Islam had spread across West Africa. Over hundreds of years, Muslim traders carried their religion into many parts of Africa. The rulers of Ghana had allowed Muslims to trade in their lands, but most rulers kept their traditional religious beliefs.

Mansa Musa adopted the new faith. Many officials and other Mandingos also converted to Islam, although large numbers of people continued to follow their old beliefs.

Under Mansa Musa, the influence of Islam increased. The emperor based his system of justice on the Koran, the Muslim holy book. As a faithful Muslim, he made a pilgrimage to Mecca. The journey earned him worldwide fame and respect. It also led to increased contacts between West Africa and the Muslim world of North Africa and the Middle East. Mansa Musa sent ambassadors abroad and invited Muslim scholars to his lands. From Spain came the architect As-Sahili. He built many mosques, or Muslim houses of worship, in Mali. A wall of one of these mosques still stands in Timbuktu.

Decline. Mansa Musa's successors were less skillful rulers. By the early 1400s, power struggles had weakened the empire. Towns

The Great Mosque in Mali Islam spread to West Africa from the Arab world as early as A.D. 800. Some rulers of Mali and other African societies accepted the Muslim faith. They built mosques such as the Great Mosque at Mopti in Mali, shown here. ***Diversity*** (a) What part did Arab traders play in spreading Islam to West Africa? (b) How is the spread of Islam an example of cultural diffusion?

and cities broke away from Mali's control. Although Mali existed as a state for another 200 years, it covered a much smaller area.

Rise of Songhai

As Mali declined, a new empire arose in West Africa. Songhai (SAWNG hī) followed the pattern of earlier states. From the trading city of Gao (gaw), powerful rulers extended their control over other lands. By 1464, Sunni Ali, an able leader, had gained power in Gao. Because of the weakness of Mali, traders could no longer travel safely. Sunni Ali set out to restore order. For 35 years, he led his armies across West Africa. He captured Timbuktu and other centers of trade. Although he spent a lifetime at war, he also worked hard to govern his empire well.

Not long after the death of Sunni Ali, a new ruler, Askia Muhammad, helped Songhai to reach its peak of power. Like Mansa Musa of Mali, Askia Muhammad followed the teachings of Islam. He, too, made a pilgrimage to Mecca. On his return to Songhai, he encouraged Islamic teachers and writers to settle in Timbuktu. As a result, Timbuktu became the center of learning described at the beginning of this section.

Songhai fell in 1591 to invaders from Morocco. The ruler of Morocco had heard of Mali's wealth, so he sent an army across the Sahara. Exhausted by the long march, the invaders faced a much larger army from Songhai.

In the battles that followed, however, the Moroccan soldiers won because they had guns and cannons. With the new technology, they overpowered the soldiers of Songhai, who fought with spears and arrows.

MAP STUDY

Strong kingdoms led by powerful rulers rose in several parts of Africa in the years after A.D. 400.

1. **Place** (a) Name three kingdoms that developed in West Africa. (b) Which kingdom was located in the Niger River delta?
2. **Location** (a) Which African kingdom was located southwest of a group of independent city-states? (b) In what region of Africa were all of these city-states?
3. **Analyzing Information** Why did many powerful African kingdoms grow up around trading cities?

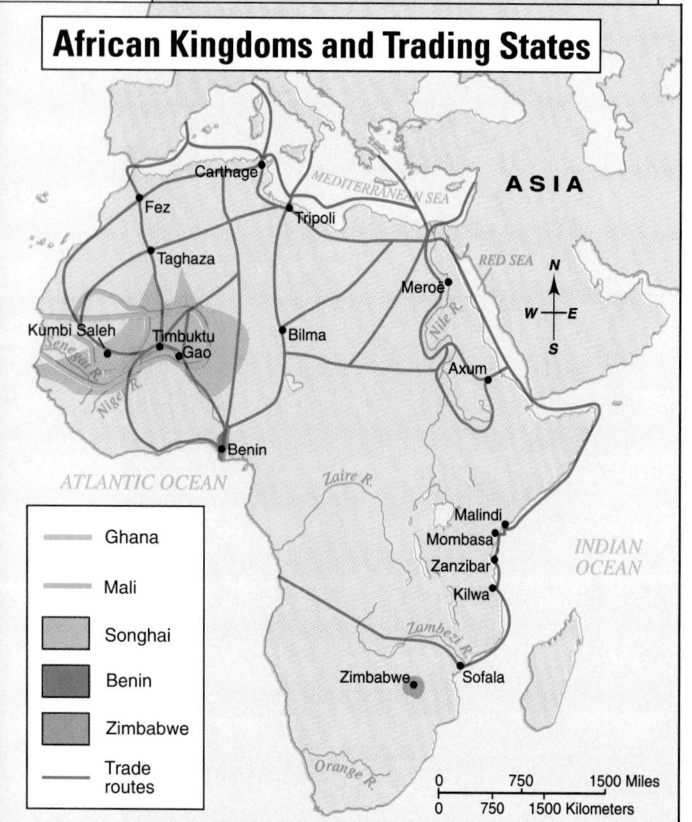

The Forest Kingdom of Benin

Other states arose in the thickly forested areas near the Equator. Among these forest kingdoms was Benin. It developed in the delta region of the Niger River. From this location, Benin controlled trade over a large area.

As in many African societies, the people of Benin preserved their history through their oral traditions. Many oral histories of Benin tell of its most glorious *oba*, or ruler. Ewuare (ay WHAR ay) "captured 201 towns and villages in Ekiti, Ikara, Kukuruku, Eka, and Ibo country. He took their rulers captive, and he caused the people to pay tribute to him." Ewuare then set up a central government to rule his lands.

Benin City, the capital, was a center of industry with broad avenues and intersecting streets. Benin craftworkers produced fine woven goods as well as elegant brass, wood, and

Ancient Bronze Art Unlike much African art made of wood, Benin bronzes have survived the centuries. Benin sculptors used advanced methods of casting metal. The largest figure on the panel is the *oba*, or king. Here, he holds the head of an animal, perhaps used in a religious ceremony. ***Fine Art*** What does the existence of this bronze panel reveal about Benin society?

ivory objects. Artists also learned to work with bronze. They probably learned this art from the Ife (EE fee), a neighboring people. In time, Benin bronze workers developed their own style.

Cities of East Africa

Since ancient times, trade had linked the coastal peoples of East Africa to other parts of the world. As you read in Chapter 3, the Egyptian pharaoh Hatshepsut sent trading voyages to Punt. At sites where the East African coast offered good harbors, small villages expanded into busy cities.

Many of these trading centers grew into independent city-states. A city-state is a large town that has its own government and usually controls the surrounding countryside. East African city-states such as Malindi, Mombasa, Kilwa, and Sofala were busy marketplaces. Traders brought slaves, ivory, gold, and animal skins from the interior of Africa to the coast. Arab traders bought these slaves and goods and carried them north.

Some traders sailed across the Indian Ocean. They took advantage of the seasonal monsoon winds. For several months each year, the winds blew northeast, carrying ships toward India. Later in the year, the winds

Mombasa Coastal cities of East Africa have long been important trading centers. Mombasa, shown here, was founded by Arab traders in the 1000s. Controlled in turn by Arabs, Persians, Portuguese, Turks, and the British, Mombasa is now Kenya's major port. ***Diversity*** Why are multicultural influences often present in port cities?

reversed direction, allowing ships to return to Africa.

Trade shaped the city-states of East Africa in other ways. Arab traders brought their culture to the region. As a result, Islam took root in parts of East Africa. On the East African coast, the contact among Arab and African peoples led to the use of Swahili. As you read in Chapter 3, this language blended Arab words with local African languages.

The East African city-states thrived for hundreds of years. In the early 1500s, however, the Portuguese attacked and occupied many of them. The newcomers wanted to build their own trading empire, but trade soon fell off. The cities declined as many people left rather than submit to Portuguese control.

Zimbabwe

Much of the gold that reached Sofala came from Zimbabwe (zihm BAH bweh) in the interior. Various migrating peoples had settled in this region of Southern Africa between the Zambezi and Limpopo rivers. By 1300, the rulers of Zimbabwe had organized a large kingdom. Control of the gold mines gave the rulers of Zimbabwe their power. With that power, they imposed a degree of unity on the diverse peoples of the region.

Zimbabwe means "great stone house." Today, the region is dotted with the remains of palaces and other buildings made of stone. Expert builders made these structures without mortar. The stones were laid so skillfully that they held together by themselves. Some of the stone walls measure up to 16 feet (4.8 m) thick and more than 30 feet (9 m) high. They have withstood the weathering of centuries.

Most of the people of Zimbabwe were farmers and herders. However, they probably also benefited from the gold trade that made their rulers wealthy. Among the stone ruins of Zimbabwe, archaeologists have found trade items such as porcelain from China and beads from India.

Power struggles weakened Zimbabwe in the 1500s. Soon, the kingdom broke apart.

SECTION 1 REVIEW

1. **Locate:** (a) Timbuktu, (b) Ghana, (c) Mali, (d) Songhai, (e) Benin, (f) Sofala, (g) Zimbabwe.
2. **Identify:** (a) Mansa Musa, (b) Sunni Ali, (c) Askia Muhammad.
3. **Define:** (a) mosque, (b) city-state.
4. How did trade help shape the city-states of East Africa?
5. How did Islam influence African societies?
6. **Understanding Causes and Effects** How did trade contribute to the rise of strong states in Africa?
7. **Writing Across Cultures** Many African traditions have been passed on through oral histories. List ways American traditions have been passed on to you.

2 PATTERNS OF LIFE

FIND OUT

What cultural ties united people in African societies?

How did the role of women vary in different African cultures?

How did religion reflect the cultural diversity of Africa?

Vocabulary lineage, consensus, subsistence farmer, polygamy, age grade

"When the day dawns, the trader
takes himself to his trade;
The spinner takes her spindle, the
warrior takes his shield;
The weaver bends over his sley
[a weaving reed];
The farmer awakes, he and his
hoe-handle;
The hunter awakes with his quiver
and bow."

This proverb described the daily activities of the Yoruba (YOH roo buh) people of Nigeria and Benin. It also reveals something about their values. Clearly, the Yoruba felt that everyone had a job to do.

The Yoruba were one of the many peoples who developed their own culture in Africa. Because cultures varied so greatly across the continent, we have to be very careful when making general statements about how people in Africa lived.

Africans had to adapt to a variety of climates and landforms, and they developed many different arts and sciences. Although patterns of life differed, many societies shared similar basic values. They found strength in their family structure, communities, and religious beliefs.

Family Ties

In Africa, as elsewhere around the world, family loyalty was a bond that held a society together. Family patterns varied, however. Areas where food was scarce could support only small numbers of people. Therefore, members of hunting and gathering societies usually lived in small groups. Most hunting bands consisted of a few nuclear families. (See page 14.)

Extended families. In farming and herding societies, people were more likely to live in extended families. Members of the extended family included parents, unmarried children, married children and their spouses, and other relatives. In a farming village, several families pooled their labor. They worked together on projects such as clearing land, building homes, and harvesting crops, which demanded a large labor force.

In villages, extended families often shared a common living area, or compound, that contained separate homes for different family members. The eldest male led the family. From an early age, children learned that their work was needed by the family. (See Connections With Literature, page 804, "Forefathers.")

Lineage and clan. Ties of kinship united people even beyond the extended family.

Farming Societies Mutual need helps forge strong ties among members of extended families in herding and farming societies. Here, family members work together in Burkina Faso. In the proven and inexpensive way of traditional farming, they harvest grain by cutting and bundling dry stalks by hand. ***Culture*** What other tasks might members of this family share?

In many societies, a group of distant kin would trace their descent back to a common ancestor. Such a lineage might link several different families. Sharing a common lineage created bonds of loyalty and responsibility.

Several lineages formed a clan, which traced its roots to an even earlier ancestor. Members of a clan also shared duties and obligations toward one another. Each clan had its own leaders who made important decisions for the community.

The system of lineages and clans varied across Africa and often grew very complex. The important general feature of these groupings was the sense of linkage that they created. Kinship ties encouraged a strong sense of community and cooperation. By tracing kinship, people understood that they could depend on one another. As you will read in Chapter 5, these values continue to shape African societies today.

Patterns of Government

African societies developed a variety of government patterns. Most people lived in small villages. Sometimes these villages were linked together as parts of larger governments. In empires such as those of Mali or Songhai, a powerful leader ruled a large area. Often, though, the ruler was a distant figure. Village leaders made the decisions that affected the daily life of most Africans.

In many areas, decisions at the village level required full public discussion. Village leaders would state their views and listen to what others had to say. When members of the

community disagreed, they worked out the issue through further discussion. Their goal was to reach a consensus, or common agreement. Sometimes, reaching a consensus took many days since it often called for compromises on all sides. Leaders stressed the good of the community rather than individual desires or interests.

On issues of justice, especially, the community took care to reach a consensus. Among the Ibo of West Africa, the village leader and his council of elders listened to both sides in a dispute. If, for example, two families disagreed over a boundary between areas where they farmed, the elders held a public hearing. Members of both families would speak. (See Connections With Literature, page 804, "The Cow Tail Switch.")

Before reaching a consensus, the elders would weigh many issues. How was the boundary set? Did one man have too little land to support his family? The elders might decide that the current boundary was unfair. They would then plant a row of trees to mark the new boundary. Both sides were expected to accept the verdict. Sometimes they exchanged gifts to show that trust and harmony had been restored.

Economic Organization

Many Africans lived in either farming or herding societies. Farming was common in river valleys and in the savanna. In these places, rainfall and fertile soil often allowed good harvests. Most villagers were subsistence farmers. They produced enough for their own needs with little or no surplus.

Methods of farming varied according to the environment. In forested areas, farmers had to clear the land. They created an opening in the dense forest by burning and cutting down bushes and small trees. They left larger trees standing. Using digging sticks and iron-bladed hoes, farmers cleared roots and prepared the soil for planting.

Herding Societies For centuries, the cattle herders of the African savanna have been nomadic because grasses are generally sparse and cattle must graze over a wide area. In herding societies, women garden and build the homes while men travel with the herds. ***Environment*** How does the environment influence how people live on the savanna?

After three or four crops, the soil was worn out. Then, people had to move on to clear other land. Sometimes they returned to their first plot after letting it lie fallow, or unused, for a time to regain its fertility.

In most farming societies, people saw the land as community property. Individuals did not own the land. Each family, however, had a right to use a fair share of the available land.

In drier parts of the savanna, farming was difficult. In areas free from the tsetse fly, many people were herders. Among the cattle herders of Africa were the Masai, who lived in East Africa. Cattle provided the Masai with almost everything they needed, including food and clothing. Owning many cattle gave a family high status in the community. Today, the Masai and other herding societies throughout Africa still depend on cattle or other animals to support their way of life.

Lives of Women

African women contributed to the economic well-being of the family. In farming societies, women did the planting, weeding, and harvesting. In parts of West Africa, women took any surplus crops to market.

As elsewhere, women were central to family life. They were respected because they bore the children. Moreover, they were responsible for educating young boys and girls. They also prepared their daughters for their future roles as wives and mothers.

Status. Attitudes toward women varied widely. In some areas, women held positions of power. The Wolof people sometimes chose women to serve as their leaders. The Ashanti believed that women caused the land to be fertile. As a result, Ashanti women owned the land and ruled the home. In many other places, women had little power or prestige. In patriarchal societies, men dominated the family. At marriage, a woman became the property of her husband or his family.

In some African societies, men married more than one woman. The practice of having more than one spouse is called polygamy Islamic law allows a man to have as many as four wives. In some parts of Africa, having several wives showed a man's high status.

In a polygamous family, each wife had her own household within the family compound. The first wife usually held an honored position. Ideally, a man's wives lived in friendship and harmony. Sometimes, though, a man would marry a younger wife and older wives would feel angry at being pushed aside.

Bride wealth. In much of Africa, women married at the age of 14 or 15. Men tended to marry when they were older. The young man was expected to offer a valuable gift to the bride's family. Sometimes men were 30 years old before they could afford such a gift, known as bride wealth. In a cattle-herding society, bride wealth consisted of a number of cattle. Elsewhere, it might be a quantity of cloth, tools, or goats.

Giving bride wealth was a way of recognizing a woman's importance. At the time of marriage, the bride's family lost its daughter's valuable labor. The two sides had to respect each other. By giving bride wealth, a man was honoring the bride's family. He was also promising not to mistreat his future wife. By accepting bride wealth, a woman's family acknowledged the bond that marriage created.

Inheritance and Descent

A variety of traditions governed inheritance and descent in African societies. Some West African peoples, such as the Ashanti, were matrilineal. Members of matrilineal societies traced their lineage through the female line.

The Ashanti believed that a child's blood came entirely from the mother. Therefore, the mother's brother—the child's uncle—had a closer blood relationship to the child than the father had. An Ashanti boy would inherit property from his uncle. He also lived with his uncle and took his name. If necessary, the boy's uncle defended him against his father. In the same way, the father would be responsible for his sister's children.

Many other societies were patrilineal, tracing their lineage through the male line. The

African Women As in other societies, African women contribute to the economic and social well-being of the community. Throughout Africa, women such as these in Zambia produce most of the food for consumption. They also educate children about their place in society. ***Culture*** How has the value of the contributions of women been acknowledged in some African societies?

oldest male headed the family. He would decide such questions as when to clear new land or plant seeds. When he died, his eldest son inherited his property and his responsibilities toward the family.

The Age-Grade System

Outside the family, some African societies developed ties of loyalty through a system of age grades. An age grade included all boys or girls born in the same year. Young people passed through different stages of life with other members of their age grade. Together they took part in the special ceremonies that marked each step on their way to adulthood.

Early on, children in an age grade learned the values of their society. They learned to support each other and to cooperate. As the members of an age grade grew older, their duties to one another changed. Sometimes they helped each other's children. As mature adults, some shared in the political leadership of their community.

Old Ways of Learning Together

The age-grade system was most important as a means of educating the young. The elders of a community served as teachers.

Molapatene (moh lah PAH tuh nee) grew up among the Batlokwa people of Southern Africa, where the age-grade system was strong. When he was 12, the older men of his clan led him and other boys his age away from their village. For 30 days, the boys received intense instruction in the ways of their people.

> “Beliefs and philosophies were transmitted through singing, chanting and the talking drums. I was taught respect, honor, praise, veneration, and worship of my ancestors. I have not forgotten the commandments of my ancestors. I must never forget.”

Two years later, the boys in Molapatene's age grade underwent additional instruction. They learned songs and sacred knowledge to prepare for their role as adult members of the community.

> “Every morning we were aroused to sing and chant the Bodika hymn 'Tlou Wetzee,' which was followed by instruction in wisdom and life by our elders. We chanted day and night while we underwent the tests of manhood. By midnight we fell exhausted on the cold ground to sleep a few hours before being aroused at dawn each day to undergo more rituals and to learn the chants, taboos, and values that related to actions of past rulers and heroes.”

Molapatene's sister went through other rituals with the girls in her age grade. Like the boys, the girls learned the special knowledge

Age-Grade System As the age-grade system of educating young people disappears in Africa, other ways of passing on knowledge and traditions are replacing it. For example, in this farmers' club, experienced farmers give instruction on how to raise crops successfully. ***Interdependence*** Why is education an important link among people?

of the Batlokwa people. The girls' teachers were older Batlokwa women. After three months of instruction, the girls understood the responsibilities of marrying and caring for their families.

Koranic schools. Ways of educating children varied. In Islamic societies, boys attended Koranic schools. There, they learned to read and write Arabic, the language of Islam. They also memorized parts of the Koran. ■

African Religions

Religious beliefs and practices reflect the great variety of cultures in Africa. As elsewhere, religion helped to unite a society. Through religion, people came to understand their origins. Oral traditions and myths taught important moral truths about right and wrong. Dancing, singing, and playing musical instruments have also been part of religious celebrations. Although beliefs and ceremonies varied, African religions have had some common threads.

Traditional beliefs. Most African religions were monotheistic. People believed in a Supreme Being who created the world and its inhabitants. They saw the Supreme Being as a distant figure, however, remote from their daily lives. As a result, many people turned to lesser gods and spirits. These divine figures played a role somewhat similar to that of Christian saints. Africans appealed to them through prayers and other religious rituals. They might request good health, steady rain, or a rich harvest.

Many Africans believed that their ancestors could help or harm them. To honor and please their ancestors, people said prayers and performed certain rituals. Often, the clan leader was responsible for these ceremonies. Some people believed in direct links between the living and the dead. The Baganda of East Africa, for instance, believed that their ancestors' souls were reborn in children.

Like followers of traditional religions in other parts of the world, many African peoples believed that every object on Earth is filled with a living spirit. They respected nature because they believed that the Supreme Being had created all things. If a hunter killed an animal, for example, he first explained his intentions and asked the creature's forgiveness. The animal, after all, was part of the natural world that the Supreme Being had created.

Diviners and healers. In some African societies, diviners and healers held places of honor. These men and women were well educated in the traditions of their society.

Diviners served as interpreters between people and the divine world. Their most important task was to explain the cause of misfortune. If someone fell ill, a healer would seek the cause. He or she studied how members of the sick person's family got along. Perhaps greed or selfishness was at the root of the illness. The healer would help the family become aware of the problem and find a solution.

Diviners and healers also had expert knowledge of herbal medicines. Today, African and western doctors are studying the roots and herbs used in traditional African healing.

Christianity and Judaism. Both Christianity and Judaism reached Africa in ancient times. As you will recall, Christianity spread to North Africa and up the Nile to Axum and Kush. Judaism arrived in Ethiopia from Jewish settlements across the narrow Red Sea. A large community of Ethiopian Jews was established that lasted for hundreds of years. In 1991, most members of that community moved to Israel.

Ethiopian Christians have also survived as a strong community. Christianity has been in Ethiopia for more than 1,500 years. In fact, the Ethiopian Orthodox Church claims roots dating to the time of Solomon in the Old Testament.

In the 1800s, when Europeans pushed into Africa, Christian missionaries set out to replace traditional African religions. Christianity took root in many parts of Africa. Over time, however, African Christians formed their own churches. These churches blended African beliefs, music, and dancing with western Christian beliefs.

Christianity in Africa Christianity spread into what is now Ethiopia in early times. Axum became a Christian kingdom in the A.D. 300s, and the Christian religion remained strong in the area. Members of the Ethiopian Orthodox Church, shown above, view a picture of St. George. ***Diversity*** How have religions contributed to the cultural diversity of Africa?

Islam. Earlier in this chapter, you learned that Muslim traders spread the teachings of Islam to parts of Africa. As early as A.D. 800, wealthy leaders in some African societies converted to Islam. Sometimes, they fit certain features of Islamic culture into their own cultures. In northern Nigeria, for example, some people used a form of Arabic writing for their languages. (See page 570.)

Islam spread gradually. Sometimes its influence was great, sometimes limited. In the early 1800s, Muslim leaders in West Africa felt that Islamic teachings had become corrupted. They called for a *jihad,* or holy war, to purify Islam. In what is today Nigeria, Usuman dan Fodio launched a revival of Islam. He united the nomadic Fulani herders, conquered the neighboring Hausa, and created the powerful Hausa-Fulani Empire. The revival created other strong Islamic states across the savanna.

SECTION 2 REVIEW

1. **Define:** (a) lineage, (b) consensus, (c) subsistence farmer, (d) polygamy, (e) age grade.
2. How did the extended family help to unite a society?
3. How were villages governed?
4. What did bride wealth show about African attitudes toward women?
5. How has cultural diffusion influenced religious life in Africa?
6. **Analyzing Ideas** "The ruin of a nation begins in the homes of its people." How does this proverb from Ghana reflect African attitudes toward family?
7. **Writing Across Cultures** Write a paragraph comparing traditional African government, based on consensus, with American government, based on majority rule.

3 THE SLAVE TRADE

FIND OUT

Why did Europeans become interested in Africa?

Why were millions of Africans sent as slaves to the Americas?

How did the Atlantic slave trade affect Africa?

Vocabulary abolition, diaspora

In the mid-1700s, 11-year-old Olaudah Equiano was kidnapped from his home in Nigeria and sold to slave traders. Bound in chains, he and hundreds of others like him were marched to the coast. There, a slave ship waited at anchor, ready to carry its human cargo to the Americas.

Olaudah Equiano lived many years as a slave in the Americas before he was able to buy his freedom. Later, he wrote a book describing the terrors of his voyage into slavery.

> "I was immediately handled, and tossed up to see if I were sound, by some of the crew, and I was now persuaded that I had gotten into a world of bad spirits, and that they were going to kill me. Their complexions, too, differing so much from ours, their long hair, and the language they spoke . . . united to confirm me in this belief. . . .
>
> The closeness of the place and the heat of the climate, added to the number in the ship, which was so crowded that each had scarcely room to turn himself, almost suffocated us."

From the 1500s to the 1800s, slave traders sent an estimated 10 to 15 million Africans across the Atlantic to the Americas. In some areas, the slave trade had an unsettling impact. This deadly commerce in human beings came to dominate relations among Europe, Africa, and the Americas.

Exploring the Coast of Africa

The first direct contacts between Europeans and the peoples of West Africa occurred in the early 1400s. By then, Portugal's Prince Henry was looking for a sea route around Africa to India. He sent explorers to map the coast of West Africa. Prince Henry also hoped to find the kingdoms of West Africa, which had large resources of gold.

Gradually, Portuguese sailors explored the African coast. In 1488, Bartholomeu Dias rounded the southern tip of Africa. Ten years later, Vasco da Gama followed Dias's route and reached India by sea.

The Portuguese and other Europeans built small trading stations on the coast. They traded with the peoples of West Africa, exchanging iron and copper for fish, sugar, ivory, gold, and pepper. The Europeans also brought Christian missionaries, who set out to convert Africans to Christianity.

Trade in Human Beings

During the 1400s, Europeans bought a few Africans as slaves and carried them to Europe. The demand for slaves was limited, however, until Europeans began to settle the Americas. European rulers required a large labor force to make their American colonies profitable. At first, they used Native Americans to mine gold and silver and to work their plantations, but many died. (See page 460.) Europeans then looked to Africa. They thought that Africans would be able to survive in the tropical climates of the Caribbean and Central America.

Slavery in Africa. Forcing people into slavery did not begin in the 1500s. In Africa, as elsewhere around the world, slavery had existed since ancient times. Most slaves in Africa were people who had been captured in war. Others had sold themselves into slavery during times of famine.

In many African societies, slaves were part of the community. They were treated as servants rather than property. According to an Ashanti saying, "A slave who knows how to serve inherits his master's property." In time, slaves or their children might become full members of the society.

The Atlantic slave trade. Europeans, however, introduced slavery on a massive scale. At the height of the slave trade in the 1700s, up to 60,000 Africans a year were packed into the airless holds of slave ships. Many did not live through the "middle passage" across the Atlantic. This vast, forced migration moved the surviving Africans thousands of miles from their homes.

As the demand for slaves grew, so did the profits to be made from the slave trade. By the 1600s, a trade network, with people as cargo, linked Africa, Europe, and the Americas.

Racism quickly took root. Many whites in Europe and the Americas came to look on Africans as inferior humans. Some even tried to back up their bias with so-called "scientific proof" of racial differences. Racism was used to justify treating Africans as property.

Slaves for guns. European slave traders relied on local African rulers to supply them with slaves. They paid for slaves with guns and other manufactured goods. Armed with guns, African slave traders attacked villages, taking many prisoners.

Many captives resisted, but only a few escaped. Once on board ship, some Africans tried to organize rebellions. Others jumped overboard to avoid a life of slavery. Many died of diseases that spread rapidly in the filthy, crowded conditions of a ship's hold. The Atlantic slave trade lasted about 400 years. During that time, it may have caused the deaths of as many as 2 or 3 million Africans.

Ending the Slave Trade

"It is our will that in these kingdoms there should not be any trade of slaves nor outlet for them." King Affonso, a Christian African ruler, made this proclamation in 1526 to the Portuguese government. Affonso had seen the misery of the slave trade, but his efforts to stop it failed.

Some people in Europe spoke out against slavery. However, their voices also went unheeded. In the 1700s, a few important European thinkers began to talk about human rights and to oppose slavery. Abolition, or the movement to end slavery, slowly gained force. The Quakers, a religious group, were strong supporters of abolition. Later, in Britain and the United States, many free blacks such as

The Middle Passage This painting by an English officer on a slave ship shows how Africans were crammed into the ship's hold, where they suffered horribly. In desperate attempts to escape, some Africans organized revolts while others jumped overboard. ***Human Rights*** What human rights guaranteed by the Bill of Rights of the United States Constitution were denied to those who were enslaved?

Olaudah Equiano and Frederick Douglass struggled tirelessly against slavery. By telling about their own experiences, they exposed the evils of the system.

In 1807, Britain outlawed the slave trade. Later, the British convinced other nations to accept the ban. Many people, however, broke the law and continued to ship Africans to the Americas illegally. Also, the ban on the slave trade did not end slavery. Under pressure from abolitionists, Britain outlawed slavery in its empire in 1834. Slavery, which contributed to the outbreak of the Civil War, continued in the United States until 1865.

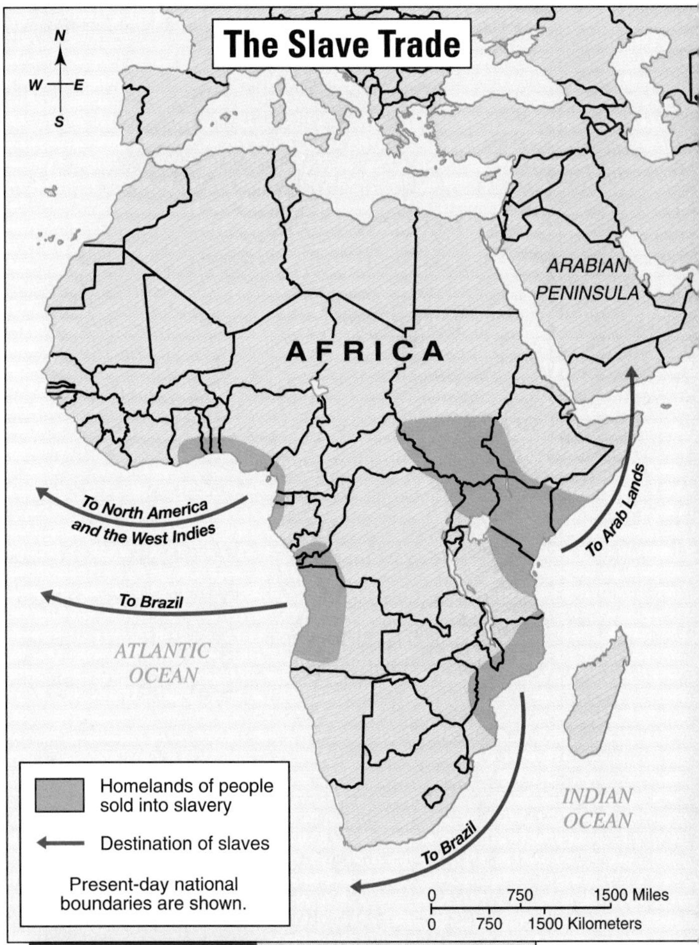

MAP STUDY

Millions of Africans were captured and sold into slavery from the 1500s to the 1800s. This trade in enslaved Africans caused great suffering and lasting hardships in African societies.

1. **Region** Which regions of Africa were the homelands of most of the people who were enslaved?
2. **Movement** (a) What were the destinations of the slave trade? (b) Describe the route of the slave trade from East Africa to Brazil.
3. **Applying Information** Why do you think that the Atlantic Ocean became the main route of the slave trade?

Effects of the Slave Trade

As European nations began to industrialize, slavery became less profitable. Instead of slaves from Africa, Europeans needed Africa's raw materials for their factories. However, 400 years of the slave trade had a lasting effect on Africa as well as on other areas of the world.

In some parts of Africa, the slave trade had little or no impact. In other areas, however, it disrupted whole societies. Sometimes the slave trade encouraged wars and increased tensions among neighboring peoples. In West Africa, for example, the rulers of the Ashanti and Dahomey attacked their neighbors to take slaves. They exchanged slaves for guns, which they used to dominate trade and build strong states.

When slave raiders attacked small communities, economic life suffered. Raiders seized healthy young men and women. Without strong hands to plant and harvest, the community faced disaster. No one knows how many small communities may have disappeared in this way.

The slave trade also thrived in East Africa. There, some African rulers delivered captives to Arab merchants, who sent their human cargoes to the Middle East and North Africa. As in West Africa, the slave trade in East Africa led to the rise of strong new states. During the late 1800s, Mirambo, ruler of the Nyamwezi, built a centralized state. He traded slaves for guns and extended his power over a large region of what is today Tanzania. At about the same time, Tippu Tib organized an empire in the eastern Congo (today Zaire). It was built on the ivory trade and the slave trade.

African diaspora. The slave trade sent millions of Africans overseas. This scattering

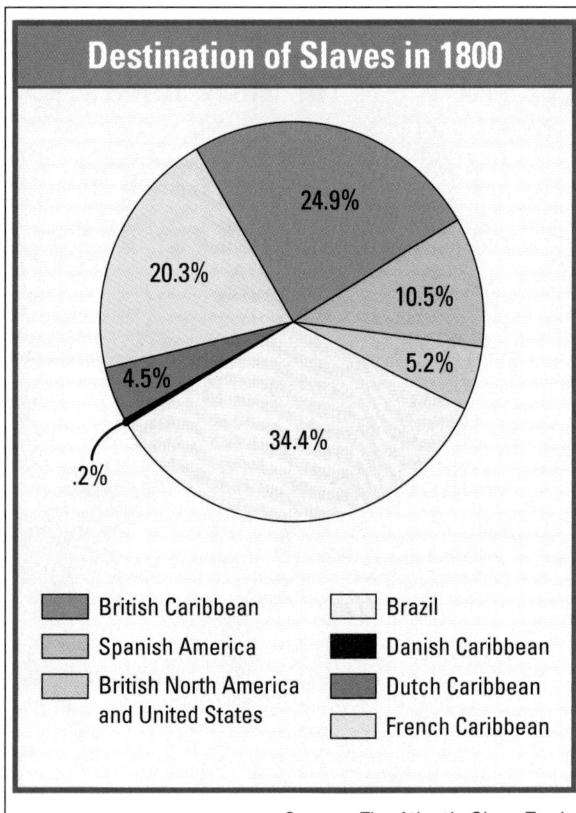

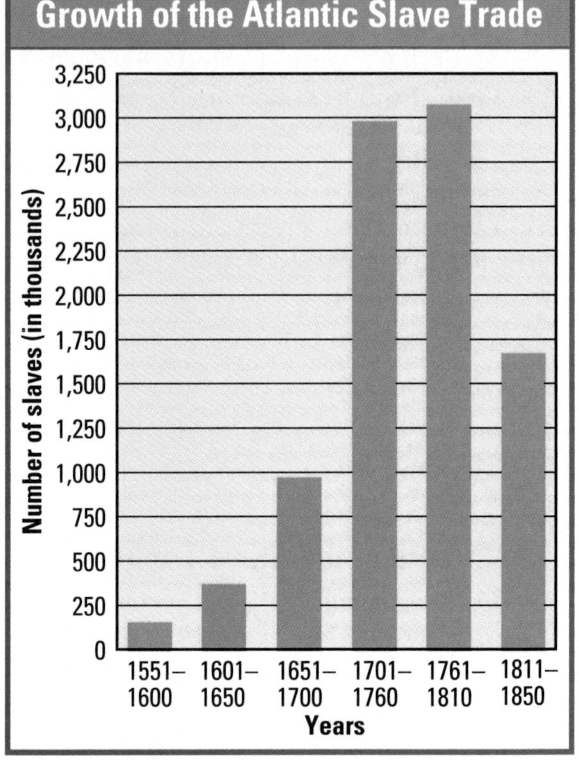

Source: *The Atlantic Slave Trade, A Census* by Philip D. Curtin, 1969.

Graph Skills Statistics about the number of enslaved Africans who were brought to the Americas are very rough estimates. Historians have worked with sketchy records to recreate a picture of the Atlantic slave trade. ▶To which three areas were the largest number of slaves sent in 1800? Approximately how many enslaved Africans were brought to the Americas between 1761 and 1810?

of people, called a diaspora (dī AS puh ruh), brought great suffering to those who were taken captive. The survivors, however, struggled to hold on to their culture. The African diaspora spread the ideas, customs, and beliefs of African peoples to other regions of the world. African musical traditions, proverbs, foods, religious beliefs, and artistic styles all enriched the cultures of these regions. (See Global Connections on page 154.)

Sierra Leone and Liberia. As slavery was abolished, some Africans returned to the continent where they or their ancestors had been born. In 1787, the British set up a colony in West Africa for freed slaves. The colony was called Sierra Leone. Later, free blacks from the United States organized Liberia. Liberia became independent in 1847, despite many obstacles. At this time, Europeans were expanding their influence all across Africa.

SECTION 3 REVIEW

1. **Identify:** (a) Mirambo, (b) Tippu Tib.
2. **Define:** (a) abolition, (b) diaspora.
3. What motives led Europeans to explore the coast of Africa in the 1400s?
4. **Understanding Causes and Effects** (a) How did scarcity of labor in the Americas encourage the Atlantic slave trade? (b) Explain one other cause of the slave trade.
5. **Writing Across Cultures** List two ways in which slavery and the slave trade affected Africa. List two ways in which they affected the United States.

4

AGE OF EUROPEAN IMPERIALISM

FIND OUT

Why did Europeans carve up Africa into colonies?
How did technology help Europeans divide Africa?
How did Africans resist European imperialism?
What groups fought for control of Southern Africa?

"We wish for peace," declared a Xhosa (KOH seh) leader to British soldiers in 1819.

> "We wish to rest in our homes; we wish to get milk for our children; our wives want to farm the land. But your troops cover the plains and swarm in the forests, where they cannot distinguish the men from the women and shoot all."

The British would not make peace, and the fighting continued.

Europeans Explore Africa

Before the 1800s, Europeans knew very little about Africa. They built trading posts along the coasts, but they relied on Africans to bring slaves and trade goods such as ivory and gold from the interior. European interest in Africa increased, however, during the Age of Imperialism.

Spurred on by trading companies and a desire for adventure, Europeans explored the rivers of Africa. In 1795, Mungo Park, a young Scotsman, set out to trace the Niger River to its source. He endured incredible hardships on a long trek inland from the West African coast. His book about his travels made him a hero in Europe.

Richard Burton and John Speke devoted years to hunting for the source of the Nile. The French explorer René Caillié searched for the famous city of Timbuktu. In books and lectures, these explorers painted vivid pictures of Africa for European audiences. Their views of Africa, however, reflected European attitudes. They made little effort to understand African cultures.

More than anyone else, David Livingstone, a British doctor and missionary, captured the imaginations of Europeans. Livingstone spent much of his life in Africa. He wanted "to open up highways for commerce and Christianity to pass into the vast interior of Africa." Europeans credited Livingstone with "discovering" the huge waterfalls on the Zambezi River. He named them Victoria Falls, after Britain's Queen Victoria. The Africans who lived nearby, however, had long known the falls as Mosi oa Tunya, "the smoke that thunders."

European Motives

Following the paths of these explorers, Europeans extended their influence in Africa. By the outbreak of World War I in 1914, European nations claimed all of Africa except Liberia and Ethiopia. Britain controlled most of the continent. Belgium, France, Germany, Italy, Portugal, and Spain were also represented.

Economic motives. Europeans took over lands in Africa for a number of reasons. Economic competition was a major motive. By the late 1800s, the nations of Western Europe had industrialized. They competed for control of raw materials for their factories. Africa was a source of palm oil for soaps, cotton for textiles, and gum for paper and fabrics. The rain forests provided rubber, ivory, and rare hardwoods. In addition, Europeans looked on African societies as possible markets for the goods produced by European factories.

Political motives. Economic competition went hand in hand with political rivalries. Nationalism was sweeping through Europe in the late 1800s. European powers built vast empires to boost their place in the world. Rivalries fueled the scramble for colonies. Britain, for example, claimed lands in Africa to prevent German or French expansion.

"The Smoke That Thunders" The British explorer David Livingstone marveled at the beauty of this waterfall on the Zambezi River. He called it Victoria Falls, but Africans called it Mosi oa Tunya. Today, the river provides hydroelectric power to two bordering countries, Zambia and Zimbabwe. ***Culture*** What do the two names for the falls tell you about the different cultures?

Religious motives. Some people went to Africa for religious reasons. Christians believed that it was their duty to spread the benefits of western civilization. They thought their religion and civilization were superior, so they expected Africans to adopt European ways. Many Christian missionaries supported the colonial governments by introducing western values among the people, but some, such as David Livingstone, also campaigned against the slave trade. Livingstone and others worked to improve health care and set up schools.

The Scramble for Colonies

Two innovations helped Europeans advance into Africa. New medical knowledge improved treatment for diseases such as malaria and yellow fever, which let Europeans survive in Africa. In addition, the British had developed the Maxim gun. This early machine gun gave them an advantage over Africans armed with muskets or spears.

Europeans pushed their claims in all parts of Africa. France and Britain competed for power in Egypt. A French company completed the Suez Canal in 1869. Soon after, the British gained control of the canal. They regarded it as a key link to the empire they had established in India. Elsewhere in North Africa, France and Italy gained influence. (See the map at right.)

The scramble for colonies in Central and West Africa began when King Leopold II of Belgium gained control of the Congo basin (present-day Zaire). Britain and Germany supported his claims in order to stop French expansion in the region. Tensions mounted quickly as European rivals sent agents to negotiate treaties with African leaders. To ease the crisis, 14 European nations met in Berlin, Germany, in 1884.

Berlin Conference. At the Berlin Conference, Europeans made decisions about dividing Africa. No Africans were invited to the meeting. The European powers recognized Leopold's personal claim to the Congo Free State. They accepted boundaries already set up by the French, German, and Portuguese in other parts of Africa.

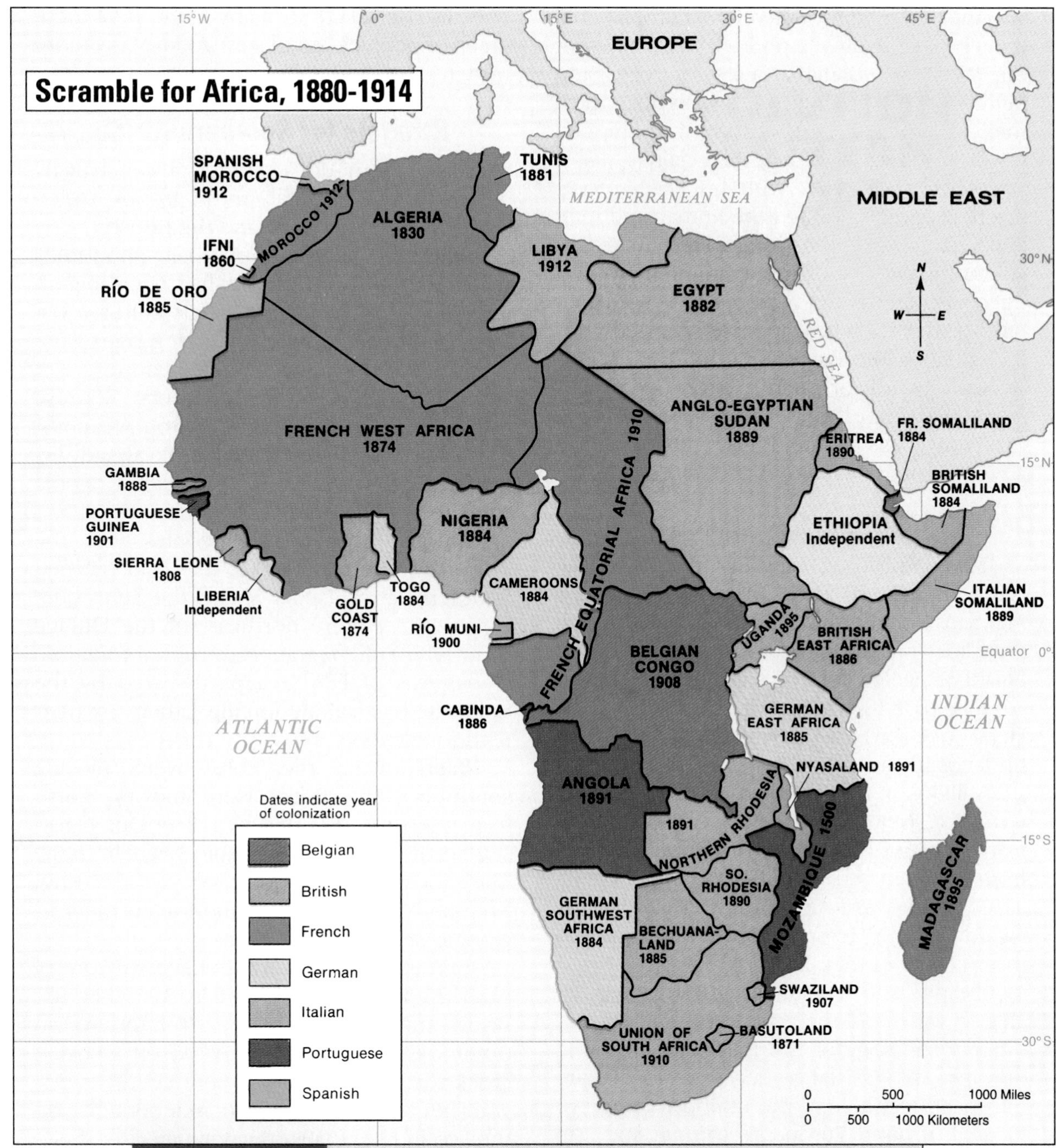

MAP STUDY

In the late 1800s, European nations scrambled to claim territory in Africa. By 1914, almost the entire continent had been partitioned.

1. **Movement** (a) Which African land became the first European colony? (b) Which European nation controlled it?
2. **Region** Name the European powers that controlled most of North Africa.
3. **Comparing** How were the boundaries of Europe's African colonies different from those of earlier African kingdoms?

After the Berlin Conference, European nations began solidifying their claims. They sent out surveyors to map routes for roads and railroads. They appointed officials to govern their colonies. When necessary, they shipped troops to Africa to enforce their claims.

Congo Free State. With his claim recognized, Leopold exploited the human and mineral resources of the Congo Free State. His agents forced each African community to produce a set amount of rubber or ivory without paying them. When people resisted this forced labor, the Belgians cut off their hands or ears. Word of such horrors eventually reached Europe. Under pressure, Leopold turned over his private domain to the Belgian government.

African Resistance

Many Africans resisted European imperialism with military force. In North Africa, the Algerians fought the French expansion with great loss of life. In West Africa, the Ibo and Fulani struggled for years against the British advance. For 10 years, Mkwawa, leader of the Hehe, opposed the German advance across his lands in East Africa.

Millions of Africans died as a result of the wars of resistance. During 20 years of fighting in the Congo Free State, the population fell from an estimated 20 million to about 8 million. In southwest Africa, the Germans nearly wiped out the Herero people, who opposed the takeover of their land.

Despite stiff resistance, Africans were unable to withstand the advanced weapons and other technology of the Europeans. Only in Ethiopia did resistance succeed. To acquire European technology, the Ethiopian emperor Menelik II hired Europeans to train and arm his forces. The policy worked. At the Battle of Adowa in 1896, he defeated an Italian army and preserved Ethiopia's independence.

Natural disasters such as disease sometimes helped the Europeans. Matabele armies in present-day Zimbabwe suffered from a smallpox epidemic at a crucial moment in their struggle against the British. In the late 1880s, Europeans accidentally introduced rinderpest, a cattle disease, into East Africa. The disease killed so many cattle that thousands of people died of starvation. Many more were too weak to fight.

Struggle for Southern Africa

In Southern Africa, a bitter power struggle developed among local African groups, Dutch settlers known as Boers, and the British.

Migrating peoples. For many hundreds of years, groups of Africans had been migrating into Southern Africa. Their cultures differed, although some of their languages were related to a root language called Bantu.*

The newcomers were farmers. Because they were better armed with iron weapons, they seized the lands of the people already living in Southern Africa. The defeated people retreated into less desirable lands.

Among the migrating peoples were the Zulus. By the early 1800s, they had reached Southern Africa. Under Shaka, the Zulus built a powerful empire northeast of the Orange River. The Zulu migration disrupted traditional patterns of life. Groups defeated by the Zulus fled to safety, forcing others in their path to move on.

Boers. While the Zulus were moving southward, the Boers were moving north from the tip of South Africa. The Dutch had settled at what is now Cape Town in 1652. They looked on the local people, the Khoi Khoi and San, as inferior and forced them to work as slaves on their farms.

In the early 1800s, the British won control of the Cape Colony from the Boers. When the British tried to end slavery and interfered in other ways, the Boers retreated on a "Great Trek" northward.

The Boers set up two independent republics in the 1850s, the Orange Free State and the Transvaal, in lands which the Zulus had recently conquered. Battles between Boers and Zulus continued for decades. Finally, the British joined the struggle and defeated the Zulus. As elsewhere in Africa, the

* Just as many languages in Europe, Iran, and India can be traced to a common root called Indo-European (see page 643), many languages of Africa have Bantu as a common root.

Builders and Shapers

Shaka: King of the Zulu Nation

> " The nations, Shaka, have condemned
> you,
> Yet still today, they speak of you,
> Still today their books discuss you,
> But we defy them to explain you. "

With these words, Zulu poet B. W. Vilakazi expressed his pride in the achievements of Shaka. To Zulus, Shaka is as much a hero today as he was 140 years ago. As the leader of one small clan, he rose to conquer a huge empire in Southern Africa.

Shaka was born around 1787, the son of the Zulu chief Senzangakona and his wife Nandi. As a boy, Shaka was rebellious. He angered his father by refusing Senzangakona's gift of a warrior's lion skin. Then Shaka learned the arts of war from Dingiswayo, king of the more powerful Mtetwa people.

When Senzangakona died in 1816, Dingiswayo helped Shaka become king of the Zulus. The two kings remained allies and friends. After Dingiswayo's death, the Mtetwa placed themselves under Shaka's command.

Shaka introduced new methods and techniques of fighting. He reorganized the Zulu army into regiments called *impi* and replaced their throwing spears with assegais, short-handled stabbing weapons. He also developed a form of attack that allowed his forces to surround and crush any enemy. Under Shaka's brilliant leadership, the Zulu army became an outstanding fighting force. Within four years, he conquered dozens of smaller kingdoms and united them into a single powerful nation. The Zulu empire helped slow down British advances into South Africa.

Shaka's triumphs came at a great price. Millions of people died as a result of his conquests. In 1828, his two half brothers killed him. Although Shaka has been called a tyrant, generations of Zulus have honored his name. One *izibongo,* or poem of praise, refers to the king as "he who beats but is not beaten."

1. What changes did Shaka make in the Zulu army?
2. **Making Inferences** Why do you think later Zulus have honored Shaka despite his reputation as a harsh ruler?

Maxim gun and other weapons enabled Europeans to win key battles.

Diamonds and gold. The discovery of diamonds in 1867 and gold in 1884 sent Europeans into the Boer republics. Eager to expand their empire, the British fought to control the rich area. By 1902, the British had defeated the Dutch settlers in the Boer War.

Eight years later, the British created the Union of South Africa out of various colonies in the region. They granted self-government to the new nation. Under the constitution, however, only white men had the right to vote. Because the Boers made up a majority of the white population, they gained control of the South African government.

SECTION 4 REVIEW

1. **Locate:** (a) Cape Town, (b) Union of South Africa.
2. **Identify:** (a) David Livingstone, (b) Leopold II, (c) Menelik II, (d) Shaka, (e) Boer War.
3. (a) Why did European explorers take an interest in Africa in the 1800s? (b) Why did Europeans want colonies in Africa?
4. How did the Berlin Conference change the map of Africa?
5. Why did African efforts to resist European imperialism fail?
6. **Making Inferences** "When you first came, you had the Bible and we had the land," noted a Zimbabwean during the Age of Imperialism. "Now we have the Bible and you have the land." What does this imply about the impact of missionaries?
7. **Writing Across Cultures** Write a dialogue between a Native American and an African in which they discuss the arrival of Europeans in their land.

5 EFFECTS OF EUROPEAN RULE

FIND OUT

What methods did Europeans use to rule their colonies?

What economic changes did European rule bring to Africa?

How did European rule affect African cultures?

What material improvements did Europeans introduce?

Vocabulary elite

> "If you woke up one morning and found that somebody had come to your house, and had declared that the house belonged to him, you would naturally be surprised, and you would like to know by what arrangement."

Jomo Kenyatta posed the question above, one that many people in Africa asked. What right did Europeans have to walk in and take over African lands?

Kenyatta was born in Kenya several years after the British took control in 1886. He lived to become the first president of Kenya in 1963. Although colonial rule was relatively brief, its effects are still felt today. (📖 See World Literature, "The Gentleman of the Jungle," by Jomo Kenyatta, page 152.)

New Political and Economic Systems

In their African colonies, European nations set up governments that reflected their own traditions. They introduced European legal systems that differed greatly from those of the people they ruled. European law codes were impersonal. Unlike African forms of justice that emphasized discussion and consensus, European justice relied on abstract principles of right and wrong. Africans saw these principles as unjust, especially when Europeans used those laws to take African lands.

Colonial governments. European nations developed two methods of ruling their colonies—direct and indirect rule. Direct rule meant that the colonial power controlled the government at every level. It appointed officials from colonial governor to village leader. France, Portugal, Germany, and Belgium practiced direct rule.

Britain had a huge worldwide empire to govern. It did not have enough officials to send to every colony, so the British relied on indirect rule. They left traditional rulers in place. British officials made the decisions but expected local rulers to enforce them.

Under both types of government, the result was the same. Traditional African rulers no longer had power or influence.

New economic patterns. The Europeans expected their colonies to be profitable. European companies exploited the mineral resources of Africa, sending raw materials to feed European factories. White settlers also sought to make the land profitable. They set up plantations to produce cash crops such as cocoa, cotton, peanuts, and coffee.

The new ways upset traditional patterns of life. African communities had been largely self-sufficient. Villagers bartered, or traded, for goods they needed. Europeans introduced a money economy. They required Africans to pay taxes in cash instead of goods.

Money economy. To make money, Africans sold their labor. Men had to leave home to take jobs as farm workers and miners. Because they were away for long periods, the close-knit life of villages changed. In South Africa, men who worked in mines lived in large dormitories with other workers. Such arrangements undermined family life. Others became migrant workers, leaving their homes to work in faraway places 11 months of the year.

The money economy created differences in wealth as some people accumulated capital and property. It also changed attitudes toward the land. In the past, land belonged to the community. European rulers encouraged individual ownership of land, especially by Europeans.

As you read in Chapter 2, the export of cash crops and raw materials made the less-developed world dependent on the markets in the industrial world. The new money economy also encouraged many farmers to grow cash crops instead of food. In some areas, Africans even had to import food. In other areas, however, new seeds and the use of fertilizers led to greater output of food.

French Colonial Rule In North Africa, the French extended their rule over Algeria, Tunisia, and Morocco. Here, a French official greets the sultan of Morocco. Although the sultan headed the government, the French were the real rulers. ***Power*** Why might some European countries have chosen to leave local African rulers in place?

Material Improvements

Colonial rule brought new systems of transportation and communication. The Europeans invested money to build roads and railroads and to set up telegraphs. These improvements had advantages and disadvantages. They made travel easier. Many Africans, however, were forced to work on building projects for very low wages.

Roads and railroads were built to connect plantations or mines to the coast. They also allowed colonial governments to extend their control. The new transportation systems encouraged the migration of workers, further weakening family and village ties.

Other improvements contributed to population growth. Missionaries set up hospitals, and doctors introduced better medical care. In towns and cities, improved sanitation and water systems helped people live healthier lives. Colonial governments also battled diseases that had killed many people in the past.

Currents of Change

Europeans set up elementary schools for Africans. In colonial schools, African students

British Colonial Rule During the Age of Imperialism, a British tobacco company used this advertisement to sell tobacco from Nyasaland (present-day Malawi). British companies set up plantations in Africa to grow cash crops, including tobacco, coffee, and cotton. ***Change*** How did colonial rule affect African societies and disrupt their economies?

learned European history and culture along with basic skills. A few Africans had the opportunity to attend secondary schools. They formed an educated elite in the colonies. An elite is a small group of people with high social status. Some young men went to schools in Europe. On their return home, however, they often found that higher-level jobs were closed to Africans.

Some western-educated Africans rejected their traditional cultures. They discovered that the only way to get ahead was to become like their rulers. Others saw serious flaws in European culture. Africans read the works of John Locke. His ideas about equality had encouraged democratic revolutions in Europe. How could Europeans praise Locke, they asked, and refuse Africans their basic rights?

By the early 1900s, new African leaders were emerging. They called for Africans to reexamine their heritage and to take pride in their past. They were laying the basis for independence movements that would follow.

SECTION 5 REVIEW

1. **Define:** elite.
2. What was the difference between direct and indirect rule?
3. How did a money economy affect Africans?
4. How did colonial rule affect agriculture?
5. Why did European rule lead to economic dependence in Africa?
6. **Applying Information** How did colonial rule influence traditional African cultures?
7. **Writing Across Cultures** Write a paragraph comparing the 13 British colonies in the Americas and Britain's colonies in Africa.

Chapter 4 Review

Understanding Vocabulary

Match each term at left with the correct definition at right.

1. lineage	**a.** common agreement
2. consensus	**b.** small group of people with high social status
3. diaspora	**c.** Muslim house of worship
4. mosque	**d.** group that traces its descent to a common ancestor
5. elite	**e.** scattering of people

Reviewing the Main Idea

1. (a) Describe the pattern of trade in the kingdoms of West Africa. (b) Describe the pattern of trade in East African city-states.

2. What role did women play in traditional African societies?

3. How did the age-grade system help maintain African traditions and unite some societies?

4. (a) What were the traditional religious beliefs of African cultures? (b) How did Christianity and Judaism reach Africa?

5. (a) Why did Europeans turn to Africa for slaves? (b) How did the slave trade affect both Africa and the Americas?

6. (a) Who attended the Berlin Conference? (b) What did the conference decide?

7. (a) Why were Europeans able to defeat Africans who resisted colonial rule? (b) Why was Ethiopia able to remain independent?

8. (a) How did economic patterns introduced by Europeans affect African families? (b) What were some material improvements brought by European imperialism?

Reviewing Chapter Themes

1. Trade supported large states and empires in parts of Africa. Describe how trade contributed to the rise of three of the following: Ghana, Mali, Songhai, Benin, Zimbabwe.

2. People in Africa organized their societies in different ways. Choose four of the following social institutions and explain the role of each in uniting African communities: extended families, clans, consensus, matrilineal lineage, patrilineal lineage, the age-grade system.

3. The Atlantic slave trade caused great upheaval. Explain how slavery disrupted traditional patterns of life in some parts of Africa.

4. Europeans brought their culture and ideas to Africa; their legal system; government; money economy; cash crops; new systems of transportation and education. Choose four of these topics and explain how each affected the African cultures.

Thinking Critically

1. Defending a Position Do you think the missionaries' desire to spread Christianity in Africa was ethnocentric? Explain.

2. Making Global Connections Why are many African Americans interested in tracing their African roots?

Applying Your Skills

1. Analyzing a Quotation "What happiness have they brought us?" asked a ruler in the Congo. "They have given us a road we do not need, a road that brings more and more foreigners." How did the speaker view the material improvements brought to Africa by the Europeans?

2. Understanding Sequence European imperialism reached its peak by the early 1900s. In chronological order, list four events that marked the interaction between European imperialists and Africans.

Chapter 5

AFRICA IN TRANSITION

Independence Day in Namibia When Namibia became independent in 1990, its people celebrated their freedom from colonial rule. After a century of domination by Germany and then by South Africa, Namibians now control their nation and its government. ***Change*** What are some challenges that Namibia faces as a newly independent nation?

CHAPTER OUTLINE

1 Winning Independence

2 Steps Toward Development

3 Changing Patterns of Life

4 Nigeria

5 Zimbabwe

With a flourish, the bandmaster raised his hand. The crowd rose to its feet. Trumpets and drums began to play "N'Kosi Sikelel'I Afrika" ("God Bless Africa").

> "God bless Africa,
> Let her fame spread far and wide;
> Hear our prayer,
> May God bless us.
> Come, Spirit, come,
> Come, Holy Spirit,
> Come and bless us, her children."

As the stirring anthem drew to a close, thousands cheered. After years of struggle, Namibia finally won independence in 1990.

Mankayi Sontanga wrote "N'Kosi Sikelel'I Afrika" in 1897, when Europeans were extending their rule across Africa. Nationalists in Southern Africa soon adopted the song as their unofficial anthem. After independence, countries such as Tanzania, Zambia, and Namibia made it their national anthem. In 1994, South Africa, too, adopted this anthem as its own. The words differ from nation to nation, but each version echoes a deep love for Africa.

CHAPTER PERSPECTIVE

In the 1950s, African nations began to cast off colonial rule and take charge of their own destinies. Like emerging nations everywhere, they have faced many challenges.

As you read, look for these chapter themes:

- Since winning independence, African nations have taken different routes toward modernization.
- Patterns of colonial rule and the diversity of people on the continent have shaped developments there.
- Natural forces such as drought as well as rapid population growth pose problems for the developing nations of Africa.
- Urbanization and modern technology are changing African societies.

Literature Connections

In this chapter, you will encounter passages from the following works.

"God Bless Africa," Mankayi Sontanga

"Black Woman," Léopold Sédar Senghor

"My People," Christy Essien-Igbokwe

"Take Up Arms and Liberate Yourselves," Zimbabwean folk song

For other selections, see Connections With Literature, pages 804–808.

1 WINNING INDEPENDENCE

FIND OUT

How did nationalism help shape modern Africa?

How did African nations win independence?

How does the colonial past affect modern African nations?

Vocabulary boycott, guerrilla warfare

"Freedom for the Gold Coast will be the fountain of inspiration from which other African colonial territories can draw when the time comes for them to strike for their freedom."

Kwame Nkrumah's prediction came true. In 1957, Nkrumah (en KROO muh) led the Gold Coast to independence. The nation then changed its name to Ghana. With Nkrumah as prime minister, Ghana served as a model for many other African nations that wanted to shake off colonial rule.

African Nationalism

By the early 1900s, nationalism had taken root in Africa. Nationalism, as you will recall, is a sense of pride in and devotion to one's country. Gradually, it became a powerful force.

Nationalism grew out of European rule. Colonial powers had drawn boundaries that included diverse ethnic groups. In the Gold Coast (present-day Ghana), the British created a colony that put longtime rivals such as the Ashanti and Fante under the same government. The colony also included other groups, such as the Ewe, Dagomba, and Tallensi. African nationalists realized that they had to create a sense of unity among diverse groups if they were to win independence.

Pan-Africanism. Many nationalists embraced the idea of Pan-Africanism, which called for unifying all of Africa. Pan-Africanism began in the early 1900s with the slogan "Africa for the Africans."

Prominent African Americans supported the movement. Leaders such as W.E.B. Du Bois and Marcus Garvey called for a sense of unity among all people of African descent.

Léopold Sédar Senghor. During the 1930s, a Senegalese poet, Léopold Sédar Senghor, took the lead in the *négritude* movement. The movement encouraged Africans to value their heritage, and it strengthened Pan-Africanism. Senghor rejected the negative view that colonial powers held about African cultures. Instead, he urged both Africans and Europeans to take a new look at African traditions. In poems such as "Black Woman," he praised the beauty and vitality of African culture:

> "... black woman,
> Clothed in your color which is life,
> your form which is beauty!
> I grew in your shadow, the sweetness
> of your hands bandaged my eyes,
> And here in the heart of summer and
> of noon, I discover you, promised
> land from the height of a burnt
> mountain,
> And your beauty strikes my heart, like
> the lightning of an eagle."

Like many nationalists, Senghor had completed his education in Europe. There he saw European strengths and weaknesses. He was horrified by the racism of German dictator Adolf Hitler, who attacked Jews and other minorities. Returning to Africa, Senghor became politically active. He served as Senegal's representative to the French National Assembly. After Senegal became independent in 1960, he served for 20 years as its president. Today Senghor ranks among the greatest leaders of Pan-Africanism.

New Nations Emerge

As World War II ended, independence movements gained strength in both Africa and Asia. The war weakened colonial powers such as Britain and France. The Cold War also helped nationalists. The Soviet Union condemned imperialism and aided some nationalist movements. At the same time, the United States spoke out against colonialism. Slowly, some European nations saw that they must give up their colonial empires.

In 1950, Africa contained only four independent nations—Liberia, Ethiopia, Egypt, and South Africa. (In South Africa, a small white minority ruled over the black majority, who were denied the right to vote.) During the 1950s and 1960s, African demands for freedom led to the birth of many new nations.

Ghana. Most African nations won independence through largely peaceful means. In the Gold Coast, for example, Kwame Nkrumah organized strikes and boycotts to protest British rule. A boycott is a refusal to buy certain goods or services. Although the British jailed him for his actions, he achieved his goal. In 1957, Ghana became the first black African nation to win independence. Over the next decade, many former British and French colonies gained freedom. (See the map on page 110.)

North Africa. During the 1950s, the nations of Libya, Tunisia, and Morocco also won independence in a generally peaceful manner. By contrast, in 1954 a bitter war broke out in Algeria. Many French people had settled in Algeria. They considered Algeria to be a part of France. Algerian nationalists rejected this idea and fought hard for freedom. More than 100,000 Algerians and 10,000 French died in the eight-year struggle. In 1962, Algerians forced the French to withdraw.

Kenya. Fighting also broke out in other areas where large numbers of whites had settled. In Kenya, Jomo Kenyatta demanded political and economic reforms from the British. White settlers, however, wanted to protect their own rights. They opposed giving rights to blacks. Slowly, some Africans moved toward armed resistance, known as Mau Mau.

A Presidential Visit As the first president of Senegal, Léopold Sédar Senghor was one of the strongest supporters of African nationalism and independence. Here, citizens in Abidjan, the capital of Côte d'Ivoire, are welcoming President Senghor on a state visit. ***Interdependence*** Why are international relations important in Africa today?

The British accused Kenyatta of leading secret Mau Mau groups that attacked white settlers. Kenyatta was imprisoned, but bloody fighting continued. Both sides committed acts of brutal violence. Most of the 1,300 people killed were Kikuyu, whose ancestors had migrated to the region in the 1400s. In 1964, the British finally agreed to withdraw. Kenyatta became the first president of Kenya.

Southern Africa. In Southern Africa, Portugal refused to give up its colonies of Angola and Mozambique. Nationalist groups in both colonies waged guerrilla wars against the Portuguese. In guerrilla warfare, small bands of fighters stage hit-and-run attacks against a larger power. Angola and Mozambique finally won independence in 1975. In Chapter 6, you will read how blacks struggled for freedom in white-ruled South Africa.

The Colonial Legacy

The effects of colonial rule lasted long after African nations won independence. Europeans left behind a legacy of anti-colonialism. They had ruled their colonies in the belief that European cultures were superior. Colonial rule also created in Africans the desire for modern technology and the same standard of living that Europeans enjoyed.

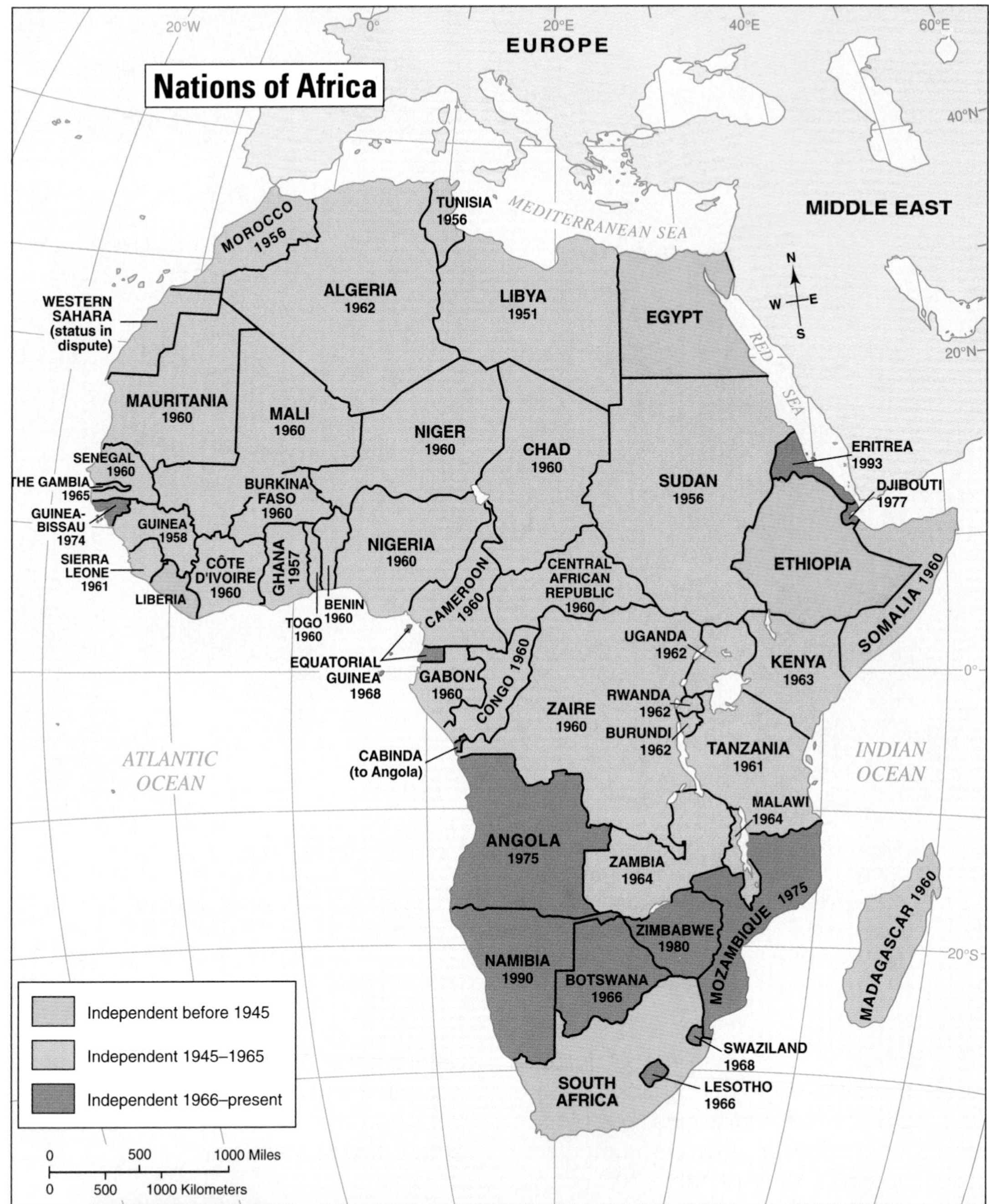

MAP STUDY

Today, Africa is a continent of 55 independent nations, most of which gained their independence in 1960 or soon thereafter.

1. **Place** Which nation was the first to win its independence after 1945?
2. **Region** In which region of Africa did most nations become independent after 1965?
3. **Drawing Conclusions** What changes transformed Africa into a continent of free and independent nations?

While creating high expectations, colonial rulers did little to prepare Africans for independence. They had replaced or weakened local leaders and disrupted the traditional economy. Although colonial rulers helped Africans set up the outward forms of democratic government, most new African nations had few experienced leaders.

As you have read, the new national boundaries were artificial creations of colonial powers. They included many rival ethnic groups. Sometimes borders divided people belonging to the same ethnic group. The Ewe people, for example, were split between Ghana and Togo. In addition, many new nations were small, with fewer than 10 million people. These nations would have difficulty meeting the economic needs of their people.

Colonial rulers had made some positive changes. As you have read, they built roads, bridges, and railroads, and they dredged harbors for seagoing ships. They set up schools and introduced new crops and farming methods. Although these changes were made for the benefit of the colonial powers, they did give the new nations a framework on which to build.

SECTION 1 REVIEW

1. **Locate:** (a) Ghana, (b) Algeria, (c) Kenya, (d) Angola, (e) Mozambique.
2. **Identify:** (a) Pan-Africanism, (b) Léopold Sédar Senghor, (c) négritude movement, (d) Kwame Nkrumah, (e) Jomo Kenyatta.
3. **Define:** (a) boycott, (b) guerrilla warfare.
4. What were the goals of African nationalist leaders?
5. Why were many African nations able to win independence after World War II?
6. Describe three effects of colonial rule on African nations.
7. **Understanding Causes and Effects** How did the négritude movement encourage African independence?
8. **Writing Across Cultures** Imagine that you are W.E.B. Du Bois, an African American fighting for civil rights. Write an editorial explaining your support for Pan-Africanism.

2 STEPS TOWARD DEVELOPMENT

FIND OUT

What political challenges do African nations face?

How have African nations tried to solve their economic problems?

How has the population explosion strained Africa's resources?

Vocabulary secede, democratization, socialism, multinational corporation

"While the United States is trying to reach the moon, Tanzania is trying to reach its villages," observed Julius Nyerere (nyuh RAIR ay) in the 1960s. Nyerere was Tanzania's first president. Like other African leaders, he wanted to unite the people of his nation, provide basic services, and end foreign influence.

At independence, Africans looked forward to a bright future. In cities, workers expected wages to rise. They wanted to be able to buy the goods that westerners enjoyed. In farming villages, people hoped that freedom would mean lower taxes and the chance to improve their lives. In the next decades, however, a number of forces created major stumbling blocks to progress. Yet, African nations remained determined to make good on the promises made at independence.

Building Governments

After independence, African governments faced the challenge of building national unity. By tradition, Africans valued ties to families, villages, and ethnic groups. They felt little loyalty to distant national governments. Economic differences created further divisions. Some Africans lived in areas rich in resources. Others struggled to survive in poor farming or herding regions. Such ethnic and economic divisions led to war in the Congo.

Civil war. In 1960, the Congo won independence from Belgium. The new nation included 14 million people from more than 200 separate groups. Under a hastily written constitution, six provinces of the former Belgian Congo were joined together. Each had its own economic interests, political parties, and leaders.

Regional and ethnic rivalries plunged the nation into civil war. Copper-rich Katanga province chose to secede, or break away, from the Congo. Cold War rivalries added to the conflict as the United States and the Soviet Union supported rival groups. United Nations forces tried to restore peace. In 1965, military strongman Mobutu Sese Seko (moh BOO too SAY say SAY koh) seized power. He gave the country an African name, Zaire. He also took steps to unify the rival groups.

Other African nations have suffered the effects of civil war. In Ethiopia, Somalia, Liberia, and Rwanda, internal struggles created huge numbers of refugees. Fighting disrupted farming, which in turn contributed to famine. In the early 1990s, rival groups kept food from reaching starving people in Somalia. In response, a United Nations peacekeeping force, including thousands of Americans, landed in Somalia to oversee food distribution.

One-party rule. The need to build national unity led some African leaders to set up one-party rule. They felt that having many parties encouraged divisions and wastefulness. One-party rule also reflected traditional African values of discussion and consensus within a community. In Tanzania, for example, Julius Nyerere argued that one-party rule could achieve democracy. Nyerere set up a system of choice within a single party. In each election district, voters could choose between two or more very different candidates from the same party.

Military rule. In a number of African nations, the military has stepped in to restore order and get rid of corrupt civilian leaders. Such military rulers often silence dissent and use harsh measures to stay in power.

Many Africans have welcomed military rule. To them, the test of government is not its support for democracy. Rather, the test is the government's success in developing the nation's economy. Does the government help workers earn more? Has it improved health care, set up schools, and provided seeds on time to farmers?

Stability and progress. Countries that have made the most economic progress since independence are those with stable governments. For 33 years, President Félix Houphouët-Boigny (fay LEEKS OO FWAY bwah NYEE) has ruled the Côte d'Ivoire (KOHT dee VWAH) with a strong hand. During much of that time, the economy grew. Under tight political control, Gabon, Cameroon, and Kenya also made economic gains.

Beginning in the late 1980s, many African nations joined the worldwide trend toward democratization, or the move toward multiparty systems. Several nations held multiparty elections. In Benin, a civilian candidate defeated the general who had ruled for 19 years. Elsewhere, voters returned longtime leaders to power.

Economic Systems

As they experimented with various forms of government, independent nations of Africa also experimented with various economic systems. One key issue has been how much control the government should have over the economy.

African socialism. Some African nations, such as Tanzania, set up socialist governments. Under socialism, the government owns and operates major businesses and controls other parts of the economy. Many Africans felt that the state could direct the economy to meet the basic needs of food, housing, and health care. They also saw socialism as a way to end special privileges and bring about equality. Just as important, socialism rejected colonialism.

The socialist experiment had few successes. In the 1970s, Nyerere set up a socialist system in Tanzania. He tried to achieve equality

Building New Nations After independence, African countries had to establish national governments and set up schools, hospitals, and other services for their people. Villagers in Zambia (above) learn about nutrition. Voters in Namibia (right) take part in electing government leaders. ***Choice*** Why do political systems differ among the many nations of Africa?

and self-reliance through strict government control of the economy. Although Tanzania did avoid the corruption that plagued other nations, its economy suffered because world market prices for its exports dropped.

Mixed economies. Today, most African nations have mixed economies. The governments exercise control over many aspects of business, but they also encourage private investment.

A major goal of African nations is to build factories and produce goods for their own use. In this way, they hope to reduce dependence on foreign imports. To obtain capital, they have turned to multinational corporations, huge enterprises with branches in many countries. Multinational corporations have invested in mining and large agricultural operations. Some people see them as simply replacing colonial powers in the economic system. They make profits from exporting African crops and commodities.

Most of those profits, however, flow out of Africa. Government leaders want to limit the amount of money leaving their countries. Therefore, some nations keep at least 51 percent of control over key industries.

Economic Choices and Challenges

As you read in Chapter 2, developing nations everywhere share similar economic goals. They want to improve agriculture and build modern industrial economies. They also want to become economically self-sufficient and to end foreign domination.

Developing agriculture. Although most Africans are subsistence farmers, government programs often neglect their needs. Instead, most programs focus on cash crops for export. As a result, farmers have stopped planting food crops and have grown crops for export. Governments also have kept prices for food crops low. This policy helps poorly paid city workers to buy food. Farmers, however, suffer from low prices. Many have left the land to join swelling city populations.

Rapid population growth and unpredictable rainfall also cause problems for farmers. In the past, farmers cleared and planted the same land for a number of years. They then moved on to other land, leaving the soil to renew itself. With a growing population, pressure on the land is constant. Land is

Industrial Development The developing nations of Africa have worked steadily to industrialize. Ghana built the huge Volta River Dam project to generate electricity. With that energy source, it could then develop industries like the aluminum-producing complex shown here. ***Choice*** How does a nation benefit by developing its industries?

quickly exhausted and there are fewer areas to plant.

After years of good rainfall, much of Africa was hit by a series of severe droughts beginning in the 1970s. Crops withered and herds died or were killed because there was no food for them. Millions of people faced starvation. In drought-stricken countries such as Ethiopia and Somalia, civil war further disrupted life.

Economic dependence. A major goal of African nations is reducing economic dependence. Because they rely heavily on the export of a single crop or commodity, they are at the mercy of world market prices. African nations, such as Egypt and Kenya, have tried to diversify their exports, but they face stiff competition from developing nations in Asia and Latin America.

African nations have tried to limit costly imports, which cut into their national earnings. Only a few African nations produce enough oil for their factories and transportation systems. The other nations must spend large sums on imported oil. When world oil prices soared in the 1970s, most African nations had to pay huge sums for imported oil. At the same time, prices fell for many African exports. To make up the difference, African nations borrowed heavily. They expected to repay their debts once prices for their exports recovered, but prices remained low. Then in the 1980s interest rates rose, leading to a severe debt crisis. (See page 40.)

African consumers want western-made goods such as cars and televisions. Factories, too, need parts and machines made in industrial countries. In the 1990s, some African nations took steps to limit foreign imports and support local industries.

The Population Explosion

Since independence, birth rates in Africa have risen. At the same time, better health care has slowed the death rate. The result is soaring populations in some countries. By the mid 1990s, the population of Africa was approaching 680 million. At the current growth rate, it will double by the year 2020.

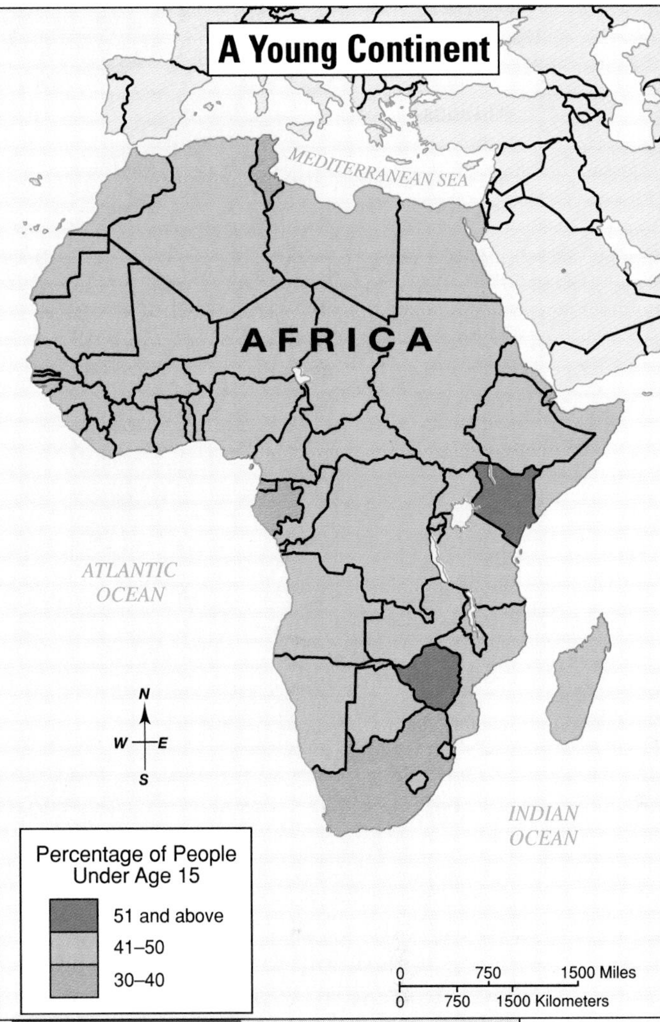

MAP STUDY

The population of Africa numbers about 680 million and is expected to double in less than 30 years. Today, nearly half the people of Africa are under the age of 15.

1. **Location** (a) What percentage of people are under the age of 15 in most of Africa? (b) In what regions of Africa are people generally older?
2. **Place** (a) Using the map on page 57, in what two countries are more than 50 percent of the people under 15? (b) In what countries are 30–40 percent of the people under the age of 15?
3. **Forecasting** (a) What challenges may face African nations because of the population explosion? (b) How do you think these nations might meet those challenges?

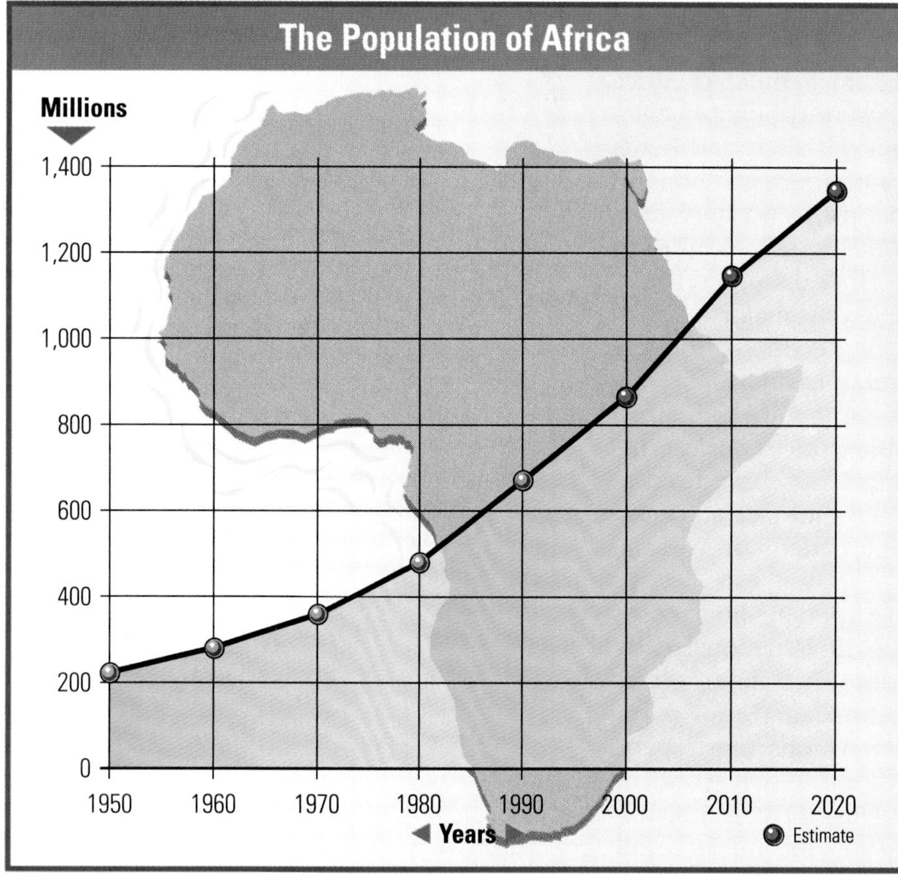

Source: *Population Reference Bureau*

Graph Skills Africa's population is increasing rapidly and now has one of the fastest growth rates in the world. ▶Study the graph and make a generalization about population increase in Africa from 1950 to 1990. Make a generalization about the estimated future increase from 1990 to 2020. Why do you think these statistics are important to government planners?

African traditions encourage large families. Children are seen as a valuable resource to the family. "Each extra mouth comes attached to two extra hands," notes a West African saying.

The population explosion in Africa has created many problems for government leaders and economic planners. Half of the people of Africa are under 15 years old. Governments have to find money for schools, housing, and jobs for these young people. Also, because good farmland is scarce in Africa, more and more people are crowding into cities.

The strains caused by the population boom are leading some people to change their ideas about family size. In cities, people may choose to have fewer children. Some governments are providing family planning information and health services. Economic hard times in the 1990s, however, have forced governments to spend less on such programs.

SECTION 2 REVIEW

1. **Locate:** (a) Zaire, (b) Tanzania, (c) Côte d'Ivoire.
2. **Identify:** (a) Mobutu Sese Seko, (b) Julius Nyerere, (c) Félix Houphouët-Boigny.
3. **Define:** (a) secede, (b) democratization, (c) socialism, (d) multinational corporation.
4. Describe two political problems facing African nations.
5. Why did socialism appeal to many Africans?
6. Describe how rapid population growth strains limited resources in Africa.
7. **Defending a Position** Would you agree that developing agriculture is as important as building industry? Why or why not?
8. **Writing Across Cultures** Reread the quotation at the beginning of this section. Write a paragraph explaining what Julius Nyerere meant.

3

CHANGING PATTERNS OF LIFE

FIND OUT

How is urbanization affecting African societies?

How are the lives of women and rural people changing?

Why are schools a source for cultural change?

"At first I couldn't keep the tractor going in a straight line," recalled Gilda Mohlanga. "But each day I got a bit better." Soon, Mohlanga was plowing fields. "I got very excited and I would think: 'Goodness, I can drive a tractor! We women can do this kind of work!' "

Mohlanga works on a state-owned farm in Mozambique. Women have traditionally done most of the farm work in Africa. Under European rule, however, African men raised cash crops. Women still grew food for the family. After independence, men guarded their jobs in the cash economy. To encourage equality between men and women, Mozambique hired women to work on farms.

Modern technology, such as tractors, is bringing change to African societies. The greatest changes are occurring in the growing cities.

Growth of Cities

The population explosion and the growth of industry have contributed to rapid urbanization. Although some African cities have existed for hundreds of years, they remained relatively small. Today, city populations are soaring. In 1990, only 22 percent of Africans lived in cities. By 2025, about 54 percent of Africans will live in urban areas.

Cairo, Egypt, had a population of 3.7 million in 1960. By 1995, the population topped 11 million. Dakar, Senegal, is expected to grow from 1 million people in 1990 to 5 million by 2000. During the same period, the population of Nairobi, Kenya, will grow from 2 million to 5 million.

Why do people migrate from farms to cities? Rural poverty is driving millions of people to give up farming. These displaced farmers want the benefits of urban life such as better jobs, improved housing, better schools, and more health care. Cities also offer a wide range of activities, from markets and stores to sporting events and discos. Young people enjoy greater freedom in cities than in villages.

Despite their attractions, cities have a bleak side. Jobs are scarce. Many people do not have money to buy the goods shown in stores or to see the movies advertised on billboards. They live in sprawling shantytowns that have grown up around the cities.

A Long Trek to Work

Six days a week, Mutombo Kinaoudi sets out on foot for work. Mutombo* lives in a shantytown outside Kinshasa, Zaire's capital city. "I walk because I can't afford 25 zaires [about 12 cents] to pay for the bus," says Mutombo. With his weekly earnings of $9, he must buy food, clothing, and other necessities for himself and his family.

For almost two hours, Mutombo treks along dirt roads. Government-owned buses stuffed to overflowing pass him by. Because the government cannot buy more buses, owners of private vehicles fill in. Trucks, called *fula-fulas,* load up with dozens of passengers. The last riders to squeeze onto the truck stand on the bumpers.

As Mutombo nears the city, the dirt roads become paved streets. Here, he walks by the heavily guarded homes of Kinshasa's rich. As in cities everywhere, the wealthy people of

* In some African societies, a person's family name is given first. Mutombo is this man's family name.

Commuting Workers Demand for public transportation has outstripped the government's ability to provide it. As a result, some workers must take the "fula-fulas," trucks converted into buses by private individuals. Many workers can barely afford the fare, which amounts to pennies a day. ***Change*** What problems face workers newly arrived in the city from the countryside?

Kinshasa live in fine homes. They have green lawns, shade trees, and well-lighted streets.

Finally, Mutombo reaches the international hotel where he works as a car-park attendant. He has walked six miles.

Like all African cities, Kinshasa has grown rapidly. By the mid 1990s, its population topped 4 million people. The Zairean government cannot afford to pave roads or extend sewers, water, and electricity outside the city. In the shantytowns, people like Mutombo build homes out of scrap metal, cardboard, and dried clay bricks. A family may live in one or two rooms. They rent space to others, often relatives newly arrived from the country.

Like his neighbors, Mutombo dreams of moving into a better neighborhood. The next step up might be a government-built bungalow with a water spigot outside. Such a home would be an improvement. Most shantytown residents get their untreated water from shallow wells. ■

Effects of Urbanization

The growth of cities is helping to reshape African societies. A new urban elite has emerged. In colonial days, the elite were the white colonial officials and business owners. Today, the elite are Africans with top jobs in government and business. Wealth, education, and power set them apart from others.

Most cities have a small middle class that includes people with a high school education.

They might be clerks in government offices or factory supervisors. The great majority of city dwellers, however, are poor workers who earn barely enough to get by.

Changes in the family. Urbanization is changing family life. In cities, people tend to live in nuclear families rather than in extended families. Traditional bonds of lineage and kinship are weakening. The longer people live in cities, the less attached they feel to their ancestors and to the land.

Despite changes, the old bonds remain strong. Often a family member goes to the city and finds a job. Soon, other family members follow. The newcomers add a strain because they have no money or jobs, but their relatives feel responsible for helping them.

Among the wealthier and better educated, marriage customs are changing. Instead of accepting arranged marriages, as was common in the past, more young people choose their own mates. Such marriages further weaken family ties.

Westernization. Many young people in Africa dream of romantic marriages like those shown in western movies and soap operas. Western culture and technology are everywhere in the cities. Many Africans welcome the benefits of western technology but warn against the dangers of westernization. To

Nairobi, Kenya Urbanization is bringing many changes to African societies. Nairobi, shown here, is Kenya's capital and largest city. Its location and mild climate have contributed to its rapid growth. Today, the city has a population of 2 million people and is a hub of commerce and industry. ***Change*** Describe ways in which cities like Nairobi are transforming Africa.

them, western culture glorifies individual desires and material goods at the expense of the community. They urge Africans to preserve traditional values of family and group loyalty.

Religion. Those who reject westernization include many Islamic leaders. In the 1980s, a religious revival swept across the Islamic areas of Africa as well as the Middle East. This revival called for strict obedience to the laws of the Koran. The Islamic revival has had a great impact on North African nations such as Libya, Sudan, and Egypt. It has not, however, gained much support in sub-Saharan Africa.

Since the early 1900s, numerous "independent" Christian churches have arisen in Africa. These churches blend Christian and local African religious beliefs. They have great appeal to many Africans. Religious groups have sometimes mobilized their followers to achieve important social reforms.

The growth of Christian churches has been rapid. By the next century, Africa may have more Christians than any other continent.

Women's Lives

Throughout Africa, women are gaining legal rights. In Ethiopia and Kenya, new laws allow women to own and inherit property. Recent laws in the Côte d'Ivoire outlawed polygamy and payment of a bride price.

Governments are also beginning to support programs to help women obtain technical training and jobs. Women in cities have an opportunity to enter the money economy. A growing number are taking jobs as clerks, salespeople, and bankers. In Zimbabwe and several other African nations, a few women have risen to high-level government jobs.

Despite new laws, however, most women's lives have changed little. In rural areas, women are still the main food producers. In much of Africa, they raise two thirds of the food.

Today, as in the past, a woman rises at dawn and spends 10 to 15 hours completing basic tasks. She feeds her children, weeds the fields, chases off animals that raid crops, and collects wood for fuel. Besides raising food for her family, she helps her husband grow cash crops.

Preparing food takes hours. Women must pound millet or sorghum into flour. Even though packaged foods are available, few rural women can afford them. Women must spend much time getting water. One man in Tanzania noted,

> "Water is a big problem for women. We can sit here all day waiting for food because there is no woman at home. Always they are going to fetch water."

As this quotation shows, attitudes about the role of women are very slow to change. African women today are organizing politically to change such attitudes.

Rural Patterns

Despite the migration to the cities, most Africans still live in rural areas. Many farmers continue to use non-mechanized farming tools such as hoes, but they want the benefits of technology. "My biggest desire is to acquire a seeding and weeding machine," remarked a man in Gambia. A Nigerian woman said, "If I could have modern implements to clear, till, and plant my farm, I would have more energy and time for house chores."

Technology is changing herding and fishing societies, too. Owners of meat-packing factories are trying to convince herders to sell more of their cattle for cash. Some herders have done so, but many refuse. They view cattle, not money, as a symbol of wealth. People in fishing societies are using motorized boats to fish on lakes and along seacoasts. With refrigeration, their catches can be sent to distant markets.

Schools and Universities

Schools are another force for cultural change. All African governments support programs to increase literacy and to give people job skills. Through education, too, leaders

A Planned Village In most African villages, people follow traditional ways of life. Some governments created new forms of villages. In these, distribution of farmland, houses, roads, and railroads was designed to benefit the village as a whole. ***Culture*** What goods and services did the government have to supply if planned villages were to be successful?

hope to encourage a sense of national unity. Before the 1960s, only a small percentage of African children went to school. By building schools and training teachers, governments have made progress toward increasing literacy.

Schools face many challenges, however. Many students drop out after a few years. Recently, economic hardships have forced governments to cut spending on schools. A teacher might have 100 students in a classroom without enough desks, chairs, books, or chalkboards. Many teachers themselves have little training beyond elementary school.

Only a few students attend high schools or universities. Most African governments, however, pay the cost for each student. These governments recognize the need to educate future leaders.

The number of universities in Africa has risen from 6 in 1960 to 80 in 1990. Most universities lack adequate equipment, libraries, and supplies. Professors earn from $15 to $85 a week. Students live in crowded, tiny dormitory rooms since most cannot afford private housing off campus. Despite the difficulties, students share a sense of community and are determined to get an education.

SECTION 3 REVIEW

1. Describe three changes brought about by rapid urbanization.
2. Why do some Africans oppose westernization?
3. (a) How are women's lives changing? (b) How do traditional ways still shape their lives?
4. How can education lead to social change?
5. **Analyzing Information** An African saying states, "An old man is one who remembers when people were more important than machines." What does this saying show about the changes taking place in African societies?
6. **Writing Across Cultures** Write a paragraph describing the similarities between the effects of urbanization in the United States and in African countries.

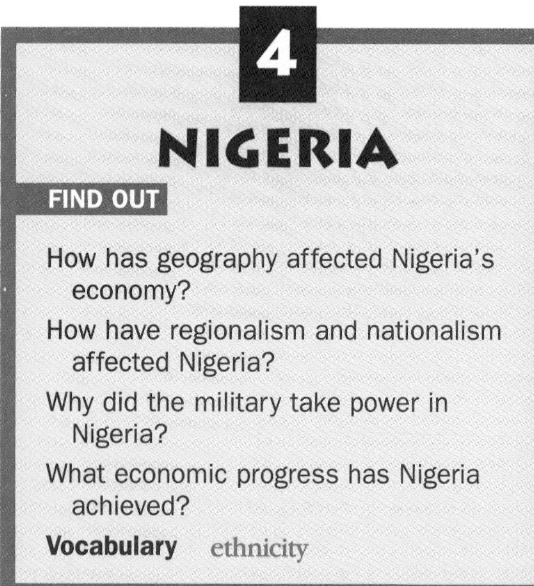

4 NIGERIA

FIND OUT

How has geography affected Nigeria's economy?

How have regionalism and nationalism affected Nigeria?

Why did the military take power in Nigeria?

What economic progress has Nigeria achieved?

Vocabulary ethnicity

Christy Essien-Igbokwe is Nigeria's most popular woman singer. On stage, she sometimes sings in French. Then she switches to one of the four Nigerian languages she speaks. (Like most Africans, she is fluent in several local languages.) At other times, she sings in a form of English used by some Nigerians. In her song "My People," she urges:

> "No matter who you be
> Ooooh
> No matter your job
> Ooooh
> Come on everybody
> Let we build Nigeria now."

Nigeria is one of the largest and richest nations in Africa. It is also the most populous. In fact, one out of every five Africans is Nigerian. Size, resources, and population combine to make Nigeria a powerful force in West Africa. By looking at Nigeria's experience since independence, you can see many of the challenges facing the nations of Africa.

Geography and People

Nigeria lies in the tropics, just north of the Equator. The hot, wet climate of southern Nigeria supports large rain forests. This resource gives Nigeria an active lumber industry. Farther north, the forests give way to wooded savanna and grasslands. There, people have developed farming and herding societies.

Nigeria has mineral resources such as gold, tin, and iron. Its most valuable resource, though, is oil. Machines work night and day pumping oil from wells along the coastal lowlands and offshore. Oil has brought both wealth and troubles to Nigeria, as you will read.

Nigeria takes its name from the Niger River. Along with the Benue River, the Niger provides water for irrigation and serves as a transportation route. The rivers also divide the country into three regions, roughly matching its largest ethnic groups. Northern Nigeria is home to the Muslim Hausa and Fulani people. In the southwest are the Yoruba, and in the southeast live the Ibo. Many southerners are Christians or follow traditional religious beliefs.

Many smaller ethnic groups are scattered throughout the country. In all, Nigeria is home to 250 ethnic groups who speak 12 different languages. **Ethnicity**, or attachment to one's own ethnic group, and regional loyalties play an important role in shaping Nigeria today.

Political Development

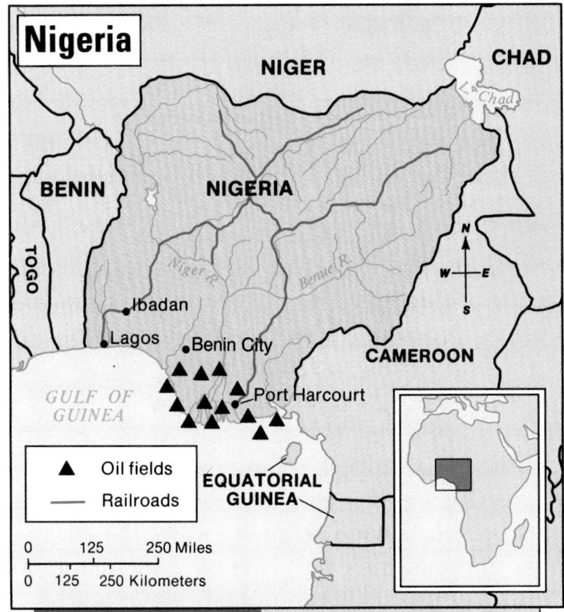

MAP STUDY

Nigeria is one of Africa's largest nations and has the largest population, with at least 125 million people. Nigeria also has rich natural resources of oil, coal, iron ore, and tin.

1. **Location** (a) Describe the location of Nigeria's main cities. (b) Which two cities are less than 100 miles apart?
2. **Interaction** Why have railroads been important in developing Nigeria's economy?
3. **Applying Information** What advantages does Nigeria's location offer in developing its resources and promoting world trade?

Before the Age of Imperialism, many diverse groups lived in what is today Nigeria. Some, such as the Yoruba, Hausa, and Fulani, created powerful states. As you read in Chapter 4, the forest kingdom of Benin flourished in this region. Other people, such as the Ibo, lived in small, self-governing villages.

In the late 1800s, the British annexed lands in West Africa. Many local rulers strongly resisted British rule. Eventually, the British set up the colony of Nigeria. They carved out plantations to produce cash crops such as cocoa, cotton, palm oil, and peanuts.

The road to independence. Despite British domination, resistance continued. In 1929, market women in eastern Nigeria led violent protests against foreign rule. After World War II, Nigerian nationalism grew stronger. Each main region had its own political party, representing the region's major ethnic group. The nationalist leader Nnamdi Azikiwe (ehn NAHM dee ah zee KAY way) called for regional parties to unite and form a national party. Slowly, Nigerians gained greater rights. In 1960, they finally achieved independence.

Tragic divisions. Religious, economic, and ethnic divisions flared after independence. These divisions led to a tragic civil war. The Ibo in the southeast felt that the Muslim Hausa-Fulani dominated Nigeria. The Ibo also wanted to keep control of the rich oil fields in their region. In 1967, the Ibo seceded. They set up the independent Republic of Biafra.

In the brutal war that followed, Nigeria's central government blockaded Biafra. More than 1 million Biafrans may have died of starvation. In 1970, a defeated Biafra rejoined Nigeria. Today, despite efforts to build national unity, regional loyalties remain strong. Nigerians do not, however, foresee another civil war. (📖 See Connections With Literature, page 804, "Civil Peace.")

Civilian and military rule. Since independence, Nigeria has moved back and forth between civilian and military rule. The military first seized power in 1966. It won popular support by promising to end corruption and mismanagement. The military turned the government back to civilian leaders in 1979. Four years later, unrest and new charges of corruption led to another period of military rule.

Why did corruption occur? During the 1970s, oil prices soared. Government officials and business leaders used their positions to make huge personal fortunes. In the 1980s, oil prices fell, bringing hard times to Nigeria. Ordinary citizens grew angry about the extravagant spending of the rich.

Under pressure, the military government of General Ibrahim Babangida agreed to hold elections in the early 1990s. Nigerians awaited a return to democracy, but the promise was not fulfilled. Although Babangida resigned, a new military leader, Sani Abacha, took power and continued to campaign against corruption.

Economic Development

Since gaining independence, Nigeria has had mixed success in developing its economy. The civil war disrupted the economy. Then, in the 1970s, the oil boom brought spectacular riches to Nigeria. The government borrowed heavily to develop industry and agriculture. It built schools and raised its literacy rate.

Oil wealth had its negative side, though. As you have read, it contributed to corruption. It also helped to increase the gap between the wealthy elite and the poor majority. Massive borrowing from western banks and governments also left Nigeria $30 billion in debt. When oil prices plunged, Nigeria did not have money to repay the loans.

In the late 1980s, Babangida made difficult economic reforms. To save money, he banned imports of wheat, rice, and other goods. He then renegotiated the loans, gaining additional time to repay the nation's debt.

Industry and agriculture. The Nigerian government plays a large role in the economy through its ownership of key industries. Private businesses also operate throughout the country. During the oil boom years, Nigeria developed a range of industries from automobile assembly plants to steel mills and petrochemical plants.

Despite the growth of industry, most Nigerians still make a living from the land. Farmers produce cash crops such as cotton, palm oil, cocoa, and kola nuts. Nigeria also exports rubber, coffee, and timber.

Babangida's ban on imported wheat was meant to help farmers. As in many African nations, city dwellers in Nigeria preferred wheat and rice to locally grown foods like millet and sorghum. Imports of wheat and rice hurt local farmers who could not sell their food crops.

Nigerian Oil Drilling Nigeria has the largest oil deposits of any African nation. Oil produced from wells, like the one offshore shown here, accounts for more than 90 percent of the nation's exports. Nigeria has used its oil wealth to begin to industrialize its economy. ***Choice*** How might the people and the government disagree about how income from oil should be spent?

Although the ban on imports was unpopular in the cities, the government hoped it would stimulate food production.

Population Growth

Nigeria needs to increase food output to feed its soaring population. Nigeria's population numbers 125 million. Experts predict it may triple by the year 2020. Like much of Africa, a large percentage of Nigeria's population is under 15 years old. In the years ahead, Nigeria must not only feed but also educate and provide jobs for these young people.

Many younger Nigerians prefer to live in cities such as Lagos. The government, however, is trying to encourage people to remain on farms. Michael Ibru, the son of a privileged family, is setting an example for others. He founded a huge fish business to provide a source of low-cost protein to city dwellers. He has also diversified his business by producing poultry.

Music and Literature

The many traditions of Nigeria's diverse people are evident in the arts. Today, artisans in Benin City turn out fine bronze sculptures similar to those their ancestors made hundreds of years ago.

In dance halls and on street corners, bands play juju music based on the traditional "talking drums." A talking drum has special features that allow the drummer to vary the pitch. In that way, the drummer can imitate the tones of African languages.

Nigerian band leaders such as King Sunny Ade (AH day) and Fela Anikulapo Kuti have won international fame. Ade's music weaves together the sounds of steel guitars, rhythm guitars, synthesizers, maracas, and talking drums. Kuti's band blends traditional African rhythms and American jazz.

Novelists and playwrights have also found inspiration in traditional cultures. *Things Fall Apart,* a novel by Chinua Achebe (CHIHN wah ah CHEE bee), reveals the tragic effects of European rule on a Nigerian village. (See page 144.) In 1986, Nigeria's leading playwright, Wole Soyinka, became the first African to win the Nobel Prize for Literature. His play *A Dance of the Forests* tells of the relationship between spirits, ghosts, and Ogun, one of the powerful gods of the Yoruba people. (📖 See Connections With Literature, page 804, "Civilian and Soldier.")

Contemporary African Music Music has always been a vital part of Africa's heritage. Today, African musicians play for a worldwide audience. Nigerian band leader King Sunny Ade, shown here, combines the music of traditional instruments like "talking drums" and maracas with the sounds of high-tech synthesizers and steel guitars. ***Culture*** How can music bring better understanding among peoples?

SECTION 4 REVIEW

1. **Locate:** (a) Nigeria, (b) Niger River, (c) Benue River, (d) Lagos.
2. **Identify:** (a) Nnamdi Azikiwe, (b) Biafra, (c) Ibrahim Babangida, (d) Chinua Achebe.
3. **Define:** ethnicity.
4. How have natural resources played a role in Nigeria's development?
5. Why have some Nigerians welcomed military rule?
6. What steps has the government of Nigeria taken to solve economic problems?
7. **Linking Past and Present** Why do you think Nigerians feel more loyalty to ethnic groups than to the national government?
8. **Writing Across Cultures** Write a paragraph explaining a similarity or difference between a cause of civil war in Nigeria and a cause of the American Civil War.

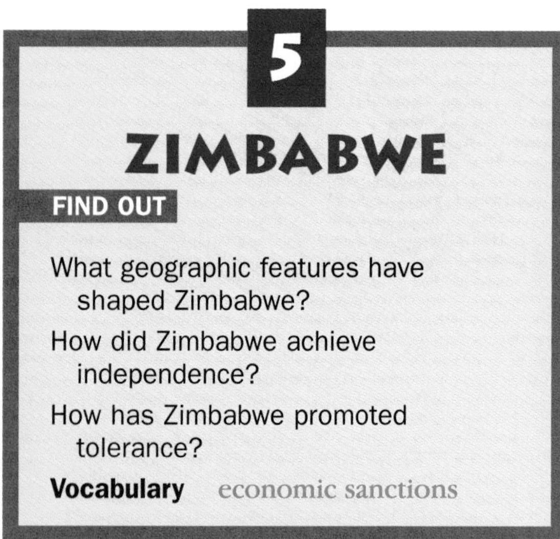

5 ZIMBABWE

FIND OUT

What geographic features have shaped Zimbabwe?

How did Zimbabwe achieve independence?

How has Zimbabwe promoted tolerance?

Vocabulary economic sanctions

"Our ancestor Nehanda died with
these words on her lips,
'I'm dying for this country.'
She left us one word of advice,
'Take up arms and liberate
yourselves.'"

In the 1890s, Nehanda and her husband were captured and executed for resisting British rule. Her courage inspired young freedom fighters in the 1970s. Like Nehanda, they wanted to end white rule over what is today Zimbabwe. The poem "Take Up Arms and Liberate Yourselves" became their anthem. As you will read, modern-day Zimbabweans succeeded in winning independence in 1980.

Compared to Nigeria, Zimbabwe is a small country. Its population numbers about 8.8 million. In area, it is less than half the size of Nigeria. Yet today Zimbabwe is as important to Southern Africa as Nigeria is to West Africa.

Geography and People

Zimbabwe is a landlocked nation. Goods must be sent overland through neighboring countries. In colonial days, most trade passed through white-ruled South Africa. Since independence, Zimbabwe has tried to reopen rail and road routes through Mozambique. It has also sent troops to help Mozambique defeat rebels who have damaged roads and railroads.

Resources. Geography has influenced Zimbabwe in many ways. The country is mostly high plateau with a mild climate and regular wet and dry seasons. In level areas, Zimbabweans grow cash crops such as tobacco and cotton. They also produce food crops such as corn. Unlike other African nations, Zimbabwe has faced the threat of drought only once. In the early 1980s, drought greatly reduced food output for two seasons.

Zimbabwe has rich mineral deposits, including chromium, coal, copper, nickel, and gold. Those resources have helped the country to develop economically. An excellent system of roads and railroads links different parts of the country. In addition, Zimbabwe uses the Kariba Dam to harness the energy of the Zambezi River.

Ethnic groups. Zimbabwe has fewer ethnic divisions than Nigeria. About 80 percent of the people are Shona. Another 19 percent are Ndebele (ehn duh BEH leh). Each group has its own language. Whites, Asians, and people of mixed race make up a small portion of the population.

Although ethnic rivalries exist, Zimbabwe's leaders have limited their effects. The goal of the independence struggle was to force the minority white rulers to turn over the government to the majority black population.

The Road to Independence

Zimbabwe was the center of an ancient gold-trading kingdom. In the period between 800 and 1300, local people traded with the cities of East Africa. (See page 84.) In the 1500s, the Portuguese tried unsuccessfully to set up a colony and mine gold in the region. Not until the late 1890s did the British manage to build a colony in what is today Zimbabwe.

Rhodesia. The British called their colony Rhodesia, after Cecil Rhodes. Rhodes was a businessman who promoted imperialism in Africa. Thousands of white settlers migrated to Rhodesia. They took over the best land and set up large plantations to grow cash crops. The British also used African labor to develop the mineral resources of Rhodesia.

In the 1960s, independent nations were emerging across Africa. Britain took steps to move Rhodesia toward black majority rule. White Rhodesians objected to these moves. They were determined to hold onto power even though they made up less than 5 percent of the population. In 1965, they issued their own declaration of independence.

Taking action. No nation except white-ruled South Africa recognized the independence of Rhodesia. The United Nations condemned the actions of the white-led government. The UN imposed economic sanctions. That is, they called on member nations to stop trading with Rhodesia. Despite the sanctions, the minority government clung to power.

By the 1970s, several black nationalist groups had launched a guerrilla war to win freedom. The fighting continued through the decade, taking more than 20,000 lives. Finally, all sides agreed to negotiation. In 1980, the nationalists achieved their goal. Rhodesia was renamed Zimbabwe.

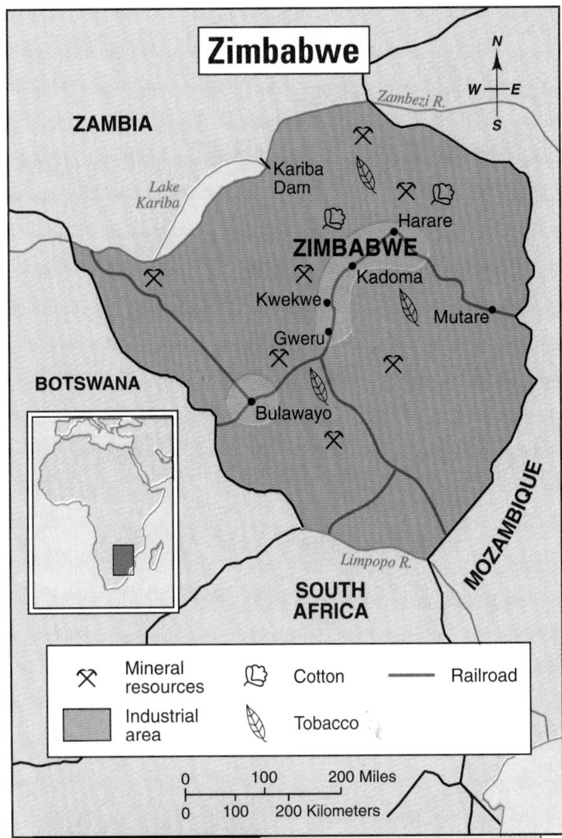

MAP STUDY

Zimbabwe is a small nation in Southern Africa, with a population of less than 10 million. It has abundant mineral resources of chromium, copper, gold, nickel, and coal, as well as fertile farmland.

1. **Location** Describe the relative location of Harare.
2. **Interaction** (a) What cash crops are grown in Zimbabwe? (b) How are crops and mineral resources transported to the industrial areas?
3. **Drawing Conclusions** (a) Why is Zimbabwe described as a "landlocked country"? (b) What are the disadvantages of such a location?

Rebuilding the Nation

A leader of the independence struggle was Robert Mugabe (moo GAH beh). After his party won a majority in the national elections, he formed a government. Mugabe urged blacks and whites to set aside differences and

Linda Mutondoro, Guerrilla Commander

Many women took an active part in the struggle to win independence for Zimbabwe. Linda Mutondoro, a guerrilla leader, rose to become a skillful company commander. Commitment to her country's freedom propelled her far beyond the traditional role of a woman in Africa.

In 1976, thousands of Zimbabweans traveled to neighboring Mozambique. There, men and women were trained in guerrilla warfare to fight the army of Rhodesia. Although she was only 15 years old, Mutondoro left school to join the struggle. She walked for days to reach the military camps in Mozambique. Twice during her training, Mutondoro survived massacres by Rhodesian forces. Artillery and aircraft fire killed thousands of Zimbabwean soldiers and refugees.

At the time, traditional attitudes kept women in jobs such as carrying supplies and cooking. Only the most outstanding and bold women could overcome discrimination and receive promotions. Mutondoro rose to the rank of commander, with three platoons under her command. She successfully led her company against the enemy within Rhodesian territory. In 1979, just as the war was ending, she was captured and beaten in prison.

After independence in 1980, Mutondoro was released. She joined Zimbabwe's ministry of foreign affairs, working in embassies in Sweden, Germany, and Senegal. Linda Mutondoro's plans include earning a doctorate in political science. Someday, she will teach a new generation of Zimbabweans about the struggle for freedom.

Leaders such as Linda Mutondoro help change women's role in society. Traditionally, women were seen as inferior to men politically, although they were respected as mothers and teachers. During the colonial period, the status of women fell. Today, women in Zimbabwe are gaining access to jobs and positions formerly reserved for men.

1. What risks did Linda Mutondoro face in becoming a guerrilla commander?
2. **Drawing Conclusions** How did the contributions of Zimbabwean women to the struggle for independence help them win greater political rights?

work together to rebuild the nation. He spoke out strongly against racism in any form:

> “The wrongs of the past must now stand forgiven and forgotten. . . . If ever we look to the past, let us do so for the lesson the past has taught us, namely that oppression and racism are [injustices] that must never again find scope in our political and social system.”

Restoring unity. Zimbabwe's constitution included a number of protections for the white minority. Leaders of the former white government held seats in Zimbabwe's parliament. Mugabe also appointed two whites to positions in his cabinet.

At the same time, Mugabe tried to ease political tensions among Zimbabwe's ethnic groups. His own party was made up largely of Shona. The rival party was dominated by the Ndebele. In 1987, these two parties merged. Nonetheless, Zimbabwe remains a multiparty democracy.

Improving services. Mugabe's goals included providing basic services to all citizens. Before independence, the Rhodesian government had favored whites. White children attended better schools and white farmers received more aid. Whites also received better health care. At independence, Mugabe set out to improve services to blacks.

The number of children in elementary school more than tripled in the last decade. The government has pledged to provide eight years of schooling to all children. Although education is costly, people in local communities give their time and work to setting up schools.

Schools are not segregated officially, although most students are black. Textbooks promote unity by discussing the contributions of all ethnic groups, not just Europeans as they did in the past.

Economic Development

Besides working toward national unity, Mugabe sought to reform landholding patterns and develop agriculture. In Zimbabwe, the best land belongs to about 4,000 big farmers, most of them white. About 7 million black farmers are crowded onto rocky, dry land.

Under a 1992 law, the government started buying land to transfer to peasants. Tensions rose because white landowners objected to having to sell their land at prices set by the government. Another problem emerged when reports suggested that the government had sold some lands to powerful supporters.

Education in Zimbabwe Public schools are the key to a better future everywhere. They provide skilled workers needed for a productive society. These Zimbabwean students are learning English, the official language of their country. ***Diversity*** In what ways can Zimbabwe's schools strengthen its diverse society?

Zimbabwe Industry Zimbabwe has used its hydroelectric power, iron ore, coal, and other resources to become one of the most industrialized nations of Africa. These skilled foundry workers produce machine parts. About one fourth of the population works in manufacturing. ***Choice*** Why does the government control some of the economy but also allow private enterprise?

Both large plantations and small family farms are common in Zimbabwe. In the 1980s, the small farms outproduced large plantations. The government has set up programs to provide seed, fertilizer, and technological help to farmers. As a result, food output has increased.

Unlike many African nations that have to import manufactured goods, Zimbabwe has a number of industries. During the years of UN sanctions, Rhodesians built factories to produce goods that had once been imported. Today, those factories produce steel and heavy industrial equipment along with textiles and consumer goods.

As in most developing nations, the government of Zimbabwe maintains a large degree of control over the economy. Mugabe has, however, encouraged private investors to develop new businesses. Multinational corporations operate many mines as well as other industries. Private companies compete with government-run enterprises, encouraging diversity.

SECTION 5 REVIEW

1. **Locate:** (a) Zimbabwe, (b) Zambezi River.
2. **Identify:** (a) Rhodesia, (b) Robert Mugabe.
3. **Define:** economic sanctions.
4. Describe one advantage and one disadvantage of Zimbabwe's geography.
5. Why did Zimbabweans have to fight for independence?
6. What economic successes has Zimbabwe had?
7. **Applying Information** "An evil remains an evil whether practiced by white against black or by black against white," said Robert Mugabe at Zimbabwe's independence. How has Mugabe tried to end the evil of racism?
8. **Writing Across Cultures** The civil rights movement in the United States occurred at about the same time as nations in Africa were gaining their independence. Write a paragraph explaining how the movements might be connected.

Chapter 5 Review

Understanding Vocabulary

Match each term at left with the correct definition at right.

1. guerrilla warfare	**a.** move toward multiparty system of government
2. democratization	**b.** huge enterprise with branches in many countries
3. multinational corporation	**c.** refusal to buy certain goods or services
4. boycott	**d.** attachment to one's own group
5. ethnicity	**e.** hit-and-run attacks by small bands of fighters

Reviewing the Main Ideas

1. What means did Kwame Nkrumah use to help Ghana win its independence?
2. (a) Why is economic dependence a problem for African nations? (b) What steps have leaders taken to end economic dependence?
3. Describe three changes that are taking place in family life in Africa.
4. How has technology affected the lives of rural people in African nations?
5. Describe the achievements of Nigerians in (a) art, (b) music, (c) literature.
6. What steps did Robert Mugabe take to ease political tensions in Zimbabwe?

Reviewing Chapter Themes

1. At independence, African nations moved to modernize their economies. Explain how each of the following has affected economic development: (a) socialism, (b) multinational corporations, (c) development projects.
2. Colonial rule and ethnic diversity have shaped African nations. Explain how these two forces have affected Nigeria and Zimbabwe.
3. Many African nations have faced severe challenges to development. Describe how the population explosion and drought hinder economic progress.
4. Various forces are bringing change to African life. Choose three of the following and describe how each has affected life in Africa: (a) urbanization, (b) education, (c) westernization, (d) technology.

Thinking Critically

1. **Analyzing Ideas** Kwame Nkrumah said of Ghana in 1957, "Our independence is meaningless unless it is linked up with the total liberation of the African continent." (a) How does Nkrumah's statement reflect the idea of Pan-Africanism? (b) How did Ghana pave the way for other African nations?
2. **Making Global Connections** Why do you think many African students study in American universities?
3. **Defending a Position** Some African nations have adopted one-party rule or military rule. Give arguments to support or oppose these forms of government in Africa.

Applying Your Skills

1. **Analyzing Literature** Reread the lines from Senghor's poem "Black Woman" on page 108. (a) How does Senghor show pride in Africa? (b) How does this poem reflect the goals of the négritude movement?
2. **Constructing a Time Line** Use the map on page 110 to construct a time line showing when African nations won independence. Then answer these questions: (a) When did Guinea win independence? Botswana? (b) When did the greatest number of African nations win independence? (c) Which nations did not achieve independence until after the 1960s?
3. **Ranking** List six political, economic, and cultural challenges facing African nations. (a) Which two do you think are the most important? (b) Give reasons for your answer.

Chapter 6

AFRICA IN THE WORLD TODAY

CHAPTER OUTLINE

1 Regional and Global Issues

2 The Republic of South Africa

3 Literature and the Arts

Modern African Art African artists have influenced the development of modern art around the world. Senegalese artist Serigne N'Diaye paints on glass. This detail of his painting, *The City*, shows the artist's impression of life in Dakar. ***Fine Art*** Why are artists, musicians, and writers important to a society?

The magical beat of a talking drum pounds. Electric guitars run riffs up and down the scale. Above these sounds, Youssou Ndour sings in the Wolof language of Senegal. Ndour is among the most popular singers of West Africa. In the late 1980s, he gained worldwide fame during the "Human Rights Now!" tour. Along with other international stars like Bruce Springsteen and Sting, Ndour carried the message of human rights to audiences around the world.

Ndour's music, known as *mbalax,* is one of many African musical styles. African popular music is as diverse as its people. Today, musicians from Senegal to South Africa are creating exciting new music by blending African sounds with western jazz, gospel, rock, and Latin beats.

"I'm an ambassador for African music throughout the world," says Ndour. "If people become more interested in Senegal and if there is more interaction between people of different cultures because of my music, that will be very good."

In the arts, as in politics, people recognize the growing interdependence of the world. Through international concert tours, musicians raise money for causes such as famine relief and campaign for social and political change.

CHAPTER PERSPECTIVE

In the 1990s, music was just one way that Africans were taking their place on the world stage. The 55 independent nations of Africa make up a major part of the "global village."

As you read, look for these chapter themes:

- Through regional and international organizations, the nations of Africa have worked for peace and economic development.
- Although African nations generally remained nonaligned, Cold War politics had an impact on them.
- Under internal and external pressures, South Africa has taken steps to end its policy of racial segregation.
- African arts and literature blend traditional and modern influences.

Literature Connections

In this chapter, you will encounter passages from the following works.

"Africa and Freedom," Albert J. Luthuli

"Song for the Lazy," Central African poem

Things Fall Apart, Chinua Achebe

For other suggestions, see Connections With Literature, pages 804–808.

1

REGIONAL AND GLOBAL ISSUES

FIND OUT

How do the goals of the Organization of African Unity reflect the interdependence of African nations?

Why do African nations take an active role in the United Nations?

How did African nations respond to Cold War issues?

How are Africans using science and technology to solve problems?

Vocabulary nonalignment

"Anyone who wants to participate in a peaceful and democratic transition in our country is welcome," said an Ethiopian government leader in 1991. After almost 30 years of civil war, peace was returning to the battered land. A center of fighting had been Eritrea, a region on the Red Sea that finally won independence. War had also raged in the Ogaden region, where people of Somali descent fought Ethiopian rule. During the long war, each side had received aid from one of the superpowers. After the Cold War ended, peace seemed possible.

While Ethiopians welcomed peace and planned elections, wars flared in other African countries. To resolve such conflicts, African nations turned to regional and international organizations.

Regional Cooperation

As you read, in the 1950s Kwame Nkrumah called for a politically united Africa, like the United States. Although this goal of Pan-African unity was never reached, the dream never died. Even as individual nations won independence, Pan-Africanism remained a strong force.

Organization of African Unity. In 1963, the independent nations of Africa formed the Organization of African Unity, or OAU. By 1991, all African nations except South Africa had joined the OAU. Through the OAU, they have supported independence movements and promoted peace. In 1963, the OAU stopped a brief war between Algeria and Morocco. It also helped settle a border dispute between Kenya and Somalia. Bringing peace to nations that are torn by civil war has proved difficult, however. Many nations do not want the OAU to meddle in their internal affairs.

In spite of differing interests, the members of the OAU have developed programs for economic cooperation. The OAU was largely responsible for the Lomé Agreement in 1975. Under it, African countries could sell goods free from tariffs in Europe's Common Market countries without being obliged to buy European goods.

In addition to promoting peace and economic cooperation, OAU members have worked together to fight disease, encourage cultural links, and develop agriculture. They also have pushed to achieve majority rule in South Africa.

Other regional groups. Many African nations belong to regional groups. Like the OAU, these groups encourage economic development. Because many African nations are small and have limited resources, these efforts are meant to strengthen their position in the world.

The nine-nation Southern African Development Coordination Conference (SADCC) helped members reduce their dependence on South Africa. For example, Zimbabwe, Zambia, and Botswana, which are landlocked, used to ship goods through South African ports. By improving rail links through Mozambique and Tanzania, SADCC gave the three landlocked nations another route for trade. The 16-nation Economic Community of West African States (ECOWAS) helped members by ending customs duties and supporting joint transportation and energy projects.

International Ties

At independence, each African nation joined the United Nations (UN). Since then, Africans have taken an active role in that world body. They have worked for policies favorable to developing nations. For example, developing nations want access to new technology. They also want to be able to sell their manufactured goods in markets traditionally controlled by the industrial world. Although African nations agree on some issues, they do not always vote the same way in the UN.

Through the UN, African nations seek international cooperation on issues such as the environment, education, and agricultural development. UN agencies send farm experts, engineers, and teachers to help developing nations. They have also provided emergency relief to areas faced with famine. In Africa, as elsewhere, UN peacekeeping forces have at times tried to restore order in war zones such as Somalia or Rwanda.

African nations belong to a variety of other international organizations. Algeria, Libya, Nigeria, and Gabon are members of OPEC, the Organization of Petroleum Exporting Countries. OPEC includes major oil-exporting nations from Africa, the Middle East, and Latin America. It was set up to regulate oil prices.

Many African nations also have strong economic and cultural ties to former colonial powers. Most former British colonies belong to the Commonwealth of Nations. This group includes more than 40 countries that Britain once ruled. Many African nations once ruled by France have linked their currencies, or money, to the French franc. They also give preference to French products. Nearly all the cars in Senegal, for example, are French.

Relations With the Superpowers

African nations won independence during the Cold War. Because Africa is rich in mineral resources and is centrally located, both the United States and the Soviet Union wanted to win allies among the new nations.

Famine Aid Workers, below right, unload food sent by the International Red Cross. Above, other aid workers distribute food to refugees who had fled the fighting during the civil war in Ethiopia. War combined with severe drought caused crop failures and famine in both Ethiopia and Somalia. ***Human Rights*** What responsibility, if any, do people have to help those in need?

Like other developing nations, however, most African countries chose a policy of nonalignment—that is, they did not favor either side in the Cold War. Ghana's Kwame Nkrumah wrote:

> "Our attitude, I imagine, is very much that of America looking at the disputes of Europe in the 19th century. We do not wish to be involved."

Although they remained nonaligned, many African nations looked to the superpowers for aid. The Soviet Union provided arms and economic aid to African countries that adopted socialist systems. At the same time, the United States supported governments that were friendly to its interests. Sometimes, that meant backing a harsh dictator like Mobutu Sese Seko in Zaire.

Foreign intervention. In order to promote their interests, the superpowers often involved themselves in the internal affairs of African countries. For example, the Soviet Union and the United States backed rival groups in civil wars in Ethiopia and Somalia. They did this because they wanted to build naval bases along the Red Sea, where these two nations were located.

Former colonial powers also remained involved in African affairs. In the 1960s, Belgium sent troops into the Congo when civil war broke out there. On many occasions, France has flown in troops "to protect French citizens." Today, France has permanent military forces in six West African nations.

Easing tensions. In the late 1980s, Cold War tensions eased around the world. The United States and Soviet Union both backed peace efforts in Namibia, Angola, and elsewhere.

In Southern Africa, Namibia finally won independence. For years, South Africa had controlled this mineral-rich country. Namibians waged a long war for freedom. The UN, too, pressed South Africa to withdraw. Finally, South Africa agreed to leave, and Namibians elected their own government in 1990.

In Ethiopia, once Soviet aid was withdrawn, the harsh military government fell in 1991. Elections were scheduled, but long-standing conflicts among many rival groups posed obstacles for establishing a democratic government. The people of Eritrea, however, gained their independence, becoming the fifty-fifth African nation.

Continuing Concern Over Debt

In the early 1990s, a worldwide economic slowdown hurt African nations. Developed nations cut back on aid. The UN reduced spending on important projects, too. In addition, as prices for export goods dropped and oil prices rose, African nations were forced into debt. Many African governments found it hard to pay even the interest on loans.

Like debtor nations elsewhere, African nations turned for help to the International Monetary Fund (IMF) and the World Bank. Both those international lending agencies demanded that debtor nations make major economic changes. For example, they told debtor nations to increase exports of raw materials. That policy, however, led to a greater supply of goods on the international market. As a result, prices fell even further, hurting the African producers.

The IMF and World Bank also required debtor nations to move toward free market economies. To qualify for help, debtor nations had to reduce government controls over the economy and sell some industries to private investors. Many African nations saw this as interference in their internal affairs and decided to solve their debt problems without international help. As you have read, Nigeria's military ruler set up his own program to reduce costs and repay loans.

Despite these measures, the debt problems remain. African nations, like many other developing nations, continue to face the heavy burden of debt repayment.

Looking to the Future

African countries face a variety of issues for the future. They are searching for solutions appropriate for their societies.

Limiting family size. The population explosion is straining the economies of African nations. The UN and industrial nations are working with African governments to set up programs to teach about family planning.

The traditional view that African men should father many children works against family planning. Many nations are trying to combat this way of thinking. In Zimbabwe, social workers like Apollonia Chirimuta speak to groups of men in the villages. She asks them: "What do your children want? Land?" The men answer yes. "Well," she continues, "there won't be enough land for them because your families are too big." Officials are spreading a

Making the Desert Bloom Using a mixture of fertilizers and products that help soil retain moisture, scientists in Africa have had some success in making dry soil productive. Experiments conducted on the dry volcanic soil of the Cape Verde Islands have shown that unproductive soil can be made to support crops. ***Technology*** What impact might such an innovation have on nations in arid regions of the world?

similar message in countries from Egypt to Kenya to Mozambique.

Science and food production. African nations are also finding ways to increase food production. A successful program has introduced dry-season farming. By digging wells and irrigation ditches to link ponds and fields, farmers can grow corn and wheat during the dry season. Dry-season farming has allowed farmers to produce two crops a year. Says Adamou Sani, a farmer in Niger:

> “Dry-season crops are such a normal practice now that everyone grows them. Before, each year after the harvest I went to the city to look for work. But today, with the dry-season crops, I have work in the village. Truly it is a good thing.”

Researchers have worked to save the important cassava (kuh SAH vuh) crop, which was threatened by insects. About 200 million Africans depend on cassava as their main source of calories. (Many Americans know this plant as the source of tapioca.) In the 1970s, mealybugs attacked the cassava crop, causing crop losses of up to 80 percent. To solve the problem, scientists bred wasps that eat mealybugs and then released the wasps from airplanes. This method of using insects to fight other insects is called biological pest control.

Farm experts are developing new kinds of crops, such as corn and sorghum, that yield larger harvests. Ordinary farmers are experimenting with new crops and new techniques, too. In Burkina Faso, Halodou Sawadogo wanted to grow and store potatoes. He dug a 10-foot-deep storage pit and devised a system to keep it cool and dry. “The agricultural experts told me, ‘It's impossible to store potatoes in this climate without them sprouting.’ Well, I've proved you can,” said Sawadogo proudly.

Scientists are working with farmers to stop soil erosion. Nigerian farmers are trying “alley-cropping.” They plant long rows, or

Trapping the Tsetse Fly

SCIENCE AND TECHNOLOGY

Members of the research team paused on the trail, deep in Kenya's Rift Valley. Above the usual forest noise, the African scientists picked out a dim sound—the menacing buzz of the tsetse fly.

The bite of the tsetse can cause sleeping sickness—a disease often fatal to humans and cattle. The tsetse fly thrives in some parts of the African savanna. Each year, the flies cause more than 20,000 new cases of sleeping sickness among people. The disease also kills thousands of cattle, causing the loss of 3 billion pounds of beef annually. Sometimes, people have had to abandon their communities because of the tsetse fly.

The high cost in human life and great economic losses have spurred scientists to hunt for ways to control the tsetse fly. Kenyan scientist Thomas Odhiambo founded the International Centre of Insect Physiology and Ecology (ICIPE) in Nairobi, Kenya. The ICIPE is the only scientific institution in the world devoted solely to the study of insects and the control of insect-related problems.

In the past, people used drastic measures against insect populations. A common tactic was to set fire to large areas to destroy insect breeding grounds. The only alternative was to spray highly toxic pesticides. Yet these killed many other things besides "pests." Neither of these destructive measures solved the insect problem.

Today, ICIPE scientists use techniques that destroy tsetse flies without harming the environment. One research team invented a simple trap that can catch more than 20,000 tsetse flies in a week. Constructed of some blue cloth, a few staples, and a plastic bag, the trap uses no poisons at all. Tsetses just cannot resist the trap's bait—ox-breath perfume.

Thomas Odhiambo hopes that the next step will be to discover ways in which seemingly harmful insects can serve useful functions. He poses the question, "Did you know that termites make excellent chicken food?"

1. What is the function of the International Centre of Insect Physiology and Ecology (ICIPE)?
2. **Applying Information** How might worldwide benefits be gained from insect research in Africa?

alleys, of crops such as corn and yams. In between, they plant rows of fast-growing trees and vines that can be harvested for firewood.

Fighting disease. As you read in Chapter 3, many diseases flourish in the tropical climates of Africa. Researchers have curbed tropical diseases such as malaria and sleeping sickness. (See the feature above.)

Since the late 1970s, AIDS has swept across much of the continent, infecting millions of African men and women. AIDS has hit urban areas the hardest. Many victims are between the ages of 19 and 40. Because of the worldwide impact of the disease, scientists in many countries are seeking vaccines or cures for the AIDS virus.

SECTION 1 REVIEW

1. **Identify:** (a) Organization of African Unity, (b) International Monetary Fund.
2. **Define:** nonalignment.
3. (a) How is the OAU an example of Pan-Africanism? (b) How do regional organizations help African nations strengthen their economies? Give an example.
4. What role do African nations play in the UN?
5. (a) How did the Cold War affect African nations? (b) What effect has the end of Cold War tensions had on Africa?
6. How do science and technology offer Africans hope for the future?
7. **Synthesizing** How is the debt crisis an example of global interdependence?
8. **Writing Across Cultures** Reread the statement by Kwame Nkrumah, on page 135, comparing African attitudes during the Cold War to American attitudes toward foreign involvement in the 1800s. Write a paragraph explaining what Nkrumah meant by this statement.

2 THE REPUBLIC OF SOUTH AFRICA

FIND OUT

What was the purpose of apartheid?

How did apartheid affect the lives of South Africans?

Why did South Africa move toward democracy?

Vocabulary apartheid

"Free at last," proclaimed Nelson Mandela in 1994 as South Africa held its first ever all-race elections. In a landslide victory, Mandela became the first black president of South Africa. The elderly leader had spent 27 years in prison for opposing the racial policies of the old white-dominated South African government.

"Let there be justice for all. Let there be peace for all," declared Mandela as he took office. "The time for the healing of wounds has come." South Africans of all races hoped that healing would take place.

A Policy of Forced Segregation

In 1910, Britain granted South Africa self-rule. Until 1994, a small white minority governed the nation. Whites make up about 16 percent of South Africa's population. The majority of South Africans—70 percent—are black. Other groups include people of mixed racial background (11 percent) and Asians (3 percent).

Origins of apartheid. In 1948, the Nationalist party came to power in South Africa. It drew support from conservative white farmers. Many of them were descended from Dutch settlers who held strong views on white superiority. South Africa was already segregated along racial lines, and the Nationalists strengthened the divisions. They set up the strict legal system of apartheid (uh PAHRT hayt), or rigid separation of races.

Under apartheid, the government classified all South Africans as white, black, "coloured" (people of mixed race), or Asian. It then passed laws to keep the races separate. Nonwhites could not vote. They were also restricted as to where they could live and work.

The government assigned black ethnic groups, such as the Zulus and Xhosas, to live in a number of bantustans, or homelands. Supporters of apartheid claimed that separation allowed each group to develop its own culture. The homelands, however, were located in dry, infertile areas. Four fifths of South Africa, including its rich mineral resources and fertile farmlands, remained in white hands.

Strict laws. Because South Africa needed black workers, the government allowed some blacks to live outside the homelands. To control their movement, it enacted pass laws. The pass laws required all black South Africans living in a town or city to carry a passbook. The

MAP STUDY

South Africa is the largest nation in Southern Africa and the most industrialized in all of Africa. Its natural resources include gold, diamonds, iron ore, chromium, and coal.

1. **Location** Describe the relative location of South Africa.
2. **Location** In what areas of South Africa are the major cities located?
3. **Making Global Connections** Why do you think economic sanctions by other nations have helped pressure South Africa to end apartheid?

passbook included a record of where they could travel or work, their tax payments, and a record of any criminal convictions. It had to be carried at all times and produced upon demand.

Pass laws divided families. A man might have a job in town, while his wife had to remain in the homeland. One South African newspaper reported how Mathilda Chikuye was fined $25 for letting her husband live with her. She had permission to be in town, but he did not.

Apartheid enforced a system of inequality. Blacks were forbidden to ride on "white" buses, swim at "white" beaches, or eat at "white" restaurants. Apartheid also extended to education. Black schools received much less money and other support than white schools. As a result, literacy remained low among black students, and many dropped out of school. Only a very few black African students received higher education.

Struggle Against Apartheid

From the start, blacks and some other South Africans opposed apartheid. Leaders such as Albert J. Luthuli (luh TOO lee) urged nonviolent resistance. Luthuli won the Nobel Peace Prize in 1960. In his acceptance speech, he stated,

> "[Apartheid] is a museum piece in our time, a hangover from the dark ages . . . a relic of an age that everywhere else is dead or dying. . . . These ideas survive in South Africa because those who sponsor them profit from them."

Later, another black South African leader, Archbishop Desmond Tutu, won the same prize. Like Luthuli, Tutu strongly opposed apartheid but rejected violence. (See Connections With Literature, page 804, "The Ultimate Safari.")

The South African police and government forces used violence, however. In 1960, protesters staged a peaceful demonstration in Sharpeville, a township near Johannesburg. The police opened fire, killing more than 60 people. The "Sharpeville massacre" aroused anger worldwide. As protests continued, the government banned opposition groups, such as the African National Congress (ANC). Black leaders, including Nelson Mandela, went into hiding. Mandela was captured and sentenced to life in prison in 1964.

Women and students. Many South African women joined the struggle against apartheid. At one rally, more than 20,000 women marched through Pretoria to demonstrate against the pass laws. During the years of struggle, many women lost their lives or went to prison for their beliefs.

In 1976, students in Soweto (suh WEE toh), a black township located outside Johannesburg, protested a new law requiring the use of Afrikaans in all public schools. Afrikaans is the language of white South Africans who are descended from Dutch settlers. When the government responded with violence, the protests spread.

Pressure grows. While South Africans demanded change from within, international pressure grew. From its founding, the OAU had worked to end apartheid. It urged members to boycott South Africa. Other groups also pressed for change in South Africa. The United Nations placed an arms embargo on South Africa. International sports organizations such as the Olympic Committee barred South African athletes from competition.

During the 1980s, many nations, including the United States, imposed economic sanctions. This meant that they cut off trade in many items and ended financial dealings with South African businesses.

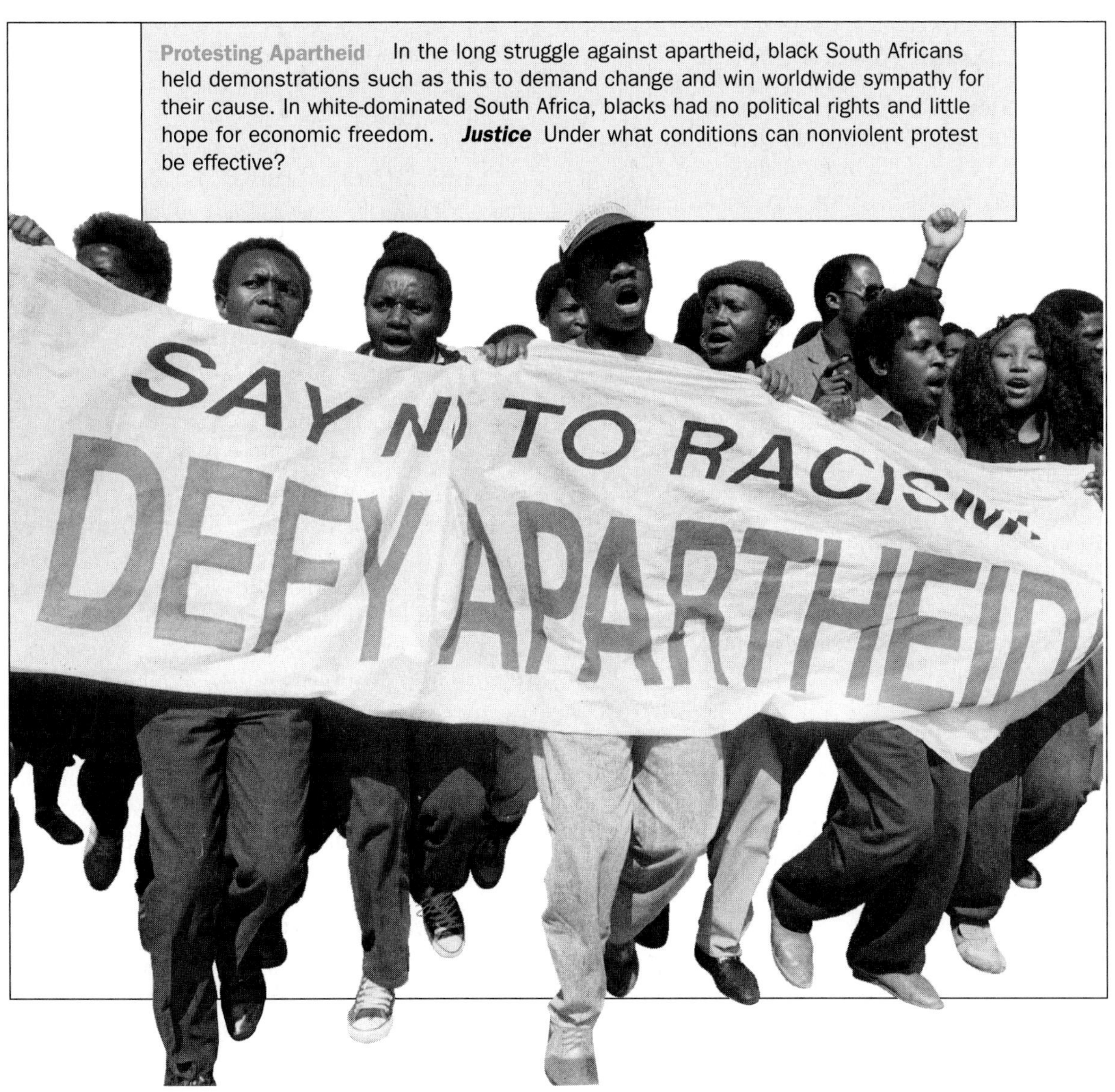

Protesting Apartheid In the long struggle against apartheid, black South Africans held demonstrations such as this to demand change and win worldwide sympathy for their cause. In white-dominated South Africa, blacks had no political rights and little hope for economic freedom. ***Justice*** Under what conditions can nonviolent protest be effective?

The Dawning of a New Era Supporters of Nelson Mandela celebrate his election as South Africa's first black president. The relatively peaceful election raised hopes that South Africa could make a smooth transition to a non-segregated society. ***Justice*** What obstacles still stand in the way of blacks becoming equal members of South African society?

Steps Toward Change

Protests and economic sanctions had an effect. The sanctions slowed the South African economy, causing white business leaders to press the government for change. The ending of the Cold War also played a part. A growing number of white South Africans came to feel that apartheid must end.

In the mid-1980s, the South African government began to make changes. It repealed the hated pass laws and opened some segregated facilities to all South Africans. In 1989, South Africa's president, F. W. de Klerk, lifted the ban on the ANC and other groups opposed to apartheid. A year later, the government released Nelson Mandela from prison and began to hold talks with black leaders.

A new constitution. In the early 1990s, the de Klerk government slowly moved to end white-minority rule in South Africa. A new constitution was drawn up to give blacks basic rights. In 1994, elections were held to create a coalition government that would remain in office until 1999.

The historic election in which black South Africans voted for the first time swept Mandela into office. As he cast his ballot, Mandela noted:

> “We have moved from an era of pessimism, division, limited opportunity, and turmoil. We are starting a new era of hope, of reconciliation, of nation-building.”

South Africa's future. As Mandela campaigned for office, he made many promises. He wanted to "heal the wounds of the past" by building a new order "based on justice for all." That task meant bringing basic services such as electricity and housing along with decent schools and other improvements to millions of black South Africans.

The challenge was enormous. After years of hardship under apartheid, many blacks were eager to see rapid change. Yet Mandela also vowed to keep the economy from faltering. Even though foreign countries ended economic sanctions, the new South Africa could not afford to outspend its income.

Mandela faced other problems. A small but determined group of whites, particularly in rural areas, strongly opposed the new government of national unity. Ethnic and political tensions between Mandela's ANC and the Inkatha Freedom Party led by Chief Mangosuthu Buthelezi (boo tuh LEE zee) had flared into violence during the election campaign.

Many South Africans admired Mandela and respected his efforts to create a nation "at peace with itself." Yet Mandela was 75 years old, and no one knew who might be able to replace this strong leader in the future.

SECTION 2 REVIEW

1. **Identify:** (a) Nelson Mandela, (b) Albert J. Luthuli, (c) Desmond Tutu, (d) Sharpeville massacre, (e) F. W. de Klerk.
2. **Define:** apartheid.
3. (a) How did apartheid divide South African society? (b) How did it promote social inequality?
4. Why did the South African government change its racial policy?
5. **Applying Information** How has the legacy of the pass laws contributed to violence among black South Africans today?
6. **Writing Across Cultures** Write a letter to Nelson Mandela congratulating him on his election as president. Explain why you think the victory against apartheid in South Africa is important to people in the United States.

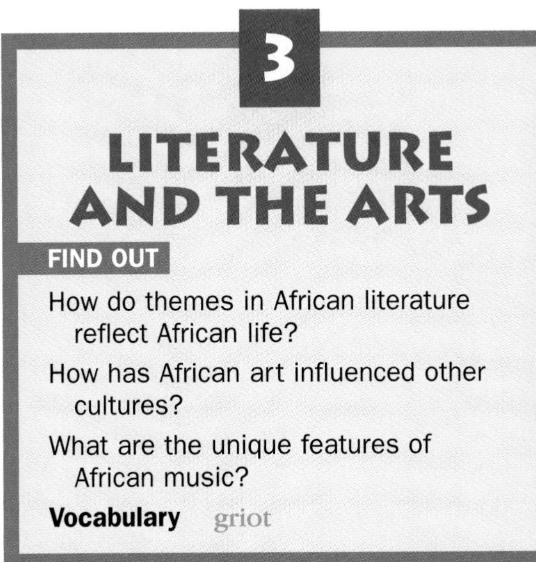

3 LITERATURE AND THE ARTS

FIND OUT

How do themes in African literature reflect African life?

How has African art influenced other cultures?

What are the unique features of African music?

Vocabulary griot

Captain Africa is a superhero. In popular comic books, he fights a constant battle against evildoers and ignorance. In one story, a college graduate learns that her parents have arranged for her to marry "the notorious Chief Eza." In the nick of time, Captain Africa arrives to right the wrong that has been done.

"We have our own culture, our own heritage," says Mbadiwe Emelumba, head of the Nigerian firm that publishes the Captain Africa comics. The comics deal with current issues, but also include themes from the past. Above all, they tell a good story, and storytelling has long been a feature of African culture.

We can understand a people's culture by looking at their literature, music, and other arts. Through these forms of expression, people communicate their feelings, beliefs, and ideas to other members of their culture and to the rest of the world.

African Literature

The peoples of Africa have developed a rich oral and written literature. Oral literature includes poems, histories, folk tales, and myths that were passed on by word of mouth from one generation to the next. Written literature began with ancient Egyptian works.

Oral literature. In traditional African societies, the storyteller, or griot (GREE oh), held a place of honor. The griot spoke the praises of the ruler and recited events from history. Storytellers also recited riddles, poems, and tongue-twisters. Many of the stories or poems that griots told contained a moral, or lesson, such as this "Song for the Lazy" from Central Africa:

> "If you are hungry
> Use your hoe,
> The only drug
> The doctors know."

Some themes appear in many stories. One favorite theme is that the universe has a moral order. If people disturb that order, they will suffer misfortune. Another common theme is that people must respect the environment if they wish to prosper. "If one wants to catch a large fish," states a West African proverb, "one must give something to the stream."

In villages today, people gather around the storyteller to hear familiar tales and poems. They can also hear storytellers on the radio. Tapes with poets reading both new and old poems are also available.

Written works. Modern African writers often write about the conflict between old and new ways. Some focus on how Africans can preserve what is good in traditional societies while moving ahead with technological progress. Others examine the problems faced by villagers who move to cities.

In the years after independence, writers such as Hamidou Kane (KAH nuh) of Senegal wrote about the effect of western culture on Africa. In *Ambiguous Adventure,* Kane's hero is a Fulani boy who goes to study in France. There, he loses touch with his Islamic faith and his Senegalese roots. "The cannon compels the body," notes the author, "the school bewitches the soul."

Nigerian novelist Chinua Achebe writes of problems created by imposing European culture on traditional African values. One of his best-known novels, *Things Fall Apart*, shows how the arrival of the British in Nigeria disrupted the age-old patterns of African village life. The novel's main character, Okonkwo says:

> "[The white man] is very clever. He came quietly and peacefully with his religion. We were amused at his foolishness and allowed him to stay. Now he has won our brothers, and our clan can no longer act like one. He has put a knife on the things that held us together and we have fallen apart."

Storytelling in Africa Storytelling has long been an important tradition in Africa. As these children of the Cote d'Ivoire listen to the storyteller's tales, they learn about the history, customs, and values of their society. ***Change*** How may the use of books and television affect the ancient art of storytelling?

Film in Africa This dramatic scene is from the film *Yaaba,* which is based on a tale that its director, Idrissa Ouedraogo, heard as a child. The movie has been widely praised for its compelling portrayal of the lives of people in a West African village. ***Culture*** Why do you think many Africans would enjoy movies such as *Yaaba*?

Things Fall Apart was both a critical and popular success. Translated into more than 40 languages, it has sold more than 2.5 million copies worldwide. Other novels by Achebe include *No Longer at Ease* and *Arrow of God*.

African women have also written about the conflict between traditional customs and modern ways. In *So Long a Letter* by Mariama Bâ, a Senegalese woman writes a letter to her daughter in which she describes how society has changed. In *The Bride Price,* Nigerian author Buchi Emecheta tells of a young woman who escapes from an arranged marriage because she is in love with someone else. (See Connections With Literature, page 804, *Things Fall Apart* and "Snapshots of a Wedding.")

Drama and Film

African playwrights and filmmakers have built on the tradition of the griots, who acted out the characters in their tales by putting on masks or using puppets. Today's plays address modern issues but use traditional methods. A popular playwright from Ghana is Ama Ata Aidoo. In *The Dilemma of a Ghost,* she shows what happens when a student returns to his village with an African American wife.

African filmmakers reach a wide audience in the cities. Like filmmakers everywhere, they sometimes use historical events as subjects. In *The Camp at Thairoye,* Senegalese director Sembene Ousmane examines a massacre of African soldiers by the French army in 1944. The soldiers, who had fought for France during World War II, are waiting in a camp in Senegal to leave the army. When they learn that the French do not plan to pay them as promised, the soldiers revolt. In response, the French fire on the men during the night, as they sleep, killing the entire force.

Other films retell popular village tales. In *Yaaba* ("Granny"), director Idrissa Ouedraogo captures the story of two children who make friends with an old woman whom people think is a witch.

Visual Arts

In African cultures, as elsewhere, art has served both religious and practical purposes. A bronze figure of a king is a symbol of the ruler's divine nature. It also is a decorative work. Beautifully carved masks also have a dual purpose. A dancer wears a mask to represent a spirit in a religious ceremony. According to traditional beliefs, the mask gives the dancer the powers of that spirit.

African artists are probably best known for their fine sculpture. In forested areas, artists carved green wood into human figures, masks, and everyday objects. Unfortunately, termites and other insects attack wood, and only a few examples of ancient wood carvings have survived. Other African sculptors created excellent works in bronze. Benin craftworkers cast bronze heads and wall plaques that showed important events in history.

African art has a long history. Ancient Egyptian art influenced the art of many societies. In the early 1900s, westerners began to study other African art styles. The Spanish artist Pablo Picasso admired the unique

Ndebele Houses Traditional African art takes many forms. Ndebele women in South Africa paint their houses and the clay walls around them in bold geometric designs. The colors and shapes express their individuality. They use materials ranging from natural dyes to acrylic paints. ***Fine Art*** In what similar ways do people around the world express their individuality in visual arts?

features of African masks and statues. He applied similar techniques to his own paintings and sculptures. Other European and American artists also found inspiration in African art.

African Art Today

African artists today produce a wide variety of art that is both new and uniquely African. One area in which they are experimenting is painting. In the past, Africans reserved color for fabrics, building decoration, and body painting. In recent years, however, more and more African artists have been painting pictures. Among the most popular are Gora Mbengue (ehm BEHN gay) from Senegal, known for his painting on glass, and Cheri Samba of Zaire, who uses a cartoon style to explore social and political themes.

Much African art is both useful and decorative. Many artists create works for everyday use. Sometimes these practical creations gain such acclaim that they end up in museums as well. Such has been the fate of the work of Kane Kwei (KAH nuh KWAY).

Kane Kwei: Carpenter Artist

An unusual exhibit has intrigued museum goers in New York, San Francisco, and around the world. In galleries, amidst paintings and sculpture, rests a coffin shaped like a boat. According to its creator, Kane Kwei,

> “When people die, they like to travel to heaven in different ways—some by land, some by sea, some by air.”

The effort of the artist to fulfill people's wishes has brought him attention far beyond his small village in Ghana.

As a boy, Kwei went to work for a local carpenter, who taught him to build and repair wooden homes and furniture. From the carpenter, Kane Kwei learned to make coffins.

One day, an ailing uncle asked him a favor. The uncle knew he was dying and wanted his nephew to build him a special coffin. By now an experienced carpenter, Kwei gave the request serious thought. He had an idea. His uncle was a fisherman. Why not build the coffin in the shape of a boat?

Kane Kwei's boat coffin created a stir in the village. Other people asked him to build coffins for them. For a local farmer, he created a colorfully painted onion-shaped coffin, such as the one on page 148. For the wealthy owner of a fleet of taxis, he built a car coffin. The coffin of the grandmother of a large family

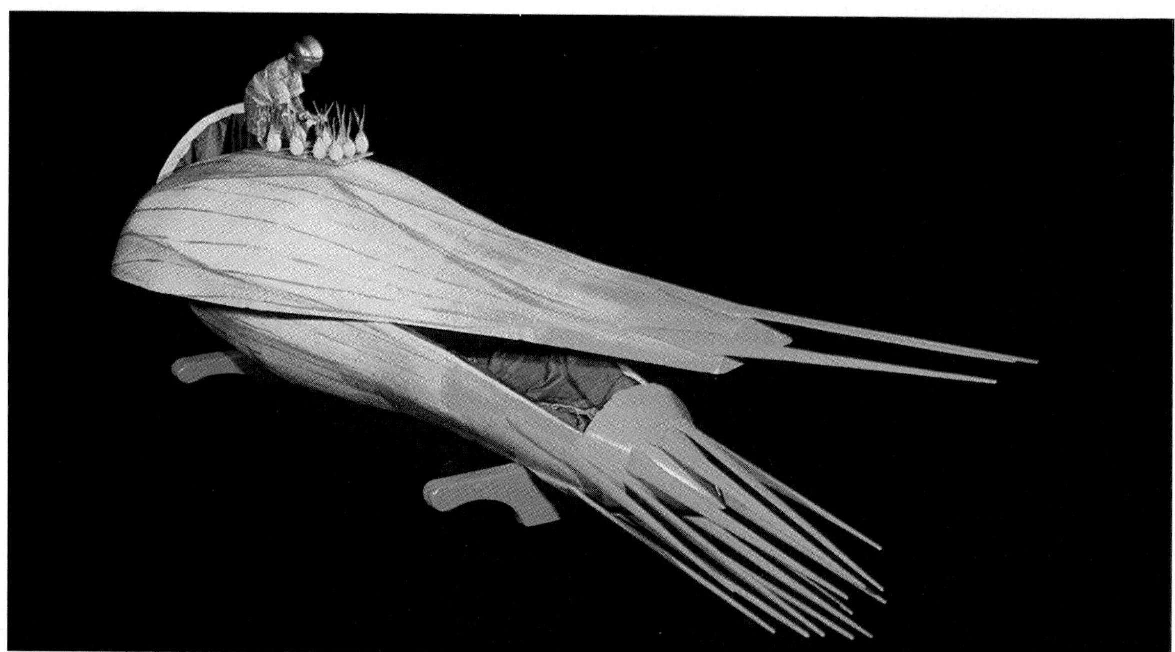

Onion Coffin Present-day African artists are exploring new forms of art. Kane Kwei's coffins have caught the imagination of people around the world. A farmer's family asked Kwei to design the coffin shown here. The artist used enamel paint on wood and carved a farmer planting onions. ***Fine Art*** How can an item made to serve some practical purpose also be considered a work of art?

was a hen accompanied by her chicks. A coffin could cost an amount equal to one year's wages. Sometimes, entire extended families contributed money to pay for one.

As Kwei's reputation spread, people from other villages came to admire his work. Today, Kwei heads a large workshop that produces coffins for local people and for tourists. Even international art critics have come to recognize the artistic value of his work. ■

Music

As you have read, popular music in Africa builds on many traditions. Styles and instruments vary from region to region. In Southern Africa, the *mbira,* or thumb piano, is popular. Stringed instruments are also widely used. In Botswana, cattle herders use cowbells to create music.

Much African music relies on percussion instruments, such as xylophones and drums. "Talking drums" imitate human speech and have many functions, including religious ones. Among the Akan people of West Africa, drummers create music that sounds like poetry. On important occasions, drum-poets play special greetings to leaders. For example, the drums might suggest the message: "I am addressing you, and you will understand."

SECTION 3 REVIEW

1. **Identify:** (a) Hamidou Kane, (b) Mariama Bâ.
2. **Define:** griot
3. Describe three concerns of Africans today that are reflected in African literature.
4. How has African art served more than one purpose?
5. **Synthesizing** Why do you think that the arts and music of Africa are so varied?
6. **Writing Across Cultures** Jot down five things that an African might learn about your culture from American popular music.

Chapter 6 Review

Understanding Vocabulary

Match each term at left with the correct definition at right.

1. nonalignment	**a.** storyteller
2. apartheid	**b.** cutoff of trade and financial aid
3. alley-cropping	**c.** method of limiting soil erosion
4. economic sanction	**d.** system of rigid separation of races
5. griot	**e.** policy of favoring neither side

Reviewing the Main Ideas

1. How did superpower rivalries affect African nations?
2. How did the economic downturn of the early 1990s affect African nations? (b) What measures are they taking to cope with the effects?
3. Describe three ways that African nations are working to solve their problems.
4. (a) Describe the system of apartheid. (b) List the events that led to the end of apartheid and the establishment of democracy in South Africa.
5. Describe three themes that are found in African literature.
6. How have the works of African artists influenced European artists?
7. How do playwrights and film makers build on the tradition of the griots?

Reviewing Chapter Themes

1. Interdependence is drawing regions and countries closer together. Describe a goal of each of the following organizations: OAU, SADCC, ECOWAS.
2. The Cold War affected developing countries throughout the world. Describe two events in Africa that were influenced by rivalry between the superpowers.
3. Historians describe events and developments in terms of cause-and-effect relationships. (a) Describe the causes of apartheid. (b) Discuss the effects of apartheid on South Africa.
4. The literature, music, and art of a region often blend traditional and modern influences. Choose an example of modern African literature, music, and art, and explain how each blends old and new ideas.

Thinking Critically

1. **Making Global Connections** How have relations between the United States and the nations of Africa been affected by the end of the Cold War?
2. **Linking Past and Present** Describe two ways in which present-day Africa is affected by its past.
3. **Applying Information** South African President F. W. de Klerk stated, "One cannot build security on injustice." To what groups in South Africa do you think this remark would appeal? Why?

Applying Your Skills

1. **Reading a Map** Look at the political map of Africa on page 110 or the physical map of Africa on page 62. (a) Locate a landlocked nation in East Africa, West Africa, and Southern Africa. (b) Through what nations must the goods of these landlocked nations pass to reach the nearest ocean? (c) What do the nations of Africa gain by cooperating with one another?
2. **Using Your Vocabulary** Use the Glossary on pages 794–803 to review the meaning of the following terms: *export, racism, democratization.* Use each term in a separate sentence about South Africa.

SKILL LESSON 3

Reading a Time Line: Events From Modern African History

Time lines are useful tools for understanding the sequence in which events occurred. By placing events in chronological order, or the order in which they occurred, it becomes easier to see how certain events are related.

The time line below shows important dates in Africa's history. Study the time line, using the following steps to guide you.

1. **Identify the time period covered in the time line.** (a) What is the earliest date shown on the time line? (b) What is the latest date? (c) What is the period covered by the time line?
2. **Determine how the time line is divided.** Time lines are always divided into equal parts or time periods. Some are divided into 10-year periods called decades. Others are divided into 100-year periods called centuries. The period between 1800 and 1899, for example, is called the nineteenth century. (a) How many years are there between the dates on the top of the time line? (b) What events occurred during the decade of the 1980s? (c) Part of what century is shown on the time line?
3. **Examine the time line for events that span a period of time.** Some events do not occur on a specific day. They may span, or last, months or years. (a) What event on the time line below occurred between 1954 and 1962? (b) What other events took place during this time span? (c) When was Nelson Mandela first imprisoned? (d) How long was he in jail?
4. **Study the time line to discover how events are related.** (a) How many nations listed on the time line have become independent since 1950? Name them. (b) Which nation won its independence most recently? (c) How long after white Rhodesians declared independence did Rhodesia change its name to Zimbabwe? (d) Based on your reading of Chapter 5, was there a relationship between these two events? Explain the reasons for your answer. (e) Was Nelson Mandela released from prison before or after South Africa's racial classification laws were repealed? Based on your reading of Chapter 6, what was the relationship between these two events?

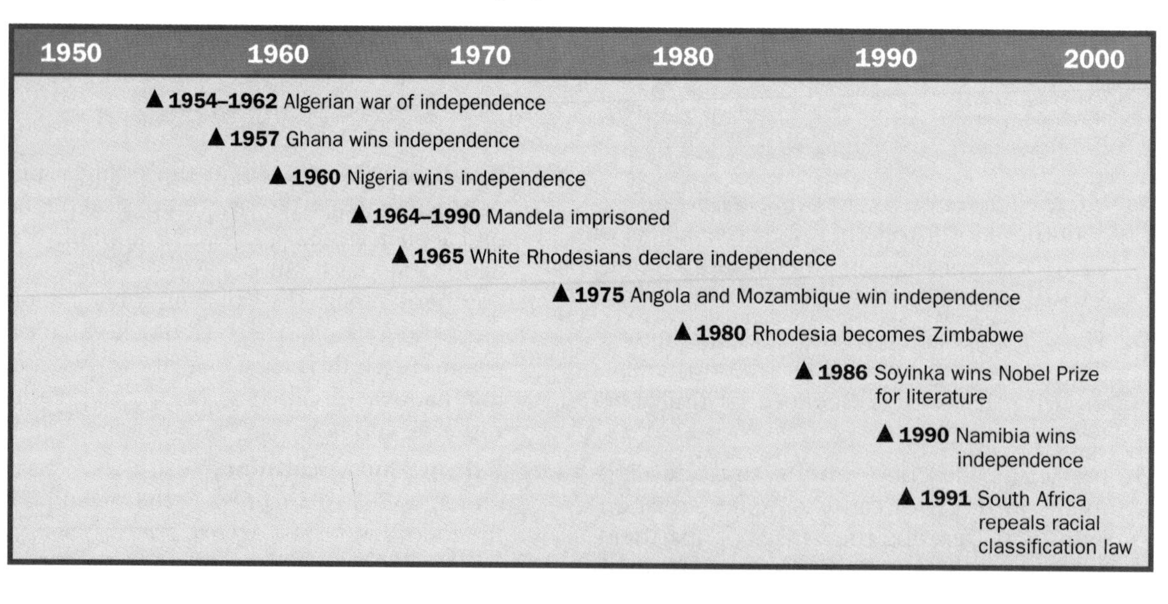

SKILL LESSON 4

Recognizing Facts and Opinions: Lifting Sanctions Against South Africa

Facts and opinions are very different things. Facts are actual events or situations that can be proven to have occurred. Opinions are judgments formed by people about a particular matter. They may or may not be provable.

In the 1980s, many nations imposed economic sanctions on South Africa. They hoped to force South Africa's white government to end its policy of apartheid.

The speeches at right were given in 1990, after President F. W. de Klerk began to undo South Africa's system of racial segregation. De Klerk also released leaders of the African National Congress from prison, including Nelson Mandela. Analyze the speeches, using the following steps to guide you.

1. **Identify the facts.** To identify facts, look for situations or events that have occurred and can be checked. **(a)** What fact does Boesak present about the Bush administration's policy toward lifting sanctions on Eastern Europe? On South Africa? **(b)** What fact does Duigan present about reforms that South Africans have made?
2. **Identify the opinions.** To identify an opinion, ask yourself what the writer thinks or believes. Sometimes, the speaker or writer uses phrases such as *I think, I believe,* or *in my view*. **(a)** In Boesak's opinion, what two sets of rules about sanctions did the Bush administration have? **(b)** In Duigan's opinion, should the United States lift sanctions? Why or why not?
3. **Determine whether the facts support the opinions.** Do you think that Boesak and Duigan have supported their opinions with facts? Explain.

Allan A. Boesak, a black South African and president of the World Alliance of Reform Churches:

> " I was amazed to see that all of a sudden there emerges now a new set of rules. There is one set of rules for democracy in Eastern Europe . . . and another set of rules for South Africa.
>
> The same [Bush] administration here [in the United States] who would say to Eastern Europe, 'We will not even think of lifting sanctions or think of giving aid . . . [until] we . . . see a free and fair election in which people can express their will,' is the same government who simply wanted to lift sanctions on South Africa without even talking about free and fair elections in South Africa. "

Peter Duigan, an American:

> " The freeing of Nelson Mandela from prison on February 11 opened a new era in South Africa's troubled history. . . . Mandela's release signaled that the white government of recently elected President de Klerk was serious about ending apartheid and negotiating with black leaders over some form of power sharing. A peaceful and prosperous era may conceivably have begun in South Africa, and at least Prime Minister Thatcher [of Great Britain] recognized this and wanted to reward the South Africans for these reforms by reducing some of the sanctions imposed on that besieged society. . . . I believe, like Mrs. Thatcher, that we [the United States] need to use the carrot, now, more than the stick, to keep the reform process going. "

The Gentlemen of the Jungle

Jomo Kenyatta

INTRODUCTION Jomo Kenyatta (1893–1978) was a leader in Kenya's struggle against British rule. In 1964, he became the first president of an independent Kenya. Through this fable, Kenyatta describes how the Europeans took control of much of Africa during the Age of Imperialism.

Vocabulary Before you read the selection, find the meaning of these words in a dictionary: turmoil, intricacy, relevant, verdict.

Once upon a time an elephant made a friendship with a man. One day a heavy thunderstorm broke out. The elephant went to his friend . . . and said to him: "My dear good man, will you please let me put my trunk inside your hut to keep it out of this torrential rain?" The man . . . replied: "My dear good elephant, my hut is very small, but there is room for your trunk and myself. . . ." But what followed? As soon as the elephant put his trunk inside the hut, slowly he pushed his head inside, and finally flung the man out in the rain. . . ."

The man . . . started to grumble; the animals . . . heard the noise and came to see what was the matter. . . . In this turmoil the lion came along roaring, and said in a loud voice: "Don't you all know that I am the King of the Jungle! . . . I command my ministers to appoint a Commission of Enquiry to go thoroughly into this matter and report accordingly." . . .

The elephant, obeying the command of his master, got busy with other ministers to appoint the Commission of Enquiry. . . . On seeing the personnel, the man protested and asked if it was not necessary to include in this Commission a member from his side. But he was told that it was impossible, since no one from his side was well enough educated to understand the intricacy of jungle law. . . .

The Commission sat to take the evidence. The Rt. Hon. Mr. Elephant was first called. He came along with a superior air, . . . and said: "Gentlemen of the Jungle, . . . I have always regarded it as my duty to protect the interests of my friends. . . . He invited me to save his hut from being blown away by a hurricane. As the hurricane had gained access owing to the unoccupied space in the hut, I considered it necessary, in my friend's own interests, to turn the undeveloped space to a more economic use by sitting in it myself. . . ."

After hearing the Rt. Hon. Mr. Elephant's conclusive evidence, the Commission . . . then called the man, who began to give his own account of the dispute. But the Commission cut him short, saying: "My good man, please confine yourself to relevant issues. . . . All we wish you to tell us is whether the undeveloped space in your hut was occupied by anyone else before Mr. Elephant assumed his position?" The man began to say: "No, but—" But at this point the Commission declared that they had heard sufficient evidence from both sides. . . . After enjoying a delicious meal at the expense of the Rt. Hon. Mr. Elephant, they reached their verdict. . . . "In our opinion this dispute has arisen through a regrettable misunderstanding due to the backwardness of your ideas. We consider that Mr. Elephant has fulfilled his sacred duty of protecting your interests. As it is clearly for your good that the space should be put to its most economic use, and as you yourself have not reached the stage of expansion which would enable you to fill it . . . Mr. Elephant shall continue his occupation of your hut, but we give you permission to look for a site where you can build another hut more suited to your needs. . . ."

The man, having no alternative, and fearing that his refusal might expose him to the teeth and claws of members of the Commission, did as they suggested. But no sooner had he built another hut than Mr. Rhinoceros charged in with his horn lowered and ordered the man to quit. . . . This procedure was repeated until Mr. Buffalo, Mr. Leopard, Mr. Hyena and the rest were all accommodated with new huts. Then the man decided that he must adopt an effective method of protection, since Commissions of Enquiry did not seem to be of any use to him. He sat down and said, "Ng' enda thi ndagaga motegi," which literally means "there is nothing that treads on the earth that cannot be trapped," or in other words, you can fool people for a time, but not forever.

Early one morning . . . he went out and built a bigger and better hut a little distance away. No sooner had Mr. Rhinoceros seen it than he came rushing in, only to find Mr. Elephant was already inside, sound asleep. Mr. Leopard next came to the window, Mr. Lion, Mr. Fox and Mr. Buffalo entered the doors, while Mr. Hyena howled for a place in the shade and Mr. Alligator basked on the roof. Presently they all began disputing about their rights of penetration . . . and while they were all embroiled together the man set the hut on fire and burnt it to the ground, jungle lords and all. Then he went home, saying: "Peace is costly, but it's worth the expense," and lived happily ever after.

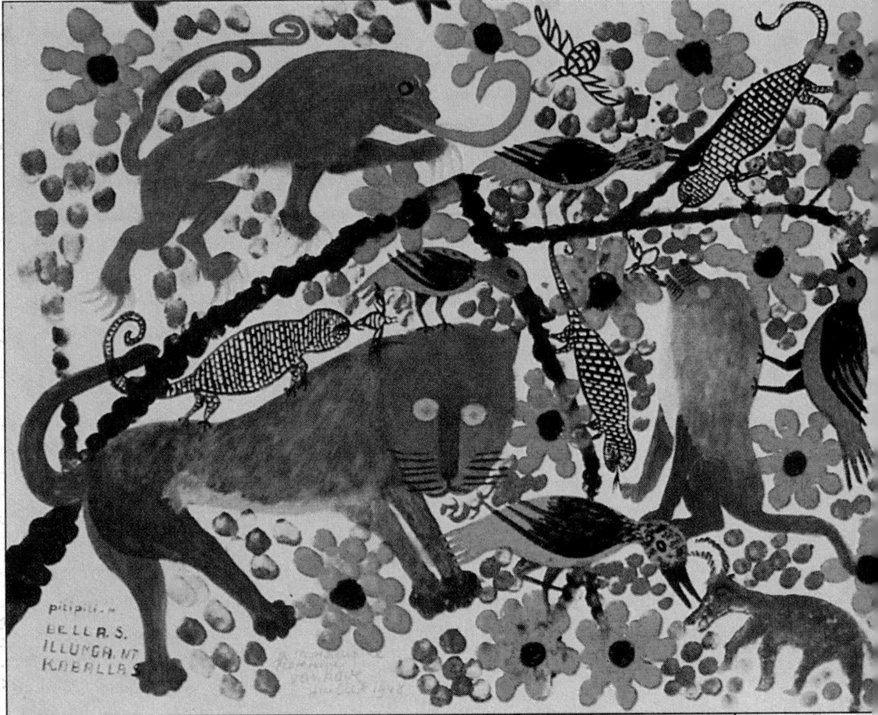

Four artists in Zaire collaborated on this drawing, "À Monsieur le Professeur Van Hove," done in 1948. Compare the way these painters use birds and animals in their drawing with the writer's use of animals in this fable.

Source: Jomo Kenyatta, from *Facing Mount Kenya,* selected and edited by Chinua Achebe and C. L. Innes. Reprinted by permission of Martin Sesker and Warburg Limited.

THINKING ABOUT LITERATURE

1. What is the Commission's explanation for siding with the elephant in the dispute?
2. How does the man solve his problem with the animals?
3. **Synthesizing Information** Explain how the story illustrates the relationship between Africans and Europeans during the Age of Imperialism.

Africa and Modern Art

The young Spanish artist had never seen anything like it. He was dining at the home of Henri Matisse, the great French painter. During the evening, Matisse showed his guests an African woodcarving he had just bought. It was one of the first examples of African art in Paris.

The young Spaniard was fascinated. Another guest later recalled:

> “He held the statuette in his hands all evening. The next morning, when I came to his studio, the floor was covered with sheets of drawing paper. Each sheet had virtually the same drawing on it, a big woman's face with a single eye, a nose too long that merged into the mouth, a lock of hair on the shoulder. Cubism was born.”

The Spanish painter was Pablo Picasso. He and the school of art he helped found, cubism, changed the course of art.

Africa and Cubism

In the early 1900s, as European powers were colonizing Africa, European artists began to collect African art objects. They admired the bold curves and geometric shapes. The African artists did not try to create an exact copy of nature. Their goal was to capture the inner spirit of an object. To artists like Picasso, African art offered a fresh way to see and portray the world.

The cubists blended African techniques with those of earlier European painters. By using geometric forms such as cubes, triangles, and cylinders, cubists created startling images.

Picasso's 1907 painting *Les Demoiselles d'Avignon* (The Young Ladies of Avignon) featured five women with distorted, geometric faces. They resembled the masks used in religious rituals in the Congo. Picasso may have modeled two of the faces on actual masks he had seen. His *Bust of a Sailor*, (far right) bears an even closer resemblance to African masks. Paintings like these shocked viewers into a new way of seeing.

Other painters and sculptors adopted the new techniques. In the following years, "modern art" blossomed into a wide variety of styles. Many artists acknowledged their debt to Africa. Jacques Lipschitz, a Latvian sculptor who later emigrated to America, remarked:

> “African artists have been a great example to us. Their very real understanding of proportion, their feeling for design and acute sense of reality has led us to perceive . . . to dare, many things.”

In 1913, the 69th Regiment Armory in New York City housed the first American exhibition of the new European

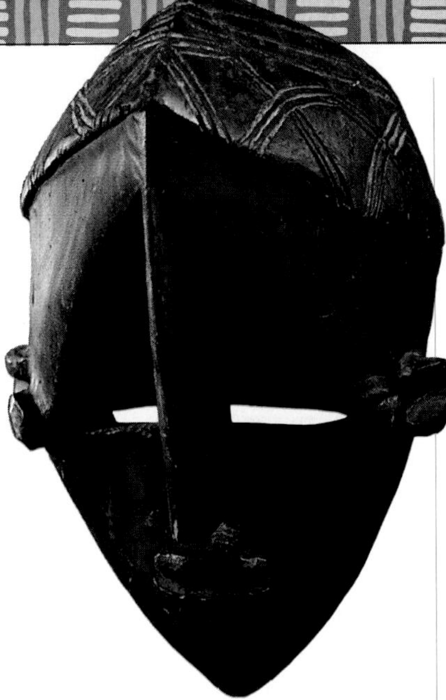

styles. Although many condemned or ridiculed the Armory Show, American artists gradually began to experiment with modern art.

African Influence

The next year, a New York gallery held the first American showing of African art. African American artists were proud of this display of their African heritage. Yet some feared that if they put too much emphasis on African techniques and themes, art critics would dismiss their work as "ethnic."

During the 1920s, the Harlem Renaissance—a flowering of African American literature and art—began in New York. The philosopher Alain Locke urged other black Americans to enrich American culture by drawing inspiration from their African roots.

African American artists took Locke's words to heart. Aaron Douglas produced exuberant murals that portrayed the joys and anguish of African American heritage. Works such as *Aspects of Negro Life* featured geometric motifs and stylized figures. Douglas used the techniques of African art in a way that was totally different from that of the cubists.

North Carolina artist Romare Bearden saw a New York exhibit of African art in the 1930s. He used African techniques and themes in his works. In *The Prevalence of Ritual* (bottom left) a series of collages, he broke faces and bodies into planes. He also blended modern and ancient symbols. "African art appeals to me," Bearden said, "because it has offered another dimension, a way of looking at the world."

Past and Present

African traditions had first influenced American art during the days of the slave trade. Enslaved workers recreated many themes and shapes of African art. In South Carolina, African artists made stoneware vessels shaped like suffering human faces. In Missouri, at the time of the Civil War, Henry Gudgell carved a walking stick with reptiles, a human figure, and abstract designs. His work was similar to that of the Bakongo people of what is now Angola.

Today, many African American artists travel to Africa to study African art firsthand. African American sculptor Barbara Chase-Riboud noted that "the African dancing mask (wood) is always combined with other materials: raffia, hemp, leather, feathers, cord, metal chains or bells." This style influenced her statue, *Monument to Malcolm X*. The body of the statue is bronze, while the lower portions feature contrasting textures of wool and silk. Chase-Riboud and others continue to seek new ways to adapt African techniques to modern materials and themes.

1. How did African techniques influence the rise of modern art?
2. **Making Inferences** Why do you think that both African art and European modern art shocked many Americans?
3. **Writing Across Cultures** Write a speech giving reasons for painters and sculptors to study African art.

Reviewing the Main Ideas

1. (a) Describe the major climate zones of Africa. (b) How have Africa's climate zones increased cultural diversity? (c) How has climate influenced the economy of the savanna region?
2. (a) What was the earliest African civilization? (b) Describe two of this civilization's major achievements. (c) Choose two other ancient African civilizations and describe one achievement of each.
3. (a) Identify three characteristics of traditional religions in Africa. (b) How did traditional religious beliefs work to unify African societies?
4. (a) Why did Europeans begin to explore Africa? (b) What effects did contact with Europeans have on the peoples of Africa?
5. (a) How did World War II and the Cold War help nationalist causes in Africa? (b) What problems do many African nations face today in creating unity among their peoples?
6. How has urbanization affected traditional patterns of life in Africa?
7. (a) List two regional organizations that were formed by African nations. (b) Describe how one problem has been solved with the help of a regional organization.
8. (a) What traditional art forms are still popular in Africa today? (b) How have they been adapted to modern life?

Thinking Critically

1. **Making Global Connections** Rainfall is a crucial factor in determining food production in Africa. How does rainfall affect how people live and earn a living in your region of the United States?
2. **Understanding Causes and Effects** (a) Explain how the gold-salt trade created interdependence between the peoples of the Sahara and the peoples of the savanna. (b) How did this pattern of trade lead to the development of powerful kingdoms in West Africa?
3. **Comparing** Compare the experiences of Ghana, Algeria, and Kenya in their struggles for independence.

Applying Your Skills

1. **Analyzing a Quotation** Study the Egyptian hymn quoted on page 74. How does the hymn express the ancient Egyptians' dependence on the Nile River?
2. **Identifying the Main Idea** Reread the first paragraph on page 136 under the heading "Continuing Concern Over Debt." What is the main idea of the paragraph?
3. **Reading a Map** Study the map below and answer the following questions. (a) What cash crops does Tanzania grow? (b) Which of Tanzania's neighboring nations might benefit from its railroads? Explain. (c) Which of the elements shown on the map are probably leftovers from Tanzania's days as a British colony? (See Skill Lesson, page 48.)

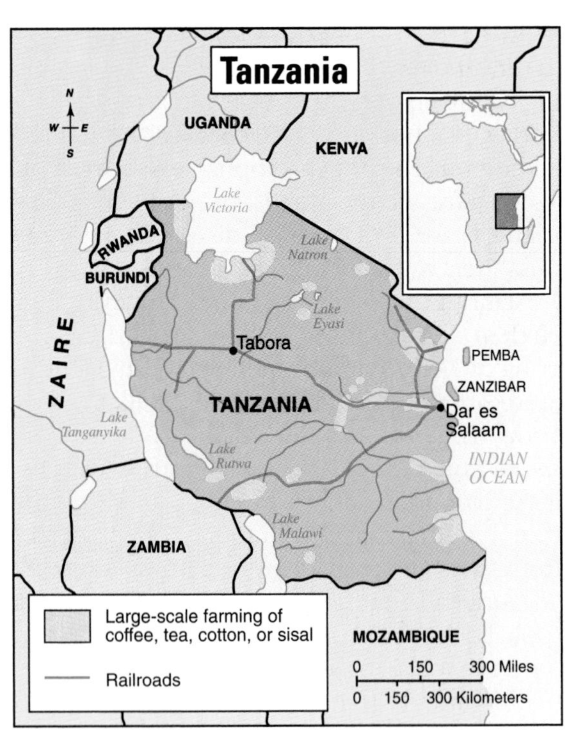

Learning by Doing

1. **Creating a Map** On an outline map of Africa, label the landforms, islands, deserts, rivers, lakes, oceans, seas, gulfs, and straits. Draw and label the Equator and a directional arrow. Using a color key, identify the eight climate regions of Africa. Key the colors to the map. See the maps on pages 62 and 65.
2. **Creating an Illustration** Choose an African culture that you read about in Chapter 3 or 4. Compose a sentence that describes an aspect of that culture. Then, using the information in the text or other sources, illustrate the sentence.
3. **Making a Chart** Make a chart listing the African nations that gained independence after World War II. Divide the paper into three columns: Year of Independence, Country, and Former Colonial Ruler. List the countries in chronological order. See the maps on pages 99 and 110.
4. **Drawing a Cartoon** Draw a political cartoon that protests the injustice of apartheid. First, choose the specific message you would like your cartoon to express. Then, brainstorm images that would best express that message. To make your point, you may want to exaggerate or distort a certain image such as a passbook. Include a caption.

WRITER'S Workshop

Rewording a Question as a Topic Sentence

The topic sentence in a one-paragraph answer states the main idea of the answer. A topic sentence can be written by rewording the question.

Read the following question: *How did European rule affect African cultures?* To write a topic sentence, reword the question: *European rule affected African cultures in several ways.*

Note that the topic sentence includes the clues in the question. The phrase *several ways* covers what the key word *How* in the question tells you to do. The words *European rule* and *African* are clues that limit the topic to a specific time and place.

You may reword the question as a topic sentence without covering the key word *How*. For example: *European rule affected African cultures.* Later, when you select information for detail sentences, be sure to keep the key word in mind.

Practice Reword each of the following questions as a topic sentence for a one-paragraph answer.

1. How is urbanization affecting modern African societies?
2. Why did black South Africans work to end apartheid?

Writing to Learn

1. Imagine that you are an African whose village has been raided by slave traders. Describe the raid and what life in your village was like before and after the raid. Begin by freewriting about your village, the raid, and its effects on the village and its inhabitants. Include facts, sense impressions, and reactions. In your first draft, try to capture the reader's interest with a dramatic topic sentence. Organize details in time order or in order of importance. Revise your description, checking for logical organization, and make a final copy. Then, share your account with a classmate.

2. Write a short biography about one of the people who is mentioned in Chapter 6. Use an encyclopedia or another library source to research and record details about the person's life. Begin your first draft with a topic sentence that states the main reason the person you are writing about is important. Next, arrange the details in time order. Be sure to include all of the person's accomplishments. Revise the biography for clarity and accuracy. Then, proofread and make a final copy of the biography. Help to publish a collection of historical biographies written by your classmates.

SOUTH ASIA

INDIA, PAKISTAN, BANGLADESH

UNIT OUTLINE

1 These women in a village in central India are carrying water to their homes. They wear the traditional clothing and jewelry of South Asian women.

3 During the reign of Asoka, Indian artists carved huge stone pillars such as these. The three lions appear as symbols on stamps and coins in India today.

2 Young women in Nepal are playing a game using stone marbles. They live in Katmandu, their nation's capital city, located in the majestic Himalaya Mountains.

	Early History	1400
History and Politics	▲ 321 B.C. Maurya dynasty emerges in India	▲ 1398 Mongols reach India
Society and Culture	▲ 1500s B.C. Hinduism develops; ▲ 500s B.C. Buddhism spreads; ▲ 1200s–1500s Muslim rulers govern much of northern India	
Economics and Technology	▲ 2500 B.C. Indians build cities in Indus Valley	▲ 1351–1388 Sultan Firuz Tughlak expands Delhi

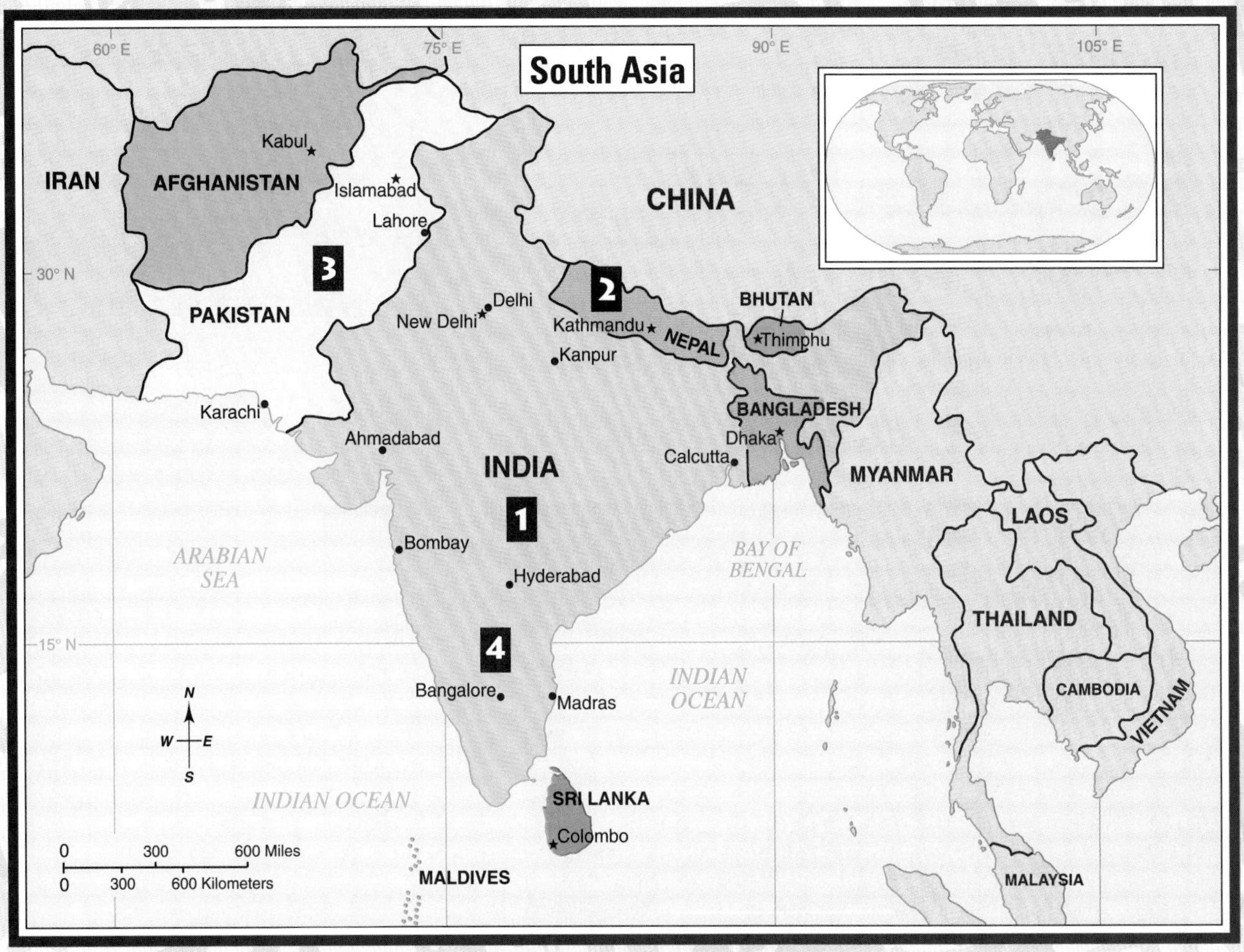

South Asia

60° E
75° E
90° E
105° E
30° N
15° N
IRAN
AFGHANISTAN
Kabul
Islamabad
Lahore
PAKISTAN
Karachi
CHINA
NEPAL
Kathmandu
BHUTAN
Thimphu
BANGLADESH
Dhaka
Calcutta
Delhi
New Delhi
Kanpur
Ahmadabad
INDIA
Bombay
Hyderabad
Bangalore
Madras
SRI LANKA
Colombo
MALDIVES
MYANMAR
LAOS
THAILAND
CAMBODIA
VIETNAM
MALAYSIA
ARABIAN SEA
BAY OF BENGAL
INDIAN OCEAN
INDIAN OCEAN
N
W
E
S
0 300 600 Miles
0 300 600 Kilometers
1
2
3
4

4 Farmers in southern India and in other fertile areas of the subcontinent grow grain and other food products needed to feed the nation's large population.

1600 — 1800 — 2000

- ▲ **1526–1700s** Hindu and Islamic art and architecture blend
- ▲ **1600** British set up East India Company
- ▲ **1630s–1650s** Shah Jahan builds Taj Mahal
- ▲ **1700s** Mughal Empire declines
- ▲ **1700s** East India Company reaps enormous profits
- ▲ **1857** Sepoy Rebellion breaks out
- ▲ **1858–1947** British modernize transportation and communications in India
- ▲ **1913** Rabindranath Tagore wins Nobel Prize for literature
- ▲ **1947** India gains independence
- ▲ **1980s** Farm production increases

Chapter 7

Geography and Early History of South Asia

Origin of the Ganges A culture's beliefs are often reflected in its art. This stone carving, "The Descent of the Ganges," portrays a scene from an Indian legend about the origin of the Ganges River. It shows figures moving toward the sacred river, represented by a cleft in the rock. ***Fine Art*** Why is art an important element of culture in South Asia as elsewhere?

Chapter Outline

1 The Shape of the Land

2 Climate and Resources

3 Early Civilizations of India

Long ago, begins an Indian legend, two sisters went walking in the hills on a hot April day. The younger one, Nuengi, complained endlessly of thirst. Finally, her sister, Tuichang, demanded, "Would you rather have water than me, Nuengi?" Nuengi replied, "If I don't get any water to drink now, I shall die in any case, and then what use would you be to me?"

Tuichang responded by turning herself into a river so that her sister could quench her thirst. In this way, says the legend, the Tuichang River, in northeastern India, was formed.

The appearance of the new river created great interest. The local king sent explorers to find its source, and they came upon Nuengi, lost and helpless. They took her back to the king, who fell in love with the young woman and married her.

The river continued to play a role in Nuengi's life. When she bore a son, the king's chief wife was jealous. She had the baby thrown in the Tuichang River. The ever-caring Tuichang saved the boy and raised him and his six brothers who were also cast into the river by the jealous chief wife.

When the seven boys grew up, Tuichang sent them to meet their father. After hearing their story, he had his wicked chief wife executed and put Nuengi in her place.

CHAPTER PERSPECTIVE

Legends such as this one show the importance of rivers and their life-giving waters to India. India is the largest nation in the giant peninsula known as South Asia. More than a billion people live in South Asia. The region has an immense variety of landscapes and cultures. Geography has contributed to the differing ways of life there.

As you read, look for these chapter themes:

- South Asia is a well-defined region with geographic features that set it apart from the rest of Asia.
- Geographic features have contributed to cultural diversity in the region.
- The earliest civilization in South Asia developed in the Indus Valley.

Literature Connections

In this chapter, you will encounter passages from the following works.

"Hail Motherland" ("Vande Matarum"), Bankim Chandra Chatterjee

Poems From the Sanskrit, Amaru

"Hymn of the Primeval Man," *Rig Veda*

For other suggestions, see Connections With Literature, pages 804–808.

1

THE SHAPE OF THE LAND

FIND OUT

How did geography help South Asia develop separately from the rest of Asia?

What are the three major physical regions of South Asia?

What river systems are important to South Asia?

Vocabulary subcontinent

Millions of years ago, a huge landmass in the Southern Hemisphere known as Gondwanaland began to break up and its parts drifted away from each other. One part drifted slowly northward until it eventually collided with another vast landmass—the mainland of Asia. The force of the collision was enormous. The earth buckled and broke, pushing up the Himalaya and Hindu Kush mountains.

The Himalayas and Hindu Kush formed barriers separating South Asia from the rest of Asia. Although people kept moving through the passes in the mountains, South Asia developed its own identity.

The Indian Subcontinent

South Asia is a large triangular peninsula that juts southward from the continent of Asia. (See the map on page 164.) South Asia is bounded on the north by the Hindu Kush and Himalaya mountains. The rest of South Asia is surrounded by water. The Arabian Sea lies to the west, the Indian Ocean to the south, and the Bay of Bengal to the east. These bodies of water set the region apart from other regions but have not isolated it. For thousands of years, these seas have served as highways. They have linked the peoples of South Asia with other parts of the world.

Another name for South Asia is the Indian subcontinent. A subcontinent is a large landmass that is smaller than a continent. Today, eight independent nations occupy this region. Although India is by far the largest, South Asia also includes Pakistan, Bangladesh, Nepal, and Bhutan and the island nations of Sri Lanka and the Maldives. Afghanistan, in the northwest, is also often considered part of South Asia.

At its widest, the subcontinent stretches about 2,500 miles (4,023 km) from east to west and nearly the same distance from north to south. This vast region contains a variety of landforms. Three of these landforms shape the major geographic regions of South Asia: the northern mountains, the northern plains, and the Deccan Plateau.

Northern Mountains

As you have read, mountains separate South Asia from the rest of the continent. Stretching 1,500 miles (2,414 km) from east to west, the snow-capped peaks of the Himalayas rise above the clouds. They create a massive wall that separates the Indian subcontinent from the interior of Asia. Many of the world's tallest mountains are found in the Himalayas. At least 50 of the mountains are more than 5 miles (8 km) high, including Mount Everest, on the border of Nepal and Tibet.

To the northwest lie the Hindu Kush. While smaller in area than the Himalayas, the Hindu Kush are nearly as high and certainly as rugged. Indeed, the word *kush* means "death," and the mountains were probably given this name because of the danger they posed to people crossing them.

Mountain passes. Although the mountains form a barrier, they can be crossed. In the west, several passes cut through the mountains, making movement possible between the Indian subcontinent and other parts of Asia. Among the best known is the Khyber (KĪ ber) Pass through the Hindu Kush. For thousands of years, traders and invaders have made their way through mountain passes and descended into India.

Mountain valleys. The northern mountains are important for other reasons. The great river systems of the subcontinent have their sources in streams fed by melting snows from the mountains. Also, among the mountains lie high valleys, where farmers grow crops such as wheat and rice and herders raise goats. People living in these isolated valleys have developed their own ways of life. In one of these valleys, the Kashmir Valley, the goats produce a fine wool, known to the western world as cashmere.

Northern Plains

Just south of the Himalayas and the Hindu Kush is the northern, or Indo-Gangetic, plain. It stretches in a great curve from Pakistan across India into Bangladesh. Much of the area benefits from the three large rivers of the subcontinent that have their source in the Himalayas: the Indus, the Ganges (GAN jeez), and the Brahmaputra (brahm uh POO truh). These rivers and their many tributaries carry silt from the mountains that fertilizes the farmland on the plains. They also provide a reliable source of water for irrigation.

A steady source of water, fertile soil, and a long growing season combine to make the Indo-Gangetic Plain densely populated. Hundreds of millions of people live in the cities and on the farms on the northern plains. Throughout the region, farmers raise rice, wheat, and jute (a plant used to make twine and burlap).

A popular national hymn, "Hail Motherland," celebrates the riches of the Indian land.

> "I bow to thee, Mother,
> richly watered, richly fruited, cool
> with the winds of the south, dark
> with the crop of the harvests, the
> Mother!"

Rivers. The Indus River empties into the Arabian Sea. The Indus is the principal river of Pakistan, and a majority of Pakistanis live in the Indus River basin. The Indus is also important in South Asia's history. The region's earliest civilization developed in the Indus Valley. The word *indus*, which means "river," is the source of the name India.

A Varied Landscape The people of India must adapt to many different kinds of environments. In the Thar Desert of Rajasthan, above, people adapt to desert conditions by using camels for transportation. In the fertile Kulu Valley, known as the "Valley of the Gods," at right, they use the rich soil for raising many crops. ***Environment*** How do people in your area adapt their lives to the environment?

The Ganges River has its beginnings in an ice cave high in the Himalayas. The river flows eastward across India and then, near its mouth, joins the Brahmaputra, in Bangladesh. Together, the two rivers create an enormous delta on the Bay of Bengal. The delta region, located in Bangladesh, has very fertile soil but is subject to terrible flooding. (See Up Close on pages 167–168.)

Rivers are sacred to most of the people of South Asia. The most holy river is the Ganges, and shrines and temples line its banks. Each year, thousands of pilgrims come to purify themselves in the river and to take home some of its waters for ceremonies. Even though rivers may cause great flood damage, their waters are essential to life.

Thar Desert. At the western end of the northern plains lies the Thar Desert. This vast desert covers 100,000 square miles (259,000 sq km) of India and Pakistan, an area about the size of Colorado. The Thar features a barren landscape of sand dunes, sandy plains, and low hills. While rainfall is scarce, some grasses do grow here. Nomadic herders graze flocks of sheep and goats in the Thar Desert.

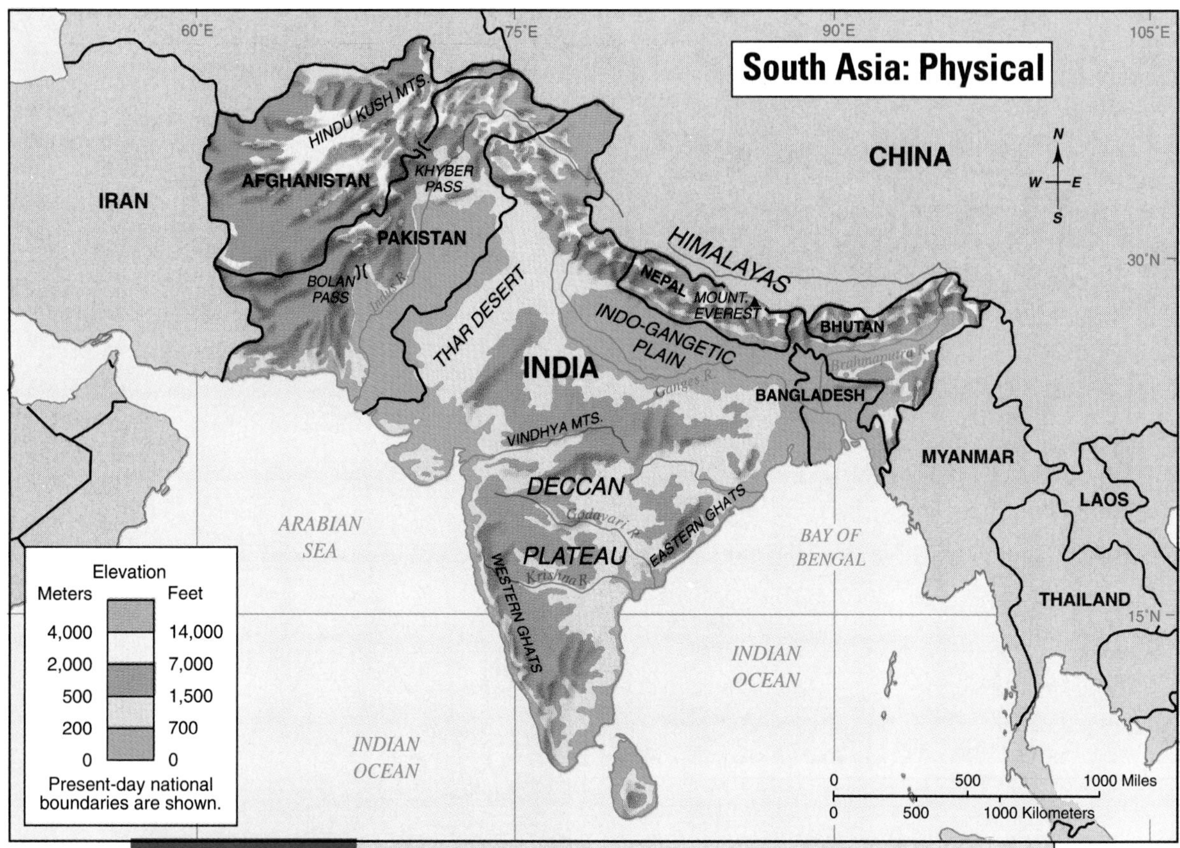

MAP STUDY

South Asia is a huge, triangular region that juts southward from the continent of Asia. It includes varied landforms, from the towering Himalaya Mountains to low-lying delta land along the Bay of Bengal.

1. **Location** Name and describe the location of two major mountain ranges in India.
2. **Place** (a) Which rivers flow through the plains of northern India? (b) Which of these rivers meet? (c) Where do they form a delta?
3. **Applying Information** How has India's geography protected the people living in the Deccan Plateau?

Deccan Plateau

South of the great plains lies the triangular Deccan Plateau. It is a region of high, flat land crossed by many rivers and broken by low, rolling hills. The Deccan occupies nearly half of South Asia. Millions of tiny farms dot the countryside. Farmers there raise millet, cotton, wheat, and rice.

Vindhya Mountains. Mountains border the Deccan Plateau on three sides. In the north, the Vindhya (VIHND yuh) Mountains separate the plateau from the Indo-Gangetic Plain. The Vindhyas are rugged but low compared to South Asia's other mountain ranges. Their highest point is about 3,600 feet (1,097 m).

According to an Indian myth, the Vindhya Mountains were once much higher. But Vindhya, the spirit of the mountains, became puffed up with pride. At last, he became so big that he kept the sun from reaching the Himalayas, the home of the gods. Angered, the gods sent Agastya, a well-known wise man, to warn Vindhya of their displeasure. Seeing Agastya, Vindhya bowed as a sign of respect.

"Stay that way until I return," advised Agastya. The wise man never returned, which is why the Vindhya Mountains are much lower than the Himalayas.

The Vindhya Mountains mark the boundary between northern and southern India. For centuries, they made travel and communication difficult and contributed to the development of regional cultures. People did migrate south, however. From time to time, invaders from the north conquered the Deccan as well. The arrival of newcomers added to the diversity of the region.

The Ghats. In the east and west, two other low-lying mountain ranges fringe the Deccan Plateau. The Ghats (gahts) are named for the many ghats, or passes, that cut through them. The Western Ghats border on the Arabian Sea. When Europeans reached South Asia in the 1500s, these mountains helped prevent their movement into the interior. The Eastern Ghats are a disconnected range of hills that face the Bay of Bengal. Near the city of Madras are broad valleys through which Europeans entered southern India and acquired territory in the 1700s.

SECTION 1 REVIEW

1. **Locate:** (a) Himalayas, (b) Hindu Kush, (c) Arabian Sea, (d) Indian Ocean, (e) Bay of Bengal, (f) Khyber Pass, (g) Vindhya Mountains, (h) Eastern and Western Ghats.
2. **Define:** subcontinent.
3. Describe the three main regions of South Asia.
4. (a) What rivers flow across the northern plains? (b) How do these rivers affect the people?
5. **Understanding Causes and Effects** How did geography help South Asia develop a distinct identity?
6. **Writing Across Cultures** Write a paragraph comparing the effects of the Himalayas on the history of India with the effects of the Rocky Mountains on the development of the United States.

2 CLIMATE AND RESOURCES

FIND OUT

How do the monsoons affect South Asia?

Why is water supply a problem in many parts of the subcontinent?

How does South Asia reflect the influences of many cultures?

Vocabulary monsoon, dialect

"A line of spectators had formed behind the Kovalam beach road. They were dressed with surprising formality, many of the men wearing ties and the women fine saris which streamed and snapped in the wind. . . . Thunder boomed. Lightning went zapping into the sea. . . . 'The rains!' everybody sang. The wind struck us with a force that made our line bend and waver. Everyone shrieked and grabbed at each other. . . . The deluge began."

A reporter described a familiar scene in Trivandrum, a town at the southwestern tip of India. Each year, huge crowds gather to look for the first signs of the summer rains. Millions of other people of South Asia listen closely to the reports from Trivandrum's weather center. This widespread interest shows the importance of rain to the people of South Asia.

The Monsoons

Some people consider monsoon forecasts the most important weather predictions on Earth. The monsoon is a seasonal wind that dominates the climate of South Asia. The word *monsoon* means "season" in Arabic. Two monsoons define the seasons of South Asia:

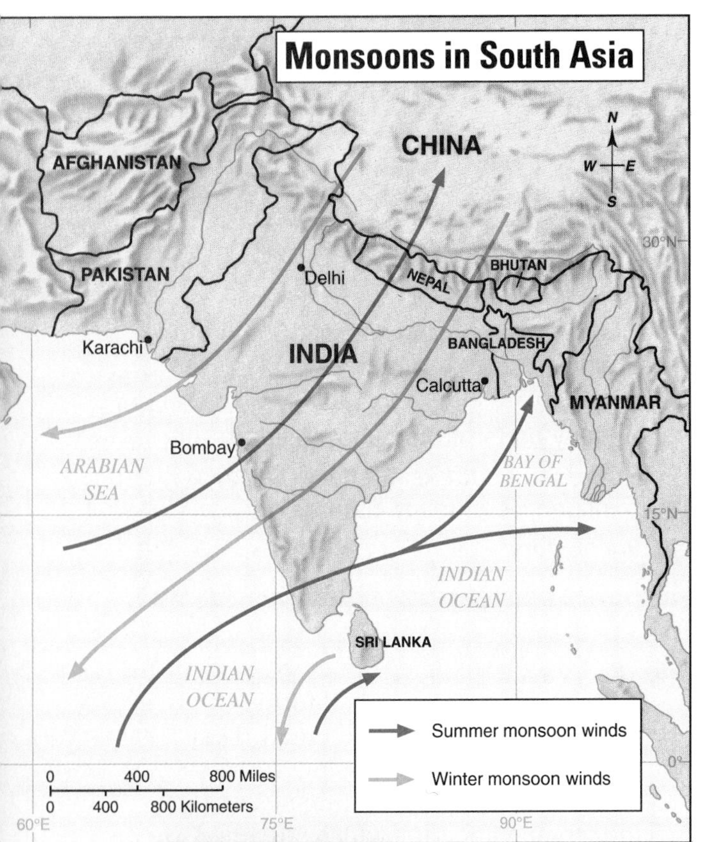

MAP STUDY

The monsoons profoundly affect the climate in South Asia. They determine the duration of this huge region's two seasons—summer and winter.

1. **Movement** (a) Where does the summer monsoon originate? (b) In which directions does it move?
2. **Movement** (a) Where does the winter monsoon originate? (b) In which directions does it move?
3. **Forecasting** (a) Which parts of South Asia do you think receive the largest amount of rainfall? (b) In which season does this rainfall occur?

the wet monsoon of summer and the dry monsoon of winter.

The monsoon cycle. The wet monsoon arrives in late May or early June. At this time, temperatures may reach as high as 120°F (45°C) in places like Trivandrum or Delhi. Little or no rain has fallen for eight or nine months, and the ground is parched and cracked. The land heats the air, causing it to rise. Cool, moist air from the sea flows in across the land, bringing the hoped-for rains.

By October, cool air masses from the northern mountains sink, creating winds that blow back toward the sea. These monsoon winds carry dry air across the subcontinent. They bring a season of clear skies, mild temperatures, and low humidity.

In March, however, temperatures rise. The cycle that leads to the wet monsoon begins again.

Importance of the monsoon. The monsoons are key to the life of farmers in South Asia. In the months before the wet monsoon, farmers plant seeds in the dry, sunbaked earth. The seeds must take root before the summer downpours begin. If the monsoon is late, the tiny plants wither and die, and famine results.

On the other hand, the monsoon can bring too much rain. Some years, heavy rainfall causes rivers to overflow and wash away crops. Still, the people of South Asia welcome the arrival of the wet monsoon. Within hours after the rains begin, the parched earth springs to life with green plants.

Monsoons have influenced the art and literature of South Asia. More than 1,000 years ago, an Indian poet sang the praises of the monsoon:

> “The summer sun, who robbed the
> pleasant nights,
> And plundered all the water of the
> rivers,
> And burned the earth, and scorched
> the forest-trees,
> Is now in hiding; and the rain-clouds,
> Spread thick across the sky to track
> him down,
> Hunt for the criminal with lightning
> flashes.”

Flooding and Storms in Bangladesh

Bangladesh is one of the most densely populated nations in the world. Most of its population is crowded into the delta formed by the Ganges and Brahmaputra rivers. The delta soil is extremely fertile, and Bangladeshi farmers can plant and harvest three crops of rice a year. Still, the land can barely support such vast numbers of people, and Bangladesh is among the world's poorest countries.

The concentration of people in the delta creates problems. Because much of the land is barely above sea level, flooding during the wet monsoons is common. In addition, every five to seven years, fierce tropical cyclones sweep in from the Bay of Bengal. The storms whip up waves that submerge the low-lying land and take a huge toll in lives and property.

More than 50 cyclones have struck the coast of Bangladesh since 1900. One of the worst was on April 29, 1991.

Waves As High As Mountains

> "The waves were so high and intense, the five of us on board could not remain on deck. So we climbed up the crane to a protected area. We could not see anything, not even the person next to us. Completely shattered, we really did not know whether we were alive or dead."

When the cyclone struck, Zaheer Ahmed was on board the ship *Comfort Marie*. For seven hours, he and his shipmates clung to the ship as the storm raged. Finally, at six o'clock the next morning, the winds died down and the crew climbed ashore. Only then did they discover that the waves had carried the *Comfort Marie* onto shore and left it by the side of a road.

Zaheer Ahmed was lucky. He survived the terrible cyclone of 1991. About 140,000 other people of Bangladesh died in the storm.

During the cyclone, the last thing Mufizur Rahman remembered before he was knocked unconscious was seeing waves "as high as mountains." When he opened his eyes several hours later, his wife, son, and three daughters had disappeared. Rahman's family and his home had been swept away by the giant waves that crashed over his village. In his grief, Rahman cried out, "I have lost everything. God, why has it happened to me?"

Winds of 150 miles (241 km) an hour pushed waves 20 feet (6 m) high over the land. The storm released other dangers. One man, caught in the swirling flood, tried to find a safe place for his infant son. He grabbed at an uprooted banana tree as it floated by. Quickly, he pulled back his hand in horror. He had been bitten by a poisonous snake nestled in the branches. Both father and son lost their lives.

Whenever possible, the government of Bangladesh sends its citizens advance warning of cyclones. However, people often ignore the warnings. Many have no safe place to go. The government has built some dikes and cyclone shelters, but Bangladesh is poor and lacks the funds to protect all parts of the country.

Cyclone in Bangladesh Cyclones often bring death and destruction to South Asia. This boy is probably the only member of his family who survived the 1991 cyclone. Since the 1700s, more than 1 million people have been killed by storms in the area of Bangladesh. ***Technology*** How can technology help people survive cyclones?

After the 1991 disaster, a newspaper reporter in Dacca, the capital of Bangladesh, wrote in despair, "No country has got a worse natural and environmental deal than Bangladesh." Still, in the words of another observer, "There is a lot more going on here than just disasters." With courage and determination, the people of Bangladesh rebuilt their homes and lives, as they have so many times in the past. ■

Rainfall and Vegetation

The monsoons affect South Asia unevenly, so that climates and vegetation vary greatly. The west coast of India has heavy rainfall. Trivandrum, for example, gets 160 inches (406 cm) of rain a year. In some areas of heavy rainfall, tropical rain forests flourish. Other areas, where the monsoons bring little moisture, are desert.

Mountains and rainfall. Mountains affect rainfall. As winds from the Bay of Bengal reach the Himalayas, the warm, moist air rises and cools. The cooling air releases its moisture as rain. As a result, areas directly south of the Himalayas—such as Bhutan, Bangladesh, and northeastern India—have heavy rainfall. Cherrapunji, India, gets as much as 425 inches (1,080 cm) of rain a year, making it perhaps the wettest place on Earth. By comparison, the annual rainfall in New York City is about 45 inches (114 cm).

Some mountains create a "rain shadow." One side of the mountain receives plenty of moisture, while the other side gets almost none. Winds blowing from the Arabian Sea drop their moisture on the coastal plains as they run up against the Western Ghats. However, the mountains block the winds from reaching the Deccan Plateau. As a result, the Deccan is drier than the coastal plains. The

Harvesting Tea Many factors determine which crops grow best in a region. Tea, one of India's major export crops, grows best in a warm climate with plentiful rainfall. Also, the quality of tea improves at higher elevations. Darjeeling in West Bengal is one of India's largest tea-growing areas. ***Geography*** How do the climate and the geography of a nation affect agriculture?

dry climate of the Deccan supports only low trees and scattered grasses.

Temperature. Like rainfall, temperatures vary greatly across the subcontinent. In the northern mountains and on the upper slopes of the Western Ghats, temperatures can be cold. Much of South Asia, however, has a tropical climate with warm temperatures year-round.

From November through January, the average temperature in the Indian city of Madras is 84°F (29°C). In February, the temperature begins to climb. By May, the average temperature has reached 100°F (38°C). The weather of Madras has been described as "three months hot and nine months hotter."

Natural Resources

Parts of South Asia have fertile soil, especially the Indo-Gangetic Plain. Farmers have raised crops on these lands for thousands of years. In some places, constant cultivation has worn out the soil. In the northern plains, as you have read, rivers deposit silt that renews the soil. Yet there, as elsewhere, farmers use fertilizers to restore nutrients to the soil.

Irrigation. Water is scarce in many parts of the subcontinent. Although rain is plentiful, most of it falls during the wet monsoon. During the dry season, farmers use water from rivers to irrigate crops. They also dig wells to tap underground water.

On the Deccan Plateau, finding water is made more difficult because the water lies in rock deep below the ground. To reach water for irrigation, farmers must dig wells at least 200 feet (61 m) deep. As you will read, building dams to increase the supply of water for irrigation is a major issue in India. (See pages 228–229.)

Mineral resources. South Asia has a variety of mineral resources. Many parts of India have large reserves of high-quality iron ore. India is also rich in manganese, bauxite, and copper.

In the northern plains, coal is plentiful. The region has other resources such as mica, limestone, and gypsum. South Asia, however, has few sources of oil, a basic need for industry today. For this reason, the Indian government has supported the use of nuclear power. (See the feature on page 228.)

The Peoples of South Asia

The population of South Asia numbers more than 1.1 billion people. In other words, one out of five people in the world lives there. India alone has a population of more than 855 million people—the largest of any nation except China. Bangladesh and Pakistan also rank among the 10 most populous countries in the world.

About three quarters of the people of South Asia depend on farming to earn a living. Most people live in villages, although cities are growing rapidly.

Cultural diversity. South Asia is a region of great cultural diversity. Over thousands of years, many peoples have settled in the subcontinent. They have migrated from Europe, the Middle East, and other parts of Asia.

Geographic features have tended to separate people into regional and local groups, each with its own way of life. Throughout South Asia, the people have a wide variety of customs and practices. They eat different foods, dress in different styles, and respect different values. Even a simple activity such as making bread varies widely from place to place. In northern India, women roll dough flat and cook it on a griddle. In the south, they eat boiled rice and make pastes of rice and drop them into boiling oil.

Religious beliefs also vary. The people worship in different ways and have different ideas about what is sacred. As you will learn, India has many religious groups, including Hindus, Muslims, Christians, Sikhs, and Buddhists.

Languages. A clear sign of the cultural diversity of South Asia is language. Nepal, a country about the size of Illinois, has 13 languages. India has more than 700 languages and dialects. A dialect is a regional version of a language with its own words, expressions, and pronunciations.

The most widely spoken language in India is Hindi. Yet, fewer than 30 percent of Indians

Indian Money India is a land with hundreds of languages. Many of these languages have their own scripts, or forms of writing. These scripts include Bengali, Devanagari, Gujarati, and Telugu, among others. India's paper money, the rupee, shown here, uses many different scripts. ***Diversity*** Why do you think the rupee is printed with different scripts?

speak Hindi. To meet the needs of its varied population, India recognizes 15 official languages. In addition, it recognizes 35 other major regional languages. Often, these languages are written in different scripts. A rupee note, the Indian money, has the same words written in several different scripts.

English is not an official language, but it is used by many Indians. The English language is a holdover from a period of British colonization, as you will read in Chapter 8.

Cultural diversity has enriched the region, but it also poses a challenge to the governments of India and its neighbors.

SECTION 2 REVIEW

1. **Define:** (a) monsoon, (b) dialect.
2. (a) How do the wet and dry monsoons differ? (b) Why are monsoons so important to the people of South Asia?
3. Give two reasons why water supply is a serious problem in South Asia.
4. How does language show the cultural diversity of South Asia?
5. **Comparing** How do the seasons in South Asia differ from those in your area?
6. **Writing Across Cultures** Write an editorial for an American newspaper appealing for help for monsoon flood victims.

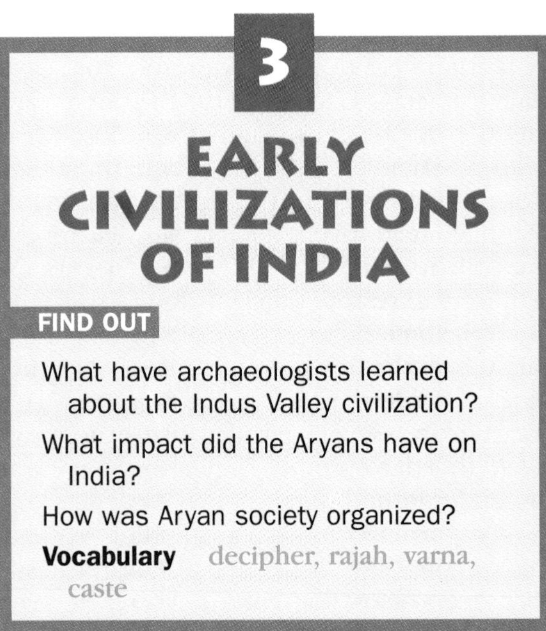

3 EARLY CIVILIZATIONS OF INDIA

FIND OUT

What have archaeologists learned about the Indus Valley civilization?

What impact did the Aryans have on India?

How was Aryan society organized?

Vocabulary decipher, rajah, varna, caste

The railroad workers needed stones to anchor the track they were laying. The line ran along the Indus Valley, linking towns and cities in the north and south. Near the town of Harappa, workers used old bricks from a local ruin in place of stones. Among the bricks, they found hundreds of tiny stone carvings. The workers threw most of the carvings away. They kept a few as curious objects.

An observer thought that the stone carvings were very old, but few people listened to him. More than 70 years later, in the 1920s, archaeologists turned their attention to the ruins at Harappa. They soon discovered that the town had once been the center of an ancient civilization. Today, this ancient culture is known as the Indus Valley, or Harappan, civilization.

Indus Valley Civilization

Like many early civilizations, India's first civilization grew up in a fertile river valley. It was the largest of the world's early civilizations, extending almost 1,000 miles (1,609 km) inland from the Arabian Sea. It lasted for about 1,000 years, from 2500 B.C. to 1500 B.C.

Planned cities. Archaeologists are still learning about this ancient civilization. They have excavated several large cities as well as many smaller towns along the Indus River and the Arabian coast. The cities of Harappa and Mohenjo-Daro, in present-day Pakistan, were the most important.

Each city was carefully laid out, with straight streets that formed a checkerboard pattern. A walled fortress protected the city, and special warehouses held food supplies. The cities had separate districts for homes and for public buildings. Some buildings had elaborate bathing facilities and drains that linked them to a city sewer system.

This level of urban planning suggests that the government was well organized. It was able to set and enforce building codes. Throughout the Indus Valley, for example, the bricks used for building were all the same size.

Archaeologists think that the cities were built as capitals of a strong empire. Harappa and Mohenjo-Daro lie about 350 miles (563 km) apart. Other towns dotted the region in between.

Farming. To support such cities, rulers of the Indus Valley civilization must have collected taxes in the form of food. Although officials, craftworkers, and merchants lived in the cities, most people were farmers. They grew barley, wheat, peas, and sesame. Many kept cattle, sheep, goats, and water buffaloes. Indus Valley farmers were probably the first people to grow cotton and to domesticate, or tame, chickens.

Trade. Merchants of the Indus Valley civilization traded with the peoples of the Middle East. Either overland or by sea, traders carried goods from Harappa to Sumer, an early civilization of the Middle East. (See page 29.) Perhaps Harappan merchants exported cotton to the Middle East. Through trade, ideas, too, passed back and forth.

Unsolved Puzzles

Archaeologists working in the Middle East have found hundreds of small clay seals that came from the Indus Valley. Indus Valley craftworkers made these seals, carving pictographic writing and figures of animals on them. Merchants probably used the seals to identify their goods. Unfortunately, scholars have been unable to decipher, or determine the meaning of, the writing.

Deciphering this ancient script might help us learn about the religion of Indus Valley people. Archaeologists have found small statues of women that suggest the people worshipped a mother goddess. Other statues suggest that animals, especially cattle, also had religious importance. That idea apparently influenced later Indian civilization.

Decline of the Indus Valley Civilization

Why did the Indus Valley civilization decline? No one knows for sure. By about 2000 B.C., the cities showed signs of decay. The bricks were no longer uniform in size. Broken streets were not repaired. Fine homes were divided into small tenement-like apartments. Some towns were abandoned.

Until recently, scholars thought that invaders had conquered the Indus Valley. New evidence, however, suggests that the decline was originally due to natural causes. Possibly the climate became too dry to support extensive farming. Without surplus crops, farmers

Digging in the Indus Valley

Railway workers found signs of an ancient civilization in the Indus Valley more than 135 years ago. Archaeologists first excavated the site in 1922. Yet today, we still know very little about the Indus Valley civilization. One reason is the geography of the valley, which poses special problems for digging.

In 1950, British archaeologist Sir Mortimer Wheeler set out to excavate the lowest level of ruins at Mohenjo-Daro. He hoped to trace Mohenjo-Daro's development over the centuries. As archaeologists dug, though, underground water from the river kept seeping into the site.

To cope with the water problem, Wheeler brought powerful mechanical pumps to the Mohenjo-Daro site. Wheeler described what happened next:

> “We struck water at fifteen feet below the . . . surface, and with mechanized pumps and careful engineering, we dived for a further ten feet into the streaming mud. . . . Then, one night, . . . a thousand jets of water burst from the sides of our cutting, and with a sullen roar it tumbled in. We had reached farther than any of our predecessors, but time and tide had beaten us.”

Wheeler refused to accept defeat. After careful study, he devised a method of digging that was suited to Mohenjo-Daro's particular geography. As a result, Wheeler was able to add greatly to our knowledge of Indus civilization and to suggest the date 2500 B.C. for its beginning. In addition, the new techniques he developed for Mohenjo-Daro were important contributions to the science of modern archaeology.

1. How did the geography of the Indus Valley create a problem for archaeologists?
2. **Making Inferences** What personal qualities do you think a successful archaeologist would need?

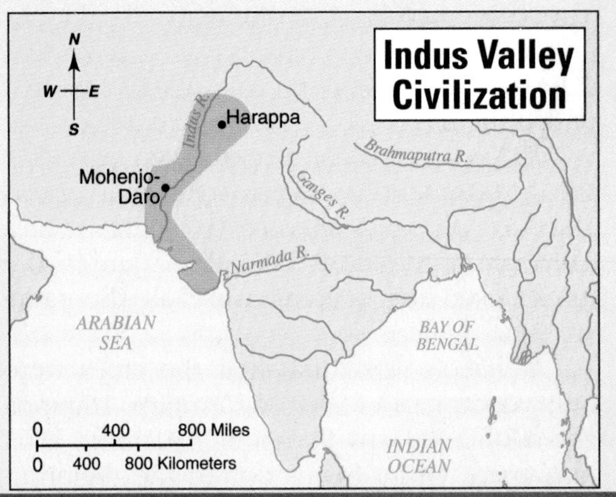

could not provide food for the cities. Perhaps the Indus River changed course, which would have affected food production. Centuries of farming may have exhausted the soil. Some evidence suggests that floods may have contributed to the decline.

As the Indus Valley civilization decayed, people migrated to other parts of the Indian subcontinent. Scholars think that the Dravidian people who live in southern India today may be descended from these Indus Valley settlers. Many centuries after the Indus

Valley civilization disappeared, the Dravidians built flourishing kingdoms in the Deccan Plateau.

Arrival of the Aryans

The arrival of a nomadic and warlike people, the Aryans, may have contributed to the final collapse of the Indus Valley civilization. Already in decline, the Indus people were probably too weak to resist the newcomers.

The Aryans swept into India through the high passes of the Hindu Kush Mountains. They came from the region of the Caucasus Mountains. As they traveled, they came in contact with the peoples of the Middle East. From them, the Aryans learned how to make iron tools and weapons.

The Aryan migration into India took hundreds of years. In time, the Aryans overran the towns and cities of the Indus Valley. Their success was due in part to their iron weapons. In addition, they were skilled charioteers who used fast, horse-drawn war chariots to overpower their enemies. Over time, the Aryans absorbed ideas from the Indus Valley civilization.

Aryan Culture

The Aryans gradually spread out across the northern plains. Much of what we know about them comes from oral religious traditions, known as the Vedas (VAY duhz). The Vedas include hymns, prayers, and rituals used in religious ceremonies. They were composed between about 1500 B.C. and 1000 B.C. Today, the Vedas are still part of Indian religious life. People recite Vedic hymns and prayers on many special occasions, such as weddings and funerals. (See Connections With Literature, page 804, "Night" from the *Rig Veda.*)

Religious beliefs. At first, Aryan priests memorized the hymns and prayers. Religious beliefs passed by word of mouth from generation to generation. Much later, the Aryans developed a written language, called Sanskrit, and their oral religious traditions were written down.

From the Vedas, we learn that the Aryans worshipped many gods. Among the most important was Indra, a warrior god. Indra had many human characteristics and enjoyed such pleasures as eating and dancing. By contrast, the god Varuna was a strict figure. He governed the workings of the universe and punished sinners.

Aryan worship centered around sacrifices to the gods. Priests performed the sacred rituals on open-air altars. They set out food and drink for the gods, while singing hymns and prayers. The Aryans believed that if the sacrifices were generous and offered correctly, the gods would reward them with wealth, healthy children, long life, and success in war.

Villages. As the Aryans moved across the northern plains, they settled into villages. The pattern of village life that developed over the centuries continues to influence India today. (See pages 214–217.)

The Aryans were both farmers and herders. They placed great value on cattle. Men received cattle as a reward when they were successful in war. People measured wealth in terms of cattle. The Vedas compare the Earth to a cow. Rain is like the cow's milk, and the sun is its calf.

Hereditary chiefs, called rajahs (RAH juhz), ruled the villages. A council of warriors assisted the rajah. The chief priest also held great power. He alone could carry out the sacrifices needed to please the gods.

Social classes. The Aryans divided people into four classes, called varna.* At the top of society were Brahmans, or priests. Next came Kshatriyas (kuh SHAT ree yuhz), or warriors. The third class, Vaisyas (VĪS yuhz), were landowners, merchants, and herders. At the bottom of society were the Sudras (SOO druhz), servants and peasants who waited on others.

The following hymn from the Vedas explains the origins of the four social classes:

* In Sanskrit, *varna* means "color." Some scholars suggest that the light-skinned Aryans wanted to distinguish themselves from the darker-skinned peoples whom they conquered.

Honoring Cattle The beliefs and customs of the early Aryans developed into the religion of Hinduism. Aryan customs that valued cattle evolved into Hindu beliefs that forbid the slaughter of cattle. Today, cows wander undisturbed even in crowded cities. This statue of a bull is at the temple at Baijnath, a major Hindu pilgrimage site.
Fine Art How are Hindu beliefs reflected in India's art?

"When the gods divided the Man,
into how many parts did they divide him?
What was his mouth, what were his arms,
what were his thighs and his feet called?
The Brahman was his mouth,
of his arms was made the warrior,
His thighs became the Vaisya,
Of his feet the Sudra was born."

Over time, the social classes of the Aryans developed into a more rigid system of caste, or social groups based on birth.* You will read about caste in Chapter 8.

* Indians use the word *jati* to describe their social system. When the Portuguese reached India, they used the word *caste*, which other Europeans adopted.

SECTION 3 REVIEW

1. **Locate:** (a) Indus River, (b) Harappa, (c) Mohenjo-Daro.
2. **Identify:** (a) Dravidian, (b) Aryan, (c) Vedas, (d) Sanskrit.
3. **Define:** (a) decipher, (b) rajah, (c) varna, (d) caste.
4. (a) What do the cities of Harappa and Mohenjo-Daro reveal about the Indus Valley civilization? (b) Why is our knowledge of the Indus Valley civilization limited?
5. How was Aryan society organized?
6. **Synthesizing Information** What can we learn about a culture by studying its hymns and other religious texts?
7. **Writing Across Cultures** Using the Vedic hymn at left as a model, write a poem explaining the structure of American society.

Chapter 7 Review

Understanding Vocabulary

Match each term at left with the correct definition at right.

1. subcontinent	**a.** determine the meaning of
2. monsoon	**b.** hereditary chief of the Aryans
3. dialect	**c.** seasonal wind
4. decipher	**d.** large landmass that is smaller than a continent
5. rajah	**e.** regional version of a language

Reviewing the Main Ideas

1. (a) What rivers are important to South Asia? (b) What role do these rivers play in South Asian culture?
2. (a) How do monsoons shape the seasons of South Asia? (b) Why do South Asians celebrate the arrival of the wet monsoon?
3. (a) How do the Himalayas affect rainfall patterns in South Asia? (b) Why is the Deccan much drier than the coastal plains?
4. Give three examples of cultural diversity in South Asia.
5. (a) What were the two main cities of the Indus Valley civilization? (b) How did farmers and merchants help support the civilization? (c) How might geography have contributed to the decline of the civilization?
6. (a) Why were the Aryans able to defeat the Indus Valley people? (b) Where does most information about the Aryans come from?

Reviewing Chapter Themes

1. The cultures of South Asia differ from those of the rest of Asia. How did its geography help South Asia to develop unique cultures?
2. Geographic features have contributed to the cultural diversity of South Asia. Choose two features and describe how each has promoted cultural diversity.
3. The people of the Indus Valley built an advanced civilization. Discuss three pieces of evidence that support this statement.

Thinking Critically

1. **Understanding Causes and Effects** (a) Why is so much of Bangladesh's population concentrated in a single region? (b) What problems has this caused? (c) How might high population density worsen the effects of flooding?
2. **Making Global Connections** (a) Why do Indians speak many different languages? (b) Why do you think there is less variation in languages spoken in the United States?

Applying Your Skills

1. **Reading a Map** Use the map on page 166 and what you have read to answer the following questions. (a) In which directions does the wet monsoon blow? (b) Which part of South Asia receives the first rainfall during the wet monsoon? (c) In which directions does the dry monsoon blow? (d) Based on the map, explain why the dry monsoon occurs in the winter. (See the Skill Lesson on page 48.)
2. **Analyzing a Quotation** A well-known Indian, Jawaharlal Nehru, once wrote: "India is like some parchment on which layer and layer of thought . . . has been inscribed, and yet no succeeding layer has completely hidden or erased what has been written previously. All of them exist together in our common selves, and . . . they have gone to build up the complete, mysterious personality of India." Based on what you have read in this chapter, explain what Nehru meant.

Chapter 8

HERITAGE OF SOUTH ASIA

The God Krishna Krishna is a god, revered by Hindus throughout South Asia. In this painting, he is shown surrounded by women playing musical instruments. Hindus believe that Krishna once lived on Earth as a great warrior and king. Stories about his brave deeds are very old, like many other aspects of South Asian culture. ***Fine Art*** Based on this picture, how do you think Hindus view the god Krishna?

CHAPTER OUTLINE

1 Religious Traditions

2 Powerful Empires

3 Patterns of Life

4 India Under British Rule

One day, Bhrigu Varuna approached his father. "Father," he asked, "can you please explain to me the mystery of brahman?" (To Hindus, brahman is the supreme force of the universe.)

His father replied, "Seek to know brahman through meditation." Only through thoughtful, focused prayer, he said, can a person come to "know" brahman.

Brighu prayed, but enlightenment did not come. He returned to his father, who simply repeated: "Seek to know braham by prayer."

Years went by. Then one day, Bhrigu had the highest vision. He saw the brahman and himself united as a single formless, nameless, limitless being. He now understood the Hindu belief that brahman underlies the universe. Everything else—food, life, mind, reason—is not real.

The story of Bhrigu appears in the Upanishads. These sacred Hindu texts originated more than 2,500 years ago. In dialogues and stories, they explain the basic ideas of Hinduism, the religion of most Indians.

CHAPTER PERSPECTIVE

In this chapter, you will learn how two world religions—Hinduism and Buddhism—developed in South Asia. Over thousands of years, many invaders swept into South Asia. They brought their own beliefs and ideas, adding to the cultural diversity of this region.

As you read, look for these chapter themes:

- India is the birthplace of Hinduism and Buddhism.
- Powerful empires united parts of South Asia, but invaders and local rulers often competed for power.
- Throughout India's long history, local cultures blended with those brought by invaders.
- The caste system, the village, and the family were the basic social units shaping the lives of ordinary people.
- British colonial rule changed the political, economic, and social structure of South Asia.

Literature Connections

In this chapter, you will encounter passages from the following works.

The Upanishads

The *Ramayana*

Shakuntala, Kalidasa

Memoirs of an Indian Woman, Shudha Mazumdar

For other suggestions, see Connections With Literature, pages 804–808.

1 RELIGIOUS TRADITIONS

FIND OUT

What are the basic Hindu beliefs?

How are Hinduism and the caste system linked?

How are Hinduism and Buddhism both similar and different?

How did Buddhism spread to other parts of the world?

Vocabulary brahman, sect, atman, reincarnation, karma, dharma, nirvana

"We worship all the Hindu gods, but our family god is Lord Venkateshwara," says Bhama Pandurang of southern India. "It is hard to explain just why a god is a family god to one family and not to another. It is inherited, and our family has worshipped Lord Venkateshwara for generations."

Bhama explains that her family sets aside a room in their house to honor the god. An altar bears a picture of Lord Venkateshwara and statues of other gods. Oil lamps burn constantly nearby. Each morning, family members pray before the altar.

Hindu customs vary greatly across the Indian subcontinent. Hinduism developed over thousands of years. It absorbed the beliefs of many different peoples. Its many gods and practices are diverse. Underlying this diversity, however, are some common beliefs.

Basic Hindu Beliefs

Hinduism is the chief religion of India. Unlike most other world religions, Hinduism has no founder or formal church. Its roots lie in ancient Aryan beliefs and practices. Over thousands of years, those beliefs and practices changed.

Hinduism is a way of life. Today, as in the past, it shapes and unifies much of Indian culture.

Sacred texts. Hindu beliefs are recorded in sacred texts. The most important texts are the Vedas and the Upanishads (oo PAN ih shadz). For Hindus, the Vedas contain eternal truths that were revealed to wise men. The Upanishads help to explain the ideas contained in the Vedas.

Hindu ideas appear in other ancient writings such as law codes and epics, or long narrative poems. The *Ramayana* (rah MAH yuh nuh) and the *Mahabharata* (muh HAH bah rah tuh) are the two most famous Hindu epics. You will read more about these poems in Chapter 10.

Brahman. Hindus worship thousands of gods. Each god is part of a single supreme force called brahman. Hindus believe that only a few people can truly understand brahman, which is nameless, formless, and unlimited. The many gods of Hinduism give brahman a concrete form that is more understandable to the average person. (See Connections With Literature, page 805, "Taittiriya Upanishad.")

The three main gods of Hinduism are Brahma, Vishnu, and Siva. Brahma is the creator, Vishnu is the preserver, and Siva is the

Bathing in the Ganges Hindus consider the Ganges River holy and pure. To bathe in its water, Hindus travel from all over India to such holy cities as Allahabad and Benares. Many pilgrims take bottles of Ganges water home with them to use in family worship. ***Comparing*** Why do you think peoples of many different religions make pilgrimages to holy sites?

destroyer. Throughout India, different sects, or religious groups, worship one or another of these gods or their many wives and children. (📖 See World Literature, "Such Perfection," by R. K. Narayan, page 240.)

Hindus believe in the unity of all life. Every person has an essential self, or atman (AHT muhn). This self is part of a universal soul, which is also called atman. The Upanishads explain:

> "The essential self or the vital essence in humans is the same as that in an ant, the same as that in a gnat, the same as that in an elephant . . . indeed the same as that in the whole universe."

To Hindus, atman and brahman are the same thing.

Because they believe that all things in nature are part of the same universal soul, Hindus stress the idea of nonviolence. To a Hindu, it is important to respect nature and not struggle against it.

Reincarnation. According to Hinduism, people suffer from pain and sorrow because they pursue false goals such as material riches and personal pleasure. The true goal of life, Hindus believe, is *moksha*, freeing of the soul from the body so that the soul can unite with brahman.

Moksha cannot be achieved in one lifetime. Thus, Hindus believe that people undergo reincarnation, or rebirth of the soul in various forms. After the body dies, the soul may be reborn as anything from a god to a flower or a snake. Each form is only temporary, however.

Karma. For Hindus, the cycle of death and rebirth continues until the individual soul achieves union with brahman. Whether a soul gains this release is governed by the law of karma.

Karma comes from a Sanskrit word meaning "to do." The law of karma holds that every deed—mental or physical—in this life affects a person's fate in a future life. In a similar way, a person's present situation is the result of his or her deeds in a past existence. Every good deed sooner or later results in happiness. Every evil deed sooner or later brings sorrow.

Hinduism and the Caste System

Hindu beliefs about rebirth and karma are closely tied to the caste system. The caste system developed in ancient times. Some scholars think that it arose when the light-skinned Aryans conquered darker-skinned non-Aryan people. Others argue that the caste system was based on occupation.

Whatever its origins, the caste system set up a strict social and religious order. A person was born into a certain caste and remained a member of that caste for life. Nothing he or she did could change that fact. (You will read more about the caste system later in this chapter.)

Most Hindus believe that a person's caste is the result of karma. Both high-caste and low-caste Hindus accept the idea that one's deeds in past lives are responsible for one's present position in society. Hindus also believe that the Brahmans, the highest caste, are closest to moksha.

Each caste has its own dharma, or duties and obligations. Among these duties are obedience to caste rules as well as to moral laws. People can improve their position in the next life by carrying out their duties in this life.

Dharma influences Indian life in many ways. It provides a guide to conduct. It also offers Hindus the hope of a better life in the future. Indeed, the knowledge that their future life depends on their past deeds encourages Hindus to behave morally.

Buddhism

By about 600 B.C., the Brahman caste had become very powerful. Brahmans claimed that they alone could perform the sacred rituals of Hinduism. Some reformers tried to limit the priests' power. Among them was Siddhartha Gautama (sihd DAHRT uh GOWT uh muh).

The Healing Buddha Paintings of the Buddha, such as this one, often show a halo above his head to represent divine radiance. The topknot stands for the wisdom of enlightenment. This painting is in a monastery at Sarnath, India, where the great religious leader preached his first sermon. ***Fine Art*** Why do you think this painting creates a feeling of calm and repose?

Gautama's enlightenment. Gautama was born in what is now Nepal in about 560 B.C. He was the son of a local ruler and enjoyed a life of luxury, unaware of human sorrow. In time, he married and had a son of his own.

One day, Gautama went beyond the palace walls. In quick order, he saw an old man, a sick man, a dead man, and a beggar. Their images haunted him. For the first time, he realized that life was full of suffering and misery.

According to legend, Gautama left his family and his life of wealth and set out to find the cause of human misery. One day, after six years of searching, he sat meditating under a sacred tree. Suddenly, he achieved enlightenment. He understood the cause of human suffering—and its cure. From then on, Gautama was known as the Buddha, or "Enlightened One." (See Connections With Literature, page 805, "Siddhartha.")

The Buddha's teachings. The Buddha spent the rest of his life teaching others what he had learned as he sat under the sacred tree. He called these ideas the Four Noble Truths.

The first truth is that suffering is universal. Everyone suffers from pain, sickness, and death.

The second truth is that the cause of suffering is desire. People desire things such as riches and long life. However, everything in life is constantly changing. Nothing is permanent. Even pleasure causes suffering, because pleasure must end.

The third truth is that the only way to end suffering is to crush desire. If people give up desire, they can achieve nirvana, the condition of wanting nothing.

The fourth truth is that the way to end desire is to follow the Noble Eightfold Path. In the Noble Eightfold Path, the Buddha set out a practical guide to right conduct. It stressed understanding of the cause of suffering, compassion for all creatures, kindness, and truthfulness.

The Buddha thought of himself as a Hindu. Like other Hindus, he believed that salvation was achieved when the individual self escaped the body. He also believed in karma and reincarnation.

Unlike most Hindus, however, the Buddha denied the existence of any gods. He also taught that priests were not necessary. Instead, people had to seek nirvana on their own by following the Noble Eightfold Path. The Buddha rejected the caste system as well.

Spread of Buddhism

The Buddha attracted many followers. He set up monasteries and convents, where monks and nuns could devote themselves to the Noble Eightfold Path. After the Buddha's death, his followers passed on his teachings by word of mouth. In time, his ideas were written down in the *Three Baskets of Wisdom.*

Buddhism spread quickly across South Asia. Buddhist missionaries also carried the new ideas to other parts of Asia. As people in other cultures adopted Buddhism, they adapted the Buddha's teachings to their own needs. (See Chapters 11 and 15.)

Over time, two main sects grew up within Buddhism—Theravada (ther uh VAH duh) Buddhism and Mahayana (mah huh YAH nuh) Buddhism. Theravada Buddhists stressed the monastic life as the way to reach nirvana. They respected the Buddha as a teacher but did not worship him as a god. This branch of Buddhism spread to Ceylon, Burma, and Thailand. Mahayana Buddhism spread to China, Tibet, Japan, and Korea. Its followers

MAP STUDY

Buddhism and Hinduism are two major world religions that began in South Asia. During many centuries, missionaries and traders spread these religions to other areas.

1. **Movement** (a) Which religion spread to both East Asia and Southeast Asia? (b) Which religion did not spread into East Asia?
2. **Region** (a) Identify the areas to which Hinduism spread. (b) Identify the areas to which Buddhism spread.
3. **Understanding Causes and Effects** In what ways do you think the spread of these two religions affected the cultures of Southeast Asia and East Asia?

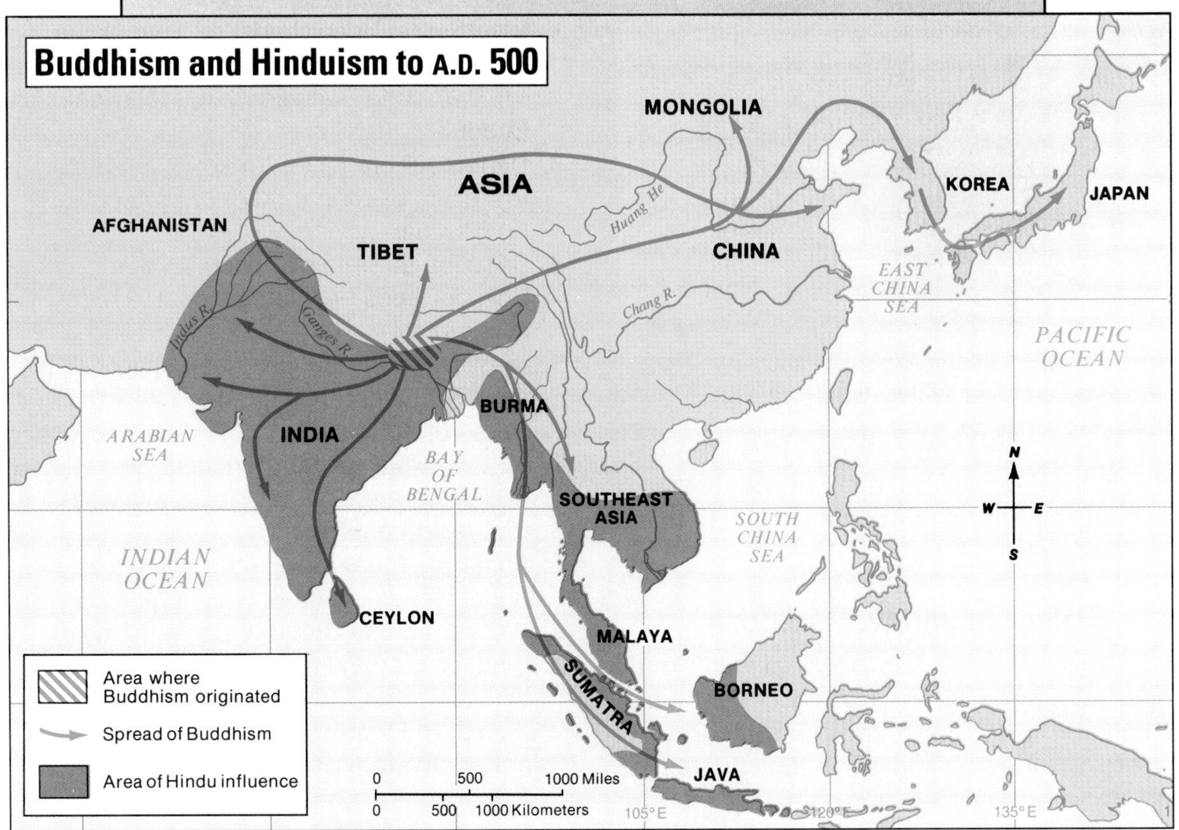

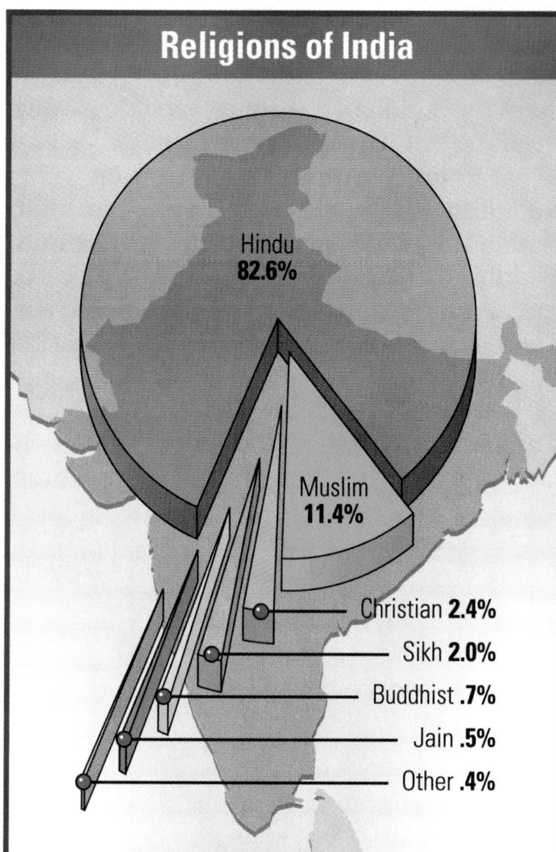

Source: *India 1990 Handbook*

Graph Skills India is the home of many religions. This religious diversity adds richness to its people's cultures. ▶According to this circle graph, which religion is dominant in India? What percentage of India's population is made up of Muslims, Christians, and Sikhs?

worshipped the Buddha and other enlightened ones as gods.

Although Buddhism began in South Asia, it almost disappeared there. Hinduism is a tolerant faith, and it slowly absorbed many Buddhist ideas.

Other Religious Traditions

Other religions also developed in South Asia. Among these was Jainism (JĪN ihz um). Like Buddhism, Jainism grew out of efforts to reform Hinduism. Mahavira, the founder of Jainism, lived at about the same time as the Buddha. Like the Buddha, he rejected the power of the Brahmans. His teachings also included Hindu ideas such as reincarnation.

Jainists emphasize *ahimsa,* or nonviolence. Mahavira taught that people should avoid harming any living creature. As a result, Jainists are strict vegetarians. A vegetarian is someone who does not eat meat. Many Jainists sweep the ground before them as they walk to avoid stepping on any living thing.

Several other religions had an impact on South Asia. As you will read later in this chapter, Muslim invaders brought the religion of Islam into the subcontinent. Over time, Islam won many converts.

In the 1500s, Sikhism emerged in South Asia. It combines features of Hinduism and Islam. About the same time, Christian missionaries began to arrive in South Asia. They, too, won converts among the peoples of the subcontinent.

SECTION 1 REVIEW

1. **Identify:** (a) Upanishads, (b) Four Noble Truths, (c) Noble Eightfold Path, (d) Theravada Buddhism, (e) Mahayana Buddhism, (f) Jainism.
2. **Define:** (a) brahman, (b) sect, (c) atman, (d) reincarnation, (e) karma, (f) dharma (g) nirvana.
3. Describe three basic Hindu beliefs.
4. How do Hindu beliefs support the caste system?
5. (a) Why did the Buddha seek enlightenment? (b) What did he believe was the cause of suffering?
6. (a) List two ways that Hinduism and Buddhism are similar. (b) List two ways that they are different.
7. **Analyzing Ideas** How is the spread of Buddhism an example of cultural diffusion?
8. **Writing Across Cultures** Speaking about Hinduism, an Indian noted: "We believe that the worst of all evils is the ego, the 'I am.' The more we can squash it, the better." Write a paragraph comparing American and South Asian attitudes toward individual wants.

2

POWERFUL EMPIRES

FIND OUT

What dynasties united large parts of India?

Why did Muslims and Hindus clash?

What were the achievements of the Mughal Empire?

How did invasions contribute to cultural diversity in South Asia?

Vocabulary dynasty, stupa, sultan

India's great epic poem, the *Ramayana,* proclaims the need for a strong king:

> "Where the land is kingless, the cloud,
> lightning-wreathed and loud-
> voiced, gives no rain to the earth.
> Where the land is kingless, the son
> does not honor his father nor the
> wife her husband.
> Where the land is kingless, men do
> not meet in assemblies, nor make
> lovely gardens and temples."

From time to time, strong rulers united the northern plain of India. More often, however, the northern plain was a battleground. Rival princes waged war with one another and with invaders who regularly swept into South Asia.

The Maurya Empire

The first ruler to unite the northern plain was Chandragupta Maurya (chuhn druh GUP tuh MAWR yah). In 321 B.C., Chandragupta founded the Maurya dynasty, or ruling family. The Mauryas ruled India for 140 years.

Government. Chandragupta conquered a large empire. It stretched across the northern plain from the Bay of Bengal to the Hindu Kush. He appointed thousands of officials to help him rule. Among them were tax collectors, who took one quarter of the farmers' crops. Herders and merchants paid taxes of cattle and trade goods.

MAP STUDY

Chandragupta founded the Maurya Empire in India. The empire reached its height under the rule of his grandson, Asoka.

1. **Location** (a) Describe the exact location of the Maurya Empire. (b) Describe the relative location of the Maurya Empire.
2. **Interaction** What landforms in South Asia limited the expansion of the Maurya Empire?
3. **Drawing Conclusions** How did the location of the Tamil kingdom probably affect its relationship with the Maurya Empire?

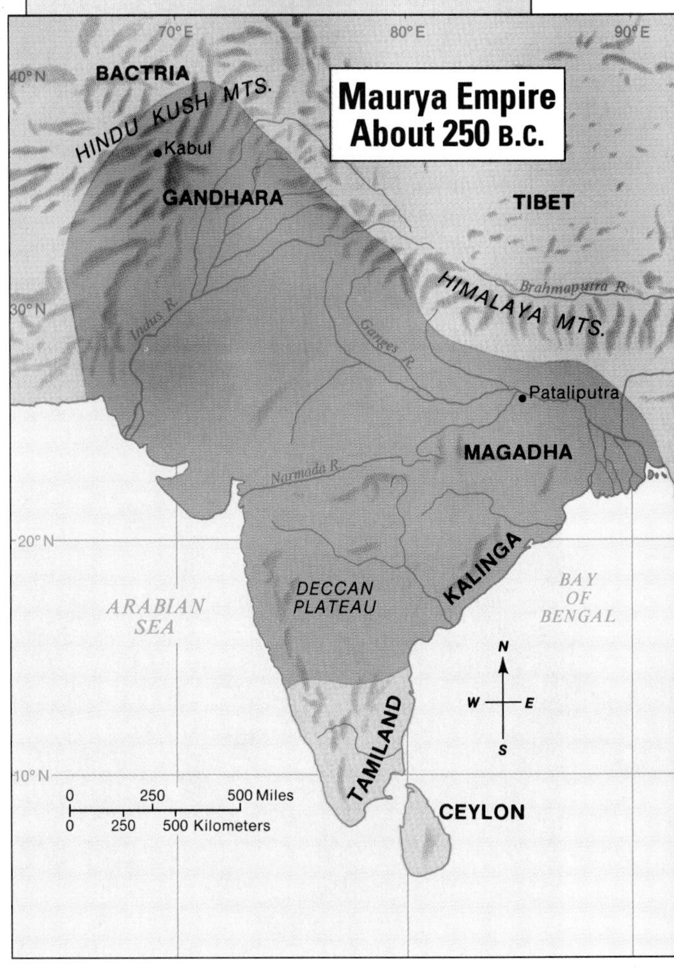

Pataliputra (pah tah lih POO trah), the Maurya capital, was a bustling city. Enclosed by a mighty wooden wall, it had 570 guard towers and 64 gates. Within the royal palace, Chandragupta protected himself against enemies. He never slept in the same bed two nights in a row, and he had someone taste his food before eating.

Under Chandragupta, the empire enjoyed peace. Trade prospered. The government saw to the building of irrigation systems and maintained roads.

Asoka's reforms. Chandragupta's successors added to his empire. His grandson, Asoka (uh SOH kuh), ruled from about 269 B.C. to 232 B.C. He brought the Maurya Empire to the height of its power.

A Soldier of the Maurya Empire During the Maurya Empire, armies of well-armed soldiers conquered most of South Asia. This sculpture of a warrior dates from the 200s B.C., when the Maurya Empire reached its height under Asoka. This work of art was used to decorate a Buddhist temple built by the Mauryas. ***Fine Art*** Why is art an important source of information about ancient civilizations?

At first, Asoka ruled harshly. For several years, he waged wars to conquer the region of Kalinga in the south. More than 100,000 people died in the fighting. The slaughter sickened Asoka. He converted to Buddhism and renounced violence. He then set out to rule his empire kindly and without force.

Asoka encouraged unity among his subjects and urged them to be tolerant of one another. "All faiths deserve to be honored for one reason or another," he declared. "By acting thus, a man exalts his own faith and at the same time does service to the faith of others." Asoka tried to rule according to Buddhist ideals, including nonviolence and the sacredness of all living creatures. His beliefs led him to give up hunting, end animal sacrifices, and become a vegetarian. He mixed justice with mercy and worked to improve the lives of his people.

Asoka had his laws carved on rocks and pillars for everyone to see. These stone carvings reveal the thoughts and beliefs of this unusual ruler.

> "All men are my children. As on behalf of my own children I desire that they may be provided by me with complete welfare and happiness in this world and in the next, so do I desire for all men as well."

Asoka's example has influenced Indian leaders down to the present. You will read in Chapter 9 how Mohandas Gandhi, like Asoka, followed the doctrine of nonviolence.

Asoka spreads Buddhism. To promote Buddhism in the empire, Asoka ordered the building of thousands of stupas (STOO puhz), or shrines containing remains of the Buddha. He made pilgrimages, or journeys, to these shrines, and encouraged others to do the same. He improved the roads and built rest houses with shade trees and water for the weary pilgrims.

Asoka also worked to spread Buddhism to foreign lands. He sent Buddhist missionaries to China and Southeast Asia. His efforts helped to make Buddhism a major world religion and to spread Indian culture throughout Asia.

Small Kingdoms

The Maurya Empire declined after Asoka's death in 232 B.C. During the next 500 years, the northern plain again became a battleground. Numerous invaders pushed into the region.

The first invaders were Greeks from Bactria, a kingdom north of the Hindu Kush Mountains. They were followed by the Pahlavas from Persia and the Kushans from Central Asia. Each group brought its own customs and ideas. In time, however, their cultures were absorbed into Hindu culture.

Southern India developed separately from the north. Its people were Dravidians, not Aryans. They spoke many languages, the most widespread of which was Tamil. Hinduism spread slowly into the south. As it did, it absorbed local gods and religious beliefs and so grew even more diverse.

In the small Tamil kingdoms of the south, trade flourished. Rulers improved harbors along the coasts and exported ivory, cotton, pepper, and gems. Tamil captains took advantage of the monsoons to sail west to Arabia. Other Tamil ships carried goods to China.

A Painting From the Ajanta Caves This detail is part of a large wall painting made at Ajanta, India, during the A.D. 400s. Here, followers of the Buddha gather to hear him speak. The artist has included monks wearing orange robes and, at top right, a horse and its rider. ***Fine Art*** What does this painting tell you about everyday life in India at that time?

The Gupta Empire

In A.D. 320, an ambitious young warrior again united the north. Taking the name Chandragupta I, he set up the Gupta dynasty. He probably chose the name Chandragupta to link himself with the ancient Maurya ruler.

The Gupta Empire lasted from A.D. 320 to A.D. 535. Under the Guptas, India enjoyed a golden age. The Guptas expanded their rule over much of northern India. They brought peace and prosperity to their empire. Trade increased, especially with China.

Achievements. Art, literature, and mathematics flourished in the Gupta Empire. On the walls of caves near Ajanta, artists painted colorful murals. The paintings illustrate Indian legends and scenes from the life of the Buddha. They also give a vivid picture of everyday life. The artists included figures of rich and poor, craftworkers and beggars, and animals and flowers of India.

In literature, Gupta writers produced fine poems and dramas. The best-known poet and playwright was Kalidasa. His play *Shakuntala* (shah KUHN tuh luh) is still performed today. It tells the story of a king who marries Shakuntala, daughter of a river goddess. An angry spirit puts a curse on Shakuntala, causing the king to forget her. After much sadness and suffering, the pair are finally reunited. In the following lines, the king expresses his joy upon seeing Shakuntala again:

> "Behold me, best and loveliest of
> women,
> Delivered from the cloud of fatal
> darkness
> That once oppressed my memory.
> Again
> Behold us brought together by the
> grace
> Of the great lord of Heaven."

In mathematics, Indian scholars developed the concept of zero and invented the decimal system, using symbols for the numbers 1 through 9. The new system let them make complicated calculations. At universities across the Gupta Empire, scholars figured the correct shape and size of the Earth. The Arabs adopted and spread the Indian system of numbers to Europe. There, these "Arabic numerals" gradually replaced Roman numerals.

Decline. As Gupta power declined, the Huns, a nomadic people from Central Asia, invaded South Asia. Their arrival marked the end of the Gupta Empire. For the next thousand years, rival Indian princes battled one another. Still, despite the turmoil, Hindu culture remained strong. The caste system and Hindu traditions gave people a sense of order.

Muslim Expansion Into India

In the mid-600s, the religion of Islam rose in the Middle East. (See Chapter 26.) In the centuries that followed, waves of Muslims swept into South Asia. They included Mongols from Central Asia, Afghans, Turks, and Persians. Muslim invaders attacked and plundered the rich cities of India. Some set up their own kingdoms.

Delhi sultans. Around 1200, Muslim rulers set up a capital at Delhi. For 300 years, these Delhi sultans, or rulers, governed much of northern and central India. Like Muslim rulers elsewhere, the Delhi sultans generally did not force their Hindu subjects to adopt Islam. Instead, non-Muslims had to pay special taxes. Some Hindus did become Muslims, however, because only Muslims could hold high-level government jobs.

Taxes on non-Muslims helped support a lavish court. The Delhi sultans introduced Persian culture into South Asia. Sultan Firuz Tughlak (fee ROOZ tuhg LAK) was a great builder. During his reign, from 1351 to 1388, he supervised the building of 30 colleges, 50 dams and reservoirs, 100 hospitals, and 200 new towns.

Mongol invasions. After the death of Firuz Tughlak, the Delhi sultanate declined. In 1398, Mongols from Central Asia descended into India. Under their leader, Tamerlane, they attacked and destroyed Delhi. The Mongol invaders killed or enslaved the entire population of the city and carried off its treasures. After Tamerlane left India to conquer other lands, the Delhi sultans were restored. The conquest had weakened them, however, and they did not retain power for long.

In 1526, another Mongol army invaded India. At its head was Babur (BAH buhr), who claimed to be Tamerlane's grandson. Babur founded the Mughal* Empire, which you will read about shortly. It was during the Mughal Empire that Islamic civilization reached its height in India.

A Clash of Beliefs

Unlike earlier invaders, the Muslim conquerors were never absorbed into Hindu society. The differences between Muslims and Hindus were too great. Islam was based on belief in one God. Hindus worshipped many gods. Islam taught that all Muslims were equal before God. Hinduism supported the caste system, which was built on inequality.

Muslims required believers to follow strictly the laws of the Koran—the holy book of Islam. Hindus had many sacred writings and tolerated many different beliefs. To Muslims, cattle were a source of food. To Hindus, cattle were sacred animals that could not be killed.

Such differences led to conflict. Muslim armies smashed Hindu temples, destroying images of Hindu gods and goddesses. In northern India, where Muslim rule was strongest, many Hindus converted to Islam. Some wanted to escape the tax imposed on nonbelievers. Others hoped to get jobs in government. Still others wanted to escape the caste system. Farther south, where Muslim rule was weaker, few Hindus changed religion.

Despite clashes between Hindus and Muslims, the two groups slowly learned to live together. Under the Mughals, a brilliant culture emerged, blending both Hindu and Muslim traditions. A new language, Urdu (UR doo), came into use. Urdu combined Persian and Hindi and was written in Arabic script. Hindu architects designed and built mosques, Mus-

---

* *Mughal* is the Persian word for "Mongol."

BUILDERS AND SHAPERS

Akbar the Great: Champion of Religious Toleration

"If men walk in the way of God's will, interference with them would be unfair," declared the Mughal emperor Akbar the Great. He was one of the few world leaders of his time to practice toleration of all religions.

Akbar could not read or write, but learned from those around him. His son wrote:

> "My father always associated with the learned of every creed and religion . . . and although he was illiterate, so much became clear to him through constant discussion with the learned and the wise . . . that no one knew him to be illiterate."

Akbar, a Muslim, invited scholars of many religions to regular Friday afternoon discussions. They included Hindus, Christians, Jains, Zoroastrians, and other Muslims. Through their debates, Akbar came to see similarities as well as differences among the religions. "Each person according to his condition gives the same Supreme Being a name," he believed.

Akbar hoped to end religious conflict by uniting the various faiths. He combined the teachings of several religions into a new religion—Din Ilahi, or "Divine Faith." Din Ilahi developed only a small following and died with its founder.

Akbar's public policies showed his belief in religious toleration. He ended the destruction of Hindu temples and gave honors to both Hindu and Muslim artists and poets.

Akbar's successors did not share his intellectual curiosity or his tolerance. They abandoned most of his reforms. As his son said, "In his actions and movements he was not like the people of the world."

1. How did Akbar overcome his handicap of illiteracy?
2. **Synthesizing Information** Read "The Mughal Empire" on pages 187–188. (a) How might Akbar's policies of religious toleration have helped strengthen his rule? (b) How did abandonment of these policies by his successors contribute to the Mughal decline?

lim houses of worship. Hindus absorbed many Persian legends and myths into their own literature.

The Mughal Empire

The Mughal Empire founded by Babur in 1526 lasted for more than 300 years. At its height, it united most of the peoples of South Asia. Its golden age occurred during the reign of Akbar, grandson of Babur. Akbar ruled from 1556 to 1605. (See the feature above.)

Akbar realized that to rule India he had to lead Hindus as well as Muslims. Adopting a policy of religious toleration, he married a Hindu princess and abolished the special tax on Hindus. He also appointed Hindus to jobs in government. Today, Indians honor Akbar as

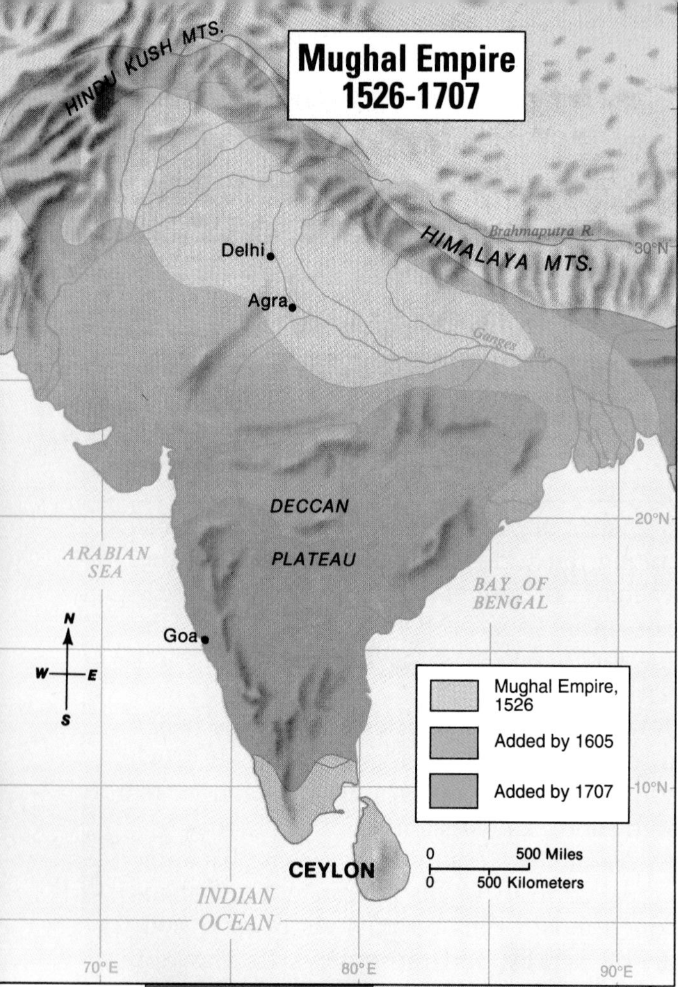

MAP STUDY

The Mughal rulers established a powerful empire that included most of the lands in South Asia.

1. **Movement** (a) In which directions did the Mughal Empire expand after 1526? (b) What large area was added by 1707?
2. **Movement** What lands were added by the great Mughal emperor Akbar, who ruled from 1556 to 1605?
3. **Comparing** Compare the lands included in the Mughal Empire with the lands in the earlier Maurya Empire. (a) In what ways were these empires similar? (b) In what ways were they different?

a master of compromise. He stands with Asoka as one of India's most brilliant rulers.

The arts. Under the Mughals, Islamic and Hindu styles of art and architecture blended to create a unique Indian style. Painters adapted Persian techniques to produce elegant miniature portraits and to illustrate Hindu stories. Hindu music borrowed from Persian and Arabic musical traditions.

Akbar's grandson, Shah Jahan, hired the best architects to build the Taj Mahal (tahzh muh HAHL) as a monument to his beloved wife Mumtaz Mahal. Overcome with grief at her death, he ordered the white marble tomb to be "as beautiful as she was beautiful." More than 20,000 artisans worked for 22 years to complete the Taj Mahal.

Decline. Mughal power weakened in the 1700s. Wasteful spending hurt the empire. Also, Akbar's successors ended his policy of toleration. They imposed heavy taxes on Hindus, closed Hindu schools, and dismissed Hindus from government. Such actions led Hindu princes to revolt. Civil wars among Muslim princes also broke out. The emperor continued to rule over a brilliant court, but his power over outlying areas declined. At the same time, a new wave of intruders—the Europeans—were arriving in growing numbers. You will read about the impact of the Europeans in Section 4.

SECTION 2 REVIEW

1. **Locate:** (a) Maurya Empire, (b) Pataliputra, (c) Delhi, (d) Mughal Empire.
2. **Identify:** (a) Asoka, (b) Kalidasa, (c) Urdu, (d) Akbar, (e) Taj Mahal.
3. **Define:** (a) dynasty, (b) stupa, (c) sultan.
4. (a) During what periods was India united? (b) How did unity under the Guptas lead to a golden age?
5. How did differences between Muslims and Hindus lead to conflict between the two groups?
6. What role did invaders play in shaping Indian culture?
7. **Synthesizing Information** Give two examples of cultural diffusion that occurred as a result of Muslim expansion into South Asia.
8. **Writing Across Cultures** Religion was a major force in keeping Indian society stable during times of turmoil. Jot down your ideas about the role of religion in the development of American society.

3

PATTERNS OF LIFE

FIND OUT

How did the caste system affect life in India?

What role did the village play in traditional Indian life?

What was the structure of the traditional family in India?

Vocabulary purdah

"It is better to do one's own duty badly," says the god Krishna in the *Bhagavad-Gita* (BUHG uh vuhd GEE tuh), "than to do another's duty well." Krishna's advice summed up the law of dharma. From an early age, Hindu children learned about duty. Doing one's duty ensured the moral order of the universe.

While rival princes waged war or made peace, millions of Indians built their lives around two basic social units—the family and the village. The caste system bound people further. It gave each person a role in society and rules to live by. Those rules governed the work people did, the tools they used, the food they ate. To ignore or change those rules was to disrupt the harmony of society.

The Caste System

Indian society developed into a complex system based on class and caste. In Aryan society, you will recall, people belonged to one of four varna, or classes. Later, a fifth group emerged. It included people known as untouchables, who lived at the lowest level of society.

Over thousands of years, the caste system grew and changed. It divided people within each class, until there were thousands of castes and subcastes. Caste is based on the idea that there are separate kinds of humans. Higher-caste people considered themselves purer—and closer to moksha—than lower-caste people.

As invaders and other people settled in South Asia, they were absorbed into the caste system. Often, they formed new castes. Since caste was based partly on occupation, additional subcastes emerged as new occupations developed.

Rules. Over the centuries, caste rules became increasingly complex. The rules were meant to help people remain spiritually pure. As a result, rules were especially strict for members of the higher castes, who were considered the purest members of society. A

Gardeners at Work This colorful painting from the 1700s shows gardeners tending an irrigated plot of land. As the caste system became more complex over the centuries, even people like gardeners became a separate caste. Nearly two thirds of the members of India's many castes worked in agriculture. ***Culture*** How would the caste system have affected the lives of these gardeners' children?

high-caste person risked spiritual pollution—becoming spiritually unclean—if he or she had contact with lower, or impure, castes. Some castes were thought to be so impure that even the shadow of a person of that caste could pollute others. Members of such low castes had to strike a wooden clapper to warn others of their approach.

Caste rules governed cooking and eating habits, marriage, and employment. A Brahman, for example, could only eat food prepared by another Brahman. Many Brahmans became cooks. Because they were the highest caste, anyone could eat the food they prepared. A Brahman, like members of other castes, had to marry someone of his or her own caste.

Each occupation had its own caste, and a person's job was determined at birth. Gardeners, jewelers, woodworkers, water carriers, and moneylenders—each formed a separate caste.

Other rules determined which gods caste members worshipped, where they lived, and what clothes they wore. Manners, too, grew out of caste. People in lower castes had to greet higher-caste people in certain ways. They could never sit in the presence of a person of higher caste. Each caste had its own council that enforced caste rules.

Interdependence. The caste system created a sense of stability and order in Indian life. Each caste looked after its own members. At the same time, different castes depended on one another. An upper-caste merchant, for example, needed the services of a lower-caste water carrier. Neither could do the work of the other.

For the lowest castes and untouchables, life was very harsh. Each day brought new reminders of their lowly position. Still, the caste system was deeply imbedded in law, custom, and religious tradition, and they accepted the view of their own unworthiness.

Village Life

For most people in South Asia, the village was the basic unit of society. A headman governed the village. He was a respected landlord who often inherited the position from his father. Usually, the headman made decisions with the help of a council of elders. Together, they organized villagers to work on local projects such as roads, irrigation ditches, and temples.

Villages varied in size, from a handful of people to hundreds of families. Each village had a variety of castes that did the jobs needed for daily life. Castes might include priests, landowners, farmers, herders, carpenters, and metalworkers, as well as such low castes as leather workers and sweepers.

Villages were generally self-sufficient. They produced most of what they needed. At regional markets and during religious festivals, however, people from different villages met and mingled.

In most villages, landlords held much of the land. Landless workers farmed plots belonging to the landlord and had to give him part of the harvest. What remained was barely enough to feed themselves and their families. In the north, people grew wheat and barley. On the well-watered plains, they grew rice. In the drier regions of the Deccan, they planted millet. Families also grew peas, beans, lentils, and cotton, which they spun into cloth.

Villagers relied on cattle for plowing, transporting goods, and milk. They also used cow's milk to make an oil called ghee (gee). Ghee had many uses in cooking. Because it contained no fat, it kept well even in the hot weather. Some scholars suggest that cattle became sacred to Hindus in part because of their economic importance.

Family Life

Indians identified first with their family, then with their village. By tradition, Indians valued the joint family.* The joint family was a form of the extended family. It included a husband, his wife, their sons with their wives and children, and unmarried daughters. The

* Although the joint family was the ideal, in fact only about half of all Indians enjoyed such an arrangement. Especially among the poor, people simply did not live long enough for several generations to be alive at the same time.

Indian Villagers Throughout history, most people in South Asia have lived in villages. The women shown here live in northwestern India. They are operating a machine that grinds up hay, turning it into fodder used to feed farm animals. Indians have long raised buffalo, goats, and sheep as well as cattle. ***Technology*** Describe the farm technology and economy of this Indian village based on this picture.

husband's brothers, uncles, and cousins might also live under the same roof or nearby.

The family was patriarchal. In the traditional view, "Father is heaven, father is religion, the gods are pleased by pleasing father." "Father" was the oldest male. He was thought to be the wisest and most knowledgeable member of the family. As a result, he had complete control over the household. He might, however, consult with his wife or brothers on issues such as arranging marriages for the children.

Strong family ties created a sense of order. Family interests, rather than those of the individual, were most important. Marriages, therefore, were a family concern. The head of the family arranged marriages to protect and benefit the family. The bride or groom had little or no say.

Often, families arranged marriages for children at an early age. The actual wedding might take place later. At marriage, a girl left her home to become part of her husband's family. Once a year, she might return to visit her family.

Families celebrated weddings with great ceremony. The bride's family paid most of the expenses. Often, they went into debt for a daughter's marriage. Her family had to provide a dowry—that is, a gift of money or goods paid to the groom. The higher a family's caste, the more costly the marriage would be.

A Traditional Marriage

Once established, marriage customs remained largely unchanged for hundreds of years. In her autobiography, *Memoirs of an Indian Woman,* Shudha Ghose Mazumdar recalled her own marriage.

> "One fine day in November of 1910 I was preparing for my annual [school] examination when I was told that I would not have to go to school any more for my marriage had been arranged."

Shudha Ghose was 11 years old at the time. The young man she would marry, Satish Chandra Mazumdar, was twice her age. Their parents had arranged the marriage after careful research. They had studied the young couple's horoscopes to be sure that the marriage would be blessed. "I did not want to get married," Shudha wrote later. "I only wanted to go to school. But my opinion did not count."

Shudha's father was a wealthy, educated landowner. He had sent his daughter to a convent school. Shudha's mother, however, strictly followed traditional customs. The bride and groom met for the first time at their wedding.

The festivities lasted for several days. In the final ceremony, Shudha and Satish Chandra stood before a statue of Vishnu. A priest lit a fire at the altar. The bride and groom poured rice and ghee onto the flame. Then, hand in hand, they circled the fire seven times. Satish Chandra recited this verse:

> "In all that I dedicate myself, offer thou
> thy heart.
> May thy mind in all consciousness
> follow mine.
> May thy speech be ever one with
> mine.
> May the Lord of Creation keep
> thee
> Ever dedicated to me."

As custom dictated, Shudha replied, "I shall try my utmost."

Indian Bride and Groom This young bride and groom are waiting for their wedding guests to arrive. Their wedding, like many Hindu marriage ceremonies, is being held in an outdoor pavilion. The bride and groom may be meeting each other for the first time. ***Culture*** Why have the parents of the bride and groom traditionally arranged most marriages in India?

Shudha did her utmost. Like all brides, she moved into the home of her husband's parents. She came to love her husband and bore him two sons. In time, her sons married and their wives joined the family, continuing traditions established over generations. ■

Women's Lives

Within the family and society, women had few rights. A woman's duties were to marry, wait on her husband, and bear sons. In Hindu tradition, only a son could perform the rituals for his dead father's soul.

Although a woman's position was inferior, she did not lack power. Hindus believed that women alone had *shakti,* or creative energy. Because men lacked shakti, they were incomplete unless they married. Women were thought to lack the knowledge to control their power. For that reason, they were seen as dangerous unless ruled by a man.

Throughout her life, a woman had to obey a man. Hindu law codes stated:

> "[A woman] should do nothing independently even in her own house. In childhood subject to her father, in youth to her husband, and when her husband is dead to her sons, she should never enjoy independence."

Higher-caste women had to obey especially strict rules. They often lived in purdah, or complete seclusion. They wore veils over their faces and rarely left home. They were kept separate from all men except for their husbands and close relatives.

As caste rules hardened, widows were forbidden to remarry. A widow was expected to give up all comforts and spend her life in prayer. A widow was considered unlucky, so other family members ignored her. Some widows threw themselves onto their husbands' funeral fires rather than endure a life of hardship. They became *sati,* or "virtuous women." In sacrificing her life, Hindus believed, a widow wiped away the sins of her husband and herself.

SECTION 3 REVIEW

1. **Define:** purdah.
2. (a) What areas of life did the caste system regulate? (b) Why were caste rules stricter for higher castes?
3. (a) How were Indian villages governed? (b) How did most villagers support themselves?
4. Describe the traditional Indian family.
5. **Applying Information** How did the number of castes reflect India's cultural diversity?
6. **Writing Across Cultures** From what you have read, you can tell that a traditional Indian marriage differs in many ways from a typical American marriage. Make a list of ways in which they are similar.

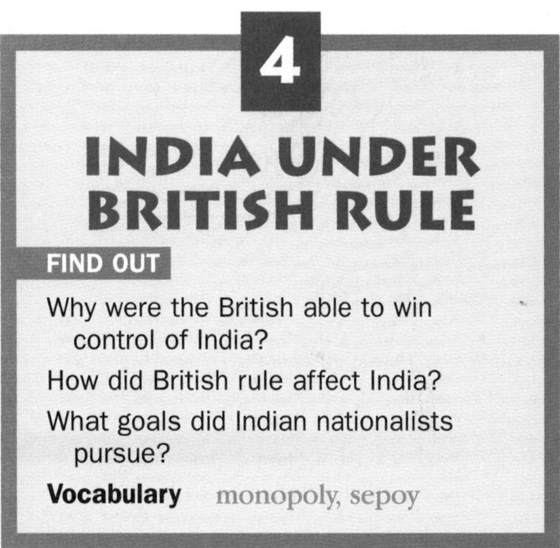

4 INDIA UNDER BRITISH RULE

FIND OUT

Why were the British able to win control of India?

How did British rule affect India?

What goals did Indian nationalists pursue?

Vocabulary monopoly, sepoy

"A lucky adventure, a lucky venture!" exclaimed a Muslim trader when Portuguese captain Vasco da Gama reached India in 1498. "Plenty of rubies, plenty of emeralds. You owe great thanks to God for having brought you to a country of such riches."

The Portuguese were the first Europeans to gain a foothold in India. The Dutch, French, and British soon followed. They were eager for a share of the rich Indian trade. At first, the mighty Mughal emperors kept tight control of European activity. In time, however, Mughal power declined. The British, who

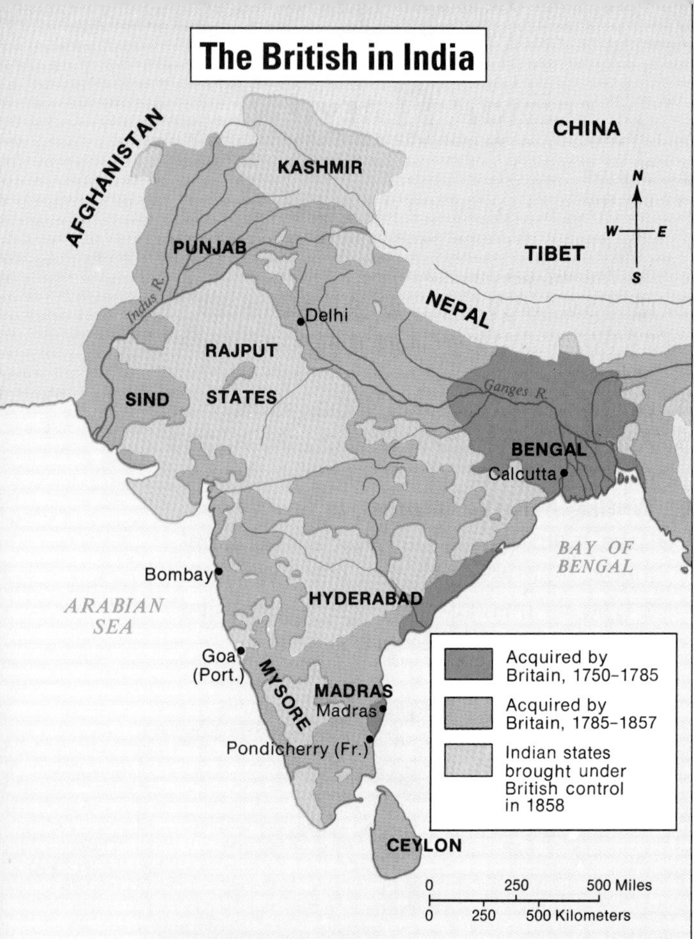

MAP STUDY

The British first gained a foothold in India by setting up a few trading posts in the 1600s. They expanded their control after 1750 until they finally ruled all of India by 1858.

1. **Region** (a) What parts of India did the British acquire between 1750 and 1785? (b) What cities in those regions probably traded earlier with the East India Company?
2. **Location** Who ruled the lands in India that the British took control of in 1858?
3. **Synthesizing Information** What generalization can you make to describe how the British established their empire in India?

had come as traders, then turned their attention to conquest.

Mughal Emperors and European Traders

After da Gama's voyage, the Portuguese quickly built a trading empire in Asia. They set up trading posts, from Goa on India's west coast to Southeast Asia. Catholic missionaries sailed with Portuguese merchants and converted many Indians to Christianity.

In the 1600s, the Dutch broke into the Portuguese trade monopoly in Asia. A monopoly is complete control over a market or a product. The English and French also sought trading rights from the Mughals.

Early trade. In 1600, England set up the East India Company. From the Mughal rulers, the East India Company won rights to build trading posts and forts at Madras, Bombay, and Calcutta. (See the map at left.) The English traded gold and silver for Indian goods such as cotton, silk, and tea.

Textiles, or cloth, were the most important goods carried to England by the East India Company. The influence of this trade can still be seen today, in the Indian words that have entered the English language. They include the words calico, dungarees, gingham, khaki, madras, and shawl.

A struggle for power. At first, the powerful Mughal rulers looked down on the Europeans. To the Indians, with their rich spices and silks, the newcomers had little of value to offer. The Mughals set the terms of trade and had the power to enforce them.

In the early 1700s, however, changes occurred in India and in Europe that would have major effects on South Asia. In India, the Mughal Empire entered its long period of decline. Emperors still ruled over a rich court, but they no longer controlled most of the subcontinent. Rival princes set up their own, almost independent kingdoms. In Europe, the British and French were competing for political and economic power. This power struggle spilled over into other parts of the world, including India.

The British* and French took advantage of the Mughal decline. They competed to control India's many small kingdoms and tap new sources of wealth. Fierce fighting broke out between the two European powers. In their

* In 1707, England and Scotland officially joined, forming the United Kingdom of Great Britain. Thus, the term England is used for the country before 1707. The term Britain or Great Britain is used after 1707.

bitter struggle, both sides found allies among local Indian rulers. By the 1760s, however, British forces had overcome the French.

East India Company Rule

Britain owed its success in India in part to Robert Clive, an administrator of the East India Company. Clive led British forces in their successful drive against the French. He also won control of the wealthy Indian state of Bengal. In Bengal and elsewhere, he appointed local rulers who favored the interests of the East India Company.

Many individual Indian rulers fought to keep the British out of their territory. Traditional rivalries, however, kept them from uniting. The British encouraged this disunity. The East India Company forced Indian rulers, one by one, to sign treaties granting it greater power.

The East India Company gained enormous wealth from India, especially after the Mughal emperor gave it the right to collect taxes. To protect its interests, the company set up a law code and a court system. It also took over more land. Some areas it ruled directly. Others, it ruled indirectly through local princes.

British Rule

The British government took steps to check the increasing power of the East India Company. Parliament passed laws to regulate

British Justice in India The East India Company set up a system of special courts for Indians. This ceramic model shows an East India Company official, seated at right, presiding over a court trial. An Indian guard, in the red-coat uniform at the far left, is employed by the company to keep order. ***Justice*** Why might the East India Company want to set up its own court system in India?

affairs. London, however, was far off, and communications were slow.

By the 1850s, Indians had many grievances against British rule. Hindus were outraged when the British outlawed ritual suicide by widows and other Hindu practices. Indian princes disliked having foreigners tell them what to do. High taxes angered farmers. Both Hindus and Muslims resented the efforts of missionaries to convert them to the Christian religion. For many Indians, foreigners were a threat to their whole way of life.

The Sepoy Rebellion. The general unrest helped spark a revolt among the sepoys, Indian troops who served in the British army. In the 1850s, sepoys heard rumors that the cartridges for their new rifles were greased with beef or pork fat. To Hindus, cows were sacred, and Muslims were forbidden to touch pork. A new law further upset the sepoys. The law required them to fight for Britain in foreign lands. Hindus believed that they would lose caste if they traveled overseas.

The Sepoy Rebellion broke out in 1857 near Delhi. It quickly spread across northern and central India. During several months of fighting, both sides committed savage acts. In the end, the British put down the uprising.

A British colony. The rebellion led to a number of political changes. In 1858, the British government took over India as a colony. They sent the last Mughal emperor into exile. In 1876, Queen Victoria of Britain took the title Empress of India.

The British ruled most of India directly, through appointed officials. About a third of the subcontinent remained in the hands of local rulers. Hindu and Muslim princes governed their own kingdoms but had to sign treaties giving the British control of their foreign and military affairs. The British reformed the law codes and controlled the court system.

The Sepoy Rebellion left lasting distrust between Indians and British. The British moved away from using Indian soldiers and set up their own civil service, or body of officials, to rule the colony. At the same time, they set out to create a new class of British-educated Indians.

Indians continued to resent efforts to change their culture. One Indian commented about widespread racism under British rule:

> “In India, every European is automatically a member of the ruling race. Railway carriages, station waiting rooms, benches in parks are marked ‘For Europeans Only.’ To have to put up with this in one's own country is a humiliating reminder of our enslaved condition.”

Effects of British Rule

British rule brought economic and social changes to South Asia. The British improved roads and modernized ports. They directed the building of railroads and telegraph systems. These modern forms of transportation and communications helped the British increase trade and control their colony. Officials could report uprisings or disasters instantly and send troops by rail to trouble spots. Improved communications also brought Indians in different regions closer together.

New economic patterns. Other changes helped to destroy the traditional Indian economy and tie India economically to Britain. By the mid-1800s, the Industrial Revolution was in full swing in Britain. British factory owners saw India as a market for their own goods. They discouraged local Indian industries and pushed for laws to limit British imports of Indian-made goods. As a result, Indian industries declined, locally made goods disappeared, and Indians had to buy expensive British-made products.

To pay for British imports, Indians had to raise cash crops such as tea, pepper, coffee, and cotton. As Indian farmers grew less food, famines became frequent and widespread. When food shortages occurred, however, rail links allowed officials to send supplies to hard-hit areas.

Social changes. Britain also introduced changes that affected Indian society. Improved health care and sanitary conditions led to population growth. Many young Indians moved to cities to find jobs.

An Indian Prince's Court British officials, shown here at left, are being received by an Indian prince, Fateh Singh. Prince Singh, dressed in white, continued to oppose the British long after they took control of his state. He refused to allow the British to build irrigation systems, roads, or a school system. ***Human Rights*** Why do you think Fateh Singh resisted British rule?

The British set up schools and colleges to educate higher-caste Indians. The course of study, which stressed English language and culture, reflected British ethnocentrism. To the British, their culture was superior to that of India. As one official boasted, the British wanted to create "a class of persons, Indian in blood and color, but English in taste, in opinions, in morals, and in intellect."

A British-educated Indian middle class emerged. For them, English became a useful common language. Hindi-speakers from the north, for example, could communicate with Tamil-speakers in the south. In studying English history, young Indians learned about political ideals such as liberty, freedom, and "rule by the consent of the governed." Educated Indians also learned more about their own cultural traditions. This awareness increased their resentment against foreign rule and contributed to the growth of nationalism.

Indian Nationalism

Indian nationalism was strongest among the British-educated elite. These people came mostly from the upper and middle classes, and they were determined to change India. At first, nationalists disagreed among themselves about what direction to take. Some wanted to adopt western ways. They wanted to modernize India and reform the system of British rule.

Other nationalists favored a return to Hindu traditions. They wanted to build a new

The British in India British officials and business people in India continued to follow their own customs. Many had little contact with the Indians whose lives they controlled. This British couple is being served English food, eating on English china, in their home filled with English furniture. ***Culture*** Why did the British in India keep many of their own ways?

India that blended the best of both Hindu and western cultures. Hindu nationalists won support among poor peasants and other working people. In time, they rejected foreign rule completely and demanded independence.

Indians formed various groups to work for change. Among the most successful was the Indian National Congress (INC), set up in 1885. Most Congress members were Hindus who lived in the cities. The INC began by calling for gradual change. At the same time, it urged the British to open more government jobs to Indians.

After World War I, however, the INC took a more forceful stand. In 1920, Mohandas Gandhi took over the leadership of the Congress movement. As you will read in Chapter 9, he united large sections of the Indian people in support of home rule. Under pressure, Britain promised self-government to India in time. It slowly turned over control of some areas to local government but kept overall power in the country.

As Hindu nationalism grew, Muslims became concerned. In 1906, they founded the Muslim League under the leadership of Muhammad Ali Jinnah. Tensions and distrust kept Hindus and Muslims apart. By the 1930s, Jinnah came to believe that the subcontinent must be divided into two separate nations—one for Hindus and one for Muslims.

SECTION 4 REVIEW

1. **Identify:** (a) East India Company, (b) Robert Clive, (c) Sepoy Rebellion, (d) Indian National Congress, (e) Muslim League.
2. **Define:** (a) monopoly, (b) sepoy.
3. What changes in South Asia helped the British conquer India?
4. What economic changes did the British bring to India?
5. What were the goals of the two major nationalist groups in India?
6. **Recognizing Bias** Some people have called the events of 1857 the Sepoy Mutiny. Others have called them the First War of Independence. (a) What does each name suggest about the revolt? (b) Who do you think used each name?
7. **Writing Across Cultures** Imagine that you are living in one of Britain's 13 American colonies during the early 1700s. Write a letter to an Indian living under British colonial rule in which you discuss Britain's regulation of colonial trade.

Chapter 8 Review

Understanding Vocabulary

Match each term at left with the correct definition at right.

1. reincarnation	**a.** Indian soldier
2. sepoy	**b.** complete control over a market or a product
3. dynasty	**c.** rebirth of the soul in various forms
4. purdah	**d.** ruling family
5. monopoly	**e.** complete seclusion

Reviewing the Main Ideas

1. (a) How is Hinduism a tolerant religion? (b) How did this tolerance contribute to India's cultural diversity?

2. How did the development of southern India differ from that of northern India?

3. Why were Muslims never absorbed into Hindu society?

4. What was the role of dharma, or duty, in Hindu society?

5. (a) Why did Indians believe they must obey caste rules? (b) How did new castes and subcastes develop?

6. (a) Describe the causes of the Sepoy Rebellion. (b) What political changes resulted from the rebellion?

7. What were the goals of the following: (a) Indian National Congress, (b) Muslim League?

Reviewing Chapter Themes

1. Two major world religions, Hinduism and Buddhism, started in South Asia. (a) What were the basic beliefs of Hinduism? (b) What were the basic beliefs of Buddhism? (c) Why did Buddhism almost disappear in India?

2. Several great empires united South Asia. Describe two achievements of each of the following: (a) Maurya Empire, (b) Gupta Empire, (c) Mughal Empire.

3. Over many centuries, various Muslim peoples invaded South Asia. Identify three cultural changes that resulted from contacts between Muslims and Hindus.

4. Traditional Indian life centered around caste, family, and village. Choose one and describe its role in people's daily life.

5. British colonial rule brought major changes to India. Describe one political, one economic, and one social change that resulted from British rule.

Thinking Critically

1. Analyzing Information How might Indians rate the effects of British rule?

2. Analyzing Ideas How did Hindu traditions support both a positive and a negative view of women?

3. Making Global Connections (a) Compare the British treatment of Indians with their treatment of Native Americans. (b) What might explain the differences?

Applying Your Skills

1. Using Visual Evidence Look at the pictures on pages 197 and 198. (a) What does the relationship appear to be between the British and the Indians in each picture. (b) How would you account for the relationship between the prince and the British officials? (c) How do you think the Indians reacted to their role as servants?

2. Constructing a Time Line Make a time line showing the major events in Section 2 and Section 4. (a) When did Mughal power weaken? (b) When did the British gain control of India? (c) How are the two events related?

Chapter 9

SOUTH ASIA IN TRANSITION

Gandhi's Teachings This mural depicts significant events in the life of Mohandas Gandhi, one of the most important Indian leaders of modern times. Gandhi, at left, is shown in meditation. During India's struggle for independence, he spread the message of nonviolent action. ***Citizenship*** How can a struggle for independence help strengthen citizenship among a nation's people?

CHAPTER OUTLINE

1 Freedom—And Partition

2 Political Challenges

3 Economic Development

4 Changing Patterns of Life

5 Other Nations of South Asia

Neatly dressed in a dark suit and turban, a young Indian lawyer named Mohandas Gandhi boarded the train at Durban, in South Africa. As he sat in the first-class compartment a train official approached him.

"Come along," the official said, "you must go to the rear compartment." At that time, in the 1890s, South Africa had laws that required "coloured" travelers to sit apart from whites.

"But I have a first-class ticket!"

"That doesn't matter. . . . I shall have to call a police constable to push you out."

"Yes, you may. I refuse to get out voluntarily."

The police forced Gandhi from the train. As he sat in the cold station, he reflected on what had happened. Now, he saw the injustices suffered by Indians living in South Africa. For 20 years, he worked without success to change laws that discriminated against Indians.

During the struggle, Gandhi developed ideas about nonviolent action as a way for people with little political power to end injustice. When he returned to India in 1914, he used this approach in the struggle for independence from Britain.

CHAPTER PERSPECTIVE

After a long struggle, two independent nations emerged in South Asia in 1947—India and Pakistan. Like developing nations elsewhere, these nations faced choices about how to achieve modernization.

As you read, look for these chapter themes:

- Gandhi urged Indians to use nonviolence and civil disobedience to win independence from Britain.
- Ethnic and cultural diversity have posed challenges for India and other South Asian nations.
- South Asian nations have pursued modernization with mixed results.
- Technology and other changes have affected the people of South Asia, but traditional patterns of village life remain strong.

Literature Connections

In this chapter you will encounter passages from the following works.

Autobiography, Mohandas Gandhi

"We Have Arrived in Amritsar," Bhisham Sahni

For other suggestions, see Connections With Literature, pages 804–808.

1 FREEDOM—AND PARTITION

FIND OUT

How did Gandhi help India win independence from Britain?

How did World War II affect the struggle for independence?

What cultural differences led to the partition of India?

Vocabulary satyagraha, civil disobedience

"The British want us to put the struggle on the plane of machine guns. . . . Our only assurance of beating them is to keep it . . . where we have the weapons and they have not."

To Mohandas Gandhi, India's struggle for freedom had to be won by peaceful means. What "weapons" could this soft-spoken Hindu use to defeat the British? Gandhi campaigned vigorously to convince Indians to achieve independence through nonviolent means.

Growing Unrest

During and after World War I, Indian nationalists increased their demands for freedom. In 1919, Britain responded with harsh new laws limiting freedom of the press and other rights in India. For weeks, nationalists protested. After five British officials were killed, General Reginald Dyer banned all public gatherings.

The nationalists determined to defy Dyer's order. On April 13, 1919, more than 10,000 Indians gathered in a public area in Amritsar, a city in northwestern India. General Dyer ordered his troops to open fire. Men, women, and children were trampled as they tried to escape. When the shooting stopped, 379 Indians lay dead and more than 1,100 were wounded.

The Amritsar Massacre was a turning point in India's struggle for freedom. It deepened distrust of the British and led to increased violence. It also stirred many Indians to call for complete separation from Britain.

Mohandas Gandhi

Mohandas Gandhi returned to India from South Africa in 1914. Within a few years, he emerged as a key figure in the Indian struggle for independence. Gandhi united many groups within the nationalist movement. He took the struggle beyond the Congress party, which was largely a middle-class organization. He inspired the common people of India to work for change. In addition, he won the backing of the Indians who had benefited most from British rule.

Gandhi's principles. Gandhi came from a middle-class Hindu family and went to England to study law. In 1891, he returned to India but had little success as a lawyer. As you have read, Gandhi then moved to South Africa to practice law. There, he developed his ideas about the use of nonviolent resistance to end injustice. Gandhi called this method satyagraha (SUHT ya gruh ha), or "truth force."

Gandhi's ideas were rooted in Hindu beliefs and in Christian traditions. From Hinduism, Gandhi absorbed ideas about nonviolence and respect for all life. (See page 179.) While studying in England, he came to admire the Christian teaching of love, even for one's enemies. The writings of American philosopher Henry David Thoreau influenced Gandhi as well. Thoreau had practiced civil disobedience, the refusal to obey unjust laws.

To Gandhi, the goal of satyagraha was to "convert the wrongdoer." He hoped to make the world aware of British injustice by accepting punishment without striking back. He also hoped to awaken in the British a sense of their own wrongdoing.

Gandhi's appeal. Gandhi's ideas were appealing to Hindus of all classes. He won support by stressing India's rich heritage. He gave up western ways and encouraged traditional Indian industries, such as spinning cotton. He lived simply, dressing in the white cotton garments worn by India's poor.

Like many devout Hindus, Gandhi was a vegetarian. He often fasted, or went without food. He emphasized Hindu virtues such as duty, morality, and self-discipline. Gandhi's followers called him Mahatma, or "Great Soul."

Like the Buddha and other reformers, Gandhi rejected some features of the caste system. He demanded better treatment for untouchables, whom he called Harijan, or "Children of God." Gandhi also reached out to Muslims, including them in his campaign to unite all Indians.

Campaign of civil disobedience. During the early 1920s, Gandhi traveled around India, urging nonviolent resistance to British rule. He supported strikes and protests. Along with other leaders, he called on Indians to boycott, or stop buying, British-made goods. A future Indian prime minister, Indira Gandhi (who was not related to Mohandas Gandhi) recalled that, as a child, she gave up her British-made doll. She took "my friend, my child" to the roof of her home and burned it, then burst into tears.

The Salt March. In 1930, Gandhi used satyagraha to protest the tax on salt. British laws forbade Indians to make salt. Indians could only buy salt heavily taxed by the government. In protest, Gandhi led followers on a 200-mile march from his home to the coast. Thousands of people joined the march along the way. At the coast, they broke the law by making salt from sea water.

The salt protest spread across India. The British arrested Gandhi and an estimated 50,000 other Indians. Although the government kept its salt tax, the campaign increased world support for Indian nationalists. Throughout the 1930s, the British responded to nonviolent Indian protest with force. In Britain, people began to debate whether their government should hold on to India.

Moving Toward Independence

When World War II began in 1939, most Indians had no desire to fight in what they saw as Britain's struggle. The Indian National

Gandhi at His Spinning Wheel Gandhi inspired the people of India to return to traditional ways such as spinning thread to make cloth. Gandhi himself spent time each day spinning and meditating. The spinning wheel soon became a symbol of India's struggle for freedom from British rule. ***Change*** Why do you think Gandhi's call to return to traditional ways appealed to Indians?

Congress refused to support the war unless Britain promised immediate independence. When the British refused, Gandhi and other Congress members organized a "Quit India" movement. They urged Indians to follow a policy of non-cooperation with the British. They also continued their campaign of civil disobedience. The British responded by arresting more than 20,000 Congress members.

By 1945, war-weakened Britain realized that it could no longer keep India. Nationalist forces were simply too strong. Also, popular opinion in Britain opposed keeping overseas colonies.

Hindu-Muslim conflict. As independence approached, a tragic conflict took shape between Hindus and Muslims. In the early days of the nationalist movement, Hindus and Muslims had cooperated. During the 1920s and 1930s, however, divisions grew between the largely Hindu Congress party and the Muslim League. The British encouraged the conflict, hoping to weaken the nationalists.

The Muslims, led by Muhammad Ali Jinnah, demanded a separate Muslim nation. As you have read, in the past, deep differences in religious beliefs had led to clashes between Hindus and Muslims. As a result, many Muslims feared that their rights would not be respected in a country dominated by Hindus.

Gandhi disagreed. He hoped that Hindus and Muslims would work together in an independent India. Many Hindus distrusted Muslims, however. They looked on Muslims as foreign conquerors. Economic and political differences between the two groups further increased tension.

The Subcontinent Divided

In 1946, widespread rioting broke out between Hindus and Muslims. Britain realized that if something were not done to resolve the problem, civil war would result. In 1947, the British parliament passed the Indian Independence Act. The act ended British rule in India. It also provided for the partition, or division, of the Indian subcontinent into two separate and independent nations. One nation was Hindu-dominated India. The other nation was Pakistan, with a Muslim majority. Jawaharlal Nehru (juh WAH huhr lahl NAY roo) became prime minister of India, while Jinnah became governor general of Pakistan.

Partition led to an explosion of violence. Although India and Pakistan each promised religious toleration, distrust and fear were deeply rooted. Violence broke out between Muslims and Hindus. More than 500,000 people died in the fighting. In his short story "We Have Arrived in Amritsar," Indian writer Bhisham Sahni described a train ride during that time of violence:

> "The whole city was aflame. . . . A deserted railway platform faced us when the train stopped at the next station. . . . A water carrier . . . came over to the train . . . and began serving the passengers with water.
>
> 'Many people killed. Massacre, massacre,' he said. It seemed as though in the midst of all that death he alone had come out to perform a good deed."

To escape death, millions of Muslims fled from India to Pakistan. At the same time, millions of Hindus left Pakistan for India. An estimated 15 million people took part in this mass migration.

Sickened by the violence, Gandhi refused to celebrate India's independence on August 15, 1947. During the months that followed, he held prayer meetings across India. At these meetings, he recited verses from the *Bhagavad-Gita,* the Koran, and the Bible. (See Connections With Literature, page 805, the *Bhagavad-Gita*.)

In January 1948, Gandhi himself fell victim to the violence. A Hindu extremist, who believed that the Mahatma had betrayed his own people, shot Gandhi. "The light has gone out of our lives," mourned Nehru. "There is darkness everywhere."

MAP STUDY

The map of South Asia was redrawn after World War II ended. The former British-ruled lands in this region then became free and independent nations.

1. **Region** Identify the two countries of South Asia that gained their independence in 1947.
2. **Place** (a) Why was the new nation of Pakistan created in two separate areas of South Asia? (b) Identify these two areas.
3. **Making Global Connections** Many African nations, too, gained their freedom after World War II. What forces were at work that promoted independence in both regions?

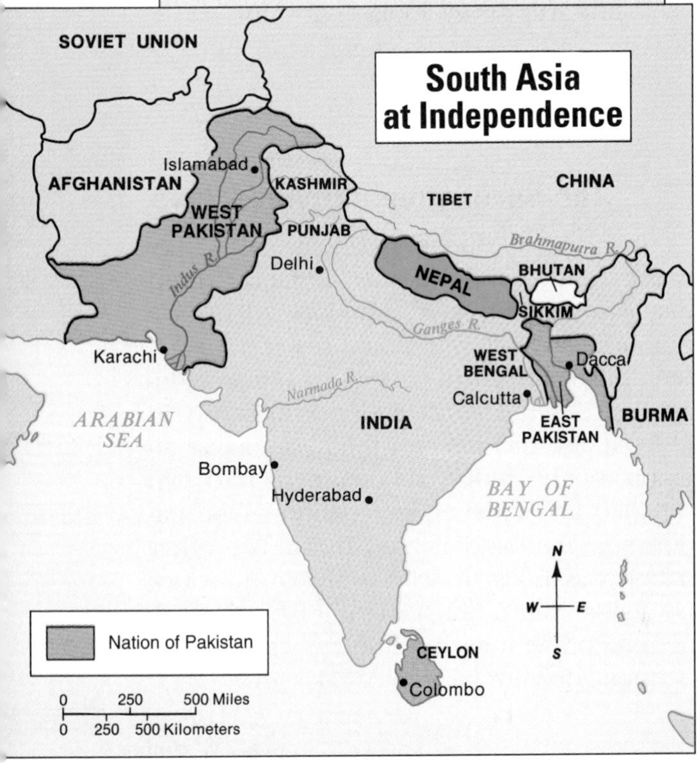

SECTION 1 REVIEW

1. **Locate:** Pakistan.
2. **Identify:** (a) Amritsar Massacre, (b) Mohandas Gandhi, (c) Jawaharlal Nehru.
3. **Define:** (a) satyagraha, (b) civil disobedience.
4. (a) How was the Salt March an example of civil disobedience? (b) What other actions against British rule did Gandhi support?
5. Why did Muhammad Ali Jinnah want a separate nation for Muslims?
6. Why were the British willing to leave India after World War II?
7. **Evaluating Information** Why do you think Gandhi was able to win the support of so many Indians?
8. **Writing Across Cultures** Write a paragraph describing how civil rights protesters or other activists in the United States in the 1960s used methods similar to those of Mohandas Gandhi.

2

POLITICAL CHALLENGES

FIND OUT

How is the government of India organized?

What forces have unified Indians and what forces have divided them?

What leaders have shaped India since independence?

Vocabulary parliamentary democracy, coalition, secular

"We, the people of India, having solemnly resolved to constitute India into a sovereign, democratic republic and to secure to all its citizens: justice . . . liberty . . . equality . . . do hereby adopt, enact and give to ourselves this constitution."

These lines from the Indian constitution sum up the goals of India's government. In the decades since independence, India—the world's largest democracy—has tried to fulfill its promises.

The Parliament Building The parliament of India meets in this building in New Delhi. Indians strongly support their democracy, and often 80 to 90 percent of all eligible voters take part in an election. Unlike many other nations that gained independence after World War II, India began as a democracy and remains a democracy. ***Political System*** Why do you think India is called "the world's largest democracy"?

India's Government

In 1949, Indian leaders gathered to write a constitution. Like the constitution of the United States, the Indian constitution created a federal system. It consists of a central government and the governments of 25 states and 7 territories.

The constitution divides power between the federal and state governments. India's central government, however, has more power than the United States federal government. The president of India appoints the state governors. In an emergency, the president also has the power to dissolve the government of a state.

Parliament. Under the constitution, India is a parliamentary democracy. This system is based on the British form of government. A president is head of state but has little power. The real power lies in the hands of the political party that wins the most seats in parliament. The leader of that party becomes the prime minister.

The Indian parliament has two houses. The upper house is called the Rajya Sabha, or Council of State. Its members are chosen by the state legislatures. The more powerful lower house is called the Lok Sabha, or House of the People. Voters elect members to the Lok Sabha directly.

Political parties. India has more than a dozen national political parties. Many more parties exist at the state level. Parties represent the interests of different caste, language, or religious groups.

The Indian constitution guaranteed every citizen over the age of 21 the right to vote. (In 1989, the voting age was dropped to 18.) Because many voters cannot read and write, parties use symbols on the ballots. A tree, ox, or cornstalk might stand for a particular party.

For many years, the Congress party dominated the national government. Indians voted for it as the party that had led them to independence. In recent years, other political parties have grown stronger. In the early 1990s, the Bharata Janata party (BJP) was gaining popular support. Its leaders stressed Hindu traditions.

If no party wins a majority in elections, a coalition government is formed. In a coalition, several parties join to rule. A coalition often has difficulty governing because the parties disagree on many issues.

Dividing and Unifying Forces

As in other developing nations, many forces have threatened to break India apart. One problem is India's large population, which has more than doubled since independence. Although the government has tried to meet the needs of its 870 million people, poverty and illiteracy are still widespread. These conditions contribute to unrest.

Caste. The caste system poses problems as India seeks to modernize. The government has sought to weaken its effects, especially in the area of economic opportunity. Yet, efforts to help lower castes and the poor often meet strong opposition from people higher in caste or in economic status.

The group that suffered most under the caste system were the untouchables, who were forced to live almost completely outside society. After independence, the Indian constitution declared untouchability illegal. It also outlawed discrimination against untouchables and set aside government jobs for people from this group. Despite the new laws, however, untouchables are still not fully accepted by other Indians. (See the feature at right.)

In 1990, the government tried to increase the number of government jobs reserved for lower-caste people. Youths in higher castes protested because they would no longer be assured of the best government jobs. Their violent protests forced the government to retreat from its policy.

Cultural diversity. Cultural diversity is another dividing force. Some ethnic and language groups have demanded their own states. Separatist violence has often resulted. For example, after independence, the Naga people in the northeast claimed the right to a separate state. They formed a small army and for many years waged bloody battles with government forces. Finally, in 1960, the government decided that Nagaland should become a separate state of India.

Sikh separatism. Another group that protested their treatment by the government were the Sikhs. As you have read, Sikhism is a religion that began in the early 1500s by blending elements of Islam and Hinduism. It teaches belief in one god and rejects the caste system. Sikhs developed a strong military tradition to defend their religion. Today, Sikhs make up about 2 percent of India's population.

In a country dominated by Hindus, Sikhs feel they do not receive a large enough share of government resources. Sikh separatists want to break away and form a separate country. In the northwestern state of Punjab, where Sikhs form a majority, protests became increasingly violent. In 1984, Sikh extremists in Amritsar occupied the Golden Temple, their holiest shrine, and refused to leave. The government ordered an attack on the temple, and many Sikhs were killed.

Hindu-Muslim clashes. Conflict between Hindus and Muslims also continue to plague

The Untouchables: Turning From the Past

TRADITION AND CHANGE

"The water hole of the untouchables is dry—we beg for water."

These words aroused no pity. Instead, upper-caste villagers reacted angrily:

"There is no water for you. This drought is your fault. The gods are angry at you for your past sins of selfishness, untruthfulness, and greed. Leave our well at once. Your presence will pollute what water we have."

For thousands of years, Indian society has subjected the untouchables to a life of denial and shame. Forced to live in separate areas outside of towns, untouchables held such jobs as street sweeping and leather working. They were barred from most schools and forbidden to enter Hindu temples.

Independence brought many changes to India. The Indian constitution made untouchability illegal. Under a quota system, the government set aside seats for untouchables in the parliament and state assemblies. Universities admitted some untouchables and some government jobs became open to them.

Although some untouchables have benefited from the quotas, discrimination remains. In rural areas, untouchables have trouble buying land. They are also frequent victims of violent crimes motivated by bias.

Untouchables have fought the caste system by becoming politically active. In the 1970s, they formed a political party to win better treatment.

Untouchable leader Henry Thiagaraj sees education as the key to change. He has set up the Education Facilitation Center in Madras. It teaches job and communications skills to untouchables, operates a home for abandoned children, and runs group camps to promote self-esteem. Mostly, Thiagaraj tries to help untouchables repair their wounded spirits. He says:

"We like to include people of all faiths in our work while expressing our deep commitment and love for our fellow untouchables who have been denied human fellowship and dignity."

1. How have untouchables tried to improve their lives?
2. **Analyzing Information** Why do you think discrimination against untouchables remains widespread?

India. Although many Muslims fled to Pakistan at the time of independence, about 100 million Muslims still live in India.

Hindus and Muslims clashed over a Muslim mosque in the city of Ayodhya (uh YOHD yuh). Hindus claimed that the site was the birthplace of the god Rama. They charged that in the past Muslim invaders tore down the temple that once stood there. The leader of the Bharata Janata party called on Hindus

A Family of Prime Ministers Nehru's daughter, Indira Gandhi, became prime minister of India in 1966. After she was assassinated, her son, Rajiv Gandhi, became leader of India's government. When Rajiv Gandhi, too, was shot during an election campaign in 1991, much of India mourned his death. ***Political System*** How can a family dynasty like the Gandhis arise in a democracy?

to destroy the mosque and build a Hindu temple in its place.

In 1990, Hindus attacked the mosque. Many shouted, "I will put a stone in that very place, even if I get a bullet in the chest." Hundreds of Hindus and Muslims were killed at Ayodhya. Political parties like the BJP have used the conflict to win popular support.

Unifying forces. Despite many threats to unity, India has survived. Millions of Indians share a common faith. Hindu traditions create important ties for the majority of Indians.

Modern communications and strong leaders have also helped to unite the country. Faced with demands from groups that want to break away, the government has tried to negotiate compromises. Most Indians are also committed to democratic traditions.

India's Leaders

Jawaharlal Nehru led India for 17 years after independence. Nehru wanted to make India a modern industrial nation. He had a vision of a casteless, secular India. A secular country is one that has no official religion.

Nehru carried India through many crises. He calmed outbreaks of regional violence in the north. His government helped resettle millions of Hindu refugees from Pakistan. Nehru also set up programs for schools and economic development.

Nehru's successors. Nehru died in 1964, and in 1966, his daughter, Indira Gandhi, became prime minister. Although she continued policies aimed at modernization, economic problems and charges of corruption weakened her government. In 1975, Gandhi declared a state of emergency. She jailed political opponents and limited freedom of the press.

In time, Gandhi restored democratic rule, but unrest among ethnic and religious groups continued. In 1984, the prime minister ordered government troops to storm the Golden Temple, which was being held by a militant group of armed Sikhs, as you have read earlier in this chapter. Later that year, two of Gandhi's Sikh bodyguards shot and killed her. Anti-Sikh rioting shook the country after her death.

Rajiv Gandhi, Indira's son, was elected to replace his mother. Violence, however, also took his life. In 1991, he was murdered while campaigning for reelection. The assassins were linked to Tamil guerrillas from neighboring Sri Lanka. You will read more about the Tamils in Sri Lanka later in this chapter.

Looking ahead. "What will happen to our country?" one Indian commented at the funeral of Rajiv Gandhi. Gandhi's death marked the end of a political dynasty. As India moved

Struggles Within India Violence between the Sikhs and the government in the Punjab has troubled India's political life. In this cartoon, an angry Indira Gandhi is shown struggling against political terrorism. Gandhi lost this struggle, and after her death, moderate Sikhs themselves became victims of attacks. ***Diversity*** Why are many Sikhs dissatisfied with the Indian government?

into the 1990s, it looked for new leaders to deal with the challenges posed by its diverse population.

SECTION 2 REVIEW

1. **Identify:** (a) Bharata Janata party, (b) Sikh, (c) Indira Gandhi, (d) Rajiv Gandhi.
2. **Define:** (a) parliamentary democracy, (b) coalition, (c) secular.
3. Describe the federal organization of the Indian government.
4. How has religion created both divisions and bonds among Indians?
5. What goals did Nehru and his successors have for India?
6. **Drawing Conclusions** Why do you think the BJP has gained popularity in recent years?
7. **Writing Across Cultures** Imagine that you are one of the delegates who framed the Indian constitution. Write a letter to an American friend comparing your government with the government of the United States.

3 ECONOMIC DEVELOPMENT

FIND OUT

What economic goals did Nehru set for India?

What progress has Indian industry made?

How has India tried to increase farm output?

Vocabulary tenant farmer, land reform

Operation Flood has lived up to its name. The flood does not refer to monsoon rains or overflowing rivers. Instead, it refers to a successful program to produce milk. Twenty years ago, India needed to import milk powder and other dairy goods. Today, it is the third-largest milk producer in the world.

Increasing food production is vital to India's economy. In the years since independence, the government has taken a major role in developing agriculture and industry.

MAP STUDY

One of the Indian government's chief goals has been to develop modern industry and end dependence on foreign imports. India has important natural resources and a skilled labor force that have helped it become more industrialized.

1. **Location** (a) What industries are located near Ahmadabad? (b) Where are most iron and steel plants located?
2. **Interaction** According to the map, what natural resources contribute to the industrialization of India?
3. **Solving Problems** How did the Indian government try to strengthen the nation's economy?

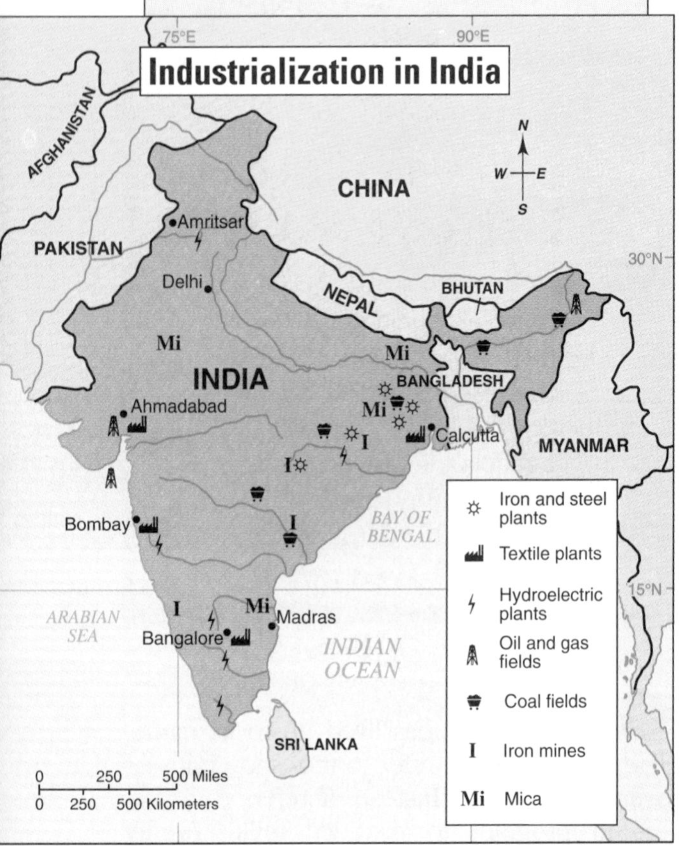

Economic Goals

In 1947, India's economy was poor and undeveloped. Although India exported raw materials, it had to import machinery and other finished goods from industrial countries. India's new leaders were determined to free their country from economic dependence.

Nehru wanted to make the nation self-sufficient. India must produce what it needs, he said, and stop importing goods. To achieve his goals, Nehru adopted many socialist principles. His government carefully regulated the economy and issued a series of five-year plans to set economic goals. Nehru also limited foreign investment to prevent foreigners from controlling Indian businesses.

Like many developing nations, India set up a mixed economy. The government took control of some industries such as steel, mining, transportation, and energy. At the same time, it allowed private ownership of smaller businesses. These businesses produced consumer goods such as bicycles, sewing machines, and hand tools.

Industrial Growth

To lessen dependence on imports, India needed factories to produce basic materials such as steel and plastics, as well as finished goods such as tractors and trucks. The government encouraged Indians to save money that could then be invested in industry. It also used income from cash crops and taxes to build industry.

As you read in Chapter 7, India has iron, coal, and other mineral resources. It used these resources to build steel factories and huge hydroelectric plants. Nehru called these plants "India's new temples."

During the early years of independence, industry made impressive gains. The output of iron ore tripled. Coal and steel production rose, and India doubled its energy output. India also set up new industries in engineering, chemicals, and textile manufacturing. By the 1960s, India ranked as the world's seventh most industrialized nation.

In the 1970s, industrial growth slowed. Because India has few oil resources, it must import oil. As a result, the worldwide rise in oil prices hurt the Indian economy. In addition, many government-run businesses were inefficient. With foreign investment limited, India also had trouble building new industries.

In the 1980s, Rajiv Gandhi called for economic reforms. He wanted to reduce government regulation and encourage private enterprise. India entered into joint projects with foreign companies. With help from Japan, India is now making and exporting cars. In the 1990s, the government took more active steps to encourage investment in industry by foreigners and by Indians living abroad. Indians welcomed the reforms, but political unrest still disrupted the economy.

Progress in Agriculture

Today, as in the past, farming is the heart of the Indian economy. About three quarters of India's people live in rural areas. Most are subsistence farmers, struggling to feed their families. At independence, India could not feed its population. Poor soil and inefficient farming methods kept farm output low. At the same time, droughts and other disasters often led to famine.

Indian leaders knew that farm output must increase in order for the nation's economy to grow. Farmers need to sell their produce in order to buy manufactured goods. To improve farming, the government invested heavily in agriculture.

Irrigation. The government set up new irrigation systems. As you read in Chapter 7, monsoons do not always arrive on time. In many areas, there is almost no rain for six to eight months of the year. By building dams and digging canals and wells, the government tries to ensure a steady water supply throughout the year.

The new programs have had a major effect. They have eased flooding caused by the monsoons. They have also allowed farmers to plant a second, dry-season crop. Much arable

Sorting Peppers This colorful harvest of red chili peppers covers a field in northwestern India. Some of this crop is consumed in India, where people use many spices in their cooking. However, a large portion of the crop is exported. These women sorting peppers earn about 12 cents a day. ***Interdependence*** Why does a largely agricultural nation like India export peppers and other cash crops?

Valley Farms in India Surrounded by the foothills of the Western Ghat Mountains, this valley in southern India has a mild climate well suited for growing vegetables. Potatoes, which flourish at high altitudes, are one of India's major cash crops. ***Geography*** Why would this mountainous area be more suited for farming than areas along India's northern borders?

land, however, still does not receive enough water. In the early 1990s, progress slowed because of a general decline in India's economy. Large projects such as dams are costly. Also, environmentalists have protested some plans to build dams.

Land reform. Another problem the government tackled was land distribution. While a few landowners had large farms, millions of Indians had only tiny plots or owned no land at all. Landless peasants worked as tenant farmers, people who rent land from large landowners and pay the owner a portion of their crops.

The government began a program of land reform, or redistributing land. State governments passed laws to limit the size of farms. They sold surplus land from large landowners to tenant farmers. Other laws kept landowners from collecting more than one fourth of a tenant's crop as rent.

Land reform had limited success. Because large landowners had political power, they blocked efforts to enforce the laws. Also, few tenant farmers had the money to buy surplus land.

Green Revolution. New technology helped improve India's farm output. Scientists from many countries developed new types of wheat and rice seeds that resulted in much larger harvests. These "miracle" crops were part of a technological advance in agriculture known as the Green Revolution.

The Green Revolution has been only partly successful, however. It has helped farmers who grow wheat and rice, but few others. The new seeds need fertilizers and irrigation, which many farmers cannot afford. In many areas of India, people continue to survive on meager harvests. Still, by the 1990s India not only produced enough food for its population, it exported some grain.

SECTION 3 REVIEW

1. **Identify:** Green Revolution.
2. **Define:** (a) tenant farmer, (b) land reform.
3. What was the chief goal of Nehru's economic planning?
4. How did natural resources help India to industrialize?
5. (a) Describe three programs aimed at helping farmers. (b) Why has each had limited success?
6. **Analyzing Ideas** What do you think Nehru meant when he called factories and power plants "India's new temples"?
7. **Writing Across Cultures** Write a letter to an Indian official explaining why you think the Indian government should encourage Americans to invest in India.

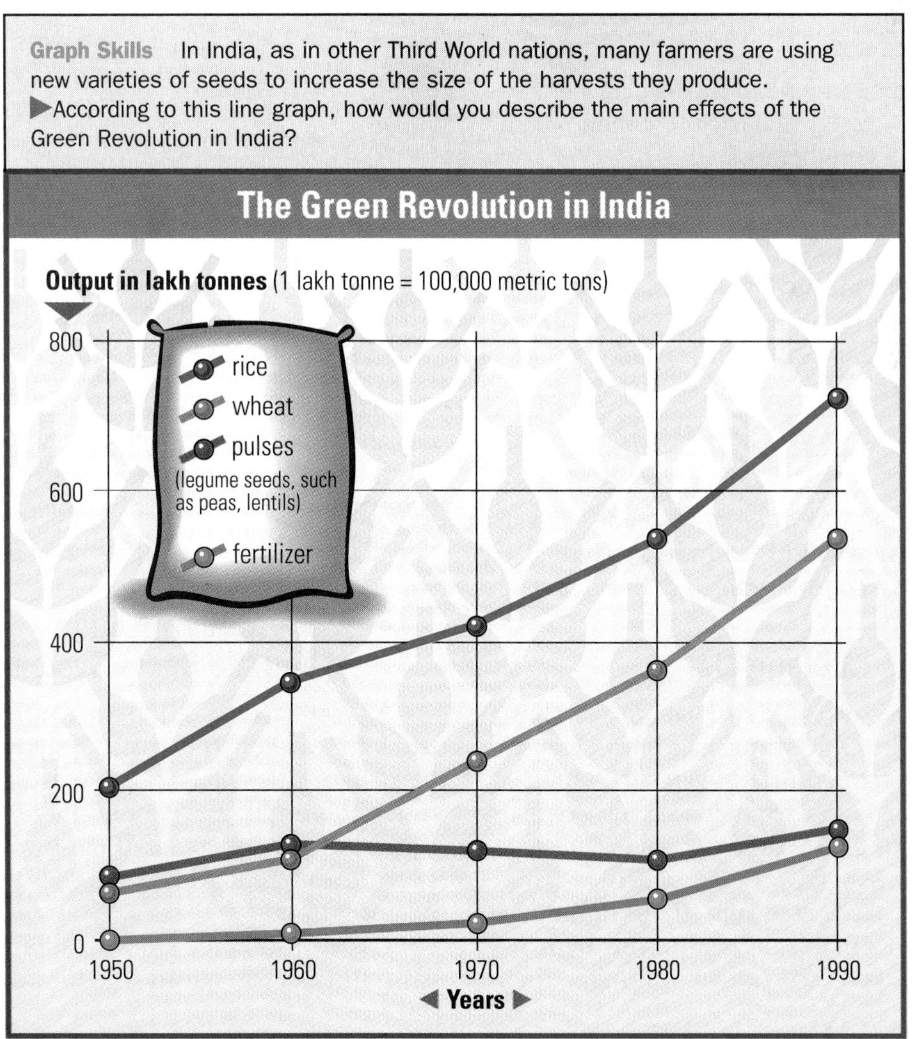

Graph Skills In India, as in other Third World nations, many farmers are using new varieties of seeds to increase the size of the harvests they produce. ▶According to this line graph, how would you describe the main effects of the Green Revolution in India?

Source: *India 1990 Handbook*

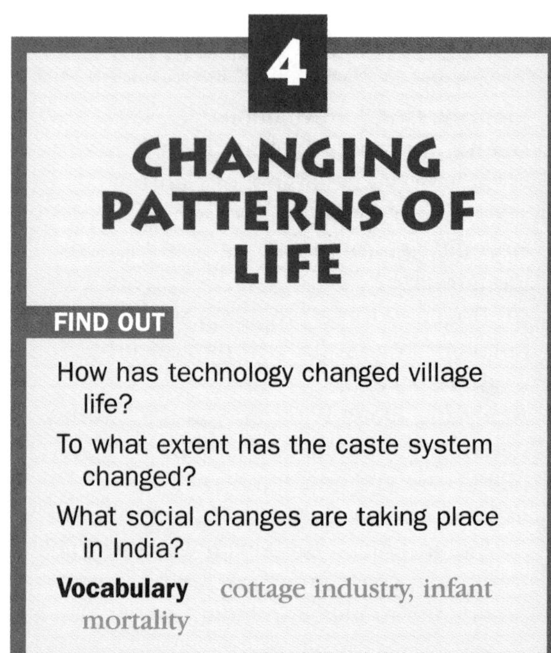

4 CHANGING PATTERNS OF LIFE

FIND OUT

How has technology changed village life?

To what extent has the caste system changed?

What social changes are taking place in India?

Vocabulary cottage industry, infant mortality

Since winning independence, villagers in India have witnessed remarkable changes. Prafulla Mohanti commented:

> "My village is changing. A straight road was built in the mid-1960s to carry iron ore from the mines to the port of Paradip, forty miles away. . . . Nylon, stainless steel, plastic, fizzy drinks have reached the village. Electricity has come too . . . there is a cinema and video hall."

As Mohanti's words show, technology is opening up new worlds to India's 500 million villagers. Even so, traditions remain strong.

Village Life

In some ways, many Indian villages have changed little. Only about half have electricity, and few have running water. Clothing is still traditional, and women wearing colorful saris walk along dirt paths carrying water jugs on their heads.

Villages have also kept their traditional economies. Farmers still plant crops by hand and guide ox-drawn plows through their fields. People produce handmade goods such as clothing, ivory carvings, and brass jugs in cottage industries, or small businesses run from the home.

Technology and change. Still, life is changing rapidly. As you have read, the Green Revolution has improved harvests in some areas. A growing number of villages have electricity, clinics, schools, and telephones. Some villagers buy factory-made goods, and a few can afford tractors.

Roads, buses, movies, and television have put village people in touch with a wider world. Today, radar dishes are sprouting up across India. At night, groups of villagers gather around a single television set to watch the news. Recently, tens of millions of Indians thrilled to a dramatic reenactment of the *Ramayana*, the great religious epic of Hinduism.

As travel becomes easier, more people move from small villages to towns and cities. As elsewhere around the world, they hope to make a better living in urban areas. You will read more about India's rapidly growing cities in the next chapter.

Improved health care. The government has taken steps to improve health care. It encourages villagers to dig deep wells that provide cleaner water. In addition, health clinics bring better medical care to rural areas. The result has been a decline in infant mortality, the rate at which babies die. Because of traditional attitudes in the villages, however, boys often continue to receive better food and care than girls. In the cities, sons and daughters are generally treated equally.

Modernization and the Caste System

As you have read, India's government has tried to weaken the caste system. Yet laws have had little effect on deeply rooted attitudes and traditions. People still tend to associate with members of their own caste. In villages, different castes still live in separate neighborhoods.

Caste also affects occupations. Higher-caste Indians can afford to educate their children. Through family connections, their children can get good jobs. As a result, higher-caste Indians dominate professions such as law, engineering, and medicine. (See Connections With Literature, page 805, "The Artist.")

Some changes have occurred, however. For example, people from different castes mix more freely. Former untouchables might be allowed to draw water from the village well and worship at the village temple. Their children attend public schools, although they often have to sit in a separate part of the classroom.

Urbanization also weakens caste distinctions. City-dwellers do not always know the backgrounds of their neighbors. As a result, lower-caste Indians are freer to move up in society. In offices and factories, caste rules are harder to maintain. Many educated, westernized Indians reject caste differences. Some even accept marriages between people of different castes.

Improving Education

When India became independent, only about 10 percent of the people could read and write. Fewer than half of all children attended school. Aware that an educated population is necessary to a modern industrial nation, India's leaders worked to improve education. In each state, governments built schools and hired teachers. Today, 80 percent of elementary-age children get some schooling, and 35 percent of Indians can read and write.

Schooling is free and required for all children up to 14 years of age. In practice, however, social attitudes affect who gets an education. More boys attend school than girls. As a result, more men than women are literate. At the same time, many poor families need their children to work in the fields. Literacy, therefore, is much lower among untouchables and lower castes.

Camel Cart Library Villages in many parts of India lack books and libraries. This traveling library offers magazines and books to villagers living in the desert area near Jaipur in northern India. People pay three rupees (about 12 cents) for the books they borrow each month.
Environment How has this library adapted its services to meet villagers' needs?

Higher-caste students are the most likely to continue their education. Yet many students who get college degrees cannot find jobs. Those who come from higher castes refuse to work in jobs requiring manual labor. These restless youths pose a problem for the government. As you have read, they have protested government efforts to open more jobs to the lowest castes. In the Punjab, joblessness among young Sikhs also has fueled separatist violence.

Family Life

Marriage customs are changing in India. Most people today marry at a later age than in the past. Parents still arrange about 95 percent of all marriages, however. Among upper-class city-dwellers, the young couple will often meet before the wedding. They may even reject their parents' choice. If they accept the arrangement, the couple may meet once or twice under the supervision of an adult. (See the Skill Lesson on page 239 for a description of a modern courtship, from R. K. Narayan's novel *The World of Nagaraj*.)

Family structures are also changing. Although most Indians still consider the joint, patriarchal family the ideal, more city-dwellers are living in nuclear families. Educated young couples set up their own homes rather than move in with the husband's family.

The role of women. Women are still subordinate to men, but they have gained some legal rights since independence. They have the right to vote, to own property, and to get a divorce. Widows can also remarry.

A few women have achieved high positions in government. Women hold about 10 percent of the seats in the parliament. Vijaya Pandit, Nehru's sister, was the first woman president of the UN General Assembly. His daughter, Indira Gandhi, served as India's prime minister.

In the villages, most women still accept traditional ideas that require them to be modest and silent. A few women, however, have become village leaders. One of these is a Brahman widow named Saroj.

The "Village Indira"

"Of course, I am the cleverest woman in the village," Saroj notes. At age 60, she occupies an unusual place in her village in northern India. She takes an active role in political and economic affairs.

Saroj's early life followed traditional patterns. Married at the age of nine, she faced hard times. She gave birth to 14 children. "My first children did not live long," she recalled. "Later on seven more were born. And they are alive up to now. So again I became happy."

Although she and her husband were Brahmans, they were poor. However, they worked hard and prospered. At night, Saroj secretly helped her husband build a new brick home. As a Brahman woman, she was not supposed to work outside the home. "Brahman women can do any work inside the house," she explained, "whether the work of the spinning wheel or weaving."

When her husband died, Saroj still had to educate her two youngest children. "My older son began to live out of the joint family," she explained. He did not want to have to pay for the weddings of his younger brother and sister.

Traditional views. As a Brahman, Saroj accepts Hindu beliefs about her family's superiority. "If Brahmans act properly according to their fate . . . if they do good work, they are devata [gods]," she declares.

Saroj also holds traditional views on the status of women. She plainly states, "The woman is inferior. . . . She can never leave the customs." Saroj links the tradition of purdah to family honor:

> "Women who used to live inside the house, in purdah, nowadays those very women are wandering outside on the road and in the fields to collect fuel or cut grass. . . . Does honor lie in these activities?"

Modern actions. Despite her traditional views, Saroj's actions reflect modern goals.

A Woman Villager Speaks Out Saroj makes use of modern communications in this interview with a reporter. Her role in politics and village affairs sets her apart from most Indian women. However, her simple clothing and her hands held in a traditional Hindu greeting show that in many ways Saroj is like them. ***Culture*** Why does a woman like Saroj win respect among her people?

She made sure that her four daughters completed school. When the government set up programs to educate rural women, Saroj was chosen to head the group in her village. She joined the Congress party and organized villagers to attend political rallies in Delhi. There she met leaders such as Indira Gandhi and Rajiv Gandhi.

Other villagers called her the "village Indira." The name suggested that she had no modesty and no honor. Saroj shook off the criticism. "People call me Indira. . . . It doesn't affect me. No defect comes to me if they call me Indira." ■

SECTION 4 REVIEW

1. **Define:** (a) cottage industry, (b) infant mortality.
2. Describe three changes that are affecting village life in India.
3. (a) Why has India emphasized education? (b) How has education created problems for the government?
4. How is modernization affecting Indian families?
5. **Applying Information** (a) How do traditional views place limits on Indian women? (b) Why might an older, widowed Brahman like Saroj have more freedom than other women in an Indian village?
6. **Writing Across Cultures** Write a paragraph comparing the efforts to improve opportunities for lower castes in India with efforts to provide equal opportunities for people in the United States.

5 OTHER NATIONS OF SOUTH ASIA

FIND OUT

How were Pakistan and Bangladesh created?

What economic progress has Pakistan made?

Why does geography pose problems for Bangladesh?

How has ethnic diversity affected Sri Lanka?

On independence day in 1947, Muhammad Ali Jinnah, the founder of Pakistan, addressed the people:

> "If we want to make this great state of Pakistan happy and prosperous, we should wholly and solely concen-

trate on the well-being of the people, and especially of the masses and the poor. ”

Like other developing nations, Pakistan has had a mixed record in achieving its goals of modernization. Pakistan is one of eight nations of South Asia. In this section you will read about Pakistan. You will also read about several other South Asian nations, including Bangladesh, Sri Lanka, Nepal, and Bhutan.

Benazir Bhutto of Pakistan Benazir Bhutto became the first woman to head a modern Muslim state when she was elected prime minister in 1988. Although the military forced her from office two years later, Bhutto was elected again in 1993. Her father, Zulfikar Ali Bhutto, had also been prime minister. ***Political System*** In what ways was Benazir Bhutto's career like Indira Gandhi's?

Pakistan Since Independence

At independence, British India was divided into India and Pakistan. In 1947, Pakistan was made up of two regions: West Pakistan and East Pakistan. The two areas were separated by 1,000 miles (1,610 km) of Indian territory. (See the map on page 204.)

Conflict and division. West Pakistan and East Pakistan had large Muslim populations. Otherwise, they had little in common. They had different geography, languages, and cultural traditions. West Pakistan bordered the Middle East and was subject to droughts. East Pakistan bordered Southeast Asia, and its low-lying delta plain suffered from frequent floods.

West Pakistan dominated the government. It used government funds and foreign aid to promote industry in the west. Pakistanis in the east, who received much less funding, resented the inequality. In 1970, a cyclone caused enormous damage to East Pakistan. When the government was slow to send aid, the people of East Pakistan were furious.

That year, East Pakistanis won a majority of seats in parliament, but the government refused to accept the election results. A civil war broke out. With the help of Indian troops, East Pakistan won. In 1971, it became the independent nation of Bangladesh. (See page 219.)

Economic development. After the civil war, Pakistan pushed ahead with plans to modernize. Because most Pakistanis live in rural areas, the government devoted much of the nation's resources to developing agriculture. It invested heavily in irrigation and enforced land reform programs. Aided by the Green Revolution, these efforts increased Pakistan's farm output.

The government tried to reduce its dependence on foreign aid by developing local industries. It built chemical, auto, and steel factories. As farmers increased cotton production, Pakistan also developed a booming textile industry.

Forces for change. Although it has enjoyed some successes, Pakistan today faces many economic and political challenges. Like other developing nations, its population and cities are growing rapidly. Illiteracy is high, and many people live in poverty.

Pakistan has experienced long periods of military rule. Even when elections are held, the government has sometimes blocked candidates from running for office.

Like other Muslim countries, Pakistan has felt the effects of Islamic fundamentalism. The leaders of this movement have called for strict obedience to the Koran as a way of improving people's lives. In response to the movement, Pakistan amended its constitution in 1991. The amendment made the Koran the supreme law of the land. Muslims disagree strongly about how to implement Koranic law, however. As a result, the amendment remains largely unused. (You will read more about Islamic fundamentalism in Chapter 27.)

Bangladesh

As you read in Chapter 7, Bangladesh is a densely populated country. More than 120 million people live in an area about the size of Wisconsin. The land is fertile and has abundant water, but it is also subject to terrible flooding.

Natural disasters and a huge population have limited progress in Bangladesh. The people farm every bit of land. They grow food crops such as rice and wheat, as well as cash crops such as jute and tea. The Green Revolution has helped to increase output. Despite larger harvests, however, the population keeps growing at a faster rate than the food supply. As a result, millions of people are hungry each day.

The government faces many obstacles in its struggle to improve conditions. World prices for cash crops have declined. As a result, Bangladesh has little money for development. It has tried to diversify its economy, setting up small industries. It has also called on neighboring India to build flood control projects that would reduce the yearly monsoon flooding.

To add to its problems, Bangladesh has few roads or bridges. Most travel is by boat along its many waterways. Without massive aid, Bangladesh cannot improve its communications and transportation systems.

Conflict in Sri Lanka

Like other South Asian nations, the island nation of Ceylon won independence from Britain after World War II. In 1972, Ceylon changed its name to Sri Lanka.

Since independence, Sri Lanka has developed its economy based on exporting crops such as tea, rubber, and coconuts. It has also built local industries. A literacy rate of more than 75 percent offered hope for a bright future.

Ethnic tensions. Ethnic and religious divisions brought serious problems, however. About 70 percent of Sri Lankans speak Sinhalese and practice Buddhism. Their ancestors migrated to the island long ago from northern India. Another 18 percent of the people came from southern India more recently. They speak Tamil and practice Hinduism.

Tamil-Sinhalese tensions grew in the 1970s. The Tamil minority claimed that the Sinhalese majority discriminated against them. Tamils demanded equal rights to education, jobs, and land ownership. When the government failed to make changes, angry Tamils called for a separate, independent state. Then they launched a guerrilla war that disrupted the entire country.

Indian involvement. In the early years of the conflict, India supported the Tamil separatists. Later, however, Indian prime minister Rajiv Gandhi changed course. He sent Indian troops to help Sri Lanka fight the Tamil minority. The Tamil guerrillas responded by assassinating Gandhi in 1991. Despite efforts at a negotiated settlement, the fighting in Sri Lanka continues. Tens of thousands have died in the decade-old civil war.

In the Mountains of Nepal This Nepalese woman, wearing American-style sneakers, carries a heavy load as she trudges along a mountain pass. Her people, the Sherpas, are skilled mountaineers. Many of them make a living by guiding climbers through the challenging terrain of their country. ***Diversity*** How does the clothing of this Sherpa show a blending of two cultures?

Tamil extremists felt betrayed by India. They were probably responsible for the assassination of Rajiv Gandhi in 1991. Since then, new outbreaks of violence have clouded hopes for peace in Sri Lanka.

Small Nations of the Subcontinent

Two other nations occupy the northeastern corner of the subcontinent. Bhutan and Nepal are landlocked countries in the Himalayas. Bhutan is a monarchy and most of its people are Buddhist.

Most people in Nepal are Hindu. Until recently, they were ruled by a king who held almost absolute power. Under pressure for reform, he permitted elections in 1991, moving Nepal toward democracy.

Most people in both Nepal and Bhutan are farmers. The mountainous geography of these nations, however, limits where people can farm. In Nepal, the growing population is causing serious deforestation. People clear land for farming and burn wood for fuel. Without tree roots to hold the soil in place, erosion occurs. Farmers then must move on to clear new land.

SECTION 5 REVIEW

1. **Locate:** (a) Bangladesh, (b) Sri Lanka, (c) Bhutan, (d) Nepal.
2. Why did Bangladesh break away from Pakistan?
3. How did Pakistan develop its economy after independence?
4. What effect has geography had on life in Bangladesh?
5. How have Tamil-Sinhalese tensions led to violence in Sri Lanka?
6. **Understanding Causes and Effects** How did the partition of British India create problems that led to unrest in Pakistan?
7. **Writing Across Cultures** Imagine that you are a Peace Corps volunteer in one of the nations you read about in this section. List three ways in which you might help people in your new home.

Chapter 9 Review

Understanding Vocabulary

Match each term at left with the correct definition at right.

1. civil disobedience	**a.** redistribution of land
2. boycott	**b.** refusal to obey unjust laws
3. coalition	**c.** small business run from the home
4. land reform	**d.** joining of several parties
5. cottage industry	**e.** to stop buying

Reviewing the Main Ideas

1. How did the Amritsar Massacre affect the movement for Indian independence?
2. Describe three ideas behind Gandhi's method of satyagraha.
3. Why does India sometimes have a coalition government?
4. How is India's economy "mixed"?
5. What factors have weakened the caste system in India?
6. (a) What challenges do farmers in Bangladesh face? (b) In Nepal?

Reviewing Chapter Themes

1. Nationalism was a major force in the struggle of India and Pakistan for independence. Explain the role of nationalism and one other factor in the independence movements.
2. Ethnic and cultural diversity have led to conflict in many parts of South Asia. Describe the causes and effects of two of the following: (a) conflict between Hindus and Muslims at the time of independence, (b) Sikh separatism in India, (c) Tamil-Sinhalese tensions in Sri Lanka.
3. Modernization involves building a stable government and producing a high level of goods and services. Describe how two nations of South Asia have tried to modernize.
4. Despite many changes, traditional forces remain strong in Indian life. Describe how both tradition and change have affected two of the following: (a) the caste system, (b) family life, (c) the status of women.

Thinking Critically

1. **Applying Information** In a 1937 speech, Indian author Rabindranath Tagore wrote that Gandhi "has never, for the sake of immediate results, advised or approved any departure from the standard of universal morality." How does this statement apply to Gandhi's methods for protesting British rule?
2. **Making Global Connections** (a) Why do you think Indians used the British system of government as a model in 1950? (b) How did Americans in 1789 use British traditions in designing their government?
3. **Comparing** Nehru wanted India to become a secular nation. How does this attitude toward religion differ from the attitude of Pakistan's leaders?

Applying Your Skills

1. **Using Your Vocabulary** Use the glossary on pages 794–803 to review the meanings of the following terms: *republic, privatization, socialism*. Use each term in a separate sentence about India.
2. **Analyzing a Quotation** Indira Gandhi once said, "It is absolutely necessary that agricultural productivity is improved to a point where . . . we have a reasonable margin of safety. We simply cannot afford another gamble with the rains." (a) What did Gandhi mean by a "reasonable margin of safety"? (b) How could low agricultural productivity hurt India's drive to modernize?

Chapter 10

SOUTH ASIA IN THE WORLD TODAY

Bombay, India India is the world's most populous democracy and an important leader among developing nations. Like other developing nations, India is building a modern society on an ancient culture. Regal Circle, in the center of Bombay, reflects India's accomplishments and its forward-looking plans. ***Choice*** What choices must Indians make as their nation modernizes?

CHAPTER OUTLINE

1 Regional and Global Issues

2 Looking to the Future

3 Art and Literature

When the British still ruled India, Jawaharlal Nehru served several prison terms for civil disobedience. Once, a British friend visited him in jail. She noticed the hornets that buzzed about his cell.

"Don't they bother you?" she asked the Indian leader.

With a slight smile, Nehru answered:

> "At first they bothered me a great deal. The window seemed alive with them. I kept killing them, but always new ones flew in to take the place of the slaughtered. After days of this warfare, I decided to try nonviolence. I pronounced a cease-fire, vowing to kill no more and telling them to keep to their part of the cell—the window. It worked. I've had no further trouble."

Although Nehru was joking, he took nonviolence seriously. An admirer of Gandhi, Nehru shared both his principles and his goal of independence. Indians honored Nehru with the title "Pandit," meaning "Teacher."

Unlike Gandhi, Nehru wanted India to take a major role in world affairs. He went on to become India's first prime minister. In that role, he directed the new nation's foreign policy.

CHAPTER PERSPECTIVE

Under Nehru, India became a modern industrial state and a leader among developing nations. While India and other nations of South Asia have worked to meet pressing domestic needs, they have also faced a wide variety of regional and global challenges.

As you read, look for these chapter themes:

- Geographic and political concerns helped shape the foreign policies of India and Pakistan.
- Rapid population growth has put severe strains on South Asian nations.
- The peoples of South Asia draw strength from their rich cultural heritage, which blends Hindu, Buddhist, and Islamic traditions.

Literature Connections

In this chapter, you will encounter passages from the following works.

"A Fight for Truth Has Begun," Ghahshyam "Shilani"

Ramayana, Hindu epic

"Thou art the ruler of the minds of all people," Rabindranath Tagore

For other literature suggestions, see Connections With Literature, pages 804–808.

1 REGIONAL AND GLOBAL ISSUES

FIND OUT

What issues have affected relations between India and Pakistan?

How did India take a leading role in world affairs?

How have local and regional concerns shaped Pakistan's foreign policy?

Vocabulary plebiscite, buffer state

"Love your neighbor, but do not throw down the dividing wall," advises an Indian proverb. It suggests combining respect for others with caution. This same attitude has guided South Asian nations in their dealings with one another and with the world.

India and the Subcontinent

In size and strength, India dominates the subcontinent. As a result, its neighbors watch its actions with some concern. Since 1947, relations between India and Pakistan have remained tense. The terrible violence following partition left a legacy of bitterness and distrust. Partition also created territorial disputes that remain unresolved.

Conflict over Kashmir. Kashmir, a region of India, is a source of conflict between the two nations. Kashmir is located in the mountains that border India, Pakistan, and China. The Indus River and many of its tributaries flow through the region. As a result, the nation that controls Kashmir controls the source of irrigation water.

In 1947, the rulers of India's many princely states had to decide whether to become part of India or part of Pakistan. Kashmir had never been under British control. It was ruled by a Hindu prince, but most of the people were Muslim. At first, the ruler tried to

Rivalry Over Kashmir Kashmir has been a source of conflict between India and Pakistan since 1947. Yet this peaceful scene of people tending their boats on Dal Lake in Kashmir gives little hint of the bitter rivalry over this beautiful land. ***Human Rights*** In what ways has the conflict over Kashmir affected the rights of the people of that land?

remain independent of both nations. When his Muslim subjects rebelled, however, he asked India for help. At the same time, Pakistan sent troops into Kashmir to support the Muslim rebels.

In 1949, the United Nations arranged a cease-fire and divided Kashmir. About one third went to Pakistan. The rest eventually became part of India. The solution satisfied no one, so clashes continued. Heavy fighting broke out in Kashmir between Indian and Pakistani forces in 1965, and again during the Pakistani civil war of 1971.

In the late 1980s, Muslim groups in Indian Kashmir began to demand independence. As new violence broke out, the Indian government took strong action against separatists. In response, Pakistan charged India with violating human rights. India accused Pakistan of sending arms to the rebels.

Pakistan wants a plebiscite, or popular vote, to let the people of Kashmir decide their future. It feels sure that Muslims in Kashmir would vote to join Islamic Pakistan. India has opposed the vote. It is unwilling to give up a territory in which it has invested heavily. Indian leaders also fear that the loss of Kashmir would encourage separatist groups in other parts of India.

Nuclear weapons. Nuclear weapons are also a source of tension between India and Pakistan. In 1974, India tested a nuclear device. Pakistan also entered the race for nuclear technology. Both nations deny that they have nuclear weapons. Yet both have refused to sign the Nuclear Non-Proliferation Treaty. In that 1968 treaty, more than 40 nations agreed to limit the spread of nuclear weapons.

Relations with Bangladesh. As you have read, India sent troops to help the people of East Pakistan win independence. Pakistan deeply resented this intervention by India, which led to the creation of Bangladesh.

Despite India's support, relations between India and Bangladesh are sometimes strained. Economics is at the root of some problems. Floods in Bangladesh contribute to poverty there. Bangladesh wants India to build more flood control projects on the Ganges and Brahmaputra rivers to reduce flooding in the delta where Bangladesh is located. (See the map on page 164.) When Bangladeshi refugees have streamed into India to escape poverty, India has built fences to close off its border.

India and the World

Although India has worked to develop nuclear weapons, its leaders seek peaceful solutions to world problems. India gained independence just as the Cold War was beginning.

As you read in Chapter 2, the United States and the Soviet Union headed rival blocs, or groups of nations. The Cold War influenced India's foreign policy.

Nonalignment. In 1947, Prime Minister Nehru announced a policy of nonalignment. He felt that India could help ease international tensions by following an independent course. Under Nehru, India helped form a bloc of nonaligned developing nations. In that role, India arranged prisoner-of-war exchanges after the Korean War. India has also played an active part in the UN. Indian troops have served with UN peacekeeping missions in trouble spots around the world.

Relations with the superpowers. While India rejected any military alliance with either the United States or the Soviet Union, it welcomed economic aid from both superpowers. Because the United States provided much aid to Pakistan, India looked on the United States with some distrust. As a result, India and the Soviet Union developed close ties.

Early in the Cold War, American leaders tended to view India and other nonaligned nations as pro-communist. Nehru's criticisms of United States policies toward China and other nations seemed to support this view. Gradually, however, the United States realized that nonaligned nations wanted to stay out of superpower conflicts.

Relations with China. After winning independence, India sought friendly relations with its powerful neighbor, China. In the 1950s, however, Chinese forces occupied Tibet, a nation in the Himalayas to the north of India. The occupation of Tibet strained relations between India and China.

In 1962, a border dispute between China and India flared into war. Chinese troops invaded India, forcing the Indian army to retreat. India asked for and received aid from the United States. Although peace was quickly restored, India has continued to keep a close watch on its northern border. In the mid-1970s, fear of Chinese aggression led India to take control of the tiny Himalayan kingdom of Sikkim.

Pakistan and the World

Unlike India, Pakistan took a strong anti-communist stand during the Cold War. It saw the nearby Soviet Union as a possible threat to its independence. As a result, Pakistan joined military alliances set up by the United

Chinese Rule in Tibet After Chinese troops seized Tibet, the people rose in rebellion. When Chinese forces crushed this uprising, the spiritual leader of Tibet, the Dalai Lama, fled. He then appealed to the world's nations to restore freedom to his land. His efforts earned him the Nobel Peace Prize in 1989. In this 1987 demonstration in Lhasa, Tibetans protest continued rule by China. ***Power*** How do you think China maintains control of Tibet?

Afghan Refugees More than 3 million Afghanis fled their war-torn land after it was invaded by the Soviet Union in 1979. They make up the largest refugee population in the world. This Afghan father and his son, shown in a refugee camp in Pakistan, reflect the weariness and despair of refugees everywhere. ***Human Rights*** Why are the lives of refugees in all parts of the world so difficult?

States to stop Soviet expansion. Because of its anti-communism, Pakistan received massive military and economic aid from the United States. Yet Pakistan also accepted Soviet economic aid. The Soviet Union, for example, helped Pakistan build its first steel mill.

Soviet invasion of Afghanistan. In 1979, a Soviet invasion of Afghanistan increased tensions between Pakistan and the Soviet Union. Afghanistan shares borders with Pakistan, Iran, the former Soviet Union, and China. It has long been a battleground for foreign powers. In the 1800s, it was a buffer state between Russia and the British in India. A buffer state is a small country located between two large, hostile powers.

From 1979 to 1989, the Soviet Union sent troops to back a pro-Soviet government in Afghanistan. During that time, more than 3 million Afghans fled into Pakistan. Pakistan and the United States helped arm and train Afghan resistance fighters. The guerrillas slipped through mountain passes to attack the Soviet and Afghan government forces.

The Soviet Union finally withdrew its forces in 1989. Fighting continued, however, among various groups in Afghanistan. As a result, many Afghan refugees remained in Pakistan.

Ties to the Middle East. Geography and culture help create close ties between Pakistan and the Middle East. As an Islamic state, Pakistan has sought friendship with Iran and Turkey. It has accepted aid from oil-rich countries in the Persian Gulf. Also, thousands of Pakistanis work in the Middle East and send their earnings home. These earnings are an important source of revenue for Pakistan.

During the Gulf War of 1991, the government of Pakistan backed the coalition led by the United States. Many Pakistanis, however, favored Iraq. They viewed Iraqi leader Saddam Hussein as a defender of Islam who was standing up to the strong powers of the West.

SECTION 1 REVIEW

1. **Locate:** (a) Kashmir, (b) Tibet, (c) Afghanistan.
2. **Define:** (a) plebiscite, (b) buffer state.
3. Why have India and Pakistan clashed over the region of Kashmir?
4. What foreign policy did India follow during the Cold War?
5. How did the Soviet invasion of Afghanistan affect Pakistan?
6. **Drawing Conclusions** Why do you think other nations of South Asia might view India with distrust?
7. **Writing Across Cultures** Write a letter to a newspaper expressing concern over a nuclear arms race in South Asia. Consider how the existence of nuclear weapons might affect United States relations with India and Pakistan.

2 LOOKING TO THE FUTURE

FIND OUT

What environmental issues are affecting South Asia?

How does rapid population growth affect South Asia?

What are some results of urbanization in South Asia?

"A fight for truth has begun . . .
A fight for rights has begun . . .
Sister, it is a fight to protect our
mountains and forests . . .
Hug the life of the living trees and
streams to your hearts
Resist the digging of mountains
which kills our forests—and our
streams
A fight for life has begun."

Indian folk poet Ghahshyam "Shilani" wrote those lines to inspire the Chipko, or "Hug-the-Tree," Movement. Women in northern India launched the movement to save Himalayan forests from destruction. In the 1970s, Chipko activists used Gandhi's philosophy of satyagraha, or nonviolent resistance, to alert Indians to threats to the environment. When contractors arrived to cut trees, they found women protecting the trees with their bodies.

Today, Chipko activists have also begun efforts to protect other threatened environments. Protection of the environment is only one of the pressing issues facing South Asia in the 1990s.

Protecting the Environment These young Indians are members of the Chipko Movement, a group founded in 1972 to prevent the destruction of the nation's forests. Chipkos are helping Indians to become aware of the need to conserve their resources and use them wisely. ***Environment*** How can people in developing nations help save their environment?

Nuclear Power in India

SCIENCE AND TECHNOLOGY

For Hindus, the Ganges is the most sacred of all rivers. Many Indians were therefore horrified when their government announced plans to build a nuclear power plant at Narora, on the banks of the holy river. Outraged citizens' groups fought bitterly against the plant. Their protests, though unsuccessful, marked a new stage in the history of nuclear power in India.

From the first days of its independence, India worked hard to develop nuclear power. Homi Bhabha, a brilliant scientist, convinced Prime Minister Nehru to start a nuclear program. Bhabha felt that India's other energy sources, such as coal, could not meet the demands of modernization in the years ahead.

Critics felt that the cost of developing nuclear power was too high. As head of the Department of Atomic Energy (DAE), however, Bhabha was able to control information about nuclear power. Without information, critics won little support. India forged ahead with its nuclear program. Today, India has four operating nuclear power stations, with more under construction. India has more nuclear power plants than such nations as China and Australia.

The program has been costly, though. India has spent huge sums on nuclear power. Yet the plants provide less than 10 percent of India's power needs. Many Indians are also concerned over possible harm to the environment. In the late 1980s, a group of scientists formed an organization called the Indian Nuclear Society (INS). The purpose of the INS is to keep an eye on the DAE. The INS hopes to inform the Indian people about both the benefits and the disadvantages of nuclear power.

The scientists of the INS still see nuclear power as an important resource. They insist, however, that the Indian people should have the information they need to plan for the future.

1. How did the DAE help India to develop nuclear power?
2. **Forecasting** How might public involvement in nuclear issues affect the government's plans to build more power plants? Explain.

Environmental Issues

In South Asia, as elsewhere, people are concerned about the effects of modernization on the environment. In India, the government wants to develop resources and improve the standard of living for the people. Many kinds of development, however, have negative as well as positive effects.

Narmada Valley Project. The Narmada Valley Project (NVP) has angered environmentalists. The Narmada River flows through central India. The NVP calls for the building of 30 major dams and more than 3,000 smaller dams. Supporters argue that the project will provide water to irrigate millions of acres of land. Also, the dams will produce electric power for thousands of villages and towns.

Critics point out that the dams will flood fertile farmland. In addition, the NVP will destroy valuable wildlife, force almost 200,000 people to move, and submerge many sacred shrines. One critic said:

> “In India, we call our rivers lok-mata—mother of the people. Like a great lady, certainly she can put on small ornaments, like bangles and rings, like dikes and small pumps. But don't bind her up in cement and chains. This will draw off her great power.”

Despite such criticism, work has begun on the dams.

Accident at Bhopal. In December 1984, a terrible accident increased concern about industrial pollution. Workers at an American-owned chemical plant in Bhopal, India, made a mistake while cleaning a storage tank. As a result, clouds of deadly gas leaked into the atmosphere, killing more than 2,000 people. Although Indians want foreign investment and modern industries, many fear the lack of controls that have led to accidents like that at Bhopal.

Other issues. Elsewhere in India, activists have protested large-scale limestone quarrying. The quarrying has destroyed forests and topsoil, damaged farmlands, and worsened water shortages. Protesters also oppose the building of nuclear power plants. They fear India might suffer a disaster like that at the Chernobyl nuclear power plant in the Soviet Union. (See page 44.)

People in rural areas also damage the environment. They clear forests to increase farmland or to sell the wood. The expanded use of chemical insecticides and fertilizers resulting from the Green Revolution is also an environmental issue.

Crisis in Numbers

Many threats to the environment are closely linked to the population explosion. Today, growing numbers of people compete for scarce resources such as land, water, and building materials.

By the early 1990s, South Asia had more than 1.1 billion people. At the current growth rate, its population will soon overtake that of China. India's population has more than doubled since 1947, while Pakistan's has more than tripled. About 26 million more people are added to the population of South Asia each year.

MAP STUDY

India's population reached 870 million people in 1990. By the year 2050, experts believe it will be 1.6 billion, surpassing the population of China, a nation much larger in size. Then India will be the world's most densely populated nation.

1. **Place** Which areas of South Asia have the greatest population density?
2. **Location** (a) Name three Indian cities with populations of more than 3 million people. (b) Where are most of these cities located?
3. **Forecasting** How do you think rapid population growth will affect living conditions among the people of South Asia?

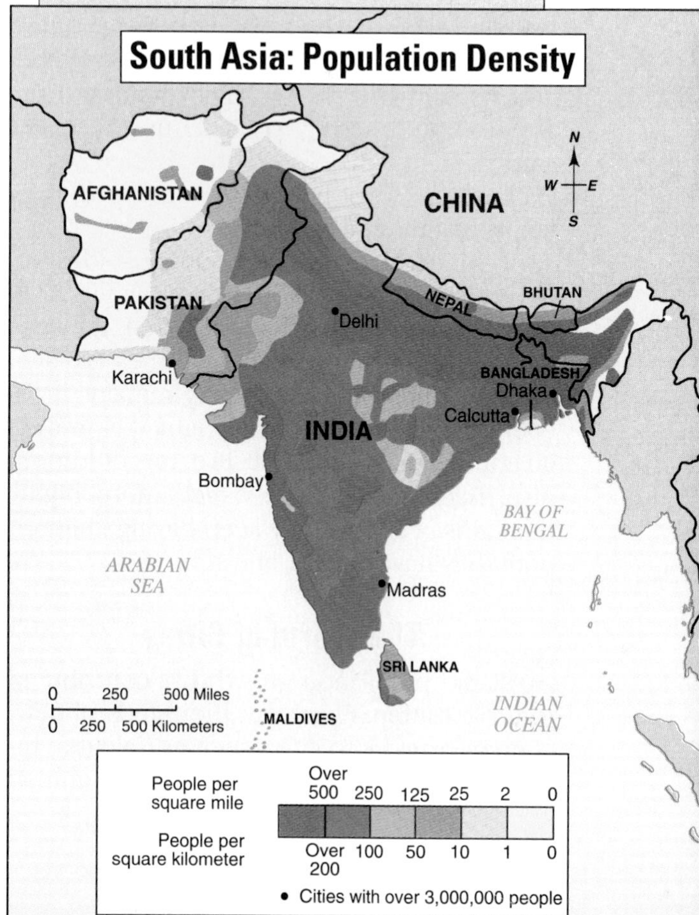

Causes and effects. In South Asia, as elsewhere, rapid population growth has several causes. In the past, diseases like cholera, malaria, and smallpox killed large numbers of people. Today, medical care means that more people live longer. Thus, more people have survived to bear children of their own. Also, infant mortality has declined.

Rapid population growth has had a tremendous impact on South Asian nations. Even though a country's population grows, its land area remains the same. The result is greater population density. In agricultural countries like India and Pakistan, high population density puts strains on limited resources. In addition, more than a quarter of the people in South Asia are under 15 years of age. These young people must be fed, clothed, educated, and, in time, employed.

Limiting growth. South Asian governments see the need to limit population growth. They encourage family planning through various educational programs. The Indian government promotes slogans such as "A Small Family Is a Happy Family."

These efforts have had mixed success. People in cities tend to have smaller families. In rural areas, too, large landowners have begun to limit the size of their families. They want to avoid having to divide up their land among many children. Poorer farmers, however, often do not have access to appropriate family planning resources.

People's attitudes based on age-old traditions also hamper efforts to limit family size. Many farmers depend on children to work the land and to support them in their old age. In areas where infant mortality remains high, couples might have six or eight children to guarantee that some will live to adulthood. Also, because boys are valued more highly than girls, a couple may keep having children until they have at least one son.

The World of Cities

Rapid population growth has contributed to urbanization. Every day, thousands of newcomers crowd into cities such as Calcutta, India, or Karachi, Pakistan. Streets are jammed with buses, cars, and bicycles. Sidewalks overflow with people. Vendors cram into any available space, offering a wide array of goods and services. In India, cows often wander among the throngs, a symbol of Hindu tradition.

Most newcomers to the cities are landless peasants who had no way to make a living in their villages. In the cities, however, there are not enough jobs or housing for everyone. Hundreds of thousands of people live in makeshift slums. Many find no shelter at all. They live and die on the city streets.

Cities offer sharp contrasts between the worlds of the rich and of the poor. The rich live in luxury apartment buildings, drive imported cars, and dine at elegant restaurants. The poor live in crowded slums, walk or ride bicycles, and struggle to get enough food for themselves and their families. In between is a small but growing middle class.

In Bombay, India, about half of the 8 million residents are poor. There, people like Ashok struggle to improve their lives.

Indiranagar, Near Bombay Many of India's landless farmers have moved to Bombay and other large cities, where they live in sprawling slums. Rural settlers first moved into Indiranagar, shown here, in the 1950s and 1960s. Over the years, they established a thriving community where families have worked hard to improve their lives. ***Change*** How are the lives of rural people changed by living in large cities?

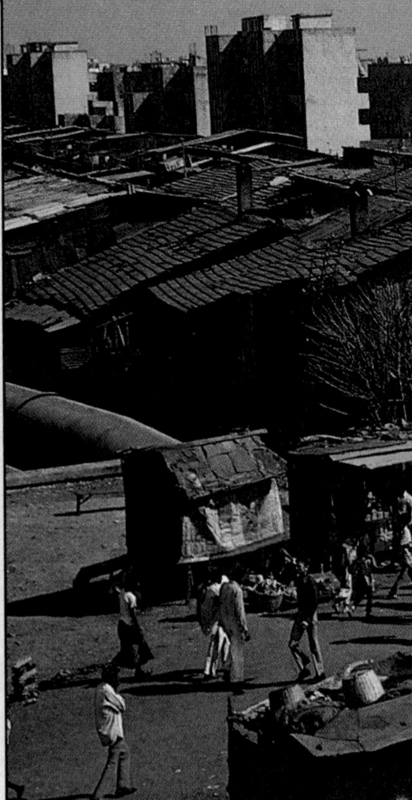

Building a Better Life

Things are better now, but Ashok knows the hardship of city life from his own experience. When Ashok first arrived in Bombay, he had no job and no place to live. Like his neighbors, he has struggled to survive.

> “People who come to the city come because they are paupers; they're forced off their land by debt or family quarrels or making bad marriages. People don't come to Bombay for an easy life or to see the lights. What drives them is poverty and hunger. Nobody who has learned to live in this city will tell you how easy it has been.”

Ashok managed to find part-time work in a factory. At first, he claimed a spot on nearby pavement where he could sleep. In three years, Ashok saved enough to build a tar-paper shack in Indiranagar, a slum on the outskirts of Bombay.

More than 30,000 people call Indiranagar home. Most live in flimsy shanties. Only a few families have electricity. None have running water. Residents line up at shallow wells to hoist buckets of brownish water for cooking and washing. During the dry season, the treeless streets swirl with dust. During the wet monsoon, they ooze mud.

Indiranagar is seeing changes for the better, however. In 1985, residents managed to get Indiranagar recognized as a community by the city of Bombay. Official status meant that Bombay could not bulldoze the settlement out of existence—at least not without warning and compensation.

Since then, Bombay has dug deep wells with water taps that provide clean water to residents. Concrete channels drain off wastes along the streets. The people of Indiranagar are making other improvements themselves. They have enlarged their homes and made them sturdier.

Over the years, the community has acquired a mixed population of skilled and unskilled workers. Hindus and Muslims live side by side. Most people do not move from Indiranagar. In overcrowded Bombay, they have nowhere to go. Also, they feel attached to their community. The people of Indiranagar help each other in times of trouble.

Like his neighbors, Ashok has improved his life. Using the skills he learned from his father, he began to make jewelry for a rich store owner. Ashok now makes a good living—$200 a month. He is married and has three children. He and his wife have added a room to their house and put on a corrugated iron roof. He hopes for an even better life for his children:

> “I'm with my family all the time. I see the children grow. I can talk to them, I can teach them. . . . I want them to get educated, but if everything else fails, they will have a skill to fall back on.”

SECTION 2 REVIEW

1. **Identify:** (a) Narmada Valley Project, (b) Bhopal.
2. What benefits and problems has modernization brought to South Asia?
3. How does rapid population growth contribute to scarcity in South Asia?
4. Why have cities in South Asia grown rapidly?
5. **Understanding Causes and Effects** (a) Why are the populations of South Asian nations growing so rapidly? (b) What are two effects of this population growth?
6. **Writing Across Cultures** Write a paragraph comparing a recent environmental issue in the United States to the conflict over the Narmada Valley Project. Conclude by making a generalization about the conflict between economic development and the environment.

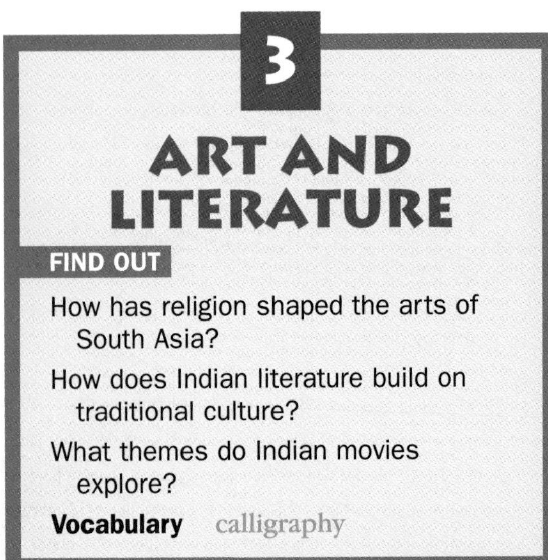

3 ART AND LITERATURE

FIND OUT

How has religion shaped the arts of South Asia?

How does Indian literature build on traditional culture?

What themes do Indian movies explore?

Vocabulary calligraphy

The goddess Lakshmi, says a Hindu story, once watched her husband, the god Vishnu, kill two demons. His movements were so graceful that she asked him what they meant. Vishnu explained that he was performing the art known as dancing. Lakshmi then persuaded him to teach the movements to the gods Brahma and Siva. Siva learned to dance so well that he became Lord of the Dance. Every night, the gods and goddesses assemble in their Himalayan mountain home. Siva dances while the others sing.

As the story suggests, dancing and other arts have their roots in religious traditions. The three major religions of South Asia—Hinduism, Buddhism, and Islam—each helped to shape the region's rich culture.

The Visual Arts

The earliest remains of Indian art and architecture date from the Indus Valley civilization. (See page 171.) Archaeologists in the Indus Valley found figures made by ancient carvers. The tiny figures of people and animals probably had religious importance. Later Indian art showed the influence of these ancient carvings.

Stupas. By the reign of Asoka, Buddhism had emerged as a vital religion. Buddhist traditions helped shape the arts of India. Asoka was the first great patron, or supporter, of the arts. He had builders construct tall columns inscribed with messages praising peace and nonviolence. As you have read, to strengthen Buddhism, he ordered the building of stupas, or dome-shaped burial mounds. The stupas housed remains of the Buddha or other holy persons. They became sacred sites visited by pilgrims.

Like most religious art, each feature of the stupa has symbolic meaning. The dome shape stands for the dome of heaven. On top of the dome is a square structure that represents the world. Rising above the square is an umbrella, a symbol of royalty. The railings and gateways that surround stupas seem alive with carvings. Some show life in princely courts. Others illustrate daily life, scenes from stories, animals, monsters, and spirits.

Temples. Both Buddhists and Hindus carved huge temples into hillsides. The Buddhist cave temple at Karli, built around A.D. 50, has a vast hall that is 124 feet (38 m) long and almost 50 feet (15 m) high. At Ellora, Hindu workers built an immense temple 96 feet (29 m) high by chiseling from the top of a hill down to its base.

Later, Hindus built large temple towers above the ground. In some places, they built clusters of temples. Cities often grew up around the temples. (📖 See Connections With Literature, page 805, "Old Man of the Temple.")

Sculpture. Sculptors decorated every inch of temples with rich carvings. Through carvings, people learned Hindu stories and traditions.

Indian artists often mingled Buddhist and Hindu themes. A Hindu temple carving might include the lotus flower, a symbol of the Buddha. The wheel is important in both Hindu and Buddhist art. It stands for the unending cycle of reincarnation and for the teachings of the Buddha.

At first, Buddhist artists did not show the Buddha as a human figure. They used symbols such as the sacred tree under which the Buddha sat when he achieved enlightenment. Later, sculptors and painters created thousands of images of the Buddha. He is shown with a lump on his head that represents his supreme wisdom. The Buddha's face always has a calm, peaceful expression, a sign of his perfection. His positions and hand gestures also have special meanings.

Hindus recognize hundreds of gods and goddesses. Each may appear in many forms, giving sculptors a vast choice of subjects. A common image of the god Siva shows his many aspects. He has four hands. In one hand, he holds the drum of creation. In another, he carries fire—the flame of destruction. A third hand is raised to carry the message "Fear not." The fourth points to the demon that he is crushing underfoot. The demon stands for the evils that Siva dispels.

Islamic art. As you have read, Muslims introduced new styles of art to South Asia. They built graceful mosques and tombs that

The Taj Mahal The Taj Mahal, at Agra, India, is one of the most beautiful buildings in the world. It is also one of the greatest works of Indian architecture. The Mughal emperor Shah Jahan built this dazzling white marble structure, completed in 1648, as a tomb for his beloved wife. ***Fine Art*** What do you think buildings from the past reveal about a society?

reflected Persian, Greek, and Roman influences. In time, Islamic and Hindu styles mingled to create a rich new Indian art.

Islam forbids the use of images of people or animals. Instead, Muslim artists created elegant designs using fruits, flowers, and leaves. They decorated buildings with passages from the Koran, written in an ornate form of writing called calligraphy.

Wealthy Mughal emperors supported the arts. Akbar had a gleaming new capital city built, with palaces, schools, and public buildings. At his court, painters produced beautiful miniatures that illustrated Persian poems and myths. In these works, artists showed people and animals despite Islamic law. These miniatures remain one of the most important artistic contributions of the Muslims in India.

Literature

Religion inspired Indian literature as well as art. The great sources of Indian literature are two epic poems, the *Mahabharata* ("The Great Story") and the *Ramayana* ("Rama's Way").

Hindu epics. The *Mahabharata* has 100,000 verses and contains many basic Hindu ideas. This long poem tells about a 12-year war between two branches of a royal family. (📖 See Connections With Literature, page 805, "Sibi.")

The *Ramayana* also contains Hindu teachings. The story concerns Rama, his faithful wife, Sita, and his brother Lakshmana. By rights, Rama should inherit his father's throne, but to save his father's honor, he accepts exile rather than fight for the throne. Lakshmana protests the decision, but Rama replies:

> “You know very well that I shall obey my father to the last word. It is my first and foremost duty. Let us therefore do what father bids cheerfully and with a smile on our lips.”

Lakshmana is not convinced. He wants to fight to help his brother gain the throne. "It is the dharma of a Kshatriya to fight evil and establish good," he cries. Rama refuses the offer.

> “So long as our parents are alive, it is our foremost duty to obey them. Let us not be swayed by emotion. Let us think clearly and follow the path of dharma.”

The *Ramayana* continues to be popular in India today. The main characters are considered to be models of correct behavior. Brides recite verses from the epic during their weddings. Some actors who performed in a television reenactment even became popular political figures.

Diffusion and diversity. The epic poems and many early stories began as part of oral tradition. Eventually, they were written down in Sanskrit. Through cultural contacts, stories spread to other parts of the world. The *Panchatantra* is a famous collection of Indian stories, many of them featuring animals as characters. Arab traders carried the stories west to Baghdad and Cairo. From there, the tales entered Europe, where they inspired writers such as Hans Christian Andersen. (📖 See Connections With Literature, page 805, "Numskull and the Rabbit.")

Over the centuries, writers produced fine works in many regional languages, such as Hindi, Bengali, Tamil, and Urdu. The British introduced English, as well as new forms of literature such as novels and autobiographies.

Tagore. Among India's most famous modern writers is Rabindranath Tagore. He wrote poems, short stories, essays, fables, and plays in both Bengali and English. In 1913, Tagore was the first Asian writer to win the Nobel Prize for literature.

One of Tagore's poems celebrated the cultural and ethnic diversity of India. The poem later became India's national anthem:

> “Thou art the ruler of the minds of all
> people,
> Thou Dispenser of India's destiny. . . .
> Day and night, thy voice goes out
> from land to land,
> Calling Hindus, Buddhists, Sikhs and
> Jains round thy throne and Parsees,
> Mussalmans [Muslims] and
> Christians.

A Story From the *Ramayana* Indian art often portrays Hindu teachings. This painting, created for the royal court in Punjab in the 1700s, illustrates part of the epic poem the *Ramayana*. It shows Sita, the wife of Rama, held prisoner by the demon-king Ravana in his garden at Lanka. ***Fine Art*** Why are religious themes often the subjects of art and literature?

Offerings are brought to thy shrine by
the East and the West to be woven
in a garland of love.
Thou bringest the hearts of all peoples
into the harmony of one life. ❞

Novelists. Modern Indian writers have gained worldwide audiences. They draw on many themes, including the struggles of the poor in both villages and cities. In his novel *Untouchable,* Mulk Raj Anand re-creates a day in the life of a young sweeper, an outcaste in Indian society. In *Nectar in a Sieve,* Kamal Markandaya tells of a woman's struggle to hold her family together in the face of desperate poverty.

The Performing Arts

In the performing arts, classical styles continue to influence modern performers. Indian music combines traditional melodies, or *ragas,* with traditional rhythms, or *talas*. Today, as in the past, Indian musicians improvise freely, building on basic melodies and rhythms to create their own performances.

Dance and theater. Dance and music are closely linked. Every movement in Indian dancing has meaning. Through their eye, head, and hand movements, dancers tell a story. Dancers train for years to learn hundreds of hand gestures, called *mudras*. The audience knows the emotion or idea suggested by each movement.

Indian theater combines music, dance, pantomime, and dialogue. Many dramas are based on episodes from the *Mahabharata*, the *Ramayana*, or other well-known tales.

Movies. Today, movies are India's most popular performing art. India has the largest motion-picture industry in the world. Its studios turn out more than 900 films each year.

Movie Billboards in Bombay Movies are the most popular form of entertainment in India's popular culture. Most films portray well-known and accepted patterns of behavior in Indian society. The actors in these films often become famous throughout the cities and villages of India. ***Culture*** Why are movies and pop music popular in so many societies?

Most Indian movies are made in Bombay with actors who speak Hindi. Some of these movies build on familiar stories of warrior heroes and gods and goddesses. Modern love stories are also popular. The movies feature improbable plots, gorgeous costumes, and exotic sets. Most include dancing and singing. The music combines classical ragas and folk tunes with popular western music.

Other movies are made in India's many languages. Those made in Calcutta feature actors speaking Bengali. These works tend to have more serious themes. They are less popular in India than the Bombay movies but have won praise from western viewers. The most famous Bengali director is Satyajit Ray. His best-known work is the *Apu Trilogy.* In this series of three movies, Ray traces the life of a boy named Apu who grows to manhood in rural Bengal.

SECTION 3 REVIEW

1. **Identify:** (a) *Mahabharata,* (b) *Ramayana,* (c) *Panchatantra,* (d) Rabindranath Tagore, (e) Satyajit Ray.
2. **Define:** calligraphy.
3. Give three examples of how religion and the visual arts are linked in South Asia.
4. What traditional values do the *Ramayana* and other works of literature teach?
5. How do movies made in Bombay differ from those made in Calcutta?
6. **Synthesizing** How have diffusion and cultural diversity enriched the arts of South Asia?
7. **Writing Across Cultures** Jot down a list of popular American stories and characters that teach American values in the way that characters from the *Mahabharata* and the *Ramayana* teach Indian values.

Chapter 10 Review

Understanding Vocabulary

Match each term at left with the correct definition at right.

1. plebiscite	**a.** country located between two large, hostile powers
2. buffer state	**b.** symbolic hand gesture
3. stupa	**c.** ornate form of writing
4. calligraphy	**d.** dome-shaped burial mound
5. mudra	**e.** popular vote

Reviewing the Main Ideas

1. (a) How did India take a leading role in world affairs? (b) Why did nonalignment put a strain on relations between India and the United States?
2. (a) Why has Pakistan forged close ties to the Middle East? (b) How did Pakistanis feel about the Persian Gulf War of 1991?
3. (a) How did the industrial accident at Bhopal increase concerns about modernization? (b) List three other environmental issues that the peoples of South Asia face.
4. What attitudes hamper efforts to limit family size in South Asia?
5. (a) Why did Asoka have stupas built throughout India? (b) How do stupas express religious ideas?
6. What are some of the themes of modern Indian literature?

Reviewing Chapter Themes

1. Tensions between neighboring countries often have complex causes. Describe the issues that cause conflicts between two of the following: (a) India and Pakistan, (b) India and Bangladesh, (c) India and China, (d) Pakistan and the Soviet Union.
2. Urbanization, modernization, and rapid population growth pose challenges to developing nations. Give four examples of how these changes have strained resources and caused controversy in South Asia.
3. South Asia is home to many cultural traditions. Describe how cultural traditions have shaped three of the following creative arts: (a) architecture, (b) sculpture, (c) literature, (d) dance, (e) movies.

Thinking Critically

1. **Making Global Connections** Why do you think the United States gave economic aid to India despite India's policy of nonalignment?
2. **Forecasting** (a) How might the end of the Cold War benefit South Asia? (b) How might it be a disadvantage?
3. **Linking Past and Present** Why do you think movies based on the ancient Indian epics are usually more popular than realistic movies like those of Satyajit Ray?

Applying Your Skills

1. **Understanding Sequence** Review the discussion of the Cold War (Chapter 2) and Indian independence (Chapter 9). List these events in time order and explain how they are related: (a) Nehru adopts a policy of non-alignment, (b) World War II ends, (c) India wins independence, (d) Cold War begins.
2. **Analyzing a Poem** Reread the excerpt from the Tagore poem on pages 234–235. (a) What picture of India does Tagore present? (b) Why do you think he does not mention the conflicts among the various groups in India? (See Skill Lesson, page 541.)

SKILL LESSON 5

Reading a Graph: Average Rainfall in Calcutta

Graphs are diagrams, or drawings, that contain statistical information. When information is put into a diagram, it is often easier to understand and interpret. Graphs are often used to illustrate changes that occur over time.

The graph on this page is a line graph. Study it. Then use the following steps to read the graph.

1. **Identify the subject of the graph.** The title of the graph gives you a general idea of the information to be found in the graph. Line graphs also have a horizontal axis and a vertical axis. Each axis is labeled with numbers or dates. These labels give you more specific information about the time period being covered and the measurement being used. **(a)** What is the title of the graph? **(b)** What do the numbers on the vertical axis show? **(c)** What time period does the horizontal axis cover?

2. **Practice reading the information on the graph.** The intervals, or spaces, between the numbers and dates on a graph are always equal. **(a)** What is the average monthly rainfall in Calcutta in May? **(b)** How many months of the year does Calcutta receive less than two inches of rain? **(c)** In what two months is Calcutta's rainfall the greatest? **(d)** In what two months month is its rainfall the least?

3. **Study the graph for evidence of a trend.** A trend is a general movement over time in the subject being measured. **(a)** During which months does Calcutta's rainfall demonstrate a sharp upward trend? **(b)** What kind of a trend do you see in Calcutta's rainfall between September and December?

4. **Draw conclusions.** (a) During which months do you think tourists would be most likely to visit Calcutta? Why? **(b)** When do you think farmers in Calcutta would plant their crops? Why?

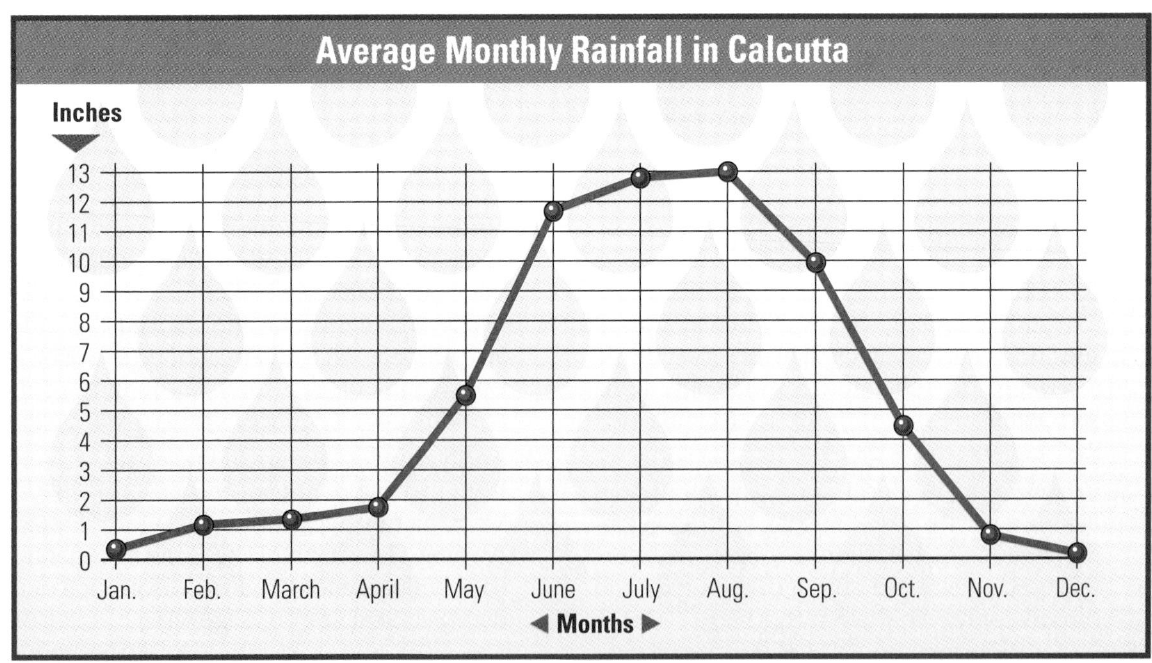

SKILL LESSON 6

Analyzing Fiction: Learning About Indian Culture

Novels, short stories, and other works of fiction can reveal a great deal about a culture. Keep in mind, however, that the author may present a limited view. All members of a culture do not live and think the same.

The excerpt below is from *The Tale of Nagaraj,* a 1990 novel written by the Indian author R. K. Narayan. In the excerpt, Tim, Gopu, and Nagaraj visit the home of Saroja to determine if she will be a suitable wife for Tim. Gopu is Tim's father. Nagaraj is Tim's uncle.

Analyze the excerpt for cultural information. As you read, look up cultural terms you do not know.

1. **Analyze clothing.** (a) What traditional clothing are Gopu and Saroja wearing? (b) What is Tim wearing? (c) How do Tim's clothing and appearance suggest that traditional Indian culture might be changing?

2. **Analyze the role of women.** (a) What is the role of Saroja's mother during the visit? (b) What talents and education does Saroja have? (c) Based on your answers, do you think the role of women in India might be changing? Explain.

3. **Analyze customs.** (a) Who speaks for Saroja during the visit? (b) Who seems to make the final decision for Tim? (c) What does Nagaraj think will be the main attraction? (d) Based on your answers, explain how Indian marriages such as this one are decided.

"Tim wore a blue shirt over his jeans and had tousled his hair to look like an off-stage film actor. . . . His father, Gopu, had donned a silk shirt, wrapping a gaudy shawl around his shoulders.

Fruits and refreshments were served. . . . When it was finished and the dishes were carried away, a silver plate with betel leaves to chew was brought in by a lady and placed before them with a flourish. She was middle-aged and Nagaraj guessed she must be the mother of the bride-to-be. . . . She suddenly stooped low and whispered in her husband's ear, and he laughed artificially and said, 'Of course, if she is ready.' And he turned to the visitors and said, 'Saroja is ready, says my wife.'

Presently, . . . led by her mother the bride-to-be appeared: a thick-set girl in a blue lace sari, bedecked with jewelry head to foot. She shyly entered, with eyes fixed on the ground. . . .

Gopu was staring at her unabashedly to evaluate her personality. Nagaraj commented to himself, 'Whatever she may be, the ten-thousand [rupee] dowry is the real attraction for Gopu. . . .'

The girl's father induced her to sit down with a harmonium [reed organ] and sing. She protested coyly at first, but yielded. . . .

Her father said, 'She is singing a famous song from the latest Hindi film. She has learnt it by herself. . . . Gramophone companies want her to record but I say, "Not yet." She must complete her M.A. [graduate degree] first. . . .'

Tim was not only impressed but overwhelmed. As he told his father later, 'In Delhi, girls are smart. . . . ' Gopu kept talking about the Delhi family and made several complimentary remarks about it. Nagaraj asked, 'When will you get the dowry in hand?'

'Right away, as soon as we give the approval.'"

Such Perfection

R. K. Narayan

INTRODUCTION R. K. Narayan (1906–) is considered to be one of the foremost Indian writers today. Through this story, Narayan describes some of the beliefs about Siva, one of the three great Hindu gods. Hindus often call Siva the Destroyer because they believe that he is capable of destroying the universe through fire and flood. "Such Perfection" is about an image of Siva called Nataraja.

Vocabulary Before you read the selection, find the meaning of these words in a dictionary: auspicious, consecrated, vouchsafed, ruminating, prostrated.

A sense of great relief filled Soma as he realized that his five years of labor were coming to an end. He had turned out scores of images in his lifetime, but he had never done any work equal to this. . . . He sat back, wiped the perspiration off his face and surveyed his handiwork with great satisfaction. . . . The sculptor stood lost in this vision. A voice said, "My friend, never take this image out of this room. It is too perfect. . . ." Soma . . . looked round. He saw a figure crouching in a dark corner of the room—it was a man. . . . "Such perfection is not for mortals." . . .

On an auspicious day, Soma went to the temple priest and asked, "At the coming full moon my Nataraja must be consecrated. Have you made a place for him in the temple?" The priest answered, "Let me see the image first. . . ." He went over to the sculptor's house, gazed on the image and said, "This perfection, this God, is not for mortal eyes. He will blind us. At the first chant of prayer before him, he will dance . . . and we shall be wiped out. . . ." The sculptor looked so unhappy that the priest added, "Take your chisel and break a little toe or some other part of the image, and it will be safe. . . ." The sculptor replied that he would sooner crack the skull of his visitor. . . . "Get out, . . ." Soma shouted. "I don't care to bring this Nataraja to your temple. I will make a temple for him where he is. You will see that it becomes the greatest temple on earth. . . ."

[At Soma's invitation, people poured in from nearby villages at the next full moon to see the Nataraja consecrated.]

The screen which covered the image parted. A great flame of camphor was waved in front of the image, and bronze bells rang. A silence fell upon the crowd. . . . In the flame of the circling camphor Nataraja's eyes lit up. His limbs moved, his anklets jingled. The crowd was awe-stricken. The God pressed one foot on earth and raised the other in dance. . . . The crowd stood stunned by this vision vouchsafed to them.

At this moment a wind blew from the east. The moon's disc gradually dimmed. The wind gathered force, clouds blotted out the moon. . . . Lightning flashed, thunder roared and fire poured down from the sky. It was a thunderbolt striking a haystack and setting it ablaze. . . . Another thunderbolt hit a house. Women and children shrieked and wailed. . . . It rained as it had never rained before. The two lakes, over which the village road ran, filled, swelled and joined over the road. "This is the end of the world!" wailed the people through the storm.

The whole next day it was still drizzling. Soma sat before the image, his head bowed in thought. . . . Some of his friends came wading in water, stood before him and asked, "Are you satisfied? . . . God has shown us only a slight sign of his power. Don't tempt Him again. Do something. Our lives are in your hands. Save us, the image is too perfect."

After they were gone he sat for hours in the same position, ruminating. . . . Tears gathered in his eyes. "How can I mutilate this image? Let the whole world burn, I don't care. I can't touch this image." . . . Far off the sky rumbled. "It is starting again. Poor human beings, they will all perish this time." . . . Outside, the wind began to howl. People were gathering in front of his house and were appealing to him for help.

Soma prostrated before the God and went out. He stood looking at the road over which the two lakes had joined. Over the eastern horizon a dark mass of cloud was rolling up. . . . "Nataraja! I cannot mutilate your figure, but I can offer myself as a sacrifice if it will be any use. . . ." He checked himself. "I must take a last look at the God before I die." He battled his way through the oncoming storm. The wind shrieked. . . . Men and cattle ran about in panic.

He was back just in time to see a tree crash on the roof of his house. "My home," he cried, and ran in. He picked up his Nataraja from amidst splintered tiles and rafters. The image was unhurt except for a little toe which was found a couple of yards off, severed by a falling splinter.

"God himself has done this to save us!" people cried.

The image was installed with due ceremonies at the temple on the next full moon. Wealth and honors were showered on Soma. He lived to be ninety-five, but he never touched his mallet and chisel again.

Source: "Such Perfection" from *Malgudi Days* by R. K. Narayan. Copyright 1982 by R. K. Narayan. Reprinted by permission of Viking Penguin Inc. and William Heinemann Ltd.

This bronze statue of the god Siva was made in the 1200s. Hindus worship Siva as both a destroyer and a creator of life. Here, Siva is shown as lord of the cosmic cycle. In one hand he holds a drum, the symbol of creation. In the other hand is a flame, the symbol of destruction. With his foot, Siva crushes a dwarf, which represents the human illusions that he destroys. Why do you think many artists and writers use religious subjects for their works?

THINKING ABOUT LITERATURE

1. Why does Soma refuse to break off a piece of the statue?
2. What happens after Soma ignores the warnings and tries to consecrate the statue?
3. **Evaluating Information** What Hindu beliefs concerning Siva are revealed in this story?

Champions of Nonviolence

The police surge forward into the mass of demonstrators. Clubs smash against skulls. Men, women, and children cry out in pain. Some run, but none strike back. Many submit peacefully to arrest.

The scene might be India in the 1930s. Or it might be the United States in the 1960s. In both places, people used a technique known as nonviolent resistance to fight oppression and end injustice.

Mohandas Gandhi

Mohandas Gandhi developed nonviolence as a political weapon in South Africa and later used it to lead India to freedom from British rule. In the United States, Martin Luther King, Jr., drew inspiration from Gandhi and adapted his nonviolent methods to the American civil rights movement.

Gandhi's ideas reflected both eastern and western thought. From Hinduism, he learned respect for all life. From Christianity, which he encountered as a young man in England, he absorbed the idea of love for one's enemies.

Gandhi also admired the American writer Henry David Thoreau. A strong abolitionist, Thoreau spent a night in jail for refusing to pay taxes to a government that captured runaway slaves. In his 1849 essay "On the Duty of Civil Disobedience," he urged people to defy any law that was unjust.

"When I saw the title of Thoreau's great essay," Gandhi said, "I began the use of his phrase to explain our struggle to the English readers." Civil disobedience—the deliberate and public refusal to obey an unjust law—was a central part of Gandhi's philosophy. A spectacular example of Gandhi's use of civil disobedience was the Salt March that he led during India's struggle for independence. (See page 202.) Later, it was eagerly embraced by King.

Gandhi's philosophy of nonviolence and the success of his civil disobedience campaigns won him a small but dedicated following in the United States. Howard Thurman, an African American professor, visited Gandhi in 1935 and appealed to him to visit the United States. Gandhi turned down the request but encouraged African Americans to use nonviolent techniques in their struggle for equal rights. "It may be through the Negroes that the unadulterated message of nonviolence will be delivered to the world," Gandhi told Thurman.

Martin Luther King, Jr.

Martin Luther King, Jr., was a young student preparing for the ministry when he first became acquainted with Gandhi's philosophy. King had journeyed to Philadelphia

to hear a sermon by Mordecai Johnson, the president of Howard University. Just back from India, Johnson spoke of Gandhi's life and teachings. King later wrote:

> “His message was so profound and electrifying that I left the meeting and bought a half-dozen books on Gandhi's life and works. . . . It was in the Gandhian emphasis on love and nonviolence that I discovered the method for social reform that I had been seeking.”

In 1955, King had his first chance to put Gandhi's ideas to work. That year, the black residents of Montgomery, Alabama, organized a boycott of city buses. They were protesting a law that required blacks to give up their seats on the bus when a white person wanted to sit down. Montgomery's black leaders chose King to head the boycott.

King was determined to keep the boycott nonviolent. Once a week, he held meetings to teach Montgomery blacks nonviolent techniques.

Borrowing from Gandhi, King advised the protesters:

> “We must meet the forces of hate with the power of love; we must meet physical force with soul force. Our aim must never be to defeat or humiliate the white man, but to win his friendship and understanding.”

For more than a year, thousands of blacks boycotted the buses. At last, in 1956, the United States Supreme Court ordered Montgomery to provide equal, integrated seating on public buses.

Spreading Influence

Headed by King, nonviolent resistance against racism and discrimination spread rapidly across the segregated South. Like Gandhi, King did not try to evade unjust laws. Rather, he confronted them openly. He and his followers refused to be segregated from whites on public transportation or in public buildings. They went proudly to jail, winning widespread publicity and support for their defiance of segregationist laws.

The civil rights movement that King helped to inspire brought sweeping changes to life in the United States—changes as momentous as those Gandhi's civil disobedience movement had sparked in India.

Today, the philosophy of nonviolent resistance continues to exert its power. Throughout the world, oppressed people look to Gandhi—and to King—as symbols in their struggle against injustice.

1. (a) In what cause did Mohandas Gandhi use the techniques of nonviolence? (b) In what cause did Martin Luther King, Jr., use them?
2. **Defending a Position** Critics of nonviolent resistance argue that it takes too long to achieve results. (a) How might Gandhi or King respond to this argument? (b) What do you think? Defend your position.
3. **Writing Across Cultures** Write a dialogue between Gandhi and King in which they discuss their use of nonviolent resistance.

UNIT 3 REVIEW

Reviewing the Main Ideas

1. (a) What are the main landforms of South Asia? (b) How have they contributed to cultural diversity on the subcontinent?
2. (a) What factors may have led to the decline of the Indus Valley civilization? (b) What have scholars learned about the Aryan civilization from the Vedas?
3. (a) Which two major world religions developed in India? (b) What are the main differences in the beliefs of these two religions? (c) What other religions had an impact in South Asia?
4. (a) How was government organized in traditional Indian villages? (b) What were a woman's duties in traditional Indian society? (c) How has the status of women changed in recent years?
5. (a) List three main events that led to the independence of India. (b) Why did the British try to encourage conflict between Hindus and Muslims during India's struggle for independence?
6. (a) What steps did India's leaders take to modernize their country's economy after independence? (b) How did the worldwide rise in oil prices affect the Indian economy?
7. (a) Why did Tamils in Sri Lanka demand a separate state? (b) Why did India become involved in this conflict?
8. What environmental issues must India consider as it industrializes?
9. Describe how religion has inspired literature and the visual arts in South Asia.

Thinking Critically

1. **Analyzing Information** (a) What is purdah? (b) Why might women of higher castes be expected to obey the rules of purdah more strictly than women of lower castes? (c) Why might it be impractical for lower-caste women to obey these rules?
2. **Making Global Connections** Both Americans and Indians fought against the British to gain independence. (a) Describe another similarity between the American Revolution and the Indian War for Independence. (b) Describe one difference between the two events.
3. **Relating Past to Present** Review the conflict between Hindus and Muslims that is discussed in Chapters 8, 9, and 10. Why do you think hostility between the two groups persists today?

Applying Your Skills

1. **Analyzing a Quotation** Reread the quotation on page 179. Which aspect of Hinduism does the quote express?
2. **Reading Maps** Study the maps on pages 159 and 204. (a) What is West Pakistan called today? (b) What was Sri Lanka called before it gained independence? (c) Why was it difficult for East Pakistan and West Pakistan to remain a unified country?
3. **Analyzing a Primary Source** The wooden carving shown below depicts a tiger attacking a British soldier. It was made for Tipu Sultan, an Indian ruler of the late 1700s. (a) What were the sultan's feelings about the British? How do you know this? (b) What impression do you think this carving created when it was sent to England?

Learning by Doing

1. **Creating a Map** On an outline map of South Asia, label all countries, oceans, seas, rivers, and mountains. Include a directional arrow. Using a color key, identify the six climate regions and the January and June monsoon winds. Key that information to the map. (See the maps on pages 164 and 166 and the Atlas map on page 778.)
2. **Making a Presentation** Form two groups of five students to make a presentation on Hinduism and Buddhism. Use the information in Chapter 8 and other sources. The group that focuses on Hinduism should include an introduction that states how, when, and why Hinduism was founded; an explanation of brahman; karma; reincarnation; and dharma. The group that focuses on Buddhism should include a brief introduction that states how, when, and why Buddhism was founded; an explanation of nirvana; the Middle Way; the Four Truths; and the Noble Eightfold Path.
3. **Making a Model** Make a paper model of the flag of Bangladesh, Bhutan, India, Nepal, Pakistan, or Sri Lanka. Begin by consulting an encyclopedia for illustrations of flags and for additional information. Prepare a brief presentation to explain your model. Tell which country the flag represents, and describe its colors, symbols, and the significance of its design. Based on information you read in the chapters, explain how the flag stands for the country's land, government, people, culture, or ideals.

WRITER'S Workshop

Selecting Supporting Information

In a one-paragraph answer, detail sentences give information that supports the main idea. Supporting information may consist of details, facts, examples, reasons, or incidents.

Look at this topic sentence: *Under the Gupta dynasty, India enjoyed a golden age.* The information that you must supply are details about the Guptas's achievements. For example: *The Guptas extended their rule over much of northern India. Peace and prosperity united their empire. Trade increased, especially with China.*

Make sure that the supporting information you have selected completely supports the main idea. For example, the following information would not support a statement about why Britain was able to win control of India: *British factory owners regarded India as a market for their own goods.*

Practice Study this topic sentence for a one-paragraph answer: After independence, Jawaharlal Nehru guided India through many crises. List the details that should be included in your answer.

Writing to Learn

1. Imagine that you are a newspaper reporter interviewing Mohandas Gandhi. Brainstorm questions about Gandhi's accomplishments. You may want to consult other sources for additional information. Your article will be composed of the answers to your questions. Begin the article with an engaging topic sentence. Organize the information in time order. (See page 319.) Revise your first draft, checking for coherence. Then, proofread and make a final copy of it. Finally, publish the interview in a class newspaper.

2. Write an essay explaining the causes and effects of Indian independence. First, state the main points in a topic sentence. Then, explain the causes in time order, followed by the effects. Words such as *reason, result, because, since,* and *consequently* will help you to distinguish cause and effect. Revise the first draft of your essay, checking for logical organization and factual accuracy. Then, proofread and make a final copy of it. Read your essay to the class.

UNIT 4

SOUTHEAST ASIA, AUSTRALIA, AND OCEANIA

UNIT OUTLINE

1 This bronze head of the Buddha, from the 1600s, is in a temple in Thailand. Buddhism has had a major impact on life in Southeast Asia.

2 Ranchers in Australia and New Zealand raise cattle and sheep for a living, and sell wool and meat products to many other nations.

3 Dancers in colorful costumes take part in traditional religious ceremonies on the island of Bali in Indonesia.

	1200	1400
History and Politics	▲ **1287** Mongols overrun Pagan	▲ **1400s** Burmans no longer under Mongol rule
Society and Culture	▲ **900s** Arab traders introduce Islam to Southeast Asia	
Economics and Technology	▲ **1100s** King Suryavarman II builds Angkor Wat	▲ **1400s** Demand for goods from Southeast Asia increases in Europe

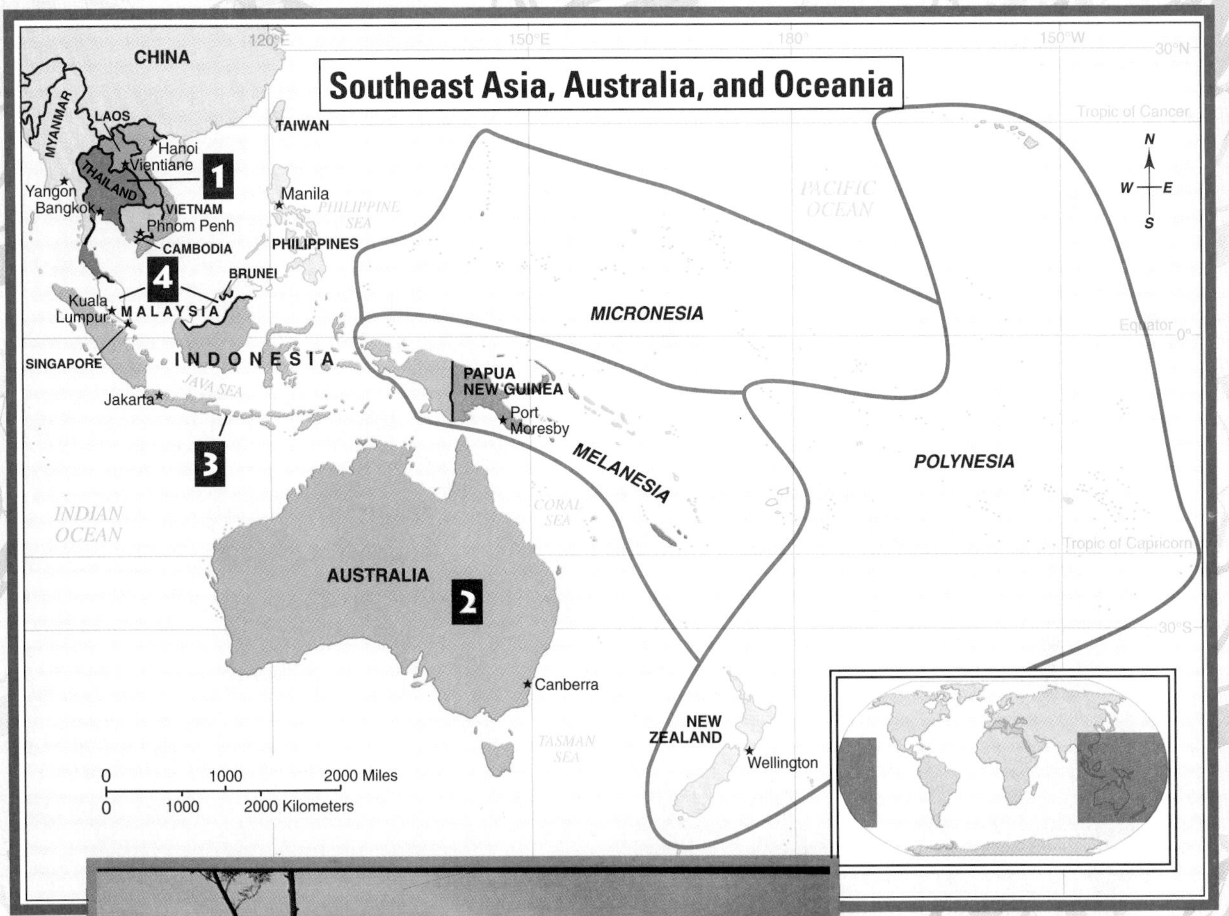

Southeast Asia, Australia, and Oceania
CHINA
MYANMAR
LAOS
Hanoi
Vientiane
THAILAND
Yangon
Bangkok
VIETNAM
Phnom Penh
CAMBODIA
TAIWAN
Manila
PHILIPPINE SEA
PHILIPPINES
BRUNEI
Kuala Lumpur
MALAYSIA
SINGAPORE
INDONESIA
JAVA SEA
Jakarta
PAPUA NEW GUINEA
Port Moresby
MICRONESIA
MELANESIA
POLYNESIA
PACIFIC OCEAN
INDIAN OCEAN
CORAL SEA
AUSTRALIA
Canberra
TASMAN SEA
NEW ZEALAND
Wellington
Tropic of Cancer
Equator
Tropic of Capricorn
120°E
150°E
180°
150°W
30°N
0°
30°S
N
S
W
E
1
2
3
4
0 1000 2000 Miles
0 1000 2000 Kilometers

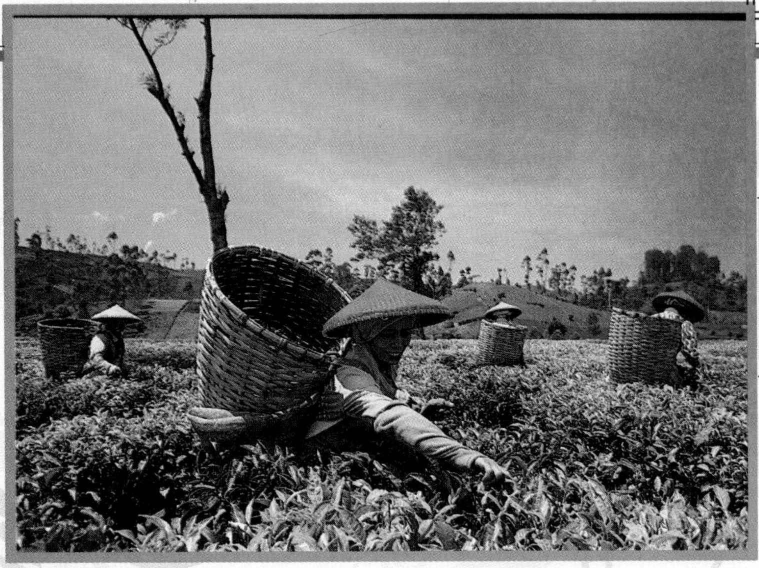

4 Farmers in Malaysia harvest tea, one of the major cash crops produced in Southeast Asia.

1600 — **1800** — **2000**

▲ **1521** Magellan claims Philippines for Spain

▲ **1769** Captain Cook arrives in New Zealand

▲ **1800s** France and Britain colonize most of mainland Southeast Asia

▲ **1900s** Nationalism spreads in Southeast Asia

▲ **1983** Benigno Aquino assassinated in Philippines

▲ **1500s** Christian missionaries arrive in Southeast Asia

▲ **1787** First convicts arrive in Australia

▲ **1800s** Dutch set up Cultural System in Java

▲ **1600** Spanish abandon encomienda system in Philippines

▲ **1782** New Thai capital of Bangkok constructed

▲ **1850s** Gold discovered in Australia

▲ **1990s** Vietnam moves to a market economy

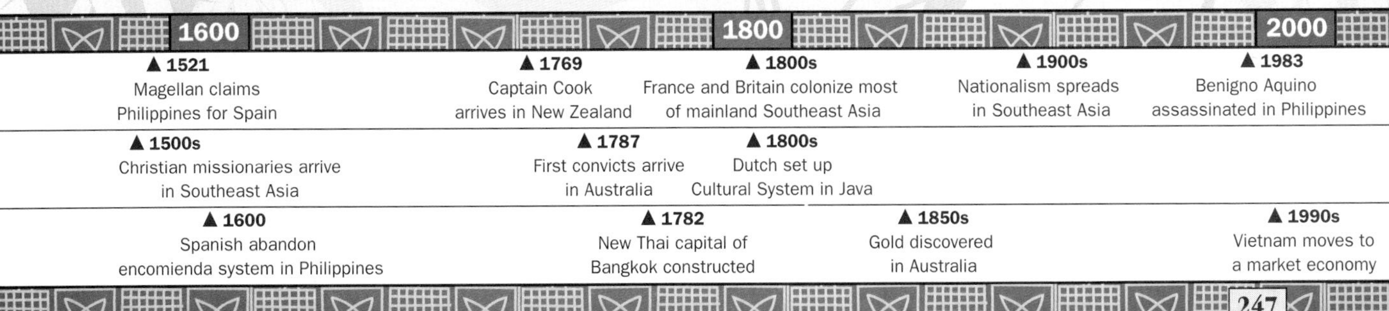

Chapter 11

GEOGRAPHY AND HERITAGE OF SOUTHEAST ASIA

Buddha and Monks This smiling head of Buddha is part of a giant reclining figure. Buddhism, an important religion in Southeast Asia, was brought from South Asia by monks like those shown here as well as by merchants. Most parts of Southeast Asia are near major trading routes. ***Interdependence*** How did Buddhism link the peoples of Southeast Asia and South Asia?

CHAPTER OUTLINE

Pysit Charoenwongsa and Chester Gorman were in a race against time. Farmers at Ban Chiang in Thailand had uncovered ancient pottery, and they were selling pieces to art dealers. Pysit, a Thai museum official, and Gorman, an American professor, went to Ban Chiang to study the findings.

Some scientists said that Thailand had no ancient civilization to compare with those of China and Egypt. Pysit and Gorman, however, found evidence that it had.

They examined jars that were more than 5,000 years old. Embedded in the ancient pottery were rice husks, suggesting that early residents of Ban Chiang were rice farmers. Farming could have spread from Thailand to China rather than the other way around.

Soon, old theories suffered another blow. Pysit and Gorman dug up bronze bracelets dating from about 3600 B.C., before bronze was invented in the Middle East.

The discoveries at Ban Chiang convinced scientists that Thailand was a cradle of ancient civilization.

Local farmers also saw their village in a new light. "The pottery was not just something to sell to rich foreigners," said one farmer. "What was in our soil held great meaning for our country."

CHAPTER PERSPECTIVE

Discoveries like those at Ban Chiang proved that the people of Southeast Asia had developed their own advanced cultures. Much later, they absorbed ideas from India and China and adapted these ideas to fit their own societies.

As you read, look for these chapter themes:

- Geography has contributed to the immense cultural diversity of Southeast Asia.
- The ancient kingdoms of Southeast Asia borrowed ideas from other civilizations and adapted them to their own needs.
- Hinduism, Buddhism, and other religions had a major impact on the cultures of Southeast Asia.
- Agriculture has helped shape the patterns of life in rural Southeast Asia.

Literature Connections

In this chapter, you will encounter passages from the following works.

"The King and the Poor Boy," Cambodian folk story

"All the Male Heroes Bowed," Vietnamese poem

"A Farmer's Calendar," Vietnamese poem

For other suggestions, see Connections With Literature, pages 804–808.

1 THE SHAPE OF THE LAND

FIND OUT

How have landforms and climate influenced the cultures of Southeast Asia?

What are the major resources of Southeast Asia?

Why is Southeast Asia an ethnically diverse region?

Vocabulary archipelago

"God has made the earth and the seas, has divided the earth among mankind, and given the sea in common. It is a thing unheard of that anyone should be forbidden to sail the seas."

The ruler of Makassar (muh KAS er), an Indonesian seaport, spoke these words in the 1600s. For many people living among the islands of Southeast Asia, the "common" seas have served as highways for trade and travel. Yet millions of people in this vast region never see the ocean. They spend their lives among the rugged mountains on the mainland. This contrast shows an important division between the two main regions of Southeast Asia: mainland and islands.

Southeast Asia lies east of India and south of China. It consists of a giant peninsula and a mass of islands. For a thousand years or more, the Chinese called the region the Southern Islands. Not until World War II was the region referred to as Southeast Asia.

Mainland Southeast Asia

Mainland Southeast Asia is a peninsula that lies between the South China Sea and

A Lake in Myanmar These people are fishing in the clear, shallow waters of Inle Lake in central Myanmar. They have a special method of moving their boat as they fish. Standing up, they watch for air bubbles that show where fish are. Then, they use one arm and one leg to steer their boat and use the other arm to throw their net into the water. ***Environment*** How does this way of fishing protect the environment?

the Indian Ocean. Today, it includes five independent nations: Myanmar (MEE uhn mahr), formerly Burma; Cambodia;* Laos; Thailand; and Vietnam.

Mountains cover much of mainland Southeast Asia. Lying among them are highland plateaus that stretch from the Himalayas across southern China. These mountains and plateaus separate Southeast Asia from the rest of Asia. Despite this barrier, invaders and traders from the north have crossed into Southeast Asia since early times.

The mountain ridges run roughly north and south. In between lie a series of valleys. Four vast river systems—the Irrawaddy, Salween, Chao Phraya (CHOW prah YAH), and Mekong—flow south through the valleys. A fifth river, the Red River, flows east into the Gulf of Tonkin.

* In 1975, communist rebels took over the government of Cambodia. They renamed the country Kampuchea. After the rebels were overthrown, most governments returned to using the name Cambodia.

The rivers deposit soil from the mountains across the valleys. As a result, the river valleys and their deltas are fertile farmlands. They have supported large populations for thousands of years.

Island Southeast Asia

Southeast Asia includes a mass of islands scattered across thousands of miles of ocean. In addition to many small island nations, the islands make up five major independent nations: Malaysia, Brunei (bru NĪ), Singapore, Indonesia, and the Philippines.

These nations vary greatly in size. Malaysia lies partly on the mainland and partly on the island of Borneo. Tiny Brunei is also on Borneo. Singapore is a small island at the tip of the Malay Peninsula. Indonesia and the Philippines are made up of archipelagos, or chains of islands. Indonesia includes more than 13,500 islands, while the Philippines has more than 7,000 islands. (See Connections

With Literature, page 805, "The Ebb-Tide" and "In the South Seas.")

Island Southeast Asia is located on the Ring of Fire, a line of volcanoes around the Pacific Ocean. When volcanoes erupt, they often spread ash over nearby land. Since volcanic ash is rich in minerals, the soil becomes fertile. Because of this fertile soil, many people farm near active volcanoes, especially on the Indonesian island of Java.

The volcanoes pose very real dangers, however. Mount Pinatubo, on the island of Luzon (loo ZAHN) in the Philippines, erupted in 1991. A thick layer of volcanic ash destroyed crops and caused buildings to collapse. Hundreds of people died. Many more were left homeless.

Climates of Southeast Asia

Most of Southeast Asia lies in the tropics. The climate of the region is hot and humid for most of the year. As in South Asia, monsoons affect climate. (See Chapter 7.) From June to September, wet monsoon winds from the southern seas bring heavy rains to the

MAP STUDY

Southeast Asia is a region that includes the large peninsula between the Indian Ocean and the South China Sea as well as a large group of island nations.

1. **Region** (a) Name three nations of mainland Southeast Asia. (b) Name three island nations of Southeast Asia.
2. **Location** (a) What is the largest nation of Southeast Asia? (b) What is the relative location of this nation?
3. **Applying Information** What generalization can you make about the landforms of Southeast Asia?

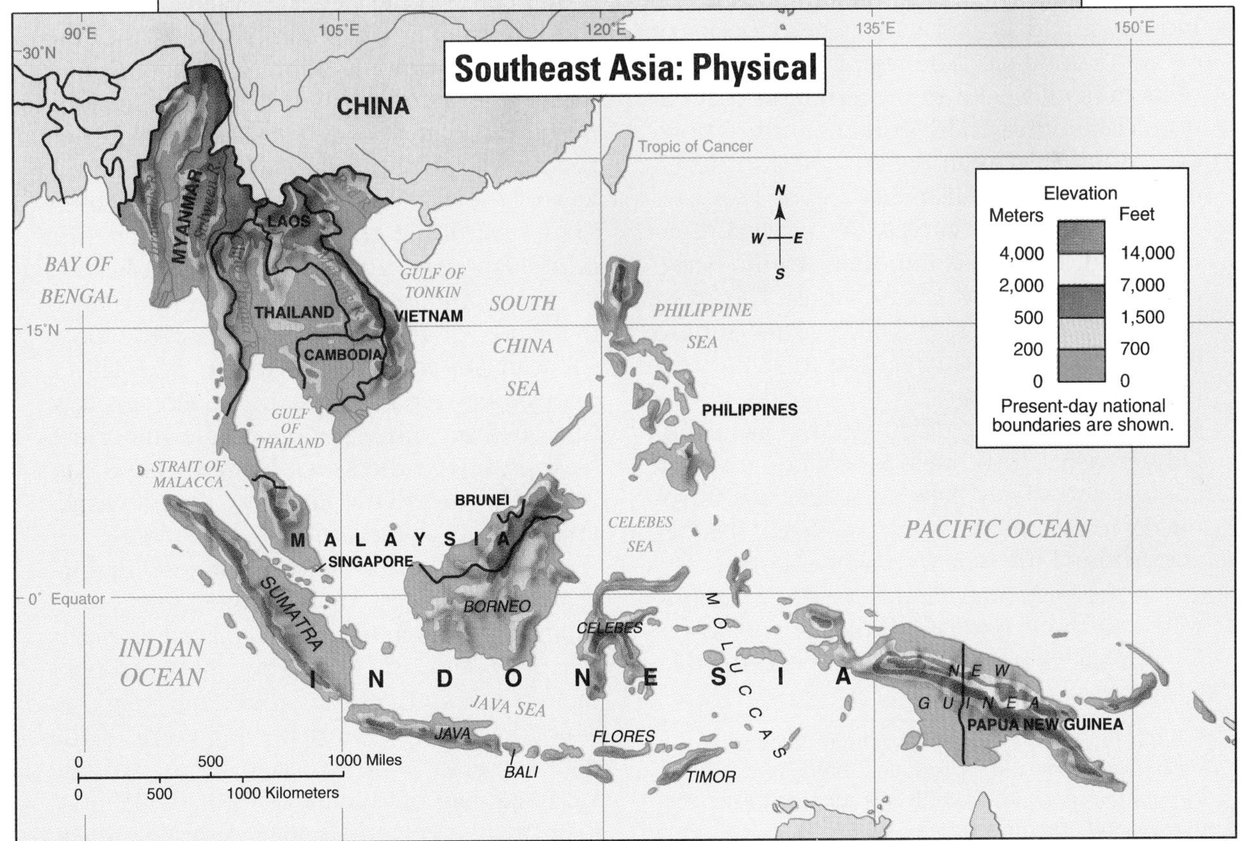

mainland. Later, the winds reverse direction, bringing drier weather, although the temperature remains high.

Monsoons have shaped the patterns of life in Southeast Asia since earliest times. In the 700s, the Malays developed the lateen sail, which allowed sailors to take advantage of the seasonal wind.* Traders planned their voyages to coincide with the expected arrival of the monsoon. Today, as in the past, farmers depend on the wet monsoon to water their crops. Each June, they anxiously watch the skies for signs that the rainy season will begin on time.

Southeast Asia is also subject to typhoons, fierce tropical storms that can strike with little warning. Their high winds often kill many people and cause massive damage, especially in the island regions.

Natural Resources

Southeast Asia is rich in natural resources. It supplies about half of the world's tin, as well as metals such as aluminum and nickel. Indonesia and Brunei have large deposits of oil and natural gas. The region exports much of its mineral wealth to western industrial nations. Like other Third World countries, however, Southeast Asian nations are also developing their own industries.

Agricultural resources. As elsewhere in the world, farming is important to the economies of Southeast Asian nations. The most important crop is rice, which farmers raise both to feed their families and to sell for export. About one third of the world's rice is grown in the river deltas of the mainland. Other cash crops include coffee, tea, coconuts, and spices. Rubber, which was introduced to Southeast Asia from Brazil, has become one of the region's major exports.

In the past, many Southeast Asian nations relied on the export of just one or two crops. As a result, they suffered if the price for that crop fell on the world market. Today, most countries have diversified their economies. They try to export a variety of crops.

Lumber. Parts of both mainland and island Southeast Asia have dense tropical rain forests. These forests contain teak, mahogany, and other trees that are prized for their hard woods. In many areas, loggers are cutting down the rain forests at a rapid rate.

Like countries around the world, the nations of Southeast Asia face a difficult choice. They need the income from exporting lumber. At the same time, the destruction of the rain forests is taking a huge toll. Logging threatens the environment and destroys the cultures of people who have lived in the forests for centuries.

A Diverse Region

The geography of Southeast Asia has contributed to ethnic and cultural diversity. The mountains cut groups of people off from one another. In many countries, a majority ethnic group controls the rich river valleys as well as the government. For example, Laos is home to Lao, Tai, Hmong, Yao, Mon, and Khmer (kuh MEER) peoples, as well as to many Chinese and Vietnamese. The Lao make up 48 percent of the population and occupy the valleys of the Mekong River and its tributaries. They control the government, determine the official language, and set education policies.

Ethnic minorities often live in the rugged highlands of the mainland. Since the poor soil can support only a sparse population, highlanders tend to live in smaller groups. Cut off from other people, these minorities have preserved their own languages and customs. Many feel little kinship to the lowlanders or loyalty to the central government.

Highland people are not the only minorities in Southeast Asia. Immigrants from China and India have also played a major role in Southeast Asia. They have brought their arts, languages, literature, and religions, which have helped enrich the culture of the region. Today, nearly one third of all Malaysians are of Chinese descent, while more than 10 percent are Indian. Although these

* Later, the Arabs learned about the technology of the lateen sail from the Malays and brought it to the Mediterranean world, where it was adopted by the Portuguese and other Europeans.

In a Malaysian Market The diversity of Malaysia is shown in this market. The two women at left are Malays, the largest ethnic group in Malaysia, which makes up 59 percent of the population. The woman behind them is Chinese. The Chinese constitute 32 percent of Malaysia's population. ***Diversity*** The Chinese and Indians have lived in Malaysia since the 1800s. How might this have affected their cultures?

minorities have added to the cultural diversity of Southeast Asia, they have also experienced discrimination.

As in other parts of the world, the nations of Southeast Asia are struggling to create unified nations from diverse peoples. In recent years, governments have gained control over people in remote areas.

SECTION 1 REVIEW

1. **Locate:** (a) South China Sea, (b) Myanmar, (c) Thailand, (d) Vietnam, (e) Malaysia, (f) Indonesia, (g) the Philippines.
2. **Identify:** (a) mainland Southeast Asia, (b) island Southeast Asia, (c) Ring of Fire.
3. **Define:** archipelago.
4. Describe one way that life in Southeast Asia has been affected by (a) mountains, (b) rivers, (c) volcanoes, and (d) monsoons.
5. **Understanding Causes and Effects** How has the geography of Southeast Asia contributed to cultural diversity?
6. **Writing Across Cultures** List the major resources of Southeast Asia. Jot down a reason why each resource would be important to the United States.

2 EARLY TRADITIONS

FIND OUT

What effect did geography have on the history of Southeast Asia?

How did the kingdoms of Southeast Asia differ from one another?

How did other civilizations influence Southeast Asian kingdoms?

Vocabulary tributary state

A Cambodian folk tale tells of a poor boy who goes to work in the palace of the king. One day, the king comes upon the boy sweeping the floors of the palace. The king asks the boy whether he is rich or poor. The boy replies, "I think that I am as rich as a king."

Surprised, the king asks the boy what he means. The boy explains:

“Your Majesty, I may receive only six *sen* each month, but I eat from one plate and you also eat from one plate. I sleep for one night and you also sleep for one night. We eat and sleep the same. There is no difference. Now, Your Majesty, do you understand why I say that I am as rich as a king?”

Like many Southeast Asian folktales, this one carries a Buddhist message. Through such tales, Buddhism influenced both rulers and subjects in Southeast Asia.

River Valley Civilizations

Because of geography, no single ruler could conquer the diverse lands and peoples of Southeast Asia. Instead, most rulers controlled relatively small areas.

Powerful leaders built their kingdoms in fertile river valleys. They organized strong armies and collected taxes from farmers. They also set up the complex irrigation systems that were needed for rice farming. Through warfare, they extended control over neighboring groups.

To the north lay the powerful civilization of China. The Chinese conquered parts of Southeast Asia. With the exception of Vietnam, however, most Southeast Asian regions remained independent from China.

Pagan

An early civilization grew up along the Irrawaddy River in what is today Myanmar. There, in about 849, the Burmans built the kingdom of Pagan (pah GAHN). By controlling the fertile rice-growing lands of the

Pagan Painting Elephants and marching figures enliven this colorful painting from Burma's Pagan kingdom. The most famous Pagan ruler, Anawrata, not only dominated the Irrawaddy Valley, but also led his armies into what are now Bangladesh and Thailand. Anawrata's rule ended when he was killed in a hunting accident in 1077. ***Fine Art*** What does this painting suggest about the riches of the Pagan kingdom?

Irrawaddy, the rulers of Pagan grew rich and powerful.

King Anawrata ruled Pagan during the eleventh century. According to tradition, Anawrata brought Buddhism to his people. Long before, Buddhist missionaries had carried their religion to the Mon, people who lived south of Pagan. When Anawrata invaded the Mon kingdom, he took possession of statues of the Buddha and sacred Buddhist writings. Both Pagan and its neighbors maintained links with Buddhist centers in India and Sri Lanka.

In 1287, Mongol armies from China overran Pagan. As a result, Pagan became a tributary state of China. As a tributary state, Pagan recognized the superiority of the Chinese emperor by giving tribute, or gifts, to him. By the 1400s, however, the Burmans had thrown off Chinese rule.

Vietnam

The Vietnam kingdom in the Red River delta also came under Chinese domination. In A.D. 39, the Trung sisters, daughters of a Vietnamese noble, led the struggle against the invaders. Their armies freed 65 towns from Chinese rule. In the end, though, a Chinese general captured and executed the Trung sisters. Ever since, the Vietnamese have celebrated these women for their bravery. As a poet of the 1400s wrote:

> “All the male heroes bowed their
> heads in submission;
> Only the two sisters proudly stood up
> to avenge their country.”

The Chinese ruled Vietnam for more than 1,000 years. During that time, Chinese culture greatly influenced the language, art, poetry, and customs of Vietnam. From China, the Vietnamese absorbed Confucian philosophy and Mahayana Buddhism, which you will read about in Chapter 15. The Vietnamese finally regained their independence from China in 939.

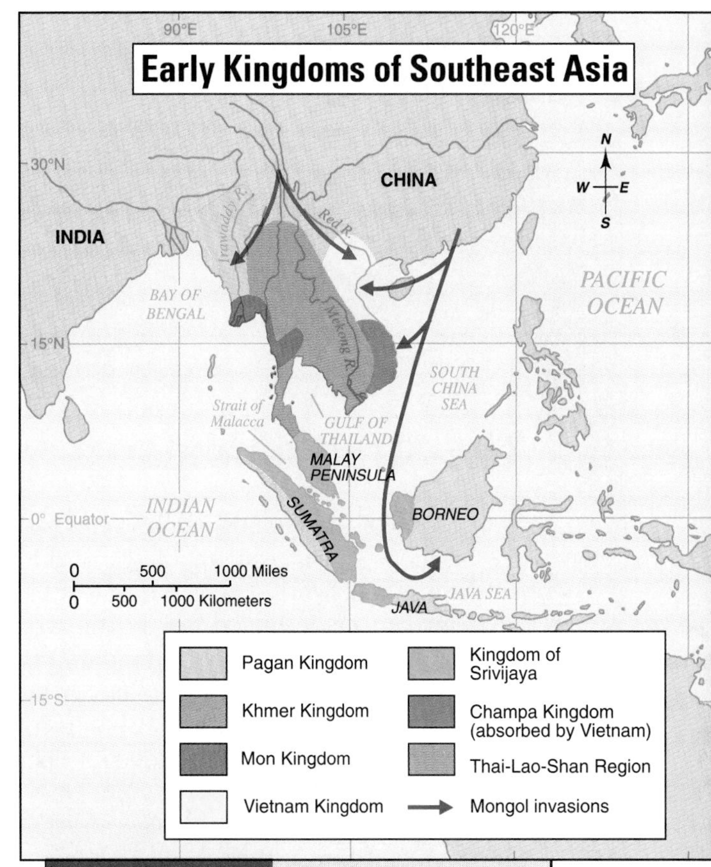

MAP STUDY

In Southeast Asia, as in other regions, early civilizations developed in river valleys. Among these civilizations were the Pagan kingdom in the Irrawaddy River valley and the Vietnam kingdom in the Red River valley.

1. **Location** What kingdom developed along the Mekong River delta?
2. **Interaction** What nation attacked several of these early kingdoms of Southeast Asia?
3. **Drawing Conclusions** Why do you think no kingdom was able to establish an empire to rule most of Southeast Asia?

Khmer Kingdom

Among the most powerful kingdoms of Southeast Asia was the Khmer kingdom. It controlled the Mekong River delta in what is today Cambodia and the southern part of Vietnam. By about A.D. 85, the Khmer had built a prosperous kingdom.

The Strait of Malacca

The pace of bargaining picked up as traders haggled with merchants. A ship from China had just anchored in port. Heavy crates of fine porcelain made it ride low in the water. On shore sat sacks of cloves, cinnamon, and pepper. Nearby, traders looked over swords from Damascus, precious jewels from Sri Lanka, and cashmere from Bengal. The time was the 1400s. The place was the busy port of Malacca on the Strait of Malacca.

Since ancient times, the Strait of Malacca had been a vital waterway because it offered the shortest water route between the Pacific and Indian oceans. (See the map at right.) Through its narrow channel sailed Chinese junks, Arab dhows, and South Sea outriggers. At Malacca, traders exchanged goods from China, India, the Middle East, Southeast Asia, and the Mediterranean world.

By the late 1400s, Europeans wanted to find a direct sea route to the rich "Spice Islands" of Southeast Asia. In time, the Portuguese and then the Dutch built huge trading empires among the islands.

Whoever ruled the Strait of Malacca waged constant war with pirates. Lurking in the coastal mangrove swamps, pirates looked for easy targets. In small, light ships, they attacked and plundered trading ships. Not until the 1800s did steam-powered warships control this threat.

Today, the Malaysian cities of Kuala Lumpur and George Town are major ports on the strait. From there, ships carry rubber, copra, and tin from Malaysia to world markets. Huge oil tankers also sail the strait, cruising between the Middle East and East Asia. Recently, however, the strait has become more than a passage route. Oil companies have begun drilling, hoping to find a new source of wealth under the sea floor.

1. Why did the Strait of Malacca become a well-traveled sea route?
2. **Drawing Conclusions** Why has the Strait of Malacca continued to be important in the modern world?

For centuries, the Khmer had close contact with Indian traders. From these Indians, the Khmer learned much about government and literature. In time, the Khmer created a writing system for their language based on Indian scripts. Khmer rulers also absorbed Hindu beliefs and built temples to honor Hindu gods.

Successful farming allowed hundreds of thousands of Khmer to live in large cities.

Engineers built water systems with canals and reservoirs. These systems prevented floods during the rainy season. They also stored water for use in farming during the dry months.

In the 1100s, King Suryavarman II built Angkor, a vast capital city dedicated to the Hindu god Vishnu. The ruins of Angkor survive today as a monument to the engineering and artistic skills of the Khmer people. (See page 2.)

The golden age of Angkor was brief. In 1177, the Cham people attacked and looted the rich city. The Cham continued their attacks throughout the next century. Eventually, the Khmer again built a strong kingdom. King Jayavarman VII founded a new capital dedicated to a new protector, the Buddha.

The Khmer conversion to Buddhism was part of a larger movement in which many mainland peoples converted from Hinduism to Buddhism. Elements of Hinduism, however, remained in Cambodian culture.

Tai Kingdoms

The many peoples of Southeast Asia each have their own histories, which have helped to shape the present-day nations of the region. The people of Thailand today have their roots in several early kingdoms. They are descended from the Tai, a group that included the Thai, Lao, Shan, Black Tai, and Red Tai peoples.

By the 1200s, the Tai kingdom of Lanna had become powerful. The Mongols invaded Southeast Asia in 1287. The fighting greatly weakened the Khmer, the Burmans, and the Mon, giving the Tai an opportunity to expand. In 1782, the Chakkri (chahk kree) family set up a new Thai dynasty with Bangkok as their capital. Today, the people of Thailand still recognize the Chakkris as their royal family.

An Island Empire

Many small kingdoms developed on the islands of Southeast Asia. Some island kingdoms profited from the spice trade. The rulers of Srivijaya (shree vah JĪ yah) on the island of Sumatra controlled the Strait of Malacca, a vital waterway connecting the Indian Ocean and the Pacific Ocean. From there, they controlled a flourishing island empire. (See the feature on page 256.)

The religion of Srivijaya's rulers changed several times, reflecting different outside influences on Southeast Asia. By the 900s, the rulers worshipped Hindu gods. Later, Buddhist missionaries from China won many converts. After the 1200s, Arab and Indian Muslims introduced Islam, which most people throughout the region gradually adopted.

Europeans sailed into the Strait of Malacca in the 1500s. By then, the Srivijaya Empire had collapsed into many rival kingdoms. Through bargaining and force, European traders won the right to set up trading posts in the region. Much later, Europeans would turn these outposts into colonies, as you will read.

SECTION 2 REVIEW

1. **Locate:** (a) Pagan, (b) Khmer kingdom, (c) Srivijaya, (d) Strait of Malacca.
2. **Identify:** (a) Anawrata, (b) Trung sisters, (c) Suryavarman II, (d) Angkor, (e) Chakkri family.
3. **Define:** tributary state.
4. Why was it difficult for Southeast Asian rulers to control large areas?
5. (a) How did Chinese civilization influence Vietnam? (b) Name two kingdoms influenced by Indian civilization.
6. (a) Describe two achievements of the Khmer kingdom. (b) Why was the Tai kingdom able to expand in the late 1200s?
7. **Synthesizing Information** How did technology help people like the Khmer build a powerful kingdom?
8. **Writing Across Cultures** Brainstorm a list of American women who have been admired for their courage. Then, write a paragraph comparing one of these women with the Trung sisters.

3

PATTERNS OF LIFE

FIND OUT

What different religious traditions have influenced Southeast Asia?

Why does rice play a major role in Southeast Asian life?

What family patterns are found in Southeast Asia?

Vocabulary animism

The two reporters paddled their dugout canoe toward the remote interior of the island of Borneo. They had traveled there to visit the Iban people and write about how the Iban survived with little or no contact with the modern world. To their surprise, the reporters found the Iban wearing baseball caps and T-shirts with pictures of American rock stars. Iban homes had plastic chairs and pink linoleum floors.

Modern technology and the influence of western culture are rapidly changing life in Southeast Asia, yet many traditions remain strong. Despite their baseball caps and T-shirts, some Iban still live by hunting and food gathering, and they continue to honor traditional spirits.

The Importance of Religion

A plume of steam rises from the crater of Gunung (GYOO nyuhng) Agung, on the island of Bali. Otherwise, the volcano is quiet. The people of Bali believe that Gunung Agung is the center of the world. There, life begins and ends. Like their ancestors, the Balinese bring offerings to the edge of the steaming volcano. They leave rice, fruit, flowers, and eggs to please the spirit that dwells in Gunung Agung.

The practices of these Balinese are based on animism, the belief that spirits live in the natural world. Mountains, streams, trees, rocks, and even dreams have spirits. Over the centuries, many elements of animism have blended with religious beliefs that were brought to Southeast Asia.

Hinduism. The earliest world religion to influence Southeast Asia was Hinduism. Indian traders spread Hindu beliefs throughout the region. Many peoples of Southeast Asia blended Hindu gods and goddesses with their own spirits.

They also accepted the Hindu belief in reincarnation, but rejected other ideas such as the rigid caste system. Despite its early influence on Southeast Asia, Hinduism later declined. Today, Hindus are found in Bali and parts of Malaysia.

Buddhism. Buddhism had a far greater impact on Southeast Asia than Hinduism. Buddhist missionaries carried the religion east from India in the early centuries A.D. By then, two schools of Buddhism were emerging.

Theravada Buddhism took root in Myanmar, Thailand, Laos, and Cambodia. Local people built Buddhist monasteries, and Buddhist traditions shaped their culture. Boys entered a monastery at an early age. They learned to read and write and became monks. Most of them left the monastery to marry. Some women also joined Buddhist orders as nuns.

Chinese Buddhists carried Mahayana Buddhism into Vietnam. Mahayana Buddhists place less emphasis on monastic life. They believe that ordinary men can achieve nirvana, the condition of wanting nothing, by meditation. Women, however, cannot reach nirvana.

Buddhist influences remain strong in much of Southeast Asia. In mainland countries, Buddhist monasteries and temples are centers of village life. Farmers turn to Buddhist monks for advice on daily life and sometimes for political leadership.

Local people often blend Buddhist and animist beliefs. A Buddhist farmer in Thailand does not ask the Buddha to help him raise a good crop. Instead, he turns to the *nats,* or spirits in the natural world. He builds a small

Different Religious Traditions Most Malays are Muslims, like this woman in silent prayer at a mosque. Elsewhere in Southeast Asia, many people believe in spirits known as nats. In the photo below, a family has built a spirit house dedicated to the nat that protects newly planted rice fields. ***Culture*** How is animism reflected in the religious practices of some Southeast Asians?

shrine on top of a pole in his rice field. There, he puts food, incense, and other offerings.

Spread of Islam and Christianity

Two other religions have shaped beliefs in parts of Southeast Asia. By 900, Arab traders had brought Islam to the Malay Peninsula and the islands of Sumatra, Java, and Borneo. Many people converted to the new religion. Today, Islam is the official religion of Malaysia, and Indonesia has one of the largest populations of Muslims in the world.

Islam has created strong ties among the peoples of Malaysia, Indonesia, the southern Philippines, and other Muslim lands. Millions of Muslims from Southeast Asia make the pilgrimage to Mecca in Saudi Arabia. Like all Muslims, they accept the Koran as the holy book of Islam and accept its laws.

During the 1500s, Christian missionaries accompanied European traders to Southeast Asia. When Spain conquered the Philippines, the missionaries set out to convert the people to the Roman Catholic faith. Within 50 years, they had converted most of the Filipinos in the lowlands. In remote highland areas, however, people kept their local beliefs. Many did not become Catholic until the twentieth century.

Today, most Filipinos are Catholics. Other Southeast Asian countries contain smaller groups of Catholics and Protestants.

Economic Patterns

In most parts of Southeast Asia, people make a living as their ancestors did—by farming the land or by fishing. Most people are subsistence farmers, although an increasing number sell their surplus crops for cash.

Rice. Throughout Southeast Asia, rice is the major food crop. People eat rice at every meal. "Don't let rice fields lay fallow," warns a Vietnamese proverb. "An inch of soil is an inch of gold."

Depending on where they live, farmers in Southeast Asia grow rice in one of two ways. Farmers in the lowlands grow "wet rice." Wet rice requires flat land and large amounts of water. Farmers soak the rice fields, or paddies, with water before planting the seedlings. The paddies remain covered with water until almost harvest time. Wet-rice farming is difficult work, usually requiring the labor of an entire family.

In drier highland areas, farmers plant "dry rice." Farmers burn brush and small trees on a few acres of land. They then plant rice. The first year's crop is usually good because ashes from the burned plants nourish the soil. In most places, however, the soil wears out quickly. Farmers must then move on to other areas while the land renews itself. Governments today are trying to discourage this wasteful "slash-and-burn" agriculture.

Other farm products. Farmers grow other crops, such as corn, peanuts, and sweet potatoes. Coconut trees grow in coastal regions. Copra, or dried coconut meat, is an important source of oil, soap, and margarine. However, demand for coconut oil has decreased as people in industrialized countries have become more concerned about saturated fats in their diet.

Fishing. Fish is an important source of protein in all parts of Southeast Asia. Fish are especially plentiful in coastal regions and on the islands, where many people depend on fishing for their livelihood. In the interior regions, families fish in rivers and even catch eels in irrigation canals and rice paddies. People eat both fresh and dried fish. They also produce fish sauce to season their food.

Village Life

Most people in Southeast Asia live in villages. Villages dot the banks of rivers and canals. Other villages are found on hillsides and in forests. Homes are often built of bamboo, clay bricks, or concrete blocks. As a protection against monsoon flooding, some homes are built on stilts.

A village might have anywhere from 50 to 200 families. Village leaders may inherit their post or may be elected or appointed. They enforce the law and supervise work on canals and roads. In Buddhist areas, the village leader is also responsible for maintaining the temple.

Today, many forces are affecting village life. Cities are growing, and many young people leave their villages to find jobs in cities. Farmers buy tools and clothing in local stores instead of making them. Farmers who sell their surplus crops for cash also buy televisions or build homes of cement and wood.

Family Life

In much of Southeast Asia, people live in nuclear families. In Vietnam, however, Chinese influences helped shape the culture. Chinese tradition supports the extended family. As a result, in Vietnam the extended family is the ideal. The Vietnamese also adopted the Chinese tradition of reverence for ancestors.

The rights of women. Despite strong Chinese influence, the Vietnamese kept many of their own cultural traditions. Among them was respect for the rights of women. In traditional Chinese culture, women were seen as inferior to men, but in Vietnam, the law code gave women and men nearly equal rights. Women could own property and marry without parental approval.

Today, women in Southeast Asia enjoy many rights that other Asian women have traditionally lacked. "By law and custom," noted a scholar in Myanmar, "Burmese women are equal. We couldn't have one law for women and another for men, could we?" In Thailand, sisters share with their brothers in the inheritance of valuable rice fields. Women run most of the stores in Vietnam.

Division of labor. In farm families, each person has a job. Men plow the paddies, operate rice-planting machinery, and harvest the rice crop, while women plant rice by hand and husk the cut rice. In addition, men build homes and make furniture, pottery, baskets, and fish traps. Women take care of the house and the children. Women also cook, tend the livestock, gather firewood, fetch water, and make clothing.

A Vietnamese folk poem, "A Farmer's Calendar," shows that men and women have worked side by side in the rice fields for centuries.

> "In the third month, we break the land
> to plant rice in the fourth while the
> rains are strong.
> The man ploughs, the woman plants,
> and in the fifth: the harvest, and the
> gods are good—
> an acre yields five full baskets this
> year. . . .
> In plenty or in want, there will still be
> you and me,
> always the two of us.
> Isn't that better than always prospering, alone?"

Education. Children begin to help their parents at a young age. Today, most children also go to elementary school at least, if not to high school. In countries where Buddhism is strong, boys learn to read and write at Buddhist temples. In Malaysia and Indonesia, many children attend schools run by Muslim teachers.

Although girls attend elementary school, many leave school when they reach their teens. Their mothers train them at home for their future roles as wives and mothers. Some women, however, complete high school and even college. Banyen Phimmasone of Laos was one of these women.

Working Together In Myanmar, villagers pitch in to repair a roof. Their simple, lightweight clothing is common throughout Southeast Asia. Both men and women wear a skirt-like garment called a *longyi*. Sandals are common, and everyone removes footgear before entering a temple or house. ***Environment*** How have these villagers adapted to their environment?

Two Kinds of Healing

Banyen was born in Vientiane, the capital of Laos. Her father, a doctor, had learned "all there was to be known about the art of healing." He knew the properties of medicinal plants and how to use them to cure various diseases. He also knew how to deal

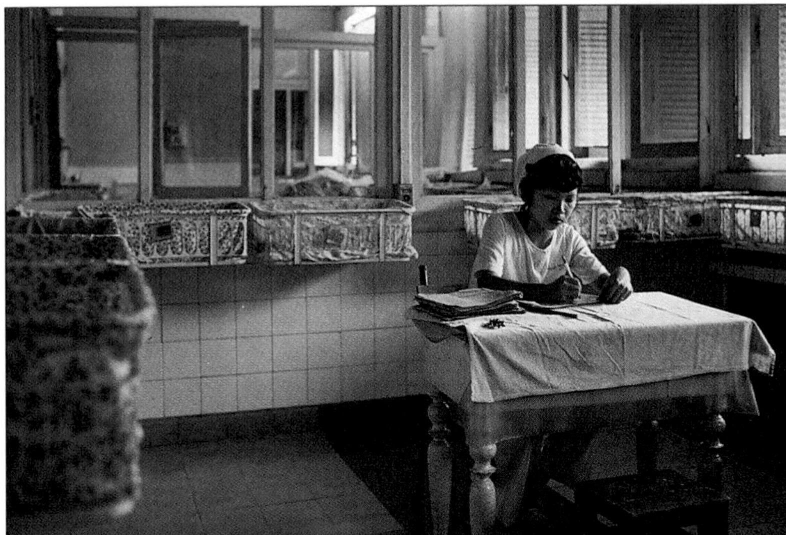

A Nurse in Vietnam This nurse keeps records at a hospital nursery in Ho Chi Minh City. Health care in Vietnam has improved in recent decades. In the 1960s, the average Vietnamese had a life expectancy of 34 years. By the early 1990s, people's life expectancy had increased to about 60 years. ***Change*** How does this increase in life expectancy affect a nation's population?

with *phipops,* evil spirits whose anger was believed to be one of the causes of disease.

Once, Banyen secretly watched as her father cast a female phipop out of a woman in the neighborhood. He demanded that the phipop leave, but the phipop refused. Banyen recalled:

> " Then they brought my father some pepper and he took her hands away from her face and threw the pepper in her eyes. She began to cry. Again he asked her who she was and this time she told him her name. She promised that she would go away and never return. Suddenly the woman sat up. . . . My father uttered certain formulae, breathed on her, and the pain disappeared. It was as if nothing had happened. "

Watching and listening to her father, Banyen came to admire his great knowledge and healing skill. When she went to school, Banyen was an excellent student. At a time when few girls finished elementary school, she and her sisters went on to high school, then to college. Banyen recalled:

> " We were the first women students. My mother did not see any reason why I should waste four more years at college when I might have made myself useful at home and learned to cook and weave. "

However, Banyen had a secret goal. Remembering how her father had healed the sick, she decided to become a doctor. She transferred to a college in Phnom Penh, Cambodia. From there, she won a scholarship to study in Hanoi, Vietnam, and became the first Laotian woman to enroll in medical school. ■

SECTION 3 REVIEW

1. **Define:** animism.
2. Describe how Hinduism, Buddhism, Islam, and Christianity reached Southeast Asia.
3. How does geography affect the ways in which rice is grown?
4. How did Chinese traditions influence family life in Vietnam?
5. **Applying Information** How did the peoples of Southeast Asia adapt ideas from other cultures to their own needs?
6. **Writing Across Cultures** Write a paragraph comparing the life of women in Southeast Asia with that of women in the United States.

Chapter 11 Review

Understanding Vocabulary

Match each term at left with the correct definition at right.

1. archipelago	**a.** rice field
2. copra	**b.** country that recognizes the authority of an overlord
3. tributary state	**c.** dried coconut meat
4. animism	**d.** chain of islands
5. paddy	**e.** belief that a spirit lives in every object

Reviewing the Main Ideas

1. (a) What are the two regions of Southeast Asia? (b) How are they different?
2. (a) List two mineral and two agricultural resources of Southeast Asia. (b) Why does the use of forest resources cause problems?
3. Why have Southeast Asian nations had difficulty achieving unity?
4. (a) Why were river valleys important to the development of kingdoms in Southeast Asia? (b) How did India influence the region?
5. (a) How did animist beliefs blend with Hinduism and Buddhism? (b) How did Islam and Christianity arrive in Southeast Asia?

Reviewing Chapter Themes

1. Geography has contributed to cultural diversity in Southeast Asia. Explain how two of the following have encouraged this diversity: (a) location, (b) topography, (c) waterways.
2. The ancient kingdoms of Southeast Asia were influenced by neighboring civilizations. Describe how outside influences affected two of the kingdoms.
3. Many religious traditions have influenced Southeast Asia. Choose two religions and describe: (a) how they were introduced to Southeast Asia, (b) how they were adapted, (c) how they influence life today.
4. Most people in Southeast Asia are farmers. Describe how agriculture affects the economies, ethnic makeup, and family life of Southeast Asian nations.

Thinking Critically

1. **Making Global Connections** (a) Why does cultural diversity pose a challenge to the nations of Southeast Asia? (b) What similar challenges does the United States face?
2. **Comparing** Compare and contrast the effects of Mongol invasions of Southeast Asia on Pagan and the Tai kingdoms.
3. **Applying Information** War and trade are two of the common methods of cultural diffusion. Explain how one of these contributed to cultural diffusion in Southeast Asia.
4. **Making Inferences** Why do women in Southeast Asia have political rights, yet often receive less schooling than men?

Applying Your Skills

1. **Identifying the Main Idea** Reread "A Diverse Region" on pages 252–253. (a) Which sentence expresses the main idea? (b) List three facts that support the main idea.
2. **Constructing a Time Line** Use the information in this chapter to construct a time line of events relating to the ancient kingdoms of Southeast Asia. Use different-colored markers to show the periods during which each kingdom was independent.
3. **Analyzing a Poem** Reread "A Farmer's Calendar" on page 261. (a) Who is speaking? (b) What does the poem say about rural life? (c) What does the poem show you about relationships in farming families? (See Skill Lesson 12 on page 541.)

Chapter 12

Southeast Asia in Transition

Old Ways and New This contemporary Vietnamese print shows how important both the past and the present are in Southeast Asia. The elderly man, dressed in traditional clothes, is next to his son or grandson, dressed in western-style clothes. The print says, "The old bamboo and the young bamboo each have their time." ***Fine Art*** What does this art suggest about culture and change in Southeast Asia?

Chapter Outline

1 European Influence

2 A New Political Map

3 War in Southeast Asia

The novel had the innocent title *The Lost Eden.* Yet Filipinos had to read it in secret. Mere possession of the book could lead to imprisonment.

Written by a young Filipino poet and doctor named José Rizal, *The Lost Eden* was published in 1887. By then, Spain had ruled the Philippines for more than 300 years. In the book, Rizal showed how Spanish officials abused their power. He called for reform but condemned revolution.

To show his loyalty, Rizal volunteered as a doctor in the Spanish army. In 1896, he set out to join the Spanish fighting in Cuba. On the way, Spanish police arrested him and sent him back to the Philippines to be tried for rebellion. "I never sought the liberty to rebel . . . only political liberties," said Rizal at his trial. The judges, however, ignored his words and sentenced him to death.

While awaiting execution, Rizal wrote "My Last Farewell":

“Land I adore, farewell! . . .
Joyous, I yield up for thee
my sad life, and were it
far brighter,
Young, or rose-strewn, for
thee and thy happiness
still would I give it.”

To Filipino nationalists, Rizal became a symbol of their struggle for independence from Spain.

CHAPTER PERSPECTIVE

Throughout Southeast Asia, years of European rule sparked nationalist movements. During the mid-1900s, Southeast Asians fought wars for independence whose effects are still felt today.

As you read, look for these chapter themes:

- Desire for profit led Europeans to take colonies in Southeast Asia.
- The growth of nationalism in Southeast Asia led to struggles for independence.
- The newly independent nations of Southeast Asia faced many challenges as they tried to create unified nations.
- Cold War tensions led to a long struggle between communist and non-communist forces in Vietnam.

Literature Connections

In this chapter, you will encounter passages from the following works.

"My Last Farewell," José Rizal

"Who Am I?" Tru Vu

For other suggestions, see Connections With Literature, pages 804–808.

1 EUROPEAN INFLUENCE

FIND OUT

Why did European powers want to set up colonies in Southeast Asia?

How did European interest in Southeast Asia grow during the 1800s?

How did colonial rule affect the peoples of Southeast Asia?

Vocabulary protectorate, encomienda

“This city of Malacca is the richest trading port and possesses the most valuable merchandise . . . that is known in all the world.” That was how Malacca looked to Duarte Barbosa, a Portuguese sailor.

The city sat at the narrowest point on the Strait of Malacca. Each year, as many as 15,000 merchants sailed into Malacca from Southeast Asia, China, India, and the Middle East. They traded silks, iron, silver, pearls, and precious spices. During the 1500s, though, Europeans battled to control this rich port.

Arrival of the Europeans

For centuries, Arab traders carried spices, silks, and other goods from Asia to the Middle East. There, the Arabs sold these goods at a profit to traders from Venice and Genoa. In turn, these traders sold the goods throughout Europe at even higher prices.

European rulers and merchants envied the huge profits made by these traders. They wanted to gain a share of the spice trade for themselves. To do so, they had to bypass the Mediterranean and find an ocean route to the "Spice Islands." Spain and Portugal sent explorers like Christopher Columbus and Vasco da Gama to hunt for such a route. In 1498, da Gama sailed around Africa and reached the

The Dutch in Java Dutch artist Aelbert Cuyp painted this portrait in the 1600s. It shows a Dutch merchant and his wife at the port of Batavia in Java, a city founded by Dutch traders. Now called Djakarta, it is the capital city of Indonesia. ***Fine Art*** How does the artist suggest the important role of early Dutch settlers in this region of Southeast Asia?

west coast of India. The Portuguese then pushed farther east and captured Malacca in 1511. From there, they built trading posts throughout island Southeast Asia. Europeans called this region the East Indies.

The next Europeans to gain power in Southeast Asia were the Dutch. In 1596, they set up a trading post on the island of Java. From there, they seized Malacca from the Portuguese in 1641. During the following decades, the Dutch pushed the Portuguese out of the region.

Taking advantage of rivalries among many small kingdoms, the Dutch gained control over almost all of what is now Indonesia. They set up plantations for the production of cash crops. For the next 200 years, the Dutch were the main European traders in Southeast Asia.

European Power Grows

During the 1700s and 1800s, changes in Europe affected events in Southeast Asia. First, Europeans acquired a taste for products such as sugar, coffee, and tea that grew in tropical climates. Second, the population of Europe grew rapidly, increasing the demand for these goods. Third, the Industrial Revolution led Europeans to look to Southeast Asia for raw materials for their factories and mills as well as markets for the products of these factories and mills.

The Dutch in Java. To meet the growing demand for coffee and other crops, the Dutch set up a Culture System on Java during the 1800s. Under this system, they forced villages to set aside one fifth of their land to grow cash crops. Each year, local farmers had to sell a certain amount of their harvest to the Dutch at a low price.

The Culture System greatly benefited the Dutch government. It gained about one third of its total income from the export of these cash crops. On Java, however, local farmers suffered. They made no profit from the sale of their crops. If harvests fell short, farmers were forced to make up the difference by paying taxes or providing free labor. Worse, they often were forced to neglect their own rice fields to work for the Dutch. As rice production fell, Java was struck by famine.

The British in Malaya. While the Dutch concentrated on Java, Britain slowly gained control of the Malay Peninsula. In 1786, a British trading company acquired Penang Island. Nine years later, the British captured Malacca from the Dutch. Then, in 1824, British traders bought Singapore from the sultan who ruled it. From these three possessions, Britain gradually extended its influence into Malaya. In the 1890s, Britain combined several lands ruled by sultans to form the Federated Malay States.

To supply their industries, the British promoted production of tin and rubber in Malaya. For centuries, Malayans had mined tin by hand. The British introduced machinery to increase tin production. They also brought rubber trees from Brazil. The trees thrived in tropical Malaya, creating a booming rubber industry. To meet their labor needs, the British imported hundreds of thousands of Indian and Chinese workers to Malaya.

The island of Singapore had an excellent location on the Strait of Malacca. Its deep harbor could handle modern steamships, and under British rule, Singapore became the busiest trading port in Southeast Asia.

Scramble for Colonies

By the early 1800s, rivalry between Britain and France led to a scramble for colonies on mainland Southeast Asia. Both powers wanted colonies that would provide raw materials for their factories and markets for their manufactured goods. Both nations also wanted bases from which to increase trade with China.

From India, the British pushed into Burma. In a series of wars with Burmese rulers, the British took over the area piece by piece. By 1890, Britain ruled Burma as a province of India.

Vietnam. During the 1800s, the French carved out an empire that became known as French Indochina. It included what is today Vietnam, Cambodia, and Laos. Since the 1600s, French missionaries had traveled to Vietnam to convert people to Catholicism. One French missionary also developed a western alphabet for Vietnamese to replace the existing one based on Chinese characters. This alphabet, *quoc-ngu* (kwahk-noo), is still used throughout Vietnam.

Vietnamese rulers, however, viewed the missionaries as a threat to their own authority. The Vietnamese grew more concerned as European powers began to carve up China. (See Chapter 15.) In an effort to end foreign

MAP STUDY

During the 1800s, many western nations built colonial empires in Southeast Asia. By 1914, these nations controlled nearly all of the region.

1. **Place** Which Europeans claimed land in New Guinea?
2. **Region** Which imperialist power ruled the largest empire in island Southeast Asia?
3. **Synthesizing Information** (a) Why did Britain and France become rivals for overseas colonies in Southeast Asia? (b) How did this affect the nations there?

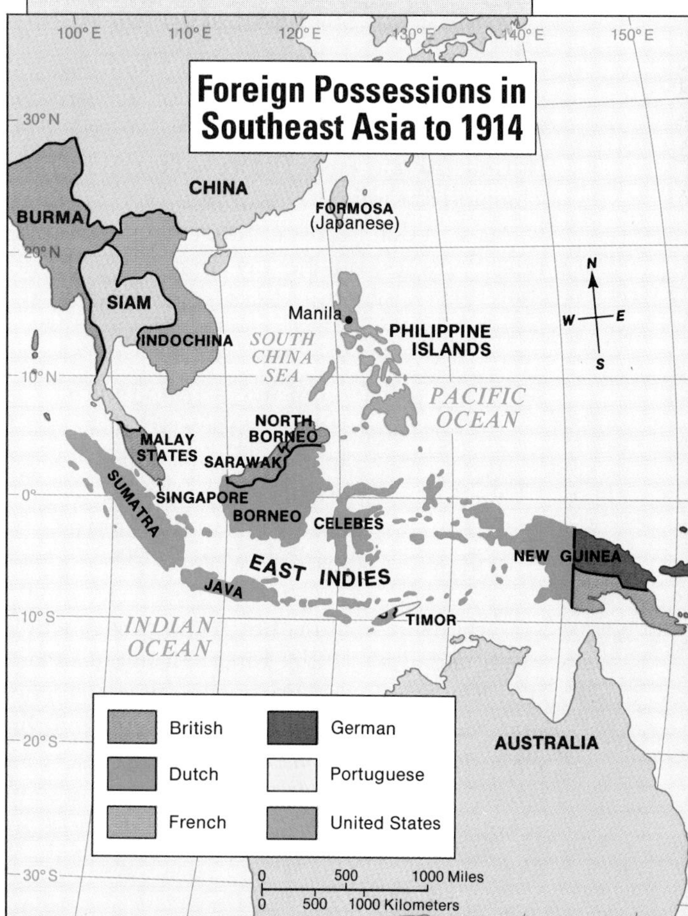

influence, Vietnamese officials used harsh measures against the missionaries. During the 1840s, Emperor Thieu Tri expelled most of the missionaries. A number of missionaries and many Vietnamese Christians were executed.

Using this persecution as an excuse, French forces invaded Vietnam in 1858. Although they met strong resistance at first, the French gradually conquered the land. In 1884, France made Vietnam part of its empire.

Cambodia and Laos. For centuries after the fall of the Khmer Empire, Cambodia resisted efforts by Thailand and Vietnam to conquer it. In the 1860s, the French intimidated the Cambodian king into signing a treaty that made Cambodia a protectorate of France. A protectorate is a country that has its own government but whose policies are directed by an outside power. Much of Laos had been under Thai control. When the Thais withdrew, the French moved in. By 1893, most of present-day Laos had been added to French Indochina.

Thailand Escapes European Rule

Thailand, then known as Siam, lay between the growing spheres of British and French influence. To the west, Britain held Burma. To the east, France ruled Indochina. Thailand's King Mongkut was a realist. He wanted to defend his country from the imperialist powers, but he saw that he could not fight the powerful European armies and navies. He wrote:

> “Being, as we are now, surrounded on two or three sides by powerful nations, what can a small nation like us do? . . . The only weapons that will be of real use to us in the future will be . . . sense and wisdom.”

To ensure that no European power would dominate his land, King Mongkut made treaties with several European nations. France and Britain cooperated. They recognized that an independent Thailand would reduce the danger of conflict between them. At the same time, Mongkut hired European experts to help Thailand modernize. Mongkut's successors followed his policies and succeeded in protecting Thai independence.

The Philippines Under Foreign Rule

Long before Europeans reached Southeast Asia, the Philippines had been a cultural crossroads. Chinese, Japanese, Malays, Arabs, and Indians traded there. In 1521, explorer Ferdinand Magellan claimed the Philippines for Spain. Later, Spain made the Philippines part of a vast Spanish empire that stretched from Manila to Mexico.

A Spanish colony. In the Philippines, as in its American colonies, Spain at first granted encomiendas to settlers. An encomienda was a right to demand taxes or labor from the people living on the land. In theory, the encomienda system was supposed to protect Filipinos and provide for teaching them Christianity. In practice, most settlers took advantage of the Filipinos. They also failed to provide religious instruction. By the late 1600s, the Spanish government had abandoned the encomienda system. Instead, the king of Spain appointed officials to rule the Philippines directly.

Spanish missionaries spread Catholicism throughout the islands. They set up schools and introduced many Spanish customs. The Catholic archbishop of the Philippines also gained enormous political power.

Rebellion and defeat. By the 1800s, Spanish power had declined around the world. In the Philippines, however, the wealth and power of Catholic religious orders were growing. Many Filipinos, like José Rizal, accused the Church of abusing its power. Their anger fueled a growing Filipino nationalism.

During the 1890s, the Filipinos rebelled against Spanish rule. A young soldier and politician, Emilio Aguinaldo (ahg ee NAHL doh), led the rebels. Their hopes for victory rose when the United States declared war on Spain in 1898. Filipinos declared independence and helped the Americans surround Spanish troops in Manila. The war ended when the Spanish surrendered to the Americans.

Emilio Aguinaldo, Freedom Fighter

BUILDERS AND SHAPERS

On July 4, 1946, Filipinos joyously prepared to celebrate their independence. In Manila, 77-year-old Emilio Aguinaldo carefully put on his black bow tie for the last time. For almost 50 years, he had worn this tie as a symbol of grief—grief that the Philippines were not free.

Aguinaldo had devoted his life to the struggle for Philippine independence. As a young man, he led rebel forces against Spanish rule. In 1896, Aguinaldo attacked the Spanish garrison in his hometown of Kawit. Victorious, he then led more raids against the Spanish. He urged his followers:

> "Filipino citizens! Now is the occasion for shedding our blood for the last time, that we may achieve our beloved freedom. . . . The time has come. Let us march under the Flag of the Revolution whose watchwords are Liberty, Equality, and Fraternity!"

In 1898, Aguinaldo joined forces with the Americans against Spain. He declared Philippine independence and, after the Spanish defeat, took office as the nation's first president. He was so popular that young men all over the islands imitated his close-cropped hairstyle, the "Aguinaldo cut."

The struggle for independence did not end in 1898. When the Americans tried to assert control of the islands, Aguinaldo again took up arms. For two years, he led guerrilla forces against the Americans. Then, betrayed by an informer, he was captured. Reluctantly, Aguinaldo swore allegiance to the United States. "I believe I am serving thee, my beloved country," he said.

Now, in 1946, nearly 50 years after Aguinaldo first proclaimed Philippine independence, the Philippines were free. Proudly, the old rebel leader marched down Dewey Boulevard in Manila. As the crowd cheered, Emilio Aguinaldo took off his black bow tie.

1. Why did nearly 50 years pass between Aguinaldo's declaration of Philippine independence and the first celebration of independence?
2. **Drawing Conclusions** What character traits and beliefs do you think helped Aguinaldo work for his goals?

Filipinos expected the Americans to recognize their independence. Instead, the treaty between Spain and the United States placed the islands under American control. Bitterly disappointed, Filipino nationalists renewed their struggle, this time against the United States. About 100,000 Filipinos died before American forces crushed the rebellion in 1901.

American rule. Unlike the European imperial powers, the United States allowed Filipinos to hold high government office. The Americans also built schools, hospitals, and roads. They did little to change the Philippine economy, however. A few wealthy landlords owned huge estates, while most Filipinos lived in poverty.

Filipino nationalists continued to make demands for freedom. In 1934, the United States promised the Philippines independence within 10 years.

Impact of Colonial Rule

In Southeast Asia, as elsewhere, colonial rule altered the economy. In Java, Malaya, and Indochina, Europeans set up plantations to produce cash crops or other export commodities. The economies of those areas thus came to depend on European markets.

Europeans also sold factory-made goods to their colonies. By selling cloth, tools, and other products cheaply, they undercut local crafts. Local artisans could not compete with factory-made goods and were forced out of business. As a result, the economies of Southeast Asia became dependent on the industrialized nations for manufactured goods.

Foreign rulers built modern transportation systems to make their colonies profitable. They also built schools and universities to train local people for careers such as administration, teaching, and medicine. Education had unforeseen results, however. As in Africa and India, it created an educated middle class and contributed to the growth of nationalism.

Colonial rule had little impact on the cultures of Southeast Asia. Except in the Philippines and Vietnam, most people did not become Christians. Europeans did, however, bring many Chinese and Indian workers to Southeast Asia, adding to its cultural diversity. In Malaya, a system of separate schools for Malay, Chinese, and Indian students helped to create long-lasting ethnic divisions.

Tapping a Rubber Tree Workers, such as the man shown here, must collect raw latex from rubber trees by hand, without machinery. When Indonesian rubber production began to decline in the 1970s, the government began a tree replanting program. By 1990, total output of rubber had increased by nearly 20 percent, to more than 1 million tons a year. ***Technology*** Why can rubber be an expensive crop to grow?

SECTION 1 REVIEW

1. **Locate:** (a) Java, (b) Malaya, (c) Singapore, (d) Manila.
2. **Identify:** (a) Culture System, (b) French Indochina, (c) Mongkut, (d) Emilio Aguinaldo.
3. **Define:** (a) protectorate, (b) encomienda.
4. (a) What resources attracted Europeans to Southeast Asia in the 1500s? (b) In the 1800s?
5. How did the Dutch, British, and French extend their power in Southeast Asia?
6. Describe three effects that European colonization had on Southeast Asia.
7. **Defending a Position** (a) How did King Mongkut's actions show that he was a realist? (b) Do you agree with his policy? Why or why not?
8. **Writing Across Cultures** Imagine that you are a Filipino in the time following the Spanish-American War. Write a letter to an American senator explaining why the United States should grant the Philippines independence.

2

A NEW POLITICAL MAP

FIND OUT

Why did nationalism grow in Southeast Asia?

How did the nations of Southeast Asia win independence?

What problems did the new nations face?

Vocabulary nationalize, martial law

A young Indonesian named Sukarno* stood before the Dutch court. He faced a prison sentence for plotting to overthrow Dutch rule. "Yes, we are revolutionaries," Sukarno told the court. "Even when a worm is hurt, it squirms and turns. So do we."

In 1930, the Dutch felt sure that they could put down any rebellion in their colony. They imprisoned Sukarno and ignored his words when he warned:

> "A nation can exist without tanks and guns. A nation cannot exist without faith. That is what we have. That is our secret weapon."

Growing Nationalism

By the early 1900s, nationalist movements were taking root throughout Southeast Asia. Nationalists took pride in the history and traditions of their people. Everywhere, they organized forces to win independence.

In 1905, nationalist hopes surged when Japan crushed Russia in the Russo-Japanese War. For the first time, an Asian nation had defeated a major European power. In the 1930s, however, the Japanese conquered much of China and threatened Southeast Asia. During World War II, Japan overran most of Southeast Asia from Indochina to the Philippines.

At first, some Southeast Asian nationalists welcomed the Japanese advance. They were glad to see the French, British, and Dutch forced to retreat. The Japanese tried to encourage local support. They emphasized the need for "co-existence and co-prosperity" among Asian peoples. In Buddhist countries, they stressed their shared religion.

Japanese troops, however, tortured and killed people who opposed their presence. They tramped through Buddhist temples and seized food and fuel from the people to support their war effort. Nationalists who had opposed the European colonial powers soon switched to fighting the Japanese. The Allies sent arms to local groups that resisted the Japanese. As a result, by 1945, many Southeast Asians were well-armed, experienced guerrilla fighters.

Japanese Conquest The Japanese seized most of Southeast Asia during World War II. They wanted the region's natural resources to help fuel the Japanese economy. This photograph shows Japanese troops as they prepared to invade Burma. ***Power*** Why did Southeast Asian nationalists support Japan's invading armies at first?

* Like many Indonesians, Sukarno used a single name.

An Appeal to Nationalism This World War II poster urged the people of Southeast Asia to resist the Japanese "octopus." With its message in Dutch, it appealed to people living in Dutch-ruled territories. ***Choice*** Why is a Dutch message to resist foreign rule ironic?

The Road to Independence

After the defeat of Japan, European powers planned to return to Southeast Asia. Nationalist leaders were equally determined to win independence. Some countries won freedom peacefully. In others, the struggle for independence involved violence.

Peaceful transitions. In the Philippines, the United States finally made good on its promise of independence. On July 4, 1946, Filipinos celebrated independence.*

After the war, the British returned to Burma. They found Burmese nationalists armed and well organized. Aung San, the leader of Burma's main political party, called for immediate independence. Weakened by the war and fearing that communist forces might seize power, the British agreed. Although Aung San was murdered, Burma won its independence early in 1948.

Conflict in Malaya. In 1957, after a long struggle between communist rebels and Malay supporters of Britain, Malaya gained independence from Britain. It took the name Malaysia in 1963, when it joined with Singapore, Sabah, and Sarawak.

Malaysia faced severe problems among its three major ethnic groups. Malays, mostly farmers and fishers, made up 50 percent of the population but were among the poorest people. The Chinese and Indians, on the other hand, dominated business and the professions. Although the government promoted education and found jobs for Malays, ethnic unrest continued.

Indonesia and Indochina. After World War II, the Dutch returned to Indonesia to find that Sukarno had declared Indonesia's independence. For four years, the Dutch fought to regain control of their colony. In the end, they were forced to give up all of Indonesia except West Irian, the western half of New Guinea. In 1949, Sukarno became president of an independent Indonesia. Twelve years later, after further armed clashes, West Irian also became part of Indonesia.

Like the Dutch, the French sought to regain control of their colonies in Indochina. Although France granted limited independence to Laos in 1949, it fought to hold on to Vietnam and Cambodia. As you will read later in this chapter, Vietnamese nationalists were determined to end French rule.

Challenges for the New Nations

Like emerging nations everywhere, the new nations of Southeast Asia faced many challenges. Under colonial rule, they had little experience with self-government. After independence, leaders had to forge diverse groups into unifed nations committed to the achievement of common goals. To make matters worse, almost all of these new nations faced severe economic problems.

* Since 1962, Philippine Independence Day has been celebrated on June 12 to commemorate the day in 1898 when Emilio Aguinaldo declared independence. July 4 is Philippine-American Friendship Day.

Burma becomes Myanmar. After independence, Burma had trouble achieving unity. Minority ethnic groups such as the Karen and the Shan demanded their own countries. At the same time, Burmese communists fought to overthrow the new government.

Like other new nations, Burma had to decide how to develop its economy. At first, it moved toward a limited form of socialism. The government nationalized, or placed under state control, British-owned plantations. It made rice growing a state monopoly. When these measures failed to improve the economy, the Burmese army seized power. In 1962, General Ne Win became dictator and set up a one-party socialist state.

For almost 30 years, Ne Win kept Burma isolated from the rest of the world. During the late 1980s, however, Burmese students and others demanded democratic elections. The army opened fire on the demonstrators, killing thousands. In 1990, the government finally held elections. Opponents of the military dictator won by a landslide. The army responded by jailing the winners and forcing others to flee the country.

Under Ne Win, Burma changed its name to Myanmar. The new name comes from the Burmese words for "country" and "the people." The name change recognizes that the nation contains many ethnic groups besides the dominant Burmans.

Singapore. In 1963, Singapore achieved independence from Britain. At first, as you have read, it joined Malaya, Sabah, and Sarawak to form Malaysia, but this union did not work. Two years later, Singapore, with its Chinese majority, was forced out of the union.

Like Myanmar, Singapore fell under the control of a strongman, Lee Kuan Yew. Although Singapore had a parliament and held elections, Lee ruled the one-party state like a dictator. To stay in power, Lee controlled the press and the labor unions. He also rallied popular support by playing on the Singaporeans' fear of invasion by Malaysia and Indonesia.

Despite harsh rule, Singapore prospered economically. Lee provided stable government. Also, by limiting the power of labor unions, he kept wages low and attracted foreign business. Still, many people felt that Singapore's economic success did not make up for lack of freedom. In 1990, Goh Chok Tong replaced Lee as prime minister. Elections were held in 1991.

The Philippines After Independence

During the years after independence, the Philippines faced serious challenges to their democracy. Some problems grew out of centuries of Spanish rule. Under the Spanish, a small upper class had controlled the wealth and power of the islands. The gap between rich and poor grew even wider after independence. Another problem was widespread corruption in government.

The Huk rebellion. Filipino communists, known as Huks, fought against the government during the 1950s. By promising land reform, they won the support of many peasants. Because the United States feared a communist revolution, it helped the Philippine government crush the Huk rebellion.

Speaking Out Daw Aung San Suu Kyi, the daughter of Burmese nationalist leader Aung San, won a free election in Myanmar in 1990. However, the military government then placed her under house arrest. Because she continued to oppose the government's oppression, Suu Kyi won the Nobel Peace Prize in 1991. ***Human Rights*** How did Myanmar's military government violate democratic principles?

The Philippine government then took steps to improve conditions for peasants. It built health clinics and schools and dug wells. It also made some effort to end corruption and to redistribute land. However, rich landowners used their power to block most land reform programs.

Ferdinand Marcos. In 1965, Ferdinand Marcos was elected president. A smart politician, he won popular support by extending programs to help the poor. At the same time, Marcos used government money to enrich himself and his supporters. When anti-Marcos protests broke out in 1972, Marcos imposed martial law, or temporary rule by the military. He shut down newspapers and jailed opponents. Although Marcos ended martial law in 1981, he kept tight control over the country.

In 1983, Benigno Aquino (buh NEEN yoh ah KEE noh), a popular reformer, returned to Manila from exile. As he stepped off the plane, he was murdered by supporters of Marcos. Aquino's death set off massive protests. To restore calm, Marcos finally agreed to hold elections in 1986. His chief opponent was Corazon Aquino, the widow of the slain reformer.

After a campaign marked by fraud and violence, Marcos declared himself the winner even though Aquino won a majority of the votes. Filipinos then took to the streets, demanding that Aquino be put in office. When the military gave its support to Aquino, Marcos fled to Hawaii.

Marcos's Millions By the time Ferdinand Marcos was forced to leave the Philippines in 1986, he had amassed a fortune abroad. He had drained millions from the Philippine treasury and deposited it in Swiss banks, as this cartoon shows. ***Power*** Why would a powerful ruler like Marcos steal from his nation's treasury?

Aquino in power. Corazon Aquino entered office on a tremendous wave of "people power." After her election, a columnist in the *Philippine Daily Enquirer* wrote:

Aquino Campaigning Corazon Aquino generated great enthusiasm during her 1986 campaign to become president of the Philippines. She had decided to enter politics after her husband's murderers were freed by Marcos. Her campaign ended in victory when Marcos fled the country. ***Political System*** How did Aquino's victory strengthen democracy in the Philippines?

"We voted in the past for Presidents for all sorts of reasons, but those who voted for you in the last elections did so because they also *loved* you."

Once in office, Aquino faced severe tests. The government was challenged by army leaders who tried to seize power and, in some areas, by communist rebels. Aquino made little progress in ending corruption or pushing land reform programs. Millions of Filipinos continued to live in desperate poverty. In 1992, General Fidel Ramos was elected to succeed Aquino.

Both Aquino and Ramos had to balance strong anti-American feeling in the Philippines against the aid provided by the United States. Many Filipinos campaigned fiercely to remove American military bases from their country. They considered the bases a symbol of colonial rule. In late 1992, American forces withdrew from the bases. The Philippine government, however, agreed to allow the United States to have access to the installations.

SECTION 2 REVIEW

1. **Identify:** (a) Aung San, (b) Sukarno, (c) Ne Win, (d) Lee Kuan Yew, (e) Huk, (f) Ferdinand Marcos, (g) Corazon Aquino.
2. **Define:** (a) nationalize, (b) martial law.
3. How did World War II affect nationalist movements in Southeast Asia?
4. Describe how the following nations became independent: (a) Burma, (b) Malaysia, (c) Indonesia.
5. What problems have the Philippines faced since independence?
6. **Making Inferences** What does Burma's change of name to Myanmar suggest about the role of ethnic groups in Southeast Asia?
7. **Writing Across Cultures** Singapore has encouraged foreign businesses to invest in its economy. Write a newspaper editorial explaining whether or not you believe American businesses should invest in Singapore even though Singapore limits the freedom of its citizens.

3 WAR IN SOUTHEAST ASIA

FIND OUT

What role did Ho Chi Minh play in Vietnam?

How did the United States become involved in the war in Southeast Asia?

What were the short-term and long-term effects of the war?

Vocabulary domino theory, genocide

World War I had ended at last. In 1919, United States president Woodrow Wilson joined the leaders of Britain, France, and Italy at the Versailles peace conference. Wilson wanted a peace treaty that would guarantee all people the right to determine their own future.

A young Vietnamese nationalist took Wilson seriously. He went to Versailles and called on France to grant independence to Vietnam. France refused, however. Disappointed, the young man left Versailles, vowing to help his people win their freedom. During the struggle that followed, he would take the name Ho Chi Minh—"He Who Enlightens."

Struggle Against France

During the years after World War I, Vietnamese nationalists pushed for changes. France responded with force, crushing all attempts at reform.

Ho Chi Minh. Ho Chi Minh emerged as a leader of the independence movement in Vietnam. After his bitter experience at Versailles, Ho helped to found the Communist party in France. Communism appealed to many nationalists because it rejected colonialism. When Ho returned to Vietnam, he had two goals—to build a communist movement and to win independence.

The French in Indochina The French made themselves at home in Vietnam. In this photo, French officials relax on a hotel terrace in Saigon. Saigon's broad, tree-lined avenues and handsome parks reminded them of Paris. In addition, French was used as the language of business and government. ***Power*** In what ways did the French try to impose their culture on the Vietnamese people?

During World War II, Ho and other Vietnamese nationalists formed the Viet Minh. They used guerrilla warfare against the Japanese occupation forces. By 1945, the Viet Minh occupied parts of northern Vietnam, including the city of Hanoi. Ho wrote a declaration of independence for Vietnam that echoed the American Declaration of Independence. It proclaimed:

> "All men are created equal. The Creator has given us certain inviolable Rights: the right to Life, the right to be Free, and the right to achieve Happiness."

In 1946, however, France set out to regain control of Indochina. For eight years, French forces battled Vietnamese nationalists.

Cold War issues. By this time, the struggle in Vietnam had become part of the Cold War. The Soviet Union and China supported Ho's communist forces. Although the United States opposed colonialism, it supported the French. American leaders believed in the domino theory. According to the theory, if one nation fell to communist forces, neighboring nations would also become communist, like a row of falling dominoes.

In 1954, the Viet Minh trapped a French army at Dienbienphu, forcing it to surrender. Later that year, France withdrew from both Vietnam and Cambodia under a peace agreement drawn up in Geneva, Switzerland.

A Divided Nation

The Geneva agreement temporarily divided Vietnam at the seventeenth parallel. Ho Chi Minh and the communists controlled North Vietnam. A non-communist government led by Ngo Dinh Diem (ngaw dihn dzee EHM) ruled South Vietnam. Within two years, the Vietnamese were to hold elections to reunite the country. However, thousands voted with their feet. They fled either south or north to the area of Vietnam where they felt politically most comfortable.

In North Vietnam, Ho put a communist system firmly into place. He limited freedom of the press and silenced opponents. Still, he won the support of poor peasants by redistributing land taken from large landowners.

In South Vietnam, the fighting continued among various groups opposed to Diem. In 1956, Diem blocked the scheduled elections, fearing that the communists would win. By 1960, communists in the south had formed an underground army known as the Viet Cong. With arms from the north, the Viet Cong fought a guerrilla war to overthrow Diem. (See World Literature, "Thoughts of Hanoi," by Nguyen Thi Vinh, page 314.)

Diem had the support of the United States. However, he steadily lost popular support in Vietnam by failing to end corruption or set up land reform programs. Also, Diem, a Roman Catholic, angered the Buddhist majority by favoring Catholics. As protests increased, Diem cracked down harshly. His actions increased support for the Viet Cong and led to his assassination in 1963.

American Involvement

As the Viet Cong expanded their power, the United States took a more active role in the war. It sent thousands of military advisers to South Vietnam. In response, North Vietnam stepped up its involvement. Ho Chi Minh sent North Vietnamese troops to help the Viet Cong. To reach the south, they used routes that ran through Laos and Cambodia. These routes became known as the Ho Chi Minh Trail.

Gulf of Tonkin Resolution. In 1964, two small American patrol ships in the Gulf of Tonkin claimed that North Vietnamese gunboats had attacked them. In response, the United States Congress passed the Gulf of Tonkin Resolution. It gave President Lyndon Johnson the power to "take all necessary steps including the use of force" to help South Vietnam.

MAP STUDY

The struggle against French rule led to the creation of Vietnam, Laos, and Cambodia. During the 1960s, the conflict between North and South Vietnam became a major war.

1. **Interaction** How might the climate of the region have affected the fighting in the war? See the climate map on page 778.
2. **Place** In which capital city was the last battle of the Vietnam War fought?
3. **Drawing Conclusions** How did North Vietnam's use of the Ho Chi Minh Trail help spread the war to other nations?

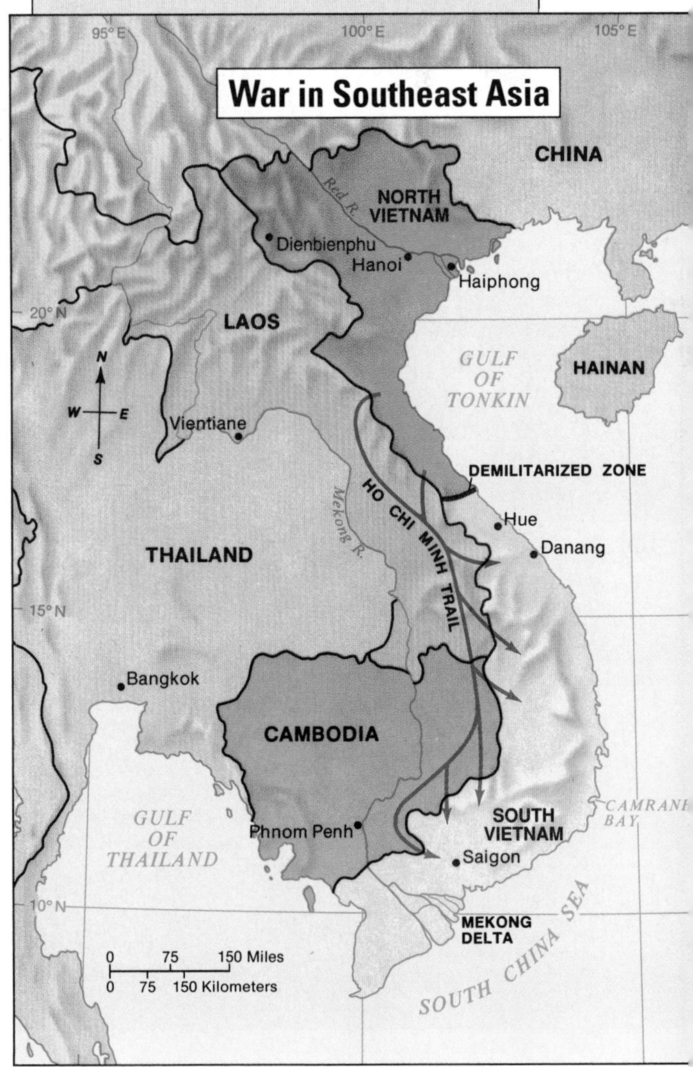

In 1965, Johnson sent American combat forces to South Vietnam and began to bomb towns and cities in the north. Within three years, 500,000 American troops were fighting in Vietnam. Despite the American buildup, the Viet Cong continued to fight effectively.

Young Soldiers The long war in Vietnam devastated that small nation. More than 1 million people in North Vietnam and South Vietnam died in the conflict. Even young boys like these fought. For the United States, the Vietnam War was the longest war in its history. ***Choice*** Why did many Americans oppose the war in Vietnam?

The Soviet Union and China supported Viet Cong efforts with arms and supplies.

The war spreads. The American buildup spread the war to Laos and Cambodia. In 1964, the United States sent planes to bomb the Ho Chi Minh Trail in Laos. Despite heavy attacks, the supply route remained open. Also, the bombing angered many Laotians and increased support for the Pathet Lao, the local communist guerrillas.

For years, Cambodia tried to stay out of the war. The North Vietnamese and the Viet Cong, however, had bases inside Cambodia. In 1969, the United States began bombing these bases. The next year, American and South Vietnamese troops invaded Cambodia to destroy the bases. As in Laos, the bombing of Cambodia increased support for the local communist guerrillas, the Khmer Rouge.

A Slow Return to Peace

By the 1970s, Vietnam had been at war for more than 30 years. In the following poem, Tru Vu expressed the weariness and suffering of the people of Vietnam:

> “I am neither a communist
> nor a nationalist:
> I am Vietnamese.
> Is it not enough?
> For thousands of years
> that's what I've been:
> Don't you think that's enough?
> And Vietnam in flames
> and mother who weeps
> and youngsters who suffer
> and all the words we use to kill each
> other!
> O river
> we stand on our respective banks
> our fallen tears mingling.”

End of American involvement. The Vietnam War sparked loud protests in the United States. Antiwar demonstrators called for withdrawal of American troops. In 1969, President Richard Nixon began to withdraw the troops and to seek peace talks. Four years later, a peace treaty ended American involvement in the war. It did not, however, end the war in Southeast Asia. (📖 See Connections With Literature, "Fallen Angels," page 805.)

Vietnam reunited. After the Americans left, South Vietnam was unable to hold back the Viet Cong and North Vietnamese. In 1975, communist forces surrounded Saigon, the capital of South Vietnam, and the government surrendered. Vietnam was finally united.

The victors renamed Saigon Ho Chi Minh City, after Ho, who had died in 1969. The new name symbolized their goal—to build a socialist state such as Ho had imagined. The communist government took over private businesses and farmlands in the south. It sent thousands of South Vietnamese to reeducation camps for forced study and labor.

Years of war had left the economy of Vietnam in shambles. Under communist rule, the country remained poor. Government controls and a United States ban on trade with Vietnam kept foreigners from investing in the country. In the late 1980s, to increase production and encourage investment, the government relaxed some controls. The economy improved as the government moved toward a market economy and the United States lifted its trade ban in 1994.

Tragedy in Cambodia

Soon after Saigon fell, the Khmer Rouge swept to power in Cambodia. The Khmer Rouge leader, Pol Pot, renamed the country Kampuchea. He set out to destroy all traces of foreign influence in Cambodia. Since most city dwellers had come in contact with foreigners, Khmer Rouge soldiers forced people out of the cities and resettled them in the country. There, many died of starvation. The Khmer Rouge also tortured and murdered anyone it suspected of being disloyal.

The actions of the Khmer Rouge are an example of genocide, or the deliberate killing of an entire national or ethnic group. Executions and famine killed more than 1 million Cambodians out of a population of 7 million. (📖 See Connections With Literature, page 805, Haing Ngor: A Cambodian Odyssey.)

Although both Cambodia and Vietnam were communist nations, old rivalries resurfaced between them. In 1979, Vietnamese forces invaded Cambodia and overthrew Pol Pot. Many Khmer Rouge soldiers escaped to remote areas and continued to fight. Under pressure from world powers, the Vietnamese withdrew their forces in 1989. In 1991, the United Nations negotiated a peace settlement in Cambodia. Despite the peace agreement, fighting between rival groups continues.

Escape From the Killing Fields

"They killed my family, they took my brother away," said Chhean Im. "They were always looking for some reason to kill us." Chhean Im was among those who survived the brutal Khmer Rouge reign of terror in the "killing fields" of Cambodia.

Like other Cambodians, Chhean Im had to return to her village. There, the Khmer Rouge forced her to work in the fields. For four years, she worked seven days a week and barely had enough to eat. She recalled:

> "A few grains of rice in a bowl of water, that's all the Khmer Rouge would ever give me to eat. A few times I stole a vegetable or some plant and hid it in my pocket, even though I knew they would kill me if they saw."

Chhean Im faced death every day. She watched as soldiers killed people for the most minor crimes. "They would beat the person terribly. Then four of the Angka [secret police] would pick him up by the arms and legs and throw him alive on a big fire."

When the Vietnamese invaded in 1979, Chhean Im took advantage of the confusion in her village. "There was a lot of shooting," she recalled, and many villagers tried to

Life in Cambodia In 1975, the Khmer Rouge took control of Cambodia and forced the people to leave the capital city of Phnom Penh. In 1979, when the Vietnamese captured the city, the survivors were allowed to return. Here, a Cambodian woman trudges along a road near a poster praising communism. ***Human Rights*** How did the Khmer Rouge deprive Cambodians of their freedom?

escape. "Some people helped me and I followed them." During her flight, she was lucky to avoid land mines, starvation, and capture. Many others were not so lucky.

After two weeks of running, hiding, and walking, she reached a refugee camp in Thailand. Eventually Chhean Im managed to join relatives who lived in the United States. Like many survivors of the killing fields, she now lives in southern California.

Effects of the War

Today, people in Vietnam, Cambodia, and Laos still feel the effects of war. The fighting killed millions of people and disrupted the lives of many others. Massive bombing destroyed villages, bridges, roads, and irrigation systems. In parts of Vietnam, the United States used deadly chemicals to destroy trees, making the land unusable. Everywhere, unexploded land mines still pose danger.

After the communist victory, many Vietnamese tried to escape the harsh political and economic conditions at home. Some left in leaky, unsafe boats. At sea, these "boat people" faced starvation, drowning, and attacks from pirates. The lucky ones reached harbors and found temporary homes in refugee camps.

Thailand, Hong Kong, and other countries reluctantly took in refugees from Vietnam, Cambodia, and Laos. Today, hundreds of thousands still live in refugee camps. Many are afraid to return home.

SECTION 3 REVIEW

1. **Locate:** (a) Dienbienphu, (b) Ho Chi Minh Trail, (c) Saigon.
2. **Identify:** (a) Ho Chi Minh, (b) Ngo Dinh Diem, (c) Viet Cong, (d) Gulf of Tonkin Resolution, (e) Pol Pot.
3. **Define:** (a) domino theory, (b) genocide.
4. How was France's fight to regain control of Indochina part of the Cold War?
5. How did the war in Southeast Asia spread after the United States became involved?
6. Describe three results of the war in Southeast Asia.
7. **Defending a Position** Do you think Diem should have allowed elections in 1955, even if it meant the communists might win? Why or why not?
8. **Writing Across Cultures** Write a list of questions about how the war in Southeast Asia affected people in the United States. Then, ask a parent or older friend your questions and write down their answers. Conclude by writing a one-paragraph summary of what you have learned.

CHAPTER 12 REVIEW

Understanding Vocabulary

Match each term at left with the correct definition at right.

1. protectorate	**a.** deliberate killing of an entire national or ethnic group
2. encomienda	**b.** temporary rule by the military
3. martial law	**c.** country whose policies are directed by an outside power
4. domino theory	**d.** right to demand taxes or labor from people living on the land
5. genocide	**e.** idea that if one nation fell to communist forces, neighboring nations would also become communist

Reviewing the Main Ideas

1. How did the Industrial Revolution spur colonialism in Southeast Asia?

2. How did Thailand avoid European domination during the 1800s?

3. (a) Explain how the Philippines came under the rule of Spain. (b) Of the United States.

4. How did Japanese occupation strengthen nationalist movements in Southeast Asia?

5. (a) What were Ho Chi Minh's goals for Vietnam? (b) How did the Geneva peace agreement lead to further conflict in Vietnam?

Reviewing Chapter Themes

1. After the 1500s, European nations gradually gained control of Southeast Asia. Explain how two of the following extended their power: (a) the Dutch in Java, (b) the British in Malaya, (c) the French in Indochina, (d) the Spanish in the Philippines.

2. Some Southeast Asian nations gained independence by peaceful means, while others had to fight for freedom. Choose two nations and explain how each won independence.

3. Many Southeast Asian nations faced problems forming unified governments. Describe the challenges faced by Myanmar, Singapore, or the Philippines since independence.

4. Cold War tensions played a major part in the Vietnam War. (a) Explain how the Cold War influenced American policies in Vietnam. (b) Describe three results of the Vietnam War.

Thinking Critically

1. Understanding Causes and Effects (a) How did the British increase ethnic diversity in Malaya? (b) How did this affect Malaya after it gained independence?

2. Analyzing Ideas Why do you think that many newly independent nations fall under the control of dictators?

3. Making Global Connections Do you agree or disagree with President Johnson's decision to bomb North Vietnam? Give reasons to support your opinion.

Applying Your Skills

1. Reading a Map Study the map on page 267. (a) Which independent state existed between British and French territory? (b) Which European country held the least territory by 1914? (c) How does the map reflect the history of Southeast Asia?

2. Using Your Vocabulary Use the Glossary on pages 794–803 to review the meaning of the following terms: *export, imperialism, modernization, buffer state*. Use each term in a separate sentence about European influence in Southeast Asia.

3. Constructing a Time Line Use the information in the chapter to construct a time line of events relating to the Vietnam War. (a) Which events on the time line are related to the spread of the war to other parts of Southeast Asia? (b) How are Southeast Asians still feeling the effects of this war?

Chapter 13

Southeast Asia in the World Today

The Skyline of Singapore Modern skyscrapers tower over Singapore, the busiest port city in Southeast Asia. This prosperous capital of the island nation of Singapore is a major center of trade, industry, and banking. Like Singapore, other nations of Southeast Asia are working to develop their economies. ***Geography*** How do you think its location has helped Singapore prosper?

Chapter Outline

Manto and Suminten were shocked when they first arrived at their new home in Rimba Ayu. "The land was so overgrown, we couldn't see the house," Manto recalled. "I said to my wife, 'We'd better get to work.' We've been working ever since."

Manto and Suminten took part in a special program of the Indonesian government. The government gave them five acres of land, a small house, tools, seeds for crops, and other supplies. In return, they gave up their home on crowded Java and moved to Rimba Ayu, a jungle outpost on the sparsely settled island of Kalimantan. All in all, the government has relocated more than 700,000 families.

Indonesia began the resettlement program to redistribute its population. Although Indonesia includes more than 13,500 islands, most people live on just two islands—Java and Bali.

Rapid population growth and overcrowding pose obstacles to

development. Sometimes, the people living on outlying islands object to having people from other religious or ethnic groups resettled onto their islands. However, the program continues in an effort to relieve overcrowding on Java and Bali. While resettlement causes hardships for many families, the program shows that Indonesia is determined to forge ahead on the road to modernization.

CHAPTER PERSPECTIVE

Like Indonesia, the other nations of Southeast Asia face many challenges as they seek to modernize. In Chapter 12, you read about the political developments that have shaped the region since independence. In this chapter, you will look at economic developments.

As you read, look for these chapter themes:

- The nations of Southeast Asia have developed their economies in different ways.
- Thailand and Indonesia have adopted development policies suited to their special geographic and political needs.
- The arts of Southeast Asia reflect a blend of foreign and local traditions.

Literature Connections

In this chapter, you will encounter a passage from the following work.

The Tale of Kieu, Nguyen Du

For other literature suggestions, see Connections With Literature, pages 804–808.

1 ECONOMIC DEVELOPMENT

FIND OUT

How have Southeast Asian countries developed their economies?

How has the Green Revolution affected Southeast Asia?

What is life like in modern cities of Southeast Asia?

Faulizah binti Mat Yatin pleaded with her parents. She badly wanted to take a job at a factory some distance from her village. Her parents resisted. They did not want their 21-year-old daughter living alone so far from home.

At last, Mat Yatin's parents gave in, and Mat Yatin moved into an apartment with four other women who worked at the factory. "We all live here like one happy family," she reported. "Most of us send some money back to our families."

The desire to earn money and to experience city life is causing many young people in Southeast Asia to leave their villages. Many, however, do not find factory life as pleasant as Mat Yatin did. As more and more people migrate to cities, both rural and urban areas are changing.

Economic Choices

As you have read, Southeast Asians won political independence after World War II. Economically, however, they remained dependent on the industrial world. Like other developing nations, they exported raw materials or cash crops and imported most manufactured goods. To reduce this dependence, Southeast Asian nations have diversified their crops, invested in factories, and built modern transportation and communications systems.

Each country has made choices about how to develop its economy. Under commu-

Power Shovels in Indonesia Made in Japan, these giant earth-moving tractors are used to build factories and offices in Indonesia. Japan is Indonesia's most important trading partner. Indonesia sells more than 40 percent of its exports to Japan and imports nearly 25 percent of its goods from Japan. ***Interdependence*** Why does Southeast Asia have close trading ties with Japan?

nist rule, Vietnam, Cambodia, and Laos set up command economies. The socialist government of Myanmar also has a command economy. In these countries, the state has nationalized major industries and taken over the land. The government decides what to produce, how much to produce, and what prices to charge.

By contrast, the Philippines has a market economy. Private individuals own factories and farms and make economic decisions. The government promotes economic growth but does not control the economy directly.

Finally, Singapore and Indonesia chose mixed economies. In these countries, the government owns major industries and takes a strong role in the economy. On the other hand, private individuals own most smaller businesses.

Developing Industry

Southeast Asian nations are working to develop industry for several reasons. Many manufactured goods sell at higher prices than farm products and mineral resources. Also, factory workers earn more money than most farmers. With the extra money, they buy a variety of goods, which in turn encourages factories to produce more and hire more workers. Finally, by increasing local manufactured products, a country reduces its dependence on imported goods.

Singapore's economic success. The tiny island nation of Singapore has made great progress in industrializing. With its few natural resources, it set out to produce manufactured goods for export. Singapore's former leader Lee Kuan Yew pushed through laws favorable to foreign investors. By keeping wages low, he attracted foreign companies eager to produce goods cheaply. Lee also took steps to bring high-tech companies to Singapore. Since these companies need highly skilled workers, Singapore built a modern educational system.

Lee's policies made Singapore a major exporting nation. People's incomes rose, making Singapore's workers among the highest paid in Asia. The government also set up a national health care system and built housing for most people.

New directions in Vietnam. After years of war, Vietnam faced the massive job of rebuilding its economy. As you read in Chapter 12, the communist government took over the nation's land and businesses. Under government control, production in factories and output on farms decreased. In recent years,

Vietnam has moved away from a command economy and has reduced government controls. In that way, it hopes to encourage private enterprise, increase production, and attract foreign investors.

Changes in Agriculture

Most Southeast Asians still support themselves by farming. Many are subsistence farmers, growing just enough rice and vegetables to feed themselves and their families. As Southeast Asian nations modernize, governments are encouraging commercial farming. Commercial farmers raise cash crops to be sold on world markets. The export of cash crops provides income that can be invested in building new industry.

The Green Revolution. In Southeast Asia, as in India, the Green Revolution has greatly improved food production. The Green Revolution, you will recall, involves the use of new seeds, fertilizers, pesticides, and irrigation to increase harvests.

In fact, the Green Revolution began in Southeast Asia. In the early 1960s, scientists working in the Philippines developed a new kind of high-yield rice seed. With this seed, farmers could double the amount of rice they harvested. Since then, scientists have developed other high-yield seeds suited to different environments around the world.

In Southeast Asia, most farmers gradually switched to the new rice seed. Many farmers had to borrow money to buy fertilizers and pesticides needed to grow the improved rice. Still, by selling the surplus rice they raised, these farmers usually earned money to repay loans and buy other goods. Some became small-scale commercial farmers.

Unforeseen effects. The Green Revolution has helped to reduce food shortages and

Chart Skills The nations of Southeast Asia are working to build their economies and to provide better lives for their people. ▶According to this chart, which nation of Southeast Asia has the highest standard of living? What information on the chart supports your answer?

Economic Development in Southeast Asia

	Thailand	Malaysia	Singapore	Indonesia	Philippines
Population (in millions)	57.2	17.9	2.7	179.3	61.5
People per doctor	5,576	2,853	837	7,318	1,062
People per auto	67	12	10	198	161
People per personal computer	296	140	18	N.A.	N.A.
McDonald's restaurants	6	23	37	1	34
GNP* (billions of U.S. dollars)	$79.3	$40.4	$35.2	$105.3 (est.)	$44.0
Source of most imports	Japan	Japan	Japan	Japan	Japan
Destination of most exports	United States	Japan	United States	Japan	United States

*Gross national product: total value of goods and services produced by a nation in a year

Source: *Fortune*, October 7, 1991

Harvesting Rice by Machine The peoples of Southeast Asia depend on rice as their most basic food. Farmers drain rice paddies about two weeks before they harvest the rice. As this photo shows, rice growing is changing as farming becomes more mechanized. ***Change*** How has the Green Revolution changed agriculture in Southeast Asia and fostered the use of farm machinery?

hunger in Southeast Asia. However, it has upset traditional patterns of rural life. In the past, villagers helped each other harvest rice when it matured. Today, farmers hire landless workers or rent tractors to do the job. Also, as the cost of fertilizer rises, some farmers cannot repay their loans. They then must sell their land and join the ranks of landless farm workers or move to the cities.

Another unforeseen effect of the Green Revolution is the damage caused by the widespread use of fertilizers, pesticides, and weedkillers. These chemicals drain into streams, polluting water supplies and killing wildlife.

Urbanization

The urban population of Southeast Asia is soaring. As commercial farming expands, fewer people are needed to work the land. Many move to cities to find jobs. Manila has grown from a city of 1.5 million in 1950 to about 8.5 million today. Bangkok, Thailand, has seen its population climb from 1.4 million in 1950 to more than 7 million today.

Within the cities, a middle class is growing. Middle-class people work in stores, banks, government offices, and hospitals. Many are well educated, with college degrees. Like middle-class city dwellers in other countries, they live in high-rise apartments and own washing machines, cars, and VCRs.

The class of urban poor is growing even more rapidly than the middle class. Although many poor people have low-paid jobs in factories, thousands of others cannot find work. Many are newcomers from rural areas, with few job skills. They often depend on friends and relatives to help them survive.

Making Ends Meet in Klong Toey

It is daybreak in Klong Toey, a slum on the outskirts of Bangkok. Phen prepares breakfast for her husband Lop and their three-year-old son Mong. By 7:00 A.M., Lop must catch a ride to the outskirts of Klong Toey. From there, he can get a bus to his job in Bangkok.

Lop works as a driver and watchman for a Japanese construction company. Phen also works to help support the family. Each week, she brings home jackets from a nearby clothing factory and embroiders designs on them. Together, Lop and Phen earn enough to survive.

Like others in Klong Toey, Phen and Lop rely on friends and family for help. When they were first married, they moved into a tiny shack. In time, they saved enough money to improve their home. One Saturday morning, Lop's friends came by. Phen served them food, and then they all set to work to expand the dwelling. When they ran out of lumber, Lop rushed to his mother's house and borrowed money to buy more wood.

To officials who gather statistics about Thailand's population, Phen and Lop are poor. By Klong Toey standards, they are doing

Life Along the River The capital of Thailand grew up along the banks of the Chao Phraya River. Since office buildings and homes of wealthy Thais are built on higher ground, most people live along the river, where floods often occur. These makeshift wooden houses are raised on stilts, as this photo shows. ***Geography*** Why are many of the world's major cities built on rivers?

quite well. Within the community, however, differences in wealth exist. As one resident observed:

> "If you look into the houses, some people have a television set, a stereo, and a refrigerator. These people cannot be very poor. If you compare these families with others, who have nearly nothing, you notice the difference."

The poorest residents of Klong Toey can barely afford basic necessities. Some spend their days scouring a nearby garbage dump for discarded plastic. They cut the plastic into chips to sell to a plastic factory for recycling. Others buy bamboo, soak it in water, and then cut it into thin sticks that are sold as skewers for grilling meat and fish. If they are lucky, these hardworking poor might find factory jobs like Phen's and begin to save money for a tiny dwelling of their own.

SECTION 1 REVIEW

1. (a) Why do the nations of Southeast Asia want to develop industry? (b) What steps has Singapore taken to become an exporter of manufactured goods?
2. (a) How has the Green Revolution helped to reduce food shortages and hunger in Southeast Asia? (b) How has it affected rural life?
3. (a) Give one reason for the rapid growth of cities in Southeast Asia. (b) What problems do newcomers from rural areas face in the cities?
4. **Defending a Position** Which do you think is more important, economic security or political freedom? Explain your answer.
5. **Writing Across Cultures** Make a list of economic choices that must be made by people and governments in Southeast Asia that are similar to choices that must be made by people in the United States.

2

TWO NATIONS OF SOUTHEAST ASIA

FIND OUT

What natural resources have helped Thailand and Indonesia to develop?

What steps have Thailand and Indonesia taken to modernize their economies?

How has modernization affected traditional ways of life in Thailand and Indonesia?

Each nation of Southeast Asia has developed its own policies for modernization. In this section, you will read how one mainland nation, Thailand, and one island nation, Indonesia, are going about the task of modernizing.

Thailand

Thailand is in the heart of mainland Southeast Asia. It shares borders with four countries and has long had to protect itself against powerful invaders. The Thais compare themselves to the slender bamboo plant, which bends in the wind so that it does not break. As you have read, Thailand "bent" in the "wind" of imperialism in the 1800s. In this way, it managed to avoid colonial rule. It was the only Southeast Asian nation to do so.

Ethnic diversity. Like other nations of Southeast Asia, Thailand has a majority ethnic group. About 85 percent of Thailand's 56 million people are Tai—that is, Thai, Lao, Shan, and related groups. The Thais live in the Chao Phraya River valley and in Bangkok. The Lao and the Shan live in northern Thailand. Cambodians, Chinese, Malays, and other ethnic groups also live in Thailand.

Thailand also has a large population of refugees. During and after the Vietnam War in Southeast Asia, thousands of Vietnamese, Cambodians, and Laotians fled their homes. Today, many of them remain in refugee camps in Thailand. The refugees pose a difficult political and social problem for Thailand. Even though most refugee camps are run by international agencies, the government of Thailand would like to see the refugees leave.

Economic development. Thailand is an agricultural nation. The long growing season and fertile soil enable Thai farmers to produce a variety of tropical crops. In the south, many small farmers cultivate rubber trees. Many other Thais who live along the country's long coastline earn a living by fishing.

Thailand has tried to diversify its exports. Traditionally, Thailand exported mainly rice and rubber. Today, the government encourages farmers to grow corn, sugarcane, pineapples, and cassava for sale on the world market. It has also built factories and expanded older industries, such as the textile industry. Today, Thailand is a leading exporter of textiles.

Thailand has benefited from a major discovery of natural gas, located offshore in the Gulf of Thailand. As a result, Thailand no longer has to depend on expensive imported oil to power its factories.

Under Thailand's market economy, most businesses are privately owned. Thailand has noted Singapore's success in attracting foreign investment. It, too, has begun to offer low taxes and other benefits to foreign companies that set up their factories in Thailand.

Foreign policy. During the Vietnam War, Thailand sided with the United States. Today, the two nations remain on friendly terms. Thailand has also sought good relations with China. Thailand's relations with Vietnam were strained after the Vietnamese invaded Cambodia in 1979. By the early 1990s, relations had improved. Thailand and Vietnam agreed on economic cooperation in 1991.

Thailand backs the UN peace agreement on Cambodia. It hopes that the agreement works so that the Cambodian refugees in Thailand can return home.

Daily life. In general, farmers in Thailand have a higher standard of living than many other people in Southeast Asia. As the popu-

A Floating Market This outdoor market is near Bangkok, Thailand. Free enterprise flourishes here as buyers and sellers meet on this busy waterway. Notice the passenger in the boat at the upper left, probably a tourist. Thailand attracts more tourists than any other Southeast Asian nation. ***Choice*** Why do many countries like Thailand encourage tourism?

lation grows, however, pressure on limited land resources will increase.

Despite the rapid growth of Bangkok and other cities, most people live in villages. There, traditions are stronger than in the cities. Life centers around the *wat,* or Buddhist temple. People go to the wat on holy days, as well as for medical aid, to learn the latest news, and to visit with their friends.

Until recently, most children in Thailand went to school in Buddhist temples. Today, most children attend public schools, but the temple still holds an important place in the people's lives.

Indonesia

Like many other countries, Indonesia faces the challenge of building a unified nation out of many ethnic groups. The dominant ethnic group is the Javanese. About 300 other groups, speaking more than 200 languages and dialects, also live in Indonesia.

Geography makes the task of building unity even more difficult. Indonesia includes more than 13,500 islands, 6,000 of which are inhabited. The islands stretch in a great arc across 3,200 miles (5,149 km) of water, a distance equal to the width of the United States.

Unifying forces. Some forces do help to unite Indonesians. Nearly 90 percent of the people are Muslims. In fact, Indonesia has one of the largest Muslim communities in the world. Also, although Indonesia includes thousands of islands, most people live on either Java or Bali.

Strong leadership has been another unifying factor. Since independence, Indonesia has had only two presidents—Sukarno and

Suharto. Sukarno, viewed as a national hero, was a champion of nonalignment. Suharto, who took office in 1967, opposed communism. He put to death an estimated 500,000 suspected communists. Both men were backed by the military and ruled as dictators, stressing economic development over political freedom. Democracy, they argued, encourages ethnic divisions and disunity.

Economic development. Indonesia has a mixed economy, with the state owning a number of industries. Recently, the government has made reforms aimed at increasing private investment.

Vast natural resources have helped Indonesia to develop. The country has large supplies of oil, natural gas, and tin. Its fertile soil supports plantations of rubber, rice, coffee, and sugar.

Despite these resources, many Indonesians are poor. A major problem is rapid population growth. Indonesia is the fifth most populous country in the world. It must find jobs for the 2.3 million young people who reach working age each year.

Oil boom and bust. Indonesia was caught in the same cycle that affected many other oil-producing nations. In the 1970s, world oil prices quadrupled. Indonesia used its huge oil earnings to build roads, schools, and factories. Then, in the early 1980s, oil prices plunged, and Indonesia had to borrow large sums to continue to develop its economy. Today, like other developing nations, Indonesia

Street Scene in Java Crowds jam a street market in the city of Malang in eastern Java. Two thirds of Indonesia's population live on the island of Java. In fact, Java is one of the world's most densely populated areas, with an average of more than 1,700 people per square mile. ***Political System*** How is the Indonesian government trying to reduce the population density in Java?

spends much of its income to repay the large debt it owes foreign nations.

To avoid another boom-and-bust cycle, Indonesia has taken steps to limit its dependence on oil. It has diversified its agriculture and increased exports of rice, coffee, and sugar. The government has sought foreign investors to build factories. Today, Indonesian factories produce textiles, lumber, plastics, and cement.

Foreign policy. During the Cold War, Indonesia was a leader of the nonaligned nations. Later, it supported the United States. In 1967, Indonesia joined Malaysia, Singapore, Thailand, and the Philippines to form the Association of Southeast Asian Nations (ASEAN). ASEAN has worked to solve regional disputes and promote trade. When Vietnam invaded Cambodia in 1979, ASEAN backed trade sanctions against Vietnam.

Daily life. Indonesia's booming population is causing other serious problems. Although most Indonesian farmers own their own land, their plots are small. As families further divide their land among the growing population, many people can no longer produce enough to support themselves.

To escape this situation, more and more people are moving to the cities. There, many face unemployment and a desperately hard life in overcrowded slums. As you have read, the government is trying to relocate people to some of the less-crowded islands. (See pages 282–283.)

Most Indonesians are Muslims. Many have adapted the religion to their own way of life. In Java, for example, Muslims have blended Islam, Hinduism, and Buddhism into a religion they call Agama Java. In this version of Islam, the Javanese use Hindu names to refer to Allah.

Islamic fundamentalism has affected some parts of Indonesia. Islamic fundamentalists call for strict obedience to the Koran as a way of improving people's lives. In Aceh, a state in northern Sumatra, the government is based on traditional Islamic law. Islamic fundamentalism has wide appeal to the poor and unemployed in the cities.

SECTION 2 REVIEW

1. **Identify:** (a) Suharto, (b) ASEAN, (c) Agama Java.
2. (a) Describe how natural resources have affected economic development in Thailand. (b) In Indonesia.
3. (a) List two forces that hinder Indonesian unity. (b) List two forces that help unite Indonesians.
4. What problems does rapid population growth cause in Thailand and Indonesia?
5. (a) What is the major religion in Thailand? (b) In Indonesia? (c) What role does religion play in the daily life of each country?
6. **Comparing** Compare the economies of Thailand and Indonesia. (a) How are they similar? (b) How are they different?
7. **Writing Across Cultures** Like Indonesia, the United States includes many diverse ethnic groups. List three forces that help to unite these diverse Americans.

3 LITERATURE AND THE ARTS

FIND OUT

What cultures have influenced the arts of Southeast Asia?

How does the literature of Southeast Asia reflect both traditional and modern values?

What performing arts are important in Southeast Asia?

According to legend, the god Sang Hyang Guru was the first king of Java. One day, Sang Hyang Guru wanted to summon the other gods to a meeting, so he made a gong and tuned it to a special pitch. The gong worked well for calling the gods, but Sang Hyang Guru had other messages to send. He made a second gong, and then a third. He tuned each to a different pitch. In time, says the legend, the three gongs, with their varying pitches, became the basis for the traditional Indonesian orchestra known as the gamelan (GAHM uh lahn).

In Southeast Asia, the arts grew out of religious traditions. Hindu and Buddhist traditions from India greatly influenced the arts. However, local peoples blended these outside elements with their own traditions to create a uniquely Southeast Asian art.

Literature

For many centuries, Indian literature influenced the poetry, plays, and stories of Southeast Asia. Southeast Asian scholars translated and adapted the great Hindu epics of the *Ramayana* and the *Mahabharata*. In Thailand, the Rama epic is called the *Ramakien,* and singers and dancers perform popular stories from the work.

Each nation of Southeast Asia has its own rich tradition of folktales; epics about kings, queens, and heroes; and love poems. Today, as in the past, village storytellers recite these ancient tales and poems from memory, handing on oral traditions that are hundreds of years old. In monasteries and convents, Buddhist monks and nuns preserve stories about the life of the Buddha.

The Tale of Kieu. Vietnam's most famous poem is *The Tale of Kieu*. Written in the early 1800s, the poem blends Confucian and Buddhist ideas. Kieu (kyoo) is a beautiful young woman who falls in love with a student, Kim Trong. While Kim is away, Kieu's father and brother are arrested. To save her family, Kieu sells herself into slavery. After 15 years of hardship, she is reunited at last with Kim and her family:

> "She glanced and saw her folk—they
> all were there.
> Father was still quite strong, mother
> quite spry.
> Both sister Van and brother Quan
> grown up.
> And standing to one side was Kim,
> her love.
> Where was she now? And was this
> moment real?
> Was she dreaming awake, with open
> eyes?
> Tear-pearls dropped one by one and
> damped her robe;
> Her heart was filled with joy and grief
> alike."

The Tale of Kieu is so popular that many Vietnamese can recite passages of it from memory. Its sympathetic view of Kieu suggests the special status of women in Southeast Asia.

Modern writers. Novels and short stories are popular in Southeast Asia today. Some writers use fictional works to examine social issues. In *Arjuna Searching for Love,* the Indonesian novelist Yudhistira Ardi Noegraha uses the story of a high school student to criticize the gap between rich and poor.

Arjuna is a rebellious young man who decides to teach a rich classmate a lesson. He leaves her alone in the city to ride a bus and come into contact with the common people. Only in this way, he believes, can she appreciate the daily struggle for survival of ordinary people.

The Performing Arts

Music, dance, and drama are closely linked in Southeast Asia. The three are often combined to present stories based on ancient myths or historical events.

Music. Traditional Southeast Asian music sounds unfamiliar to most westerners. That is because it uses a different scale than western music. Also, Southeast Asians use mainly percussion instruments—gongs, drums, or other instruments that produce sounds when they are tapped or struck. Western music, on the other hand, relies heavily on stringed and wind instruments.

A popular example of traditional Southeast Asian music is the gamelan music of Java, which you read about earlier. The gamelan orchestra is composed of gongs of various

Gamelan Music The traditional orchestra of Java and Bali consists of two sets of instruments, one tuned to one scale and the other tuned to a different scale. Above the rhythmic percussion sound, listeners hear a melody of music provided by a flute, a stringed instrument called a *rebab*, or a singer. ***Culture*** What instruments does a gamelan usually include?

sizes and pitches, drums, brass kettles hung from strings, and xylophone-like instruments with bars of bronze or wood. Flutes and two-stringed lutes are also part of the group. A gamelan may have from 12 to 40 players. The leader plays the largest drum. Gamelan music is almost always used to accompany dance or drama.

Dance. Classical dance in Southeast Asia is performed both for religious purposes and for entertainment. Compared to western dancers, Southeast Asian dancers move very little. Instead, they use highly symbolic gestures and facial expressions to convey meaning. For example, dancers may express the idea of clouds, woods, river, night, or sparkling water by the manner in which they hold an outstretched hand. Dancers train for years before they can perform the required subtle movements of arms, hands, and fingers.

In Cambodia, the Khmer Rouge, under Pol Pot, destroyed Cambodian dance groups. The few older surviving dancers are now struggling to teach the new young generation of dancers the ancient traditions. What they do not have the time to pass on will die with them.

Shadow plays. In many parts of Southeast Asia, especially Indonesia, shadow-puppet plays are popular. These plays are based on the Hindu epics and, more recently, on political events. (See the feature at right.)

Art and Architecture

Scattered across Southeast Asia are great monuments that testify to the wealth and artistic skill of ancient civilizations. The finest surviving buildings are temples and stupas. Each is decorated with lively sculptures that portray episodes from the lives of Hindu gods and goddesses or teach about the life of the Buddha.

Angkor Wat. In Cambodia, the ancient temple of Angkor Wat reflects Hindu influences. The Khmers built Angkor Wat in the 1100s. Like temples in India, Angkor Wat has three tiers surrounded by rectangular walls. Along the walls, sculptors carved thousands of figures, illustrating both Hindu myths and scenes from daily life. The walls of one gallery contain more than a mile of carvings. (See page 2.)

Ananda. As you have read, the kingdom of Pagan, in present-day Myanmar, flourished as a center of Buddhism between the 1100s and 1300s. The people of Pagan did a vast amount of building. Today, more than 2,000 Buddhist temples and stupas from that period dot the landscape. The largest is the

The Temple of Borobudur While the lower levels of this famous Buddhist temple in Java are richly decorated, the very top is plain. It displays a single figure of the Buddha. Experts believe that the temple's builders wished to symbolize the difference between the lower world of the senses and the upper world of the mind. ***Fine Art*** What other carvings does this temple contain?

Shadow Theater of Indonesia

TRADITION AND CHANGE

In a village on Java, a roving *dalang* sets up a white cotton screen in front of a flickering oil lamp. The news of his arrival spreads quickly, and excited villagers soon crowd around, waiting for the show to begin. The dalang is a master puppeteer. From midnight until dawn, his leather puppets will perform a *wayang kulit,* the traditional Indonesian shadow play.

Wayang kulit is an ancient and popular form of entertainment. No one knows whether it was brought from India or originated on Java, but Indonesians have enjoyed shadow theater for 1,000 years. Traditionally, shadow plays dramatized episodes from the Hindu epics or recounted the adventures of well-known heroes and their evil enemies. Recent plays, however, deal with current political events.

Tonight, the dalang performs a story from the *Mahabharata.* Sitting cross-legged behind the cloth, he begins telling this ancient Hindu tale. As he talks, he moves the puppets. Each gesture is determined by tradition. At the same time, he conducts the gamelan gong and cymbal orchestra that accompanies a wayang kulit performance.

On the other side of the screen, the audience sees only the puppets' shadows. The villagers know the story, but they watch and listen eagerly just the same. They laugh when the dalang improvises a joke, shiver when he recalls the fury of a great battle. In the end, they cheer when the hero finally triumphs over evil.

Shows like this are repeated all over Indonesia, where thousands of dalangs practice their art. Many Indonesians see the puppets dance several times a year. Recently, the Indonesian government set up a school for dalangs. In this way, they hope to preserve a vital part of Indonesian cultural heritage.

1. How does the dalang create shadows with his puppets?
2. **Making Inferences** How might modernization affect an ancient art like wayang kulit?

temple at Ananda. Its gilded spire rises 163 feet (50 m) into the air. Towering above the temple, four colossal statues of the Buddha look out over the surrounding plain. Unlike most temples in Myanmar, Ananda is still in use.

Borobudur. The island nations of Southeast Asia have their own ancient monuments. In Java, the temple of Borobudur is an immense artificial mountain. Built in the 800s, it rises five tiers above the ground level. At the top of the temple is a central stupa with an unfinished statue of the Buddha.

More than 400 images of the Buddha adorn Borobudur. All sit cross-legged, with only their hand gestures varying to indicate different moods.

Borobudur's galleries contain thousands of carvings illustrating Buddhist texts. While

A Woodcarver at Work The people of Bali are noted for their beautifully intricate carvings in wood. Many of these carvings adorn Balinese temples and houses. The religion of the people of Bali combines Hinduism, Buddhism, animism, and reverence for ancestors. ***Change*** How do you think industrial development may affect traditional arts and crafts in Indonesia?

these carvings, and the temple itself, reflect Indian influences, local artists also left their mark. Javanese sculptors carved detailed scenes of everyday life in early Java. For example, the carvings show Javanese boats, with outriggers and sails, that carried people among the islands of Indonesia in the 800s.

Popular Arts

For centuries, artisans of Southeast Asia have produced fine handicrafts including textiles, woodcarvings, and metalwork. In textiles, artists developed a technique of dyeing known as batik (buh TEEK). Batik artists use wax to paint a design on cloth. Then they dye the cloth. The dye colors the cloth but cannot penetrate the wax, and the design under the wax remains uncolored. For a multicolored design, the artist repeats the process several times.

In Thailand, sculptors produce beautiful teak carvings and fine furniture. Because teakwood is hard and fine-grained, craftworkers can create delicate designs.

Many Indonesian craftworkers specialize in metalwork. In Java, artisans hammer scenes from Hindu myths into trays and plates. In the Molucca Islands, they make delicate silver necklaces and bracelets.

Today, industrialization is threatening the traditional arts of Southeast Asia. Few people make batik fabrics by hand anymore. Even machine-made batik is uncommon. Instead, people buy imported mass-produced printed fabrics, which are cheap and available everywhere. Deforestation endangers the sources of hardwoods used by carvers and woodworkers.

SECTION 3 REVIEW

1. **Identify:** (a) gamelan, (b) *The Tale of Kieu,* (c) Ananda, (d) Borobudur, (e) batik.
2. (a) How did Hindu and Buddhist traditions influence Southeast Asian literature? (b) How did they influence Southeast Asian art and architecture?
3. Why are village storytellers important?
4. (a) How are music, dance, and drama linked in Southeast Asia? (b) How did the Khmer Rouge affect Cambodian dance?
5. **Evaluating Information** How do the arts of Southeast Asia reflect cultural diffusion?
6. **Writing Across Cultures** Write a letter to a student in Southeast Asia describing your favorite kind of music.

Chapter 13 Review

Understanding Vocabulary

Match each term at left with the correct definition at right.

1. command economy	**a.** technique for dyeing cloth
2. wat	**b.** traditional Indonesian orchestra
3. gamelan	**c.** state nationalizes major industries and takes over land
4. percussion instrument	**d.** musical instrument that produces sounds when it is tapped
5. batik	**e.** Buddhist temple

Reviewing the Main Ideas

1. What steps have Southeast Asian nations taken to reduce their dependence on industrialized countries?
2. (a) What three types of economy are found in Southeast Asia? (b) Why is Vietnam changing its form of economy?
3. (a) How did Singapore become a major exporting nation? (b) What impact has this had on life in Singapore?
4. (a) How did the Green Revolution help Southeast Asian farmers? (b) What are some negative effects of the Green Revolution?
5. Explain how economic modernization has disrupted traditional patterns of life in Southeast Asia.
6. (a) How has Thailand benefited from a discovery of natural gas? (b) How have rich oil resources both helped and hurt Indonesia?
7. How is modernization changing the traditional arts of Southeast Asia?

Reviewing Chapter Themes

1. Since independence, the nations of Southeast Asia have worked to modernize their economies. Give two examples of how Southeast Asian nations are modernizing in each of the following areas: (a) industry, (b) agriculture.
2. The governments of Thailand and Indonesia must make choices about how to develop their economies. (a) What economic resources does each nation have? (b) What obstacles does each face?
3. Southeast Asia has a rich cultural heritage. Give three examples of how the arts and literature of Southeast Asia blend foreign and local traditions.

Thinking Critically

1. **Making Global Connections** Today, Americans import a variety of manufactured goods from Southeast Asia. These goods compete with American-made goods. What are the advantages of a free exchange of goods to the American economy? What are the disadvantages?
2. **Defending a Position** As you have read, some Indonesian leaders feel that democracy encourages ethnic divisions and disunity. Do you agree or disagree? Why?

Applying Your Skills

1. **Reading a Chart** Use the chart on page 285 to answer the following questions. (a) What is the subject of the chart? (b) Which nation has the highest gross national product? (c) How many people per doctor are there in Singapore? In Indonesia? (d) How does this information relate to what you have learned about Singapore and Indonesia?
2. **Identifying the Main Idea** Reread the subsection "Economic Choices" on pages 283–284. What is the main idea of the subsection?

Chapter 14

AUSTRALIA AND OCEANIA

CHAPTER OUTLINE

1 Geography of Australia and New Zealand

2 Growth of Australia and New Zealand

3 Oceania—Islands of the Pacific

Sydney Opera House Australians often think of this building as the symbol of Sydney, the nation's busiest port. It reminds many Australians of giant wind-filled sails. In fact, sails and ships are fitting symbols for the vast region of Australia, New Zealand, and Oceania. ***Geography*** All the peoples in this region live on islands. How might this affect their lives?

"Once a jolly swagman
camped by a billabong
Under the shade of a
coolibah tree,
And he sang as he watched
and waited till his billy
boiled,
'Who'll come a-waltzing
Matilda with me?' . . .

Down came a jumbuck to
drink at the billabong,
Up jumped the swagman and
grabbed him with glee,
And he sang as he shoved
that jumbuck in his
tucker-bag,
'You'll come a-waltzing
Matilda with me!' "

A. B. "Banjo" Paterson, an Australian poet, wrote the words for "Waltzing Matilda." The song tells of a *swagman,* or tramp. Carrying his *swag* (knapsack), the swagman camps by a *billabong* (water hole) under a *coolibah* (eucalyptus) tree. There, he boils water in a *billy* (tin can). When a *jumbuck* (sheep) appears, the swagman grabs it and stuffs it into his *tucker* (food) bag. *Waltzing Matilda* itself means "carrying the swag."

This colorful language developed when British settlers adopted some words from the original inhabitants of Australia and made up others. The result is Australian English, sometimes called Strine.

CHAPTER PERSPECTIVE

In the late 1700s, Australia became an outpost of European settlement in the Pacific. There, and in New Zealand to the southeast, Europeans overwhelmed the original people and set up their own cultures. Despite their remoteness, the people of the region, including Oceania, are part of today's interdependent world.

As you read, look for these chapter themes:

- Geographic isolation allowed the peoples of Australia and Oceania to develop their own distinct cultures.
- The migration of westerners to the Pacific region changed the ethnic and cultural patterns of the region.
- Australia and Oceania are linked to the world economy and have taken an active role in world affairs.

Literature Connections

In this chapter, you will encounter passages from the following works.

"Waltzing Matilda," A. B. Paterson
"A Drought Idyll," George Essex Evans
"Look, Koori," Kevin Gilbert
My Place, Sally Morgan

For other literature suggestions, see Connections With Literature, pages 804–808.

1

GEOGRAPHY OF AUSTRALIA AND NEW ZEALAND

FIND OUT

How have geography and climate affected Australia?

What natural resources have influenced the economic development of Australia and New Zealand?

Vocabulary geothermal energy

"It was the middle of the drought; the ground was hot and bare,
You might search for grass with a microscope, but 'nary grass was there
The hay was done, the cornstalks gone, the trees were dying fast.
The sun o'erhead was a curse in red, and the wind was a furnace blast;
The waterholes were sun-baked mud."

These lines from "A Drought Idyll" by George Essex Evans suggest the harsh climate of Australia's vast interior. Called the Outback by Australians, the dry, sunbaked interior remains almost as much of a challenge to people today as it did 150 years ago. Despite air travel, modern methods of irrigation, and satellite communications, the Outback remains Australia's unconquered frontier.

An Isolated Continent

Australia is the world's largest island and its smallest continent. The nation of 16 million people occupies nearly 3 million square miles (7.8 million sq km), an area that's about the size of the mainland United States.

A world apart. Australia was once part of Asia. About 25 million years ago, it broke off from the mainland and drifted south. Plants

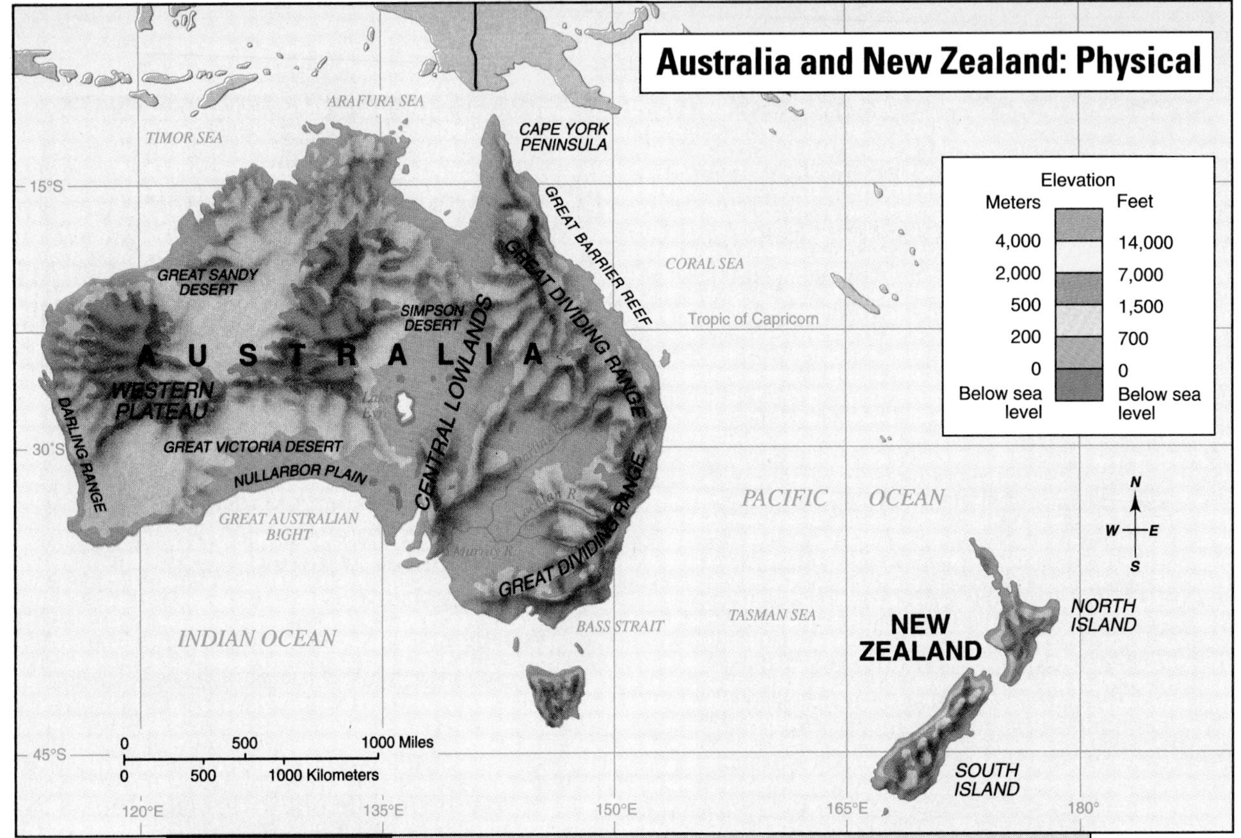

MAP STUDY

Australia is a vast continent nearly equal in size to the mainland United States. The geography of both Australia and New Zealand is marked by a wide variety of landforms.

1. **Location** Name three landforms in Australia shown on the map.
2. **Region** (a) Identify two mountain ranges in Australia. (b) In what area are most of Australia's rivers located?
3. **Synthesizing Information** Write a sentence or two describing the geography of Australia and New Zealand.

and animals developed there, isolated from the rest of the region. As a result, only Australia is home to the kangaroo, koala bear, and duck-billed platypus.

Great distances separate Australia from other centers of population. Its nearest mainland neighbors are the nations of Southeast Asia. In the past, the distances meant that Australian societies developed with little outside contact. It took modern transportation and communications to bring Australians closer to the rest of the world.

Landforms. Australia is made up of a plateau, lowlands, highlands, and a coastal rim. The Western Plateau covers most of western Australia. It is broken up by huge outcrops of bare rock. The largest, Ayers Rock, juts 1,143 feet (348 m) above the surrounding land. The Central Lowlands lie east of the plateau. Running north to south along the eastern coast is the Great Dividing Range.

East of the Great Dividing Range lies a narrow coastal rim. Never more than 248 miles (400 km) wide, this coastal rim is home to Australia's largest cities and most of its population. Today, about 87 percent of Australians live in cities on or near the coasts. Few live in the Outback.

Climate and Resources

The climate of Australia is generally warm. The northern third of the continent lies in the tropics, while the rest of Australia lies in the temperate zone. The major differences in the climate of Australia are caused by the amount and distribution of rainfall.

Rainfall. The Great Dividing Range forms a "rain shadow" in eastern Australia. Winds blow moist air in from the Pacific. As the air reaches the mountains, it rises and cools, releasing its moisture on the eastern side. As a result, the eastern coastal rim receives an abundance of rainfall. The coastal areas are the only parts of Australia that can support large-scale farming.

Grasslands lie to the west of the Great Dividing Range. Farther into the interior, the grasslands gradually become drier. Much of the Outback is sand and gravel desert. From time to time, heavy seasonal rains pound the interior and fill dry riverbeds to overflowing. After the rains stop, however, the water rapidly dries up. This repeated cycle of flood and drought has leached nutrients from the soil.

Agricultural resources. Australians have struggled to overcome a scarce water supply, poor soil, and rugged land to develop the resources of their land. Huge herds of sheep graze on the grasslands of the interior. With more than 150 million sheep, Australia produces more than one fourth of the world's wool and exports large quantities of meat. The northern and eastern parts of the Outback have enough moisture to support large herds of beef cattle. In other areas, Australians irrigate the land so they can grow wheat, sugarcane, cotton, and other crops.

Mineral resources. Australia has benefited from a variety of mineral resources. During the 1850s and 1880s, the discovery of gold brought floods of settlers to the continent. Coal, iron ore, copper, zinc, uranium, and lead supported economic development. Australia is a leading exporter of bauxite, which is used to make aluminum. It also has large oil and natural-gas deposits both in the interior and offshore.

New Zealand

The island nation of New Zealand lies about 1,200 miles (1,931 km) southeast of Australia. It consists of two large islands,

Herding Sheep in New Zealand A rancher, aided by sheep dogs, moves his flock across a valley slope. As the seasons change, ranchers change their pastureland. The animals graze at low elevations in the winter and in the highlands in the summer. In the spring and fall, they graze on the lands in between. ***Geography*** How does the geography of New Zealand foster raising sheep?

North Island and South Island. In contrast to the generally flat, dry landscape of Australia, New Zealand is mountainous and green. As in Australia, however, most New Zealanders live in urban areas along the coasts. About 70 percent of New Zealanders live on North Island, which has warmer weather, more rainfall, and fewer high mountains than South Island.

Resources. The coastal rims of both islands are fertile and have plenty of water. The sloping lands provide excellent pasture for sheep and cattle. Much of New Zealand's foreign earnings comes from exporting wool and meat. Many American markets sell frozen New Zealand lamb. New Zealand also exports vegetables, fruits, and grains. Many of these crops are grown on the Canterbury Plain of South Island.

New Zealand has limited mineral resources, with only small deposits of coal, natural gas, and gold. Because it has no oil resources, New Zealand has tried to develop sources of geothermal energy. This energy comes from heat that is released naturally in geysers, hot springs, and volcanoes.

SECTION 1 REVIEW

1. **Locate:** (a) Australia, (b) Western Plateau, (c) Great Dividing Range, (d) New Zealand, (e) North Island, (f) South Island.
2. **Identify:** Outback.
3. **Define:** geothermal energy.
4. (a) How has location affected the development of Australia? (b) How has climate influenced population and economic patterns?
5. List the major natural resources of Australia and New Zealand.
6. **Comparing** Describe two similarities and two differences between the geography of Australia and that of New Zealand.
7. **Writing Across Cultures** Write a letter to a sheep rancher in the interior of Australia asking for a summer job. Describe why you would like to visit the rugged interior of Australia.

2 GROWTH OF AUSTRALIA AND NEW ZEALAND

FIND OUT

How did Australia's location affect the Aborigines?

What changes did Europeans bring to Australia and New Zealand?

How have European ideas shaped the government and economies of Australia and New Zealand?

What roles have Australia and New Zealand played in international affairs?

Vocabulary penal colony, suffrage, nuclear free zone

"Look to the dawn, dark brother . . .
Rise to the call of justice . . .
Rise to the call of land right
Rise to the blackman's song
Rise to the blood-red dawn of truth
At last to right the wrongs."

Kevin Gilbert is an outspoken Aboriginal poet. In "Look, Koori,"* he urges Australia's Aboriginal people to take pride in their ancient heritage and demand justice from the government that denied them rights for so long.

The First Migrations

Australia was peopled by two waves of migrations. The first Australians arrived about 40,000 years ago, probably from Southeast Asia. They spread across the continent, where they lived in isolation from the rest of the

* When Europeans reached Australia, they called the dark-skinned people they met Aborigines, which means the earliest people to live in a place. Today, many Aborigines call themselves Kooris.

Aboriginal Art The art of Australian Aborigines often combines colorful realistic and abstract elements, as seen in this painting. Many Aboriginal paintings, drawings, and carvings also have religious meaning and are done as part of religious rites. ***Culture*** Why does the Aborigines' art often depict animals and other aspects of nature?

world. A little more than 200 years ago, a second wave of immigrants began to settle the continent, forcibly displacing the original inhabitants.

Adapting to the environment. The Aborigines were nomadic hunters and gatherers. Along the coastal rim and river valleys, they hunted small game and gathered berries, nuts, and eggs. Some learned to hunt and find water in the forbidding dry lands of the Outback.

The Aborigines lived in small groups and spoke as many as 250 distinct languages. While customs varied from one group to another, they had some common features. Aborigines felt a deep religious bond with nature. "We see all things natural as part of us," explained a present-day Aborigine. "All the things on Earth we see as part human."

The Aborigines had few material possessions, but they had a rich oral tradition that preserved their religious beliefs and explained how their ancestors created the world. According to tradition, long ago in "Dreamtime," the ancestors of the Aborigines roamed the Earth, forming mountains, valleys, and rivers as well as plants and animals. Aboriginal artists have left records of these and other stories and dances on rock paintings and carvings. Today, Aborigines have adapted ancient artistic traditions to modern ideas and methods.

The Maoris of New Zealand. Compared with the Aborigines, the Maoris of New Zealand are relative newcomers. Their ancestors were seafaring people from Southeast Asia. About 800 years ago, these seafarers reached New Zealand in 100-foot-long oceangoing canoes.

Unlike the nomadic Aborigines, the Maoris were farmers who settled in villages. The center of village life was the *marae*. At this ceremonial gathering place, the Maoris celebrated religious occasions with song and dance. The Maoris decorated the marae with intricate woodcarvings. (📖 See Connections With Literature, page 805, "Land of the Long White Cloud: Maori Myths, Tales and Legends.")

The First European Settlers

In 1769, British explorer Captain James Cook landed in New Zealand. The next year, he explored the east coast of Australia and claimed the land for Britain.

The British first used Australia as a **penal colony**, a place where they could send people who had been convicted of crimes. In 1787, the first shipment of convicts set sail for Australia. The First Fleet, as it was later called, included 776 men, women, and children. More than 160,000 more would follow before the British government ended its transportation policy in 1867. People were transported for a variety of crimes ranging from murder and robbery to stealing bread or failing to repay a debt.

Condemned to Transportation

On a hot July day in 1784, a frightened boy stood before the judge in London's Old Bailey court. The government accused 14-year-old Matthew Everingham of stealing two books for the purpose of pawning, or selling, them.

"The prisoner's defense?" asked the judge.

"I was in great distress," the defendant replied in a whisper.

"Guilty," the judge proclaimed. He sentenced the boy to seven years' transport to Australia.

Matthew was one of countless people trapped in the harsh poverty of Britain's growing cities. Some, like Matthew, turned to crime to survive. After his conviction, Matthew spent three years on a prison ship on the Thames River. Then, in June 1787, he was forced on board the ship *Scarborough,* part of the First Fleet. Packed into airless holds, many prisoners died on the brutal eight-month voyage to Australia.

When Matthew staggered ashore at Botany Bay, he faced a hard life as part of a work gang. Despite hunger, illness, and brutal beatings by overseers, however, he held on to his hopes for the future.

> "I have now two years and seven months to remain a convict and then I am at liberty to act as a free-born Englishman ought to. . . . I am yet but young, only 19. If my health is spared, I shall not be one jot the worse for being transported."

The next year, the Second Fleet brought 700 more convicts. Among them was 17-year-old Elizabeth Rimes, transported for stealing a blanket and a sheet. Within a year, she and Matthew married.

When Matthew's term of punishment ended, the couple decided to stay on in Australia as settlers. He and Elizabeth suffered incredible hardships. "The first six months," he wrote, "everything seemed to run against me. My crop failed. My daughter died, and my wife hung on my hands very ill."

Matthew and Elizabeth moved farther into the highlands. There, they farmed, and raised nine children in a rough hut. Despite floods and conflicts with Aborigines, they survived and prospered.

Today, more than 7,000 Australians, including an Aboriginal branch, trace their family roots to Matthew and Elizabeth Everingham.

Convicts Arriving Beginning in the 1780s, Britain sent many convicts to Australia. It did this mainly to ease overcrowding in English prisons. The problem had become worse after the Revolutionary War, when Britain lost its American colonies, where it also had shipped convicts. ***Citizenship*** Why are many Australians proud to trace their ancestry to convict immigrants?

Impact of European Settlement

During the 1800s, an increasing number of free men and women emigrated to Australia. Settlers fanned out along the eastern rim of the continent. Slowly, they learned to make the land productive. Many raised merino sheep, prized for their fine wool. On widely scattered ranches in the Outback, settlers respected the frontier virtues of individualism and self-sufficiency.

The gold rush in 1851 brought tens of thousands of people to Australia. The eastern colonies of Victoria and New South Wales boomed. Many gold seekers stayed on to build farms and sheep ranches. Others tried their luck in new settlements on the west coast, around Perth. (See Connections With Literature, page 805, "The Boy in the Bush.")

An outpost of British culture. Most settlers who poured into Australia and later New Zealand came from Great Britain. They brought the English language to the new lands. They also transplanted British customs, holidays, and ideas about government. Despite vast distances, they maintained strong family and economic ties to Britain.

Impact on the Aborigines. British colonization spelled disaster for the Aborigines. Their Stone Age weapons were no match for European military technology. The newcomers drove the Aborigines off the best lands and into the arid interior. Many Aborigines were forced to work on white-owned sheep ranches. About 10,000 Aborigines died in wars. Many more died from European diseases such as smallpox and measles.

Until recently, many white Australians looked down on the Aborigines. In her autobiography, *My Place,* Sally Morgan, who is part Aborigine, related a conversation with a white woman at a bus stop.

> "'You're very beautiful, dear,' she said.
> 'What nationality are you, Indian?'
> 'No,' I smiled, 'I'm Aboriginal.'
> 'Oh you poor thing,' she said . . .
> 'what are you going to do?'"

Today, the remaining 200,000 Aborigines make up only about 1 percent of the Australian population. Modern Aboriginal leaders and writers are struggling to protect their rights and preserve their rich heritage.

In New Zealand, the Maoris also lost their lives and land in wars with white settlers. By the 1870s, their numbers had shrunk from 250,000 to fewer than 50,000. Today, the population has recovered somewhat. Maoris are fighting in court to regain lands illegally taken by British settlers.

Political and Economic Development

By the mid-1800s, settlers in both Australia and New Zealand were calling for greater self-government. At first, Britain granted them some rights, but by the early 1900s, both nations had won complete independence. They kept close ties with Britain, and in time joined the British Commonwealth of Nations.

Democratic traditions. Australia and New Zealand set up governments that reflected European traditions of democracy. Both countries adapted British models, but they also borrowed ideas from the United States. Each developed a written constitution that set up a federal system of government. Power rests in the hands of a parliament, made up of a senate and a house of representatives. Members of the majority party in the parliament choose the prime minister, who is the chief executive.

Australia and New Zealand have made their own contributions to democratic traditions. For example, Australia introduced the secret ballot. New Zealand and later Australia were also the first nations to grant women suffrage, or the right to vote.

Economic patterns. Economic interests link Australia and New Zealand to the world economy. As you have read, both nations export agricultural products such as wool, lamb, and beef. Australia is also the world's largest producer of coal, and it exports huge amounts of iron ore. It calls itself the "Quarry and Mine of the World."

Most people in Australia and New Zealand enjoy a high standard of living, thanks in part to the widespread use of machinery in farming and mining. Success has had its drawbacks, however. Overgrazing threatens some lands. Growing demands on scarce water resources create frequent water shortages. Intensive mining has caused pollution and stripped the land of many resources. Mining also threatens lands that the Aborigines hold sacred. In both nations, conservationists have taken active stands.

Regional and Global Issues

With their strong ties to Britain, both Australia and New Zealand joined the Allied powers in World War I and World War II. After 1945, however, British influence in the region as well as in the world declined. During the Cold War, both nations developed closer ties with the United States. Australian troops helped battle communist forces in the Korean and Vietnam wars.

In recent years, Australia and New Zealand have worked more closely with their Pacific Rim neighbors. Both countries recognize that their economic and political futures are linked to those of Asian nations. Japan, for example, is Australia's chief trading partner. Japan needs Australian mineral resources, while Australia benefits from Japanese investment.

Australia has helped Vietnam and other Southeast Asian nations to rebuild after many years of war. It has backed projects to promote regional cooperation and economic growth. Students in Australian high schools learn about Southeast Asian history and culture so that they can recognize the importance of that region to their lives.

SCIENCE AND TECHNOLOGY

Scanning the Stars From the Land "Down Under"

Are there other civilizations in the universe? Can we communicate with them or at least detect their presence? Astronomers hope to answer these and many more questions as they probe the universe. Their tool is a new and extremely powerful radio telescope called the Australia Telescope, or AT. The AT consists of a series of radio dishes spread out over 180 miles (290 km). The signals or waves collected at separate dishes are combined to produce a single image.

Australia, or the land "down under" the Equator, offers the best vantage point in the Southern Hemisphere from which to gather information about the universe. Far from car phones, electric motors, and radar from airfields, the vast, rugged Australian interior provides a perfect setting for the AT. The AT can collect data from 16 billion light-years away without interference. (One light-year equals 5.7 trillion miles.)

It is still too early to say what impact the AT will have. Currently, scientists are using the new telescope to study the radiation both in areas where stars are born and in areas where they are dying. They hope to learn how stars are formed. Astronomers are also collecting long-hidden facts about the workings of our own galaxy, the Milky Way. Aimed at the stars in distant galaxies, the AT also awaits a signal from other living beings.

1. Why is the Australian Outback an ideal place in which to build a radio telescope?
2. **Drawing Conclusions** Why do you think scientists want to find out more about distant parts of the universe?

Mining in Australia Minerals are one of Australia's major exports. Australian mines also produce nearly all of the world's finest opals—semiprecious stones used in jewelry. To strengthen its economy, the government requires that Australians own at least 50 percent of every mining operation. ***Change*** How did the gold rush of the 1850s affect Australia?

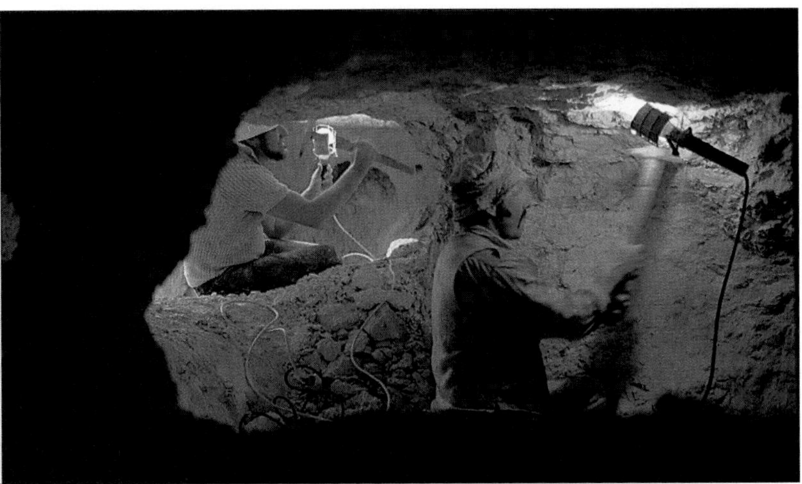

Immigration. For most of its history, Australia welcomed Europeans but excluded Asians and other nonwhite immigrants. The government has eased this policy somewhat. Many Asians have sought safety in Australia, including "boat people" from war-torn mainland Southeast Asia. Other immigrants have come from Hong Kong, Singapore, Thailand, the Philippines, and Indonesia. These newcomers are often skilled people seeking greater economic opportunities.

Nuclear tensions. New Zealand has declared itself a nuclear free zone, an area where nuclear weapons are banned. This policy created tensions with its longtime ally, the United States. New Zealand banned American warships armed with nuclear weapons from its harbors. As Cold War tensions eased during the 1990s, the United States removed nuclear weapons from its ships, ending the dispute.

SECTION 2 REVIEW

1. **Define:** (a) penal colony, (b) suffrage, (c) nuclear free zone.
2. (a) How did the Aborigines adapt to the Australian environment? (b) How did the Maoris live in New Zealand?
3. (a) How did Britain colonize Australia? (b) What effect did colonization have on the Aborigines?
4. How did Australia and New Zealand adapt British democratic traditions?
5. What ties have Australia and New Zealand developed with other nations?
6. **Drawing Conclusions** Why do you think the people of Australia and New Zealand came to prize individuality and democracy?
7. **Writing Across Cultures** Jot down arguments that you might give in a debate if you had to defend or criticize New Zealand's decision to ban American warships from its harbors.

3 OCEANIA—ISLANDS OF THE PACIFIC

FIND OUT

How has geography influenced the peoples of Oceania?

What different traditions have shaped Pacific island cultures?

How have world events affected the peoples of Oceania?

Bellona is one of the thousands of islands that make up Oceania. On a map, it looks like a tiny dot in the South Pacific. For centuries, its people had a subsistence economy. Today, mining companies are eager to exploit the resources of the island.

Some people on Bellona welcome modernization. Others view mining as a threat to their way of life. "We had our own political system, we had our own religion, we had our own economic system," protested one critic. "Now we are living in an era of changes."

Geographic Setting

Oceania is made up of more than 25,000 islands scattered across the Pacific Ocean. While some lie north of the Equator, many more lie in the Southern Hemisphere. All are far from the world's great continental landmasses. Oceania is divided into three regions, Melanesia, Micronesia, and Polynesia.

Three regions. Melanesia includes the islands in the western Pacific that extend from New Guinea to Fiji to the Solomons. New Guinea is the largest and most populous of these Pacific islands. The name Melanesia, from the Greek meaning "black islands," probably refers to the dark skin of the islands' peoples.

Micronesia, meaning "tiny islands," lies to the north of Melanesia. As the name suggests, most of the 2,000 islands in this region are small. The largest, Guam, covers only 210 square miles (544 sq km).

Polynesia, or "many islands," lies to the east. This region covers a huge 15-million-square-mile region (39 million sq km) of the Pacific Ocean, including the Hawaiian Islands, New Zealand, Easter Island, and Tahiti.

Landforms. Oceania is made up of two types of islands: high islands and low islands. Both are formed by mountains, but they differ in elevation. High islands are actually the tops of volcanic mountains. They rise far above sea level. Volcanic ash has covered the islands, leaving fertile soil that supports lush vegetation. Major volcanic islands include New Guinea, Fiji, Samoa, and Hawaii.

In contrast, low islands lie barely above sea level. They are made up of coral reefs that have attached themselves to undersea mountains. Most of the Micronesian islands are coral islands.

Climate and resources. Most of Oceania lies in the tropics, giving the islands warm temperatures all year round. Rainfall varies. In general, high islands have more rain, which favors agriculture. Copra, the meat of the coconut, is a major agricultural product of high islands. Other exports include sugar and tropical fruits such as bananas and pineapples.

Many low islands lack moisture, so the people there have depended on fishing for their livelihood. They became skilled seafarers. A brisk trade developed among the farmers of high islands and the fishing people of low islands. In their huge oceangoing canoes, seafaring peoples traveled vast distances across the ocean. They faced many dangers, including severe tropical storms called typhoons.

Differing Traditions

People probably first migrated from Southeast Asia to New Guinea about 30,000 years ago. Over thousands of years, people spread across Melanesia, northward into Micronesia, then eastward to Polynesia. People from mainland Asia may also have reached the islands of Polynesia by sea.

Living on widely scattered islands, the many peoples of Oceania developed their own distinct and complex cultures. Religious and artistic traditions differed throughout the vast region, and people spoke hundreds of different languages. The peoples of Polynesia seem to have had contact with South American cultures. From South Americans, apparently, they learned to grow potatoes.

Impact of Europeans. European explorers first reached the islands of the Pacific during the 1500s. By the 1700s, France and Britain had begun to claim various islands. Later, Christian missionaries began to win converts among some island peoples. These missionaries convinced many people to reject their own traditions and adopt western values and beliefs.

During the Age of Imperialism, European nations and the United States competed for colonies in Oceania. Eventually, they divided the entire region among themselves. The colonizers profited from trade in copra, coconut oil, and sandalwood. White settlers set up plantations and forced local people to grow cash crops such as coffee, bananas, and rubber. On some islands, such as Fiji, they brought thousands of laborers from as far away as India. These Indian immigrants, in turn, brought their Hindu culture to Fiji.

Regional and Global Concerns

World War II gave the islands of Oceania new importance in the world. In 1941, Japan occupied many islands in the Pacific. Allied forces fought bloody battles to dislodge the Japanese at Guadalcanal, the Solomon Islands, New Guinea, Saipan, and Guam.

Developing nations. Since 1945, nine island nations have won independence. Others are self-governing territories of New Zealand. New Caledonia remains a French territory. Guam and American Samoa are United States territories, while Hawaii became a state in 1959.

The developing nations of the region have tried to diversify their economies.

MAP STUDY

Oceania consists of three main groups of islands scattered across the vast Pacific Ocean. Oceania includes nine island nations and many other islands with distinct cultures.

1. **Location** Describe the relative location of Micronesia and identify three of its main islands.
2. **Region** (a) In which region of Oceania is the largest island found? (b) Which region of Oceania extends across the largest area of the Pacific Ocean?
3. **Understanding Causes and Effects** Why do you think the island nations of Oceania formed the South Pacific Forum to help their people deal with world problems?

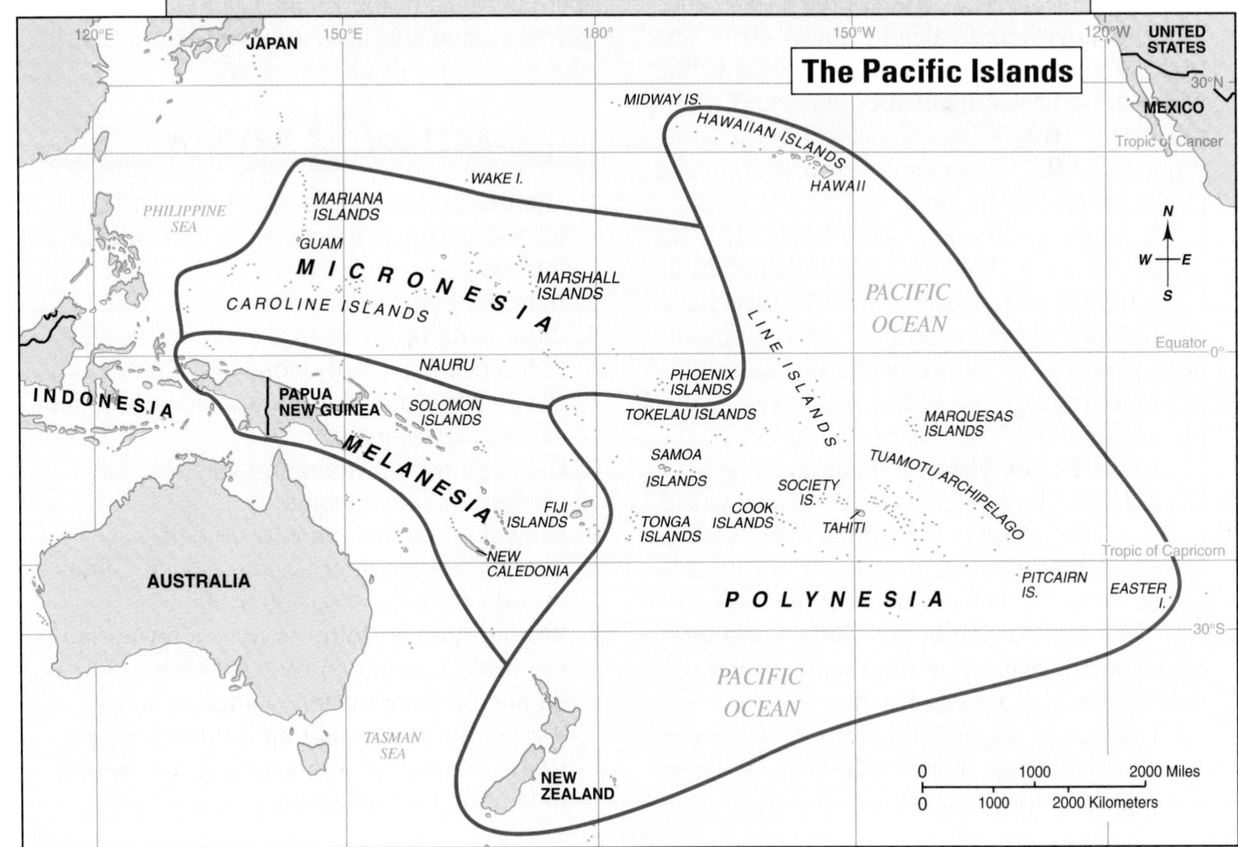

An Island of Samoa Samoa, a part of Polynesia, is made up of 15 islands. The nine western islands form the nation of Western Samoa. The six islands to the east make up American Samoa, a territory of the United States. Almost all of the islands are ringed by coral reefs and shallow lagoons. ***Geography*** What are the two main forms of islands in Oceania?

Mining has offered a new source of income, but the environmental and social costs are high. Mining introduces a cash economy, but when mineral resources are exhausted, people are left with no way to make a living. Also, the extraction of mineral resources causes great damage to the land.

Tourism has brought the islands into the global economy. Foreign investors have built huge hotels and resorts, which in turn have created jobs for islanders. Such development, however, takes a toll on the environment. For example, tourism has strained the water supply on some islands.

South Pacific Forum. The remoteness of Oceania no longer protects it from world events. The 15-nation South Pacific Forum takes a stand on issues of concern to the people of Oceania. It has opposed nuclear testing. The United States and Britain stopped testing such weapons in the Pacific during the 1960s. France, however, has not.

The use of huge fishing nets by Japanese and Korean fishing ships threatens sea life in the region. Global warming is another issue of concern. Said one Pacific island leader, "We will be asking the industrialized countries to take it easy and think about us."

SECTION 3 REVIEW

1. **Locate:** (a) Melanesia, (b) New Guinea, (c) Micronesia, (d) Polynesia, (e) Hawaiian Islands.
2. **Identify:** South Pacific Forum.
3. What roles do landforms and climate play in the economies of Oceania?
4. How did the arrival of Europeans affect the cultures of Oceania?
5. Describe two environmental issues that concern Pacific nations.
6. **Drawing Conclusions** Why do small nations like those of Oceania join together to form regional associations?
7. **Writing Across Cultures** As you have read, the United States and Britain have stopped testing nuclear weapons in the Pacific, but France has not. Write a letter to the premier of France urging the French to join the nuclear-test ban in the Pacific.

CHAPTER 14 REVIEW

Understanding Vocabulary

Match each term at left with the correct definition at right.

1. geothermal energy	**a.** island formed by the top of an active volcano
2. penal colony	**b.** heat released naturally in geysers, hot springs, and volcanoes
3. suffrage	**c.** place where people convicted of crimes are shipped
4. high island	**d.** island formed by a coral reef
5. low island	**e.** right to vote

Reviewing the Main Ideas

1. (a) Describe the major physical regions of Australia and New Zealand. (b) What areas of these nations are most heavily populated?
2. (a) How did the Australian Aborigines preserve their beliefs? (b) How did the Aborigines of Australia differ from the Maoris of New Zealand?
3. (a) Who were the first British settlers in Australia? (b) What traditions did they bring?
4. (a) Why do Australia and New Zealand have a high standard of living? (b) Describe two problems that prosperity has brought.
5. Describe the three main regions of Oceania.
6. (a) How did imperialism affect the peoples of Oceania? (b) How did World War II affect the Pacific islands?

Reviewing Chapter Themes

1. Geographic factors have played a key role in the development of Pacific cultures. Describe the relationship between: (a) geographic isolation and the cultures of Australia and Oceania, (b) rainfall and the economic development of Australia, (c) different landforms and the islands of Oceania.
2. Europeans had settled Australia, New Zealand, and Oceania by the 1800s. Describe three effects European colonization had on the region.
3. Modern transportation and communications have contributed to interdependence. Explain how economic or political ties have affected the relations of Australia, New Zealand, and Oceania with: (a) Southeast Asia, (b) Japan, (c) the United States.

Thinking Critically

1. **Forecasting** Do you think the Australian Outback is likely to remain sparsely populated in the future? Why or why not?
2. **Making Global Connections** Compare the settlement of Australia by Europeans with the settlement of the United States.
3. **Drawing Conclusions** (a) Why do you think tourism has become a major source of income for many Pacific islands? (b) What are the advantages and disadvantages of an economy that is based on tourism?

Applying Your Skills

1. **Analyzing a Poem** Reread the excerpt from the poem by Aboriginal poet Kevin Gilbert on page 302. (a) What is the subject of this poem? (b) How does Gilbert express pride in being an Aborigine? (c) What actions might he support? (See Skill Lesson, page 541.)
2. **Recognizing Points of View** Reread the quotation on page 310. (a) What attitude does the speaker express toward industrialized nations? (b) What do his words suggest about the nations of Oceania? (c) Why might some Pacific island leaders disagree with his point of view?

SKILL LESSON 7

Using a Primary Source: Life Under the Khmer Rouge

Primary sources are firsthand accounts of events. Letters, diaries, newspaper accounts, and autobiographies are all examples of primary sources. They provide us with details that are often missing from secondhand descriptions. Remember, however, that a writer's point of view can influence what he or she emphasizes.

The excerpt below is from Haing Ngor's autobiography, *A Cambodian Odyssey,* published in 1987. Haing Ngor and his wife, Huoy, were sent to a forced labor camp after the Khmer Rouge took power in Cambodia in 1975. In the excerpt, Haing Ngor writes of his experiences in the camp. Read the excerpt, using the following steps to guide you.

1. **Analyze details that the author provides.** (a) What details does Haing Ngor give about camp life in the morning? At lunch time? In the afternoon? In the late afternoon? (b) Based on Haing Ngor's details, how would you describe the quality of life in the camp?

2. **Identify the author's point of view.** (a) What does Haing Ngor think people taken as prisoners might have done wrong? (b) What statements does he make about laws and courts under the Khmer Rouge? (c) Based on your answers, what is his view of rule by the Khmer Rouge?

3. **Decide whether the source is reliable.** (a) Do you think that Haing Ngor gives an accurate view of the labor camp? (b) Do you think he gives an accurate view of the Khmer Rouge? Explain.

> "They [the labor camp leaders] rang the first bell at four o'clock in the morning. . . .
>
> By the second series of bells, Huoy and I had joined our separate groups, 10 people in each. Different groups joined together, depending on their work sites, and set off across the landscape in long, single-file lines. . . .
>
> When we reached the canal my group . . . went to its site. . . . I climbed down to the bottom of the canal, sighed and swung my hoe. . . .
>
> At lunch time they rang the bell. . . . Before the first bell had stopped, we fell into a line and trudged off, merging with other lines that converged on the common kitchen. . . .
>
> Nine of us sat on the ground in a circle while the tenth, our group leader, went to the kitchen to get our rations. . . . By the time he returned to the circle with the pan [of watery rice] and a stack of rusted bowls, the rest of us were sitting expectantly on our haunches with our spoons out. . . .
>
> The afternoon was the same as the morning, only longer. . . . The worst part of the day was late afternoon. That was when the soldiers came to take prisoners. We never knew ahead of time whether they would come, or who they would choose, or how many. The uncertainty made the waiting worse. . . .
>
> What had the prisoners done wrong? We knew not to ask. Asking wouldn't bring them back. It only endangered those who dared to question. There were no laws under the Khmer Rouge except the law of silence. There were no courts except Angka Leu [the higher levels of the Khmer organization]. Maybe the prisoners hadn't worked hard enough. Or they stole food. Or a *chhlop,* a spy, overheard them making remarks about Angka. People disappeared. That's all we knew. And I knew that someday I would be one of them."

SKILL LESSON 8

Reading a Thematic Map: Religions of Southeast Asia

Thematic maps provide specialized information about a geographic area. Examples of thematic maps include population maps, resource maps, and language maps. These maps can tell you a great deal about the people and customs of other cultures.

The map below shows the religion of the majority of the population in each nation of Southeast Asia. The map key contains important information that will help you to interpret the map. Practice reading a thematic map, using the following steps as a guide.

1. **Identify what the map shows.** (a) What land area does the map include? (b) What is the subject of the map? (c) What do the different colors represent?

2. **Analyze the information on the map.** (a) What color represents Protestantism? (b) What religion do most people in Thailand practice? (c) Name two countries in which Islam is the main religion.

3. **Synthesize the information and draw conclusions.** According to what you have read in Chapter 11, people from India, China, and the Middle East brought their religious beliefs to Southeast Asia. The Indians and the Chinese brought Buddhism, and the Arabs brought Islam. (a) In what countries of Southeast Asia did Indian and Chinese beliefs have the greatest influence? How do you know this? (b) In what countries of Southeast Asia did Islamic beliefs have the greatest influence? Explain. (c) Based on what you have read in Chapter 11, how did Roman Catholicism come to be the major religion of the Philippines?

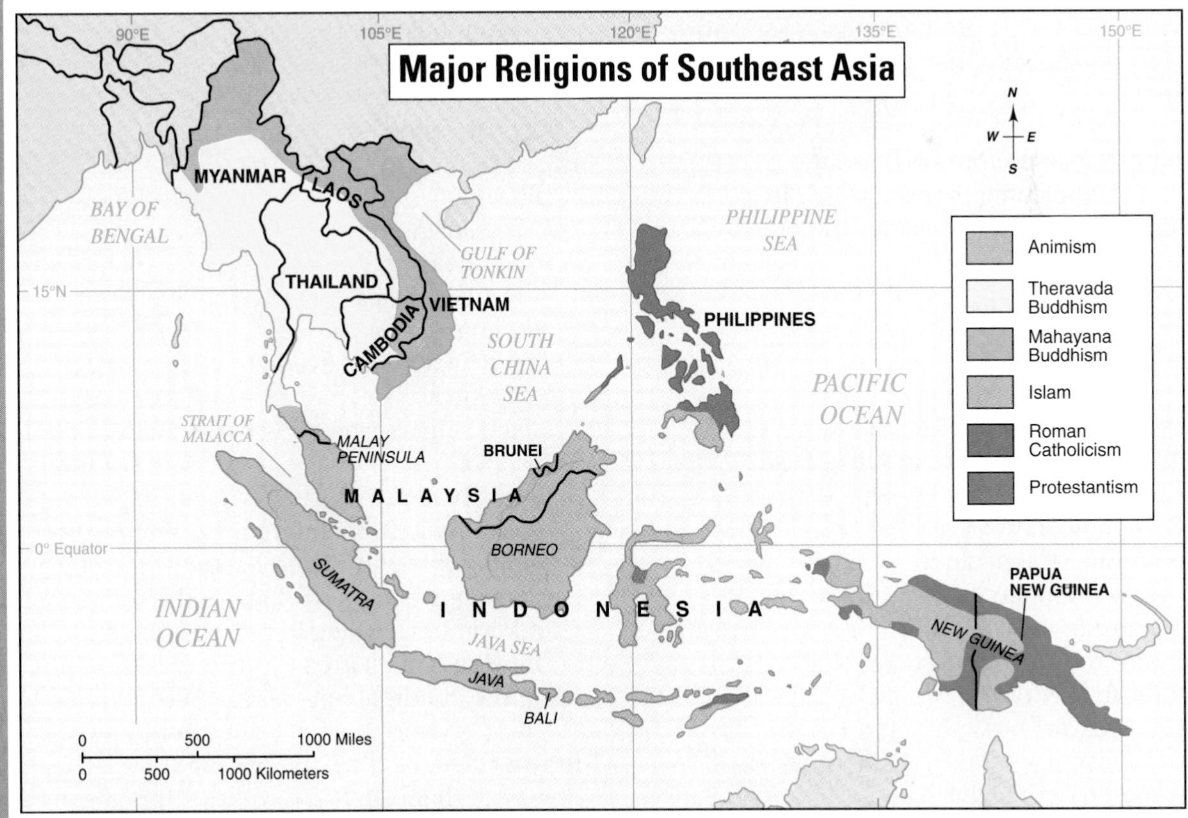

Thoughts of Hanoi

Nguyen Thi Vinh

INTRODUCTION In 1954, when Vietnam was divided into two countries, nearly 1 million people fled North Vietnam because they did not want to live under communist rule. Many prominent political leaders, business executives, and artists—including Nguyen Thi Vinh—were among the refugees. Those who had fled to South Vietnam faced particular hardships. The South was quite different from the North in climate, cuisine, landscape, and customs.

When civil war broke out, the North Vietnam that the refugees had known was gone forever. It was in this climate that Nguyen Thi Vinh (1924–), a prominent novelist, short-story writer, and poet, wrote "Thoughts of Hanoi."

Vocabulary Before you read the selection, find the meaning of these words in a dictionary: yearn, jubilant, obsolete.

The night is deep and chill
as in early autumn. Pitchblack,
it thickens after each lightning flash.
I dream of Hanoi:
Co-ngu Road
ten years of separation
the way back sliced by a frontier of
  hatred.
I want to bury the past
to burn the future
still I yearn
still I fear
those endless nights
waiting for dawn.

Brother,
how is Hang Dao now?
How is Ngon Son temple?
Do the trains still run
each day from Hanoi
to the neighboring towns?
To Bac-ninh, Cam-giang, Yen bai,
the small villages, islands
of brown thatch in a lush green sea?

The girls
  bright eyes
    ruddy cheeks
  four-piece dresses
    raven-bill scarves
  sowing harvesting
    spinning weaving
  all year round,
the boys
  plowing
    transplanting
  in the fields
    in their shops
  running across
    the meadow at evening
  to fly kites
    and sing alternating songs.

Stainless blue sky,
  jubilant voices of children
stumbling through the alphabet,
  village graybeards strolling to the temple,
grandmothers basking in twilight sun,
  chewing betel leaves
while the children run—

Brother,
how is all that now?
Or is it obsolete?

Are you like me,
reliving the past,
imagining the future?
Do you count me as a friend
or am I the enemy in your eyes?
Brother, I am afraid
that one day I'll be with the March-North
Army
meeting you on your way to the South.
I might be the one to shoot you then
or you me
but please
not with hatred.
For don't you remember how it was,

you and I in school together,
plotting our lives together?
Those roots go deep!

Brother, we are men,
conscious of more
than material needs.
How can this happen to us
my friend
my foe?

Source: "Thoughts of Hanoi," by Nguyen Thi Vinh (translated by Nguyen Dgoc Bich with Burton Raffel and W. S. Merwin), from *A Thousand Years of Vietnamese Poetry*, edited by Nguyen Ngoc Bich. Copyright 1962, 1967, 1968, 1969, 1970, 1971, 1974 by the Asia Society and Nguyen Ngoc Bich.

An unknown Indonesian artist created this imaginative batik design. First, the design was painted on cloth with wax. When the cloth was dyed, the wax was removed, leaving the design. Like the writer of "Thoughts of Hanoi," the artist expresses powerful feelings. How does the artist's view of the beauty and serenity of this peaceful scene compare with the poet's description of the violence of civil war?

THINKING ABOUT LITERATURE

1. (a) How does the speaker in the poem feel about Hanoi? (b) Who does he mean when he says "brother"?
2. (a) What is the speaker afraid of? (b) What does he mean when he says, "How can this happen to us/my friend/ my foe?"
3. **Recognizing Point of View** (a) How does the speaker feel about being involved in a civil war? (b) What statements in the poem support your answer?

Pepper Fever

Rome trembled. Barbarian Visigoths, led by the ruthless Alaric, had sacked the once-proud city. Now Alaric threatened to slay the defenseless citizens unless they paid an outrageous ransom. One of Alaric's demands was a great treasure from the East. Yes, said Alaric, he would spare the lives of the Roman people, but only if they gave him 3,000 pounds (1,361 kg) of pepper!

That deal, in A.D. 410, is one of the only times that a claim can be made that pepper saved lives. For the most part, the history of pepper is violent and bloody. As pepper traveled from India (right), Java, and the Spice Islands to the dinner tables of Europe, each mile along the route was paved with great hardship and even death. It is estimated that during the Middle Ages, each ship's cargo of pepper cost 1,000 lives.

Pepper, Then and Now

Today, we take pepper for granted. At your local supermarket, a typical spice section contains enough pepper to have paid a year's rent or have provided a bride's dowry during the Middle Ages.

Pepper is common today because world travel time has shrunk dramatically. Pepper harvested in the Spice Islands can appear on an American dinner table in a matter of days rather than years. To people in the past, however, the place where the pepper vines (below, right) grew seemed as distant as the moon.

For centuries, the Arabs controlled the key points on the spice trade routes from Asia to Europe. These traders made up fantastic stories about monsters that supposedly guarded the lands where the spices grew.

In Rome, the great scholar Pliny the Elder scoffed: "All these tales . . . have been evidently invented for the purpose of enhancing the values of these goods." Indeed, they had been. At one point, Romans paid the equivalent of $125 for 12 ounces (340 g) of pepper. The stories also kept Europeans from seeking out the source of pepper.

In the first century A.D., the Arabs lost their monopoly. Taking advantage of the monsoon winds, Roman ships sailed east during the summer from Egypt's Red Sea coast to India. There, the ships were loaded with pepper and other spices. When the winter winds blew west, the ships returned home.

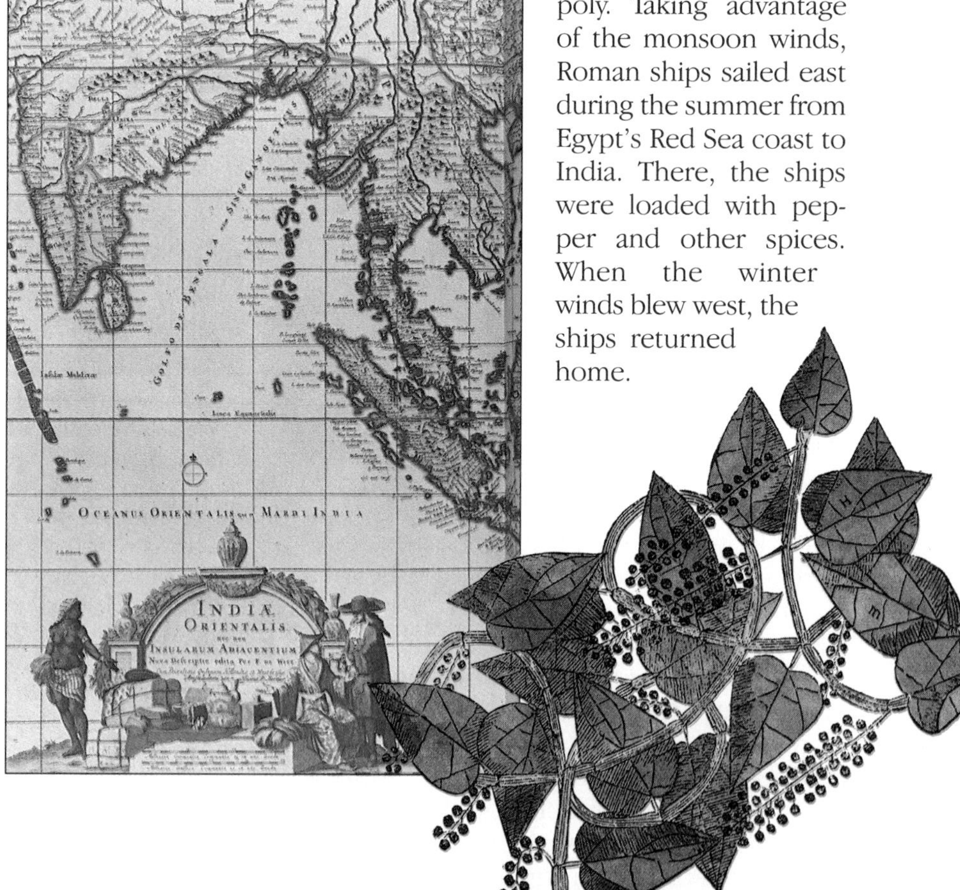

The brisk trade in pepper drained India of its supply. Soon, traders began to look for pepper in Southeast Asia. By the 300s, however, trade between Asia and Europe had ground to a halt. Rome's reserves of gold had been so greatly reduced that a financial crisis resulted. Western Europe's passion for pepper and other spices had helped to destroy the Western Roman Empire.

Trade Revives

Not until the 1100s did the glorious flavor of pepper once more delight the taste buds of Europeans. Knights who had fought in the Crusades came back from the Holy Land with luxuries from Asia. Pepper fever again gripped Europe. This time, however, the spice would come by land rather than by sea.

The sea route had been dangerous, but the overland route was even worse. Caravans loaded with spices had to cross the grim mountain ranges and bleak, forbidding deserts of Asia. Bandits lay in wait for travelers who had been lucky enough to survive nature's hardships.

When Constantinople fell to the Ottoman Turks in 1453, the overland trade in pepper was cut off. Europe still wanted pepper in its food, however, and Europeans were not alone in their longing for the spice.

During the early 1500s, a Portuguese priest on a trip to Ethiopia reported that pepper was an absolute necessity for doing business in that country. On a visit to a town called Ingabelu, he wrote:

> "We found in this town an infinite quantity of fowls, of which 100 could be bought at leisure, if one wanted so many in exchange for a little pepper, so little do they value the hens and so highly do they value pepper."

Ferdinand Magellan's explorations finally opened the treasures of the fabled Spice Islands to Europeans. Magellan's ships reached these islands shortly after he was killed in the Philippines. His crew found one island where pepper berries grew on tall vines.

By the 1800s, England and Holland were fighting to control the trade in pepper and other spices, but Europe never gained a monopoly. The United States, too, took part in the pepper trade. Ships that sailed from Salem, Massachusetts, to Sumatra returned with cargoes that made the pepper merchants rich beyond imagination. The taxes Salem paid on its pepper were equal to 5 percent of the money spent by the United States government during the early 1800s.

At one time, nations rose and fell because of pepper. Great battles were fought over it. Now, pepper is so readily available that there is no such thing as pepper fever. Still, it is fascinating to consider that pepper lent spice to human history for hundreds of years.

1. (a) How did pepper reach Europe? (b) Where did pepper come from?
2. **Making Inferences** Why was pepper so valuable?
3. **Writing Across Cultures** List hardships you might have faced if you had traveled in a spice caravan.

Unit 4 Review

Reviewing the Main Ideas

1. (a) List the physical characteristics of mainland Southeast Asia and island Southeast Asia. (b) How did geography influence the organization of early civilizations in Southeast Asia?
2. (a) Identify three early kingdoms of Southeast Asia. (b) Describe the major achievements of the Khmer kingdom.
3. (a) Name three events in Europe that caused changes in Southeast Asia during the 1700s and 1800s. (b) How did European rule affect traditional economies in Southeast Asia?
4. Explain how two of the following foreign powers influenced events in Vietnam: (a) China, (b) France, (c) the United States.
5. (a) Describe the modern-day economies of Cambodia, the Philippines, and Singapore. (b) Why is industrialization important to the economies of Southeast Asian nations?
6. (a) How does Southeast Asian music differ from western music? (b) How does Southeast Asian classical dance compare with western dance?
7. (a) Describe the traditional cultures of the Aborigines and the Maoris. (b) How did European settlement of Australia and New Zealand affect the Aborigines and the Maoris?
8. (a) Name the three regions of Oceania. (b) How have the developing nations of Oceania tried to diversify their economies?

Thinking Critically

1. **Drawing Conclusions** (a) Why was the Strait of Malacca important to traders in Southeast Asia? (b) How did internal rivalries within the Srivijaya Empire on Sumatra help Europeans gain control of the Strait of Malacca? (c) If the people had been united, do you think they could have fought off the Europeans? Explain.
2. **Making Global Connections** In 1848, gold was discovered in California, sparking a gold rush to the American West. Compare California's gold rush with Australia's gold rush in 1851. How did mining for gold affect settlement of the American West and Australia?
3. **Comparing** Compare European colonies in Southeast Asia and Oceania with European settlements in Australia and New Zealand. (a) What brought Europeans to each of these regions? (b) In which of these regions did Europeans have a more lasting impact socially, politically, and economically? Explain.

Applying Your Skills

1. **Analyzing a Poem** Reread the excerpt from José Rizal's poem "My Last Farewell" on page 265. (a) Which phrase describes the Philippines? (b) Why do you think this poem would inspire other nationalists in their struggle for independence? (See Skill Lesson, page 541.)
2. **Analyzing a Political Cartoon** Review the information about war in Cambodia on pages 279–280 and the Skill Lesson on page 540. Then, study the cartoon below. (a) Whom do the figures represent? (b) What does the expression "bury the hatchet" mean? (c) How have the figures waving the hatchets decided to "bury the hatchet"? (d) What reason do they have for their action?

3. **Identifying the Main Idea** Read the subsection "Impact of European Settlement" on page 305. (a) Write a sentence expressing the main idea of this subsection. (b) List two facts that support the main idea.

Learning by Doing

1. **Creating a Map** On an outline map of Southeast Asia, label all countries and their capitals. Label all oceans, seas, straits, gulfs, rivers, and mountains. Using a color key, identify the seven major religions of this region. Key the colors to the map. (See the maps on pages 247 and 251 and the Skill Lesson on page 313.)
2. **Drawing a Cartoon** Draw a political cartoon that reflects opposition to imperialism in Southeast Asia during the early 1900s. You may want to focus on a particular country and foreign power, or you may decide to focus on all of the colonial powers and how they scrambled for dominance and territory in Southeast Asia.
3. **Giving an Oral Report** Using encyclopedias or other sources, research information about Angkor Wat. Focus on the history of the temples and why they are of artistic and architectural importance. Organize your information in time order and write it on note cards. Be sure to practice your report several times before presenting it to the class.

WRITER'S Workshop

Arranging Information in Time Order

Arranging supporting information in time order means arranging it in the order of occurrence. Time order should be used when the supporting information in an answer is based on the events or steps in a process.

Read this topic sentence: *Powerful Southeast Asian rulers sometimes attacked neighboring groups.* Detail sentences supporting this topic sentence should be presented in time order. For example: *In 111 B.C., a Chinese army invaded Vietnam. In A.D. 1177, the Cham people attacked and looted the Khmer's temples in Angkor. In 1287, Mongol armies from China overran Pagan.* Note that the dates show the time order.

It is not always necessary to provide dates. You may use other **transitions,** or connecting words or phrases, to show time order. Here are some common time-order transitions: *after, afterward, at last, before, earlier, eventually, finally, first, formerly, last, later, meanwhile, next, now, previously, soon, then, ultimately, until,* and *while.*

Practice Rewrite each of the detail sentences stated above. Use transitions other than dates to show time order. For example: *First, a Chinese army invaded Vietnam.* Underline the transition in each sentence.

Writing to Learn

1. Write a brief newspaper account of the 1991 Mount Pinatubo volcanic eruption. First, research the topic in periodicals. In your first draft, write a topic sentence that summarizes the significance of the event. Organize the account in time order. Make sure that your information covers *who, what, where, when, why,* and *how.* Revise your account, checking for accuracy and thoroughness. Give the account a title. Proofread and make a final copy of it. Post your account on the class bulletin board.

2. Imagine that you are the leader of a Southeast Asian nationalist movement during the early 1900s. Write a short speech that defends your cause. Begin by brainstorming a list of the reasons you object to foreign rule. Then, make a list of the virtues of independence. In your first draft, write a topic sentence that states why foreign rule is unacceptable to the peoples of Southeast Asia. Use detail sentences, organized in order of importance, to support your topic sentence. In closing, state why independence is necessary. When you revise your speech, be sure that all of your points support the topic sentence. Proofread and make a final copy of your speech. Read your speech to the class.

UNIT 5

EAST ASIA
CHINA, KOREA, JAPAN

Unit Outline

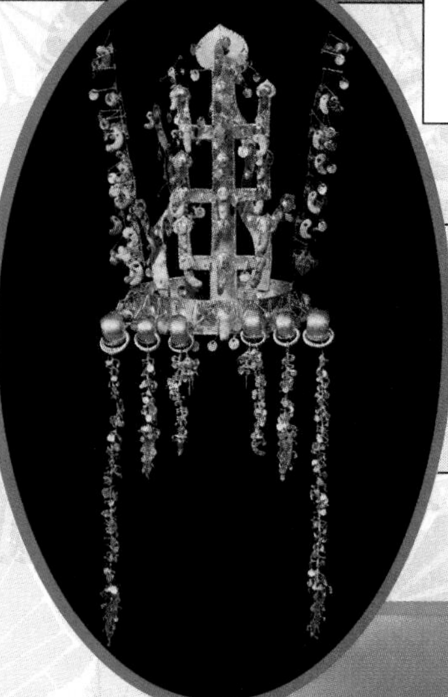

1 Rulers of the ancient Silla kingdom in Korea wore this magnificent crown. Royal artisans fashioned the crown, using gold and precious jade ornaments.

2 This Shinto shrine is in Hiroshima Bay bordering Japan's main island of Honshu. Shintoism and Buddhism are important religious traditions in Japan.

3 More than 1.1 billion people live in China today, making it the most populous nation in the world. Although China's urban population is growing, most of the Chinese people are farmers.

	Early History			1600		1700
History and Politics			▲ 1275 Marco Polo arrives in China	▲ 1600s Manchus overrun Korea and China		
Society and Culture	▲ 500s B.C. Confucianism emerges	▲ 1008 *Tale of Genji* written	▲ 1500s Kabuki theater develops		▲ 1639 Shogun closes Japan to the world	
Economics and Technology	▲ 400 B.C. Construction begins on the Great Wall of China	▲ 1050 Chinese develop movable type				

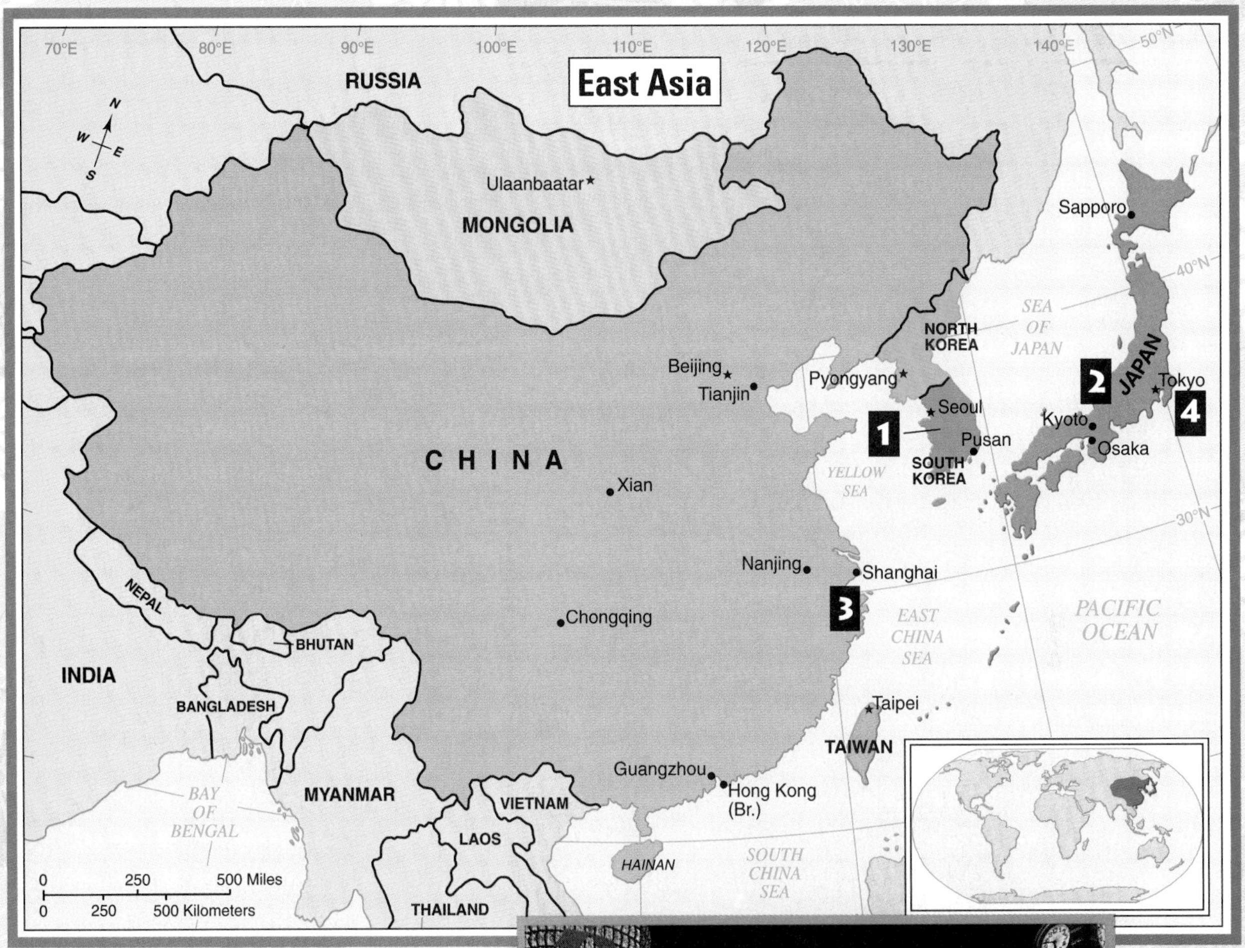

East Asia

70°E 80°E 90°E 100°E 110°E 120°E 130°E 140°E
50°N 40°N 30°N
N S E W
RUSSIA
MONGOLIA
Ulaanbaatar
CHINA
Beijing
Tianjin
Xian
Nanjing
Shanghai
Chongqing
Guangzhou
Hong Kong (Br.)
HAINAN
NORTH KOREA
Pyongyang
SOUTH KOREA
Seoul
Pusan
JAPAN
Sapporo
Tokyo
Kyoto
Osaka
TAIWAN
Taipei
SEA OF JAPAN
YELLOW SEA
EAST CHINA SEA
SOUTH CHINA SEA
PACIFIC OCEAN
BAY OF BENGAL
INDIA
NEPAL
BHUTAN
BANGLADESH
MYANMAR
VIETNAM
LAOS
THAILAND
1 2 3 4
0 250 500 Miles
0 250 500 Kilometers

4 Tokyo, Japan's capital, is one of the world's leading business, financial, and commercial centers. Nearly destroyed by an earthquake in 1923 and by bombing in World War II, Tokyo today is home to more than 8 million people.

1700 | 1800 | 1900 | 2000

- ▲ **1700s** Opium introduced to China
- ▲ **1800s** Japan becomes a unified nation
- ▲ **1839** Opium Wars
- ▲ **1900** Boxer Rebellion
- ▲ **1950–1953** Korean War

- ▲ **1925** All Japanese men gain the right to vote
- ▲ **1966** Mao launches Cultural Revolution

- ▲ **mid-1700s** Industrial Revolution begins in Europe
- ▲ **1854** Japan opens ports to foreign trade
- ▲ **1899** China agrees to "Open Door" policy
- ▲ **1980s** Japan emerges as economic superpower

Chapter 15

GEOGRAPHY AND HERITAGE OF CHINA

Rearing Dragon This mythical creature has always had special meaning for the Chinese. They regarded it as a helpful animal that brought moisture to the earth. Like water itself, which, sometimes came as floods and at other times came as much-needed rain, a dragon could signify both good and bad. ***Fine Art*** How does the artist suggest the dragon's great power over the Chinese people's lives?

CHAPTER OUTLINE

The attendants of the emperor pushed toward the palace gate, eager to get their first glimpse of a *qilin.* According to Chinese legend, the beast could walk without crushing the grass and had a single horn to strike evildoers. More important, its appearance was a sign that a ruler was just and virtuous.

To mark the occasion, a court poet, Shen Du, composed an ode:

> "A qilin has in truth been produced, some fifteen feet in height,
> Its body that of a deer and with the tail of an ox, with a fleshy horn without bone,
> And luminous spots like a red cloud, a purple mist."

The qilin described by Shen Du was a real creature. During the early 1400s, Chinese fleets had sailed around Southeast Asia to India and Africa. They returned with a gift for the emperor's zoo—a giraffe.

To the Chinese, the giraffe was more than an exotic animal from a distant land. It was a symbol that suited perfectly their beliefs about the emperor and his rule.

CHAPTER PERSPECTIVE

For much of its history, China had little to do with the rest of the world. Located far from other civilizations, the Chinese viewed their land as the center of the world and their civilization as superior.

As you read, look for these chapter themes:

- China's civilization influenced East Asia for thousands of years.
- Traditions based on family and Confucian teachings helped to shape ancient China.
- Chinese advances in science and technology later spread to other parts of the world.
- European imperialism and crises in China led to a long process of revolutionary change.

Literature Connections

In this chapter, you will encounter passages from the following works.

"How glorious is the Sacred Emperor," Shen Du

Analects, Confucius

The Way of Virtue, Lao Zi

"Work, work—from the rising sun," Chinese folk verse

The Travels of Marco Polo, Marco Polo

"Fighting South of the Ramparts," Li Bo

For other literature suggestions, see Connections With Literature, pages 804–808.

1 GEOGRAPHIC SETTING

FIND OUT

How did location shape China's view of the world?

Why is China's population unevenly distributed?

How have rivers influenced the lives of the Chinese?

Vocabulary loess

A Chinese historian guides a visitor to the highest terrace of the Temple of Heaven in Beijing* (bay jihng), China's capital. The tourist gazes at a stone. The guide explains that the ancient Chinese believed the stone was the center of the Earth. The guide notes,

> "We Chinese call our country Zhongguo [Middle Kingdom]. . . . The Chinese for centuries knew no other world than China, for thousands of years no other highly developed culture than their own. . . . The realm of the Han [Chinese] was the center of civilization, the center of the Earth."

Location

China's location helps to explain why the Chinese thought they lived at the center of the Earth. As the map on page 324 shows, China covers a huge area. Long ago, distance and physical barriers limited contact between China and other centers of civilization.

The physical barriers of China are varied. They include the vast Gobi Desert, the rugged Mongolian and Tibetan plateaus, and the towering Himalaya Mountains. Mountains

* Most Chinese names in this book are spelled according to the Pinyin system established in China in 1979.

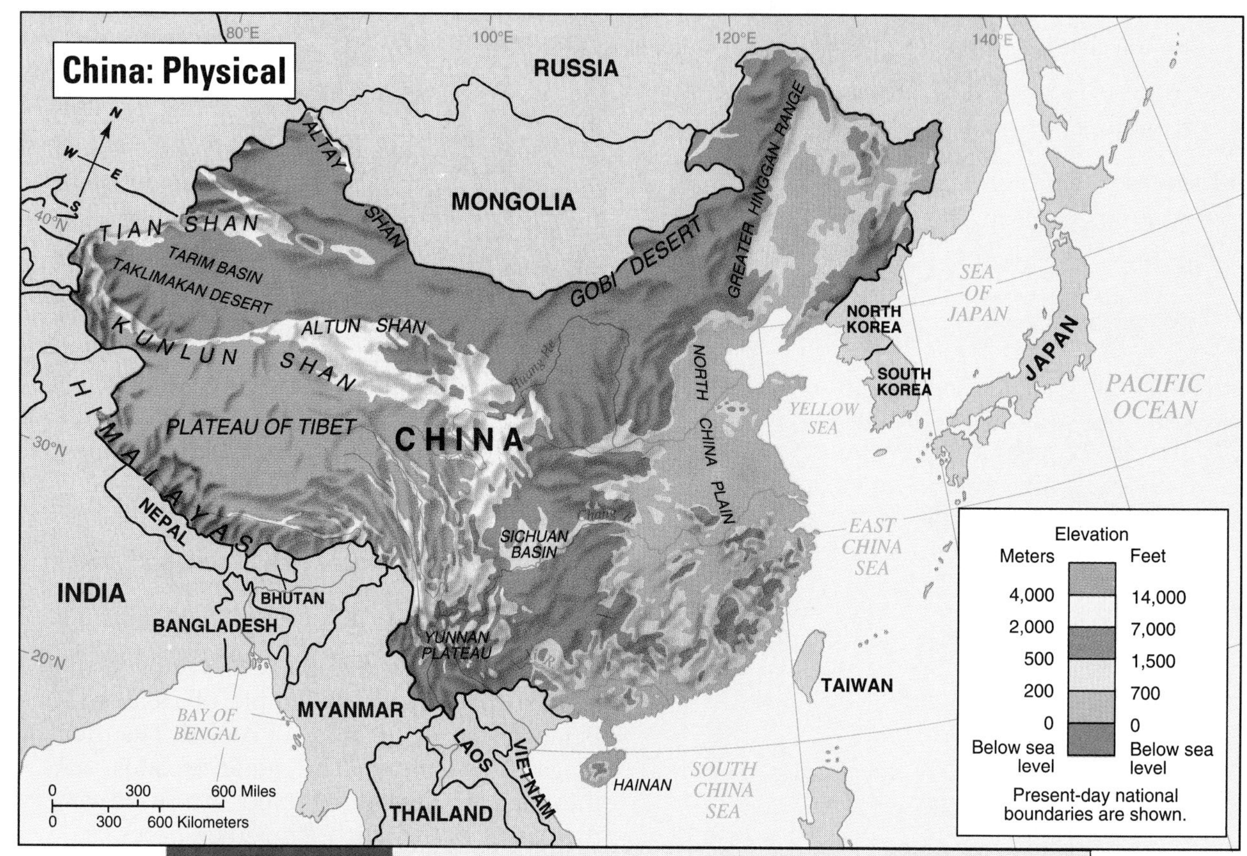

MAP STUDY

China's vast landmass extends from the Pacific Ocean into the heart of Central Asia. China is the third largest nation in the world. Eighty percent of its land is mountains and plateaus.

1. **Location** Identify and give the location of China's three main rivers.
2. **Region** (a) Describe the relative location of the North China Plain. (b) What is the elevation of most of its land?
3. **Understanding Causes and Effects** Why does most of China's population live in the eastern part of the nation?

and rain forests also separate China from Southeast Asia. To the east lies the Pacific Ocean.

Despite physical barriers, China did have some contact with other peoples. Trading caravans trekked great distances, carrying goods between China, India, and the Middle East. Buddhist missionaries carried their religion into China. Invaders, too, swept into China, helping to spread ideas and technologies.

Today, China is one of the largest nations in the world. Modern forms of transportation and communication link China to other parts of the world.

Landforms

China is home to more than 1.1 billion people, or more than one fifth of the world's population. It covers a huge area—3.7 million square miles (9.6 million sq km). Yet most Chinese are crowded into the eastern third of the country. Why do most Chinese live in an area that is about half the size of the United States?

The answer lies in part with China's topography and in part with its economy. Today, as in the past, most Chinese are farmers. They live wherever they can find land that will support them.

Mountains and plateaus cover about 80 percent of China, including much of western China. Because of the rugged terrain and cold, dry climate, the highlands are not suited to farming. As a result, western China has a scattered population, and many people are nomadic herders.

About 20 percent of China is level land, including the coastal plain and the river valleys. Yet only about half of the level land is good for farming. Because there is so little arable land elsewhere, people crowd into eastern China.

To create more farmland, people have constructed terraces, or small, flat fields built into the sides of hills and mountains. The terraces hold the soil in place so that farmers can plant crops.

Regions

China has six main regions. Two regions, which lie in densely populated eastern China, are known as the Chinese heartland. As you will read, the heartland was home to China's first civilization.

The heartland. The two regions of the heartland are North and South China. Together, they stretch from Beijing in the north to China's border with Vietnam in the south. Because North China and South China have different climates, they produce different crops.

North China has warm or hot summers and cold winters. Rainfall varies greatly, and farmers never know how much to expect. Years of floods may alternate with years of severe drought. The chief food crops of North China are wheat and millet.

The cities of Beijing and Tianjin (tyehn jihn) are manufacturing centers in North China. As China's capital, Beijing has had a major impact on cultural and political affairs.

South China is a much richer farming and industrial region than North China. The mild, humid climate allows farmers to grow rice, cotton, tea, vegetables, and many other crops. Because much of South China is hilly, people are packed onto farmland in the river valleys and around lakes.

Outlying regions. Four regions lie beyond the heartland: the Northeast, Mongolia,* Xinjiang (sheen jee ahng), and Xizang (shee dzahng). They are home to diverse ethnic groups. Some areas are rich in natural resources.

* One part of Mongolia is an independent country. The other part is under Chinese control.

Terrace Farming Chinese farmers began terracing hills and mountains at least 700 years ago. Terraces are still needed today because only 7 percent of China's land is arable. ***Technology*** Why must sloping land be terraced before crops can be grown on it?

The Northeast was once known as Manchuria. As you will read, the Manchu (man choo) people who lived there conquered China during the 1600s. Today, the Chinese government is working to develop the region's many resources, including oil, iron, aluminum ore, coal, lead, and zinc. Because of its cold climate, the Northeast is sparsely populated. The government offers special rewards to attract people to the region.

Lying in the parched Gobi Desert, Mongolia, too, has a harsh climate. Summers are extremely hot, and winters are bitterly cold. The government has tried to improve irrigation and thereby promote farming.

The desert basin of Xinjiang is an important oil-producing region. If the government's plans for irrigation succeed, the region may also produce wheat and cotton. Xinjiang is home to many non-Chinese peoples, including Muslim Uighurs, Kazakhs, and Kyrgyz. Although it has been isolated for a long time, Xinjiang is now linked to the heartland by railroads.

Xizang, also known as Tibet, sits among several mountain ranges, including the world's highest mountains—the Himalayas. Much of the region is barren and treeless, but farming is possible in some valleys. Since taking over Tibet in 1958, China has tried to develop its rivers for hydroelectric power. The region may also have mineral wealth that could help China in the future.

Rivers

Since ancient times, three rivers have held an important place in Chinese life: the Huang He (hwahng huh), Chang (jahng), and Xi (shee). Today, as in the past, these rivers serve as both transportation routes and sources of irrigation water.

Despite the ever-present danger of flooding, hundreds of millions of Chinese work the fertile land in the river valleys. Earlier, the Chinese had developed the technology to build dikes and canals to help control floods.

Huang He. The Huang He (Yellow River) wanders for thousands of miles across North China before emptying into the Yellow Sea. Its name comes from the yellow-brown soil, called loess (LOH ehs), that winds carry across the North China Plain and into the river. This windblown soil is quite fertile and enriches the land.

In China, the Huang He has earned the name "River of Sorrow" because it floods frequently, causing terrible destruction. In 1931, for example, a flood destroyed China's crops and almost 4 million people died of starvation.

Boat on the Chang Asia's longest river, the Chang, is also China's busiest shipping lane. It carries three fourths of the country's waterborne traffic. Dams like the one shown here help control the flow of the Chang and also provide hydroelectric power. ***Geography*** Which river in China is known as the "River of Sorrow"? How did it get that name?

Flooding occurs because loess clogs the riverbed. After heavy rains, the river overflows its banks. In Chinese writing, the character for "misfortune" is 𡿧. The symbol is a river with a barrier that causes flooding. Yet the flooding provides one important benefit to the Chinese. The flood waters leave behind a fertile layer of silt after they dry up.

Chang River. The Chang, also known as the Yangzi (yang zih), carries much of China's trade. For centuries, large ships have sailed hundreds of miles upriver. At the mouth of the Chang lies the busy port city of Shanghai, from which China ships many of its goods to countries overseas.

In recent years, the government has built dams to develop hydroelectric power along the Chang. However, the Three Gorges Dam has sparked furious debate. Government planners say the dam will produce such abundant electric power that the environmental damage it may cause will be acceptable. Critics point out that it will flood farmland and force more than 1 million people to leave their homes.

Xi River. China's third major waterway is the Xi Jiang, or West River, which flows through South China. Oceangoing vessels can navigate this river to reach Guangzhou (Canton). From this major port, China ships the riches of its southlands to the world.

Tens of millions of Chinese are crowded into the Xi delta. There, ample water, a favorable climate, and good soil enable farmers to produce two or even three crops a year.

People

About 95 percent of the people who make up China's huge population are Han, or ethnic Chinese. Ethnic minorities such as the Mongols, Tibetans, and Tajiks live in the remote regions of the interior.

Even though most people who live in China are Chinese, they speak different dialects, or regional forms, of Chinese. Dialects differ so much that Chinese from one area cannot understand people from other areas. To promote unity, the government has made Mandarin, which is spoken in North China, the country's official language.

SECTION 1 REVIEW

1. **Locate:** (a) Himalayas, (b) Gobi Desert, (c) Huang He, (d) Chang River, (e) Xi River.
2. **Define:** loess.
3. (a) Why did the Chinese call their land Zhongguo? (b) How did China's location contribute to Chinese ethnocentrism?
4. (a) Describe the six regions of China. (b) Why do most people live in the Chinese heartland?
5. (a) What are the three main rivers of China? (b) How have they influenced Chinese life?
6. **Understanding Causes and Effects** How have topography and climate influenced population patterns in China?
7. **Writing Across Cultures** Write a dialogue in which an American and a Chinese discuss how geography has affected contact between their nation and other civilizations.

2 ENDURING TRADITIONS

FIND OUT

What were the achievements of the Shang civilization?

How did the Mandate of Heaven explain changes in dynasties?

What three schools of thought emerged in China?

How did the Chinese adapt Buddhism to their own society?

Vocabulary ideograph, dynastic cycle, filial piety

In a great flood, begins a Chinese legend, the waters of the Huang He swirled across the North China Plain. The flood lasted for seven years. Finally, a young man named Yu set out to master the waters.

For 13 years, Yu dug canals and planted trees along the river. Not once did he stop working, even to visit his family. In the end, Yu calmed the Huang He, which did not flood again for 1,600 years. As a reward for his labors, Yu became the founder of the Xia (shee ah) dynasty, or ruling family.

The story of Yu may be a legend, but it shows the standard by which the Chinese judged their rulers. A ruler who worked hard to provide good government, including relief from floods, deserved the support of the people.

China's Earliest Civilization

Archaeologists have not yet found any proof that the emperor Yu or the Xia dynasty actually existed. They have, however, uncovered a great deal of evidence about early civilization in China.

In China, as elsewhere, the agricultural revolution led to the rise of civilization. (See Chapter 2.) Using hoes and digging sticks, early farmers planted crops in the rich loess of the Huang He Valley. By about 1650 B.C., strong rulers had extended their power over a number of farming villages by defeating their rivals. They set up the Shang dynasty.

Under the Shang dynasty, Chinese civilization took shape. Ideas evolved that would influence later Chinese history. The idea of dynastic rule, for example, lasted until 1911—more than 3,500 years.

Government. At Anyang, the Shang dynasty capital, archaeologists have found palaces, temples, and royal burial sites. With a well-organized army of nobles, peasants, and slaves, the Shang battled nomadic invaders. Nobles fought from wheeled chariots, an invention that may have come to China from the Middle East.

Shang rulers supervised irrigation and flood control projects. Because these projects benefited the people, they helped to strengthen the ruler's power.

Religion. An important duty of the king was performing rituals to please the gods. The Chinese believed that heaven was the home of many gods and spirits. Shang Di was the chief god. If the gods were pleased, they sent good harvests and victory in war. If they were not, they could cause floods and famine.

Shang Bronze Figure This vessel, cast from a mold, was probably used to make ritual offerings of wine. The animal's feathered hind legs, which face backward, are those of an owl. A dragon coils along the animal's back, raising its head above the ears.
Fine Art Why do you think the artist created an animal that does not exist in real life?

Through his ancestors, the king—the Son of Heaven—served as the link between heaven and Earth. To find out the gods' will, the king consulted the spirits of his ancestors. After offering the correct sacrifices, he asked them questions about problems he faced.

Priests used "oracle bones" to consult the ancestors. (An oracle is a person or agency that communicates with the gods.) Priests wrote the ruler's questions on the bones of sheep or goats. A typical question might be, "Will the royal baby be a boy?" or "Will the king succeed in battle today?" After heating the bones, the priests interpreted the cracks that appeared as answers from the gods.

Achievements. By the time of the Shang dynasty, the Chinese had developed their own form of writing. As with other early people, Chinese writing was based on pictographs, or pictures of objects such as trees, animals, and weapons. The Chinese also used ideographs, or symbols, to express ideas such as beauty, joy, and justice. Through conquest, trade, and other contacts, the Chinese system of writing spread to Korea, Japan, and Vietnam.

The Shang used about 3,000 characters in their system of writing. As their civilization advanced, the Chinese added more characters. In later times, students had to memorize at least 10,000 characters to be literate. Because the writing system was so complex, only the children of wealthy families had the time to learn to read and write.

Under the Shang, the Chinese made advances in many other areas. By carefully recording their observations of the heavens, priests developed an accurate calendar. This knowledge was essential to farming people, who needed to know when to plant and harvest their crops.

Chinese craftworkers improved the art of bronze making. Out of bronze, they created weapons, vessels for religious rituals, and everyday objects such as cooking pots. Craftworkers also developed methods of making silk and pottery. Much later, Chinese potters perfected their methods and produced the fine chinaware that is so valued by foreigners.

Ideas About Government and Society

In 1027 B.C., the Zhou (joh) people invaded from the northwest and overthrew the Shang dynasty. The Zhou dynasty ruled China for almost 900 years. During this long period, ideas emerged that would shape many of China's basic traditions.

The Mandate of Heaven. One key idea was the Mandate of Heaven. The Chinese believed that heaven granted a ruler the mandate, or right, to rule. The people, in turn, owed the ruler complete loyalty and obedience.

The Mandate of Heaven linked power and responsibility. In exchange for their loyalty, the people had the right to expect good government. If a ruler failed to maintain harmony and order, the people had the right to rebel. War, floods, and famine were signs that the ruler had lost the Mandate of Heaven.

The Zhou used the Mandate of Heaven to justify their rise to power. The last Shang ruler, they said, was wicked and corrupt. "Our kings of Zhou . . . treated the people well and were able to sustain the burden of virtuous government." Heaven, therefore, had "made choice of them to rule over many regions."

During its long history, China had many ruling dynasties. The Mandate of Heaven helped to explain the dynastic cycle, or the rise and fall of ruling families. (See the diagram below.)

Three schools of thought. After about 700 B.C., the Zhou had little control over powerful

Graph Skills The Chinese believed that their emperor had received the Mandate of Heaven to rule his people. However, they also believed that the emperor must govern wisely and preserve order in China. ▶ According to this flow chart, what events or developments showed that a dynasty had lost the Mandate of Heaven?

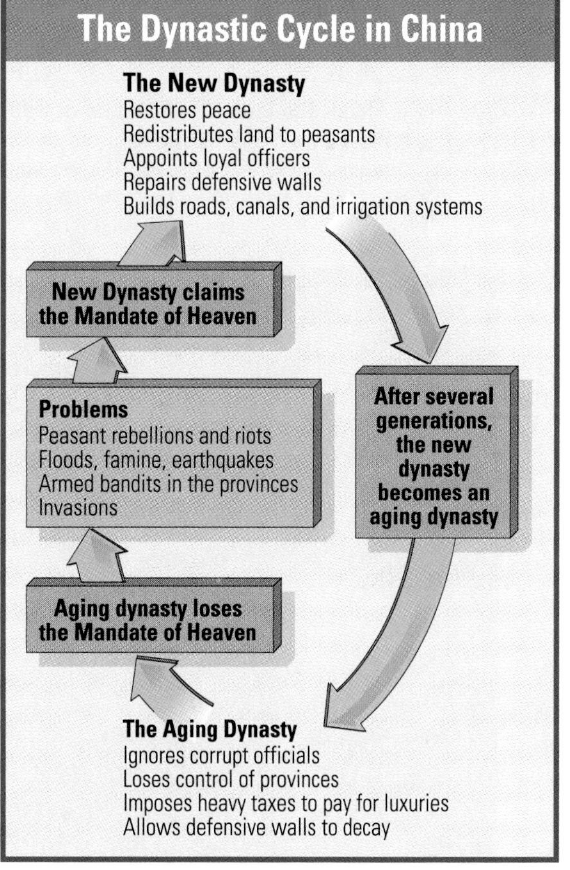

lords who set up their own independent states. Rival states constantly battled for power.

Some of China's greatest thinkers lived during those centuries of chaos and uncertainty. They developed three philosophies, or schools of thought: Confucianism, Daoism, and Legalism.

Each philosophy differed from the others, but all of them had a similar concern: What principles should guide human conduct and ensure order in society? The answers to this question have guided Chinese life to the present.

Teachings of Confucius

Confucius (kuhn FYOO shuhs),* China's best-known philosopher, was born in about 551 B.C. The disorder and suffering caused by constant warfare disturbed Confucius. He developed ideas about how to restore peace and ensure harmony.

* When Europeans reached China, they heard about the thinker Kong Zi (kuhng dzuh), or Master Kong. They pronounced the name Confucius.

Confucius visited the courts of various princes, hoping to convince them to put his ideas into practice. Disappointed, he returned home, where he taught a small but loyal group of followers. After his death, his followers collected his teachings in the *Analects.*

Five relationships. To restore order, Confucius taught that five relationships must govern human society. They are the relationships between ruler and ruled, father and son, older brother and younger brother, husband and wife, and friend and friend. In all but the last relationship, one person has authority over another. In each, said Confucius, the superior person should set an example for the inferior one.

> "If a ruler himself is upright, all will go well without orders. But if he himself is not upright, even though he gives orders, they will not be obeyed."

According to Confucius, the superior person is also responsible for the well-being

A Chinese Emperor The emperor was the supreme ruler of Chinese society. Although he had great power, this power was based on Confucian principles. In practice, this meant that Confucian advisers helped the emperor rule and also served as a check on his actions. ***Political System*** What were the obligations of the ruler and the people in Chinese society?

of the inferior person. A supporter of the Mandate of Heaven, he said that the ruler must provide good government for his subjects. The ruler's subjects, in turn, owed the ruler loyalty and obedience.

To Confucius, relationships involving the family are the key to an orderly society. One of those relationships—the relationship between father and son—is very much like that between the ruler and the ruled.

Like a ruler, the father must set an example for his son and look after his family. The father takes the credit—or blame—for his children's actions. The son, in turn, is expected to honor and obey his father. Confucius stressed this idea of filial piety, the duty and respect that children owe their parents.

Influence. Confucius created a guide to proper behavior based on ethical, or moral, principles. In his teachings, he placed the family and the good of society above the interests of the individual. He also stressed loyalty, courtesy, hard work, and service.

Confucius placed great emphasis on education. "By nature, men are pretty much alike," he said. "It is learning and practice that set them apart." The importance of education as well as other Confucian ideas would shape Chinese government, as you will read.

In time, Confucian ideas came to dominate Chinese society. As China expanded across Asia, Confucianism influenced the cultures of Korea, Japan, and Vietnam as well.

Daoism

Like Confucius, the philosopher Lao Zi (low dzuh) studied human society. He, too, searched for ways to establish an orderly society. The founder of Daoism, however, emphasized the link between people and nature rather than the importance of proper behavior. Lao Zi's thoughts are contained in *The Way of Virtue.*

The natural way. Daoists believed that the best way to live was the natural way. In Chinese, the word *dao* means "the way." Daoists did not define "the way," however. It is said, "Those who know the Dao do not speak of it; those who speak of it do not know it."

Lao Zi on a Water Buffalo Scholars know little about Lao Zi, the founder of Daoism. For centuries, Chinese artists have depicted him as a kindly sage who embodies the ideal at the heart of Daoism. "Reveal thy simple self, embrace thy original nature, check thy selfishness, curtail thy desires," he advised. ***Diversity*** How does Daoism differ from Confucianism?

To Daoists, Confucian rules for society were useless. A society with rules was an artificial creation that disturbed the natural order. People should do nothing that was contrary to nature.

> "The duck's legs are short, but if we try to lengthen them, the duck will feel pain. The crane's legs are long, but if we try to shorten them, the crane will feel grief. Therefore we are not to cut off what is by nature long, nor to lengthen what is by nature short."

Daoists believed that the best government was the one that had the fewest rules and laws. They valued simplicity. "The wise man," said Lao Zi, "keeps to the deed that consists in taking no action and practices the teaching that uses no words."

Influence. From their study of nature, Daoists made advances in science and technology. By recording the movement of the planets, they increased their knowledge of astronomy. They may have developed the magnetic compass to determine favorable places for graves. Their observations of natural forces led to discoveries in chemistry and biology. Some scholars think Daoists invented gunpowder, which they used to frighten ghosts.

Yin and Yang Symbol The concept of yin and yang has shaped Chinese thinking for more than 2,000 years. Yin and yang are the forces in nature that are thought to balance each other. Yin (here in blue) is regarded as female, passive, and earthly. Yang (in red) is considered to be male, active, and heavenly. ***Culture*** Why might both Confucianists and Daoists accept the yin-yang principle?

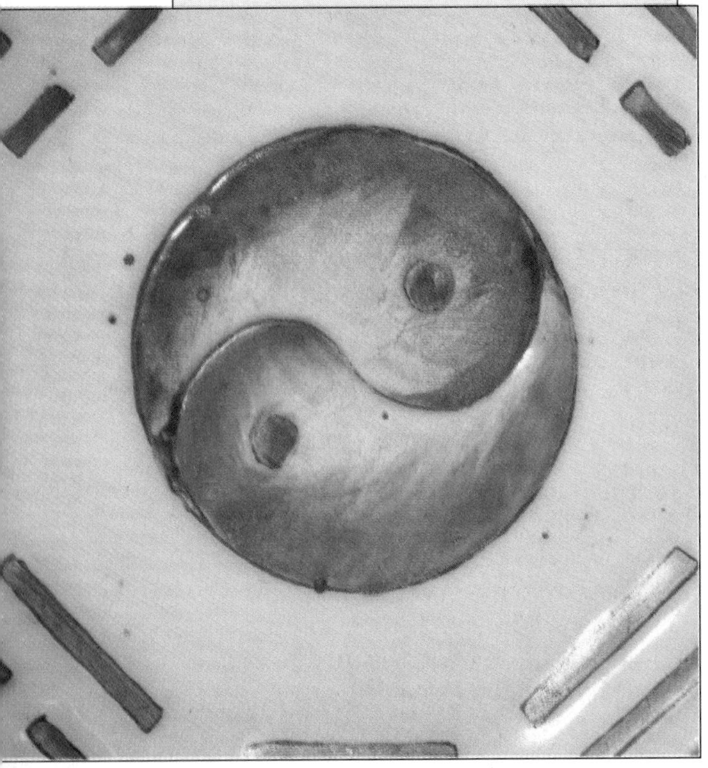

Daoism developed links with folk religion. Peasants believed that gods and spirits controlled the unseen but powerful forces in nature. To find out what would please the spirits, they turned to Daoist priests for help. Priests used all kinds of magic to determine lucky days for weddings and the best placement of graves.

Daoist ideas influenced the arts of China, as you will read. In Chinese painting and poetry, for example, nature dominates. The individual has only a small role.

Legalism

A third school of thought, Legalism, shaped China's early history. The most famous Legalist writer was Han Feizi (hahn fay dzuh). In his book, *Han Feizi,* he rejected Confucian ideas about proper behavior. He believed that people acted out of self-interest. They would respond to rewards and punishments, not to good examples.

To Legalists, only harsh laws imposed by a strong ruler would ensure order in society. "The ruler alone possesses power," noted Han Feizi, "wielding it like lightning or like thunder." In 221 B.C., the Qin (chihn) emperor Shi Huangdi (sher hwang dee) used Legalist ideas to unite China.

Buddhism

During the first century A.D., Buddhism reached China from India. Buddhism was one of the few foreign influences that had a deep impact on Chinese life. It spread along caravan trade routes that linked India to China. Later, Buddhism—and the culture of China—was taken to Korea, Japan, and Vietnam.

Appeal. The Chinese found a great deal of comfort in Buddhism. The three Chinese schools of thought—Confucianism, Daoism, and Legalism—dealt with life on Earth. Buddhism was a religion that offered an escape from the suffering of earthly life. It promised salvation for the good—those who lived moral lives—and punishment for the wicked. It stressed mercy and compassion. Buddhist monks and nuns built hospitals and helped the poor.

When Buddhism first reached China, many Chinese saw it as a foreign religion. They could not understand the vague concept of nirvana. Also, they criticized people who abandoned their families to become monks and nuns.

In time, Buddhism blended with Chinese beliefs and values. Nirvana became the Western Heaven, reflecting Chinese ideas about the afterlife. Chinese Buddhists emphasized Confucian ideas of proper behavior and respect for family and ancestors. They also absorbed Daoist views of nature. (See Connections With Literature, page 805, "Poems by Wang Wei.")

Diverse beliefs. The Chinese could accept diverse ideas. As a result, many Chinese followed Buddhist, Daoist, and Confucian beliefs at the same time. Confucianism and Daoism were concerned with ethics and living in harmony with nature, including the gods and spirits that were believed to be everywhere. Although temples and ceremonies developed around both schools of thought, neither of them was a true religion as Buddhism was.

SECTION 2 REVIEW

1. **Identify:** (a) Mandate of Heaven, (b) Lao Zi, (c) Han Feizi.
2. **Define:** (a) ideograph, (b) dynastic cycle, (c) filial piety.
3. What were three achievements of the Shang civilization?
4. How did the Mandate of Heaven explain the rise of the Zhou?
5. (a) What were the three main schools of thought that developed in China? (b) What values did each school emphasize?
6. Why did Buddhism appeal to the Chinese?
7. **Synthesizing Information** How is the spread of Buddhism to China an example of cultural diffusion?
8. **Writing Across Cultures** Write a dialogue in which the speakers debate whether Confucian ideas would support American democracy.

3 PATTERNS OF LIFE

FIND OUT

What factors affected a person's status in Chinese society?

How did the lives of gentry and peasants differ?

What values did Chinese families teach?

What attitudes did the Chinese have toward women?

"Work, work—from the rising sun
Till sunset comes and the day is done
I plow the sod
And break up the clod,
And meat and drink both come to me
So what care I for the powers that
be?"

This folk verse suggests the gulf that separated China's rulers from the peasants. For peasants, survival was a constant struggle. They worked very hard to make a living from the land. Wars, famine, earthquakes, and taxes added to their hardships. When those hardships became unbearable, the peasants rose in revolt.

In general, Chinese peasants were self-sufficient and self-reliant. They had little contact with distant rulers. "Heaven is high and the emperor is far away," was a common saying. Peasants relied on their families rather than their rulers to solve the problems of survival.

Social Classes

In traditional Chinese society, all people were not equal. According to Confucian ideas, a person's age, sex, education, and occupation all affected his or her place in society.

Young people had to respect their elders. Women were inferior to men. Scholars held the highest positions in society. Peasants who worked the land were more valuable than people who simply traded goods or fought China's battles.

These beliefs shaped the social system of traditional China. At the top of China's society were the gentry, followed by the peasants. Below them were the artisans and merchants. Soldiers had very low status in this society.

Gentry. The gentry were wealthy landowners who had been educated in the Confucian classics. They were the leisure class, and they looked down on those who did physical labor. To show that they did not have to work with their hands, the gentry allowed their fingernails to grow very long.

The gentry produced most of the scholars, who became government officials. They collected taxes, kept the peace, and advised the emperor. In theory, if not always in practice, the scholar officials admired the Confucian virtues of respect, obedience, and service to the state.

The gentry had the time and wealth to support the arts. They often painted or composed poems. In lavish ceremonies, they carried out the traditional rituals required to honor their ancestors.

Peasants. The vast majority of people were peasants. Some owned and worked small plots of land, and a few were comparatively rich. Others were tenant farmers who had to pay part of each harvest to the landowners. Still others were landless laborers. Besides working the land, many peasants made and sold simple tools, furniture, and cloth.

Peasants lived in villages surrounded by farmland. Most of the time, the emperor's officials did not interfere with their affairs. The village headman, together with heads of families, kept order and resolved disputes. Most peasants paid their taxes but otherwise avoided contact with the imperial government. They feared its harsh system of justice and punishment.

Tea Farmers In this vase painting, women and men are tending tea plants. Tea cultivation probably began in China and then spread to Japan and Southeast Asia. The first description of tea appears in a Chinese dictionary of the A.D. 300s. Buddhist priests encouraged people to drink tea instead of alcoholic drinks. ***Interdependence*** How might the use of tea have been spread from China to other lands?

Despite the hardships of their lives, peasants did have some leisure. They celebrated festivals such as the New Year and enjoyed tales told by wandering storytellers. Events such as marriages, funerals, and religious festivals also enlivened country life.

Social mobility. Although they had low status in Confucian society, artisans and merchants played an important role in China. They produced the goods demanded by both the wealthy and foreign traders. Sometimes, they gained great wealth.

Artisans, merchants, and even peasant families could move up in society. To do so, they used their wealth to educate their sons. If these young men passed the examinations, they might become government officials. Sometimes a village supported an intelligent young boy so that he could get an education. In this way, lower-class families could rise in society.

Family Life

In the *Analects,* Confucius stressed the importance of family, respect for elders, duty, and harmony. These values reflected China's needs as a farming society. Only by working together could a Chinese family produce what it needed to survive. To help the family, younger members had to respect their elders, and women had to obey men. Although women had an inferior position, they deserved the loyalty and respect of their children. (📖 See Connections With Literature, page 806, "The Analects.")

Joint family. The joint family was the ideal in China. It included many generations. The oldest male had the most authority. Few families achieved the ideal, however. Poor families lost many people to death and disease, and many children died young. Only the strongest family members survived to old age.

Among the gentry, families might include several generations. When the head of the family died, his sons and their wives often moved away to set up their own households.

Filial piety. From birth, children learned to put the family's interests before their own wishes. Parents expected complete obedience and respect. "The bamboo stick makes a good child," advised an old saying.

Folktales supported the ideal of filial piety. One story records the actions of a dutiful son, Koh Ku. During a famine, Koh Ku is willing to let his child starve in order to feed his mother. "We may yet have another child," he said, "but never another mother." The story has a happy ending, however. Pleased with Koh Ku's filial piety, the gods reward him with a pot of gold.

Respect for ancestors. Filial piety included reverence for the family's ancestors. In memorial services, the Chinese paid respect to their ancestors. Westerners who did not understand the practice called it ancestor worship.

People believed that the extended family included the living, the dead, and all future generations. Ancestors lived in another world but depended on their descendants to provide them with food and clothing. Without these necessities, the ancestors would become ghosts and their descendants would suffer. Throughout the year, the family offered food and clothing to their ancestors. A family must have sons to carry on such rituals.

Marriage. In traditional China, as elsewhere around the world, parents arranged marriages for their children. Through marriage, the gentry strengthened their position in society. A boy's family would examine the resources of a possible bride's family. Among peasants, a man looked for a woman who could work hard and bear him many children.

Before a marriage took place, the families consulted their ancestors for approval of their choice. A go-between worked out the details of the marriage, such as the dowry that the bridegroom would pay the bride's family. Priests studied the birth dates of the girl and boy to determine a marriage day that would bring good fortune.

Role of Women

The Chinese believed that women were inferior to men. They valued girls for their work and for the children they would bear. They did not celebrate the birth of a daughter,

A Chinese Wedding
A bride and groom often met for the first time at their wedding. Usually, their parents had made all the arrangements. A Chinese proverb, using buildings to symbolize families, sums up this tradition in these words: "When doorways match and houses pair, a marriage may be settled there." ***Culture*** How did arranged marriages suit the ideals of Chinese family life?

however. When she married, she left the family and became a part of her husband's family.

A young bride had to obey her husband's mother. Under the guidance of her mother-in-law, she learned the ways of her new home. If she gave birth to a son, she gained respect. Some mothers-in-law were harsh and cruel to their sons' wives. Because of filial piety, neither a son nor his wife could criticize his mother's behavior. In time, however, a woman became the head of her own household.

Sometime in about A.D. 950, the Chinese adopted the practice of binding women's feet to keep them small. The custom probably began at court, but it spread to many parts of China. Peasants also accepted the custom, even though it limited their freedom of movement.

Only women with bound feet were thought to be beautiful. Parents knew that foot-binding caused pain. However, they feared that they would not be able to find a husband for a daughter who had large feet.

SECTION 3 REVIEW

1. What were the main social classes in traditional China?
2. Describe three ways in which the life of the gentry differed from that of the peasants.
3. (a) List three values of the traditional Chinese family. (b) How did these values reflect the needs of a farming society?
4. How did the Chinese show respect for their ancestors?
5. What role did a young bride play in her husband's family?
6. **Analyzing Information** "In education there are no class distinctions." How does this statement by Confucius reflect Chinese attitudes about social class and education?
7. **Writing Across Cultures** The folktale about Koh Ku supported the Chinese ideal of filial piety. Write a story that supports an American ideal of family life.

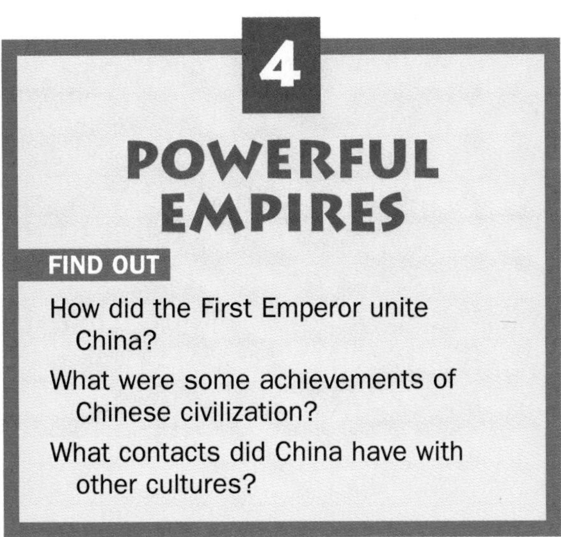

4 POWERFUL EMPIRES

FIND OUT

How did the First Emperor unite China?

What were some achievements of Chinese civilization?

What contacts did China have with other cultures?

"Let me tell you next of stones that burn like logs," wrote Marco Polo, a European who spent 17 years in China during the late 1200s. The stone, he said, was dug "out of the mountains, where it runs in veins. When lighted, it burns . . . and retains the fire much better than wood." The stones were coal, a fuel that was unknown to Europeans at the time.

In *The Travels of Marco Polo,* Marco Polo described the wondrous sights of China. He told of the emperor's huge palaces and great wealth. His reports that the Chinese used paper money and bathed frequently were especially shocking to Europeans. Both of these practices were unheard of in Europe at that time.

Most Europeans refused to believe any of Polo's stories. Yet in 1276, China probably had the richest and most advanced civilization in the world. By then, the Chinese civilization was already 3,000 years old.

The First Empire

China owed its success in part to energetic and ruthless leaders who made it a strong, unified empire. Under the Zhou dynasty, you will recall, China broke up into warring states. By 221 B.C., the ruler of the state of Qin had conquered his neighbors and overthrown the Zhou dynasty. He then took the name Shi Huangdi (sher hwang dee), or "First Emperor."

Shi Huangdi believed in Legalist principles. He used harsh means to centralize power in his own hands. In doing so, he laid foundations for Chinese rule that would last until 1911.

Uniting China. To unite the empire, Shi Huangdi imposed several measures. Among them were a single law code, uniform standards for weights and measures, and currency regulations. To improve transportation, he forced peasants to build roads across the empire. Good roads allowed him to move troops quickly to any trouble spot.

The First Emperor also took steps to control knowledge and ideas. He banned all books except Legalist works, and he persecuted Confucian scholars. Qin officials collected and burned books of Confucian teachings. Only books on medicine, agriculture, and technology were spared.

The Great Wall. Shi Huangdi extended Chinese power to the south and west. Using forced labor, he built the Great Wall. In the past, local lords had built walls to defend their lands against nomadic invaders. Shi Huangdi joined and extended these walls across northern China.

Hundreds of thousands of peasants labored under brutal conditions to build the Great Wall. "Every stone cost a human life," wrote a later Chinese historian.

The Great Wall extended 1,500 miles (2,414 km) from east to west. It seldom kept invaders from attacking. It did, however, become a symbol to the Chinese. South of the wall lived the "civilized" farming people of China. North of it lived the nomadic "barbarians."

Expansion Under the Han

Shi Huangdi wanted his dynasty to rule forever, but his harsh policies sparked deep anger. When he died, revolts broke out. Within eight years, Liu Bang (lyoh bong), a peasant leader, had overthrown the Qin and set up a new dynasty, the Han.

Under the Han dynasty, which ruled from 202 B.C. to A.D. 220, China expanded across

The Silk Road

Along the ancient highway flowed riches of the great empires of the East and West. They included Roman glass, Persian coins, and Chinese silk. The demand for Chinese silk in the West was so great that the route was called "the Silk Road."

The great Silk Road stretched halfway across Asia and linked East Asia and the Mediterranean world. For thousands of years, camel caravans plodded for months on end across shifting desert sands and over icy, barren mountains. A Chinese historian described travel on the desert:

> "You see nothing in any direction but the sky and the sands, without the slightest trace of a road, and travelers find nothing to guide them but the bones of men and beasts and the droppings of camels. . . . You hear sounds, sometimes of singing; and it has often happened that travelers going aside to see what these sounds might be have strayed from their course and been entirely lost."

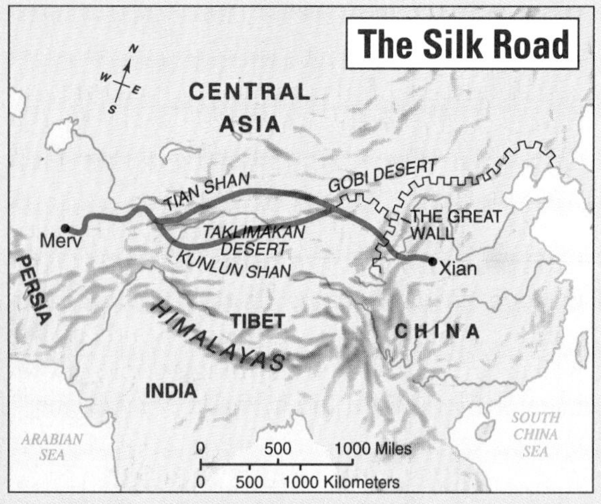

In addition to the menace of natural forces, bands of raiders lurked along the route, ready to descend on careless travelers.

Despite the dangers, traders and travelers moved along the Silk Road. They brought new products to China, such as oranges, peaches, and pears. The wheel, writing, weaving, gunpowder, religions, paper, and printing were among the inventions and ideas that spread along the Silk Road.

Throughout its history, China sought to keep peace along the eastern half of the Silk Road, which extended about 5,000 miles (8,000 km) from Xian (sī ahn) to Persia. However, local rulers often asserted their independence. Still, the good profits from trade lured people to risk the journey.

1. Why was the Silk Road more than a highway for trade?
2. **Forecasting** How do you think the European discovery of sea routes to Asia affected the Silk Road?

Asia. Powerful emperors used their armies to keep the peace and protect trade. During this period, caravans plodded the length of the Silk Road. They carried Chinese jade, bronzes, and silk westward in exchange for the goods of India and the Mediterranean world. (See the feature above.)

Chinese travelers returned home with new seeds such as grape and alfalfa. Trade within China expanded, and tea growing spread from the south to other parts of China. Travelers and merchants also introduced new ideas, such as Buddhism, into China.

Civil service system. Han rulers continued the First Emperor's policy of central control, but they restored Confucian learning. Under the Han, the Chinese developed the idea of a government run by the most talented and learned men.

The Chinese set up an examination system to choose civil servants, or government officials. To pass the exam, candidates for office had to know Confucian teachings as well as Chinese law, history, and traditions. The government set up a university to train scholars for the highest offices. By A.D. 100, about 3,000 students were studying at the university.

The civil service system strengthened China. Under the system, officials gained jobs through merit, not by birth or wealth. Also, the Confucian-educated officials shared the same values and traditions. The common bond helped to unite the vast empire and hold it together as dynasties changed. This system of choosing officials lasted until the early 1900s.

Exam Time

The doors are sealed. Soldiers stand guard from watchtowers. Trembling men, young and old, sit in their cells and read the themes the examiners have selected:

> "He who is sincere will be intelligent, and the intelligent man will be faithful.
>
> In carrying out benevolence, there are no rules."

The fate of the men depends on the answers they compose for such essay topics.

For more than 2,000 years, scholars endured the agony of the civil service exams. People from any class could take the exams, but only the cleverest and best-educated succeeded.

Candidates had to pass grueling exams at the local and the provincial levels before they could take the imperial civil service test. To pass, they had to know the more than 400,000 characters in the Confucian texts by heart. They also had to be able to compose elegant poetic essays on the exam themes.

At exam time, candidates gathered in the "examination hall," which was actually rows and rows of mud-brick cells. Each cell was barely the height of an average-size man. Candidates brought their own bedding as well as enough food and fuel for the three-day ordeal.

Before candidates entered their cells, guards searched them and their belongings. Day and night, soldiers remained on the lookout for cheating. A cheater brought dishonor not only on himself but also on his family and his tutor.

Was it worth it? One scholar, Ye Shih, wrote of his feelings:

Examination Cells During the 1870s, students took their civil service exams in these huts. Historians believe that only about 1 percent of the students who studied so long and hard for these difficult tests passed them. Those who did pass the exams became respected lifetime civil servants known as mandarins. ***Culture*** How did the civil service system strengthen China?

> “Beginning with childhood, all of a man's study is centered on one aim alone: to emerge successfully from the three days' examinations, and all he has in his mind is what success can bring to him in terms of power, influence, and prestige.”

Although Ye Shih was critical of the exams, most candidates accepted them. Those who failed returned again and again. One candidate finally succeeded at the age of 83. ■

Achievements of the Han

Under the Han, Chinese civilization advanced on many fronts. Han astronomers improved the calendar. Other scientists invented a seismograph, or a machine that records the direction of earthquakes.

Medical colleges flourished. Doctors made advances in medical treatment. For example, doctors began to time a patient's pulse to diagnose illnesses. They developed acupuncture. In this medical treatment, the doctor uses needles inserted under the skin to relieve pain and cure various illnesses. Also, doctors wrote about typhoid fever and the use of anesthetics.

In farming, the Chinese used complex flood control systems, fertilized the soil to increase crop yields, and planted drought-resistant rice. They developed practical tools such as the wheelbarrow, mill wheel, water clock, and sundial.

In addition, the Chinese improved on ideas from other civilizations. For example, they developed the foot stirrup, an advance over stirrups brought from India. They also learned to make paper, an invention that would not reach Europe for another 1,000 years.

Golden Ages in China

Invaders helped to destroy the Han Empire. For the next 1,000 years, various dynasties reunited China. Under the Tang dynasty (618–906) and the Song dynasty (960–1279), China enjoyed long periods of peace. During these golden ages, the economy prospered and the arts flourished.

Expanding horizons. Under the Tang and Song dynasties, China's trade increased. Chinese goods and ideas traveled to India and the Persian Empire. Trade brought new goods to China, including cotton, pepper, and dates.

To protect its trade, the Song dynasty built a navy, making China a great sea power. Chinese ships used the sternpost rudder and the magnetic compass. These two inventions would later reach Europe by way of Arab traders.

Foreign merchants and missionaries settled in China's busy cities. They included Muslims from Persia and Arabia, along with Jews and Christians.

During this time, the Chinese conquered Vietnam. The conquerors carried Chinese ideas about government and society as well as inventions such as printing. Chinese influence also spread to Korea and Japan.

Literature. The Chinese invented block printing and later movable type. The new technology led to greater literacy and an outpouring of books. Poetry was especially popular.

The Tang poet Li Bo (lee bwaw) is one of China's best-known writers. Li Bo served as court poet for a time. He later spent many years wandering about China. During his travels, he absorbed Daoist teachings about the value of nonaction and detachment from life. In “Fighting South of the Ramparts,” he captures the sadness of war.

> “Last year we were fighting at the source of the Sang-kan;
> This year we are fighting on the Onion River road. . . .
>
> Where the house of Qin built the Great Wall that was to keep away the Tartars [invaders],
> There, in its turn, the House of Han lit beacons of war.
> The beacons are always alight, fighting and marching never stop.
> Men die in the field, slashing sword to sword;

The horses of the conquered neigh
piteously to Heaven . . .

Know therefore that the sword is a
cursed thing
Which the wise man uses only if he
must. ❞

Painting. Many paintings illustrated a line or thought from a poem. Artists also used nature as subjects and perfected the art of landscape painting. In works of great beauty, Song artists celebrated the grandeur of nature.

Steeped in Daoist traditions, an artist might study a scene in nature for hours or days. Then, with a few strokes of the brush, the artist would suggest the essence, or meaning, of the scene. Artists also painted just a single element of nature, such as a flower or the branch of a tree.

Mongol Conquest

The Song dynasty battled constantly to protect China's borders from invaders. During the late 1100s, Song rulers faced a powerful new threat when the Mongols burst onto the world scene.

Under their fierce leader Genghiz Khan (GEHNG gihs kahn), the Mongols conquered a vast empire. It extended from the Pacific Ocean to the Danube River in Europe. After the death of Genghiz Khan, the huge Mongol Empire was divided among his sons and grandsons.

China under foreign rule. By 1279, Kubilai Khan (KOO bih lī kahn), grandson of Genghiz Khan, had extended Mongol power over all of China. At first, the Mongols tried to reduce the role of Confucian scholars and preserve their own culture. For example, Kubilai Khan appointed only Mongols and other foreigners to positions of power.

Kubilai Khan could not resist powerful Chinese influences, however. In the end, he gave his dynasty a Chinese name, the Yuan (yoo ahn). Also, he left Confucian officials in lower-level jobs.

Mongol achievements. During the reign of Kubilai Khan, Marco Polo visited China. For many years, Polo worked as an official of the Mongol ruler. As you have read, Europeans found Polo's stories about Chinese wealth and practices hard to believe.

Polo described, for example, the efficient transportation system the Mongols had set up to unite their empire. From Beijing, they built roads to every province. A system of relay riders allowed messengers to carry news across China.

Along the roads flowed trade goods and technical information. Much useful knowledge moved west, including such Chinese

The Poet Li Bo One poem by Li Bo, shown here, begins: "My friend is lodging in the Eastern Range,/Dearly loving the beauty of valleys and hills./A pine-tree wind dusts his sleeves and coat;/A pebbly stream cleans his heart and ears." This famous poet, a great traveler, wrote many verses about the beauties of nature. ***Choice*** Why might a writer be especially interested in travel?

inventions as the magnetic compass, sternpost rudder, mechanical clock, gunpowder, and printing.

Chinese Revival

Marco Polo described Mongol rule at its height. As the Yuan dynasty declined, Chinese resentment against foreign rule led to revolts.

The Chinese finally found a leader in a poor peasant, Zhu Yuanzhang (joo yoo ahn jahng). He drove the Mongols from South China and in 1368 captured Beijing. The peasant general then claimed the Mandate of Heaven. He called himself Ming Hung Wu and set up the Ming dynasty.

The Ming dynasty ruled China from 1368 to 1644. Ming emperors wanted to restore China to the greatness it had achieved under the Tang and Song dynasties. The Ming revived Confucian learning and expanded the civil service. They built a new imperial palace called the Forbidden City in Beijing.

Voyages overseas. Between 1405 and 1433, the Ming dynasty sent several huge fleets to restore Chinese authority at sea and to renew trading ties. Ming ships explored Southeast Asia, India, and the coast of East Africa.

Suddenly, the Ming voyages ended. Historians are not sure why this happened. Perhaps some officials were jealous of the Ming

The Forbidden City The Ming dynasty's complex of palaces and government buildings in Beijing was called the Forbidden City. Only members of the imperial household were allowed to enter it. At the center of this photograph is the Hall of Great Harmony, where the emperor received visitors. ***Political System*** How did Ming rulers isolate China from the world after the 1430s?

admirals. Perhaps the emperor needed the money to fight invaders. At the same time, the Chinese cut off contact with the outside world. They placed limits on foreigners and stopped Chinese citizens from traveling abroad.

Isolation. The Ming dynasty isolated China at a time when Europeans were beginning to develop new technologies and explore other lands. As the Chinese turned inward, Europeans slowly advanced and posed a threat to the Middle Kingdom.

Invaders From the Northeast

In 1644, China once again fell under foreign rule. This time, the invaders swept in from Manchuria. The Manchus set up the Qing (chihng) dynasty, which ruled China until 1911. The Qing claimed authority over many states, including Burma, Thailand, Laos, Nepal, Vietnam, and Korea.

Like the Mongols, the Manchus did not want to be absorbed into Chinese civilization. They passed laws forbidding Manchus to marry Chinese people or wear Chinese clothing. Unlike the Mongols, however, Manchu rulers kept Confucian ideas. The Manchus also accepted that the Chinese wished to limit contact with foreigners.

SECTION 4 REVIEW

1. **Identify:** (a) Shi Huangdi, (b) Great Wall, (c) Li Bo, (d) Kubilai Khan.
2. Describe three ways in which the First Emperor united China.
3. How did Chinese civilization advance under the Han?
4. Why are the Tang and Song dynasties considered to be China's golden ages?
5. How did Mongol rule affect China?
6. **Drawing Conclusions** What effect did political unity have on the Chinese civilization?
7. **Writing Across Cultures** Write three history questions each for a civil service exam taken in China and in the United States.

5 ROOTS OF REVOLUTION

FIND OUT

How did China's relations with the West change in the 1800s?

Why were European nations able to gain influence in China?

What were the causes and effects of the "revolution" of 1911?

Vocabulary kowtow, extraterritoriality, sphere of influence

"As your Ambassador can see for himself, we possess all things. I set no value on objects strange and ingenious and have no use for your country's manufactures." With these words, the emperor Qianlong firmly turned down Britain's request for more trading rights in China in the 1700s.

The Chinese felt satisfied that their civilization was superior to any other. After all, their neighbors had adopted Chinese culture. Foreigners were seeking to buy silk, tea, porcelain, and other Chinese goods. Secure in their own world, what did the Chinese need from the "barbarians"?

Qianlong's refusal to end trade restrictions came at a critical moment. By the late 1700s, powerful nations were emerging in Europe. They would soon challenge China's proud image of itself.

A Position of Strength

By the 1500s, the Portuguese had reached India and Southeast Asia. They then sailed on to China, hoping to expand their trading empire.

In China, the powerful Ming emperors placed strict limits on foreign traders. They allowed foreign ships to unload cargoes only at the ports of Macao and Guangzhou. Traders could sell their goods only to certain Chinese merchants. The Ming and later the Qing were strong enough to enforce these laws.

By the late 1700s, two developments were underway that would have major effects on China's relations with the West. First, the Qing dynasty entered a long period of decline. Burdened with high taxes and limited land, the increasing peasant population had a hard time growing enough food to survive. When floods and droughts caused famine, peasant revolts broke out.

A second development was the Industrial Revolution in Western Europe. The Industrial Revolution increased the military power of European nations. With modern fleets, these strong nations could reach distant places. The British used their military strength to back their demands for expanded trading rights with China.

European Imperialism

By the late 1700s, Europeans refused to kowtow, or bow low, to the Chinese emperor. The kowtow was a symbol which showed that foreigners accepted their inferior status. Also, Europeans resented being restricted to Macao and Guangzhou. They wanted to be accepted as equal partners in trade, and they demanded the right to trade at other Chinese ports.

Opium War. When diplomacy failed to bring change, the British resorted to other means. During the late 1700s, Britain began to sell opium that was grown in India to

A Sea Battle in the Opium War In this clash, a British warship (at left) destroys a fleet of junks, as Chinese sailing ships were called. China's only weapons in this unequal conflict were burning rafts, which the Chinese sent against the British fleet. ***Power*** How did the war show that the Qings had lost the Mandate of Heaven?

China. Other western nations also entered the opium trade. By the early 1800s, many Chinese had become addicted to the drug. The opium trade also drained China's supply of silver, which was used to pay for the drug.

The Chinese government tried to stop the illegal drug trade by passing harsh laws. Users and smugglers who were caught faced the death penalty. In 1839, the Chinese destroyed a British shipment of opium, and war broke out.

In the Opium War, the Chinese were no match for the British. Even though the Chinese had invented gunpowder and cannons, their weapons were outdated. Also, they lacked modern warships. With their superior military technology, the British soon defeated the Chinese.

The unequal treaties. The Treaty of Nanjing, which ended the Opium War, was the first of many "unequal treaties." In it, the Chinese had to accept British terms for peace. The emperor agreed to pay for the opium that had been destroyed. He also agreed to give Britain the island of Hong Kong and to open other ports to British trade.

The Treaty of Nanjing showed that the Chinese could no longer set the terms of trade. Before long, France, Russia, Germany, and the United States concluded similar treaties with the Qing emperor.

Westerners also won the right to extraterritoriality. Under this authority, westerners accused of a crime in China could be tried in their own courts instead of in Chinese courts.

Increased foreign influence. By the late 1800s, the western powers had carved up China into spheres of influence. (See the map at right.) A sphere of influence is an area in which a foreign nation has special economic privileges, such as the right to build railroads and factories. Economic rights also gave westerners political influence.

Japan, too, expanded into China. During the late 1800s, Japan adopted western technology and modernized its industries. By 1895, a strong Japan was able to defeat China in the Sino-Japanese War. As a result, Japan won Formosa (present-day Taiwan) and also extended its influence over Korea.

Open Door policy. The United States feared that European nations might set up colonies in China. To prevent this outcome, it called on European nations to support

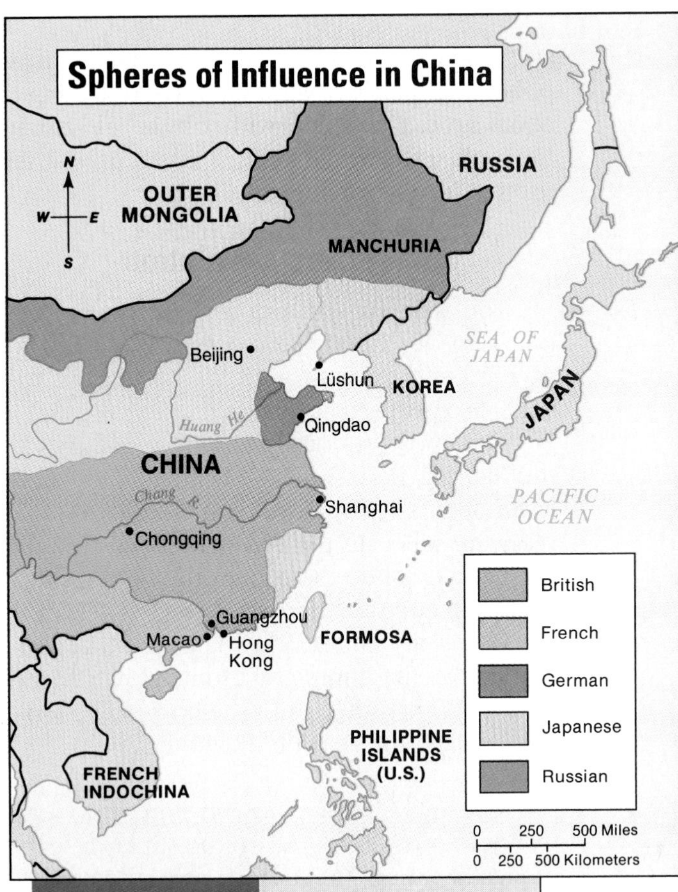

MAP STUDY

Foreign nations began to force China to open its ports to their trade in the mid-1800s. By the late 1800s, foreign powers had carved up large parts of China into spheres of influence.

1. **Region** Which nation of East Asia established a sphere of influence in China?
2. **Interaction** Identify major Chinese ports that were controlled by foreign nations. Explain why these cities became the centers of their spheres of influence.
3. **Comparing** Compare the role of foreign nations in China and in Africa during the Age of Imperialism. (a) In what ways were their policies similar in both places? (b) In what ways were their policies different?

an "Open Door" policy in China. Under this policy, all nations were supposed to have equal access to trade with China. Although this policy failed, the United States used it to protect its own trade with China.

Unrest and Revolution

The loss of territory to foreigners was one sign of China's weakness under the decaying Qing dynasty. A series of peasant revolts also erupted at this time.

The most serious peasant uprising was the Taiping Rebellion. It began in 1851 and lasted for 14 years. More than 50 million people were killed in this struggle. Even though the Qing crushed the rebels, the fighting further weakened the dynasty.

Efforts at reform. The Taiping Rebellion marked the beginning of a long, slow revolution in China. After the rebellion, some Chinese called for reforms in government and society.

Reformers wanted to introduce modern technology to China. "Learn the superior techniques of the barbarians to control the barbarians," they declared. Although the reformers saw the need for western technology, they also wanted to preserve Confucian culture.

Under pressure, the government began a series of reforms. It set up factories and dockyards to produce modern weapons and ships. It sent young men abroad to study. In 1898, the young emperor Guang Xi (gwahng shee) supported the Hundred Days of Reforms. He issued laws to update the civil service exam, organize western-style schools, and promote economic changes.

Led by Ci Xi (tsuh shee), the widow of a former emperor, conservatives opposed the reforms. They believed that the changes threatened the traditional Confucian order. In 1898, Ci Xi seized power as empress and ended the influence of the moderate reformers. More radical reformers, however, stepped up their demands for an end to the Qing dynasty.

Boxer Rebellion. While the reform effort was underway, a growing number of foreign missionaries and business people were settling in China. The Chinese people's hostility to foreigners and to the Qing increased.

Anti-foreign Chinese soon took strong action. They formed the Fists of Righteous Harmony, called Boxers by westerners, to expel all foreigners. Empress Ci Xi secretly encouraged the Boxers. In 1900, the Boxers attacked and killed many Chinese Christians and foreigners. Boxer forces surrounded the foreign diplomatic quarter in Beijing.

The western powers then quickly organized an international army, which crushed the Boxers. As a result of the Boxer Rebellion, China was forced to allow foreign troops on Chinese soil and foreign warships in Chinese waters.

Revolution of 1911. Ci Xi remained in power after the uprising, but the Qing dynasty collapsed soon after her death. In 1911, China declared itself a republic, ending the ancient system of imperial rule.

In 1911, China had no well-organized government to replace the Qing dynasty. From 1911 to 1928, the country seemed ready to break into many pieces. Civil war raged, with many people claiming the right to rule China.

Struggles of the Republic

For a brief time in 1911, Dr. Sun Yatsen (soon yaht sehn) served as president of the new republic. Sun had helped to organize the Guomindang (gwoh mihn dang), or Nationalist party, and had struggled against the Qing dynasty. When the Qing dynasty collapsed, Sun was living in the United States. He returned to China at once.

Sun Yatsen set out his goals for China in "Three Principles of the People." First, he called for nationalism, which meant making China a unified nation and ending foreign domination. Second, he supported democracy, or representative government. Third, he spoke of "livelihood," or ensuring a decent living for all Chinese.

Sun had little chance to achieve his goals, however. A powerful general, Yuan Shikai, forced Sun out of office in 1912. Soon warlords, or regional leaders with their own armies, were battling for power in China.

The Boxer Rebellion To show their hatred of all things from foreign lands, the Boxers burned trains and railroad stations, destroyed telephone lines, and wrecked factories. This drawing of a captured foreigner kneeling before a group of Boxers suggests their deep resentment of westerners. ***Change*** What were two important results of the Boxer Rebellion?

Nationalists and Communists

During the years of turmoil, Sun Yatsen rallied followers to his Three Principles. From his base in Guangzhou, he organized an army to restore unity.

Sun appointed Chiang Kai-shek, an energetic young officer, to command the Nationalist army. When Sun died in 1925, Chiang took over as the leader of the Nationalist party. By 1928, Chiang had brought China under his control.

Attack on the Communists. The Nationalists faced challenges to their authority. Most Chinese felt strong ties to their own families but had little loyalty to a national state. China had no experience with representative government, and the nation's economy was badly depressed.

Chiang was especially concerned about the Chinese Communist party (CCP), which a group of young Chinese had formed in 1921. The CCP joined forces with the Nationalists to expel foreigners and fight the warlords. They hoped to win control of the Nationalist party by working from within.

In 1927, Chiang moved against the Communists. He expelled them from the Guomindang and killed thousands of their supporters. The Communists who survived fled to the mountains of southeastern China.

Long March. During the late 1920s and the 1930s, Mao Zedong (mow dzoo doong) emerged as the leader of the Chinese Communists. Mao believed that the Communists would succeed in China only by winning the support of the peasants. (See Chapter 16.) He insisted, therefore, that Communist forces treat the peasants fairly and politely. Unlike other Chinese armies, the Communists paid peasants for the food their forces required. With the support of the peasants, Mao's army grew in numbers.

Chiang launched a fierce campaign against the Communists. Greatly outnumbered, the Communists fled from Chiang's armies in 1934. Led by Mao, they trekked more than 6,000 miles (9,656 km) from southeastern China to the remote northwestern province of Shaanxi. The chase lasted more than a year.

The Long March Mao Zedong, shown here on horseback, spent years in Shaanxi training his forces and developing theories about revolution. The peasants, Mao predicted, would "rise like a tornado or a tempest" and become a force so powerful that no one could suppress them. ***Political System*** How did Mao's Communists win the peasants' support for their cause?

About 90,000 Communists with their families set out on the dangerous "Long March." Only about 7,000 survived. The Long March became a symbol of the bitter hardships the Communists would endure before they finally gained power in 1949.

Japanese invasion. While Chiang battled the Communists, the Japanese pushed into China. In 1931, the Japanese seized Manchuria. Many Chinese called on Chiang and Mao to set aside their differences and fight their common enemy.

In 1937, the Japanese launched an all-out war against China. Japanese planes bombed Chinese cities, and Japan's armies overran the most heavily populated regions of China. During World War II, Nationalists and Communists joined together to battle the Japanese. At the same time, each side kept a close watch on the other.

With the defeat of Japan in 1945, Mao's forces held much of northern China, while the Guomindang ruled in the south. Both sides then prepared to renew their struggle for power, as you will read in Chapter 16.

SECTION 5 REVIEW

1. **Locate:** (a) Guangzhou, (b) Hong Kong, (c) Japan.
2. **Identify:** (a) Taiping Rebellion, (b) Hundred Days of Reforms, (c) Ci Xi, (d) Boxer Rebellion, (e) Guomindang, (f) Three Principles of the People, (g) Chiang Kai-shek, (h) Mao Zedong, (i) Long March.
3. **Define:** (a) kowtow, (b) extraterritoriality, (c) sphere of influence.
4. What two developments of the late 1700s affected China's relations with the West?
5. (a) What was the outcome of the Opium War? (b) What did Britain gain in the Treaty of Nanjing?
6. Why did civil war break out after the Revolution of 1911?
7. **Understanding Causes and Effects** What steps toward reform did the Chinese take as a result of western imperialism?
8. **Writing Across Cultures** Write a newspaper editorial to persuade American readers that an Open Door policy in China would benefit the United States.

Chapter 15 Review

Understanding Vocabulary

Match each term at left with the correct definition at right.

1. loess
2. ideograph
3. dynastic cycle
4. sphere of influence
5. extraterritoriality

a. authority under which foreigners accused of a crime can be tried in their own nation's courts
b. rise and fall of ruling families
c. yellow-brown fertile soil carried by winds
d. symbol used to express an idea
e. area in which a foreign nation has special economic privileges

Reviewing the Main Ideas

1. (a) What are the physical barriers of China? (b) How did they affect China's contact with other ancient civilizations?
2. (a) What five relationships did Confucius think should govern human society? (b) Describe the role of superior and inferior persons in these relationships.
3. Describe the role of each of the following in family life: (a) joint family, (b) filial piety, (c) respect for ancestors.
4. (a) What was the civil service system? (b) How did it strengthen China?
5. (a) Why did unrest grow in China during the 1800s? (b) What reforms did the government undertake?
6. (a) What were Nationalist goals for China? (b) What challenges did Nationalists face?

Reviewing Chapter Themes

1. Chinese civilization influenced East Asia for thousands of years. (a) What ideas, inventions, and achievements contributed to China's strength? (b) How did China influence Korea, Japan, and Vietnam?
2. Traditions based on family and Confucian teachings helped to shape ancient China. Explain two ways in which these traditions and teachings affected the role of women.
3. Chinese advances in science and technology later spread to other parts of the world. Choose two of these achievements and describe their importance.
4. About 200 years ago, China began a long process of revolutionary change. Describe the role of the following in that process: (a) Taiping Rebellion, (b) Qing dynasty, (c) Chiang Kai-shek, (d) Mao Zedong.

Thinking Critically

1. **Making Global Connections** Compare the latitudes and climates of North China and South China with those of the northeastern and southeastern United States.
2. **Analyzing Ideas** An ancient Chinese scholar wrote: "I am happy because I am . . . a Chinese, and not a barbarian." How does this statement reflect the view the Chinese had of their civilization?
3. **Synthesizing Information** Why were European powers able to carve up China?

Applying Your Skills

1. **Analyzing a Quotation** "The goodness of the superior man is like the wind and the goodness of the people is like the grass. The grass bends in the same direction as the wind blows." Which Chinese philosophy does this statement reflect? Give reasons for your answer.
2. **Making a Review Chart** Make a chart listing the names, dates, and achievements of four Chinese dynasties.

Chapter 16

CHINA TODAY

The Changing Face of China This scene dramatizes some of the great changes that are transforming China. China is becoming urbanized, women enjoy greater equality, and families are now smaller in size. Even the sea of bicycles conveys this sense of rapid change. ***Change*** What features of traditional Chinese society do you think might hinder these changes?

CHAPTER OUTLINE

After years of struggle, Happy Boy had finally saved enough money to buy a rickshaw. Now he could earn a living by pulling passengers through the streets of Beijing.

Happy Boy's joy did not last. Soldiers kidnapped him and forced him to transport them through the mountains. Everything he had was lost.

> "The more Happy Boy thought of what had already gone by, the more he hated the soldiers who had taken him. They had robbed him of his clothes, his shoes, his hat, his rickshaw, and even of the strip of cloth that he wound around his waist as a belt. They had left him nothing but black and blue bruises."

In *Rickshaw Boy,* Lao She tells the tragic tale of a young Chinese during the 1930s. Happy Boy's sufferings were not unique. Between 1911 and 1949, China experienced civil war and foreign invasion. For most Chinese, the turmoil led to hunger and injustice.

CHAPTER PERSPECTIVE

In 1949, the Chinese Communists won power by promising a new order. In the years that followed, they introduced changes that completely transformed China's political, economic, and social life.

As you read, look for these chapter themes:

- The Chinese Communists set out to revolutionize government, the economy, and society.
- During the 1950s, China tried to replace the old Confucian order with a new system of thought based on the teachings of Mao Zedong.
- After 1949, many obstacles stood in the way of China's becoming a modern world power.
- Because of its vast size and rapidly developing economy, China today ranks as a world leader.

Literature Connections

In this chapter, you will encounter passages from the following works.

Rickshaw Boy, Lao She

Quotations From Chairman Mao

Son of the Revolution, Liang Heng

Chinese Lives, Zhang Xinxin and Sang Ye

The People's Comic Book

For other suggestions, see Connections With Literature, pages 804–808.

1 THE PEOPLE'S REPUBLIC OF CHINA

FIND OUT

Why did many Chinese people support the Communists?

What ideas influenced Mao Zedong?

How did the Communists achieve order?

Vocabulary proletariat, totalitarian state, propaganda

"A revolution is not a dinner party, or writing an essay, or painting a picture, or doing embroidery; it cannot be so refined, so leisurely and gentle," wrote the Chinese Communist leader Mao Zedong in 1927. "A revolution is an . . . act of violence by which one class overthrows another."

During the 1930s and 1940s, Mao rallied supporters to free China from the forces of oppression—greedy landlords, corrupt officials, and foreign imperialists. By 1949, the Chinese Communists had gained control. They then built a powerful state to push through revolutionary changes.

Communist Victory

Even before World War II ended, the Nationalists and Communists had resumed their bitter struggle for control of China. Backed by the United States, Chiang Kai-shek and his Nationalist forces battled the Communists, who were led by Mao Zedong.

Mao's peasant armies were highly disciplined. The Nationalists, on the other hand, suffered from low morale. Soldiers were poorly paid and underfed. Massive corruption among Chiang's officials further undermined the Nationalist cause.

By 1949, the Communists had swept into Beijing. To throngs of cheering supporters, Mao Zedong announced the birth of the People's Republic of China.

Chiang retreated with his forces to the island of Taiwan, off the coast of China. There, he set up a government and vowed to regain control of the mainland.

Appeal of communism. Why did the Communists succeed? Mao preached a philosophy that appealed to China's poor. He promised to end many years of oppression by landlords and government officials. The Communists, he said, would set up a "dictatorship of the people" and introduce land reform. He denounced imperialism and called for China to industrialize so that it could take its place as a leading world power.

The Communists also won the support of many educated and middle-class Chinese. They welcomed Mao's pledge to end China's humiliation at the hands of the imperial powers.

Marxism and Maoism. The writings of Karl Marx, a German philosopher, shaped Mao's ideas about class struggle. During the mid-1800s, Marx had predicted that the proletariat, or industrial working class, would rise up against the ruling class. The proletarian revolution would spread around the world and create a new, classless society.

Mao adapted Marxism to Chinese conditions. He put his faith in China's poor, landless peasants to carry out the revolution, because China had only a small industrial working class. The 1917 Communist revolution in Russia also inspired Mao. It showed him that a strong Communist party could lead the people. (See Chapter 33.)

Creating a New Order

Once in power, the Chinese Communists wrote a new constitution. On paper, it set up a National People's Congress, permitted free elections, and protected other democratic rights. In practice, China became a one-party dictatorship.

Communist party members held all the important jobs and controlled the government and the economy. Supported by the People's Liberation Army (PLA), the Communists silenced critics and enforced their own views. As head of the Chinese Communist party, Mao Zedong became chairman of the People's Republic of China.

The new Chinese leaders faced many pressing political and economic problems. Years of war had created chaos and caused much suffering. In both cities and rural areas, millions of people faced starvation. Beggars and criminal gangs roamed the land.

To restore order and achieve their revolutionary goals, the Communists turned China into a totalitarian state. In a totalitarian state, the government controls every aspect of citizens' lives through a single-party dictatorship.

Mao's Leadership

Through huge propaganda campaigns, the Communists made Mao Zedong a popular hero. Propaganda is the spread of ideas to promote a cause or damage an opposing cause. Children and adults were taught that Chairman Mao had all the answers to China's problems. They memorized his sayings from *Quotations From Chairman Mao,* better known as the Little Red Book.

In school, in the workplace, and at home, the Chinese learned obedience and loyalty to Mao. A three-year-old boy who ran away from a child-care center was scolded, "You are not Chairman Mao's good little boy. You haven't upheld revolutionary discipline." Years later, Liang Heng recalled how the scolding hurt:

> "I had been taught that Chairman Mao was like the sun itself. At home, 'Mao' had been my first word after 'Mama,' 'Baba' [father], and 'Nai Nai' [grandmother]. . . . Later I had learned to say, 'I love Chairman Mao' and 'Long Live Chairman Mao.'"

Under Mao, China restored order and ended foreign influence. Mao insisted that China become self-sufficient. He promoted programs to increase food production and protect people from periodic famines. Under Mao's leadership, the Chinese built schools

End of the Long March This poster, made in 1973, shows Mao Zedong at the end of the Long March in 1936. It glorifies Mao and other revolutionary leaders who survived The Long March. Since most of the Chinese people were illiterate, the Communist government made wide use of colorful posters. ***Political System*** How might propaganda such as this strengthen Communist control?

and extended basic health care services to the huge population.

Mao launched massive drives to build a "New China." In Section 2, you will read about the Great Leap Forward and the Cultural Revolution, Mao's programs to transform China's economic structure and social attitudes. Both programs had ambitious goals—and both ended in failure.

New Directions

Despite the growing discontent with his policies, the Chinese continued to honor Chairman Mao until his death in 1976. Then, in the late 1970s, China's new leader, Deng Xiaoping (duhng syow ping), turned away from some of Mao's ideas. Deng eased some of the government's strict economic controls. He also sent Chinese students to study abroad, and he welcomed foreign investment in China.

Encouraged by Deng's moderate policies, many of the better-educated Chinese, especially those living in the eastern coastal cities, pressed for democratic reforms. In early 1989, students in Beijing and elsewhere organized huge rallies to demand political freedom.

The pro-democracy movement received wide publicity in the world press. Reporters compared events in China with those in Eastern Europe, where nations were rejecting communism in favor of democracy. (See Chapter 34.)

At first, China's leaders allowed students to gather in Tiananmen Square in central Beijing. Then, in June 1989, the government ordered the students to return home. When the protesters refused to leave, the army opened fire on them. Several thousand people were killed or wounded. In a harsh crackdown, the government arrested, tortured, and even

Tiananmen Square Protests In June 1989, Chinese students brought a large "goddess of liberty" into Tiananmen Square during pro-democracy demonstrations in Beijing. This figure, modeled on the Statue of Liberty, became a symbol of the demands for greater freedom in China. ***Human Rights*** What freedoms did the Chinese government deny by suppressing this protest?

executed leaders of the pro-democracy movement. The "Beijing massacre" showed that China's leaders would not allow their authority to be challenged. To them, the protests were a threat to the Communist order.

SECTION 1 REVIEW

1. **Identify:** (a) Karl Marx, (b) People's Republic of China, (c) Deng Xiaoping.
2. **Define:** (a) proletariat, (b) totalitarian state, (c) propaganda.
3. (a) What goals did Mao support? (b) How did these goals appeal to different groups of Chinese?
4. Describe two ways in which the Communists restored order in China.
5. **Making Inferences** How did Communist propaganda about Mao Zedong help to unite China?
6. **Writing Across Cultures** List three examples of propaganda about a person or event that you have seen on television or in a newspaper or magazine.

Free Enterprise in China Under Deng Xiaoping, citizens were allowed to operate small businesses. Many Chinese earned extra income by selling products at city market stands such as this one. ***Choice*** Why might people prefer to buy things from private businesses?

2 ECONOMIC DEVELOPMENT

FIND OUT

What obstacles stood in the way of the modernization of China?

What were the Great Leap Forward and the Cultural Revolution?

How did economic policies change after Mao's leadership ended?

Vocabulary collective farm, commune, capitalism

From a street stall, Shang Jinxi (shahng jeen shee) sells tea broth to people passing by. "These last couple of years, while the nation's been trying to rev up the economy, I've retired," Shang explained. "I thought about it awhile, then dug out this big old kettle of mine. . . . I can make over 100 yuan [$20] a month from it, on top of my pension. I've got it made."

Under Mao, the government ended private ownership of land and businesses. People like Shang Jinxi worked at government-owned farms, businesses, and factories. During the 1980s, however, Deng Xiaoping introduced new economic policies. Some private businesses such as Shang's tea stall were allowed to flourish once more.

Revolutionary Goals

As you have read, Mao proclaimed three main goals for China's Communist revolution. He promised a better life for the poor. He called for development of a modern economy. He pledged to restore China's position as a major world power.

When the Communists took over in 1949, many obstacles prevented them from achieving these goals. China's huge population needed to be fed, clothed, housed, and educated. Yet years of war had destroyed China's few industries and disrupted its farming. China's geography, too, limited the amount of land that could be used to produce food. Floods, earthquakes, and droughts had further hampered its agriculture. As for modernization, China lacked the technology and capital to industrialize quickly. China's isolation from the world community added to its problems.

For the Communists, economic and political goals could not be separated. To build a strong economy, they believed, they had to destroy the old class system. In the past, landowners and other wealthy Chinese had controlled the means of production—that is, land, labor, and capital. The Communists wanted to place the means of production under central government control. In this way, they hoped to end inequality and increase output. As output increased, China could sell its goods on the world market and use the income to invest in industry.

Reorganizing Agriculture

Once in power, the Communists quickly introduced land reform. They took land from large landowners and divided it among landless farm families. Many landlords faced harsh punishments for their past mistreatment of the peasants.

During the early 1950s, the government set up new programs, ending private ownership of land altogether. The government forced peasants to pool their land, tools, and labor to form collective farms. The members of collective farms worked for the state and received a share of the harvest. The rest of the harvest went to the government. The government believed that collective farms would be more efficient and result in greater food production.

Great Leap Forward. In 1958, Mao introduced another program. He called on the Chinese to make a superhuman effort to achieve modernization through one "Great Leap Forward." As part of this program, he divided China into communes. A typical commune included several villages, thousands of acres of land, and as many as 20,000 people.

Working on a Commune Under Mao, all Chinese farmers had to live and work in communes. More than 50,000 communes were established to produce the nation's crops. By the late 1970s, however, the government had begun to move away from commune farming. Peasant families were then allowed to lease farms. Farm output nearly doubled in value between 1978 and 1985. ***Change*** Why did communes fail to produce enough food?

The commune controlled the land and peasants' lives. At first, families were split up. Men, women, and children slept in separate dormitories and ate in large dining halls. The commune assigned jobs to each worker. In turn, it provided all workers with food, clothing, housing, medical care, child care, schooling, and even recreation.

The commune system was a way to mobilize the Chinese people to build bridges, dams, irrigation systems, and other projects needed for a modern China. Mao expected to increase food output through large-scale farming.

Effects. The Great Leap Forward led to disaster. Peasants resisted the commune system, sometimes even destroying crops. Food production fell because the government assigned millions of farm workers to projects such as building schools and roads. Since everyone was guaranteed a living, many workers did not work very hard.

Floods and droughts added to China's problems. Millions of people died in the famine that swept China from 1959 to 1961. Finally, during the early 1960s, Mao had to abandon the Great Leap Forward in favor of less ambitious plans.

Cultural Revolution

Many Chinese blamed Mao for the disaster that followed the Great Leap Forward, and a power struggle broke out among the top Communist leaders. Mao grew concerned about factions, or rival groups, within the Communist party. He also believed that China's new generation had to experience revolution firsthand. In 1966, to renew the revolutionary spirit, he launched the "Great Proletarian Cultural Revolution."

Methods. Mao stressed the class struggle. He urged young people to root out "capitalist roaders," or followers of capitalism, as he called his critics. Capitalism is another term for a free market economy, in which the means of production are owned and operated by individuals for profit.

Students and young factory workers responded to Mao's call by organizing the Red Guards. The Red Guards held mass rallies to support Mao. They traveled around China attacking government officials and others who did not fully support the chairman.

Quoting the Little Red Book, Red Guards heaped abuse on people with "bad class backgrounds"—those whose families had been landlords, rich peasants, or supporters of the Nationalists before 1949. In public "struggle meetings," they forced teachers, factory managers, and even Communist party members to confess to "crimes" against Mao. Victims of the abuse were then sent to distant rural areas to do manual labor.

Effects. The Cultural Revolution created chaos in China. Schools closed. In factories, disputes between rival factions slowed production. Finally, in 1969, the Chinese army restored order, sending millions of young Red Guards to work in faraway rural areas. The emphasis on political struggle continued, however, until Mao's death. The Cultural Revolution left deep wounds. Many people had been tortured, imprisoned, or killed. The lives of millions of young Chinese had been disrupted. They never completed school. Many lost faith in their hero, Mao Zedong, and in the Communist party.

A Doctor's Story

"I was not a Communist [in 1949]," the elderly Chinese man told a visiting journalist, "but I admired what they were trying to do. Old China was so backward, so poor, and so corrupt, there were beggars who starved to death in the streets every day."

In 1949, the man returned to China from the United States, where he had graduated from Harvard Medical School. Full of hope, he took a job in a Shanghai hospital.

The young doctor's optimism faded in the 1950s. In 1957, Mao encouraged people to freely express their suggestions for improvement. The doctor suggested that doctors themselves, not Communist party officials, should run the hospital. "I took Mao at his word, I thought he was sincere," he explained. Mao soon changed his policy about openness, and the doctor was harshly punished.

Dragged before his colleagues, the doctor was beaten and accused of crimes against the revolution. "They called it a 'self-help meeting,' to help me improve my attitude," he said. The doctor was then sent to a labor reform camp, where he spent his time breaking rocks in a quarry.

After nearly 10 years, the doctor was released just as Mao launched the Cultural Revolution. The doctor was arrested again. His family suffered, too. Red Guards forced his wife, who was also a doctor, to sweep floors and clean toilets. They made his son leave medical school to work in a remote peasant village. His young daughter was expelled from junior high school because of her father's past.

Life improved for the doctor after 1976. He returned to his old job, where he worked with the people who had attacked him in the past. To the journalist, he confided:

> "It's funny, some of them now fall asleep at political study sessions from boredom. For all of us, the revolution is over. What is left is doubt and disbelief. It is very sad for China." ■

Four Modernizations

After Mao's death in 1976, a power struggle took place. On one side was the "Gang of Four," Jiang Qing (jee ahng ching), Mao's widow, and her top supporters. They favored the radical policies of the Cultural Revolution. On the other side were moderate leaders. The moderates, who made up the vast majority, won. They had Jiang Qing and her supporters arrested and put on trial. (See Connections With Literature, page 806, "Homecoming Stranger.")

By 1978, Deng Xiaoping had emerged as China's leader. Deng's goals were similar to Mao's—to help China achieve wealth and power. However, he stressed economic reform instead of class struggle as the way to achieve those goals. Deng named his program the Four Modernizations. It called for modernizing agriculture, expanding industry, developing science and technology, and upgrading China's defense forces.

Deng wanted to increase mechanization, or the use of machines, in farming. He also hoped to make China self-sufficient in food production. To help achieve these goals, Deng introduced the responsibility system. Under this system, each farm family was responsible for making its own living. The government leased land to peasant households.

Study Groups During the Cultural Revolution, people everywhere, in cities and on farms, had to attend meetings to study and discuss the benefits of communism. The government supplied the approved texts to teach correct Communist thinking. Here, groups discuss their "lesson." ***Citizenship*** How were study groups an effective means of propaganda?

Each householder raised crops and sold a certain amount of the harvest to the government at a set price. Peasants could sell any surplus for profit—on the open market.

The new system used profits to encourage farmers to produce more goods. Private enterprise reappeared. Some peasants did well, and the standard of living in many areas rose. Although the profit motive replaced Mao's emphasis on moral goals, China had not adopted a capitalist system. The responsibility system was simply a new program to raise production and strengthen the government's power.

Despite increased prosperity, the more conservative members of the government decided to restore some collective farming in 1991. They insisted that only collective farms could produce enough food for China's population. They also argued that only collectives could organize the work force needed to repair canals, dikes, and dams.

The City of Shenzhen The Special Economic Zone (SEZ) at Shenzhen, the largest in China, covers more than 130 square miles (337 sq km) near Hong Kong. Shenzhen spurred China's economy by bringing in foreign businesses. These businesses have invested more than $2 billion in Shenzhen. ***Interdependence*** How does China encourage foreigners to build businesses in SEZs?

Building Industry

Under Mao, China poured resources into developing industry. At first, Mao stressed heavy industry, such as mining and military weapons. During the Great Leap Forward, he called on China to become self-sufficient. To meet this goal, communes built small factories to make farm tools, furniture, and clothing. Products made in these factories were often poor because managers emphasized quantity rather than quality. Many communes also set up "backyard furnaces" to make steel, but most of it was unusable.

Under Deng Xiaoping, China shifted its emphasis to light industry, such as manufacturing consumer goods. To make factory managers more efficient, Deng extended the responsibility system to industry. Managers were allowed to make decisions about what was produced, but they were also responsible for making a profit.

Although many factories remain inefficient, industrial output has grown. Today, China is one of the world's most rapidly developing countries. It has benefited from the discovery of new mineral resources. By developing its oil resources, China expects to increase economic growth and rival other major industrial powers. On the negative side, China faces serious pollution problems as it struggles to expand its industries.

Opening the Door to Trade

Deng Xiaoping ended Mao's policy of self-reliance and isolation. He realized that China needed foreign technology and capital in order to modernize. He called for an "open door" to foreign trade and sent Chinese students abroad to study science and technology.

To attract foreign capital, Deng set up Special Economic Zones (SEZ) in southeastern China. In an SEZ, foreign companies enjoy tax benefits and private free enterprise flourishes. The SEZ at Shenzhen, near Hong Kong, has grown from a small fishing village into a modern city of 500,000. There, foreigners have set up about 600 businesses, ranging from toy factories to hotels and banks.

After the 1989 crackdown on student protesters, foreign investment slowed. China, however, kept its doors open. In the early 1990s, some foreigners, especially the Japanese, seemed ready to renew investment in China. China's poor human rights record, however, continued to hold back others.

SECTION 2 REVIEW

1. **Identify:** (a) Great Leap Forward, (b) Cultural Revolution, (c) Red Guards, (d) Jiang Qing, (e) Four Modernizations, (f) responsibility system.
2. **Define:** (a) collective farm, (b) commune, (c) capitalism.
3. (a) List two economic goals that China has pursued since 1949. (b) What problems has China faced in achieving those goals?
4. Describe two results of each of the following: (a) Great Leap Forward, (b) Cultural Revolution, (c) Four Modernizations.
5. (a) Describe two ways in which the economic policies of Mao Zedong and Deng Xiaoping are similar. (b) Describe two ways in which they are different.
6. **Applying Information** Deng Xiaoping has responded to critics of his economic reforms with this traditional saying: "It doesn't matter if the cat is black or white as long as it catches mice." What does he mean by this?
7. **Writing Across Cultures** Jot down some ideas about how the economy of the United States differs from that of China.

3 CHANGING PATTERNS OF LIFE

FIND OUT

How does Communist ideology differ from Confucianism?

What social changes did the Communists introduce?

What is China doing to limit population growth?

What role does education play in China today?

"My main worry was getting into the Communist Youth League. It looks good if you can. . . . Universities will judge you by whether you're a member and whether you're a 'three-good' student. That means good health, good politics, and good marks."

In China today, as in the past, education is the path to advancement. As 17-year-old Wu Liyao (woo lee ow) points out, getting into a university takes more than good grades. Coming from a family of good Communists and supporting the Communist party are also key requirements. For the Chinese, education is an opportunity to help China, not the individual, to develop.

A New Philosophy

When the Chinese Communists gained power, they tried to replace the old Confucian traditions with a new, revolutionary philosophy. That philosophy combined the ideas of Marx and Mao.

The new ideology, or official way of thinking, emphasized the values and goals of China's new leaders. *Quotations From Chairman*

In a Shanghai Park This group is practicing an ancient Chinese discipline called *tai chi.* Using tai chi, people combine slow, graceful body movements with silent meditation. The goal of those who practice tai chi is to increase and direct the flow of their natural energy to improve their health and well-being. ***Culture*** Why might a student like Wu Liyao practice tai chi?

Mao took the place of the Confucian classics. Instead of filial piety, the Communists called for loyalty and service to China. "Serve the People," declared posters and loudspeakers throughout the land. By stressing this idea, the Communists encouraged a sense of national unity.

China's new heroes were workers like Wang Qinxi, the head of an oil-drilling team who risked his life to limit the damage to an oil rig after an explosion. Children learned to admire the four-year-old boy who gave up his playtime to gather fertilizer for the commune vegetable fields. Traditional fairy tales were rewritten to teach the value of physical labor rather than riches.

Social Changes

The Communists set out to build a classless society in which everyone was equal. They did away with the landowning class and mocked the scholars who had once ruled China. "Learn from the peasants," declared Mao.

The government tried to ensure equality by outlawing private property. In theory, everyone had equal access to education, health care, housing, and jobs. In practice, a new elite emerged. Communist party members and leaders of the People's Liberation Army lived in the best apartments. They had cars and drivers to take them to work and could buy hard-to-find consumer goods. Their children won places in the universities and got good jobs.

By the 1980s, Deng's economic reforms were creating new differences in wealth. Some peasants and business people were making profits from private enterprise. With the money they earned, they bought luxuries such as refrigerators, television sets, and motorbikes.

Under Deng, the old division between rural and urban China also has deepened. Cities in eastern China modernized and adopted western technology and ideas. In remote rural areas, peasants had fewer opportunities to make money and move ahead. These areas remained less developed than the urban areas.

Family Life

After 1949, China's leaders tried to weaken the influence of the family. They reversed the Confucian teaching of respect for elders and put their faith in young people. During the Cultural Revolution, Mao encouraged children to criticize their parents for clinging to the old ways. Today, institutions outside the family, such as day-care centers and schools, have great influence on the young.

The Communists also tried to destroy the traditional reverence for ancestors. To get more farmland, communes took over grave sites. Officials forbade families to hold traditional funerals or make offerings to their ancestors. During the Cultural Revolution, the Red Guards ransacked homes and destroyed family shrines. Even having a list of one's ancestors was considered a crime.

Traditions survive. Despite such attacks, respect for elders and other traditions survived, especially in rural areas. Families still scraped together enough money to bury their dead in expensive coffins. Although the old religions were banned, people hired Daoist priests to perform the required ceremonies. Even Communist party leaders sometimes held lavish funerals or memorial services for their parents or grandparents. Today, family members still get together to celebrate the Spring Festival, the traditional time for honoring their ancestors.

Marriage. In 1950, China passed a marriage law that provided for freedom of choice in marriages. Under the law, women and men were equal. In the family, therefore, the man was no longer dominant.

Young people no longer had to accept the marriage partner chosen by their parents. However, most young Chinese still rely on a third party, such as a co-worker or a family friend, to help them find a mate. (See the feature on page 362.)

Family size. China's huge population is a major threat to modernization. In the years of Communist rule, the population has doubled. The government has taken strong measures to limit population growth. As part of its program, the government has encouraged young women and men to delay marriage until they reach their mid- or late twenties. It has also adopted a one-child-per-family policy. To enforce the policy, the government mixes penalties and rewards. Families that accept the one-child limit receive wage raises and other benefits, such as first chance at scarce apartments. Those who insist on having more than one child are fined or receive only limited food rations for the second child.

China's family planning program has had mixed success. In cities, where housing is scarce, many families follow the government's strict guidelines. In rural areas, however, peasant families still want large families. They can use the extra labor. Also, if the first child is a daughter, many parents will try again, hoping for a son.

"I've borne nine children," admitted one peasant woman in 1987. "The first was a boy, but he died. Then I had seven girls. . . . Only the ninth time did heaven send another son." She paid increasingly large fines for each child.

A Changing Role for Women

Before 1949, women were considered inferior to men. They could not own property, and were expected to serve and obey their husbands and to remain secluded inside the home. Few received an education. "An ignorant woman is virtuous," advised an old saying.

Chinese Marriage Customs

The wedding took place during the 1980s, but the wedding feast in the village of Maoping (mow ping) continued traditions that had been part of Chinese culture for centuries. Round balls of sweetened rice symbolized a life of harmony. Pieces of sugarcane stood for a sweet future. Fish signified abundance, and date soup meant hope for the early birth of a son.

After taking power in 1949, Chinese Communist leaders tried to end many traditional customs. They outlawed the binding of women's feet and encouraged women to work outside the home. They also tried to do away with religious rituals. Marriages, for example, were performed in government offices or in the commune.

The Chinese, especially in rural areas, have resisted efforts to change traditional marriage feasts. Today, rural Chinese combine the old and new ways.

Although parents no longer arrange their children's marriages, most matches are still arranged with the help of friends or relatives. For example, the young couple in Maoping met at work and decided to marry. Still, they wanted the approval of the woman's mother. In accordance with custom, they hired a go-between to get the mother's permission.

The Chinese government has tried to convince people to be thrifty in planning weddings. Despite these efforts, the groom in Maoping spent about five years' income on the wedding arrangements. The couple were married first in a government ceremony. Then they held a traditional wedding ceremony and feast in their native village. In addition to the traditional foods, the groom provided cash, sweets, and other gifts for the members of the bride's family.

1. What changes did the Communists try to make in Chinese marriage customs?
2. **Evaluating Information** Why do you think the Chinese government has been unable to end many traditional customs?

Under China's 1950 constitution, the Communists introduced major changes for women. The constitution declared, "Women enjoy equal rights with men in all spheres of political, economic, cultural, social, and family life. Men and women enjoy equal pay for equal work." China's marriage law also gave women the right to own property and to keep their family name.

Today, Chinese women have become more independent. Almost all women work outside the home, and many hold high-level jobs in the Communist party or as factory managers. The government has set up day-care centers and nurseries so that young mothers can be free to work outside the home.

Although the law states that women and men are equal, most women do a greater share of housework as well as most of the shopping and cooking. An equal number of girls and boys attend elementary school, but far fewer girls complete high school and enter college. Also, despite the law, men are usually paid more than women for the same job.

Education and Technology

Since 1949, China's Communist leaders have emphasized literacy. They saw the need for educated workers in a modern industrial society. The government opened schools throughout China. It also set up adult education centers to teach older men and women to read and write. Through education, the government tried to mold people's beliefs. In political study classes, for example, students learn correct Communist thinking.

The government made Mandarin China's official language. It also took steps to make Chinese script easier to learn. Traditionally, each Chinese character was made up of a number of strokes. To become literate, a person had to memorize at least 3,000 characters, compared to 26 letters in the English alphabet. To promote literacy, the government simplified 2,000 of the most commonly used characters.

The quality of schools varies throughout China. Schools in eastern cities are generally better than elsewhere. Students must take competitive exams to win places in the universities. Because they receive better training, city dwellers pass the exams more easily. Uneven education tends to widen the gap between China's rural and urban areas.

Science and technology. Throughout its long history, China has achieved an impressive record of inventions and scientific advances. (See Chapter 15.) Many of these Chinese ideas were later adopted by the rest of the world. By the 1700s, China fell behind the West technologically. Today, however, it is again putting great resources into scientific research.

The Chinese stress practical uses for science. For example, Chinese engineers have designed a small "walking tractor" that looks like a giant lawn mower. The "grasshopper," as it is called, is better suited to China's small fields and terraced farmland than are large tractors.

Operating a "Grasshopper" This handy machine, called a "grasshopper," is widely used in Chinese farming. Its chassis, or body, can also be separated and used as a form of transportation. China now manufactures 1 million of these machines each year. It exports many of them to Southeast Asia and Latin America. ***Technology*** Why might Chinese farmers prefer this machine to a full-size tractor?

Studying a Foreign Language Students like these at Beijing University use technology to study English and other foreign languages. However, only about 1 percent of all Chinese students attend college or receive higher education. Moreover, nearly 20 percent of all adults still cannot read or write. ***Interdependence*** Why is education so important in China as it prepares for the world of the next century?

SECTION 3 REVIEW

1. (a) What actions did the Communists take to create a classless society? (b) Were they successful? Explain.
2. How has the Communists' effort to replace Chinese traditions met with mixed success?
3. (a) Why has China adopted a one-child-per-family policy? (b) How does the government enforce this policy?
4. (a) Why have the Communists stressed literacy? (b) What steps have they taken to make it easier to write Chinese script?
5. **Comparing** Describe two similarities and two differences between Confucianism and Communist ideology.
6. **Writing Across Cultures** On a sheet of paper, jot down one fact from Section 3 about each of the following: social classes, women, marriage, family, and education in China. Then, next to each item, jot down one fact about each in the United States.

4 CHINA AND THE WORLD

FIND OUT

How has China's role in the world changed since 1949?

Why did China regard itself as a model for developing nations?

What policies has China adopted toward its neighbors?

Herds of Asian elephants, sheep, and buffaloes graze peacefully in the fields. Nearby, spectacular palaces and temples dot the land. The herds are mechanical, not real, while the palaces and temples are tiny copies of the originals. All are part of a 100-acre park called Splendid China in Shenzhen.

In a joint venture with western companies, the Chinese developed this center to attract tourists. It features 20 villages that represent the cultures of ethnic groups from all over China. In addition, it displays—in miniature—the splendid monuments of China's past.

Shenzhen lies in one of the Special Economic Zones set up under Deng Xiaoping. In these SEZs, more than elsewhere, China's new "open door" policy is evident. Since 1949, China has moved from a policy of strict isolation to one of active involvement in the global economy. Because of its size, resources, and rapidly developing economy, China is emerging as a major power both among nations of the Pacific Rim and in the world.

Relations With the Soviet Union

During the 1950s, the Soviet Union was the chief ally of the People's Republic of China. The Soviets had provided training and

MAP STUDY

Despite its rapidly developing economy, China remains a largely agricultural nation. It produces several major food crops. China also has important natural resources that strengthen its economy.

1. **Region** (a) Name a food crop that is grown in many regions of China. (b) Where is most rice grown?
2. **Location** What important food source is provided by China's location along the Pacific Ocean?
3. **Analyzing Information** Give evidence to support this generalization: China has the natural resources needed to build basic industries.

weapons to the Chinese Communists during the civil war. After 1949, they helped China with loans and technical advice.

The alliance was an uneasy one. China's Mao Zedong and the Soviet leader Joseph Stalin had different ideas about the best way to build a communist state. The Chinese and the Soviets had long been rivals for power in Asia. In the late 1950s, both also competed for influence in developing countries.

By the late 1950s, friendship between China and the Soviet Union had turned to hostility. China expelled its Soviet advisers. Border disputes along the Amur River in the northeast and in Mongolia threatened to erupt into war.

Gradually, relations between the two countries improved. However, the breakup of the Soviet Union in 1991 caused concern in China. China's northern and western regions are home to diverse ethnic groups who are related to peoples in neighboring states. As Soviet republics gained freedom, Beijing worried that its own minorities might demand independence.

Influence in the Developing Nations

After 1949, China became a leader among the developing nations. Mao's outspoken anti-imperialism and his call for socialism found many supporters in these countries. At the same time, China supported nationalist movements in Africa and helped to arm and train communist guerrillas fighting in Southeast Asia.

China offered itself as a model to developing nations. Like them, it wanted to modernize its agriculture and build industry. Mao encouraged developing nations to set up collective farms, as China had. Few nations adopted the Chinese model, but China did send some technical advisers and workers, especially to Tanzania. There, they built an important railroad.

New Ties With the West

Cold War attitudes shaped relations between China and the West. Mao condemned the imperialist nations and called for the overthrow of capitalism. To western powers, Mao's victory in China was one more sign of the communist threat to democracy.

Led by the United States, most western nations refused to recognize the People's Republic of China. They supported Chiang Kai-shek's Nationalist government on Taiwan. The United States hoped to weaken the mainland government by isolating it. It also blamed China for supporting the aggressive wars waged by Communist North Vietnam and North Korea. (See Chapters 12 and 17.)

China remained isolated from the West until the early 1970s. Then, as the Cultural Revolution slowed, moderate Chinese leaders began to renew ties with western industrial powers. By 1971, the United Nations had recognized the People's Republic of China. A year later, the United States president, Richard Nixon, visited China. The two countries set up trading ties, and finally, in 1979, the United States officially recognized the People's Republic of China.

China has encouraged foreign investment and vastly increased its trade with the West and with Japan. However, the massacre of student protesters at Tiananmen Square in 1989 soured relations. Western nations criticized China for human rights abuses such as using forced labor in factories. Chinese leaders rejected these criticisms as efforts by outsiders to interfere in China's internal affairs.

China and Its Pacific Rim Neighbors

The nations of the Pacific Rim are emerging as a major force in the global economy during the 1990s. Relations between China and its Pacific Rim neighbors will shape developments in this region in the years ahead.

Hong Kong. By 1997, China will regain control of Hong Kong, which Britain acquired after the Opium War. This colonial outpost has long been a bitter reminder of western imperialism in China.

Under Britain, Hong Kong has been a major center of trade, manufacturing, shipping, and finance. Until 1990, its capitalist economy was booming. While Hong Kong Chinese welcome an end to colonial rule, many feel uneasy about the future. As a result, economic growth there has slowed.

China has promised not to change Hong Kong's economy for at least 50 years after 1997. Despite that assurance, many wealthy Hong Kong Chinese have emigrated to other countries. Most of Hong Kong's 6 million people cannot afford to leave and have nowhere to go. Their only hope is that China will want to benefit from Hong Kong's economic strength and therefore will not make any drastic changes.

Japan. The Japanese invasion and occupation of China during the 1930s and 1940s left bitter memories among the Chinese. Since the 1970s, however, China and Japan have improved relations and developed many economic ties. (See Connections With Literature, page 806, "My Old Home.")

Both nations favor increased contacts. Through Japan, China gains access to advanced science and technology. At the same time, Japan sees China as both a vast new market for its goods and a source of much-needed raw materials.

Vietnam. China's relations with Vietnam have often been strained. In imperial times, China conquered and ruled present-day Vietnam. Many Chinese settled in Vietnam, and Chinese culture influenced the Vietnamese.

During the Vietnam War in the mid-1900s, the Chinese helped North Vietnam by providing arms and other supplies. After the war, old conflicts surfaced, however. China even invaded Vietnam briefly in 1979. Many people of Chinese descent have fled Vietnam, claiming persecution by the Vietnamese government. Full diplomatic relations between Vietnam and China were restored in 1991.

Downtown Hong Kong Britain and China have agreed that Hong Kong will be restored to China in 1997 under a plan for "one country, two systems." Hong Kong will be allowed to keep its capitalist economy, and its people will continue to enjoy the political freedoms they had under British rule. ***Human Rights*** What does this agreement on Hong Kong's future mean by "one country, two systems"?

Taiwan. The Nationalist government on Taiwan faced the threat of an invasion by Communist forces on the mainland for years after 1949. Today, economic and political changes on both the mainland and Taiwan have eased that threat.

With military and economic aid from the United States, Taiwan prospered. Building on industries set up by the Japanese during the early 1900s, Taiwan developed a strong manufacturing economy. It exported goods worldwide and achieved a high standard of living.

Taiwan's economic success has strengthened the long-standing desire of many of its people to remain independent. Others,

China and Vietnam China blamed Vietnam for numerous border clashes during the 1970s. In 1979, Chinese troops pushed 30 miles (48 km) into Vietnam. Two weeks later, China pulled back its troops, declaring that it had taught Vietnam a "lesson." ***Power*** How did China's action in 1979 recall its earlier relationship with Vietnam?

however, want to see the island united with the mainland. Beijing favors that goal. Both sides are quietly working behind the scenes to explore ways to achieve closer ties.

SECTION 4 REVIEW

1. **Locate** (a) Taiwan, (b) Hong Kong, (c) Japan, (d) Vietnam.
2. (a) How did the Soviet Union help China during and after the Chinese revolution? (b) Why do events in the Soviet Union cause concern in China?
3. Why did China find many supporters in developing nations?
4. (a) Why did the United States want to isolate China after 1949? (b) How did China's relations with western nations change in the 1970s?
5. Why do the Chinese regard Hong Kong as an important symbol?
6. **Synthesizing** List three adjectives that describe China's relations with its neighbors. Explain why you chose each.
7. **Writing Across Cultures** Some Americans believe that the United States should not trade with China until the Chinese government ends human rights abuses. Express your view in an editorial.

5 LITERATURE AND THE ARTS

FIND OUT

How have political changes affected the arts?

What traditions remain strong in the arts?

How do the Communists use the arts to teach values?

"Although Lei Feng's life is over, his spirit continues to shine forth undiminished. Rivers have their source, trees their roots. The source and the roots of Lei Feng's spirit lie in Mao Zedong's thought. . . . Let us forever remember Comrade Lei Feng's promises: to study for the people, to serve the people, and to fight for the people to the end."

During the Cultural Revolution, millions of Chinese read the stirring story of Lei Feng in a comic book. As a child, Lei Feng was cruelly beaten by the wife of a landlord. The Japanese killed his father during World War II. His brother died of starvation. By studying the thoughts of Chairman Mao, however, Lei Feng overcame his bitterness about the past. A truck driver in the army, this soldier-hero was killed while serving the people.

Lei Feng is propaganda literature. It shows how the Chinese Communist government used the arts to further promote their revolutionary goals.

Old and New Traditions

The Chinese have excelled in the arts, sciences, and technology for thousands of years. As you read in Chapter 15, several traditions, including Confucianism, Daoism, and Buddhism, influenced the arts and sciences in the past. During the 1800s and 1900s, the Chinese absorbed ideas from the West that produced new traditions. For example, to help modernize China, they adopted western approaches to science and technology.

After 1949, the Communists set out to reform the arts. "All art is politics," declared Mao. He believed that the government must control painting, literature, and music and make the arts serve the people. He rejected much of China's cultural heritage because it reflected the old society, which was based on classes.

During the Cultural Revolution, the Red Guards smashed temples, statues, and other

Serious Comic Books Chinese of all ages like to read about heroes like Lei Feng. Although Lei Feng died in 1962, his memory lives on. After the Tiananmen Square uprising in 1989, the government issued 300,000 copies of Lei's diary in order to encourage "a new upsurge in learning from Lei Feng." ***Citizenship*** What aspects of Lei's life make him a good propaganda hero?

Porcelain From the Tang Dynasty A kneeling woman at the imperial court holds a bamboo flute. Most of the ceramic art from the Tang dynasty has been found in tombs, some as far away as the Middle East. An Arab traveler in China during the A.D. 800s described the porcelain he saw as "vessels of clay as transparent as glass." ***Fine Art*** What does this figure suggest about China during the Tang dynasty?

works of art from the past. They burned books and family records. They did not destroy China's ancient culture, however. Interest in the past remained. In the arts and sciences today, the Chinese are seeking to create a new identity that blends old and new traditions.

Visual Arts

Today, as in the past, the arts reflect how people see the world and their place in it. You have read that Shang craftworkers produced fine bronze vessels. The bronzes were used to hold offerings of food or drink for the spirits of respected ancestors. Some of these bronzes were richly decorated. Among the most common decorations are monsters with curled tails and gaping jaws, tigers, snakes, birds, and elephants.

Porcelain. By the Tang dynasty, Chinese artisans had perfected the art of making porcelain. Porcelain is a hard, smooth, shiny pottery. Its special qualities are the result of mixing a pure white clay called kaolin with petuntse, a mineral found only in China. Objects made of the clay mixture are then baked at high temperatures. Tang artists made lovely porcelain figures of servants, musicians, dancers, camels, and horses. They colored these figures with distinctive yellow, green, and blue glazes.

Chinese porcelains were in great demand as articles of trade. Archaeologists have found Chinese pottery from Southeast Asia to East Africa. During the Ming dynasty, the Chinese produced the blue-and-white porcelains that later became popular in Europe and the United States.

Painting. In traditional China, painting was an art of the gentry class. They treasured works painted in ink on silk or paper scrolls. The scrolls were rolled up for storage and safekeeping. The wealthy brought out and unrolled their scrolls when they had time to study them at leisure.

Chinese landscape paintings reflected Daoist ideas. Many paintings showed rugged mountains and rushing rivers. In them, the artists conveyed the vastness of the universe and the harmony of nature. Painters used a wide variety of symbols. The plum blossom in winter, for example, suggested the hope of spring.

Under western influence, Chinese artists began to paint scenes that included realistic human figures. After the Communists won power, the government encouraged artists to use their works to promote the goals of the revolution. Painters depicted life on communes and in factories. Some artists still drew on scenes from nature, but in these paintings nature was simply a background for soldier-heroes and model workers. Such heroes, the

Communist party believed, would stir the masses to great deeds.

Modern Chinese artists use symbols from the past and the present. Red has long been a symbol of joy in China. Today, many paintings include a red sun rising to celebrate the victory of communism in China. (In the western world, red was a symbol of communism.)

Literature

Confucianism influenced traditional Chinese literature. Among the educated, scholars wrote poetry that followed strict literary forms. The common people preferred legends and folktales recited by wandering storytellers. These tales of emperors, scholars, gods, demons, and magicians taught strict moral lessons. The disobedient son is always punished, and the good son is always rewarded. Many stories also carried the Buddhist message that people should accept their fate.

Early novels. For the most part, the Chinese have always regarded fiction as inferior to poetry. Despite this attitude, the Chinese have produced a number of notable novels.

An outstanding early novel was Wu Chengen's *Journey to the West,* written during the 1500s. In English, it is known as *Monkey.* A fabulous and funny adventure story, it describes the pilgrimage of a Buddhist monk to India during the A.D. 600s. Monkey, the spirit guardian who protects the monk during the journey, is one of the most popular figures in Chinese literature.

Among the most famous Chinese novels is *A Dream of the Red Chamber,* written in the 1750s by Cao Xueqin (tsow shweh cheen). This popular novel describes the tragic decline of a large and wealthy family.

Modern writing. During the late 1800s, Chinese writers adapted western forms of literature to their own uses. Modern writers, such as Lao She in *Rickshaw Boy,* use novels to criticize society and call for change.* Lu Xun's widely read *The True Story of Ah Q,* published in 1921, ridicules people who still accepted Confucian values.

After 1949, Chinese writers emphasized new themes such as the dignity and strength of the common people. Their stories told of the superhuman efforts of peasants and

* At first, the Communists praised the works of Lao She and encouraged people to read them. During the Cultural Revolution, however, the Red Guards drowned him in a lake.

Peasant Painter at Work Peasant painting emerged as a new form of art during the years of the Great Leap Forward. Mao strongly supported it, saying, "Everyone may participate in artistic creation." Peasant paintings, like those shown here, use bright colors and are highly stylized. ***Political System*** Why might the Chinese Communist government encourage peasant art?

Classical Chinese Dance China's most popular form of drama is opera, which combines singing, dancing, and the use of symbolic movements. This performer at the Beijing Opera is dancing while moving long ribbons of silk cloth to form constantly changing patterns. ***Culture*** Why do you think opera is popular in China?

workers who triumphed over evil. Using stories like that of Lei Feng, the government created positive role models and glorified the values of the Communist system.

Performing Arts

China has a long tradition of opera, dance, theater, and other performing arts. In classical Chinese theater, elaborate traditions governed performances. Each movement of a dancer's head, hand, or arm expressed a particular action or suggested an emotion or attitude.

In Confucian China, actors and other performers had low status. They formed wandering troupes that were regarded as rootless and lacking in family ties. Desperately poor families sometimes sold their children to acting troupes.

During the 1950s, China set new standards for performing artists. Actors, singers, dancers, and composers carried the message of revolution to audiences. The ballet *The Red Detachment of Women,* for example, shows the courage and cooperation of women soldiers during China's civil war. In operas like *Taking Tiger Mountain by Strategy,* the Communists rewrote traditional stories. They set them in the modern period and used them to teach Communist ideology.

Chinese movies also build on colorful traditions from the past. They illustrate themes such as the conflict between good heroes and evil villains. Movies often portray rural life.

Government policy toward the arts has alternated between relative freedom and strict censorship. Recently, China entered the movie *Ju Dou,* about a family conflict, in an international film festival. The government later tried to withdraw the movie because it presented a negative view of Chinese life.

SECTION 5 REVIEW

1. **Identify:** (a) Lei Feng, (b) porcelain, (c) *Monkey*, (d) Lao She, (e) *Red Detachment of Women.*
2. (a) What Confucian traditions influenced Chinese arts in the past? (b) How do Communist values affect the arts today?
3. Why did Mao reject China's old culture?
4. How did Chinese artists promote the goals of the revolution in their work?
5. **Applying Information** Mao Zedong once said, "Weed through the old to bring forth the new, and make things foreign serve things Chinese." Explain how China has applied Mao's advice to the arts.
6. **Writing Across Cultures** Write the text for a story in comic book form that expresses an important value of American society. When you have finished writing, illustrate the comic book story.

Chapter 16 Review

Understanding Vocabulary

Match each term at left with the correct definition at right.

1. proletariat	**a.** market economy
2. totalitarian state	**b.** nation where the government controls every aspect of life
3. propaganda	**c.** large state-run farm
4. collective farm	**d.** spread of ideas to promote a cause or damage an opposing cause
5. capitalism	**e.** working class

Reviewing the Main Ideas

1. Why were the Communists able to defeat the Nationalists in 1949?

2. (a) What steps did Mao take to modernize China's economy? (b) How did Mao's successors modify his policies?

3. Describe the goals and results of the Cultural Revolution.

4. How did the government respond to the call for democracy in 1989?

5. How did policies toward women change under the Communists?

6. (a) What values does traditional Chinese literature express? (b) What values does Communist literature promote?

Reviewing Chapter Themes

1. The Communists set out to transform China. Describe one change they made in each of the following areas: (a) government, (b) economy, (c) society, (d) the arts.

2. The Communists' efforts to create an orderly society in China differed greatly from those of the Confucianists. (a) Describe three ways in which the Communists tried to establish order. (b) Describe how the two philosophies differ.

3. Deng Xiaoping instituted new economic reforms to meet the needs of Chinese society. (a) Describe the main features of the Four Modernizations program. (b) Discuss the extent to which the system was successful or unsuccessful in meeting its goals.

4. China has moved from a policy emphasizing self-sufficiency to one of interdependence. (a) What steps has China taken to end its isolation? (b) How do China's policies reflect its acceptance of global interdependence?

Thinking Critically

1. Making Global Connections In 1957, Mao noted: "There is a Chinese saying, 'Either the East Wind prevails over the West Wind or the West Wind prevails over the East Wind.' I believe . . . that the East Wind is prevailing over the West Wind." (a) What did Mao mean by this statement? (b) Do events today support this view? Explain.

2. Solving Problems Why are the performing arts a good way for a government to spread its message to the people?

Applying Your Skills

1. Using Your Vocabulary Use each of the following terms in a sentence about the economy and politics of modern China: *command economy, modernization, elite, land reform.* See the Glossary, pages 794–803, to review the meaning of the terms.

2. Analyzing a Painting Study the painting on page 353. Based on the painting, what conclusions can you draw about how the government wanted the people to view the Communist revolution? (See Skill Lesson 9, page 428.)

Chapter 17

KOREA

Olympics in South Korea Massed drummers added a colorful note to the opening ceremonies at the 1988 Summer Olympics held in Seoul. Koreans spent $2 billion to build a huge new stadium and other facilities. A record number of countries and their best athletes took part in these games. ***Interdependence*** Why was South Korea proud to be the site of the Olympics?

CHAPTER OUTLINE

Korean poets praised it. Chinese visitors admired it. Families jealously guarded the secret of how to make it. All agreed that Korean porcelain had a rare beauty. Most highly prized were pieces glazed in the color known as celadon, or "kingfisher green." In his poem "Koryo Celadon," Pak Chong-hwa displays the pride Koreans feel in this porcelain:

> "Depth of color, softly shaded;
> Iridescent kingfisher;
> Blue sky glimpsed through
> autumn clouds
> As the rain squall passes on;
> Or a white cloud, fresh with
> dew,
> Wings its way on high.
> But wake!—for this is Koryo
> celadon,
> This was ours for a thousand
> years."

In the 1200s, the Mongols overran Korea. Many Koreans died in the fighting and its aftermath. The Mongols destroyed the kilns, or ovens used for baking clay pottery. In the chaos of war, the secret of Korea's special celadon was lost. Although Korean potters make fine celadon today, they have never been able to re-create the wonderful glazes of the "kingfisher" pottery.

CHAPTER PERSPECTIVE

Korea has long had close ties to its powerful neighbor, China. From China, Koreans learned to make porcelain, but the Koreans perfected the art of making celadon. Although Chinese civilization influenced Korea, Koreans adapted many of these ideas to their own uses. Later, they passed many Chinese traditions along to Japan.

As you read, look for these chapter themes:

- Geography has influenced the population patterns and economy of Korea.
- Though strongly influenced by Chinese traditions, Koreans developed a distinct language and culture.
- Since the mid-1800s, imperialism, Japanese colonialism, Korean nationalism, and the Cold War have shaped developments in Korea.
- The division of Korea after World War II has led to the emergence of two sharply contrasting nations.

Literature Connections

In this chapter, you will encounter passages from the following works.

"Koryo Celadon," Pak Chong-hwa

Songs of Flying Dragons, Korean poem cycle

Lost Names, Richard Kim

For other suggestions, see Connections With Literature, pages 804–808.

1 GEOGRAPHIC SETTING

FIND OUT

How has location affected Korea?

How have physical and climate features influenced Korean life?

What resources support the economies of North and South Korea?

Vocabulary homogeneous society

Almost no one visits Korea without being introduced to kimchee. Kimchee is made of cabbage and other vegetables, heavily spiced with garlic, onions, ginger, red pepper, and shellfish sauce. Koreans eat it with breakfast, lunch, and dinner. Koreans make several months' supply at harvest time and store it in huge jars that can be seen on the balconies of city apartments and in country courtyards.

Preserving vegetables as kimchee is just one way Koreans developed to meet their food needs. Geography limits the amount of land that Koreans can farm. Koreans have used their land resources carefully to provide plenty of rice and vegetables.

Location

Korea is a peninsula attached to the eastern mainland of Asia, between China and Japan. The Yellow Sea is to its west. To the east are the Korea Strait and the Sea of Japan.* (See the map on page 376.) Today, the peninsula is divided into two nations, North Korea and South Korea. South Korea is slightly smaller than North Korea, but has twice as many people.

Because of its location, Korea has served as a cultural bridge between China and Japan.

* Koreans call the Sea of Japan the East Sea.

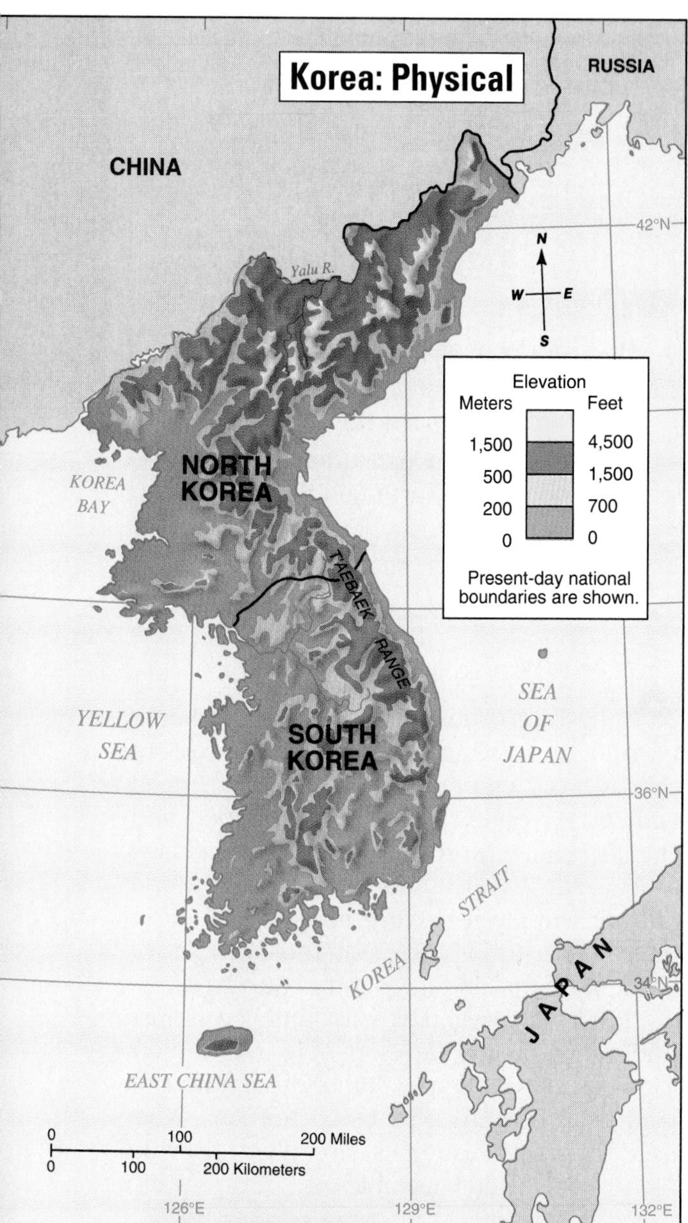

MAP STUDY

The Korean peninsula juts southward from East Asia. Most of Korea is mountainous, but plains stretch along much of its long coastline.

1. **Place** What river separates Korea from China?
2. **Location** (a) Name the bodies of water that surround the Korean Peninsula. (b) Name and give the relative location of the body of water that separates Korea from Japan.
3. **Analyzing Information** Why do you think China has had a strong impact on Korean history? (See the map on page 321.)

As early as 100 B.C., Chinese civilization began to spread to Korea. The Koreans transformed Chinese civilization and passed it on to Japan. This peaceful transmission of Chinese traditions had a major influence on Korean culture.

Location has also made Korea a frequent battleground for forces seeking control of East Asia. In the 1950s, Korea became a battleground in the Cold War struggle between the United States and the Soviet Union.

Landforms

The two major physical features of Korea are its mountains and its plains. Because it is a peninsula, Korea also has a long coastline.

Mountains. A Korean proverb says, "Over the mountains, mountains!" Steep, but low, mountains cover nearly 70 percent of the Korean peninsula. The most important mountain chain, the T'aebaek Range, runs from the north to the south. Smaller ranges branch off to form hilly areas, especially in the southwest. Because farming on the steep slopes is difficult, only about 25 percent of Koreans live in the mountains or in mountain valleys. North Korea is more mountainous than South Korea, which is one reason it has fewer people.

Plains. Most Koreans live on the coastal plains. There are three separate areas of plains: in the northeast, along the west coast, and at the southern end of Korea. The west coast plain is Korea's major farming region. Pyongyang (pee AWNG yahng), the capital of North Korea, and Seoul (sohl), the capital of South Korea, are also located along the west coast plain.

A long coastline. The Korean peninsula has a 6,000-mile (9,656-km) coastline with many good harbors. In addition, about 3,000 islands dot its offshore waters. Many Koreans make a living by fishing. South Korea has the world's third-largest fishing industry, after Japan and China. Korean and Japanese fishing boats compete fiercely in the waters between the two nations.

Climate and Resources

Korea has a temperate climate, with hot summers and cold winters. Compared to the south, North Korea has harsher winters, with heavy snows and bitter winds.

Differences in climate affect crop production. In the north, farmers can harvest only one crop a year. In the south, the milder climate offers a longer growing season. As a result, farmers produce some crops twice a year. South Korea's rice yields are among the highest in the world.

Korean Landscape This valley in southeastern Korea forms part of the coastal plain near the city of Pusan. Even here, however, mountains are nearby, as the photograph shows. One early foreign visitor to Korea compared the peninsula's mountainous land to "a sea in a heavy gale." ***Geography*** What part of the coastal plain is the major farming region of Korea?

Natural resources. South Korea is less mountainous than the north, giving it more arable land. About 60 percent of the land in the south is suited to farming, compared with only about 20 percent in the north.

The mountains of North Korea, however, are rich in mineral resources. They contain large amounts of coal, iron, lead, copper, and zinc. Rivers flowing out of the mountains also offer excellent sources of hydroelectric power.

People. Korea's most valuable resource is its skilled and educated population. Korea has a literacy rate near 95 percent. Almost all Korean children attend elementary school. Most complete high school.

Korea is a homogeneous society—that is, the people share a common ethnic and cultural background. They speak their own language, which differs from both Chinese and Japanese. For much of its long history, Korea was united. Despite the present-day division between the north and south, Koreans consider themselves one people.

SECTION 1 REVIEW

1. **Locate:** (a) Yellow Sea, (b) Korea Strait, (c) Sea of Japan, (d) North Korea, (e) South Korea, (f) T'aebaek Range, (g) Pyongyang, (h) Seoul.
2. **Define:** homogeneous society.
3. Describe two ways in which location has affected Korean life.
4. How does geography influence population patterns in Korea?
5. How have differences in climate and resources led to different economic patterns in North Korea and South Korea?
6. **Applying Information** Is the geography of North Korea or South Korea more favorable? Give reasons to support your answer.
7. **Writing Across Cultures** Look up the word "pluralistic" in a dictionary. Then jot down some of the advantages and disadvantages of living in a homogeneous society, such as Korea, as compared with a pluralistic society, such as the United States.

2

DYNAMICS OF CHANGE

FIND OUT

How did Chinese culture influence Korea?

What are some achievements of Korean civilization?

How did imperialism affect Korea?

Vocabulary isolationism, annex

In *Songs of Flying Dragons,* Korea's leading poets celebrated the achievements of the great general Yi Song-gye (ee song keh). They portrayed him as a model ruler who practiced Confucian virtues:

> "Though he was busy with war,
> He loved the way of the scholar.
> His work of achieving peace
> Shone brilliantly. . . .
> Upon receiving an old scholar
> He knelt down with due politeness."

Like most peoples of East Asia, Koreans looked on China as the center of civilization and absorbed many of its traditions. At the same time, they developed their own distinct identity. In fact, *Songs of Flying Dragons,* though influenced by Chinese ideas, was the first work written by Koreans in their own alphabet.

Early Traditions

In ancient times, small bands of nomadic hunters migrated to Korea from Central Asia. They settled in villages and began to grow rice. Over thousands of years, Koreans developed their own culture.

From about A.D. 100 to A.D. 668, three kingdoms dominated Korea. Koguryo (koh guh ree oh) dominated in the north, Paekche (pehk chay) in the southwest, and Silla (shil lah) in the southeast. During this period, Korea absorbed many ideas and customs from China, including Buddhism, Confucianism, and Chinese written script. Through trade and other peaceful contacts, elements of Chinese culture were transmitted from Korea to Japan.

Chinese culture spread into Korea in several ways. At times, China ruled parts of northern Korea. During periods of turmoil at home, Chinese refugees fled to Korea, bringing their customs with them. Also, Buddhist missionaries carried Mahayana traditions and other Chinese ideas to Korea. Finally, many Koreans went to study in China, where they learned the Chinese language and read Confucian texts. These scholars brought home knowledge of Chinese achievements as well as political and social ideas.

Koreans adapted Chinese traditions to their own beliefs. An example is the belief that spirits resided in natural objects such as rocks and trees. Among the most revered spirits was the mountain god. In Korea, Buddhism absorbed this belief, and Korean Buddhist temples include a shrine to the mountain god. (See Connections With Literature, page 806, "The Silence of Love.")

Powerful Dynasties

In 668, the Silla kingdom united all of Korea. Korea then remained a single, unified state until 1945. Unlike China, with its many dynasties, Korea had only three periods of dynastic rule—the Silla, Koryo (kor ee oh), and Choson (choh suhn).*

Silla. During the Silla dynasty (668–918), Korea enjoyed a golden age. Traders flocked to Korean ports from all parts of Asia—even the Middle East. The Silla capital at Kyongju grew into a large city with fine palaces and tall pagodas, or Buddhist temples. Buddhist beliefs influenced architecture, sculpture, and literature and helped to unite the people.

Koryo. Korea takes its name from the Koryo dynasty, which ruled from 918 to 1392. The first Koryo ruler was a soldier named

* Many scholars outside Korean refer to this as the Yi dynasty.

Wang Kon. He built a capital at present-day Kaesong (keh song) and encouraged culture and the arts. As you have read, potters perfected the making of celadon porcelain during this period.

In 958, the king introduced the Chinese system of civil service examinations to attract the most talented scholars to government service. (See page 339.) Koreans modified this system to suit their own culture. Korea had a strong tradition of aristocratic rule. As a result, only the sons of aristocrats were allowed to take the civil service exams.

Buddhist influence reached its height during the Koryo dynasty. Temples flourished, and religious writings multiplied. The royal family had printers carve more than 81,000 wooden blocks containing the entire Buddhist scripture. The blocks can still be seen in a Buddhist temple today. The Koreans later improved printing by developing movable metal type.*

The Koryo kingdom had to fight off constant invasions from the mainland and defend its coasts against Japanese pirates. In the 1200s, the Mongols conquered Korea. Although Mongol rule was harsh, the Koreans learned from the invaders how to grow cotton and use gunpowder.

Choson. In 1392, an able Korean general, Yi Song-gye, set up the Choson dynasty. With its capital at Seoul, the Yi royal family ruled Korea until 1910.

During the Choson dynasty, Confucianism replaced Buddhism as the dominant system of social ethics. Koreans adopted Confucian teachings on moral conduct and the duties of the superior and the inferior person. These teachings guided Koreans' relationships in the family, community, and government.

At this time, Korea acknowledged China's superior power. As a result, for nearly 500 years, relations with countries other than China were discouraged, and Korea came to be known as the "Hermit Kingdom."

Following Confucian teachings, Koreans treated China with the respect that a younger brother owed to an older brother. Yet, Koreans maintained their own identity. The Choson ruler Sejong (say jong) showed this independence when he called on scholars to develop *han'gul,* a phonetic alphabet suited to the Korean language. (See the feature on page 380.)

Celadon Porcelain This pitcher in the shape of a tortoise dates from the early 1100s, when Korean artisans produced some of their finest works. When a Chinese scholar of the Sung dynasty listed the ten most wonderful things in the world, nine of them, including books and tea, were Chinese. The tenth thing he listed was Koryo celadon. ***Fine Art*** Why did Koreans lose the secret of making celadon?

Invasions and Isolation

In 1592, a powerful Japanese ruler tried to attack China by way of Korea. For the next six years, the Koreans fought off the Japanese invaders. A Korean admiral invented "turtle boats," the first metal-plated ships, to defeat the Japanese navy. Finally, with Chinese help, the Koreans drove off the invaders. The war, however, destroyed much of Korea.

Greatly weakened, the Koreans were unable to fight off the Manchus, who invaded in the early 1600s. The Manchus overran first Korea and later China, as you have read. Although the Choson dynasty remained in power, to secure peace, Korea paid tribute to the Manchu rulers of China.

* Although the Chinese invented movable type in about 1045, they did not at first use metal pieces.

King Sejong, Father of the Korean Alphabet

South Korea is the only country in the world that has dedicated a national holiday to its alphabet. More than that, Han'gul Day—October 9—is a tribute to Korea's greatest ruler, King Sejong.

During his reign (1418–1450), Sejong encouraged advances in agriculture, government, science, music, medicine, and astronomy. He ordered scholars to invent a rainfall gauge and publish a 112-volume encyclopedia. His highest achievement, however, was the development of a simple Korean alphabet.

Until the 1440s, Korean scholars used a form of Chinese writing. To be literate, a person had to learn at least 20,000 Chinese characters. King Sejong wanted a simpler and more efficient method of writing the Korean language. He asked scholars to invent a writing system based on the way Korean was pronounced. The result was an alphabet with 17 consonants and 11 vowels. King Sejong called it han'gul, or "Korean Script."

Many Koreans who had become Confucian scholars scorned han'gul. They warned against "dragging the Chinese classics in the dust of vulgar script." King Sejong, though, was pleased with han'gul. He said:

> "A wise person can learn han'gul in a few hours. Even a foolish person can learn it in ten days."

King Sejong used different methods to popularize the alphabet. According to one story, he had the alphabet written in honey on the leaves of trees in his garden. Overnight, insects chewed through the leaves as they ate the honey. The next day, visitors to the garden were startled to see han'gul inscribed on the leaves of the trees!

Today, Koreans have simplified han'gul even further, to 14 consonants and 10 vowels. Its use has helped make Korea one of the world's most literate nations.

1. Why did King Sejong encourage the invention of a Korean alphabet?
2. **Applying Information** King Sejong had poems, Buddhist scriptures, and Chinese classics written in han'gul. How might this new literature have promoted use of the new script?

In response to these attacks, Korea turned to further isolationism. Isolationism is a policy of avoiding foreign involvements and contacts. For almost 200 years, Korea closed its ports to foreign ships and resisted foreign ideas. Korean rulers also banned Christianity, which reached Korea by way of China in the 1700s. Korean Christians then had to worship in secret.

Imperialism and Nationalism

The Age of Imperialism put Korea at the center of a new struggle. By the mid-1800s, western powers wanted the Hermit Kingdom to open its ports to foreign trade. With the Choson dynasty in decline, Korea could not resist the imperialist powers.

In the past, China had supported Korea's isolation. However, China could no longer help itself, let alone Korea. As in China, imperialist powers forced Korea to sign "unequal treaties." In this way, foreigners won trading rights and special privileges, such as extraterritoriality.

Japanese rule. As Japan modernized and expanded its power, it competed with China and Russia for control of Korea. By 1905, Japan had defeated its rivals and won control over Korea. Five years later, it ousted the Choson dynasty and annexed Korea. To annex means to add a territory to one's own country.

The Japanese imposed harsh rule on Korea. Like other imperialist powers, Japan introduced modern improvements to serve its own interests. The Japanese forced the Koreans to build factories, roads, and railroads for Japan's benefit. They encouraged education to make Korean workers more productive. The Japanese also improved farming methods, but then took half of Korea's yearly rice crop to support Japanese expansion.

Korean nationalism. Koreans bitterly resented Japanese rule. Nationalists campaigned to win freedom for their country. On March 1, 1919, Korean nationalists held a huge, peaceful demonstration to demand independence. The Japanese responded by killing 2,000 Koreans and jailing 19,000 others.

During the years that followed, the Japanese hunted down leaders of the March 1st Movement, as the Korean nationalist movement was called. Many nationalist leaders fled to the United States, China, and the Soviet Union.

In the 1930s and 1940s, Japan expanded its empire across much of Asia. During World War II, it forced Koreans to fight in its armies and used Korean resources to power its war machines. The Japanese also tried to suppress Korea's identity. They forbade Koreans to speak their own language in public and made them take Japanese last names. Writer Richard Kim described this attempt to erase Korean culture in his autobiographical novel *Lost Names*.

Lost Names

Young Richard Kim never forgot that day in school. The teacher, a young Japanese man, came into the freezing classroom before the bell rang. The boys knew something was about to happen.

The bell rang. The boys rose, bowed to the teacher, and resumed their seats. Then, without looking at the students, the teacher spoke:

> "Today, I must have your new names. . . . I shall call your old names, and those who are called will be excused from the class immediately, so that they can go home and return with their new names, which have been properly registered with the proper authorities."

Students in Seoul These young women attend Ewha University, one of the largest women's universities in the world. Koreans, who have always placed a high value on education, preserved their cultural identity even when the Japanese tried to weaken it. ***Culture*** What steps did the Japanese take to suppress Koreans' sense of identity?

Young Kim ran home to find out his new name. All the way, the same thought pounded in his head: "I am going to lose my name; I am going to lose my name, we are all going to lose our names."

Kim and his father had to go to the police station to register the family's new name. It sounded strange to his ears.

> "'Iwamoto.' I mouth the name. Our new name. My new name. 'Iwa'—rock. 'Moto'— . . . foundation. 'Rock-Foundation.' So this is our 'new' surname, our Japanese 'family' name."

Later, the boy went with his father and grandfather to visit the graves of their ancestors. His father brushed off the snow, and the three knelt. His grandfather said to the ancestors, "We are a disgrace to our family. We bring disgrace and humiliation to your name. How can you forgive us?" With tears spilling from their eyes, the two older men bowed to their ancestors.

Scenes like this one occurred throughout Korea during the years of Japanese rule. Yet, the harder the Japanese tried to undermine Korean culture, the stronger the Koreans felt attached to their own ways.

SECTION 2 REVIEW

1. **Identify:** (a) Silla, (b) Koryo, (c) Yi Song-gye, (d) han'gul, (e) Hermit Kingdom, (f) March 1st Movement.
2. **Define:** (a) isolationism, (b) annex.
3. How did Buddhism and Confucianism affect Korean culture?
4. Describe two achievements of Korean civilization.
5. What happened to Korea during the Age of Imperialism?
6. **Making Inferences** How do you think Japanese efforts to undermine Korean culture contributed to Korean nationalism? Why?
7. **Writing Across Cultures** Imagine that you are a member of the March 1st Movement who has fled to the United States. Write a speech urging Americans to support Korean nationalism.

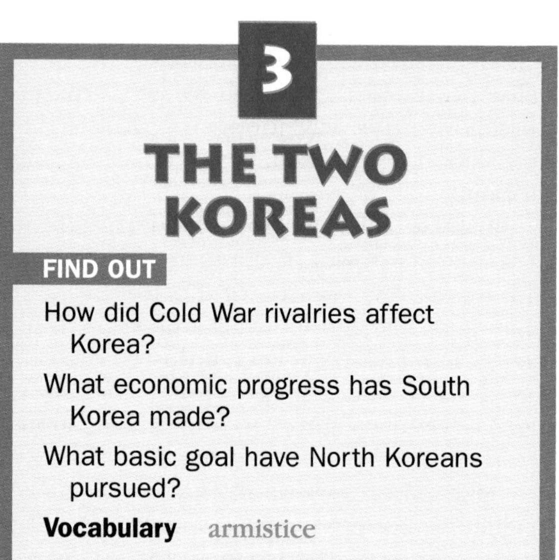

3 THE TWO KOREAS

FIND OUT

How did Cold War rivalries affect Korea?

What economic progress has South Korea made?

What basic goal have North Koreans pursued?

Vocabulary armistice

> "The whole atmosphere was forbidding and ugly. I could very well imagine how the mood sometimes explodes into violent incidents."

A Korean-born journalist was describing tensions at Panmunjom, on the dividing line between North Korea and South Korea. For almost 40 years, this artificial line has separated families as well as governments. Yet, Koreans cherish the hope that someday their country will be reunited.

A Divided Land

In 1945, Koreans celebrated the Japanese defeat in World War II with joy and great hope for the future. Soon, however, Korea again became a battleground between strong powers. As the war ended, the United States and its wartime ally, the Soviet Union, agreed that Korea should regain its independence. Both nations sent troops to Korea to accept the Japanese surrender. Soviet troops occupied the region north of the 38th parallel. American troops occupied the southern part of Korea. The occupation was to last only until elections could be held.

Cold War rivalries led to a permanent division of Korea. During the Japanese occupation, Korean nationalists had split into communist and non-communist factions. In 1945, the Soviet Union helped Korean communists gain power in the north. At the same time, the United States backed non-communist Koreans in the south. By 1948, Korea officially split into the Democratic People's Republic of Korea, or North Korea, and the Republic of Korea, or South Korea.

War in Korea

After the split, clashes occurred between North Korean and South Korean troops along the 38th parallel. In 1950, North Korea launched an all-out invasion of South Korea to reunite the country by force. Surprised and poorly equipped, South Korean soldiers retreated.

UN involvement. The United States and its allies saw the North Korean invasion as part of a worldwide communist threat. China had been taken over by communist forces the year before. The Soviet Union had armed and trained the North Koreans. At the urging of the United States, the United Nations voted to send troops to South Korea. An American general, Douglas MacArthur, took command of the combined UN and South Korean troops. In the end, more than 15 nations sent troops to Korea. American and South Korean soldiers, however, did most of the fighting.

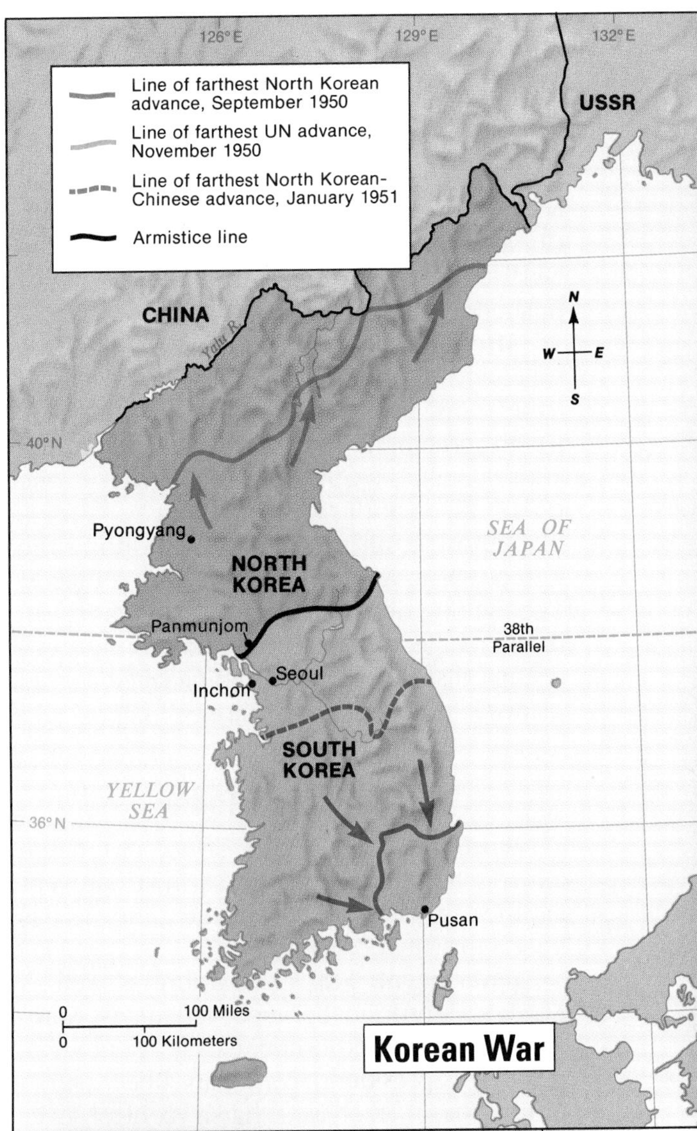

MAP STUDY

In 1950, communist North Korean armies invaded South Korea. The UN sent an army largely made up of American troops to aid South Korea. After three years of bitter fighting, the war ended in a stalemate.

1. **Interaction** What geographic features made fighting in the Korean peninsula difficult for both sides?
2. **Movement** (a) Describe the position of the UN forces' deepest advance into North Korea. (b) Describe the position of North Korea's deepest advance into South Korea.
3. **Drawing Conclusions** (a) Which side seemed to be winning the war in September 1950? In November 1950? (b) How do you explain this great change?

Effects of War The war in Korea brought bloodshed to towns and villages in all parts of the Korean peninsula. As this photograph shows, the war and everyday life were closely intertwined. ***Power*** What were the economic results of the Korean War?

The fighting seesawed back and forth across the peninsula. At first, the North Koreans pushed deep into the south. Then, UN forces landed behind enemy lines at Inchon and swept into North Korea. At this point, Chinese troops crossed the Yalu River to help North Korea. The Chinese and North Koreans pushed the UN forces back to the south.

Aftermath of the war. The war ended in a stalemate. In 1953, both sides finally agreed to an armistice, or an end to fighting. The truce agreement left Korea divided at the 38th parallel, with a demilitarized zone (DMZ) along both sides of the line.

Almost 4 million people died during the Korean War. Many more became refugees. The fighting destroyed factories and farms. In the north, as well as in the once communist-occupied south, heavy bombing by American planes left most cities in ruins.

South Korea Today

Since the war, South Korea has maintained a large, well-equipped army to prevent another invasion. At the same time, it has built a thriving economy.

Government. Fear of invasion, as well as Korea's Confucian heritage, led many Koreans to accept authoritarian rule. South Korea's first president, Syngman Rhee (SIHNG muhn REE), exercised harsh control over people's lives. He and his successors, beginning with President Park Chung Hee, cracked down hard when South Koreans demanded greater freedom. They believed strong measures were needed to maintain stability and promote rapid economic growth.

Despite this repression, demands for democratic freedoms continued. In 1960, massive protests by students and other groups forced Rhee to resign. In the 1980s, the government gave in to demands for more democratic elections. Today, the government remains powerful and restricts human rights, although opposition groups have won some rights.

Economic growth. In 1953, South Korea faced the enormous task of rebuilding its shattered villages and cities. As you have read, it has only limited natural resources. Also, it had to absorb millions of refugees who had fled the fighting or escaped from North Korea. With massive United States aid, South Korea made progress.

Since the 1960s, South Korea's economic success has been spectacular. Today, it ranks with Taiwan, Hong Kong, and Singapore as one of the "four Asian tigers" that have rapidly industrialized.

Although South Korea has a free market economy, the government has kept tight control over it. South Korea stresses manufacturing for export. Its skilled work force produces

Downtown Seoul Modern buildings surround the South Gate, which dates from the founding of Seoul in the late 1300s. South Korea's capital, which has a metropolitan population of more than 16 million, is the world's fourth-largest city. Nearly 25 percent of the population of South Korea lives in Seoul. ***Environment*** Why might the government wish to discourage Seoul's further growth?

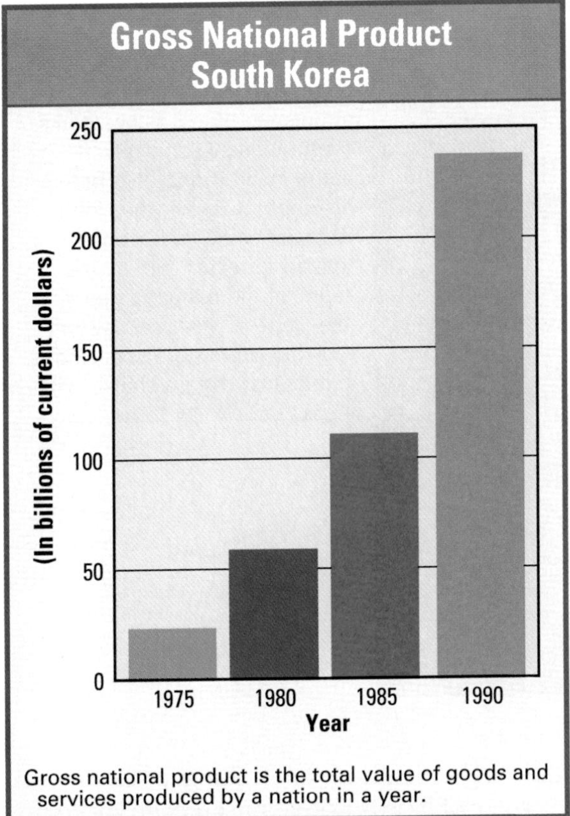

Source: *Statistical Abstract of the United States.*

Graph Skills South Korea's economy developed rapidly after the devastation of the Korean War. Today, South Korea is an industrial nation whose products are sold throughout the world. ▶According to this bar graph, how did South Korea's GNP in 1990 compare with its 1975 GNP?

goods, such as textiles and electronics equipment, that are sold on the world market. Businesses reinvest their profits in other industries. Because of its reliance on exports and its need for raw materials and foreign capital, South Korea is interdependent with the world economy.

South Koreans enjoy a rising standard of living, but they have paid a price for progress. They work long hours for low pay. The environment has suffered tremendous damage. Chemicals pollute the air and water around Seoul. In recent years, labor unions have demanded and won higher wages. As wages rise, however, some foreign businesses are moving to other countries, where they can produce goods more cheaply.

Social changes. Economic progress also brought major social changes. Industry has drawn people away from farms to jobs in urban areas. Today, about 75 percent of South Koreans live in cities. A new and growing middle class has emerged.

Urbanization has affected families. In cities, nuclear families are more common than extended families—the Confucian ideal. Women have won more rights, and many have taken jobs in factories.

Confucian traditions still influence Korean life, however. Close ties bind families together. Families look after the old and ill at home. Most marriages are still arranged, although usually with the couple's consent. Confucian values such as respect for elders and for the well educated remain strong. Religions such as Buddhism and Christianity also play an important role in people's lives.

North Korea Today

Unlike South Korea, with its many outside ties, North Korea is a closed society with few links to the world. North Korea is a communist dictatorship. From 1948 to 1994, North Korean leader Kim Il Sung (kihm ihl soong) built a totalitarian state. Through a huge propaganda campaign, North Koreans learned to express loyalty and obedience to the man they called "Great Leader." After Kim Il Sung died in 1994, his son, Kim Jong Il, succeeded him as ruler of North Korea.

Kim Il Sung preached the goal of *juche* (JOO chay), or self-reliance. To achieve this goal, he avoided dependence on foreign countries, even other communist states. Kim's policies also focused on making the North Korean economy self-sufficient. North Korea has built heavy industry to supply its own needs. It imports and exports few goods.

Like South Korea, North Korea has also made economic progress. It has industrialized and become more urbanized. Although its standard of living has risen, North Korea still lags far behind South Korea.

A North Korean Rally A giant portrait of North Korea's strongman, Kim Il Sung, looms over a massive student gathering in Pyongyang. Before his death in 1994, the North Korean people had been trained to regard Kim as the "sun" of the nation, a near-god-like figure. ***Political System*** How did North Korea become a communist dictatorship?

Under Kim Il Sung, North Korea outlawed all religions. It tried to replace Confucian values with communist beliefs. Because of its closed society, we know little about life in North Korea. Some visitors suggest that beneath the surface of the communist society, ancient Korean traditions survive.

Outlook for the Future

With their common history and culture, Koreans cling to the hope of reunification. In recent years, some promising signs have appeared. Both countries have offered plans for reunification, and in late 1991, they signed a nonaggression pact. Both countries have cooperated with the International Red Cross to arrange meetings between members of separated families. The reunification of Germany in 1990 raised hopes that someday Korea will again become one country.

Yet, many obstacles stand in the way of this goal. The chief problem is the different directions the two Koreas have taken since 1945. Each country believes that the other wants to overthrow its system of government. In the early 1990s, North Korea's suspected nuclear program heightened tensions. In addition, the death of Kim Il Sung, after 46 years as ruler of North Korea, raised even more uncertainty about Korea's future.

SECTION 3 REVIEW

1. **Locate:** (a) 38th parallel, (b) Inchon, (c) Yalu River
2. **Identify:** (a) Syngman Rhee, (b) "four Asian tigers," (c) Kim Il Sung.
3. **Define:** armistice.
4. (a) Why did the United States and the Soviet Union divide Korea in 1945? (b) How did the division become permanent?
5. In what three ways is South Korea linked to the world economy?
6. How did Kim Il Sung pursue the goal of juche in North Korea?
7. **Analyzing Ideas** How do you think Confucian traditions contributed to authoritarian rule in both South Korea and North Korea?
8. **Writing Across Cultures** Write an editorial for or against sending United States troops to Korea in 1950. You should consider what the results might have been if UN forces had not intervened.

CHAPTER 17 REVIEW

Understanding Vocabulary

Match each term at left with the correct definition at right.

1. homogeneous society	**a.** phonetic alphabet suited to the Korean language
2. han'gul	**b.** end to fighting
3. isolationism	**c.** culture in which people share a common background
4. annex	**d.** add on
5. armistice	**e.** policy of avoiding foreign involvements and contacts

Reviewing the Main Ideas

1. (a) What are the two main landforms of Korea? (b) How does each affect people's lives?
2. Describe two geographic differences between North Korea and South Korea.
3. How did Chinese culture spread into Korea?
4. (a) Why did Korea enter a period of isolation in the 1600s? (b) How did this isolation affect the spread of Christianity in Korea?
5. (a) What economic progress has South Korea made since the Korean War? (b) What have been some costs of this rapid progress?
6. (a) Why do Koreans hope for the reunification of North and South Korea? (b) What obstacles to reunification exist?

Reviewing Chapter Themes

1. Geography has influenced Korea's history and economy. Describe the effects of two of the following: (a) its location between China and Japan, (b) its major landforms, (c) its long coastline.
2. For centuries, China strongly influenced Korean culture. (a) Describe three practices or ideas that Koreans borrowed from Chinese culture. (b) Describe one way in which Koreans adapted Chinese traditions.
3. Outside influences have affected Korea since the 1850s. Describe the effects of two of the following: (a) imperialist rivalries, (b) Japanese expansionism, (c) World War II, (d) Cold War tensions.
4. North and South Korea have followed different paths. Compare North Korea and South Korea in terms of: (a) government, (b) economy, (c) foreign policy.

Thinking Critically

1. **Analyzing Ideas** Korea has been both a cultural bridge and a battleground in Asia. (a) Give examples that support this statement. (b) Why do you think Korea has maintained its unique identity despite foreign influence?
2. **Making Global Connections** Since the 1950s, the United States has given economic aid to South Korea and kept military bases there. Why do you think the United States continues to support South Korea?
3. **Forecasting** (a) Do you think Korea will eventually reunite? (b) If it does, do you think the reunited country will have an economy and government more like that of North Korea or that of South Korea? Why?

Applying Your Skills

1. **Recognizing Points of View** (a) What does the nickname "Hermit Kingdom" show about the attitude western nations have toward Korea? (b) What name might Koreans have given to outsiders?
2. **Understanding Causes and Effects** Create a cause-and-effect chart for the Korean War. (See Skill Lesson 13, page 628.)

Chapter 18

GEOGRAPHY AND HERITAGE OF JAPAN

Imperial Court Official This Japanese official was a powerful member of the imperial court and a scholar of Chinese literature in the late 800s. Chinese culture greatly influenced Japan during this period. ***Fine Art*** How does this painting reflect a respect for nature, a common feature in Chinese art?

CHAPTER OUTLINE

"The Mongols are ready to sail!" Japanese spies sent word from Korea. The Japanese knew that the Mongol emperor Kubilai Khan wanted to add their lands to his empire. They built walls along the coast and placed warriors on alert. They prayed to the *kami,* or spirits, for protection.

In June 1281, the invasion began. For seven weeks, Japanese warriors battled the mighty Mongol fleet. On the fiftieth day, thick clouds blotted out the sun, making the sky as dark as night. A howling typhoon whipped up the coast. For two days, the histories relate,

> "The wind blew fiercely, the . . . billows surged up to heaven, the thunder rolled and the lightning dashed against the ground so that it seemed as if mountains were crumbling down and high heaven falling to the Earth."

When the storm quieted, the Mongol fleet lay in ruins. The Japanese rejoiced that the kami had sent a divine wind—a *kamikaze*—to destroy the invaders. They came to believe that the gods would always protect them from invasion.

CHAPTER PERSPECTIVE

The island nation of Japan sits off the coast of East Asia. It is close enough to feel the influence of China but far enough away to remain independent. During the 1800s, Japan again borrowed foreign ideas when it set out to become a modern industrial power.

As you read, look for these chapter themes:

- Japan's island setting and scarcity of raw materials have affected its relations with the outside world.
- Geographic isolation helped the Japanese to develop a strong sense of themselves as a separate people.
- The Japanese have selectively borrowed ideas from other cultures.
- During the Age of Imperialism, Japan modernized rapidly.

Literature Connections

In this chapter, you will encounter passages from the following works.

The Tale of Genji, Murasaki Shikibu

"Looking at Mount Fuji in the Distance," Yamabe No Akahito

The Autobiography of Fukuzawa Yukichi, Fukuzawa Yukichi

For other suggestions, see Connections With Literature, pages 804–808.

1 A WORLD APART

FIND OUT

What geographic features have shaped Japanese life?

How has the scarcity of some resources influenced Japan's relations with the world?

How did the Japanese develop a sense of their own special identity?

According to a Japanese legend, male and female gods created the islands of Japan by throwing a jeweled spear into the sea. The salt water that dripped from the spear hardened to form islands. Only then did the gods descend to Earth and create the rest of the world.

A Chain of Islands

Japan is an archipelago, or chain of islands, that lies about 100 miles (161 km) off the coast of East Asia. The stormy Korea Strait and the Sea of Japan separate Japan from the mainland. Japan consists of four main islands and more than 3,000 tiny islands. Of the main islands, Kyushu (kee oo shoo) lies closest to Korea and the mainland of Asia. Just east of Kyushu lies tiny Shikoku (SHEE koh koo). Honshu (hahn shoo) is the largest and most populous island. Hokkaido (hoh KĪ doh), in the north, is the most isolated of the main islands.

In the past, the seas surrounding Japan isolated and protected it from invaders. Yet, when the Japanese chose, they could cross the seas to make contact with other societies. The seas also provided links within Japan. Honshu, Kyushu, and Shikoku surround a body of water known as the Inland Sea. Sheltered from dangerous Pacific storms, the Inland Sea has served as a major highway between islands.

Location has affected Japanese life in other ways. Japan lies on the Pacific Ring of Fire, a region of earthquakes and volcanoes. (See page 251.) As many as 1,500 tremors shake the islands each year. The islands also contain 30 active volcanoes. Fierce typhoons from the southern Pacific pound the islands from August to October. The Japanese have constant reminders of the menacing forces of nature.

Landforms and Climate

Japan is a relatively small country. In size, it is equal to the state of Montana, but larger than such European countries as Italy or Great Britain. Its population, however, is large. With more than 125 million people, Japan's population ranks seventh in the world.

Mountains and plains. As in China, Japan's large population is packed onto a tiny fraction of the land. More than four fifths of Japan is mountainous. The rugged terrain limits the amount of arable land to coastal plains and narrow river valleys. As a result, fertile lowland areas such as the Kanto Plain on Honshu are densely populated, with more than 20,000 people per square mile. By comparison, New York State has a population density of 360 people per square mile.

Mild climates. The climates of Japan are similar to those found along the east coast of the United States, but the summers are not as hot nor the winters as cold as they are in the eastern United States. A warm ocean current moderates summer and winter temperatures in most coastal areas. As a result, Japan has a long growing season that averages between 200 and 260 days. In addition, rainfall is plentiful.

Intensive land use. The Japanese developed methods of intensive farming, using every available piece of land. To create land, they carved terraces into steep hillsides and drained marshes, swamps, and deltas. A favorable climate helps the Japanese make the most of their limited farmland. In much of Japan, farmers harvest two crops a year.

Japan's major crop is rice. Wet-rice agriculture came to Japan from South China. Like their mainland neighbors, the Japanese have built complex irrigation systems to flood their rice paddies with water. In small, crowded farming villages, people worked together to plant, irrigate, and harvest rice.

Living Along the Coast Mountains cover so much of Japan that the country's population must live crowded together in the coastal plains, as shown here. Japan's coast also is dotted with more than 2,000 fishing ports. Their fleets bring the world's largest catch of fish to Japan. ***Scarcity*** Why is fish so important in the Japanese diet?

Those activities gave them a sense of closeness and shared purpose.

Until modern times, the Japanese produced all the food they needed. Today, they produce about three quarters of their food needs, even though only 8 percent of the people work in agriculture. They are successful farmers in part because they have used technology to develop high-yield types of rice.

Harvests from the sea. Partly because farmland is so limited, fish is the major source of protein in the Japanese diet. In the rich waters off the coasts, the Japanese catch sardines, tuna, herring, salmon, cod, and halibut. They also raise fish in flooded rice paddies and harvest shellfish and vitamin-rich seaweed in inlets and bays.

Limited Mineral Resources

Japan has few mineral resources. Until the late 1800s, this scarcity had little effect on Japan. As a nation of farming and fishing people, it had enough coal, copper, iron, and other resources to meet its needs. As Japan industrialized, however, it needed to import many raw materials. As a result, Japan became increasingly dependent on world trade.

Today, ships from the Philippines, Malaysia, Australia, and India unload iron ore at Japanese ports. From North America, South Africa, and Australia comes coal. Since it has no oil resources, Japan imports nearly all of its oil from nations of the Middle East. As a result, world events that disrupt the flow of oil from the Middle East have threatened and can again threaten Japan's busy industrial economy.

People of Japan

Japan is a homogeneous society. The people speak the same language and share the same culture. Unlike most nations around the world, Japan has almost no ethnic minorities.

Japan's isolated island setting helped to shape its society and its view of the world. From earliest times, the Japanese had a sense of their own separate, special identity. This sense of specialness has in turn encouraged ethnocentrism. Today, as in the past, the

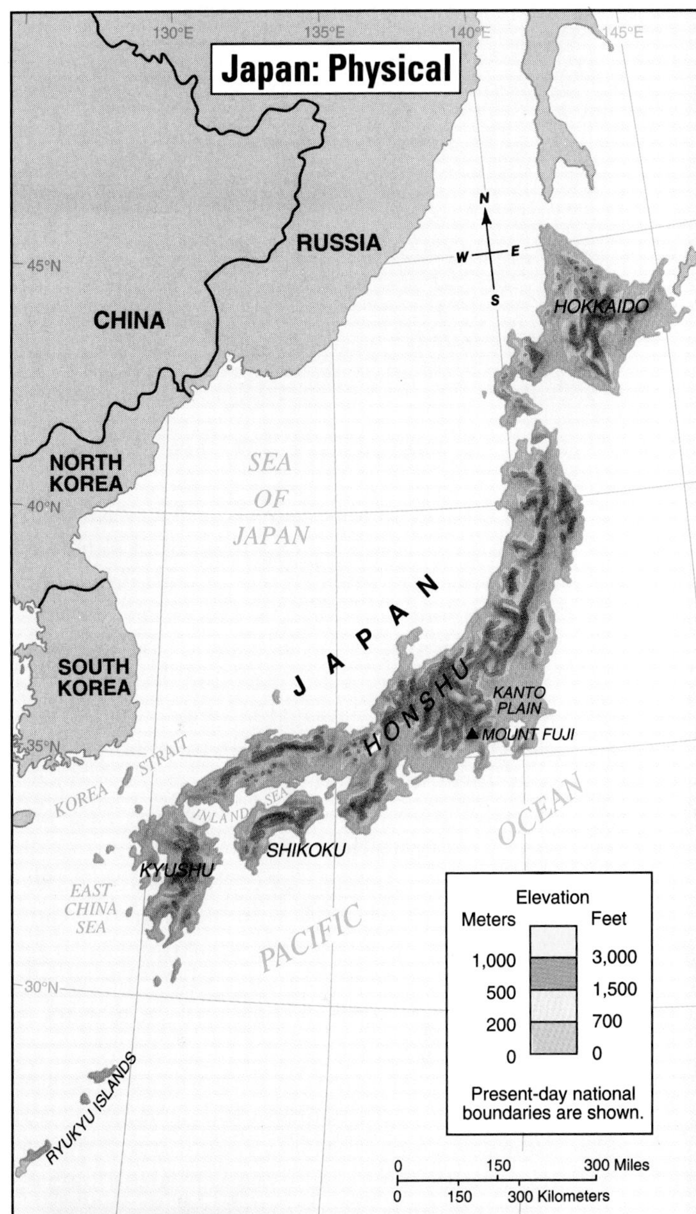

MAP STUDY

Japan is an island nation in East Asia. Its four main islands extend about 1,300 miles (2,080 km) along the East Asian mainland. Most of the landscape of Japan's islands is mountainous, with an area of coastal plains.

1. **Location** (a) Describe the exact location of Japan. (b) Describe the relative location of Japan.
2. **Place** Rank Japan's main islands by size, from the largest to the smallest.
3. **Understanding Causes and Effects** (a) As an island nation, how is Japan separated from other nations? (b) How is it linked to other nations?

Crowded in Tokyo

The alarm clock sounds at 5 A.M. Kirasake Toshiro rises and dresses in a white shirt and blue suit like millions of other commuters who stream into Tokyo each day. Monday through Saturday, he spends six hours a day on high-speed trains traveling to and from work. At every stop along the way, white-gloved station attendants help push passengers into the packed trains.

Like many other city workers, Kirasake must commute because he cannot find or afford comfortable living quarters in Tokyo. Living in Tokyo with his wife and family would mean living in a cramped apartment with no closets. To keep a car in Tokyo, he would have to prove that he had a place to park it off the street.

Part of the problem is simply Japan's size and growing population. With less land than California, Japan has a population half that of the entire United States. As an island nation, Japan has little room to expand.

Because most people have jobs in cities, they have been forced to respond resourcefully to overcrowding. On the top of department stores and office buildings, Tokyo residents practice golf on miniature putting greens or swing at baseballs on tiny fields. When Japanese businessmen must stay overnight in Tokyo, they take "rooms" in inexpensive "capsule hotels." The rooms, in fact, are fiberglass bunks that are built in rows.

Tokyo city planners are discussing solutions. They talk about filling in part of Tokyo Bay. Others want to buy land from the national railroad. Yet, even these proposals can barely keep up with the ever-growing demand for space.

1. Why are some people willing to endure a long commute rather than live in Tokyo?
2. **Solving Problems** Imagine that you are a Tokyo city planner. What recommendations could you make to help relieve overcrowding?

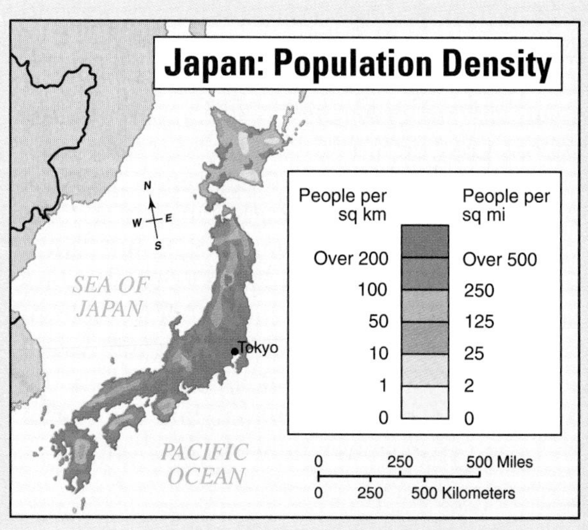

Japanese make a distinction between "we Japanese" and foreigners. They rarely grant citizenship to immigrants. Even Koreans whose families have lived in Japan for generations remain "foreigners."

A strong sense of national identity has strengthened Japan but has also contributed to prejudice against the Ainu and the *burakumin.* The Ainu were early inhabitants of northern Japan who were excluded from Japanese society. The burakumin are descendants of butchers and leather tanners who lived during feudal times. The Buddhist view against the taking of life made the burakumin outcasts. Both the Ainu and the burakumin suffer from discrimination today.

SECTION 1 REVIEW

1. **Locate:** (a) Korea Strait, (b) Kyushu, (c) Shikoku, (d) Honshu, (e) Hokkaido, (f) Inland Sea, (g) Kanto Plain.
2. **Identify:** Ainu.
3. Describe two ways in which the seas have affected Japan.
4. How has geography affected population patterns in Japan?
5. How did Japan's island setting influence its sense of itself?
6. **Applying Information** How have the Japanese used technology to make up for limited land?
7. **Writing Across Cultures** Write a sentence summarizing the Japanese attitude toward foreigners. Write another sentence describing what you think is the American attitude toward foreigners. Then, write a generalization comparing the two attitudes.

2 EARLY HISTORY

FIND OUT

How did the Japanese adapt Chinese culture to their own needs?

How did a feudal society develop in Japan?

How did centralized feudalism change Japan?

Why did Japan isolate itself from the world during the 1600s?

Vocabulary samurai, feudalism, shogun, daimyo

Everyone was talking about the new book, *The Tale of Genji*. As each chapter appeared, members of the court eagerly read the latest episode in the life of young Prince Genji:

> ❝ From this time, the young prince took up residence in the Imperial palace; and next year, at the age of seven, he began to learn to read and write under the personal supervision of the Emperor. . . . Everyone was pleased to greet him, and there was already a winning friendliness in his manners, which amused people, and made them like to play with him. We need not refer to his studies in detail, but on musical instruments such as the flute and the zither he also showed great skill. ❞

Murasaki Shikibu, the author of *The Tale of Genji,* had a favorable position at the Japanese court. She completed her book—the world's first novel—around the year 1008. Although *The Tale of Genji* is fiction, it reveals much about the elaborate ceremonies and manners of Japanese court life. By the time of Murasaki, the Japanese had successfully blended ideas borrowed from China to enrich their own culture.

Early Japanese Society

Life in early Japan was very different from the elegant world of Murasaki Shikibu. The earliest Japanese society was organized into clans, or groups of families descended from a common ancestor. Each family inherited its position within a clan. Some families were warriors. Others might be farmers, weavers, or potters.

By A.D. 400, several clans formed a union and settled in the district called Yamato. They united much of Japan and even governed a small area of southern Korea. The Tenno clan led the union and claimed to be descended from the sun goddess Amaterasu. Through the goddess, legends relate, the Tenno clan received the three symbols of imperial power: a bronze mirror, an iron sword, and a jeweled necklace. In time, the Tenno set up Japan's first and only ruling dynasty. Japan's present emperor traces his descent to the Tenno clan.

Adapting Chinese Patterns

During the 500s, missionaries from Korea introduced Buddhism and Chinese culture to Japan. They brought Chinese script, which

Todaiji Temple at Nara Built to house a colossal statue of the Buddha, this temple was originally constructed in the 700s. It reflects the Chinese influence on Japanese architecture during this period. Later destroyed by fire, the temple was rebuilt in about 1700. It is believed to be the largest wooden building in the world. ***Interdependence*** How did Japanese culture in the 600s and 700s reflect Chinese influence?

became Japan's first written language. These early contacts with China's advanced civilization impressed the Japanese. Between 550 and 850, they set out on a course of deliberate cultural borrowing from China.

In 607, Prince Shotoku of the imperial family sent a group of Japanese nobles to China. The young men spent years at the Chinese court, studying government, art, literature, science, and philosophy. They returned home eager to share their new knowledge. In the years that followed, other Japanese visited China.

Cultural diffusion. Chinese influences reached every level of Japanese life. The Japanese modeled their government on Chinese ideas. They increased the authority of the state and set up elaborate court ranks like those in China. Japanese scholars studied Confucian and Daoist philosophies. In addition, Confucian ideas about family and reverence for ancestors helped shape Japanese society.

Peasants learned to use Chinese tools and farming methods and to raise Chinese crops. Japanese potters and weavers modeled their wares on Chinese samples. The Japanese also absorbed Chinese ideas about music, dance, sculpture, and architecture. In the past, Japan moved the capital whenever an emperor died. Under Chinese influence, the emperor built a capital city at Nara, modeled on the Tang capital.

Selective borrowing. Despite the massive borrowing, the Japanese preserved their own identity. After the first enthusiasm for Chinese ideas faded, the Japanese selected the ideas that worked for them. They tried and then discarded the Chinese civil service system. The idea of choosing officials by merit did not fit the Japanese belief that people inherited their position in society.

The Japanese never accepted the idea of the Mandate of Heaven. (See page 329.) Unlike the Chinese, the Japanese did not change dynasties. To them, the emperor was a divine figure, descended from the sun goddess. The Japanese accepted Buddhism, but they kept their traditional beliefs as well.

Heian Court

In 794, the emperor moved his court to Heian, present-day Kyoto. At Heian, the Japanese showed their genius for creative adaptation. There, they blended Chinese and Japanese ideas, creating a rich new culture.

A system of writing. A major achievement of this new culture was the development of a Japanese system of writing. Chinese script was not well suited to spoken Japanese. In time, the Japanese developed *kana,* a set of written symbols that represent syllables. Although educated Japanese men continued to use Chinese writing, women like Murasaki Shikibu adopted the new system.

Powerful families. Although the emperor ruled over a brilliant court at Heian, his power over the country was declining. By the 800s, great court families controlled Japan. They divided the land into private estates, which they assigned to local strongmen. Peasants worked the land on these estates. Slowly, a single family, the Fujiwara (foo jee WAH rah), gained great land wealth and concentrated power in their own hands.

For 200 years, the Fujiwara ruled Japan. The emperor became a figurehead. He carried out religious duties but had no real power. The Fujiwara strengthened their position by marrying their daughters to the heirs to the throne. Other noble families occupied government positions, which they tried to make hereditary. They also devoted themselves to the hundreds of ceremonies and festivals that regulated court life. (📖 See World Literature, "The Pillow Book," by Sei Shonagon, page 430.)

Japanese Feudalism

During the 1100s, turmoil rocked Japan. Strong warrior families on the frontier challenged the power of the Heian court. These samurai, or warrior knights, waged fierce battles for control of the land. Out of the struggles emerged a new system of government known as feudalism. Under feudalism, local lords ruled the land, but they were bound to higher lords and to the emperor by ties of loyalty. This pattern was similar in some ways to European feudalism. (See Chapter 29.)

Feudal society. By 1192, Minamoto Yoritomo* had emerged as the strongest military figure in Japan. The emperor gave him the title shogun, or chief general of the army. Under Minamoto and his successors, a feudal class system emerged.

* Traditionally in Japan, family names precede given names.

Samurai Warrior on Horseback This samurai in battle was protected by armor made of hide and lacquered iron as well as by a gilt helmet. In his left hand, he carries a bamboo bow, and in his right hand, a steel sword. A samurai regarded his sword as his soul. If he gave up his sword, he was giving up his life. ***Citizenship*** Where did the samurai rank in Japanese feudal society?

The emperor stood at the head of feudal society, but he remained a figurehead. The shogun, who was the most powerful samurai, exercised more power. Like other great samurai, the shogun controlled land and the people living on it. Moreover, the shogun commanded an army composed of samurai of lesser rank.

Samurai of all ranks formed a small class of noble warriors that dominated feudal society. Below them were commoners including peasants, artisans, and merchants. Peasants worked the land for the great samurai, providing wealth to support the nobility. Sometimes, peasants served as foot soldiers.

Frequent warfare. In theory, the shogun commanded the complete loyalty of his lords. In practice, these samurai lords and their followers battled for power with the shogun and with one another. At times, the shogunate passed from one military family to another. By the 1400s, Japan was in a constant state of war.

Achieving Unity

During the 1500s, several strong military leaders pushed to reunite Japan. The most successful was an able general, Hideyoshi (hee day HOH shee). By 1590, he had converted his rivals into his subordinates and brought all of Japan under his control. He then invaded Korea, hoping in time to conquer China. Although Hideyoshi failed in these goals, he did build the foundations for a united Japan.

Centralized feudalism. In 1600, Hideyoshi's successor, Tokugawa Ieyasu (toh kuh GAH way ee YAY yah soo), claimed the title of shogun. He set up the Tokugawa shogunate, which lasted until 1868. During that time, the shoguns created a peaceful, orderly society under a system of centralized feudalism.

The Tokugawa shoguns left feudal classes in place, but they brought the great samurai, now called daimyo (DĪ myoh), under their control. The shogun required the daimyo to spend every other year in Edo, present-day Tokyo. To guarantee their good behavior, the daimyo had to leave their wives and children in Edo as permanent hostages. Meanwhile, the emperor remained a powerless figurehead ruler at his palace.

Economic and social changes. The new system of centralized feudalism brought unexpected changes. Edo grew from a small fishing village into a bustling city. Roads improved as the daimyo and their servants traveled back and forth between Edo and their estates in the country.

More peaceful conditions led to increased trade and travel on rivers or roads. Cities and towns sprang up by harbors and along the roads to provide goods and services to travelers. The growth of cities created new markets. During this period of expansion, a money economy developed. Some merchants became rich through trade. Many set up banks to lend money at interest.

The daimyo and their samurai followers had to adapt to the changing conditions. Under the Tokugawas, this military class no longer spent its time fighting as it had in the past. Some samurai became government officials. Others managed the estates of the daimyo or shogun. As Japanese society changed, education became more widespread. The children of wealthy merchants, as well as those of samurai, began to attend school.

By the early 1800s, Japan had become a unified nation in many ways. In addition, the expansion of trade created economic links within Japan.

An Isolated Nation

These changes occurred during a remarkable period of isolation. Early on, the Tokugawas felt threatened by the growing number of westerners who were arriving in Japan. The Portuguese had reached Japan in 1543. Spanish, Dutch, and English traders soon followed. An active trade arose—Chinese silk and European firearms, textiles, and glassware for Japanese copper and silver.

Along with traders came Catholic missionaries. Their success in winning converts an-

Dutch Traders in Nagasaki Japan's isolation in the 1600s and 1700s was never complete. Foreigners continued to interest the Japanese. This scroll shows Dutch merchants dining, at upper right, while servants entertain other merchants with music, at upper left. On the street below is a turkey, an animal that the Dutch brought to Japan. ***Choice*** Why did Japan keep out most foreigners for two centuries?

gered the shogun. He did not want Japanese Christians to pledge loyalty to a foreign ruler—the pope. The shogun's hostility to Catholic countries increased when he heard about the Spanish conquest of the Philippines. He acted to protect Japan from a similar fate.

During the early 1600s, the government began persecuting foreign missionaries and Japanese Christians. This anti-Christian drive grew into a general expulsion of foreigners. In 1639, the shogun closed Japan to the world. Foreigners were forbidden to enter the country. Any Japanese who left the islands could not return. The government even outlawed the building of oceangoing vessels.

The isolation was not complete, however. The government did permit a few contacts with Korea and China. The Dutch, too, were allowed to keep a tiny trading post at Nagasaki. Two ships a year could unload their goods there.

Like Korea, Japan enforced its policy of isolation for 200 years. By the mid-1800s, however, the United States and the industrialized nations of Europe had begun to pressure Japan to open its ports to the world.

SECTION 2 REVIEW

1. **Identify:** (a) Tenno, (b) Prince Shotoku, (c) Heian, (d) kana, (e) Fujiwara, (f) Minamoto Yoritomo, (g) Hideyoshi, (h) Tokugawa Ieyasu.
2. **Define:** (a) samurai, (b) feudalism, (c) shogun, (d) daimyo.
3. (a) List three ways in which Chinese culture influenced Japan. (b) Give one example of how the Japanese adapted Chinese culture to their own traditions.
4. Describe the structure of Japanese feudal society.
5. How did the Tokugawa shoguns isolate Japan?
6. **Understanding Causes and Effects** (a) Why did the Tokugawa shoguns create the system of centralized feudalism? (b) How did this system produce economic and social changes?
7. **Writing Across Cultures** Like Japan, the United States has borrowed ideas from other cultures. List four examples of American cultural borrowing. Describe how each idea or item has been adapted to American use.

3

JAPANESE TRADITIONS

FIND OUT

What religious traditions shaped Japanese culture?

How did Confucian ideas influence the Japanese?

What values governed relationships in feudal Japan?

Vocabulary bushido

Mount Fuji, Japan's highest mountain, soars 12,389 feet (3,776 m) into the air. On one side, it rises directly from the sea. To the early Japanese, Mount Fuji was a sacred place, linking heaven and Earth. Japanese poet Yamabe No Akahito celebrated the beauty of the mountain in his poem "Looking at Mount Fuji in the Distance":

> "Since heaven and Earth parted,
> godlike, lofty, and noble
> in Suruga, Fuji the lofty peak—
> as I turn and look at the Plain of Heaven,
> the light of the coursing sun is hidden
> behind it,
> the shining moon's rays can't be seen,
> white clouds can't move, blocked
> and regardless of time, the snow's
> falling."

Respect for the beauty and power of nature is central to Japanese culture. These ideas are closely linked to Japan's religious traditions.

Religious Traditions

Two religious traditions, Shinto and Buddhism, have influenced the beliefs and practices of the Japanese. Because each religion met different needs, many Japanese followed both Shinto and Buddhist practices. Although it was not a religion, Confucianism also helped to shape Japanese ethics, or beliefs about right and wrong.

Shinto. Like many religions of early peoples, Shinto has neither sacred writings nor an organized set of beliefs. For centuries, it did not even have a name. When Buddhist missionaries reached Japan, it was they who called the local Japanese beliefs Shinto, or "the way of the gods."

The early Japanese believed that spirits, or kami, lived in everything from plants and animals to rocks and mountains. Spirits also controlled natural forces such as earthquakes and typhoons. Through prayer and offerings, the Japanese tried to win the favor of the kami. Peasants, for example, appealed to friendly spirits to send good harvests.

Shinto created a link between people and the awesome forces of nature. Shared beliefs

Shinto Shrine at Ise This temple complex dates from very early times. The Shinto shrine was dedicated to the sun goddess. Japanese emperors journeyed here to perform rites designed to ensure the nation's prosperity. Like most early temples, this shrine was constructed of wood. ***Culture*** What was the relationship between the sun goddess and the imperial family?

in the gods encouraged a sense of closeness among people and later helped to unite all of Japan. Shinto did not, however, answer questions about life after death or proper behavior. The Japanese had to turn to other religious traditions to find the answers to those questions.

Buddhism. In 552, the first of many Buddhist missionaries arrived in Japan. Buddhism gave the Japanese a new set of beliefs. It taught them about the cycle of birth and rebirth and the goal of enlightenment. It also taught that people could move closer to salvation through meditation and good deeds. Buddhism supported virtues such as friendliness and compassion.

By the time Buddhism reached Japan, it had divided into many sects. Commoners favored a sect that believed anyone could enter paradise through faith. The samurai followed Zen Buddhism, which came from China during the 1100s and 1200s. Zen Buddhism emphasized meditation and self-discipline as the way to achieve salvation. To the samurai, it offered a way to develop the mental and physical self-control that their way of life demanded. Zen also had a lasting influence on Japanese art, as you will read in Chapter 19.

Confucianism. Japanese visitors to China studied Confucian ideas. The Japanese adopted Confucian teachings about the five basic relationships and the duties and obligations of superior and inferior persons. (See page 330.) During the late 1600s, the Tokugawa shoguns placed new emphasis on the Confucian values of filial piety and loyalty to the ruler. Those ideas supported their efforts to unite Japan. The Tokugawa also stressed other Confucian virtues, such as hard work and the importance of education.

Family

Confucian traditions guided Japanese family life. Men were superior to women. Older brothers outranked their younger brothers. Family members owed complete obedience to the head of the household. His duty, in turn, was to provide for the family, give moral leadership, and protect the family honor.

In the Kitchen One woman cares for a child, while the other prepares the family's meal. Though considered to be socially inferior, Japanese women performed vital labor. Only women raised silkworms and wove silk cloth. They also worked in rice fields and on tea plantations. Some operated shops, small hotels, and teahouses.
Human Rights How was the role of women in Japan similar to that of women in China?

A man chose an heir, usually his eldest son, to succeed him. If he did not have a son, he might adopt an heir. That person might be his son-in-law or even the child of another family. An adopted son took his new family's name and honored its ancestors as his own.

Marriage. The head of the family arranged marriages for his children as well as for unmarried brothers and sisters. Marriages were family alliances, not love matches. At the time of marriage, a young woman became a part of her husband's family. Like an adopted child, she was expected to be loyal to her new family.

After marriage, a younger son might set up a separate branch of the family, but only with his family's permission. Although he might live apart in his own household, he shared the same ancestors and usually followed the same occupation as other family members.

Women. In ancient Japan, women had certain rights. Early records suggest that some clans had women leaders. Women could inherit property, and there were periods when empresses ruled Japan. As Confucian beliefs became more widespread, however, the status of women gradually declined.

At the Heian court, women still exercised some influence. Women like Murasaki Shikibu could read and write. In her diary, Murasaki recorded that she could read ancient Chinese texts faster than her brother. "If only you were a boy," sighed her father.

The frequent warfare of the feudal period brought great hardships to women. Because feudal Japan relied on men to fight, women were ignored. The wives of samurai were expected to show the same bravery and discipline as their husbands. Further, they had to sacrifice their comforts to serve their husbands and his lord.

Hard at Work These two women use a special device to prepare cotton for spinning, while the man at right carries bundles of cotton fiber. At the time this screen was painted, in the 1800s, many artisans belonged to craft guilds. These guilds limited the production of cloth and regulated prices. ***Technology*** Look at the pictures in this chapter and list other kinds of work artisans performed.

Feudal Traditions

Like the Chinese, the Japanese stressed loyalty to the family. However, they put a different emphasis on that bond. In China, loyalty to the family came before all other ties. In Japan, loyalty to one's feudal lord overshadowed family ties.

For more than 700 years, feudalism shaped Japanese society. Just as everyone in a family had a rank and duties to fulfill, so every class in feudal society had its rank and certain responsibilities.

Bushido. Throughout the centuries, the samurai class developed a code of behavior that came to be called bushido (BOO shee doh), "the way of the warrior." Bushido governed the relationship between a lord and his samurai. It emphasized loyalty above all else. A samurai supported his lord during times of both war and peace.

Bushido encouraged respect for other military virtues such as bravery, self-discipline, and honor. If a warrior brought dishonor to his lord or to his family, he was expected to perform an honorable penalty, that is, to commit *seppuku* (seh POO koo), or ritual suicide. In one tragic event in feudal Japan, 47 loyal samurai committed seppuku after killing the official who had wronged their feudal lord. Today, thousands of Japanese still visit the graves of these highly honored samurai.

Other feudal values. Although feudal culture emphasized military service and personal loyalty, the samurai were more than warriors. Especially during the Tokugawa era, samurai respected education and took pride in their artistic abilities. Samurai, for example, wrote poetry and spent hours producing fine calligraphy.

Lives of Commoners

In Tokugawa Japan, everyone had a well-defined place. Each of the three classes of commoners—peasants, artisans, and merchants—played a role within the larger social order. Peasants played a key role by supporting the samurai class. Artisans and merchants had lower status, but contributed to the economy.

The growing prosperity the Japanese experienced under the Tokugawa shoguns allowed some commoners to grow rich. Yet wealth did not improve a family's status. Nobles expected even wealthy peasants to show respect for people of higher rank. As daimyo and their samurai traveled to Edo, peasants along the road had to bow low. In 1649, the government issued an order forbidding peasants to wear silk clothes. Also, only nobles could carry two swords.

Artisans and merchants also had to show respect for their superiors. Merchants paid an annual fee to a daimyo, who, in turn, gave them permission to do business on their land. The daimyo also agreed to protect merchants during times of war.

Wealthy merchants could spend their money on luxuries and entertainment, though not on silk clothes. Some rich merchants married their daughters into the families of poor samurai. In that way, they tried to rise in society. The shoguns disapproved of such changes, however. As a result, they passed laws to protect the old social order.

SECTION 3 REVIEW

1. **Identify:** (a) Shinto, (b) Zen Buddhism, (c) seppuku.
2. **Define:** bushido.
3. (a) What were the basic beliefs of Shinto? (b) How did Buddhist sects followed by commoners and samurai differ?
4. How did Confucianism affect the Japanese family?
5. (a) What values did the samurai respect? (b) What restrictions governed the lives of commoners?
6. **Synthesizing Information** Choose three values or traditions and describe how they helped to ensure order in Japanese society.
7. **Writing Across Cultures** Make a list of 10 qualities that were admired in feudal Japan. Place a check beside the three that you think were most important. Then, rank these qualities in order of their importance in modern American society.

4 JAPAN BECOMES A WORLD POWER

FIND OUT

Why was Japan able to modernize rapidly after 1868?

How did Japan build an overseas empire?

How did Japanese expansion lead to war?

Vocabulary zaibatsu, militarism

Japanese leaders were expecting the foreigners. In 1853, four American warships anchored in Tokyo Bay. The American commander demanded that Japan open its ports to trade. Some Japanese favored upholding strict isolation. Others, like Lord Koroda, urged that Japan learn from the foreigners:

> "The condition of foreign states is not what it once was; they have invented the steamship and introduced radical changes in the art of navigation. They have also built up their armies . . . and risen to be formidable powers. If, therefore, we persistently cling to our outdated systems, heaven only knows what disaster may befall our Empire."

Under outside pressure, Japan finally ended 200 years of isolation. To defend itself against the foreigners, Japan chose to modernize by adapting western technology. As they had done over 1,000 years before (see page 394), the Japanese went abroad with the aim of borrowing from other cultures.

An End to Isolation

By the mid-1800s, western nations were competing to expand trade in Asia. In 1853, the United States sent a fleet commanded by

Perry's Visit A Japanese artist created this print to commemorate the American expedition of 1853. Below the world map, on which North America is labeled as California, is a procession of Americans. Admiral Perry, wearing a green polka-dot shirt, strides behind musicians and the ship's crew. ***Power*** Why did the shogun sign a treaty with the United States?

Commodore Matthew Perry. Perry's goal was to force Japan to end its policy of isolation.

Unequal treaties. The Japanese realized that their weapons were no match for Perry's cannons and steam-powered warships. In 1854, the shogun signed the Treaty of Kanagawa with the United States. It granted American ships the right to stop at two Japanese ports for supplies. It also gave the United States the right to send a diplomatic representative to Japan.

Before long, the United States and other western nations won additional rights. Like China, Japan had to sign "unequal treaties." Under these agreements, Japan had to give foreigners extensive trading rights as well as the right of extraterritoriality. (See page 345.) Many Japanese were angry that their leaders had signed these treaties.

Growing unrest. Even before Perry's arrival, people of all classes had become unhappy with Tokugawa rule. Wealthy merchants resented the strict laws that kept them in a lowly social position. At the same time, the growing money economy hurt the samurai class. To get more money, many samurai increased the taxes their peasants had to pay. High taxes only added to the general discontent.

Reform-minded samurai looked to the emperor at Kyoto as a symbol of a new order. They urged him to take his rightful place as Japan's ruler. In this atmosphere, feelings against foreigners and the shogun grew. Reformers took up the battle cry, "Honor the emperor and expel the barbarians."

Meiji restoration. In 1868, rebels forced the shogun to step down. They then restored the emperor to power. The 15-year-old emperor moved from Kyoto, the old imperial capital, to Tokyo, where the shogun had ruled. He called his reign Meiji (may jee), meaning "enlightened rule."

Under the Meiji restoration, samurai reformers set Japan on a new course. They realized that Japan had to modernize before it could "expel the barbarians." Their new motto became, "Enrich the country, strengthen the military." Meiji reformers then sent hundreds of Japanese to Europe and the United States to study western government, industry, and military organization.

A Visit to the "Western Barbarians"

"Even high-ranking officials do not show contempt towards men of lower classes. Neither do they act in a domineering manner. Therefore the ordinary people need not flatter high officials."

The lack of strict social class divisions surprised early Japanese visitors to the United States. In their diaries, they recorded this and other responses to the unfamiliar culture. Their comments reveal as much about themselves as about their hosts.

Notes on the president. In 1860, the president of the United States, James Buchanan, received the samurai diplomats on their first visit to the West. The Japanese noted that he "wore a simple black costume of coat and trousers in the same fashion as any merchant and had no decoration or sword on him." Some of the visitors approved of this informality. At the same time, they were amazed by the Americans' lack of respect for their founders. One young scholar, Fukuzawa Yukichi, noted:

> " One day, on a sudden thought, I asked a gentleman where the descendants of George Washington might be. He replied, 'I think there is a woman who is directly descended from Washington. I don't know where she is now, but I think I have heard she is married.' His answer was so very casual that it shocked me. "

Manners and customs. American social customs both bewildered and amused the visitors. At a hotel, they noticed that the floor was covered with "valuable carpets and rugs, which in Japan only the wealthy could buy." Yet Americans walked on this valuable carpet without removing their shoes! The Japanese also attended dances, where "the ladies and gentlemen seemed to be hopping about the room together." The visitors could barely keep from laughing at the hilarious sight, but they did not wish to appear rude.

Studying industry. Of course, a major purpose of the visit was to observe modern industry. At factories, the Japanese watched in awe as steam-powered machines cranked out goods. "The introduction of such machinery into our country," wrote a young Japanese, "would contribute greatly to the enhancement of our national interests."

Fukuzawa admired much of what he saw, but he was shocked at the enormous waste of iron:

> " In garbage piles, on the seashores—everywhere—I found lying old oil tins, empty cans, and broken tools. This was remarkable to us, for in Edo, after a fire, there would be hundreds of poor people swarming in the ruined district, looking for nails in the charred wood, so valuable was metal in Japan. "

Although they appreciated many American achievements, the Japanese ambassador himself noted that Americans lacked etiquette. "We had not entirely been wrong to call them western barbarians," he wrote. Still, he added, "I would forgive their impoliteness because of their friendliness." ■

Departing for the West This Japanese trade mission, shown here leaving Yokohama in 1871, spent nearly two years in Britain. A member of this mission described London in these words: "Black smoke rises to the sky from every possible kind of factory. . . . This is a sufficient explanation of England's wealth and strength." ***Choice*** Why did the Meiji government send missions abroad to study western ways?

Government Under the Meiji

Meiji leaders wanted to create a strong central government. They convinced the feudal lords to give up their power and return their lands to the state. In exchange, the daimyo received high positions in government.

The reformers wrote a constitution, which the emperor presented to the people in 1889. The constitution adapted western ideas to Japanese needs. It preserved the idea of imperial rule, however, and gave the emperor great power. At the same time, the constitution set up a two-house Diet, or parliament, modeled on the German system. The Diet had limited power, however.

Other reforms included a court and legal system that was based on European ideas. New laws abolished torture and set out rules regarding evidence and court procedures. The government also organized departments, such as ministries of education, finance, and the military. These departments undertook ambitious policies to increase education, set up a new tax system, and strengthen the military.

The new government was not intended to bring democracy to Japan. Its goal was to unite Japan and make it the equal of western powers.

Economic Modernization

While strengthening the government, the Meiji reformers also worked to modernize Japan's economy. They realized that Japan could compete with western powers only by industrializing.

To learn new technologies, Japanese students visited factories and shipyards in the West. Japan also invited foreign engineers and other experts to teach its people how to build railroads and make machines such as

Mitsui Bank in Tokyo After the Meiji restoration, the Mitsui family received permission to establish Japan's first private bank. Out of this main building in Tokyo, it operated 30 branches. This bank became the cornerstone of Mitsui, one of the most powerful companies in Japan. ***Change*** Why did Japan need to develop a modern banking system in order to build an industrial economy?

steam engines. The government improved ports, built weapons factories, and set up modern transportation and communications systems.

Need for capital. To raise money, the government continued to tax peasants and borrow from merchants. In addition, a natural disaster gave the economy an unexpected boost. During the 1860s, disease destroyed most of the silkworms in Europe. As a result, silk prices soared, and the Japanese silk industry boomed. Japanese silk makers used their profits to mechanize silk factories. Even after the European silk industry recovered, silk remained Japan's leading export.

The government aided industrial growth by building and equipping many factories and mills. To raise money for more reforms, it later sold these plants to private owners. While some business leaders were commoners, the most influential leaders came from former samurai families.

Zaibatsu. With government help, powerful families used traditional ties of loyalty and modern business methods to build huge companies. These large family organizations became known as zaibatsu (zī baht soo). By the late 1800s, zaibatsu controlled large parts of the economy.

The government encouraged cooperation rather than competition among companies. For example, Mitsubishi, a successful shipping company, merged with Mitsui in 1885. The giant new company that resulted could now compete with western shipping interests.

Social Changes

The Meiji reformers believed that modernization should include social changes. They abolished feudal classes and made everyone equal before the law. Samurai were forbidden to wear swords, a traditional symbol of their special privileges. Other laws required all men, rather than just the sons of samurai, to serve in the military.

Industrialization brought many changes to Japan. Millions of people moved from rural farms to take jobs in the cities. Many women began to work outside their homes, earning money in factories. By the early 1900s, almost half of all factory workers were women.

The government required all children to attend elementary school. Some went on to high school and college. As literacy increased, so did the number of newspapers and magazines. The press gained influence in shaping public opinion. New political parties were formed, and Japan took steps toward making its government more democratic. In the late 1800s, less than 4 percent of adults had the right to vote. By 1925, all Japanese men had that right. (Women did not win the right to vote until 1947.)

Japanese Expansion in Asia

By 1900, Japan had become a modern industrial nation. In a short time, it had rapidly absorbed western technology and built a well-governed society. Japan's rapid success was due in part to its strong sense of national unity and its tradition of self-sacrifice and hard work. These changes enabled Japan to negotiate new agreements with western nations, replacing the "unequal treaties" of the past.

Rivalry over Korea. Following the example of western nations, Japan set out to gain an overseas empire. It competed with China and Russia for influence in Korea. In 1895, Japan defeated China in a war and forced the Chinese to give up their claims to Korea. Japan also gained Taiwan, known as Formosa, and won the same special privileges in China that western nations enjoyed.

In 1904–05, Japan fought Russia in the Russo-Japanese War. The Japanese victory stunned western nations. For the first time in modern history, an Asian nation had defeated a major European power. The treaty ending the war forced Russia to leave Korea and gave Japan a foothold in Manchuria.

Benefits of expansion. By expanding, Japan sought equal political standing with western powers. It also gained scarce raw materials for its industries. These included coal and iron from China. During World War I, Japan took over Germany's holdings in northern China, setting the stage for further expansion.

Growth of Extreme Nationalism

During the 1920s, Japan benefited from years of peace and prosperity. Business leaders favored strengthening Japan by peaceful means rather than by military expansion. As a result, Japan backed international efforts to ensure world peace. It signed agreements with the United States and Britain to limit the size of their navies. Japan also reduced the size of its army.

Effects of depression. In 1929, the Great Depression began in the United States and spread around the world. Japan was also hit by this worldwide economic slowdown. Japan's prosperity depended heavily on trade, but the depression forced other countries to cut back on imports. In addition, many countries raised tariffs on imports to protect their own industries. Between 1929 and 1931, the value of Japanese exports fell by 50 percent. As Japan's trade declined, factories closed and unemployment rose.

The government's failure to solve the crisis led to domestic unrest. As elsewhere, extremist groups attracted large followings. In Japan, extreme nationalists argued that Japan should not have stopped its overseas expansion. They pointed out that western powers had grabbed a large part of the world. They also bitterly criticized the exclusion of Japanese immigrants by nations such as Australia and the United States.

Military dictatorship. Backed by extreme nationalists, military leaders, who had held a respected place in Japanese society since the days of the samurai, gained more power. In 1931, a group of army officers created a crisis in Manchuria, a province of China. They then used the crisis as an excuse to seize the entire region. Most Japanese approved of the conquest of Manchuria. When the prime minister opposed the move, he was assassinated.

During the 1930s, Japan gradually became a military dictatorship. The new leaders promoted militarism, the glorification of the military and a readiness for war. Military officers revived samurai traditions and emphasized loyalty to the emperor, Hirohito. They encouraged people to believe that Japan had a special mission in the world—to free Asian nations from western imperialism.

The War in the Pacific

During the 1930s, the military continued to expand into China. Some Japanese felt this expansion was necessary to protect Manchuria against the Chinese, who wanted to regain control of the region. The Japanese argued that they had won Manchuria in the same way that westerners had gained their colonies. They looked on China as both a source of raw materials and a market for Japanese goods. In 1937, the Japanese launched a major drive into China, forcing Chinese armies to retreat.

World War II begins. While Japan was conquering China, aggressive actions by Germany and Italy plunged Europe into World War II. In 1940, Japan joined an alliance, known as the Axis, with Germany and Italy. The opponents of the Axis, which included Britain, France, and the Soviet Union, were known as the Allies. As German armies overran France, Japanese forces seized the French colony of Indochina.

The United States responded to this latest Japanese expansion by cutting off oil and other supplies that were vital to Japan's military-industrial complex. Japanese diplomats then negotiated with the United States to avoid war. At the same time, the Japanese military was preparing for war. It planned a surprise attack to destroy the American fleet in the Pacific.

War against the United States. On December 7, 1941, Japanese planes bombed Pearl Harbor, Hawaii, the chief American naval base in the Pacific. The surprise attack destroyed or badly damaged eight battleships and killed more than 2,500 Americans.

The Japanese followed up this attack by conquering Hong Kong and much of Southeast Asia, including the Dutch East Indies, Burma, and the Philippines. The conquests gave Japan vital sources of raw materials, including rubber, oil, and tin. By 1942, Japan ruled a vast empire stretching from Southeast Asia across the western Pacific.

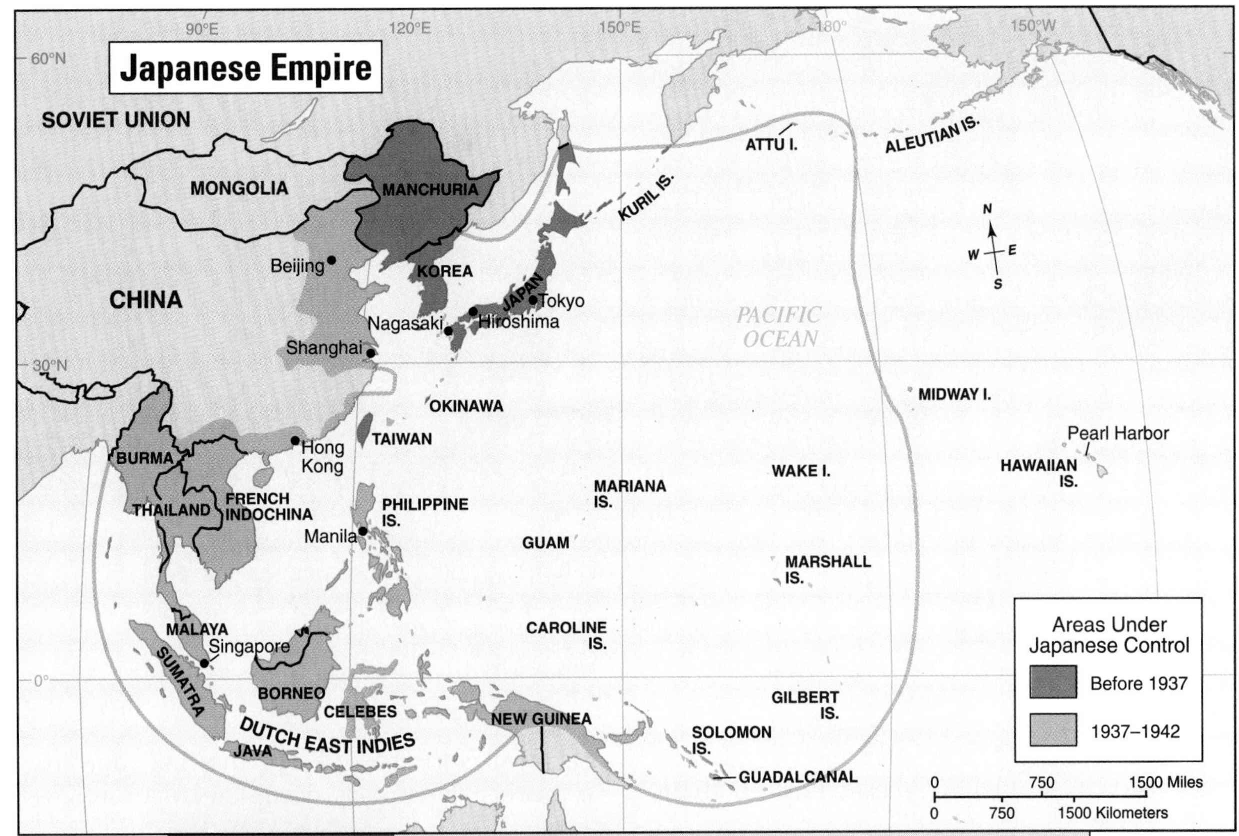

MAP STUDY

During World War II, Japanese forces conquered a vast empire in the Pacific. At its height in 1942, Japan's new colonial empire extended from Manchuria and Burma to islands off the coast of Alaska.

1. **Region** Name the three world regions in which Japan conquered lands that became part of its empire.
2. **Movement** (a) What conquered islands marked Japan's farthest advance into the southern Pacific? (b) What areas in mainland Southeast Asia did Japan conquer?
3. **Analyzing Information** The fighting in the Pacific between Japan and the Allies was called an "island-hopping" campaign. Why do you think this term was used to describe the conflict?

After the attack on Pearl Harbor, the United States joined the Allies. Allied forces rallied to slow the Japanese advance. By mid-1942, they had begun to turn the tide. In bitterly fought battles, the Americans forced the Japanese to retreat from one Pacific island after another.

From island bases in the Pacific, the United States began bombing Japan's cities. At the same time, American submarines destroyed Japanese ships carrying supplies to Japan from Southeast Asia and China. By early 1945, the Japanese economy had collapsed.

Defeat. After the defeat of Germany and Italy in Europe, the Allies called on Japan to surrender. Japan's military leaders refused. The United States then decided to use a deadly new weapon against Japan—the atomic bomb. On August 6, 1945, an American bomber dropped an atomic bomb on Hiroshima. The single bomb killed more than 80,000 people and leveled 42 square miles (109 sq

Nagasaki, Before and After The photo at left shows this port city in peacetime. The atomic bomb dropped on Nagasaki was more powerful than the bomb at Hiroshima. The devastation at Nagasaki is shown at right. Nearly 40,000 people were killed, and half of the city was destroyed. Today, the site where the bomb was detonated is a peace park. ***Choice*** Why was a second atomic bomb dropped on Japan?

km) of the city. Hiroko Nakamoto, who was 15 years old at the time, recalled the bombing of her city:

> "In one quick second, my world was destroyed. . . .
>
> Suddenly, from nowhere, came a blinding flash. It was as if someone had taken a flashbulb picture a few inches from my eyes. There was no pain then. Only a stinging sensation, as if I had been slapped hard in the face. I tried to open my eyes. But I could not. . . .
>
> I saw dead bodies all about me. The buildings were in ruins, and from the ruins I could hear people crying for help. But I could not help them. Some people were trying, as I was, to walk, to get away, to find their homes. I passed a streetcar that was stalled. It was filled with dead people."

In spite of the bombing of Hiroshima, the Japanese military government refused to surrender. Three days later, American planes dropped a bomb on Nagasaki, which killed more than 40,000 people. Finally, on August 14, Japan surrendered. For the first time in its history, Japan was occupied by a foreign power.

SECTION 4 REVIEW

1. **Locate:** (a) Manchuria, (b) Hiroshima, (c) Nagasaki.
2. **Identify:** (a) Treaty of Kanagawa, (b) Meiji, (c) Pearl Harbor.
3. **Define:** (a) zaibatsu, (b) militarism.
4. (a) Why did Japan decide to modernize? (b) What steps did it take to achieve this goal?
5. Why did Japan want an overseas empire?
6. What events led Japan into war with the United States?
7. **Understanding Causes and Effects** Describe economic factors that led to Japanese expansion and extreme nationalism.
8. **Writing Across Cultures** President Harry Truman said he decided to drop the atomic bomb on Japan in order to end the war and "shorten the agony of young Americans." Write a speech in which you either defend or criticize the bombing of Hiroshima and Nagasaki.

Chapter 18 Review

Understanding Vocabulary

Match each term at left with the correct definition at right.

1. feudalism	**a.** Japanese military lord
2. daimyo	**b.** glorification of the military and readiness for war
3. bushido	**c.** large family-business organizations
4. zaibatsu	**d.** system in which local lords are bound to higher lords by ties of loyalty
5. militarism	**e.** samurai code of behavior

Reviewing the Main Ideas

1. (a) What are the four main islands of Japan? (b) Describe two ways in which location has affected Japan.

2. What role did each of the following play in feudal Japan: (a) emperor, (b) shogun, (c) daimyo, (d) peasants, (e) merchants?

3. How did centralized feudalism under the Tokugawa shoguns unite Japan?

4. How did Buddhism develop in Japan?

5. Describe two reforms that were adopted by the Meiji leaders after 1868.

6. How did Japan win an overseas empire?

Reviewing Chapter Themes

1. Japan's development has been shaped in part by geography. Describe how two of the following features affected Japan: (a) landforms and climate, (b) geographic isolation, (c) scarcity of mineral resources.

2. During two different periods, the Japanese consciously borrowed ideas from other cultures and creatively adapted them to their own use. (a) Describe the two periods of cultural borrowing. (b) Give an example of creative borrowing from each period and explain how it affected Japan.

3. Confucian ideas and feudal values influenced Japanese culture for centuries. Describe how these systems affected two of the following: (a) government, (b) social relations, (c) family life.

4. In less than 50 years, Japan changed from an isolated nation of farmers into a major industrial power. Describe three effects of this rapid development on Japan and its relations with the world.

Thinking Critically

1. Comparing (a) How did centralized feudalism differ from early feudal society in Japan? (b) Describe one way in which they were similar.

2. Making Global Connections Review "A Visit to the 'Western Barbarians,'" on pages 402–403. (a) What did the Japanese visitors admire about American life? (b) What did they condemn? (c) What do these judgments reveal about Japanese ideas and values? (d) About American ideas and values?

Applying Your Skills

1. Analyzing Fiction Review the excerpt from *The Tale of Genji* on page 393. (a) According to this passage, what qualities were admired at court? (b) Do you think this novel is a reliable description of court life? Why or why not? (See Skill Lesson, page 239.)

2. Understanding Causes and Effects Construct a cause-and-effect chart for the overthrow of the Tokugawa shogunate. The chart should include both long-term and short-term causes and effects. (See Skill Lesson, page 628.)

Chapter 19

Japan Today

Osaka Skyline In Japan's third-largest city, high-rise buildings frame Osaka Castle, built by Hideyoshi, a powerful general, in the 1580s. He encouraged merchants to settle in Osaka by making the city his headquarters. Like the rest of Japan, Osaka preserved many reminders of the past as it modernized. ***Geography*** How did Osaka's location make it an important city?

Chapter Outline

Tradition demanded that the emperor write a poem at the end of each year. The year 1945, however, had brought only disaster. No "divine wind" arrived to save Japan from United States bombers. Millions of Japanese had died during eight years of war. Japanese cities lay in ruins, and the economy was at a standstill. For the first time in history, foreigners occupied Japan.

Emperor Hirohito wanted to reassure the Japanese people that although Japan had been beaten, it would recover. He wrote:

> "Under the weight of winter
> snow
> The pine tree's branches
> bend
> But do not break."

Like the pine tree in Hirohito's poem, Japan did not break. Indeed, by 1989, when Emperor Hirohito died, Japan had become a respected economic superpower. Besides the Japanese mourners, representatives from 163 nations attended the emperor's funeral. Among the 10,000 guests were kings, queens, prime ministers, and presidents.

CHAPTER PERSPECTIVE

During his 62-year reign, Emperor Hirohito witnessed many changes in Japan. At the outset, Japan acquired a vast overseas empire. Imperialist expansion led to a war that ended in the horrors of Hiroshima and Nagasaki. In the postwar years, Japan rebuilt its economy and introduced major social and political changes. The Japanese adapted western ideas and used them to enrich their own distinct culture.

As you read, look for these chapter themes:

- Since 1945, Japan has achieved a stable democratic government.
- Today, as in the past, Japan has selectively borrowed ideas and technologies from other cultures.
- As an economic superpower, Japan has worldwide influence, but its dependence on the world economy has increased.
- Today, Japanese culture blends both ancient and modern traditions.

Literature Connections

In this chapter, you will encounter passages from the following works.

"Under the Weight of Winter Snow," Emperor Hirohito

A Half Step Behind, Jane Condon

"Poverty's Child," Matsuo Basho

"Summer Grasses," Matsuo Basho

For other suggestions, see Connections With Literature, pages 804–808.

1

GOVERNMENT AND SOCIETY

FIND OUT

How did the American occupation affect Japan?

How did Japan build a democratic system?

What changes have shaped Japanese society since 1945?

Japan's surrender in 1945 left many Japanese feeling deeply betrayed. For years, their leaders had glorified Japanese military efforts and urged further sacrifices. In the end, however, those leaders had brought Japan not victory, as promised, but almost total destruction.

Out of the misery of defeat, the Japanese looked for a better future. In 1947, the new Japanese constitution expressed the people's goals for the future:

> "We, the Japanese people, desire peace for all time. . . . We desire to occupy an honored place in international society, striving for the preservation of peace, and the banishment of tyranny and slavery, oppression and intolerance, for all time from Earth."

During the years that followed, the Japanese worked to fulfill these goals.

Postwar Reforms

In 1945, the United States and its allies wanted to make sure that Japan would never again threaten world peace. In their view, the chief causes of the war were Japanese militarism, which had encouraged overseas expansion, and the Japanese tradition of undemocratic rule. The Allies appointed an American general, Douglas MacArthur, to command the occupation forces in Japan. Through MacArthur, they introduced sweeping reforms to destroy Japanese militarism and build a democratic government and society in Japan.

Ending militarism. To achieve the first goal, MacArthur disbanded the Japanese armed forces. At the same time, Japan's overseas empire was dismantled and its wartime military and civilian leaders put on trial. Those found guilty of war crimes were either imprisoned or executed.

Building democracy. Under MacArthur's guidance, the Japanese adopted a new constitution in 1947. The chief purpose of the constitution was to make Japan a democratic society. The constitution stripped the emperor of all his power. Instead, it gave power to the Diet, an elected legislature. (See Chapter 18.) The emperor remained as a figurehead, a symbol of national unity.

A key feature of the document was a list of rights, similar to the American Bill of Rights. It protected freedom of speech, religion, and the press. In addition, it gave women the right to vote, established the equality of men and women, and guaranteed the right of all Japanese to an equal education.

Finally, the constitution made it illegal for the Japanese to wage war. In the words of Article 9, "The Japanese people forever renounce war as a sovereign right." The constitution also forbade the Japanese government to maintain military forces.

In the past, large landowners and the zaibatsu had exercised great influence over the government. To make Japan more democratic, the Americans tried to weaken the power of these groups. The government passed land reform laws that required large landowners to sell their holdings to tenant farmers. Other laws divided the zaibatsu into smaller, separate companies.

Occupation ends. In 1952, the occupation forces withdrew from Japan, and the Japanese regained control of their own affairs. The Cold War helped bring about this change. In 1949, the Communists won power in China. The following year, the Korean War broke out. As a result, the United States came to look on Japan as a key ally in the battle against communism in Asia rather than as a former enemy.

Political Patterns

After 1952, the Japanese modified some of the reforms that had been introduced by the Americans. Unlike the Americans, the Japanese did not feel that large companies posed a danger. They saw the zaibatsu as partners in rebuilding the economy. As a result, the government permitted the zaibatsu to reorganize and even worked closely with them.

The Japanese have developed their own democratic processes. One political party, the Liberal Democratic party (LDP), dominated the Japanese government for 38 years. Differences among opposing political parties limited their ability to defeat LDP candidates. A series of scandals, however, finally toppled the LDP. In 1993 elections, the LDP failed to win a majority of seats in the Diet. A coalition government was formed. It promised political reform and stable foreign and economic policies.

Changing Social Patterns

During and after the occupation, Japanese society became more democratic. As you have read, women won the right to vote. In addition, the old military elite lost its power, and tenant farmers were able to buy the land they worked.

Family. Changes reached into the family as well. Today, for example, the head of the household no longer has legal authority over other family members. Nor can a man leave his entire estate to one child at the expense of his other children.

Arranged marriages based on family interests or social class are less common today than they were in the past. The present emperor, Akihito, for example, chose his own bride. Her family belonged to the business class. He met her while playing tennis.

Urbanization and economic growth have affected families, too. Today, about 76 percent of the Japanese people live in cities. Because

Dinner Time This family eats a meal in their small city apartment. They sit on the floor around a traditional low table, which uses space efficiently. Other space savers include bedrolls and movable screens to create separate areas. Some rooms may also have western-style furniture. ***Change*** How has westernization affected traditional patterns of life?

many people now live in tiny city apartments, the nuclear family has replaced the extended family. Often, older relatives remain on family farms while younger family members move to the cities. Also, the role of mothers has increased because of the long working hours of many Japanese men in urban society.

Despite the changes that have taken place, the family remains the center of Japanese life. It is there that children learn basic values such as discipline, hard work, harmony, and loyalty. (See Connections With Literature, page 806, "The Jay.")

Role of women. As you have read, the 1947 constitution gave Japanese women the same rights enjoyed by men. Traditional attitudes remain strong, however. Though both men and women have a hard time getting into the top universities, women have a harder time advancing and are paid less than men once they enter the work force.

Still, almost half of Japan's workers today are women. Most work in factories or as waitresses, salespeople, clerks, or secretaries. The situation is changing rapidly, however. Increasing numbers of women are completing college and entering professions. Masako Owada, who married Japan's crown prince in 1993, studied at several universities and had a career in international relations. Other women have advanced in politics. In 1993, Japan's Diet elected its first woman speaker.

One out of every three Japanese working women is an OL, or "office lady." Every day, in offices and factories throughout Japan, these women answer phones, greet customers, and pour tea. Most Japanese think of OLs as young, single women who take on the job because of the freedom it gives them. Today, however, many OLs are married women with children. They work because their family needs the income. Like Takahashi Etsuko, most of these women have two jobs—one at the office and one at home.

Life of an "Office Lady"

Every morning at 6:30 A.M., Takahashi Etsuko gets up and makes breakfast for her husband and three-year-old son. When breakfast is over and she has prepared lunch boxes for her family, she takes her son to her mother's house across the street. Then, at exactly 8:05 A.M., Takahashi climbs into the family car. Ten minutes later, her husband drops her off at a nearby soy-sauce factory, where she works as an OL.

After changing into her crisp blue company uniform, Takahashi starts work. She tidies the office and brews tea for the men who work there.

“ We have seven girls and eighteen men in my section. The OLs are supposed to start cleaning the room from 8:30, but I get there a little early, so I start dusting and wiping off desks as soon as I've changed into my uniform. And I serve tea. My hours are 8:30 to 5:00. ”

Takahashi joined the company at age 18. At age 30, her duties are mainly the same. Besides dusting and pouring tea, she does general office work such as typing and filing. Over the years, her pay has been raised and her responsibilities have increased. She has no hope for promotion, however. "I could never be a manager," she says. In Takahashi's mind, managing is men's work.

After work, Takahashi drives home with her husband. She prepares dinner, washes the dishes, and unrolls the futons, or beds. At last, when their son is asleep, she has a cup of coffee and talks with her husband. She still has laundry to do, however, and often talks while she is hanging out the wash on the balcony or doing the ironing. "I'd like my husband to help with the housework, but he doesn't," she says. "That's natural with husbands, isn't it?"

An "Office Lady" at Work The Japanese are hard workers who put in many overtime hours, sometimes without pay. Women such as "office ladies" are essential to the labor force. However, women are paid only half the wages received by men doing the same jobs. ***Choice*** Why would employees work extra hours without pay?

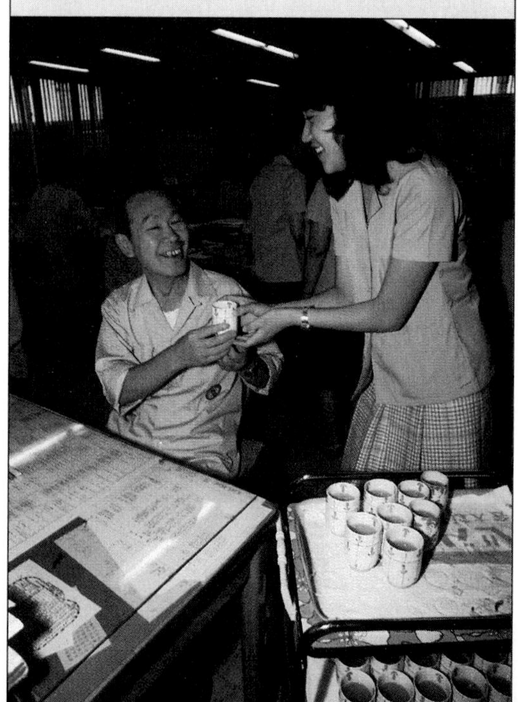

Like most Japanese, Takahashi works on Saturdays. Sunday, her day off, is reserved for housecleaning, grocery shopping, and visiting her parents and other family members. Takahashi wishes she had more time for herself. She would also like to spend more time with her son. In the meantime, however, she tries to make the best of her situation. As she explains:

“ What I really want is to do two jobs well: at home and at the office. I'm trying to do both perfectly. ” ■

Education

Once Takahashi's son starts school, she will have the additional responsibility of helping him to succeed. Japanese families firmly support education, and every child has the chance to attend school. During the occupation, the Americans set up a school system like the one in the United States. Accordingly, all children had to attend school for at least nine years. Today, more than 94 percent of Japanese students complete high school, and about 40 percent go on to college.

In Japan, the competition to get into the best schools is fierce. Indeed, many students attend *juku,* special "cram" schools that prepare them to take the entrance exams for elite high schools or universities. A diploma from a top university such as Tokyo University—called simply Todai by the Japanese—is the key to success in business and government.

Western Influences

Western styles and customs, which had begun to appear in Japan before World War II, gained popularity after the war. More and more Japanese adopted western clothing, filled their homes with western appliances, and turned to western forms of entertain-

Accepted! Friends celebrate with a high school senior who has just been accepted at Tokyo University. Getting into a top university requires very intensive study. Yet students know that when they graduate from a good university, they will be successful in society. ***Culture*** Why is it so important for a Japanese student to be accepted by a school like Tokyo University?

ment. In addition, as the economy prospered, many Japanese traveled abroad, where they developed a strong taste for western ideas and products.

SECTION 1 REVIEW

1. Identify the two main goals of the American occupation of Japan.
2. How did the 1947 constitution help build democracy in Japan?
3. How did the Cold War affect relations between Japan and the United States?
4. (a) Describe three ways in which Japanese society changed after 1945. (b) List three values that survived from earlier times.
5. **Analyzing Information** Japan's new constitution in 1947 declared that men and women were equal. Has this guarantee been carried out? Explain.
6. **Writing Across Cultures** Write a description of one way Japan's constitution is different from the United States Constitution and one way it is similar to it.

2 ECONOMIC GROWTH

FIND OUT

How did Japan rebuild its economy after World War II?

What factors helped Japan to become an economic superpower?

What challenges does the Japanese economy face today?

Twice a year, delivery trucks loaded with gifts rumble through the streets of Tokyo and other major Japanese cities. The gifts include candy, imported fruits, and other delicacies. During gift-giving season, employees give presents to their supervisors, students bring gifts to their teachers, and large companies send gifts to important customers. The gifts show appreciation for daily services and for special favors. Although the gifts are usually not expensive, they are always beautifully wrapped and thoughtfully chosen.

Centuries ago, strict rules governed the giving of gifts. Today, those rules have relaxed somewhat, but the custom of gift giving survives. In Japan, a gift given at the right time builds loyalty and friendship. These values play an important role in the way the Japanese do business.

The Economic Miracle

After World War II, Japan, with American aid, set out to rebuild its shattered economy. The government at first guided the development of basic industries and then helped develop more advanced industries. The Korean War, which took place in the early 1950s, helped to stimulate economic growth. Japan sold $4 billion worth of supplies to United Nations forces fighting in Korea.

During the 1950s and 1960s, Japan's economy raced ahead. Most factories had been totally rebuilt with the latest technology imported from abroad. As a result, Japanese factories outproduced the older factories of the United States. The Japanese recaptured old markets and opened new ones. This rapid recovery is often called the Japanese economic miracle.

From the 1960s through the 1980s, the Japanese economy experienced almost uninterrupted expansion. In the early 1990s, however, a severe economic slowdown occurred. Despite this, Japan is an economic superpower with worldwide influence. Its products dominate markets in many parts of the world.

Industrial Development

Before World War II, Japan was the most industrialized nation in Asia. After the war, the Japanese were determined to regain their economic position.

Japan built a diversified industrial economy geared both toward exports and its home market. At first, the Japanese rebuilt industries such as textiles in which they had been strong before the war. When they encountered stiff competition from textile manufacturers in other parts of Asia, however, they moved some factories to South Korea, Taiwan, Hong Kong, and Singapore, where wages were lower than they were in Japan.

During the 1960s, the Japanese further boosted economic growth by developing heavy industry. Japan turned its lack of natural resources into an advantage. It combed the world for the cheapest sources of iron, coal, and other raw materials. Then, using these imported materials, it moved ahead to become the world's leading shipbuilder and a major steel producer.

The oil shock. As Japan's economy expanded, it became increasingly dependent on oil imports. Then, in 1973, the Organization of Petroleum Exporting Countries (OPEC) quadrupled the price of oil. Japan experienced an oil "shock" as soaring oil prices almost brought its economic boom to a halt.

The Japanese responded to the crisis by increasing conservation efforts. With a long tradition of thrift and careful use of resources, the Japanese were able to reduce their consumption of oil. They increased the number of nuclear power generators and used more non-petroleum fuels.

Shift to high-tech industries. The oil crisis spurred another change. The Japanese shifted from industries that used large amounts of energy to new, "high-tech" industries based on highly specialized technologies, such as electronics. Since the 1970s, Japan has become the leading producer of televisions, radios, videocassette recorders (VCRs), compact disc (CD) players, and stereo equipment.

Also, during the oil crisis the Japanese developed fuel-efficient cars that soon found buyers around the globe. Today, Japan is the world's largest producer of automobiles. One out of three automobiles bought in the United States was made in Japan.

Electronic Traffic Reports A small computer screen provides drivers with up-to-date traffic news. Japan's electronics industry exports nearly half of its output and is the most profitable segment of its economy. Japanese-owned factories in other Asian nations manufacture many of these electronics products. ***Change*** Why did Japan change its emphasis from heavy industry to high-tech industry?

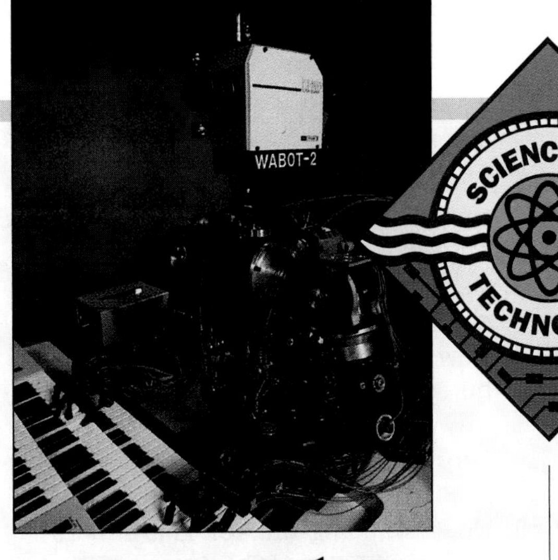

Japan's Robots Come to Life

In the fish section of a Tokyo supermarket, a "sushi robot" methodically molds rice balls. A human worker tops the rice with a strip of raw fish. The robot then wraps the finished product—a popular Japanese food known as sushi—in cellophane and places it on a conveyor belt that carries it to the selling floor.

In a single day, the sushi robot, assisted by eight human helpers, makes 8,000 pieces of sushi. "This volume of business would not have been possible without the robot," says manager Fusada Kohji. "One sushi chef could never make 8,000 pieces, and hiring two or three chefs would not have been profitable."

The sushi robot is a forerunner of a new generation of Japanese robots. Since the 1970s, the Japanese have pioneered the use of industrial robots to perform repetitive tasks in factories. Today's researchers, however, are building more advanced robots. In particular, the new robots are intended for jobs that are dangerous or for which there is a shortage of workers.

Some new-style robots are already at work. In Tokyo, a fire-department robot measures temperatures in burning rooms, checks for toxic gases, and searches for victims. In Osaka, "robo-cops" print out local maps and give directions in tinny voices in both Japanese and English. In Japan's construction industry, where there is a severe shortage of human workers, robots have proved to be invaluable.

The Japanese companies that built these "smart machines" are now working on an even more ambitious project—a service-oriented, humanlike robot for use in homes and hospitals. Creating such a robot, which must be kind and gentle as well as functional, "is much more difficult than making one for a nuclear power plant," says one researcher. Still, Waseda University's Kato Ichiro predicts that Japan will have such a robot within another 10 to 15 years. Eventually, he prophesies,

> "People will be able to live like people by turning robots humanlike and using them in place of humans working like robots."

1. How are Japan's new robots different from the first generation of robots?
2. **Synthesizing Information** (a) What kind of work are the new robots being designed to perform? (b) Why do you think the Japanese want robots to do these jobs?

Reasons for Success

Japan's success in the years following World War II can be traced to several causes. Since the Meiji period, Japan has borrowed western technology and improved on it. For example, Japanese companies bought the rights to the VCR technology developed by American companies, improved it, and produced easy-to-use, affordable VCRs.

To remain competitive, the Japanese have encouraged their own inventors. High-speed color printers, CD players, and floppy disks for computers are among Japan's best-selling inventions.

Traditional values such as loyalty and hard work have contributed to productivity. Employers and employees work as a team. Workers rarely change companies. The companies, in turn, do their best to reward this loyalty.

Respect for education, too, has played a role in creating a skilled work force. In addition, businesses have benefited because Japanese workers save a large percentage of their income. As a result, Japanese banks have money to lend to businesses. Also, because Japan spends little on defense, it has money to develop new industries.

Close ties between business and government have further helped Japanese companies. The government gives businesses special tax breaks and loans. In addition, Japanese businesses cooperate among themselves. Groups of businesses that have common interests form alliances to share information and plan for the future. Agricultural production has also been protected by high tariffs, which help shut out foreign competitors.

Challenges for the Future

Today, Japan is a prosperous country that enjoys one of the world's highest standards of living. However, with industrial growth has come air, water, and noise pollution. Urbanization and limited space have created incredible overcrowding in cities like Tokyo.

Japan also faces a serious labor shortage. This is due in part to an aging population and a low birth rate. To ease the labor shortage, Japan is encouraging more women to take jobs outside the home and is building factories abroad where it can hire foreign workers. It is also using robots and other mechanical "workers." (See the feature on page 417.)

Japan's aging population will need costly services. Many Japanese workers have limited retirement benefits. In the past, children took care of their aging parents, but today many children are unable to do so. The government has begun to provide pensions for disabled and retired workers, nursing homes, and medical care.

SECTION 2 REVIEW

1. What was Japan's economic miracle?
2. How did the Japanese build their economy after World War II?
3. Describe three reasons for Japan's economic success.
4. How has industrial growth both helped and hurt Japan?
5. (a) Why does Japan face a serious labor shortage? (b) What steps are the Japanese taking to solve this problem?
6. **Understanding Causes and Effects** (a) Why did the 1973 increase in oil prices have such a strong impact on Japan? (b) What steps did Japan take to avoid another oil shock?
7. **Writing Across Cultures** Jot down a list of items in your house that were made in Japan. Write a generalization about the kinds of products Japan produces for export.

3

JAPAN AND THE WORLD

FIND OUT

What concerns have shaped Japan's foreign policy?

How is Japan linked to the global economy?

What issues have strained Japan's relations with its trading partners?

What issues affect Japan's relations with its Asian neighbors?

Vocabulary pacifism, trade imbalance, reparations

A Japanese boy returned home from his first trip to the United States. He told his friends about life in California: *"America ni mo Makudonarudo ga aru!"* "Even in America, they have McDonald's!"

Interaction between Japan and other cultures has reached an amazing level. The Japanese have absorbed the foods and styles of many nations. At the same time, the names of Japanese producers—Sony, Toyota, Nikon—are known throughout the world.

Security and Defense

In reaction to World War II, the Japanese embraced a policy of pacifism, or opposition to the use of force under any circumstances. As you have read, the 1947 Japanese constitution renounced war and forbade the government to maintain a military force.

For protection, Japan aligned itself with the United States. As Cold War tensions grew, the United States urged Japan to build its own defensive forces and to rearm. Japan's economy had recovered, and Americans felt that it was only fair for the Japanese to share in the cost of their own defense. Japan resisted the pressure to rearm. In time, however, it did set up a Self-Defense Force despite widespread objections among the Japanese.

Some Japanese feared that alliance with the United States might drag their country into war. In 1960, violent protests broke out when Japan and the United States negotiated a Mutual Security Treaty. During the late 1960s, many Japanese bitterly protested the Vietnam War. They compared American activities in Vietnam with Japan's own efforts to conquer China during the 1930s.

During the 1970s and 1980s, international concerns slowly shifted away from the Cold War. Increasingly, attention focused on Japan's place in the global trading network. Still, international conflicts such as the Persian Gulf War created problems for Japan. In 1990, the United States established a multinational force to oppose Iraq's invasion of Kuwait. (See Chapter 28.) When asked to support the alliance, Japan agreed to send money but did not send troops.

Antiwar Demonstrators Both left-wing and right-wing groups have criticized government policies in Japan. The protesters shown here attacked Japan's support of the United States during the Vietnam War. Conservatives have opposed Japan's modernization as a threat to traditional culture. ***Citizenship*** Why might the Japanese have opposed the Vietnam War?

Japan and the Global Economy

Japan has carved out a unique place for itself in the global economy. In the past, it borrowed and then adapted ideas, first from China and later from the West. Today, people from both western and nonwestern nations are traveling to Japan. They are eager to study Japanese business methods and to learn from Japan's successes.

Interdependence. Foreign trade is critical to Japan's general prosperity. Japan imports most of its energy resources, including oil from the Middle East. It buys food from the United States, Canada, and Australia. In exchange, Japan exports a variety of manufactured goods.

Because trade is central to the country's economic well-being, Japan's foreign policy has focused on trade issues. It has sought favorable trading terms with its neighbors in Asia as well as with developed nations in the West. Japan is particularly sensitive to issues that might affect shipping or the availability of resources.

The trade imbalance. One issue that is of concern today is the trade imbalance between

Japan's Trade Lifeline The rows of trucks awaiting export, at left, and stacks of imported Canadian lumber, at right, show how important foreign trade is to Japan. Japan must import many raw materials, but the high value of its exports provides the nation with a favorable balance of trade. ***Interdependence*** Why do nations want to export more than they import?

Japan and its trading partners, including the United States and the nations of Western Europe. This trade imbalance has occurred because Japan exports more goods to those nations than it imports from them.

Japan's success in selling goods abroad has created frustration and anger among its competitors. They complain that Japan's success is the result of unfair trade policies. They argue, for example, that Japan profits from the fact that most nations have few barriers to trade. Yet, Japan's home markets have been very difficult for foreign competitors to reach.

Foreign companies complain that complex Japanese licensing and customs rules prevent them from doing business in Japan. In addition, the close ties among Japanese businesses and the deeply ingrained attitude of "we Japanese" against "the foreigners" have made it difficult for outsiders to compete with Japan.

Leaders from the industrial nations have met to discuss ways to close the trade gap. Under pressure, Japan has made some efforts to ease trade barriers and increase imports.

Aid to developing nations. As an economic superpower, Japan has faced criticism for doing little to help less-developed nations. In response, the government set up a Peace Corps. Under this program, the Japanese help people in developing nations to gain skills in modern technology and farming methods. Japan has also brought students from developing nations to study at its universities and has provided economic aid to these countries.

Japan and Its Asian Neighbors

In the past, most of Japan's trade was carried on with Asian nations. After World War II, it gradually rebuilt that trade. In doing so, it had to overcome the bitterness and hostility of countries that suffered during the Japanese invasion and conquest. Today, Japan is the major trading partner of many East Asian and Southeast Asian nations. (See the chart on page 285.) This gives it a position of influence in the Pacific Rim, a region of the world that is undergoing a major economic expansion.

China. To Japan, China represents a huge untapped market. Because of Japan's close ties to the United States during the Cold War, it did not recognize the People's Republic of China until 1972. Today, Japan has undertaken joint economic ventures with the Chinese and has invested more in China than any other industrial nation.

Korea. In the mid-1990s, the uncertainties raised by the death of North Korean leader Kim Il Sung and North Korea's nuclear program posed possible threats to Japan's security. In addition, Japan's relations with both North and South Korea remain strained. Koreans have not forgotten the hardships of Japanese colonial rule. They also resent the discrimination experienced by Koreans living in Japan. Despite these tensions, Japan and South Korea have extensive trade ties.

South Korea and the other Asian "tigers," Taiwan, Hong Kong, and Singapore, have modeled their own economic development on that of Japan. As a result, they have become major competitors of Japan.

Soviet Union. Japan and the Soviet Union long disagreed over the fate of the Kurile Islands, north of Hokkaido. The Soviet Union seized the islands in 1945. After the breakup of the Soviet Union in 1991, Japan continued to negotiate with the Russian Federation to settle the territorial dispute. It also established contacts with other former Soviet republics to develop joint projects. Japan sees much economic opportunity in the region.

Southeast Asia. Southeast Asian nations still distrust Japan, despite extensive Japanese investment in the region. Many nations feel that Japan is using its economic power to dominate the region. For example, Japan provided reparations, or payments for damages, to nations it conquered during World War II. The payments, however, were made not in cash but with Japanese goods. To many Southeast Asians, that policy showed that the Japanese were more interested in promoting their own industries than in making up for the damage they had done.

Japan is sensitive to such criticisms, and it has made efforts to be a good neighbor. The Japanese government has provided billions of dollars in loans and grants to Southeast Asian nations. At the same time, it has helped Japanese companies to invest in the region.

Japanese Store in Hong Kong Sogo, a Japanese firm based in Osaka, owns a chain of department stores. As businesses profited from Japan's "economic miracle," many branched out into foreign countries. They invested not only in Asian nations but in Europe and the United States. ***Power*** Why do Korea and some other Asian nations resent Japan's investment in their countries?

SECTION 3 REVIEW

1. **Define:** (a) pacifism, (b) trade imbalance, (c) reparations.
2. (a) Why did Japan rely on the United States for military protection after World War II? (b) Why did some Japanese protest the alliance with the United States?
3. Explain the role that trade has played in Japan's economy.
4. (a) Describe the trade imbalance that exists between Japan and its trading partners. (b) Why do many nations blame Japan for the trade imbalance?
5. Describe two issues that affect relations between Japan and its Asian neighbors.
6. **Defending a Position** Does an economic superpower like Japan have an obligation to provide aid to developing nations? Give reasons for your answer.
7. **Writing Across Cultures** Some American businesses have urged our government to restrict imports from Japan in order to protect American industry. Write an editorial defending or opposing such a move.

4 LITERATURE AND THE ARTS

FIND OUT

What traditions have shaped the arts in Japan?

How does Japanese culture today blend old and new traditions?

How have Japanese artistic traditions influenced other cultures?

Vocabulary haiku, Kabuki

Tucked away in a garden off a crowded street sits a traditional tea hut. The doorway is so low that guests must enter on their hands and knees. Doing so shows humility, one of many traditional values involved in Japan's ancient tea ceremony.

Inside, the tea master and a few guests sit on the floor of a small, bare room. The fragrance of incense fills the air. The tea master, following elaborate, age-old rules, prepares the tea. The guests sip the tea slowly. They comment on the beauty of a scroll painting and on the flower arrangement, which are the only decorations in the room.

Even in the rush of modern city life, the tea ceremony remains popular in Japan. Business executives and housewives find the slow, formal ritual relaxing. For a few hours, they put aside everyday problems in order to refresh their senses and nourish their souls.

Deeply rooted in the Japanese culture is an appreciation of beauty and simplicity. Today, as in the past, these traditions help to mold and enrich Japanese life.

Visual Arts

Like other aspects of Japanese life, the visual arts reflect a variety of local and foreign traditions. Shinto beliefs about the forces of nature, Buddhist teachings about the impermanence of life, and western styles have all played a role in shaping the arts of Japan.

Chinese influence. During the great period of cultural borrowing from China, the Japanese learned a variety of skills in painting, architecture, and the decorative arts. The Japanese, however, adapted these art forms to their own circumstances. The Chinese preferred art that was massive, evenly balanced, and realistic. In their crowded cities and limited rural spaces, the Japanese created art styles in miniature.

Zen traditions. During the feudal period, you will recall, many samurai adopted the values of Zen Buddhism. Zen emphasized simplicity, self-discipline, and closeness to nature. In accordance with Zen teachings, artisans and artists learned to suggest an idea, a thought, or a feeling with a minimum of detail. A few bold lines, for example,

A Tea Ceremony Because serving tea is an ancient ceremony, traditional kimonos are often worn. This ritual continues to be popular because it is a time when all social barriers are relaxed. All participants, no matter what their status in society, must follow the same formal customs. ***Culture*** What traditional values are part of the tea ceremony?

could suggest to the viewer the artist's impression of a mountain. A tiny garden could be created with sand, a single rock, and a twisted tree.

Zen taught that beauty can be found in ordinary objects and in daily tasks. Those ideas influenced such Japanese traditions as landscape gardening, flower arranging, and the elaborate tea ceremony. Even today, the Japanese can transform a bowl of flowers or a plate of food into a work of art.

Woodblock prints. During the Tokugawa period, Japanese artists developed new styles that reflected the interests and tastes of the growing middle class. Among the best-known works of this period are brilliantly colored

Mount Fuji The artist Hokusai made this woodblock print of Mount Fuji in the early 1800s. Mount Fuji is Japan's highest mountain, and it was long considered to be a sacred place. The beauty and unusual composition of woodblock prints influenced many western artists. ***Fine Art*** How was this woodblock print probably created?

woodblock prints of city life called *ukiyoe* (OO kih yah yeh). During the late 1800s, ukiyoe influenced art styles in Europe.

Unlike many art forms, ukiyoe was not the work of a single person. Instead, an artist worked with a woodcarver, a colorist, a printer, and a publisher to produce multiple copies of the finished woodblock print. Today, most Japanese printmakers work on their own, but they add traditional themes to their work.

Decorative arts. In the decorative arts, the Japanese borrowed from the Chinese but displayed their own genius in developing distinct new styles. The Chinese, and later the Europeans, imported Japanese lacquerware, porcelain, folding fans, screens, and swords.

Literature

The Japanese have an ancient tradition in literature. In the Heian court, men and women competed to write elegant poetry. There, too, Murasaki Shikibu wrote the world's first great novel. Through the story of Prince Genji and his children, *The Tale of Genji* captures the complex human relationships of Japanese court life.

Poetry. Since early times, the Japanese have used poetry to express emotions and create a particular mood. Among the samurai, the ability to write fine poetry was valued as highly as skillful sword handling.

By the 1700s, the haiku (HĪ koo) had become the most popular type of poem. A haiku is a short poem of only 17 syllables, divided into three lines of five, seven, and five syllables each. Using just a few words, the haiku poet suggests an entire range of feelings or ideas. Although the images appear to be simple, they may carry several levels of meaning. (See Connections With Literature, page 806, Selected Haiku.)

Matsuo Basho ranks among Japan's greatest poets. In his haiku, he used the first two lines to set a scene and the last line to give the poem a larger meaning. In the following haiku, for example, Basho captures the soothing effect of nature on the human spirit by contrasting the image of a boy grinding rice with his observation of the moon:

> “Poverty's child—
> He starts to grind the rice
> And gazes at the moon.”*

The Japanese still place great value on poetry. Each year, many people enter the national poetry-writing contest, contributing short poems on a given theme. The winners' poems are read aloud before the emperor. He, in turn, contributes his own poem.

Fiction. Japanese writers have continued to develop fiction since the days of Murasaki. After the Meiji restoration, Japanese writers began to read western literature. They experimented with new ideas and forms. At the same time, they often looked back to Japanese traditions for the subjects of their novels and short stories.

Today, people in the United States and Europe read the works of many Japanese writers in translation. Kawabata Yasunari was the first Japanese to receive the Nobel Prize for literature. His novels, which include *Snow Country* and *The Sound of the Mountain,* are distinguished by a masterful use of imagery.

Performing Arts

Japanese audiences have been enjoying music, dance, and drama for at least 600 years. Many traditional forms of theater are still popular today.

No plays. The No (noh) play, the oldest surviving form of Japanese theater, originated during the 1300s. No plays combine music, dance, and acting to communicate religious themes. Wearing traditional masks and elaborate costumes, the actors slowly move about a nearly bare stage in highly stylized ways that suggest emotions or events. A seated chorus chants the story as musicians solemnly beat drums and play bamboo flutes. The No play has almost no plot and unfolds without much action. During intermission, other

---

* This is a translation. Like all haiku, this one has 17 syllables in the original Japanese.

Kabuki Actor In Kabuki theater, actors wear colorful costumes and fantastic, masklike makeup. During the performance, actors address the audience directly and often make their costume changes onstage. A Kabuki actor usually comes from a family of performers and often starts training for the theater as a child.
Culture Why do you think Kabuki became more popular than No plays?

actors performing short comical skits known as *kyogen* provide comic relief. (See Connections With Literature, page 806, "The Deserted Crone.")

Kabuki. During the 1500s and 1600s, livelier forms of entertainment developed in the cities. One of these was *bunraku,* or puppet theater. The other was Kabuki, exciting and colorful dramas that dealt with themes such as love and revenge.

Unlike No plays, Kabuki requires elaborate stage settings. The costumes and makeup are also spectacular. Dancing, acrobatics, and swordplay add to the excitement. Kabuki does share some features of No, however. For example, as with the No drama, a Kabuki chorus chants the story with musical accompaniment. Also, in both No and Kabuki, male actors play female as well as male roles.

Popular Culture Today

Although traditional arts, literature, and theater have a firm place in Japan today, Japanese spend their leisure time watching television, going to the movies, or attending sports events. The Japanese enjoy many of the same television shows and movies as do people in the United States. Other popular programs, however, have Japanese themes and re-create important events in Japanese history.

Rooftop Golf Japan has few golf courses since space is so limited and land is so expensive. These players enjoy a game on a rooftop putting green provided by their employer. Baseball, too, faces a similar problem. With little space for athletic fields, local teams often play their games on the grounds of temples or shrines. ***Scarcity*** Why is open space so limited in Japan?

Japan's best-known movie director is Kurosawa Akira (koo roh SAH wah ah KEE rah). In *The Seven Samurai,* he re-creates the exciting story of warriors who defend a village against bandits. Kurosawa's filming techniques—especially his epic battle scenes—have inspired both European and American directors.

Reading is a popular pastime in Japan, especially for long-distance commuters. Bestsellers include comic books, which are read by adults as well as children. The Japanese devour the adventure and love stories portrayed in these picture books. Indeed, booksellers chalk up sales of more than 5 million comic books each week.

Today, styles and ideas are just as likely to spread from Tokyo to New York and Paris as in the other direction. The Japanese have adopted many western sports, such as baseball, golf, skiing, and volleyball. On the other hand, sushi bars, certain architectural styles, and landscape gardening are popular Japanese "exports" to the West. Japanese musicians perform in orchestras all over the world. Japanese designers rival the French, Italians, and Americans in the world of fashion.

SECTION 4 REVIEW

1. **Identify:** (a) Matsuo Basho, (b) Kawabata Yasunari, (c) Kurosawa Akira.
2. **Define:** (a) haiku, (b) Kabuki.
3. (a) What Zen values influenced Japanese artists? (b) How did the growth of a middle class affect the arts?
4. Give some examples of how Japanese culture today reflects both old and new ideas.
5. What is one similarity and one difference between No and Kabuki theater?
6. Give two examples of the influence Japan has had on the arts of other cultures.
7. **Synthesizing Information** Reread the following statement from the beginning of Section 4: "Deeply rooted in Japanese culture is an appreciation of beauty and simplicity." Select one of the art forms discussed in the section and explain how it illustrates this statement.
8. **Writing Across Cultures** Review the discussion of haiku on page 424. Then, using the haiku on that page as an example, write a haiku expressing an aspect of American life.

Chapter 19 Review

Understanding Vocabulary

Match each term at left with the correct definition at right.

1. pacifism
2. reparations
3. trade imbalance
4. haiku
5. Kabuki

a. 17-syllable poem
b. situation that occurs when one nation exports more goods than it imports
c. form of Japanese theater
d. opposition to the use of force
e. payment for damages

Reviewing the Main Ideas

1. How did the United States influence Japan after World War II?
2. (a) What steps did the Japanese take to rebuild their economy after 1945? (b) How did traditional values help Japan's recovery?
3. (a) After World War II, why did Japan have no military forces? (b) How did this policy change during the Cold War?
4. How has Japan reacted to criticism of its role in the global economy?
5. Why has poetry been important in Japanese culture?

Reviewing Chapter Themes

1. Since 1945, Japan has worked to build both a democratic government and a democratic society. (a) Describe two reforms that made the government more democratic. (b) Describe two ways in which Japanese society became more democratic.
2. Throughout its history, Japan has selectively borrowed and then adapted foreign ideas and technologies. How has selective borrowing helped Japan to become an economic superpower?
3. Japan has carved out a major place for itself in the global economy. Describe two ways in which the country's economic success has increased its dependence on the rest of the world.
4. The arts in Japan reflect ancient and modern traditions. Describe one literature form and one art form that have endured in Japanese culture.

Thinking Critically

1. **Understanding Causes and Effects** How did Japan's experience in World War II influence its postwar foreign policy?
2. **Analyzing Information** Based on what you have learned about literature and the arts in Japan, list three values important to Japanese culture. Which value do you think has had the greatest influence on Japan's success?
3. **Making Global Connections** American businesses have valued competition. How does this view differ from the Japanese view?

Applying Your Skills

1. **Analyzing a Poem** Read the following haiku by Matsuo Basho: "Summer grasses—/All that remains/Of soldiers' visions." (a) What images does the poet use? (b) What idea is the poet trying to convey? (c) How does the haiku form reflect Japanese emphasis on simplicity and suggestion? (See Skill Lesson 12, page 541.)
2. **Ranking** Make a list of the reasons for Japan's economic success since 1945. Then rank the reasons according to their order of importance.

SKILL LESSON 9

Analyzing a Painting: Chinese Art and the Cultural Revolution

Paintings are valuable sources of historical and cultural information. They often depict life as it was at the time the artist lived. They also reveal what the artist's culture thought was an acceptable subject for a work of art. Keep in mind, however, that an artist's beliefs, opinions, and culture influence what he or she paints and how it is painted.

The painting below is by an unknown Chinese artist. It was probably done in the late 1960s or early 1970s, shortly after the Cultural Revolution began in China. During the Cultural Revolution, Chinese artists were no longer free to paint what they wanted to paint. Their work had to have a political or patriotic theme. It had to promote the ideals and goals of a Communist society. Study the painting carefully, using the following steps to guide you.

1. **Identify the painting.** (a) Who painted the picture? **(b)** When was it painted? **(c)** During which period of Chinese history was it painted?
2. **Analyze the information in the painting.** **(a)** Describe the workers in the painting and what they are doing. **(b)** What kinds of jobs do the workers seem to have? How can you tell? **(c)** Do the workers seem happy? How does the artist convey this? **(d)** What do you think the red flag represents? **(e)** What agricultural tools and machinery do you see?
3. **Draw conclusions from the painting.** Based on what you read in Chapter 16, how does the painting promote the ideals and goals of the Chinese Communists?

SKILL LESSON 10

Synthesizing Information: The Japanese Economy

In order to understand world issues, you must be able to synthesize information. Synthesizing involves putting various pieces of information together to form a complete picture. The process requires you to analyze the information, compare the data, and then draw conclusions.

To practice the skill of synthesizing information, use the chart and line graph below, the political cartoon on page 434, the photographs on page 420, and the text material in Chapter 19. Study all the information carefully, using the following steps to guide you.

1. **Analyze each piece of information.** (a) According to the graph below, when did Japan's exports begin to significantly exceed its imports? (b) According to the chart below, which nation is Japan's leading export trade partner? (c) According to the political cartoon on page 434, what are the Japanese farmers represented by Mount Fuji trying to stop? Why? (d) According to the photographs on page 420, what product does Japan import? What does Japan export? (e) According to the text on pages 419–421, why are foreign countries critical of Japan's trade policies?

2. **Compare the information.** (a) What do the photographs on page 420 tell you about Japan's import and export of raw materials and manufactured goods? (b) How does the text support your findings? (c) What does the chart below tell you about Japan's prosperity and its standard of living today? (d) What other pieces of information support your findings?

3. **Synthesize the information in order to draw conclusions.** (a) If you looked only at the graph below, what would you conclude about Japan's trade balance in recent years? (b) How would the political cartoon help you to understand why Japan has a trade imbalance? (c) How does the text add to your understanding of the Japanese trade imbalance issue? (d) Write a paragraph explaining why Japan's trading partners are concerned about the Japanese trade imbalance.

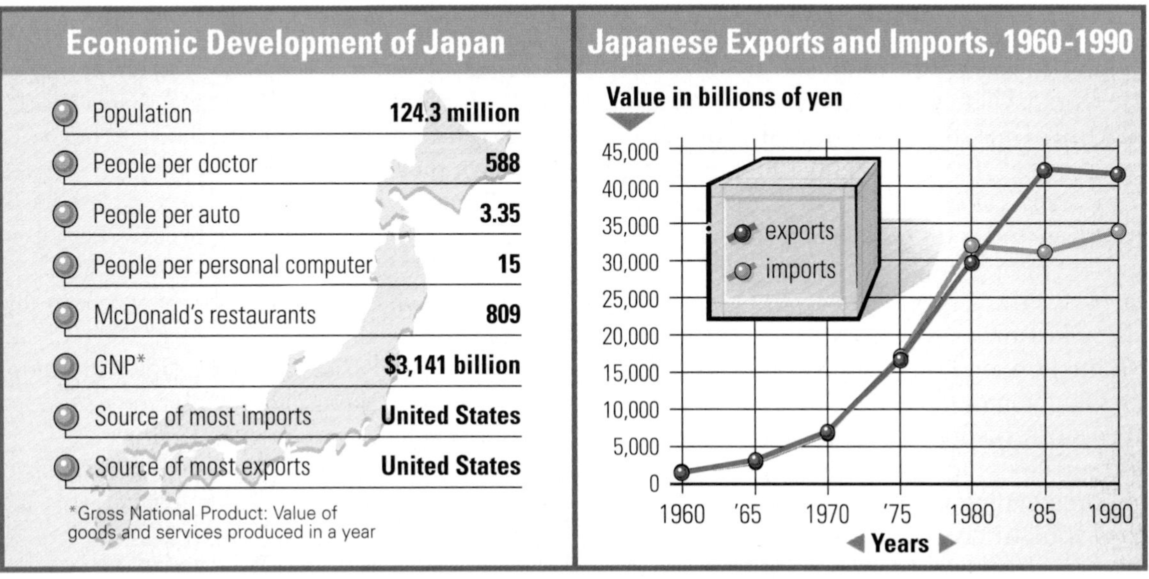

Economic Development of Japan

Population	124.3 million
People per doctor	588
People per auto	3.35
People per personal computer	15
McDonald's restaurants	809
GNP*	$3,141 billion
Source of most imports	United States
Source of most exports	United States

*Gross National Product: Value of goods and services produced in a year

WORLD

The Pillow Book

Sei Shonagon

INTRODUCTION Perhaps the two most important writers of the Heian court in Japan were women. Both Lady Murasaki Shikibu's *The Tale of Genji* and Sei Shonagon's *The Pillow Book* are treasured records of court life. Written during the 10 years in which Shonagon was a lady-in-waiting to Empress Sadako, *The Pillow Book* is filled with descriptions, anecdotes, character sketches, and personal insights. The following story, called "The Cat Who Lived in the Palace," is about two royal pets.

Vocabulary Before you read the selection, find the meaning of these words in a dictionary: veranda, chastised, reproached, bemoaning, loathsome, ablutions.

The cat who lived in the Palace has been awarded the headdress of nobility and was called Lady Myobu. She was a very pretty cat, and His Majesty saw to it that she was treated with the greatest care.

One day she wandered onto the veranda, and Lady Uma, the nurse in charge of her, called out, "Oh, you naughty thing! Please come inside at once." But the cat paid no attention and went on basking sleepily in the sun. Intending to give her a scare, the nurse called for the dog, Okinamaro.

"Okinamaro, where are you?" she cried. "Come here and bite Lady Myobu!" The foolish Okinamaro, believing that the nurse was in earnest, rushed at the cat, who, startled and terrified, ran behind the blind in the Imperial Dining Room, where the Emperor happened to be sitting. Greatly surprised, His Majesty picked up the cat and held her in his arms. He summoned his gentlemen-in-waiting. When Tadataka, the Chamberlain, appeared, His Majesty ordered that Okinamaro be chastised and banished to Dog Island. The attendants all started to chase the dog amid great confusion. His Majesty also reproached Lady Uma, "We shall have to find a new nurse for our cat," he told her. "I no longer feel I can count on you to look after her." Lady Uma bowed; thereafter she no longer appeared in the Emperor's presence. . . .

It was about noon, a few days after Okinamaro's banishment, that we heard a dog howling fearfully. How could any dog possibly cry so long? All the other dogs rushed out in excitement to see what was happening. Meanwhile a woman who served as a cleaner in the Palace latrines ran up to us. "It's terrible," she said. "Two of the Chamberlains are flogging a dog. They'll surely kill him. He's being punished for having come back after he was banished. . . ." Obviously the victim was Okinamaro. I was absolutely wretched and sent a servant to ask the men to stop; but just then the howling finally ceased. "He's dead," one of the servants informed me. "They've thrown his body outside the gate."

That evening, while we were sitting in the Palace bemoaning Okinamaro's fate, a wretched-looking dog walked in; he was trembling all over, and his body was fearfully swollen.

"Oh dear," said one of the ladies-in-waiting. "Can this be Okinamaro? We haven't seen any other dog like him recently, have we?"

We called to him by name, but the dog did not respond. Some of us insisted that it was Okinamaro, others that it was not. "Please send for Lady Ukon," said the Empress, hearing our discussion. "She will certainly be able to tell." We immediately went to Ukon's room and told her she was wanted on an urgent matter.

"Is this Okinamaro?" the Empress asked her, pointing to the dog.

"Well," said Ukon, "it certainly looks like him, but I cannot believe that this loathsome creature is really our Okinamaro. When I called Okinamaro, he always used to come to me, wagging his tail. But this dog does not react at all. No, it cannot be the same one. And besides, wasn't Okinamaro beaten to death and his body thrown away? How could any dog be alive after being flogged by two strong men?" Hearing this, Her Majesty was very unhappy.

When it got dark, we gave the dog something to eat; but he refused it, and we finally decided that this could not be Okinamaro.

On the following morning I went to attend the Empress while her hair was being dressed and she was performing her ablutions. I was holding up the mirror for her when the dog we had seen on the previous evening slunk into the room and crouched next to one of the pillars. "Poor Okinamaro!" I said. "He had such a dreadful beating yesterday. How sad to think he is dead! I wonder what body he has been born into this time. Oh, how he must have suffered!"

At that moment the dog lying by the pillar started to shake and tremble, and shed a flood of tears. It was astounding. So this really was Okinamaro! On the previous night it was to avoid betraying himself that he had refused to answer to his name. We were immensely moved and pleased. "Well, well, Okinamaro!" I said, putting down the mirror. The dog stretched himself flat on the floor and yelped loudly, so that the Empress beamed with delight. All the ladies gathered round, and Her Majesty summoned Lady Ukon. When the Empress explained what had happened, everyone talked and laughed with great excitement.

The news reached His Majesty, and he too came to the Empress's room. "It's amazing," he said with a smile. "To think that even a dog has such deep feelings!" . . . Before long, Okinamaro was granted an Imperial pardon and returned to his former happy state. Yet even now, when I remember how he whimpered and trembled in response to our sympathy, it strikes me as a strange and moving scene; when people talk to me about it, I start crying myself.

"The Lady Fujitsubo Watching Prince Genji Departing in the Moonlight" was painted by an unknown Japanese artist in 1853. It illustrates a scene from Japan's most famous novel, *The Tale of Genji. The Pillow Book* also told stories about life in the royal palace at Heian. Why do you think early Japanese literature focused on the imperial court?

Source: "The Cat Who Lived in the Palace" reprinted from *The Pillow Book of Sei Shonagon,* translated and edited by Ivan Morris. Copyright Ivan Morris 1967, published by Columbia University Press.

THINKING ABOUT LITERATURE

1. Why did the emperor banish Okinamaro?
2. Why was Okinamaro granted a pardon?
3. **Comparing** (a) What does this story reveal about attitudes toward pets among the Japanese nobility? (b) Compare their attitude with that of Americans.

Japanese Architecture

"Young architects, forget Rome! Go to Japan!"

When Walter Gropius gave this advice, architects all over the world listened. After all, the German-born genius was one of the founders of modern architecture. Yet, Gropius was only saying what Americans had already discovered.

A Startling Exhibition

The year 1876 marked the 100th birthday of the United States. To celebrate, Philadelphia hosted a gala Centennial Exhibition. Nations from all around the world were invited to send exhibits in a friendly competition of technology and culture.

Japan eagerly accepted the invitation. Only 23 years earlier, American warships had ended Japan's isolation. Now, the Japanese and the Americans were curious to learn more about each other. Japan sent some of its finest architects and workers to Philadelphia, along with building materials that filled 50 railroad cars.

As the Japanese workers built their exhibit hall, observers scoffed. At the time, American tastes favored massive, ornate mansions. This Japanese building did not even have a foundation—just wooden posts pounded into the earth! The framework, said one American, looked like "a crib to store corn."

When the building was done, most of the scoffers changed their tune. One guidebook called the Japanese exhibit "the best-built structure on the centennial grounds . . . as nicely put together as a piece of cabinet-work."

Early Asian Influence

Before this time, American architects had looked to Europe for inspiration. True, there had been some earlier interest in East Asian design. In the early 1800s, Thomas Jefferson, for example, copied Chinese architectural style for the railings and stairways of the University of Virginia. Later, Frederick Law Olmstead modeled New York City's Central Park on Chinese gardens. In each case, however, the influence had come from China to the United States by way of Europe.

On the other hand, Japan's influence came directly across the Pacific. It had a lasting effect on American architecture and design.

Japanese Styles Spread

In the late 1800s, Americans liked their buildings cluttered with ornaments. Japan's ornate "imperial style" appealed to them. Some architects enthusiastically loaded American buildings

with Japanese decoration, whether it fit the style or not.

Other Americans, however, appreciated the simple elegance of traditional Japanese design (bottom, far left). One of these people was Edward Morse. In 1877, on a visit to Japan, he made detailed sketches of homes, workplaces, and other buildings. He published his sketches in a book, *Japan Day by Day.* Americans read the book eagerly. A critic said the book was "well worthy of study, by every architect and decorator, because of its fresh ideas in design and construction."

At the time, young American architects were looking for ways to break with European styles. They felt that a building's style should be "organic"—that is, it should grow naturally out of the function and setting of the building (bottom, left). The Japanese style, with its simple lines and lack of ornamentation, was just what they were looking for.

One young midwestern architect, Frank Lloyd Wright, began to collect Japanese art. He remarked:

> ❝ Japanese art and architecture have organic character. Their art is more nearly modern . . . than that of any European civilization alive or dead. ❞

Inspired by the Japanese, Wright created the "prairie style" of architecture. He designed eye-catching homes with long horizontal lines, low roofs, and windows arranged in banks (above). Inside, the rooms were wide open, flowing into one another rather than being separated by walls and doors.

Today, the prairie style is considered America's greatest contribution to world architecture. Ironically, one of Wright's most famous buildings was the Imperial Hotel—in Tokyo.

A Wealth of Styles

A group of architects in California turned to Japan for different reasons as well. One of them, Clarence Mayhew, explained:

> ❝ The problems of topography and climate conditions of Japan and California are very much the same. . . . The Japanese have been designing for these conditions for so long . . . they have reached many admirable solutions which are easily adapted to our local conditions. ❞

The result was called the "California bungalow." Like Japanese homes, the bungalow was constructed of plain wood and followed a simple design of low walls, wide overhanging roofs, and large porches. California bungalows soon sprang up all over the country.

Even the skyscraper felt the imprint of Japan. Early skyscrapers had been ornate. After the 1940s, a new "international style" developed, with simple lines, lack of ornamentation, and uninterrupted interior space. From desert homes in the Southwest to the skylines of the largest cities, Japanese styles have influenced the very look of America.

1. How did Americans become acquainted with Japanese architecture?
2. **Comparing** How did Frank Lloyd Wright's reasons for adopting Japanese styles differ from those of the California architects?
3. **Writing Across Cultures** Write a letter inviting the leader of a foreign nation to send an exhibit to an American exposition. Outline some of the benefits of sharing cultures and technologies.

UNIT 5 REVIEW

Reviewing the Main Ideas

1. (a) How has geography influenced population distribution in China? (b) What methods have the Chinese developed to help them adapt to their land?
2. (a) When did European powers begin to dominate China? (b) What treaties and conditions were the Chinese forced to accept? (c) What Asian power attacked China? (d) When did foreign influence in China decline?
3. (a) Why did communism appeal to many Chinese? (b) After the Communist revolution, how was Mao Zedong's image glorified through the use of propaganda? (c) How did the Communists try to reform Chinese art?
4. (a) Describe Korea's two main physical features. (b) How has geography affected Korea's economy?
5. (a) How did Manchurian control affect Korea? (b) How did Japanese control affect Korea?
6. (a) How was Japanese society organized after the 1100s? (b) What effect did the early Tokugawa shoguns have on Japan? (c) When did the power of the Tokugawa shogun decline?
7. How did modernization provoke Japanese expansion?
8. How did a worldwide economic slowdown contribute to the rise of a military dictatorship in Japan during the 1930s?

Thinking Critically

1. **Making Inferences** Some scholars say that it was not the Mongols who conquered the Chinese but the Chinese who conquered the Mongols. What did these scholars mean?
2. **Making Global Connections** Compare the Opium War, which was fought to control drug use in China in 1839, and the current war on drugs in the United States today.
3. **Relating Past to Present** (a) Why do you think the Ming and Qing dynasties confined foreign trade to Macao and Guangzhou? (b) How have attitudes toward foreign trade changed in China?

Applying Your Skills

1. **Understanding Causes and Effects** Read Section 3 in Chapter 17, "The Two Koreas," pages 382–386. (a) List two causes and two effects of the Korean War. (b) Under what conditions might North Korea and South Korea be reunited?
2. **Analyzing a Quotation** Reread the quotation on page 403. (a) What did Fukuzawa Yukichi ask the American gentleman? (b) Why was he shocked at the American's response? (c) What do you think the American might have written about his encounter with Fukuzawa?
3. **Analyzing a Cartoon** Study the Japanese cartoon below. The caption warns, "Stop the increasing liberalization of importation limits on farm products. Support Japanese farming, forestry, and fishing." (a) Which figure represents Japan? (b) Which foreign country is represented? (c) What is the goal of the protest? (d) Do you think the protest is justified? Explain.

Learning by Doing

1. **Creating a Map** On an outline map of China, label all mountain ranges, landforms, rivers, seas, and oceans. Create symbols for the main resources of China. Use the symbols to locate the resources on the map. See the maps on pages 324 and 365.
2. **Writing Headlines** Write a brief but informative headline for an article about each of the following topics: Mao's land reform, Mao's Great Leap Forward, Mao's Cultural Revolution, and Deng's Four Modernizations and "open door" trade policy. As you reread this material in the textbook, extract the key information about the topic. After the headline, write the approximate year in which the event occurred in parentheses. For example: *Chinese Government Restores Profit Motive to Raise Crop Production (1978).*
3. **Making a Chart** Create a comparison chart based on information you read in Chapter 17 titled "North Korea and South Korea." Make three columns. In the first column, write Dates. Beneath it write: 1945, 1948, 1950, 1953, and Today. Title the remaining two columns: North Korea, South Korea. Fill in the chart with information about events that took place in the country during these time periods. Compare your entries with those of a classmate.
4. **Making a Diagram** Make a diagram titled "Feudal Society in Japan." Box the following: emperor, shogun, daimyo, samurai, artisan, peasant, and merchant. Arrange each category according to the rank each individual held in society. Write a one-sentence description for each category in the box. Using arrows, indicate the direction in which power flowed within the society.

WRITER'S Workshop

Arranging Information for Comparison

When you arrange supporting information in comparison order, you are arranging it according to similarities and differences.

Look at this topic sentence: *The philosophy of Confucianism is different from the philosophy of Daoism.* In detail sentences, present all the information you can find about the first subject. For example: *According to Confucianism, the family and the good of society are more important than the interests of the individual. Loyalty, hard work, courtesy, and service are emphasized.*

Then, using a transition, present all the information you can find about the other subject. Arrange the information in the same order (the role of the individual, the type of behavior that is encouraged).

Common transitions for differences include *but, however, by contrast, instead, on the contrary, on the other hand,* and *unlike.* For similarities, common transitions include *both, like, similarly,* and *similar to.*

Practice Using the example above, write detail sentences about Daoism.

Writing to Learn

1. Write an essay in response to Confucius's vow "to bring comfort to the old, to have trust in friends, and to cherish the young." List the three topics and jot down the virtues and rewards of each. Begin the first draft of your essay with a topic sentence that clearly states your reaction to Confucius's ideas. Then, devote a paragraph to each topic. When you revise, be sure that your points support your topic sentence. Proofread and make a final copy of the essay. Read your essay to the class.
2. Write a haiku about a season. First, brainstorm a list of vivid images. Refer to your list and write your haiku, which should be three lines of a set length. The first line is five syllables long. The second line has seven syllables. The third line has five syllables. Focus on clear, spare, precise, and suggestive images. Avoid using any abstract or unnecessary words. As you revise, make sure that your haiku evokes emotion and stimulates thought. Replace any vague words. Post your final version on the bulletin board.

UNIT 6

LATIN AMERICA AND CANADA

UNIT OUTLINE

1 This dancer in Ecuador is taking part in a fiesta, a public celebration of a local religious holiday.

2 Native Americans in southwestern Canada used this painted mask of the sun spirit during winter religious ceremonies.

3 Yves Phonard, a modern Haitian artist, painted this scene of women workers harvesting corn in a field.

4 Nearly one third of Chile's population lives in Santiago, the nation's capital and largest city. Founded in 1541, Santiago was an important city in Spain's empire in Latin America.

	Early History			1500		1600
History and Politics		▲ 1000 Vikings land in Newfoundland		▲ 1492 Columbus reaches Americas	▲ 1550s Spanish Empire stretches from present-day Oregon to Chile	
Society and Culture		▲ 300s–600s Maya civilization flourishes	▲ 1400s Inca Empire expands	▲ 1500s Aztec and Inca civilizations flourish		▲ 1660s Sor Juana Inés de la Cruz writes poetry
Economics and Technology	▲ 3000s B.C. People in Mexico begin to farm				▲ 1521 Magellan's expedition sails around the world	▲ 1600s Mercantilism develops in Europe

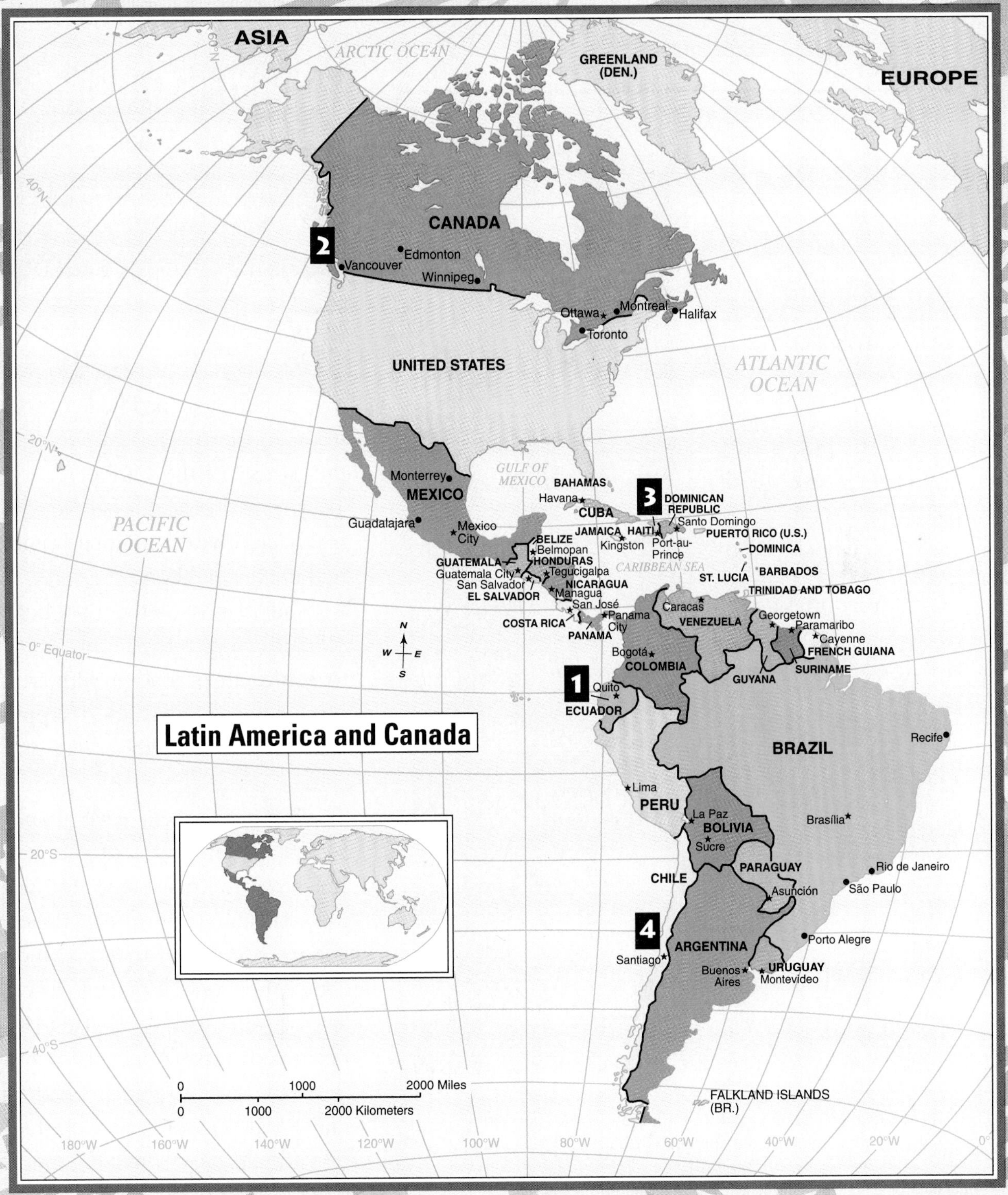

Latin America and Canada

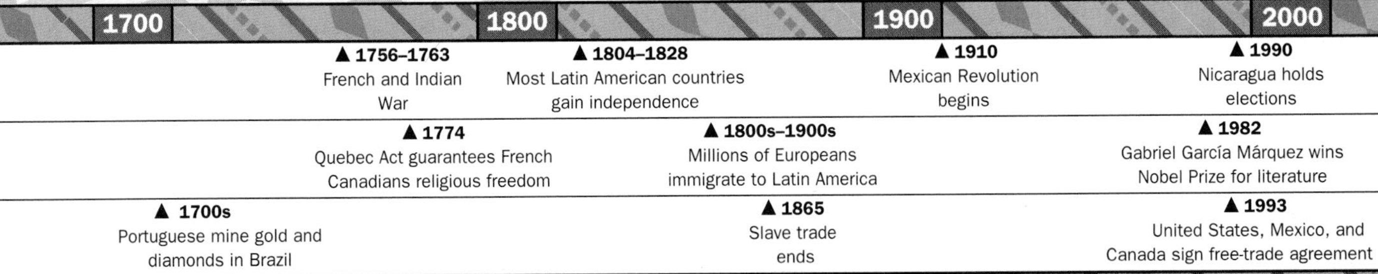

Chapter 20

GEOGRAPHY AND EARLY HISTORY OF LATIN AMERICA

Ancient Mexican Art These stone carvings from early Mexican civilizations are in an outdoor park. The giant head was made by the Olmecs in about 900 B.C. The standing figure, from the Maya civilization, dates from A.D. 800. These ancient civilizations had a lasting influence on the diverse cultures of the Americas. ***Fine Art*** Why do you think these artworks are on display in a public park?

CHAPTER OUTLINE

Thousands of years ago, Native Americans paddled canoes from northern South America to the islands of the Caribbean Sea. They were a peaceful people who had been driven from their homes by warlike neighbors.

The islands of the Caribbean seemed a perfect place in which to settle. Trees loaded with fruit offered an abundant food supply. The coastal waters abounded with fish.

The newcomers gave thanks to their many gods—of the sun, the sea, the rain—who favored the islands with their riches. Soon, however, they learned about the god Hurakan. During late summer and early fall, Hurakan sent terrible storms to the islands. Howling winds, blinding rains, and 50-foot waves crashed over the beaches, wrecking everything in their path.

The fearful islanders prayed to this dreaded god of storms:

> “Oh dread wind of the sea,
> please stay away from
> our shores.”

Later, when Europeans reached the islands of the Caribbean, they, too, felt the fury of tropical storms. They called the storms hurricanes, after the islanders' fierce god Hurakan.

CHAPTER PERSPECTIVE

Today, hurricanes still rip across the land bordering the Caribbean Sea. These storms are one of the many ways geography affects Latin America. Latin America is a vast cultural region that stretches from Mexico to the tip of South America. A variety of landforms and climates have helped to shape the cultures of this huge region.

As you read, look for these chapter themes:

- Latin America is a region of widely diverse physical features, climates, and cultures.
- Physical features and climate have influenced the patterns of settlement in the region.
- Latin American cultures are a mixture of Native American, African, and European traditions.
- Advanced civilizations, including those of the Mayas, Aztecs, and Incas, emerged in the Americas.

Literature Connections

In this chapter, you will encounter passages from the following works.

Prayer to Hurakan, islanders of the Caribbean Sea

The Incas, Pedro Cieza de León

For other suggestions, see Connections With Literature, pages 804–808.

1 THE SHAPE OF THE LAND

FIND OUT

What regions and landforms does Latin America include?

How have geographic features contributed to regionalism?

What river systems are important to Latin America?

Vocabulary pampas, regionalism

Two high peaks guard a rugged valley in the mountains of Mexico. From time to time, wisps of smoke rise from the one called Popocatépetl (poh poh kah TEH peht ' l), or Smoking Mountain. Snow blankets a companion mountain, Ixtacihuatl (eehs tah SEE waht ' l), or Sleeping Woman.

An Indian legend tells the origins of the two peaks. Long ago, a prince left his beloved wife and went off to war. After a time, word reached the princess that her husband had been killed in battle. Grief-stricken, she lay down, covered herself with a white robe, and died.

The prince, however, had not been slain in battle. When he returned to find his wife in the sleep of death, he knelt beside her and burned incense to her memory. The smoke rising from Popocatépetl reminds people today of this ancient tale. Throughout Latin America, legends such as this expressed people's feelings about the lands in which they lived. (See Connections With Literature, "Popocatépetl and Ixtlaccihuatl," page 806.)

A Vast Region

The term Latin America refers to a vast cultural region. It includes the lands in the Western Hemisphere that were influenced by Spanish and Portuguese settlers. The word

MAP STUDY

Latin America includes Mexico, Central America, the islands of the Caribbean, and South America. This region has a varied topography, but mountains and highlands are its dominant landforms.

1. **Place** Identify the mountains that run the length of western South America.
2. **Location** (a) Identify the largest area of lowlands in South America. (b) Describe the relative location of these lowlands.
3. **Solving Problems** What river systems have the nations of South America probably used for transportation and trade?

Latin refers to the language that is a common root for Spanish and Portuguese.

Subregions. Latin America stretches for about 5,500 miles (8,851 km) from the Rio Grande in Mexico to Cape Horn at the tip of South America. This vast area has two main subregions: Middle America and South America.

Middle America lies in the Northern Hemisphere. It includes Mexico, the 7 nations of Central America, and 13 island nations and Puerto Rico in the Caribbean.*

Much of South America lies in the Southern Hemisphere. South America has 12 independent countries and two foreign-ruled territories, the Falkland Islands and French Guiana. One country, Brazil, covers half the land and has half the population of the entire continent.

Location. Latin America lies between the Atlantic and Pacific oceans. These oceans link countries within Latin America and connect Latin America to other regions. For centuries, the Atlantic Ocean has served as a highway between Europe, Latin America, and Africa. Today, the Pacific Ocean is increasingly important as a trade route. Nations on the west coast of Latin America are developing close ties with Pacific Rim countries of Asia.

Latin America shares the Western Hemisphere with the United States and Canada. In Chapter 23, you will read about the great influence the United States has exercised over Latin America since the 1800s.

* After the voyages of Christopher Columbus, Europeans called these islands the West Indies.

Major Landforms

Latin America, which covers one sixth of the world's land surface, has a great variety of landforms. Much of the land consists of rugged mountains or highlands.

Mountains and highlands. Perhaps the most striking physical feature of Latin America is the backbone of high mountains, called La Cordillera, that run the length of the region. These mountains actually begin in the Rocky Mountains of western Canada and the United States. In Mexico, the mountains split into two ranges. The Sierra Madre West (see EHR uh MAH dray) rise along the Pacific coast, while the Sierra Madre East stand near the

Mount Aconcagua, Argentina This towering snowcapped peak is in the Andes, the highest mountains in Latin America. Few people live in the cold, rugged Andes terrain. Most of the population in the western region of Latin America live in lowlands at the foot of the Andes. ***Geography*** What are three important highland regions in South America?

Atlantic coast. Between them lies the Central Plateau. Mountains and highlands also cover most of Central America. Many Caribbean islands also have rugged terrain.

Running the length of western South America are the snowcapped Andes Mountains. The towering Andes have dozens of peaks that rise more than 20,000 feet (6,096 m) high and are second in height only to the great mountain ranges in Asia. Other highlands are found in eastern South America. They include the Guiana Highlands in Venezuela and the Brazilian Highlands.

Earthquakes and volcanoes. Mountains have created problems for Latin America. The mountains along its western edge are part of the Ring of Fire that encircles the Pacific Ocean. Along this ring, pressure builds up deep inside the Earth and causes frequent earthquakes and volcanoes. Some volcanoes explode almost without warning and rain destruction on nearby areas.

Lowlands. Lowlands are found along the coasts of Mexico, Central America, and South America. Most of these coastal plains are narrow. On the Pacific side of South America, for example, the Andes Mountains extend almost to the sea.

Several wide lowland areas lie in eastern South America, as you can see from the map on page 440. The largest of these is the great Amazon Basin. It occupies 40 percent of South America and has the world's largest rain forest. Another major lowland area is the pampas, the grassy plains that stretch from Argentina into Uruguay. There, wheat farmers and cattle ranchers have created one of the most productive farming regions in Latin America.

Regionalism. Mountains, along with tropical forests in the lowlands, created barriers to the movement of people. These features limited contact among areas and contributed to regionalism, or strong local traditions that divide people within a country or region.

The Brazilian Rain Forest A hiker moves through the world's largest rain forest, located in Brazil's Amazon Basin. The rain forest supports a variety of plants and animal life. It also has many resources, including valuable mahogany, cedar, rosewood, and rubber trees. ***Environment*** Why is the rain forest a difficult environment for humans?

Great Rivers

Because Middle America has a rugged landscape, it has few rivers wide enough or deep enough for ships to travel on. By contrast, South America has three major river systems that provide important transportation routes.

The mighty Amazon. Beginning in the snowy Andes Mountains in Peru, the mighty Amazon River flows eastward across Brazil. At least 1,100 tributaries pour into the Amazon on its 4,000-mile (6,437-km) journey to the Atlantic Ocean. Because the Amazon is both wide and deep, oceangoing ships can sail 1,000 miles (1,609 km) upriver, as far as Manaus, Brazil. Smaller vessels carry cargoes as far as Iquitos, Peru, which is 2,300 miles (3,701 km) from the mouth of the Amazon.

Until the 1950s, few people lived along the river. The hot, humid climate as well as seasonal flooding and thick vegetation made settlement difficult. Since then, many settlers have moved into the region to develop its rich resources. Today, ships haul lumber, minerals, and livestock along the Amazon from the interior to the coast.

Orinoco. In northern South America lies the Orinoco (or uh NOH koh) River. It starts in the Guiana Highlands and flows northward through Venezuela to the Atlantic Ocean. Like the Amazon, the Orinoco carves a path through rain forests and open plains. Freighters on the Orinoco carry iron ore, bauxite, and forest products to the Atlantic and then to overseas markets.

Río de la Plata. The Río de la Plata (REE oh deh lah PLAH tah), or River of Silver, forms the border between Uruguay and Argentina. Fed by several rivers in the interior, the Río de la Plata serves as a major shipping route. Farmers and ranchers on the pampas use the waterway to send grain, meat, and hides to markets around the world. Buenos Aires, at the mouth of the river, has become the world's second-busiest port.

SECTION 1 REVIEW

1. **Locate:** (a) Rio Grande, (b) Cape Horn, (c) South America, (d) Caribbean Sea, (e) Andes Mountains.
2. **Define:** (a) pampas, (b) regionalism.
3. (a) What are the two main subregions of Latin America? (b) What areas are included in Middle America?
4. (a) Name two landforms found in Latin America. (b) How have landforms contributed to regionalism?
5. (a) What are three major river systems in South America? (b) List two products that people ship on each river.
6. **Applying Ideas** (a) Why is Latin America called a cultural region? (b) What physical regions does it include?
7. **Writing Across Cultures** List two geographic features that the United States shares with Latin America. Write a paragraph describing each feature.

2 CLIMATES AND PEOPLE

FIND OUT

Why does Latin America have many different climates?

What are the chief resources of Latin America?

What ethnic groups have contributed to the culture of Latin America?

How has geography affected population patterns in Latin America?

Vocabulary tierra caliente, tierra templada, tierra fría, mestizo

Waves thunder against the Pacific shore of northern Chile. Nearby lies the Atacama Desert, one of the driest places on Earth. In some parts of the desert no rain has fallen for 400 years. A few areas get as much as half an inch of rain each year.

The long, narrow Atacama Desert lies between the Andes Mountains and the Pacific Ocean. The Andes are one reason for the extreme dryness of the Atacama, as you will read.

Varied Climates

If you walked the 5,500-mile (8,851-km) length of Latin America, you would pass through many climate zones, ranging from lush tropical rain forests to frozen wastelands not far from Antarctica. Factors affecting the climates of Latin America are distance from the Equator, elevation, wind patterns, and ocean currents.

Tropical climates. Three fourths of Latin America lies in the tropics. Within the tropics, climates vary greatly. Some areas have a tropical wet climate. They include the Amazon Basin, some Caribbean islands, and parts of Central America. There, warm temperatures and plenty of rainfall all year support huge rain forests.

El Niño Strikes

GEOGRAPHIC CONNECTION

Who would believe that a change in an ocean current near Peru could cause drought in Australia and flooding as far away as India? Yet these events occur every few years when the warm Pacific Ocean current called *El Niño* strikes.

Normally, the cool Peru current flows northwestward along the Peruvian coast. The cool surface water is a good environment for many plants on which small fish, such as anchovies, feed. The abundance of fish benefits Peru's fishing industry.

Every few years, a current of warm water flows south from the Equator, forcing the Peru current to the west. This change in ocean current usually occurs close to Christmas. As a result, the warm current is known as El Niño, Spanish for "the Christ child."

El Niño can bring disaster. The warm waters of El Niño kill the small plants on which the fish feed. The fish either die or migrate to other areas.

In 1972, El Niño destroyed a large part of the anchovy population. Sardines moved in to replace the anchovies and thrived for 10 years. In 1982, however, El Niño began to affect the sardines as well. The fishing industry of Peru suffered greatly.

El Niño also leads to drastic changes in the weather. Coastal Peru usually gets 1 to 5 inches (2.5 to 12.5 cm) of rain each year. When El Niño arrives, as much as 12 feet (3.6 m) of rainfall may result in some areas. The downpours erode land, wash away homes and roads, and kill hundreds of people.

In both 1982 and 1983, El Niño caused droughts in Australia, India, and Africa, and cyclones across the Pacific. California had three times its normal amount of rainfall. El Niño may strike at Christmas, but it is no gift.

1. What is El Niño?
2. **Solving Problems** Why do you think scientists are trying to learn more about El Niño?

Much of tropical Latin America, however, has a wet and dry climate. In these areas, temperatures are warm all year, but half of the year is rainy while the other half is dry. A tropical wet and dry climate is found in the lowlands of Mexico, as well as in western Central America and southern Brazil.

Temperate climates. Several regions have temperate climates, as you can see from the Atlas map on page 778. Paraguay, Uruguay, and northern Argentina have a humid subtropical climate. There, a warm season alternates with a cool season, much as in South Carolina or Georgia in the United States. The grasslands of this region provide excellent grazing for livestock, as well as good farmland.

Dry climates. Parts of Latin America have dry climates. Northern Mexico and part of Argentina have a semiarid climate. Very light rainfall throughout the year allows some grasses to grow in these dry areas.

Bordering these semiarid areas are deserts. The Baja Peninsula of northeastern Mexico is a sunbaked desert. The windswept Patagonian Plateau at the tip of South America receives barely enough moisture to support stunted trees and scattered grasses. Neither of these areas is as dry as Chile's Atacama Desert, however.

The extreme dryness of the Atacama is due in part to the "rain shadow" created by the Andes. Winds blow west from the Atlantic across South America, dropping their moisture as they reach the Andes. As a result, the eastern slopes of the Andes and the Amazon Basin receive drenching rains. The western side of the Andes, however, remains very dry.

Ocean currents also affect the Atacama. Warm winds that blow east from the Pacific Ocean pass over the icy Peru current, which runs up the west coast of South America. These winds drop their moisture at sea, so only dry winds reach the land.

Elevation and Climate

In much of Latin America, the chief influence on climate is elevation above sea level. Within a single country, the climate can vary enormously, depending on whether you are in the lowlands or the highlands. People in Latin America have their own terms for these variations in climate.

Closest to sea level is the tierra caliente, or hot land. Lowlands such as the Yucatán Peninsula of Mexico and the Amazon Basin are located in the tierra caliente. In these regions, tropical crops such as bananas and sugarcane flourish.

The next zone, the tierra templada, or temperate land, includes areas that lie above 3,000 feet (914 m). There, the days are hot, but the nights are cool. The Central Plateau and the valleys in the Andes are part of the tierra templada. Many cities are also found in this temperate zone. Coffee and tobacco thrive at this altitude.

The third zone is the tierra fría, or cold land. This zone includes highlands that are at least 6,000 feet (1,829 m) above sea level. There, nighttime and winter temperatures can be quite cool. Major cities such as Mexico City and Bogotá lie in the tierra fría. Farmers who live in this zone grow wheat, barley, and potatoes.

Natural Resources

Parts of Latin America are rich in natural resources. Some of its countries have valuable mineral or agricultural resources. Others, especially the islands of the Caribbean, have relatively few resources. Most Latin Americans have not benefited from the vast resources of Latin America. As you will read, the Spanish, and later the wealthy ruling groups, exploited these resources in order to promote their own interests.

Minerals. Gold and silver are the minerals that lured many Europeans to the Americas. Today, Brazil, Mexico, and Peru are still producing large quantities of these precious metals.

Latin America has other minerals, too. Chile is the world's leading producer of copper. In Bolivia, miners extract huge amounts of tin each year. Jamaica, Guyana, and Suriname have major deposits of bauxite, the claylike ore from which aluminum is extracted.

Energy resources. Some Latin American countries have abundant supplies of oil and natural gas. Mexico and Venezuela have experienced the "boom and bust" of rising and falling oil prices. Bolivia, Ecuador, Colombia, and Peru also have large oil deposits.

In parts of Latin America, heavy rains fill rivers that cascade down from the highlands. Countries from Mexico to Paraguay have harnessed the force of these rivers to produce hydroelectric power. Brazil, for example, has seven of the world's largest hydroelectric plants.

Agricultural resources. The economies of many Latin American countries depend on the export of cash crops such as bananas, sugar, tobacco, coffee, and rubber. In addition, the rain forests of Brazil and Central America provide the world with valuable lumber.

Problems of economic dependence. The export of farm products and minerals has contributed to economic dependence in Latin America. Countries that rely on single crops or goods are at the mercy of world demand. Also, natural disasters such as hurricanes and frost can destroy an entire harvest. Since the 1950s, Latin American countries have worked to achieve greater independence by diversifying their economies.

Peoples of Latin America

In Guatemalan villages, many children speak their local Indian language before they learn Spanish. In Buenos Aires, people speak Spanish with an Italian accent, a reminder of the millions of Italians who settled in Argentina. In Brazil and the Caribbean, people tell folktales based on stories brought from Africa. These facts suggest the variety of people who live in Latin America and have contributed to the cultures of this region.

Native Americans. Before Christopher Columbus reached the Americas, about 80 million Native Americans lived in the Western Hemisphere. They spoke a variety of languages and had many different cultures. Some lived in large cities. Others were farmers or hunters and food gatherers. Although the arrival of Europeans led to the death of millions of Native Americans, their cultures survived in many parts of Latin America.

Europeans and Asians. After 1492, Europeans began to settle in Latin America. They included Spanish and Portuguese as well as French, Dutch, and English settlers. Many Spanish and Portuguese settlers married Native Americans. Their children formed a new ethnic group called mestizos, people of mixed European and Native American ancestry.

During the 1800s, thousands of Asians settled in Latin America. They included Indians and Chinese who took jobs on plantations after the abolition, or end, of slavery. During the same period, European immigrants flocked into Latin America, as they did to the United States. Many Italians went to Brazil, Uruguay, Argentina, and Chile. Germans, British, and other Europeans settled elsewhere in South America.

Africans. Many people in Latin America trace their roots to Africa. Between about 1500 and 1800, slave traders carried millions of Africans to the Americas. Africans were forced to work as slaves on plantations and in mines in the Caribbean, Brazil, and elsewhere.

Ethnic and cultural mix. Latin American countries have a mixture of ethnic groups. In some countries, such as Mexico, Chile, and Colombia, most of the people are mestizos. Guatemala, Bolivia, Peru, and Ecuador all have a large population of Native Americans. Many Brazilians, Cubans, Puerto Ricans, Dominicans, and Jamaicans have African ancestors, while large numbers of people of European background live in Costa Rica, Argentina, and Uruguay.

Population Patterns

Geography has influenced where people in Latin America live. A few areas are densely populated, while many others are sparsely settled. Few people can live in the rugged mountains, deserts, or rain forests because

Lunch Break at Ponce Students in Ponce, Puerto Rico's third-largest city, pose for their picture. Their faces suggest Latin America's ethnic diversity. The facial features and skin color of the population reflect Native American, European, and African backgrounds. ***Diversity*** What ethnic group in Latin America has both European and Native American ancestry? In which nations does this group make up the majority?

these areas are so unfavorable to farming. Instead, people are concentrated in temperate highland areas and along the coastal plains. In Brazil, for example, the largest cities are Rio de Janeiro and São Paulo on the coast. The area between the Atlantic Ocean and the Andes Mountains has few cities. In the 1950s, the government of Brazil tried to open up the interior by building a new capital city at Brasília. (See the feature on page 6.)

Limited farmland. Climate and rugged terrain do more than limit where people live. They severely limit the amount of arable land that is available. Only about 6 percent of Latin America is suitable for farming, compared with 20 percent of the United States.

Through irrigation, however, people in Latin America have created farmland in desert areas. Mexico has built water projects that now make it possible to channel water from mountain streams to the northern desert. In these irrigated desert lands, farmers produce crops of cotton, wheat, and vegetables.

In Central America and Brazil, developers have cleared the rain forests to open up new farmland. The soil in the rain forests, however, is not very fertile. These cleared lands support crops for only a few years before they wear out, forcing farmers to move on. As in tropical Africa, leaching and erosion damage the land.

Difficult communication. Landforms and climate have limited contact between people in coastal areas and the interior. During colonial times, cities such as Buenos Aires had closer ties to Spain, across the Atlantic, than to the interior of Argentina. (📖 See Connections With Literature, page 806, "The Handsomest Drowned Man in the World.")

Differences in culture also contributed to the gap between coastal cities and the interior. Often, the interior was a stronghold of Native American or mestizo cultures, in contrast to the European culture of the cities.

Today, radio, television, telephones, and air travel link cities and rural areas in a way that was not possible in the past. Despite the changes brought by modernization, differences between urban and rural areas are greater in Latin America than in countries such as the United States.

SECTION 2 REVIEW

1. **Locate:** (a) Atacama Desert, (b) Yucatán Peninsula, (c) Buenos Aires, (d) Rio de Janeiro.
2. **Define:** (a) tierra caliente, (b) tierra templada, (c) tierra fría, (d) mestizo.
3. Name one area of Latin America that is in each of the climate zones created by elevation.
4. What resources are important to Latin America?
5. Give two examples of how geography has affected where people live in Latin America.
6. **Synthesizing** Why are few major cities located in the interior of Brazil between the Atlantic Ocean and the Andes Mountains?
7. **Writing Across Cultures** Write a dialogue in which students discuss the similarities between the peoples of Latin America and the peoples of the United States.

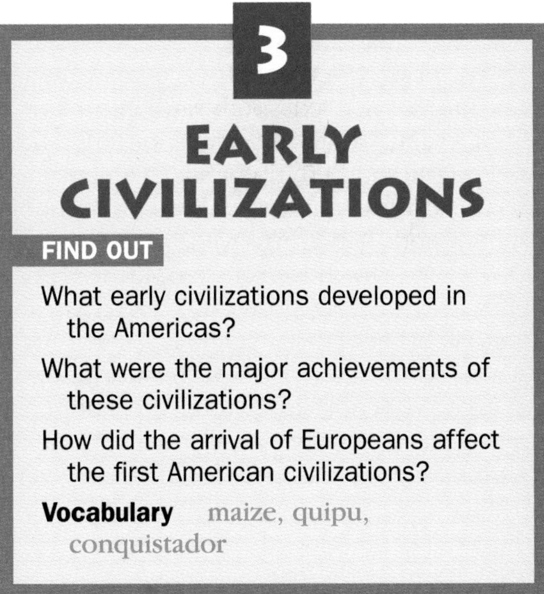

3 EARLY CIVILIZATIONS

FIND OUT

What early civilizations developed in the Americas?

What were the major achievements of these civilizations?

How did the arrival of Europeans affect the first American civilizations?

Vocabulary maize, quipu, conquistador

The desperate inhabitants of the parched lands of northern Mexico struggled to survive. Over several centuries, these people, later known as the Aztecs, slowly moved southward onto the Central Plateau. In 1325, according to legend, the Aztec god Uitzilopochtli (wee tsee loh POHCH tlee) told the people where to settle: "Search until you find this sign—an eagle perched atop a cactus holding a snake in its beak."

Soon afterward, the Aztecs found the sign on an island in Lake Texcoco. There, they built the city of Tenochtitlán (tay nawch tee TLAHN). Today, Mexico City stands on the spot where the Aztec capital once flourished. The eagle, snake, and cactus have become the national symbols of Mexico, as shown in the Mexican flag.

The Aztecs were one of many Native American civilizations that emerged in what is today Latin America. Like people everywhere, they built on the successes of earlier civilizations.

The First Americans

Thousands of years before the Aztecs built Tenochtitlán, nomadic people migrated from Asia into North America. During the last Ice Age, huge glaciers froze so much water that ocean levels dropped, exposing a land bridge that connected Siberia to Alaska. The first people to cross that land bridge may have reached the Americas about 50,000 years ago. Slowly, some groups moved southward into Central America and South America. In time, they reached the southern tip of South America.

The earliest Americans lived by hunting, fishing, and gathering wild plants. About 5,000 years ago, however, people in Mexico began to farm. They grew maize, or corn, and planted other crops such as beans and squash. As in other parts of the world, farming allowed people to give up their nomadic way of life and settle in villages. As farming methods improved, people in some areas produced the food surpluses that were needed to support advanced civilizations.

Maya Cities

> "Their books were written on large sheets of paper doubled in folds, which were enclosed entirely between boards which they decorated, and they wrote on both sides in columns following the order of the folds. And they made this paper from the roots of a tree."

A Spanish priest wrote that description of the books kept by the ancient Mayas. Writing, books, and paper were a few of the remarkable achievements of the Mayas. By the time the Spanish reached the Americas, Maya civilization was more than 2,000 years old.

The ancient Mayas lived in the dense, lowland rain forests of Central America. Between about A.D. 300 and A.D. 900, their civilization reached its peak. Prosperous Maya cities ruled the lands from the Yucatán Peninsula to what is today Guatemala. A network of roads linked cities such as Tikal (tee KAHL) in Guatemala and Palenque (puh LEHN kay) in Mexico. Merchants did a brisk trade carrying goods, such as cotton cloth and ornate gold jewelry, from one city to another. They shipped other goods to distant lands in oceangoing canoes.

Farming. How did these cities thrive in the difficult tropical environment? Scientists have only recently learned how the Mayas developed complex farming methods to produce enough food to support city life.

In low-lying areas, Maya farmers cleared the dense forests and then built raised fields for crops. These platforms caught and held rainwater. If too much rain fell, farmers opened channels to drain the fields. The system worked so well that farmers produced corn and other crops to feed themselves plus a surplus to feed cities that had as many as 20,000 people.

Government and society. Trade, language, and a common culture linked the Mayas, although they had no single, unified empire. Instead, each Maya city-state had its own king, who was the most important military and religious leader. Below him, nobles and priests helped to govern the city. Artisans and merchants were next in the social order. They supplied the ruling class with fine cloth, gold ornaments, and feathered cloaks, and benefited from trade with other city-states.

The largest group of people included peasants and laborers. They grew food and hauled stone to build splendid temples and palaces. At the lowest level of Maya society were slaves, usually people captured in war or criminals.

Religion. Like other ancient peoples, the Mayas believed that gods controlled the powerful forces of nature. Each day, priests performed the rituals they believed would please the gods. Without those ceremonies, the gods might send storms, drought, or other disasters.

At the center of Maya cities were huge pyramid-temples built to honor different gods. Some pyramids towered 20 stories above the ground. On the walls of the temples, artists painted brilliantly colored murals. These scenes recorded historical events or told ancient legends. Surrounding the temples were the stone palaces of priests and nobles.

Maya cities had a large rectangular stone court that was used for a ball game called pok-a-tok. Like modern basketball, the game involved sending a ball through a hoop. Unlike basketball, the ball was about the size of a softball, and the hoop was set vertically 30 feet (9 m) above the ground. Also, players were not allowed to use their hands to catch or throw the ball. Ordinary people played the game for fun. When nobles played the game, however, it took on religious meaning. Priests then watched the game carefully, believing that the gods sent messages by allowing one side or another to win.

Maya Warriors This wall painting on a Maya temple shows warriors in combat using deadly sharp knives and spears. Other wall paintings show the bright colors of clothing worn by the Mayas and their fine ornaments made of feathers, gold, copper, and jade. ***Fine Art*** How do wall paintings help us learn about early civilizations?

Maya Achievements

The magnificent buildings the Mayas erected are proof of their great skills in architecture. The Mayas also left evidence of many other achievements. Maya priests developed a system of writing, using hieroglyphics. Scholars are just beginning to decipher Maya "glyphs." Most glyphs carved on temples and stone pillars seem to concern religious and historical events.

Maya priests made important advances in the sciences. Priest-astronomers studied the sky in order to measure the passage of time. As in other ancient societies, the priests needed to know when they should tell peasants to plant and harvest crops.

Based on careful observation and years of records, the priests developed a $365\frac{1}{4}$-day calendar—the most accurate calendar in the world at the time. From their study of the stars, the priests also developed complex mathematics. They learned to use zero, a breakthrough that allowed them to express numbers of any size.

Maya cities began to decline in about 800. Historians do not know why this happened. Disease or war may have weakened Maya society. Some experts think that high taxes may have led peasants to rebel against their rulers. By 900, most people had abandoned the cities, but Maya culture survived and influenced other people, from Central America to Mexico.

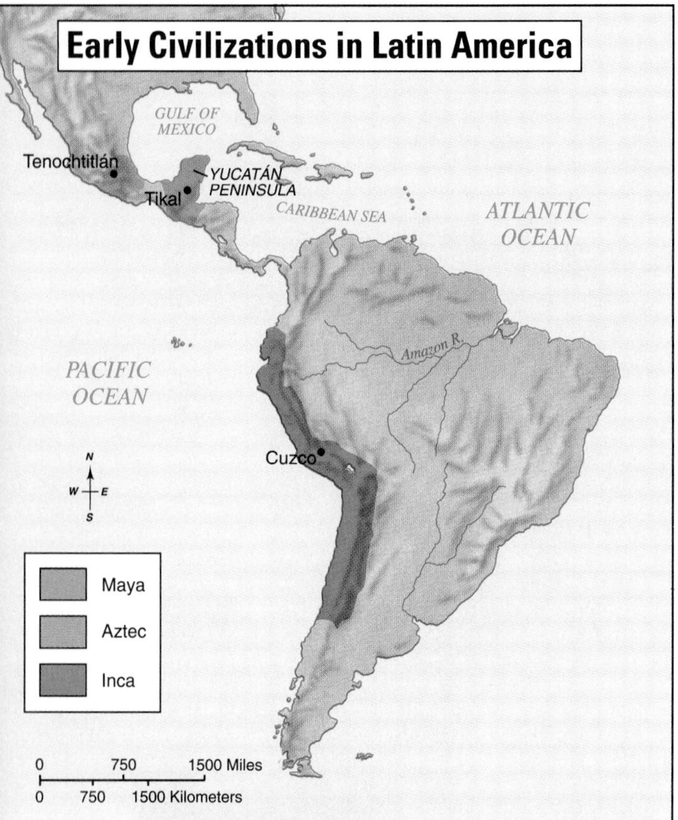

MAP STUDY

Several great civilizations developed in Latin America. These early civilizations were established in South America, Central America, and Mexico.

1. **Location** (a) Which early Native American empire was located in the Yucatan Peninsula? (b) What was its capital city?
2. **Interaction** Among which Native American cultures would you expect to find the most similarities? Explain
3. **Analyzing Information** What challenges might the Incas have faced in keeping their empire united?

The Aztec Empire

Long after the Maya cities had declined, the Aztecs built an advanced civilization to the north and west of Maya lands. The Aztecs moved into the Central Plateau of Mexico in about 1200. There, they came into contact with people like the Toltecs, who had absorbed ideas from the Mayas. From the Toltecs, the Aztecs learned to build pyramid-temples and indirectly absorbed other ideas from the Mayas.

Government. After settling in Tenochtitlán, the Aztecs embarked on a course of conquest. Unlike the Maya city-states, each of which had its own king, the Aztecs had only one ruler. He was chosen by a small group of priests, nobles, and warriors. With their help, the Aztec ruler gained control of a vast territory.

By about 1450, Aztec warriors began to attack and defeat the city-states that bordered Tenochtitlán. When the Aztecs defeated a nation, they left its rulers in place. However, the defeated nation had to pay tribute to the Aztecs in the form of maize, tobacco, gold, precious stones, and jaguar skins. By 1500, the Aztecs were collecting tribute from about 500 city-states.

As the Aztecs expanded, they took thousands of prisoners of war. They kept some captives as slaves, but they sacrificed many others to their god of war. The Aztecs believed that their success in war depended on such human sacrifices. The slaughter of captives made the Aztecs feared and hated throughout Mexico.

Religion. Like the Mayas, the Aztecs worshipped many gods. Priests had a powerful place in Aztec society. Priests were the guardians of the many huge temples in Tenochtitlán. Only they could perform the rituals that were thought to please the gods. They also recorded knowledge of science, mathematics, and medicine in books.

Among the chief Aztec gods was Quetzalcoatl (keht suhl koh AHT l), who they believed had brought maize to the Earth. According to legend, Quetzalcoatl had once taken human form and ruled the land. Then, disaster struck his kingdom, and this light-skinned, bearded ruler was banished. As he sailed off into the "eastern sea," he vowed to return one day. The legend of Quetzalcoatl would have tragic consequences for the Aztecs, as you will read.

Tenochtitlán. At the heart of the Aztec empire was the bustling city of Tenochtitlán. By 1500, it was home to 150,000 people, making it the largest city in the world at the time. To provide food, the Aztecs developed ways to farm the swampy land of Lake Texcoco.

Farmers filled large reed rafts with earth and anchored them in the lake bed. On these small floating islands, or *chinampas,* they planted their crops.

In Tenochtitlán's busy central market, merchants sold goods from all over the empire. A Spanish soldier described the many activities of the market:

> “There is an orderly arrangement of wares so that each kind is sold separately in its proper place. . . . [Here] they sell mantles and various kinds of men's dress, while women's dresses are sold elsewhere. There is a place for the sale of shoes, another for tanned deer hides. . . . Cotton is sold in yet another place, and grain here and bread there, of various kinds.”

Education. The Aztecs were among the first people to educate both boys and girls. Aztec children studied civics, history, and religion. To prepare for their future, boys received training in the arts of war. Girls studied homemaking skills and learned herbal medicine.

Women. Aztec women had certain rights. A woman could own property, and she could remarry if her husband died. Some women became priestesses, weavers, musicians, and midwives. Most of them spent their days at the time-consuming tasks of preparing food and making clothing for the family. One father's advice to his daughter shows what was expected of an Aztec woman:

> “How will you fulfill your womanly duties? Will you not prepare the food, the drink? Will you not spin and weave? Look well how are the food and drink, how they are made, that they should be good, know how good food and drink are prepared.”

The Inca Empire

Far to the south of the Aztec Empire lay the powerful Inca civilization. From their capital at Cuzco, the Incas built a vast empire in the fertile valleys of the Andes. Like the

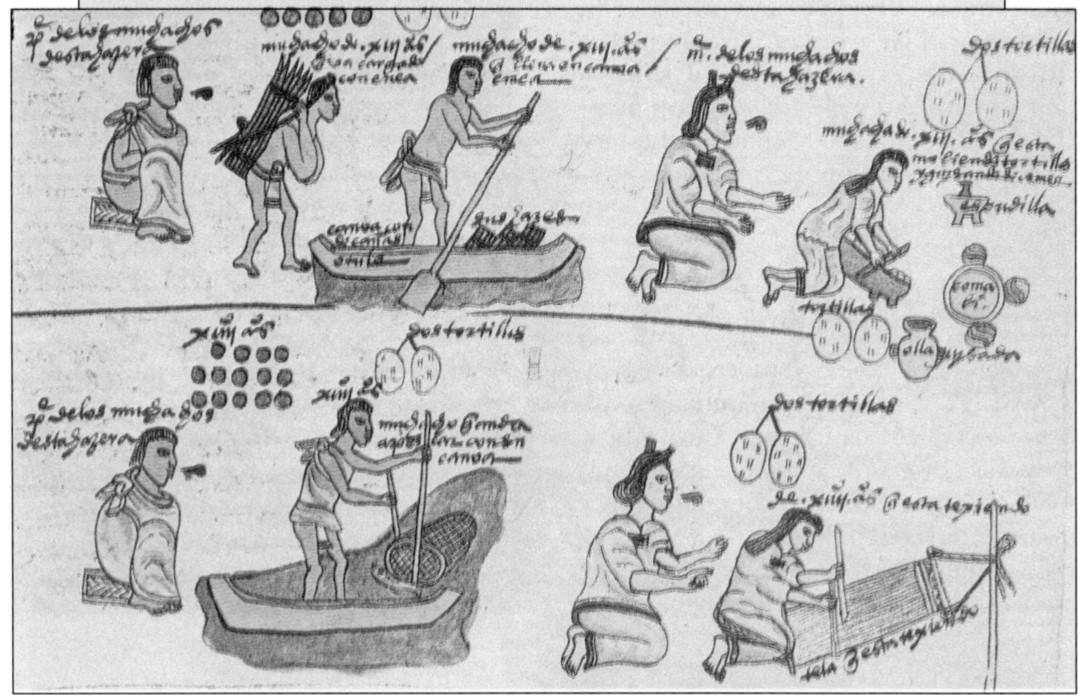

Aztec Education Pictures in an Aztec book show how the Aztecs taught their children. At left, a father teaches his son how to gather firewood, canoe, and fish. The mother, at right, instructs her daughter in grinding grain and weaving cloth. ***Technology*** What items of Aztec technology are shown here?

Aztecs, the Incas acquired skills and learning from earlier peoples in the area. By the late 1400s, the Inca Empire stretched 2,500 miles (4,023 km) across what is today Peru, Ecuador, Bolivia, and Chile.

Farming. The Incas were able to feed a population of 9 million people in part because they developed skilled farming methods. From earlier civilizations in the region, they learned to build complex irrigation systems that channeled water from mountain streams into the dry lowlands. They created farmland by carving terraces on steep mountainsides. By using fertilizer, they produced huge crops of corn, potatoes, and beans. Modern scientists have studied Inca farming methods to improve crop production today.

Religion. Like the Mayas and the Aztecs, the Incas worshipped many gods. Chief among them was the sun god. In fact, the word Inca means "children of the sun." The Inca royal family claimed to be descended from the sun god.

The center of Inca worship was the Temple of the Sun in Cuzco. Sheets of gold covered the temple walls, flaming in the Andean sun. To the Incas, gold was "the sweat of the gods." Priests and priestesses performed ceremonies to honor the sun god.

Government. The Inca emperor owned all the land, mines, and wealth of the empire. He ruled with the aid of nobles and priests. Officials told the people where to live and what jobs to do. They assigned plots of land to peasants to farm and collected taxes on peasants' crops. The smooth running of the empire also depended on an elaborate communications network.

The Efficient Incas

A young Inca crouched by the side of a mountain road. Let us call him Cusi Puma. His body was tense as he watched a point 100 yards (91 m) down the road. There, the highway disappeared over a ridge.

The young man was a *chasqui,* or runner. Assigned to this stretch of the highway, he was one of hundreds of messengers who helped to carry news across the Inca Empire.

To keep order in their empire, the Incas improved and extended the network of roads built by earlier people. The roads provided a

An Inca Highway A winding road crosses a small valley high in the Andes. The mountain highways of the Inca Empire stretched thousands of miles from north to south. To construct these roads, Inca engineers cut steps into steep mountainsides. They also used rope cables to build bridges across deep gorges. ***Power*** Why did the Incas need this vast network of roads?

route for armies and messengers. Pedro Cieza de León, a Spanish soldier and writer of the time, marveled at one of these Inca roads:

> "It passes over deep valleys and lofty mountains by snowy heights, over falls of water, through living rocks and edges of tortuous currents. In all these places, it is level and paved, along mountain slopes well excavated, by the mountains well terraced . . . along the river bank supported by walls, in the snowy heights with steps and resting places."

Cusi Puma's job began the moment another chasqui appeared on the road. He would dash out to meet him. Falling in stride alongside the tired runner, he would memorize the message he was given. Sometimes the messenger had to carry a quipu, or knotted string, to the next chasqui. The Incas, lacking a system of writing, used the quipu to keep records and accounts of such things as the size of a harvest.

With a fresh burst of speed, the young runner would race off, following the road as it zigzagged uphill. After three miles, the runner reached the next relay stop. There, he would pass the message on to another chasqui.

Through this efficient system of relays, a message could travel as far as 200 miles (322 km) a day. If a revolt occurred in one part of the empire, the ruler would learn of it quickly and send his armies to crush the rebels. Officials, too, used the roads for business, but the common people could not. ■

The Great Empires Fall

Both the Inca and the Aztec empires reached the peak of their power in about 1500. By then, Columbus had claimed the islands of the Caribbean and the nearby mainland for Spain.

Within a few years, conquistadors, or Spanish conquerors, were following Columbus to the Americas. They fanned out across Middle America and South America, hunting for the gold kingdoms that rumor described. "We came here to serve God and the king, and also to get rich," declared one conquistador about his motives for going to the Americas. Many Catholic priests went with the Spanish to the Americas. Once on shore, they set out to convert the Native Americans they found there to Christianity.

Cortés in Mexico. Hernando Cortés (kor TEHZ) landed on the coast of Mexico in 1519. As soon as he heard about the fabulous riches of the Aztec Empire, he made a daring plan to conquer it. With about 400 Spanish soldiers, 16 horses, and 14 cannons, he marched on Tenochtitlán. Within two years, the Spanish destroyed the powerful Aztec Empire. How did a tiny Spanish force defeat the Aztecs?

Many factors helped Cortés. First, the Aztec emperor, Moctezuma (mok tuh ZOO muh), hesitated to fight the Spanish. He believed that Cortés was the god-king Quetzalcoatl, returning as he had promised he would. Second, Cortés won allies among the people the Aztecs had conquered. Their armies strengthened the Spanish forces. Third, smallpox and other diseases that Europeans brought to the Americas killed thousands of Aztecs.

In addition, the Spanish rode horses, animals the Aztecs had never seen before. These strange animals terrified many Aztec soldiers. The metal armor, muskets, and cannons of the Spanish only increased the Aztecs' fears.

Pizarro in Peru. Similar events soon took place in South America. Like Cortés in Mexico, Francisco Pizarro had heard rumors of the great wealth of the Inca Empire. In 1532, he landed on the coast of Peru. There, Pizarro learned that the Incas had just emerged from a terrible civil war. Although the emperor Atahualpa (ah tah WAHL pah) retained his power, the fighting had weakened the empire.

Once again, a handful of Spanish soldiers riding horses and armed with muskets spread terror among the Indian armies. Disease, too, killed many of those who might have fought the invaders.

Pizarro used trickery to capture Atahualpa. The Inca emperor then offered to buy his freedom by filling a room with gold treasure.

Gold Ceremonial Weapon A gold-and-turquoise Inca knife is one of the few early Native American art objects that survived the Spanish conquest. Priceless works of art, such as golden ears of corn in silver baskets, were seized by Cortés and his army and destroyed. ***Fine Art*** Why did the Spanish melt down many gold and silver art objects?

Pizarro agreed to this, but then seized the treasure and murdered Atahualpa. Without a strong leader, organized Inca resistance faltered. By 1535, Pizarro controlled the vast Inca Empire.

Resistance and Survival

Intent on gaining riches and converting the Native Americans, Spanish soldiers and priests destroyed much of the material wealth of Native American cultures. The invaders melted down gold and silver objects of great beauty. They burned books and smashed sculptures and temples. Only a few ornaments and manuscripts survived the destruction.

Throughout the Americas, Native Americans fought against the invaders. Even after the Spanish completed their conquest, rebellions were frequent. Among the most famous was the 1780 uprising led by Tupac Amaru II, a descendant of the last Inca emperor.

Native Americans who survived the conquest preserved much of their cultural heritage. Today, millions of people in Peru, Ecuador, and Bolivia speak Quechua, the language of the Incas. In Guatemala and Mexico, Indian groups speak many languages that are of Maya origin. Temples, pyramids, and terraced hillsides stand today as evidence of the great Native American civilizations.

SECTION 3 REVIEW

1. **Locate:** (a) Tenochtitlán, (b) Tikal, (c) Cuzco.
2. **Identify:** (a) Quetzalcoatl, (b) Hernando Cortés, (c) Moctezuma, (d) Francisco Pizarro, (e) Atahualpa.
3. **Define:** (a) maize, (b) quipu, (c) conquistador.
4. (a) What three civilizations developed in the Americas? (b) Where was each located?
5. Describe two achievements of each of the early American civilizations.
6. Give three reasons why the Spanish were able to defeat the Aztecs and the Incas.
7. **Linking Past and Present** "As long as the world may endure, the fame and glory of Tenochtitlán will never perish," claimed an Aztec carving. Do you agree with this statement? Explain.
8. **Writing Across Cultures** Write a brief paragraph comparing the purpose of roads in the Inca Empire with the purpose of roads in the United States.

Chapter 20 Review

Understanding Vocabulary

Match each term at left with the correct definition at right.

1. pampas	**a.** Spanish conqueror
2. regionalism	**b.** hot land
3. tierra caliente	**c.** grassy plains south of the Amazon
4. mestizo	**d.** person of mixed Native American and European ancestry
5. conquistador	**e.** strong local traditions that divide people

Reviewing the Main Ideas

1. (a) Describe the location of Latin America. (b) How have the oceans affected Latin America?
2. (a) List the three major river systems of Latin America. (b) Briefly describe the location and importance of each.
3. Why is the Atacama Desert extremely dry?
4. Identify the major mineral resources, energy resources, and agricultural resources of Latin America.
5. How have people in Latin America created more farmland?
6. (a) How did the Maya religion contribute to advances in science and mathematics? (b) What role did disease play in the conquest of the Aztecs and Incas?

Reviewing Chapter Themes

1. Latin America is a region of diverse physical features, climates, and cultures. Give one example of diversity for each of these.
2. Geography has influenced population patterns in Latin America. Describe how physical features and climate have affected settlement in the region.
3. Latin Americans come from a variety of ethnic groups. Briefly describe how and when three of these groups reached Latin America.
4. In early times, three advanced civilizations emerged in the Americas. Briefly describe one of those civilizations.

Thinking Critically

1. **Making Global Connections** How do the agricultural resources of Latin America link it to the rest of the world?
2. **Understanding Causes and Effects** How do you think the geography of Latin America has affected the following: (a) communication, (b) differences among cultures, (c) relations with other nations?
3. **Evaluating Information** (a) What subjects did Aztec children study? (b) Do you think Aztec education prepared children for their roles in society? Explain.
4. **Synthesizing Information** How did the Incas keep control over their vast empire?

Applying Your Skills

1. **Outlining** Outline the subsection "Major Landforms" on pages 441–442. Make a generalization based on the outline.
2. **Identifying the Main Idea** Reread the paragraphs about Aztec government on page 450. List two main ideas from these paragraphs.
3. **Making a Review Chart** Make a chart that lists the names, dates, location, and achievements of the three major Native American civilizations of Latin America. (a) Which civilization was earliest? (b) Which civilizations were located in Central America? (c) Which civilization created farmland by carving terraces on steep mountainsides?

Chapter 21

HERITAGE OF LATIN AMERICA

A Country Church in Mexico The Catholic Church spread Christianity throughout Latin America, where it won millions of converts. The Church played an important role in the lives of the people of Latin America, both under Spanish rule and after independence. ***Culture*** What other elements of Spanish culture were adapted by Native Americans and influenced how they lived?

CHAPTER OUTLINE

In the pale light of dawn, an Aztec peasant named Juan Diego hurried along a dusty trail toward Mexico City. According to Diego's story, he suddenly heard a voice. Looking up, he saw the image of the Virgin Mary—a dark-skinned Native American woman—on Tepeyac Hill. "Go to the bishop of Mexico," the vision said, "and tell him that I wish a church to be built on this spot." Startled, Juan Diego did as he was told.

The year was 1531, only 10 years after Cortés had conquered Mexico. As word of Diego's story spread, Indians flocked to Tepeyac Hill. It was well known to them because a temple to the Aztec goddess Tonantsi had once stood there. The story of the appearance of the Virgin of Guadalupe led thousands of Aztecs to become Christians. Yet, when they prayed to her, they kept alive the spirit of their old religion. Some even called her Tonantsi.

The story of the Virgin of Guadalupe continues to inspire Christians. Each year, thousands of pilgrims visit the shrine.

CHAPTER PERSPECTIVE

This story suggests the enormous power and influence that the Roman Catholic Church has had in Latin America. It also shows the blending of Spanish and Native American cultures. In time, that culture would reflect African traditions as well.

As you read, look for these chapter themes:

- Spain and Portugal built rich empires in Latin America based on the labor of Native Americans and enslaved Africans.
- During the colonial period, a rigid class structure developed in which a privileged few controlled economic and political life.
- The Roman Catholic Church dominated life in Latin America and served as a unifying force.
- In the 1800s, Latin American countries won independence but many had trouble building stable governments.

Literature Connections

In this chapter, you will encounter passages from the following works.

"The Fall of Tenochtitlán," Aztec poem

A General History of the Indies, Bartolomé de las Casas

"Letter to the Bishop of Puebla," Sor Juana Inés de la Cruz

For other suggestions, see Connections With Literature, pages 804–808.

1 EUROPE'S COLONIES IN THE AMERICAS

FIND OUT

How did Spain and Portugal rule their empires in the Americas?

How did Europeans make their colonies profitable?

What were the effects of the Columbian exchange?

Vocabulary viceroy, cabildo, mercantilism, hacienda, donatario

A few years after Cortés captured Tenochtitlán, an Aztec poet wrote:

> “How can we save our homes, my
> people?
> The Aztecs are deserting the city:
> the city is in flames, and all
> is darkness and destruction. . . .
> Weep, my people:
> know that with these disasters
> we have lost the Mexican nation.”

The Spanish conquest ushered in a new era in the Americas. New governments replaced the great Native American empires. A new culture also evolved, blending the traditions of the Americas, Europe, and Africa.

Europeans Explore the Americas

By the late 1400s, Spain and Portugal were seeking an ocean route to Asia. While Portuguese explorers plotted a sea route around Africa, Christopher Columbus looked for a westward route across the Atlantic Ocean. He persuaded the rulers of Spain to pay for his voyage.

Columbus set sail on August 3, 1492, expecting to reach Asia within a few weeks.

When he sighted land on October 12, he was sure he had reached the East Indies off the coast of Asia. Columbus claimed the land for Spain. He called the people he met there Indians. However, Columbus had not reached the East Indies, but was in the islands of the Caribbean. Although Europeans soon realized Columbus's error, they continued to call the people of those islands Indians.

Dividing up the world. Columbus's voyage heightened tensions between Spain and Portugal. Both nations claimed the right to any lands they explored. To avoid war, they signed the Treaty of Tordesillas (tor day SEE yahs) in 1494. The treaty drew a Line of Demarcation that ran from north to south, about 1,100 miles (1,770 km) west of the Azores in the Atlantic. It gave Spain the right to claim all non-Christian lands west of the line. Portugal claimed lands east of the line.

Spanish claims. Under the Treaty of Tordesillas, Spain claimed most of the Americas. Hundreds of explorers and conquistadors followed in the path of Columbus. They hunted for gold and for a sea route around or through the Americas to the riches of Asia. In doing so, they mapped vast areas of the Americas.

One Spanish explorer, Vasco Núñez de Balboa, led an expedition across the mountains and jungles of Panama in 1513. Finally, Balboa reached a great body of water that he called the South Sea. Before long, another explorer, Ferdinand Magellan, renamed it the Pacific Ocean.

Magellan. In 1519, Magellan set out from the busy port of Seville, Spain, with 5 ships and 268 sailors. He hoped to find a passage around South America. After much hardship, he sailed around the stormy Cape Horn at the southern tip of the continent and into the Pacific Ocean. Magellan himself died fighting local people in the Philippines. In 1521, 18 sailors aboard one ship arrived back in Spain—the first Europeans to sail around the world.

Magellan's route around Cape Horn was too long and difficult to become a profitable trade route to Asia. By the 1530s, however, Spain was more interested in profiting from the enormous wealth of the Aztec and Inca empires.

Other claims to the Americas. Spain was not the only country to claim lands in the Americas. In 1500, Portuguese explorer Pedro Cabral landed on the east coast of South America in what is today Brazil. Because this land lay east of the Line of Demarcation, Cabral claimed it for Portugal.

During the 1500s and 1600s, French, English, and Dutch explorers tried to find a wa-

A Remarkable Voyage This map of the Americas was made in 1590 and notes Magellan's achievement in charting a route around the tip of South America. After reaching the Pacific, Magellan and his crew spent 98 days without touching land. After Magellan's death in the Philippines, the surviving crew members made their way to Spain. ***Geography*** How did Magellan's voyage succeed in achieving Columbus' goal?

ter passage through the Americas, connecting the Atlantic and the Pacific Oceans. These nations soon challenged Spanish and Portuguese claims. For almost 300 years, European powers battled for control of the Americas. Some Caribbean islands, such as Hispaniola and Jamaica, passed back and forth between Spain and France or Britain.

Spanish Rule in the Americas

By the mid-1500s, Spain ruled an empire that extended from Mexico to Peru. At first, the king of Spain divided his huge empire into two kingdoms and appointed a viceroy to rule in each. A viceroy is an official who rules in place of a king. One viceroy ruled New Spain, which had its capital in Mexico City. The other viceroy ruled Peru, which had its capital in Lima.

In Spain, the king set up the Council of the Indies. This powerful council made all the laws for the colonies. It also regulated the Church, the courts, and trade with Spain's American empire. The viceroys carried out the laws made by the Council of the Indies. Through these laws, the Council transferred Spanish ideas about government, law, and justice to the Americas.

Most Spanish settlers lived in towns. Spain set up cabildos (cah BEEL dohz), or councils, to govern towns and their surrounding lands. Cabildos usually were made up of wealthy landowners. The cabildos punished criminals, sent troops to hunt runaway slaves, and set the price of bread and other items.

Mercantilism. Like other European countries, Spain believed that the purpose of colonies was to enrich the parent country. This belief was based on the principles of mercantilism. According to mercantilists, a country's economic strength depended on increasing its gold supply by exporting more goods than it imported.

Under mercantilism, colonies had two roles. They supplied the parent country with raw materials such as lumber, cotton, sugar, and precious metals. They also served as a market where the parent country sold its manufactured goods, such as furniture, clothing, and tools.

MAP STUDY

In the 1500s, Spain and Portugal built empires in the Americas. This map shows European colonies in the late 1700s.

1. **Region** (a) Which European nation set up the largest empire in the Americas? (b) Name four of its colonies.
2. **Location** Which European nations had colonies in South America?
3. **Forecasting** Based on geography, what problems do you think European powers had ruling colonies in the Americas?

A colony could trade only with its parent country and was not allowed to manufacture finished goods. Thus, mercantilism made the colonies economically dependent on Spain for trade and manufactured goods. In return,

Silver Mining in Bolivia The Spanish founded the town of Potosí in the high Andes in the early 1500s. This sketch shows llamas carrying silver from the mines and Native American workers processing the ore. The Potosí mines were the world's richest source of silver for more than half a century. ***Power*** Why was silver mining important to Spain's mercantilist policy?

the colonies received protection from the parent country.

Treasure from the Americas. The first raw materials shipped from the Americas to Spain were the treasures of the Aztec and Inca empires. The conquistadors melted down tons of fine gold and silver jewelry and magnificent ornaments created by Aztec and Inca artisans. Each year, huge fleets set sail for Spain, loaded with bars of gold and silver. Pirates lurked in the sea lanes around the Caribbean, eager to seize these treasure ships.

The Spanish also forced the Indians to mine gold and silver. Mines such as Potosí (poh toh SEE) in the Andes produced tons of silver ore. Treasure from the Americas helped to make Spain the richest and most powerful nation in Europe at this time.

Plantation economy. Agriculture in the Americas was another source of wealth for Spain. Spanish colonists set up plantations to grow cash crops that were shipped to Spain. Each plantation was a large tract of land operated by the owner or an overseer and farmed by workers who lived on the land.

A plantation usually grew a single crop. Many plantations in the West Indies produced sugar cane, which was made into refined sugar for easy shipping. Most plantations in Central and South America produced coffee or fruit crops such as bananas. In Mexico and Argentina, colonists turned large tracts of land into cattle or sheep ranches. These ranches provided meat, hides for leather, and wool for textiles.

The Search for Labor

Spanish settlers needed workers for their mines, plantations, and ranches. As a result, they tried various sources of labor.

Encomienda system. During the early 1500s, the king of Spain rewarded the conquistadors with encomiendas. An encomienda gave a Spanish settler the right to demand taxes or labor from the people living on the land. The settler given an encomienda was supposed to pay the Native Americans for their work, look after their health, and teach them about Christianity.

In many places, settlers forced Native Americans to labor in mines under dangerous and unhealthy conditions. The backbreaking work, poor food, and frequent epidemics killed thousands of Indians. Four out of every five Indians died during their first year in the mines. On the sugar plantations of Hispaniola, harsh conditions and brutal treatment led to the destruction of the entire population of the Arawak people.

Bartolomé de las Casas. A few Spanish settlers spoke out against the mistreatment of the Indians. Bartolomé de las Casas (las KAH sahs) briefly held an encomienda in Cuba. His disgust at the cruel system led him to become a Dominican friar. He then went to Spain to plead with the king to stop the misuse of the Indians. In detailed reports, he told of the horrors he had seen and the desperation of the Indians.

In his *General History of the Indies,* Las Casas told of a Native American prince who was named Hatuey. Condemned to be burned at the stake for leading a rebellion, Hatuey asked a Spanish monk if heaven was open to the Spanish.

> “The monk replied that it was open to those who were good. With no more thought, Hatuey said he had no mind to go to heaven, for fear of meeting with such cruel and wicked people as they were; he would much rather go to hell. This is the renown and honor that God and our religion have acquired because of the people who have gone to the Indies.”

New laws. The reports from Las Casas caused a scandal in Spain. In 1542, the Spanish government passed the New Laws of the Indies. They reformed the encomienda system and banned Indian slavery. By then, however, most Indians in the Caribbean had died from mistreatment and diseases brought by the Europeans, and Indian populations elsewhere had fallen dramatically.

The death of so many Native Americans opened new lands for the Spanish to settle. By the late 1500s, many newcomers from Spain owned haciendas, or large plantations. The haciendas were located on the best farmland, leaving the Indians only the least productive lands.

A Slave System

In his desire to protect the Indians, Las Casas gave advice that he later regretted. He suggested that Spain use Africans instead of Indians to work the mines and plantations. He thought that Africans could survive the harsh conditions in the tropics.

Roots of slavery. During the 1500s, slavery existed in Europe as it did elsewhere around the world. Europeans bought slaves from Russia and Eastern Europe as well as from Africa. In fact, the word slave comes from Slav, the name of an ethnic group that includes Russians and Poles. During the mid-1500s, however, the expanding Ottoman Empire cut off the supply of slaves from Eastern Europe. By that time, the Portuguese were increasing their trade with Africa, exchanging cloth and weapons for gold, salt, and slaves.

Spread of African slavery. Several factors encouraged the growth of African slavery. For one thing, the Spanish were already using Africans to work their plantations on the Canary Islands off the northwest coast of Africa. When colonists in the Americas needed laborers, Europeans were ready to send Africans across the Atlantic.

A New Settlement In the 1500s, the Spanish built towns across Mexico. This painting shows the founding of San Crístobal de las Casas in southern Mexico. It lies in a high, fertile basin and is ringed by the Chiapas Mountains.
Choice Why do you think the Spanish moved quickly to build settlements like this one?

Spanish colonists valued African slaves over Native Americans because Africans knew how to plant and raise crops. Except for the Aztecs and the Incas, most Native Americans did not live in settled farming villages. Also, Africans were better able to resist diseases brought by Europeans such as smallpox and measles. As a result, fewer Africans died of these diseases than Indians did.

As you read in Chapter 4, European and Arab slave traders sent millions of Africans to the Americas. Many Africans died during the terrible voyage across the Atlantic. Others died from overwork, poor food, and unhealthy living conditions. As late as 1850, a slave in Brazil could be expected to live for about 35 years. As a result, the demand for slaves continued.

The Portuguese in Brazil

At first, the Portuguese were slow to develop their American colony in Brazil. They were busy building a trading empire in Africa and in the Spice Islands of Southeast Asia. (See Chapter 12.)

In the 1530s, the king of Portugal began to encourage settlement. He was afraid the French or English would seize Brazil. As a result, he divided the colony into 15 regions and distributed them among the nobles at his court. Each donatario, as these landowners were called, was the lord of a huge area. The donatarios, in turn, brought over colonists from Portugal to settle their lands.

Sugar and slavery. To make the colony profitable, the Portuguese turned to growing sugar. Between 1550 and 1605, the number of sugar plantations grew from 5 to 350. Like the Spanish, the Portuguese, too, enslaved the Native Americans at first, but then turned to slaves from Africa. Nearly 40 percent of all Africans taken to the Americas were sent to Brazil. By 1860, when the slave trade finally ended, slave traders had carried 3.5 million Africans to Brazil.

In addition to sugar cane, Brazil produced cotton and coffee. Colonists built plantations in a narrow strip along the coast at the mouths of rivers. Port cities such as Bahia, Pernambuco, and Rio de Janeiro grew as the plantation economy prospered.

During the 1630s, the Dutch seized lands in Brazil and learned to grow sugar. When the Portuguese expelled them, many Dutch moved to the Caribbean. There, they set up sugar plantations like those they had left in Brazil. English, French, and Danish settlers also seized islands in the Caribbean. They then learned from the Dutch how to produce sugar.

New treasures. During the 1690s, the Portuguese discovered gold and diamonds in the Brazilian Highlands. Thousands of colonists deserted the coastal cities to seek their fortunes in the interior. New settlers, eager to find gold, poured in from Portugal. They took many slaves to work in the gold fields, further expanding settlement in Brazil.

The Columbian Exchange

The European exploration and conquest of the Americas created important links between the Eastern and Western hemispheres. These links changed both regions forever. Europeans and Africans brought plants, animals, and knowledge to the Americas. In turn, products and ideas from the Americas spread around the world. This global exchange of people, goods, and ideas is called the Columbian exchange. It is named after Christopher Columbus.

Movement of peoples. The Columbian exchange involved the movement of millions of people. Settlers flocked to the Americas from all over Europe, carrying their ideas about government, law, and religion. Enslaved Africans also brought their own cultures to the New World. Through their folktales, music, and beliefs, they helped to reshape the cultures of the Americas.

Foods. The Spanish introduced many new foods from the Americas to Europeans. These included corn, potatoes, squash, chocolate, peanuts, and tomatoes. From the Americas, Europeans carried sweet potatoes to Africa and pineapples, papaya, and chili peppers to Asia. The new foods enriched the diets of people around the world. Italians, for exam-

Potato Farming Andean people first raised potatoes about 2,000 years ago. The Spanish took this vegetable back to Europe. At first, because the Bible did not mention potatoes, some clergy warned Europeans not to eat them. In time, however, potatoes became an important part of people's diet. ***Interdependence*** How did the Columbian exchange help enrich the food supply of the world?

ple, invented many dishes that included tomatoes. People in India used chili peppers to spice their curry dishes.

At the same time, Europeans introduced new crops such as wheat, barley, and chick-peas to the Americas. Columbus brought horses, cows, sheep, chickens, and pigs from Europe. Horses and cattle thrived in parts of Mexico and Argentina. From Asia, Europeans brought rice and bananas to the Americas, while from Africa, they carried yams, sugar cane, coffee, and coconuts.

Disease. From the Incas, Europeans learned to use quinine, from the bark of the cinchona tree, to treat malaria. At the same time, however, the Spanish carried diseases such as smallpox, measles, and influenza to the Americas. Because they had no resistance to these diseases, Native Americans died in great numbers. An Aztec described a smallpox epidemic that struck Tenochtitlán during the 1520s:

> "The illness was so dreadful that no one could walk or move. . . . A great many died from this plague and many others died of hunger. They could not get up to search for food, and everyone else was too sick to care for them."

Disease, along with war and mistreatment, changed the population patterns of the Americas. The Indian population of Central Mexico, for example, was about 25 million when Cortés arrived in 1519. It fell to 6 million by 1550 and to a little more than 1 million by 1605.

SECTION 1 REVIEW

1. **Locate:** (a) Hispaniola, (b) New Spain, (c) Peru, (d) Brazil.
2. **Identify:** (a) Vasco Núñez de Balboa, (b) Ferdinand Magellan, (c) Pedro Cabral, (d) Bartolomé de las Casas, (e) Columbian exchange.
3. **Define:** (a) viceroy, (b) cabildo, (c) mercantilism, (d) hacienda, (e) donatario.
4. How did the king of Spain control his empire in the Americas?
5. How did Europeans get the workers they needed to make their colonies profitable?
6. Describe three results of the Columbian exchange.
7. **Understanding Causes and Effects** How did sugar encourage the growth of the slave trade between Africa and the Americas?
8. **Writing Across Cultures** Write a list of ways in which European exploration and conquest of the Americas have affected your life.

2

PATTERNS OF LIFE

FIND OUT

What social classes developed in Latin America?

How did the Catholic Church influence colonial life?

What were the main features of family life?

Vocabulary peninsular, creole, peon

"At the age of six or seven, when I already knew how to read and write, as well as to sew and do other women's tasks, I heard that in Mexico City there was a university, and schools where the sciences were taught. No sooner had I heard this than I began to badger my mother with pleas that she let me put on men's clothing and go to Mexico City."

Juana Inés de la Cruz was brilliant. Still, officials refused to admit her to the university because she was a woman. To pursue a life of study, she became a nun. In the convent, she wrote poems and essays on topics ranging from music to mathematics. At a time when few women in Latin America learned to read, Sor (Sister) Juana won great fame for her clever writings and her vast knowledge.

Sor Juana lived in Mexico during the 1600s. There, as elsewhere in the Americas, certain patterns of life emerged. The three most powerful forces that shaped colonial life were the social system, the Roman Catholic Church, and the cities.

A Rigid Class System

A rigid social structure governed colonial life. Although conditions varied from one region to another and changes occurred over time, the social system was basically the same throughout Latin America.

Peninsulares. The highest class were the peninsulares (peh NIHN suh LAHR ays), officials sent from Spain to rule the colonies. Peninsulares included viceroys as well as high government and Church officials. This small but powerful group controlled the economic and political life of the colonies. Proud of their Spanish birth, the peninsulares looked down on people who were born in the colonies.

Creoles. Ranked below the peninsulares were the creoles, who were American-born descendants of Spanish settlers. By law, creoles had the same rights as peninsulares. In practice, however, the king did not appoint creoles to top jobs in government or the Church. Educated and wealthy creoles bitterly resented the privileged peninsulares.

Mestizos. Far below the peninsulares and creoles were the mestizos, people of mixed Indian and European descent. Their numbers grew over the years until they became the majority in some areas. Most mestizos were shop owners, artisans, farmers, and overseers at mines or on plantations.

Native Americans. Lower on the social scale were the Native Americans. Some worked as farmhands on haciendas owned by peninsulares and creoles. Others lived in their own villages, raising crops on lands that they held in common. In most villages, Native Americans spoke their own languages and preserved their own traditions. Nearly all became Christians, however.

Free blacks. Over time, the number of free blacks grew. Both Spain and Portugal allowed slaves to buy their freedom. A few owners freed their slaves in their wills. In the Caribbean islands ruled by the British or French, slaves had a much harder time winning freedom.

Most free blacks became farm workers and laborers. Some, especially in Brazil, earned a living in skilled trades. They worked as barbers, shoemakers, goldsmiths, sculptors, and musicians.

Slaves. At the lowest level of society were the slaves. Planters deliberately bought slaves from different parts of Africa so that their slaves would not have a common language or religion. They would then have to adopt the language and customs of their owners. Most slaves became Christians, although a few Muslim Africans held on to their beliefs.

Under colonial law, slaves were considered to be property. Even so, slaves in Latin America had certain rights. They could marry and own property, unlike slaves in the English colonies. They could also buy their freedom.

The Roman Catholic Church

The social system divided people along class lines. By contrast, the Roman Catholic Church was a unifying force. From the very beginning, the Church played a major role in shaping colonial life. The missionaries who came with the conquistadors set up churches in towns and cities. They also traveled to remote areas, where they built missions.

At first, the missionaries tried to protect the Indians from harsh rule by the Spanish. But they also wanted Native Americans to give up their religious beliefs, which the missionaries believed were evil. For this reason, they destroyed Native American temples, statues, and sacred objects. In writing about his travels to Maya lands, the bishop Diego de Landa said, "We found a large number of books . . . and we burned them all."

Indian influences. The Church replaced Native American beliefs with those of European Christians. In the process, the Church absorbed some Indian customs. In Mexico City, Cuzco, and elsewhere, Christian churches were built on the ruins of Indian temples. In Mexico, Indian stonemasons decorated the new churches with both Christian figures and Aztec symbols. Offerings of maize and other local products filled the churches during religious festivals. The story of the Virgin of Guadalupe, which you read earlier, is an example of the blending of Indian and Christian traditions.

Social Classes At top, a peninsular and his family are out for a walk near their home. The family's fine clothing and servants attest to their high status in society. In contrast, the people in the picture below rank lower on the social scale as their clothing and heavy loads suggest. ***Diversity*** Name and rank the six main social classes in colonial Latin America.

Africans and the Church. The Church also spread Christianity among the Africans who had been brought to the Americas. To teach Christian beliefs, missionaries told stories about saints. Africans often saw similarities between their traditional gods and Catholic saints. Most Africans converted to Christianity,

Life in Havana Wealthy women had the advantage of shopping from their carriage in Cuba's capital city. When these women returned home, they may have enjoyed a popular beverage made of chocolate, or cacao, and some pastry. A variety of fresh fruit, including figs, bananas, grapes, and oranges, was also available. ***Culture*** What were some of the activities of upper-class women?

but many retained some elements of their traditional beliefs.

A powerful force. Because it had close ties to the government, the Church enjoyed great power and wealth. It received huge grants of land from Spain and Portugal, as well as gifts from wealthy colonists. Like other landowners, Church officials taxed the Indians and others who worked the land. In time, the Church became the largest and richest property owner in Latin America.

The Church controlled many aspects of life, including education, hospitals, and services to the poor. It set up schools and trained teachers. By the 1550s, it had built universities in Santo Domingo, Mexico City, and Lima. There, the sons of wealthy creoles and even some mestizos studied to become priests, doctors, and lawyers. The Church spent large sums on charity and on the many religious festivals that were celebrated throughout the year.

Family Life

Family ties were strong throughout Latin America. Among Spanish and Portuguese colonists, the extended family was the ideal. On many haciendas, several generations lived under one roof. Servants, slaves, and even skilled craftworkers might also live with the extended family. In towns and cities, however, many colonists lived in nuclear families, although they maintained close ties to relatives.

Padrinos, or godparents, played an important role in the family. They made sure that their godchildren received proper religious instruction. Often, padrinos were friends or relatives who helped the family in time of need.

By tradition, families were patriarchal. The oldest male made the important decisions. When a man died, most of his lands and property went to his eldest son. Women and younger family members were expected to obey the head of the household. Parents arranged marriages. Sometimes, a young couple would not meet each other until the day of their wedding.

Women in the Spanish colonies had few rights. The Spanish believed that teaching women to read and write would corrupt them. Therefore, most women received little or no formal education. Sor Juana was an exception. She struggled hard to educate herself. Even then, officials refused to admit her to the University of Mexico.

Women from the middle and upper classes were carefully guarded when they went outside the home. Unmarried women had to travel with dueñas, or chaperones. In wealthy households, women occupied their time with music, embroidery, or religious matters. Some did charity work at hospitals and orphanages. Servants or slaves did the housework.

Lower-class women often worked outside the home. In cities and towns, some women ran taverns or small stores, especially if they were widowed. In rural areas, a widow might manage a farm or ranch if she had no male relative nearby.

Life in the Cities

Cities were the center of power and wealth in Latin America. Most peninsulares and many creoles lived in towns or cities. Owners of plantations and mines also spent long periods in their city homes, leaving overseers to look after their properties in the country.

Town layout. Colonial towns and cities had the same layout as those in Spain or Portugal. At the center was a large plaza, with a cathedral or church on one side and government buildings, a monastery, or a school on the other. Wide streets led out from this central plaza. Wealthy families lived along these streets. Beyond were the homes of artisans and small merchants. The poorest people lived on the outskirts of the town.

Rich and poor. In colonial cities, the wealthy copied the styles of the upper class in Spain and Portugal. Architects designed stone and brick houses like those in Madrid or Lisbon. The rich imported furniture, rugs, and paintings from Europe. They dressed lavishly to show off their great wealth. "A hat-band and rose made of diamonds in a gentleman's hat is common," noted one visitor.

In contrast, the poor lived in homes made of adobe, or sun-dried brick, with straw roofs. In the Caribbean, they lived in shacks made of planks or sugar canes and thatched with palm leaves. They wore simple, homespun clothes. Both rich and poor, however, enjoyed the many public celebrations and fiestas. To mark occasions such as the arrival of a new viceroy, towns and cities held bullfights and grand processions.

Life in the Countryside

Some Latin American cities grew to be very large by the early 1600s, but most people lived in the countryside. Native Americans and mestizos lived in villages and on haciendas. A hacienda was like a small town owned by one person. The largest haciendas covered many square miles of territory. The *hacendado,* or landlord, ruled his estate with a firm

Country Life This drawing shows the society of Mexico's rural areas. Hunting and riding were favorite pastimes of the rich hacendados. The landless peasants who farmed these estates worked long, hard hours in the fields. However, they, too, enjoyed amusements such as family weddings and christenings. ***Power*** How did the estate owners control the peasants who worked for them?

hand. He acted as both judge and jury if someone was accused of a crime.

Life on the hacienda. Haciendas might be either farms or ranches. They were largely self-sufficient. They produced crops, meat, and leather for their own use and for sale to outside markets. Haciendas in north Mexico, for example, provided for the needs of the silver mining center at Zacateces.

Workers on haciendas made their own clothing, candles, and other everyday goods. A blacksmith made farm tools and horseshoes. On religious holidays, people held their own celebrations and might have their own rodeos.

Most hacienda workers were Native Americans. Often, haciendas included one or more Native American villages. The hacendados sought to hold Indian workers in debt in order to ensure a steady source of labor for their land. They would give workers advances on their wages and require them to stay on the hacienda until they had paid back what they owed. Indians or mestizos who were forced to work for someone else in order to pay off a debt were called peons.

Native American men did the heavy outdoor work. Women were usually cooks and servants in the hacendado's house. In addition, Native Americans also grew their own food on small plots of land.

Haciendas were frequently so large and self-sufficient that many people spent their entire lives on these estates. As a result, haciendas contributed to regionalism within Latin America. (See Connections With Literature, page 806, "Bread.")

Maroon colonies. Another type of rural settlement was the maroon colony.* Maroon colonies were villages built by escaped slaves. They were found in Brazil, the Guianas, Haiti, and Jamaica. Runaways faced the constant risk of attack by soldiers. To planters, the maroons set a dangerous example for their own slaves, who might be inspired by them to dream of freedom.

Escape to the Woods In Brazil, the Caribbean, and elsewhere in Latin America, escaped slaves hid and formed their own communities, or maroons. One maroon settlement in Brazil lasted for more than 65 years. Another, in Ecuador, escaped discovery by the Spanish for nearly three centuries. ***Human Rights*** What benefits did escaped slaves hope to gain by living isolated from others?

Life in a Maroon Colony

Louis and his father carefully planned their escape. All week, they saved and hid food. Early one morning, they stole a small canoe. They paddled upstream, away from the town of Cayenne in French Guiana. With luck, they might reach a maroon colony, high in the hills.

After paddling beyond the last houses, Louis and his father hid in the forest. Eventually, they met another escaped slave who told them how to reach the nearest maroon village. Louis recalled:

> "We slept in the forest that first day and arrived at the village on the following day at about noon, after having taken several detours and passed many streams and mountains."

---

* Maroon comes from the Spanish word *cimarrón,* meaning wild or untamed.

More than 70 runaways lived in the maroon colony. They welcomed and fed the two newcomers. The gardens that surrounded the village, said Louis, "are almost completely filled with manioc, millet, rice, sweet potatoes, yams, sugar cane, bananas, and other crops, and a lot of cotton." Women first spun the cotton into yarn and then wove it into clothing.

The villagers gave land to Louis and his father. "Everyone is allotted a plot according to the needs of his family," Louis noted. "Whenever land has to be cleared, everyone works together." Still, life was not easy. The maroons had few tools or pots and pans. They had some weapons but little gunpowder.

The villagers were devout Christians who recited prayers each morning and evening. In addition, Louis noted, "They maintain strict observance of Sundays and feast days by refraining from work and reciting the rosary."

After a year and a half of freedom, Louis and many other villagers were captured by French soldiers. The French executed the colony's leaders in front of their children. Louis and his father were sent back to their owners. ■

SECTION 2 REVIEW

1. **Define:** (a) peninsular, (b) creole, (c) peon.
2. (a) Describe the main social classes in colonial Latin America. (b) Why did creoles resent the peninsulares?
3. What are three ways the Catholic Church influenced colonial Latin America?
4. (a) Who had most power in the traditional family? (b) How did social class affect women's lives?
5. **Comparing** (a) How did city life differ from rural life in colonial Latin America? (b) In what ways were they similar?
6. **Writing Across Cultures** In both Latin America and the United States, runaway slaves took enormous risks. Write a diary entry in which a slave explains why he or she is willing to face these dangers.

3 WINNING INDEPENDENCE

FIND OUT

Why did the people of Latin America seek independence?

How did events in Europe influence the wars of independence?

What role did individual leaders play in winning independence?

Before dawn on September 16, 1810, ringing church bells woke the Indian peasants of Dolores, a small town in Mexico. The people hurried to their church. Their creole priest, Father Miguel Hidalgo, was waiting for them. He spoke urgently:

> "My children, will you be free? Will you make the effort to recover from the hated Spaniards the lands stolen from your forefathers 300 years ago?"

Startled at first, the people soon responded to Father Hidalgo's call. His words echoed throughout the Spanish colonies in Latin America. *"El grito de Dolores"*—the cry of Dolores—became the rallying cry for many people unhappy with Spanish rule. Today, Mexicans celebrate September 16 as their Independence Day.

Unrest in the Colonies

By the late 1700s, many groups had begun to demand freedom from Spanish rule. Creoles often led the struggles for independence. The creoles felt that they had built the colonies and deserved to rule them. Getting rid of royal officials would open new opportunities.

Mestizos, too, hoped to move up in society once the peninsulares were gone. Many Indians, remembering that the Spanish had taken their lands 300 years earlier, also sought freedom from Spanish rule. In 1780, the Indian leader Tupac Amaru led a revolt against the Spanish in Peru. After a brief success, the revolt was crushed and Tupac Amaru and all his family were executed or imprisoned. Finally, slaves saw independence as a way to gain freedom.

Spread of revolutionary ideas. Radical new ideas from Europe fueled the growing discontent. During the period known as the Enlightenment, thinkers in France and Britain argued that people had natural rights to life, liberty, and property. These thinkers supported freedom of speech, an end to slavery, and the idea that people had the right to rebel against unjust rulers. You will read more about the Enlightenment in Chapter 30.

Ideas like these encouraged colonists in North America to throw off British rule in 1776. When the French Revolution broke out in 1789, creoles and mestizos watched events in Europe with interest. Some took up the cry of the French revolutionaries—"Liberty, Equality, Fraternity."

Toussaint L'Ouverture As ruler of an independent Haiti, L'Ouverture kept strict control over his people. The freed slaves who worked on the plantations now received some of the profits. L'Ouverture, a deeply religious man, dealt fairly with the French, who had oppressed his people. ***Change*** Why did Haiti's independence alarm creoles in other Latin American colonies?

Revolution in Haiti

Revolutionary ideas touched off a revolt in French-ruled Haiti. Located on the island of Hispaniola, Haiti was the world's leading sugar producer. A few French families made huge profits from sugar, while most Haitians lived in misery as slaves.

When the French Revolution began, white settlers called for independence. Slaves had their own goal—freedom. In 1791, they rebelled. They burned the sugar cane in the fields and killed hundreds of slave owners. The uprising touched off 13 years of terrible civil war in which both sides suffered massacres.

Toussaint L'Ouverture. The rebels found a remarkable leader in Toussaint L'Ouverture (too SAN loo vehr TYOOR), a self-educated former slave. L'Ouverture organized the rebels into an effective fighting force. By 1800, this able but ruthless leader had driven all foreign forces out of Hispaniola.

When the ambitious general Napoleon Bonaparte took power in France, he decided to reclaim the rich sugar plantations of Haiti for France. In 1802, he sent a French army to the island. L'Ouverture urged Haitians to fight to the death against the invaders.

The French captured L'Ouverture and sent him to an icy prison in France. There, the Haitian leader died in 1803. Before his death, however, he warned the French:

> "In overthrowing me, the French have only felled the tree of black liberty in Saint Domingue [Haiti]. It will shoot up again for it is deeply rooted and its roots are many."

Independence at last. In Haiti, meanwhile, thousands of French soldiers died from yellow fever. The survivors fled the island. In 1804, Haiti declared its independence. It became the first independent nation in Latin America and the second in the Western Hemisphere, after the United States.

Haiti's success frightened many creoles in Spanish America. They wanted independence, but not a revolution that might upset the social order. The Haitian slave revolt roused fears about what actions other black populations in the Americas might take.

Liberty for South America

Events in Europe triggered revolts in most of Spanish-ruled America. During the early 1800s, Napoleon plunged all of Europe, including Spain, into years of war. The fighting weakened Spain's hold on its colonies and increased demands for independence.

With the defeat of Napoleon in 1815, Spain set out to restore its authority in its colonies. By then, however, the colonists had found strong leaders who were determined to win freedom.

Simón Bolívar. In South America, Simón Bolívar (see MOHN boh LEE vahr) earned the title "the Liberator" for his role in the wars of independence. Energetic and brilliant, Bolívar came from a wealthy creole family in Venezuela. As a young man, he studied in Europe. There, his love of freedom was strengthened by the ideas of the French Revolution. Before returning, Bolívar vowed:

> "I will never allow my hands to be idle nor my soul to rest until I have broken the chains laid upon us by Spain."

In 1807, Bolívar joined revolutionaries in Venezuela who were plotting to end Spanish rule. They faced a long struggle against the peninsulares and other royalists, or supporters of the monarchy. Twice, Bolívar had to flee to Haiti. Haitian leaders gave him ships, guns, money, and a printing press. In return, Bolívar promised to free all slaves once Venezuela gained independence.

The rebels were not strong enough to defeat the royalists, who held forts along the coast. Instead, Bolívar came up with a bold plan. He would march his army inland and over the Andes to attack Bogotá, capital of the viceroyalty of New Grenada. Bolívar won the backing of the *llaneros* (yahn AYR ohs), the cowboys of the plains. They held down Spanish forces in Venezuela. Meanwhile, Bolívar led his ragged army up the Orinoco River, through dense jungles, and over the icy peaks of the Andes. In 1819, they surprised and defeated the Spanish defenders of Bogotá.

"The Liberator" In a daring move, Simón Bolívar and his ragged army scaled the Andes. They suffered great hardships before they triumphed over the Spanish defenders of Bogotá. After 1819, the Liberator's successes increased as he helped other areas gain freedom from Spain. ***Power*** How do you think a bold move like crossing the Andes inspired confidence in Bolívar's leadership?

Bolívar then set up the Republic of Gran Colombia, which included Venezuela, Colombia, and two areas yet to be freed from Spanish rule—Ecuador and Peru. In the fight to free those colonies, Bolívar joined forces with another Latin American hero, José de San Martín.

José de San Martín. Like Bolívar, José de San Martín was a creole. His family lived in

MAP STUDY

During the early 1800s, most of Latin America gained its independence from European rule.

1. **Region** (a) Name the nations of Central America that gained their independence from Spain. (b) Which lands in Central America and the Caribbean remained European colonies?
2. **Interaction** How did geography affect the struggle for independence?
3. **Comparing** Compare this map with the map on page 459. Then write two generalizations about the changes that occurred in the Americas by the early 1800s.

Argentina but sent him to Spain to serve as an officer in the Spanish army. In 1812, San Martín returned to Argentina to fight for freedom. By 1816, Argentina had won independence.

San Martín then vowed to liberate Chile. With the help of Chilean patriot Bernardo O'Higgins, San Martín led his army across 12,000-foot (3,657 m) snow-clogged passes in the Andes. Troops dragged heavy cannons up dangerous, icy trails. Caught unprepared, the Spanish soon surrendered. Chile declared its independence in 1818.

San Martín left O'Higgins in charge of Chile. He then headed north to help Bolívar free Ecuador and Peru. By 1825, South America had thrown off Spanish rule. The British, French, and Dutch, however, still held their colonies on the northern coast of South America.

Mexico's Struggle for Freedom

With the "grito de Dolores," in 1810, Father Miguel Hidalgo touched off a long struggle for independence in Mexico. There, as elsewhere in Latin America, many groups had grievances against Spain.

Division between rich and poor. At first, the creoles supported Hidalgo and his army of Native Americans and mestizos. However, they soon turned against the rebellion. As the rebels marched toward Mexico City, they seized the estates of wealthy creoles and peninsulares. Hidalgo announced liberal reforms such as an end to slavery and to the tribute that Indians had to pay. He also promised to return lands to the Indians. This frightened creole landowners, who withheld their support from the rebels.

That decision had tragic consequences. Peninsulares, rich merchants, Church officials, and even many creoles were loyal to Spain. Their well-trained, well-armed forces soon forced the rebels into retreat. In 1811, the Spanish captured Hidalgo. Just 10 months after uttering the "grito," Hidalgo died before a royalist firing squad.

José Morelos. The rebels found a new leader in a mestizo priest named Father José Maria Morelos. He brought discipline to the rebel army and won some successes. In 1815, however, he, too, was captured and executed. For a time, the revolution had no army or strong leaders, just loosely organized guerrilla bands.

Independence. In 1820, events in Europe again influenced Mexico. Reformers took power in Spain. They wrote a liberal constitution for Mexico that gave creoles more rights to rule the colony. In this way, the reformers hoped to win favor with the creoles. The plan backfired, however. Wealthy creoles feared that the new constitution would take away their privileges. They decided to fight for independence.

Their leader was a creole army officer, Agustín de Iturbide (ee toor BEE thay). Although he had long fought against the rebels, Iturbide now joined forces with the Indians and mestizos. In 1821, Iturbide declared Mexican independence and made himself emperor. After two years, he was forced to step down. In 1823, creole leaders wrote a constitution that made Mexico a republic.

Independence for Central America. Inspired by Iturbide, leaders in Central America declared independence. Most of Central America joined Mexico. Panama, however, chose to become part of Gran Colombia.

After Iturbide's downfall, Central America left Mexico to form the United Provinces of Central America. This republic included El Salvador, Guatemala, Honduras, Nicaragua, and Costa Rica. The union lasted about 15 years before it began to break up into five separate nations.

Independence for Brazil

During this period, Brazil also gained independence, but through mostly peaceful means. Once again, Napoleon's actions in Europe affected the Americas. When Napoleon invaded Portugal in 1807, King John VI and 15,000 members of his court fled to Rio de Janeiro, Brazil. There, the needs of the newcomers stimulated farming, trade, and industry. Brazilian creoles, however, wanted self-rule. They demanded a constitution, even independence.

In 1821, King John returned to Portugal, but left his son Pedro to rule Brazil. Before sailing, the king advised Pedro, "If Brazil demands independence, proclaim it yourself and put the crown on your own head."

Pedro took his father's advice. In 1822, urged on by Brazilian patriots, he declared, "Independence or Death!" Pedro made himself emperor of the new country but agreed to accept a constitution. It gave most Brazilians basic rights and set up an elected legislature. Unlike many other new nations of South America, Brazil did not abolish slavery. Freedom for slaves would not come until the late 1800s. Brazil remained a monarchy until 1889. That year, Brazilians forced the emperor to step down and proclaimed a republic.

Father Hidalgo This mural by Juan O'Gorman shows the Mexican leader, Father Miguel Hidalgo, uttering his famous "cry of Dolores." Although Hidalgo failed as a military leader, he aroused the spirit of revolt against Spanish rule. ***Fine Art*** According to this mural, what groups of people supported the Mexican struggle for independence.

SECTION 3 REVIEW

1. **Identify:** (a) Miguel Hidalgo, (b) Toussaint L'Ouverture, (c) Simón Bolívar, (d) Republic of Gran Colombia, (e) José de San Martín, (f) Agustín de Iturbide, (g) Pedro.
2. Explain why the following groups wanted independence from Spain: (a) creoles, (b) mestizos, (c) Indians, (d) slaves.
3. Describe two ways that Napoleon's actions in Europe affected the struggle for independence in Latin America.
4. Why did Miguel Hidalgo lose the support of the creoles in Mexico?
5. **Analyzing Ideas** (a) How did Simón Bolívar earn the nickname "the Liberator"? (b) Why do you think he was so successful?
6. **Writing Across Cultures** Write a letter from a creole to a friend in the United States. Discuss how United States independence inspired your colony to resist European rule.

4 THE NEW REPUBLICS

FIND OUT

Why did the new nations of Latin America have trouble building stable governments?

How did the ideas of conservatives and liberals differ?

What economic ties bound Latin America to Europe?

Vocabulary caudillo, oligarchy

During the wars of independence, Simón Bolívar had great hopes for Latin America:

> ❝ I desire to see America fashioned into the one greatest nation in the world, greatest not so much by virtue of her area and wealth as by her freedom and glory. ❞

Bolívar's hopes were later shattered, however. In 1829, the year before his death, he wrote, "America is ungovernable. He who serves a revolution plows the sea."

What happened to disappoint him so completely?

Obstacles to Progress

Like Bolívar, people throughout Latin America hoped that independence would bring justice and new economic opportunities. Leaders wrote constitutions modeled on that of the United States. The new constitutions did not bring democracy, however. Instead, the new nations suffered civil wars and dictators rose to power. A number of reasons help explain why Latin American nations failed to establish stable, democratic governments.

Geographic barriers. Despite years of hard work, Bolívar failed to achieve his dream of unity among American nations. Gran Colombia split into separate countries, as did the United Provinces of Central America. By the 1830s, Latin America was divided into 18 independent nations.

Geography created barriers to unity. The Andes Mountains divided Colombians and Venezuelans. The Atacama Desert cut Chile off from Peru. Border disputes between the new nations erupted into war.

Within individual countries, geographic barriers and limited communications also divided people. For example, farmers and ranchers on the pampas of Argentina had different interests from those of the merchants of Buenos Aires. Such divisions created strong regional loyalties and prevented national unity.

Deep divisions. Social and economic divisions also contributed to instability. After independence, the old social system remained. The peninsulares were gone. In their place, the creoles dominated society. As in colonial times, a tiny wealthy elite controlled the land and mines while most people—laborers and peasants—lived in poverty.

Independence did end slavery in Spanish America. Native Americans, however, did not regain lands that had been taken from them. Also, most peasants were peons, tied to the land. The gap between rich and poor, between wealthy landowners and the landless, contributed to unrest.

Lack of experience. Under Spanish rule, colonists had little experience with representative government. The new constitutions set up elected legislatures, but people were unfamiliar with how such a system should work. Only men with property or money had the right to vote.

Power Struggles

"Many tyrants will arise on my tomb," Bolívar had predicted. In the turbulent years after independence, his words came true.

Rise of caudillos. Within each country, power struggles often erupted between rival groups. In this atmosphere of violence, military leaders known as caudillos seized power and ruled as dictators. Often a caudillo held power for only a short time before another military strongman overthrew him.

In Mexico, for example, General Antonio López de Santa Anna seized power six times between 1832 and 1855. In Argentina, Juan Manuel de Rosas was head of the army. Rosas seized power in 1835 and used the army to enforce his will. Rosas remained in power for 17 years, until another caudillo overthrew him.

Many caudillos were heroes of the wars of independence in Latin America. They won popular support by promising democratic reforms or land reform. Once in office, however, they rewarded their friends with jobs and land. They put their own interests ahead of those of the country.

Oligarchies. By the late 1800s, the central government in most republics had gained control over the country. Most governments became oligarchies. Under an oligarchy, a small elite has ruling power. The oligarchies included wealthy landowners, merchants, and mine owners. The Catholic Church and the military also exercised great power.

Christ of the Andes A huge bronze statue of Jesus Christ stands in the high Andes, on the border between Chile and Argentina. After the two nations finally ended their bitter quarrels over their Andes border in the early 1900s, they erected this statue as a symbol of peace. ***Geography*** Which countries of South America have borders crossed by the Andes? Why might it be difficult to draw boundaries there?

Conservatives and liberals. The ruling groups divided into conservatives and liberals. Conservatives wanted to preserve the old social order and the power of the Catholic Church. They wanted the Church to continue to run the schools. Conservatives opposed freedom of speech and freedom of the press. They viewed such liberties as a threat to law and order.

Liberals wanted to limit the influence of the Church, end its power over education, and reduce its vast landholdings. By redistributing Church land among the poor, they hoped to reduce the gap between rich and

Making Sugar Workers, at left, tend large vats where sugar cane was boiled. When the water boiled off, the sugar was stored in the bins at the right. This view shows a sugar cane refinery on the Caribbean island of Antigua in the early 1800s. Cash crops, like sugar or bananas, long dominated the economies of many Latin American nations. ***Interdependence*** Why might the economy of a developing country be based on a cash crop?

poor. Liberals supported religious toleration and freedom of the press. Unlike the conservatives, who accepted change slowly, liberals called for rapid reform.

Conservatives and liberals found supporters among every level of society. Usually, conservatives included wealthy landowners, high Church officials, and top-ranking military officers. Liberals included doctors, lawyers, artisans, and people from the lower ranks of the Church and the military. The poor—mestizos and Indians—remained largely outside the debate between the ruling groups.

The power of wealthy members of society and the military over the government slowed the growth of democracy. The gap between rich and poor and the lack of modern industrial development added to the problem.

Economic Dependence and Growth

During the 1800s, Latin American countries faced the challenge of developing their economies. Independence meant that they no longer had to limit trade to Spain and Portugal. The new nations, however, remained economically dependent on Europe.

Trade. Latin American countries exported raw materials such as sugar, beef, copper, and coffee to Europe and the United States. In exchange, they imported manufactured goods.

Spain had prevented its colonies from developing industries because it wanted the colonists to buy its own manufactured goods. Even so, by the early 1800s, some colonies had small workshops that produced textiles and metal goods. After independence, however, cheap British imports flooded into Latin America, forcing these local manufacturers out of business.

In Argentina, the gauchos, or cowboys of the pampas, had been symbols of freedom and independence. By 1837, however, even the gauchos depended on imports from Britain. A British observer wrote:

> “Take his whole equipment—examine everything about him—and what is there not of raw hide that is not British? If his wife has a gown, ten to one it is made in Manchester; the camp-kettle in which he cooks his food, the earthenware he eats from, the knife, his poncho, spurs, bit, are all imported from England.”

Foreign investment. Many Latin Americans, especially liberals, wanted their countries to modernize. They looked to foreigners for the capital to build steamboats, railroads, and telegraphs. During the late 1800s, foreigners, especially the British and Americans, invested heavily in Latin America. They dredged harbors and laid out railroad systems. They developed gold, silver, and copper mines.

Improved transportation boosted trade and made some Latin Americans rich. Yet the railroads and harbors did little to create new industries or improve communications. Instead, they made it easier to ship raw materials to Europe. Most railroads ran from the interior to the nearest harbor. They seldom linked areas within a country.

Economic imperialism. Foreign investment did not cover all the costs of modernization. Many Latin American countries borrowed large sums. When they did not repay

Benito Juárez: Mexican Hero

"To Mexicans," said a recent Mexican president, "Benito Juárez (buh NEE toh WAHR ehz) is Mexico." Juárez is a national hero because he fought to win a better life for Mexico's poor.

Juárez was a Zapotec Indian who grew up in poverty in a remote mountain village. At the age of 12, unable even to speak Spanish, he came to the city of Oaxaca (wah HAH kuh) as a household servant. His employer, however, recognized the boy's bright mind and helped him to gain an education.

In 1831, Juárez began to practice law. He soon earned a reputation as a defender of the poor. Juárez also entered politics and was elected to a number of local and state posts.

As a politician, Juárez joined with other Mexican liberals in calling for democratic reforms. These reformers seized control of the government in 1855, and Juárez became minister of justice. He helped to write laws that would reduce the wealth and power of the Catholic Church and the army. These laws called for Church lands to be sold. They also gave Mexicans the freedom to practice religions other than the Catholic faith. In 1857, the reformers incorporated these laws into a new Mexican constitution.

Mexico's conservatives were outraged. They called on Mexicans to resist, and in 1858, civil war broke out. It was called the War of the Reform.

The War of the Reform ended in 1861 with victory for the reformers. Juárez was elected president of a new constitutional government. He was the first Native American to become president of Mexico.

Juárez continued to fight for reform, but he faced many problems. Years of war had left Mexico divided and in ruins. It also owed large sums of money to foreign powers. For a brief time, France even sent an emperor to rule the country, forcing President Juárez to flee.

Juárez died in 1872, during his fourth term in office. He never achieved all the reforms that he dreamed of. His contribution, however, goes beyond that. Mexicans remember him because he gave the common people new hope. *El Indio*—"the Indian"—as Mexicans call Juárez, also helped restore self-esteem to Mexico's Indians.

1. What reforms did Juárez call for?
2. **Making Decisions** Do you think that the liberals were justified in seizing power in 1855? Explain.

Manaus Opera House, Brazil Manaus, a city deep in the interior, first prospered from 1890 to 1920, during the rubber boom in the Amazon rain forest. Many European immigrants flocked to Manaus, and some made fortunes there. The town grew into a large city with expensive homes, a cathedral, and a majestic opera house (shown here). ***Environment*** How might the arrival of many newcomers affect the Amazon region?

these debts, foreign governments threatened military action. In 1861, Mexico suspended payment of its foreign debts. Napoleon III of France then sent 40,000 French troops to Mexico. He installed an Austrian duke, Maximilian, as emperor of Mexico. Supported by French forces, Maximilian ruled Mexico for three years.

During the late 1800s, foreign investment and debts led to economic imperialism. Although foreigners no longer ruled Latin American nations, they still had great influence over their economies, as you will read in Chapter 23.

Limited progress. Foreign investment did help some countries to develop agriculture, mining, and transportation. Argentina prospered from the export of beef and wheat. Chile benefited from a strong demand for copper and for nitrate, which is used in fertilizer. Mexico increased its exports of minerals, sugar, and henequen, a fiber used to make rope.

The arrival of millions of Europeans also spurred economic growth. During the late 1800s and early 1900s, immigrants from Italy, Germany, and Switzerland settled in Argentina, Uruguay, Brazil, and Chile.

Economic development contributed to the growth of a middle class. Although the gap between rich and poor remained, some people hoped that the new middle class would help to create stable government. (See Connections With Literature, page 806, "The Glass of Milk.")

SECTION 4 REVIEW

1. **Identify:** (a) Antonio López de Santa Anna, (b) Juan Manuel de Rosas, (c) conservative, (d) liberal, (e) Maximilian.
2. **Define:** (a) caudillo, (b) oligarchy.
3. Describe three problems that the new nations of Latin America faced after independence.
4. (a) How did political rivalries allow caudillos to gain power? (b) How did the goals of conservatives and liberals differ?
5. How did foreign debts lead to economic imperialism in Latin America?
6. **Distinguishing Fact and Opinion** (a) What do you think led Simón Bolívar to declare that "America is ungovernable"? (b) Is his statement a fact or an opinion? Explain your answer.
7. **Writing Across Cultures** The British colonies in North America had a history of electing legislatures to manage colonial affairs. Write a sentence or two explaining what advantage this may have given the United States over Latin America.

Chapter 21 Review

Understanding Vocabulary

Match each term at left with the correct definition at right.

1. cabildo	**a.** town council
2. hacienda	**b.** military strongman
3. peninsular	**c.** official sent from Spain to rule the colonies
4. creole	**d.** American-born descendant of Spanish settlers
5. caudillo	**e.** large plantation

Reviewing the Main Ideas

1. (a) Why did Spain and Portugal sign the Treaty of Tordesillas? (b) How did the treaty affect their claims in the Americas?

2. What effect did the encomienda system have on the Native Americans?

3. (a) How did the Catholic Church spread European ideas in Latin America? (b) How did the Church absorb ideas from other cultures?

4. Why were towns and cities important centers of power in colonial Latin America?

5. (a) Why did creoles want independence from Spain? (b) What Enlightenment ideas influenced the struggle for independence?

6. What economic progress had Latin American nations made in the 1800s?

Reviewing Chapter Themes

1. Mercantilism ruled the economic life of the colonies. (a) Explain how Spain and Portugal tried to benefit from their colonies. (b) Describe how mercantilist goals affected the growth of slavery.

2. Social and economic forces affected colonial life in Latin America. Describe the effects of three of the following: (a) social classes, (b) the Roman Catholic Church, (c) family structure, (d) the hacienda system.

3. Events outside Latin America often influenced its history. Describe how events in Europe affected the independence movements in three Latin American nations.

4. Most events in history have many causes. (a) Describe the causes of unrest in newly independent countries in Latin America. (b) Describe the causes of their economic dependence on Europe.

Thinking Critically

1. Making Global Connections (a) How was the Columbian exchange an example of cultural diffusion? (b) Describe two ways in which it affected all parts of the world.

2. Comparing (a) How did the lives of the rich and poor differ in colonial Latin America? (b) How did these differences affect the struggle for independence in Mexico?

3. Analyzing Information Explain why each of the following groups opposed change in Latin America: (a) oligarchies, (b) Roman Catholic Church, (c) military.

Applying Your Skills

1. Analyzing a Quotation Reread the quotation on page 461. (a) What point was Las Casas trying to make by telling this story? (b) Why might the story have shocked and shamed many Spanish Catholics?

2. Reading a Map Study the maps on pages 459 and 472. (a) Which independent nations were carved from La Plata? (b) Which former Spanish territory is now part of the United States?

Chapter 22

LATIN AMERICA IN TRANSITION

Celebrating Democracy Joyful demonstrators greeted the election of Argentina's new president in 1989. Such peaceful changes in government have been an important trend among Latin American nations in recent years. Free elections are replacing revolts and military coups. ***Political System*** How were most Latin American countries governed after independence?

CHAPTER OUTLINE

Thousands of worshippers listened as Archbishop Oscar Romero spoke the words of the Catholic Mass. Suddenly, gunfire echoed through the cathedral. The congregation watched in horror as a masked gunman fled down the aisle. The archbishop was dead.

The murder of Archbishop Romero in 1980 drew world attention to the civil war that was destroying El Salvador. The gunman belonged to one of the "death squads" that used terror to support the country's military rulers.

When the civil war began, Romero supported the military government. He believed it would act fairly to restore order. One day, however, he saw soldiers massacre peaceful demonstrators. Later, the government began to arrest and torture priests who it claimed were helping the rebels. These actions led Romero to speak out for human rights. When asked where he found the courage, Romero replied:

> “What sustains me in the struggle is my love for my God, . . . and my love for the Salvadoran people—particularly the poor.”

Not long after that interview, Archbishop Romero lay dead.

CHAPTER PERSPECTIVE

El Salvador was one of many Latin American countries that experienced violence during the 1970s and 1980s. In many countries, the military crushed demands for social justice and change. Although many governments have decided to restore democracy, economic and social problems remain.

As you read, look for these chapter themes:

- Poverty, social inequalities, and rapid population growth have contributed to unrest in Latin America.
- Efforts to achieve economic growth have met with mixed results.
- Urbanization and industrialization are changing life in Latin America.
- Developments in Mexico, Argentina, and Brazil show how different nations have tried to modernize.

Literature Connections

In this chapter, you will encounter passages from the following works.

"I'm Gonna Win," Ignacio Copani

"The Bosses," Mariano Azuela

For other suggestions, see Connections With Literature, pages 804–808.

1 POLITICAL AND ECONOMIC DEVELOPMENT

FIND OUT

How have economic and social problems contributed to instability in Latin America?

What were the causes and effects of revolutions in Cuba and Nicaragua?

What steps have Latin American nations taken to end economic dependence?

Vocabulary coup d'état, embargo

"Our primary objective is to move from misery to dignified poverty," declared Jean-Bertrand Aristide as he campaigned for the presidency of Haiti. A parish priest, Aristide had worked among the poor people of Haiti for years. During the campaign, he survived six assassination attempts. Aristide promised justice and openness, and he encouraged Haitians to participate in government. Haitians responded by electing him president, with 67 percent of the vote.

Haiti, the poorest country in the Western Hemisphere, has often suffered under military rule. Aristide's election in 1990 was part of the move toward democracy throughout Latin America. Less than a year after Aristide took office, however, the military overthrew him. His election and overthrow illustrate the ongoing struggle for democracy in much of Latin America.

Sources of Instability

By the 1960s, Latin American nations had made little progress toward improving the lives of most of their people. Social inequality and economic hardship led to unrest and instability.

Social and economic divisions. The social class structure created deep divisions. Old landowning families and rich industrialists, who dominated society, opposed change. In rural areas, a few families owned the best farmland. Poor peasants and Indians either scratched a living from tiny plots or worked on the estates of large landowners.

As Latin American nations modernized their economies, the gap between the rich and the poor widened. In the growing cities, the middle class often allied itself with the wealthy ruling class. The urban working class, like the rural poor, had little or no education. Wages were low, and jobs and basic services were scarce.

Political divisions. Political parties reflected the social and economic divisions. Parties on the political left demanded radical change. Most leftists supported socialism. They wanted to redistribute land to peasants, nationalize industries, and improve conditions for the working class. Leftists found support among urban workers, landless peasants, students, and intellectuals.

By contrast, the political right favored preservation of the traditional social order. Rightists wanted to protect the wealth and power of landlords and industrialists. The right won support among business leaders, large landowners, and military officers.

When unrest threatened law and order, the military would often stage a coup d'état (koo day TAH). A coup d'état is a revolt, usually by military leaders, against a nation's government.

Efforts at Land Reform

As Latin American nations modernized, land reform became a major issue. Reformers insisted that poverty was the result of uneven distribution of land. In Guatemala, for example, 2 percent of landowners held two thirds of the land. In Honduras, two thirds of the fertile land was in the hands of just 5 percent of landowners.

Nonetheless, only a handful of countries undertook major land reform programs. During the 1950s, Bolivia redistributed land to thousands of peasant families. At the same time, reformers in Guatemala began a land reform program. That nation's powerful landowning class resisted this effort. The United Fruit Company, which owned huge tracts of land in Guatemala, also opposed land reform. The United States branded the leftist government in Guatemala as communist and supported its overthrow.

Chile's attempts at land reform also failed. In 1969, the socialist president, Salvador Allende (ah YEHN day), increased the pace of land reform that was already underway. A military government seized power in 1973, killed Allende, and reversed most of the reforms.

A Farmer and His Sons in Nicaragua Fertile farmland is scarce in Latin America. Governments in some nations seized the land of large estate owners and gave it to landless peasants. Brazil, Colombia, and other nations used another method, opening up new land for farming. ***Interdependence*** How might land reform help cities as well as rural areas?

In El Salvador, the "Fourteen Families" held the best land. Much of the land was unused. Demands for land reform were a key cause of El Salvador's civil war, which raged during the 1970s and 1980s. In 1980, El Salvador divided certain large estates among some of the tenants who had worked the land. However, the political right remained firmly in control of the government. (See Connections With Literature, page 806, "Salvador.")

Even when successful, redistribution of land solved only part of the problem. For land reform to work, farmers needed seeds, tools, and fertilizer. Otherwise, the breakup of large estates often caused farm output to drop.

Revolutionary Change

Protest and economic pressure forced some Latin American governments to make limited reforms. Only Mexico, Cuba, and Nicaragua, however, had social revolutions that brought about basic changes. (You will read about the Mexican Revolution in Section 3.)

Revolution in Cuba. As elsewhere in Latin America, rural poverty, illiteracy, and high unemployment fueled discontent in Cuba. During the 1950s, Fidel Castro, a young Cuban lawyer, led a handful of rebels in a long guerrilla struggle against a corrupt dictatorship. In 1959, Castro seized power and then maintained rule for more than 30 years.

Soon after he took control, Castro declared himself a Marxist and set up a one-party state. Under Castro, Cuba became a socialist nation. He took control of foreign-owned sugar plantations and other businesses. These actions led to conflict with the United States. (See Chapter 23.) With aid from the Soviet Union, Castro set up state-owned farms, developed industry, and built housing, schools, and hospitals to improve the lives of the poor.

The costs of the revolution were high. Castro imprisoned or exiled his opponents. Thousands of Cubans fled their homeland to escape political repression and loss of personal wealth. In addition, the United States imposed a strict embargo, or complete halt to trade, on Cuba. Cuba then turned to the Soviet Union for aid and for a place to sell its exports.

When the Soviet Union collapsed in the early 1990s, Cuba lost its most important trading partner. With the Cuban economy in chaos, Castro introduced a number of minor economic reforms. Despite these reforms, Cuba's outlook looked grim unless further steps were taken to move the country toward a market economy.

Sandinistas in Nicaragua. Rebels in Nicaragua overthrew longtime dictator Anastasio Somoza in 1979. Peasants, urban workers, and some business and Church leaders supported the rebel forces. The leftist Sandinistas, who had led the struggle, soon gained control of the government. Under Daniel Ortega, the Sandinistas introduced major land reform, took over many businesses, and organized social programs for the poor. Their actions angered the wealthy elite.

With the help of the United States, the contras, or forces that opposed the Sandinistas, fought a long guerrilla war against the Nicaraguan government. The war cost many lives and disrupted the economy. As the economic situation worsened, the Sandinistas held free elections. In 1990, a new government headed by Violeta Chamorro won power. For the first time in the history of Latin America, a revolutionary leader peacefully gave up power to the winner of a democratic election.

Dictators and Democracy

During the 1960s and 1970s, the Cuban Revolution inspired leftist groups throughout Latin America. Some leftists sought power through democratic means. Others sought power through guerrilla warfare.

In almost every Latin American nation, the military and the right wing responded by seizing power. In Chile, in 1973, General Augusto Pinochet (pee noh SHAY) overthrew that nation's democratically elected president, Salvador Allende. Pinochet accused Allende,

A Coup in Haiti. After the overthrow of a dictator in 1989, Haitians destroyed his supporters' property. Until the end of the 1980s, many Latin American nations were ruled by military leaders. People in most nations were denied free elections, and democracy was weak. ***Political System*** Why were military takeovers common in the 1960s and 1970s?

a socialist, of leading Chile toward communism. In a brutal crackdown, the military ended freedom of speech and arrested, tortured, and murdered many citizens. (📖 See World Literature, "The House of the Spirits" by Isabel Allende, page 542.)

During the 1980s, Chile's military rulers came under increasing pressure to give up power. Despite the danger of arrest, women's groups, human rights activists, and the Catholic Church pushed for democratic elections. Throughout Latin America, new leaders emerged who declared their commitment to democratic rule. Even Haiti and Paraguay, where dictators had ruled for decades, held elections. To succeed, however, the new governments first had to achieve economic growth and address basic social problems.

Economic Growth

Since the 1900s, most Latin American economies have grown, although progress has been made at different rates. World events have had a major impact on their economic development.

Impact of World War II. During World War II, the demand for copper, wheat, beef, and other goods from Latin America soared. Latin American nations invested profits from their exports in developing basic industries. Large countries such as Mexico, Brazil, and Argentina constructed steel mills, chemical plants, and oil refineries. They also built factories to produce tools, appliances, and other consumer goods.

Economic nationalism. After World War II, a wave of nationalism led to independence movements throughout Africa and Asia. At the same time, economic nationalism grew in Latin America. Although Latin American nations had long been politically independent, they were still economically dependent on industrial nations. A major goal of economic nationalism, therefore, was to replace foreign imports with locally made goods.

To strengthen local industries, governments began to play a major economic role. They placed high tariffs on imports. Then they built and operated many new factories. They also nationalized a number of foreign-owned companies. Despite state ownership of many key industries, most Latin American governments were not socialist. Private enterprise continued alongside state-owned industry.

As industries grew, Latin American nations reduced their dependence on foreign imports. At the same time, they remained dependent on world demand for cash crops such as sugar and coffee, as well as for raw materials such as tin and copper.

Challenges to Economic Development

What stood in the way of greater economic progress? Many state-owned industries were run inefficiently and produced inferior goods. In addition, foreign-owned corporations took their profits out of the country instead of using them to improve local industries. Also, the national market for manufactured goods was small. When Latin American nations tried to sell their manufactured goods on the world market, they faced stiff competition from more efficient producers. Inflation and rising oil prices created additional problems.

Population explosion. The population boom further slowed development. Between 1950 and 1985, the population of Latin America more than doubled. Forecasters predict that it will reach 570 million by 2000. In order to feed their rapidly growing populations, some countries must import basic foods. Governments do not have enough money to spend on schools, housing, medical care, and other vital services.

Debt crisis. During the 1980s, rising interest rates triggered a crisis that slowed development. Like developing nations elsewhere, many Latin American countries had borrowed heavily to build industries. When a worldwide recession slowed economic activity, the demand for goods fell. The nations of Latin America earned less, but they still owed huge interest payments. They had to spend as much as one third of their foreign earnings on interest payments. As a result, they had less money for new development. (See the chart on page 786.)

Recovery. To recover from the economic crisis of the 1980s, Latin American governments lowered tariffs and encouraged foreign investment. They reduced government spending and sold state-owned industries to private investors. They also negotiated with the industrialized nations to cancel much of the debt they owed. Slowly, some Latin American nations began to make economic progress.

An Outdoor Health Clinic
This traveling medical team is providing health care for the growing population of Honduras. Honduras also is working to prevent disease by immunizing people and destroying mosquitoes that carry malaria. ***Scarcity*** Why do rural people often lack proper health care?

SECTION 1 REVIEW

1. **Locate:** (a) Guatemala, (b) Chile, (c) El Salvador, (d) Cuba, (e) Nicaragua.
2. **Identify:** (a) Salvador Allende, (b) Fidel Castro, (c) Sandinistas, (d) contras, (e) Augusto Pinochet, (f) economic nationalism.
3. **Define:** (a) coup d'état, (b) embargo.
4. Describe two causes of unrest in Latin America.
5. How did Castro's revolution affect Cuba?
6. How have Latin American nations tried to achieve economic independence?
7. **Drawing Conclusions** Why do you think attempts at land reform have failed in many countries?
8. **Writing Across Cultures** United States aid to the contras became a subject of debate during the 1980s. Write a letter to your representative in Congress opposing or defending United States support of rebels in other countries. Give three reasons for your position.

2 CHANGING PATTERNS OF LIFE

FIND OUT

What are some effects rapid urbanization has had on Latin America?

How has life in rural areas changed?

How are women's lives in Latin America changing?

What role does the Roman Catholic Church play in Latin America today?

Vocabulary liberation theology

In Buenos Aires, a teenage girl listens eagerly to the latest song by Ignacio Copani. Copani's songs provide more than entertainment. Many protest government corruption, overemphasis on material goods, and other social ills. In "I'm Gonna Win," Copani offers a message of hope to young people. He urges them to look

> "For an exit not through the airport,
> or through drugs or death,
> or stealing from others,
> I'm gonna win,
> I'm gonna win . . .
> Laughing at those I don't trust,
> Joining those who tell the truth."

For many people in Latin America, the "airport"—migration to the United States—offers an escape from a harsh life. Yet others are determined to seek justice and opportunity at home. Protest singers like Ignacio Copani express the people's desire to build a better future at home.

Move to the Cities

As in other developing nations, modernization and the population explosion in Latin America have led to rapid urban growth. Population growth indicates progress. As a result of improved health care, people live longer and more children survive to become adults. The population boom, however, strains scarce resources. In rural areas, there is neither enough fertile land for peasants to farm nor enough jobs for young people. As a result, many young people move to the cities to find work.

In the larger, more industrial countries of Latin America, more people live in urban areas than in the countryside. People flock to the large capital cities. With a population of 19 million people, Mexico City is the largest city in the world. The population of São Paulo, Brazil, is expected to grow from 18.4 million in 1990 to 24.4 million by 2000. Today, one out of every five Brazilians lives in either São Paulo or Rio de Janeiro.

Finding work. People who move to the cities often have more education than those who remain in rural areas. Still, finding a job is difficult. Modernization has created jobs in offices and industry, but city populations are growing faster than the number of new jobs. The cost of making interest payments on foreign debt cuts into the amount of money available for investment. Because so many people are in search of work, wages remain low.

Many newcomers earn their living as street vendors, selling food, drinks, and lottery tickets. Others drive taxis. Still others, especially women, turn their homes into workshops where they make clothes, repair shoes, and produce handicrafts. A Colombian woman, Maria Agudelo, described the long hours she worked in her home.

> "When everybody else went to bed, I stayed up at my sewing machine. I learned to do without sleep. Sometimes I would fall asleep when I was sewing, but then I woke up and thought, 'No, I have to get this done before morning.'"

Self-help housing. The flood of newcomers has created a severe housing crisis. Sprawling slums have sprung up around every city. They are known by different names, such as *villas miserias* (cities of misery) in Colombia, *pueblos jovenes* (young towns) in Peru, or *favelas* (shantytowns) in Brazil.

Often, groups of poor people claim vacant land that is too swampy, hilly, or dry to attract housing developers. Using scraps of wood and metal, they build makeshift homes. At first, these self-help settlements lack electricity, running water, sewers, and services such as health clinics or schools. In time, however, the residents improve their homes. They might then set up schools and a police force, or apply to the government for water and other services. Some of these self-help settlements eventually develop into stable communities.

Despite the difficulties of urban life, people continue to flock to the cities. As bad as the slums are, they are often better than the rural life that farmers leave behind.

Caracas, Venezuela Makeshift houses cluster in the shadow of modern apartment buildings. In 1930, only three Latin American cities had more than 1 million people. Today, more than 30 cities are this large. In some cities, as many as one fourth of the people live in slums. ***Change*** Why have cities grown so rapidly in recent years?

Rural Life

In very poor countries, such as Bolivia and Guatemala, the majority of the people still live in rural areas. For most farmers, life is extremely hard. On small, half-acre plots, they raise chickens and grow corn, beans, and squash. Their homes are one-room shacks with thatched or tin roofs. Hunger and disease are constant threats. Children attend school for only a few years, if at all. Many never learn to read and write.

Tenant farmers. Landless peasants work on large estates either as tenant farmers or as house servants. In exchange for the labor they provide, they get a small plot of land to farm for themselves. Often, they receive little or no pay. If they need money, they must borrow it from the landowner. As a result, many tenant farmers remain permanently in debt to the landowner.

Effects of modernization. Modernization has brought changes to rural areas. In Mexico and Central America, for example, multinational corporations have bought much of the land. They then set up huge cotton and coffee plantations or cattle ranches. Because they are efficiently operated, these large operations have increased the output of both food and export crops.

These changes have had some negative effects, however. Many commercial farms produce foods for export rather than for home markets. Locally grown food is often scarce, which results in higher food prices. Governments tend to use their limited financial resources to help city dwellers. As a result, they have neglected the needs of rural peasants. The growing gap between rural and urban conditions encourages still more people to migrate to the cities.

Elvia Alvarado—Peasant Organizer

Elvia Alvarado is typical of many *campesinos,* or rural peasants, of Honduras. Even as a child, she was aware of her family's daily struggle to survive:

> "My father was a campesino. He didn't have any land of his own, so he worked for the big landowners as a day worker. . . . My mother worked like a mule to take care of us, and we all helped out. We'd get up at three in the morning, in the dark, to help bake bread, make tortillas, feed the pigs, and clean the house. All my brothers and sisters worked hard—the boys in the fields of the big landowners, the girls in the house."

Alvarado's mother wanted her daughter to get an education. The village school had only two grades. "But I really wanted to learn, so I kept repeating second grade over and over again."

Despite her eagerness to learn, Alvarado was soon trapped in poverty like so many others in her village. She eventually had six children. At one point, she left her children with her mother and went to Tegucigalpa (tuh goo see GAHL puh), the capital of Honduras. There, she worked as a maid for a rich couple. She earned $15 a month, which she sent home to her mother and children. Part of her job was feeding the family's dog.

> "My boss would give me meat, tomatoes, and oil and tell me to cook it up for the dog. And every time I fed that dog, I'd think of my own children. My children never got to eat meat. The

The Campesinos Life is often difficult for Hondurans. About one third of the people are unemployed, and the average worker earns only about $850 a year. The diet of most poor people consists of tortillas and beans. Malnutrition is a constant threat. ***Scarcity*** Why might people who live in rural areas lack proper food?

$15 I sent them was hardly enough to buy beans and corn. But that dog got meat every day. ”

Alvarado eventually returned to her village. One day, she joined a mothers' club that her church organized. There, women met to talk about problems such as getting food and medicine for their children. Although her husband objected, Alvarado began to help other villages to set up similar women's groups. Through her work, she realized that all of the campesinos had the same problem—lack of land.

> “ If they have any land at all, it's usually the worst land—hilly with poor soils. Because the best land is the flat land the big landowners own. . . . I felt that without land, we'd never get out of our poverty. ”

Alvarado soon became active in a movement to recover land that large landowners had taken from the campesinos in the past. Because she stood up to these landowners, she was arrested and tortured. Alvarado knows that her life is in danger. "The only way they can stop me from what I'm doing," declares Alvarado, "is by killing me. But that won't stop the others from following my path. In that sense, I'm stronger than they are." ■

Changes in Family Life

Throughout Latin America, family ties remain strong in both rural and urban areas. In rural areas, parents, children, aunts, uncles, and cousins usually live nearby. If a relative is sick or hurt, other family members are there to help. They take care of the young children and provide food and other support. Today, as in the past, the man still dominates the family. However, in families where men have died or left the village to find work, women take full responsibility for the family.

In cities, newcomers often find they are completely on their own. If they have an accident or lose their jobs, they face disaster. Some people, though, move to cities where family or friends have already settled.

Godparents. The custom of godparents helps families to forge new links in the harsh urban environment. Frequently, parents ask wealthier or better-educated people to serve as *padrino* and *madrino*—"godfather" and "godmother"—to their children. These godparents provide their godchildren with advice and support.

Parents and children. Traditionally, parents have expected complete obedience from their children. At an early age, a boy either learned his father's trade or worked with him in the fields. Girls worked with their mothers both in the fields and at home. They prepared food, carried water, and looked after the younger children. Those traditions survive in rural areas.

In cities, children have more freedom while their parents are away at work. They also have greater opportunities, because urban schools are better equipped than rural schools. Still, child labor is common among poor urban families. Instead of working in the fields, children work in factories or set up street stands. Some poor children even rummage through the garbage from wealthy neighborhoods in search of food or other useful objects that have been discarded. In the cities, crime and drugs tempt children with the lure of easy money.

Changing Lives of Women

In rural areas, the custom of *machismo,* or male domination, remains strong. A woman is not expected to question her husband's decisions. Many parents raise their daughters to marry and have children. Because they do not think girls need an education, illiteracy is higher among women than among men in rural areas.

At the same time, women like Elvia Alvarado have helped to organize peasant groups in rural areas. By speaking out on issues, women have gained confidence in their ability to make changes. As a result, a growing number of women now urge their daughters as well as their sons to attend school.

Women at Work The teacher at left is instructing pupils in an elementary school in Brazil. At right, a woman in rural Mexico cooks tortillas over a fire. Although more women now work outside the home, the number of women wage earners in Latin America is small compared with the number in Africa and East Asia. ***Culture*** Why might relatively few Latin American women work outside the home?

In the cities, many women have jobs outside the home. This increases their contact with new ideas and opportunities. Furthermore, their earnings give them a sense of independence. One Peruvian woman noted that in cities, "both spouses express opinions about life in their home."

As more women earn university degrees, they enter professions such as law and medicine. Yet, they often have a hard time finding jobs in societies dominated by men.

Changing Role of the Church

Today, as in the past, the Catholic Church is a powerful force in Latin America. About 90 percent of the people are Catholic. Traditionally, the Church supported the ruling elite. As a large landowner, it opposed reforms that might threaten its power.

As people moved to cities, their ties with the Church weakened. During the 1960s, popular support for Marxism and revolutionary movements alarmed Church leaders. In response, Church leaders called for new efforts to help the poor. They set up programs to build schools and clinics in poor neighborhoods.

Liberation theology. Some members of the clergy felt that those programs did not go far enough. Poverty, they said, is caused by people, not by God. Therefore, they called on the Church to take a more active role in changing the conditions that contributed to poverty. This doctrine became known as liberation theology.

Thousands of priests, nuns, and Church workers moved into shantytowns and peasant villages. There, they helped the poor to organize for change. They also asked the governments of these nations for sweeping reforms to end social and economic inequalities.

However, liberation theology created divisions within the Church. Many bishops argued that the Church should keep out of politics. The pope ordered priests not to become political leaders. Despite official disapproval, however, many clergy continue to organize programs for social reform.

Migration to *El Norte*

Millions of Latin Americans have reacted to political violence and economic hardship by leaving their homes. Many headed to *El Norte* (The North), their name for the United States.

TRADITION AND CHANGE

Carnival!

> “This is real happiness,
> Not a soul with prejudice,
> Play your ‘mas’ as you like. . . .
> When the steel orchestra
> Blast the rhythm in your ear,
> From Monday ’til
> Ash Wednesday morning.”

Ash Wednesday marks the beginning of Lent, the 40 days of penitence and fasting before the Christian celebration of Easter. Each year in the Caribbean and Brazil, the 48 hours before Ash Wednesday become one big party. This tradition is called Carnival.

The Caribbean island nation of Trinidad and Tobago is host to one of the wildest, splashiest celebrations. Its Carnival blends the European, African, and American roots of the “Trinis,” as the people of the nation are called.

The celebration began as a festival of French aristocrats. It was a dignified affair, with carriage promenades and fancy dress balls. After the emancipation of enslaved Africans in 1834, the tempo quickened. The aristocratic Carnival was then combined with the former slave festival of *canbou-lay.* From this blend of traditions evolved today’s yearly series of parades, music, and outdoor dances.

During Carnival, tourists flock to Trinidad and Tobago. The islands hum to the sounds of music. Neighborhood pan-bands, playing specially tuned oil drums, compete for prizes. Other singers perform in a musical style known as *soca,* or social calypso. These songs often criticize government officials or address pressing social problems. For the poor, Carnival is a time to blow off steam by mocking the rich and powerful.

Perhaps Carnival is most memorable for its elaborate “mas,” or masquerade. Some costumes take weeks to make and can weigh as much as 150 pounds. “I guess it’s still an art,” remarked one tired seamstress, “but more and more I think the art has become structural engineering.”

1. How does Carnival represent the mixed European and African heritage of the Trinis?
2. **Making Inferences** How might a celebration such as Carnival benefit the people of a nation or community?

Political refugees. Some immigrants were political refugees who sought safety from harsh governments. Hundreds of thousands of Cubans have migrated to the United States since Fidel Castro took power in 1959. Many people from El Salvador and Guatemala fled to the United States to escape civil war and right-wing death squads. During the 1970s, immigrants from Chile, Argentina, and Haiti also headed north to escape brutal military regimes.

Economic refugees. Other immigrants were economic refugees who sought a better life. Some had legal papers that entitled them to work in the United States. Others entered the United States illegally. They had to take whatever jobs they could find no matter how low the pay.

Economic refugees send a large part of their earnings to their families at home. In Jamaica, Haiti, the Dominican Republic, and other countries, the money sent home by migrants in El Norte is vital to the nations' economy.

SECTION 2 REVIEW

1. **Identify:** (a) machismo, (b) El Norte.
2. **Define:** liberation theology.
3. Describe two effects of urban growth in Latin America.
4. (a) What traditions affect the lives of women in rural areas? (b) How has urbanization changed the lives of women in Latin America?
5. How has the role of the Catholic Church changed in Latin America?
6. **Evaluating Information** (a) What are the benefits and disadvantages of commercial agriculture in Latin America? (b) Have the benefits outweighed the disadvantages? Explain.
7. **Writing Across Cultures** Write a letter that a Latin American immigrant to El Norte might send to a friend back home. Explain why you left your country and whether you are meeting your goals in the United States.

3 MEXICO

FIND OUT

What were the causes and results of the Mexican Revolution?

How has Mexico tried to build a stable government?

What economic progress has Mexico made?

Vocabulary ejido, free trade, maquiladora

"First, a distant shot; then another, nearer, sharper, echoing like the explosion of a rocket. Then shots in all directions. Round a corner galloped a body of horsemen, their carbines raised. Hoofs struck sparks from the paving stone. Bullets passed whining."

In the short story "The Bosses," the Mexican writer Mariano Azuela described the arrival of revolutionary forces in a small Mexican city.

For years, the Del Llano family has used its control of the bank and land to destroy many people. Esperanza and Juanito seize the moment to take revenge. As his sister watches, Juanito sprinkles oil on the store the Del Llanos stole from their father.

"They heard an explosion and black smoke was soon pouring from the doors and windows. . . . from the top floor spirals of smoke rolled up to the clouds. The house of Del Llano Bros., Inc, burned very well."

Azuela had witnessed violence as a doctor in a revolutionary army. His stories captured the bitterness and anger that led to the Mexican Revolution. The revolution, which lasted from 1910 to 1920, ended years of dictatorship and brought about social reforms.

Geography and People

Mexico is a varied land. In the north, rugged mountains contain a wealth of minerals. The coastal lowlands and vast Central Plateau provide fertile farmland, as well as rain forests and deserts. In the past, foreigners often controlled key Mexican resources. After the revolution, however, Mexico took control of its own resources.

Location. Mexico shares a long border with the United States. Mexicans have mixed feelings about their larger, more powerful neighbor. A Mexican saying laments, *"Pobre Mexico, tan lejos de Dios, y tan cerca de los Estados Unidos!"* ("Poor Mexico, so far from God, and so near the United States!") The two nations have clashed over land in the past. In 1848, Mexico was forced to give up large areas to the United States. During more recent times, Mexicans have faced economic domination by the United States.

People. With a population of 88 million people, Mexico is the world's most populous Spanish-speaking country. Although most Mexicans are mestizos, the country's Native American heritage is still strong. The name Mexico, for example, comes from the Aztec god Mexìtli. More than 60 Native American groups, speaking 40 languages, live in rural areas of Mexico. Several million Native Americans speak Na-huatl, the language of the Aztecs.

Rapid population growth poses serious problems for Mexico. About 38 percent of all Mexicans are under the age of 15. As they grow up, they will need jobs, housing, and land, all of which are scarce. As elsewhere, the lack of jobs contributes to poverty and malnutrition.

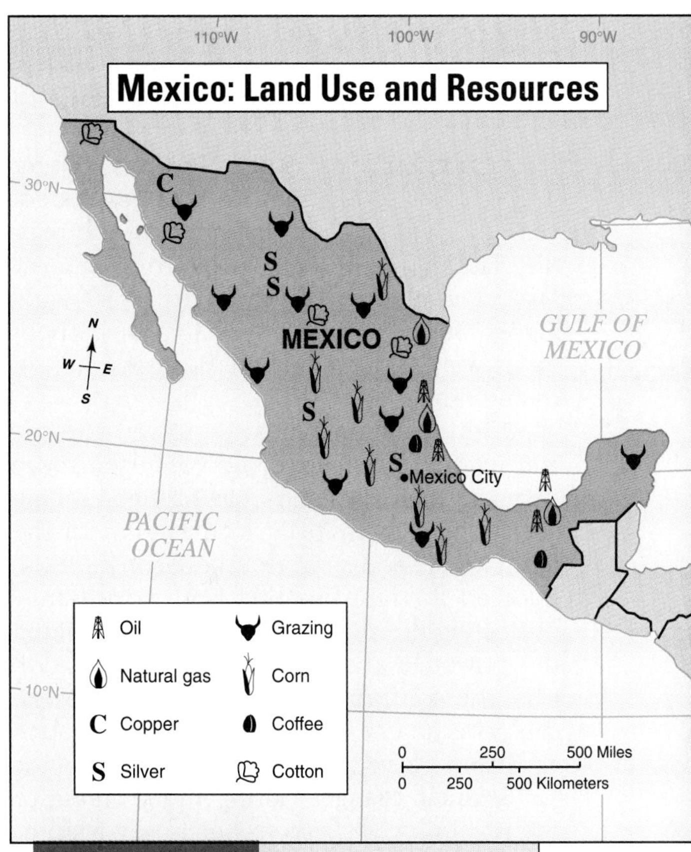

MAP STUDY

Although Mexico is mainly an agricultural country, it has important mineral resources that have helped its economic growth.

1. **Location** (a) What two major sources of energy does Mexico possess? (b) Where are these resources found?
2. **Interaction** What evidence does this map provide about Mexico's farming economy?
3. **Forecasting** As Mexico becomes more industrialized, what effect do you think this will have on people's lives?

Achieving Stability

As in other Latin American nations, caudillos often took power in Mexico during the 1800s. From 1876 to 1911, the dictator Porfirio Díaz ruled Mexico.

Díaz. Under the motto "Order and Progress," Díaz introduced programs that were intended to strengthen and modernize Mexico. He invited foreigners to invest in Mexico. They built railroads, developed mines, and bought land in Mexico. Production of silver, copper, coffee, and sugar soared. At the same time, Díaz set up a strong police force that destroyed rural bandits and political opponents.

Economic growth benefited foreign investors and wealthy Mexicans as well as Díaz and his supporters. For most Mexicans, however, life remained unbearably harsh. Nearly

90 percent of Mexican peasants owned no land at all. They worked on large estates for tiny wages. Many lived on the verge of starvation.

Revolution. In 1910, Mexicans' anger against Díaz and foreign investors exploded. Peasants, workers, and members of the middle class joined in the struggle to overthrow Díaz. For almost 11 years, civil war raged across Mexico as various rebel groups fought for power. About 1 million Mexicans died in the fighting.

The revolution almost destroyed Mexico. Yet, in the end, it gave the country a more democratic government and brought lasting social changes. In 1917, in the midst of the fighting, Mexicans wrote a new constitution. It called for redistributing land to peasants, protecting the rights of workers, and limiting the power of the Catholic Church. In addition, the constitution of 1917 gave the Mexican government control over resources such as oil and silver.

Gradual change. During the years since the revolution, Mexico has gradually tried to fulfill the promises of the constitution. During the 1930s, President Lázaro Cárdenas (CAR thay nahs) took bold steps toward achieving reform. He broke up large estates, giving small farms to about one third of Mexico's peasants. He also nationalized foreign oil companies and recognized the power of labor unions.

After Cárdenas, the pace of reform slowed. Economic hard times and pressure from right-wing groups have forced some presidents to retreat from reform.

Although Mexico is a democracy, one party, the Institutional Revolutionary party (PRI), has dominated the country since 1929. The PRI has succeeded in part by paying attention to the needs of many groups, including farmers, industrialists, labor unions, and the middle class. Critics, however, claim that the PRI has used fraud and violence to stay in power.

Challenges. In 1968, just as the Olympic Games were scheduled to begin in Mexico City, students and workers launched a massive strike. Government troops fired on peaceful protesters, killing hundreds of students. The Olympics took place as planned, but Mexicans were shocked by the massacre.

During the late 1980s, a rival political party mounted the most serious challenge the PRI had ever faced. In a close election campaign, the PRI candidate barely won the presidency. One reason many voters turned against the PRI was the economic crisis that gripped Mexico.

An Oil Refinery After Mexico nationalized its petroleum industry in 1938, Britain and the United States boycotted Mexican products. Mexico finally eased this crisis by paying foreign companies for oil wells and refineries.
Justice Why did Mexico feel justified in nationalizing its oil industry?

Economic Development

After the revolution, Mexico developed a mixed economy. The government owned key industries, such as oil. Private companies owned other businesses and industries. However, the government limited foreign ownership in any company to less than 50 percent of it.

Mexico has sought to achieve balanced growth by developing both agriculture and industry. Despite setbacks, its economy has grown at a steady pace. Food production has increased, and many people now enjoy a higher standard of living than they did in the past. The benefits have not reached everyone, however. According to one estimate, for each Mexican who lives well, six still live in poverty.

Agriculture. Under its land reform program, the government divided many large haciendas into ejidos (eh HEE dohs), or agricultural communities. Today, about half of Mexico's farmers live in ejidos. They raise crops on the land but cannot sell the land because it is owned by the community. Most people on the ejidos are subsistence farmers. They produce enough for their families but have little left over to sell.

The government encouraged the growth of commercial farming. It provided irrigation to open arid areas in the north for farming and ranching. Large companies, many of which are foreign-owned, set up commercial farms there. Using modern farm machinery, they produced a variety of crops such as fruits and tomatoes for shipment to the United States.

As commercial farming grew, farmers no longer produced enough food for local markets. To feed its booming population, Mexico had to import food. The government further contributed to the problem of falling food production. It kept prices for wheat and corn low so urban dwellers could afford to buy bread and tortillas. The low prices discouraged farmers from growing those crops.

Industry. For many years, Mexico followed a policy of economic nationalism. The government imposed high tariffs to protect local industries. By the 1960s, Mexican factories were producing cars, refrigerators, appliances, and many consumer goods. Many state-owned factories were inefficient and unprofitable. The government, however, could afford to keep them going because of an oil boom.

Growing Tobacco in Veracruz Commercial farms like this use modern methods to raise cash crops. They are more efficient than ejidos, where small plots of land are farmed and technology is often out of date. Even so, most peasants still prefer to farm their own land. ***Choice*** Why has commercial farming increased Mexico's dependence on imports?

In 1974, large new oil reserves were found in Mexico. As oil prices soared, Mexico borrowed and spent billions of dollars to build refineries and modernize its industries. It also borrowed heavily from foreign nations for various development projects.

Debt crisis. During the early 1980s, plunging oil prices ended the oil boom. At the same time, rising interest rates on its loans put Mexico into a major debt crisis. To avoid economic collapse, Mexico had to make painful reforms. As a result, it cut spending on education, health care, and other services. It also laid off thousands of government workers and sold state-owned industries to private investors.

Recent trends. Mexico also moved toward free trade, or trade that had low tariffs and no restrictions. Mexico, Canada, and the

United States—already major trading partners—signed the North American Free Trade Agreement (NAFTA) in 1993. NAFTA will create a common market with 365 million consumers. It will abolish most tariffs on goods traded among the three countries. In the future, the economies of these three North American nations are likely to become increasingly interdependent.

Many Mexicans hope that free trade will attract foreign investment and create new jobs. Others worry that the United States, Japan, and other countries might dominate Mexico's economy.

Increased free trade has encouraged the growth of maquiladoras (mah kee luh DOHR uhs). A maquiladora is a foreign-owned plant in which local workers assemble parts into finished goods. American and Japanese companies built maquiladoras in Mexico to take advantage of workers' lower wages. Mexicans flocked to the plants, which sprang up along the border with the United States. Despite overcrowded living conditions near the plants, workers were glad to have jobs.

SECTION 3 REVIEW

1. **Identify:** (a) Porfirio Díaz, (b) constitution of 1917, (c) Lázaro Cárdenas, (d) PRI, (e) NAFTA.
2. **Define:** (a) ejido, (b) free trade, (c) maquiladora.
3. Describe three changes that resulted from the Mexican Revolution.
4. What role has the PRI played in Mexican politics?
5. (a) How did nationalism affect Mexico's economic policies? (b) What economic changes has Mexico made since the debt crisis of the 1980s?
6. **Defending a Position** Do you agree that revolution was the only way to bring about reform in Mexico? Give reasons for your answer.
7. **Writing Across Cultures** Reread the Mexican saying about the United States on page 493. List three facts that might explain why many Mexicans feel this way.

4 ARGENTINA

FIND OUT

Why were Juan Perón and Eva Perón popular figures?

What role has the military played in Argentina?

What economic challenges does Argentina face?

Vocabulary inflation

Waving torches above their heads, thousands of workers marched behind a flatbed truck. On it, a huge movie screen showed pictures of a lovely blonde woman wearing elegant silk dresses and diamond jewelry. As the images flashed across the screen, the workers chanted, *"Eva es mi alma y mi corazón."* ("Eva is my heart and soul.")

Every year, on July 26, workers march through downtown Buenos Aires to honor Eva Perón, the former First Lady of Argentina. "Evita" had risen from poverty to riches. She tried to help the *descamisados*—"shirtless ones"—as working-class people were called. "You, too, will have clothes as rich as mine," she told the poor women of Argentina.

Although she died more than 40 years ago, Eva Perón remains a symbol of hope to many of Argentina's poor. Today, as in the past, the nation's leaders face the challenge of meeting the needs of its large working class.

Geography and People

In area, Argentina is one of the 10 largest countries in the world. The pampas, a vast fertile plain, stretches across east-central Argentina. There, farmers grow wheat, corn, and sorghum. Huge cattle ranches, called *estancias,* are also scattered across the grasslands. The riches of the pampas make Argentina a leading exporter of food. In addition to its agricultural resources, Argentina has deposits of lead, zinc, and tin.

Argentina's Gauchos Gauchos, or cowboys, tend livestock on ranches throughout the pampas, a vast region of fertile grasslands in South America. Argentina is a leading exporter of food, and its meatpacking is a major industry. ***Interdependence*** How do cattle ranches like this one link the economy of Argentina to the world economy?

For its large size, Argentina's population is relatively small—only 32 million people. Few people live in the towering Andes in the west or in the bleak southern region of Patagonia. Most people live in the cities. Almost a third of them crowd into Buenos Aires, the capital.

Unlike Ecuador, Peru, and other Latin American nations, Argentina has few Native Americans. Almost all of them were killed in wars with European settlers during the 1800s. Today, about 95 percent of the people in Argentina are of European origin. Most have Spanish or Italian roots. Others trace their families to Germany, Britain, and Eastern Europe. Some immigrants came from Syria, Lebanon, and other parts of the Middle East.

About half of Argentina's population belongs to the middle class, a large percentage for Latin America. Members of the middle class are highly educated and have helped the economy to develop. Many other Argentinians, however, live in poverty in urban or rural areas.

Political Development

Unlike most countries in Latin America, Argentina enjoyed fairly stable governments from the 1850s to 1930. Since 1930, however, it has faced problems that are common to much of Latin America, including political violence and military rule.

Perón. In 1946, a former army colonel, Juan Perón, was elected president. Perón appealed to urban workers by promising higher wages. He won the support of other groups by promoting economic nationalism. As president, he nationalized the railroads, reduced foreign control of businesses, and increased workers' wages.

Eva Perón did much to increase her husband's popularity among the working class. She used persuasion and threats to get "donations" from rich landowners and industrialists. She then gave the money to the poor or used it to build schools and hospitals, as well as to enrich herself. A strong supporter of women's rights, Eva Perón helped women in Argentina win the right to vote in 1947.

Under Juan Perón, the lives of working-class people improved. However, the costly new programs brought the nation to the point of bankruptcy. In addition, Perón severely restricted civil rights and his government was corrupt. Eva Perón's early death in 1952 was an added blow to her husband's popularity. Even as working-class people mourned Evita, the Church and other groups were attacking Juan Perón. As his popularity faded, the army seized power in 1955 and forced Perón into exile.

The military in power. Between 1955 and 1983, the military ruled Argentina—sometimes directly and sometimes by controlling elected leaders. The military regularly overthrew civilian governments.

Like other Latin American countries, Argentina suffered from political turmoil during the early 1970s. Left-wing terrorists kidnapped government officials and business leaders. Right-wing death squads killed labor and student leaders. To stop the violence, the army invited an aging Perón to return from exile. He won office in 1973. When he died the following year, his vice president—and new wife—Isabel Perón, assumed office. She became the first woman in the Americas to become a nation's president.

The "dirty war." In 1976, as terrorist attacks worsened, the army again seized power. It launched a brutal campaign, known as the "dirty war," against workers, students, and anyone else it decided was an "enemy of the state." Soldiers arrested and tortured thousands of men and women. As many as 30,000 people "disappeared." They were taken from their homes and never seen again.

The violence turned many people against the nation's military leaders. As the economy faltered, the military launched a different kind of war to regain popular support. In 1982, they seized a cluster of windswept islands about 300 miles (500 km) off the coast of Argentina. Since the 1830s, Britain had ruled the Falkland Islands. Argentina argued that it had an earlier claim to the islands, which they called Las Malvinas.

At first, nationalism led the people to rally behind their leaders. When the British quick-

At the Plaza de Mayo In the early 1980s, families of the "disappeared" gathered each week to ask for news. As one mother explained, "When Jorge vanished, my first reaction was to rush out desperately to look for him. . . .Then I realized we had to look for all of them and that we had to stand together because together we were stronger." ***Human Rights*** Why did these protesters wear masks?

ly regained control of the islands, however, the military lost all popular support.

Return to democracy. In 1983, the military permitted free elections. Under President Raúl Alfonsín, democracy was restored in Argentina. At the same time, pressure from the families of those who had "disappeared" mounted. Each Thursday, the Mothers of the Plaza de Mayo marched in the main plaza of Buenos Aires. Holding photographs of their sons and daughters, they demanded to know what had happened to them. The new government prosecuted some army leaders for the murders that were committed during the "dirty war."

In 1989, voters returned to the polls and elected a new president, Carlos Menem. For the first time since 1928, power passed from one civilian leader to another without interference from the military.

Economic Challenges

Although Argentinians had demonstrated their commitment to democracy, they faced severe economic challenges during the 1980s. Runaway inflation hurt workers and employers alike. Inflation is an economic cycle marked by a sharp increase in prices. In 1985, inflation reached almost 1,000 percent in Argentina. Because prices rose from one day to the next, families could not even afford food. People often paid their bills in person because they were afraid prices might rise while their payments were in the mail.

Like Mexico and other Latin American countries, Argentina also owed foreign banks and governments billions of dollars. To combat inflation and ease the debt crisis, the government took drastic steps. It imposed wage and price freezes and laid off thousands of government workers. In addition, it sold the national airline, railroad, and telephone companies to private industries.

By the early 1990s, these harsh economic reforms seemed to be working. Inflation fell to its lowest level since the 1960s. With a stable government and a recovering economy, the people of Argentina hoped for renewed economic growth.

SECTION 4 REVIEW

1. **Locate:** Falkland Islands.
2. **Identify:** (a) Juan Perón, (b) Eva Perón, (c) "dirty war," (d) Raúl Alfonsín, (e) Mothers of the Plaza de Mayo, (f) Carlos Menem.
3. **Define:** inflation.
4. What actions did the Perón government take to help the poor?
5. (a) Why did the military seize control in Argentina? (b) What events led to the restoration of democracy?
6. Describe two steps that Argentina has taken to overcome its economic problems.
7. **Forecasting** (a) Do you think that democracy will survive in Argentina? (b) What events might endanger democratic rule?
8. **Writing Across Cultures** In the past, the United States, like Argentina, faced severe inflation. Interview a parent or an older relative about the inflation of the 1970s. Write a paragraph summarizing what you learn about the effects of inflation.

5 BRAZIL

FIND OUT

Why is Brazil an ethnically and culturally diverse country?

What political and economic problems has Brazil faced since the 1930s?

What difficult choices does Brazil have to make?

Like many Brazilians, Benedita da Silva came from a poor family. When she was a child, she and her family migrated from the country to a favela, or shantytown. While living in the favela, da Silva held a variety of jobs, from market porter to house servant. At the same time, she worked to improve conditions where she lived. She said:

Carnival in Rio Many Cariocas, as the people of Rio are called, have black ancestors. African rhythms and music inspired Brazil's national dance, the samba. During a four-day carnival each year, "samba societies" parade into the city's Sambadome. These societies spend all year preparing their costumes and floats. ***Diversity*** What are the four main ethnic groups of Brazil?

> "As a black and a woman, I have a special responsibility to speak out on subjects that I know about—against racial discrimination, against the unequal rights of women, and against the injustices suffered by the poor."

In 1987, da Silva became the first black woman elected to Brazil's Congress. There, she continued to press for programs that would meet the needs of both Brazil's many poor and its culturally diverse population.

Geography and People

Brazil is a huge country that covers half of South America. Size and differences in resources have contributed to regionalism.

Regions and resources. The first Portuguese colonists settled along the fertile northeastern coast. Today, that region still produces important export crops such as coffee, cocoa, and sugar. Farther inland in the northeast lies the *sertão* (sair TOWNG), a dry region covered with scrub. Most of the people who live here are desperately poor. The huge Amazon Basin, as you have read, is heavily forested and sparsely settled.

The southeast is rich in mineral resources such as iron, nickel, and tin. Its coastal industrial cities, São Paulo and Rio de Janeiro, have huge populations. Every year, millions of Brazilians migrate to the cities of the south hoping to find jobs.

Diversity. With more than 150 million people, Brazil has the fifth-largest population in the world. Its people belong to four main groups. Indians, the original inhabitants, today make up less than 1 percent of the population. Many live in isolated communities in the northern interior.

Blacks, the descendants of enslaved Africans, make up half of Brazil's population. Their religious beliefs, food, and music have enriched Brazilian culture. Portuguese colonists and later European immigrants added to the cultural diversity of Brazil. In more recent times, many Japanese have arrived. Today, Brazil has the world's largest Japanese community outside of Japan.

Inequalities. Brazil is a land of extremes. It has the world's ninth-largest economy. In gleaming cities, the rich and middle class live in comfortable houses and apartments, attend excellent schools and universities, and get medical treatment at modern hospitals. Nearby, millions of people in the favelas suffer desperate poverty. Another huge gap divides the rural poor and the city dwellers.

Although the Brazilian constitution forbids discrimination, racism exists. Darker-skinned people have a more difficult time getting jobs than whites. People of mixed descent experience less discrimination than blacks do.

Dictatorship and Development

According to a popular Brazilian saying, "Brazil is a country of the future, and always will be." This saying expresses both the great potential of Brazil and its failure to achieve its promise. Over the years, both military dictators and democratically elected leaders have tried to develop Brazil's economic resources.

Economic diversity. Brazil has taken steps to diversify its economy. Until the 1930s, it depended on a single export crop—coffee. The dictator Getúlio Vargas, who ruled from 1930 to 1945, set up programs to promote industrial growth. Since then, with strong government support, Brazil has developed into a major industrial nation.

During the 1950s, Brazilians elected Juscelino Kubitschek (KOO bih chehk) as their president. He promised to pack "fifty years of progress in five." Kubitschek undertook an ambitious program to build highways, universities, airports, factories, and hydroelectric plants. He also created the new capital city of Brasília to encourage settlement of the interior. (See the feature on page 6.)

Kubitschek's programs created massive debts. In 1964, as the economy faltered, the army stepped in. The new military government outlawed political parties and crushed opponents.

Brazilian miracle. At the same time, the generals encouraged foreign investment and developed new industries such as steel, chemicals, and heavy machinery. They promoted efforts to develop Brazil's vast interior, including the Amazon rain forest. To end dependence on foreign oil, they encouraged the building of hydroelectric plants. Brazil also pioneered in developing gasohol, an alcohol fuel made from sugar cane. These policies created an economic boom known as the "Brazilian miracle."

The Brazilian miracle brought prosperity to people in the middle and upper classes, but most Brazilians benefited little. The government kept wages low to attract foreign investors. While investors made good profits, urban workers barely earned enough to survive. Although the government introduced several programs to help the poor, they were too limited to have much effect. In the favelas, people suffered from widespread disease, malnutrition, and illiteracy.

Difficult Choices

During the 1980s, the military slowly turned the government over to elected officials. In 1990, Fernando Collor de Mello became Brazil's first directly elected president in 29 years.

Debt and spending. By the early 1990s, Brazil's foreign debt had reached a staggering $110 billion. Interest payments alone took a large share of the nation's earnings. To reduce the debt, the government had to make drastic and painful reforms such as cutbacks in spending.

Today, more than half of Brazil's population is under the age of 20. Many never attend school. Even those who do often cannot find jobs or lack the skills needed in an increasingly industrialized economy. The government faces a difficult choice. Should it spend scarce resources for schools and services to the poor? Or should it invest in programs designed to expand the economy, which, in turn, would provide jobs for the urban poor?

Environment. Brazil hopes to reduce population growth through family planning. The government has also encouraged people to move from the crowded coastal cities into the

Off to Work at a Paper-Making Factory The Brazilian government encourages new settlements in the Amazon Basin, the site of the factory where these men work. The rain forest environment is fragile, however. Clearing land for farms reduces the rain forest, and farming wears out the soil quickly. New logging and lumber mills are destroying large parts of the rain forest. ***Choice*** Why do you think Brazil encourages its people to settle in the Amazon Basin?

interior. There, they can help to develop Brazil's rich forests and mineral resources. Development of the interior has improved Brazil's economy. Minerals, beef, and timber from the Amazon region can be sold on the world market.

Development has environmental costs, however. Farmers have cut down and burned forests, causing damage to the Earth's atmosphere. In some areas, efforts to farm unsuitable soil has created desertlike conditions. Settlers have spread diseases to the Indians of the rain forest and undermined their cultures. José Antonio Lutzenberger, a Brazilian specialist on the environment, has warned:

> "We are demolishing, poisoning, destroying all life systems on the planet. We are acting as if we were the last generation on the planet."

Today, Brazilians are looking for ways to modernize without taking such a high toll on the environment.

SECTION 5 REVIEW

1. **Identify:** (a) Juscelino Kubitschek, (b) Brazilian miracle.
2. Describe two ways in which geography has affected Brazil.
3. (a) What groups make up the population of Brazil? (b) What problems do darker-skinned people in Brazil face?
4. (a) How has Brazil tried to develop its economy? (b) How has economic development brought both benefits and disadvantages?
5. **Evaluating Information** (a) What do Brazilians mean when they call Brazil "a country of the future"? (b) What obstacles does Brazil face in achieving its potential?
6. **Writing Across Cultures** Like Brazil, the United States must make painful choices on how to spend its limited funds. Write an editorial explaining whether you think the government should cut aid to schools to reduce its debt. Give reasons for your opinion.

Chapter 22 Review

Understanding Vocabulary

Match each term at left with the correct definition at right.

1. coup d'état
2. embargo
3. liberation theology
4. maquiladora
5. inflation

a. doctrine that calls for the Church to take a more active role in changing the conditions that contribute to poverty
b. complete halt to trade
c. economic cycle marked by a sharp increase in prices
d. foreign-owned plant where local workers assemble parts
e. revolt by military leaders against a government

Reviewing the Main Ideas

1. (a) How do the goals of leftists and rightists differ? (b) Why did the military seize power in many Latin American nations?

2. (a) What were the goals of land reform? (b) What groups opposed land reform efforts?

3. What conditions contribute to rural poverty in Latin America?

4. How has its location affected Mexico's economic development?

5. (a) How did the military violate human rights in Argentina? (b) What challenges did democratic governments in Argentina face in the 1980s?

Reviewing Chapter Themes

1. Mexico, Cuba, and Nicaragua experienced revolutions that led to major social change. (a) Explain the causes and goals of the revolution in one of these countries. (b) Describe the results of the revolution, evaluating whether or not it achieved its goals.

2. Latin American nations have met with limited success in their efforts to develop their economies. (a) Describe the goals and results of economic nationalism. (b) Explain one obstacle to economic growth.

3. Modernization is changing life in Latin America. Explain how the growth of cities and other developments have affected two of the following: (a) the family, (b) women, (c) the Catholic Church.

4. The nations of Latin America have taken different paths to modernization. (a) Describe one political or economic challenge that has faced either Mexico, Argentina, or Brazil. (b) Explain what steps that country took to meet that challenge.

Thinking Critically

1. Analyzing Ideas "Our economy is doing well, but our people are not," said the leader of one Latin American nation. Why do many people in Latin America continue to live in poverty despite economic progress?

2. Making Global Connections (a) Why do many people in Latin America migrate to El Norte? (b) Compare their reasons with the reasons that have led other immigrants to come to the United States.

Applying Your Skills

1. Using Your Vocabulary Use the Glossary on pages 794–803 to review the meaning of the following terms: *land reform, nationalize, privatization, democratization.* Use each term in a separate sentence about Latin America.

2. Analyzing a Quotation During the Díaz era, a Mexican saying stated, "Mexico is the mother of foreigners, and the stepmother of Mexicans." (a) Restate the main point of this saying. (b) What situation gave rise to this saying? (c) How did the Mexican Revolution change that situation?

Chapter 23

Latin America in the World Today

A Swirling Crowd Drumming musicians seem to disappear in this crowd of Haitians. Painters from Haiti, many of them self-taught artists, have become famous for their imaginative style and colorful scenes. ***Fine Art*** Why do you think the artist has not shown individual faces or expressions?

Chapter Outline

Day after day, the workers sweated in the tropical heat. They blasted through mountains and hacked through jungles. More than 25,000 workers from Central America and the West Indies helped clear a "path between the seas." On August 15, 1914, the Panama Canal opened.

In the United States, people hailed the Panama Canal. The United States had organized and financed the project. It had even engineered a revolution to win rights to the land where the canal was dug.

Latin Americans had mixed feelings about the canal. Fifty years after it opened, Pablo Neruda, Chile's Nobel Prize–winning poet, wrote:

> "Panama, your geography granted you
> a gift that no other land was given:
> two oceans pushed forward to meet you . . .
> And what happened? little sister, they cut
> your figure as if it were cheese
> and then ate and left you
> like a gnawed olive pit."

In "History of a Canal," Neruda criticized the United States for using its power and wealth to carve up Panama. The building of the Panama Canal, however, was only one action of the United States that provoked fierce debate in Latin America.

CHAPTER PERSPECTIVE

Since the 1800s, the United States has taken an active role in Latin America. Latin Americans have struggled to limit North American influence in their lands. Today, the nations of the Western Hemisphere emphasize cooperation over conflict as they try to solve urgent problems and build a better future.

As you read, look for these chapter themes:

- Differing interests have sometimes led to conflict between Latin American nations and the United States.
- Through regional organizations, nations of the Western Hemisphere have worked to resolve issues and promote cooperation.
- The literature and arts of Latin America blend Indian, African, and European traditions.

Literature Connections

In this chapter, you will encounter selections from the following works.

"History of a Canal," Pablo Neruda

"Sensemayá," Nicolás Guillén

"Social Commitment and the Latin American Writer," Mario Vargas Llosa

"Flowers and Songs of Sorrow," Aztec poet

For other suggestions, see Connections With Literature, pages 804–808.

1 LATIN AMERICA AND THE UNITED STATES

FIND OUT

How has United States influence in Latin America grown since the 1800s?

What economic interests have shaped relations between the United States and Latin America?

How did the Cold War affect relations between Latin America and the United States?

What ties link Puerto Rico and the United States?

When the nations of Latin America won their freedom, they looked to the United States as a model for democratic government. Simón Bolívar called the United States a "model of political virtues and moral enlightenment unique in the history of mankind." Yet, by the early 1900s, Latin American admiration for the United States had turned to resentment. To many Latin Americans, the United States had become the "Colossus of the North"—a giant power that threatened their independence.

An Expanding Power

In the 1820s, Spain prepared to reconquer its former American colonies. The new nations of Latin America therefore welcomed the Monroe Doctrine, issued by United States President James Monroe in 1823. In it, Monroe declared that "the American continents are henceforth not to be considered as subjects for future colonization by any European powers."

As the United States expanded, Latin Americans no longer saw the United States as a defender of their liberties. Instead, they began to fear its power in the hemisphere.

Mexican War. In 1845, the United States annexed Texas, which had once belonged to Mexico. A year later, war broke out between Mexico and the United States. When the Mexican War ended in 1848, Mexico had to give up almost half of its territory to the United States. The war left Mexicans with a lasting bitterness toward the United States.

Spanish-American War. As the United States industrialized, it extended its influence in the Caribbean and Central America. During the 1890s, Cuban patriots were battling for independence from Spain. In 1898, the United States declared war on Spain and joined the fighting. It promised that once peace was achieved, it would "leave the government and control of Cuba to its people."

The Spanish-American War ended in victory for the United States. Cuba did gain its independence, but the United States forced Cuba to include the Platt Amendment as part of its new constitution. Under the Platt Amendment, the United States claimed the right to intervene in Cuban affairs.

As a result of the war, the United States also gained Puerto Rico and the Philippines

MAP STUDY

After the Spanish-American War, the United States played a major role in the affairs of the Caribbean nations.

1. **Region** Which two areas were acquired by the United States?
2. **Interaction** (a) In what part of Central America did the United States acquire land? (b) Why did the United States want this area?
3. **Understanding Causes and Effects** How did growing United States investments in the Caribbean and in Central America result in increased intervention in those areas?

from Spain. Many Latin Americans felt that the United States had fought the Spanish-American War to win new territories.

"Yankee Imperialist" or Good Neighbor?

During the early 1900s, the United States continued to intervene in Latin America. Its actions increased Latin Americans' distrust and fear of their northern neighbor.

Panama Canal. From the late 1800s, the United States had expressed an interest in digging a canal across Panama, which was then part of Colombia. President Theodore Roosevelt offered Colombia $10 million for a strip of land across the Isthmus of Panama. When Colombia rejected the offer, Roosevelt encouraged rebels in Panama to declare Panama's independence. In 1903, the new nation of Panama granted a 10-mile-wide "canal zone" to the United States. Roosevelt's actions heightened Latin American fears of the "Yankee menace." *

Investments and intervention. In the years that followed, United States investments in Latin America soared. North Americans bought sugar cane plantations in Cuba and copper mines in Chile. They built railroads and factories in Brazil and Argentina. In Mexico and Venezuela, they invested in oil wells. These investments benefited the wealthy, but not the majority of people in Latin America.

Financial interests led the United States to intervene in Latin America. In the early 1900s, the Dominican Republic was unable to pay its debts to American banks. The United States occupied the island, took over collection of its customs duties, and repaid the loans. United States marines remained in the Dominican Republic until 1924.

American forces also occupied Nicaragua and Haiti, and intervened in the affairs of Honduras six times. In each case, they stepped in to protect American lives and property or to support a government that favored American interests.

* In 1978, the United States agreed to a series of treaties that would grant Panama control over the canal zone by the year 2000.

In a Caracas Neighborhood Today, brightly colored signs advertising fast food restaurants rise against the background of Caracas's green hills. The United States is a major trading partner of Venezuela, Brazil, Argentina, Mexico, Chile, and most other Latin American nations. ***Culture*** Why might Latin Americans dislike signs like these?

Most Latin Americans resented "Yankee imperialism." A plantation owner in Nicaragua wrote to officials in Washington:

> "Today we are hated and despised. . . . This feeling has been created by employing American marines to hunt down and kill Nicaraguans in their own country."

Changing directions. The growth of anti-American feelings and the beginning of the Great Depression led the United States to seek better relations with Latin America. In

1933, President Franklin D. Roosevelt announced the Good Neighbor Policy. He withdrew American marines from Haiti and agreed that "no state has the right to intervene in the internal or external affairs of another state."

The United States, however, remained the dominant economic power in the region. American companies owned huge tracts of land, commercial farms, mines, and other valuable resources there. The United States was also the chief trading partner of most Latin American nations.

Cold War Politics

After World War II, the Cold War added a new issue to relations within the Western Hemisphere. The United States wanted to create a solid anti-communist bloc in the Americas. Many people in Latin America, however, saw socialism as the answer to pressing economic and social problems. At the same time, growing nationalism spurred Latin Americans to try to end economic domination by the United States.

Battling communism. To keep leftists from gaining power in Latin America, the United States backed anti-communist forces throughout the region. Often, that meant supporting corrupt dictators or harsh military governments.

The United States also returned to a policy of intervention. In 1950, it helped to overthrow a leftist government in Guatemala. It plotted against Fidel Castro in Cuba during the 1960s. It sent troops to the Dominican Republic in 1965, to the island of Grenada in 1983, and to Panama in 1989. During the early 1970s, the United States helped to pave the way for a military coup against the leftist government of Chile's Salvador Allende.

Alliance for Progress. To counter communist influence, the United States increased its aid to Latin America. In 1961, President John F. Kennedy launched the Alliance for Progress. Under this program, Kennedy encouraged Latin American countries to undertake reforms to raise the standard of living for their people. Countries that made reforms would receive United States aid to build schools, hospitals, roads, and water systems.

The Alliance for Progress was an ambitious program that produced few results. Although it improved housing, education, and health care in some countries, it did not end the causes of poverty.

Containing Castro

Castro's revolution in Cuba alarmed the United States. As a communist nation, Cuba not only became an ally of the Soviet Union but also gave support to revolutionaries in other Latin American countries.

Bay of Pigs invasion. In 1961, the United States tried to overthrow Castro. It secretly trained and equipped Cuban exiles and set them ashore at the Bay of Pigs, off the southern coast of Cuba. The exiles hoped to lead a general uprising against Castro. Instead, Cuban forces quickly defeated them. Many Latin Americans criticized the United States for plotting the invasion.

Cuban missile crisis. The Bay of Pigs invasion led Castro to seek even closer relations with the Soviet Union. Castro allowed the Soviets to build missile bases in Cuba. In response, the United States set up a naval blockade of Cuba.

These actions set off a major superpower crisis in October 1962. With Soviet ships steaming toward Cuba, some carrying atomic missiles, the world seemed on the brink of war. In the end, the Soviet Union agreed to remove its missiles if the United States pledged not to invade Cuba.

Trade embargo. In 1977, Cuba and the United States set up limited diplomatic relations, but tensions remained. While Castro denounced North American imperialism, the United States continued its trade embargo against Cuba. Many Latin American nations opposed the United States policy. As a result, they continued to trade with and extend aid to Cuba, especially after the collapse of communism ended Soviet support for the island nation in the early 1990s.

Recent Trends

In recent years, the United States has encouraged the move toward democracy in Latin America. Although it continued to aid anticommunist forces, it also pressed rightist governments to make reforms.

El Salvador. During the 1970s and 1980s, the United States gave massive military aid to El Salvador to help its government battle leftist guerrillas there. At the same time, it pressured the government to introduce land reform and hold free elections. Years of terror and turmoil had taken an enormous toll on the tiny country. In the early 1990s, the United Nations helped the rebels and government forces in El Salvador to negotiate a peace agreement.

Nicaragua. As you read in Chapter 22, leftist Sandinistas gained power in Nicaragua after the overthrow of Anastasio Somoza. Fearing that Nicaragua would become another Cuba, the United States aided the contras in their guerrilla war against the Sandinista government. (See page 483.) The United States also imposed a trade embargo that crippled the Nicaraguan economy. The United States lifted the embargo and restored aid after Nicaragua held free elections and the Sandinistas lost.

The shadow of a giant. As the Cold War ended, the fear of Soviet influence faded. Other issues, such as foreign debt and the illegal drug trade, became important in relations within the hemisphere.

Today, as in the past, Latin Americans have mixed feelings about the United States. They admire the rich material culture of their northern neighbor. At the same time, they resent its economic domination of the Western Hemisphere. The Mexican poet Octavio Paz summed up the feelings of many Latin Americans when he wrote:

> “North Americans are always among us, even when they ignore us or turn their back on us. Their shadow covers the whole hemisphere. It is the shadow of a giant.”

Puerto Rico: A Special Case

Puerto Rico has lived under the shadow of the United States since 1898. At first, the United States controlled its government and economy. To counter an independence movement, the United States gave Puerto Ricans United States citizenship in 1917.

The Mariel Boatlift
In 1980, Cuba briefly relaxed its ban on Cubans leaving their country. In just four months, 120,000 Cubans—many of them penniless—fled to Florida in boats. ***Power*** What two actions has the United States taken since 1960 against Castro's dictatorship?

San Juan, Puerto Rico Busy highways and towering buildings suggest the prosperity of Puerto Rico's capital city. The people of the commonwealth have a higher standard of living than most Latin Americans. The average income in Puerto Rico, however, is still only about one third that of people in the United States. ***Change*** How has Puerto Rico's economy changed since the 1950s?

Puerto Rico became a self-governing commonwealth of the United States in 1952. This means that Puerto Rico has its own constitution and elects its own governor and legislature. As citizens of the United States, Puerto Ricans must obey that nation's laws, but they do not have to pay taxes to the federal government. They enjoy most of the rights of citizens, although they cannot vote for the United States president or be represented in Congress.

Economic development. Until the 1950s, Puerto Rico's economy depended on a single crop—sugar. Large United States corporations owned huge sugar plantations on the island, and most Puerto Ricans lived in poverty.

In the 1950s, Luis Muñoz Marín (loo EES moon YOHS mah REEN) became Puerto Rico's first elected governor. He supported a program to encourage tourism and develop industry on the island. Known as Operation Bootstrap, the program offered United States companies tax savings to build plants in Puerto Rico.

Hundreds of American businesses set up factories to produce shoes, clothing, chemicals, and electronics. In addition to receiving tax breaks, these companies also benefited because wages in Puerto Rico were lower than those on the mainland United States. Even so, incomes for Puerto Ricans rose as the economy developed.

Despite economic progress, unemployment remained high. Many Puerto Ricans migrated to the mainland United States to find jobs. Today, about 2.7 million Puerto Ricans live on the mainland, and 3.5 million live on the island.

Future status. Puerto Ricans are divided about the future of their island. Some call for independence. Others want the island to become the fifty-first state of the United States. A majority of the people of Puerto Rico have voted to remain a commonwealth.

SECTION 1 REVIEW

1. **Locate:** (a) Panama Canal, (b) Puerto Rico.
2. **Identify:** (a) Monroe Doctrine, (b) Mexican War, (c) Spanish-American War, (d) Platt Amendment, (e) Good Neighbor Policy, (f) Alliance for Progress, (g) Bay of Pigs invasion, (h) Cuban missile crisis, (i) Operation Bootstrap.
3. (a) How did Latin American nations first react to the Monroe Doctrine? (b) Identify two events that changed their view of the United States.
4. What was one result of increased United States investment in Latin America during the early 1900s?
5. Give two examples of how the Cold War affected relations between the United States and Latin America.
6. (a) How has Puerto Rico encouraged economic development? (b) Have these programs been successful? Explain.
7. **Identifying Alternatives** (a) What choices must Puerto Ricans make about the future of their island? (b) What reasons might some Puerto Ricans have for becoming an independent nation? (c) What reasons might they have for wanting to keep their present status?
8. **Writing Across Cultures** Some people say that the Monroe Doctrine protected Latin America from Europe but not from the United States. Do you agree or disagree with this opinion? Write a paragraph explaining your answer.

2 REGIONAL AND GLOBAL ISSUES

FIND OUT

What role have regional organizations played in Latin America?

Why have Latin American debt and the drug trade become global issues?

What environmental issues are important in Latin America?

Why has human rights been an issue in Latin America?

Vocabulary default

In 1992, nations around the world marked the 500th anniversary of the voyage of Christopher Columbus to the Americas. The anniversary sparked bitter debate. Some people wanted to celebrate the heroic achievements of Columbus and other European explorers. Others pointed to the destruction of Native American cultures and other tragic effects of European expansion. In the end, many people used the occasion to evaluate the past and set goals for the future.

In Latin America, a group of concerned writers drew attention to an urgent issue:

> "On the eve of the 500th anniversary of the meeting of two worlds . . . the Earth is experiencing its worst ecological crisis in history—a crisis that not only threatens thousands of plant and animal species but the survival of the human species as well."

The writers called on Latin American leaders to work together to meet the crisis. They noted, however, that environmental concerns were not limited to Latin America. "We are part of a global problem which requires global solutions," they declared. The environment

Medicines From the Rain Forest

SCIENCE AND TECHNOLOGY

In a rain forest in South America, a young boy cries with pain from an earache. Quickly, his parents prepare a cure. First, they squeeze the juice from a local plant. Then, rolling a leaf into the shape of a funnel, they drop the juice into the boy's ear. The medicine works quickly. In a few hours, the pain is gone and the boy is laughing and playing with his friends.

Thousands of species of plants and animals are found in the world's tropical rain forests. Over the centuries, the peoples of the rain forests have learned how to use these resources not only for food but as medicine. Like the South American parents mentioned above, they cure earaches with the juice of a plant. They use other plants to treat centipede bites, to get rid of head lice, and to reduce fevers.

Modern scientists have come to respect the medical knowledge of rain forest peoples. They also have learned to value the rain forests as an important source of medicines. Today, about one quarter of all the ingredients in prescription drugs comes from the rain forests. Researchers have identified 1,400 plants that have the potential to fight cancer. Thousands more have not yet been studied.

Today, the knowledge of rain forest peoples, as well as the rain forests themselves, is threatened by development. About 100 species of plants and animals from the rain forests become extinct every day. Scientists and other groups are campaigning to preserve the rain forests. They point out that in terms of medicine alone the loss of these resources is something the world cannot afford.

1. List three ways that rain forest peoples use local plants to treat illness or disease.
2. **Defending a Position** Some people argue that development would benefit rain forest peoples because it would give them access to things like modern medical care. Do you agree or disagree? Explain.

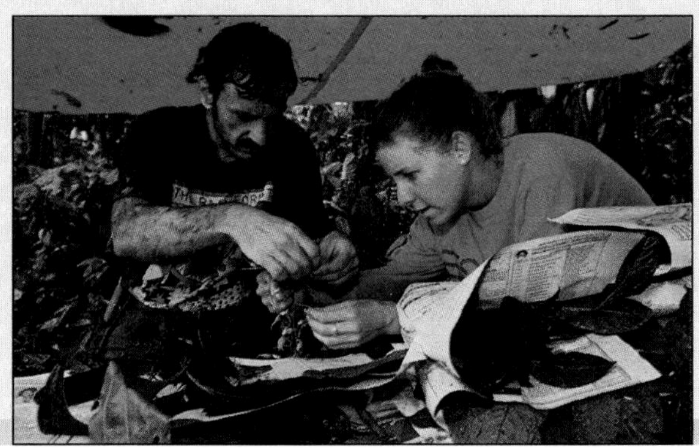

is just one of many issues that require regional and global cooperation.

Regional Cooperation

Because many Latin American nations are relatively small, they have limited national markets for their goods. During the 1960s and 1970s, some nations organized regional common markets. Through these organizations, they created larger markets for the sale of their products.

In 1969, Colombia, Ecuador, Peru, Bolivia, and Chile organized the Andean Pact. Venezuela joined four years later. Members of the Pact agreed to lower their tariffs and promote economic development. The Caribbean Community and Common Market and the Central American Common Market had similar goals. These groups had limited success, however. Often, political differences and economic hard times prevented members from agreeing on a common policy.

OAS. The largest regional organization is the Organization of American States (OAS). It was set up in 1948 to help members settle disputes through peaceful means, discourage foreign intervention in the region, and promote economic development and democracy. The OAS includes the United States, which has tended to dominate the organization.

The OAS has successfully resolved disputes among Latin American nations. In 1969, for example, it helped to end a war between Honduras and El Salvador. In 1991, it worked to restore Haiti's democratically elected president after he was overthrown in a military coup. It has channeled large amounts of aid from the United States to member nations and helped poorer nations to improve health care, transportation, and education.

The United States and other OAS members have disagreed on various issues. In 1962, for example, the United States pressured the OAS to expel communist Cuba, an original member of the organization. Several member nations, including Mexico, opposed the move. In the 1982 Falklands war, Latin American nations in the OAS supported Argentina. The United States, however, condemned Argentina's invasion of the islands and supported its longtime ally, Britain. This policy angered many Latin Americans.

Free trade. During the 1990s, interest in free trade revived. Latin Americans watched closely as Mexico, the United States, and Canada negotiated the North American Free Trade Agreement (NAFTA). Many wondered whether Mexican industry could compete with United States and Canadian goods without the protection of high tariffs. If Mexico benefits from NAFTA, other Latin American countries may then seek similar agreements.

Ties With the World

Latin American nations are active in several world organizations, including the United Nations. Although 20 Latin American nations belong to the UN, they do not vote as a bloc.

Links to Europe. Latin Americans have strong cultural ties with European nations, especially Spain and Portugal. Although Spain refused to recognize many Latin American nations during the early years after independence, relations slowly improved. Portugal and Brazil, on the other hand, kept close contact from the beginning.

In 1991, Spain, Portugal, and the nations of Latin America held their first summit meeting in Mexico City. There, leaders discussed issues of common concern.

Expanding horizons. In recent years, Latin American nations have expanded contacts with other parts of the world, especially Japan. A number of Latin American countries have begun to benefit from Japanese investment and technology. Nations on the west coast of Latin America are also eager to join in the growing trade with other Pacific Rim countries.

Global Issues

In recent years, several issues have increased world focus on Latin America. They have highlighted the interdependence of the region and the rest of the world.

The debt problem. Like other Third World nations, most Latin American nations have borrowed heavily from foreign banks and governments. They used the money to develop agriculture and industry. During the 1980s, however, interest rates rose and the world economy slowed. Debtor nations faced a crisis. (See the chart on page 786.)

Some Latin American nations threatened to default, or stop repaying the loans. Default could cause lending banks to fail, so they searched desperately for solutions. Banks lowered interest rates and extended the repayment period. They also canceled some debt in exchange for partial ownership of local companies. In "debt-for-nature swaps," foreign lenders agreed to cancel a small part of a nation's debt if it agreed to support local conservation projects.

Today, Latin American nations owe foreign countries about $420 billion. Under international pressure, Latin American governments have cut spending on services to the poor, laid off workers, and sold state-owned industries. Although these policies saved money, they also caused the standard of living among Latin America's poor to fall even lower than it was.

Drug trade. Another issue of global concern is the drug trade. Many illegal drugs such as cocaine, heroin, and marijuana are smuggled from Latin America into the United States and Europe. This illegal trade is fueled by two forces: a strong demand for drugs in the United States and Europe and poverty in Latin America.

The drug trade is big business in parts of Latin America. In Colombia, Bolivia, and Peru, poor farmers can earn more growing coca—the plant from which cocaine is made—than any other crop. Thousands of other people, from cocaine processors to smugglers, also earn their living from the drug trade.

During the 1980s, the drug trade led to widespread corruption and violence in Colombia and elsewhere. Drug lords bribed government officials and murdered anyone who opposed them. In the early 1990s, Colombia reduced the level of violence somewhat by convincing several major drug figures to surrender.

The United States gave aid to Colombia, Bolivia, and Peru to combat drug production. In 1988, the United States charged Panama's president, General Manuel Noriega, with drug trafficking. A year later, it invaded Panama and seized Noriega for trial. He was found guilty and sentenced to 40 years in prison.

Solving the drug problem requires international cooperation. Latin Americans have called on the United States to curb the demand for drugs. They have also requested economic aid in order to offer poor farmers who raise coca other ways to earn a living.

Environmental Issues

In Latin America, as elsewhere, the population explosion and the need to develop resources threaten natural environments. Latin Americans have harvested lumber from the rain forests, cut strip mines in wilderness areas, and overfished coastal waters. Air pollution endangers people's health in crowded urban areas such as Mexico City; São Paulo, Brazil; and Santiago, Chile.

International efforts are underway to educate the people of Latin America about environmental threats. Under strong pressure, some countries, such as Costa Rica and Brazil, have acted to slow the destruction of rain forests by setting aside large areas as protected preserves. Most Latin American nations, however, need the income produced from their forests.

Experts are seeking ways to combine economic growth with environmental protection. For example, scientists have studied the methods that Mayas still use to farm in the rain forests of Central America. By working small plots of land for brief periods and then leaving the land uncultivated for long periods, the Mayas produce plentiful crops without destroying the soil.

Human Rights

The turmoil of the 1960s and 1970s led to widespread human rights abuses in Latin America. Military governments in Argentina,

Armed Villagers Peruvian farmers have few weapons to oppose the Shining Path, an extreme left-wing group. Since 1980, the Shining Path has waged warfare against the government as well as against relief organizations trying to improve farmers' lives. ***Human Rights*** How might relief efforts weaken the Shining Path's efforts to gain control of the government?

Chile, and Uruguay tortured and killed citizens who opposed their leaders. In Cuba, Castro imprisoned citizens who spoke out against his regime. The governments of Guatemala and El Salvador allowed right-wing death squads to assassinate farmers, priests, nuns, students, and labor leaders.

Human rights groups and the United Nations condemned these abuses, with little effect. Finally, as democracy was restored in Latin America during the 1980s, much of the killing stopped. In Peru, however, violence continued. Both government forces and an extreme left-wing group known as the Shining Path resorted to torture and murder in their ongoing struggle to control the country.

In Guatemala, too, human rights abuses continued. For almost 30 years, the military and its death squads terrorized the country. More than 100,000 people disappeared. To prevent Indians from supporting rebel guerrillas, the government forced them out of their villages and massacred thousands of Indian men. Although the killings have slowed, death squads have recently targeted Indians working for human rights and land reform.

SECTION 2 REVIEW

1. **Identify:** (a) Andean Pact, (b) OAS, (c) Shining Path.
2. **Define:** default.
3. (a) Why did Latin American nations form regional common markets? (b) Why have they had limited success?
4. Describe three goals of the OAS.
5. (a) How does foreign debt tie Latin America to the global economy? (b) How have lenders tried to ease Latin America's debt problem?
6. What are two causes of environmental problems in Latin America?
7. **Analyzing Information** Why do you think that many experts consider the drug trade to be an economic problem?
8. **Writing Across Cultures** List three steps the United States might take to help end human rights abuses in Latin America.

3 LITERATURE AND THE ARTS

FIND OUT

What traditions have influenced the arts in Latin America?

What themes have Latin American writers explored?

How are music and dance linked in Latin America?

How do crafts preserve ancient traditions?

"Mayombe-bombe-mayombe!
Mayombe-bombe-mayombe!
The snake has eyes of glass
The snake comes and winds round a stick."

These lines come from "Sensemayá," a poem by the popular Afro-Cuban writer Nicolás Guillén. The poem re-creates a traditional snake dance that enslaved Africans brought to Cuba. In "Sensemayá," Guillén combines African and Spanish words and rhythms to create a poem that is uniquely Latin American.

Like "Sensemayá," much of the literature and arts of Latin America reflect a blend of traditions. Native Americans, Africans, and Europeans have all contributed to the rich cultural heritage of the region.

Literature

Writers hold a respected place in Latin American societies. Many novelists and poets are national figures who speak out on social and political issues. Often, they also take an active part in government. The Nicaraguan poet Ernesto Cardenal served as a cabinet minister in the Sandinista government. Chilean poet Pablo Neruda and Peruvian novelist Mario Vargas Llosa each ran for office as president of his country. Vargas Llosa explains:

A View of Aztec Civilization This mural, painted by Diego Rivera in 1942, hangs in the Presidential Palace in Mexico City. In it, Rivera creates a picture of Aztec life. At left, the rulers are being dressed in elaborate costumes. The artisans at bottom use feathers and gold to create fine works. ***Technology*** What other activities are shown in this mural?

> "In Peru, in Bolivia, in Nicaragua, et cetera, to be a writer means . . . to assume a social responsibility; . . . There is no way to escape this obligation. If you tried to do so, if you were to isolate yourself and concentrate exclusively on your own work, you would be severely criticized . . . as an accomplice to all the evils—illiteracy, misery, exploitation, injustice, prejudice—of your country and against which you refused to fight."

Early writings. Scholars believe that the Mayas produced the first books in the Americas as early as A.D. 300. The Mayas had a well-established bookmaking tradition. Few Maya books survived, however. Spanish priests burned whatever books they found, calling them works of the devil.

The Spanish also destroyed Aztec books. An unknown Aztec poet recorded the sense of loss that resulted from the conquest:

> "Nothing but flowers and songs of sorrow
> are left in Mexico and Tlatelolco,
> where once we saw warriors and wise men."

The earliest writings in Spanish were the diaries and reports of the conquerors. Among the most notable was Bartolomé de Las Casas's *General History of the Indies.* It gives a vivid picture of the clash of Native American and Spanish cultures. An early mestizo writer was Garcilaso de la Vega, who wrote during the late 1500s. In *Royal Commentaries of the Inca,* he portrays the loneliness and pain of someone torn between the values of an Incan mother and a Spanish father.

The epic poem *La Araucana* continues the theme of the clash of cultures. In it, Alonso de Ercilla y Zúñiga describes the courage of the Araucanian Indians of Chile in resisting the Spanish invaders.

A distinct voice. Much colonial writing imitated European styles. By the late 1800s, however, bold young writers such as the Nicaraguan poet Rubén Darío were developing a distinct Latin American voice. In his early poems, Darío created an exotic fantasy world that celebrated art and beauty. Later, he became concerned with social issues. Darío's unusual style has influenced Latin American writers to the present.

Common themes. Modern Latin American writers have explored a number of themes, including small-town life and the clash of cultures. Miguel Angel Asturias, a Nobel Prize–winning poet and novelist from Guatemala, wrote about the experience of living under a dictatorship. In *Mr. President,* Asturias recreates a world in which a tyrant rules through fear, killing anyone who opposes him. The dictator-president becomes a larger-than-life figure with almost magical powers.

Another Nobel Prize-winning author, Gabriel García Márquez of Colombia, writes in a style called magical realism—a blend of fact, fantasy, and humor. One of his most popular novels, *One Hundred Years of Solitude,* recounts the history of an imaginary town called Macondo and its leading family. The novel is full of strange miracles, flying carpets, and odd dreams. Yet it captures basic human experiences. Latin American readers have told the author how closely his imaginary setting and characters resemble their towns and families. (See Connections With Literature, page 807, "A Very Old Man With Enormous Wings.")

Not all Latin American writers dealt with social themes. The blind poet and short story writer Jorge Luis Borges (BOR hays) of Argentina was part of a movement called *ultraismo.* He and his fellow writers believed that art should exist for its own sake, not for any social or political reasons. Borges is probably best known for his highly imaginative short stories, which range from fantasies to detective yarns.

Poetry. In Latin America, poetry is a part of daily life. Children recite poems in grade school. Teenagers take pride in writing poetry. A young man might send love poems to a local newspaper to tell a particular woman of his interest in her. In Cuba, workers in a cigar factory pooled their money to hire readers to entertain them with stories and poems.

Poets such as Pablo Neruda have achieved international reputations. The poem "History of a Canal," which appears at the beginning of this chapter, comes from his epic work, *General Song.* In it, Neruda gives his view of the people who shaped Latin America, including the Incas, conquistadors, and liberators.

Women's voices. The first woman writer of the Americas was Sor Juana Inés de la Cruz, whom you read about in Chapter 21. During

Memory of Cuernavaca A popular tourist town in Mexico is the subject of this painting by Mexican artist Juan O'Gorman. O'Gorman blends realistic elements, such as the houses, trees, and laundry, with fanciful images of a bird and a hot-air balloon. ***Fine Art*** Why do you think the artist has not included any human figures?

the late 1600s, she fiercely defended a woman's right to receive an education and to participate in a free expression of ideas.

In recent years, Latin American women writers have gained recognition. Like many male writers, women joined in movements for social change and had to flee when harsh dictators threatened their safety. Isabel Allende, for example, escaped from Chile after the military overthrew her uncle, Salvador Allende. Her best-selling novel, *The House of the Spirits,* portrayed the hardships she suffered while living in exile. (📖 See World Literature, page 542, "The House of the Spirits.")

Music and Dance

Latin America has produced a variety of popular music and dance styles. Often, a certain kind of music is linked to a particular dance step. In Argentina, for example, the tango is both a sad song and a complex dance. In Brazil, people both dance and sing the bossa nova, samba, and lambada.

The Caribbean islands have produced many music-and-dance forms, including the rumba from Cuba, calypso from Trinidad, merengue from the Dominican Republic, and salsa from Puerto Rico. Many of these styles have influenced jazz and rock musicians around the world.

Popular singers such as Rubén Blades of Panama blended traditional poetry with the fast-paced music of salsa and merengue. Folk singers such as Chile's Violeta Parra collected rural songs and dances and popularized them among urban audiences. Other musicians created new sounds by using Native American bamboo flutes, African percussion instruments, and European guitars.

Architecture and Painting

The ancient civilizations of the Americas excelled in architecture as well as in other arts, such as sculpture. The Spanish destroyed most Aztec and Inca temples and built churches on the ruins. The remains of Maya temples and statues, however, still dot the landscape in Mexico and Central America.

Modern buildings. Today, the cities of Latin America boast colonial-style churches alongside towering high-rise buildings. Brazil is especially proud of the modern buildings in its well-planned capital city, Brasília.

Mexican architects designed a new university in the 1950s. In form, some of the buildings resemble ancient Aztec structures. The outer walls are decorated with mosaics—designs made from colored stones—that recall Mexico's Native American past.

The muralists. The Mexican Revolution inspired an exciting new school of artists–the muralists. During the 1920s and 1930s, Diego Rivera, José Clemente Orozco (oh ROHS koh), and David Alfaro Siqueiros (see KEH rohs) created mural paintings that portrayed the struggles and achievements of the Mexican people. Their vivid, bold work influenced artists around the world.

Rivera had studied in Europe and had seen murals painted by the great Italian artists. He noted that they had used their work to communicate Christian themes to ordinary people. In the same way, Rivera decided to carry the message of the Mexican Revolution to Latin America's uneducated masses. In European museums, Rivera also saw Aztec paintings that had been brought back by the conquistadors. In his murals, he combined the techniques of the Italian painters with the bold figures and bright colors of Aztec artists to bring the revolution to life. (See page 516.)

Frida Kahlo: Reflection of Mexico

"It was a strange collision," Frida Kahlo recalled. "It was not violent, but rather silent [and] slow." Kahlo, 18 years old, was riding a bus in Mexico City in 1925 when a streetcar smashed into its side. "The crash bounced us forward and a handrail pierced me the way a sword pierces a bull," she said. The accident broke Kahlo's spine, leg, foot, and collarbone.

The bus crash changed Kahlo's life. She would never again be free of physical pain.

Yet the tragedy also opened a new door. Lying in a hospital bed, Kahlo became restless. "I was young. . . . I felt I had energies enough to do anything. . . . And without paying much attention, I began to paint."

As soon as she could walk, Kahlo took an armful of her paintings to Diego Rivera, Mexico's most famous artist. She found him high on a scaffold, painting a mural. Kahlo called to Rivera to climb down. When he did, she announced boldly:

> "Look, I have not come to flirt or anything. . . . I have come to show you my painting. If you are interested in it, tell me so; if not . . . I will go to work at something else to help my parents."

Rivera praised the young woman's work. Soon after, the two artists fell in love and married.

At first, Kahlo imitated Rivera's painting. In time, however, she found her own style. Kahlo was inspired by *retablos,* religious paintings offered as thanks for escape from misfortune. Kahlo used the vibrant colors and bold lines of retablos in her own work. Her images, too, were often fantastic. In one self-portrait, she is sleeping under a grinning skeleton. In another, her arms and legs are roots that disappear into the ground.

At a time when well-to-do Mexicans admired European traditions, Kahlo was a champion of Mexican culture. In public, she proudly wore the long, colorful dresses favored by Native Americans in Mexico. When she taught art, she led her students out of the studio and into the streets. There, they painted food peddlers, cactus flowers, and Aztec sculptures. One student remarked:

> "She made us feel and understand a certain kind of beauty in Mexico that we could not have realized by ourselves."

Although Kahlo loved Mexico, it took Mexico years to appreciate her talent. By the time she had an art show of her own in Mexico City in 1953, she was near death. On opening night, she arrived in an ambulance, with its siren screaming. Nurses carried Kahlo inside on a stretcher. "I am broken," she said. "But I am happy to be alive as long as I can paint."

Today, Kahlo's work is more widely admired than ever before. The rock star Madonna is one of the many people who collect

A Self-Portrait Frida Kahlo used her remarkable talent as an artist to inspire pride in Mexican culture. Although she lived in the shadow of her famous husband, Diego Rivera, Kahlo developed her own artistic style, as shown in this self-portrait. ***Choice*** How do you think Kahlo's accident may have affected her work as an artist?

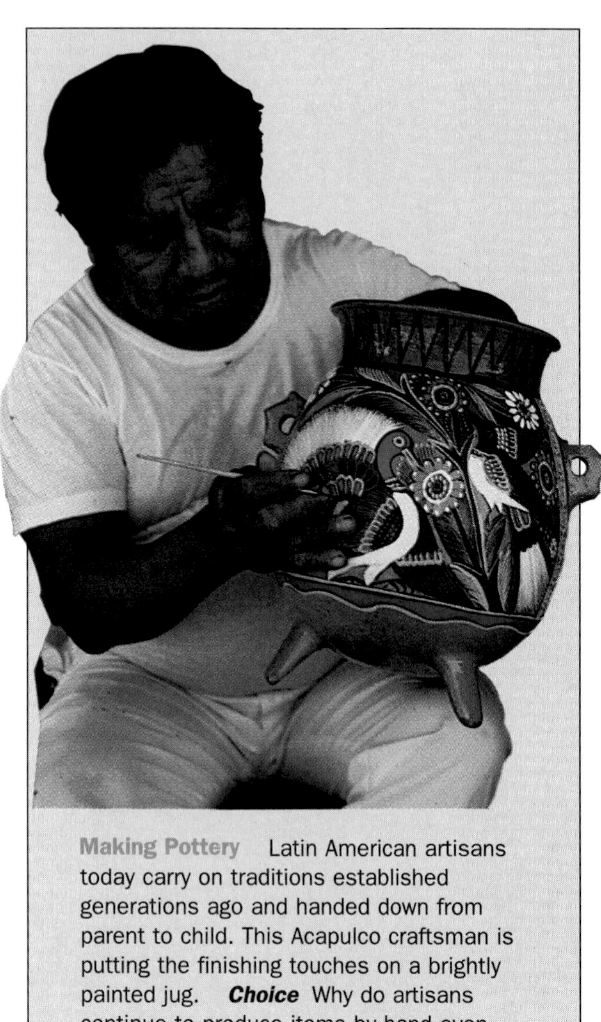

Making Pottery Latin American artisans today carry on traditions established generations ago and handed down from parent to child. This Acapulco craftsman is putting the finishing touches on a brightly painted jug. ***Choice*** Why do artisans continue to produce items by hand even when machines can make them?

Kahlo's paintings. Although highly personal, Kahlo's portrayal of the hardships of human life gives her work universal appeal. ■

Crafts

Throughout rural Latin America, artisans still practice traditional crafts. In the Caribbean, craftworkers produce fine wood carvings, ceramics, and textiles. In rural villages in Mexico, Guatemala, Bolivia, and Peru, Native American women weave and make pottery much as they have done for centuries.

In Guatemala, women weave cloth to make the huipil (wee PEEL), a simple tunic that they wear over a long wrapped skirt. The many patterns in their weaving date from before the Spanish conquest. Diamond-shaped patterns represent the universe and figures of ancestors emerging from the underworld. Similar figures appear in ancient Maya sculptures, painting, and pottery. Although all weavers use the same basic designs, each adds her own touches. During the six months it takes to weave a huipil, a woman produces not only a piece of cloth but also a fine work of art.

Until recently, the weavers spun their own cotton by hand and used natural dyes. Today, they use machine-made yarns and chemical dyes. Yet, peering out of the modern weavings are traditional figures such as Toad, who symbolizes femininity, and Earthlord, who lives in a cave and controls the growth of plants.

SECTION 3 REVIEW

1. **Identify:** (a) Pablo Neruda, (b) Mario Vargas Llosa, (c) Rubén Darío, (d) Gabriel García Márquez, (e) magical realism, (f) Isabel Allende, (g) David Alfaro Siqueiros, (h) Frida Kahlo.
2. (a) What three traditions have contributed to the cultural heritage of Latin America? (b) Give an example of the influence each has had.
3. How has Latin American music influenced musicians around the world?
4. What was the goal of Diego Rivera and other Mexican muralists?
5. How do woven fabrics in Central America combine traditional and modern elements?
6. **Analyzing Information** Why do you think Latin American artists and writers feel the obligation to work for social change through their art?
7. **Writing Across Cultures** Many Latin American music forms and dances are popular in the United States. Write a description of one dance or music form that you like. Illustrate your description with a drawing or a picture taken from a magazine.

Chapter 23 Review

Understanding Vocabulary

Match each term at left with the correct definition at right.

1. default	**a.** fail to repay a debt
2. magical realism	**b.** design made from colored stones
3. tango	**c.** writing style that blends fact, fantasy, and humor
4. mosaic	**d.** sad song and complex dance from Argentina
5. huipil	**e.** simple tunic worn in Guatemala

Reviewing the Main Ideas

1. What economic ties link Latin America and the United States?
2. Describe Puerto Rico's status as a commonwealth of the United States.
3. (a) What were the goals of regional groups such as the Andean Pact? (b) Why did these groups have only limited success?
4. (a) List two achievements of the OAS. (b) What issues caused disagreement among the members?
5. What role does the illegal drug trade play in the economies of Latin American nations?
6. (a) Describe the role of writers in modern Latin American society. (b) What themes do these writers explore?

Reviewing Chapter Themes

1. Many Latin Americans have mixed feelings about the United States. Discuss why the Latin American view of the United States changed from that of a defender of liberty to one of "Yankee imperialist." Give at least three examples to support your answer.
2. Today, the nations of the Western Hemisphere emphasize cooperation as the way to solve problems and build a better future. Select two of the following problems and describe regional or global efforts to resolve them: (a) economic development, (b) debt crisis, (c) illegal drug trade, (d) threats to the environment, (e) human rights abuses.
3. Latin America has a rich cultural heritage. Describe three traditions that have influenced the arts and literature of Latin America.

Thinking Critically

1. **Defending a Position** In Chile and Argentina, some people have demanded that former military leaders who are accused of human rights abuses be put on trial. Others oppose this as reopening old wounds. Should the new democratic governments of those nations hold such trials? Explain.
2. **Making Global Connections** How can the United States help Latin America to solve its economic and political problems?

Applying Your Skills

1. **Analyzing a Poem** Read the poem by Pablo Neruda on page 504. (a) What is the subject of the poem? (b) According to Neruda, what unique geographic feature did Panama have? (c) What happened to this feature? (d) Based on the excerpt, what is Neruda's opinion of the building of the Panama Canal? (e) Do you think the poem is a reliable source of information about Latin American attitudes toward the United States? Explain. (See Skill Lesson, page 541.)
2. **Ranking** List the problems that Latin Americans face today. Then rank the problems in order of their importance. Give reasons for your ranking.

Chapter 24

CANADA

Shooting the Rapids The birchbark canoe in this painting carries people from three groups who shaped Canada's culture. Native American and French fur traders paddle the canoe through river rapids. The English artist, Frances Ann Hopkins, also included herself in the painting, in the straw hat. ***Fine Art*** How does the painting suggest that the life of fur traders was dangerous?

CHAPTER OUTLINE

Day after day, the ice held the French ships in its grip. On board, Jacques Cartier and his crew struggled to stay warm. Daylight was short, and each night's darkness brought still more bitter cold. Some of the sailors went onshore to hunt game. Many, however, were too ill to move.

Cartier was icebound on the St. Lawrence River in eastern Canada. During the winter of 1535–1536, members of his crew suffered from a mysterious disease. At first, their legs became swollen. Then the disease afflicted the rest of their bodies. Finally, the victims' teeth fell out. At least 25 crewmen died.

Cartier did not know that this disease, called scurvy, was caused by a lack of vitamin C. For months, the sailors had not eaten fresh fruits or vegetables. The Indians of what is now Nova Scotia, however, were familiar with the disease. They taught Cartier how to treat his men:

> "They told us how to strip off the bark and leaves from

a certain tree, boil them in water, and drink the liquid . . . while placing the boiled bark and leaves on swollen and afflicted legs. ”

The men who drank the brew recovered their health.

CHAPTER PERSPECTIVE

During the 1500s, French and English explorers began to tap the rich resources of Canada. From the Indians whose land they claimed, they learned how to survive in the cold. Later, French and English settlers helped to shape Canada's unique character. Today, immigrants continue to add to the cultural diversity of Canada.

As you read, look for these chapter themes:

- Although geography has posed severe challenges to Canadians, it also provides rich resources.
- The diverse population of Canada includes Indians, Inuits, and immigrants from around the world.
- French and English colonists settled eastern Canada and expanded westward, contributing two separate cultural traditions to Canadian life.
- Canada is an urban, industrial nation with a democratic political system and a distinct identity.

Literature Connections

In this chapter, you will encounter a passage from the following work.

"The Cremation of Sam McGee,"
Robert Service

For other suggestions, see Connections With Literature, pages 804–808.

1 GEOGRAPHIC SETTING

FIND OUT

What are the main physical and climate regions of Canada?

What natural resources have enriched the Canadian economy?

Why is the Canadian population so diverse?

Vocabulary multiculturalism

In 1896, the discovery of gold in the Yukon Territory sent a flood of miners into northwestern Canada. The Gold Rush inspired the poet Robert Service, a British immigrant, to write "The Cremation of Sam McGee." It tells a humorous "tall tale" of two miners in the icy Yukon. Sam McGee, an immigrant from Tennessee, dies of the bitter cold. His friend cremates him in a furnace. After a while, the friend looks inside the furnace:

> “ And there sat Sam, looking cool and calm, in the heart of the furnace roar;
> And he wore a smile you could see a mile, and he said: 'Please close that door.
> It's fine in here, but I greatly fear you'll let in the cold and storm—
> Since I left Plumtree, down in Tennessee, it's the first time I've been warm.' ”

Since the 1500s, settlers have flocked to Canada to profit from resources such as fish, fur, gold, and land. Often, settlers had to adapt to severe geographic conditions. Vast distances and rugged terrain also posed a challenge to Canada's development. Natural barriers divide the country into regions, each

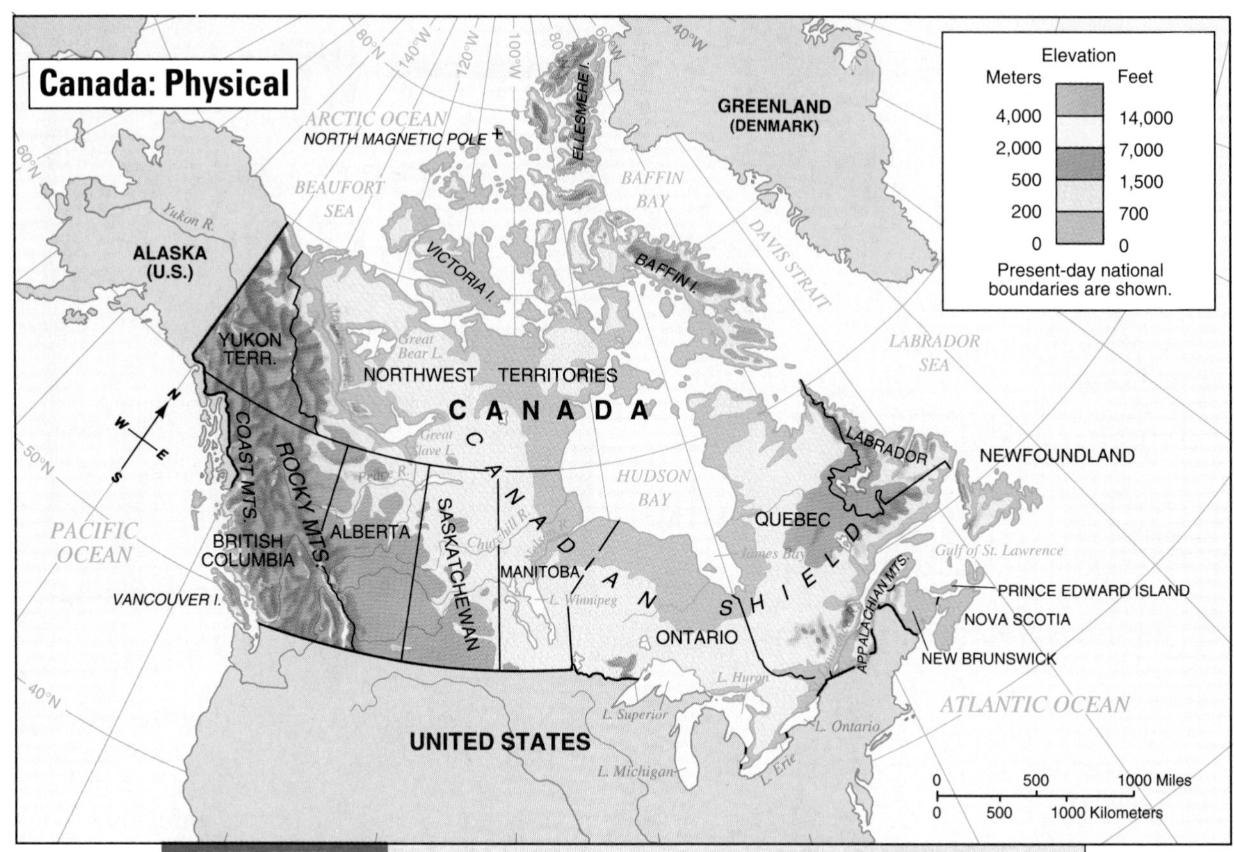

MAP STUDY

Canada is the second largest country in the world. Its huge landmass includes five major geographic regions.

1. **Location** (a) What is Canada's largest province? (b) Describe the relative location of this province.
2. **Movement** What waterway provides a major route for trade by connecting the interior of Canada with the Atlantic Ocean?
3. **Drawing Conclusions** Why do you think Canada's geography has limited the size of its population and determined where most people live?

with its own interests. At times, these regional interests clash with national goals, threatening Canada's fragile unity.

The Shape of the Land

Canada sprawls across the northern half of North America, from the Atlantic Ocean in the east to the Pacific in the west. Its border to the north is the frozen Arctic Ocean. To the south, Canada borders the United States. This boundary line, which is 3,000 miles (4,828 km) long, is the longest undefended border in the world. Covering an area of 3.8 million square miles (9.8 million sq km), Canada is one of the world's largest countries.

Canada has clearly defined political and physical regions. It is divided into ten provinces and two territories.* Excluding the Arctic Islands, Canada's many landforms shape five distinct geographic regions.

Appalachian region. The most eastern region of Canada lies between the Atlantic

* In 1991, the Canadian government reached an agreement with the native arctic people, or Inuits, granting them control of a political subdivision to be carved out of the Northwest Territories.

Ocean and the heavily forested Appalachian Mountains. This region of low hills, plains, islands, and peninsulas includes the Atlantic Provinces of Newfoundland, Nova Scotia, Prince Edward Island, and New Brunswick.

The sea has long shaped the life of the Appalachian region. Early Europeans built small fishing settlements along the rocky coast. From there, they fished in the Gulf of St. Lawrence and on the Grand Banks off Newfoundland, one of the world's richest fishing areas. Since the 1960s, however, fishing has become less profitable because the region has been overfished. Discoveries of offshore oil and natural gas promise to revive the region's economy.

Great Lakes–St. Lawrence lowlands. To the north and west of the Atlantic Provinces is a region of fertile lowlands that stretches along the St. Lawrence River and the Great Lakes. The St. Lawrence Seaway, a system of locks and canals, links the river to the lakes. Together, they form a 2,000-mile (3,219-km) water highway that connects the Canadian interior to the Atlantic Ocean.

Good transportation, fertile soil, and a mild climate have helped to make this region the agricultural and industrial center of Canada. Six out of ten Canadian people live there in its two provinces, Quebec and Ontario.

Canadian Shield. Covering almost half of Canada, the Canadian Shield stretches west and north from the Atlantic Ocean to the Arctic Ocean. It consists of low hills, swamps, lakes, and streams. Because the soil is poor and the climate is cold, few people live in this region.

To Canadians, the Shield is both a curse and a blessing. It cuts the country in half and contributes to divisions between easterners and westerners. At the same time, the Shield is rich in mineral resources. Its forests once supported huge numbers of fur-bearing animals. Hardy trappers and traders once paddled up its rivers and streams to trap animals or trade skins.

Great Plains. Farther west lie the Great Plains, part of the vast interior plains that stretch from the Gulf of Mexico to the Arctic Ocean. Because of its rich soil, this region is known as Canada's breadbasket. In the moist eastern plains, Canadian farmers grow grains. The drier western area supports cattle ranching.

Western Mountain region. The fifth region is a mountainous strip of land about 500 miles (805 km) wide. It stretches from the towering Rocky Mountains to the Coastal Ranges along the Pacific. Between the mountains lie rugged plateaus.

The Western Mountains form an imposing barrier. Until the late 1800s, the province of British Columbia was isolated from the rest of Canada. Even today, people in the far west have an intense regional pride and sense of independence. Distance also affects trade patterns. Vancouver, British Columbia, is closer to Tokyo, Japan, than to Halifax, Nova Scotia. As a result, British Columbia has developed trade ties with the countries of the Pacific Rim.

Climates and Vegetation

Climates vary greatly across Canada. This affects both the vegetation and the wildlife. In the far north, the climate is dry and icy. During the brief arctic summer, the top layer of ground thaws, creating vast marshes. Mosses, flowers, and berries flourish then, attracting large flocks of migrating birds and huge herds of caribous. In the past, the Inuit* (IH noo wiht) people hunted caribous for food and clothing.

A vast subarctic climate zone stretches across most of northern Canada. Winters are severe and summers are short, but there is enough moisture to support vast forests.

Most Canadians live in the humid-continental climate zone that extends from Newfoundland on the Atlantic coast to Alberta on the Great Plains. This climate is similar to that of the northeastern United States, with long, snowy winters and short, warm summers.

Part of the Great Plains has a semiarid climate. There, huge herds of buffaloes once

* Inuit, meaning "the people," is the name these arctic people called themselves. The Indians called them Eskimos, meaning "eaters of raw meat."

A Snowy Harbor in Newfoundland Most of Canada has snowy winters. In the Rocky Mountains, snowfall may total 240 inches (600 cm). Areas near the Atlantic and Pacific coasts have less severe weather. ***Geography*** Why do coastal regions have milder winters than interior areas?

fed on prairie grasses. Few trees grow there because of the lack of water. Winters are long and bitterly cold. Summers are hot. On the plains, warm air currents from the Gulf of Mexico clash with cold air from the north, creating sudden changes in the weather.

Canada's west coast has a mild marine climate. Pacific winds dump huge amounts of rain on the western slopes of the Coastal Ranges. Vast forests of fir, cedar, and spruce grow in the warm, wet region. The Indians of the Northwest Coast used those resources to build their homes and their canoes for fishing. Today, the forests support a thriving lumber industry.

Natural Resources

Despite the harsh climates and poor soil in many regions, Canada has rich agricultural resources. The fertile soil of the Great Plains supports large commercial wheat farms. Using irrigation and hardy seeds, farmers have overcome some disadvantages of the climate. Other fertile regions include the "fruit belt" of southern Ontario and Quebec. In valleys of the Atlantic Provinces and British Columbia, farmers grow potatoes and tend orchards.

Mineral resources. Canada has a variety of mineral resources. During the 1800s, the search for copper, gold, and silver brought settlers to western and northern Canada. Today, Canada is the world's leading exporter of minerals, such as the nickel, cobalt, tungsten, and silver that are found in the Canadian Shield. In eastern Canada, deposits of iron ore and coal have promoted the growth of industry.

Energy resources. Besides coal, Canada has other energy resources. The discovery of huge oil and natural-gas fields under the Great Plains has brought refining and chemical in-

Wheat Fields Saskatchewan produces twice as much wheat as all other Canadian provinces combined, even though only the southern half of the province is farmed. The growing season is short, but long summer days provide lots of sunshine for crops. ***Geography*** Why do you think farming is concentrated in southern Saskatchewan?

Bilingual Traffic Sign Below the English word "stop" is its equivalent in Inuktitut, the language of the Inuit. The Inuit, who number about 27,000 people, live in Canada's far north. Inuits are served by special government radio and television broadcasts in their own language. ***Culture*** In what way is broadcasting in Inuktitut an example of multiculturalism?

dustries to Alberta. Uranium from Saskatchewan supplies fuel for nuclear power plants.

Today, people are more aware of the environmental limitations of relying on oil and coal. As a result of this growing awareness, Canadians are taking steps to exploit a renewable energy resource—water. Canada has one third of the world's fresh water. Canada has built several hydroelectric plants, which supply nearly 75 percent of the nation's electrical needs. Canada also exports water to dry regions of the United States.

People

Despite its vast size, Canada has a population of only 26 million people. Due to difficult climates and terrains, much of Canada is sparsely populated. Most Canadians live in urban areas within 100 miles (161 km) of the United States border.

Canadians include people from many ethnic and cultural groups. The first people to reach Canada crossed the land bridge from Siberia more than 15,000 years ago. Today, Canada's Indians make up about 1.4 percent of the total population, and these Native American groups take great pride in their ancient cultures.

Two European nations, France and Britain, provided large numbers of settlers for Canada. More than 40 percent of Canadians are of British origin. About 24 percent are descended from French colonists who arrived during the 1600s and 1700s. Other immigrants came from Germany, Italy, Ukraine, and the United States. More recently, Canada has accepted many immigrants from Asia, Africa, and Latin America.

The Canadian government follows a policy of multiculturalism. It encourages people to preserve and maintain their distinct cultural traditions. This policy grew out of Canada's past, in which both French and English settlers played significant roles.

SECTION 1 REVIEW

1. **Locate:** (a) Arctic Ocean, (b) Appalachian Mountains, (c) St. Lawrence River, (d) Great Lakes, (e) Canadian Shield, (f) Great Plains, (g) Rocky Mountains.
2. **Define:** multiculturalism.
3. (a) Describe the five main physical regions of Canada. (b) How has the Canadian Shield affected Canada's development?
4. How has Canada benefited from its natural resources?
5. (a) What ethnic groups live in Canada? (b) Why does the Canadian government encourage cultural diversity?
6. **Synthesizing Information** Review the information in this section and study the maps on pages 524, 778, and 782. How have landforms and climates affected population patterns in Canada?
7. **Writing Across Cultures** Make a list of the geographic features of your region, including landforms, climate, vegetation, and resources. Then write a sentence explaining which region of Canada seems most similar to where you live.

2

DYNAMICS OF CHANGE

FIND OUT

What distinct societies did Indians develop in Canada?

Why did Europeans go to Canada?

How did Canada become a united, self-governing nation?

How did Canada expand during the late 1800s?

> "Go return peacefully to your farms. Stay in the arms of your wives. Give this example to your children. But watch us act. We are going ahead to work and obtain the guarantee of our rights and yours."

Louis Riel spoke these words to his followers, the Métis. The Métis were descended from French fur traders and Indian women. They were Catholic and spoke French. For generations, they had hunted buffaloes on the Great Plains. By the 1860s, however, large numbers of English-speaking Protestant settlers had begun to head west, threatening the Métis way of life. Led by Riel, the Métis fought to protect their language, religion, and land.

The Métis uprising reflected several themes in Canada's history. One is the division between French-speaking Catholics and English-speaking Protestants. Another is the role French fur traders played in opening Canada to European settlement. A third is the westward movement of European settlers during the 1800s.

The First Canadians

The first Canadians were the Inuits and the Indians whose ancestors had migrated to North America from Asia. Most of them lived along the Pacific coast and in the Great Lakes–St. Lawrence lowlands. These first Canadians developed stable societies and adapted to a variety of environments.

Distinct societies. An abundance of resources allowed the Northwest Coast Indians to live in settled villages. They used wood from the forests to build their homes and canoes. The Northwest Coast people fished in bays and rivers. Their chiefs led whale hunts in the nearby ocean.

Many Native American groups were nomadic hunters and food gatherers. In the harsh, arctic climate, the Inuits hunted seals, walruses, and sea otters. In the subarctic climate of the Canadian Shield, small bands of Indians hunted caribous and moose. On the Great Plains, Indians such as the Blackfeet, Crees, and Assiniboines followed the great buffalo herds. A European fur trader noted the importance the buffalo had for the Assiniboines:

> "The buffalo alone supplies them with everything which they are accustomed to want. The hide of this animal, when dressed, furnishes soft clothing for the women; and, dressed with the hair on, it clothes the men. The flesh feeds them; the sinews afford them bow-strings; and even the paunch . . . provides them with that important utensil, the kettle."

The Great Lakes–St. Lawrence lowlands region was home to the Eastern Woodlands Indians. They hunted in the vast forests of the region. Some groups, such as the Hurons and the Iroquois (IHR uh kwoi), cleared trees and farmed the land. They lived in settled villages, often in wooden buildings called long houses.

Interaction with Europeans. When Europeans arrived in Canada, they adopted many skills and technologies from the Indians. They used Native American toboggans to transport heavy loads over long distances in the snow. Europeans learned to make snowshoes and valued the Indians' lightweight

Huron Encampment Native Americans of the Eastern Woodlands, such as the Huron in this painting by Paul Kane, were among the first people Europeans encountered. The English language has adopted many Native American words for things distinctly American (raccoon, chipmunk) and things distinctly Native American (moccasin, tomahawk). ***Fine Art*** What evidence does this painting provide about Eastern Woodland culture?

birchbark canoe, which could carry two adults and 300 pounds (136 kg) of furs. Europeans, in turn, brought the Indians new tools, weapons, and religious beliefs.

As elsewhere in the Americas, the arrival of Europeans brought disaster to the Indians. Huge numbers died of diseases brought by the Europeans. The way of life of those who survived was changed forever.

Europeans Reach North America

The first Europeans to reach Canada were the Vikings from Scandinavia. In about 1000, they built settlements on the coast of Newfoundland, but the people living there soon drove them away.

No other Europeans arrived for almost 500 years. Then, they crossed the Atlantic in their search for a northwest passage to the Indies.

Cabot. In 1497, John Cabot, an Italian sailing for England, explored the coasts of Nova Scotia and Newfoundland. Like Columbus, he was seeking a sea route west to Asia. On his return to England, Cabot told of the rich fishing waters off the Grand Banks of Newfoundland. Soon, fishing fleets from France, Portugal, and England began to sail to the Grand Banks each year to catch cod and herring and to hunt whales.

Cartier. In 1534, the king of France sent Jacques Cartier (kahr tee YAY) across the Atlantic to look for a northwest passage. The king also ordered Cartier to search for gold, just as the Spanish were doing so successfully in Mexico and Peru.

Cartier explored the St. Lawrence River, but he found no water route to the Pacific and no gold. He did, however, claim the lands he explored for France. He adopted the Iroquois word *kanata,* meaning "settlement," for the vast region.

A rival claim. In 1610, England sent Henry Hudson to find a northwest passage. He explored the huge northern inland bay that bears his name, but found no outlet to the Pacific. Still, Hudson's voyage led England to claim the vast territory surrounding Hudson Bay—an area that is half the size of Europe.

By the 1600s, both France and England wanted to profit from the furs that Indian trappers were willing to trade. As the two nations pushed to expand this valuable trade, they met on a collision course.

Building New France

To defend their interests in Canada, the French sent Samuel de Champlain (sham PLAYN) to build the colony of New France. In 1608, Champlain founded Quebec on a cliff above the St. Lawrence River.

Champlain made friends with the Algonquins and Hurons, who supplied furs to the French. He also helped them to fight their long-time rivals, the Iroquois. As a result, the Iroquois became lasting enemies of France. Wars with the Iroquois threatened the early French settlements.

Because of the harsh climate and poor soil, few French families wanted to move to New France. French missionaries, however, arrived to convert the Indians to Christianity.

Exploring the continent. French fur traders ranged deep into the interior of North America. These hardy adventurers were called *voyageurs* (vwah yah ZHERS), from a French word meaning "traveler." They learned Indian languages and adopted Indian customs. Many married Indian women. Montreal, founded in 1642, became the center to which they brought furs from the interior.

Led by Indian guides, voyageurs explored as far west as the Rocky Mountains and south to the Gulf of Mexico. Accompanying them were "black robes," as French priests were called. In 1673, Louis Joliet, a fur trader, and Jacques Marquette, a priest, paddled from Lake Michigan to the Mississippi River. Nine years later, Robert de la Salle followed the Mississippi to the Gulf of Mexico. He claimed the surrounding lands for France, naming the vast region Louisiana after King Louis XIV.

French settlements. New France grew slowly. By 1680, only about 10,000 colonists lived in scattered settlements along the St. Lawrence. *Habitants*, as French farmers were called, made a meager living from the land. The fur trade, however, brought prosperity to some. French priests and nuns set up schools, hospitals, and churches and helped to plant French culture firmly on Canadian soil.

By the 1700s, France had built a string of forts along the Ohio and Mississippi rivers. These outposts, defended by the voyageurs and their Indian allies, would soon become the center of a major conflict.

MAP STUDY

French explorers, missionaries, and fur traders helped France claim a large empire in North America by the 1700s.

1. **Region** What nations claimed territories bordering New France?
2. **Location** Where did the French build forts to protect their colony?
3. **Applying Information** Why do you think the Mississippi River was important to French colonists?

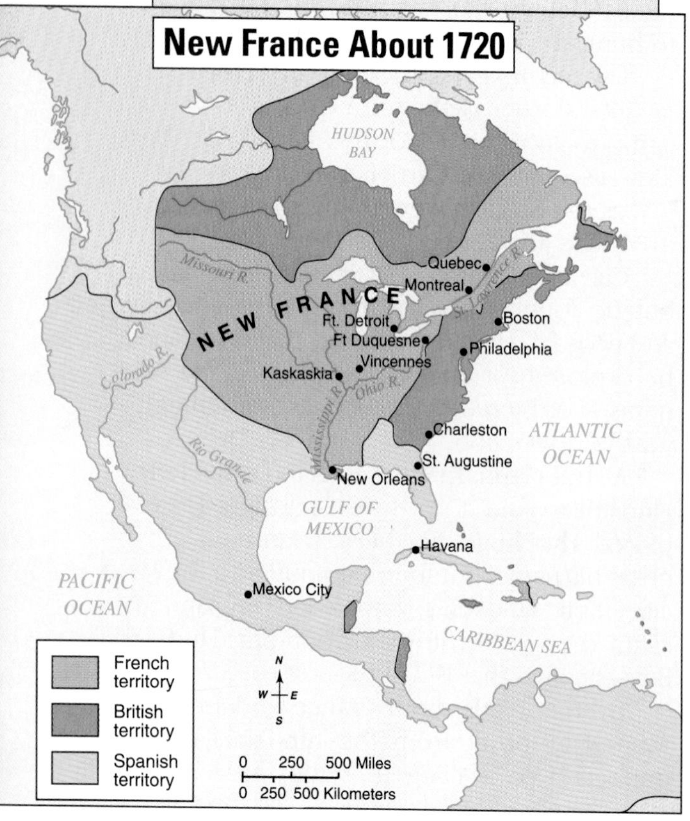

New France About 1720

Struggle for North America

During the 1700s, rivalry between France and Britain grew. The British forced the French to give up their claims to the rich fur-trading region around Hudson Bay. They also gained Newfoundland and Acadia, a French settlement in what is today Nova Scotia and

Settlement on the Plains Fort Garry (present-day Winnipeg) was a major trading post on the Red River in western Canada. This painting shows Fort Garry and its people in the 1800s. ***Fine Art*** What does this scene reveal about who visited the fort and what activities went on there?

New Brunswick. The westward expansion of the 13 English colonies along the Atlantic coast posed a threat to New France as well.

French and Indian War. By the mid-1700s, the British were seeking to control the fur trade in the Ohio River valley. With the aid of the Iroquois, they attacked French trading posts. In 1754, the conflict flared into the French and Indian War. The war was part of a worldwide struggle between Britain and France for trade and empire. The two nations were fighting for power in India and Europe. In North America, the French and their Huron allies battled the British and their Iroquois allies. In 1759, the British captured Quebec. Although fighting continued, the loss of Quebec destroyed France's power in Canada.

By the terms of the Treaty of Paris, which finally ended the war in 1763, New France became a British colony. The British victory turned out to be costly, however. When Britain raised taxes in its 13 colonies to pay for the war, the colonists rebelled. The American Revolution greatly affected Canada.

British rule. After the French defeat, many wealthy settlers left Quebec for France. Farmers, artisans, trappers, priests, and nuns remained. In 1774, Britain passed the Quebec Act. It granted the French in Quebec the right to keep their language and religion. The act also recognized French civil law in the colony.

In the late 1700s, the English-speaking population of Canada grew. During the American Revolution, thousands of colonists who remained loyal to England fled to Nova Scotia and Ontario. After the revolution, many more settlers moved north from the United States. During the mid-1800s, escaped slaves from the southern United States and free African Americans fleeing racial violence in Ohio found safety in Canada.

Faced with a growing number of English-speaking colonists, Britain divided Canada into two provinces. Lower Canada (now Quebec) kept its French language and culture as well as its Catholic religion. Upper Canada (now Ontario) followed British law and traditions and the Protestant religion. The cultural and political differences between the two provinces fueled tensions.

The Making of a Nation

By 1800, Britain had six colonies in Canada—Lower Canada, Upper Canada, and the Atlantic Provinces of Nova Scotia, Prince Edward Island, New Brunswick, and Newfoundland. Each colony had an elected assembly, but officials appointed by Britain had final authority. During the 1800s, Canada slowly moved toward greater self-rule.

Two rebellions. Discontent with British rule sparked two rebellions in 1837. In Lower Canada, French-speaking Canadians were angry because most of the appointed officials were British and the British dominated their economy. "The descendants of the French have no equal rights with their masters of British origin," complained their leader, Louis Joseph Papineau.

In the same year, William Lyon Mackenzie, a political activist, urged rebellion in Upper Canada. He and his supporters resented the power that a small British elite held over Upper Canada's government and economy. "Put down the villains who oppress and enslave our country," he cried.

Lower and Upper Canada united. The uprisings convinced the British Parliament to make changes. It sent Lord Durham to study Canadian grievances. He urged Parliament to unite Lower and Upper Canada into a single province and to give its elected assembly greater power. In 1840, Britain passed the Act of Union, creating the United Province of Canada. However, it did not follow Durham's recommendation to include the Atlantic Provinces in the union. In 1849, Britain granted Canada the right to some self-government in internal affairs. External issues such as trade would be handled by Britain.

Dominion of Canada. As Canada expanded westward, the need for a strong central government grew. Two Canadians, John Macdonald and George-Etienne Cartier, convinced the provinces to accept confederation, or unification of all Canada's provinces. Largely as a result of their efforts, Britain passed the British North America Act in 1867. It united Ontario, Quebec, Nova Scotia, and New Brunswick to create a self-governing nation—the Dominion of Canada. Later, Prince Edward Island, Manitoba, Alberta, Saskatchewan, British Columbia, and Newfoundland joined the new nation. The British officially recognized Canada's control over its foreign affairs in 1931.

Building a Rail Line These workers on the White Pass and Yukon Railway pause for lunch. The railroad, Canada's most northern, was built in the 1890s to connect Whitehorse in the Yukon Territory with Skagway, Alaska. The many bridges and the tunnels that had to be blasted through mountains of solid rock made the work very dangerous. ***Change*** How did railroads change Canada's population patterns?

Expansion and Immigration

John Macdonald became Canada's first prime minister. As part of his plan to strengthen the new nation, he set three main goals. First, he called for the building of a transcontinental railroad that would unite the East and the West. Second, he wanted to place a high tariff on foreign-made goods to protect Canada's own industries. Finally, he promoted western settlement. He believed that settlers would then produce products for export and create a strong demand for Canadian goods.

Macdonald's expansionist policy threatened the way of life of the Indians and the Métis on the Great Plains, however. During the 1870s, most Indian nations were forced to sign treaties surrendering their lands to the government. The government crushed the Métis uprising and executed its leader, Louis Riel. French-speaking Canadians in the East felt that Riel was killed because he was a Frenchman and a Catholic.

By 1885, the Canadian Pacific Railway was completed, linking the nation from the Atlantic to the Pacific. The transcontinental railroad carried timber and other raw materials to markets in the East and West. It also brought immigrants to the plains and supplied them with manufactured goods.

Before confederation, most Canadians were of either French or British descent. Between 1885 and 1914, however, millions of Germans, Poles, Scandinavians, Ukrainians, Italians, and Russians arrived in Canada. Many Chinese workers went to Canada to build the transcontinental railroad and stayed on to work in the mines. Japanese immigrants settled on the west coast to fish and farm. All these newcomers made Canada a country of many ethnic groups.

SECTION 2 REVIEW

1. **Locate:** New France.
2. **Identify:** (a) Jacques Cartier, (b) Samuel de Champlain, (c) voyageurs, (d) Quebec Act, (e) Act of Union, (f) John Macdonald, (g) British North America Act.
3. (a) Describe how the lives of Indian groups differed in various regions of Canada. (b) How did the Indians' knowledge help the first Europeans in Canada?
4. What caused tensions between France and Britain in North America?
5. What steps led to greater self-rule in Canada?
6. **Understanding Causes and Effects** (a) List John Macdonald's three goals for Canada. (b) Explain how each goal helped Canada to grow and develop during the late 1800s.
7. **Writing Across Cultures** Write a paragraph explaining why French Canadians may have not wanted to join the Americans in their revolution against British rule.

3 CANADA TODAY

FIND OUT

What type of government does Canada have?

What economic progress has Canada made since 1900?

What interests affect Canadian foreign policy?

Vocabulary bilingual, service economy

"This is not the last stand," declared Georges Erasmus, an Indian leader, in the summer of 1990. "This could be the first stand."

For seven weeks, Mohawk Indians confronted Canadian government troops near Oka, Quebec. The immediate issue was Oka's plan to build a golf course on land that the Mohawks claimed was theirs. The underlying issue was the Indians' demand for recognition of their own laws, customs, and traditions. The standoff at Oka is one of many crises that Canada has faced in its efforts to balance the demands of the country's diverse population.

A Parliamentary Democracy

Canadians borrowed ideas about government from Britain and the United States, but shaped them to fit their own needs. Today, Canada has a parliamentary system of government similar to that of Britain. It is made up of three branches—executive, legislative, and judicial.

The executive branch includes the prime minister and the cabinet. The prime minister is the leader of the majority party in Parliament. Queen Elizabeth II of Britain is also Queen of Canada, but she is a symbolic figure and has no ruling power.

The legislative branch consists of a two-house parliament, the House of Commons and the Senate. Members of the House of Commons are directly elected by voters.

BUILDERS AND SHAPERS

Emily Murphy, Crusader for Women's Rights

"I'm sorry, you must leave the court." The evidence is "not fit for mixed company." With these words, the members of the Edmonton Council of Women were sent from the room. Concerned about the harsh treatment poor women received in the courts, they had tried to attend a police hearing. In 1916, however, "ladies" were not supposed to be interested in crime.

The council turned to Emily Murphy, a popular journalist and a champion of women's rights. According to Murphy, "She who would put on gloves must learn how to fight." She lobbied for a special women's court, presided over by a woman. When the government agreed, it appointed Murphy herself to the post. She became the first woman police magistrate, or judge, in the British Empire.

Murphy's battle wasn't over, however. On her first day as a judge, a lawyer objected that women could not serve as magistrates. According to the language of Canada's constitution, he said, women were not legally "persons." Murphy kept her post but realized that she would have to continue to fight for equality.

One of Murphy's tactics was to join with several other women and submit their names as Senate candidates. When they were rejected on the legal grounds that they were not persons, they then petitioned Parliament for a ruling. To their shock, the Canadian Supreme Court ruled against them.

Still, the "Alberta Five," as Murphy and the other women came to be called, would not give up. "I know of no way of driving a nail other than by hammering it," Murphy declared. In July 1929, the women carried their case all the way to London, where cases of this nature were decided at the time.

After a three-month hearing, the verdict finally came. Women, said the British court, were indeed persons under the law. Thanks to Emily Murphy and the "Alberta Five," Canadian women won recognition as full citizens.

1. How did Emily Murphy become a police magistrate?
2. **Analyzing Ideas** Why do you think Murphy and her colleagues worked so hard to get a ruling on the wording of the constitution?

Elections must take place at least once every five years. The House of Commons has far more power than the Senate, whose members are appointed by the prime minister. The members of the Senate are usually respected business leaders, lawyers, and people who have experience in government.

Like the United States, Canada has a federal system. Authority is divided between the central federal government in Ottawa and the governments of the 10 provinces. The territories have a separate and much less powerful government. The national government oversees matters that affect the entire nation, such as defense, foreign affairs, and finances. The provincial governments control such matters as education, housing, highways, and social welfare. Originally, the federal government was stronger than the provinces. Today, however, provincial governments have gained greater control over their affairs.

Unity and Diversity

Within Canada, regional feelings remain strong. Because Ontario and Quebec have large populations, they have many representatives in the House of Commons. People in other provinces and the territories complain that they have too little say in the government. Also, farmers and oil producers in western Canada resent the power that financial leaders in eastern Canada have over prices and taxes. Still, Canadians have tried to protect diverse interests within their federal framework.

Quebec nationalism. A major challenge to unity has come from French-speaking Canadians, most of whom live in Quebec. They have struggled to keep their culture from being swallowed up by English-speaking Canada. Today, Quebec license plates carry the motto "*Je me souviens*" ("I remember"). It reflects the desire of French-speaking Canadians to preserve their distinct culture.

Quebec nationalism has also focused on economic issues. Until the 1950s, English-speaking businesses dominated the economy. French-speaking Canadians were thus excluded from many jobs. The French-speaking majority moved to improve education and take a larger role in Quebec's economy. In 1977, the provincial government made French the official language of Quebec. By requiring all government offices and businesses to use French, the government opened new opportunities to French-speaking people.

The separatist debate. Despite these changes, some French-speaking Canadians support separatism. They want Quebec to separate from Canada and to become an independent nation. One separatist recently noted, "Many have long thought that our culture would be better served by our own independent political institutions. The difference [today] is that more and more people believe that Quebec—economically—is a feasible country."

The federal government has worked hard to keep Quebec in Canada. It has recognized Quebec as a distinct society. It has also met demands to make Canada bilingual, that is, having two official languages—French and English. Other provinces, however, have objected to Quebec's special status, so tensions remain.

Up Close: Canada's Cultural Mosaic

Vancouver, British Columbia, has one of the two largest Chinese communities in North America. The bulblike spire of a Russian Orthodox church rises above wheat fields in Saskatchewan. An "oompah" band plays German songs at an Oktoberfest celebration in Kitchener, Ontario. The spicy aromas of Indian food waft from a restaurant in Montreal. Sights, sounds, and smells like these give a hint of Canada's cultural diversity.

In Quebec City, Marco Nolasco belts out songs with the Son del Pacifico Latin band. Nolasco fled El Salvador after his uncle was killed by death squads. "We went to Mexico. We thought it would last only a few months," he explained. When the violence in his

A Mix of People This street scene reflects Canada's ethnic diversity. Note that the signs in the store window include both French and English words. About 20 percent of Canada's population today was born abroad. ***Diversity*** What do you think is meant by the term "cultural mosaic"?

homeland continued, Nolasco looked for another place to call home. "United Nations officials told us that Canada had programs to help immigrants."

Like immigrants everywhere, Nolasco had to make many adjustments. After the tropical climate of El Salvador, the Quebec winter was a shock:

> " We are not accustomed to such bad temperatures and having to wear so many clothes. But Quebecers are a nice people, with a culture and a language that Spanish speakers can identify with. "

Montreal The second-largest French-speaking city in the world, Montreal is a modern industrial center. It specializes in oil refining and the manufacturing of clothing. Montreal is also a railroad and highway hub, and its busy harbor handles one fourth of all the nation's waterborne goods. ***Change*** How has the growth of Montreal reflected Canada's economic development?

Finding a job was another challenge. Nolasco's law degree from El Salvador was useless. He could only find work washing windows or shoveling snow. Then he formed a band with three other Salvadorans, a Quebecer, and a Swiss immigrant. Music was part of his culture and offered "a way of working and of sharing my emotions with Quebec."

After six years in Canada, Nolasco felt that he still belonged to two worlds. "Every immigrant thinks that his native country is the best in the world," he noted. Yet the longer he lives in Canada, the more Nolasco becomes a part of its life. ■

A Growing Economy

Immigrants have contributed to Canada's economic development. Today, Canadians enjoy a high standard of living, thanks largely to the country's abundant natural resources and the industries it has developed to exploit them.

Like the United States, Canada has a free-market economy. Its government, however, plays a more active role in the economy than does that of the United States. Canada has a system of national health insurance that pays all of its citizens' medical costs. The national and provincial governments own broadcasting companies and public utilities, such as gas and electric companies. They also play a large role in deciding how natural resources such as oil and gas will be developed.

Economic growth. Before 1900, the work most Canadians did was connected to farming, mining, fishing, or lumbering. Canada exported farm products and raw materials, and imported manufactured goods.

Today, Canada has developed an urban, industrial economy. The two world wars spurred the growth of Canadian industries. Canadians built factories to transform mineral resources into steel and finished goods such as cars. They set up plants to make paper and other products from raw lumber. Meat processing became another important industry. Oil resources in the west supported refining and chemical industries.

Like many older industrial nations, Canada is now moving from a manufacturing to a service economy. In a service economy, most people have jobs that provide services to individuals, communities, and businesses. Service industries include hospitals, restaurants, and banks. More than 60 percent of all Canadians hold jobs in service industries. Another 30 percent work in manufacturing. Only about 7 percent work in farming, forestry, mining, and fishing.

Importance of trade. Canada's economic success is based on foreign trade. Because it has a small population, Canada has only a limited market at home and must sell to foreign customers. Three quarters of all Canadian exports go to the United States. About 20 percent of United States exports go to Canada. In 1993, Canada, the United States, and Mexico signed the North American Free Trade Agreement (NAFTA). By abolishing most trade barriers, NAFTA will create a common market among the three countries.

A World Power

Canada emerged as a major power during the two world wars. Canadian troops fought with the Allies. Canadians also used their resources and industries to produce food and weapons. By 1945, Canada ranked as the fourth-most-powerful military and industrial nation in the world.

Since then, Canada has taken a leading role in world organizations. Canadians are part of United Nations peacekeeping forces in the Middle East, Asia, and Africa. Canada provides technical and economic aid to developing nations. It is also a member of the Commonwealth of Nations, an association that includes Britain and the independent nations that were once part of its colonial empire.

During the Cold War, Canada stood with the United States. Canadians fought in the Korean War. Canada also joined NATO, a defensive alliance that you will read about in Chapter 31.

An Uneasy Friendship

Although Canada and the United States are friendly neighbors, the friendship has undergone strains. During the War of 1812, United States troops invaded and burned the city of York, present-day Toronto. Canadians still learn about this attack in school. During the mid-1800s, border disputes were settled peacefully. Since then, the two countries have cooperated on many programs, including building the St. Lawrence Seaway, which created a shipping channel between the Great Lakes and the Atlantic.

Canadians sometimes feel dwarfed by their southern neighbor. The population of the United States is nearly 10 times greater than that of Canada. Pierre Trudeau, a former prime minister, once compared Canada's situation to that of a mouse trying to coexist with an elephant. Many Canadians fear that their economy is too dependent on the United States. According to one popular saying, "When America sneezes, Canada catches pneumonia."

Environmental problems have created tensions between the two nations. Air pollution from American factories in the Midwest falls as acid rain. This rain falls on Canadian lakes and forests, damaging fish, wildlife, and trees. As a result, Canada wants the United States to enforce stricter pollution controls. The United States, in turn, wants Canada to limit the amount of sewage it dumps into waterways shared by both nations.

Recognizing the interdependence of the two countries, Canadian and American leaders meet frequently to discuss various issues. In addition to trade agreements, they have signed agreements to limit pollution.

Canadian Culture

Canadians take great pride in their many cultural achievements. The most famous school of Canadian painters in the 1920s was the Group of Seven. Their works celebrated the Canadian wilderness and still shape people's views of Canada. In recent years, art collectors have come to value the fine wood, stone, and ivory carvings made by Inuits and Indians.

Literature. In literature, Canada has strong traditions in both French and English. Writers from both cultures have reflected Canadian experiences such as frontier life and the wilderness environment.

Inuit Carving A polar bear grips the hood of a man's parka in this soapstone carving. Early Inuit carvings were small animal figures that hunters carried for good luck. Today's Inuit artists create larger, more complex works of art. ***Fine Art*** How is art affected by environment? Compare this work to other carvings in this book.

Well-known Canadian writers include Lucy Maud Montgomery, Marshall McLuhan, and Anne Hébert, an award-winning French Canadian writer. Montgomery's novel *Anne of Green Gables* is as popular today as it was when she wrote it in 1908. Writer Marshall McLuhan promoted the idea that the world is a "global village." Hébert's works include *Kamouraska* and *Selected Poems*. Each of these writers has helped make Canadians aware of their unique literary heritage, distinct from those of Europe and the United States. (See Connections With Literature, page 807, "Significant Moments in the Life of My Mother.")

Performing arts. Toronto and Montreal are major centers for the performing arts. They rival each other with theaters, symphonies, ballet troupes, and opera companies. The government-sponsored National Film Board of Canada has developed many excellent, low-budget movies. Today, filmmakers from around the world flock to Canada to study its original and successful filmmaking techniques.

Sports. Canadians enjoy a variety of recreational activities that their land offers. Canada's many lakes and rivers, vast national park system, and broad wilderness make boating and camping popular during the summer. In the winter, Canadians enjoy skiing, tobogganing, and ice fishing.

Canada's national sport is ice hockey. On frozen ponds and indoor rinks, well-organized hockey leagues help young players to perfect their moves. Young Canadians dream of playing for professional teams such as those in Toronto, Edmonton, Calgary, or Montreal.

SECTION 3 REVIEW

1. **Identify:** (a) Group of Seven, (b) Lucy Maud Montgomery, (c) Marshall McLuhan, (d) Anne Hébert.
2. **Define:** (a) bilingual, (b) service economy.
3. How is power divided in Canada's federal system?
4. How has Canada's economy changed since 1900?
5. (a) What problems have caused tensions between Canada and the United States? (b) How have the two countries cooperated to resolve these problems?
6. **Applying Information** In 1907, a Canadian noted: "There is Ontario patriotism, Quebec patriotism, or Western patriotism . . . but there is no Canadian patriotism, and we can have no Canadian nation when we have no Canadian patriotism." (a) In what way does this statement still apply to Canada today? (b) What steps has Canada taken to solve this problem?
7. **Writing Across Cultures** Write a brief statement supporting or opposing the elimination of tariffs on goods traded between the United States and Canada.

CHAPTER 24 REVIEW

Understanding Vocabulary

Match each term at left with the correct definition at right.

1. multiculturalism
2. federal
3. voyageur
4. bilingual
5. service economy

a. having a division of power between a central government and local governments
b. having two official languages
c. system where most people work in jobs that provide services
d. encouraging people to preserve their distinct cultural traditions
e. French fur trader

Reviewing the Main Ideas

1. Describe two geographic features of each of the following regions: (a) Appalachian, (b) Great Lakes–St. Lawrence lowlands, (c) Canadian Shield, (d) Great Plains, (e) Western Mountains.
2. What energy and mineral resources does Canada have?
3. (a) What did Europeans seek in Canada in the 1600s and 1700s? (b) How did the arrival of Europeans affect Canada's Indian population?
4. (a) Why did Canadians grow discontented with British rule during the 1800s? (b) What steps did Britain take in response?
5. How is Canada's government organized?
6. What themes have Canadian artists and writers explored?

Reviewing Chapter Themes

1. Geography has influenced Canada's development. (a) Give three examples of how climate, landforms, and resources affect Canadian life. (b) How does geography contribute to regionalism in Canada?
2. The population of Canada includes people of many ethnic backgrounds. (a) Describe how three groups have enriched Canadian culture or society. (b) Give one example of how cultural diversity has led to conflict.
3. How has Canada developed since 1900 into a major world nation (a) politically, (b) economically, (c) culturally?

Thinking Critically

1. **Comparing** (a) How did the Canadian Pacific Railway and the St. Lawrence Seaway serve similar functions? (b) Why was the building of each important to Canada?
2. **Evaluating Information** (a) What was the purpose of the Quebec Act of 1774? (b) What actions has the modern Canadian government taken to satisfy demands of Quebec nationalists? (c) Why do you think these actions have not been completely successful?
3. **Making Global Connections** (a) How do environmental issues make Canada and the United States interdependent? (b) How have the two nations tried to cooperate? (c) What are some obstacles to cooperation?

Applying Your Skills

1. **Identifying the Main Idea** Reread the subsection "People" on page 527. Write a sentence that summarizes the main idea of the subsection.
2. **Analyzing a Painting** Study the painting on page 522. (a) What groups of people does the painting represent? (b) What does the painting reveal about Canadian rivers? (c) How does it show the influence Indians had on the French? (d) What title might you give to this painting? (See Skill Lesson, page 428.)

SKILL LESSON 11

Analyzing a Political Cartoon: A View From Developing Nations

Political cartoons present a particular point of view on a current issue or event. They often appear in newspapers and newsmagazines. Political cartoonists not only express an opinion but also try to influence the readers' views on an issue. Using exaggeration and humor, cartoonists can make powerful statements.

Most political cartoons contain few written words. Instead, cartoonists use symbols. A symbol is a concrete object that represents, or stands for, something else. The American flag, for example, often is used as a symbol of the United States. In analyzing a political cartoon, look at all the images and words. They are the keys to understanding the cartoonist's point of view.

The political cartoon at right appeared in a Costa Rican newspaper, *La Nación,* in 1991. The cartoonist, Arcadio, has used the term Third World to represent developing nations. Study the cartoon, using the following steps to guide you.

1. **Identify the symbols in the cartoon.** (a) Whom do the three children on the far side of the fence represent? (b) What does the dollar sign represent? (c) Whom does the boy looking over the fence represent? (d) Why are his clothes patched and worn? (e) What are the other boys' clothes like?
2. **Determine the meaning of the cartoon.** During holidays in Mexico, blindfolded children take turns trying to break open a piñata filled with toys and candy. In this cartoon, the three boys labeled North America, the East Asian nations, and Europe are trying to break open a piñata that is in the shape of a dollar sign. (a) What do you think will happen when the piñata is broken open? (b) Why does the Third World figure seem confused?
3. **Draw conclusions about the cartoonist's point of view.** (a) What nation is the cartoonist from? (b) Is his country a Third World, or developing, nation? (See the map on page 39.) (c) Why do you think the Third World is not involved in breaking open the piñata? (d) What do you think the cartoonist would like North America, the East Asian nations, and Europe to do? (e) Does the cartoon present a balanced view of the issue? Explain.

SKILL LESSON 12

Analyzing a Poem: The Life of an Argentinian Cowboy

Like novels and other works of fiction, poems can provide useful information about cultures. Remember, however, that a poet may exaggerate, either to make the writing more powerful or to make a point.

The verses at right are from "The Gaucho Martín Fierro," a lengthy poem written by the Argentinian poet José Hernández in 1872. In the poem, Hernández describes the life of the gaucho—the South American cowboy. He also describes many changes that took place in the lives of gauchos when the government encouraged people to settle cattle lands and introduced crop farming. Read the verses carefully, using the following steps to guide you.

1. **Identify the subject of the poem.** (a) What is a gaucho? (b) What is the subject of the verses? (c) Why do you think Hernández wrote the verses?
2. **Analyze the content of the poem.** (a) When did the gauchos start their day? (b) What kind of equipment did they use? (c) What kinds of work did the gauchos do? (d) Did the gauchos enjoy their work? How do you know? (e) How does Hernández describe the gauchos "these days"?
3. **Draw conclusions from the poem.** (a) Do you think Hernández might be exaggerating about some aspects of the gauchos' lives? Explain. (b) What do you think Hernández thought of the government's attempt to colonize cattle lands? How do you know? (c) In what ways do you think the histories and cultures of the United States and Argentina during the 1800s are similar?

"And as soon as the dawn
started to turn red
and the birds to sing . . .
it was time to get going
each man to his work.

One would be tying on his spurs,
another go out singing;
one choose a supple sheepskin,
one a lasso, someone else a whip—
and the whinnying horses
would be calling them from the
hitching-rail.

The [gaucho] whose job was
horse-breaking
headed for the corral
where the beast was waiting,
snorting fit to burst—
wild and wicked as they come
and tearing itself to bits.

. . .

Ah those times! . . . you felt proud
to see how a man could ride.
When a gaucho really knew his job,
even if the colt went over backwards,
not one of them wouldn't land on his
feet
with the halter-rein in his hand.

And while some were breaking-in,
others went out on the land
and rounded up the cattle
and got together the horse-herds—
and like that, without noticing,
they'd pass the day, enjoying themselves.

. . .

I remember—ah, that was good!
how the gauchos went around,
always cheerful and well mounted
and willing to work. . . .
But these days—curse it!
you don't see them, they're so beaten
down."

The House of the Spirits

Isabel Allende

INTRODUCTION Isabel Allende (1942–) fled Chile in 1973 when the military overthrew her uncle, Salvador Allende. Her novel, *The House of the Spirits,* is her memorial to "the house that I lost, the people that are dead . . . the friends that were scattered." This excerpt, titled "Uncle Marcos," captures the atmosphere of small-town life and the connection between the people and their religion.

Vocabulary Before you read the selection, find the meaning of these words in a dictionary: dialect, decipher, speculate, disconsolately, accessible, intrepid, grandiose, surreptitiously, lineage, ingenuity.

Each time Uncle Marcos had visited his sister Nivea's home, he had stayed for several months, to the immense joy of his nieces and nephews, particularly Clara. . . . While the rest of the household tried to sleep, he dragged his suitcases up and down the halls, practiced making strange, high-pitched sounds on savage instruments, and taught Spanish to a parrot whose native language was an Amazonic dialect. During the day, he slept in a hammock that he had strung between two columns in the hall, wearing only a loincloth that put Severo [Nivea's husband] in a terrible mood but that Nivea forgave because Marcos had convinced her that it was the same costume in which Jesus of Nazareth had preached. . . .

[After an extended trip around the world, Uncle Marcos returned with a shipment of enormous boxes.] Marcos spent two weeks assembling the contents according to an instruction manual written in English, which he was able to decipher thanks to his invincible imagination and a small dictionary.

When the job was finished, it turned out to be a bird of prehistoric dimensions, with the face of a furious eagle, wings that moved, and a propeller on its back. . . . Marcos announced that as soon as the weather cleared he planned to take off in his bird and cross the mountain range. The news spread, making this the most talked-about event of the year. . . .

The appointed day dawned full of clouds, but so many people had turned out that Marcos did not want to disappoint them. He showed up punctually at the appointed spot and did not once look up at the sky, which was growing darker and darker with thick gray clouds. . . .

The bishop himself, accompanied by two incense bearers, appeared to bless the bird without having been asked. . . . The police, on horseback and carrying lances, had trouble keeping the crowds far enough away from the center of the park, where Marcos waited dressed in mechanic's overalls, with huge racer's goggles and an explorer's helmet. . . .

Against all logic, on the second try the bird lifted off without mishap and with a certain elegance, accompanied by the creaking of its skeleton and the roar of its motor. It rose flapping its wings and disappeared into the clouds, to a send-off of applause, whistlings, handkerchiefs, drumrolls, and the sprinkling of holy water. . . .

After a week with no word from the flying uncle, people began to speculate that he had gone so high that he had disappeared into outer space, and the ignorant suggested he would reach the moon. With a mixture of sadness and relief, Severo decided that his brother-in-law and his machine must have fallen into some hidden crevice of the cordillera [a mountain chain], where they would never be found.

Nivea wept disconsolately and lit candles to San Antonio, patron of lost objects. Severo opposed the idea of having masses said, because he did not believe in them as a way of getting into heaven, much less of returning to earth. . . . Because of his attitude, Nivea and Nana had the children say the rosary behind their father's back for nine days. Meanwhile, groups of volunteer explorers and mountain climbers tirelessly searched peaks and passes, combing every accessible stretch of land until they finally returned in triumph to hand the family the mortal remains of the deceased in a sealed black coffin.

The intrepid traveler was laid to rest in a grandiose funeral. His death made him a hero and his name was on the front page of all the papers for several days. The same multitude that had gathered to see him off the day he flew away in his bird paraded past his coffin. The entire family wept as befit the occasion, except for Clara, who continued to watch the sky with the patience of an astronomer.

One week after he had been buried, Uncle Marcos, a bright smile playing behind his pirate's mustache, appeared in person in the doorway of Nivea and Severo del Valle's house. Thanks to the surreptitious prayers of the women and children, as he himself admitted, he was alive and well and in full possession of his faculties, including his sense of humor. Despite the noble lineage of his aerial maps, the flight had been a failure. He had lost his airplane and had to return on foot, but he had not broken any bones and his adventurous spirit was intact. This confirmed the family's eternal devotion to San Antonio, but was not taken as a warning by future generations, who also tried to fly, although by different means.

Legally, however, Marcos was a corpse. Severo del Valle was obliged to use all his legal ingenuity to bring his brother-in-law back to life and the full rights of citizenship.

Colombian artist Fernando Botero completed this painting titled *The Pinzon Family* in 1965. Botero shows a sense of humor as well as serious purpose in his art. Isabel Allende, too, displayed a similar point of view in her story about Uncle Marcos. Compare the way in which Botero satirizes the people in his painting with the way Allende describes the villagers' actions when Uncle Marcos made his "flight."

When the coffin was pried open in the presence of the appropriate authorities, it was found to contain a bag of sand.

Source: "Uncle Marcos" from *The House of the Spirits* by Isabel Allende, copyright 1982 by Isabel Allende. Published by Alfred A. Knopf, subsidiary of Random House, Inc., 1985. Reprinted by permission of the author.

THINKING ABOUT LITERATURE

1. What did Uncle Marcos propose to do that caused such an uproar in the village?
2. Why was Uncle Marcos legally a corpse?
3. **Analyzing Information** What does this excerpt reveal about the role of religion in Latin American life?

The Tuneful Influence of Latin America

The young American bandleader could not shake the syncopated rhythm out of his head. W. C. Handy—known later as the "Father of the Blues"—visited Havana, Cuba, in 1900. He later recalled:

> "I sought out the small, shy bands that played behind closed shutters on dark out-of-the-way streets. . . . They were playing a strange native air new and interesting to me. More than thirty years later I heard that rhythm again. By then it had gained respectability in New York and had acquired a name—the Rumba."

When Handy wrote his famous "St. Louis Blues," he remembered the wonderful sounds he had heard in Havana. He blended a Cuban musical form known as the habanera with the African American blues.

Today, an endless stream of music still flows from the back streets and night spots of Latin America to the jukeboxes and CD players of the United States. Latin American styles have helped to shape rhythm and blues, jazz, rock-and-roll, and disco. In fact, few forms of "American music" have been untouched by the "Latin beat."

Roots of Latin American Music

The origins of these musical crosscurrents were not in the Western Hemisphere. Latin American music traces its roots back to the colonial nations of Europe—especially Spain and Portugal, and to Africa.

Strains of African music are strongest in areas where large numbers of captured Africans were imported as slaves.

The complex drum beats and overlapping call-and-response singing of Africa have enriched the music of Brazil, Cuba, Jamaica, and Haiti. In countries where African slavery played a smaller role—such as Argentina and Mexico—the European musical strains are stronger. For example, European forms like the waltz and the polka helped to shape Mexican music.

The Sound Travels North

American fascination with Latin American music began early. Victor Herbert's *Cuban Song* introduced Latin themes to Broadway musicals as early as 1897. By 1900, John Philip Sousa was weaving Mexican and Native American elements into his military marches.

In 1913, dancers Vernon and Irene Castle performed an Argentinian step called the tango in a Broadway show. "Tango fever" quickly swept the nation. Waiters at fancy restaurants complained about couples getting up to tango between courses. Preachers denounced the tango as "immoral." When a high school student died after dancing for seven hours, headlines screamed, "Death Attributed to Tango."

In the following years, dozens of Latin American musicians visited the United States. In Spanish-speaking sections of American cities, musicians from Cuba and Puerto Rico performed in the raw, exuberant styles they had learned in their homelands. In the ballrooms of major hotels, musicians like Xavier Cugat and Desi Arnaz played a smoother, more middle American version of the Latin styles.

Cole Porter and other popular songwriters adapted Latin rhythms, such as the rumba and the beguine. At the same time, pop singers turned Latin tunes into hits by giving them English lyrics. "Cuando Vuelvo a Tu Lado," for example, hit the charts as "What a Difference a Day Makes."

Cubop, a fusion of Cuban and North American jazz styles, influenced the development of progressive jazz in the 1940s and 1950s. In the 1960s, "The Girl From Ipanema" by Stan Getz and Astrud Gilberto brought the Brazilian bossa nova north.

The Beat Goes On

Music from the English-speaking islands of the Caribbean also became popular. In Trinidad, calypso musicians used homemade steel drums. Their lyrics featured social and political comment. Harry Belafonte, a Brooklyn-born singer, helped popularize calypso in the United States.

Jamaican reggae made an even bigger splash in the 1970s. It was itself influenced by the music of the United States. Reggae superstar Bob Marley grew up listening not only to island music but to singers such as "Fats" Domino and rock singers like Elvis Presley: He noted:

> "You have a jukebox, and you always have music going on. . . . I used to hear things like 'Jim Dandy to the Res-cue!' 'A-Bonie Maronie.' . . . Heavy music."

Transformed by the genius of Marley, these sounds later reentered the United States as reggae.

In recent years, a flood of immigration has increased the Latin American influence. Salsa, a rousing blend of Caribbean styles, was perfected in the dance halls of New York and Miami. In Texas, Mexican-born guitarist Carlos Santana brought the Latin influence to hard rock.

From Tito Puente to Linda Ronstadt, from Gloria Estefan to Ruben Blades, performers of Latin American heritage help to produce the music that makes us sing and dance.

1. What cultures have influenced Latin American musical styles?
2. **Analyzing Information** How do you think geography and technology affected the spread of Latin American music to the United States?
3. **Writing Across Cultures** W. C. Handy said that "music needs no interpreter when it speaks." Restate Handy's main idea in your own words. Jot down two or three examples that illustrate his point.

UNIT 6 REVIEW

Reviewing the Main Ideas

1. (a) Identify three physical characteristics of Latin America. (b) Describe why the population of Latin America is diverse. (c) Describe one way in which the people have interacted with their environment.
2. (a) Compare how the Maya, Aztec, and Incan empires were organized and governed. (b) What was the role of priests in each of these cultures?
3. (a) How did the Catholic Church become an instrument of colonial power? (b) What role has the Church played in modern times?
4. Choose three economic issues and describe how they have influenced Latin American history.
5. (a) Identify how the illegal drug trade has affected the economy and government in some Latin American nations. (b) What difficulties do drug enforcement officials face in their war against illegal drugs?
6. How have the works of Latin American writers reflected the issues and tensions in Latin American society? Give specific examples.
7. (a) Describe the major climate zones of Canada. (b) How have they affected Canada's economy?
8. (a) List the main events from 1837 to 1931 leading to Canada's independence from Britain. (b) Describe Canada's relationship with Great Britain today.

Thinking Critically

1. **Comparing** Compare the effects of regionalism in Latin America and Canada. (a) How has regionalism affected nationalism in each area? (b) Why do you think Canada was able to develop as one country while Latin America developed into more than 25 countries?
2. **Making Global Connections** Although they are politically independent, most Latin American nations were influenced by and continue to be influenced by the United States. Describe three examples of interaction between the United States and a Latin American country.
3. **Forecasting** What long-term effects do you think the NAFTA free-trade agreement will have on the economies of the United States, Canada, and Mexico? (b) Why are other Latin American nations interested in the results of this agreement?

Applying Your Skills

1. **Identifying the Main Idea** Reread the first paragraph on pages 446–447, under the subsection "Population Patterns."(a) What is the main idea of this paragraph? (b) List two facts that support the main idea.
2. **Reading a Graph** Answer the questions based on the graph below. (a) What was

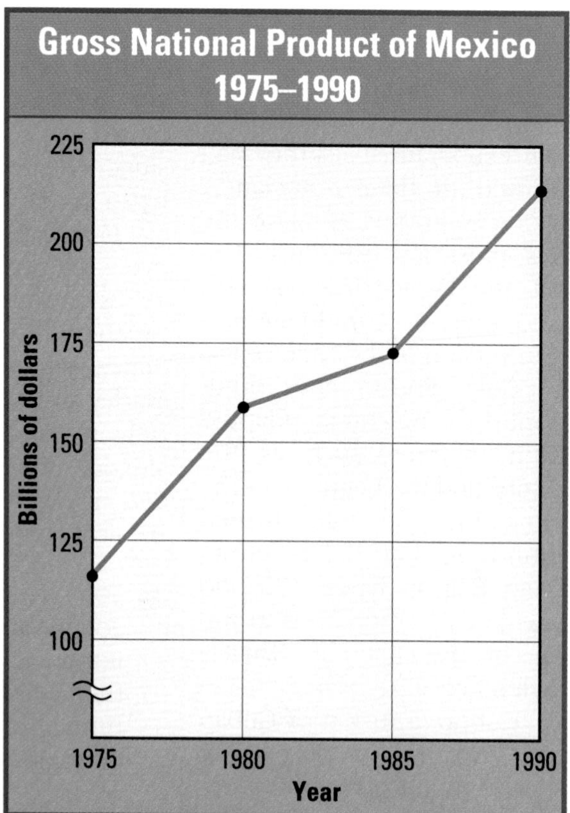

Source: *Statistical Abstract of the United States* (1990 and 1991); *Encyclopaedia Britannica, 1993 Book of the Year.*

Mexico's Gross National Product in 1985? (b) In which five-year period did the Gross National Product increase the least? (c) Make a generalization based on the information in this graph. (See Skill Lesson, page 238.)

3. **Analyzing a Poem** Reread the poem on page 457. (a) What event does the poem describe? (b) How might a Native American living in Mexico today feel about the last line of the poem? (c) How might a Mexican of Spanish origin feel about that same line? (See Skill Lesson, page 541.)

Learning by Doing

1. **Creating a Map** On an outline map of Latin America, label the countries, oceans, gulfs, mountain ranges, major rivers, and the Caribbean Sea. Draw and label the Equator, Tropic of Capricorn, Tropic of Cancer, and include a directional arrow. Use different colors to show the eight climate regions: tropical wet, tropical wet and dry, semiarid, arid, mediterranean, humid subtropical, marine, and highlands. Make a key for the climates. (See the World Climate Region Map on page 778.)

2. **Making a Travel Plan** Make a travel plan that covers 8 of Canada's 10 provinces. Work with a partner or in a small group. First, consult the map on page 524. Plot out a course of travel from east to west or west to east. Try to include a range of sights (cities and natural wonders) and modes of travel (land, air, water). Consult an encyclopedia to identify and locate historical landmarks and provincial parks.

WRITER'S Workshop

Arranging Information in Order of Importance

Order of importance means arranging supporting information from most important to least important, or vice versa. In ranking information, you will often have to use your own judgment.

Look at this topic sentence: *After independence, Latin American nations failed to establish democracies.* In detail sentences, you might begin by describing the less important obstacles and end with the most important obstacle in your judgment. For example: *First, Latin American nations had little experience with representative government. Second, social, economic, and geographic divisions created barriers to unity. Most important, civil wars broke out and dictators rose.*

Transitions for order of importance include *also, even more serious, finally, first, for one reason, furthermore, more important, moreover, most important, one, perhaps the greatest reason,* and *second.*

Practice: Look at this topic sentence: *The nations of Latin America have tried to develop modern industries to strengthen their economies and lower their need to import manufactured goods.* Write detail sentences that support this statement. Present your information in order of importance.

Writing to Learn

1. Imagine that you are an Aztec youth. Write a description of Cortés's forces marching into Tenochtitlán. First, freewrite about the event. Include facts, sense impressions, and reactions. Organize details in order of importance. Revise your description for unity. Make a final copy that you can share with a classmate.

2. Write an editorial supporting or opposing Quebec separatism. Include information about the economic, political, social, and cultural impact of the separatist movement. Consult current sources of information such as news magazines. Organize your arguments in order of importance. Make a recommendation in your closing statement. Revise for clarity and coherence. Proofread, make a final copy, and publish it in the school newspaper.

UNIT 7 THE MIDDLE EAST

UNIT OUTLINE

1 Muslims in Iran worship at this famous mosque in the city of Isfahan. The mosque has a dome of blue ceramic tile, and its exterior walls and arches are decorated with intricate geometric patterns.

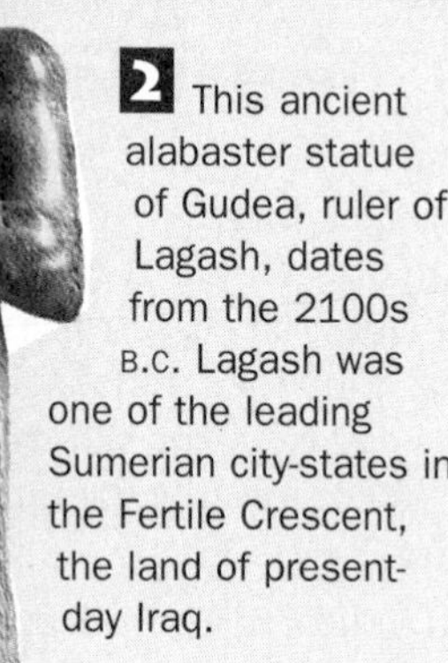

2 This ancient alabaster statue of Gudea, ruler of Lagash, dates from the 2100s B.C. Lagash was one of the leading Sumerian city-states in the Fertile Crescent, the land of present-day Iraq.

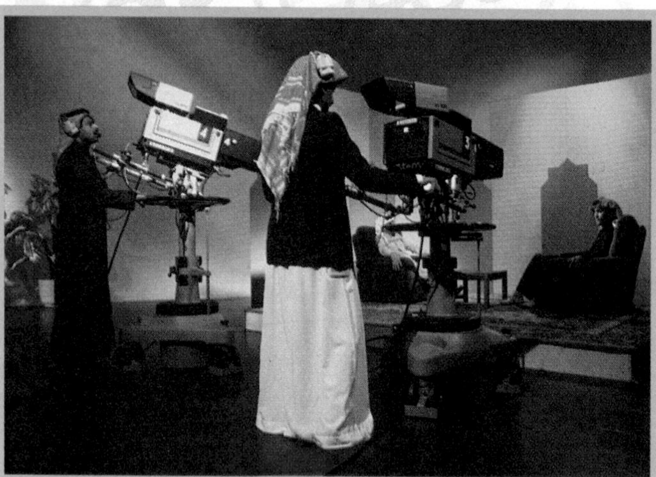

3 Saudi Arabian TV cameramen are televising a press conference in Riyadh. They wear traditional Saudi clothing but make use of the latest technology in electronic communications.

	Early History	1200	1400
History and Politics	▲ **1025 B.C.** Hebrews organize kingdom of Israel	▲ **1187** Saladin recaptures Jerusalem from Christians	
Society and Culture	▲ **First Century** Christianity spreads; ▲ **600s** Islam founded	▲ **1258** Golden Age of Islam ends; ▲ **1300s** *One Thousand and One Nights* written	
Economics and Technology	▲ **750s** Abbassids build Baghdad		

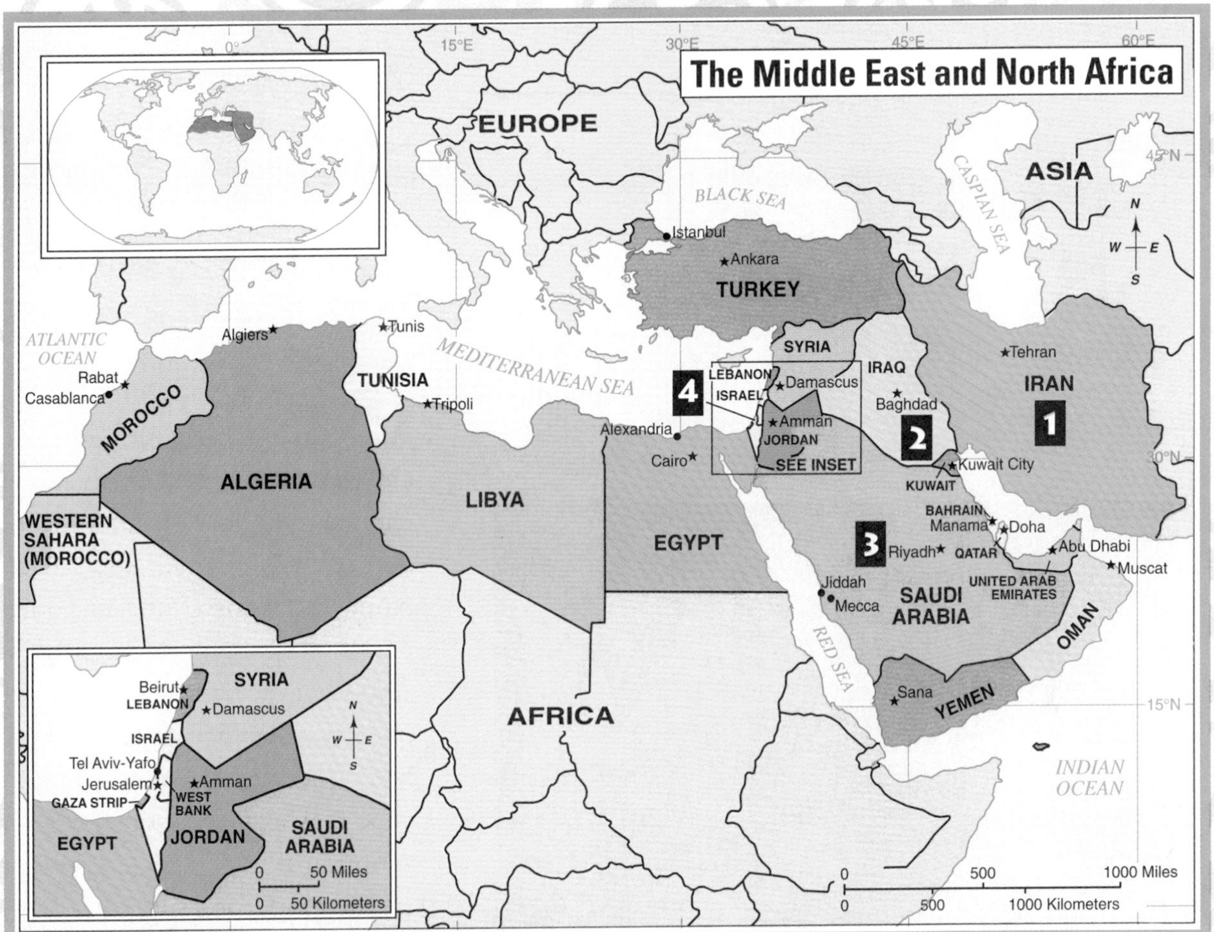

The Middle East and North Africa

EUROPE
ASIA
AFRICA
ATLANTIC OCEAN
MEDITERRANEAN SEA
BLACK SEA
CASPIAN SEA
RED SEA
INDIAN OCEAN
MOROCCO
WESTERN SAHARA (MOROCCO)
ALGERIA
TUNISIA
LIBYA
EGYPT
TURKEY
SYRIA
LEBANON
ISRAEL
JORDAN
IRAQ
IRAN
KUWAIT
BAHRAIN
QATAR
UNITED ARAB EMIRATES
SAUDI ARABIA
OMAN
YEMEN
Rabat
Casablanca
Algiers
Tunis
Tripoli
Alexandria
Cairo
Istanbul
Ankara
Damascus
Amman
Baghdad
Tehran
Kuwait City
Manama
Doha
Riyadh
Abu Dhabi
Muscat
Jiddah
Mecca
Sana
SEE INSET
0° 15°E 30°E 45°E 60°E
45°N 30°N 15°N
0 500 1000 Miles
0 500 1000 Kilometers

Inset:
SYRIA
Beirut
LEBANON
Damascus
ISRAEL
Tel Aviv-Yafo
Jerusalem
GAZA STRIP
WEST BANK
Amman
JORDAN
EGYPT
SAUDI ARABIA
0 50 Miles
0 50 Kilometers

4 Members of this kibbutz, or collective farm, in Israel are harvesting grapefruits. Israeli farmers have developed new methods of irrigation to grow a variety of fruits and vegetables in their dry desert land.

▲ **1453** Constantinople falls to Ottomans

▲ **1566** Ottoman Empire flourishes under Suleiman I

1948 ▲ Israel created

▲ **1994** Israel and PLO reach accord on Gaza

▲ **1500s** Persians develop the art of miniature painting

▲ **Late 1800s** Zionist movement develops

▲ **1988** Naguib Mahfouz wins Nobel Prize for Literature

▲ **1450s** Ottomans establish European and Asian trade routes

▲ **1598–1629** Safavid Shah Abbas builds magnificent capital in Isfahan

▲ **1869** Suez Canal completed

▲ **1960** OPEC formed

Chapter 25

GEOGRAPHY AND EARLY HISTORY OF THE MIDDLE EAST

The Death of Darius By the time he died, Darius I had expanded the Persian Empire across the Middle East as far as the Indus Valley. He had also sent expeditions to explore the Indian Ocean and the Mediterranean Sea. ***Fine Art*** Although this drawing was done 2,000 years after Darius' rule, how does it show continued respect for him?

CHAPTER OUTLINE

1. The Land and the People
2. Early Civilizations
3. Judaism and Christianity

Day after day, stone masons chipped away at the rock cliff. High above the surrounding land, they carved the great figure of the emperor Darius I. Smaller figures, hands tied behind their backs, stood before him. They were conquered rulers whose lands Darius had added to the Persian Empire. Dust flew as the masons cut an inscription into the rock. It recorded the emperor's successes.

> "I am Darius, the great King, the King of Kings . . . . These are the countries which have fallen into my hands—by the grace of Ormuzd I have become king of them—Persia, Susiana, Babylonia, Assyria, Arabia, Egypt; . . . Sparta and Ionia; Armenia, Cappadocia, Parthia, Zarangia, Aria, Chorasmia, Bactria, Sogdiana, the Sacae, the Sattagydes, Arachosia, and the Mecians, the total being twenty-one countries."

By 516 B.C., Darius ruled an empire that stretched from the Nile River to the Indus Valley.

Within its borders lived dozens of different peoples. To rule such a diverse empire, Darius developed an efficient system of government. He then ordered the creation of great carvings and statues to remind his subjects of his power.

CHAPTER PERSPECTIVE

The Persians were one of many peoples who ruled the region we call the Middle East. Located where Europe, Asia, and Africa meet, the Middle East is a cultural crossroads. Throughout history, traders and invaders crossed the region, promoting a constant flow of knowledge and ideas between the Middle East and the rest of the world.

As you read, look for these chapter themes:

- Geographic factors, including scarcity of water, have influenced the cultures of the Middle East.
- Location has made the Middle East a meeting ground for many peoples and a center from which ideas have spread around the world.
- Ancient civilizations developed in the Tigris-Euphrates and Nile river valleys.
- The Middle East is the birthplace of Judaism, Christianity, and Islam.

Literature Connections

In this chapter, you will encounter passages from the following works.

The Epic of Gilgamesh

Zend-Avesta

Exodus

For other suggestions, see Connections With Literature, pages 804–808.

1

THE LAND AND THE PEOPLE

FIND OUT

How has location affected the peoples of the Middle East?

What are the main physical regions of the Middle East?

What geographic factors influence population patterns in the Middle East?

Which ethnic and religious groups live in the Middle East?

Vocabulary oasis

What is the Middle East? Europeans invented the term to describe the region that lies between Europe and distant parts of Asia—what they once called the Far East. In fact, the Middle East lies in southwestern Asia. Today, some people use the term Southwest Asia instead of the term Middle East. The Middle East, they point out, is "Middle" only in relation to Europe. Still, most Americans, including the United States government, continue to refer to the region as the Middle East.

Often, the Middle East includes North Africa. North Africa has a double heritage. It is part of Africa, but it also has strong ties to the Middle East. As you will read in this unit, the religion of Islam and the use of the Arabic language make North Africa part of the cultural region known as the Muslim world.

Crossroads of the World

The Middle East stands at the crossroads of three continents: Africa, Asia, and Europe. Since ancient times, it has connected major trade routes, both overland and on the seas. Caravans from India and China brought goods to the busy markets of the Middle East. From there, traders carried the goods across the Mediterranean into Europe. Other routes took traders across the Red Sea or down the coast of East Africa.

Cultural diffusion. Over thousands of years, migrating peoples, traders, and conquerors crossed the Middle East. They spread the ideas, inventions, and achievements of many civilizations. Some of these ideas, such as iron making, the alphabet we use today, and the religious traditions of Judaism, Christianity, and Islam, originated in the Middle East. Others started in Asia and traveled to Europe by way of the Middle East. Examples include Arabic numerals from India and the lateen sail from Southeast Asia.

Strategic location. Today, Middle Eastern nations command vital sea routes. Some sit atop vast reserves of oil. As a result, the Middle East has strategic importance—that is, it is important to the world for military and economic reasons.

Egypt, for example, operates the Suez Canal. The canal links the Mediterranean Sea and the Red Sea, creating a water route to the Indian Ocean. Turkey controls the Bosporus and the Dardanelles, two vital straits that link the Black and Aegean seas. Geographers call these two waterways the Turkish Straits. The Strait of Hormuz at the mouth of the Persian Gulf is another strategic waterway. Through its waters travel huge tankers loaded with oil for industries and homes half a world away.

MAP STUDY

The Middle East is a region in Southwest Asia that is located at the crossroads of three continents.

1. **Location** (a) Name the three continents that meet in the Middle East. (b) What bodies of water border the Middle East?
2. **Region** (a) In which two countries are plateaus the dominant landform? (b) Which mountain ranges have elevations over 7,000 feet (2,000 m)?
3. **Understanding Causes and Effects** Why do you think early civilizations arose in the valleys of the Nile and of the Tigris and Euphrates rivers?

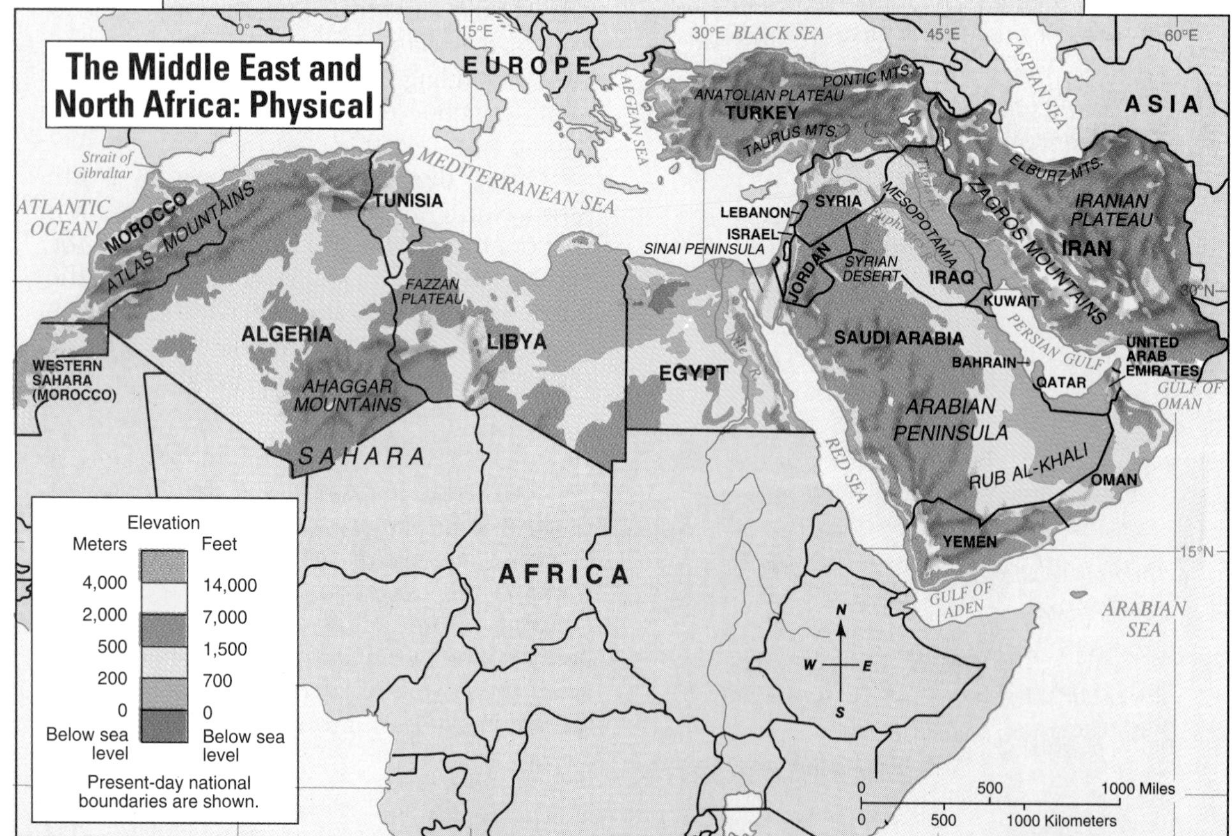

Major Regions

As elsewhere around the world, physical features have affected human settlement in the Middle East. The five main physical regions of the Middle East are the Northern Tier, Arabian Peninsula, Fertile Crescent, Nile Valley, and the Maghreb.

Northern Tier. The Northern Tier stretches across present-day Turkey and Iran. It is a region of mountains and plateaus. In the west lies the Anatolian Plateau, ringed by the Pontic and Taurus mountains. The Anatolian Plateau has fertile soil and receives enough moisture to support farming. As a result, it has a large population.

The Anatolian Plateau is located in Asia Minor, a large peninsula that connects Asia and Europe. As you will read in Chapter 26, the Ottoman Empire flourished in this region for hundreds of years.

To the east lies the Iranian Plateau. Like Anatolia, it is ringed by mountains, including the Elburz and Zagros ranges. Unlike Anatolia, however, most of the region is dry and the population remains small. Still, several major empires, such as the Persian Empire, were founded on the Iranian Plateau. These empires controlled large parts of the Middle East.

Arabian Peninsula. The Arabian Peninsula is a vast plateau that is about one third the size of the United States. It borders on several important bodies of water, including the Red Sea, the Arabian Sea, and the Persian Gulf. Saudi Arabia is the largest nation in the region.

Despite its size, the Arabian Peninsula has a small population. The reason is lack of water. Except for some fertile areas on the mountainous southern coast, the peninsula is a barren desert. Most people in the region live around scattered oases. An oasis is a fertile desert area that has enough water to support plant and animal life.

The Arabian Peninsula plays a major role in the world economy. Beneath its desert surface lie huge amounts of oil. Due to the growing demand for oil, some countries in the region have gained great wealth.

The Arabian Peninsula is important for other reasons, too. It is the birthplace of Islam, and the holy city of Mecca attracts Muslims from around the globe.

Farming in a Dry Land The Elburz Mountains along Iran's northern border block winds that carry moisture from the north. Thus, the land south of the mountains is generally dry. However, melting snow from the hillsides provides enough water for farmers to grow limited crops of wheat and barley. ***Geography*** What other geographic features shown in this photograph would make farming difficult?

Fertile Crescent. The Fertile Crescent is an arc-shaped region that stretches from the eastern Mediterranean along the Tigris and Euphrates rivers to the Persian Gulf. Rich soil and abundant water have made it a major population center. One of the world's earliest civilizations emerged in the fertile Tigris-Euphrates Valley.

The Fertile Crescent has few natural barriers. Throughout history, invaders have conquered its fertile lands and rich cities. The wealthiest settlements lay in Mesopotamia, the "land between the rivers." Other cities grew up in Syria and Palestine, along the Mediterranean coast.

GEOGRAPHIC CONNECTION

Clash Over the Euphrates

A narrow band of green borders the rivers in the Middle East. Beyond the reach of the waters lies barren desert. Without water, the desert will expand its hold on the land.

For nearly 6,000 years, the Euphrates River, which rises in the mountains of eastern Turkey and flows south through Syria and Iraq, has been the source of life along its fertile banks. Today, it is also a source of strife.

One day in January 1990, the president of Turkey proudly began the process of filling the new Atatürk Reservoir with water from the Euphrates. For several weeks, Turkey siphoned off 75 percent of the water that usually flowed through Syria and Iraq. Syria and Iraq reacted angrily to this move, which they said endangered both their agriculture and their industry.

Water security is a vital issue in the Middle East. One country's source of water often lies in another country. In the case of the Euphrates, it is Turkey that has the upper hand. Turkey's plan to turn its southeastern provinces into the breadbasket of the Middle East threatens Syria's supply of drinking water as well as its irrigation systems and hydroelectric power plants.

As population grows in the Middle East, the demands will become even greater and the shortages more acute. Tensions in the region, already high because of political differences and age-old rivalries, will be heightened.

1. Why will the question of water rights continue to be an issue in the Middle East?
2. **Synthesizing Information** Using the map and the information in the text, explain why Syria is concerned about the security of its water supply.

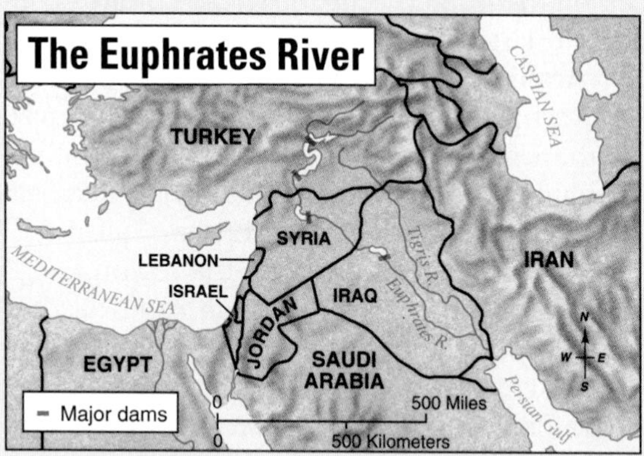

In the spring or early summer, melting snows from surrounding mountains sometimes cause the Tigris and Euphrates rivers to flood. The flood waters spread fertile soil over Mesopotamia. The flooding is unpredictable, however. Some years, tremendous flood waters sweep over farmlands, bringing disaster and death. In other years, the rivers carry little water, which makes irrigation difficult and causes crops to wither. Today, as in the past, governments help farmers to build dikes and canals to control the flooding.

Nile Valley. As you have read, the fertile Nile Valley in northeastern Africa was a cradle of ancient civilization. The Nile Valley enjoyed geographic advantages that Mesopotamia did not possess. Forbidding deserts in the east and west protected it from invaders, and the flooding of the Nile River was both predictable and dependable.

In ancient times, trade and other contacts linked Egyptians in the Nile Valley with the peoples of the Fertile Crescent. From Egypt, caravans and armies crossed the Sinai Peninsula, while ships sailed from Nile delta ports to lands adjoining the Mediterranean.

The Maghreb. The Maghreb includes the North African nations of Algeria, Tunisia, and Morocco. Five other African nations—Libya, Chad, Niger, Mali, and Mauritania—share geographic and cultural links with the Maghreb.

Maghreb comes from an Arab term meaning "western isle." To the early Arabs, this region, which lies west of the Arabian Peninsula, seemed like an isolated land surrounded by water, mountains, and deserts. During the 600s and 700s, Arab armies carried the religion of Islam to this "western isle."

Among the chief features of the Maghreb are the vast Sahara and the rugged Atlas Mountains. Because of the scarcity of water, both areas have few inhabitants. Most people live along the Mediterranean coast, which has fertile soil and plenty of rain.

The Maghreb has long been a major crossroads. It commands the southern rim of the Mediterranean as well as the gateway to the Atlantic. Traders from the Maghreb exchanged goods from West Africa, Europe, and the Middle East.

Climate and Resources

Climate has dictated where people live in the Middle East. Nearly all of the region is desert. People have clustered in well-watered areas along the coasts and in river valleys where they irrigate and farm the land. Settlements were scattered. Many separate nations developed throughout the Middle East.

Adapting to scarcity. Lack of rainfall and scarcity of water have shaped the cultures of the Middle East. Less than 10 percent of the land receives enough water to make farming possible.

From earliest times, people built irrigation systems to carry water from rivers to crops. Ancient Egyptians used the shaduf, a simple water hoist, to transfer water from ditches and canals to their fields. Modern technology has improved on older irrigation methods, and people have developed new ones such as drip irrigation, which delivers a measured amount of water to each plant. The nations of the Arabian Peninsula also have invested huge amounts of money in desalination plants, which convert the water from the surrounding seas into fresh water. (See the feature on page 613.)

Oil. The Middle East has a variety of resources, including salt, phosphate—which is used in fertilizers—and copper. The most valuable resource, however, is oil.

Oil is unevenly distributed across the region. As a result, great economic differences exist between oil-rich countries and those that lack oil.

Peoples

The Middle East is home to many different peoples with a variety of languages, religions, and traditions. Among the major languages of the region are Arabic, Turkish, Hebrew, Kurdish, Persian, Greek, and Armenian. Religions

Water in Saudi Arabia Sections of a pipeline are waiting to be hooked up to carry fresh water from a desalination plant. Pipelines carry millions of gallons of treated water to such inland cities as Riyadh. ***Scarcity*** How has scarcity of water affected the development of nations in the Middle East?

include Islam, Christianity, and Judaism. The region—including the Maghreb—consists of 19 countries and almost 350 million people.

Ethnic diversity. Arabs are the majority group in most Middle Eastern countries. But what is an Arab? Beginning in the mid-600s, Arabs from the Arabian Peninsula conquered many different peoples in the Middle East and North Africa. Over time, the conquered peoples adopted the Arabic language as well as the religion of Islam. They, too, became known as Arabs. Today, the term Arab is used to describe anyone whose native language is Arabic. Within this large group, however, Arabs may differ greatly from one another.

Besides Arabs, the Middle East is home to other ethnic groups such as Turks, Iranians, and Kurds. Most of these groups migrated to the Middle East from other parts of Asia. They all have their own languages and traditions.

Religious diversity. Islam is the religion observed by the majority of people in the Middle East. Most Arabs are Muslims. Many non-Arabic people are also Muslims. For example, most Iranians, Turks, and Kurds are Muslims. Yet Islam itself is divided into different sects, or groups. (See Chapter 26.)

A significant number of Christians live in Egypt, Lebanon, and Syria. Like Muslims, these Christians belong to different sects. They include Coptic, Greek Orthodox, and Maronite Christians.

Judaism is the most ancient of the three religions of the Middle East. In Israel, the majority of the people are Jewish. Many are descended from recent European, Asian, and North African immigrants.

SECTION 1 REVIEW

1. **Locate:** (a) Red Sea, (b) Persian Gulf, (c) Tigris River, (d) Euphrates River, (e) Nile River.
2. **Identify:** (a) Suez Canal, (b) Strait of Hormuz, (c) Asia Minor, (d) Fertile Crescent, (e) Mesopotamia.
3. **Define:** oasis.
4. Why does the Middle East have strategic importance?
5. (a) What are the five main physical regions in the Middle East? (b) Describe two features of each region.
6. (a) Where do most people in the Middle East live? (b) Why is the population so unevenly distributed?
7. **Understanding Causes and Effects** How has location contributed to cultural diversity in the Middle East?
8. **Writing Across Cultures** Keep a record of your use of water for one day. Then list five ways in which your life would be different if water were as scarce in your area as it is in parts of the Middle East.

2 EARLY CIVILIZATIONS

FIND OUT

What civilizations developed in the Tigris-Euphrates Valley?

What were the major achievements of ancient Mesopotamian civilizations?

How did trade and warfare affect Middle Eastern civilizations?

How did the Greek and Roman cultures blend with the culture of the Middle East?

Vocabulary ziggurat, scribe, cuneiform, satrap

"Whatever I had of gold I loaded
aboard the ship;
Whatever I had of the seed of all
living creatures I loaded aboard.
After I had caused all my family and
relations to go up into the ship,
I caused the game of the field, the
beasts of the field, and all the
craftsmen to go into it. . . .
I entered the ship and closed my
door."

These lines are from an ancient poem called the *Epic of Gilgamesh.* The poem was composed in about 2000 B.C. and includes many stories and myths from the Middle East. In the episode quoted here, Utnapishtim tells how he and his family escaped by boat from a savage flood that swept across the delta of the Tigris and Euphrates rivers.

Devastating floods were a frequent occurrence in the Tigris-Euphrates Valley. Controlling these floods required large-scale cooperation. This need to work together contributed to the rise of the earliest civilizations in the Middle East.

Sumerian Civilization

The first civilization in the Middle East was that of Sumer, in the fertile Tigris-Euphrates delta. As in other early civilizations, rich soil, rivers filled with fish, and a ready source of water for irrigation attracted early settlers. They lived by raising grain and dates. Working together, farmers drained swamps and controlled flood waters by building dikes and canals.

City-states. By about 3500 B.C., the most successful farming settlements had grown into powerful city-states. Each city-state controlled the farmlands that surrounded it. It had its own ruler as well as its special god or goddess, laws, and army. Rival city-states such as Erech, Ur, and Kish often fought each other. (See Connections With Literature, page 807, "Prologue" and "The Battle With Humbaba.")

Religion. Sumerians believed that the gods were all-powerful. If the gods were angry, they sent disasters such as floods and disease. As a result, Sumerian priests were very important. Only they knew the prayers, hymns, and other rituals that were needed to keep the gods happy.

The chief building in each city-state was the ziggurat, a huge, many-tiered temple. From the ziggurat, priests controlled the daily lives of the people. They collected taxes in the form of crops. They used grain as offerings to the gods and to support the many activities of the temple. At temple schools, young men learned to read and write. They then became scribes, who kept the temple records.

A system of writing. Like other advanced ancient peoples, the Sumerians developed a system of writing. Writing enabled people to record information pertaining to trade, government, and ideas. Writing was also an important tool for cultural diffusion. With a writing system, the Sumerians could transfer ideas to other people and places.

A Sumerian Ziggurat
Large temple complexes were the center of life in the Sumerian city-states. A modern artist drew this picture of the ziggurat at Ur based on the discoveries of archaeologists and historians. ***Technology*** What evidence do ziggurats provide about Sumerian building skills?

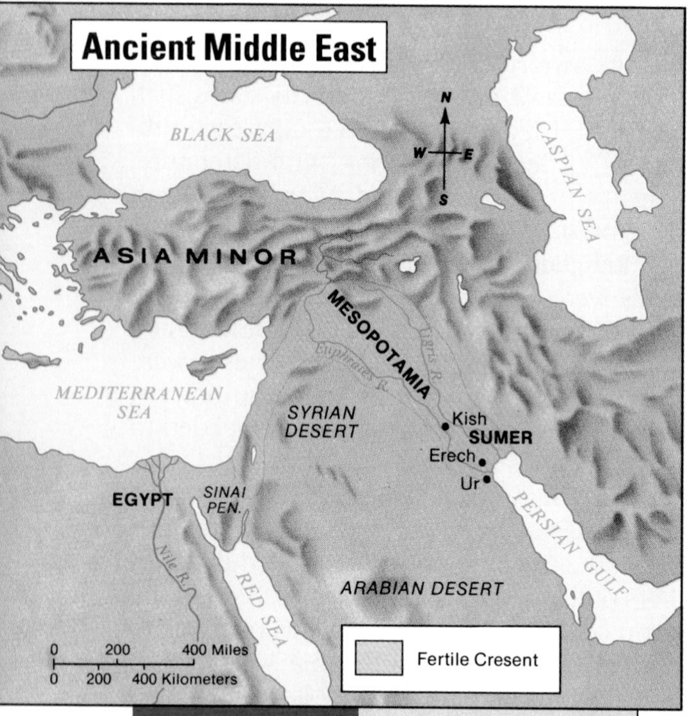

MAP STUDY

Several important early civilizations developed in the Fertile Crescent of the Middle East. The contributions of these cultures also spread to other world regions.

1. **Location** (a) What was the earliest civilization in the Middle East? (b) Describe its relative location.
2. **Interaction** How might you explain the location of the cities shown on the map?
3. **Synthesizing Information** How did trade and warfare encourage cultural diffusion among the peoples of the ancient Middle East?

At first, Sumerian writing was in the form of pictographs. To write "ox," for example, the scribe would draw an ox head. In time, the Sumerians added phonetic symbols to represent sounds. This made it possible for them to represent both objects, such as tables and chairs, and ideas, such as heaven, distance, and anger.

Sumerians wrote on clay tablets. They used a stylus, or sharpened reed, to cut wedge-shaped symbols into wet clay. The clay was then hardened by baking. The Romans, who conquered the Middle East much later, called this ancient writing cuneiform (kyoo NEE uh form), from the Latin word *cuneus,* meaning "wedge."

Cuneiform gradually spread across the Fertile Crescent. Archaeologists have found thousands of cuneiform tablets that record laws, prayers, treaties, medical knowledge, and other information. Some tablets date from Sumerian times. Others are the records of later civilizations.

Other achievements. The Sumerians made many advances that influenced later peoples. They were the first people who were known to have used the wheel, and they invented the sail. Sumerian wheeled carts and sailing ships carried trade goods and knowledge across the region and even beyond, to the Indus Valley in South Asia.

The Sumerians also invented the plow and developed an accurate calendar. They used arithmetic and geometry to survey fields. They set up a system of measurement based on the number 60. Because of the Sumerians, people today use the 60-second minute, 60-minute hour, and 360° circle.

Warfare and Trade Spread Culture

The Fertile Crescent has few natural barriers, and throughout its long history, a pattern emerged. Nomadic people from the highlands were attracted to the fertile river valleys and rich cities of the plains. They conquered the settled lands. Over time, they adopted the advanced civilization of the peoples they defeated, adding their own ideas and beliefs to those they found.

Despite the frequent turmoil of the region, trade flourished across wide areas. Over thousands of years, warfare and trade created a rich blend of cultures in the Middle East.

A code of law. In about 1700 B.C., the Babylonians, under King Hammurabi (hah moo RAH bee), conquered much of the Fertile Crescent. To provide justice throughout his large empire, Hammurabi drew up a single code of law, replacing the many law codes of earlier peoples.

Hammurabi's Code included 282 laws. They regulated economic, social, and moral affairs. The purpose of the code, Hammurabi declared, was:

> "to cause justice to prevail in the land, to destroy the wicked and the evil, to prevent the strong from oppressing the weak . . . and to further the welfare of the people."

The code distinguished between major and minor crimes. It also tried to make the punishment fit the crime. The basic principle of punishment was "an eye for an eye and a tooth for a tooth." If one person blinded another, he or she would be blinded as punishment.

Hammurabi had these laws carved in stone and placed where everyone could read them. His law code became an example for later peoples and served as a foundation for future codes of law.

The spread of iron. In about 1500 B.C., the Hittites marched into the Fertile Crescent from their homeland in Asia Minor. After they conquered the region, they adopted cuneiform and absorbed other ideas from the Babylonians. The Hittites carried Mesopotamian culture back to Asia Minor, where it later influenced the Greeks.

The Hittites are best known in history for their mastery of iron. In fact, iron helped them win their empire. Their strong iron weapons gave them an advantage over enemies armed with soft bronze spears and shields. The Hittites tried to keep the technology of iron making a secret, but it soon spread to other peoples.

The Phoenician alphabet. While the Hittites ruled the Fertile Crescent, the Phoenicians (fuh NEE shuhns) moved into what is now Lebanon. They set up small city-states along the eastern Mediterranean coast and earned a living through commerce and trade. They never built an empire, but hardy Phoenician traders sailed the Mediterranean Sea, planting colonies from North Africa to Spain. Today, the Phoenicians are known as the "carriers of civilization" because they spread the culture of the ancient Middle East across a wide area.

The Phoenicians developed an alphabet that eventually evolved into the one we use today. Unlike the many signs in Egyptian hieroglyphics, the Phoenician alphabet used just 22 symbols and was easy to learn. About 800 B.C., the Greeks adopted the Phoenician alphabet and added four symbols. Later, the Romans adapted the Greek alphabet, which was then passed on to the western world. The Phoenicians also passed their alphabet to other peoples of the Middle East, including the Hebrews, Persians, and Arabs.

The Persian Empire

By 500 B.C., the Persians had conquered a vast empire that stretched from Asia Minor to the Indus Valley. As you have read, the emperor Darius I developed an efficient system of government to rule the diverse peoples of his empire. Later rulers modeled their governments on the Persian system.

Government. Darius divided his empire into 20 provinces. Each province roughly corresponded to the homeland of a particular group of people. The Persians tolerated diversity among the peoples they conquered, allowing them to keep their own languages, customs, and religions.

The governor, or satrap, of each province was responsible for collecting taxes and for keeping order. To check on the satraps, Darius sent special inspectors, known as the "eyes and ears of the king," on regular tours of the empire.

Communications and trade. The Persians improved and expanded the road system built by earlier peoples. On the main roads connecting the four capital cities of the Persian Empire stood relay stations. There, royal messengers could get fresh horses as they quickly spread news and information across the empire.

Peace and good roads encouraged trade. To further promote trade, Darius set up a uniform system of coinage—that is, he established a standard value for each coin. Metal coins were first introduced to the Middle East by the Lydians, who lived on the Anatolian

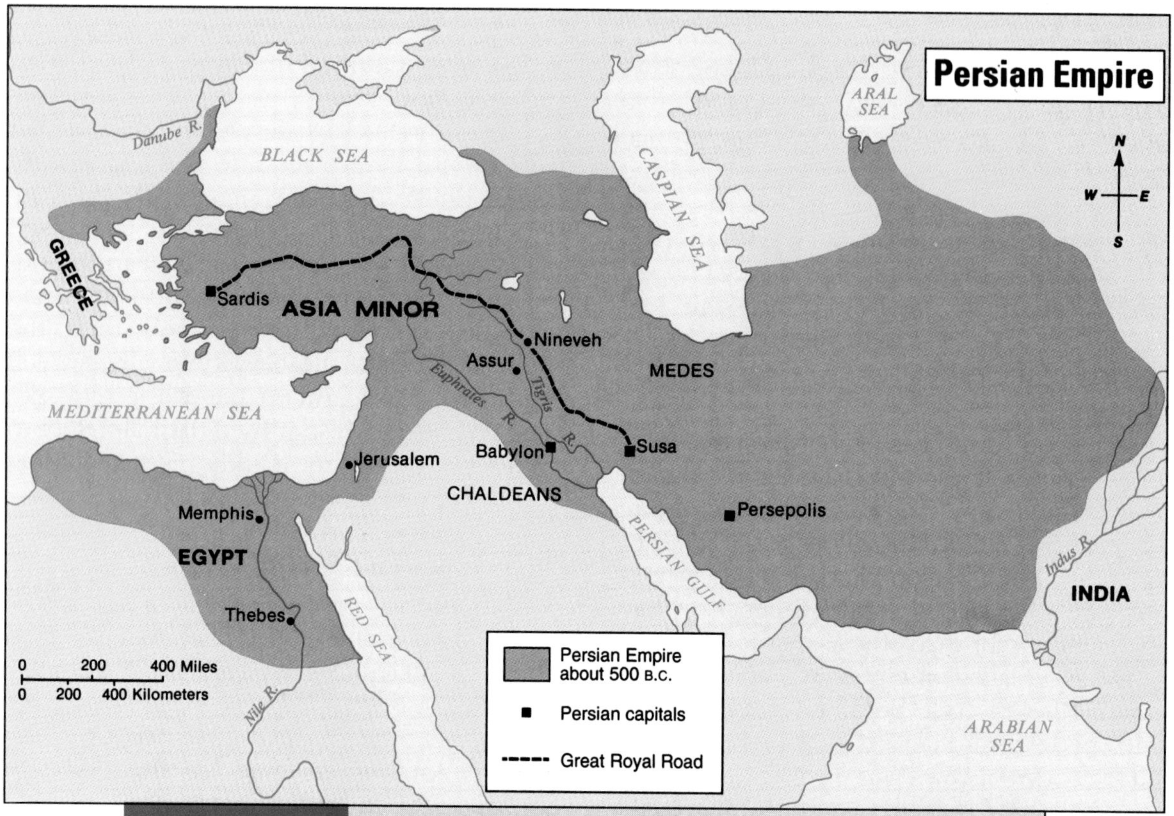

Persian Empire

MAP STUDY

At its height, the Persian Empire extended into Europe, Africa, and Asia.

1. **Place** (a) What river bordered the empire on the east? (b) What body of water bordered it on the west?
2. **Movement** (a) Name the two capitals that were connected by the Great Royal Road. (b) Why do you think the road was important?
3. **Comparing** Like the Persians, the Incas in South America built roads to unite their empire. (a) In what ways were the roads of these two civilizations similar? (b) In what ways were they different?

Plateau. The idea of coined money soon spread. Merchants found coins easier to count, store, and carry than the bulky goods they had been using for barter, or trade.

Zoroaster and the Forces of Good and Evil

Zoroaster (zoh roh AS tuhr), the founder of the ancient Persian religion Zoroastrianism, is a figure shrouded in mystery. Scholars think he lived in about 600 B.C. Although we know little about him, his ideas influenced many peoples, including the ancient Greeks, Hebrews, and Christians.

In ancient Persia, farmers and herders believed that many gods controlled the forces of nature. They relied on priests, called Magi (MAY jī), to win the favor of these gods.

According to legend, the Magi learned that a child named Zoroaster* had been born who would destroy their idols and magic. They seized the child and placed him on a burning altar, but the fire did not harm the boy. They then left him in the path of a herd of cattle, but the cows turned aside, leaving him unharmed.

* In Persian, he was called Zarathustra.

When the child grew up, he became a healer, visiting the poor and the sick. Like the Buddha and other great thinkers of the ancient world, Zoroaster sought to understand why misery and suffering existed alongside good in the world. One day, Zoroaster had a vision that proclaimed:

> “From good must come good; and from evil must come evil.”

As a result of this vision, Zoroaster became convinced that the world was a battleground between good and evil. The forces of good were led by the god Ahura Mazda (ah HOO ruh MAHZ duh). The god Ahriman (AH rih muhn) commanded the forces of evil. Ahura Mazda appeared to Zoroaster many times. Each person must choose whether to fight on the side of good or evil, Ahura Mazda instructed.

For 10 years, Zoroaster traveled the land, spreading the message of Ahura Mazda. Few people listened, however.

At last, Zoroaster reached the kingdom of Bactria. There, he asked to see King Vishtaspa.

A Golden Bull In Zoroastrianism, the bull was linked with Ahura Mazda. Priests carried this bull's head on a staff to symbolize their leadership in the war against the forces of evil. Priests encouraged people to perform good deeds, such as giving alms and protecting animals. ***Choice*** How do you think Vishtaspa's conversion strengthened Zoroastrianism?

> “'And who are you?' asked the guard.
> 'Go, and tell King Vishtaspa that I, [Zoroaster], have come to preach the True Religion, the religion of the Holy One, Ahura Mazda, and to turn him and his court away from the worship of idols to the worship of the Beneficent One.'”

For three days, Zoroaster spoke to the king and his court about the struggle between the forces of good and evil. Said Zoroaster:

> “'There will come a day, the Judgment Day, when Ahura Mazda will conquer and banish Ahriman.'
> 'And when will that be?' asked the king's chief priest.
> 'When man allies himself with Ahura Mazda and helps him to banish all that is evil, all that is darkness, and all that is death.'”

In the end, King Vishtaspa had his scribes write down everything Zoroaster had said. These writings became known as the *Zend-Avesta.* Vishtaspa then made the teachings of Zoroaster the official religion of the land. These teachings played a major role in encouraging the Persians to treat conquered peoples in a humane way. ■

Greek and Roman Influences

The civilizations of Greece and Rome added to the rich blend of cultures in the ancient Middle East.* In 334 B.C., Alexander of Macedonia set out to conquer the world. Macedonia is a mountainous region north of Greece. Alexander led his armies into Asia Minor, Syria, Palestine, and Egypt. He defeated the powerful Persian Empire and pushed as far east as the Indus Valley.

Hellenistic civilization. Alexander died in 323 B.C., and his empire was divided among his generals. Alexander's most lasting achievement, however, was not military but cultural.

* You will read about the Greek and Roman civilizations in Chapter 29.

Alexander the Great This drawing of Alexander with his troops is from a French manuscript of the Middle Ages. Alexander, wishing to unite the peoples he ruled in Greece and Persia, married a Persian princess. His soldiers also had Persian wives. ***Power*** Why might Alexander's marriage have helped unite his empire?

His conquests paved the way for the blending of Greek civilization with the cultures of the ancient Middle East. That new culture is known today as Hellenistic civilization.

One center of Hellenistic civilization was Alexandria, Egypt. There, merchants and scholars gathered from all over the Mediterranean world as well as from distant parts of the Middle East. In Alexandria's great library, scholars pursued research in science, mathematics, medicine, and philosophy that continues to influence the world today.

Roman conquest. From its base in Italy, the powerful Roman Empire expanded eastward. By A.D. 115, it ruled much of the Middle East, including Asia Minor, the Nile Valley, and the Fertile Crescent.

Under Roman rule, trade flourished across a huge area that stretched from the Persian Gulf to the Atlantic. The movement of people and goods that resulted increased the spread of ideas and technologies. The Romans carried their ideas about law and government as well as their engineering and building skills eastward. At the same time, Egyptian and Persian styles, beliefs, and traditions flowed westward. As you will read, followers of a new religion, Christianity, also spread their beliefs across the vast Roman Empire.

Byzantine Empire. By A.D. 330, the Roman Empire had split into two parts. The eastern half, which became known as the Byzantine Empire, included Greece, Asia Minor, Egypt, and the eastern Fertile Crescent. From their capital at Constantinople, Byzantine emperors ruled much of the Middle East for the next 1,000 years. Their rich civilization blended Middle Eastern, Roman, Greek, and Christian ideas.

SECTION 2 REVIEW

1. **Locate:** (a) Sumer, (b) Persian Empire, (c) Alexandria.
2. **Identify:** (a) Hammurabi, (b) Hittites, (c) Phoenicians, (d) Zoroaster, (e) Hellenistic civilization, (f) Byzantine Empire.
3. **Define:** (a) ziggurat, (b) scribe, (c) cuneiform, (d) satrap.
4. What conditions favored the development of civilization in the Tigris-Euphrates Valley?
5. Describe four achievements of ancient Middle Eastern civilizations.
6. Give one example of how trade spread cultural ideas and one example of how warfare spread ideas.
7. **Applying Information** How is Hellenistic civilization an example of cultural diffusion?
8. **Writing Across Cultures** The Phoenicians were "carriers of civilization" because they spread ideas through commerce. List five ways in which Americans have been "carriers of civilization."

3

JUDAISM AND CHRISTIANITY

FIND OUT

What were the main religious beliefs of the ancient Hebrews?

How did Judaism influence Christianity?

What were the teachings of Jesus?

Why did Christianity attract a large following?

Vocabulary messiah, parable, martyr, pope

In about 1800 B.C.,* drought and famine drove some nomadic Hebrews from Canaan (later called Palestine), on the eastern Mediterranean coast. They migrated to Egypt, where they were eventually enslaved. After many years, a great leader, Moses, helped the Hebrews escape from Egypt. He led them into the Sinai Peninsula. There, according to Hebrew tradition, Moses heard the voice of God:

> “‘Now therefore, if ye will hearken unto My voice indeed, and keep My covenant, then ye shall be Mine own treasure from among all peoples; for all the Earth is Mine; and ye shall be unto Me a kingdom of priests, and a holy nation.’”

The Hebrews believed that God had made a covenant, or binding agreement, with Moses. Under this agreement, the Hebrews accepted God as the ruler of heaven and Earth. In return, God made the Hebrews the chosen people on Earth.

The Hebrews set up a small state in the area of Palestine. The Hebrew political state lasted for a relatively short time. Hebrew religious and cultural beliefs, however, still influence the world today.

The Kingdom of Israel

After the Hebrews emerged from the Sinai Peninsula, they migrated into the Fertile Crescent. In about 1025 B.C., they formed the kingdom of Israel. Ancient Israel was located in Palestine, at the crossroads between Egypt and Mesopotamia. As a result, it was frequently threatened by invaders. Under its two greatest kings, David and Solomon, however, Israel flourished.

King David was a skilled general. He unified Israel and made it a power in the Middle East. David's son, Solomon, was noted for his wisdom, and his reign was marked by peace. Solomon transformed the city of Jerusalem

Ancient Jerusalem The tower and city wall beyond this gateway are among the few remains of ancient Jerusalem. Only one wall of the great temple built by Solomon still stands. ***Culture*** Why do you think many Jews visit these ancient monuments?

* Many scholars use the terms B.C.E., before the common era, and C.E., common era, instead of B.C. and A.D.

into a magnificent capital. There, he built palaces and a great temple dedicated to God. The outer walls of the temple were made of stone, but inside the walls were made of wood covered with gold.

Conquest. To pay for his many building projects, Solomon taxed the people heavily. Discontent grew, and after Solomon's death in 930 B.C., revolts weakened the kingdom. Foreign rulers soon conquered Israel and forced the Hebrews into exile.

When the Persians conquered the Fertile Crescent in 500 B.C., they allowed the Hebrews to return to Israel. The Hebrews rebuilt Solomon's temple in Jerusalem. However, they came under the rule of one foreign people after another. After the Persians, the Greeks and then the Romans ruled Palestine.

The diaspora. In A.D. 70, the Jews, as the Hebrews came to be called, revolted against Roman rule. In a savage war, many Jews were killed. The Romans forced the survivors out of Palestine. The scattering of Jews throughout the world is called the diaspora.

In their scattered communities, Jews preserved their religious and cultural traditions. Throughout the centuries, they made important contributions to science, medicine, business, and the arts in Europe, Africa, Asia, and the Americas.

Menorah in Stained Glass The menorah, a seven-branched candleholder, was used in Jewish worship by the time of the exodus from Egypt. The menorah became a symbol of both the Jews' exile and their freedom from captivity. Today, it appears on the coat of arms of the Jewish state of Israel. ***Culture*** What teachings of Judaism set Jews apart from other early Middle Eastern peoples?

Teachings of Judaism

Hebrew beliefs developed slowly over time. Unlike nearby peoples, the Hebrews were monotheistic—that is, they believed in one God. The Hebrews called their God Yahweh. He was the Creator and ruler of the universe. The Hebrews recorded their early history as well as the moral and religious laws of God in their sacred book, the Torah.*

The importance of law. The Hebrews believed that God had chosen them as a special people. In the Torah, they recorded how God gave them the Ten Commandments while they were wandering in the Sinai Peninsula. The Ten Commandments are religious and ethical, or moral, laws. They urge people to respect and honor God. They also forbid stealing, lying, cheating, and murder.

The Torah recorded many other laws and set out the duties that people owed to God and to their fellow human beings. Like Hammurabi's Code, the laws of the Torah outlined standards of conduct for everyday life. The Torah differed from Hammurabi's Code in significant ways, however. For example, although slavery was accepted everywhere at that time, the Torah required Hebrews to treat slaves with kindness.

Ethical world view. The religious beliefs of the Hebrews came to be called Judaism. A major feature of Judaism is its ethical world

* Much later, Christians adopted the Torah as the first five books of the Bible.

view—that is, the belief that people and their rulers should lead moral lives.

Religious teachers, called prophets, reminded the Jews of their duties. Whenever Jews strayed from God's laws, the prophets warned of God's anger and punishment. They insisted that rulers, as well as common people, must obey God's laws. Unlike many other Middle Eastern peoples, the Jews did not regard their rulers as gods.

Judaism also taught that individuals were responsible for their actions. The teachings of Zoroaster influenced the Jews. Like Zoroastrians, Jews believed that people had to choose between good and evil.

Rise of Christianity

Palestine, the homeland of the Jews, gave rise to another major religion—Christianity. Christianity grew out of Hebrew traditions.

Life of Jesus. Jesus, the founder of Christianity, was born in Palestine while it was under Roman rule. The story of the life of Jesus comes from Christian sources called the Gospels, which were written by his followers after his death. According to the Gospels, Jesus was born in Bethlehem, a small town near Jerusalem. As a young man, he learned carpentry and studied with rabbis—Jewish scholars and teachers.

When he was about 30 years old, Jesus became a preacher, teaching the poor about God's goodness and mercy. The Gospels record that he performed miracles such as healing the sick and raising the dead.

Jesus attracted many disciples, or followers. The Jewish prophets had predicted that a messiah, a savior chosen by God, would deliver the Jews from foreign rule and restore the kingdom of Israel. Some Jews believed that Jesus was the Messiah. Most Jewish leaders, however, rejected that view. They saw Jesus as a troublemaker who opposed traditional laws.

As Jesus' popularity grew, Roman officials became worried. To them, Jesus was a rebel. Although Jesus taught respect for the Roman emperor, he refused to accept the emperor as a god. In A.D. 33, Jesus was arrested. He was sentenced to die by crucifixion, a Roman method of execution. Jesus was nailed to a wooden cross and left to die of exposure.

Teachings of Jesus. The teachings of Jesus were rooted in the Jewish tradition of monotheism. Jesus preached belief in one God, the God of the Hebrews. He also upheld the Ten Commandments of the Hebrews as God's law.

At the same time, Jesus put special emphasis on certain beliefs. He stressed love for God and compassion for other people. He offered his followers a forgiving God who was the loving father of all people, rich and poor, Jew and non-Jew. In the eyes of God, said Jesus, everyone was equal. He taught that people who were humble, merciful, and unselfish would be rewarded with eternal life.

Jesus used parables, or short stories with simple moral lessons, to teach people to be kind to one another. He warned that acquiring wealth on Earth did not guarantee salvation.

Spread of Christianity

Jesus' followers believed that he was the Son of God, and in the years after his death, they preserved his teachings. In time, these teachings were collected in the New Testament. The followers of Jesus became known as Christians, from the Greek word *Christos,* meaning "messiah."

From its small beginnings in Palestine, Christianity spread across the Roman world. Missionaries like Peter and Paul worked hard to spread Jesus' message. In their travels, they benefited from the good roads and peaceful conditions that existed under Roman rule.

Persecution. In general, the Romans tolerated the religious beliefs of the diverse peoples they ruled. They looked on Christians, however, with suspicion because Christians refused to show respect for Roman gods. As a result, Christians were often persecuted. During the early centuries of Christianity, thousands of Christians became martyrs, people who suffer or die for their beliefs.

Persecution failed to destroy Christianity, however. Instead, its numbers grew. As one Roman observed, "The blood of the martyrs is the seed of the Christian Church." Finally, in A.D. 313, the Roman emperor Constantine

Jesus as the Good Shepherd The image of Jesus as shepherd comforted early Christians and strengthened their faith, especially during the Roman persecutions. In the Bible, Jesus tells the parable of the good shepherd protecting his flock, and adds, "I am the good shepherd. The good shepherd lays down his life for his sheep." ***Culture*** Why might parables be a good way to teach moral lessons?

converted to Christianity and ended the persecution of Christians. By A.D. 395, Christianity had become the official religion of the Roman Empire.

Appeal of Christianity. Why did Christianity appeal to people? For many people, both rich and poor, the new religion offered hope of salvation and eternal life. The Christian belief that each person could achieve salvation through moral choices gave people a sense of control over their destiny. The poor found comfort in Jesus' teaching that all believers were equal in the eyes of God.

The Christian Church. Christian ideas developed over a period of centuries. In time, a formal church was organized. At first, the highest Church officials were bishops. Eventually, the bishop of Rome became the head of the Church. He took the title pope, or father of the Church.

The Byzantine Church. As you have read, the Roman Empire was divided in A.D. 330, and the eastern half eventually became the Byzantine Empire. The Byzantine emperor refused to recognize the pope in Rome as the head of the Christian Church. Instead, the emperor controlled the Church himself. In time, the Christian Church also split into two parts: the Roman Catholic Church, with its center in Rome, and the Eastern Orthodox Church, which was centered in Constantinople.

SECTION 3 REVIEW

1. **Identify:** (a) Moses, (b) Solomon, (c) Torah, (d) Ten Commandments, (e) Jesus, (f) Gospels, (g) Eastern Orthodox Church.
2. **Define:** (a) messiah, (b) parable, (c) martyr, (d) pope.
3. (a) List three beliefs that were held by the ancient Hebrews. (b) What was the ethical world view of Judaism?
4. (a) How did Christian beliefs reflect Hebrew traditions? (b) What ideas did Jesus emphasize?
5. Give three reasons for the spread of Christianity.
6. **Analyzing Ideas** Review this statement by an early Roman: "The blood of the martyrs is the seed of the Christian Church." (a) What do you think he meant? (b) Why might this be true?
7. **Writing Across Cultures** List five teachings from Judaism and Christianity that influence the values of Americans in their everyday lives.

Chapter 25 Review

Understanding Vocabulary

Match each term at left with the correct definition at right.

1. oasis	**a.** savior chosen by God
2. ziggurat	**b.** many-tiered temple of the Sumerians
3. cuneiform	**c.** short story with a simple moral lesson
4. messiah	**d.** fertile area in a desert
5. parable	**e.** Sumerian writing

Reviewing the Main Ideas

1. Why has the Middle East been called "the crossroads of the world"?

2. (a) Compare the geography of the Fertile Crescent with that of the Iranian Plateau. (b) How did geography influence each region's history?

3. (a) Why are Arabs the majority group in most of the Middle East? (b) Which religion is observed by the majority of people?

4. Why are the Phoenicians known as the "carriers of civilization"?

5. (a) What were the basic beliefs of Zoroastrianism? (b) How did the teachings of Zoroaster influence Judaism?

6. What is the Jewish diaspora?

7. (a) Why did the Romans distrust Jesus? (b) How did they treat the early Christians? (c) How did the Eastern Orthodox Church come into being?

Reviewing Chapter Themes

1. Geographic factors played an important role in the development of Middle Eastern cultures. Discuss two ways in which each of the following helped to shape the cultures of the Middle East: (a) location, (b) water resources.

2. The Middle East was the home of several early civilizations, including Sumer, Persia, and Egypt, which you read about in Chapter 3. Select two civilizations and describe each in terms of the following: (a) government, (b) religion, (c) achievements, (d) cultural diffusion.

3. Judaism and Christianity first arose in the Middle East. (a) Describe the basic beliefs of Judaism. (b) Explain how Christianity is rooted in Hebrew traditions. (c) Discuss two ways in which Christianity differs from Judaism.

Thinking Critically

1. Synthesizing Give three examples of cultural diffusion in the ancient Middle East.

2. Linking Past and Present King Hammurabi drew up his code of laws to provide justice in his empire. How does Hammurabi's concept of justice compare with our concept of justice today? Give examples to illustrate your answer.

3. Making Global Connections Describe three achievements of Middle Eastern civilizations that play a role in your life today.

Applying Your Skills

1. Reading a Map Study the map on page 560. (a) What is the subject of the map? (b) How many miles did the Persian Empire extend from east to west? How many kilometers? (c) What were the capitals of the Persian Empire? (d) Why do you think the Persians created four separate capitals? (See Skill Lesson, page 48.)

2. Understanding Causes and Effects List two causes and two effects of the development of ancient civilizations in the Middle East. (See Skill Lesson, page 628.)

Chapter 26

HERITAGE OF THE MIDDLE EAST

Islam's Holiest Shrine Muslim pilgrims from all over the world travel to Mecca in Saudi Arabia. This ceramic tile shows a plan for Mecca's holiest site, the Kaaba. A cubelike black structure, the Kaaba is in a courtyard that can hold 300,000 worshippers. ***Diversity*** Why is Mecca such an important center of Islam?

CHAPTER OUTLINE

1 The World of Islam

2 Centuries of Turmoil

3 Patterns of Life

4 Imperialism and Nationalism

"I left Tangier [Morocco], my birthplace, on Thursday, 2nd Rajab, 725 [June 14, 1325], being at that time 22 years of age, with the intention of making the Pilgrimage to the Holy House at Mecca and the Tomb of the Prophet at Medina."

For almost 30 years, Ibn Battuta traveled around the world. During the course of his travels, he met at least 60 monarchs and hundreds of governors and other dignitaries. Traveling both on foot and by camel caravan, he covered more than 75,000 miles.

Alone or in the company of merchants and pilgrims, Ibn Battuta visited the Nile Valley, the Fertile Crescent, Asia Minor, India, China, and West Africa. Almost all the lands he visited were under Muslim rule. His colorful book, *Travels in Asia and Africa,* provides a fascinating record of his adventures. It is also an invaluable source of information about the diverse cultures and peoples of the Muslim world.

CHAPTER PERSPECTIVE

By the early 1300s, the religion of Islam had spread to many parts of the globe. Trade and travel flourished as Muslim pilgrims like Ibn Battuta made the pilgrimage to Mecca. Although the people of the region shared a common religion, the peoples and cultures of the Middle East remained as diverse as they had been in ancient times.

As you read, look for these chapter themes:

- Islam was the third major religion to emerge in the Middle East and to spread its message throughout the world.
- Islamic civilization preserved the cultures of the ancient world and also made important contributions of its own.
- The Arabs and later the Ottomans created vast empires that ruled diverse peoples in the Middle East and North Africa.
- European imperialism fueled nationalist movements among the peoples of the Middle East.

Literature Connections

In this chapter, you will encounter selections from the following works.

Ibn Battuta, *Travels in Asia and Africa*

Koran

Ibn al-Athir, *Sum of World History*

For other suggestions, see Connections With Literature, pages 804–808.

1 THE WORLD OF ISLAM

FIND OUT

What are the basic teachings of Islam?

Why did Islam spread rapidly?

Why did Islam split into different branches?

What were some achievements of Islamic civilization?

Vocabulary hejira, hajj, caliph

Muhammad grew up during an age of violence and lawlessness. Troubled by the evil and corruption he saw in the world, he often withdrew to a cave to fast and pray. According to Muslim belief, one day, while praying, Muhammad heard a voice call out, telling him to "Proclaim." The voice was that of the angel Gabriel. Alarmed and puzzled, Muhammad asked, "What shall I proclaim?" The angel replied:

> "Proclaim—in the name of your God, the Creator,
> Who created man from a clot of congealed blood.
> Proclaim! Your God is most generous,
> He who has taught man by the pen
> Things he knew not."

Gabriel then told Muhammad that he was to be a prophet of God. Deeply shaken, Muhammad returned home. Encouraged by his wife, Khadija, he began telling people about the religion of Islam. The words Gabriel spoke became part of the Koran, the holy book of Islam.

During the 600s and 700s, Islam spread across the Middle East and beyond, into Africa, Asia, and Europe. Today, Islam remains a powerful influence in the world. Almost one fifth of the world's people are Muslims.

The Rise of Islam

Islam emerged in the Arabian Peninsula. The region is largely a desert. Unlike the rich plains of the Fertile Crescent, the harsh environment of Arabia could not support large empires. The region was an important crossroads for trade, however.

The setting. At the time of Muhammad, some Arabs lived as nomadic herders. Others lived in towns located at some oases and along the coasts. The two leading towns were Mecca and Yathrib. Located on the busy caravan route that linked the southern tip of Arabia with the Mediterranean Sea, these towns prospered as centers of trade.

Mecca also benefited from a constant flow of pilgrims. They came to worship at the Kaaba, a sacred shrine that housed the images of the many Arab gods. Also in the Kaaba was the sacred Black Stone, a meteorite that Arabs believe was sent from heaven.

Muhammad Journeys to Paradise According to legend, Muhammad ascended to heaven on a horse with a human head. Note that the prophet's face is veiled. Muslims believe Muhammad was human. Yet in this and other paintings, his face is covered to signify his greatness as the messenger of God.
Change How did Muhammad build on the teachings of Judaism and Christianity?

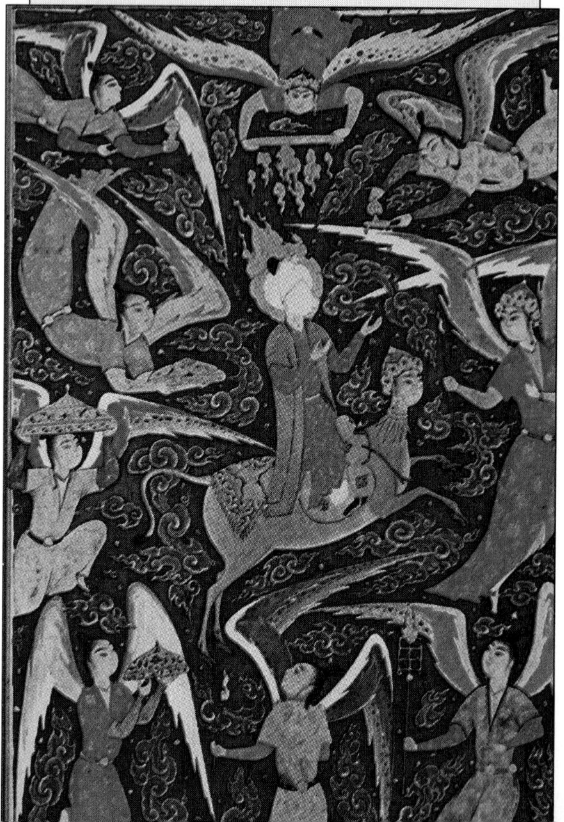

The prophet Muhammad. Muhammad was born in Mecca in about 570. His parents died when he was still a child, and he was raised by an uncle. As a young man, Muhammad worked for a wealthy widow named Khadija (kah DEE jah), leading trade caravans across the desert to Palestine and Syria. When he was about 25, he and Khadija married.

Khadija recognized that Muhammad had deep spiritual qualities. She encouraged him to spend time away from the world in prayer and fasting. During one of these retreats, when Muhammad was about 40 years old, he heard the voice of Gabriel ordering him to "proclaim," or preach, to all people.

The experience frightened Muhammad. When he returned home, he confided in Khadija. She urged him to accept the mission that God had entrusted to him. Determined to do his duty as God's prophet, Muhammad set out to spread the message of the one God.

At first, Muhammad won few converts. The Arabs of Mecca rejected the idea that there was only one God. Muhammad's message also angered the town's merchants and innkeepers. They were afraid that if they gave up their traditional gods, the profitable pilgrim traffic to Mecca would end.

In 622, after Khadija's death, Muhammad and his followers were forced to leave Mecca. They went to Yathrib, where Muhammad was welcomed as a respected leader. Later, the name Yathrib was changed to Medina, or "city of the prophet."

The hejira. The migration of Muhammad and his followers from Mecca to Medina became known as the **hejira** (hih JĪ ruh). The hejira was a turning point in Islam. It marked the beginning of the expansion of Islam. After Muhammad's death, his followers chose the year of the hejira as the first year of the Muslim calendar.

In Medina, Muhammad increased his following. In 630, he returned to Mecca with a strong army and captured the city. "Truth has come and falsehood has vanished," Muhammad declared as he smashed the images of the gods in the Kaaba. He then dedicated the Black Stone to God. Before his death in 632, Muhammad had carried Islam across the Arabian Peninsula and brought most of the region under his control.

Teachings of Islam

The basic message of Islam is summed up in the Arabic expression *La ilaha illa Allah: Muhammadun rasulu Allah*—"No god but Allah: Muhammad is the prophet of Allah." The word Islam means "submission." A Muslim is someone who submits to God.

Five Pillars. In submitting to God, Muslims accept five duties, known as the Five Pillars of Islam. As their first duty, Muslims proclaim their belief in one God. Further, they accept that God revealed his message to Muhammad. Muslims honor many prophets, including Abraham, Moses, and Jesus. To Muslims, Muhammad is the last and most important prophet. Although Muslims honor Muhammad, they do not worship him as a god.

A Muslim's second duty is prayer. Five times a day, Muslims face the holy city of Mecca and pray. Charity to the poor and the aged is the third duty. The fourth duty is fasting during the holy month of Ramadan. Ramadan, the ninth month in the Muslim calendar, is the month when Gabriel spoke to Muhammad as well as the month of the hejira. During Ramadan, Muslims may neither eat nor drink from dawn to sunset. A Muslim's fifth duty is the hajj, or pilgrimage to Mecca. All Muslims who are able are required to make the journey at least once in their lives.

Some Muslims look on jihad, or struggle in God's service, as a sixth pillar. Jihad includes a person's inner struggle to achieve spiritual peace as well as any battle in defense of Islam.

The Koran. The sacred book of Islam is the Koran. Muslims believe that the Koran contains the exact word of God as revealed to Muhammad. For Muslims, it is the authority on all subjects, including religion, politics, and law as well as economic and social life.

For a long time, Muslims were forbidden to translate the Koran from Arabic. As a result, Arabic became a universal language, uniting Muslims around the world. (See Connections With Literature, page 807, "The Opening," "Power," and "Daybreak.")

The Koran Borders of gold and decorative patterns called arabesques surround the Arabic script on this page of the Koran. Some devout Muslims memorize the entire Koran. ***Fine Art*** Why is religion the subject

People of the Book. Muhammad had met many Jews and Christians on his travels. Their beliefs influenced Islam. All three religions are monotheistic. Muslims believe that Allah is the same God as the God of the Jews and the Christians. Like Jews and Christians, Muslims also believe in a final day of judgment. On this day, it is believed, the wicked will be punished with suffering and the faithful will be rewarded with eternal life in heaven.

Muhammad accepted the original teachings of the Jewish and Christian scriptures as God's word. He called Jews and Christians "people of the Book" because they followed God's teachings in the Bible. The "people of the Book" had a special status as *ahl al-dhimma,* or protected people, and Muslims were required to treat them with tolerance.

Ethical conduct. Like Judaism and Christianity, Islam sets ethical, or moral, standards. Muslims must honor their parents, be honest and kind, and protect the weak and helpless. Islam also teaches that all people are equal. "Know that every Muslim is a brother to every other Muslim, and that you are now one brotherhood," declared Muhammad. This idea has helped unite Muslims throughout the world.

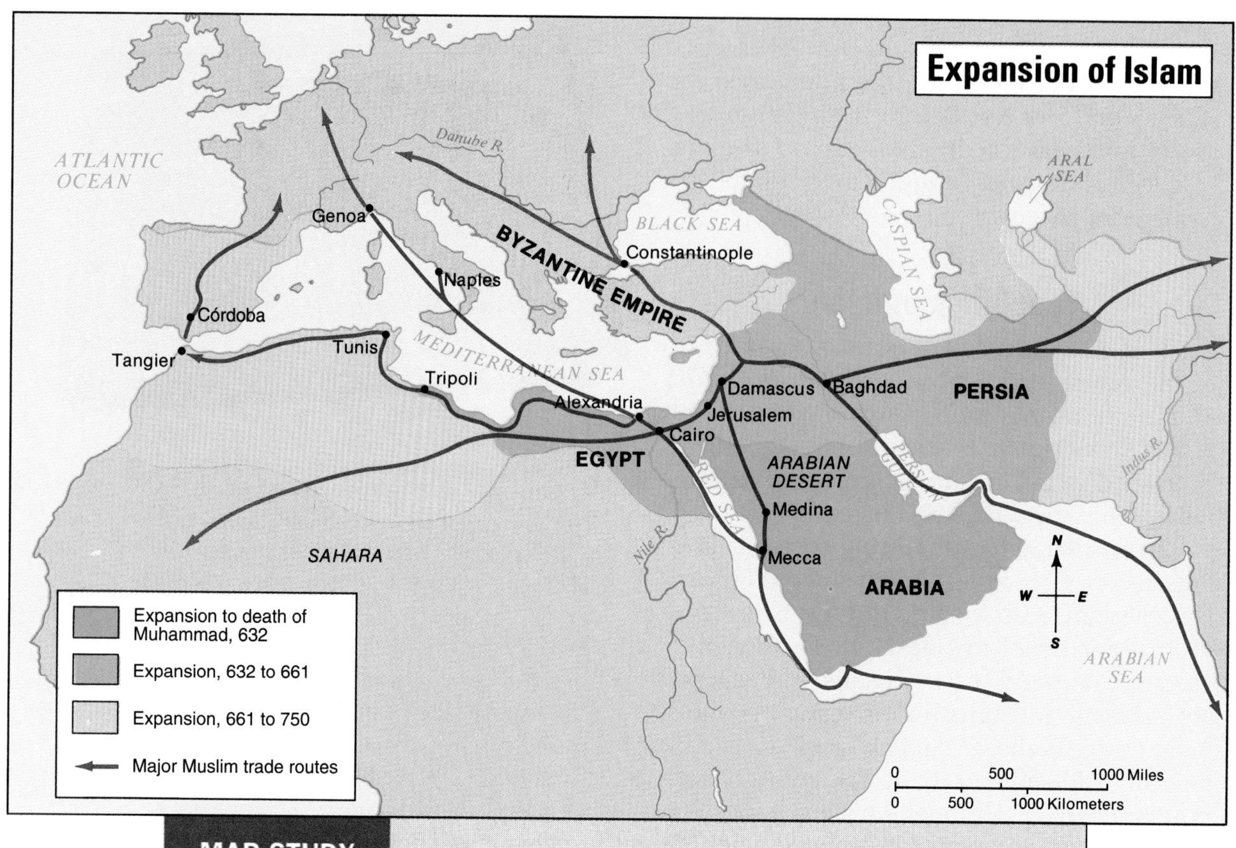

MAP STUDY

After Muhammad's death, Muslims spread the Islamic religion to the peoples of many lands. By 732, the Arab Empire extended from the Atlantic Ocean to the Indus River.

1. **Location** (a) During which period did Egypt become part of the Arab Empire? (b) In which period was the Arab Empire largest?
2. **Movement** (a) During Muhammad's lifetime, where did Islam spread? (b) When did Islam spread across North Africa?
3. **Synthesizing Information** How might trade have helped spread Islam?

Expansion of Islam

Islam spread rapidly during the 100 years after Muhammad's death. By 732, the Muslim Arabs had conquered an empire that reached from the Indus River to the Atlantic Ocean. It included the peoples of Persia, Arabia, Palestine, Egypt, North Africa, and Spain. At its height, the Arab Empire was larger than any previous empire in the region.

Reasons for success. Why did Islam expand so swiftly? One reason is that the Arab armies were united by their beliefs. Islam taught that Muslim warriors who died in the service of Islam would win a place in paradise. The idea of jihad also motivated many Muslim soldiers. The lure of riches to be won in the conquered lands was another powerful incentive.

In some places, people welcomed the Arabs. The Persian and Byzantine empires, for example, ruled diverse peoples who resented foreign control. Some of these peoples looked on the Arabs as liberators. Furthermore, many conquered peoples found the message of Islam appealing. They eagerly accepted its emphasis on human equality.

The Muslims were tolerant conquerors. They did not force "people of the Book" to convert to Islam. Jews and Christians were free to worship as they pleased, make money in trade, own property, and hold government office. However, they had to pay a special "nonbeliever tax." Some people converted to Islam in order to escape the tax.

Divisions within Islam. Within 30 years of Muhammad's death, a serious dispute permanently split Islam into two separate branches: Sunni (SOO nee) and Shiite (SHEE īt). The dispute concerned who should become caliph, or successor to the prophet.

After Muhammad's death, several able caliphs led Islam. The fourth caliph was Ali, Muhammad's cousin and son-in-law. In 661, Ali was murdered. A rival leader claimed the office of caliph and set up the Umayyad (oo MĪ ad) dynasty. When Ali's son challenged the authority of the Umayyads, he, too, was murdered.

These murders caused the followers of Ali, the Shiites, to break away. They claimed that only descendants of Ali could become caliphs. However, the majority of Muslims, the Sunni, believed that any devout Muslim could become a caliph.

Over time, the two branches developed other differences. The split between Sunni and Shiite Muslims affects Islam to this day.

The Arab Empire

As Islam expanded, the Arabs had to organize their vast empire. Under the Umayyads and later the Abbassids (uh BAS ihdz), the Arab Empire enjoyed periods of stable, orderly government.

Umayyad dynasty. The Umayyads (661–750) made Damascus, Syria, the capital of their empire. Even though the Umayyads adapted ideas from the Byzantines and Persians, they emphasized Arab culture. Arabic was the language of the empire. Also, the highest jobs in government and the army went to Arabs.

Non-Arab Muslims, such as the Persians, resented this discrimination. They insisted that being a Muslim was more important than being an Arab. In 750, Shiites and other discontented groups overthrew the Umayyads and set up the Abbassid dynasty.

Abbassid dynasty. The Abbassids (750–1258) built a magnificent new capital city at Baghdad, on the banks of the Tigris River. Baghdad, which means "God-given," flourished. At its height, the city was home to more than 1 million people.

Damascus in the 1600s The Syrian capital is one of the oldest cities in the world. The open courtyard in the middle of this painting shows the Great Mosque of Damascus, built in the early 700s. The picture below shows a mosque lamp made of enameled and gilded glass. ***Power*** Why was Damascus an important city in the Arab Empire?

Muhammad al-Razi, Islamic Physician

Abu Bakr Muhammad ibn Zakaria al-Razi, known in the West as Rhazes, was a man of many talents. One of the most original thinkers and physicians of the Middle Ages, he studied philosophy, music, and medicine. His interest in all of these fields lasted his entire life.

Al-Razi was born in Persia in about 865. He received his medical training in Baghdad and later became head of that city's chief hospital. Patients knew Al-Razi as a kind and generous physician who cared for rich and poor alike. Under his leadership, the Baghdad hospital became one of the leading medical centers of the world.

A free thinker, Al-Razi challenged accepted medical practices. He encouraged patients to eat a balanced diet in order to maintain good health—a revolutionary idea at that time. He also recognized the link between mental and physical health and urged young doctors to treat the mind as well as the body. He set the example, making hopeful comments to his patients as he made his hospital rounds. If patients had a positive outlook, he believed, they would recover more rapidly.

Calling for high professional standards for physicians, Al-Razi urged doctors to continue their education by studying medical treatises, attending lectures, and training at hospitals. He himself taught at the Baghdad hospital, and his skill as a physician-educator attracted many students.

Al-Razi's devotion to medical education led him to write more than 50 books on medicine. His most important work was *al-Hawi,* "Comprehensive Work on Medicine," an encyclopedia that summed up the medical knowledge of the time. Translated into Latin in 1279, the book remained a standard medical textbook in Europe until the 1700s.

1. How did Al-Razi contribute to medical knowledge?
2. **Linking Past and Present** Do Al-Razi's ideas about the study and practice of medicine still apply today? Explain.

The Abbassids supported many building projects, including mosques, irrigation systems, libraries, hospitals, public baths, and schools. Under their rule, not only Arabs but Persians, Syrians, Egyptians, Turks, and Indians held high jobs in government and became religious leaders.

Although the Abbassid dynasty lasted for 500 years, many kingdoms broke away. Despite political divisions, religion and culture united the peoples of the Muslim world.

Golden Age of Muslim Civilization

Through trade and conquest, Muslim civilization spread across a large area. It blended Greek, Persian, and Indian influences and also built on the heritage of ancient Egypt and Mesopotamia. Over time, it adapted all of these traditions to its own needs.

Trade and commerce. Wealth from trade and commerce helped make Muslims' golden age possible. Muslim fleets controlled the Mediterranean and sailed the Indian Ocean. Caravans carried textiles, steel, and glazed tiles from Baghdad to China. They returned with silk, paper, and porcelain. From India and Southeast Asia, they brought spices. In the markets of Baghdad, Cairo, and Córdoba, buyers could purchase rubies from Central Asia, honey and furs from Scandinavia and Russia, and ivory and gold from East Africa.

As trade grew, Muslim merchants developed new business practices. They set up banks at different trading centers. They issued letters of credit, which were easier and safer to carry than coins. They wrote receipts for payment and used bills of lading that listed all of the goods included in a shipment. Europeans later adopted many of these practices, which are still used by businesses today.

Advances in learning. Respect for learning led to a flowering of Islamic civilization. Islamic scholars translated ancient works from Persian, Sanskrit, and Greek into Arabic. In 830, the caliph Al-Mamun set up the House of Wisdom in Baghdad. It served as a library, university, and translation center. At centers like this, Muslim scholars preserved the learning of earlier civilizations. They also made many contributions of their own.

Brilliant Muslim scholars boasted accomplishments in many fields. The astronomer Al-Khwarizimi, for example, made advances in the field of algebra. The mathematician and astronomer Omar Khayyám (OH mahr kī YAHM) developed an accurate calendar, but he is best known to the western world as the author of the poem *The Rubáiyát.* The physician Ibn Sina—known in the West as Avicenna—wrote more than 100 books on subjects ranging from astronomy, music, and philosophy to medicine and poetry. His medical textbook influenced Europeans for hundreds of years.

Today, western languages use many technical terms that are of Arabic origin. This lasting mark of Arab learning on the West includes terms like zenith in astronomy, alcohol and alkali in chemistry, and soda and syrup in medicine.

SECTION 1 REVIEW

1. **Locate:** (a) Mecca, (b) Medina, (c) Damascus, (d) Baghdad, (e) Córdoba.
2. **Identify:** (a) Muhammad, (b) Khadija, (c) Kaaba, (d) "people of the Book," (e) Umayyads, (f) Abbassids, (g) Ibn Sina.
3. **Define:** (a) hejira, (b) hajj, (c) caliph.
4. What are the Five Pillars of Islam?
5. Give three reasons for the rapid spread of Islam.
6. What issue divided Sunni and Shiite Muslims?
7. **Analyzing Ideas** Muhammad taught that "the ink of the scholar is holier than the blood of the martyr." (a) What do you think he meant? (b) How do you think this teaching contributed to Islamic civilization?
8. **Writing Across Cultures** Consult a dictionary. Write a sentence using each of the following words of Arabic origin: *algebra, genius, henna, mohair, mufti, sandal, sherbet.*

2 CENTURIES OF TURMOIL

FIND OUT

What changes did foreign invaders bring to the Middle East?

What were the strengths of the Ottoman Empire?

Why were the Ottoman and Safavid empires rivals?

Vocabulary crusade, millet, shah

By 900, the great Arab Empire forged in the years after Muhammad's death had broken up into many kingdoms. However, these kingdoms continued to develop as centers of Islamic civilization. Although foreign invaders set up their own kingdoms in the Middle

East, most of these invaders converted to Islam. Islamic civilization flourished despite the turmoil of war.

Foreign Invaders

Beginning in about 1000, waves of nomads from Central Asia overran the Middle East. Like earlier invaders, they sought to control the fertile lands of the Anatolian and Iranian plateaus and of Mesopotamia.

Seljuks. The Seljuks, a Turkish-speaking people, had converted to Islam in Central Asia before migrating to the Iranian Plateau. In 1055, the Seljuks seized Baghdad, but allowed the Abbassid caliph to remain on the throne as a figurehead. Moving west, they then captured Anatolia from the Byzantines. Their success weakened the Byzantine Empire and frightened the Christian rulers of Europe.

Mongols. During the 1200s, horse-riding Mongols charged out of Central Asia and swept westward into Russia and the Middle East. In 1258, Hulagu (hoo LAH goo), a grandson of the great Mongol leader Genghiz Khan, captured Baghdad from the Seljuks. The Mongols looted and destroyed the city, burning its palaces, mosques, and libraries and killing the last of the Abbassid caliphs.

The Mongol invasions continued on and off for more than 100 years. Their armies destroyed many cities and irrigation systems. Millions of people were killed. Some areas of the Middle East did not fully recover from the effects of the Mongol invasions until many centuries later.

Despite the terrible destruction, the Mongol conquests spurred international trade. Mongols controlled the major trade routes between China, India, and the Middle East. Eventually, the Mongols converted to Islam and were absorbed into the cultures of the Middle East.

Crusaders

A third group of outsiders invaded the Middle East from Europe. As the Seljuks advanced into Asia Minor, the Byzantine emperor called on the Christian states of Western Europe for help. Despite the differences within the Christian Church, Pope Urban II responded. In 1095, he called for a crusade, or holy war, against the Muslims. "It is the will of God," cried Christian warriors from France, England, Germany, and Italy as they advanced into the Middle East. Their goal was to capture Palestine. Christians called it the Holy Land because Jesus had lived and died there.

For almost 200 years, Christians poured into Palestine in a movement that became known as the Crusades. On the First Crusade in 1096, crusaders helped the Byzantine emperor recover much of Anatolia. They went on to conquer Jerusalem, slaughtering Mus-

Crusaders Attacking Jerusalem European rulers answered the pope's call for a crusade to reconquer the Holy Land. In 1099, crusaders finally reached Jerusalem, where they besieged the Muslims and Jews. In this painting, Christian armies storm the city. ***Power*** Why were the European soldiers unable to win a lasting victory in the Middle East?

lim and Jewish residents. They then set up four small Christian kingdoms along the Mediterranean coast.

The Crusades had only a limited effect on the Middle East. At the time, the civilization of Western Europe was less advanced than that of the Islamic world. In 1187, a brilliant Muslim general, Salah-al-Din—better known in the West as Saladin—drove the Christians out of Jerusalem. Christian armies managed to hold on to a few coastal cities for another century, but they never again posed a serious threat to Muslim lands. The Crusades did, however, have a major impact on Europe. (See Chapter 29.)

Saladin: A Noble Warrior

During the late 1100s, the Muslim world was united under a new leader, Saladin. Muslims and Christians alike came to respect Saladin as a noble knight. He was God-fearing, courteous, and generous to friends and enemies—traits admired by warriors of both religions.

For the Muslims, Saladin was a badly needed leader. He united Muslims from Syria and Egypt, surrounded the crusader kingdoms, and forced the foreigners to retreat. As he approached Jerusalem, the Christians determined to stop him.

In July 1187, the crusaders gathered on the Horns of Hattin, a dry, rocky pass. The dust and intense summer heat choked both men and horses. Without water, they suffered terribly from thirst.

Under cover of darkness, Saladin moved his forces into the pass. At dawn, the Christians found themselves surrounded and greatly outnumbered. Saladin's forces set grass fires to smoke out the enemy. Then they attacked. The battle raged all day. Finally, exhausted by heat and thirst, the crusaders surrendered.

Saladin rejoiced, knowing that he had destroyed the crusaders' strength. Saladin's son, who was with him at Hattin, later recorded:

Saladin When this great Muslim military leader recaptured Jerusalem in 1187, he dealt fairly with Christians and Jews there. However, European rulers soon sent another army to recapture the holy city. This Third Crusade ended in failure. Saladin then ruled Palestine as well as Egypt and Syria. ***Fine Art*** How has the artist suggested Saladin's character?

> "My father immediately got down from his horse, prostrated himself before God and gave thanks to Him, weeping tears of joy."

Saladin pressed forward. By October, he stood outside Jerusalem, a city as sacred to Muslims as it was to Jews and Christians. Christian forces knew that they could not hold out, so they surrendered.

Saladin's entrance into Jerusalem differed completely from the Christian conquest of the city 88 years earlier. A crusader who had witnessed the savage massacres in 1099 said that "men rode in blood up to their knees and bridle reins." Saladin, by contrast, forbade his soldiers to kill the inhabitants of the city or steal from the defeated crusaders. He also issued orders against burning Christian homes or churches.

In Muslim lands, as elsewhere, it was the custom for people who had been defeated in war to become the slaves of the victorious army. Yet, Saladin treated his former enemies well. He freed old people and allowed other Christians to buy their freedom. He even used money from his own treasury to help the widows and orphans of crusaders who had been killed in battle.

As Christians marched out of Jerusalem, Muslims raised the golden banner of Saladin above the city walls. They joyfully reclaimed the Dome of the Rock, the holy mosque that Christians had converted into a church. Ibn al-Athir, who witnessed the event, described the great rejoicing that occurred:

> “There was on the dome . . . a great cross of gold. The day the town surrendered, many Muslims climbed up to pull it down. . . . When the cross fell, cries arose from everyone in the town and the surrounding districts. . . . The noise was such that one might have thought that the end of the world had come.”

Thanks to Saladin, Muslims were once more masters of the holy city of Jerusalem. ■

Ottoman Empire

During the early 1300s, a powerful people, the Ottomans, emerged in Anatolia. Like the Seljuks, the Ottomans were a Turkish-speaking people from Central Asia who had converted to Islam. The Ottomans conquered an enormous empire that extended from central Europe across much of the Middle East and North Africa.

In 1453, the Ottomans stunned Christian Europe by capturing Constantinople, ending the 1,000-year-old Byzantine Empire. The Ottomans renamed the city Istanbul and made it the capital of their expanding empire.

The Ottoman Empire reached its height under Suleiman I (soo lay mahn), who ruled from 1520 to 1566. Suleiman made Istanbul one of the world's most splendid cities, adorning it with large, beautiful mosques and filling it with art treasures. He also introduced many reforms to ensure justice and good government for the 50 million people under Ottoman rule. His reforms earned him the title the Lawgiver.

Government. The Ottoman Empire lasted for more than 500 years. During this time, the Ottomans held their diverse empire together with a strong but flexible government.

At the head of the government was the sultan, who ruled with absolute power. He relied on a large number of officials to supervise the government of the vast empire. These officials came from two groups, the "men of the pen" and the "men of the sword." The first group included lawyers, judges, mathematicians, and poets. Some were experts in Islamic law who ruled on religious and legal matters. The second group were soldiers who guarded the sultan and fought in his armies. The men of the sword were made up of slaves.

Role of slaves. The Ottomans looked on the peoples they conquered as slaves. They took young Christian boys from their families to be trained for jobs in government and the military. When a slave converted to Islam, he gained his freedom.

When the training was over, those who had displayed a talent for book learning and mathematics were trained in the palace school as royal pages. The brightest moved up in the sultan's service and became provincial governors or even grand vizier, as the chief minister was called. Those who excelled in sports and the martial arts became cadets in the Janizary corps, elite military units that guarded the sultan and his palace.

The millets. Within the Ottoman Empire, each province had its own local government. Non-Muslim communities, called millets, owed loyalty to the sultan but were ruled by their own religious leaders. Jews, Armenian Christians, and Greek Orthodox Christians were among the many millets that made up the Ottoman Empire.

The Safavid Empire

By the 1500s, the chief rival of the Ottoman Empire in the Middle East was the Safavid Empire in what is today Iran. The two powers waged bloody battles for control of Mesopotamia. Religious disputes added to the conflict. The Safavids were fiercely loyal to Shiite traditions, while the Ottomans were Sunni Muslims.

Abbas the Great. The Safavid Empire reached its height under Abbas the Great, who ruled from 1587 to 1629. Earlier Safavid shahs, or kings, had despised non-Shiites. However, Abbas welcomed them to his court.

Safavid Court Musicians Playing a lute, panpipes, and a large tambourine, these musicians welcome a Mughal ruler from India. Foreigners admired the culture, prosperity, and toleration of the Safavid Empire under Abbas the Great. One French visitor later wrote, "When this great prince ceased to live, Persia [Iran] ceased to prosper." ***Change*** Was the French visitor's observation accurate? Explain.

European rulers were eager to make alliances with the shah against the Ottomans. For example, one group of English experts helped Abbas train an army to use muskets and also taught the Iranians how to make cannons.

Shah Abbas encouraged trade and commerce. Like the Ottoman rulers, he built a network of roads that had inns for travelers and rest stops for caravans. To take advantage of the growing demand for Chinese porcelain in Europe, he brought hundreds of Chinese potters to his capital at Isfahan (ihs fuh HAHN). Under Abbas, Iranians produced fine-quality goods such as silk, woolen carpets, steel, porcelain, and glassware.

Decline. After Abbas, the empire declined. In 1736, the last of the Safavids was overthrown. Other dynasties gained power for short periods. Iran remained under the rule of a shah, however, until 1979. Today, it survives as a major Shiite state, the Islamic republic of Iran.

SECTION 2 REVIEW

1. **Locate:** (a) Jerusalem, (b) Constantinople, (c) Iran.
2. **Identify:** (a) Seljuk, (b) Holy Land, (c) Saladin, (d) Suleiman I, (e) Abbas.
3. **Define:** (a) crusade, (b) millet, (c) shah.
4. (a) List three groups of outsiders who invaded the Middle East. (b) Describe one change that was brought by each group.
5. Describe how the Ottomans treated the diverse groups who made up their empire.
6. What two issues led to war between the Ottoman and Safavid empires?
7. **Drawing Conclusions** How do you think centuries of invasion by outsiders contributed to cultural diffusion in the Middle East?
8. **Writing Across Cultures** Are officials of the United States government divided into "men of the pen" and "men of the sword"? Write a paragraph explaining your answer.

3

PATTERNS OF LIFE

FIND OUT

What were the main patterns of life in the Middle East?

What was the typical Middle Eastern city like?

What roles did women have in Islam?

Five times a day, from the top of mosques throughout the Muslim world, the muezzin (myoo EHZ ihn), or crier, calls the faithful to prayer:

> " God alone is great.
> I testify that there is no god but God.
> I testify that Muhammad is the messenger of God.
> Come to prayer.
> Come to success.
> God alone is great.
> There is no god but God. "

Since the 600s, Islam has been a major force in shaping the patterns of life in the Middle East. However, as everywhere in the world, geography has played a role in shaping people's lives. Across the Middle East, people adapted to the resources available in the places where they lived. There were farmers in the villages, nomadic herders in the deserts, and merchants and traders in the towns and cities.

Village Life

Most people in the Middle East lived in small farming villages that grew up around sources of water. From one generation to the next, villagers cultivated the land and raised wheat, barley, and olives. In places with a good supply of water, they also grew vegetables and fruits. Some villagers tended herds of sheep and goats in nearby pasturelands.

Farm families divided their labor. Men and boys did the plowing, harvested the crops, and built the houses. Women drew water from the well, fed the animals, gathered wood for fuel, did the spinning and weaving, and cared for the children. Women also worked in the fields. For example, they walked behind the plow and broke up clods of dirt that the plow missed.

Villages included a mosque and a few stores that sold spices, sugar, and other goods that people did not produce themselves. Most houses were made of sun-dried mud, clay bricks, or timber and had only one or two rooms. A section of every house, no

Plowing Fields Middle Eastern farmers made important contributions to agriculture. For example, when the Arabs conquered Spain, they introduced sugar cane into Europe. Arabs also were the first to grow coffee as a crop. ***Technology*** Do you think this painting tries to show a real Arab farmer at work? Explain.

matter how small, was set aside as the women's quarters. When men outside the immediate family visited, the women remained secluded in their quarters.

Villagers distrusted outside authority. A story from Ottoman times tells what happened when the tax collector arrived in a village. When the tax collector summoned a resident, the village leader instructed the man's son:

> "Go to your father, my lad, and tell him that the tax collector is waiting here for him. If your father isn't there, tell him to come all the same, for the tax collector knows that he is there."

Nomadic Life

Lack of water made much of the Middle East unsuitable for farming. In the desert and dry plateaus, nomadic herders learned to live with scarce water resources. Nomads were constantly on the move with herds of camels, goats, and other livestock. Their movements were purposeful. They traveled to areas where seasonal rains caused plants to grow.

The Bedouins. In Arabia, desert nomads were called Bedouins (BEHD oo ihnz), or "people of the tent." They lived in small, tightly knit tribal groups that competed for pastures and water holes. They spent the hot, dry summer at oases. During the winter, when there was some rainfall, they migrated in search of pastureland for their herds of sheep, goats, and camels.

Highland nomads. In the mountains and plateaus of the Northern Tier, nomads followed a different pattern. During the summer, they moved with their herds from the parched plains into cool upland pastures where they could find water and grass for their flocks. During the winter, when snows covered the uplands, they returned to the plains.

Conflicts with settled peoples. Many villagers and traders regarded the Bedouins and other nomadic herders as lawless warriors. Groups of nomads sometimes raided houses and shops in nearby towns. Their herds often grazed on villagers' crops or trampled them. Some nomads required trade caravans to pay tribute before they could pass through certain territories.

Nomads also aroused the anger of powerful central governments. Officials found it difficult to collect taxes from people who were always on the move. At times, governments used harsh measures to force nomads to settle permanently in one place.

City Life

Many cities flourished in the powerful empires of the Middle East. These cities developed for different reasons. Jerusalem had been the capital of ancient Israel. Damascus was a trading center on a key caravan route. Powerful caliphs built Cairo and Baghdad as their capitals. Mecca remained the religious center of Islam. Beirut was a prosperous seaport.

Like most other cities of the time, Middle Eastern cities were protected by high walls. The city streets were dark, narrow, and winding, the houses densely packed together. Shuttered upper stories often jutted out over the streets, blocking sunlight. The ground floors of many houses served as shops. Owners painted pious Muslim phrases, such as "May God forgive the faithful of Islam," above doorways.

Mosques were at the center of life in Muslim communities. The mosques served as meeting places, centers of study, and inns for travelers.

The commercial heart of the city was the *suq* (sook), or marketplace. It included a network of covered streets filled with shops. Often, each trade had its own section, and streets were named for the goods that were made and sold there. *Suq as suf*, for example, was the wool market, while *suq an nahas* was the copper market. On any day of the year, women, farmers from mountain villages, and nomadic Bedouins, as well as merchants and traders, flocked to the suq.

Family Life

As in many other cultures around the world, the family in the Middle East was patriarchal. The father had the final say on all

A Family Celebration A wealthy Muslim family is celebrating a special occasion—the birth of a child. At the top, women care for the new mother and her child. Below them are musicians, a servant with food, and a man handing out coins. At the bottom, a crowd gathers to receive alms. ***Fine Art*** What does this painting tell you about social classes in Muslim society?

matters. Women usually sought their husband's approval, and children were expected to obey their parents.

The Koran acknowledges the authority of parents. Only obedience to God is considered more important than the respect that children owe their parents.

Marriage. As elsewhere in the world at this time, marriages were arranged. They usually occurred between families that belonged to the same social class or between families that followed the same trade or profession. Although a Muslim man could marry a Christian or Jewish woman, tradition forbade a Muslim woman to marry a non-Muslim.

The Koran permits a man to have as many as four wives, as long as he treats each of them equally. This means that he must give them all the same material benefits, the same amount of love, and the same degree of respect. Since few men could afford to support several wives, most men had only a single wife.

Divorce. Divorce was easier for men than for women. To divorce his wife, a man had to recite on three separate occcasions, "I divorce you." He also had to make a payment to her or to her family. By contrast, a woman who wanted a divorce had to take her case before a judge. Both divorced men and women could remarry, however.

Lives of Women

Among Muslims, tradition and customs made women subordinate to men. According to the Koran, "Men are the managers of the affairs of women." During childhood, a girl had to obey her father. After marriage, she had to obey her husband and her husband's father.

Muslims believed that women were more likely than men to bring dishonor on the family. Women were expected to be modest and to remain secluded within the home. They wore veils to conceal their faces from men who were not members of their family. In some Muslim homes, women used separate entrances and ate their meals only in the company of other women.

The system gave women security. Women in Islamic societies knew that their fathers, brothers, or husbands would protect and provide for them. Also, within their homes and with their children, many women exercised considerable influence. According to an Arab proverb,

> "If a woman loves you, she can open countless doors to you, but if she hates you, with a spider's web she can build an iron wall across your path."

Rights. Islam gave women protections that they had not had in the past. During pre-Islamic times, for example, poor Arab families frequently killed unwanted girl babies. The Koran outlawed this practice. Under Islamic law, women also gained the right to an education and to own or inherit property. Finally, although the Koran made women subordinate to men, women, like all believers, were equal in the eyes of God.

In early Islamic societies, women had enjoyed greater freedom than they sometimes did at a later time. Customs such as wearing a veil, living in seclusion, and separating men and women in all activities came into practice gradually. In fact, some scholars think the Arabs adapted some of those practices from the Byzantines whose lands they conquered. In many Muslim lands outside the Middle East, women did not observe these customs.

SECTION 3 REVIEW

1. **Identify:** (a) Bedouin, (b) suq.
2. Describe three different ways of life that developed in the Middle East.
3. (a) Why did nomads come into conflict with settled peoples? (b) With the central government?
4. (a) Name three Middle Eastern cities and give the reasons they developed. (b) Describe a typical Middle Eastern city.
5. (a) Identify two ways in which Islam expanded women's rights. (b) Identify two ways in which it restricted them.
6. **Defending a Position** Explain why you agree or disagree with the following statement: "By and large, women benefited from the rise of Islam."
7. **Writing Across Cultures** Compare the role of women in early Islam to the role of women in the United States today. Write a paragraph noting similarities or differences.

4 IMPERIALISM AND NATIONALISM

FIND OUT

What challenges did the Ottoman Empire face?

How did imperialism spur the growth of nationalism in the Middle East?

What reforms did nationalist leaders introduce?

Vocabulary mandate, anti-Semitism

Ismail, the ruler of Egypt, beamed with pleasure. The lavish spectacle was going exactly as planned. Cannons roared, bands played, and the crowd cheered. Dozens of ships bearing monarchs and diplomats steamed into the waterway. At 8 A.M. on November 17, 1869, the Suez Canal was officially opened.

In ancient times, Egyptian pharaohs began digging a canal that would link the Mediterranean with the Red Sea. More than 2,000 years later, a French company finally completed the task. Under the supervision of Ferdinand de Lesseps, Egyptian workers labored for nearly 11 years to dig the 100-mile (160-km) Suez Canal. Even more than Egyptians, Europeans welcomed the canal because it reduced the ocean voyage to Asia by thousands of miles.

By the late 1800s, European influence in the Middle East was growing. The Suez Canal was a symbol of that influence. During the Age of Imperialism, European interference in the Middle East would spur the growth of nationalist movements whose effects are still being felt today.

Challenges to Ottoman Power

During the 1700s and 1800s, European imperialism and growing nationalism posed major challenges to the Ottoman Empire. Russia and Austria-Hungary nibbled away at Ottoman provinces in Europe. At the same time, national groups within the empire sought independence from Ottoman rule. The Greeks revolted and won freedom in 1832. Later, other ethnic groups, including the Serbs, Romanians, and Bulgarians, won independence or at least some degree of self-rule.

Russia encouraged these groups to revolt against their Ottoman rulers. It hoped to gain more lands from a weakened Ottoman Empire. France and Britain, however, became alarmed at Russia's ambitions. They tried to prevent the breakup of the Ottoman Empire. Noting the many troubles of the Ottoman Empire, Europeans began to call it the "sick man of Europe."

Reform efforts. During the 1800s, powerful sultans tried to strengthen the empire. They introduced reforms to modernize the government and the army along western lines. They also set up secular, or nonreligious, schools to teach students western ideas in science and technology.

Reform did not go smoothly, however. Some sultans refused reformers' demands for a constitution. Corrupt officials, religious leaders, and other groups opposed changes that threatened their power.

Turkish nationalism. In the late 1800s, a number of young army officers formed a revolutionary group known as the Young Turks. The Young Turks wanted to strengthen the Ottoman Empire and end western imperialism. In 1908, they overthrew the sultan. They placed a new sultan in power, and forced him to carry out their program.

The Young Turks supported a policy of Turkish nationalism. They abandoned traditional Ottoman tolerance of diverse cultures and religions. Instead, they persecuted non-Muslim communities. For example, the Young Turks greatly distrusted Armenian Christians, who had ties with Russia. The Young Turks followed a brutal policy of genocide that caused the death of hundreds of thousands of Armenians.

Despite their shared religion, the Young Turks stressed differences between Turks and Muslim Arabs within the empire. They tried to impose the Turkish language on Arabs and mistreated Arabs in many other ways. These actions fueled growing Arab nationalism.

World War I. During World War I, the Ottoman Empire sided with Germany against Russia, Britain, and France. Defeat brought disaster to the empire. In 1919, at the Versailles peace conference, the Allies stripped the Ottoman Empire of its Arab provinces. Britain received Iraq, Transjordan, and Palestine as mandates. A mandate was a territory that was administered but not owned by a member of the League of Nations. France gained a mandate in Syria and Lebanon.

Republic of Turkey

Shortly after World War I ended, Greece seized land that was ruled by the Turks in Anatolia. A brilliant general, Mustafa Kemal, rallied Turkish resistance to the Greek advance. After bloody clashes, the Turks succeeded in driving the Greeks out of Anatolia. By 1923, Kemal had become strong enough to overthrow the sultan, abolish the Ottoman Empire, and make Turkey a republic. He later took the name Kemal Atatürk, or "father of the Turks."

Atatürk's reforms. As president of Turkey, Atatürk continued the reforms begun under the Ottomans. He was determined to make Turkey a modern secular state. To encourage economic development, he used government funds to build industries. He also insisted on the separation of religion and the government. For example, he replaced Islamic law with a new law code based on western models. Under the new laws, women won the right to vote and hold public office. He also set up a system of public schools that were separate from religious schools.

To Atatürk, modernization meant adopting many features of western culture. Turkey began to use the western calendar and the metric system of weights and measures.

Atatürk replaced Arabic script with the western alphabet. As a symbol of change, he encouraged western-style clothing. Men were forbidden to wear the fez, their traditional brimless felt hat. Also, women were forbidden to veil their faces in public.

Atatürk's reforms brought many important changes. They were not always popular, however. He had the support of Turkish nationalists, but many Muslims opposed his policies. They feared that western ways would destroy their traditions and values.

Rise of Modern Egypt

During the Age of Imperialism, other parts of the Ottoman Empire came under European control. Egypt became the focus of imperialist rivalry between Britain and France. Both nations wanted to dominate Egypt and build a canal across the Isthmus of Suez. Whoever held the canal would control shipping and trade between Europe and Asia.

In 1798, the French general Napoleon Bonaparte invaded Egypt. Joining forces, the British and Ottomans forced the French to retreat. French influence, however, remained strong in Egyptian culture.

Muhammad Ali. In 1805, Muhammad Ali, an Albanian soldier who had fought against the French, became governor of Egypt. Officially, Egypt was still a part of the Ottoman Empire. In fact, Ali pursued his own policies.

Ali introduced many reforms to modernize Egypt. He invited French experts to train Egyptians in the latest European military and scientific techniques. He also introduced new farming methods, improved irrigation, and promoted the growing of cash crops such as cotton, sugar, and tobacco. Before long, cotton exports were booming, and Egypt itself was setting up textile mills.

Growing foreign influence. Ali's successors continued his policies, but they had to borrow money from European banks in order to pay for them. The increasing debts gave France and Britain an excuse to interfere in Egypt's internal affairs.

Atatürk and His Wife Atatürk broke with the tradition of arranged marriages by choosing his wife himself. His wife, Latifah, accompanied him on many official trips in Turkey. Among the changes supported by Atatürk were new laws that discouraged the practice of segregating women in public places. ***Change*** Why did Atatürk's reforms stir controversy?

During this period, the French won the right to build the Suez Canal. Faced with huge debts, the Egyptian ruler, Ismail, sold his shares in the canal to the British. As Egypt's financial problems worsened, Britain and France took control of its economy.

Outraged at this foreign intervention, Egyptians rebelled. British forces crushed the rebels and occupied the country in 1882. Both Muslims and Egyptian Christians, known as Copts, supported efforts to end British

Opening Day of the Suez Canal The Egyptians celebrated the opening of the canal in 1869 as a symbol of progress. Yet, the canal led to British occupation of Egypt in 1882. ***Power*** How was the canal a symbol of European imperialism in the Middle East?

control. Although Egypt declared its independence from Britain in 1922, the Suez Canal remained in British hands until 1956. (See Chapter 27.)

Struggle for Iran

Like the Ottomans, the rulers of Iran faced the challenge of European imperialism. Both Russia and Britain acquired spheres of influence in Iran. Both nations were competing for influence elsewhere in Asia, and each sought access to the Persian Gulf.

During the Age of Imperialism, the shahs who ruled Iran were weak, and their governments lacked the power to resist European expansion. By the early 1900s, however, Iranian nationalists were demanding reform. In 1925, Reza Khan, an army officer supported by some nationalists, seized power. He set up the Pahlavi dynasty and made himself shah.

Like nationalist leaders elsewhere, Reza Khan set out to end foreign control and create a modern industrial state. He built roads and factories, modernized the army, and reduced the power of the Muslim clergy.

Under the Pahlavis, westernization increased. In the cities, men and women adopted western clothing. Women gained more freedom to move about in public. In addition, schools emphasized western courses of study, and the government used western models for its law code.

Arab Nationalism

World War I fueled Arab nationalism in the lands controlled by the Ottomans. During the war, some Arabs helped the British fight the Ottomans. In return, they expected the British to help them set up independent kingdoms after the war.

The Arabs felt betrayed by the peace settlement that ended World War I. Britain and France gained control of many Arab lands that had been part of the Ottoman Empire. Only in Saudi Arabia did an Arab ruler gain independence.

Throughout the 1920s and 1930s, Arab nationalists continued their demands for self-rule. The growing importance of oil from the Middle East, however, made Britain and France unwilling to withdraw from the region. Still, in 1932, Iraq gained independence. Lebanon won its freedom in 1943, and Syria became independent in 1945.

Conflict Over Palestine

During the 1920s and 1930s, the British mandate of Palestine became the center of conflict between Jewish and Arab nationalists.

Zionism. During the late 1800s, persecution of Jews led to the modern form of Zionism. This movement sought to reestablish a Jewish state in Palestine. As you read in Chapter 25, the Romans had expelled the Jews from Palestine in A.D. 70. Since then, Jews had dreamed of returning. The desire for a Jewish homeland grew as anti-Semitism, or hatred and fear of Jews, increased. In Eastern Europe and Russia, thousands of Jews were killed in organized massacres. The violence led many European Jews to migrate to Palestine.

In 1897, Theodor Herzl (HER tsuhl), an Austrian Jew, formed an organization to promote Zionism. With his encouragement, Jews from Eastern Europe began to migrate to Palestine. They set up communities there and called on Britain and other European powers to support them. In 1917, the British government issued the Balfour Declaration. The key paragraph declared:

> "His Majesty's Government views with favour the establishment in Palestine of a national home for the Jewish people . . . it being clearly understood that nothing shall be done which may prejudice the civil and religious rights of existing non-Jewish communities in Palestine. . . ."

MAP STUDY

After the Ottoman Empire was defeated in World War I, Britain and France gained control of lands in the Middle East.

1. **Location** (a) Where were the British mandates? The French mandates? (b) Which Middle Eastern countries or territories did each nation rule?
2. **Region** How did Palestine became a center of conflict between the Arabs and European Jews?
3. **Applying Information** "During the early 1900s, Arab nationalism became a powerful force that reshaped the Middle East." Explain the meaning of this statement.

Early Jewish Settlers in Palestine In 1922, two years after this photograph was taken, Palestine's first census recorded a Jewish population of 84,000—11 percent of the total. Many early immigrants set up cooperative farms, called *kibbutzim*, where people owned all property in common. ***Human Rights*** What were the roots of Zionism?

Arab response. The "existing non-Jewish communities" were those of the Palestinian Arabs. At the time, Arabs—both Christian and Muslim—greatly outnumbered Jewish settlers in Palestine. Like other Arabs, Palestinians wanted their own independent state.

During the 1930s, Jewish immigration increased as anti-Semitism worsened in Europe. As a result, tensions between Arabs and Jews in Palestine heightened. Zionist groups helped Jews to buy land from Arab landowners. Often, these Arab landowners lived in the cities. They did not farm the land and were happy to make a good profit by selling it.

Arabs who worked the land as tenant farmers were suddenly forced to leave. Many migrated to the cities. Since they had no money or education and few skills beyond farming, they faced severe hardship.

Angry, landless Arab peasants joined other Arabs in attacking Jewish settlements. In response, Jewish settlers struck back. Eventually, the conflict in Palestine erupted into war, as you will read in Chapter 28. (See Connections With Literature, page 807, "The Diameter of the Bomb.")

SECTION 4 REVIEW

1. **Identify:** (a) Zionism, (b) Theodor Herzl, (c) Balfour Declaration.
2. **Define:** (a) mandate, (b) anti-Semitism.
3. (a) How did European imperialism affect the Ottoman Empire? (b) What happened to the Ottoman Empire after World War I?
4. What developments encouraged the rise of nationalism in (a) Egypt, (b) Iran, (c) Arab lands?
5. How did each of the following leaders try to modernize his country: (a) Atatürk, (b) Muhammad Ali, (c) Reza Khan?
6. What two groups claimed the right to live in Palestine?
7. **Understanding Causes and Effects** How did Turkish nationalism fuel the rise of Arab nationalism?
8. **Writing Across Cultures** Imagine that you are a Panamanian. Write a letter to a friend in Egypt comparing the role of the United States in building and controlling the Panama Canal with that of European nations in building and controlling the Suez Canal.

CHAPTER 26 REVIEW

Understanding Vocabulary

Match each term at left with the correct definition at right.

1. hejira
2. hajj
3. crusade
4. mandate
5. anti-Semitism

a. hatred of Jews
b. pilgrimage to Mecca
c. Christian holy war against the Muslims
d. territory administered but not owned by a member of the League of Nations
e. Muhammad's migration to Medina from Mecca

Reviewing the Main Ideas

1. Why did the people of Mecca oppose Muhammad at first?

2. What were three major contributions of Muslim civilization?

3. (a) Why did Christian crusaders invade the Middle East? (b) Why did the Crusades have a limited effect on the Middle East?

4. Describe the contributions of (a) Saladin, (b) Suleiman I, (c) Abbas.

5. (a) What way of life did most people in the Middle East follow? (b) How was work divided among family members?

6. Why did Europeans call the Ottoman Empire the "sick man of Europe"?

7. How did Britain and France gain power in Egypt?

8. Why did many Arabs feel betrayed by the peace settlement that ended World War I?

9. (a) How did Jewish immigration cause tension in Palestine? (b) What was the result of this tension?

Reviewing Chapter Themes

1. Islam arose in the Middle East during the 600s and spread rapidly. Discuss the reasons for Islam's appeal.

2. Islam united and shaped the culture of the Arab Empire. How did each of the following contribute to the unity of Islam: (a) Arabic language, (b) Koran, (c) Five Pillars?

3. Non-Arab invaders brought many changes to the Middle East. Describe two changes caused by each of the following: (a) Mongols, (b) Ottomans, (c) Safavids.

4. After World War I, nationalism became a major force in the Middle East. Choose one country discussed in the chapter. For that country, (a) identify a nationalist leader or group, (b) describe one nationalist goal, (c) describe an action taken to achieve that goal.

Thinking Critically

1. Making Global Connections Islam has been a unifying force in the Middle East. (a) What force or forces unified the United States during its early history? (b) Is there a unifying force in the United States today? Explain.

2. Analyzing Information Why do you think religious leaders in the Middle East objected to some programs for westernization?

Applying Your Skills

1. Analyzing a Painting Study the painting of Damascus on page 573. What impression does the artist convey about life in a Middle Eastern city? (See Skill Lesson, page 428.)

2. Using Your Vocabulary Use the Glossary on pages 794–803 to review the meaning of the following terms: *imperialism, nationalism, westernization, secular, mandate.* Use each term in a separate sentence about the Middle East after World War I.

Chapter 27

The Middle East in Transition

Chapter Outline

Istanbul This city, which lies partly in Europe and partly in Asia, has a long, rich history. More than 2,500 years ago, Greeks founded a colony called Byzantium on the site of present-day Istanbul. It was later the capital first of the Byzantine Empire and then of the Ottoman Empire. Today, Istanbul is the largest city and seaport in Turkey. ***Geography*** What makes Istanbul's location so strategic?

Despite the July heat, thousands of Egyptians crowded into the main square of Alexandria. They cheered as their president, Gamal Abdel Nasser, denounced European domination of Egypt. Then, as he complained that the Suez Canal was still controlled by Britain and France, Nasser seemed to lose his place. "Lesseps, Lesseps," he said, loudly repeating the name of the French engineer who had designed the canal.

The Frenchman's name was a signal. Egyptian troops, listening on the radio, swung into action when they heard it. Soldiers burst into the canal offices and ordered French and British officials to turn on the radio. The astonished officials heard Nasser thunder:

> "The sovereign state of Egypt will run the canal. The Suez Canal belongs to us. . . . The canal was built by Egyptians. . . . The canal will be run by Egyptians, Egyptians, Egyptians!"

Egypt's seizure of the Suez Canal in 1956 led to war. British, French, and Israeli armies invaded Egypt, but in the end Egypt kept control of the canal. Nasser's bold action made him a hero in the Arab world. By taking over the canal, he toppled the last symbol of European imperialism in the Middle East.

CHAPTER PERSPECTIVE

During the 1950s, nationalism was a powerful force in the Middle East. Although many Middle Eastern nations had won their political independence, they resented economic domination by foreign powers. Strong-willed leaders like Nasser moved forcefully to erase all traces of colonialism and set their countries on the road to modernization.

As you read, look for these chapter themes:

- Arab nationalism and Islamic fundamentalism reflected the desire of the Muslim nations of the Middle East to end western domination.
- Middle Eastern governments have taken a strong role in planning and supervising economic development.
- Oil wealth has divided the Middle East into rich and poor nations.
- Rapid population growth and urbanization have brought changes to the Middle East.
- Iran, Egypt, and Turkey each followed its own route toward modernization.

Literature Connections

For literature suggestions, see Connections With Literature, pages 804–808.

1 POLITICAL DIRECTIONS

FIND OUT

What role has pan-Arabism played in the Middle East?

What different kinds of government have emerged in the Middle East?

Why did civil war break out in Lebanon?

What changes do Islamic fundamentalists seek?

As a high school student, Gamal Abdel Nasser worked actively in Egypt's nationalist movement. He believed nationalism would help "rebuild the country so that the weak and humiliated Egyptian people [could] rise up again and live as free and independent men."

After World War II, a strong sense of national pride emerged among the newly independent nations of the Middle East. Nationalists revived memories of the great Arab empires that had ruled the Middle East in the centuries after Muhammad. They called on Arabs to join forces and free themselves of domination by the West.

Pan-Arabism

By 1950, most Middle Eastern nations had won independence. Yet, they still felt the effects of western imperialism. Their borders had been drawn by Europeans, and their economies depended on the West. Although Muslims wanted western technology, some bitterly opposed the growing influence of western culture.

Goals. During the early years after independence, some nationalists turned to pan-Arabism. This movement sought to unite all Arabs based on their common language and culture. To promote Arab unity, nationalists formed the Arab League in 1945.

Arab nationalists believed that a unified Arab state would be a major world power. Such a state would be strong enough to end European domination of the Middle East.

Various Arab leaders tried to make pan-Arabism work. In 1958, Egypt's president, Gamal Abdel Nasser, organized Egypt and Syria into the United Arab Republic. The new nation was short-lived, however. Within three years, Syria broke away, charging that Egypt was dominating the union.

Obstacles to unity. Although many leaders talked about a shared Arab culture, state nationalism proved to be stronger than pan-Arab unity. In Syria, Lebanon, Jordan, Egypt, and Iraq, people felt greater loyalty to their own country than to an ideal Arab state. Each state pursued its own national goals.

Pan-Arabism faced other obstacles. Arab lands included many ethnic and religious groups that opposed the creation of an Arab state. In addition, Arab lands had no geographic unity. They included settlements scattered across a wide area. An economic gap between rich and poor nations as well as rivalries within the Arab world created other stumbling blocks.

Although Arab states failed to unite, pan-Arabism remains a goal of some Arab leaders. Calls for Arab unity continue to be heard in the Middle East.

Political Traditions

In general, the period after independence was a time of experimentation as Middle Eastern nations struggled to define their individual identities. Most states built powerful central governments. In some, strongman rulers emerged.

Forms of government. Most Middle Eastern nations today are republics, though in some dictators hold power. At independence, many nations were monarchies. Some, like Egypt, Iraq, and Iran, later became republics. Others retained monarchies. Saudi Arabia and Jordan, for example, are ruled by kings.

The degree to which citizens participate in government varies greatly from one country to another. Saudi Arabia has a king who has absolute power. Although the king consults with members of the royal family, his decrees are law. Saudi Arabia has never held elections. On the other hand, Jordan is a constitutional monarchy. It has an elected parliament, although the king holds most of the power.

Turkey and Israel are multiparty states that hold free elections. However, in these countries, as elsewhere, certain groups are denied civil or human rights. By contrast, in both Syria and Iraq, a strongman ruler and a single party, the Baath party, dominate. Iraqi president, Saddam Hussein, has brutally si-

King Fahd of Saudi Arabia The king, at left, holds *majlis,* or audiences, where his subjects can ask for assistance. Royal princes and government officials grant similar audiences to as many as 300 people a day. Requests might involve a daughter's dowry or arranging a trip abroad for medical treatment. ***Political System*** How might majlis help the king protect his absolute power?

lenced critics and crushed opposition groups. Although the Baathists have used terror to stay in power, they also have the support of some groups who have benefited from their social and economic policies.

Islamic law. In the past, Islam was both the religion and, in theory, the basis of government in the Middle East. The Koran is the highest authority for the *Shariah* (shuh REE uh), or sacred law of Islam. The Shariah claimed to govern all aspects of Muslim life. It sought to set rules for political, social, and economic behavior.

Today, the Shariah remains the law code in a few Middle Eastern countries, including Saudi Arabia and Iran. Countries such as Egypt, Syria, Turkey, and Iraq have adopted western-style, secular law codes. Even so, the Shariah has shaped legal ideas in these countries, too. Since the early 1970s, Muslim religious leaders have become a powerful political force that can influence governments and public opinion.

Beirut Under Siege More than 150,000 were killed in Lebanon's long civil war. The fighting devastated the capital city of Beirut, the home of half of the population. Constant fighting between Muslims and Christians reduced entire neighborhoods to rubble. ***Diversity*** How did Lebanon's ethnic diversity lead to civil war?

Challenges to Stability

Most Middle Eastern governments have faced many challenges to their rule. The causes of unrest vary. In Iran, Iraq, and Turkey, for example, minority ethnic groups like the Kurds have demanded self-rule. Religious diversity has fueled turmoil in some countries. Rapid population growth and urbanization also have created severe strains on limited government resources. In many countries, the majority of people are under the age of 18. Widespread poverty and illiteracy have added to discontent in many countries as well.

Conflict in Lebanon. In 1975, a bitter power struggle among rival groups plunged Lebanon into a bloody civil war. The conflict grew out of the constitution drawn up by the French before they left Lebanon in 1943.

The constitution divided power among the various Christian and Muslim groups that made up Lebanon's population. Christian groups included Maronite, Greek Orthodox, and Armenian Christians. Muslims were divided among the Sunni, Shiite, and Druse sects.

At independence, Maronite Christians were in the majority in Lebanon. The Sunni were the second-largest group, while Shiites ranked third. Under the constitution, Maronites were guaranteed the presidency and the largest number of seats in the legislature. The prime minister was a Sunni, and the speaker of the legislature was a Shiite.

Changing population. By the 1970s, Lebanon's population had changed. Shiites outnumbered Sunni, and Maronites had slipped to third place. Maronites, however, were determined to hold on to their power.

Other problems sharpened the conflict. Thousands of Palestinians who had fled their homeland in Israel lived in Lebanon. Most were Muslims. Some supported the Palestine Liberation Organization (PLO), which waged a guerrilla war against Israel from bases in Lebanon.

When Maronites attacked Palestinians in Lebanon, civil war broke out. Syria, Israel,

Iran, and even the United States became involved in the long struggle. The fighting destroyed Lebanon's once-prosperous economy. In the late 1980s, the Maronites finally agreed to a compromise that gave more power to the country's Muslim majority. Many Lebanese who had left during the fighting began to return to rebuild their war-torn country.

Islamic Fundamentalism

As Middle Eastern nations adopted western technology, they also adopted many elements of western culture. Many countries set up secular governments. They established secular schools and replaced Islamic law with law codes based on western principles. In cities, especially, many young people adopted

TRADITION AND CHANGE

A Pilgrimage to Mecca

The pilgrimage to Mecca is one of the five pillars of Islam. All Muslims who can do so are expected to make the journey at least once during their lifetime.

Geography, war, and other factors once made the journey long and dangerous, and thousands of people and camels died along the way. In 1784, a group of pilgrims from India traveled so slowly that they arrived late for the hajj of 1785! Once pilgrims reached Mecca, crowded and dirty conditions bred disease. One pilgrim of the 1800s described the "suffocating heat, deadly wind, and clouds of flies" in the desert city.

Today, the hajj continues to bring together Muslims from all corners of the world. Every year during Dhu'l Hijja, the month of pilgrimage, an estimated 2 million Muslims stream into Mecca. Jets have reduced the travel time to a matter of hours. In addition, the Saudi Arabian government has spent billions of dollars to improve health facilities, transportation, and water supplies in the holy city.

The meaning of the hajj, however, remains unchanged. For devout Muslims, the hajj is the greatest moment of their life. It is an act that will count in their favor on Judgment Day.

Today, as in the past, hundreds of thousands of pilgrims travel to Mecca each year. They come by plane, car, and bus. On the outskirts of Mecca, pilgrims purify themselves by washing from head to foot. Then, they wrap themselves in identical seamless white garments as a reminder that all people are equal before God. Together, they proclaim:

> "Here am I, O my God, here am I; no partner hast Thou, here am I; verily the praise and the grace are Thine and the empire."

Upon entering Mecca, the thousands of white-clad pilgrims go directly to the Kaaba. They circle the holy shrine seven times, reciting prayers glorifying God. Some pilgrims touch or kiss the Black Stone, which they believe was sent by God.

1. What is the significance of the hajj to Muslims?
2. **Analyzing Information** How would the hajj encourage cultural diffusion?

western music, clothing, food, and cultural values. Women gained more freedom to go out in public, and some stopped veiling their faces.

Some Muslims saw westernization as a dangerous force that was undermining Islamic society. They supported a movement known as Islamic fundamentalism. Fundamentalists demanded a return to the values set out in the Koran. Governments, they said, must use the Shariah as the basis of all law. Authority must be restored to religious leaders and Islamic governments must enforce the strict separation of men and women in public.

Fundamentalists gained influence in many Muslim nations. To many people, from Algeria to Iran, fundamentalism offered a way of coping with rapid social and economic changes. In Iran, an Islamic revolution brought fundamentalists to power, as you will read in Section 3.

SECTION 1 REVIEW

1. **Identify:** (a) pan-Arabism, (b) Shariah, (c) Islamic fundamentalism.
2. (a) What was the goal of pan-Arabism? (b) What obstacles did it face?
3. (a) What different kinds of governments are found in the Middle East? (b) Which countries are multiparty states that hold free elections?
4. (a) Which religious groups shared power in Lebanon before 1975? (b) Why did fighting erupt among these groups?
5. What are the goals of Islamic fundamentalists?
6. **Analyzing Ideas** How were both Arab nationalism and Islamic fundamentalism a response to western domination?
7. **Writing Across Cultures** Review the obstacles to the creation of a united Arab state. Then list some of the obstacles that might exist if the United States considered uniting with Canada, Australia, and New Zealand. Write a paragraph explaining why it may be difficult for several independent nations to form a single unified nation.

2 CHANGING ECONOMIC AND SOCIAL PATTERNS

FIND OUT

What economic goals have Middle Eastern nations pursued?

How have Middle Eastern nations improved their agriculture?

How has oil affected Middle Eastern nations?

What are some effects of rapid population growth and urbanization?

Vocabulary desalination

In Arab nations like Syria, the middle class is growing. In 1962, Riyadh Seif and his brothers bought some sewing machines and set up a workshop. In time, the shop grew into a real factory. By 1989, Seif had become Syria's largest private employer and was making women's clothing for export. Seif credits his success to his policy of distributing profits among workers.

"I take the workers' youth and their labor," he says, "so why shouldn't I pay them as well as possible? Every worker who stays five years at my company will be able to buy an apartment. And they will return their wages with even bigger efforts."

Syria is a socialist country in which the state controls most basic industries. At the same time, it supports private enterprise. People like Seif operate manufacturing businesses that produce consumer goods such as clothing, shampoo, and toys. Often, these workshops employ mostly family members. Taken together, however, they provide jobs for a large number of people.

Economic Goals and Growth

After independence, a major goal of Middle Eastern nations was to reduce European economic influence. Most nations relied on Europe for manufactured goods. Foreigners owned key industries. They also controlled the region's greatest asset—its oil resources.

Arab socialism. Some Arab nations turned to socialism as a way of taking charge of their own destinies. Under socialism, governments took control of large sections of their economies.

In the 1950s, a number of Middle Eastern countries nationalized foreign-owned companies in industries such as banking, oil, and food processing. This nationalization reduced reliance on the West to some degree. However, most countries still depended on Europe, Japan, and the United States for both high-technology goods and technological know-how.

Government's key role. Throughout the Middle East, governments have taken a leading role in promoting industrial growth. In socialist countries like Iraq and Syria, the state owns nearly all businesses. Even in nonsocialist countries, the government owns most medium-size and large industries, including transportation, telephone, and utility companies. Smaller businesses, however, remain in private hands.

Some governments believe that centralized control is necessary to achieve modernization. Only governments can raise the capital to invest in factories, steel mills, roads, irrigation systems, and schools. Also, governments are able to make long-term plans. In Turkey, for example, the government has designed a huge project to turn the southeast into a rich agricultural region. (See the feature on page 554.)

Recent trends. Government control of the economy has had mixed results. Industrial output has grown since the 1950s, but state-run factories are often inefficient. By the 1990s, some countries had begun to move

Fertilizer Plant in Jordan The economy of Jordan is based on free enterprise, but government plays a key role as well. Public funds helped build this factory at the port city of Aqaba on the Red Sea. It processes phosphate, Jordan's main mineral resource, into fertilizer. ***Choice*** What are two advantages of centralized control of the economy?

away from strict government control toward a free market economy. They privatized some government-owned industries by selling them to private investors.

The Population Challenge

In the Middle East, as elsewhere in the developing world, rapid population growth poses a challenge to modernization. Egypt's population has tripled since 1962, jumping from 17 million to more than 58 million in 1993. In the same period, Iraq's population grew from less than 7 million to 19 million. At the current growth rate, the population of the Middle East will double in 24 years.

The population explosion puts a huge strain on the region's resources. Limited farmland and the scarcity of water make population growth an especially critical problem in the Middle East.

Some governments have tried to slow the population boom. Egypt encourages couples to delay marriage in the hope that they will have fewer children.

Urban dwellers tend to have smaller families because of the cost of raising children. In rural areas, however, the tradition of large families remains strong because farm families need children to help work the land and support aging family members. As a result, family planning has had only limited success.

Harvesting Avocados in Israel Mechanized farming helps produce bumper crops. Less than 5 percent of Israel's labor force works in agriculture, but fruit and vegetables are an important source of foreign earnings. Israel's major crop is citrus fruit, which is exported mainly to Britain, Germany, and Italy. ***Technology*** How does Israel's work force differ from that of other Middle Eastern nations?

Developing Agriculture

Most people in the Middle East still earn a living from the land. Yet, as populations grow, governments have had to import more food. To improve food production, governments have poured resources into modernizing agriculture. They have also tried to increase the output of cash crops that earn much-needed income.

New water supplies. Governments have worked to increase the amount of farmland that can be cultivated. In the Middle East, this means developing dependable water supplies such as irrigation systems.

Many countries have constructed dams, such as the Aswan High Dam in Egypt and the dams built by Syria and Turkey on the Euphrates River. Dams provide water for irrigation as well as hydroelectric power. Iraq and Iran have restored and modernized networks of irrigation canals.

Modern technology has allowed people to tap other water sources. They have dug deep wells and carried out specialized scientific studies to find underground reservoirs. In the Arabian Peninsula, governments have built huge plants for desalination, or converting sea water into fresh water for drinking and irrigation. (See the feature on page 613.)

Improved farming methods. Farmers have increased crop yields by using better seeds and fertilizers, which were developed during the Green Revolution. Machines such as seed drills, tractors, and threshing machines have also helped increase output.

Israel has pioneered new farming methods such as "fertigation," a method for pumping water and fertilizer directly to the roots of plants. Computers control the flow of liquid, enabling farmers to raise bumper crops of grain, fruit, and vegetables. The high cost of fertigation, however, puts it beyond the reach of many developing countries.

Land reform. In the 1950s, countries such as Iran, Turkey, and Syria undertook land reform programs. By redistributing land to poor farmers, the governments of these countries hoped to increase food output, end rural poverty, and reduce the power of landlords.

Under Nasser, Egypt forced large landlords to sell much of their land to landless peasants. The government set up programs to teach peasants modern farming methods and provide them with fertilizers and other basic supplies. Land reform was politically popular, but it had limited economic success because farmers still lacked the training and supplies they needed to produce efficiently.

The Role of Oil

The Middle East has 60 percent of the world's oil reserves. Saudi Arabia, Iran, Iraq, Kuwait, Libya, and several small states along the Persian Gulf are rich in oil. Except for Iran, all of these states have small populations. A clear division exists between them and their more densely populated, poorer neighbors.

Oil-rich nations have enjoyed remarkable growth. Using the enormous profits from oil, they have developed industries, built handsome new capital cities, invested in modern hospitals, and raised the standard of living of their people. Kuwait, for example, provides free education and health care for all its citizens. Oil-producing nations have also built pipelines, ports, and refineries to handle their oil exports.

Oil resources are unevenly distributed, but since the late 1960s, the entire Middle East has benefited from oil wealth. Oil-rich nations have given money and loans to poorer neighbors. More important, in the 1970s and 1980s, several million workers from Egypt, Jordan, Yemen, and other Muslim countries found jobs in oil-producing countries. These "guest workers" sent much of their earnings to families back home. In this way, they helped spread the oil wealth to poorer nations.

Urban Growth

Modernization and the population explosion have contributed to the rapid growth of Middle Eastern cities. Baghdad, Iraq, has grown from a city of 550,000 people in 1965 to one that has more than 5 million today. The population of the Iranian capital, Tehran, soared from nearly 2 million to more than 13 million in the same period. Many newcomers are landless farmers looking for work. Others are young people from prosperous rural families who move to the cities seeking higher education and better jobs.

Adjusting to city life. Cities are bewildering places for newcomers. They often live packed together in crowded neighborhoods and compete for scarce jobs. Some find only part-time or short-term work. Others become peddlers, selling bread, fruit, tea, clothing, and hundreds of other goods on the streets.

Because housing is limited, millions of people live in flimsy shacks on the edge of the city. In Turkey, these shantytowns are called *gecekondu,* which means "houses built overnight." Moroccans call them *bidonvilles,* or "tin-can cities." In Egypt, nearly a million residents in Cairo have crowded into makeshift houses built among the tombs and monuments of the City of the Dead, a cemetery outside the capital.

In cities, people from the same village often cluster together in the same neighborhoods. They worship at the same mosque and gather at the same coffeehouse to exchange news and gossip. Networks of families and friends help each other find jobs and housing. A Lebanese engineer who worked for an airline proudly noted the help he had given family members. "About 40 of my relatives work for the airline," he said.

Conflict between generations. Children usually adapt to city life more quickly than do their parents. One reason is that children attend school and learn to read, while their parents often remain illiterate. Differences in education and attitudes can create conflict between the generations.

Cairo's City of the Dead Living space is so limited in Cairo that people have put up small houses among the tombs of this ancient cemetery. Many newcomers from rural areas who cannot afford the scarce and expensive apartments in Cairo live here. ***Scarcity*** Why is decent housing unavailable in many Middle Eastern cities?

Many young people want fashionable clothing, cassette tapes, and other items that their parents think are foolish luxuries. Teenagers watch music videos and go to see foreign films. Parents worry that foreign ideas are undermining traditional values. Some Middle Eastern governments agree. Saudi Arabia and Iran have banned western music, television shows, and movies.

Dating is rare in much of the Middle East. In many families, parents still arrange marriages for their children. Today, however, most young women and men expect to have some say in choosing their marriage partner.

Women's Lives

The status of women varies from one country to another in the Middle East, depending on each nation's government, laws, and social traditions. In conservative places like Riyadh, Saudi Arabia, or Tehran, Iran, the law requires women to be veiled when they go outside their homes. In other Middle Eastern cities, such as Ankara, Cairo, Damascus, and Amman, most women walk along the streets freely and remain unveiled.

Education and work. Everywhere, the number of women completing high school and earning university degrees is growing. Women are entering the work force as doctors, lawyers, journalists, and government officials.

Whether or not they work outside the home, women are responsible for the housework and child care. Hadiya, a factory worker in Cairo, gets up at 5 A.M. to prepare food for her husband and son. She takes the boy to nursery school, works a full day on the job, then returns home to cook, clean, and take care of her son until he goes to bed. She says:

> "Sometimes my husband will shop or take the boy out if he sees me tired. But all of this is a matter of whim. If I complain, he tells me to leave work and get along without my pay. But he knows we couldn't do that, not in today's conditions."

Recent trends. The spread of Islamic fundamentalism has affected Muslim women from all social classes. Many women are choosing to return to traditional dress—a floor-length garment and a scarf that covers the head and neck. To them, these clothes reinforce their identity as Muslims and women in the face of growing western influence. "This dress is to protect my dignity as a woman," says an Egyptian journalist. Another Egyptian woman, who disagreed with the fundamentalists, observed:

> " As long as women are covering their heads and not their minds, it is an individual expression. "

In Arab countries, some women have organized themselves to challenge the social patterns of the past. They argue that Islamic law regarding women was developed to protect women in the 600s. Islam, they say, must adapt to the modern world. Muslim women often face difficult choices, however, as they try to change social attitudes inherited from the past.

Boutaina Shaaban Ever since she made the difficult decision to break with tradition in her own life, Boutaina Shaaban has encouraged other Arab women to do the same. Now a professor at Damascus University, Shaaban has written a book describing her talks with Arab women about their lives. ***Change*** Why do most Arab women continue to follow Islamic traditions?

Pioneering Change

Boutaina Shaaban faced a difficult dilemma—to live her own life or obey her parents' wishes. Shaaban and her eight brothers and sisters grew up in a Syrian village. Her father "did his utmost to ensure his daughters had an equal education to his sons."

Shaaban did brilliantly in high school. However, when she graduated, everyone urged her to get a two-year teaching certificate, she said, "so that I could help my father bring up my younger brothers and sisters." Shaaban wanted to study English literature at the university. With her father's help, she managed to fulfill her dream. She became the first young woman to leave her village on her own to study at the University of Damascus in the Syrian capital. From there, she went to England for a graduate degree.

In England, Shaaban fell in love with an Iraqi named Khalil Jawad. She returned home to get her parents' approval before marrying. But her parents rejected the young man.

> " The real problem was that I was the first woman they had known to choose her husband quite independently of her father's and brothers' wishes. My father [repeated] that people in the village were going to say I had brought my husband with me and that, like a coward, my father had to endorse my choice. Although all my older brothers got married to women of their own choice, . . . they all denied me the same right because . . . I was a woman. "

Shaaban angrily rejected the double standard that gave men rights that were denied to women. Yet, she loved her family and felt great pressure to obey them. Eventually, her father told her to either leave Jawad or leave home and never see her parents again. Sadly, she said goodbye to her family and has not seen them since.

In Arab countries, as well as elsewhere, families are closely knit. Children learn to respect male authority and preserve the family honor. Shaaban recalls that when she married in 1981 some people thought she was ungrateful. After all, her family had given her an excellent education, and she had abandoned them to marry as she wished.

Yet, Shaaban does not regret her decision. Today, she says, women feel more free to "marry men of their choice, regardless of family pressures or social considerations."

> "In a way, I became a pioneer for a younger generation which reaped the fruits of my sacrifice. One of my younger sisters, for example, just had to name the man she chose to be given my father's blessing and many wonderful presents besides."

Unlike Shaaban, many women have made the choice to follow traditional social customs. They make that decision to preserve family life. They believe that crime, drugs, alcoholism, and other problems in western society are the result of the failure of the family. They accept Muslim traditions as a guide for contemporary behavior. ■

Education

Middle Eastern nations have placed great emphasis on education. At independence, the new nations of the Middle East depended on foreign engineers and skilled workers. "Almost all the architects who build new houses, new factories, and new schools are foreigners," complained an Iranian. "In the secondary and high schools, courses are given by . . . French, German, and American professors!"

In most Middle Eastern countries, few people had the technical training needed to run modern factories. Literacy rates were low, and most children had little if any schooling.

Since the 1950s, Middle Eastern nations have made rapid progress toward expanding education. Oil-rich countries like Kuwait as well as poorer countries like Turkey have invested millions in building schools and training teachers. Other countries have not only raised literacy rates but also doubled and tripled the number of high school graduates.

A Classroom in Yemen Middle Eastern countries with low literacy rates are working to improve education. When Yemen first began public education in the 1950s, only 5 percent of its people could read and write. Today, this figure has increased to almost 40 percent and is steadily growing. ***Change*** Why do you think these men and women are attending school?

Despite great progress, education is uneven. Literacy varies from one country to another, between urban and rural areas, and between social classes. For example, the adult literacy rate in Yemen is less than 40 percent, and in Israel it is 90 percent.

Although most boys attend school, education for girls lags in many countries. In rural families, where a child's labor is needed, one or more boys may go to school, but the girls do not. Many parents think girls do not need to learn to read and write. Still, the enrollment of girls is growing. In Iraq, Jordan, Lebanon, Israel, and the United Arab Emirates, for example, all girls attend school.

The population explosion has created problems in education. Each year, the growing number of school-age children outpaces the number of schools and teachers. Countries must spend an ever-larger part of their limited budgets on education. They do so, however, because a skilled and literate population is essential to a modern nation.

SECTION 2 REVIEW

1. **Identify:** fertigation.
2. **Define:** desalination.
3. (a) List three economic goals of Middle Eastern nations. (b) Give an example of how they have tried to achieve one of these goals.
4. Describe three ways in which Middle Eastern nations have tried to expand agriculture.
5. (a) How have oil-rich nations benefited from oil profits? (b) How has oil wealth affected the poorer nations of the Middle East?
6. What social changes has urbanization brought to the Middle East?
7. **Analyzing Ideas** Why is a skilled and literate population essential to a modern nation?
8. **Writing Across Cultures** Write a paragraph comparing the issues that create conflicts between generations in the United States and in the Middle East.

3 THREE NATIONS ON THE ROAD TO MODERNIZATION

FIND OUT

What were the causes of the Islamic revolution in Iran?

What economic policies have Egyptian leaders followed?

How has Turkey progressed toward modernization?

Vocabulary theocracy

In 1971, Iran's ruler, Shah Muhammad Reza Pahlavi, organized a fantastic spectacle to celebrate 2,500 years of Persian (Iranian) monarchy. His own family was a newcomer among the many dynasties that had ruled Iran. Yet, the shah turned to Iran's splendid past to strengthen his own image in the eyes of his people and the world.

Eight years later, the shah and his family had to flee their homeland as religious revolutionary forces swept into power. The new rulers of Iran also appealed to the past. Their Islamic revolution grew out of deep attachments to Muslim traditions dating from the time of Muhammad.

In this section, you will read about three of the largest and most influential nations of the Middle East: Iran, Egypt, and Turkey. Each has a history that is rooted in ancient civilizations. Each has followed its own path to modernization.

Iran

In both size and population, Iran is the second-largest country in the Middle East. Its huge oil resources, strategic location on the

Nomads in Iran The mountainous land of south-central Iran is the home of the Qashqai, a nomadic group of about 400,000 people. In search of pasture lands for their sheep, Qashqai often travel several hundred miles between summer camps in the highlands and winter camps in the lowlands. ***Environment*** Why might the Qashqai have to travel so far to find pastures?

Persian Gulf, and Islamic revolution have made it a focus of world attention.

Land and resources. Much of Iran is a dry, rugged plateau. Most Iranians live in the northeast, where the rainfall is adequate for farming. Tehran, the capital, is located in this fertile region. Like other Iranian cities, Tehran has grown rapidly. Still, about one third of Iranians are farmers who produce a variety of crops.

Oil plays a dominant role in Iran's economy, accounting for more than 25 percent of the national income and 98 percent of the value of its exports. Iran's oil reserves are the third largest in the Middle East and the fourth largest in the world. Output decreased sharply after the 1979 revolution and a long war with Iraq. Today, the country is struggling to return to prewar levels of oil production.

The people. Iran is home to more than a dozen ethnic groups, including Persians, Kurds, Baluchis, and Armenians. Only a small percentage of the people are Arabs. Most Iranians speak Persian, a modern form of the language of ancient Persia. Most Iranians are Muslims, but Iran is the only Middle Eastern nation where Shiites are in the majority.

Modernization. As elsewhere in the developing world, nationalism fueled a drive to modernize. Iran was the first Middle Eastern country to end western control of its oil resources. In 1951, it nationalized its oil wells and refineries. During the 1950s and 1960s, the shah used wealth from oil to launch sweeping economic and social reforms. His goal was to make Iran "comparable to the most developed countries in the world."

Under a land reform program, the shah broke up large estates and distributed the land to peasants. He improved health care and education. The government financed water projects and new roads and encouraged industrial growth. The shah's social reforms also gave women new rights, including the right to vote.

The reforms provoked loud protest, especially from religious leaders. They condemned the shah's efforts to replace Islamic traditions with secular western ideas. Other critics denounced government corruption and the shah's failure to help the poor. They bitterly criticized Iran's alliance with the United States. The shah used secret police to silence protesters, forcing many into exile.

Islamic revolution. The shah's policies failed to improve life for many Iranians. Instead, a growing gap separated the small, westernized middle and upper classes from the rest of the people. Also, nationalists' anger increased over Iran's dependence on the West. These conditions led many Iranians to embrace the ideas of an outspoken Muslim fundamentalist, the Ayatollah* Ruhollah Khomeini (ī uh TOH luh roo HOH luh koh MAY nee). From his exile in France, Khomeini condemned western influences on his country. "In Iran, until something has a western name it is not accepted," he declared. He called on Iranians to defend their values. "An enlightened heart cannot stand by silently and watch while traditions and honor are trampled upon," he said.

In 1979, growing unrest forced the shah to flee. Khomeini returned to Iran to lead the Islamic revolution. He and his supporters made Iran a theocracy, a nation ruled by religious leaders. They made the Koran the basis of all law. They replaced secular courts with religious courts and enforced Muslim traditions, such as requiring women to wear veils in public. Strict new laws banned western music and movies. As part of their antiwestern campaign, revolutionaries in Iran held 52 American citizens as hostages for more than a year.

Revolutionaries saw themselves as leaders of a spiritual revolution that would sweep the Muslim world. This Islamic religious revival had an impact outside Iran. However, it did not trigger Islamic revolutions elsewhere because other countries had different political and social conditions.

Demonstration in Tehran These Iranians are carrying pictures of the Ayatollah Khomeini. Islamic fundamentalists like these strongly supported his rule. Iran today seeks closer ties with other nations, but not with the United States, which it calls "the symbol of bullying . . . and cruelty to the weak nations of the world." ***Culture*** Why does Iran accept some western practices but reject others?

Economic patterns. Economic development slowed after the Iranian revolution. Because of a United States trade boycott, Iran could not get spare parts for its factories. Many plants eventually closed. Internal turmoil and war with Iraq further disrupted Iran's economy. The Iran-Iraq War lasted from

* *Ayatollah* is a Persian word that means "sign of Allah." It is the highest title that can be held by a Shiite Muslim religious leader.

1980 to 1988. It led to an estimated 1 million casualties, slowed oil production, and caused enormous destruction.

Like the shah, the new Islamic government extended land reform and pressed ahead with irrigation projects. When the Iran-Iraq War ended, the government transferred resources from war industries to rebuilding the nation's economy. Today, a variety of industries, ranging from food processing to automobile assembly plants, have resumed operation.

After Khomeini's death in 1989, Iran's new leader, Ali Akbar Rafsanjani, began to renew ties with western nations that had been cut during the revolution. In 1991, Iran used its influence with Islamic fundamentalists in Lebanon to help win freedom for western hostages held in Beirut. Iran remains committed to Islamic principles, but it is also determined to push ahead with modernization. Although Iranians are prepared to use western technology, they reject what they see as dangerous western cultural values.

Egypt

As in Iran, nationalism helped shape modern Egypt. Egypt, however, lacks Iran's vast oil resources, and its geography poses obstacles to development.

Land and people. In size and population, Egypt ranks third in the Middle East. Because most of Egypt is desert, about 95 percent of Egyptians live on just 5 percent of the land. Cities, towns, and villages alike border a narrow strip of land along the Nile River. Almost 12 percent of Egypt's people live in Cairo.

Despite urban growth, about 40 percent of the Egyptian people are still farmers. Today, as in the past, the fertile Nile Valley is Egypt's greatest natural resource. Developing

Downtown Cairo With a rapidly growing population, Egypt is troubled with high unemployment. As a result, many young men travel to other Arab countries in search of jobs. In the early 1990s, over 2 million Egyptians were working abroad and sending money home to support their families. ***Geography*** How might Egypt's geography contribute to unemployment?

agriculture is a major goal of the government's economic policies.

Nasser's policies. In the 1950s, President Gamal Abdel Nasser promoted Arab socialism. He increased the economic power of the government by nationalizing industries and taking control of foreign-owned businesses, including the Suez Canal. He redistributed land to poor farmers and increased the wages of urban workers. Nasser's goal was to expand farm output and end economic dependence on the West by developing Egypt's industry.

With foreign loans and grants, first from the United States and then from the Soviet Union, Nasser financed the building of the Aswan High Dam. This huge dam allowed Egypt to irrigate more farmland, control Nile flooding, and produce low-cost hydroelectric power for factories and homes. Lake Nasser, which formed behind the dam, also supported a fishing industry.

The dam has had environmental costs, however. It ended the annual Nile flood, which brought fertile soil to the valley. Today, Egyptian farmers must buy costly chemical fertilizers. Without new deposits of soil at the Nile delta, coastal erosion has increased. Also, changes in the Nile water led to reduced fish life in the Mediterranean.

Economic patterns. Under Nasser, Egypt made some economic progress. It built new industries, such as textiles, chemicals, and steel. However, Arab-Israeli tensions led to two disastrous wars. Also, Egypt had trouble getting the capital it needed to invest in industry. Western nations distrusted Nasser's socialist economic policies and feared they would not be repaid if they lent money to Egypt. In addition, they were concerned about Nasser's close relationship with the Soviet Union.

Nasser's successor, Anwar Sadat, moved away from Arab socialism. However, the government continued to play a major role in the economy. Sadat encouraged an economic "open door" policy. He welcomed foreign investment and supported private industry. He also took Egypt on a new course in foreign affairs and became the first Arab leader to make peace with Israel. (See Chapter 28.) Other

The Port of Alexandria
Much of Egypt's trade passes through Alexandria. Egypt remains an agricultural nation, whose main export is cotton. However, Egypt also is building steel mills, light industries, and food processing plants as it becomes industrialized. ***Choice*** How does the rapidly growing population of Egypt encourage the growth of industry?

Arab nations condemned his action and expelled Egypt from the Arab League.

In 1981, Sadat was assassinated by Islamic fundamentalists, and Hosni Mubarak became president of Egypt. Mubarak focused on the nation's pressing economic problems. He sought to balance the needs of a growing population with the need to repay foreign debts. Foreign lenders urged the government to cut spending on food, housing, and other social programs. Such cuts, however, would hurt millions of poor Egyptians.

In foreign affairs, Mubarak took a cautious approach. He honored Egypt's treaty with Israel. At the same time, he quietly restored ties with other Arab nations. During the 1991 Persian Gulf War, he negotiated western aid in return for Egypt's support for the coalition that opposed Iraq.

Turkey

Turkey links the worlds of the Middle East and Europe. Most of Turkey, including the capital, Ankara, lies in Asia Minor. A tiny area of Turkey is located in Europe. Since 1973, several bridges across the Bosporus have linked Europe and Asia.

Turkey's location also gives it control of the vital shipping route that connects the Black Sea with the Mediterranean. Ships from the former Soviet Union and parts of Eastern Europe must pass through the Turkish Straits to reach the Mediterranean, Africa, and the rest of the world.

During the Cold War, Turkey developed economic and military ties with Western Europe. It is a member of the North Atlantic Treaty Organization (NATO), a western military alliance.

In recent years, Turkey has applied for membership in the European Community (EC). Membership would help Turkey increase its trade with Europe. However, many Europeans oppose opening their borders to Turkey's large Muslim population.

Land and people. Unlike other Middle Eastern countries, Turkey has no deserts. Like Iran, however, it has high, arid plateaus. Its land varies from a tropical southern coast to cooler interior highlands. In these diverse climates, farmers cultivate a variety of cash crops, ranging from bananas, sunflowers, tobacco, and olives to wheat and potatoes.

Turkey has the largest population of any country in the Middle East. Although nearly all Turks are Sunni Muslims, they are not Arabs. Turks take pride in their distinct language, culture, and history. For hundreds of years, their huge Ottoman Empire dominated the Middle East and parts of Europe.

About 10 percent of Turkey's population are Kurds. Most of them live in the mountains of the southeast. As in nearby Iran and Iraq, Kurds living in Turkey face discrimination. The government censors pro-Kurdish publications and has imprisoned some Kurds for their political activities. The Kurds' demands for self-rule have led to battles between Kurds and government forces throughout the region.

Economic patterns. In the 1920s, Kemal Atatürk set out to make Turkey a modern, secular state. Since then, the country has made steady progress toward that goal. Turkey has one of the most balanced economies in the Middle East today. New irrigation systems and the use of fertilizers, pesticides, and improved seeds have helped farmers increase their output. At the same time, Turkey has developed manufacturing. To make up for its lack of oil, Turkey has built dams that provide hydroelectric power.

In the past, the government exercised substantial control over the economy. Although it permitted private enterprise, it also owned many industries. More recently, the government has reduced its role in the economy, privatized some industries, and sought joint ventures with European companies. Today, Turkey's first woman prime minister, Tansu Ciller, is pressing forward with reforms despite opposition.

Challenges. Despite progress toward modernization, Turkey still faces many challenges. The population is growing faster than the economy's ability to create new jobs. In the past, many Turks found work in Western Europe, especially in Germany. The money they

Kurdish Farmers in Turkey About half of the world's 17 million Kurds live in Turkey. The Kurds have always resisted foreign rulers. For centuries, they have tried to establish their own nation in the mountainous region where the borders of Turkey, Iran, and Iraq meet. ***Human Rights*** Why might Turkey, Iran, and Iraq discriminate against the Kurds?

sent home helped both their families and the economy in general. The economic slowdown in Western Europe and growing anti-foreign feeling there have forced many Turks to return home.

At times, economic and political crises have contributed to unrest and violence. Turkey has many political parties, and competition among rival parties has also caused instability. On several occasions, the military has seized power, suspended basic rights, and crushed protests. The military has always returned the government to civilian hands, however. Today, Turkey has a relatively stable, democratic government. (See Connections With Literature, page 807, "Selected Poetry.")

In both rural and urban areas, there are supporters of an Islamic revival who have rejected western, secular values. At universities, some women fundamentalists have challenged laws that forbid them to veil their heads and faces in class. Islamic political parties have made some recent gains in Turkey. Still, fundamentalists remain a small but outspoken minority. Most Turks accept the idea of separating government and religion.

SECTION 3 REVIEW

1. **Locate:** (a) Iran, (b) Egypt, (c) Turkey, (d) Ankara, (e) Istanbul.
2. **Identify:** (a) Muhammad Reza Pahlavi, (b) Ayatollah Ruhollah Khomeini, (c) Ali Akbar Rafsanjani, (d) Gamal Abdel Nasser, (e) Aswan High Dam, (f) Anwar Sadat, (g) Hosni Mubarak, (h) Kurds.
3. **Define:** theocracy.
4. (a) What economic and social reforms did the shah of Iran introduce? (b) Why did many Iranians support the Islamic revolution?
5. (a) What economic policies did Nasser introduce? (b) How did Sadat and Mubarak change Nasser's policies?
6. (a) Describe three steps that Turkey has taken toward modernization. (b) Describe three challenges that Turkey faces today.
7. **Comparing** (a) What goals do Iran, Egypt, and Turkey have in common? (b) Compare the ways in which each nation has pursued its goals.
8. **Writing Across Cultures** In a brief paragraph, describe how your life might be different if you lived in Iran.

Chapter 27 Review

Understanding Vocabulary

Match each term at left with the correct definition at right.

1. pan-Arabism
2. Shariah
3. fertigation
4. desalination
5. theocracy

a. method of pumping water and fertilizer to the roots of plants
b. nation ruled by religious leaders
c. movement to unite all Arabs based on their common language and culture
d. Islamic law
e. process of converting sea water into fresh water

Reviewing the Main Idea

1. How has Islamic law influenced Middle Eastern governments?
2. Describe three causes of instability in the Middle East.
3. What steps have Middle Eastern governments taken to promote economic growth?
4. How has rapid population growth in the Middle East affected agriculture?
5. How did the shah try to modernize Iran?
6. Why has Egypt had difficulties in its efforts to modernize?
7. (a) How is Turkey similar to other Middle Eastern nations? (b) How is it different?

Reviewing Chapter Themes

1. The nations of the Middle East looked for ways to end western domination. Discuss how the following steps were intended to reduce economic dependence on the West: (a) nationalization of industries, (b) increased spending on education.
2. Oil has divided the Middle East into "have" and "have-not" nations. (a) How have oil-rich nations used their wealth to modernize? (b) How have poorer Middle Eastern nations benefited from the oil wealth of their more prosperous neighbors?
3. Rapid population growth poses a challenge to modernization. Describe what problems the population boom creates in (a) food production, (b) cities, (c) education.
4. Middle Eastern governments have taken a strong role in planning and supervising economic development. (a) Describe the steps taken by the governments of Iran, Egypt, and Turkey to encourage modernization. (b) What challenges did each country face as it modernized?

Thinking Critically

1. **Analyzing Ideas** How does Islamic fundamentalism offer an alternative to westernization in some nations of the Middle East?
2. **Making Global Connections** If the population of the United States were distributed like that of Egypt, most Americans would live in an area the size of Montana. (a) How has geography created hardships for Egypt? (b) How has it favored the United States?

Applying Your Skills

1. **Comparing Points of View** Review the section titled "Women's Lives" and the Up Close, "A Bitter Choice," on pages 600–601. (a) What different points of view about women are presented? (b) What arguments does each side use to support its point of view? (c) With which side do you agree? Explain. (See Skill Lesson, page 629.)
2. **Making a Generalization** Make a generalization about the challenges Middle Eastern societies face as they try to modernize. Then give at least two facts to support your generalization.

Chapter 28

THE MIDDLE EAST IN THE WORLD TODAY

Oil Refinery People in desert lands in the Middle East wear clothing well suited to the climate. White reflects the sun's heat so it is cooler than darker cloth. Loose robes also are cooler. The head covering, called a *keffiyah,* provides protection from the sun. Here, two oil company executives inspect a refinery. ***Geography*** Why is oil so vital to some Middle Eastern economies?

CHAPTER OUTLINE

"Jerusalem is a golden basin filled with scorpions," an Arab philosopher observed centuries ago. Today, Jerusalem is still a place of religious treasures and dangerous conflicts. This ancient city is a holy place to Jews, Christians, and Muslims.

In the past, all three groups have fought for control of Jerusalem. During the Crusades, Christians conquered the city for a time until the Muslims recaptured it. In modern times, Israel gained control of the city after several wars with Arab neighbors. In *Songs of Jerusalem and Myself,* the Israeli poet Yehuda Amichai tells of the constant conflict over the city:

> "All the Nations (united) will
> stream into Jerusalem
> to see if the Law went
> forth from Zion, and
> meanwhile
> seeing it's now spring
> they'll pick flowers,
> and beat sword into
> plowshare and plowshare
> into sword
> then back again, and again

and again, without
 stopping.
Maybe, from so much
 beating and grinding,
the iron of war will die
 out. ”

CHAPTER PERSPECTIVE

Since World War II, the conflict between Arab nations and Israel has erupted into four wars. These wars and other events in the Middle East have had global significance because of the region's oil resources and its command of vital shipping lanes. During the Cold War, the United States and the Soviet Union competed for allies in the Middle East. After the Soviet Union collapsed, new peace efforts raised hopes for reducing tensions in the region.

As you read, look for these chapter themes:

- After World War II, the Middle East became a focus of Cold War rivalries.
- Tensions among neighboring Muslim nations have sometimes erupted into war.
- Conflicting historical claims and nationalism led to wars between Arab nations and Israel.
- Since ancient times, the peoples of the Middle East have produced outstanding works of literature and art.

Literature Connections

In this chapter, you will encounter passages from the following works.

Songs of Jerusalem and Myself, Yehuda Amichai

Shah-nama, Firdawsi

For other suggestions, see Connections With Literature, pages 804–808.

1 REGIONAL AND GLOBAL ISSUES

FIND OUT

Why does the Middle East have global importance?

How did the Cold War affect the Middle East?

How did the actions of OPEC affect nations around the world?

What were the results of the Iran-Iraq and Persian Gulf wars?

Black, greasy rain fell on Tehran, Iran, in February 1991. Hundreds of miles away across the Persian Gulf, fires raged through the oil fields of Kuwait. Winds carried soot-laden air from Kuwait eastward as far as Iran. In somber warnings, scientists predicted that the burning oil would damage the environment far beyond the Middle East.

Most of the fires had been set deliberately by Iraqi troops, who had invaded the small nation of Kuwait. When an international force defeated the Iraqis, retreating Iraqi soldiers set fire to Kuwait's oil wells.

Damage to the environment was only one aspect of the Iraqi invasion of Kuwait. The conflict began as a local dispute. But because it threatened the flow of oil from the Middle East, it exploded into a world crisis.

The Middle East and the Cold War

Since World War II, nations in both the developed world and the developing world have become increasingly dependent on oil from the Middle East. As a result, events in the region have taken on global importance.

Superpower rivalry. The United States and the Soviet Union recognized the strategic importance of the Middle East. The region not only controlled the oil needed for industry, but also commanded vital waterways such as the the Suez Canal, the Turkish Straits, and the Persian Gulf. During the Cold War, the superpowers competed for power and influence in the Middle East.

Turkey. An early Cold War crisis centered on Turkey. In 1945, the Soviet Union pressed territorial claims against Turkey, its neighbor to the south. It supported communist rebels in Turkey. It also sought to win control of the Turkish Straits, through which ships from the Soviet Union and Eastern Europe had to pass to reach the Mediterranean. Determined to stop Soviet expansion, the United States offered economic and military aid to Turkey. By 1947, the United States had moved a strong naval fleet into the eastern Mediterranean to show its willingness to defend Turkey. In the end, the Turks resisted Soviet pressure.

Later, Turkey joined the North Atlantic Treaty Organization (NATO), placing itself firmly in the western camp against the Soviet Union. NATO built air bases in Turkey, giving the United States an important stronghold in the Middle East.

Economic and military aid. During the Cold War, many Middle Eastern nations tried to remain nonaligned. They accepted aid from both superpowers. Egypt was a founder of the nonaligned movement. During the mid-1950s, however, relations between the United States and President Nasser of Egypt soured. Nasser then relied on Soviet loans and experts to help build the Aswan High Dam. Later, Egyptian leaders sought better relations with the United States and accepted aid from it.

The superpower rivalry continued for more than 40 years. Both sides sought allies among the nations of the Middle East. Both supplied enormous quantities of arms as well as economic aid to their clients, or nations dependent on them, in the region. The weapons strengthened the military forces of Middle Eastern nations but also added to instability in the region.

Afghanistan. In 1979, the Soviet Union sent troops into Afghanistan to support a communist government that had gained power there. The invasion raised fears that the Soviet Union might try to extend its influence over neighboring Iran and threaten shipping in the Persian Gulf.

The United States supplied arms to the Afghan rebels who were fighting Soviet troops. The fighting in Afghanistan helped to weaken the Soviet Union. Finally, in 1988, the Soviets withdrew their troops.

MAP STUDY

Oil and gas are the most valuable resources of many Middle Eastern nations.

1. **Region** Which nations are major producers of oil and gas?
2. **Movement** Which transportation routes are used to send oil and gas around the world?
3. **Solving Problems** What are some problems Middle Eastern nations have in developing oil and gas resources?

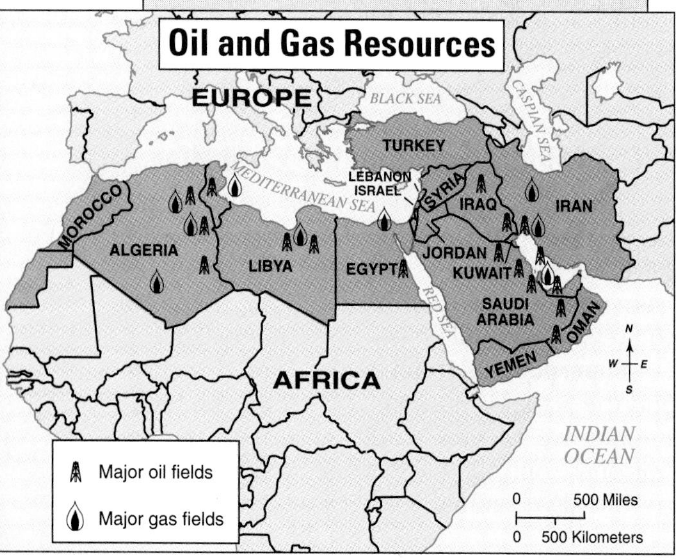

The Power of OPEC

In 1960, the major oil-producing countries of the Middle East signaled their determination to control their own destinies. That year, Iran, Iraq, Kuwait, and Saudi Arabia joined with Venezuela to form the Organization of Petroleum Exporting Countries (OPEC). Members of OPEC wanted to end the power western oil companies had over oil prices. OPEC members met regularly to decide how much oil to produce and at what price to sell it. Later, OPEC expanded to include 13 more

Fresh Water From Salty Seas

"Not oil again!" exclaimed the hydrologist, or water expert. He looked with disgust as the oily drill surfaced from underground. All too often, scientists have found "black gold"—oil—when they were desperately searching for water, the "white gold" of the Middle East.

Constant water shortage plagues the nations of the Arabian Peninsula as well as most of the Middle East. Yet, these oil-rich nations can afford to pay for new ways to obtain water. Some have considered importing water in tankers or even towing icebergs from the Arctic. The most practical solution so far, however, has been desalination. The peninsula has a ready supply of salt water in the nearby Red Sea and Persian Gulf.

Pipelines carry the salt water to huge desalination plants. There, the water is boiled in giant vats. The water turns into steam, leaving the salt behind. The steam is then trapped, cooled, and condensed to create fresh water. This process is known as distilling.

The technology of distilling has been in use for 2,000 years. Greek sailors distilled sea water into drinking water during voyages around the Mediterranean. The main obstacle to large-scale desalination is the cost of fuel. Most nations on the Arabian Peninsula, however, have abundant supplies of oil and gas.

Saudi Arabia and other Persian Gulf nations have invested huge sums of money in desalination plants. Saudi Arabia alone has about 800 plants. One plant in Jubail, Saudi Arabia, produces 250 million gallons (950 million liters) of fresh water a day. The tiny country of Qatar produces as much as 30 million gallons (114 million liters) daily through the process of desalination.

Using both technology and natural resources, nations of the Arabian Peninsula have moved toward solving a pressing problem. Through desalination, they have been able to provide their people with water that is suitable for drinking, washing, and farming.

1. Why is desalination important to nations of the Arabian Peninsula?
2. **Applying Information** Why might an oil spill in the Persian Gulf pose a threat to desalination efforts?

nations from Africa, Latin America, and the Middle East.

OPEC actions. As world demand for oil rose, OPEC's power increased. During the 1970s, the Middle Eastern members of OPEC showed how that power could be used. In 1973, Arab nations were at war with Israel. Using oil as a political weapon, OPEC stopped oil shipments from the Middle East to countries that supported Israel.

From the start, OPEC's main goal had been to increase its members' profits. The price of oil soared from less than $2 per barrel in the 1960s to $14 in the mid-1970s. In 1980, prices were as high as $44 per barrel. Profits also rose.

Global effects. Rising oil prices sent shock waves through the world economy. Developing nations were especially hard hit. Many had to cut their spending on social programs in order to pay for oil. In industrial countries, higher oil prices caused runaway inflation. Factories passed along increased costs for fuel by charging more for their products. In the Middle East itself, nations without oil, such as Egypt and Turkey, suffered hardships while their oil-rich neighbors reaped huge profits.

Many nations looked for ways to end their dependence on oil. They turned to conservation and alternative energy sources such as nuclear power. Although oil prices fell during the 1980s, OPEC still had power and influence.

Burning Oil Wells in Kuwait In 1991, retreating Iraqi troops set fire to more than 700 oil wells in Kuwait. The United States and other nations immediately sent experts to fight the devastating fires. More than 10,000 workers from 34 nations took part. Their skillful efforts put out the last fire eight months later. ***Technology*** Why were the Kuwait oil well fires so destructive?

Two Wars in the Persian Gulf

Oil has been a major factor in two regional conflicts: the Iran-Iraq War and the Persian Gulf War. The conflicts had other causes, such as border disputes. Because they involved oil-producing nations, however, they took on global importance.

Iran-Iraq War. After the Islamic revolution in Iran, long-standing disputes increased tensions between Iran and Iraq. In 1980, clashes along the border flared into war. Iraqi leader Saddam Hussein invaded Iran, seizing the Shatt-al-Arab, a key waterway into the Persian Gulf. Hussein also wanted to end Iran's support of Iraqi Shiites.

During the Iran-Iraq War, both sides used air strikes and missiles to attack each other's cities, ports, and oil fields. Casualties mounted. Inspired by the Ayatollah Khomeini, tens of thousands of young Iranians joined in the battle, often with few weapons and little training. More than a million people died in the fighting.

The war raised international concerns when Iran and Iraq attacked tankers and set mines in the Persian Gulf. The United States sent warships to the Gulf to protect oil tankers that belonged to its allies in the region. Both the Soviet Union and the United States offered aid to Iraq, but the United States also secretly sold arms to Iran.

By 1988, despite massive economic and human losses, neither Iran nor Iraq had accomplished its goal. Exhausted, they accepted a UN cease-fire. Despite heavy damage caused by the war, the two nations remained strong military powers in the Middle East.

Persian Gulf War. Faced with huge debts and public unrest, Saddam Hussein used his army to settle arguments with Kuwait. Saddam claimed that Kuwait belonged to Iraq. The claim dated from the Ottoman Empire. In August 1990, Iraqi armies invaded Kuwait and appeared to threaten Saudi Arabia.

The Iraqi invasion of Kuwait touched off an international crisis. The United Nations condemned Hussein's aggression and imposed a trade embargo against Iraq. With UN support, the United States then assembled a coalition of American, Arab, and other forces against Iraq. In January 1991, planes took off from bases in Saudi Arabia to bomb targets in Iraq. Coalition ground forces moved to drive Iraqi forces out of Kuwait in February, and within days, Iraqi forces surrendered.

With American encouragement, Kurds and other groups in Iraq rebelled against Saddam Hussein, but the uprisings were crushed. Even though Iraq suffered enormous damage, Hussein managed to hold on to power. (📖 See Connections With Literature, page 807, "Letters From the Sand: The Letters of Desert Storm and Other Wars.")

A turning point. By 1991, the collapse of the Soviet Union and the end of the Persian Gulf War had created a new situation in the Middle East. Middle Eastern nations could no longer look to the Soviet Union for aid. The United States emerged as the only superpower. With Russian cooperation, the United States and other nations pushed efforts to resolve the long-standing Arab-Israeli conflict. By the mid-1990s, peacemakers had brought Arabs and Israelis into face-to-face talks that resulted in major breakthroughs.

SECTION 1 REVIEW

1. **Locate:** (a) Persian Gulf, (b) Turkey, (c) Iran, (d) Iraq, (e) Kuwait.
2. **Identify:** (a) OPEC, (b) Saddam Hussein.
3. Why did the United States and the Soviet Union compete for allies in the Middle East?
4. (a) How did OPEC increase the power of Middle Eastern nations? (b) How did rising oil prices affect nations around the world?
5. Describe one cause and one result of the Iran-Iraq War.
6. **Applying Information** Why did the Iraqi invasion of Kuwait become an issue of global concern?
7. **Writing Across Cultures** Although the United States has reduced its dependence on oil from the Middle East, it still imports much oil from the region. Make a list of suggestions on how Americans might reduce their dependence on imported oil.

2 THE ARAB-ISRAELI CONFLICT

FIND OUT

Why was Israel founded?

Why have Arab nations attacked Israel?

What issues have made the Arab-Israeli conflict hard to resolve?

Vocabulary refugee, occupied territory, reprisal, intifada

October 30, 1991, was a historic date. After more than 40 years of hostility, Arab and Israeli leaders met in face-to-face peace talks. The meeting took place in Madrid, Spain. As the world watched, leaders from both sides presented their positions. As expected, the Madrid peace conference produced no solutions. Although the two sides had agreed to talk, they remained far apart. Peace would be a long, slow process because difficult issues, hatred, and mistrust separated the two sides.

The Founding of Israel

After World War II, violence between Arabs and Jews in the British mandate of Palestine increased. Thousands of Jewish refugees left Europe for Palestine. Refugees are people who flee their homeland to seek safety elsewhere. Most of the Jewish settlers were survivors of Hitler's death camps. Together with earlier settlers, they were determined to set up a Jewish state. To both Jews and many non Jews, Hitler's murder of 6 million European Jews showed the need for a homeland where Jews could live in safety. (See Chapter 26.)

Palestinian Arabs bitterly opposed the arrival of Jewish immigrants. They had no desire to lose any of their homeland to make up for wrongs done to Jews in Europe. Fighting intensified as both sides battled for control of towns and villages. Unable to end the violence, and exhausted by World War II, Britain withdrew from Palestine and turned the area over to the UN.

Partition and war. In 1947, the UN recommended that Palestine be partitioned, or divided, into a Jewish state and an Arab state. Zionists accepted the plan. Arabs, however, objected to giving up any territory to Jews. They regarded the plan as a violation of their right to self-determination.

When the last British troops left Palestine in May 1948, Jews announced the creation of the state of Israel. It occupied the area set aside for a Jewish state under the UN partition plan. Israel won recognition from the major world powers. Some nations, however, refused to recognize Israel. To neighboring Arabs, Israel was a creation of the western powers who wanted to continue their domination of the Middle East. Vowing to destroy Israel, Arab nations declared war at once.

Egypt, Jordan, Syria, Iraq, and Lebanon sent separate military forces against Israel. Despite suffering heavy losses, Israel defended itself and defeated the divided Arab forces. It then annexed almost half the area set aside for an Arab state under the UN partition plan, as well as half of Jerusalem. Jordan took the rest of Arab Palestine, and Egypt occupied the Gaza Strip.

Palestinian refugees. More than 500,000 Arabs fled or were driven out of Palestine during and after the 1948 war. Many Palestinian refugees settled in UN refugee camps in nearby Arab nations. The camps were supposed to be temporary. Despite their makeshift housing and poor sanitation, they soon became the permanent home for several generations of Palestinians.

Britain Leaves Palestine In 1948, this British unit in Haifa lowered the British flag as they prepared to leave Palestine. Soon afterward, Israel was established, but the Arab nations refused to recognize the new nation. ***Power*** Do you agree or disagree with the Arab view that Israel was a creation of the western powers? Explain your answer.

Arab and Palestinian leaders resisted abandoning the camps. They felt that doing so would be interpreted as a willingness to give up the goal of regaining a Palestinian homeland. Bitterness and frustration festered in the camps for decades.

Continued Conflict

Since the 1948 war, the conflict between Israel and its Arab neighbors has erupted into three more wars. In 1956, Israel, Britain, and France attacked Egypt after Nasser nationalized the Suez Canal. Israeli troops occupied but later withdrew from the Sinai Peninsula.

In 1967, a third Arab-Israeli war occurred. The fighting lasted six days. In the Six Day War, Israel made major territorial gains. Its forces took the Sinai Peninsula and the Gaza Strip from Egypt. Israel also captured the Golan Heights from Syria and the West Bank from Jordan. In addition, Israel seized East Jerusalem from the Arabs.

In 1973, Syria and Egypt attacked Israel in a partially successful attempt to regain the lands they had lost during the Six Day War. Israel pushed back the invaders, and the UN soon negotiated a cease-fire.

Superpower involvement. The Cold War fueled the Arab-Israeli conflict. For years, the United States has firmly backed Israel, giving it military and economic aid. Many Arab nations, especially Syria, Iraq, and Egypt, turned to the Soviet Union for arms and other assistance. After each war, the two superpowers rearmed their allies in the Middle East.

Both the United States and the Soviet Union realized that the tensions in the Middle East could trigger a major war. Peace efforts, however, met with fierce resistance. Arab nations refused to recognize Israel, and they knew they could rely on Soviet support. At the same time, the United States was unwilling to press its ally, Israel, to make concessions to the Arabs on the issues of Palestinian refugees.

The PLO. The fate of Palestinian Arabs was key to any lasting peace. Their numbers grew in the crowded refugee camps outside Israel. Many other Palestinians lived in the occupied territories, the lands seized by Israel during the 1967 war. Palestinians were determined to win self-rule.

In 1964, Palestinian leaders formed the Palestine Liberation Organization (PLO). Its

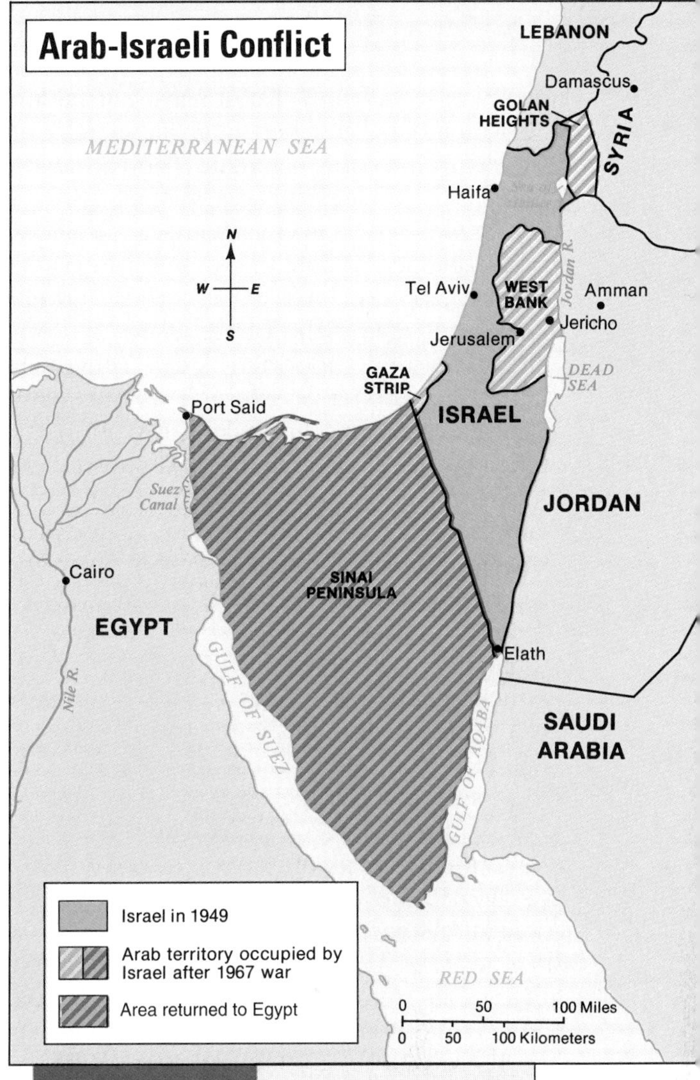

MAP STUDY

Between 1948 and 1973, Israel and its Arab neighbors fought four wars. Tensions remained high in the area until peace talks finally brought some progress in the 1990s.

1. **Location** (a) What territories did Israel gain in the 1967 war? (b) From which Arab nations did Israel take these lands?
2. **Region** What was the largest territory won by Israel?
3. **Making Decisions** Why do you think Israel agreed to sign a peace treaty with Egypt to return most of the Sinai?

goal was to set up a Palestinian state. Some PLO members launched guerrilla attacks on Israelis from bases in Jordan. They hoped to bring about the destruction of Israel.

Actions by the PLO and other radical Arab groups helped to spread the Arab-Israeli conflict beyond the Middle East. These groups lashed out against the United States and other nations that supported Israel. They committed acts of terrorism such as bombings, airplane hijackings, and taking hostages. The terrorists received training and funds from Iran, Syria, and other Middle Eastern nations. Libya's Muammar Qaddafi (kuh DAH fee), a strong supporter of the Palestinians, was often accused of backing PLO terrorist activities.

PLO attacks brought Israeli **reprisals**, or forceful acts in response to an injury. Israel struck back at PLO bases in Jordan. To stop the reprisals, Jordan's King Hussein ousted the PLO from his country in 1970. The PLO then set up bases in Lebanon and launched new raids on Israel. Their conflicts contributed to the outbreak of civil war in Lebanon.

To halt the continued PLO threat and consolidate power in the occupied territories, Israel invaded Lebanon in 1982. Israeli forces repeatedly returned to attack bases from which the PLO and other groups attacked northern Israel.

Building a Nation

Israel is one of the two democracies in the Middle East. Since its founding, it has made great progress in developing its economy.

The people. Israel is a small nation about the size of New Jersey. About 90 percent of Israelis live in urban areas, mainly along the Mediterranean coast. To strengthen Israel and further the Zionist ideal, the government has encouraged Jews to immigrate from Europe, Africa, Asia, and the Americas. Many newcomers were refugees from persecution.

Although Jewish settlers who went to Israel shared a common religion, they came from diverse cultures. The two main groups were the Ashkenazim, or Jews from Europe, and the Sephardim, or Jews from other parts of the Middle East and Africa.

At first, the more numerous and better-educated Ashkenazim dominated the government and economy. Today, Sephardim are in the majority and have increased their influence in the government. The two groups often disagree on the policies Israel should follow toward the Arab nations.

Other divisions exist among Israeli Jews. Orthodox Jews, who follow Judaic law strictly, want the government to enforce religious laws. Nonreligious Jews, who are in the majority, oppose such moves.

About 15 percent of Israelis are non-Jews. Most are Arab Muslims and Christians. Arab citizens of Israel have full political rights, but many feel discriminated against in education, employment, and other areas.

Israel's Arab population is growing rapidly. This trend worries Jews, who fear that Arabs may someday outnumber Jews in Israel. However, the recent tide of Jewish refugees from the former Soviet Union has helped to offset such Arab population growth.

Economic development. Like most of its neighbors, Israel has a mixed economy. Although the government owns some businesses, many remain in private hands. The lack of natural resources and water in Israel has been offset by hard work, inventiveness, and large amounts of capital from the United States and from Jews living outside of Israel.

Israel has expanded industry as well as agriculture. Israelis are using advanced technology to irrigate desert areas and increase food production. They have also taken advantage of the warm climate to grow fruit crops for export. Today, most Israelis enjoy a fairly high standard of living.

Despite its diversified economy, Israel remains dependent on imports for many basic goods, including oil and coal. Because of the constant threats to its security, it also has had to spend much of its budget on defense.

The intifada. Starting in 1987, Israel faced yet another challenge. That year, Palestinians in the occupied lands began a mass uprising known as the **intifada**, or "the shaking."

Frustrated by years of Israeli military rule, Palestinians attacked Israeli soldiers and civilians and organized strikes against Israeli businesses. Israelis responded to the intifada by arresting and imprisoning many Palestinians. They deported, or forced into exile, Palestinians who were suspected of leading the uprising. Troops destroyed the homes of suspected rebels and closed Arab schools on the West Bank for a while.

Israel came under increasing world criticism for violating the rights of Palestinians. Israeli leaders defended the harsh measures as necessary to protect national security. Within Israel, however, divisions deepened as many Jews urged the government to solve the problem of the occupied territories. They pointed out that violence and deaths would continue as long as Palestinians lived under Israeli occupation without hope for the future.

Peace Efforts

The Arab-Israeli conflict has been very difficult to resolve. For years, Arab nations refused to recognize or negotiate with Israel. They supported terrorist activities against the Jewish state and publicly called for its destruction. At the same time, Israeli leaders rejected the idea of a Palestinian state which they felt would threaten Israel's security. Nor would they discuss the status of the occupied territories until their Arab neighbors had made peace treaties with Israel.

A first step. A breakthrough toward peace occurred in 1977 when the Egyptian president, Anwar Sadat, agreed to peace talks with Israel. Two years later, with the help of the United States, Egypt and Israel signed a peace treaty. Under the agreement, Israel withdrew its forces from the Sinai Peninsula. The agreement also called for Palestinian self-rule in the occupied territories.

That breakthrough brought few additional gains, however. Other Arab nations condemned Egypt for making peace with Israel. Tensions remained high, and the outlook for a general peace was a distant dream.

New talks. The Persian Gulf War and the collapse of the Soviet Union led the United States to make new peace efforts in the Middle East. In the autumn of 1991, Arab and Israeli leaders finally met face-to-face in Madrid, Spain. Other peace talks followed, but they bogged down over the many difficult issues.

Surveying the Wreckage
During the Persian Gulf War, Iraq launched 39 long-range missile attacks against Israel. This young Israeli looks over the damage caused by one such attack. The boy is carrying a gas mask kit because it was feared that some of the missiles carried poison gas.
Power What might Iraq have hoped to gain by attacking Israel during the Persian Gulf War?

Israel was surrounded by hostile neighbors, including Syria, Jordan, and Lebanon. Any agreement had to settle longstanding disputes with each of these nations.

Equally important was the future status of the occupied territories. More than 1.7 million Palestinians live in the West Bank and the Gaza Strip. Many have grown up in poverty-stricken refugee camps. For years, Palestinians in the occupied territories demanded their own homeland. Many supported the PLO leader Yassir Arafat who called for the destruction of Israel and the establishment of a Palestinian state. Israel, however, refused to talk to the PLO because of its terrorist activites.

No easy solutions. During the intifada, a growing number of young Palestinians turned toward a more extreme group, Hammas. Its supporters were Islamic fundamentalists with ties to Iran.

Israelis were divided over the question of the occupied territories. The government had allowed more than 100,000 Jewish settlers to move into those lands. The growth of Jewish settlements in recent years in the West Bank and Gaza had helped spark the intifada.

Some Israelis were willing to consider giving up part of the occupied lands in return for peace. Others rejected any land-for-peace agreement. Israel, they believed, must hold onto the occupied territories for security reasons. They also claimed a historic right to these lands, which had been part of the ancient kingdom of Israel. "We are not occupying this land," declared an Israeli settler, "we are returning to it."

Added to the conflicting demands was the daily violence in the occupied lands between Israeli troops and Arab residents. Peace seemed a long way off.

The Unknown Peacemakers

On a wintry morning in 1992, two men sat across from each other in a London hotel. One was Yair Hirschfeld, a 49-year-old Israeli professor of history. The other was Ahmed Karia, also known as Abu Alaa, an official in the PLO. Hirschfeld knew that by talking to Abu Alaa he was committing a crime. Israelis were forbidden by law to meet with groups such as the PLO.

The meeting had been set up by a Norwegian sociologist. All three men hoped that the secret meeting might open the door to progress toward peace where endless talks among diplomats had failed.

A new approach. "We clicked personally," Abu Alaa later recalled about his first talk with Hirschfeld. The Israeli voiced his view another way:

> "Some of what he said was objectionable, but I liked the tone."

Back in Israel, Hirschfeld had often talked about peace with Palestinian friends. He had marched in Peace Now demonstrations. To Hirschfeld, the core issue in the Israeli-Arab conflict was the question of the Palestinians.

After meeting Abu Alaa, Hirschfeld called Ron Pundik, an Israeli friend and fellow historian. "I think we have something running," he said. Like Hirschfeld, Pundik wanted to find common ground between Israelis and Palestinians. "Let's do it," Pundik urged.

Both men were ready to break the rules to talk further with Abu Alaa. Hirschfeld recalled a story about officers in the old Austro-Hungarian army. If they ignored rules in battle and succeeded, they received a medal. But the risk was high. As he told it,

> "If you broke discipline in the Austro-Hungarian Army, you had two choices: get the Maria Theresa medal or be shot."

The Norwegian connection. Hirschfeld, Pundik, and Abu Alaa took up the offer of Norwegian officials to help them continue their talks. Starting early in 1993, they met secretly more than a dozen times in various Norwegian country homes. The peacemakers talked and shouted. They shared meals and jokes and then argued some more over drafts of a peace declaration.

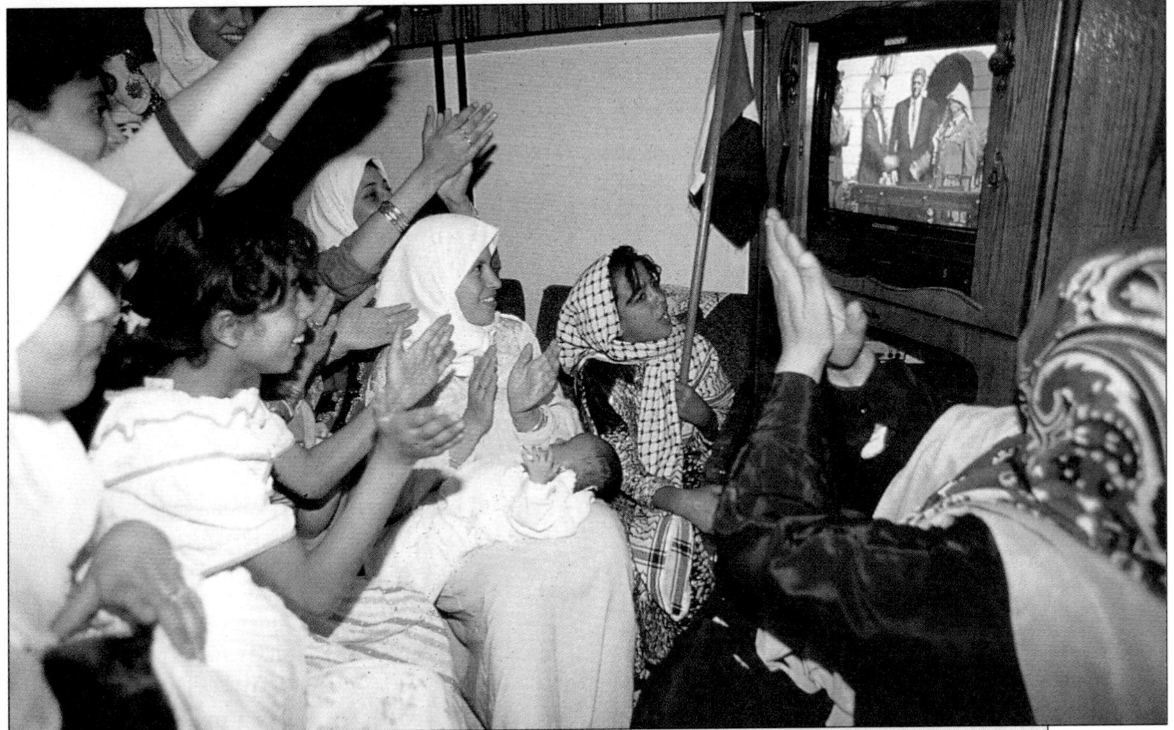

Celebrating a Historic Handshake Palestinian women and children applaud as they watch Israeli Prime Minister Yitzhak Rabin and Palestine Liberation Organization Chairman Yassir Arafat shake hands. The Declaration of Principles they had just signed led to limited Palestinian self-rule in the Gaza Strip and Jericho. ***Citizenship*** What new responsibilities for Palestinians might self-rule bring?

By 1993, the Israeli parliament had lifted the law forbidding contacts with the PLO. As the talks in Norway moved ahead, Israeli officials were brought in. Slowly, they edged toward agreement on key issues: Israel and the PLO would recognize each other; the PLO would give up attacks on Israel; Israel would withdraw its forces from parts of the occupied territories and allow limited self-rule for Palestinians in Gaza and Jericho, a town in the West Bank.

A surprised world. In August 1993, the secrecy ended, and the agreement was made public. The next month, leaders from around the world gathered in Washington, D.C. There, on the White House lawn, President Clinton of the United States watched as Israeli prime minister Yitzhak Rabin and PLO chairman Yassir Arafat shook hands after signing the agreement. The world celebrated the historic handshake.

Hirschfeld and Pundik meanwhile had a hard time rustling up tickets to the event. Among the world leaders on the White House lawn, these two remained unrecognized. Abu Alaa, however, shook hands with them. ■

Looking Ahead

Despite later difficulties, Israel withdrew from Gaza and the West Bank town of Jericho in 1994. Other issues have yet to be resolved, however. Much of the West Bank remains under Israeli control. Also, Palestinians still hope to set up an independent state, which Israel opposes.

At the same time, negotiations continue between Israel and its neighbors. In July 1994, Israel and Jordan ended the 46-year state of war that had existed between the two countries. Ongoing talks with Syria focused on the Golan Heights, which Israel occupied during the Six Day War. Problems remain, but the Gaza-Jericho agreement has led many people to hope that it is only a matter of time before these issues will be settled.

SECTION 2 REVIEW

1. **Locate:** (a) Israel, (b) Syria, (c) Jordan, (d) Egypt, (e) West Bank, (f) Sinai Peninsula, (g) Gaza Strip, (h) Golan Heights, (i) Jericho.
2. **Identify:** (a) Six Day War, (b) PLO, (c) Ashkenazim, (d) Sephardim.
3. **Define:** (a) refugee, (b) occupied territory, (c) reprisal, (d) intifada.
4. (a) Why did Jews want the state of Israel? (b) How did Arab nations respond to the founding of Israel?
5. What lands did Israel gain as a result of the war in 1948? In 1967?
6. (a) What was the cause of the intifada? (b) Why are Israelis reluctant to give up the occupied territories?
7. **Understanding Causes and Effects** How did the end of the Cold War make movement toward peace possible in the 1990s?
8. **Writing Across Cultures** Write a letter to a friend explaining why you think the United States should continue to play a role in bringing peace to the Middle East.

3 LITERATURE AND THE ARTS

FIND OUT

What traditions influenced Muslim literature?

What themes appear in the works of modern writers in the Middle East?

What art forms did Islamic civilization produce?

What are some trends in modern Middle Eastern art and music?

The audience hall of the royal palace outside Baghdad boasted a magnificent carpet. Sometime in about A.D. 500, skilled craftworkers wove the huge rug, working emeralds, pearls, and other jewels among the silk threads. The intricate weaving showed a delightful garden with winding pathways, running brooks, flower beds, birds, and fruit trees.

In rugs such as this one, craftworkers in the Middle East raised carpet weaving to a fine art. Magnificent carpets are only one of the many contributions that the Middle East has made to the arts.

Literature of the Islamic World

Islamic literature in the Middle East has been written in three languages—Arabic, Persian, and Turkish. Arabic, the language of the Koran, was used for religious and scientific works as well as for literature. By 900, Persian began to rival Arabic as the language of literature. During the Ottoman Empire, court poets produced fine works in Turkish.

The Koran and religious writings. Since the time of Muhammad, the Koran has been the model for all Arabic literature. Muslim scholars studied the Koran and wrote books explaining Islamic law. In biographies of Muhammad and his followers, they recorded the early history of Islam. By collecting and recounting the sayings of Muhammad, they helped explain the teachings of Islam.

Poetry. Poetry has long had a special place in the Arab world. Even before the rise of Islam, each tribe in Arabia had its poets. In their poems, the Arabs spoke of love, war, and courage. They praised their leaders, abused their enemies, and celebrated desert life. This rich oral literature was passed from generation to generation and later collected in books.

At the Abbassid court in Baghdad, poets writing in Persian built on Arabic forms of poetry. Court poets wrote of romantic love. They spoke of the noble, generous deeds of princes and of their own hopes and fears. Persian poets were especially noted for their mystical poetry, in which they expressed their love of God.

Among the finest Persian works were epic, or narrative, poems. Epics often drew on folklore and events from ancient Persian history. In about 1010, the poet Firdawsi composed his great work, *Shah-nama,* or "Book of Kings." In one tragic episode, Rustam, the hero of the poem, unknowingly kills his own son. When he discovers what he has done, Rustam is overcome with grief:

> "When Rustam loosed
> The armor and saw the gem, he tore
> his clothes
> And cried: 'Oh! my brave son,
> approved by all
> And slain by me!' "

The Persian poet who is best known to the western world is Omar Khayyám, who died in about 1123. More than 700 years later, the English poet Edward FitzGerald translated Omar Khayyám's poem *The Rubáiyát,* which became a major success in the West. In the Muslim world, however, Khayyám is better known for his work as an astronomer and as a mathematician, philosopher, and physician.

Folktales. As a cultural crossroads, the Middle East acquired folktales from many parts of the world. During the 1300s, some of these tales were collected and written down under the title *The Thousand and One Nights.* In that book, the princess Scheherazade (shuh hehr uh ZAH duh) uses the tales night after night to entertain the king and thereby escape execution. The stories are Persian, Indian, Egyptian, Greek, Hebrew, and even Chinese in origin. Like *The Rubáiyát* of Omar Khayyám, *The Thousand and One Nights* has enjoyed great popularity in the West. (See Connections With Literature, page 807, "The Fisherman and the Jinee.")

The Koran and Islamic Literature Artists skilled in calligraphy copied these pages of the Koran, turning them into a work of art. To Muslims, the text of the Koran contains the words of God. Thus, the holy book of Islam has long inspired Arabic, Persian, and Turkish literature. ***Culture*** Why would Muslim artists regard their work as an act of religious devotion?

Modern Writers

Today, the literature of the Middle East still reflects the region's cultural diversity. People writing in Arabic, Persian, and Turkish continue to produce outstanding works. In addition, Israeli writers have revived Hebrew literature.

Arabic literature. In an outburst of creativity, modern writers have produced novels, biographies, and histories as well as poetry in Arabic. They have explored a variety of themes, including the conflict between Arab and western cultures and the disruptions caused by modernization. (📖 See World Literature, "The Storm," by Khalil al-Fuzay, page 630.)

Among the most original writers was the Egyptian Taha Husayn, who was born in 1889. Husayn left his village to study at al-Azhar, the 1,000-year-old Islamic university in Cairo. In *al-Ayyam* (*The Days*), he gives a fascinating account of his school years.

Today, the most popular modern writer in the Arab world is Naguib Mahfouz (NAH heeb MAH fooz). Born in Cairo in 1911, Mahfouz has won fame for his novels, especially *The Cairo Trilogy.* In this series of three books, he captures the turbulence of Egyptian life during much of this century. In 1988, Mahfouz became the first Arab writer to receive the Nobel Prize for literature. He remarked:

> " Egypt and the Arab world also get the Nobel Prize with me. I believe that . . . the international doors have opened, and in the future, literate people will look for Arab literature, and Arab literature deserves that recognition. "

Israeli literature. Israel, too, has made important contributions to literature. Israelis have worked to revive Hebrew as a modern spoken language, adapting ancient words to today's uses. Israeli writers have explored such themes as the Jewish diaspora, the Holocaust, and the Arab-Israeli conflict.

A leading Israeli novelist and short-story writer was Shmuel Yosef Agnon (AGH nahn). In 1966, Agnon received the Nobel Prize for literature. In his novel *The Day Before Yesterday,* he examined the problems westernized Jews faced when they settled in Israel.

Hebrew poetry has also flourished. One well-known poet is Yehuda Amichai (yuh HOO duh AH mih kī), who wrote *Songs of Jerusalem and Myself.* In his poetry, Amichai has pioneered the use of Hebrew as an everyday language to present traditional Jewish themes. A versatile writer, Amichai has produced short stories, radio plays, and novels in addition to poetry.

Architecture and Art

During the golden age of Islam, architects and artists drew on the rich traditions of many cultures to produce some of the world's finest works. Islamic art flourished throughout the Muslim world, from Spain in the west to India in the east.

Architecture. Muslim architects designed splendid mosques and palaces that glittered with colorful glazed tiles and mosaics. From the Byzantines, Muslims acquired skills in building domes. Large domes often crowned mosques such as the Dome of the Rock in Jerusalem. The minaret, or tower, is a familiar feature of mosques. From there, the muezzin calls the faithful to prayer. Among the most famous mosques are the Suleymaniya Mosque in Istanbul, which was built during the reign of Suleiman the Magnificent, and the Mosque of Selim in Edirne, Turkey.

Muslim princes built luxurious palaces. Among the few that still exist is the Alhambra in Granada, Spain. Its sun-drenched courtyards and intricate carvings reflect Greek and Roman influences as well as Islamic traditions.

Decorative arts. Because the Koran forbids the worship of idols, many Muslims and their religious leaders opposed the portrayal of human or animal images. Despite this ban, miniature painting emerged as one of the leading artistic traditions.

Artists in Persia perfected the art of miniature painting. During the late 1400s, the brilliant court painter Kamal Ad-Din Bihzad illustrated many books with fine miniatures. From then until the 1800s, miniature painting was a respected and popular tradition.

Calligraphy, or the art of beautiful writing, became one of the highest forms of Islamic art. Arabic inscriptions with sayings from the Koran decorate the walls of such Islamic monuments as the Taj Mahal in India. Even today, calligraphy is widely used as decoration on buildings, coins, posters, and fabrics.

From the Islamic world came a variety of crafts, including pottery, textiles, and metalware. Damascus steel and damask, a figured woven cloth, were in great demand.

Weaving a Rug Turkish artisans skillfully produce this handmade carpet. Carpets originated in the Middle East as covering for earthen floors in houses and mosques. They were also used as prayer rugs, curtains, blankets, and coverings for tent openings. ***Culture*** Why is the design of this carpet appropriate for an Islamic society?

In homes and workshops, men and women perfected the art of weaving carpets. Styles and designs varied from one part of the Islamic world to another. In Persia, for example, rugs featured floral designs and curling scrolls known as arabesques. Turkish weavers used abstract or geometric designs. Today, weavers in many Middle Eastern countries continue to produce richly colored carpets for export throughout the world.

Modern artists. In modern times, western ideas have strongly influenced the arts in the Middle East. In response to western domination, however, some Arab artists are once again studying their Islamic heritage. They have developed distinctive new styles based on abstract and geometric designs as well as on traditional calligraphy.

Israel. The influence of western art is especially strong in Israel. Many Israeli artists were either born in Europe or studied contemporary western art. The Israeli artist Yakov Agam experimented with a style of modern art known as optical painting. In one painting titled *Double Metamorphosis II,* the viewer sees a huge grid with colorful geometric

Cheb Khalid, the "King of Rai" Rai is a favorite style of popular music in the Arab world. Singers like Khalid weave intricate rhythms against a solid beat produced by a combination of traditional and modern electronic instruments. Rai has been compared with American soul music because of its emotional intensity. ***Diversity*** How does rai represent a blend of musical elements?

designs. As you walk past the painting, the colors and shapes appear to shift and tilt.

Music

In the past, Muslim religious leaders disapproved of music, saying it was frivolous and turned people's minds from God. In Baghdad, Istanbul, and other cities, however, wealthy rulers supported talented musicians, and various local musical traditions developed.

Today, radio and tapes have helped to spread modern music across the Muslim world. In some ways, today's popular music—especially songs—unites Muslims, as poetry did in the past.

One of the most popular singers was Umm Kalthum, who chanted the Koran and performed songs written by Egypt's finest contemporary poets. For many years, Arabic-speaking audiences tuned in to Kalthum's Thursday evening radio show. Her death in 1975 was marked by an outpouring of grief throughout the Muslim world.

Today, singer Cheb Khalid dominates popular Arab music. Khalid is known as the "king of rai" (rī). This musical style blends traditional Arab music with rock and jazz. Khalid's concerts attract huge audiences, especially among Arab youth.

SECTION 3 REVIEW

1. **Identify** (a) *Shah-nama,* (b) Omar Kháyyám, (c) *The Thousand and One Nights,* (d) Naguib Mahfouz, (e) Shmuel Yosef Agnon, (f) Cheb Khalid.
2. (a) Describe the major themes of Arabic and Persian poetry. (b) What are three themes of modern Muslim literature?
3. (a) How did the establishment of Israel affect Hebrew literature? (b) What are three themes of modern Israeli literature?
4. (a) What were the two main types of structures in Muslim architecture? (b) Why did calligraphy become an important feature of Muslim art?
5. **Analyzing Information** How do the arts of the Middle East reflect the cultural diversity of the region?
6. **Writing Across Cultures** Does popular music help to unite Americans? Write a paragraph explaining your answer. Give examples to support your answer.

Chapter 28 Review

Understanding Vocabulary

Match each term at left with the correct definition at right.

1. refugee	**a.** forceful acts in response to an injury
2. occupied territory	**b.** person who has fled his or her homeland to seek safety elsewhere
3. reprisal	**c.** art of beautiful writing
4. intifada	**d.** land captured by Israel from Arab nations
5. calligraphy	**e.** Palestinian uprising against Israeli rule

Reviewing the Main Ideas

1. Why did the Middle East gain global attention after World War II?

2. (a) What was the outcome of the superpowers' rivalry in Turkey? (b) Why did the United States help rebels in Afghanistan?

3. (a) Why did some Middle Eastern nations form OPEC? (b) What actions did OPEC take?

4. (a) What groups does Israel's population include? (b) What progress has Israel made in its economic development?

5. (a) How did Arab nations oppose Israel? (b) How did Palestinian Arabs oppose Israel?

6. Give two examples of how Islam has influenced the arts in the Middle East.

Reviewing Chapter Themes

1. After World War II, the Middle East became a focus of Cold War rivalry between the United States and the Soviet Union. Describe two situations in which this superpower rivalry affected the Middle East.

2. Tensions among neighboring Muslim nations have sometimes erupted into war. Discuss the causes and results of the Persian Gulf War.

3. Nationalism contributed to hostility and war between Arabs and Israelis. Discuss the reasons Arab nations resented Israel.

4. The peoples of the Middle East have produced many great works of art and literature. Describe two achievements of Middle Eastern artists in each of the following: (a) literature, (b) architecture, (c) decorative arts.

Thinking Critically

1. Evaluating Information (a) Why do events in Persian Gulf nations such as Iran and Iraq have global effects? (b) How might the impact of these events on the world be lessened?

2. Synthesizing Information Why do you think the end of the Cold War has helped to ease tensions in the Middle East?

3. Making Inferences Why do you think unofficial Palestinian and Israeli negotiators were able to make progress towards peace where diplomats and superpowers could not?

4. Making Global Connections Describe the role of the United States in the Arab-Israeli conflict.

Applying Your Skills

1. Constructing a Time Line Make a time line that includes the following events: United States offers economic and military aid to Turkey; Soviet Union invades Afghanistan; OPEC is formed; Iran-Iraq War begins; Persian Gulf War ends.

2. Making a Review Chart Make a chart listing the steps toward peace that have been taken by Israel, its Arab neighbors, and the PLO. Then make a separate list of issues that remain to be resolved.

SKILL LESSON 13

Understanding Causes and Effects: The Arab-Israeli Conflict

A major event or development in history has both causes and effects. Causes are events or conditions that produced a major event. They explain why the event happened. Effects are events or conditions that the major event produced. They explain what happened as a result of the event.

Key words can provide clues in recognizing causes and effects. For example, the words *since, because,* and *due to* often indicate causes. The words *therefore* and *as a result* often indicate effects.

Causes and effects can be short-term or long-term. Short-term causes and effects happen immediately before or after an event. Long-term causes and effects take place over a long period of time.

Use the chart below and your reading in Unit 7 to study the causes and effects of the Arab-Israeli conflict.

1. **Identify the causes and effects.** (a) What were the causes of the Arab-Israeli conflict? **(b)** Which of these causes was the most long-term? **(c)** What were the effects of the conflict?
2. **Analyze the causes and effects.** (a) How did each of the following events contribute to the Arab-Israeli conflict: Israel is established as a Jewish state; Arab nations refuse to recognize Israel? **(b)** What role did the Arab-Israeli conflict play in each of the following events: Israel occupies territories that were captured from Arab nations; the Palestine Liberation Organization (PLO) attacks Israel from Arab nations?
3. **Draw conclusions based on the causes and effects.** (a) Which causes are still major issues in the Arab-Israeli conflict? **(b)** Which effects have intensified the conflict? **(c)** Why has compromise been difficult to reach in the Arab-Israeli conflict? **(d)** Write a paragraph evaluating the progress that has been made toward resolving the Arab-Israeli conflict.

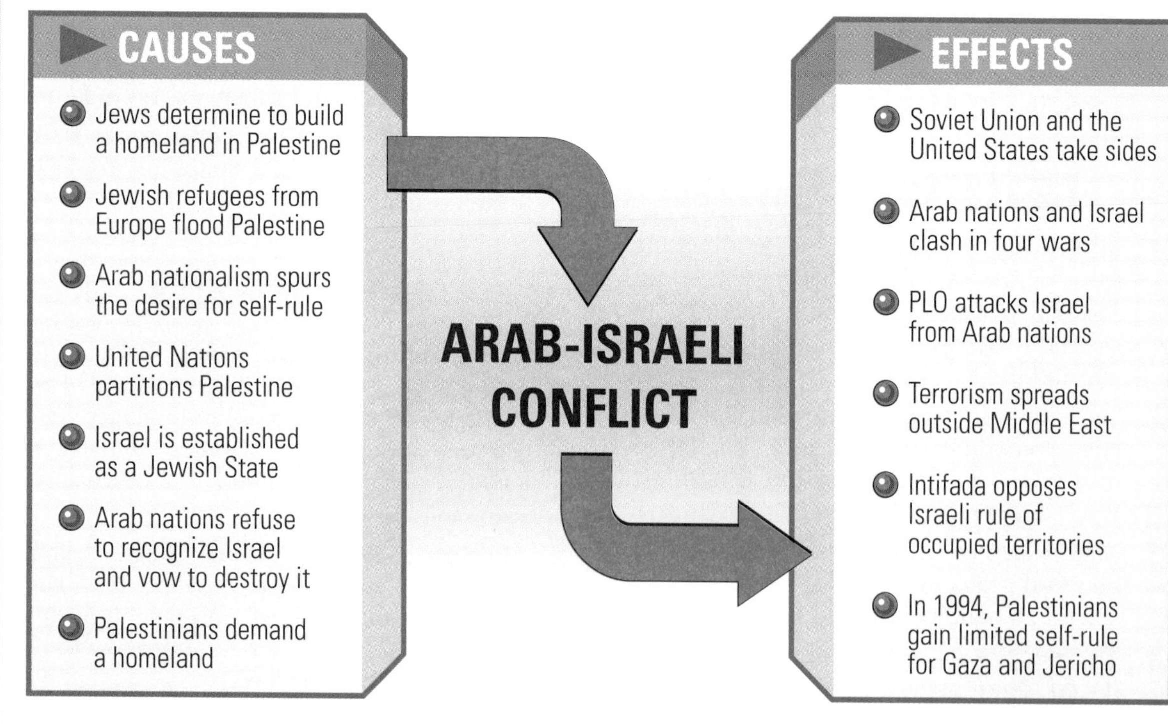

SKILL LESSON 14

Comparing Points of View: The Persian Gulf War

Some sources of information express points of view as well as provide a firsthand account of events. In many cases, two sources that have witnessed the same event present very different views of what happened.

Conflicts develop among nations when they view the same events differently. The excerpts below concern the Persian Gulf War of 1991. One excerpt is from a speech by King Hussein of Jordan, who sided with Iraq during the war. The other excerpt is from a speech by President Bush of the United States. Read the excerpts carefully, using the following steps to guide you.

1. **Identify the content of each source.** (a) According to President Bush, what event caused the Persian Gulf War? (b) What efforts does he say have been made to resolve the crisis? (c) Why does King Hussein call the Persian Gulf War the cruelest war the world has known? (d) According to King Hussein, why did diplomatic efforts fail to resolve the crisis?
2. **Compare the points of view.** (a) According to Bush, what do the United States and its allies hope to achieve by going to war with Iraq? (b) Does King Hussein agree with this view? Explain.
3. **Evaluate the sources.** (a) What do these speeches tell you about the political situation in the Middle East in 1991? (b) Do you think these speeches are reliable sources of information? Explain.

President Bush, January 16, 1991

"This conflict started August 2, when the dictator of Iraq invaded a small and helpless neighbor. Kuwait, a member of the Arab League and a member of the United Nations, was crushed, its people brutalized. Five months ago, Saddam Hussein started this cruel war against Kuwait; tonight, the battle has been joined.

This military action . . . follows months of constant and virtually endless diplomatic activity on the part of the United Nations, the United States, and many, many countries. Arab leaders sought what became known as an Arab solution. . . . Others traveled to Baghdad in a variety of efforts. . . . This past weekend, in a last-ditch effort, the Secretary General of the United Nations went to the Middle East. . . .

Now, the 28 countries with forces in the gulf area have exhausted all reasonable efforts to reach a peaceful resolution, and have no choice but to drive Saddam from Kuwait by force."

King Hussein, February 6, 1991

"The world has known cruel wars, but never one like this that is waged against Iraq. . . . The armies of the biggest and most powerful nations have gathered and unleashed their modern and dangerous weapons. . . . Fire rains down upon Iraq . . . destroying mosques, churches, schools, museums, hospitals, powdered milk factories, residential areas, Bedouin tents, electricity generating stations, and water networks. . . .

It is claimed that every effort possible was made to solve the crisis during the five months before the war. This is not true. . . . The Arab parties concerned chose from the beginning to reject any political Arab dialogue with Iraq. . . . All the good offices of Jordan and others . . . were [cut short]. Why? Because the real purpose behind this destructive war . . . is to destroy Iraq and rearrange the area. . . . This arrangement would put the [Arab world] . . . under direct foreign [influence] and would shred all ties between its parts."

The Storm

Khalil al-Fuzay

INTRODUCTION Khalil al-Fuzay (1941–) is a Saudi Arabian journalist. Many of his stories, like much of the literature from the Gulf area, focus on life in Saudi Arabia before the development of the oil industry. Stories such as "The Storm" take a nostalgic look at a past that was filled with hardship and uncertainty but was well rooted in culture and tradition.

Today is Saturday*—the beginning of the week and you are bored already. But you shouldn't be. Everyone says they come back to work full of energy after the weekend. Your work needs energy, mine doesn't. I'm the one who should be bored with this work, not you. All I do is clean the Director's office and wait for his orders. As for you, your work is always new. . . .

What? No, I don't want to sit down and chat. I know we have lots of time because the Director never gets here before eleven, but you always want me to talk about the past—about the pearl-diving days. Why do you always insist on this? . . .

Pearl-diving stories are full of sorrow. . . . But money ran through my rough hands like water then: diving brought it in heaps. And now look at me—the Director's office boy! What a world! Praise be to God the Unchanging. . . .

I had a big boat and on certain days we'd set off on our trips to the heart of the Gulf. Since I was the captain and in full charge of everything, I didn't have as hard a time as the divers. . . .

* The Muslim holy day is Friday, and the Muslim work week begins on Saturday.

Sometimes we'd come back with plenty and sometimes with hardly anything at all. But whatever we got was usually enough to hold us until the next time. . . .

One afternoon, everything was running smoothly. All our men were on deck, busy splitting the mother-of-pearl, and I was sitting there enjoying my water-pipe and quietly watching them work. Then, suddenly, the sky darkened and the sea rose. The boat lurched and everyone lost their balance. I dropped my pipe and found myself huddled in the stern with my men. Some of them were gripping the sides and voices were raised in prayers and exclamations. Water was filling the boat. I shouted at them to bail it out, grabbed the nearest bucket and started bailing. So did the others but we could not keep up with the sea. We were desperate. In those anguished moments I was not concerned for myself as much as for my men. Through the noise I realized that some had been swept overboard and were, at that very moment, battling the waves. Something told me I would lose some of them. . . .

You're letting your tea get cold, drink it. What? You don't want your tea? You want to know what happened next? Well, what happened next was enough to turn your hair white. We fought bitterly against the sea. The faster we bailed, the faster the boat filled up. The closer we came to death, the more we wanted to live. No one was speaking any more and Death himself could not have told the difference between the captain and the humblest of the men. At first I'd been thinking of my men but, in the end, I was thinking only of myself. I fiercely wanted to save the boat—not because I owned it, but because it was our only hope of survival. You know the proverbial "straw in the wind"? That's how we were. The waves played with us cruelly, tossing us here and there. One huge, monstrous wave came at us. I thought we were done for but, suddenly, we were riding it, looking down as though from a mountain-top. Then we were flung into emptiness. The boat spun and we were all beyond the point of exhaustion.

But the will to live is stronger than any storm, so we fought. We saw those who gave in being swept away to God-only-knows-where. There was a moment when I was on the point of surrendering but the image of my son Jassoum sprang into my mind and I forgot my despair. In the midst of the terrible sounds of the storm you would still hear voices raised in prayer. These urged us to even greater efforts: surely, our Maker would not desert us? Those who lost faith vanished and were swallowed up by the waves.

The storm lasted maybe an hour. It was the longest, most terrible hour in all time. Then, as suddenly as it began, it ended. The sea was covered with bodies and wrecked boats. Men were hanging on to anything to save themselves from the death they had come so close to. We finished bailing out the last of the water and started rescuing survivors. We lost some men and saved others and, as sunset approached, the world was filled with silence. All tongues praised God and that night we slept as we had never slept before. . . .

What did we do then? We did what everyone did: we went home to comfort our families, who had heard news of the storm. What? You say your own father died in that storm? God have mercy on his soul! You never told me that before. . . . So that's why you're so keen on sea stories. . . . But tell me, why are you always looking so bored? Don't you like your work? It's a comfortable job—Oh, oh. I have to leave now. The boss is here.

The peoples of the Middle East still cherish their ancient traditions and values despite the rapid change and conflicts in their region. The author of *The Storm* describes how the lives of Arabs changed when they could no longer perform their traditional occupation. Israeli artist Shraga Weil, in this painting, *Take Up the Melody,* also takes his inspiration from his people's past, depicting a verse from the Bible that celebrates a Jewish holy day. Why do you think traditions are such an important part of people's lives?

Source: "The Storm," by Khalil al-Fuzay, translated by Ahdaf Soueif and Thomas G. Ezzy. From *The Literature of Modern Arabia,* edited by Salma Khadra Jayyusi. Copyright 1988 by the King Saud University. University of Texas Press, Austin.

THINKING ABOUT LITERATURE

1. To whom does the narrator tell the story about the storm?
2. At the end of the story, what does the narrator find out about the listener's father?
3. **Making Inferences** Why do you think the listener is bored and is always asking the narrator to tell him stories about the past?

Medicine of the Muslim World

The announcement jolted the Baghdad medical community. A doctor's fatal error had caused the death of a citizen. Now, the caliph Muqtadir ordered that *all* doctors in the city be tested on their medical knowledge. The caliph's own court physician would question each doctor personally.

One by one, more than 850 Baghdad doctors submitted to the test. Most passed. Some were forbidden to perform bloodletting or prescribe harsh drugs. Others were banned from practicing medicine altogether. By the end of the year 932, Baghdad was a safer place for the sick.

The caliph's medical examination shows the high standard of medicine in the Muslim world. The ideas and practices of early Muslim physicians helped to shape the course of modern medicine.

A number of elements contributed to the major medical achievements of Muslims. One was financial support by the caliphs. They promoted public health as well as scientific discovery. Muhammad himself took a keen interest in medical matters. His medical sayings were collected in books called "The Medicine of the Prophet."

Religious toleration also helped medicine advance. At hospitals and universities, doctors of many faiths—Muslim, Christian, Jewish, Hindu, and Zoroastrian—worked side by side. They learned from each other.

Old Learning, New Discoveries

Muslim medicine was based on the knowledge of ancient Greece. Scholars translated the works of Greek medical authorities into Arabic. At a time when scholarship in Europe had nearly died out, the libraries at Baghdad, Cairo, and Córdoba preserved classic medical texts.

Starting with this knowledge, Muslim physicians made hundreds of new discoveries. The greatest medical scholars were Muhammad al-Razi (see page 574) and Ibn Sina. By the time he was 18, Ibn Sina was court physician to a sultan. Without the advantage of a microscope, Ibn Sina discovered how disease could be spread by a polluted well or river. His encyclopedia described the treatment for hundreds of diseases.

Ibn Rushd, a Spanish Muslim known in the West as Averröes, was the first to no-

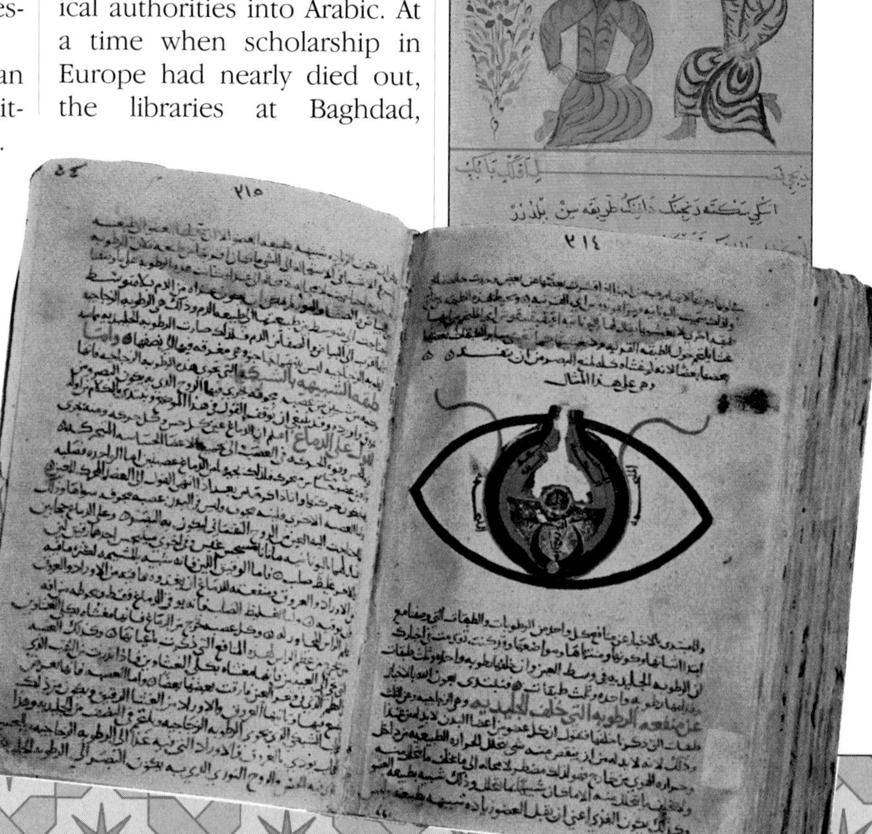

tice that smallpox never infected the same person twice. This discovery proved crucial to the development of vaccines in Britain some 600 years later. Arab surgeons performed complex operations on the head and chest. They also experimented with anesthesia, and invented new surgical instruments.

Eye disease was a common problem in the Arab world. Hunayn ibn Ishaq discovered the causes of eye diseases and made the first detailed anatomical drawings of the eye (bottom left). Eye surgeons developed a way to treat cataracts, drawing fluid out of the lens with a hollow needle. For centuries, surgeons around the world used this method to save patients' eyesight.

Hospitals and Pharmacies

Tradition says that al-Razi once had to choose the location for a new hospital. He hung up pieces of meat at various places in Baghdad and then watched them carefully. The hospital, he advised, should be built at the place where the meat rotted most slowly!

Muslim hospitals, or *bimaristans,* introduced many new practices. They had special wards for the treatment of different diseases and for the mentally ill. Injured people could get quick treatment at a department similar to today's "emergency room." Each hospital had a drug dispensary, a medical library, and a teaching staff. Traveling clinics served remote areas. Doctors would arrive by camel, set up a tent, and treat the sick. Some doctors visited jails regularly.

In addition to hospitals, major cities had drugstores. Arab traders carried healing drugs to Baghdad from all over the Arab empire. Ibn Sina's encyclopedia lists more than 4,000 prescriptions—made with such ingredients as mercury from Spain, myrrh from East Africa, and camphor from India. Arab pharmacists were the first to mix bitter medicines into sweet-tasting syrups and gums. Advances in mathematics enabled them to determine exact dosages.

The Baghdad government kept a sharp eye on pharmacies. Inspectors made surprise visits to make sure drugs were properly prepared and stored in clean jars.

Spread of Knowledge

At the time that Muslim medicine enjoyed a golden age, European doctors lived in a world full of superstition and ignorance, as expressed in the following story. During the crusades, a Lebanese doctor was successfully treating a French knight's infected leg with special herbs and oils. Suddenly, a French doctor ordered the Lebanese doctor to leave. He then tried to amputate the knight's leg. The blunt sword used for the amputation crushed the marrow of the bone, and the knight died soon after.

Slowly, however, European physicians began to attend Islamic universities in Spain. Scholars translated texts from Arabic into Latin and other languages. For 500 years, the works of al-Razi and Ibn Sina were standard textbooks at European medical schools. The rebirth of medical knowledge spread to the new universities and hospitals of France, Germany, and England—and, eventually, to the Americas.

1. Describe two contributions to the development of modern medicine made by Muslim physicians.
2. **Analyzing Information** How did the stability and size of the Arab Empire encourage diffusion of medical knowledge?
3. **Writing Across Cultures** Make a list of several ways that various federal agencies and local governments regulate medical practices and the use of medicines.

UNIT 7 REVIEW

Reviewing the Main Ideas

1. What circumstances led to the diversity of ethnic groups in the Middle East?
2. (a) How did the diaspora affect Judaism? (b) Describe the spread of Christianity after the death of Jesus. (c) Describe the spread of Islam after the death of Muhammad.
3. (a) How are Jews and Christians regarded by Islamic religious teachings? (b) How did tolerance toward other religious beliefs contribute to the spread of Islam?
4. (a) Describe the government of the Ottoman Empire. (b) Who were the "men of the pen"? (c) Who were the "men of the sword"?
5. How has contact with western nations influenced Egypt?
6. Explain the effect each of the following has had on modernization in the Middle East: (a) fundamentalism, (b) oil, (c) education, (d) population growth.
7. (a) What steps have Israel and its Arab neighbors taken toward achieving peace in recent times? (b) What issues pose a challenge to the creation of a lasting peace in the Middle East?
8. How have the cultures and concerns of the peoples of the Middle East affected the arts in that region?

Thinking Critically

1. **Linking Past and Present** Some conflicts in the Middle East are a result of cultural differences that are centuries old. Other conflicts are a result of decisions made in the more recent past by imperialist powers. Choose one of each of these types of conflict. Describe the conflict and explain how it has roots in the past.
2. **Analyzing Information** How has modernization contributed to conflict in the Middle East?
3. **Making Global Connections** After the Persian Gulf War, the United States worked to arrange meetings between Israel and its Arab neighbors. (a) Why does the United States consider peace in the Middle East to be a priority? (b) What steps do you think the United States should take to maintain peace in the Middle East? (c) What steps do you think the United States should not take? Explain.
4. **Analyzing Information** (a) How do the goals of Palestinian nationalists conflict with those of Israeli nationalists? (b) How have Palestinians tried to change their status?

Applying Your Skills

1. **Analyzing a Political Cartoon** The cartoon below from the 1980s was created by an Iranian and reflects his view of the intifada. (a) Which groups are represented in this cartoon? (b) Which groups are directly engaged in conflict? (c) Which are observing from the sidelines? (d) Do the observers appear to be completely neutral? (e) Write a caption for this cartoon that expresses the artist's point of view.

2. **Reading a Map** Study the map on page 549. (a) Which countries are in North Africa? (b) Which country is located partially in Europe? (c) How does this map illustrate the idea that the Middle East is a cultural crossroads?
3. **Analyzing a Quotation** Reread the quotation on page 590. (a) Who made this speech? (b) Why were British and French officials surprised to hear these words? (c) What national goals are expressed?

Learning by Doing

1. **Creating a Map** Make an outline map of the Middle East, labeling all countries and their capitals, major seas, and oceans. Create a map key that identifies major oil and gas fields. Key the fields to the map. (See the maps on pages 549 and 612.)
2. **Creating a Time Line** Use the time line on pages 548–549 as a model. For headings, use Early History (all the events before A.D. 600), 600, 800, 1000, 1200, and 1400. Record all important dates that are connected with Judaism, Christianity, and Islam. Begin with 1025 B.C., the year the Hebrews organized the kingdom of Israel.
3. **Creating an Illustration** Create an illustrated map that shows economic activities in the Middle East. Using an outline map as a base, illustrate the kinds of activities that are taking place in various regions. Possible examples include farms, desalination plants, industrial areas, ports, oil drilling and refining, and nomadic herding.

WRITER'S Workshop

Arranging Information to Show Causes and Effects

A **cause** is an event or a condition that produces an **effect,** or a result. Often, that effect becomes a cause that, in turn, produces another result. To show this chain reaction, you would arrange supporting information in order of causes and effects.

Consider this statement: *Muhammad Ali's attempts to modernize Egypt led to increased foreign intervention.* To explain how this happened, arrange the events in cause-and-effect order. The following diagram shows the chain reaction created by causes and effects.

Muhammad Ali borrows money to modernize Egypt

Egypt is burdened with a huge debt

Egypt sells its share of the Suez Canal to Great Britain

Transitions that show cause and effect include the words *as a result, because, consequently, therefore, thus,* and *so.*

Practice Use the preceding steps to show a cause-and-effect relationship between oil resources and a particular aspect of life in the Middle East today. (See Skill Lesson, page 628.)

Writing to Learn

1. Write a dialogue between an Israeli and an Arab in which they discuss why the Arab-Israeli conflict has been so difficult to resolve. Before you begin to write the dialogue, gather background information about the causes of the dispute. List these causes in order of importance. Write the dialogue to show the efforts made by each side to understand the other's point of view. Proofread and then make a final copy of your dialogue. Ask two classmates to read the dialogue to the class.
2. Write a report about Avicenna, the Arab physician, philosopher, astronomer, and poet. First, research his life. Write a topic sentence summarizing his accomplishments. Organize your details in time order or in order of importance. Revise the report for unity and coherence. Then, proofread and make a final copy of it. Publish your report as part of a class collection of biographies.

UNIT 8

EUROPE AND THE FORMER SOVIET UNION

UNIT OUTLINE

1 This bronze head of the goddess Aphrodite illustrates the Greek ideals of beauty and artistic expression that developed in the Hellenistic world and helped shape European civilization.

2 During the Soviet era, artists were encouraged to create paintings that glorified Soviet workers. This painting depicts industrial laborers in a factory near Moscow.

3 Fishing boats from small ports like this one in southern Portugal have long obtained a rich supply of food from the sea for themselves and other Western Europeans.

	Early History		1200	1400
History and Politics	▲ 400s B.C. Direct democracy develops in Athens	▲ A.D. 400s Roman Empire declines in the West	▲ 1215 Magna Carta limits power of English monarchs	▲ 1300s Moscow emerges as center of power in Russia
Society and Culture	▲ 750s B.C. Homer writes the *Iliad* and the *Odyssey*	▲ 1000s Feudalism develops in Western Europe		▲ 1300s Renaissance begins
Economics and Technology	▲ 200s B.C. Archimedes conducts experiments in physics	▲ 1000s Crop rotation and use of heavy plow increase food production		▲ 1200s–1480 Russians pay heavy tribute to Mongol conquerors

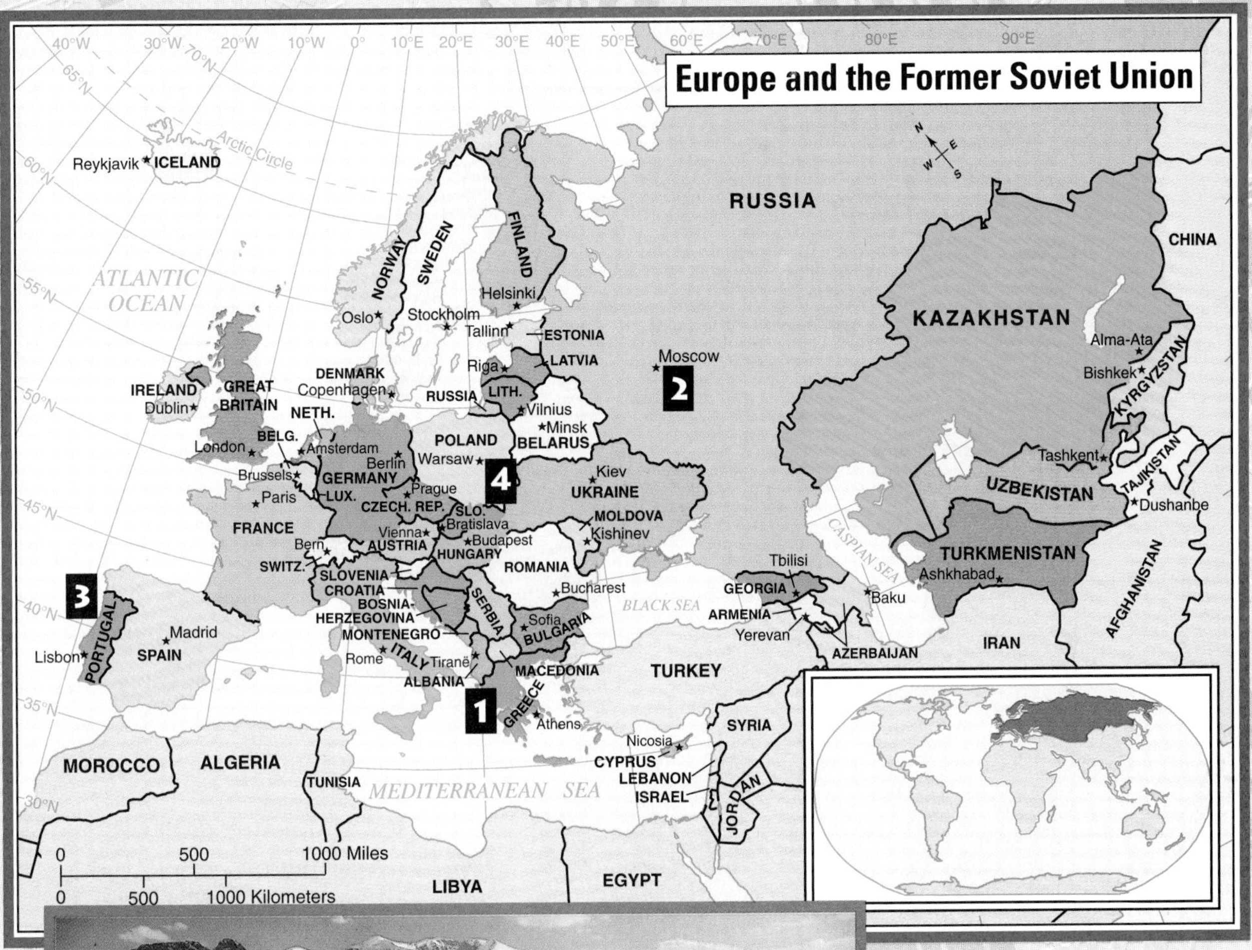

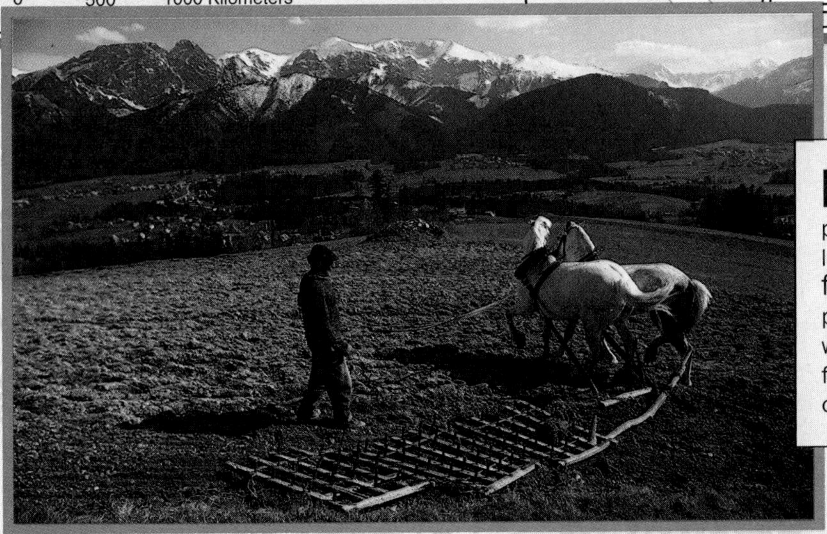

Europe and the Former Soviet Union

4 In Eastern Europe, many people continue to make their living as farmers. This Polish farmer still depends on animal power rather than machines to work the land. When they can afford it, farmers buy tractors and other modern machinery.

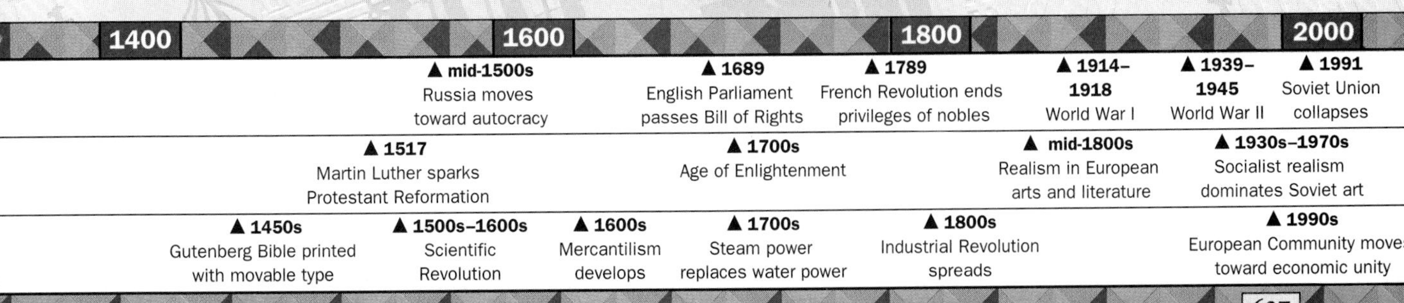

Chapter 29

GEOGRAPHY AND EARLY HISTORY OF WESTERN EUROPE

An Ancient Greek Temple Although only the ruins of this temple have survived, they suggest the beauty and simplicity of Greek architecture. For centuries, Greek achievements in the arts have served as models in the development of western culture. ***Geography*** What does this photograph suggest about the geography of Greece?

CHAPTER OUTLINE

Creon, the king of Thebes, is angry. Antigone has deliberately defied him. She has given her brother a proper burial despite Creon's order forbidding anyone to do so. Challenged to explain her action, Antigone declares:

> "It was not [the gods] who made that order. Nor did I think . . . that you, a mortal man, could overrule the gods' unwritten laws."

Creon decides to punish Antigone with death. An orderly society, he believes, is based on obedience to the king:

> "The man the state has put in place must have obedient hearing to his command, when it is right or even when it is not."

In the play *Antigone,* Sophocles portrays a tragic clash between an individual and the state. Sophocles was one of the greatest playwrights of ancient Greece.

Like other Greeks of his time, he was concerned with defining rights and responsibilities of citizens.

CHAPTER PERSPECTIVE

The civilizations of ancient Greece and Rome spread their influence from the Middle East to Europe. In Western Europe, a new civilization slowly emerged. It combined Greek and Roman traditions with the teachings of Judaism and Christianity. In time, this Western European civilization would have a major influence around the world.

As you read, look for these chapter themes:

- Geography has contributed both to intense rivalry and to economic and cultural interdependence among European nations.
- Since ancient times, Europeans have developed technologies to reshape the physical environment.
- The traditions of ancient Greece and Rome, along with the teachings of Christianity, laid the foundation of western civilization.
- During the Middle Ages, feudalism provided a stable society, but new technologies and the Crusades later changed the old feudal order.

Literature Connections

In this chapter, you will encounter passages from the following works.

Antigone, Sophocles
Aeneid, Virgil
"Funeral Oration," Pericles
"The Ruin," medieval English poem

For other suggestions, see Connections With Literature, pages 804–808.

1 GEOGRAPHIC SETTING

FIND OUT

How has location influenced the development of Western Europe?
What physical and climate features have affected Western European societies?
How have the people of Western Europe used their natural resources?

In the *Aeneid,* the ancient Roman poet Virgil tells the story of Aeneas. He and his men are sailing home after years of war. Suddenly, a violent storm in the Mediterranean Sea crashes down upon their ship:

> "The winds, wherever they could,
> came sweeping forth,
> Whirled over the land, swooped
> down upon the ocean. . . .
> Men cry; the rigging creaks and
> strains; the clouds
> Darken, and men see nothing; a
> weight of darkness
> Broods over the deep; the heavy
> thunder rumbles
> From pole to pole; the lightning rips
> and dazzles;
> There is no way out but death."

The seas have always played a major role in the life of Europeans. Since ancient times, the peoples of Europe have reached across the seas to trade and to set up colonies. Through peaceful means as well as through conquest, they have spread their cultures throughout the world. At the same time, they have brought back to Europe ideas and goods from other societies.

Location

Europe is called a continent, but it is actually part of a larger landmass that includes both Europe and Asia. In fact, Europe is a vast peninsula along the western edge of the Eurasian continent. It extends westward from the Ural Mountains to the Atlantic Ocean and southward from the Arctic Ocean to the Mediterranean Sea. Although it is only a small region—and one that at times has been remote from other centers of civilization—Europe has had a major impact on the world.

Subregions. Europe contains two main subregions, Western Europe and Eastern Europe. Although the two regions share many traditions, their histories and cultures developed differently. These differences were highlighted in the years following World War II, when the countries in Eastern Europe came under communist rule. Although the collapse of communism in the 1990s brought many changes to Eastern Europe, we still refer to Western Europe and Eastern Europe as separate subregions. (You will read about Eastern Europe in Chapters 32–34.)

Western Europe covers about one third of Europe, or 1.4 million square miles (3.6 million sq km). It contains more than 380 million people who inhabit 23 countries.

MAP STUDY

Western Europe includes the western third of the European continent. This region contains diverse landforms and is bordered by major bodies of water on the north, west, and south.

1. **Region** (a) Identify two landforms in Europe. (b) Give an example of each.
2. **Location** (a) Name three peninsulas in Western Europe. (b) Which is farthest north? (c) Which is farthest west?
3. **Understanding Causes and Effects** Europe has many navigable rivers and is surrounded by seas. (a) How have these seas helped bring the peoples of Europe together?

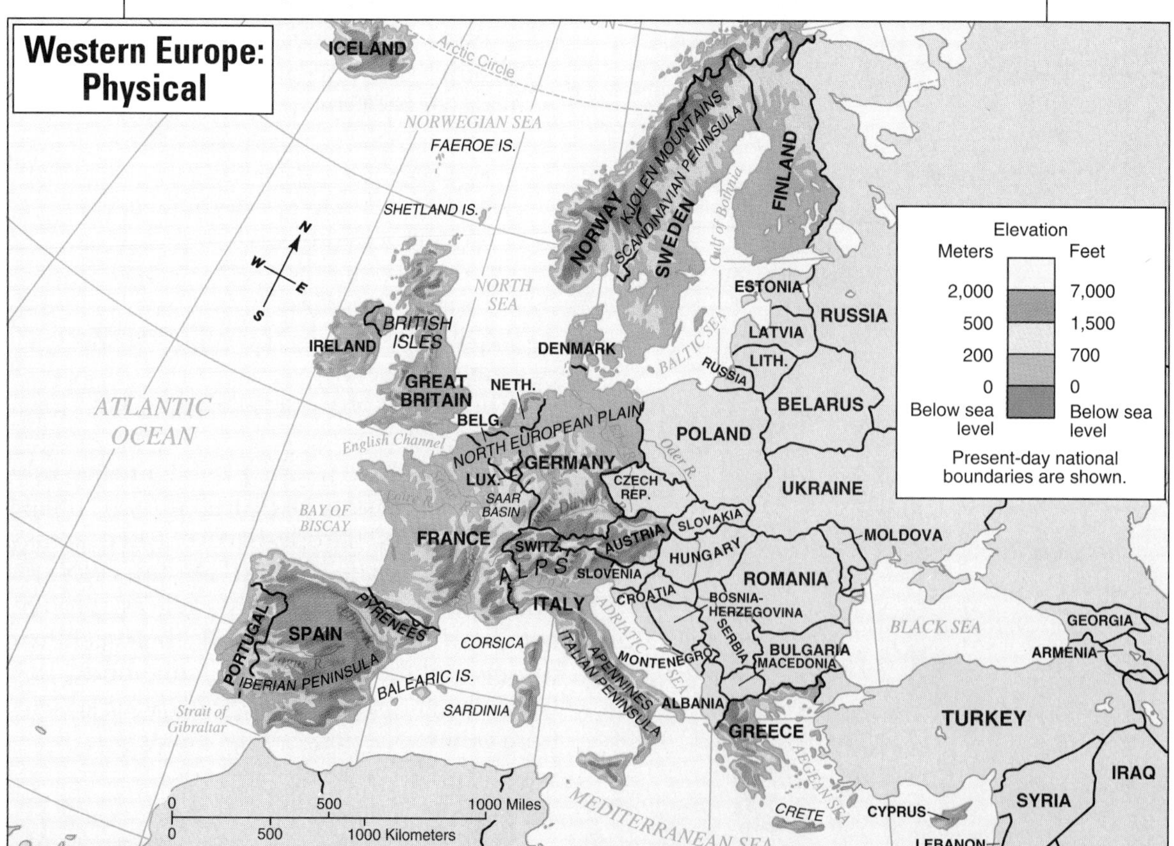

Importance of the seas. The seas have helped to shape European societies since ancient times. The region, which includes several major peninsulas that jut out into the surrounding waters, has a long coastline and countless natural harbors. For centuries, the seas around Europe have served as highways to the rest of the world. At one time, Europeans not only controlled much of the world's trade but colonized and ruled lands in Asia, Africa, and the Americas as well. The peoples of Europe have sailed to almost every corner of the globe, exchanging goods and ideas with people of other cultures.

The sea also influenced people's everyday lives. For thousands of years, coastal people have made their living from the sea. Today, fishing, shipping, and tourism at beach resorts provide major sources of income.

The Shape of the Land

Western Europe contains all the major landforms—plains, hills, plateaus, and mountains. These landforms have played an important part in influencing where people settled and how they organized their society.

Plains. One quarter of Western Europe consists of lowland plains. These plains are located along seacoasts and in river valleys. The largest and most important is part of the North European Plain, which stretches more than 1,000 miles (1,600 km) from Britain through France and Germany into Eastern Europe. Early peoples settled in the plains because the soil was generally fertile and trade and travel were fairly easy. Today, the North European Plain contains some of the world's most productive farmland as well as some of Western Europe's major cities and many of its industries.

In ancient times, many lowland areas were mosquito-ridden marshes. About 800 years ago, Europeans began to develop the technology to drain the marshlands and open up rich new lands for farming. The people of the present-day Netherlands, the Dutch, reclaimed land from the sea. They built dikes, or sea walls, to hold the sea back. They then used windmills to pump water out of the reclaimed lands that were below sea level.

The absence of natural barriers on Europe's plains has greatly affected the course of European history. For centuries, the lowlands served as the major land routes for migration and trade. In addition, the lack of barriers contributed to warfare. Rival groups and nations could invade neighboring lands with relative ease.

Highlands. Scattered across Western Europe are hills and plateaus, which are more suitable for grazing than for farming. In general, the highest of these landforms have served as barriers to migration, trade, and invaders. Major European mountain ranges include the Alps, the Pyrenees (PIHR uh neez), and the Apennines (AP uh nīnz). Because much of southern Europe is mountainous, people in Spain, Portugal, Italy, and Greece often lived in isolated communities. Unable to travel easily by land, they turned to ocean highways. For example, the Pyrenees separated Spain from France, while the Mediterranean provided a highway to North Africa. As a result, African cultures have had an important effect on Spain.

Rivers

Western Europe has many navigable rivers. Today, as in earlier times, they provide routes for transportation and trade. Rivers have encouraged economic interdependence and cultural contacts among various regions. In addition, fast-flowing streams and rivers provide hydroelectric power as well as an abundance of fish. Since the 1600s, Europeans have extended their river systems even farther by building a vast system of canals.

Many of Western Europe's major cities developed beside rivers. Paris is located on the Seine (sayn), London on the Thames (tehmz), and Rome on the Tiber. These cities became powerful because they commanded trade routes on important waterways.

The longest river located entirely within Western Europe is the Rhine. It flows 820 miles (1,310 km) from the Alps to the North Sea. Some cities along the Rhine, such as Cologne, were founded more than 2,000 years ago. Others grew up in the 1800s during the

Cologne, Germany Cologne and other European cities, including Strasbourg, Bonn, and Düsseldorf, rose along the Rhine River. For centuries, the river has served as an artery for trade and transportation as well as a source of fish and water. ***Environment*** How has industrialization brought benefits and harm to those living along the river today?

Industrial Revolution because the Rhine flowed through regions that were rich in natural resources.

Today, the Rhine Valley is one of the most densely populated and heavily industrialized areas of Europe. People and industry have contributed to major problems along the Rhine, however. The river carries toxic wastes and other forms of pollution from Switzerland, Germany, and France to the Netherlands and into the North Sea.

Climate and Resources

Climates vary across Western Europe. Much of the Atlantic coast has a mild marine climate, with warm winters, cool summers, and plentiful rainfall. The marine climate is suited to farming.

Much of southern Europe has a Mediterranean climate, with hot, dry summers and mild, rainy winters. Some areas, such as the interior of Spain, receive almost no rainfall during the winter. As a result, farmers must rely on irrigation.

Mountainous areas, such as the Alps, have a highland climate. Temperatures vary according to altitude. People make a living by farming, herding, or cutting timber in the foothills.

Agricultural resources. In ancient times, people in Western Europe drained marshlands and low-lying coastal areas bordering the Mediterranean Sea. Later, improved farming methods helped to preserve fertile soil in these areas. Despite these efforts, overuse and erosion have destroyed a great deal of farmland, especially in parts of southern Europe.

Forests once covered much of Western Europe. Over the centuries, however, people cut down forests for farmland, fuel, and building materials. Today, Western European countries are making an effort to manage their remaining forest resources.

Mineral resources. Western Europe has rich deposits of iron ore, coal, uranium, copper, and other minerals. These resources helped European nations industrialize during the 1700s and 1800s. In addition, Europeans have developed new technologies to exploit their mineral resources. During the 1700s, for example, the invention of steam-driven pumps made it possible to drain away water from flooded mines so that coal, iron ore, and other minerals could be removed.

Energy resources. During the Industrial Revolution, Europe used up much of its abundant supply of coal. Today, many European nations rely on imported oil to meet their energy needs. Since the 1970s, deposits of oil and gas in the North Sea have helped Britain and some other European nations solve their energy problems. European nations are also turning to nuclear power. France, for example, uses nuclear power to supply 35 percent of its energy needs.

People. The peoples of Western Europe belong to many different cultural groups. They speak dozens of languages, practice different religions, and follow a variety of customs.

The languages of modern Europe reflect different waves of migration that began more

GEOGRAPHIC CONNECTION

The Lost Language

All Sir William Jones wanted to do was to learn Sanskrit. While he was studying, however, he made a surprising discovery. This ancient language of India bore amazing similarities to Latin and Greek. The Sanskrit word for "mother"—*matar*—was almost identical to the Latin word, *mater*. "Father" was *pitar* in Sanskrit, *pater* in Latin and Greek. The more he studied, the more similarities he found.

How could this be? Thousands of miles and many natural barriers separated India and Europe. Still, Jones concluded, the similarities were too strong to be accidental. In 1786, he announced:

> "No one could examine them all three, without believing them to have sprung from some common source."

Since then, scholars have traced many languages to this "common source." Today, these languages are called the Indo-European family. But where did this source originate? Language and geography provide the clues. European languages have similar words for the animals and trees of northern Europe, such as oak, willow, bear, and wolf. There are no common words for the animals and trees of southern Europe.

To scholars, this suggests that the Indo-European languages began in north-central Europe. In time, some northern Europeans set out toward the east, settling in Iran, India, and Pakistan. Others migrated westward toward southern and western Europe. The root language developed into dozens of different languages, but the family resemblances remain. The word for "three" is *drei* in German, *tres* in Spanish, *tre* in Albanian, and *tri* in Russian.

Almost every language in Europe is part of the Indo-European family, but there are exceptions. Hungarian and Finnish belong to other language families. High in the Pyrenees, the Basque people speak a language that has no known relatives. Perhaps the Basques were the original inhabitants of the region. Isolated by mountains, they may have been bypassed by the spread of Indo-European culture.

1. Where do scholars think Indo-European languages originated? Why?
2. **Drawing Conclusions** Why did the root language develop into different languages as people migrated?

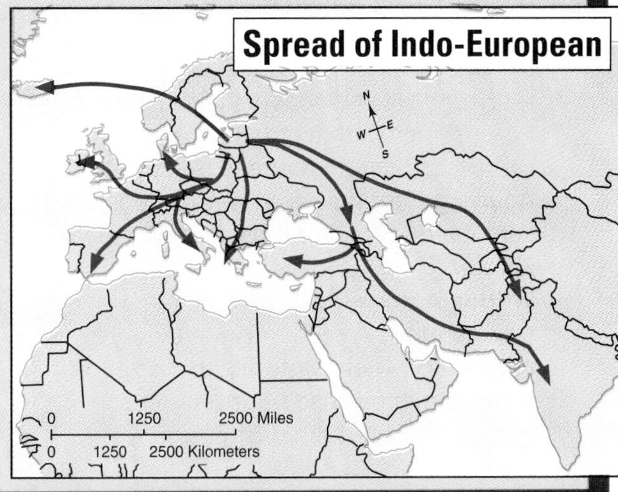

than 40,000 years ago. Some migrating peoples moved into what is today Greece and Italy. Others spread into the regions that are now Scandinavia, Germany, France, and the British Isles. The ancient Greeks traded with Egypt, Babylon, and other advanced civilizations of the Middle East. They absorbed ideas from these societies, adapting them to their own needs. Over time, the ideas from ancient peoples spread northward and westward across the continent. They helped shape the foundations of what we call western civilization.

By the 1200s, modern European nations began to emerge with their own distinct languages, customs, and cultures. As these nations expanded, they fought many wars with their neighbors. Despite long-standing religious, political, and cultural differences, Europeans are more willing than ever before to cooperate with each other. In recent years, Western European nations have opened their borders and encouraged close economic ties. Some leaders support the goal of political as well as economic union.

SECTION 1 REVIEW

1. **Locate:** (a) Europe, (b) Ural Mountains, (c) Mediterranean Sea, (d) North European Plain, (e) the Netherlands, (f) Alps, (g) Pyrenees, (h) Apennines, (i) Greece, (j) Rhine River.
2. How has the sea affected the development of Europe?
3. Describe two ways in which the geography of the North European Plain has affected the people who lived there.
4. (a) How have the peoples of Western Europe improved their land? (b) How has overuse affected European resources?
5. **Applying Information** How has geography contributed to cultural diversity in Western Europe?
6. **Writing Across Cultures** Using a map, list six important American cities that grew up near rivers. Then, write a generalization about the importance of rivers in both Europe and the United States.

2 HERITAGE OF GREECE AND ROME

FIND OUT

What ideas about government did the Greeks develop?

How did Greek culture spread throughout the ancient world?

What Roman traditions influenced Western Europe?

Vocabulary acropolis, aristocracy, direct democracy, Socratic method, patrician, plebeian

In 430 B.C., the Greek city-state of Athens was at war with its neighbor, Sparta. Pericles, a leader of Athens, spoke at a public funeral for the soldiers of his city-state who had died in battle. In his funeral oration, or speech, Pericles described the benefits of the Athenian political system:

> “Our constitution is called a democracy because power is in the hands not of a minority but of the whole people. . . . I declare that our city is an education to Greece. . . . Future ages will wonder at us, as the present age wonders at us now.”

As Pericles predicted, later ages have admired and adapted many remarkable achievements of ancient Athens.

Geographic Setting

The Greek mainland is a mountainous peninsula. Its coastline has excellent harbors. As a result, the early Greeks turned to the sea. When storms raged, Greek sailors found shelter on the many islands that dotted the Aegean Sea. Greek traders carried goods across the Mediterranean and eventually set up colonies there. The Greeks adapted many ideas from other civilizations. They adopted the Phoenician alphabet and used coins for money, as did the peoples of the Middle East.

City-states. Greece's rugged terrain made transportation and communication difficult. Because they were cut off from one another, the Greeks developed small, separate communities. In time, these communities grew into city-states. Each city-state prized its freedom and fiercely resisted outside interference.

At the center of each city-state was an acropolis (uh KRAHP uh lihs), or hilltop fortress. Public life centered around the acropolis. Because the climate of Greece is mild, men gathered in the acropolis to gossip and to discuss important religious and political events.

Harvesting Olives Most of the city-states of ancient Greece consisted of small communities surrounded by farmland. Two common crops were wheat and olives. Oil pressed from olives was used for cooking and making soap as well as for fuel for lamps. ***Fine Art*** What does this vase painting suggest about the technology used in Greek farming?

Greek Ideas About Government

The city-states developed various forms of government. At first, a monarch, or king, ruled each city-state. Gradually, aristocracies, or government by a small, privileged upper class, replaced the monarchies. As city-states grew, other classes demanded a voice in government. Slowly, ordinary citizens gained certain rights, laying the foundations for democracy. Our ideas about democracy grew out of Greek traditions.

Growth of Athenian democracy. Athens was one of the first Greek city-states to develop a democratic government. By 450 B.C., Athens was a direct democracy—that is, all citizens participated in government directly rather than through elected representatives. Under the great leader Pericles, Athenian democracy reached its height.

In his funeral oration, Pericles spelled out Athenian ideas about democracy. (See page 644.) He pointed out that power rested in the hands of individuals and that all citizens were equal before the law. Pericles also argued that each citizen had both the right and the duty to participate in government:

> “We do not say that a man who takes no interest in politics is a man who minds his own business; we say that he has no business here at all.”

The idea of individual responsibility in government became part of the tradition of Europe, the United States, and other areas of the world. (📖 See Connections With Literature, page 807, "Pericles' Funeral Oration.")

Limited democracy. Athenian democracy was extremely limited. Only citizens—free men who had been born in Athens—had the right to participate in government. The majority of Athenians, including slaves, resident foreigners, and women, had no political rights. They could not vote, own property, or hold public offices. Still, Athenian democracy, with its stress on public service and open discussion, became a model for other city-states.

The Search for Truth

Greek philosophers believed that the search for truth was a basic duty. To this end, they studied every branch of knowledge. Philosophers began to question the traditional belief that gods and goddesses controlled the forces of nature. Through observation and reason, Greek philosophers sought to discover natural laws that explained the universe.

The Greeks' search for truth influenced many fields of study. In medicine, Greek philosophers concluded that natural forces, rather than evil spirits, caused diseases. This breakthrough led them to study the human body, searching for the symptoms and causes of disease. Using reason, experimentation, and observation, Greek thinkers also made advances in mathematics, astronomy, biology, and other sciences.

Socrates. Perhaps the greatest of all the Greek thinkers was Socrates (SAHK ruh teez). He lived from around 470 B.C. to 399 B.C., about the same time as Confucius in China and the Buddha in India. Like these two philosophers, Socrates sought a code of conduct for human behavior. As a teacher, he encouraged his students to apply reason in the quest for truth. He developed a question-and-answer technique that became known as the Socratic method. By asking students one question after another, Socrates forced them to examine their beliefs and to discard any belief that could not be proved through reason.

Many Athenians saw Socrates as a dangerous troublemaker. They accused him of corrupting young people by encouraging them to doubt the wisdom of their elders and the gods. They had Socrates arrested on the charge of failing to honor the gods and corrupting Athenian youth. At his trial, Socrates argued that he was not an enemy of Athens but a friend of the truth. Still, the jury condemned him to death. His friends urged him to flee. Socrates refused, claiming that a citizen must obey the law.

Plato and Aristotle. Socrates left no writings. After his death, however, his student Plato collected Socratic ideas in the *Dialogues.* Although Socrates was his teacher, Plato developed his own ideas, especially about government. In *The Republic,* Plato described the ideal government as one that was based on justice for all. He rejected democracy because it had condemned Socrates to death. Instead, Plato proposed a state in which philosophers would rule as kings, workers would produce food, and soldiers would protect the state. Plato's ideas about justice and government have influenced western thought to the present. (📖 See Connections With Literature, page 807, "Apology.")

Plato's student Aristotle (AR ihs taht'l) sought truth from experience. The philosopher, he taught, should gather evidence from the real world and then use reason to determine the truth. He created a system of reason known as logic. Aristotle was interested in everything, and he studied a vast range of subjects, from medicine to poetry. He urged people to adopt moral behavior and to aim for moderation in all things.

Aristotle's ideas have influenced people for more than 2,000 years. Muslim scholars translated and preserved many of his works during the Early Middle Ages, when Europe was in disorder. Later in the Middle Ages, Aristotle's teachings came back to the West. European scholars turned to Aristotle as the authority in almost every field of science.

Arts and literature. The Greeks' emphasis on reason and balance shaped their arts. Architects fashioned graceful temples that reflected this interest. Sculptors carved statues that were based on an ideal notion of the human form. More than 1,500 years later, European artists continued to use Greek examples as the models for their work.

In literature, the Greeks produced epic poems, such as the *Iliad* and the *Odyssey*. In these epics, the poet Homer tells stories of how gods and goddesses interfered in the lives of human heroes. These epics have had a lasting influence on western literature. The Greeks also developed two types of drama, tragedy and comedy. Tragedies, such as *Antigone,* focused on the sufferings of the major character and usually ended in disaster. Comedies, such as Aristophanes' *Lysistrata,* ridiculed people, ideas, and social customs.

Greek historians developed a new approach to history. They treated history not as the deeds of gods but as the study of human actions. Historians such as Thucydides (thoo SIH dih deez) used evidence and impartial information to describe the wars of ancient Greece.

The Hellenistic World

Because the Greek city-states were constantly at war with one another, they could seldom unite even against a common enemy.

In the end, an outsider, Philip of Macedonia, who ruled a kingdom north of Greece, brought the fiercely independent city-states under his control.

Alexander the Great. Philip's son, known as Alexander the Great, completed the work of uniting Greece. He then conquered a huge empire that stretched from Greece and Egypt eastward to the Indus River. As a young man, Alexander had studied with Aristotle and had come to admire Greek culture. Later, he spread that culture to all of the lands he conquered.

Although Alexander's empire broke up after his death in 323 B.C., he had a lasting effect on both the European and Asian civilizations. Through conquests, he created a rich new culture known as Hellenistic civilization. It blended Greek culture with the cultures of Egypt and the Middle East.

Alexandria. The city of Alexandria in Egypt became a center of Hellenistic civilization. Scholars from Greece, Persia, and Egypt gathered in Alexandria, where they made important advances in medicine, mathematics, and the sciences. For example, the Egyptians showed Greek physicians how to perform surgery using anesthetics. Euclid summarized the mathematical learning of the ancient world in *The Elements,* which became the basis of modern geometry.

Growth of Rome

During Alexander's time, Rome was a small city-state on the Tiber River in Italy. During the Hellenistic period, it grew into a powerful empire. At its height, Rome ruled many diverse lands and peoples.

Roman Republic. In 509 B.C., the Romans set up a republic. In a republic, citizens who have the right to vote choose their leaders. As in Greece, citizenship in Rome was limited. Slaves and foreigners were not citizens. Roman women were citizens, but they could not vote or hold public office.

In the Roman Republic, a senate and an assembly made the laws. At first, patricians, or wealthy landowners, controlled the government. The plebeians (plee BEE uhnz), or common people, had no real voice in the government. They could vote, but they could not hold office. Gradually, the plebeians gained more rights, including the right to participate in the senate.

Roman expansion. During the early years of the Republic, the Romans struggled against powerful neighbors. Those early experiences helped shape Roman values. Romans emphasized duty, sacrifice, and patriotism. The Romans developed a strong, swift army, which they organized into legions, or units of about 6,000 soldiers. By 264 B.C., Roman legions had conquered all of Italy. They then won lands in North Africa, Spain, and Greece.

Expansion led to economic and social problems in the Republic. To restore order,

A Roman Woman This wall painting was found at Pompeii, a Roman city buried under lava during an eruption of Mt. Vesuvius in A.D. 79. The woman's patrician rank is indicated by her purple-and-white robes—worn only by the upper classes—and by the servant behind her. ***Citizenship*** How did the status of Roman women differ from that of Greek women?

Romans turned to military leaders. The most brilliant and powerful was Julius Caesar. Under Caesar, Rome conquered new lands in Europe and around the Mediterranean. Afraid of Caesar's growing power, a group of senators killed him in 44 B.C.

Roman Empire. Caesar's death marked the end of the Roman Republic. In 27 B.C., his adopted son Octavian declared himself emperor. He took the title Augustus Caesar.

The Roman Empire lasted almost 500 years. At its height, it stretched from Spain in the west to the Euphrates River in the east. Under the empire, Romans carried their ideas and the Latin language to diverse lands. For the first 200 years, the empire enjoyed relative peace and prosperity. This period has become known as the Pax Romana, or Roman peace.

Roman Civilization

Among the lasting contributions of Roman civilization was its system of law. During the Pax Romana, the Romans developed a legal system to meet the needs of the diverse peoples they ruled.

Under the Roman system of justice, everyone was equal before the law. The Romans introduced to Europe the idea that an accused person is innocent until proven guilty. They also allowed the use of evidence in the courtroom and set up procedures to ensure a fair trial. Roman ideas about law spread throughout Western Europe and still influence legal practices in Europe and the Americas today.

Diffusion and diversity. The Roman Empire included diverse peoples and cultures. The Romans promoted unity by offering citi-

MAP STUDY

Rome expanded from a small city on the Tiber River into a great empire. At its height, in A.D. 117, the Roman Empire extended from Asia Minor to Britain and Spain and also included parts of North Africa and the Middle East.

1. **Movement** (a) During which years did Rome add the most land? (b) What territories did Rome conquer from 44 B.C. to A.D. 117?
2. **Interaction** Explain how Rome's location helped it conquer a vast empire.
3. **Solving Problems** How did the Roman Empire strive to unify the diverse peoples it ruled?

Hadrian's Wall Among the lands ruled by Rome was England. About A.D. 123, the Roman emperor Hadrian had a wall built across northern England to keep out invaders from Scotland. Parts of the 10-foot-thick wall survive today. ***Power*** What does Hadrian's Wall reveal about Roman power?

zenship to all peoples. They also united their empire by building a vast network of roads. During the Pax Romana, trade flourished, which helped to spread goods and ideas across great distances.*

Over time, the Romans blended Greek and Hellenistic traditions with their own to create a new Greco-Roman civilization. From the Greeks, the Romans borrowed ideas about architecture, then added their own improvements such as the use of the dome. Romans were excellent engineers. They built roads and bridges that are still used today. They also built enormous aqueducts to carry water from rural areas to cities.

Spread of Christianity. The unity of the Roman Empire, its system of roads, and extensive commerce helped a new religion—Christianity—to spread. As you read in Chapter 25, Christianity began in the Roman province of Palestine. Followers of the new religion preached throughout the Greco-Roman world. The message of hope offered by Christianity won many converts.

At first, the Roman Empire persecuted Christians. Despite persecution, the religion gained in strength. The emperor Constantine tolerated Christians and converted to Christianity on his deathbed. Finally, in A.D. 395, the emperor Theodosius I made Christianity the official religion of the Roman Empire.

In time, Christians in Western Europe developed a strong church organization. At its head was the bishop of Rome, or pope. As the Roman Empire declined in Europe, the Christian Church took over many of its governing functions.

Decline of Rome. Several factors contributed to the decline of the Roman Empire. Powerful leaders competed for the throne, and civil war was frequent. The fighting disrupted trade and weakened the economy. At the same time, outside invaders frequently attacked the empire.

Occasionally, a strong ruler emerged to stem the tide of decay. Diocletian, for example, introduced reforms to restore order and

* The Pax Romana occurred at the same time that the Han rulers were uniting a huge empire in China. Through traders in the Middle East and along the Silk Road, goods passed between Rome and China.

resolve basic economic problems. Also, to govern the vast empire more effectively, he divided it into eastern and western halves. He controlled the wealthier eastern portion. A co-emperor, responsible to Diocletian, ruled the western half.

The emperor Constantine continued many of Diocletian's policies. Like Diocletian, he favored the empire's rich eastern cities, and he moved the capital to Byzantium, a city on the Bosporus. The capital was later renamed Constantinople. Moving the capital from Rome to Constantinople symbolized the declining influence of the western empire.

Despite the efforts of rulers like Diocletian and Constantine, reform failed. Weakened by internal problems and foreign invaders, the Western Roman Empire collapsed in the A.D. 400s. The Eastern Roman Empire—later known as the Byzantine Empire—survived for another 1,000 years.

SECTION 2 REVIEW

1. **Locate:** (a) Athens, (b) Alexandria, (c) Rome, (d) Constantinople.
2. **Identify:** (a) Socrates, (b) Aristotle, (c) Homer, (d) Julius Caesar, (e) Pax Romana, (f) Constantine.
3. **Define:** (a) acropolis, (b) aristocracy, (c) direct democracy, (d) Socratic method, (e) patrician, (f) plebeian.
4. How did Alexander the Great help to spread Greek culture?
5. What legal and religious traditions developed in the Roman Empire?
6. **Analyzing Ideas** A Roman poet said of Rome, "Greece has conquered her rude conquerors." How does this statement reflect the influence of Greek ideas on the Roman Empire?
7. **Writing Across Cultures** List the features of direct democracy in Athens and those of republican government in Rome. Then, write a paragraph explaining which system is closer to modern American government.

3 WESTERN EUROPE IN THE MIDDLE AGES

FIND OUT

What was the structure of feudal society?

What role did the Christian Church play during the Middle Ages?

What changes took place in Europe after the 1100s?

Vocabulary fief, vassal, knight, serf, manor, sacrament, charter

"The work of giants molders away. Its roofs are breaking and falling; its towers crumble in ruin. Plundered those walls with grated doors—the walls white with frost. Its battered ramparts are shorn away and ruined, all undermined by eating age."

The unknown poet who wrote "The Ruin" in the 600s was describing Bath, England. There, the Romans had once built huge public baths of stone. As Roman rule weakened, peasants stole the stones to build wells. They may even have taken the iron hinges from the doors to make plows.

In time, Roman officials could no longer maintain the empire's splendid buildings. Roads crumbled. Bridges collapsed. Trade and travel slowed to a trickle. Western Europe entered a long period known as the Middle Ages.

Early Middle Ages

The Middle Ages lasted from the decline of Rome to the emergence of the modern European world in about 1450. Historians usually divide the Middle Ages in Europe into two periods—the Early Middle Ages and the Late Middle Ages.

Narrowing horizons. Even before Rome fell, waves of invaders had swept into Europe, disrupting life in the Roman provinces. During the 300s, Hun warriors from Central Asia pushed Germanic peoples westward. As a result, various Germanic groups—the Vandals, Goths, and Franks—moved into Western Europe. The Angles and Saxons advanced into Britain.

During the Early Middle Ages, these invasions continued, gradually undermining orderly Roman civilization. People's horizons narrowed, as much of the learning of ancient Greece and Rome was lost. Instead of a single, unified Roman Empire, many small Germanic kingdoms appeared in Western Europe. During the invasions, trade slowed and towns declined. The money economy of Rome disappeared.

Charlemagne. Among the Germanic peoples who settled in Western Europe were the Franks. They slowly built a strong kingdom that united parts of France and Germany. The kingdom of the Franks reached its height under Charlemagne (SHAHR luh mayn). A skillful general, Charlemagne reunited much of the Western Roman Empire in about 800.

Charlemagne set up an efficient government. He helped missionaries to spread the teachings of Christianity throughout northern Europe. He also encouraged a revival of learning and the arts. Charlemagne's empire broke up after his death, but his efforts to improve education helped set the stage for medieval civilization, which grew out of Roman, Christian, and Germanic traditions.

Feudalism

For 200 years after the death of Charlemagne, Western Europe was battered by invasions. Magyars swept in from the east. Muslims controlled Spain and threatened Italy. Vikings from Scandinavia attacked communities throughout Western Europe. In response to these dangers, a military elite emerged. A feudal system slowly began to develop in Western Europe. Feudalism was a system of rule by local lords who were bound to a king by ties of loyalty. It developed into a way of life that governed the political, social, and economic order.

Structure of feudal society. In feudal society, each person had a fixed place. At the head of society was the king. He granted fiefs, or estates, to powerful lords. These lords owed him loyalty and military service in exchange. In practice, feudal kings had little power outside their own estates.

Powerful lords often acted independently of the king. The lords, in turn, divided their fiefs among vassals, or lesser lords. Vassals further subdivided their fiefs among knights, or mounted warriors. Each knight and each vassal owed his lord loyalty and service. Everyone in these groups, from feudal lord to lowly knight, was a noble.

At the bottom of feudal society were the common people, mostly peasants. They lived on lands belonging to a lord. They owed service to the lord in exchange for his protection. Most peasants were serfs, who were tied to the lord's land. Although they were not slaves, serfs were not free to leave the land.

Chart Study Under feudalism in Europe, everyone had a well-defined place in society. Nobles could be powerful lords or simple knights. Peasants and townspeople made up 90 percent of the population. ▶What was the relationshiop between these common people and the nobles?

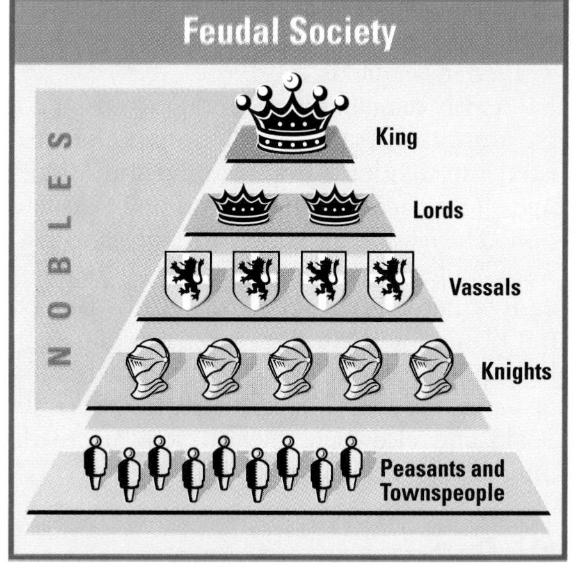

A Wedding Feast
Servants wait on nobles at this French wedding feast as musicians play in the balcony. Noblewomen sit at one table and noblemen at another. ***Fine Art*** How has the painter shown the wealth and luxury these nobles enjoyed?

Status of women. In feudal society, women were subordinate to men. A woman's father, husband, or oldest son had complete authority over her. Among the nobility, most marriages were arranged to benefit families' interests. Women who inherited land were valued for their property. A noblewoman, however, might have some influence because of her father's or husband's status.

Often, a woman looked after her husband's fief when he was away or if he was killed in battle. The chief duties of both noble and peasant women were to raise children and take care of the household. In addition to caring for their households, peasant women worked in the fields.

Jewish communities. Although most people were Christians, Jewish communities existed throughout Europe during the Middle Ages. Jews faced discrimination and persecution. They were forbidden to own land and were limited to certain professions. When disease or natural disasters struck, Christians often blamed and attacked Jews. Despite such hardships, Jews developed stable communities and preserved their ancient traditions. In Spain and elsewhere, Jewish scholars made important contributions to learning.

Feudal warfare. After the age of Charlemagne, warfare was constant as feudal lords battled for power. To protect their lands, they built fortified castles in which lords and peasants took refuge during attacks by enemy forces. As monarchs gained greater power during the Late Middle Ages, feudal warfare slowly diminished.

The Manor Economy

The economic system that supported feudalism was based on the manor. The manor included a village and the surrounding lands administered by a lord.

Each manor was a self-sufficient community. Its people produced almost everything they needed in order to survive. The peasants raised sheep for wool and spun the wool into cloth. They raised cattle for meat and milk and grew grain and vegetables. Each manor also had its own mill and blacksmith shop, as well as its own church.

Peasant life. For most peasants, life centered around the farming seasons. Peasants generally spent four days a week farming their lord's land and two days farming for themselves. They owed the lord part of their own harvest. In addition, they paid fees to use the lord's mill to grind grain and his oven to bake bread. Although peasants had a difficult life, they did have some enjoyment. They celebrated weddings and church festivals with feasts, music, singing, and dancing.

New technologies. During the Early Middle Ages, peasants produced just enough to survive. By about 1000, however, they had developed new technologies. For example, crop rotation—planting a different crop in a plot of land each year—enriched the soil and improved farming. The heavy plow allowed peasants to turn the soil more easily. Windmills provided energy for grinding grain. Such new technologies allowed peasants to produce the additional food needed to support Europe's growing population.

Role of the Church

The Catholic Church played a major role in all areas of medieval life. Faced with the hardships of everyday living, people found hope in Christian teachings. They turned to the Church for guidance and comfort.

For peasants and nobles alike, the Church offered a chance of salvation and eternal life. The path to salvation included the sacraments, the seven sacred rites that were administered by the Church. The sacraments included baptism and holy communion.

The Church also played a central role in political affairs. Because they were educated, Church officials were valued as advisers by kings and nobles. As a result, the Church was able to influence important decisions in a wide range of matters. The Church also exerted influence through its large landholdings.

At the head of the Church was the pope in Rome. The pope exercised both spiritual and political authority over everyone in feudal society—even kings. A document written in 1075 outlined some of the powers claimed by the pope, including the power to depose emperors. This claim later led to clashes between the pope and rulers of various European nations.

Peasants at Work The peasants at left straighten wool fibers and prepare them for spinning. Those at right mow wheat. Many regulations governed manor life. For example, in addition to other duties, one English lord required from each serf a "hose [long stocking] full of nuts well cleaned" each fall. ***Human Rights*** What were the main advantages and disadvantages of the manor economy?

Monasteries and convents. Many Christians joined religious orders. As monks and nuns, these men and women dedicated their lives to serving God. During the Early Middle Ages, they played an important part in spreading Christianity to northern Europe.

In monasteries, scholarly monks preserved the learning of the ancient world by carefully copying Greek and Roman manuscripts. Some religious orders founded hospitals and furnished other services for the sick and the poor.

Schools and universities. The Church provided education in Western Europe. The clergy set up schools in cathedrals to train young men for service in the Church. As interest in learning grew during the Late Middle Ages, some cathedral schools evolved into universities. The typical course of study included seven subjects—grammar, rhetoric, logic, arithmetic, geometry, astronomy, and music. Students had few books. Instead, they memorized lessons given by the teacher.

By the Late Middle Ages, new translations of Aristotle's works had reached Western Europe by way of Muslim scholars in Spain. His emphasis on reason and logic led scholars to reexamine their ideas on many subjects.

Religion and the arts. During the Late Middle Ages, the Church became the chief patron of the arts. Medieval churches were decorated with statues, paintings, and stained-glass windows. These works of art not only beautified the churches but also helped to teach Bible stories and Christian beliefs to people who could not read or write.

During the 1100s and 1200s, cities competed to build the tallest and most beautiful churches. Architects developed a style called Gothic. Gothic cathedrals were more elaborate than earlier styles. They had higher ceilings and larger windows, which created a feeling of airiness. The spires of these cathedrals, which "soared toward the heavens," were designed to remind worshipers of the power of God.

Stained-Glass Windows Building on this Gothic church in northern France began in 1211 and ended a century later. Using red-hot pokers, glassworkers cut large pieces of colored glass into smaller sections and then combined them into a beautiful window painting. ***Culture*** What purposes did stained-glass windows serve?

Expanding Horizons

By the 1100s, important changes were taking place in Western Europe that expanded people's horizons beyond the narrow world of the Early Middle Ages. The population was growing. New technologies were increasing food production. In addition, warfare declined as kings exercised more power over rival feudal lords.

Growth of towns. The decline in feudal warfare encouraged the revival of trade and travel. Some kings and feudal lords began to repair roads and bridges. Coined money slowly reappeared. At annual trade fairs, merchants and traders from all over Western Europe gathered to exchange goods.

Increased trade led to the growth of towns. Merchants set up permanent headquarters in old Roman towns. At the same time, new towns sprang up at important trade crossroads. Nobles and peasants traveled to towns to buy goods they could not produce on the manor.

Nobles controlled the land on which towns stood. Townspeople had to pay taxes to nobles and get their permission to marry, move, or own land.

As merchants gained wealth, they demanded more control over their own affairs. They negotiated with kings for charters, written documents that guaranteed certain rights to town dwellers. Slowly, townspeople began to form a new middle class.

The Crusades. As Western Europe grew stronger, Christians took part in wars of expansion. In 1095, Pope Urban II called for a crusade to take the Holy Land from the Muslims. For the next 200 years, armies of Christians left their homes in Europe to fight for lands in the Middle East. (See Chapter 26.)

The popes had several motives in calling for the Crusades. They wanted to increase the power of the Roman Church and to regain control of the Byzantine Church. They also hoped to reduce fighting in Europe by sending feudal armies to distant lands.

The crusaders, too, had mixed motives. Many believed that they were obeying God's command to reunite the Church. In this way, they hoped to achieve salvation. Others sought glory and riches. Still others were eager to escape debt and taxes at home.

Effects of the Crusades. During the First Crusade, Christian knights won control of lands in Syria and Palestine. They conquered Jerusalem, massacring its Jewish and Muslim residents. The crusaders set up four small kingdoms in the lands they seized. Later Crusades, however, failed to win additional territory. By 1291, the Muslims had recaptured all the lands taken by the Europeans.

In Western Europe, the Crusades quickened the pace of changes that were already underway. Returning crusaders brought back a taste for products from the Middle East, including sugar, spices, and silks. This demand for goods increased European trade with the Middle East. Merchants in the towns of northern Italy had built large fleets to carry crusaders to Palestine, and they benefited from the increased trade across the Mediterranean.

The Crusades also increased the desire of Europeans to learn more about the world. Crusaders brought back new knowledge and new technologies from the Muslim world. Through contact with the Arabs, Western Europeans probably learned how to make paper and use the magnetic compass. From the Middle East came Arabic works on mathematics, philosophy, and medicine, which added to the legacies of ancient Greece and Rome.

Contact with Asia greatly improved life for Europeans, but it also had a disastrous effect. In 1348, ships returning to Europe from the eastern Mediterranean brought back the bubonic plague—the dreaded Black Death.

"The End of the World"

> "Ring-a-ring o'roses,
> A pocket full of posies,
> A-tishoo! A-tishoo!
> We all fall down."

Today, young children enjoy playing "Ring Around the Rosie." But to those who first sang it, the rhyme was anything but playful. The song actually describes the deadly bubonic plague. One of the first symptoms of the disease was a circular red rash—a "ring o' roses." To ward off the disease, people carried around "posies," or bunches of herbs. The last two lines refer to the final stages of the plague. The victim suffered bouts of sneezing, then "fell down"—dead.

Bubonic plague struck Western Europe several times during the Late Middle Ages. The worst outbreak occurred during the mid-1300s, the direct result of increased trade with the Middle East. The plague had already swept through much of Asia. Flea-infested rats that carried the disease crept on board Italian trading ships in Asia Minor and spread the plague into Europe. In Genoa, Italy, sailors developed hideous swellings on their bodies. They turned black and blue all over, then died within a few hours.

From Italy, the Black Death spread across all of Western Europe. People died by the

The Plague Strikes London Bubonic plague brought death to millions of people in Europe during the Middle Ages. In this print, at left, a family is stricken by the disease. At right, armed men prevent other people from leaving. Although no one knew what caused the plague, measures like this sometimes prevented it from spreading. ***Change*** How did the Black Death change Europe?

thousands, keeping gravediggers busy night and day. In all, the plague killed more than one third of the population of Europe, an estimated 25 million people.

Punishment for "our sins." Many people viewed the plague as "just punishment for our sins." The pope called on Christians to pray for forgiveness. In 1348, more than 1 million pilgrims flocked to Rome. The crowded conditions there increased the spread of the disease. Only 1 pilgrim out of 10 survived.

Panic seized Western Europe. Fearing contagion, doctors refused to treat the sick. Priests refused to hear their confessions. Some parents even abandoned children who showed signs of the disease. In art, the "dance of death" became a common theme. Woodcuts showed the Grim Reaper dancing along a road, leading a train of victims—nobles and commoners alike.

For the Jews of Europe, the Black Death brought double trouble. They not only suffered from the disease but they also were blamed for it. In one German town, Christians walled up Jews in a wooden building and burned them alive.

Effects of the plague. In England, Henry Knighton recorded the crushing economic effects of the plague:

> "Because of the fear of death there were low prices for everything. . . . Many large and small buildings . . . collapsed and were levelled with the earth for lack of inhabitants."

The plague helped to weaken serfdom. In the chaos of the times, serfs fled without fear that anyone would capture them. Workers became so scarce that the serfs who remained could demand high wages from their lords at harvest time.

Europe did not recover from the effects of the Black Death for more than 100 years. The disease's most terrible toll, though, was on the human spirit. The Italian writer Agnioli di Tura reported simply:

> "I buried with my own hands five of my children in a single grave. No bells. No tears. This is the end of the world." ■

SECTION 3 REVIEW

1. **Identify:** (a) Charlemagne, (b) Gothic, (c) Black Death.
2. **Define:** (a) fief, (b) vassal, (c) knight, (d) serf, (e) manor, (f) sacrament, (g) charter.
3. Describe the structure of feudal society.
4. Why did the Catholic Church hold great power in medieval Europe?
5. How did the Crusades affect Western Europe?
6. **Evaluating Information** How did feudalism and the manor economy ensure order during the Middle Ages?
7. **Writing Across Cultures** Write a brief description of Americans' reactions to the AIDS virus. In what ways have they been similar to medieval Europeans' reaction to the bubonic plague? In what ways have they been different?

Chapter 29 Review

Understanding Vocabulary

Match each term at left with the correct definition at right.

1. acropolis	**a.** hilltop fortress
2. patrician	**b.** peasant tied to the land
3. vassal	**c.** wealthy landowner of ancient Rome
4. serf	**d.** written document guaranteeing rights to town dwellers
5. charter	**e.** lesser lord who owed loyalty to a more powerful lord

Reviewing the Main Ideas

1. What role did rivers and seas play in the development of Western Europe?

2. What resources helped Western Europe develop during the Industrial Revolution?

3. (a) How was Athens a direct democracy? (b) How was democracy in Athens limited?

4. (a) How did the Pax Romana affect the Roman Empire? (b) How did Rome encourage unity in its vast empire?

5. How did Germanic invasions affect the Roman Empire and Western Europe?

6. (a) Describe the role women played in feudal society. (b) How did European Jews face discrimination during the Middle Ages?

Reviewing Chapter Themes

1. Western Europe contains a wide variety of landforms. (a) Describe how geography has shaped the economic development of one region in Western Europe. (b) Describe two ways in which Europeans have used technology to reshape their environment.

2. Modern western civilization has roots in the classical civilizations of ancient Greece and Rome. Describe the influence of two of the following ideas on western civilization: (a) Greek ideas about democracy, (b) Greek philosophy, (c) Roman law, (d) Christianity.

3. Although feudalism dominated Western European society during the Middle Ages, changes gradually occurred. (a) Describe the social and economic system that developed under feudalism. (b) Describe one economic and one social change that took place during the Late Middle Ages.

Thinking Critically

1. Identifying Alternatives (a) How are modern nations of Western Europe trying to meet the need for new sources of energy? (b) What are some possible disadvantages of these alternatives?

2. Making Global Connections (a) How did ancient Greek ideas spread to Rome and then throughout Western Europe? (b) Why do you think these ideas later came to influence the United States?

Applying Your Skills

1. Identifying the Main Idea Reread the subsection "People" on page 643. Write a sentence that summarizes the main idea of the subsection.

2. Analyzing a Quotation Socrates said, "An unexamined life is not worth living." (a) What do you think Socrates meant by this statement? (b) How does this idea apply to the teachings of Socrates and other Greek philosophers?

3. Understanding Causes and Effects Construct a cause-and-effect chart for the Crusades. The chart should include both long-term and short-term causes and effects. (See Skill Lesson, page 628.)

Chapter 30

Western Europe in Transition

The Palace of Versailles The French king Louis XIV had this huge royal residence built in the late 1600s. At the time, Western Europe was enjoying great wealth and prestige. France and other countries were competing for power, both in Europe and in overseas colonies.
Power What do you think other European monarchs thought about Versailles?

Chapter Outline

1 The Renaissance and Reformation
2 Growth of Modern Nations
3 The Industrial Revolution
4 Europe in Two World Wars

Gargantua was a giant with a huge appetite. At one sitting, he could eat "a few dozen hams, smoked tongues of beef, caviar, sausages," and more. He also had a huge appetite for learning and in his youth had studied the most difficult texts ever written.

As an adult, Gargantua was deeply impressed with the interest in learning he saw everywhere. He urged his son Pantagruel to get an education. "Most dear son," he said,

> "I see such improvements [in education] that nowadays I should have trouble [keeping up with] schoolboys."

François Rabelais wrote *Gargantua and Pantagruel* in 1532. Through the two giants he created, Rabelais commented humorously on the changes taking place in France during the Renaissance.

The Renaissance lasted from about 1350 to 1600. *Renaissance* is a French word meaning "rebirth." During the Renaissance, educated Europeans like Rabelais felt they were witnessing a rebirth of civilization after the Middle Ages.

CHAPTER PERSPECTIVE

The Renaissance brought great changes to Western Europe. Trade and commerce expanded. Science and technology flourished. Soon after, modern European nations emerged. As these nations industrialized, they came to dominate the world. Two world wars, however, caused Europe's power to decline.

As you read, look for these chapter themes:

- The Renaissance, Reformation, and Enlightenment encouraged new attitudes toward learning, the individual, and government that would help shape the modern world.
- By the 1600s, strong monarchs had built the foundations of the modern nations of Europe.
- The Industrial Revolution had major effects on Western Europe, both at home and in the world.
- Two world wars had a devastating impact on Europe and helped end European domination of the world.

Literature Connections

In this chapter, you will encounter passages from the following works.

Gargantua and Pantagruel, François Rabelais

Hamlet, William Shakespeare

Lives of the Artists, Giorgio Vasari

Hard Times, Charles Dickens

Night, Elie Wiesel

For other suggestions, see Connections With Literature, pages 804–808.

1 THE RENAISSANCE AND REFORMATION

FIND OUT

What was the Renaissance spirit?

What were the results of European exploration and expansion overseas?

How did the Reformation change Europe?

Vocabulary joint-stock company, indulgence, predestination

"The natural desire of good men is knowledge," noted Leonardo da Vinci. Desire for knowledge drove Leonardo to study everything. As a painter and sculptor, he studied the human body. As an architect, he studied mathematics and engineering. As an inventor, he drew plans for a flying machine, a submarine, and a rapid-firing cannon.

During the Renaissance, Leonardo and other gifted people opened new worlds. Renaissance men and women turned to the civilizations of ancient Greece and Rome for inspiration. They reexamined ancient texts and explored new fields of study. They combined secular, or nonreligious, concerns with Christian traditions. With its emphasis on knowledge and human reason and its faith in the ability of the individual, the Renaissance helped pave the way for the modern world.

Spirit of the Renaissance

The Renaissance began in the city-states of northern Italy and later spread to northern Europe and Spain. During the Crusades, the Italian city-states had built large fleets to transport people and goods to lands bordering the eastern Mediterranean. By the 1300s, trade had made the city-states wealthy. A powerful middle class, made up of merchants and bankers, emerged. The new middle class had the time and money to seek education and support the work of artists.

Interest in the classics. The Renaissance was sparked by a renewed interest in the classics, or the learning of ancient Greece and Rome. Renaissance scholars studied the classics to learn more about the world. By reading ancient texts, they rediscovered knowledge that had been lost or forgotten during the Middle Ages.

New views of the world. During the Renaissance, Europeans began to change the way they thought about themselves and the world. As in the Middle Ages, many people had strong religious views. Scholars studied not only the classics, but also the works of early Christian writers.

At the same time, people took a greater interest in secular affairs. Some Renaissance writers focused on such practical concerns as how to behave. Niccolò Machiavelli (mahk ee uh VEHL ee) wrote *The Prince*, a handbook for rulers. He advised rulers to use whatever means were necessary to achieve their goals. "It is much safer to be feared than to be loved, if one must choose," Machiavelli explained.

Achievements of the Renaissance

The Renaissance spirit also reflected a new confidence in the ability of individuals to shape their own lives. That confidence led Renaissance artists and writers to stress the importance of individual achievement. Their work stimulated a creative spirit that revolutionized the arts and the world of learning in Western Europe.

Art. Renaissance artists turned to classical models. They studied Greek statues and Roman buildings. Their own works reflected the realism and grace of the ancient styles. Renaissance artists experimented with new kinds of paints and painting techniques. They developed perspective, a method of painting that makes objects or scenes appear three-dimensional.

Some of the world's best-known artists, including Leonardo da Vinci and Michelangelo, worked in Italy during the Renaissance. The masterpieces created by Renaissance artists have influenced painting and sculpture to the present day.

Literature. Writers in Italy, France, Spain, and England expressed the spirit of the age. They wrote on a range of religious and secular subjects.

The Italian writer Petrarch (PEE trahrk) experimented with the sonnet, which is a 14-line poem. His devotion to Laura, whose real identity is unknown, led him to write splendid love poems. Those works influenced many later poets. (See Connections With Literature, page 807, "Laura," "The White Doe," and "Spring.")

In Spain, Miguel de Cervantes (suhr VAN teez) wrote *Don Quixote,* which has remained a best-seller for almost 400 years. The novel gently mocks the ideals of medieval knights.

England's great poet and playwright, William Shakespeare, explored themes such as love, jealousy, ambition, and greed. In *Hamlet,* Shakespeare's title character expresses a typically Renaissance view of the individual:

> "What a piece of work is a man! How noble in reason! How infinite in faculties! In form and moving how express and admirable! In action how like an angel! In apprehension [understanding] how like a god!"

Hamlet and Shakespeare's other plays are still performed throughout the world today.

The printing press. During the Renaissance, Europeans applied new technologies to produce many useful inventions. Among the most important inventions was the printing press. The Chinese were the first people to invent printing. Muslim traders may have spread this technology to Europe. By the 1400s, Europeans were experimenting with new methods of printing. Johann Gutenberg of Germany developed a printing press that used movable type. In about 1455, this press was used to produce the first Bible printed by

Michelangelo: Renaissance Ideal

Michelangelo was furious. For three years, he had worked on plans for a magnificent tomb for Pope Julius II. He planned to sculpt 40 large figures to surround the giant two-story tomb. Suddenly, the pope ordered him to stop work on the tomb and paint the ceiling of the Sistine Chapel instead.

The job was awesome. The high ceiling arched across an enormous room. Michelangelo protested that he was a sculptor, not a painter. But the pope was a powerful, persuasive man. Reluctantly, Michelangelo went to work.

For four years he labored, covering the ceiling with dramatic scenes from the Bible. Each day, for hours at a time, he lay on his back atop a high scaffold, his nose just inches from the ceiling. In the end, he produced a masterpiece that many people regard as one of the most influential works in European art. On the ceiling, huge and forceful figures play out the drama of the Creation.

Michelangelo was 37 years old when he completed the Sistine Chapel. Born in Florence, Italy, he had already won attention for his drawings and carvings by the time he was 16 years old. As a young man, Michelangelo studied anatomy and ancient Roman statues so that he could create realistic figures. His most famous sculptures include Bacchus, the Roman god of wine, and figures from the Bible such as David and Moses.

A proud and arrogant man, Michelangelo was dedicated to art. His friend and biographer Giorgio Vasari describes the artist's work habits:

> “He slept very little, frequently rising in the night because he could not sleep, and resuming his labors with the chisel. For these occasions he had made himself a cap of pasteboard, in the center of which he placed a candle, which thus gave him light without encumbering his hands.”

Toward the end of his long life, Michelangelo turned to other pursuits. A brilliant architect, he designed a massive dome for St. Peter's Church in Rome. He was also a gifted poet. With his great talents and diverse accomplishments, Michelangelo represented the Renaissance ideal.

1. What challenges did Michelangelo face in painting the ceiling of the Sistine Chapel?
2. **Applying Information** How did Michelangelo's life and work illustrate the spirit of the Renaissance?

machine. Books no longer had to be copied by hand.

The printing press helped spread the new learning. From hundreds of presses came books on science, medicine, and philosophy as well as religious subjects. The ideas printed in the new books spread rapidly as more and more people learned to read.

Age of Exploration

With a boldness and curiosity that reflected the Renaissance spirit, explorers risked great hardship to expand European knowledge of the world. Their voyages dramatically changed Europe's position in the world. The Age of Exploration lasted from the 1400s to

Spanish Caravels Europeans sailed thousands of miles to distant lands in these small but sturdy vessels. Spain used caravels to bring back treasure of gold and silver from the Americas. This new wealth made Spain the world's richest nation in the 1500s. ***Technology*** What technological advances helped bring about the Age of Exploration?

the 1700s. During that time, Europe became the center of a new worldwide trading system.

Motives. Various motives lay behind overseas exploration. Portugal, Spain, France, and England searched for an ocean route to the rich spice trade of Asia. They wanted to bypass the Mediterranean routes that were controlled by the Muslims and the Italian city-states. Desire for gold and silver led Europeans to conquer the Americas. Europeans also wanted to spread Christianity to other lands.

Impact of technology. By the mid-1400s, advances in learning and technology were making long ocean voyages possible. Renaissance mapmakers began to produce more accurate maps. With the astrolabe, an instrument perfected by the Arabs, sailors could use the stars to calculate their latitude at sea. Europeans improved on the magnetic compass, a device that helped sailors determine their location.

From the Arabs, Europeans learned about the lateen sail, which allowed ships to sail against the wind. At the same time, Europeans used new shipbuilding techniques to produce the large, seaworthy ships needed for ocean voyages.

Voyages. During the Age of Exploration, Europeans charted new routes across the world's oceans. The Portuguese led the way. In 1488, Bartholomeu Dias rounded the Cape of Good Hope at the southern tip of Africa. Nearly 10 years later, Vasco da Gama sailed around Africa and on to India. That voyage led the way for Portugal to build a rich trading empire in Asia.

In 1492, Christopher Columbus sailed west across the Atlantic Ocean in search of a new route to Asia. His voyage opened the way for Spain to colonize the Americas. Later, other explorers searched for a water passage through the Americas to Asia. Ferdinand Magellan pioneered a route around the southern tip of South America and across the Pacific.

Effects of Expansion

The voyages of exploration had worldwide impact. Europeans helped to spread foods, animals, and ideas from one continent to another. Today, we call this the Columbian Exchange. Unknowingly, Europeans also introduced diseases such as smallpox to the New World. These diseases, which took a terrible toll on Native Americans, were an unintended part of the Columbian Exchange.

Colonies. European nations established colonies in the Americas and set up trading outposts in Asia. Spain and Portugal divided South America between them. Spain, France, the Netherlands, and England set up colonies in North America. These distant lands supplied Europeans with precious metals, foods, timber, and furs.

Warfare increased as European nations competed for land and power. Overseas expansion also created a legacy of resentment toward Europeans among peoples whom they ruled.

Economic impact. Overseas expansion changed the economy of Europe. Trade and commerce grew as entrepreneurs sent trading ships around the world. As trade increased, European harbor cities grew in importance.

Europeans developed new ways of doing business. They set up joint-stock companies, private trading companies that sold shares of stock to investors. Through these companies, business people could raise the capital needed for costly ventures such as trading voyages. Entrepreneurs also set up banks and insurance companies. These activities gave Europeans experience that would help them dominate world trade and finance for several centuries.

Overseas empires helped European nations increase their power. By the 1600s, European rulers had adopted the economic philosophy of mercantilism. (See Chapter 21.) They sought to strengthen their nations' economies by regulating trade with their colonies. The colonies supplied the parent country with raw materials. At the same time, the parent country expanded its industries to produce manufactured goods for its colonies.

The Protestant Reformation

During the Renaissance, many scholars and members of the clergy became concerned about the worldliness of the Roman Catholic Church. They criticized the vast sums of money that popes used to build splendid palaces and wage wars. Reformers called on the Church to return to the simple faith of early Christian times. They urged the pope and the clergy to reform corrupt practices.

Luther. Martin Luther, a German priest, was especially disturbed by the practice of selling indulgences. An indulgence was a pardon of sins. It was supposed to reduce the punishment a sinner suffered after death. By the early 1500s, the Church was selling indulgences as a means of raising money. In 1517, Luther nailed a list of questions, known as the 95 theses, to the door of the Wittenberg castle church. In the 95 theses, Luther condemned the sale of indulgences.

Printing presses quickly spread copies of the 95 theses, and Luther soon found himself at the center of a fierce religious debate. He argued that people could not achieve salvation through good works, as the Church taught, but only through God's mercy. Further, he claimed that the Bible and an individual's conscience outweighed the authority of the Church. Luther also rejected many Church

Martin Luther Preaching After Luther had harshly criticized the Church, an order went out for his arrest. A German prince protected the reformer by sheltering him in his castle. There, Luther began translating the Bible from Latin into German. ***Diversity*** How did Luther's teachings differ from those of the Roman Catholic Church?

ceremonies, as well as the authority of the pope. Luther's teachings sparked the Protestant Reformation, a movement that divided the Christian Church in Europe.

Other reformers. Protestant ideas spread rapidly, and many Protestant sects sprang up. In Geneva, Switzerland, John Calvin organized a new church that emphasized predestination, the belief that God had decided in advance whether an individual would be saved or condemned. Calvinism swept across northern Europe.

In England, King Henry VIII broke away from the Catholic Church when the pope refused to annul, or cancel, his marriage. He declared himself the head of the Church of England. Although Henry held on to many Catholic beliefs, the Church of England did adopt some Protestant practices.

Effects. The Catholic Church eventually responded to the Protestant challenge with its own internal reforms. During the mid-1500s, it ended many abuses that the reformers had criticized. Slowly, the Church regained some of the prestige and authority it had lost.

For the next 100 years, Protestants and Catholics waged bitter wars against each other. Most of the fighting took place in Germany, but civil wars also raged in France, England, Scotland, and Ireland. The wars of religion weakened some nations and led to the growth of others. The Netherlands, for example, emerged as a powerful Protestant nation.

SECTION 1 REVIEW

1. **Identify:** (a) Leonardo da Vinci, (b) Niccolò Machiavelli, (c) Miguel de Cervantes, (d) William Shakespeare, (e) Johann Gutenberg, (f) Martin Luther, (g) 95 theses, (h) John Calvin, (i) Henry VIII.
2. **Define:** (a) joint-stock company, (b) indulgence, (c) predestination.
3. (a) Why did the Renaissance begin in northern Italy? (b) Describe three ideas that were an expression of the Renaissance spirit.
4. List two causes and two results of Europe's overseas expansion.
5. (a) Why did reformers criticize the Catholic Church? (b) Describe two results of the Protestant Reformation.
6. **Understanding Causes and Effects** What role did technology play in the Age of Exploration and the Reformation?
7. **Writing Across Cultures** We use the term "Renaissance person" to describe someone who has a wide range of knowledge or skills. Identify an American public figure whom you would consider to be a Renaissance person. Write a paragraph defending your choice.

2 GROWTH OF MODERN NATIONS

FIND OUT

How did absolute monarchs increase their power?

Why did England become a limited monarchy?

What ideas did Enlightenment thinkers support?

How did the French Revolution and Napoleon change Europe?

Vocabulary absolute monarch, divine right, limited monarchy, scientific method

"*L'état, c'est moi*" ("I am the state"), declared Louis XIV, the king of France. Louis was making no idle boast. From his splendid palace at Versailles, he controlled the lives of all the French people. By the late 1600s, Louis and other strong monarchs were building the foundations for the nations of modern Europe.

Age of Absolute Monarchs

During the Early Middle Ages, monarchs had little control over their lands. Instead, powerful feudal lords exercised control over large areas.

During the Late Middle Ages, ambitious rulers worked to increase royal authority. They brought feudal lords under their control and struggled to reduce the influence of the Church. As towns grew, monarchs found ways to control trade and win the support of the growing middle class. In each country, the ruler organized a royal treasury to collect money as well as courts to administer justice. Monarchs built strong armies and enlarged their territories.

Absolute monarchs. From the 1500s to the 1700s, rulers in Spain, France, and elsewhere gained enormous power. They became absolute monarchs, or rulers who have complete authority in government and over the lives of the people they govern. (📖 See Connections With Literature, page 807, "The Prince.")

Europe's absolute monarchs believed that they ruled by divine right. According to this theory, a ruler's authority came from God. In support of divine right, the French bishop Jacques Bossuet (bah SWAY) wrote:

> "Royal authority is absolute. The prince owes an explanation to no one for what he orders. God has chosen the prince to rule over other men. Without this absolute authority, the king could neither do good nor [prevent] evil."

The Sun King. Perhaps the best example of Europe's absolute rulers was Louis XIV of France. During his long reign from 1643 to 1715, Louis XIV made himself the center of a powerful state. Louis's symbol was the sun. It suggested that just as the Earth depended on the sun for survival, so, too, did the people of France depend on their king for their well-being.

Louis XIV continued the efforts of earlier French kings to impose royal authority over local rulers. He reorganized the army so that it was loyal to him rather than to individual nobles. In a series of wars, he expanded French borders in the north, south, and east.

Economic policies. To pay for his magnificent court and the many wars he waged, Louis depended on his skillful finance minister, Jean Colbert (kohl BEHR). Colbert, a mercantilist, promoted trade and commerce so that he could tax the wealth they produced. To improve transportation and trade, Colbert

Louis XIV This painting of the proud, powerful monarch shows him dressed in royal velvet and ermine. Louis XIV enforced his authority by making nobles live at Versailles. There, they could not plot rebellions. Instead, they competed for such privileges as handing the king his gloves each morning. ***Political System*** How did absolute monarchs justify their power?

Queen Elizabeth Meets With Parliament
Elizabeth I, one of England's greatest monarchs, ruled the nation from 1558 to 1603. She was able to win Parliament's approval of her actions because of her strong will and the fierce loyalty of her subjects.
Political System What two factors helped England become a limited monarchy?

encouraged the building of roads and canals. He also improved the nation's system of tax collection.

Despite Colbert's efforts to raise money, the king's wars and court expenses drained the treasury. As a result, France was heavily in debt by the time Louis died. Convinced of their divine right to rule, however, Louis's successors refused to make desperately needed reforms. Their failure to act prepared the way for the French Revolution.

A Limited Monarchy in England

In England, monarchs tried but failed to win the same powers that Louis enjoyed in France. A government in which a monarch does not have absolute power is called a limited monarchy. Traditions dating back hundreds of years had set a number of limits on English rulers.

Magna Carta. In 1215, English nobles forced King John to sign the Magna Carta, or Great Charter. It guaranteed the nobles certain rights. For example, the king had to consult them before creating new taxes. The Magna Carta also stated that nobles accused of crimes had the right to a trial by their peers, or equals. Most important, the Magna Carta established the idea that the king had to respect the law.

Parliament. A second limit on royal power was Parliament, an assembly made up of the House of Lords and the House of Commons. Over the centuries, Parliament won certain powers, such as the right to approve new tax laws. By controlling finances, Parliament could exercise some control over the monarch.

Clashes between king and Parliament. During the early 1600s, Charles I claimed divine right to rule. When Parliament refused to recognize his authority, he tried to rule without its approval. In 1628, though, financial problems forced Charles to call Parliament into session. Parliament refused to act on his demands for money until he signed the Petition of Right. The petition asserted Parliament's authority over taxation. Once Charles got the funds he needed, however, he dismissed Parliament and ignored the Petition of Right. The king increasingly ruled on his own.

Finally, Charles's clashes with Parliament led to a civil war. The king's followers, called Cavaliers, fought Parliament's forces, called Roundheads. Many Roundheads were Puritans, or Protestants who wanted to see the Church of England "purified" of Catholic practices. Oliver Cromwell, a strong-minded Puritan, led Parliament's forces to victory. In 1649, Charles I was tried and executed. For the next nine years, until his death in 1658, Cromwell ruled England as a strict Puritan state.

In 1660, Parliament invited Charles II, the son of the executed king, to take the throne. Charles realized, however, that he owed his position to Parliament and not to divine right.

English Bill of Rights. In 1689, Parliament placed additional limits on royal power. It required King William and Queen Mary to sign the Bill of Rights, which made Parliament stronger than the monarch. The English Bill of Rights protected certain rights of individuals, such as the right to trial by jury for anyone accused of a crime.

During the 1700s, political parties began to play an important role in government. A cabinet system evolved. The cabinet was made up of a prime minister and the monarch's chief advisers, chosen from members of the party that held the most seats in Parliament. With these changes, the British government gradually took the form it has today.

The Scientific Revolution

During the 1500s and 1600s, new technology and new methods of research led to an explosion of knowledge that became known as the Scientific Revolution. The Scientific Revolution changed the way Europeans viewed the world and also laid the foundations of modern science.

During the Middle Ages, European scholars accepted the teachings of the ancient Greek philosophers and the Church. Renaissance scholars developed a new approach to scientific study that became known as the scientific method. It was a step-by-step approach that emphasized experimentation and observation. Even more significant, however, the scientific method relied on mathematics, rather than ancient principles, to test results and prove theories. It was mainly through their advances in mathematics that Renaissance thinkers revolutionized science.

Advances in astronomy. In 1543, a Polish mathematician and astronomer, Nicolaus Copernicus (koh PUR nih kuhs), challenged traditional teachings about the universe. Many ancient Greeks thought that the Earth stood at the center of the universe and all the heavenly bodies revolved around it. The Church accepted this view because it placed humans at the center of the universe. Copernicus used mathematics to show that the Earth revolved around the sun. Although many scholars and religious leaders rejected Copernicus's ideas at the time, these ideas were eventually proved correct.

In Italy, Galileo Galilei perfected the telescope. After observing the sky, he declared that the planets moved around the sun. The universe that he described was very different from the one the ancient Greeks described. Galileo's observations challenged the teachings of the Catholic Church, and Church officials put him on trial. Threatened with death if he refused to admit his errors publicly, Galileo stated that his ideas were wrong.

In England, Isaac Newton proved what Galileo had observed. He invented calculus, a new mathematical method. Using calculus, Newton showed how the sun's gravity keeps

A Scientific Experiment During the Scientific Revolution, Europeans took a new look at how and why things worked. In this painting, *An Experiment With An Air Pump*, a scientist tries out a new device. ***Technology*** What aspects of the scientific method does this painting illustrate?

the planets within their orbits. Newton helped develop a new view of the universe as a huge, well-regulated machine that worked according to natural laws. His discoveries formed the basis of much of modern science.

Medicine. During the 1500s and 1600s, scientists made advances in medicine that challenged the ideas of traditional authorities. Physicians made accurate drawings of the human body, developed new ways of treating wounds, and studied the circulation of the blood. Their discoveries slowly set the stage for the medical breakthroughs of the 1800s.

The Enlightenment

With its emphasis on natural laws, the Scientific Revolution influenced philosophers. They felt confident that they could discover natural laws that governed human behavior, just as Newton and Copernicus had discovered laws that governed physical objects.

During the 1700s, European philosophers thought that people should use reason to free themselves from ignorance and superstition. They believed that people who were "enlightened" by reason could perfect themselves and society. As a result, this period is often called the Enlightenment. Ideas discussed during the Enlightenment became the basis for today's democratic governments.

Natural rights. In the late 1600s, an English philosopher, John Locke, set out some basic ideas of the Enlightenment in his *Two Treatises on Government.* Locke regarded government as a contract between the ruler and the ruled. He believed that people everywhere had certain natural rights, including the right to life, liberty, and property. The government had a duty to protect those rights. If a ruler failed to do so, the people had the right to rebel. According to Locke, rulers should stay in power only as long as they had the consent of those they governed.

Toleration. Locke's ideas influenced many French thinkers, including Voltaire. A witty writer, Voltaire published pamphlets and essays that poked fun at France's backwardness compared with the advances being made in Britain. He urged religious toleration, as well as freedom of speech and of the press. "I do not agree with a word you say," Voltaire is supposed to have stated, "but I will defend to the death your right to say it."

Separation of powers. In *The Spirit of Laws,* the baron de Montesquieu (MAHN tuhs kyoo) discussed various forms of government. He argued that the best government was one based on the principle of separation of powers among three branches—the legislative, executive, and judiciary. If each branch had its own powers and responsibilities, Montesquieu said, then no branch could dominate any of the others.

Equality. Another French philosopher, Jean Jacques Rousseau (roo SOH), supported the revolutionary idea that all people are born equal. He opposed titles of rank and nobility. Government, he believed, belonged to the people and should represent the general will of the majority.

Impact of the Enlightenment. During the 1700s, Enlightenment ideas spread across Europe and the Atlantic to the Americas. Through books and newspapers, in coffeehouses, and at informal gatherings, people heard the call for reform. Some of Europe's rulers even supported Enlightenment ideas. In some nations, these "enlightened monarchs" ended serfdom and allowed religious freedom.

The American Revolution

Enlightenment ideas fueled a desire for freedom in Britain's 13 American colonies. In 1776, the colonists issued a Declaration of Independence. It echoed Locke's ideas in asserting people's natural rights to "life, liberty, and the pursuit of happiness." After winning their freedom, Americans wrote the Constitution of the United States. The Constitution set up a government based on Montesquieu's ideas about the separation of powers. Soon afterward, Americans added the Bill of Rights. These 10 amendments to the Constitution guarantee Americans a variety of basic civil liberties.

The Declaration of Independence, the Constitution, and the Bill of Rights became symbols of freedom to people around the world. In their own struggles for freedom, they hoped to achieve similar rights.

The French Revolution

The American Revolution and the Enlightenment helped trigger a revolution in France. By the late 1700s, France had piled up a huge national debt. A corrupt government, a weak monarch, and an outdated social and economic system added to the nation's problems.

The French people were divided by law into three estates, or classes: clergy, nobles, and commoners. The people who belonged to the first two estates paid no direct taxes. The tax burden fell on the Third Estate, which was made up of the middle and working classes. Although they paid heavy taxes, members of the Third Estate had little say in the decisions of government.

An economic crisis brought France to the edge of bankruptcy. In 1789, Louis XVI sought help from the Estates General, an assembly of the three estates that had not met for 175 years. Members of the Third Estate, along with reform-minded nobles and clergy, took the first step toward revolution when they organized the National Assembly to write a constitution for France.

Early reforms. The French Revolution passed through several stages. During the first stage, the National Assembly drew up a constitution that swept away the old feudal order and ended the many privileges of the nobles. The reformers also adopted the Declaration of the Rights of Man. It stated that all men were equal and had certain rights, such as freedom of speech, the press, and religion. The National Assembly abolished the privileges of the Catholic Church and placed the Church under government control. Under the constitution of 1791, France became a limited monarchy.

The French Republic. The revolution entered a more radical phase in 1792. By then, France was at war with Austria and Prussia. Fearing that the idea of revolution might spread, Austria and Prussia were determined to turn back the tide of revolution and restore the French king's power. During this radical phase, the revolutionaries tried and executed Louis XVI and declared France a republic.

The revolutionary government set up a Committee of Public Safety, headed by Maximilien Robespierre (ROHBS pyehr). Robespierre unleashed a brutal campaign to drive back foreign invaders and suppress uprisings at home. During Robespierre's Reign of Terror, which began in 1793, thousands of French men, women, and children were condemned to death on the guillotine. At the same time, France's armies battled against

Attack on the Royal Palace When the French Revolution began, King Louis XVI seemed to accept changes that limited the monarchy. However, when he tried to escape from France, the people turned against him. After Parisians attacked his palace in 1792, Louis XVI was tried for treason and executed. ***Change*** How did the French monarchy change between 1715 and 1792?

foreign enemies. The radical phase of the revolution ended in 1794.

The Napoleonic Age

In 1799, an ambitious young army officer, Napoleon Bonaparte, won control of the government. By 1804, he had gained enough power to proclaim himself "Emperor of the French." A majority of French voters approved his action.

Although Napoleon had gained absolute power, he did not return to the old system. Instead, he preserved many reforms of the French Revolution. He issued the Napoleonic Code, a law code that kept the most important rights won by the people during the revolution. This code recognized that all men were equal before the law, and it protected freedom of religion. Napoleon also made reforms to strengthen the French economy.

The wars of Napoleon. Napoleon conquered an empire that extended from Spain in the west to the borders of Russia in the east. These conquests helped to spread the revolutionary ideas of liberty and equality to the peoples of Europe. At the same time, Napoleon's successes encouraged the growth of nationalism among the peoples he conquered. As nationalist feelings grew, revolts against French rule erupted.

Eventually, Britain, Prussia, Russia, and Austria united to defeat Napoleon and force him into exile. The victorious allies installed the brother of Louis XVI on the French throne as Louis XVIII.

A continuing struggle. In 1814, European leaders met at the Congress of Vienna. They set out to restore order after 25 years of revolution and war. Most of them wanted to turn the clock back to the traditions that had existed before the French Revolution. Despite their efforts, they could not destroy revolutionary ideas. Throughout the 1800s, reformers in many countries demanded constitutions that protected people's basic rights. Those demands led to frequent upheavals. During this time, the Industrial Revolution was underway. It, too, contributed to the continuing turmoil in Europe.

SECTION 2 REVIEW

1. **Identify:** (a) Louis XIV, (b) Magna Carta, (c) English Bill of Rights, (d) Nicolaus Copernicus, (e) Galileo, (f) Isaac Newton, (g) John Locke, (h) Baron de Montesquieu, (i) Congress of Vienna.
2. **Define:** (a) absolute monarch, (b) divine right, (c) limited monarchy, (d) scientific method.
3. How did rulers like Louis XIV increase their power?
4. What were two limits on the power of the English monarchy?
5. What ideas about government developed during the Enlightenment?
6. **Analyzing Information** (a) How did Napoleon's conquests lead to the growth of nationalism? (b) Why do you think later European leaders were unable to destroy revolutionary ideas?
7. **Writing Across Cultures** List three ideas in the Constitution of the United States that reflect the influence of Enlightenment ideas.

3 THE INDUSTRIAL REVOLUTION

FIND OUT

How did new technologies contribute to the Industrial Revolution?

How did industrialization affect people's lives?

How did reformers try to change society in the 1800s?

Vocabulary factory system, assembly line, franchise

"It was a town of machinery and tall chimneys, out of which interminable serpents of smoke trailed themselves for ever and ever. . . . It had a black canal in it, and a river that ran purple with ill-smelling dye, and vast piles of buildings full of windows . . . where the pistons of the steam-engine worked . . . up and down, like the head of an elephant in a state of melancholy madness. ”

In *Hard Times,* the British writer Charles Dickens described life in a factory town during the Industrial Revolution. The Industrial Revolution was a long, slow process during which machines replaced hand tools and new sources of power such as steam and electricity replaced human and animal power in the production of goods.

The Industrial Revolution had two stages. From about 1750 to 1850, Britain took the lead in shifting to new methods of production. From the mid-1800s to 1914, the nations of Western Europe and the United States used these production methods to become modern industrial nations.

Beginnings of the Industrial Revolution

A revolution in agriculture during the 1700s created conditions that favored the Industrial Revolution. Small farms were combined, or enclosed, to make larger, more efficient ones. Farmers began to grow new crops and use new technologies such as the seed drill and the iron plow. Increased food production improved people's diet and health. This, in turn, contributed to rapid population growth. At the same time, better farming methods meant that fewer people were needed to farm. As a result, unemployed farmers formed a large pool of available labor.

The factory system. The Industrial Revolution began in the British textile industry. Inventors produced new machines that reduced the time required to spin and weave wool and cotton. Because running water was needed to power machines, factory owners built spinning mills near rivers. The new machines led to the growth of the factory system, which brought workers and machines together in one place to manufacture goods.

By the late 1700s, steam had begun to replace water as a source of power. The Scottish inventor James Watt improved the steam-powered engine. Steam engines gave a boost to two other industries, coal and iron. In the mid-1800s, Henry Bessemer developed a process to improve the production of steel. Better steel triggered the growth of still other industries.

The Triumph of Steam and Electricity
This English print was issued in 1897 to commemorate the sixtieth anniversary of Queen Victoria's rule. During her long reign, the Industrial Revolution transformed Britain. ***Technology*** What major changes are shown between the pictures at left and those at right?

Improved transportation and communications. The Industrial Revolution brought rapid advances in transportation and communications. Britain built a network of roads, bridges, and canals to connect all parts of the nation. By the mid-1800s, steam-powered railroads and ships were providing improved, faster transportation around the world. At the same time, inventions such as the telegraph revolutionized communications.

Why Britain took the lead. Britain took the lead in the Industrial Revolution for a number of reasons. It had the large iron and coal resources needed to provide power for machines. It was a major commercial nation where merchants had the capital to invest in new enterprises. It had an abundant supply of cheap labor. It had colonies that supplied raw materials and provided a market for finished goods. In addition, the British government encouraged improvements in transportation and used its navy to protect British trade.

The Industrial Revolution Spreads

After the 1850s, other countries industrialized. Among them were Belgium, France, Germany, the United States, and later Japan. By the 1890s, the United States had overtaken Britain as the world's leading industrial power. German industry rivaled both British and American industry by 1900.

Science and industry. By the end of the 1800s, scientists were developing many new products and methods of manufacturing goods. Physicists built electric generators that in time replaced steam engines in many factories. Discoveries in the field of electricity led to the invention of the telephone and the radio, which further improved communications. An American inventor, Thomas Edison, developed a variety of new electrical products, including the phonograph and the light bulb.

The invention of the internal combustion engine, which was used to power automobiles, set the stage for a revolution in transportation. The growth of the automobile industry, in turn, triggered booms in other industries, such as the production of steel, rubber, and petroleum.

New methods of production. To meet the growing demand for goods, factory owners developed new methods of production. At his automobile factory in the United States, Henry Ford introduced the assembly line. There, the complex job of assembling many parts was broken down into small tasks, each performed by an individual worker. The assembly line made production more efficient and reduced costs.

Changing Patterns of Life

The Industrial Revolution radically altered the patterns of life in Europe and North America. As nations industrialized, millions of people moved from rural areas into cities. By 1900, about one third of the people in industrialized countries lived in cities.

Social changes. A new social structure emerged during the Industrial Revolution. At the bottom of society were unskilled, poorly paid workers. A new middle class of factory owners challenged the old land-owning aristocracy. Women worked outside the home in growing numbers. They earned wages in factories and as domestic servants.

Life in the cities. The Industrial Revolution brought many benefits. It created millions of new jobs and produced a great variety of goods more cheaply than ever before. During this period, too, scientists made great advances in diagnosing and treating diseases.

The Industrial Revolution also created problems. Cities were filled with dark, smoky factories surrounded by rows of poorly built houses. Working-class families lived crowded together in one or two rooms in buildings that had no water or sewage system. Under these conditions, disease spread rapidly.

Working conditions. Factories, too, were dangerous and unhealthy places. Workers who were injured on the job received no sick pay. Entire families worked long hours for low pay. Even young children labored for 12 to 16 hours a day, 6 days a week. In 1832, reformers in Britain's Parliament held hearings to determine what changes needed to be made.

Evils of Child Labor

Elizabeth Bentley limped into the hearing room. Facing her sat the members of a parliamentary commission that was investigating factory conditions. Briskly, she answered their questions:

> “‘What age are you?’
> ‘Twenty-three.’
> ‘What time did you begin work at the factory?’
> ‘When I was six years old.’
> ‘What were your hours of labor in that mill?’
> ‘From five in the morning till nine at night, when they were thronged [busy].’ ”

Like many people during the Industrial Revolution, Elizabeth Bentley had worked in a textile mill since early childhood. She had no choice. Her family needed every penny she and her brothers and sisters could earn in order to survive.

Her day began at 4 A.M., when her mother shook her awake. The young girl quickly ate a bowl of thin porridge, drank a mug of tea, and then walked two miles to the factory. In the slow season, she worked a 13-hour day. Her hours increased to 16 during the busy season. At noon, she got a 40-minute break—her only time off during the day.

Bentley's first job was as a doffer. She ran from machine to machine, emptying bobbins filled with thread. At age 10, she moved on to the carding room. There, she pulled a heavy rack across linen fibers again and again. The work nearly stretched her arms out of their sockets, causing pains that wracked her body. By the time Bentley was 13 years old, her ankles, knees, and back showed signs of being deformed.

The work was not the only cause of pain, as Bentley revealed to the commission:

> “‘Suppose you flagged [slowed down] a little, or were late, what would they do?’
> ‘Strap us.’
> ‘Were the girls so struck as to leave marks upon their skin?’
> ‘Yes; they have had black marks many times, and their parents dare not come to the foreman about it, they were afraid of losing their work.’ ”

Children Working in a Coal Mine Early in the Industrial Revolution, factory owners often preferred children to adults in certain jobs. In coal mines, for example, boys and girls could crawl through tunnels more easily. In textile factories, the children could use their small fingers to handle delicate spinning and weaving machinery. ***Human Rights*** What could children do if they were mistreated on the job?

In 1842, other hearings revealed that children who worked in mines faced equally terrible conditions. Girls and boys as young as 8 years old worked 14 hours a day. Crawling on their hands and knees, they carried coal on their backs through low, damp tunnels. These reports shocked people in the middle and upper classes, who urged Parliament to pass reform laws.

Reform came too late to heal Elizabeth Bentley's broken body. Asked what she did now, she replied that she was "in the poorhouse." ■

Demands for Reform

As reformers exposed the evils of industrial society, governments slowly took responsibility for making changes. Prodded by reports of terrible conditions and by popular protests, the British Parliament passed laws that limited the work hours of children. Later, these laws applied to all workers. Other European nations eventually took similar actions.

Improvements. To press their demands for change, workers formed labor unions. At first, unions met with fierce opposition from business owners and government. Gradually, however, workers won the right to organize. Unions used strikes and other tactics to win better wages, shorter hours, and improved working conditions.

By the early 1900s, life improved for many workers. As wages rose, families no longer had to send young children to work. New regulations made factories safer and healthier. Some governments also took steps to protect workers by providing unemployment, accident, and old-age insurance.

City life also improved. Governments established building codes, improved water and sewage systems, supported hospitals, and organized police forces. In addition, all industrial nations set up free public schools.

Growth of democracy. In most nations of Western Europe, these social changes were closely linked to the growth of democracy. In Britain and elsewhere, reformers focused on extending the franchise, or right to vote.

In the early 1800s, only a small percentage of British men could vote. Prodded by reformers, Parliament passed the Reform Bill of 1832. It extended the franchise to almost all middle-class men. In 1867, urban working men won the right to vote. Eventually, Parliament passed laws that gave the vote to rural working men.

Women, too, campaigned for the right to vote. During the early 1900s, they held rallies to publicize their cause. Some even used violence to protest their second-class status. At the time, most people strongly opposed giving women the vote. In Britain, women over age 30 finally won the right to vote in 1918. Other British women, as well as women in many other Western European countries, had to wait even longer before they could enjoy this right.

A London Street Industrialization spurred the growth of cities, where the great differences between rich and poor were seen daily. Industrial progress did improve the worker's standard of living. However, it brought greater benefits to upper-class citizens, such as the mother and child at left, than to the poor, such as this flower seller. ***Change*** How did unions help workers?

New Ideas About Society

During the 1800s, philosophers studied the harsh effects of industrialization. They developed new ideas about how society should be organized. Some called on governments to protect workers and correct the worst abuses of industrial life. Others demanded more radical changes.

Socialism. Socialists argued that the capitalist system rewarded only the industrialists and not the workers whose labor supported it. They favored government ownership of land, machines, and factories. In their ideal world, poverty would not exist and all workers would share equally in the results of their labor.

Marx. Two German social philosophers, Karl Marx and Friedrich Engels, outlined their revolutionary ideas in the *Communist Manifesto.* In this pamphlet, they called for public ownership of all land as well as the means of production. This system came to be called communism.

Marx claimed that his ideas were based on a scientific study of history. He argued that history showed the struggle of two classes—the "haves" and the "have nots":

> "The history of all hitherto existing society is the history of class struggles. Freeman and slave, patrician and plebeian, lord and serf . . . in a word, oppressor and oppressed, stood in constant opposition to one another."

In industrial societies, the members of the bourgeoisie (boor zhwah ZEE), or middle class, were the "haves" and those who belonged to the proletariat, or working class, were the "have nots." Marx predicted a worldwide revolution in which the proletariat would rise up against bourgeois capitalism and form a classless society.

European history did not follow the course that Marx predicted. Working conditions improved during the late 1800s, so most workers saw no reason to overthrow capitalism. Still, Marx's idea of a classless society in which all would share equally appealed to many people. His teachings became the basis for communist revolutions in Russia, China, and Cuba. They have also inspired nationalist movements in many parts of the Third World.

SECTION 3 REVIEW

1. **Identify:** (a) James Watt, (b) Henry Bessemer, (c) Thomas Edison, (d) Reform Bill of 1832, (e) *Communist Manifesto.*
2. **Define:** (a) factory system, (b) assembly line, (c) franchise.
3. Give two examples of how inventions and new methods of production brought changes to industry.
4. Describe how the Industrial Revolution affected each of the following: (a) social structure, (b) cities.
5. (a) Why did Karl Marx oppose capitalism? (b) What solution did communism propose for the ills of modern society?
6. **Defending a Position** Do you think the positive results of the Industrial Revolution outweighed the negative results? Explain.
7. **Writing Across Cultures** In the 1860s, an underwater telegraph cable linked Britain and the United States. Write a brief statement outlining the possible benefits of improved communication with Europe during the Industrial Revolution.

4 EUROPE IN TWO WORLD WARS

FIND OUT

What were the causes of World War I?

Why did dictators gain power in Italy and Germany?

What forces contributed to the outbreak of World War II?

Vocabulary appeasement, blitzkrieg, Holocaust

"Peace remains at the mercy of an accident," declared a German diplomat early in 1914. That "accident" happened in June 1914, when an assassin shot the heir to the throne of Austria-Hungary. The assassination set off a chain of events that shattered the peace of Europe—and the world.

The period from 1815 to 1914 was a relatively peaceful one in Europe. Yet under the surface, tensions were building. As European nations dominated more and more of the globe, rivalries among colonial powers flared. Nationalism, militarism, and industrial competition also contributed to an atmosphere that led to war.

Growth of Nationalism

The wars of Napoleon helped to spark the growth of nationalism. During the 1800s, various ethnic and religious groups throughout Europe sought independence. The spirit of nationalism led to the creation of two new nations—Italy and Germany. The emergence of these nations increased tensions among the great powers of Europe.

Italy. During the early 1800s, Italy was divided into many small states. Most were under foreign rule. For decades, Italian nationalists struggled for independence and unity. Led by Count Camillo Cavour and Giuseppe Garibaldi, Italian nationalists fought to free Italy from foreign control.

By 1870, the unification of the Italian peninsula was complete. Italy then began to play an active role in world affairs. It entered the race for colonies in Africa. In addition, some Italian nationalists sought to add lands in northern Italy that remained under foreign rule.

Germany. Like Italy, Germany was divided into many separate states. During the 1860s, Count Otto von Bismarck of Prussia led the drive to unite Germany. He followed a policy of "blood and iron"—warfare and military might. Prussian armies defeated Austria, their greatest rival for control of the rest of Germany. They also defeated France in the Franco-Prussian War. France's desire for revenge fueled tensions in the years that followed.

After France's defeat in 1871, Bismarck created a united Germany that was led by Prussia. The king of Prussia was proclaimed kaiser, or emperor, of Germany. Under Prussian leadership, industry in Germany forged ahead. Germany also set out to win "a place in the sun" as a world power alongside Britain, France, Russia, and Austria-Hungary.

Unrest in Eastern Europe. In Eastern Europe, the growth of nationalism threatened to break up the large empires ruled by Austria-Hungary and the Ottomans. Both empires ruled millions of people of many ethnic groups. People like the Slavs had a strong sense of pride in their culture and resented foreign rule. As a result, during the early 1900s one crisis after another erupted in the

Garibaldi in Sicily Leading a force of volunteers called the Red Shirts, this bold military commander defeated the foreign rulers who controlled Sicily and southern Italy. The region then joined with several small states in the north to form the Kingdom of Italy. ***Choice*** Why did Italian nationalists join Garibaldi's army?

Balkans, a troubled multicultural region in southeastern Europe. Tensions there eventually flared into World War I.

The Road to War

Nationalism and the Industrial Revolution fueled a European drive to build overseas empires. Using their military and economic power, European nations carved up much of Africa and Asia for their own use.

The scramble for colonies brought European countries into conflict with one another in Asia and Africa. More than once, after 1890, Europe found itself teetering on the brink of war. Although the conflicts were smoothed over, anger and hatred grew.

Nationalism and colonial rivalries led European nations to increase military spending by enlarging their armies and building navies. In the late 1800s, all European nations, but Germany in particular, glorified war and encouraged a spirit of militarism.

Alliance system. As tensions grew, European nations sought allies that would come to their aid in case of war. Germany, Austria-Hungary, and Italy formed the Triple Alliance. In response, France joined Russia and Britain in the Triple Entente (ahn TAHNT). These two alliances only intensified tensions. A crisis that involved one of the great powers now would also affect that nation's allies.

The powder keg explodes. By the early 1900s, Europeans viewed the Balkans as a "powder keg" that was ready to explode into war. Some Slavs had won freedom from the Ottoman Empire, but others in Bosnia and Hercegovina (hehrt seh goh VEE nah) were still ruled by Austria-Hungary.

In June 1914, Archduke Francis Ferdinand, heir to the throne of Austria-Hungary, visited Sarajevo (sar uh YAY voh), the capital of Bosnia. During the visit, a Bosnian nationalist shot and killed the archduke and his wife.

The assassination triggered a major crisis. Austria accused Serbia, a nearby Slavic state, of hatching the plot, and threatened war. As diplomats rushed to resolve the crisis, the alliance system was set into motion. Germany stood by its ally, Austria. In the meantime, Russia prepared to help its fellow Slavs in Serbia. On August 1, 1914, Germany declared war on Russia. Within days, France and Britain were drawn into the conflict.

World War I

The war that broke out in August 1914 dragged on for four years. At the time, it was called the Great War. Later, it became known as World War I.

World War I involved all of the major European powers and many regions beyond Europe. On one side were the Central Powers—Germany, Austria-Hungary, and the Ottoman Empire. On the other side were the Allied Powers—Britain, France, and Russia. Eventually, more than 20 nations, including Italy and the United States, joined the Allies.

Stalemate. The war was fought on many fronts, or combat zones. On the western front—northern France and southern Belgium—France and Britain battled Germany. On the eastern front—from the Baltic to the Black Sea—Russia and Serbia battled Germany, Austria-Hungary, and the Ottoman Empire.

During much of the war, armies on the western front followed a strategy of trench warfare. Soldiers dug long trenches that were protected by mines and barbed wire. One side would shell the other and then send its troops "over the top" of the trenches to break through enemy lines. Hundreds of thousands of soldiers died in battles that won only a few dozen yards of territory. By November 1914, the war had settled into a stalemate, or situation in which no one could win.

Although Russia had the largest army in the war, its soldiers lacked weapons and skilled leadership. As a result, the Russians suffered terrible losses on the eastern front. After the Russian Revolution in 1917, Russia withdrew from the war. (See Chapter 33.)

New weapons. The Allied Powers and the Central Powers both used new weapons, such as machine guns and poison gas, that caused heavy casualties. The British introduced the armored tank. Both sides used aircraft, although mostly for observing enemy troop movements. At sea, German submarine attacks on merchant ships helped to draw the United States into the conflict in April 1917.

On the Western Front Warfare created a desolate "no man's land" littered with the bodies of the dead. During this bloody combat, a poet wrote: "In Flanders fields the poppies blow/Between the crosses, row on row." World War I cost Europe a generation of its young men. ***Technology*** What new military technology came into use during World War I?

The war ends. By the fall of 1917, large numbers of American troops were reaching Europe. Their arrival boosted the morale of Allied soldiers, who had been fighting for more than three years. When the Germans launched a final offensive in early 1918, Allied troops, bolstered by fresh American forces, beat back the attack and then pushed the Germans into retreat. On November 11, 1918, the Allies and Germany signed an armistice agreement, ending the Great War.

Peace settlements. In 1919, the victorious Allies met in Paris, France, to hammer out a peace settlement. President Woodrow Wilson of the United States had called for a "just peace." He advised the Allies not to seek revenge against Germany. He also supported the principle of self-determination, or the right of national groups to form independent nations. In the end, however, in the Treaty of Versailles, the Allies imposed harsh terms on Germany, including heavy reparations, or payments for war damages.

Under the settlements, the Allies recognized new nations in Eastern Europe, but they ignored the principle of self-determination in other regions of the world. In the Middle East, for example, parts of the Ottoman Empire became British and French mandates. The Treaty of Versailles also set up a League of Nations to settle disagreements between nations and prevent future wars.

Effects. World War I caused enormous property damage. Millions of people were killed, and millions more were seriously wounded. After the war, people lived with a sense of uncertainty. So many lives had been shattered that people could not feel secure. How could they be sure that war would never again destroy the hard-won peace? "We do not know what will be born," wrote French writer Paul Valéry, "and we fear the future, not without reason."

Rise of Dictators

During the 1920s and 1930s, the nations of Europe struggled to recover from the war. Many of them faced economic hardships and political unrest. The communist revolution in Russia created a fear that similar revolutions would take place in Western Europe.

In response to these conditions, many people turned to powerful leaders who promised their countries a glorious future. During this period, dictators emerged in Italy and Germany.

Fascist Italy. After World War I, Italy was plagued by economic and political problems. Workers in the cities went on strike. In the country, landless peasants seized the property of wealthy landowners. In addition, many nationalists denounced the government because they felt that Italy had not gained enough territory in the Paris peace settlement.

An ambitious politician, Benito Mussolini, took advantage of the turmoil to gain power. He founded the Fascist party. Fascists glorified the state and supported nationalist expansion. They defended private property, which they believed should be regulated by the government, and despised communism. They also condemned democracy. Free elections, they argued, destroyed the unity of a nation. Above all, the Fascists glorified violence and war as ways to achieve national goals.

Mussolini ruled Italy as a dictator. He silenced critics, controlled the army and the schools, and organized a secret police. Promising to make Italy a great empire like ancient Rome, he invaded Ethiopia in East Africa.

Nazi Germany. After World War I, Germany experienced frequent turmoil. Extremist groups on the far right and the far left threatened to revolt. Runaway inflation and high reparations payments weakened the economy and the new democratic government that was formed after World War I.

In the early 1920s, Adolf Hitler gained control of the National Socialist, or Nazi, party. The Nazis were fascists whose program was based on nationalism, anti-communism, and anti-Semitism. Hitler won popular support by attacking the Treaty of Versailles. He blamed the Jews for Germany's defeat in World War I and for its economic problems. He promoted racism by claiming that Germans belonged to a superior "Aryan" race that was destined to rule the world. His supporters used violence to terrorize opponents, especially the communists.

In the 1930s, the Great Depression struck around the world. Germany was especially hard hit. Faced with disastrous unemployment, desperate Germans rallied behind Hitler's promises of national greatness. In 1933, Hitler became chancellor of Germany. The chancellor was head of the German government.

Hitler moved quickly to crush opposition parties. He set up a fascist state in which he was the *Führer,* or "leader." The Nazi party controlled every aspect of German life. The secret police arrested anyone who was suspected of opposing Nazi rule. The Nazis used the press, the schools, and even churches to spread their message. They also waged a violent campaign against Jews. They sent millions of Jews, as well as other opponents, to concentration camps. These camps later became places of horrifying mass murder.

The Nazis preached the need for hard work, sacrifice, and service to the state. To end unemployment, Hitler launched a vast building program and strengthened the German military. He also embarked on an aggressive campaign to expand German territory.

Nazi aggression. "Today Germany. Tomorrow the world!" declared one Nazi slogan. In violation of the Treaty of Versailles, in 1936, Hitler boldly sent German troops into the Rhineland. Two years later, Nazi Germany annexed Austria. Britain responded with a policy of appeasement, or making concessions to an aggressor in order to preserve peace. France, which was faced with economic and social crises itself, also acted to appease Hitler.

In 1938, Hitler threatened to invade Czechoslovakia. France and Britain agreed to give Germany a part of Czechoslovakia, hoping this would end Hitler's aggression. Six months later, however, Hitler seized the rest of Czechoslovakia.

The following year, Hitler signed a nonaggression treaty with the Soviet Union. In this treaty, Germany and the Soviet Union pledged not to attack each other. The Nazi-Soviet pact allowed Hitler to invade Poland without fear of Soviet attack. At the same time, it provided the Soviet Union with at least a temporary assurance that Hitler would not attack it right away.

World War II

The German invasion of Poland in September 1939 triggered World War II. Now, at

Germany at War Soldiers give the "Heil, Hitler!" salute on this poster, printed in 1943 to mark Hitler's first 10 years in office. "One War — One Victory!" it proclaims. Yet when it appeared, the Allies had already landed in Italy and the German army was being pushed out of Russia. ***Political System*** How did Germany's economic problems aid Hitler's rise to power?

last, Britain and France declared war on Germany. The war pitted the Axis against the Allies. Germany, Italy, and Japan were the major Axis powers. The Allies eventually included Britain, France, the Soviet Union, the United States, China, and 45 other nations.

Axis advances. During the first years of the war, the Axis powers advanced across Europe. Hitler used a military strategy called blitzkrieg, or lightning war. German planes, tanks, artillery, and mechanized infantry launched a combined attack on a targeted country. By 1941, Germany had overrun Denmark, Norway, the Netherlands, Belgium, and France. Joined by Italy, it also seized the Balkans and parts of North Africa.

German planes bombed British cities, hoping to weaken the island nation before invading it. For a while, the Battle of Britain, as it was called, seemed lost. Then, in June 1941, Hitler invaded the Soviet Union. The Germans pushed deep into that country before they were stopped by the harsh Russian winter and the fierce opposition of the Russian people.

In the Pacific, the Japanese seized French, British, and Dutch colonies in Southeast Asia. (See Chapter 18.) The Japanese bombing of Pearl Harbor in 1941 brought the United States into the war. Japan, however, continued its advance, capturing the Philippines and other islands in the Pacific.

Turning the tide. Starting in 1942, the Allies slowly began to turn the tide of war. They stopped the Axis advance in North Africa and launched an invasion into Italy. Mussolini was forced out of power and eventually executed. The Soviet Union won a costly but crucial victory over the Germans in the east, at the Battle of Stalingrad, in 1942–1943.

On D-Day, June 6, 1944, the Allies landed on the coast of France, opening a new front. Despite heavy German resistance, they liberated France and pushed into Germany. At the same time, Soviet forces moved in from the east. Hitler committed suicide rather than face defeat. Finally, on May 7, 1945, Germany surrendered.

The Holocaust revealed. With the defeat of Germany, the Allies saw firsthand the atrocities committed by the Nazis. During the war, Hitler called for the extermination of all Jews in Europe. In concentration camps, the Nazis built gas chambers to carry out the genocide against Jews. About 6 million Jewish men, women, and children died in the Holocaust. Another 3 million to 6 million Poles, Gypsies, political enemies, and "undesirables" also were killed.

Elie Wiesel, a Romanian Jew, was a teenager when he was sent to a concentration camp. Years afterward, he described the horrors of the camp in his autobiographical novel *Night*:

MAP STUDY

World War II was a worldwide conflict fought in the Pacific, Europe, and North Africa. The Axis Powers and the Allies waged long, bloody campaigns by land, air, and sea that finally ended in defeat for the Axis.

1. **Region** (a) Which nation in Western Europe remained Allied territory in 1942? (b) What was the status of the countries in Eastern Europe in 1942?
2. **Movement** Describe the Allied advances on Germany from the west.
3. **Drawing Conclusions** (a) What advantages did Germany's and Italy's location give them during the war? (b) What disadvantages? Explain.

“ 'Do you see that chimney over there? See it? Do you see those flames? . . . Over there—that's where you're going to be taken. That's your grave, over there. Haven't you realized it yet? . . . You're going to be burned. Frizzled away. Turned to ashes.' . . .

Not far from us, flames were leaping up from a ditch, gigantic flames. They were burning something. A truck drove up at the pit and delivered its load—little children! ”

Holocaust Survivors These prisoners were among the few who survived at the Buchenwald concentration camp. After the war, top Nazi officials were tried and sentenced to death for committing atrocities and other war crimes. ***Justice*** Why were Nazi leaders put on trial for genocide?

Effects of the war. World War II ended with the defeat of Japan in August 1945, when the United States dropped atomic bombs on the Japanese cities of Hiroshima and Nagasaki. Japan surrendered a few days later. (See Chapter 18.)

World War II was the most destructive war in history. Some estimates say that more than 30 million people died in Europe alone, and perhaps as many as 60 million died throughout the world. Bombing destroyed or heavily damaged many cities in Europe and Asia. Throughout much of Europe, millions of homeless people wandered the streets in despair.

World War II reduced Western Europe's impact on world affairs. World leadership passed to two new superpowers—the United States and the Soviet Union. In the postwar world, European colonies in Africa and Asia sought independence. Weakened by war, the nations of Western Europe slowly gave in to the demands of nationalists.

To help prevent wars in the future, the nations of the world joined to form a new international agency, the United Nations (UN). Member nations agreed to submit disputes to the UN for peaceful settlement. They also pledged to work together to resolve the world problems of disease, hunger, and illiteracy.

SECTION 4 REVIEW

1. **Locate:** (a) Italy, (b) Germany, (c) Czechoslovakia, (d) Poland.
2. **Identify:** (a) Triple Alliance, (b) Triple Entente, (c) Treaty of Versailles, (d) Benito Mussolini, (e) Adolf Hitler, (f) D-Day.
3. **Define:** (a) appeasement, (b) blitzkrieg, (c) Holocaust.
4. Describe how each of the following contributed to the outbreak of World War I: (a) nationalism, (b) imperialism, (c) alliance system.
5. (a) Why did many Italians support Mussolini? (b) Why was Hitler popular among many Germans?
6. (a) List three events that led to the outbreak of World War II. (b) How did Western European nations respond to Hitler's aggression?
7. **Applying Information** "Everything in the state, nothing outside the state, nothing against the state." How does this statement sum up the goals of fascism?
8. **Writing Across Cultures** In 1940, as German armies marched across Europe, Americans debated whether to sell arms to the Allies or remain strictly neutral. Write an editorial taking one side or the other and explaining your reasons for doing so.

CHAPTER 30 REVIEW

Understanding Vocabulary

Match each term at left with the correct definition at right.

1. predestination	**a.** belief that God had decided in advance whether an individual would be saved or condemned
2. divine right	**b.** bringing workers and machines together in one place to manufacture goods
3. factory system	**c.** making concessions to an aggressor in order to preserve peace
4. franchise	**d.** right to vote
5. appeasement	**e.** theory that a ruler's authority came from God

Reviewing the Main Ideas

1. Describe two themes explored by Renaissance artists and writers.
2. Describe three advances made during the Scientific Revolution.
3. Why was Britain the leader in the Industrial Revolution?
4. How did democracy grow in the 1800s?
5. Why were some nations unhappy with the peace settlements ending World War I?
6. Describe two causes and two effects of World War II.

Reviewing Chapter Themes

1. The Renaissance, Reformation, and Enlightenment led to the growth of new ideas. Give examples of two of the following: (a) Renaissance ideas about learning and the individual, (b) Reformation ideas about the individual and religion, (c) Enlightenment ideas about the individual and government.
2. By the 1600s, modern states were emerging in Europe. Describe the major steps in the development of the modern nations of (a) France and (b) Britain.
3. Industrialization altered the economies and societies of Western European nations. (a) How did the Industrial Revolution strengthen European nations economically? (b) What social changes did it cause?
4. Nationalism was both a positive and a negative force in Europe during the 1800s and 1900s. (a) How did nationalism contribute to the growth of new nations? (b) What role did nationalism play in the outbreak of World War I and World War II?

Thinking Critically

1. **Making Global Connections** What political ideas and traditions did the United States inherit from Europe?
2. **Drawing Conclusions** Under what conditions do you think a dictator is most likely to gain power? Explain.

Applying Your Skills

1. **Analyzing a Quotation** The Declaration of the Rights of Man states, "The aim of all political association is the preservation of the natural . . . rights of man. These rights are liberty, property, security, and resistance to oppression." (a) How does this statement reflect Enlightenment ideas? (b) How were these ideas part of the French Revolution?
2. **Reading a Map** Study the map on page 681. (a) What was the westernmost nation to fall under Nazi control? (b) Which Western European nations remained neutral during World War II? (c) From what areas did the Allies launch their invasions of Sicily and France? (See Skill Lesson, page 48.)

Chapter 31

WESTERN EUROPE IN THE WORLD TODAY

Celebrating German Reunification In 1990, Germans celebrated the reunification of their nation, which had been divided since Germany was defeated in World War II. Germany also belonged to a regional alliance, the European Community. By the late 1990s, the European Community hoped to achieve both economic and political union. ***Geography*** What geographic features might help spur European unity?

CHAPTER OUTLINE

On the streets of Berlin, vendors sell ties of black, red, and gold—the colors of the German flag. Young people wear T-shirts that declare, *"Ein Berlin, ein Deutschland, ein Europa"* ("One Berlin, one Germany, one Europe"). The music of Germany's most famous composer, Ludwig van Beethoven, fills the air. Later, a liberty bell donated by Americans rings out over Berlin. As fireworks burst in the sky, people cry and hug one another.

The date is October 3, 1990. Germans are celebrating the reunification of their country. For nearly 45 years after World War II, the Cold War had kept Germany divided into two nations.

On that day, the president of the newly united Germany said:

> "In free self-determination, we want to complete the unity of Germany. . . . We are aware of our responsibility

for these tasks before God and the people. We want to serve the peace of the world in a united Europe. ”

CHAPTER PERSPECTIVE

After World War II, the Cold War led to the division of Europe into two hostile camps. Bitterness and fear separated the democratic nations of Western Europe and the communist nations of Eastern Europe. In the early 1990s, however, the Cold War ended. Europe then faced new challenges, especially as Eastern European nations sought to achieve their goals.

As you read, look for these chapter themes:

- For 45 years after World War II, the Cold War influenced world events.
- After World War II, Western European nations rebuilt their governments and their economies.
- Close cooperation and the use of technology helped Western Europeans advance their economies, raise their standard of living, and achieve an important role in the global economy.
- The literature and arts of Western Europe reflected the changing modern world.

Literature Connections

In this chapter, you will encounter passages from the following works:

"1914," Wilfred Owen

"My Heart Leaps Up When I Behold," William Wordsworth

A Doll's House, Henrik Ibsen

For other suggestions, see Connections With Literature, pages 804–808.

1 POLITICAL DIRECTIONS

FIND OUT

What challenges did Western Europe face after World War II?

How did the Cold War affect Western Europe?

What kinds of governments do Western European nations have?

How did Germany become a unified country during the 1990s?

Vocabulary containment

In 1945, Europeans celebrated the end of World War II. Less than a year later, however, British statesman Winston Churchill warned that Europe faced a new danger:

> “ A shadow has fallen upon the scenes so lately lighted by the Allied victory. Nobody knows what Soviet Russia and its Communist international organization intends to do. . . . From Stettin in the Baltic to Trieste in the Adriatic, an iron curtain has descended across the continent. ”

Churchill's "Iron Curtain" speech, delivered in Fulton, Missouri, made it clear that the wartime alliance of Britain, France, the United States, and the Soviet Union had ended. A new struggle—the Cold War—now pitted the western Allies against the Soviet Union. For almost 45 years, the Cold War divided Europe.

Postwar Challenges

In 1945, Europeans looked over a bleak landscape. More than 30 million people in Europe had died as a result of the war. At least half of them were civilians. The war left millions homeless, and many people faced starvation. Cities and factories, schools and hospitals, railroad lines and roads, lay in ruins.

Throughout Western Europe, many nations faced economic and political collapse. At the same time, nationalists in Africa and Asia demanded an end to colonial rule in their countries. As European nations gradually lost their colonial empires, their political power declined around the world.

The Cold War. Western Europe faced the threat of further Soviet expansion. The Soviets, for their part, feared the West. By 1949, the Soviet Union had installed communist governments in all the nations of Eastern Europe. (See Chapter 33.) The western Allies condemned the Soviet Union for its actions in crushing democratic forces in the region. They also feared Soviet support of communist movements throughout the world. (📖 See Connections With Literature, page 808, "My Melancholy Face.")

Weakened by the war, Britain and France had few resources with which to resist Soviet expansion. As a result, the United States emerged as leader of the "free world," the democratic nations of the West. On the other side were the Soviet Union and its "satellites," the communist nations of Eastern Europe. The 45-year struggle between the free world and the communist bloc became known as the Cold War.

The Two Germanies

Cold War tensions often focused on Germany. After World War II, the Allies divided Germany into four zones of occupation—British, French, American, and Soviet. Germany's capital city of Berlin, which lay within the Soviet zone, was also divided into four sectors.

The western Allies soon realized that rebuilding Germany was necessary to bring about the recovery of Europe. In 1949, they united their zones and set up the Federal Republic of Germany, or West Germany. The new nation established a democratic government. Led by Konrad Adenauer (AD ehn ow er), West Germany began to rebuild its economy.

Many countries, however, strongly opposed the reunification of Germany. They were afraid there would be a rebirth of Nazism and militarism. Joseph Stalin, the Soviet leader, feared that a united Germany might again invade the Soviet Union. He therefore set up a dictatorship led by German communists in the Soviet zone. The new country was called the German Democratic Republic, or East Germany. Berlin, too, was divided into West Berlin and East Berlin.

Crises over Berlin. During the Cold War, Berlin was the center of several crises. In 1948, Stalin set up a blockade in an attempt to stop the western Allies from uniting their portions of the city. He closed all roads and rail-

Liberation A 1945 painting by the American artist Ben Shahn contrasts a bombed-out building with the figures of children at play. World War II caused the death of more than 10 million people in Western Europe. In 1945, many experts predicted that it would take the region 20 years to rebuild. ***Interdependence*** How did the United States help Western Europe recover?

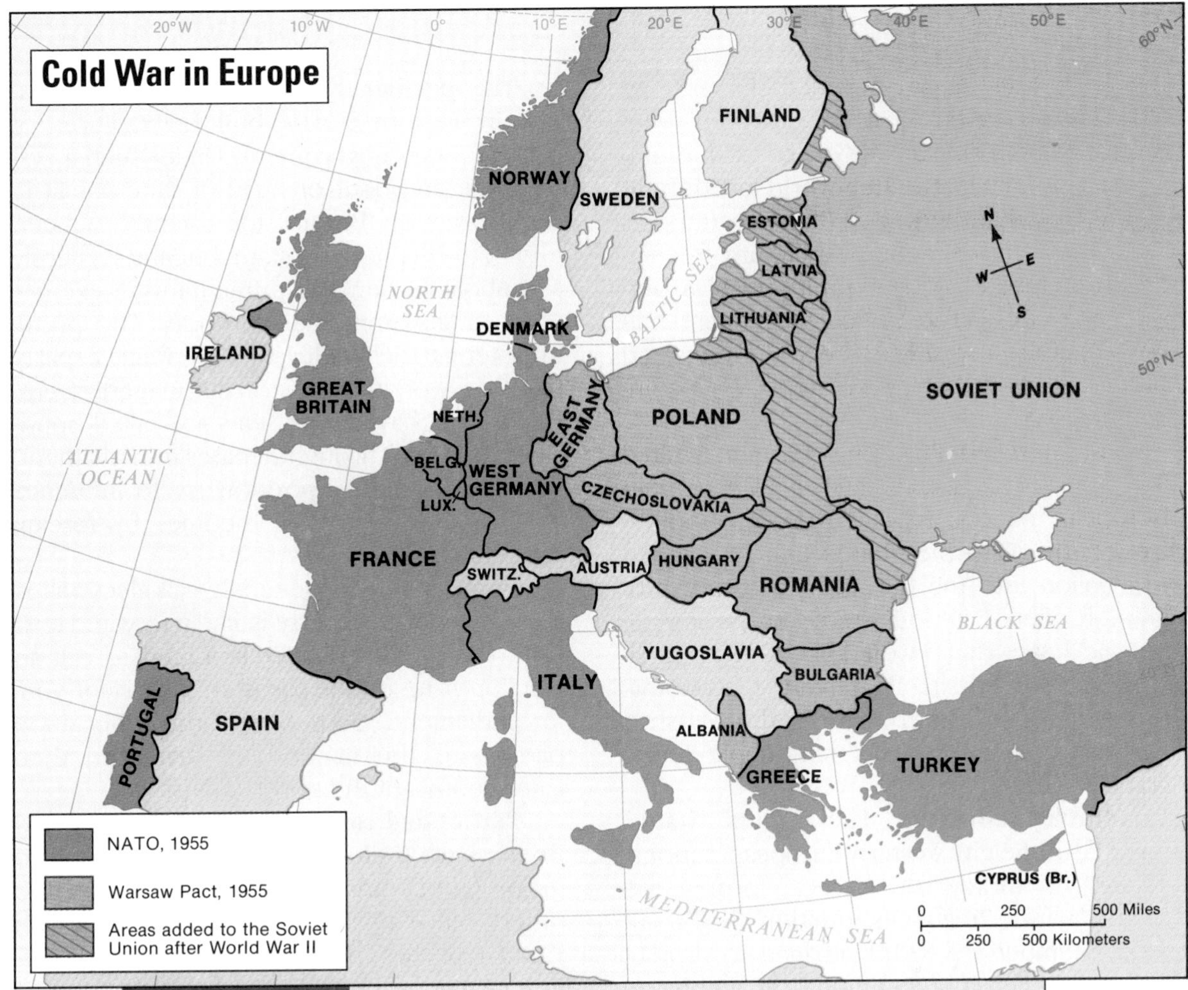

MAP STUDY

Soon after World War II ended, rivalries between the nations of the free world and the communist world led to the Cold War. Mutual distrust led to the formation of two powerful opposing alliances.

1. **Location** Which alliance included the Soviet Union and its satellites?
2. **Region** (a) Which nation was divided as a result of World War II? (b) To which alliance did each part of that nation belong?
3. **Drawing Conclusions** Why do you think that NATO maintained a large number of troops in West Germany?

road lines leading to West Berlin. The United States responded to the Soviet move by launching a massive airlift. American planes carried tons of food and fuel into West Berlin. The Berlin airlift lasted for 11 months until the Soviets finally ended the blockade.

In 1961, a new crisis arose. Thousands of East Germans were fleeing to freedom in West Berlin. To stop these flights, the East German government built a huge concrete wall to seal off East Berlin. The United States then put its military forces on alert. The crisis finally eased, but the Berlin Wall remained for 28 years—a symbol of a divided Germany and a divided Europe.

Cold War Policies

The United States launched several policies to counter Soviet influence in Europe. One of these policies, containment, was a pledge to stop Soviet expansion. In 1947,

President Harry Truman issued the Truman Doctrine, using the civil war between communists and democrats in Greece as an example of the dangers the free world faced. In it, he pledged that the United States would provide economic and military aid to any free nation threatened "by armed minorities or outside pressures." The United States sent millions of dollars in aid to Greece, Turkey, and other nations that were threatened by a communist takeover.

The Marshall Plan. In 1947, the United States announced the Marshall Plan to help European nations rebuild their economies. Under the plan, the United States pumped $13 billion into the European recovery program. It offered aid to Eastern Europe as well, but the Soviet Union would not allow its satellites to accept help. By restoring economic prosperity in Western Europe, the Marshall Plan helped the free world build stable democratic societies.

Military alliances. The United States, Canada, and eight Western European nations, as well as Turkey and Greece, formed the North Atlantic Treaty Organization (NATO) in 1949. Members of NATO pledged to protect one another from a communist attack. In response, the Soviet Union and its satellites formed the Warsaw Pact in 1955 to defend themselves from invasion.

The two rival alliances soon developed huge arsenals of tanks, airplanes, missiles, and nuclear weapons. Throughout the Cold War, NATO and Warsaw Pact forces were put on a state of alert during several crises. They also routinely conducted massive military exercises in preparation for war.

European Democracies

Following World War II, the nations of Western Europe needed to rebuild their governments quickly before conditions became so serious that people were driven to despair. Italy and West Germany, former Axis powers, wrote new constitutions. Because of the economic stability provided by the Marshall Plan, they were able to set up stable, multiparty democracies that protected the people's rights.

The parliamentary system. Most countries in Western Europe built on traditions of parliamentary government. Under such a system, the president or head of state has little real power. In Britain, for example, Queen Elizabeth II is head of state, but she is merely a symbolic leader. The prime minister exercises most governmental authority. The prime minister is the leader of the political party that has won the most seats in parliament. Parties that have fewer seats are called opposition parties. Through debates in parliament, members of the opposition try to influence government policies, sometimes by forcing new elections.

Prime ministers generally call elections at a time when their party is likely to win. However, the prime minister is forced to call an election if he or she loses an important vote in parliament. Sometimes, the opposition party wins the majority of seats and then gains control of the government.

Parties and coalitions. West Germany and Britain have multiparty systems in which two major parties are usually stronger than the others. Since 1945, the majority in the British Parliament has passed back and forth between the Labour and the Conservative parties. Labour has supported government ownership of major industries and social programs such as national health care. The Conservative party has defended private enterprise and made attempts to limit the role of government in people's lives.

By contrast, France and Italy have many different political parties. If no party wins a majority in parliament, smaller parties with similar goals join together to form a coalition government. Coalitions usually last until one party refuses to vote with the rest of the coalition. Without a majority in parliament, the government "falls" and the prime minister must call an election. Since Italy became a republic in 1946, it has had many coalition governments.

Democracy in southern Europe. After World War II, Spain and Portugal remained under the rule of longtime dictators. When both dictators died in the mid-1970s, the two countries quickly moved toward democratic governments. They wrote new constitutions and held free elections.

In Greece, the birthplace of western democratic traditions, unrest led military colonels to seize power. After the military government fell in the mid-1970s, the Greeks, too, restored democracy and civil liberties.

Germany Reunited

By the 1970s, supported by United States trade and protection, West Germany had emerged as a major economic and political power in Europe. West German leaders sought better relations with East Germany and the nations of Eastern Europe. They hoped that their country would be reunited someday.

In the late 1980s, events moved with amazing speed, largely due to great changes in the Soviet Union under Mikhail Gorbachev. (See Chapter 34.) A series of political and economic crises in East Germany led to the collapse of the communist government there. In November 1989, Berliners pushed past East German troops and smashed the huge concrete wall that divided the city.

In free elections, East Germans voted to be reunited with West Germany. In October 1990, East Germany ceased to exist when it joined the Federal Republic of Germany. A united Berlin again became the official German capital.

Germany wrestled with the problems of merging two societies and two economies. After 45 years of communist rule, East Germans faced the uncertainties of the free market system. At first, unemployment soared as many inefficient factories closed. The German government and private entrepreneurs poured large sums into modernizing plants, improving transportation, and retraining workers. Despite its problems, Germany was now in a strong position to expand trade with Eastern Europe, which had also thrown off communist rule.

For many years, Germans have had to come to terms with the crimes committed during the Nazi period. Although some Germans would rather leave the past unexamined, others would not.

Crossing the Border in 1989 As onlookers cheered, Germans traveled freely from East Berlin to West Berlin for the first time. Until then, Checkpoint Charlie, shown here, had been a heavily guarded route through the Berlin Wall. The German people faced the hard challenge of uniting two countries with distinctly different ways of life. ***Political System*** What were the main differences between East Germany and West Germany?

Up Close

The "Nasty Girl"

Growing up in the German town of Passau in the 1970s, young Anna Rosmus learned very little about World War II.

> "When I was in school, I never saw a film about a concentration camp being liberated. No one ever described the unspeakable suffering of the victims for us."

When her teacher assigned a history report, Rosmus decided to find out how the war had affected Passau. She hoped to enter her report in a national contest for high

A Scene From *The Nasty Girl* In real life, Rosmus has also spoken out against German neo-Nazis—people who are trying to revive the teachings of Nazism. This small but disturbing group has preached anti-Semitism, attacked Gypsies and Africans, and publicly celebrated Hitler's birthday. ***Choice*** Do you think *The Nasty Girl* was a good title for this movie? Explain.

school students. She had no idea that her history project would stir the anger of the entire town.

When Rosmus interviewed townspeople, she found they were reluctant to talk about the war. When she tried to find research documents, the town librarians told her that records from 1939 to 1945 were still classified, or secret. Rosmus protested that these documents were supposed to be declassified after 30 years. Officials told her the period of secrecy had just been extended to 50 years.

Still, Anna Rosmus persisted. She soon discovered some startling facts. Some leaders in her hometown had strongly supported the Nazis' persecution of the Jews. Moreover, Hitler and other leading Nazis had once lived in Passau. The teenager's discoveries and her efforts to publicize them created a furor. She received angry phone calls. Nazi sympathizers tossed stones through the windows of her home.

Eventually, Rosmus's report was published. In 1990, a German filmmaker made Anna Rosmus's story into a movie called *The Nasty Girl.* Millions of Germans saw the movie. They debated whether such films about the past should be made.

Many young Germans felt that they should not be held responsible for war crimes committed long before they were born. But Rosmus felt that it was vital for young Germans to know about the past. She said:

> "The German people have an obligation to speak out because we are responsible for the victims of those years. We need to enlighten; we need to shame people. . . . We cannot forget the wounds, so that we don't repeat them." ■

SECTION 1 REVIEW

1. **Locate:** (a) West Germany, (b) East Germany, (c) Berlin.
2. **Identify:** (a) "free world," (b) communist bloc, (c) Berlin airlift, (d) Berlin Wall, (e) Truman Doctrine, (f) Marshall Plan, (g) NATO, (h) Warsaw Pact.
3. **Define:** containment.
4. What were three problems Western Europe faced in 1945?
5. (a) Describe a parliamentary system of government. (b) What is a coalition government?
6. Describe two steps that led to the reunification of Germany.
7. **Linking Past and Present** Why do you think some Europeans might fear a united Germany?
8. **Writing Across Cultures** Interview a parent, grandparent, or other adult about how the Cold War affected his or her life. Write a paragraph summarizing what you have learned.

2

ECONOMIC AND SOCIAL CHANGE

FIND OUT

How did European economies recover after World War II?

Why did economic progress slow down during the 1970s and 1980s?

What goals has the European Community pursued?

How did life change for Europeans during the postwar period?

Vocabulary per capita income, welfare state

"The uniting of Europe will come," predicted a European leader in the late 1980s. "As far as I am concerned, it is written in the stars." Two world wars severely weakened Europe and reduced its power in the world. As Europe recovered from World War II, leaders worked toward increasing cooperation and unity. Despite setbacks, Europeans moved step by step toward the goal of building a "United States of Europe" before 2000.

Recovery and Growth

After World War II, the nations of Western Europe rebuilt their ruined economies with massive aid from the Marshall Plan. Europeans repaired war-damaged factories and transportation systems. They rebuilt their cities.

Economic expansion. West Germany led the recovery, with spectacular economic growth. By the late 1950s, German factories were booming. German exports such as cameras, electronic goods, chemicals, and automobiles gained a place in the world market.

The rate of growth varied throughout Western Europe, but the region as a whole made remarkable progress. By 1963, production far exceeded what it had been in the 1930s. Between 1950 and 1970, per capita income—the average income per person in a country or region—rose as much as it had in the preceding 150 years.

Reasons for expansion. Several conditions explain the postwar expansion. Although Europe was severely damaged by the war, it already had an industrial base and a skilled, educated labor force. Europeans were able to take advantage of the latest technology as they rebuilt their factories. The Marshall Plan encouraged European nations to cooperate closely. As a result, trade within the region flourished.

The nations of Western Europe also benefited from their diversified economies. They produced a variety of goods to meet their own needs as well as to sell in the world market.

Agriculture and industry. In the postwar boom, both agriculture and industry expanded. Western Europe has some of the world's richest farmlands. European farmers use high-yield crops, chemical fertilizers, and modern farm methods and machinery to increase farm output.

Today, the industrial output of Western Europe is greater than that of any other region in the world. Factories in Germany, France, Britain, Italy, and other countries produce a variety of manufactured goods. These range from steel and chemicals to consumer goods such as automobiles, appliances, and clothing.

In Western Europe, as in other highly industrialized areas, the number of factory and farm workers is declining. Mechanization is partly responsible. More and more people, however, now have jobs in service industries such as health care, government, recreation, and education.

Economic Challenges

Since World War II, European governments have taken a strong hand in economic planning. Most nations have an economy that mixes elements of socialism and the free market. In the postwar years, Western European governments nationalized major industries such as railroads, electric companies, and banks. (Nationalization of an industry directs its profits to the government.) The government controls costs and invests profits. At the same time, governments also supported private enterprise.

MAP STUDY

The European Community (EC) grew out of the efforts of Western European nations to work together to promote economic growth and political unity.

1. **Location** What is the relative location of the members of the EC?
2. **Movement** Why are good transportation and communications systems important to the goals of the EC?
3. **Forecasting** Which do you think will be the more powerful force among EC members in future years, nationalism or the desire for political unity? Explain.

The welfare state. In many countries, governments created a welfare state. In a welfare state, the government assumes responsibility for its citizens' social and economic well-being. The governments use tax money to support programs such as public housing for the poor and free or low-cost medical care for all citizens. They provide unemployment insurance along with pensions for the elderly. To finance these services, citizens pay very high taxes. Britain, Sweden, and Norway are among the strongest welfare states in Western Europe.

Economic slowdown. During the 1970s and 1980s, economic expansion slowed. In Western Europe, as elsewhere, rising oil prices contributed to inflation. Unemployment also soared. As inflation increased the cost of social services, governments faced severe budget crises. They had to make difficult decisions that included raising taxes.

Many voters opposed paying higher taxes to support the welfare system. To reduce inflation and ease the budget crisis, governments cut back on some social services. They also returned some nationalized industries to private ownership. State-owned industries, critics claimed, were inefficient and operated at a loss. By contrast, private industries had to be efficient to survive. Also, if they were profitable, they would pay taxes to the government.

Working Toward Unity

During the postwar years, European governments tried to reduce trade barriers in the region. Cooperation, they realized, would create larger markets for their goods and increase trade. In 1951, France, West Germany, Belgium, Luxembourg, the Netherlands, and Italy formed the European Coal and Steel Community (ECSC). They pooled their coal and steel resources and abolished tariffs on these vital materials.

European Community. By 1957, the success of the ECSC led member nations to set up the European Economic Community, which was also known as the Common Market. At first, its goal was to reduce trade barriers among member nations. By abolishing tariffs, the new organization created a large market

SCIENCE AND TECHNOLOGY

Building "Chunnel"

The giant drill roared in the underground tunnel. Stone rumbled down the conveyor belt. On December 1, 1990, French and British workers shook hands—150 feet (45 meters) beneath the English Channel. For the first time since the Ice Age, Britain was linked by land to the European continent.

The idea of building a tunnel underneath the Channel, "Chunnel," was not new. As early as 1751, a French farmer suggested such a project. One engineer even drew up plans for a stagecoach tunnel, with air supplied by chimneys rising high above the water. Technology, however, took almost 200 years to catch up with the idea.

When work began on Chunnel in 1987, British and French engineers took advantage of the latest tunnel-digging technology. The key machine was a huge drill with a rotating head. (One observer compared it to a gigantic electric razor.) Slowly and steadily, the drill sliced through the chalky rock beneath the Channel. Mechanical arms then lined the tunnel with segments of preformed cement or cast iron.

The drill was one of many new technologies that made Chunnel possible. The British and French crews were starting 31 miles (50 km) apart. Working underground, how could they avoid drilling right past each other? To solve this problem, the engineers used laser technology. With lasers to steer the drills, the two crews ended up only four inches off target. "We scored a bull's eye," boasted a British investor in the expensive project. "It's like going 'round the moon and back again and landing where you took off."

In 1994, Britain's Queen Elizabeth and French President François Mitterand opened Eurotunnel, as the channel tunnel is called. Fast trains then sped passengers, cars, trucks, and freight between France and Britain. The Paris-to-London trip fell from seven hours to less than three.

Many Britons were sad to lose their status as a separate island nation. Still, most accepted Chunnel as part of the changing world of Europe.

1. What technological advances allowed engineers to dig Chunnel?
2. **Forecasting** (a) What effects might Chunnel have on Britain and France? (b) How might it affect the unification of Western Europe?

that helped stimulate economic growth in Western Europe. By 1986, the Common Market had grown from 6 to 12 members.

Today, the Common Market is known as the European Community (EC) or the European Union. (See Skill Lesson, page 766.) Many East European nations would also like to join. The EC encourages the free movement of goods, people, and capital among member nations. By 1999, it hopes to have a single European currency. It also promotes common economic and social policies and the political unity of Western Europe.

To member nations, the EC is a way to preserve their high standard of living and protect the rights of workers who live in one country but work in another. Members also see unity as a way to compete with economic superpowers like the United States and Japan.

Skiing in the Austrian Alps Western Europeans today have one of the highest standards of living in the world. Many Europeans have leisure time to enjoy skiing and many other sports. Because distances are short, vacation travel is easy and relatively inexpensive. ***Geography*** In what other European countries would you expect to find Alpine ski slopes?

Obstacles to unity. The goal of a unified Europe faces obstacles. Nations debate how much power a European parliament should have and whether it should control foreign policy. Smaller countries, such as Portugal and Belgium, fear they might be outvoted by larger partners such as Germany and France. Europeans also differ on what political union means. Nationalism remains a powerful force, and most people have a strong sense of their national identity. In addition, economic setbacks in the early 1990s reduced popular support for the idea of unity.

Science and Technology

Cooperation among European nations led to advances in science and technology. In the 1960s, for example, Britain and France worked together to develop a supersonic jet transport. They built the *Concorde,* a passenger airplane that could fly twice the speed of sound.

In 1975, governments of Western Europe organized the European Space Agency (ESA). Scientists from member nations developed spacecraft and satellites. In 1986, ESA's space probe *Giotto* passed near Halley's comet and sent valuable photographs and information back to Earth.

Changes in Society

Since 1945, Europeans have experienced great changes in their daily lives. Large numbers of people moved from rural areas to cities. Today, three out of four people in Western Europe live in cities. In some countries, such as Britain and the Netherlands, the urban population exceeds 90 percent of the total population.

Standard of living. Advances in science and technology created many new products for consumers. At the same time, inventions and new methods of production increased agricultural and manufacturing output. These changes spurred economic growth, which enabled Europeans to achieve a high standard of living.

Western Europeans own the same kinds of appliances that Americans own. By the

1950s, Europeans could buy refrigerators, washing machines, and televisions. Automobiles, which were once a luxury, became a necessity. People enjoyed more leisure time to attend concerts, plays, and sports events, pursue hobbies, or watch movies and television. The law required most companies to give their employees a four-week paid vacation.

Social classes. European society became more democratic. Old class lines based on birth and wealth became blurred. Although differences in wealth remained, people had greater opportunities to improve their lives.

Other changes benefited people at all levels of society. Social welfare programs helped poor families to meet their basic needs. Advances in medicine and low-cost medical care increased life expectancy. Educational opportunities expanded, giving Western European nations high literacy rates. The number of students enrolled in schools and universities soared.

Changing Lives of Women

In 1949, the French writer Simone de Beauvoir (boh VWAHR) wrote *The Second Sex*. In this influential book, Beauvoir analyzed the treatment of women in western society and protested against discrimination:

> "The two sexes have never shared the world in equality. And even today woman is heavily handicapped, though her situation is beginning to change. Almost nowhere is her legal status the same as man's, and frequently it is much to her disadvantage."

New opportunities. In the years after the war, however, women won new rights. They gained new educational opportunities. More and more women worked outside the home. In the 1960s, the growing women's movement led working women to demand equal pay and an equal chance to advance in the workplace.

Women became more visible in the professions and in politics. In 1979, Margaret Thatcher became the first woman to serve as prime minister of Britain. She held office for 12 years, longer than any British leader had done in more than 100 years.

Changing family life. Although the family remained at the heart of European societies, women had fewer children than they did in the past. Also, women who worked outside the home expected their husbands to take on a larger share of household tasks and child care.

Like other advanced industrial societies, the nations of Western Europe have enjoyed great material progress. At the same time, they face serious social problems such as rising crime rates and drug addiction. Many people want to blame these problems on the breakdown of the traditional family. In Western Europe, as elsewhere, the divorce rate has risen and a growing number of children are living in single-parent families.

SECTION 2 REVIEW

1. **Identify:** (a) European Coal and Steel Community, (b) European Community, (c) Margaret Thatcher.
2. **Define:** (a) per capita income, (b) welfare state.
3. (a) Why did European economies recover quickly after World War II? (b) Why did economic progress slow down during the 1970s and 1980s?
4. (a) Describe three goals of the European Community today. (b) How is the EC helping Western Europe become a major world power?
5. Describe two ways in which life has changed for people in Western Europe since 1945.
6. **Defending a Position** Do you think governments should be responsible for the well-being of their citizens? Why or why not?
7. **Writing Across Cultures** List three ways in which Western European political and economic unity might affect the United States.

3

REGIONAL AND GLOBAL ISSUES

FIND OUT

How has the role of NATO changed?

What ties do Western European nations have with other parts of the world?

How have European nations responded to environmental issues?

How have cultural divisions and other differences created conflict within European nations?

Vocabulary détente

Inside the large United States military base at Frankfurt, Germany, American soldiers went about their daily tasks. When they went outside the gates, however, they faced the chanting and banners of thousands of protesters. "No More Nuclear Weapons!" "America Go Home!"

During the late 1960s and 1970s, young protesters throughout Western Europe gathered at American military bases. Dressed in T-shirts and jeans, with headbands and beads, they represented a new generation who were born after World War II. They condemned the United States for its involvement in Vietnam and for stockpiling, or accumulating, nuclear weapons in Europe.

By the 1990s, however, the end of the Cold War had eased fears of a nuclear war between the superpowers. Europe took steps to reduce the military power it had built up during the Cold War.

European Security

During the early years of the Cold War, tensions ran high in a divided Europe. Fearing a Soviet invasion, Western European nations welcomed United States military aid. They supported the buildup of NATO forces to protect their security. At the same time, they worried about the growing arms race between the United States and the Soviet Union.

NATO. Although NATO members joined forces against the Soviet threat, they differed on many issues. The United States felt that Western Europe should pay a larger share of NATO's costs. Many people in Western Europe feared that American policies might plunge them into another war.

A furious debate erupted when NATO decided to install nuclear missiles in Western Europe. Europeans felt trapped. If the superpowers went to war, nuclear weapons were sure to fall on European cities. As the debate raged, peace movements gained support in Western Europe.

Arms control. At times during the Cold War, relations between the superpowers improved. This relaxation of tensions was called détente (day TAHNT). During the détente of the 1970s, the United States and the Soviet Union entered into arms-control talks. Europeans welcomed these efforts to slow the arms race and reduce the threat of nuclear war. By the late 1980s, changes in the Soviet Union resulted in increased progress toward disarmament. In 1987, the Soviet Union and the United States signed a treaty banning intermediate-range missiles armed with nuclear warheads from Europe.

Recent trends. Between 1989 and 1991, the growth of democracy in Eastern Europe and the collapse of the Soviet Union created a new situation in Europe. Germany was reunited. Soviet troops withdrew from Eastern Europe, and the Soviet Union itself broke up into independent republics.

When the Cold War ended, NATO redefined its role. It reduced its forces but claimed a role in dealing with emergency situations that might arise in the Middle East or Eastern Europe. Some Eastern European nations asked to join NATO, but Russia protested. Instead, NATO agreed to form a "partnership for peace" with former Warsaw Pact members as a way to protect the security of Europe.

NATO faced a major challenge in the early 1990s as war raged in Bosnia and Herzegovina, in what was once Yugoslavia. NATO

UN Troops in Bosnia
French troops taking part in a UN peacekeeping mission are welcomed to a Bosnian town. The troops were part of the UN effort to end the bitter civil war among Serbs, Croats, and Muslims.
Interdependence
Why is it in the best interests of Western European nations to help end a civil war in Eastern Europe?

members often could not agree on a common policy.

By the mid 1990s, the European Community was also carving out a new role for itself. The EC saw the link between the security of Western Europe and Eastern Europe. The EC sought to encourage democracy and stability in Eastern Europe by extending economic aid. The expansion of EC activities raised many questions about the future of NATO and the postwar military alliance between the United States and Western Europe.

Global Ties

Europe's relationships with other parts of the world changed greatly after 1945. Nationalism in Africa and Asia forced European powers to give up their colonial empires. A few European countries made an attempt to hold on to their colonies. Only after bitter fighting did France withdraw from Vietnam and Algeria. Portugal, too, battled fiercely before it was forced to give up its African colonies in Angola, Mozambique, and Guinea.

Aid to the developing world. Some European nations maintained ties with their former colonies. Most British colonies that had gained independence joined the Commonwealth of Nations. Through the Commonwealth, Britain maintained social and economic ties with its former colonies. France, too, continued to play a role in Africa by supporting governments in several of its former colonies with economic and military aid.

Through the United Nations and other international organizations, European nations provided aid and technical experts to help developing nations. Multinational corporations based in Western Europe invested in the developing world, although industrialization has brought mixed blessings to these areas. In addition, European banks loaned money for development projects.

Competition with the United States. Since 1945, close economic and military ties have linked the United States and Western Europe. Economic aid provided by the United States helped Western Europe to rebuild after the war. As Europe recovered, United States companies set up branches there.

By the mid-1970s, Western European financial power and technology had grown strong enough for competition with the United States. In the 1980s, European companies found investment opportunities in the United States. European manufacturers sold goods such as airplanes, automobiles, and appliances to American buyers. Throughout the world, Western European manufacturers and businesses offered strong competition to the United States.

Oil from the Middle East. Although Europe gets some oil from the North Sea, it imports most of its oil from the Middle East. As a result, the decision of the Organization of Petroleum Exporting Countries (OPEC) to raise oil prices in the 1970s slowed economic growth in Western Europe.

Since then, Western European nations have tried to limit their dependence on foreign oil. Most have embarked on new energy-conservation programs. For example, many countries expanded mass transportation, especially their railroad systems. High gasoline prices also encouraged conservation. Western European countries have also turned to alternative energy sources, including coal and nuclear power. In France, more than 50 percent of electrical power is now generated by nuclear reactors. In addition, scientists are experimenting with solar and wind power.

Mining Town in Wales For centuries, Wales has provided the coal that Britain uses to fuel its industries and heat its homes. An important fuel, coal is also a major cause of air pollution. Burning coal gives off sulfur dioxide, a cause of acid rain and smog. Since the 1950s, strict laws have greatly limited the use of coal and helped reduce air pollution in Britain. ***Environment*** How might British emission controls also affect other nations of Western Europe?

Environmental Issues

In Western Europe, as elsewhere, people are becoming increasingly aware of threats to the environment. Because the region consists of more than 20 countries in a small area, pollutants can spread across national borders very quickly. In 1986, a fire at a chemical plant near Basel, Switzerland, led to massive pollution of the Rhine River, threatening the water supply of Switzerland, France, the Netherlands, and Germany. Also in 1986, an accident at the Soviet nuclear power plant in Chernobyl sent radioactive fallout across the Soviet Union and Europe. From manufacturing centers in Britain, France, and Germany, winds carry pollutants that cause acid rain in Scandinavia, especially Norway.

During the 1970s, environmentalists in West Germany formed the Green party. Other environmental parties sprang up throughout Western Europe. The leaders of these parties demanded that European governments take immediate action to protect the environment. In many countries, "green" candidates have been elected to public office and have introduced important reforms.

The members of the European Community, along with national governments, have cooperated in trying to reduce pollution. European nations have passed strict air-pollution laws for automobiles and factories. Since Chernobyl, some nations have dropped plans to build nuclear power plants. Other plants are being closed as inspectors examine them. The EC has also supported research on environmental issues such as the greenhouse effect, or global warming, and threats to the Earth's ozone layer.

Regionalism and Nationalism

Television, movies, and advertising have blunted the edge of many cultural differences among Europeans. Despite this, deep-seated cultural divisions still exist. In some regions, ancient rivalries and hatred remain strong.

In Italy, people in the north and south have cultural differences that began hundreds of years ago. In Germany, religious differences between Protestants and Roman Catholics have sometimes created tensions. Since Germany reunited, a new split has appeared between "Westies" and "Easties."

Terrorism. In Northern Ireland, social and economic issues have fueled an ancient religious conflict between Catholics and Protestants. The bitterness dates from the late 1500s, when Protestant settlers first began moving into Ireland. In 1921, Ireland gained independence from Britain. But Northern Ireland, which had a large Protestant population, remained a part of Britain. The Protestant majority controlled the government and the economy. Catholics faced discrimination.

Extremists on both sides have resorted to violence to achieve their goals. The Irish Republican Army (IRA) has used terrorism to try to end British rule in Northern Ireland. Militant Protestant forces have fought to prevent any change from taking place.

In northern Spain, the Basque people of the Pyrenees have their own language and culture. Many of them want to form a separate country, but the Spanish government has refused to recognize their demands. To gain their goals, Basque separatists have resorted to violence.

Immigration. Antiforeign nationalism has surfaced in many European countries in response to a rising tide of immigrants from the developing world and Eastern Europe. During the postwar economic boom, European nations depended on "guest workers" from Turkey, Algeria, Pakistan, and other countries. These immigrants did manual labor and filled many low-paying jobs that most Europeans did not want.

North Africans in Spain Young men from Morocco line up to obtain work visas in Barcelona. In recent years, Spain has attracted thousands of immigrants seeking jobs. These newcomers have aroused some ill feelings, however, because Spain has a fairly high unemployment rate. ***Scarcity*** Why would unemployment in Spain cause hostility toward immigrants?

When economic growth slowed, some Europeans called for the expulsion of foreigners and restrictions on immigration. Many immigrant workers had brought in their families by then and did not want to leave. As the flood of immigrants swelled during the 1980s, newcomers suffered racist attacks. Immigrants organized to protect themselves, and riots broke out in some cities.

For the first time in their history, some Western European countries, such as Britain and France, are becoming multiracial societies. These countries face the challenge of integrating newcomers into their societies while respecting the immigrants' religious and cultural traditions.

SECTION 3 REVIEW

1. **Locate:** (a) North Sea, (b) Northern Ireland, (c) Ireland.
2. **Identify:** (a) Commonwealth of Nations, (b) Green party, (c) IRA.
3. **Define:** détente.
4. (a) What was the goal of NATO during the Cold War? (b) Why has NATO had to redefine its role?
5. (a) How are Western European nations linked to the developing world? (b) Why has competition between Western Europe and the United States grown?
6. Why has antiforeign feeling grown in Western Europe?
7. **Analyzing Ideas** Why is international cooperation necessary if environmental problems are to be solved?
8. **Writing Across Cultures** Antiforeign feeling has broken out in the United States several times during the nation's history. Write a paragraph explaining how the causes of antiforeign feeling in the United States have been similar to or different from the causes in Europe.

4 LITERATURE AND THE ARTS

FIND OUT

What traditions have influenced literature and the arts in Europe?

How have individual writers and artists shaped European culture?

How have social, economic, and political conditions affected European literature and the arts?

Vocabulary romanticism, realism, impressionism

As World War I broke out in Europe, young British poet Wilfred Owen described his dismay at the coming conflict:

> "War broke: and now the Winter of the World
> With perishing great darkness closes in.
> The foul tornado, centered at Berlin
> Is over all the width of Europe whirled,
> Rendering [tearing] the sails of progress."

On November 4, 1918, Owen himself was killed in action—exactly one week before the war ended.

To Western Europeans who witnessed the slaughter of the war, civilization seemed to have collapsed. During the postwar years, European writers and artists expressed a sense of despair and hopelessness. A generation earlier, Europeans had held great faith in their civilization. Science had brought amazing progress, and people felt sure that such progress would continue to improve human society. In Europe, as elsewhere, historical developments helped shape literature and the arts.

A Rich Heritage

The many peoples of Europe have their own languages and national cultures. Yet, they share a common heritage whose roots lie in ancient Greece and Rome and in biblical traditions. Ever since the Middle Ages, Europeans have drawn on this heritage to create masterpieces in literature, music, and the visual arts. When Europeans expanded overseas, they introduced their art forms to peoples throughout the world. At the same time, Europeans absorbed important ideas from the civilizations of Africa, Asia, and the Americas.

Since the 1800s, a variety of artistic movements have emerged in Europe. These movements developed partly as a result of industrialization, urbanization, and nationalism. In this century, the mass destruction of two world wars has also helped shape European culture.

Literature

During the early 1800s, many European writers reacted against the Enlightenment, with its emphasis on reason. They created a movement known as romanticism, which valued feelings and emotions above reason. Romantic poets such as William Wordsworth and John Keats glorified nature. Wordsworth wrote:

> "My heart leaps up when I behold
> A rainbow in the sky:
> So was it when my life began;
> So is it now I am a man;
> So be it when I shall grow old,
> Or let me die!"

Romantics often glorified the Middle Ages as a heroic period. In the novel *Ivanhoe,* Sir Walter Scott created an imaginary medieval world of knights, Robin Hood, and the Crusades. The French novelist Victor Hugo used medieval Paris as the setting for his novel *The Hunchback of Notre Dame.* Romantics also reflected the spirit of nationalism. Jakob and Wilhelm Grimm roamed the German countryside collecting folktales for their famous *Grimm's Fairy Tales.*

Realism. By the mid-1800s, some writers had begun to rebel against the romantics' emphasis on emotion. They turned instead to realism, a school of writing whose goal was to describe life as it really was. Writers of realism examined social problems caused by urbanization and the evils of industrial society. In *David Copperfield, Oliver Twist,* and other novels, Charles Dickens exposed such social ills as slum conditions and the mistreatment of children.

The Norwegian playwright Henrik Ibsen was a champion of realism. In *A Doll's House*, he showed how social customs restricted the lives of middle-class women. The heroine of the play tells her husband:

> "When I lived at home with Papa, he told me all his opinions, so I had the same ones too; or if they were different I hid them, since he wouldn't have cared for that. . . . Then I went from Papa's hands into yours. You arranged everything to your own taste, and so I got the same taste as you—or pretended to; I can't remember. . . . I don't believe in that anymore. I believe that, before all else, I'm a human being, no less than you—or anyway, I ought to try to become one."

The Wounded Man Gustave Courbet, a French painter of the mid-1800s, offended many critics with his realistic works of ordinary people. People also disliked Courbet's strong views and opinions. "Show me an angel," he stated, "and I will paint one." ***Fine Art*** Do you think this painting shows life "as it really is"? Explain.

Modern writers. During the 1900s, writers experimented with new styles and forms. The ideas of the Austrian physician Sigmund Freud (froid) greatly influenced literature. Freud explored how the unconscious part of the mind affects human behavior. In *Remembrance of Things Past,* the French novelist Marcel Proust (proost) recorded the smallest details of his past in an effort to find meaning in his life. The British novelist Virginia Woolf and the Irish novelist James Joyce used inner monologues to reveal the subconscious minds of their characters. (See Connections with Literature, page 808, "The Lady in the Looking Glass: A Reflection.")

The upheaval of two world wars left many writers disillusioned. They began to reject long-held beliefs. Because of World War II, French writers such as Simone de Beauvoir, Albert Camus (ka MOO), and Jean-Paul Sartre (SAHR treh) searched for meaning in what they saw as a chaotic and meaningless world. In plays, novels, and essays, Sartre expressed his view that people were "alone, abandoned on Earth."

The Visual Arts

Like writers, artists responded to changing social conditions and values. In the early 1800s, romantic artists created huge landscapes that glorified the awesome power of nature. Painters charged their work with emotions that ranged from joy to terror.

In Britain, the painter John Constable experimented with light, shade, and vivid colors to produce realistic landscapes. After his wife's death, Constable's paintings became less colorful, reflecting his more somber emotions. The Spanish artist Francisco Goya blended romanticism and nationalism. His painting *Third of May* shows foreign invaders executing Spanish patriots, who die nobly in the cause of liberty.

By the mid-1800s, romanticism had given way to realism. Artists now depicted the everyday lives of ordinary people, such as peasants and industrial workers.

Impressionism. In the late 1800s, a school of painting called impressionism revolutionized art. Impressionists tried to capture fleeting visual "impressions" made by light and shadows. By placing bright, glowing colors side by side, they created shimmering effects to capture the viewer's eye. The European artists Claude Monet, Edgar Degas, Paul Cézanne, and Pierre Auguste Renoir were leading impressionists.

Modern art. Since 1900, artistic styles have changed rapidly. Often, artists distorted or exaggerated the real world to convey a particular feeling or an idea. After World War I, Marcel Duchamp and other painters expressed their disgust with modern society by creating works that shocked viewers. These painters came to be known as dadaists. On one occasion, Duchamp copied Leonardo da Vinci's famous portrait the *Mona Lisa* but gave the woman a mustache.

The Spanish painter Pablo Picasso was probably the most influential artist of modern times. He studied the art of other cultures, especially African art. Picasso pioneered new art forms, including the movement known as cubism. He used geometric blocks of color that showed his subject from many different angles at the same time. In a powerful mural, *Guernica,* Picasso combined cubism and other modern styles to show the bombing of a Spanish town. Jumbled images of the dead and dying capture the confusion and terror of war.

Architecture. European cities display a variety of building styles, from medieval Gothic cathedrals to towering glass skyscrapers. During the early 1800s, architects favored the graceful columns of Greek and Roman buildings. Architects influenced by romanticism preferred neo-Gothic spires and towers. By 1900, architects were using steel frames, reinforced concrete, and mass-produced glass to construct tall buildings. In Germany, the Bauhaus school emphasized functional buildings that had no ornamentation.

Music

Many European musical traditions had their origins in the Renaissance. Instruments, melodies, and musical styles evolved over the

Four Ballerinas Among the most popular impressionist works are the paintings of dancers by Edgar Degas. This French painter used pastel colors to create an impression rather than a photographic image of what he saw. His art was influenced by the style of Japanese prints. ***Fine Art*** How do you think the development of photography may have encouraged the development of impressionism?

centuries. In the late 1700s, European music reached a peak of creativity in Austria and Germany. Joseph Haydn, Wolfgang Amadeus Mozart, and Ludwig van Beethoven composed great works of classical music. The dramatic, emotional qualities of Beethoven's symphonies influenced romantic composers.

Opera. During the 1800s, opera captured the imagination of brilliant composers and of the public. Opera blends orchestral music, skilled singing, and dramatic acting to tell a story. Italian composers Giacomo Puccini and Giuseppe Verdi created many of the most stirring operas, such as *La Bohème, Madama Butterfly,* and *La Traviata*. The operas of Richard Wagner reflected German nationalism. Wagner drew on German legends to create powerful musical dramas.

Modern music. In this century, musical styles have continued to evolve. The French composer Claude Debussy produced the same effect in music that impressionist painters created in their works. In order to stir the emotions, Debussy used sounds to suggest moods and images such as moonlight or the wind.

Other composers rejected traditional styles and harmonies. In Austria, Arnold Schoenberg experimented with atonal music, or music without a key. He used his own 12-note scale, instead of the usual 8-note scale, to write symphonies. Although many people complained that his work sounded "unmusical," Schoenberg influenced many young composers.

Technology also opened up new directions for modern music. Composers can now use electronic sounds to produce effects that earlier composers could not have imagined. Through recordings and radio broadcasts, the works of both classical and modern composers now reach a new mass audience.

The Beatles The world's most famous rock group was formed in Liverpool, England, in the late 1950s. It lasted until 1970. Most of the Beatles' songs were written by Paul McCartney, far left, and John Lennon, far right. The other two members were George Harrison, center, and Ringo Starr, on drums. ***Technology*** How has electronics affected modern pop music?

Movies

Since the early 1900s, movies have become a major source of mass entertainment. European films have reached audiences throughout the world. Italian, French, and German filmmakers have portrayed a variety of themes, from the effects of the Nazi occupation on Europe to the materialism of modern society.

In Europe, directors have often been more important than film stars. Italian filmmakers such as Vittorio de Sica and Roberto Rossellini used realistic methods to convey the poverty, corruption, and violence of postwar Italy. The French director François Truffaut won international recognition for movies that examined love and human relationships. His first feature-length movie, *The Four Hundred Blows,* was a moving story of a teenage boy from a broken home who gets into trouble with the law.

The Swedish director Ingmar Bergman produced stark films that explored the nature of evil and suffering. In the 1960s and 1970s, the movies of the German directors Werner Fassbinder and Werner Herzog carried strong social messages. The works of European directors have influenced filmmakers in the United States and elsewhere.

SECTION 4 REVIEW

1. **Identify:** (a) William Wordsworth, (b) Jakob and Wilhelm Grimm, (c) Henrik Ibsen, (d) Sigmund Freud, (e) Jean-Paul Sartre, (f) Francisco Goya, (g) Marcel Duchamp, (h) Pablo Picasso, (i) Ludwig van Beethoven, (j) Richard Wagner, (k) Claude Debussy, (l) Arnold Schoenberg.
2. **Define:** (a) romanticism, (b) realism, (c) impressionism.
3. (a) How did the ideas of Sigmund Freud influence literature? (b) What effect did World War II have on literature?
4. Describe two ways in which Pablo Picasso influenced modern art.
5. How has technology affected modern music?
6. **Applying Information** (a) Give examples of how nationalism has affected literature and the arts in Western Europe. (b) Why do you think nationalism had a powerful impact on culture?
7. **Writing Across Cultures** Write a brief review of a film or play you have seen that deals with current social problems. Describe how the movie depicts the problems and explain what solutions, if any, it offers.

Chapter 31 Review

Understanding Vocabulary

Match each term at left with the correct definition at right.

1. containment
2. welfare state
3. détente
4. romanticism
5. realism

a. country in which the government assumes major responsibility for its citizens' social and economic well-being
b. artistic movement that emphasized emotions above reason
c. relaxation of tensions between the superpowers
d. policy to stop Soviet expansion
e. artistic movement that tried to show life as it really was

Reviewing the Main Ideas

1. (a) Why did Berlin become a focus of the Cold War? (b) Describe two crises that arose over Berlin.
2. How did each of the following affect Europe after World War II: (a) containment, (b) the Marshall Plan, (c) NATO?
3. (a) In what ways are the economies of Western European nations "mixed" economies? (b) How have the governments of these nations moved away from socialism?
4. How has technology helped both agriculture and industry in Western Europe?
5. Why did many Europeans support efforts to end the arms race between the superpowers?

Reviewing Chapter Themes

1. After 1945, the Cold War shaped events in Europe. (a) Describe two ways in which Cold War tensions affected Europe. (b) Describe two effects of the end of the Cold War.
2. During the postwar period, European nations moved toward greater cooperation and unity. (a) How has economic cooperation benefited European nations? (b) Describe two other ways in which European nations have cooperated.
3. Since 1945, important social and economic developments have changed people's lives in Western Europe. Describe changes in two of the following areas: (a) social welfare, (b) social classes, (c) standards of living, (d) women's rights.
4. European writers, artists, and composers have responded to social changes and world events. Choose two movements or two individuals and describe how each has influenced European literature or the arts.

Thinking Critically

1. **Making Global Connections** Compare the parliamentary system of government in Western Europe with the government of the United States. (a) How are the two systems similar? (b) How are they different?
2. **Analyzing Ideas** (a) What are some of the themes that European film directors have examined? (b) How can filmmakers have an impact on the world?

Applying Your Skills

1. **Using Your Vocabulary** Use the Glossary on pages 794–803 to review the meaning of the following terms: *interdependence, socialism, pacifism, multiculturalism.* Use each term in a separate sentence about developments that have taken place in Western Europe since World War II.
2. **Comparing Maps** Study the maps on pages 681 and 687. (a) How did the map of Europe change after World War II? (b) Which former Axis countries became members of NATO?

Chapter 32

Geography and Heritage of Russia and Eastern Europe

St. Basil's Cathedral, Moscow This ornate structure, consisting of one central church and nine smaller ones, was built in the mid-1500s. Eight of the smaller churches commemorate military victories of the Russian Empire, which stretched across Asia to the Pacific. ***Interdependence*** What benefits did the Russian Orthodox Church and the czar's government gain by working together?

Chapter Outline

The Neva River has again flooded St. Petersburg. Eugene, a poor clerk, goes mad when he discovers that his future bride has drowned. As Eugene wanders the streets, he comes upon a large bronze statue of Peter the Great, who had commanded this city to be built near the sea.

> "[Eugene's] blood boiled up. Somber, he stood before the arrogant statue. . . . 'Good! wonderworking builder!' With quivering hate, he hissed. 'You'll reckon with me yet!'"

In "The Bronze Horseman," Alexander Pushkin, one of Russia's greatest writers, creates a tragic drama that touches on important themes in Russian history. Ambitious rulers like Peter the Great sought glory for themselves and their country. Yet, their policies brought pain and suffering to the common people. Always present were the forces of nature, which added to the people's suffering.

CHAPTER PERSPECTIVE

From its small beginnings more than 1,000 years ago, Russia grew into the largest country in the world. By the 1800s, the Russian Empire stretched from Eastern Europe across much of Asia and included many ethnic, religious, and cultural groups.

As you read, look for these chapter themes:

- Severe climates, ethnic diversity, and the absence of natural barriers affected Russia's development.
- Early Russia absorbed Byzantine influences. Much later, western ideas had a major impact on Russia.
- Czarist Russia was an autocratic state built on inequality.
- In the 1800s, Russia experienced unrest as it tried to become a modern world power.
- Powerful empires competed for control of Eastern Europe, while the peoples of the region sought to maintain their independence.

Literature Connections

In this chapter, you will encounter passages from the following works.

Alexander Pushkin, "The Bronze Horseman"

Nicholas Gogol, *Taras Bulba*

The Russian Primary Chronicle

Anton Chekhov, "The House With the Mansard"

For other suggestions, see Connections With Literature, pages 804–808.

1 GEOGRAPHIC SETTING

FIND OUT

How has geography influenced Russia and the other republics that once were a part of the Soviet Union?

Why has Russia had difficulty developing its many resources?

How has ethnic diversity affected the republics of the former Soviet Union?

Vocabulary permafrost

"The whole of the country was a vast green wilderness. Never a plow had passed over its measureless waves of wild grass. . . . The whole of the surface of the earth was like a gold and green sea, on which millions of flowers of different colors were sprinkled."

With these words, the Russian writer Nicholas Gogol described the huge, open plain, often called the steppe, that stretches across parts of Ukraine and Russia. The steppe is one of many geographic regions that influenced the development of Russia.

Russia Reemerges

For most of this century, the world's largest country was the Union of Soviet Socialist Republics (USSR), or the Soviet Union. It sprawled 6,000 miles (9,700 km) across Europe and Asia, from the Baltic Sea to the Pacific Ocean. In area, it was more than twice the size of the United States. The Soviet Union included 15 republics ruled by a central government in Moscow, the nation's capital.

In 1991, the Soviet Union ceased to exist after the republics, one by one, declared independence. You will read about the breakup of the Soviet Union in Chapter 34. The chart on page 709 shows the size, population, and climate of the nations that emerged out of the Soviet Union.

Russia was by far the largest republic in the Soviet Union. It had half the country's population and about three fourths of its territory. Today, Russia, or the Russian Federation as it is known officially, remains the largest and most powerful nation in the region. If you rode the Trans-Siberian Railroad across Russia, you would cross 11 time zones.

Although the other republics operate in the shadow of Russia, they are seeking to carve out their own independent course. From tiny Estonia on the Baltic Sea to Kazakhstan in central Asia, each has its own government and pursues its own policies.

Landforms

The major landform of Russia and neighboring republics is the huge plain that stretches from the middle of Europe into Central Asia. In Europe, it is part of the North

MAP STUDY

The Russian Federation includes lands in both Europe and Asia. To the south and west lie other independent republics that once were part of the Soviet Union.

1. **Region** (a) What landform dominates much of this region? (b) Name three major mountain ranges.
2. **Interaction** (a) List the main rivers and bodies of water in the region. (b) How do you think they have helped the development of the economy?
3. **Forecasting** Which former Soviet republics would probably be most influential in a regional organization? Why?

Nations of the Former Soviet Union

	Area in thousands of square miles	Area in thousands of square kilometers	Population in millions	Climate
Russia	6,590	17,080	148	Continental, subpolar, polar
Ukraine	230	600	52	Continental
Uzbekistan	170	450	22	Semiarid, desert
Kazakhstan	1,050	2,720	17	Semiarid, desert, highlands
Belarus	80	205	10	Continental
Azerbaijan	30	80	7	Semiarid, highlands
Georgia	30	80	6	Semiarid, highlands, savanna
Tajikistan	60	140	6	Semiarid, highlands
Kyrgyzstan	80	205	5	Semiarid, highlands
Moldova	10	30	4	Continental
Turkmenistan	190	490	4	Semiarid, desert
Armenia	10	30	4	Semiarid, highlands
Total	**8,530**	**22,110**	**285**	
Baltic states				
Lithuania	30	70	4	Continental
Latvia	30	60	3	Continental
Estonia	20	50	2	Continental
Total	**80**	**180**	**9**	
Grand total	**8,610**	**22,290**	**294**	

Sources: *Encyclopaedia Britannica, 1994 Book of the Year*; *Britannica Atlas*, 1989.

Chart Skills Today, 15 independent nations occupy the land of the former Soviet Union. Locate the former Soviet republics on the map on page 708. ▶Using the information on the map and on the chart, identify the four nations with the largest population. What is the relative location of each?

European Plain. In Asia, it is called the West Siberian Plain.

In places, low hills break the seemingly endless plain. The low-lying Ural Mountains mark the division between Europe and Asia. The Urals do not form a real barrier, however. Throughout history, migrating peoples and invaders from Europe and Asia came into contact on the plain. Invaders caused great suffering among those in their paths. They also brought knowledge and ideas that deeply influenced the lands they crossed.

Plateaus and mountains. South and west of the plain are plateaus and mountains. The Caucasus Mountains lie between the Black and Caspian seas in the republics of Georgia,

Armenia, and Azerbaijan (az uhr bī JAHN) and separate Russia from Turkey and Iran. Farther east, the towering Pamir Mountains separate several Central Asian republics from Afghanistan and China. The Pamirs and other mountains block moisture from the Pacific and have created the deserts in these republics.

Seas, lakes, and rivers. Large inland seas and lakes provide nearby peoples with water, transportation routes, and food. The Caspian Sea is the world's largest inland sea. To the east, the Aral Sea is shrinking because the rivers that feed it have been diverted to irrigate farmland. In Siberia, Lake Baikal holds more water than the Great Lakes of North America combined.

Rivers were important to the development of Russia. In Europe, the first Russian state emerged at Kiev on the Dnieper (NEE puhr) River. Farther east, the Don and the mighty Volga rivers were busy highways of trade. In Asian Russia, the great rivers of Siberia, such as the Ob, Yenisei, and Lena, became important sources of hydroelectric power.

Climate, Vegetation, and Resources

Most of the republics of the former Soviet Union lie above 49° N latitude—the same line that marks the border between the United States and Canada. Because they are located so far north, the republics have a cold continental climate. Winters are long and bitterly cold, while summers are short and hot.

Because most of the republics are located inland, they do not benefit from ocean winds that carry moisture and moderate the extremes of heat and cold. Only the republics of Georgia, Azerbaijan, and Armenia in the Caucasus region have mild climates.

Harsh winters hurt the economy. They limit the growing season for crops, increase demands for energy, and create transportation problems. In Siberia, permafrost, a layer of soil below the surface that remains permanently frozen, makes building homes and factories both expensive and difficult.

Climate and location have influenced Russia's relations with other nations. Because its northern ports freeze during the winter, Russia has sought warm-water ports to the south—especially seaports on the Black Sea that have access to the Mediterranean. Over the centuries, this has led to several wars with neighboring states.

On some occasions, cold winters have helped Russia. In 1812, "General Winter" destroyed the armies of the French emperor Napoleon Bonaparte after he invaded Russia. During World War II, "General Winter" helped out once more when German troops tried to overrun the Soviet Union.

Vegetation zones. Six vegetation zones stretch across the former Soviet Union. In the Arctic north is the frozen tundra, which supports only mosses and lichens. South of the tundra is the taiga, a huge belt of evergreen forests that is larger in size than all 48 states of the continental United States. Still farther south, the taiga merges into another forest zone with broad-leaved trees such as maples, birches, and elms.

The fourth zone is the steppe, which stretches from Ukraine to Kazakhstan. With its rich black soil, the fertile steppe is the region's "breadbasket." There, farmers raise wheat, rye, barley, and potatoes. Although the steppe is similar to the American prairies, it receives less rainfall and often requires irrigation.

South and east of the steppe is the desert region of Central Asia. A sixth zone, in the mild, moist Caucasus region, supports subtropical crops such as tea, fruit, and nuts.

Resources. The republics of the former Soviet Union have a great variety of natural resources, although Russia has the greatest share. Russia has huge forests; fertile soil; enormous deposits of oil, coal, iron ore, and natural gas; and valuable minerals such as gold, platinum, and chromium.

Unfortunately, these resources are generally hard to exploit. Many mineral deposits lie in remote parts of Siberia. The best soil for farming is in regions that get only light rainfall, or even in the desert of Central Asia.

Until this century, Russia remained a relatively poor country despite its great potential. Using modern technology, the Soviet Union

Can Siberia Be Saved?

Galya Pavlikova climbs into a green van and sets out from the northern Siberian town of Norilsk, driving across the tundra. Stopping near a park, she holds a metal tube outside the van window and then checks the dials on a machine. "The air quality is acceptable," Pavlikova announces.

Pavlikova's job is to take pollution readings at 13 locations around Norilsk. Valuable metal ores were discovered there in the 1920s, and the government built factories to process them. Today, the smelting plant still pours chemical wastes into nearby rivers and its chimneys rain sulfuric acid on the tundra. On windless days, the air in Norilsk smells very much like rotten eggs. Breathing scorches the lungs.

Norilsk's environmental problems are not unique in Siberia. Sprawling across 4 million square miles (10 million sq km), Siberia is one of the world's richest storehouses of mineral wealth, including gas, oil, coal, precious metals, and metals that are of strategic importance to the military. The Soviet Union built factories and sent workers to Siberia to exploit these rich resources. But while development boosted the Soviet economy and helped meet the country's vast energy needs, it devastated the Siberian land.

Many Siberian cities rank among Russia's 70 most polluted urban centers. In some areas, lung cancer levels soared and respiratory infections among children occurred at an alarming rate. Heavy vehicles destroyed the fragile plant life of the tundra, and oil spills threatened to pollute lakes and rivers. One official complained, "They are poisoning us."

By the late 1980s, the people of Siberia had begun to protest. Residents of smokestack cities rallied to demand clean air. They called on the government to close down the worst sources of pollution. They opposed attempts to build new industries. The government made efforts to clean up the pollution, but progress was slow.

Today, the Russian Federation still faces the challenge of Siberia. Russia's new leaders must find a way to exploit Siberia's natural resources without destroying its environment.

1. What environmental problems does Siberia face?
2. **Making Decisions** What steps might the Russian government take to reduce pollution in Siberia? Explain the possible cost of such steps.

exploited its natural resources more fully. However, the rush to modernize has damaged the environment. For example, paper mills built to exploit Siberia's forests have polluted Lake Baikal.

Peoples

Before its collapse, the Soviet Union was a truly multinational nation, with people of more than 100 nationalities. Most had their own languages, cultures, and traditions. In

Ukrainian Dancers The peoples of Eastern Europe have preserved their distinctive cultures. Ukrainians like those shown here are proud of their culture, including traditional music and folk dances. ***Culture*** How does a society benefit from cultural diversity? How can it be harmed?

fact, the demands of national groups for independence helped cause the breakup of the Soviet Union.

The nationalities that live in the republics include Slavic peoples such as Russians, Ukrainians, and Belorussians. Armenians, Georgians, and Azeri live in the Caucasus. Kazakhs, Kyrgyzis, Mongols, Turkmen, and Uzbeks are among those who live in the Central Asian republics.

People in the republics follow a variety of religions. Christians include members of the Russian Orthodox, Armenian Orthodox, Protestant, and Roman Catholic churches. Thousands of Jews live in Russia and other republics. In addition, many people in the Central Asian republics are Muslims.

Today, each of the republics has a dominant ethnic group, but diversity still remains. In the Russian Federation, for example, about 80 percent of the people are Russians. The other 20 percent belong to a variety of ethnic groups.

Tangled tensions among ethnic and religious groups have led to conflict. Battles have erupted in Moldova, Tajikistan, Georgia, and other republics.

SECTION 1 REVIEW

1. **Locate:** (a) Russia, (b) North European Plain, (c) West Siberian Plain, (d) Ural Mountains, (e) Caspian Sea, (f) Dnieper River.
2. **Identify:** (a) tundra, (b) taiga, (c) steppe.
3. **Define:** permafrost.
4. (a) What is the major landform of the former Soviet Union? (b) How have landforms affected Russia in the past?
5. (a) How has climate affected the Russian economy? (b) Why did Russia seek access to ports on the Black Sea? (c) How has climate helped Russia in the past?
6. (a) What are Russia's chief resources? (b) What problems does it face in exploiting these resources?
7. **Synthesizing Information** List two geographic reasons why Russia is likely to dominate relations with neighboring countries that were once part of the Soviet Union.
8. **Writing Across Cultures** Write a paragraph comparing the climate of your region with the dominant climate of Russia. (See the map on page 778.)

2

EARLY TRADITIONS

FIND OUT

How did the Byzantine Empire influence Kievan Russia?

What were the effects of the Mongol conquest?

How did the princes of Moscow build a powerful state?

What reforms did Peter the Great introduce in Russia?

Vocabulary czar, autocrat

According to an early history of Russia, Prince Vladimir wanted a new religion for his people. He sent delegates to learn about Islam and Judaism as well as the Roman and Byzantine forms of Christianity. His ambassadors visited Constantinople, the capital of the Byzantine Empire. They returned with this report on Byzantine houses of worship:

> "We knew not whether we were in heaven or on earth. For on earth there is no such splendor or beauty, and we are at a loss how to describe it. We only know that God dwells there, and that their service is the best of all lands."

The report convinced Vladimir to adopt Byzantine Christianity. His decision, which was made more than 1,000 years ago, had major consequences. It led Russia to absorb both the religion and the culture of the advanced Byzantine civilization. By adopting Byzantine traditions, Russia would develop differently from Western Europe.

Kievan Russia

The first Russian state emerged during the late A.D. 800s in present-day Ukraine. There, Vikings from Scandinavia conquered the local Slavic people and ruled over a loose confederation of city-states. The ruler of each city-state shared power with local nobles and a city council. In time, the Vikings adopted Slavic customs and were absorbed into the local population.

This early Russian state was called Kiev, after its most important city. Because of its location on the Dnieper River, Kiev flourished. Kievan traders carried fur, honey, and farm products to the busy markets of Constantinople, the capital of the Byzantine Empire, as well as to other trading centers.

Byzantine influences. As trade expanded, Kievan Russia absorbed ideas from the Byzantine Empire, which was the most powerful and advanced civilization in Europe at the

St. George Slays the Dragon The rich colors and formal style of Byzantine art mark this work by an unknown Russian artist in the 1400s. Note the sun on St. George's shield. Pre-Christian religious beliefs in Russia focused on the sun and the forces of nature. ***Interdependence*** What were the two most important Byzantine influences on Russia?

time. Perhaps the two most important Byzantine contributions were a system of writing and the Christian religion.

In about 850, two monks, Cyril and Methodius, set out from Constantinople to spread Christianity to the Slavic peoples of Eastern Europe. At the time, the Slavs had no written language and therefore could not read the Bible and other Christian texts. To solve this problem, the monks devised an alphabet based on Greek and Hebrew letters. It was later called Cyrillic (suh RIHL ihk), after Cyril. Today, Russia and many other Slavic countries still use a form of the Cyrillic alphabet.

By 988, the efforts of missionaries as well as trading contacts convinced the ruler of Kiev, Prince Vladimir, to convert to Byzantine Christianity. As you have read, Vladimir was greatly impressed by the wealth and beauty of Byzantine civilization. He also noted that in the Byzantine Empire the emperor, not the pope, headed the Church. With Christianity, Kievan Russia also absorbed Byzantine art and architecture.

Split in Christianity. When Vladimir converted, serious disagreements divided Roman and Byzantine Christians. In 1054, Christians split into the Roman Catholic and Eastern Orthodox churches. This split in Christianity created bitter rivalries and helped cut the Russians off from developments in Western Europe. In time, the Russian church became independent of Byzantine Christianity as well, and evolved into the Russian Orthodox Church.

Mongol Rule

In the 1200s, Mongols from Central Asia conquered a huge empire that stretched from China to Eastern Europe. In 1240, a group of Mongols, called Tatars by the Russians, destroyed Kiev and other Russian cities. The invaders killed or enslaved large numbers of people.

For nearly 250 years, the Mongols controlled Russia indirectly. Russian princes acted as their agents and collected the heavy tribute, or taxes, that the Mongols forced the Russians to pay. Anyone who refused to pay the tribute was brutally punished. In general, the Mongols had little influence on Russian culture, although some Russian princes modeled themselves on the all-powerful Mongol ruler.

Although Mongol rule resulted in some trade with other Asian lands, the tribute system placed a huge economic burden on Russia. Mongol rule also reduced Russia's ties with the Byzantine Empire and Western Europe. Today, some scholars think that the terrible experience with the Mongols left the Russians with a lasting suspicion and fear of foreigners.

The Rise of Moscow

By the 1300s, the city of Moscow gained importance as Mongol power slowly declined. The princes of Moscow grew rich by keeping a share of the taxes they collected for the Mongols. Also, Moscow's location near several important rivers helped it to profit from trade. Moscow also gained in power and prestige when the head of the Russian Orthodox Church moved there from Kiev.

Ivan the Great. Ivan III, a prince of Moscow who ruled from 1462 to 1505, took steps to create a strong, unified Russian state. He conquered other lands and in 1480 ended Mongol rule by refusing to pay any more tribute. By then, the Mongols were too weak to challenge Ivan.

Ivan the Great, as Ivan III was later called, built a strong government based on Byzantine traditions. In 1472, he married Sophia, the niece of the last Byzantine emperor.* He then used the title czar (zahr), a Russian word for Caesar, or emperor. Ivan saw himself as the heir to the ancient Roman and Byzantine civilizations. Like Byzantine emperors, he was an autocrat, or a ruler who had unlimited power. He undermined the power of the nobles and destroyed the councils that had once helped rule the cities of Russia.

Ivan the Terrible. Ivan's grandson, Ivan IV, who was crowned czar in the mid-1500s,

* The Byzantine Empire ended in 1453, when Constantinople fell to the Ottoman Turks. (See Chapter 26.)

worked to strengthen the autocracy. He created a secret police force and conducted a reign of terror against powerful, independent nobles to crush them. His brutal actions earned him the nickname Ivan the Terrible. Despite his harsh rule, Ivan introduced reforms, including a new law code. He also expanded Russia's borders and renewed contact with Western Europe.

Ivan IV encouraged the growth of feudalism in Russia. He gave fiefs to loyal nobles to strengthen their bonds to him. He issued laws that bound peasants to the land. As a result, serfdom took root in Russia at a time when it was declining in Western Europe.

Peter the Great Eager to master modern technology, Peter the Great spent 15 months visiting Western Europe. In Germany, he studied how guns were made, and in Holland he worked as a ship's carpenter. Peter disguised himself as an ordinary citizen. However, his seven-foot height often gave him away. ***Technology*** Why do you think Peter the Great was selective about what he studied in each country?

A Window on the West

Despite the efforts of its rulers, Russia lagged behind the West in technology and military power, especially after the Renaissance and the expansion of Europe into the Americas, Asia, and Africa. In the late 1600s, an energetic young czar, Peter I, set out to introduce western ideas to Russia.

Peter the Great, as he is known to history, hired western engineers, shipbuilders, and other technical experts to modernize Russia's army and navy as well as build modern industries. He set up schools to teach the scientific theories being taught in the West. He introduced reforms to make his government more efficient and to increase his authority over the Church.

Peter even built a new capital, St. Petersburg, on the Baltic Sea. For him, it was "a window on the West," a city that would reflect modern European civilization rather than traditional Russian ideas. (📖 See Connections With Literature, page 808, "The Overcoat.")

Many conservative Russians resisted Peter's efforts at westernization. He overcame their opposition with force and terror. When Russian nobles at court refused to shave their beards, Peter seized a pair of scissors and did it for them. He insisted that women, who had been kept in isolation, attend public entertainments. He also forced men and women to dress in western-style clothing.

Peter's reforms strengthened Russia, but they did not close the technology gap with the West. Later rulers, such as Catherine the Great, continued Peter's reforms. Catherine encouraged Russians to adopt French culture and learning, including the ideas of the Enlightenment. (See Chapter 30.) She viewed herself as an "enlightened" ruler and even dreamed of ending serfdom. When Enlightenment ideas conflicted with her autocratic rule, however, she ignored them.

SECTION 2 REVIEW

1. **Identify:** (a) Kievan Russia, (b) Cyrillic alphabet, (c) Russian Orthodox Church, (d) Ivan the Great, (e) Ivan the Terrible, (f) Catherine the Great.
2. **Define:** (a) czar, (b) autocrat.
3. How did the adoption of Byzantine Christianity affect Russia's development?
4. Why did Moscow come to dominate Russia?
5. (a) Why did Peter the Great want to westernize Russia? (b) What steps did he take to achieve his goal?
6. **Analyzing Ideas** Autocratic rulers helped Russia make many advances. Do you think that great accomplishments justify autocratic rule? Explain.
7. **Writing Across Cultures** "Some scholars think that the terrible experience with the Mongols left the Russians with a lasting suspicion and fear of foreigners." Write a paragraph explaining what experiences in American history might have helped shape our attitudes toward foreigners.

3 PATTERNS OF LIFE

FIND OUT

How was Russian society organized?

How did religion support the social system?

What daily activities shaped peasant life?

Vocabulary icon, mir

"The peasants are oppressed by work from morning till night, and are all ill from overwork. . . . They fade early, age early, and die in filth and stench. Their children grow up and it's the same story and so it goes on for hundreds of years, millions of people living worse than animals—in constant dread, and all for a mere crust of bread."

Anton Chekhov, a great Russian writer, gave that description of peasant life in his homeland in the 1890s. For centuries, Russia's peasants lived in misery, producing barely enough to pay taxes and feed their families. At the other extreme, wealthy nobles enjoyed a life of luxury and regarded the peasants as ignorant at best. The gap between rich and poor created discontent, but the rich used their power to crush any threat to their way of life.

Russian Society

In the late 1700s, when the Enlightenment had sparked reform in Europe and America, the upper class in Russia became increasingly European. Nobles spoke French rather than Russian. They dressed in the latest French fashions and read the latest French books. Yet, Russia did not experience the revolutionary changes—improvements in farming, growth of manufacturing, and political reforms—that were paving the way for modern industrial societies in the West.

In Russia, the autocratic rule of the czars prevented any real reform. The small class of nobles owned the land. A tiny middle class existed, but it had little power. The majority of people were serfs, or peasants, who worked the land but had almost no rights. They were the property of the nobles who owned the land on which they were born.

Serfs. Nobles exercised almost absolute control over their serfs, buying and selling them as needed. Serfs who ran away faced harsh punishment if they were caught. Revolts broke out from time to time, but they were brutally crushed.

Serfdom had a deadening effect on the Russian economy. Many nobles were absentee landlords, who owned estates but did not live on them. They had no interest in improving farming tools or methods as long as they collected the rents from their estates. As a result, crop yields were small and serfs remained desperately poor.

Nobles. Wealthy families lived in comfort. They spent winters in Moscow or St. Petersburg, where they may have had as many as 100 serfs as servants. Guests arrived almost every night. Female serfs prepared meals, while male serfs served the food at dinner. Often, there were dancing parties at which serfs played music late into the night.

In summer, noble families traveled to their country estates, where more serfs attended them. In the country, serfs made everything from furniture and harnesses to clothes and shoes. Nobles maintained strict discipline by beating and flogging serfs who displeased them.

The Russian Orthodox Church

The Russian Orthodox Church supported the political and social order. By the time of Peter the Great, the Church had become a servant of the czar. The government appointed Church officials and gave them financial support. In return, the Church closely allied itself with the autocracy. In the 1800s, priests reported anyone suspected of disloyalty to the police. Members of the secret police even dressed as priests and heard confessions in attempts to get information.

Yet, the Church was a source of great comfort to both rich and poor. Peasants were baptized as infants, married according to Church law, and received the Church's blessings as they lay dying. Every peasant's home had an icon, a religious painting of Jesus, Mary, or a saint. Peasants prayed before the icons for miracles to relieve their suffering. Priests assured peasants that though their lives on Earth were hard, they would be rewarded in heaven.

Peasants welcomed holy days, and Church festivals and religious music provided some happiness. Peasants celebrated Christmas and Easter with great joy. Trinity Week, for example, marked the return of spring and the beginning of the planting season. In autumn, St. Peter's Day marked the start of the harvest, the hardest work period of the year.

Peasant Life

The life of the serf centered on the village, which was often just a few rows of houses along a road or river. Many peasants never traveled more than a few miles from the village in which they were born.

The mir. In most places, the mir (meer), or village commune, regulated village life. The mir was run by a council of men who

Rest During the Harvest The peasants in this painting look more prosperous than most actually were in real life. Most serfs on the mir lived in poverty. Since the land was redistributed from time to time, serfs had little reason to improve their strips of land. ***Fine Art*** Why do you think this artist, Alexander Morosov, painted such an idealized picture of peasant life?

were the heads of families. It controlled the village land and divided it among the villagers. Each family received scattered strips of land rather than an individual plot to farm. This gave them a certain amount of good farmland on which to grow enough crops to pay their taxes. This form of agriculture had disappeared in Western Europe hundreds of years earlier.

The mir was part of the system by which the government controlled the peasants. The mir was responsible for collecting taxes and providing recruits for the army. Young men drafted into the army served for 25 years. When a boy became a soldier, his family mourned him as if he had died. If he survived to return home, he would be an old man.

The family. Russian peasants lived in patriarchal, extended families. The oldest male headed the family, and his word was final. Women had lower status than men, and only men could inherit a share of the family land. Women were responsible for household chores as well as for tending the garden and the farm animals.

Middle-class parents, as well as those of the nobility, arranged marriages for their children based on property. Among poor peasants, property was not important because most peasants had none. A landlord, however, might either force or forbid a serf's marriage. After marriage, the couple lived with the young man's parents.

The home. A typical peasant family lived in a small wooden house that included a single large room and one or two small storage rooms. In one corner of the main room stood an enormous stove that was used for heating and cooking. In winter, older members of the family slept closest to the stove.

Peasants ate a few basic foods. The most important of these by far was dark bread, with porridge, cereal or meal boiled in water, ranking next. Cabbage, onions, and cucumbers were the main vegetables in the peasants' diet. On special occasions, peasants ate meat. From time to time, dairy products or fish caught in local lakes and streams reached the table. In the 1800s, peasants began growing potatoes, and they also added tea to their diet.

SECTION 3 REVIEW

1. **Define:** (a) icon, (b) mir.
2. (a) What were the main social classes in czarist Russia? (b) How did serfdom limit economic progress?
3. How did the Russian Orthodox Church support the government?
4. (a) How did the mir regulate village life? (b) What traditions shaped family life?
5. **Analyzing a Quotation** "Do not spare your child any beating, for the stick will not kill him but do him good. When you strike the body, you save the soul from death." This advice was taken from a Russian manual for parents. What values does it support?
6. **Writing Across Cultures** List three important events that marked the Russian calendar. Then list three events that mark the year in the United States. Write a generalization about the role of special occasions in people's lives throughout the world.

4 DYNAMICS OF CHANGE

FIND OUT

How did the Russian Empire grow?

What were the causes of discontent in Russia in the 1800s?

How did the government respond to demands for reform?

How did industrialization affect Russia?

Vocabulary: pogrom

In 1862, Nicholas Chernyshevsky, a Russian revolutionary, summed up the government's programs in this way:

"Russia's policies until recently have been directed mainly toward expansion, and this task, which has been carried out very successfully, has weakened the real strength of our people. . . . Materials needed for plows and sickles have always been used to forge swords and spears, and that is why up to now we have not been able even to cultivate our land properly. ”

For centuries, czars had concentrated on building a strong military and conquering new territories. They used their successes abroad to cover up their failures at home. In the 1800s, under pressure from all sides, the government finally took a few long-overdue steps toward reform.

Russian Expansion

From earliest times, Russian rulers followed a course of expansion. In the late 1500s, Ivan IV opened the way into Siberia. Russian explorers and fur traders pushed eastward as far as the Pacific, and by the 1680s, Russia controlled all of Siberia.

This vast frontier region was a source of fur, farmland, and mineral resources. It also became a place of punishment. Russian rulers sent political prisoners and criminals into exile in this distant land, using their labor to develop its rich resources.

Expansion in Europe. Russia also expanded into Europe. It lacked a warm-water port until Peter the Great won territory from Sweden on the Baltic Sea. The territory included the present-day independent countries of Estonia and Latvia.

Catherine the Great gained even more lands in the west. In the late 1700s, she joined Austria and Prussia in dividing Poland. (See Section 5.) Catherine also acquired the lands of present-day Belarus and Lithuania. She won a warm-water port in the south by defeating the Ottoman Empire and gaining territory on the Black Sea.

Effects of expansion. Expansion turned Russia into a multinational empire in which ethnic Russians made up less than half of the population. The new empire faced conflict among the many nationalities that lived within its borders.

In the 1800s, Russia expanded into Central Asia. Along with Western European powers, it also carved out a sphere of influence in China. Russian expansion alarmed other European powers, creating tension and eventually triggering war.

Revolt and Repression

By the early 1800s, discontent had grown at every level of Russian society. Serfs wanted their freedom and their own land to farm. At the other end of the social scale, a few nobles supported the ideas of the Enlightenment and the French Revolution. They wanted an

A Military Review Russia's autocracy was supported by the czar's police and by the army. A wide gulf separated officers like these from the troops they commanded. Most soldiers were uneducated and poorly paid. They were forbidden to enter taverns and restaurants, and they received very harsh discipline. ***Political System*** Why were a strong army and police force important to the czar?

end to autocracy. Some called for a limited monarchy like Britain's. Others wanted a republic.

As education spread, people who belonged to the tiny middle class and the working classes in the cities gained knowledge of life in the West. As a result, they demanded even faster and more radical changes than those the nobility sought.

The Decembrist Revolt. A small group of nobles and army officers tried to overthrow the czar's government in December 1825. They hoped to set up a constitutional monarchy. Czar Nicholas I quickly crushed the uprising, which was known as the Decembrist Revolt. He executed five leaders and exiled hundreds more to Siberia. Despite the Decembrists' failure, they became heroes to later generations of revolutionaries.

Reaction. Czar Nicholas I responded to the Decembrist Revolt with brutal repression. He imposed strict censorship, banned books from the West that might contain liberal ideas, and targeted schools and universities as centers of unrest. His secret police spied on students, teachers, and even government officials. More than 150,000 people were accused of treason and exiled to Siberia.

Nicholas did make reforms in the legal system. He also tried to improve the lot of the serfs by limiting their owners' power. He made no real change in his government, however. Instead, he enforced Russian nationalism and loyalty to the autocracy and the Russian Orthodox Church. By promoting these goals, he tried to unite his vast multinational empire.

Anti-Semitism. The nationalistic policies of the czar encouraged anti-Semitism. Jews had lived in Russia in large numbers since the mid-1500s, but they suffered legal discrimination. Laws forced them to live in certain areas and limited their access to education and jobs. Jews who lived in cities were often restricted to a single neighborhood, called a ghetto.

The government's anti-Jewish attitude contributed to pogroms, or organized acts of violence against Jews. The government tried to distract people from the real source of their poverty by blaming the Jews for it. A rising tide of violence forced many Jews to leave Russia in the 1800s. Many moved to Germany, where they were able to attend universities and pursue professional careers.

Limited Reform

Despite the efforts of Nicholas I to prevent change, many Russians realized that their political and economic system had slowed their nation's industrial growth. By the mid-1800s, European nations were industrializing and growing more powerful. In Russia, serfdom slowed such development. Factory owners could not find enough workers because so many people were serfs. Even conservative Russians realized that Russia had to change in order to become a modern world power.

In 1861, a new czar, Alexander II, emancipated, or freed, the serfs. The freed serfs gained a few political rights and were allowed to keep their homes and tools. Instead of being given land, however, they had to buy it at high prices. Burdened with debt and high taxes, most peasants continued to live in terrible poverty. Alexander II introduced other reforms. He relaxed censorship, encouraged the building of schools, and improved health care.

Effects of Industrialization

In the late 1800s, industry expanded. Peasants flocked to the cities, where new factories sprang up. In Moscow, St. Petersburg, and other cities, the middle class grew. Education spread as schools and universities were built in many parts of the country.

Despite the reforms that were made, life did not improve for most people. With better health care and more food, the population in the countryside soared. As a result, peasants had less land than they did before. For many, the standard of living became even worse.

For city workers, conditions in factories were similar to those in Western Europe during the early Industrial Revolution. Men, women, and children worked long hours under dangerous conditions for very low pay. If they protested, they were fired or punished. There were few laws to protect workers, and the laws that existed were seldom enforced. Workers formed trade unions even though these unions were forbidden by law. By the early 1900s, unions were organizing strikes to demand better pay and working conditions.

Revolutionary Movements

By the mid-1860s, some Russians had become frustrated by the slow pace of change. They turned to revolutionary action. Most revolutionaries came from Russia's small but growing educated classes. They wanted to overthrow the czar and establish socialism in Russia.

At first, Russian socialists tried to enlist the support of peasants in a great revolution that would end inequality and do away with private ownership of property. When efforts to win popular support failed, radical groups turned to terrorism. They killed prominent officials and even assassinated the czar, Alexander II. Alexander III, who succeeded his father, resorted to repression to stop the revolutionaries.

Despite the crackdown, unrest increased. By the 1890s and the reign of Czar Nicholas II, a new form of socialism had become popular among revolutionaries. It was called Marxism, after the German philosopher Karl Marx. (See Chapter 30.) According to Marx, factory workers, not peasants, would lead the socialist revolution. Although there were very few Marxists in Russia, they organized and slowly won support from members of the working class.

Bloody Sunday Father Gapon, his arms upraised, leads workers into a square near the Winter Palace one Sunday afternoon in 1905. The demonstrators numbered between 50,000 and 100,000. Outraged by an unprovoked attack on them by soldiers, they shouted "Murderers! You ran away from the Japanese, but you shoot at your own people." ***Change*** How were Russian workers trying to bring about change?

Bloody Sunday

In 1904, conflict with Japan over Korea and Manchuria led to the Russo-Japanese War. The war resulted in a stunning defeat for Russia and increased economic hardships at home.

A peaceful march. As the crisis at home worsened, a young priest, Father Georgi Gapon, planned a peaceful march of factory workers to the czar's palace in St. Petersburg. There, the workers would present a petition to Nicholas II, asking for better working conditions and some political freedoms. Father Gapon and the marchers believed that if the czar—whom the people called their "little father"—heard their pleas, he would respond.

On a snowy Sunday afternoon in 1905, thousands of unarmed men, women, and children joined Father Gapon. They carried banners bearing pictures of the czar and his wife. Singing the czar's hymn, "God Save Thy People," they slowly moved forward.

A massacre occurs. As the group headed toward the palace, soldiers appeared. "Surely, they would not dare to touch us," Father Gapon thought as he saw the soldiers' rifles glinting in the winter sun. He signaled the marchers to move on.

Suddenly, shots rang out.

"Down, down!" Father Gapon shouted to the frightened marchers. "What are you doing?" he cried to the soldiers. "How dare you fire on the portrait of the czar?" But the firing continued.

When the gunfire ended, Father Gapon rose. "Stand up!" he shouted to the marchers. Many obeyed, but many others remained on the ground. "Why do they lie there?" Father Gapon wondered. Then, as he saw the blood seeping into the snow, he understood. More than 100 marchers lay dead. Hundreds more were severely wounded. Father Gapon later recalled:

> " Horror crept into my heart. The thought flashed through my mind. 'And this is the work of our Little Father, the Czar.' Perhaps this anger saved me, for I now knew in very truth that a new chapter was opened in the book of the history of our people. "

Revolution of 1905

The events of Bloody Sunday, as the massacre was called, horrified Russians and sparked the Revolution of 1905. Riots and strikes swept the cities. In the countryside, peasants looted and burned the homes of landowners.

To end the violence, Czar Nicholas II finally agreed to set up an elected assembly called the Duma and to make other minor reforms. The Duma had little power, however, and the reforms failed to resolve Russia's basic problems. Since an autocratic ruler was in power, inequality and repression remained. Discontent simmered among many groups, including peasants, national minorities, middle-class liberals, and factory workers.

SECTION 4 REVIEW

1. **Locate:** (a) Siberia, (b) Baltic Sea, (c) Black Sea.
2. **Identify:** (a) Decembrist Revolt, (b) Marxism, (c) Russo-Japanese War, (d) Bloody Sunday, (e) Revolution of 1905, (f) Duma.
3. **Define:** pogrom.
4. What areas did Russia add to its empire between the 1500s and 1900?
5. (a) Which groups sought to make reforms in Russia? (b) Why did some Russians turn to revolution to achieve these reforms?
6. (a) Why was Russia slow to industrialize? (b) How did industrialization affect Russia?
7. **Applying Ideas** "Discontent only grows the more when it is repressed," warned the revolutionaries who assassinated Czar Alexander II. How does this statement reflect conditions in Russia in the 1800s?
8. **Writing Across Cultures** Write a dialogue between a Russian peasant and an American farmer in the 1800s in which they discuss ways to bring about political change.

5 GROWTH OF NATIONS IN EASTERN EUROPE

FIND OUT

How has geography influenced the history of Eastern Europe?

What empires competed to dominate Eastern Europe?

What role did nationalism play in Eastern Europe?

How did the two world wars shape developments in this region?

The opening lines of Poland's national anthem reflect the nation's long battle to protect its freedom.

> Poland is not yet lost
> While still we live.

Polish nationalists first sang these words in the early 1800s. By then, their homeland had come under the domination of powerful foreign empires. The Poles, like other peoples of Eastern Europe, have had a long history of struggle to preserve their independence against invaders from the east and west.

Geographic Setting

Eastern Europe refers to the region that lies between the former Soviet Union and Western Europe. Between 1945 and 1990, the region included East Germany, Poland, Czechoslovakia, Hungary, Romania, Bulgaria, Yugoslavia, and Albania. In 1990, East Germany was reunited with West Germany, and the Baltic republics of Estonia, Latvia, and Lithuania won their independence. In 1992, Yugoslavia splintered into separate states, triggering a brutal war in Bosnia and Herzegovina. By peaceful means, Czechoslovakia divided into the Czech Republic and Slovakia.

Eastern Europe has no clear geographic borders. It is part of the vast North European Plain that begins in Western Europe and continues into Asia as the West Siberian Plain. Its most clearly defined boundaries are the Baltic Sea in the north, the Adriatic Sea in the southwest, and the Black Sea in the southeast.

Ethnic diversity. The lack of physical barriers has contributed to conflicts in Eastern Europe. Since ancient times, migrating peoples and invaders have moved across the region. Huns, Slavs, Magyars, Ottoman Turks, and many other peoples settled there, giving the region a diverse population.

Today, Slavs make up the majority of people in Eastern Europe. However, Slavic peoples, such as Poles, Czechs, Slovaks, Bulgarians, and Serbs, each have their own history and traditions. Other groups, such as the Hungarians, are non-Slavs. Today, as in the past, conflicts among different nationalities pose problems for nations in Eastern Europe.

As new nations emerged in Eastern Europe, they struggled to protect their borders from powerful empires. The Russian, Austrian, and Ottoman empires expanded into Eastern Europe. The Germans, too, sought to control the region.

MAP STUDY

Most of Eastern Europe was dominated by the Soviet Union between 1945 and 1990.

1. **Place** (a) Name three mountain ranges in Eastern Europe. (b) In which countries are they located?
2. **Location** (a) Describe the relative location of Poland. (b) Give the relative location of Albania.
3. **Making a Generalization** Write a generalization about the geography of Eastern Europe.

Religious diversity. Location influenced the religions of Eastern Europe. During the Middle Ages, missionaries from Rome and Constantinople sought to convert the Slavs. The westernmost people, like the Poles, became Roman Catholics. Peoples farther east accepted Byzantine Christianity, which became the Eastern Orthodox Church. Albanians, who lived under Ottoman rule for centuries, adopted Islam.

Poland

In A.D. 966, the Slavic people of Poland converted to Roman Catholic Christianity and adopted the Roman alphabet. Roman Catholicism set Poles apart from other Slavic peoples, such as the Russians, who used the Cyrillic alphabet and followed Eastern Orthodox Christianity. Religious differences as well as other conflicts contributed to lasting hostility between Poles and Russians.

A large empire. The Poles first formed a unified state in the 900s. Over the centuries, Poland expanded and contracted as its rulers fought German invaders from the west or Mongols, Russians, and Ottomans from the east.

In the 1300s, Poland built a strong empire that stretched from the Baltic Sea almost to the Black Sea. As trade flourished, its cities grew. The University of Cracow became an important center of learning. There, Nicolaus Copernicus (koh PER nih kuhs) helped revolutionize astronomy in the early 1500s by showing that the planets revolved around the sun.

Partition. During the 1600s and 1700s, Poland's power declined. Because its ruler shared power with his nobles, he had never built a strong central government. In time, rivalry among nobles created chaos.

While Poland grew weaker, neighboring Prussia, Austria, and Russia grew stronger. Between 1772 and 1795, these strong powers partitioned, or divided, Poland among themselves. Polish leaders like Casimir Pulaski and Thaddeus Kosciusko (kahs ee UHS koh) tried without success to save their country, and Poland ceased to exist as an independent state.

Nationalism. During the 1800s, Polish nationalists sought to regain independence. In 1830 and 1863, Russia crushed uprisings in Poland.

A "new" Poland was born in 1919 after World War I. It survived for only 20 years. In 1939, German armies poured across the Polish border, and independent Poland vanished once more. (See Connections With Literature, page 808, "A Song on the End of the World.")

Hungary

Like Poland, Hungary has a long history. Hungarians are descended from Magyars (MAG yahrz), who migrated into Europe from the

Defeat of the Poles The histories of Poland and Russia have long been intertwined. In the early 1600s, the king of Poland negotiated to have his son become czar of Russia. Although the plan had the support of some Russian nobles, others gathered a force and drove the Poles out of Moscow. ***Power*** How did the Russians' form of government give them an edge over Poland in the 1700s?

area of the Ural Mountains. According to tradition, Stephen I of Hungary converted to Roman Catholicism on Christmas Day in the year 1000. Religion, language, and struggles against their neighbors helped Hungarians forge a distinct identity.

Hungary suffered during the Mongol invasions of the 1200s, but, unlike Russia, it was not occupied for long. During the Renaissance, Hungary's greatest ruler, Mathias Corvinus, made the country an important European power.

In the 1500s, disaster struck as the Ottomans and Austrians divided most of Hungary between themselves. By 1699, the Austrians had defeated the Ottomans and gained control of Hungary.

Despite centuries of foreign domination, Hungarians maintained their cultural identity. By the 1800s, nationalists were calling for independence. In 1848, Louis Kossuth led an unsuccessful uprising against Austrian rule.

Finally, in 1867, Austria gave in to Hungarian demands. It created the Austro-Hungarian Empire, a dual monarchy that united Austria and Hungary under a single ruler but gave Hungarians their own constitution and parliament. Hungary gained complete independence after World War I.

Struggles in the Balkans

The Balkan Peninsula lies in southeastern Europe. The dominant ethnic groups in the region are Slavs, including Bulgarians, Croats, Serbs, Slovenians, and Macedonians. The non-Slavic groups include Greeks, Turks, Romanians, and Albanians.

For 1,000 years, the Slavic peoples of the Balkans were influenced by the powerful Byzantine Empire. In 1453, the Ottomans conquered the last remnants of the Byzantine Empire and extended their rule over the Balkans. As a result, Turkish Muslims also settled in the region. By the 1800s, Austria had won control of parts of the Balkans from the Ottomans.

Throughout the 1800s, nationalist revolts erupted in the Balkans. Eventually, Romania, Bulgaria, and Albania broke free of Ottoman rule. Austria-Hungary, however, ruled many Serbs, who also sought independence. A Serbian nationalist assassinated the Austrian archduke in 1914, triggering World War I.

The Impact of Two World Wars

By 1918, the Austrian, Russian, and Ottoman empires had collapsed, leaving Eastern Europe in turmoil. At the Paris peace conference, the Allies supported the goal of self-determination for the peoples of Eastern Europe and helped set up independent, democratic states in the region. Poland, Hungary, Lithuania, Latvia, and Estonia regained their freedom. Two new states emerged. Czechoslovakia included Czechs and Slovaks, who had been ruled by Austria for centuries. Yugoslavia united Serbs, Croats, and several other Slavic groups.

Postwar problems. The new nations of Eastern Europe faced many problems. Border disputes created immediate tensions. Also, in many countries, the dominant ethnic group discriminated against national and religious minorities. Jews again suffered persecution in Poland, Hungary, and elsewhere. In addition, the Great Depression that struck in 1929 contributed to political and economic instability there and throughout the world.

Having little experience with democratic traditions, the new nations of Eastern Europe were poorly equipped to deal with economic hardship and unrest. Most of them turned to fascist dictators who promised to restore order. During the 1930s, only Czechoslovakia retained a democratic form of government.

World War II. By the late 1930s, the German dictator, Adolf Hitler, had embarked on a course of expansion into Eastern Europe. Hitler seized control of Czechoslovakia and in 1939 signed an agreement with the Soviet Union to divide Poland. The German invasion of Poland in September 1939 triggered World War II.

During the war, Albania, Bulgaria, Hungary, and Romania joined the Axis powers. Germany occupied some of the other Eastern European countries, including Poland and Czechoslovakia. People organized resistance groups against the Germans, but the war heightened tensions among various ethnic groups. In many Eastern European countries,

A Romanian Monastery The outer walls of this monastery are adorned with many fine religious frescoes, or wall paintings. Once the home of an order of monks, this building is part of Romania's cultural heritage. ***Culture*** Why would buildings like this one be important to nationalists?

local people joined the Germans in carrying out the atrocities of the Holocaust against the Jews.

In 1945, Soviet armies helped to free Eastern European nations from German occupation. However, peace brought a new threat to the freedom of these nations. For the next 45 years, the Soviet Union would dominate Eastern Europe.

SECTION 5 REVIEW

1. **Locate:** (a) Poland, (b) Hungary, (c) Czechoslovakia.
2. **Identify:** (a) Casimir Pulaski, (b) Thaddeus Kosciusko, (c) Stephen I, (d) Mathias Corvinus, (e) Louis Kossuth.
3. (a) What is the major geographic feature of Eastern Europe? (b) How has this feature affected the history of the region?
4. (a) What important contribution did Copernicus make during the Renaissance? (b) How did Poland lose its independence in the 1700s?
5. Describe the role of nationalism in each of the following regions during the 1800s: (a) Poland, (b) Hungary, (c) the Balkans.
6. (a) How did World War I affect Eastern Europe? (b) What problems did the nations of Eastern Europe face after that war?
7. **Applying Ideas** Why do you think border disputes have plagued the nations of Eastern Europe for so long?
8. **Writing Across Cultures** Imagine that you are a journalist after World War I. Write an editorial for an American newspaper supporting self-determination for the nations of Eastern Europe. Give reasons to support your point of view.

CHAPTER 32 REVIEW

Understanding Vocabulary

Match each term at left with the correct definition at right.

1. permafrost	**a.** religious painting
2. czar	**b.** absolute ruler
3. autocrat	**c.** permanently frozen ground
4. icon	**d.** title of Russian ruler
5. pogrom	**e.** acts of violence against Jews

Reviewing the Main Ideas

1. What ethnic and religious groups live in republics that were part of the Soviet Union?

2. (a) Describe the reforms of Peter the Great. (b) What effect did they have on Russia?

3. What role did the Russian Orthodox Church play in people's lives?

4. How did each of the following rulers respond to demands for reform: (a) Nicholas I, (b) Alexander II, (c) Nicholas II?

5. Why did the Decembrist Revolt and Bloody Sunday become important symbols to revolutionaries in Russia?

6. How has location contributed to ethnic and religious diversity in Eastern Europe?

7. Describe three examples of how ethnic diversity has influenced events in Eastern Europe.

Reviewing Chapter Themes

1. Geography has had a major impact on Russia. Describe two geographic features that have affected its development.

2. Russians absorbed both Byzantine and western ideas. Give two examples and discuss how each affected Russia's development.

3. Czarist Russia was built on autocracy and inequality. (a) Describe the structure of Russian society. (b) Explain how the czar and the nobles maintained their power.

4. In the 1800s, revolutionary movements increased in Russia. (a) Describe the grievances of Russian revolutionaries in the 1800s. (b) Discuss the goals and outcomes of one uprising in this period.

5. For centuries, the peoples of Eastern Europe were dominated by foreign empires. Choose one Eastern European nation and discuss its struggle for independence.

Thinking Critically

1. Understanding Causes and Effects Describe the cause-and-effect relationship between (a) growth of industrialization/end of serfdom, (b) Russo-Japanese War/Revolution of 1905, (c) Decembrist Revolt/repression.

2. Making Global Connections In the late 1700s, Polish nationalists Casimir Pulaski and Thaddeus Kosciusko came to America to help the colonists fight for independence. Why would nationalists from Eastern Europe support the colonists' cause?

Applying Your Skills

1. Reading a Map Locate the United States and Russia on the world map on pages 776–777. (a) What is the location of each country? (b) Based on this information, make a generalization about their climates.

2. Using Your Vocabulary Use the Glossary on pages 794–803 to review the meaning of the following terms: *latitude, topography, vegetation, plains, climate.* Use each term in a separate sentence about the geography of Russia and Eastern Europe.

Chapter 33

THE SOVIET ERA

Lenin Addressing a Crowd The strong-willed revolutionary leader believed that the communist government he had established in the Soviet Union would not last very long. Lenin was convinced that this government would "wither away" and be replaced by a classless society. Instead, the communist dictatorship lasted more than 70 years. ***Fine Art*** How does this painting suggest Lenin's power as a leader?

CHAPTER OUTLINE

On April 16, 1917, a crowd of people waited in the bitter cold at the train station in Petrograd. Just before midnight, a train arrived. The crowd began shouting, "Lenin! Lenin! Lenin!"

A shabbily dressed man stepped off the train. He was led to what had been the czar's waiting room. There, he addressed the crowd:

> "Dear comrades, soldiers, sailors, and workers, I am happy to greet. . . you as the advance guard of the international army of workers. . . . Any day may see the general collapse of European capitalism. Long live the International Social Revolution!"

While living in exile in Switzerland, Lenin learned that a revolution had forced Czar Nicholas II from power. Because Russia and Germany were still at war, the Germans allowed Lenin to travel through Germany to Russia. The Germans hoped that the revolution would weaken Russia and help end the war. Under Lenin's leadership, however, the Russian Revolution would have even more far-reaching effects on the world.

CHAPTER PERSPECTIVE

Discontent had been spreading in Russia since the Revolution of 1905. Under the pressures of World War I, the czarist government collapsed. Most political parties then cooperated to try to build a new, democratic government. Lenin, however, refused to support the new government. Instead, he and a small group of dedicated revolutionaries called for a new society based on equality and justice. But the society they set up was very different from what most socialists expected.

As you read, look for these chapter themes:

- Under Lenin, the Bolsheviks set up a communist state in Russia.
- Under Stalin, the Soviet Union developed into a totalitarian state.
- The Soviet economic system was based on central planning by the government.
- Although life improved for most Soviet citizens after the 1950s, shortages and limits on freedom restricted their lives.

Literature Connections

In this chapter, you will encounter passages from the following works:

"The Intelligentsia and the Revolution," Alexander Blok

Doctor Zhivago, Boris Pasternak

Blockade Diary, Elena Kochina

For other suggestions, see Connections With Literature, pages 804–808.

1 THE RUSSIAN REVOLUTION

FIND OUT

What events led to the overthrow of the czar?

How did the Bolsheviks gain power in Russia?

What were the goals of Lenin and the Bolshevik party?

What changes did the Bolsheviks bring to Russia?

Vocabulary abdicate, soviet

In 1918, Alexander Blok, a Russian poet, expressed a dream for the future of his country.

> "We Russians are living through a period that has few equals in epic scale. . . .
> To arrange things so that everything becomes new; so that the false, dirty, dull, ugly life that is ours becomes a just life, pure, happy, beautiful. . . .
> With all your body, all your heart, and all your mind, listen to the Revolution."

Revolution had brought Lenin and the Bolsheviks, a socialist revolutionary party, to power. Like many Russians, Blok believed that the Bolsheviks would build a new society based on justice and equality.

Blok's optimism did not last. The revolution led by the Bolsheviks did transform society, but not the way Blok had hoped it would.

The Strains of War

When World War I broke out in 1914, Russia joined its allies, Britain and France, in fighting Germany and Austria-Hungary. At first, each side expected that it would be able to win a quick victory.

As the war dragged on, Russia suffered a tremendous strain. Russian industries were not developed enough to meet the need for war supplies. Also, the transportation system could not supply the armies at the front. At times, only one out of three soldiers had a rifle. Unarmed soldiers were told to pick up the rifles their dead comrades had dropped. Poorly equipped troops suffered enormous losses.

Word of the terrible conditions at the front trickled back to the cities. Russians blamed the czar and his generals for disastrous defeats. In the cities especially, people faced shortages of food and other goods because of the war.

From Protest to Revolution

As shortages increased, discontent with the czar's government grew. In 1917, two revolutions took place. The first was an unplanned uprising by a huge number of people. The second was a well-planned coup d'état carried out by a small, determined group.

The March Revolution. In March 1917, riots and strikes erupted in Petrograd, the Russian capital.* Angry crowds protested the war and the shortage of food. "Bread and Peace!" they shouted. When the demonstrations began to spread, the government sent troops to restore order. Many soldiers refused to fire on the crowds, however. Hundreds even joined the protesters.

News of the events in Petrograd quickly spread by telegraph. Throughout Russia, demonstrators overthrew czarist officials. Only a week after the Petrograd riots began, Czar Nicholas II abdicated, or gave up the throne.

* Early in World War I, the Russian capital was renamed Petrograd because St. Petersburg sounded too German. Petrograd was renamed Leningrad in 1924. In 1991, the city was once again called St. Petersburg.

Soldiers Join the Revolution A Russian artist captured the spirit of the soldiers who joined the March Revolution of 1917 in Petrograd. In the following months, most soldiers on the front deserted and went home. An official report described the army as "a huge crowd of tired, poorly clad, poorly fed, embittered men." ***Change*** Why did the Russian people resort to drastic measures to bring about change?

To restore order, leaders of the Duma set up the Provisional Government. This temporary government introduced reforms such as freedom of speech and of religion. It called for an elected assembly to draw up a constitution. For the first time, Russia would have a government based on written laws rather than on the decrees of the czar.

However, the new government was powerless. It had little authority in Petrograd or elsewhere in the country. It angered peasants by refusing to redistribute land right away. The government also lost much support by continuing the war against Germany.

At the same time, socialist revolutionaries were setting up their own organizations to challenge the Provisional Government. In Petrograd and elsewhere, they formed soviets, or councils made up of workers, soldiers, and peasants. The Petrograd soviet had great influence in the capital. It acted independently and challenged the authority of the Provisional Government.

The Bolshevik Revolution. The Bolshevik party was active in organizing the soviets. The Bolsheviks called for a socialist revolution, which became known both as the Bolshevik Revolution and as the Russian Revolution. Lenin, their brilliant leader, moved swiftly to increase their power over the soviets. The Bolsheviks won increasing support among workers and soldiers in Petrograd and other cities with their slogan "Land! Peace! Bread!"

As the Provisional Government became weaker, it ordered Lenin's arrest. Lenin convinced other Bolshevik leaders that the time had come to seize power. In early November, armed Bolsheviks captured government buildings and arrested members of the Provisional Government.

Lenin immediately made two announcements that increased support for the Bolsheviks. He told peasants they could keep the land they had seized after the March Revolution. He also promised to seek an immediate peace with Germany. In March 1918, Russia and Germany signed the Treaty of Brest-Litovsk. The treaty marked the end of Russia's participation in World War I.

The Bolsheviks in Power

In the novel *Doctor Zhivago*, by the Russian writer Boris Pasternak, the title character reflects on the startling events of 1917:

> "If you charged someone with the task of creating a new world, of starting a new era, he would ask you first to clear the ground. . . . But here, they don't bother with anything like that. This new thing, this marvel of history, this revelation, is exploded right into the very thick of daily life. . . . It doesn't start at the beginning, it starts in the middle, without any schedule, on the first weekday that comes along."

With Lenin and the Bolsheviks in power, Russia entered on a new course.

Lenin. Lenin was born Vladimir Ulyanov in 1870. While he was still a teenager, his older brother was executed for plotting to kill the czar. Later, Ulyanov used the name Lenin to conceal his identity. (See Connections With Literature, page 808, "'The Bedbug' and Selected Poetry.")

As a young man, Lenin read the works of Karl Marx. He adapted Marxist ideas to suit the conditions in Russia. For example, Marx had predicted that the proletariat, or working class, would rise up, without planning, in a great socialist revolution. Lenin, however, argued that such a revolution could be successful only if it was carried out by a small, well-disciplined group of leaders.

Once in power, Lenin set out to create a Bolshevik dictatorship. He took steps to destroy all other political parties in Russia. The Bolsheviks closed down opposition newspapers and set up the Cheka, a secret police force, to end all resistance to their rule.

Civil war. The Communists, as the Bolsheviks soon began to call themselves, faced stiff opposition from many groups. Some of these groups demanded democratic socialism. Others favored capitalism. Still others wanted to restore the czar to power. In addition, national groups, such as the Uzbeks,

Georgians, and Ukrainians, sought greater freedom or even complete independence.

From 1918 to 1921, civil war raged in Russia. The Communists were better organized than the opposition groups, which were deeply divided. An energetic Bolshevik leader, Leon Trotsky, set up and trained a communist army, known as the Red Army. The Communists ruthlessly took anything they needed to build up the Red Army. They seized grain from the peasants and took control of all factories, mines, banks, and businesses. The opposing White Army was supported by British, French, and American troops for a while. However, it lost popular support as well as control of important regions. (See Connections With Literature, page 808, "The Red Cavalry.")

In the end, the Communists won control over most of the old Russian Empire. In 1922, they reorganized Russia into a union of four republics. They renamed the country the Union of Soviet Socialist Republics (USSR), or the Soviet Union. The Russian Soviet Federat-

MAP STUDY

In the 1930s, the Soviet Union was made up of 11 republics. In theory, each republic was independent. In practice, the Russian Soviet Federated Socialist Republic always dominated the Soviet Union.

1. **Location** (a) Identify the two Soviet cities that are separated by the greatest distance. (b) Approximately how far apart are they?
2. **Interaction** Why do you think the major cities of the Soviet Union are located west of the Ural Mountains? (See the map on page 708.)
3. **Applying Information** Why would governing the Soviet Union be a difficult challenge?

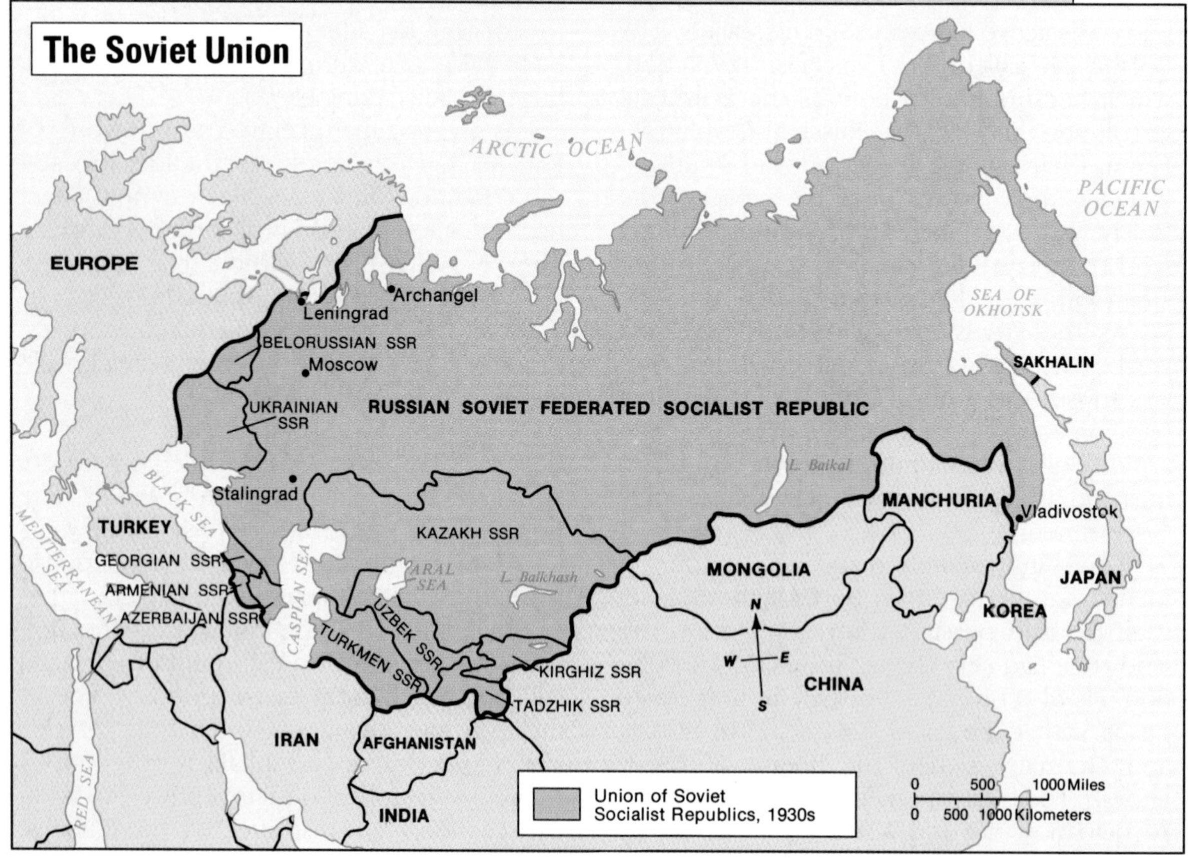

ed Socialist Republic dominated the union. Later, the USSR grew to include 15 republics that were made up of more than 100 national minorities.

New Economic Policy. The civil war took a tremendous toll. At least 7 million people died, mainly from starvation, disease, and the cold. The fighting destroyed crops, factories, and homes. When the war ended, the USSR was on the verge of economic collapse.

To ease the crisis, Lenin announced his New Economic Policy (NEP). Under the NEP, the government stopped seizing grain from peasants. It allowed them to sell their surplus crops on the open market. The government continued to control heavy industry, but it allowed some private businesses to operate in order to help the economy recover.

Although the NEP allowed some capitalist practices, Lenin still planned to set up a communist state. After Lenin died in 1924, his successor, Joseph Stalin, also tried to achieve that goal.

SECTION 1 REVIEW

1. **Locate:** Union of Soviet Socialist Republics (USSR).
2. **Identify:** (a) Provisional Government, (b) Bolsheviks, (c) Lenin, (d) Treaty of Brest-Litovsk, (e) Leon Trotsky, (f) NEP.
3. **Define:** (a) abdicate, (b) soviet.
4. How did World War I contribute to the outbreak of the Russian Revolution?
5. (a) What were the goals of Lenin and the Bolshevik party? (b) How did the Bolsheviks gain power?
6. How did Lenin organize the Soviet government and economy?
7. **Making Inferences** Why do you think the civil war in Russia was a longer and harder struggle than the Russian Revolution of 1917?
8. **Writing Across Cultures** Many Americans welcomed the overthrow of the czar but not the Bolsheviks' victory. Write a paragraph explaining why people in the United States may have felt this way.

2 A TOTALITARIAN STATE

FIND OUT

What were Stalin's goals for the Soviet Union?

How did World War II affect the Soviet Union?

What problems did Stalin's successors face?

Vocabulary kulak, dissident

Worried and weak, Lenin sat in his Moscow apartment. Seven months earlier, he had suffered the first of two strokes. Aware of his own poor health, Lenin was alarmed at the growing strength of Joseph Stalin. In a letter to the Central Committee of the Communist party, Lenin warned:

> "I propose to the comrades to find some way of removing Stalin from his position and appointing somebody else . . . more tolerant, more loyal, more polite and considerate to his comrades. . . . This circumstance may seem to be a mere trifle, but I think that it is a trifle which may acquire a decisive importance."

Despite Lenin's warning, Stalin became the leader of the Soviet Union. The new ruler set up a brutal totalitarian state.

Stalin in Power

Stalin was born Joseph Dzugashvili. As a young revolutionary, he took the name Stalin, which means "steel." When Lenin died, Stalin and Trotsky struggled for power. Stalin forced Trotsky into exile and then became dictator of the Soviet Union. Trotsky was later murdered by Stalin's agents.

A planned economy. As Lenin's successor, Stalin rejected the policy of gradual change under the NEP. Instead, he launched a campaign to turn the Soviet Union into a socialist state as quickly as possible. Under socialism, the government makes the basic decisions about the economy. Communists viewed this as a step toward a truly communist world.

Stalin believed that the Soviet Union would be unable to stand up to its capitalist rivals unless it modernized rapidly. "We are 50 to 100 years behind the advanced countries," he declared. "We must make up this gap in 10 years. Either we do it or they crush us!" In 1928, Stalin announced his first five-year plan. It set ambitious goals for developing Soviet industry and increasing food production.

Industrial development. To make the Soviet Union a world power, Stalin emphasized heavy industry over consumer goods. He poured resources into building steel mills and dams for hydroelectric power. He set high goals for coal and oil production. New factories were built to produce chemicals, tractors, and other machines.

The Soviet Union made impressive gains. Output in steel, oil, and other industries climbed rapidly. Those successes came at great human cost, however. Soviet factories and mines were operated by forced labor. Many people were worked to death. Even free workers were forbidden to strike. Workers who failed to meet quotas were severely punished. In addition, anyone who protested disappeared into Stalin's huge network of prison and slave-labor camps.

Workers who did meet their quotas were proclaimed heroes of the revolution. Propaganda in films, the press, and everywhere reinforced Stalin's power over the people.

Collectivizing agriculture. Rapid industrialization required increased food production. Food surpluses were needed to feed city workers and for export to obtain money to buy the heavy machinery needed in factories.

To increase food production, Stalin combined millions of small peasant farms into large collective farms. In theory, collective farms should have been more efficient. Many families would work together, using machinery and modern farm methods to produce food surpluses.

In fact, collectivization led to disaster. In protest, millions of peasants resisted the new system. They destroyed crops and livestock, contributing to the terrible famine that soon

A Cotton Collective This powerful painting by Alexander Volkov shows workers on a collective farm. Although collectivization had only limited success, by 1939 the government was able to transfer 20 million farmers to industrial jobs. ***Power*** How did the government enforce collectivization?

spread across the Soviet Union. Stalin responded with violence. Red Army soldiers shot peasants who refused to give up their farms. Kulaks, or prosperous peasants, were sent to brutal labor camps. Between 5 and 10 million people died as a result of collectivization and state terror.

By 1939, most peasants were working on collective farms. Food production rose slowly, however. Eventually, Stalin allowed peasants on collectives to tend small plots of land for their own use. There they grew vegetables and fruit and raised chickens, a few pigs, or a cow. Private plots made up only about 3 percent of the land. But because the peasants worked hard on them, those plots produced nearly 25 percent of the country's food.

Communist System of Government

In 1936, Stalin wrote a new constitution for the Soviet Union. It set up an elected legislature called the Supreme Soviet. All citizens were expected to vote for members of the Supreme Soviet. However, since there was only one political party, voters had no choice of candidates. In theory, the Supreme Soviet made the laws. In fact, the Communist party ran the Soviet Union. The Supreme Soviet met only once or twice a year, when it approved decisions made by Communist party leaders.

Role of the Communist party. The Communist party operated at every level of society in the Soviet Union. It controlled factories, schools, and farms. It also ran sports clubs, youth organizations, and newspapers.

At the head of the party was the Central Committee. It elected a small executive body called the Politburo, or Political Bureau. The head of the Politburo, the general secretary of the Communist party, was the most powerful person in the country. The Politburo made all important decisions in the Soviet Union.

Totalitarian rule. Under Stalin, the Communist party built a totalitarian state. Using modern technology, the government exercised complete control over the people. Radios and loudspeakers broadcast the party's message to the people. Through massive propaganda campaigns, the government convinced the people to support its goals. At the same time, the government used terror to enforce its will.

During the mid-1930s, Stalin launched the "Great Purge." Its purpose was to purge, or expel, Stalin's rivals from the Communist party. Thousands of high-ranking party members and military officers were charged with treason and were executed or imprisoned. Even many ordinary citizens faced a similar fate. Although the Great Purge increased Stalin's power, it weakened the Soviet military at a time when Hitler's activites were leading to war in Europe.

A Dishonorable Agreement

Despite their mutual hatred, Hitler and Stalin signed a nonaggression pact in late August 1939. The treaty left Hitler free to fight Britain and France without fear of attack from the Soviet Union. It gave Stalin a chance to gain territory and time to improve Soviet defenses.

A week after the pact was signed, Hitler invaded Poland from the west, while Stalin attacked from the east. The two nations then divided Poland between them. In 1940, the Soviet Union annexed the Baltic countries of Estonia, Latvia, and Lithuania.

In June 1941, Hitler turned on Stalin. He broke the nonaggression pact and invaded the Soviet Union. Within weeks, the Germans had reached Leningrad.

Life Under Siege

As the German invasion advanced toward Leningrad, a young woman began keeping a diary. Elena Kochina listened to the radio with growing alarm. "Every day," she wrote in her diary, "the Germans are swallowing up 20- to 25-mile chunks of our territory." Many people fled, but Elena Kochina and her husband, Dima, could not leave because their baby daughter was sick. As the Germans

The Siege of Leningrad During the 900-day siege, people had to carry the dead to mass graves on the outskirts of the city. Everyone who survived the terrible siege was awarded a special, highly regarded decoration. It read simply: "For the Defense of Leningrad."
Scarcity How did scarcity affect people's behavior during the siege of Leningrad?

approached, Elena Kochina joined others who were digging anti-tank trenches. "Leningraders hurriedly erected barricades out of stone, metal, all kinds of junk, and their fanatical love for the city."

By early September, the Germans had surrounded Leningrad. No one could enter or leave the city. The siege had begun.

Food supplies quickly dwindled. The city reduced bread rations to just a few ounces a day. The bread contained more sawdust than wheat. When the harsh Russian winter closed in, Leningraders ate anything they could find. Dogs and cats "disappeared" mysteriously.

One day, Kochina made a lucky find:

> "Today, in some old junk I found a box of wallpaper glue made out of macaroni waste products. It weighed over two pounds! This is terrific! We couldn't believe our eyes. Dima immediately shoved a whole handful of the glue into his mouth."

Each day, hundreds died from hunger and the cold. The living lacked the strength to remove the frozen bodies. "They just pile them up near the outer doorways," Kochina wrote.

Her husband grew too weak to get out of bed. Alone, Elena Kochina went out to find food, water, and firewood. One day, after she had waited in line for hours to get her ration of bread, a man grabbed it from her:

> "I jumped on him like a panther, grabbing him by the throat. He fell to the floor. I fell with him. Lying on his back, he tried to cram the whole piece of bread into his mouth. . . . I grabbed him by the nose. . . . Finally, I succeeded in taking everything he hadn't managed to swallow."

In the spring, the Soviet government evacuated some people across a frozen lake. At that time, the Kochinas managed to get the necessary permit to escape. At villages outside the city, they wolfed down all the food they could.

Elena Kochina and her family were lucky. More than 1 million Russians eventually died during the 900-day siege of Leningrad. As Elena Kochina discovered, the struggle to survive crushed people's sense of right and wrong.

> "Heroism, self-sacrifice, the heroic feat—only those who are full or who haven't been hungry long are capable of these." ■

Victory and Aftermath

In the same military offensive that threatened Leningrad, German troops came within 50 miles (80 km) of Moscow before the bitter

Russian winter slowed their advance in November 1941. In 1942, the German campaign reached Stalingrad on the Volga River. Fighting fiercely, the Soviets finally stopped the Germans. Slowly, Soviet forces turned the tide in the east. As Hitler's armies either froze to death, were captured, or retreated, Soviet forces occupied Eastern Europe. (See Chapter 34.)

World War II had a devastating effect on the Soviet Union. More than 20 million people, 20 percent of the Soviet population, died. Much of the western Soviet Union lay in ruins. Destroyed factories, railroads, farms, and cities had to be rebuilt.

When the war ended in 1945, Stalin wanted to make sure that Germany would never again invade the Soviet Union. To ensure this, he set up friendly communist governments in Eastern Europe.

Stalin's Successors

When Joseph Stalin died in 1953, Nikita Khrushchev (KROOSH chehf) won the struggle to succeed him.

Khrushchev. In 1956, Khrushchev shocked the world by denouncing Stalin as a tyrant who had caused the Soviet people great suffering. He introduced reforms to end the brutal terror of the Stalinist period. He also reduced censorship.

Khrushchev did not change the Soviet system of central economic planning or the Communist party dictatorship, however. He continued to work for the victory of communism over capitalism. In the Cold War rivalry that existed between the Soviet Union and the United States, Khrushchev invested heavily in arms, space technology, and heavy industry. At the same time, he tried to meet the growing demand for consumer goods. Factories increased the quantity and quality of their clothing and appliance production, while the government built more housing.

Brezhnev. Leaders of the Communist party forced Khrushchev out of office in 1964. Leonid Brezhnev (BREHSH nehf) then emerged as the new party leader. Brezhnev ended the comparative openness that had marked the Khrushchev years. He cracked down hard on dissidents, people who spoke out against the government. They were jailed, exiled, or sent to hospitals for the mentally ill.

The Soviet Economy

Under both Khrushchev and Brezhnev, the Soviet economy faced major problems. Although progress was made in agriculture, food production did not increase as fast as

Khrushchev in Iowa The Soviet leader constantly worried about his country's low crop yields. On a visit to the United States in 1959, one of the places he toured with special interest was a prosperous farm near Des Moines, Iowa. "I must admit that you are very intelligent people in this part of the world," Khrushchev remarked. "But God has helped you." ***Geography*** What do you think Khrushchev meant?

was planned. Farms planted high-yield crops and used irrigation to bring more land under cultivation. Lack of rainfall, however, limited output in areas such as Kazakhstan. Also, collective farms suffered from shortages of machinery, spare parts, and fertilizer. Food often rotted in railway cars before it reached the cities, and worker productivity remained low.

Industries, too, suffered from low productivity. The government in Moscow made economic decisions for plants that were thousands of miles away. Frequently, government planners knew little about local conditions.

Sometimes, factories had to shut down because planners had not ordered the necessary machine parts. Also, factory managers worried more about meeting government quotas than they did about the quality of the goods they produced. As a result, these goods were often poorly made.

Despite these problems, the standard of living in the Soviet Union rose. Consumers were able to buy more goods than they could during the Stalin era.

SECTION 2 REVIEW

1. **Locate:** (a) Estonia, (b) Latvia, (c) Lithuania, (d) Leningrad, (e) Stalingrad.
2. **Identify:** (a) Joseph Stalin, (b) Supreme Soviet, (c) Politburo, (d) Great Purge, (e) Nikita Khrushchev, (f) Leonid Brezhnev.
3. **Define:** (a) kulak, (b) dissident.
4. (a) Describe two goals Stalin had for the Soviet Union. (b) How did he try to achieve each of them?
5. Explain three ways in which World War II affected the Soviet Union.
6. What economic problems did the Soviet Union face after Stalin's death?
7. **Analyzing Information** How did technology contribute to the power of a totalitarian state such as the Soviet Union?
8. **Writing Across Cultures** During World War II, the United States sent food and war supplies to the Soviet Union. Write an argument for providing aid to the Soviet people during World War II and an argument against providing such aid.

3 LIFE UNDER COMMUNISM

FIND OUT

How did communism change Soviet society?

What were the economic advantages and disadvantages of the Soviet system?

How did education reflect the government's goals?

What was the government's attitude toward the family and women?

Vocabulary black market

At a Moscow department store, Nina Voronel was waiting to pay for a hand mixer she needed. She saw a sales clerk pass by carrying a box of imported lamps.

Voronel had not gone to the store to buy a lamp. In fact, she did not even need one. Yet she immediately said to the sales clerk, "I'll take one. Put me down for one and I'll go pay the cashier." While Voronel went to pay for her lamp, a long line of people formed to buy the remaining lamps.

In the Soviet Union, consumer goods were so scarce that people often bought whatever was available whether they needed it or not. They could always trade one product for another or sell what they did not need. Learning to cope with shortages was a way of life in the Soviet Union.

Social Changes

In theory, communism was supposed to create a classless society in which everyone's needs were met. After the Russian Revolution, the Bolsheviks abolished the old titles of nobility. They then set out to end the inequalities that had existed under capitalism. Czarist officials, landlords, and business owners lost their wealth and power.

Andrei Sakharov, Voice of Dissent

BUILDERS AND SHAPERS

On November 22, 1955, Soviet scientists and military leaders were celebrating the successful test of a new nuclear weapon. Andrei Sakharov, the "father of the Soviet hydrogen bomb," rose to give a toast:

> ❝ May all our devices explode as successfully as today's, but always over test sites and never over cities. ❞

A stunned silence followed. After an awkward moment, the military director of the nuclear test scolded Sakharov. Scientists, he said, should only build bombs. They should not decide how to use them.

Sakharov was a brilliant physicist. In the 1950s, he sincerely believed that building nuclear weapons would help preserve world peace. Then, he began to worry that Soviet leaders were disregarding the dangers of nuclear weapons. By the early 1960s, Sakharov had begun to call for limits on nuclear testing because it damaged the environment. His protests helped to bring about a treaty banning nuclear testing.

Sakharov emerged as an outspoken dissident. He not only rejected nuclear weapons but also denounced human rights abuses in the Soviet Union. With his wife, Yelena Bonner, Sakharov repeatedly condemned repressive government policies.

Sakharov won worldwide admiration, as well as the Nobel Peace Prize. To Soviet officials, however, he was a troublemaker. In 1980, he was arrested and exiled to Gorki, a remote city that was closed to foreigners. Despite the hardships he suffered, Sakharov continued to criticize the government and call for reform.

In 1986, as the Soviet Union entered an era of growing freedom, Sakharov was released from exile. He returned to Moscow a hero. When Sakharov died three years later, people throughout the world hailed him as a man whose vision and courage had helped to change the world.

1. (a) How did Andrei Sakharov first become famous in the Soviet Union? (b) Why did he become a critic of the Soviet system?
2. **Applying Information** (a) Why do you think the government of the Soviet Union considered Sakharov to be a troublemaker? (b) Why did it take great courage for Sakharov to defy the Soviet government?

The party elite. Before long, however, a new elite emerged. Leaders of the Communist party became a privileged class. Ordinary people waited in long lines in stores whose shelves were empty. Party leaders shopped in special stores stocked with high-quality domestic and foreign goods. Party leaders had access to the best medical care. In spite of the country's severe housing shortages, they received new apartments and enjoyed vacations in summer houses reserved for them. Their children attended top schools and were given good jobs when they graduated.

Communist party membership was limited. Less than 10 percent of the Soviet people belonged to the party. Many children joined communist youth groups that opened the way to future party membership. To join the party, people had to have recommendations from several party members and pass an investigation to make sure they held correct Communist attitudes and beliefs.

Nationalities. Other inequalities existed under the communist system. Although the Soviet Union was a multinational country, Russians held the most important positions. Other Slavic peoples, such as Ukrainians and Belarussians, also gained some key posts. The country's many other national minorities had little power or influence, however.

During the late 1800s, the czars supported a policy known as Russification. They tried to force everyone in the empire to adopt the Russian language and culture. After the Russian Revolution, the Soviet government followed a similar policy. Russian was made the official language of the Soviet Union. The government encouraged Russians to settle in the non-Russian republics. Schools emphasized communist beliefs over local traditions. Despite these efforts to weaken cultural ties, nationalism remained a strong force among the many peoples of the Soviet Union.

Attacks on religion. The communist government was hostile to all religions, since they competed with communism for the people's loyalty. Although the government did not outlaw religious observances, it did use its power to reduce the influence of religion. The government imposed tight controls on churches and delivered a constant barrage of antireligious propaganda. Stalin vowed, "Not a single house of prayer will be needed any longer in any territory of the Soviet Union, and the very notion of God will be erased."

For years after 1917, the Soviet government campaigned against the Russian Orthodox Church. It seized Church property and imprisoned and even executed some priests. Other religions suffered, too. The government destroyed churches that belonged to Catholics, Lutherans, and other Christian sects. It forced many Muslim mosques and Jewish synagogues to close. Jews faced severe persecution. By the 1960s, many Soviet Jews sought to emigrate to other countries. Until the late 1980s, the government made it difficult for them to leave the Soviet Union.

People who continued to observe their religion paid a price. No one who was openly religious could pursue a career in the Communist party. Still, many Soviet citizens maintained their religious beliefs.

Economic Life

The Soviet economic system provided its citizens with several basic benefits. Public transportation was inexpensive, and health care was free. The government kept rents and basic food prices low. It guaranteed every individual a job. Although many jobs paid low wages, most people enjoyed the security of regular employment. Unemployment was almost unknown. The government provided workers with old-age pensions. However, the pensions were so small that many elderly people lived in poverty. Also, workers on collective farms did not receive pensions until the mid-1960s.

After Stalin's death, the standard of living in the Soviet Union rose. New housing was built, and Soviet factories produced more consumer goods. By the 1970s, most urban families had radios, refrigerators, and television sets.

Shortages. Still, many goods remained in short supply, especially in comparison to Western Europe and the United States. Families in city apartments often had to share kitchens and bathrooms with their neighbors. Meat, fresh fruit, and vegetables were difficult to get and expensive when they were available. People spent much of their lives standing in lines to buy food and other goods.

The average person often spent years on a waiting list to buy a car. To make matters worse, Soviet goods were poorly made.

Because well-made goods were so scarce, a thriving black market emerged. In a black market, people trade goods and services illegally in defiance of government rules.

Shortages were common, in part because the government invested so much in military spending. Instead of making cars and appliances, for example, Soviet factories produced tanks and missiles. During the 1970s and 1980s, at least 15 percent of the total output

Goods or services	Soviet Union	United States
White bread (2.2 pounds)	17 minutes	16 minutes
Sirloin steak (2.2 pounds)	182 minutes	79 minutes
Chicken (2.2 pounds)	185 minutes	16 minutes
Fresh milk (about 1 quart)	22 minutes	6 minutes
Potatoes (2.2 pounds)	7 minutes	7 minutes
Oranges (2.2 pounds)	92 minutes	10 minutes
Bath soap	20 minutes	4 minutes
Aspirin (100 cheapest)	246 minutes	5 minutes
Lipstick	69 minutes	30 minutes
Regular gasoline (3 gallons)	210 minutes	36 minutes
Newspaper	3 minutes	3 minutes
Jeans	46 hours	3 hours
Washing machine	165 hours	47 hours
Rent (for 1 month)	12 hours	56 hours
Gas bill (for 1 month)	39 minutes	290 minutes
Telephone call (1 local)	1 minute	2 minutes
Haircut (men's)	37 minutes	63 minutes
Car (medium size)	88 months	8 months

Work Time Needed in a Major City to Buy Goods and Services, 1982

Source: *Radio Liberty Research Supplement,* 1982.

Chart Study Under communism, the Soviet government controlled the nation's products and services and determined the prices for everything. ▶Study this chart and then make a generalization about the standard of living in the Soviet Union and in the United States in 1982.

of the Soviet economy was used for military goods in the country's efforts to keep up with the arms race during the Cold War.

Education

After 1917, the Bolsheviks worked hard to provide education for everyone. By the 1960s, the Soviet Union had virtually ended illiteracy. All Soviet children received at least eight years of schooling. In large cities, children attended school for 10 years. In the fifth grade, students began an intensive study of a foreign language, often English.

Soviet schools also emphasized math and the sciences. The government felt that these subjects were essential to a modern industrial nation. By the time students completed the seventh grade, they had studied algebra and geometry, as well as biology, chemistry, and physics. Soviet students also studied warfare. In the ninth and tenth grades, male students took military training one afternoon each week during the school year. During the summer, they spent several weeks in military training.

In reality, Soviet schools were a propaganda machine for the government. Students learned about the "evils of capitalism." Teachers and textbooks presented history and economics from the point of view of Marx and Lenin. At Soviet universities, students were required to spend at least half of their time studying Marxist-Leninist ideas.

Road Construction Soviet women worked hard, but they were underrepresented in many occupations, especially in top positions. For instance, women dominated the teaching field, but relatively few of them were administrators. ***Change*** How did the status of Soviet women change after the Bolshevik Revolution?

Family Life

After 1917, the Communists simplified marriage and divorce laws. Instead of having church weddings, couples married at government offices. Getting a divorce was easy, and the divorce rate soared as a result. The government hoped to replace close family ties with loyalty to the state.

By the 1930s, however, the government realized the need for strong families. It made obtaining a divorce more difficult. The government also abandoned efforts to have families live together, sharing kitchens and other facilities. Still, the disruptions caused by Stalin's purges, collectivization, and World War II took their toll on the extended family. Many families who were separated by the war were never reunited.

Urbanization also led to smaller families. Because city apartments were so small, parents tended to have fewer children. The declining birth rate alarmed some officials. They feared that Russians would be outnumbered by other nationalities.

Women's lives. After the Russian Revolution, the Communist party passed laws guaranteeing that women and men would be treated equally. As a result, all occupations were opened to women. Soon, they were driving tractors and operating steam shovels. Women also became highly skilled professionals. About 70 percent of Soviet doctors and a large number of lawyers were women.

During World War II, millions of men were killed in the fighting. By 1945, women greatly outnumbered men in the Soviet Union. As a result, women played a large part in the task of rebuilding the nation.

By the 1980s, 85 percent of Soviet women worked outside the home. Their income was needed to support their families. However, these women had few labor-saving appliances. Neither did their husbands give them much help with household chores. In addition to their full-time jobs outside the home, married women often spent another 35 hours doing housework each week.

SECTION 3 REVIEW

1. **Identify:** Russification.
2. **Define:** black market.
3. (a) How did the Bolsheviks change the social system? (b) Did the Soviet Union achieve a classless society? Explain.
4. (a) How did the government ensure economic security for Soviet citizens? (b) What economic hardships did most people face?
5. Describe two ways in which communism affected family life.
6. **Drawing Conclusions** Why do you think the Soviet government wanted to undermine religion?
7. **Writing Across Cultures** List three ways in which Soviet schools supported the communist system. Then, list three values taught in American schools that help to support our system of government.

Chapter 33 Review

Understanding Vocabulary

Match each term at left with the correct definition at right.

1. abdicate	**a.** council of workers, soldiers, and peasants
2. soviet	**b.** illegal trade in goods and services
3. kulak	**c.** someone who speaks out against the government
4. dissident	**d.** give up
5. black market	**e.** prosperous peasant

Reviewing the Main Ideas

1. (a) What reforms did the Provisional Government introduce in Russia? (b) Why did the Provisional Government lose support?
2. Describe Lenin's New Economic Policy.
3. How did Stalin use propaganda and terror to achieve his goals?
4. (a) What progress did the Soviet Union make in agriculture after Stalin's death? (b) What problems did Soviet peasants face?
5. (a) Why did Soviet citizens face shortages of food and consumer goods? (b) How did these shortages affect people's lives?
6. (a) What gains did Soviet women make? (b) What problems did they face?

Reviewing Chapter Themes

1. In 1917, Russia experienced two revolutions. (a) Describe two causes of the March Revolution and the Bolshevik Revolution. (b) What was one difference between the March Revolution and the Bolshevik Revolution?
2. Stalin completed Lenin's goal of setting up a totalitarian state run by the Communist party. (a) How did he expand central economic planning? (b) What was the role of the Communist party in the Soviet Union?
3. Communism radically altered the lives of the Soviet people. Explain how three of the following were affected by communism: (a) human rights, (b) the social system, (c) religion, (d) education, (e) family life.

Thinking Critically

1. **Analyzing Ideas** Lenin said, "Liberty is precious—so precious that it must be rationed." (a) What was Lenin's main point? (b) Why do you think he was against allowing too much liberty all at once? (c) How did his policies reflect this idea?
2. **Making Global Connections** (a) How did the Cold War rivalry between the Soviet Union and the United States affect economic policies under Khrushchev? (b) How do you think the United States viewed the Soviet arms buildup?
3. **Linking Past and Present** (a) What problems did non-Russian peoples face in the Soviet Union? (b) How do you think their discontent contributed to the breakup of the Soviet Union in 1991?

Applying Your Skills

1. **Analyzing a Quotation** Read the excerpt from the poem by Alexander Blok on page 729. In your own words, explain why he wanted people to "listen to the Revolution." How do you think he may have reacted to the outcome of the Russian Revolution?
2. **Using Visual Evidence** Look at the pictures on pages 741 and 742. (a) What is the subject of each picture? (b) What do the pictures reveal about life in the Soviet Union? (c) Compare the life these pictures show with life in the United States.

Chapter 34

Russia and Eastern Europe in the World Today

Chapter Outline

Moscow Demonstration A flag is a powerful symbol. When the Soviet Union dissolved, the Russian people abandoned the nation's hammer and sickle flag. They returned to the tricolor flag that had been introduced by Peter the Great. This giant flag was unfurled at a celebration near the Kremlin. ***Change*** Why do you think changing the flag was so significant?

"I want to become rich, very rich. And I want all the benefits I am entitled to for my brain and my labor, like any entrepreneur in the Western industrial world."

Mikhail Dimitriev stated his goal bluntly. Like millions of people in the former Soviet Union and Eastern Europe, the enterprising St. Petersburg businessman dreamed of the wealth he would gain through his own efforts. After 74 years of communist rule, the Soviet Union and its communist government had collapsed. Many people were now eager to try capitalism—and democracy.

Many Eastern Europeans and former Soviet citizens had doubts about the new system, but most of them were ready for a change. "I cannot go back to working for the state," observed Vladimir Fedotov, a former bus driver who is struggling to become a farmer on his own plot of land. "I understand what freedom is now."

CHAPTER PERSPECTIVE

Starting in the late 1980s, revolutionary changes swept across the Soviet Union and Eastern Europe. With little bloodshed, the Soviet Union crumbled and the Cold War ended. Nations that had been locked behind the Iron Curtain for more than 40 years struggled to set up democratic governments and reform their economies.

As you read, look for these chapter themes:

- Pressures inside and outside the Soviet Union contributed to its collapse in 1991.
- As a superpower competing with the United States, the Soviet Union had great influence in world affairs.
- Although dominated by the Soviet Union, Eastern Europeans never gave up their desire for freedom.
- Shifting to free market economies has created problems for former communist countries.
- Russians and Eastern Europeans have made major contributions to literature and the arts.

Literature Connections

In this chapter, you will encounter selections from the following works.

The Song of Prince Igor's Campaign
"Pushkin," Anna Akhmatova
"The Twelve," Alexander Blok
"Babi Yar," Yevgeny Yevtushenko

For other suggestions, see Connections With Literature, pages 804–808.

1 COLLAPSE OF THE SOVIET UNION

FIND OUT

How did Mikhail Gorbachev try to reform the Soviet system?

Why did Gorbachev's reforms fail?

What problems do the former Soviet republics face?

Vocabulary bureaucracy, perestroika, glasnost, autonomy

During the 1970s, the managers of a Soviet factory designed a free-standing clothes rack. In a country where few apartments had closets, this would have been a very useful device. Under the Soviet economic system, however, the factory managers had to apply to the central government for permission to make the clothes rack. The managers filled out the required forms, then waited. A year later, they still had not received permission to make the clothes rack.

This kind of delay was just one of many problems that made the Soviet economy inefficient. During the 1980s, the Soviet leader, Mikhail Gorbachev, tried to reform the system. His reforms, however, triggered reactions that were beyond his control. One of his advisers noted:

> "Gorbachev took on this country like my wife takes on cabbage. He thought that to get rid of the dirt, he could just peel off the top layers of leaves. But he had to keep going until there was nothing left."

Gorbachev's Reforms

When Mikhail Gorbachev became head of the Communist party in 1985, the Soviet

Private Enterprise in Donetsk This woman makes and sells blini, pancakes filled with sugar and jam. Under Gorbachev, the Soviet government encouraged individuals to provide consumer goods and services. However, it tried to limit these small private businesses to students, housewives, and retired persons. ***Choice*** Why do you think the Soviet government restricted private enterprise?

Union faced severe economic problems. Central planning blocked efficient production of consumer goods such as cars, refrigerators, and even basic foods. Because all decisions were made in Moscow, change came slowly. Also, the Soviets relied on a bureaucracy, or huge system of officials and government departments, to manage the economy. This bureaucracy, with its corruption and confusing procedures, added to the general inefficiency and made change even harder to achieve.

Economic reorganization. Gorbachev recognized that the Soviet Union would need to undertake major reforms to catch up with the West. He believed this could be achieved by reforming the communist system. He therefore called for perestroika (pehr uh STROI kuh), the restructuring of the Soviet economy to make it more efficient and productive.

Under perestroika, the government began to allow factory managers rather than central planners to decide what to produce and how much to charge for goods. It then converted some factories from the production of military goods to the production of consumer goods. Improving the quality of goods became a major goal.

Also, the government gave farmers long-term leases on land they could farm as they chose. By making farmers "masters of the land," Gorbachev hoped to increase food production. For the first time since the 1920s, people were allowed to set up independent businesses.

Ending dictatorship. To achieve his economic goals, Gorbachev adopted a policy of glasnost, or openness and honesty in discussing the problems his country faced. He wanted people to speak out in favor of change and reforms. Before long, however, glasnost created greater openness within Soviet society on many topics. The government eased censorship. Newspapers and television news programs reported on sensitive issues, such as alcoholism and crime, that had been avoided in the past. The government even allowed some dissidents, such as the human rights activist Andrei Sakharov, to come out of exile.

During the late 1980s, Gorbachev quickened the pace of his reforms. He dismissed corrupt Communist party leaders and took steps to restructure the political system. Power was transferred from the Communist party to an elected legislature.

In 1990, Gorbachev ended the Communist party's monopoly on leadership. Voters now had a choice of more than one candidate for each public office. Gorbachev hoped these reforms would help people to feel that they had a stake in their country's future.

Responses to Reform

Gorbachev's reforms failed to improve the Soviet economy. In fact, conditions grew worse. The old, centrally planned economy collapsed before the new market economy could become effective. Shortages of consumer goods became more alarming. In the cities, food became scarce. Many collective farms were trading food directly for goods they needed rather than sending it to city markets. To make matters worse, factories in the cities were reducing their number of workers in an effort to improve efficiency. For the first time since the 1920s, many Soviet workers were unemployed.

The economic hardships led to strikes, and Gorbachev's policies were angrily criticized. Critics such as Boris Yeltsin, a popular Russian leader, called for more rapid and far-reaching reforms. Others thought there had already been too many changes. Many officials, for example, resisted reforms, especially those that threatened their jobs and their special privileges.

Falling Apart This Russian cartoon pictures the Soviet Union as a train hurtling off the tracks, its wheels rolling away in every direction. The emblem on the locomotive, a hammer and sickle, symbolizes the Soviet Union and communism. The wheels represent some of the republics that had declared their independence. ***Change*** How did the cartoonist view the breakup?

At the same time, Gorbachev's move toward democratic government led nationalists in the non-Russian republics to demand autonomy, or self-government. In early 1990, Lithuania challenged the Soviet Union by declaring its independence. Latvia and Estonia soon followed its example. These Baltic republics felt little loyalty to the nation that, under Joseph Stalin, had taken control of them in 1940.

Failed coup. As turmoil increased, conservative members of the Communist party removed Gorbachev from office and tried to seize power in August 1991. While most Soviet citizens watched from the sidelines, supporters of reform poured into the streets of Moscow to protest the attempted coup. Leading the resistance was Boris Yeltsin, who had just been elected president of Russia, one of the republics within the Soviet Union.

To succeed, the coup needed the support of the Soviet army. However, many army units refused to take action. Others openly supported Yeltsin. Within a few days, the coup collapsed. Although Gorbachev returned to his post as president of the Soviet Union, the unrest greatly weakened his power.

Breakup of the Soviet Union. One by one the republics declared independence, leaving the Soviet Union an empty shell. By year's end, Gorbachev resigned as head of the Soviet government. Seventy-four years after the Russian Revolution, the Soviet Union ceased to exist.

Challenges to Democracy

After declaring independence, the former Soviet republics faced enormous challenges. Some, including Latvia and Estonia, are tiny countries with limited resources. Others, such as Russia, Ukraine, and Kazakhstan, are large nations with significant resources. All, however, had been used to central economic planning, and their economies had depended on orders dictated from Moscow.

Economic crisis. In the 1990s, the republics set out to establish market economies and democratic political systems. With no experience, they had varied success. The shift from a centrally planned economy to a free market economy led to great upheavals. Some governments moved to sell factories, land, and other state-owned properties to private individuals. Many factories then closed, reducing output and creating high unemployment.

With goods scarce, prices soared. In the past, the government had kept prices for food and other consumer goods low, no matter what it cost to produce them. To achieve a market economy, however, the government had to let prices rise to reflect the actual production costs.

Although more goods gradually appeared, many were imported from abroad. Most people, especially the elderly whose incomes were limited, could not afford high-priced imports. For many, even basic goods were beyond their means.

Political problems. The economic crisis spurred unrest in some former Soviet republics. As prices rose and unemployment increased, people became impatient with democracy and market reforms. They listened to former Communist party officials or extreme nationalists who offered their own remedies to the economic problems.

Conflicts also erupted among various ethnic and national groups. Russians living in the Baltic republics and elsewhere felt threatened by local nationalist feeling. Border disputes created tensions in some areas. A long, bloody conflict raged between Armenia and Azerbaijan over Nagorno-Karabakh, an area of Azerbaijan where Christian Armenians outnumber Muslim Azeris.

Other problems rose. Corruption that had existed under the Soviet Union became more widespread. Crime, which the old Soviet government had kept hidden, seemed to be on the increase.

Struggles in the Russian Republic. Even the resource-rich Russian Republic faced endless roadblocks in its reform efforts. Russian president Boris Yeltsin had emerged from the 1991 coup a hero to democratic forces. Yet his reform program brought growing criticism and hardship to the Russian people.

Conservative foes in the Russian Parliament clashed with Yeltsin over economic and other reforms. In October 1993, the conflict erupted into bloodshed as Yeltsin forces battled foes who had barricaded themselves inside the Parliament building.

In elections held two months later, Yeltsin hoped to gain support. The new Parliament, however, included many who wanted to slow the reforms. Among them was Vladimir Zhirinovsky, who had appealed to Russian nationalism. His criticism of non Russian ethnic groups and his anti-western views reflected the anger of many Russians about the failure of reforms to bring a better life.

Much advice, few answers. When the Soviet Union collapsed, western nations offered

The White House Is Burning In October 1993, the Russian parliament building, called the White House, burned after being shelled by Russian troops loyal to Boris Yeltsin. Rebellious parliament members had barricaded themselves inside the building and formed their own government. The rebellion ended after troops stormed the building and arrested its leaders.
Political Systems What are some of the difficulties of changing from communist dictatorship to democracy?

Religious Revival

TRADITION AND CHANGE

In the days of the Soviet Union, the government-owned television network showed popular movies on the night before Easter. A rare treat, its purpose was to lure people away from midnight church services. In 1991, however, viewers watched as the Easter Mass was celebrated in Moscow's glittering Church of the Epiphany. Cameras even showed the president of the Russian Federation and other sen-ior government officials taking part in the ceremony.

As communism died, religion was reborn, or reemerged from the secrecy the government had imposed on it. In 1990, the Supreme Soviet voted to end government control of religion. For the first time in more than 70 years, churches were allowed to "carry out their activities without any outside interference."

In this new climate, churches reclaimed buildings that had been converted into offices and museums. Priests performed countless baptisms without fear of criticism, and religious organizations printed thousands of Bibles. Non-Christian religions were also revived. Muslims once again called the faithful to pray in mosques, and Jews established new synagogues and religious schools.

The religious revival brought some problems, however. Among the most disturbing was a marked increase in anti-Semitism. As religious freedom grew, so did the attacks on Jewish people and their property. One Russian Jew noted, "When the weather is good, not only children come into the sunlight but also villains."

Still, the return of religious freedom was cause for joy. One government official reported on the rebuilding of churches in Moldova:

> "The peal of bells can be heard from all over. After being silent for fifty years, the Moldovan bells have come back to life. It is hard to convey the great happiness of seeing a church restored, the joy of hearing the *tip-tap* of a tinsmith covering its dome."

1. Give three examples of changes that have taken place in the religious life of people in the former Soviet Union.
2. **Making Inferences** Why do you think greater religious freedom might encourage anti-Semitism and other forms of intolerance?

help to the new nations as they moved toward market reforms. Many western nations poured out advice to Russia and the other former Soviet republics. But no one had any proven blueprint for transforming a complex centrally planned economy like that of Russia into a successful market economy. Also, financial aid was limited as western nations faced their own economic problems in the early 1990s.

By the mid-1990s, Russians realized they must find their own solutions to their economic problems. While some wanted to move away from reform, a few Russians had successes. They made money opening banks and restaurants or starting other businesses.

SECTION 1 REVIEW

1. **Identify:** (a) Mikhail Gorbachev, (b) Boris Yeltsin.
2. **Define:** (a) bureaucracy, (b) perestroika, (c) glasnost, (d) autonomy.
3. List four economic and political reforms introduced by Gorbachev.
4. (a) How did Gorbachev's reforms affect the Soviet Union? (b) Who opposed his reforms?
5. What events led to the collapse of the Soviet Union?
6. What economic problems did the former Soviet republics face?
7. **Comparing** In the West, Gorbachev was seen as an important, courageous figure. Many Soviet citizens, however, did not regret his resignation. How would you account for this difference of opinion?
8. **Writing Across Cultures** Write a letter to someone of your age who lives in Russia. Describe, in your view, some of the advantages and disadvantages of a free market economy.

2 SOVIET FOREIGN POLICY

FIND OUT

What were the goals of Soviet foreign policy following World War II?

What issues divided the Soviet Union and the West?

Why did the collapse of the Soviet Union cause worldwide concern?

Between 1945 and 1991, the Soviet Union was one of the world's two superpowers. Along with the United States, it dominated global affairs. During the Cold War, the competition between the superpowers influenced events in distant parts of the globe, from Vietnam in Southeast Asia to Cuba in the Caribbean.

Rivalry, fear, and mistrust of the western powers shaped Soviet foreign policy. In his memoirs, the Soviet leader Nikita Khrushchev recalled Stalin's view of the world in the early 1950s:

> "Right up until his death, Stalin used to tell us, 'You'll see, when I'm gone, the imperialist powers will wring your necks like chickens.' We never tried to reassure him that we would be able to manage. We knew it wouldn't do any good."

Ensuring Soviet Security

Stalin's bitterness toward "imperialist powers" had its roots in Soviet history. After taking power in 1917, Lenin and other Bolshevik leaders called for a worldwide communist revolution against capitalism. During the civil war in Russia that followed the Bolshevik takeover, western nations, including the United States and Great Britian, supported the anti-Bolshevik forces.

Even after the Bolshevik victory, some nations refused to recognize the new Soviet Union because of its call for world revolution. The United States, for example, did not recognize the Soviet Union officially until 1933.

Effects of World War II. During the economic depression of the 1930s, the western powers feared communist revolutions directed by the Soviet Union as much as they worried about Hitler's threats of war. After Germany invaded the Soviet Union in 1941, however, the western Allies welcomed Stalin's participation in their battle to defeat Germany. During the war, Hitler became the common enemy and the old anti-Bolshevik feelings faded.

As a result of the massive destruction and huge loss of life caused by the German invasion, Stalin was determined to ensure Soviet security in the future. To Stalin, the only way to protect the Soviet Union was to control Poland, which would serve as a buffer against Germany.

The Allies met several times during the war to determine what should be done once the war ended. At those meetings, Stalin called for friendly governments to be set up in Eastern Europe after Germany was defeated. The western Allies insisted that the countries of Eastern Europe establish democratic governments and hold free elections. Stalin, however, insisted that only communist governments would safeguard Soviet interests in Eastern Europe.

The Cold War develops. When the Soviet army freed Eastern Europe from German occupation during World War II, it installed communist-led governments there. After the war, the Soviets tightened their control of the region. Disputes about the postwar world led to the Cold War.

Stalin felt that he had given the western powers freedom to deal with the defeated Axis nations of Italy and Japan. In return, he expected the West to allow him to make Eastern Europe a Soviet sphere of influence.

Stalin objected to plans to reunite Germany, fearing the revival of a strong German state. Stalin viewed the moves toward German reunification as evidence of western hostility to communism. To counter these threats, he blockaded Berlin and intensified his efforts to create a strong Soviet bloc. He also invested Soviet resources in the development of nuclear weapons and military equipment.

The communist bloc. Stalin used Eastern Europe to help rebuild the Soviet economy. In East Germany, for example, Soviet troops seized industrial machinery, including entire factories, and sent them to the Soviet Union. During the postwar years, the Soviet Union shaped the economies of Eastern Europe to fill its own needs.

In 1955, to counter NATO, the Soviet Union created the Warsaw Pact, which was a military alliance with its communist neighbors in Eastern Europe. In theory, the Warsaw Pact was formed to guarantee safety and provide defense. In practice, however, the Soviets used Warsaw Pact forces to crush democratic reform movements in Eastern Europe. (See Section 3.)

Relations With the United States

The driving force of the Cold War was the rivalry between the Soviet Union and the United States. Each side tried to outdo the other in industry, science, technology, education, and athletics, as well as in military strength.

Soviet leaders pointed to their country's achievements as proof that communism was superior to capitalism. They directed this

Armed Forces Parade
The Soviet Union used to display its military power each November on the anniversary of the Bolshevik Revolution. During the Cold War, Soviet armed forces became the world's largest military power, with nearly 6 million troops in uniform. ***Power*** Why might a country want to show off its weaponry, such as these missiles?

message to both their own citizens and people in the developing world. In 1957, Nikita Khrushchev gloated when the Soviet Union launched *Sputnik I,* the first artificial satellite to orbit the Earth. He boasted:

> “The launching of satellites is the work of the Soviet people, who, under socialism, are making fairy tales into reality.”

A time of tension. The Cold War rivalry between the United States and the Soviet Union also led to dangerous confrontations and an expensive arms race. Both sides invested huge sums of money in building large armed forces and producing weapons of mass destruction.

On several occasions, the superpowers came close to armed conflict over Berlin. (See Chapter 31.) During the Cuban missile crisis in 1963, the Soviet Union and the United States stood on the edge of nuclear war.

Other confrontations took place in Asia, Africa, and the Middle East, where both superpowers sought allies. Often, they supplied arms to rival groups, turning local conflicts into international crises. Whether in Korea, Vietnam, Afghanistan, or Nicaragua, tens of thousands of innocent people were caught in the cross-fire of the Cold War.

During the 1950s, Khrushchev tried to ease Cold War tensions. He rejected Lenin's belief that war between capitalist and communist nations was necessary and unavoidable. Instead, he supported the idea of "peaceful coexistence," arguing that the two worlds could exist side by side. In 1959, Khrushchev visited the United States and conferred with President Dwight D. Eisenhower. However, the next year an American spy plane was shot down over the Soviet Union. That event renewed distrust between the two sides.

During the following three decades, confrontation alternated with efforts to ease tensions. After the Cuban missile crisis, for example, the superpowers installed a Teletype "hot line," linking Moscow and Washington, D.C. In 1963, the Soviet Union and the United States signed a treaty that banned nuclear weapons tests in the Earth's atmosphere.

In 1964, Khrushchev's successor, Leonid Brezhnev, returned Russia to Stalin's style of government. He increased censorship, built up the Soviet military, and tightened control of Eastern Europe. Democratic movements, such as those in Hungary and Czechoslovakia, were suppressed. (See page 756.)

Brezhnev declared that the Soviet Union had the right to intervene in any socialist country and keep it from changing its government. This Brezhnev Doctrine intensified the Cold War and prolonged the economic and political suffering of Soviet citizens.

During the 1970s and 1980s, the superpowers attempted to slow the arms race. Yet, at the same time, both sides increased spending on nuclear weapons.

Gorbachev's foreign policy. An important breakthrough came after Gorbachev gained power in 1985. The new Soviet leader introduced a foreign policy based on what he called "new thinking." Using this policy, Gorbachev genuinely sought peace with the West. In 1987, the superpowers signed an agreement eliminating a major category of nuclear weapons—intermediate-range guided missiles based in Europe. Gorbachev then took other steps to end the Cold War, including withdrawing Soviet troops from Afghanistan and Eastern Europe.

The growing cooperation between the superpowers led to the settlement of various conflicts throughout the world. In Namibia and Ethiopia, for example, the superpowers supported efforts to end long-standing civil wars. In 1990, Gorbachev won the Nobel Peace Prize for his role in promoting world peace.

Relations With the Developing World

After World War II, the Soviet Union supported the goals of nationalist and communist revolutions throughout the world. It provided many countries with military and economic aid. The Soviet Union, for example, helped

Boris Yeltsin and Bill Clinton The presidents of Russia and the United States take a break from a 1994 economic summit. Yeltsin pushed to have Russia recognized as an important member of the world economic community. ***Interdependence*** How did Yeltsin's desire to be treated as an equal partner with the world's economic leaders reflect concern about global interdependence?

Egypt build the Aswan High Dam in the 1960s. In addition, many students from developing countries attended Soviet universities.

Asia. With Soviet military aid, Chinese Communists won power in 1949. During the early 1950s, the People's Republic of China relied on Soviet economic and technical aid. Later, the two nations became rivals for leadership of the world communist movement and even clashed along their border.

Elsewhere in Asia, the Soviet Union supported communist governments in North Korea and North Vietnam. To counter the spread of communism in these areas, the United States extended aid to South Korea and South Vietnam. Although Soviet ground forces did not fight in the Vietnam War, the North Vietnamese received extensive aid from the Soviet Union.

In 1979, Soviet troops invaded Afghanistan to help a communist government that had seized power there. For eight years, Soviet troops suffered heavy losses as Afghan rebels, supplied by the United States, waged a guerrilla war against the Communists. In 1988, Gorbachev finally withdrew Soviet forces from Afghanistan.

Latin America. For the Soviet Union, Cuba was an important outpost of communism in the Western Hemisphere. As a result, the government gave Cuba billions of dollars annually in economic and military aid. Between 1959 and 1990, the Soviet Union helped Cuba to introduce modern technology in its sugar industry and to set up improved health care and educational systems.

During the 1980s, the Soviet Union also sent aid to the Sandinista government in Nicaragua. The United States responded to Soviet activities in Latin America by imposing economic blockades against Cuba and Nicaragua. It also supplied arms and supplies to rebel military groups. (See Chapter 23.)

New Relations With the World

After the breakup of the Soviet Union, each of the republics struggled to set its own course in world affairs. As the largest and most powerful republic, the Russian Federation* inherited the Soviet Union's membership in the United Nations and its place on the UN Security Council. It also gained control of many of the military and industrial resources of the former Soviet Union.

Economic investment. As the former Soviet republics began shifting to free market economies, they sought closer ties with wealthy industrial nations. They turned to Japan and the West for the capital to invest in new enterprises. Some republics, such as

* The republic became known as the Russian Federation, but is often simply referred to as Russia.

MAP STUDY

The power of the Soviet government held together a vast and diverse population of European and Asian peoples. When this central power weakened, it opened the way for the breakup of the nation.

1. **Region** Which of the former republics probably identify more closely with Europe than with Asia? Why?
2. **Interaction** Choose five of the new nations and describe one favorable or unfavorable feature of its geography. (See the map on page 708.)
3. **Applying Information** (a) What benefits could the new nations gain by forming an economic community similar to the European Community? (b) Why might they hesitate to do so?

Latvia and Estonia, hoped to gain admission to the European Community.

The United States and other western powers were eager to see the former Soviet republics build free market economies and establish stable governments. Despite the economic recession of the early 1990s, the United States and other countries provided the struggling republics with limited aid and advice. Western economists shared their knowledge and experience. In addition, entrepreneurs set up joint business ventures, hoping to make profits by producing goods needed by the republics. Some early ventures included establishing hotels and restaurants, but more ambitious industrial projects were also planned. The western nations recognized that economic instability in the former Soviet Union could lead to chaos.

Dismantling nuclear weapons. A major concern of western powers was the large number of nuclear weapons that had been stockpiled by the former Soviet Union. These weapons were located in four republics—Russia, Ukraine, Kazakhstan, and Uzbekistan. Officially, the Russian Federation controlled the weapons. However, many people worried that individual republics might sell their weapons to earn desperately needed money. Partly for this reason, the United States negotiated agreements with the four republics. It provided technical and financial aid to help dismantle the weapons. It also encouraged the new republics to sign the Nuclear Non-Proliferation Treaty.

A related issue rose about nuclear weapons experts trained in the Soviet Union. It was feared that countries wanting to build nuclear weapons might hire these experts. So the United States and other nations funded a research institute in Russia. It offered jobs to these experts to work on finding peaceful uses for nuclear energy.

SECTION 2 REVIEW

1. **Identify:** (a) *Sputnik I,* (b) peaceful coexistence, (c) Brezhnev Doctrine.
2. (a) What were Stalin's goals for the Soviet Union after World War II? (b) How did he try to achieve them?
3. (a) Why did the United States refuse to recognize the Soviet Union until 1933? (b) Why did relations between the Soviet Union and the United States grow tense after World War II?
4. How did each of the following Soviet leaders try to ease Cold War tensions: (a) Nikita Khrushchev, (b) Mikhail Gorbachev?
5. What policies did the Soviet Union adopt toward developing nations?
6. (a) Why did the new republics seek ties with industrial nations after the breakup of the Soviet Union? (b) What steps did western nations take to resolve issues concerning nuclear weapons?
7. **Forecasting** Has the end of the Cold War made the world a more peaceful place? Explain.
8. **Writing Across Cultures** Write a segment for a television news program describing how the collapse of the Soviet Union has affected the lives of ordinary Americans.

3 REVOLUTION IN EASTERN EUROPE

FIND OUT

What was the relationship between Eastern Europe and the Soviet Union after World War II?

Why were some Eastern European nations able to achieve democracy in 1989?

What problems do the nations of Eastern Europe face today?

In early 1990, President Václav Havel of Czechoslovakia addressed the United States Congress. Only a few months earlier, Havel had been held in a Czech prison. His crime was speaking out against communism. He told Congress:

> “When they arrested me [in October 1989], I was living in a country ruled by the most conservative communist government in Europe, and our society slumbered beneath the pall of a totalitarian system. Today, less than four months later, I am speaking to you as the representative of a country that has set out on the road to democracy. It is very strange indeed.”

Havel was describing the remarkable revolution that swept across Eastern Europe. Within months, communist governments in the region fell to the forces of democracy. The swift changes created great opportunities for political and economic development. Yet they also presented difficult challenges for the future. By 1993, Czechoslovakia itself had split into two separate nations.

Soviet Domination of Eastern Europe

At the end of World War II, the Soviet Union imposed communist governments on the nations of Eastern Europe. In each country, the Soviet army helped the local Communists set up a system of one-party rule. To maintain their power, the Communists ended freedom of expression, attacked religion, and relied on police spies and terror to silence critics.

Economic life. The economic life of Eastern Europe mirrored that of the Soviet Union. From Poland to Hungary to Bulgaria, governments nationalized all industry and ended private enterprise. They drew up five-year plans, stressing heavy industry and military spending at the expense of consumer goods and housing. They also set up collective farms in some areas.

Eastern European nations traded with one another and with the Soviet Union on terms that favored the Soviets. Under Soviet domination, these countries ended their prewar ties with Western Europe.

Yugoslavia under Tito. The Soviet Union imposed its will on most Eastern European nations, but Marshal Josip Tito steered his own course in Yugoslavia. During World War II, Tito had led the Yugoslav resistance during the German occupation. After the war, he took power in Yugoslavia.

Although he was a communist dictator, Tito did not accept Soviet authority. During the Cold War, he declared that Yugoslavia was neutral and refused to join the Warsaw Pact. His death in 1980, however, left Yugoslavia without a strong leader.

Upheavals in the Soviet Bloc

Despite Soviet domination, the people of Eastern Europe never accepted the loss of their independence. In 1953, for example, strikes and anticommunist riots broke out in several cities in Czechoslovakia. Soviet tanks crushed similar uprisings in East Germany. By 1956, when Khrushchev eased the terror of the Stalin era, the peoples of Eastern Europe had begun to renew their demands for greater freedom.

Unrest in Poland. In Poland, workers demanding "bread and freedom" staged strikes and riots in 1956. In response to the crisis, Khrushchev allowed Wladyslaw Gomulka, a Polish Communist known for his strong nationalist feelings, to take over the Polish government. Gomulka managed to quiet the unrest and gain greater autonomy for Poland by reassuring the Soviets that Poland would remain a loyal member of the Warsaw Pact. He ended collectivization and permitted some private enterprise. He also stopped attacks on the Catholic Church.

As other Eastern European writers had done, writers in Poland joined the protest against Communist party rule. The Polish author Stanislaw Lem used satire to convey his message. Because of strict censorship, he disguised his criticism of the government by setting his novel *Star Diaries* on a distant planet. In one incident, the government of the planet sets up an irrigation system that floods the land. Instead of admitting its error, the government recommends that people learn to breathe underwater.

Hungarian uprising. Encouraged by the example set by Poland, students and workers protesting in Hungary brought Imre Nagy (noj), a liberal communist reformer, to power in 1956. Like Tito and Gomulka, the Hungarian leader was a nationalist. He forced Soviet troops to leave Hungary and ended one-party rule. But unlike Gomulka, he withdrew Hungary from the Warsaw Pact.

The Soviet Union responded by sending troops to crush the Hungarian uprising. Thousands of Hungarians died in the bitter fighting that followed, and more than 200,000 fled to the West. Nagy was arrested and later executed. Many Hungarians felt that the western powers had betrayed their democratic revolution by failing to come to their aid.

Prague Spring. In the mid-1960s, Eastern European nations followed the foreign policy set by Leonid Brezhnev in the Soviet Union, but slowly gained some power over local affairs. In the spring of 1968, reformers won control of the Communist party in Czechoslovakia. Leading the reform movement was Alexander Dubcek (DOOB chehk). He wanted to blend democracy with socialism to create what he called "socialism with a human face." Dubcek eased rigid central planning, ended censorship, and limited the powers of the secret police. This period of freedom became known as the Prague Spring, named for Prague, the capital of Czechoslovakia.

Unlike Hungary under Nagy, Czechoslovakia did not withdraw from the Warsaw Pact. Still, Dubcek's reforms disturbed hard-line Communists in Moscow and elsewhere in Eastern Europe. To them, Czechoslovakia was setting a dangerous example for other nations in the Soviet bloc.

In August 1968, the Soviet Union sent hundreds of thousands of Warsaw Pact forces to occupy Czechoslovakia. They ended the reforms of the Prague Spring and restored a hard-line communist dictatorship.

Prague Spring In the spring of 1968, people's hopes for freedom in Czechoslovakia grew. They decorated this statue of King Wenceslaus with flowers and nationalist slogans. Soon after, Soviet tanks and troops crushed the democratic demonstrations. ***Political Systems*** Why did the Soviets fear democratic movements in their satellites?

Poland's Path to Democracy

In Poland, price increases and food shortages brought renewed protests and strikes by workers. In 1980, shipyard workers in the port city of Gdańsk formed a trade union called Solidarity. Led by Lech Walesa (vah LEHN sah), Solidarity won government recognition and became the first independent trade union in any Soviet bloc nation.

With the support of the Polish people and the Catholic Church, Solidarity made demands for major political and economic reforms. Alarmed at Solidarity's growing strength, the Soviet Union pushed the Polish communist government to declare martial law. As a result, the Polish government outlawed Solidarity and arrested its leaders. The crackdown created widespread support for Solidarity and further undermined Communist party authority in Poland. Although martial law ended in 1983, the Polish government failed to improve economic conditions.

By the late 1980s, Gorbachev had renounced the Brezhnev Doctrine, leaving Eastern Europeans free to pursue their own goals. As the Polish economy collapsed, the government again legalized Solidarity.

In 1989, the Polish government agreed to hold elections. In their first free elections in 50 years, the Poles rejected communism and swept Solidarity candidates to victory. The newly elected government then set out to dismantle socialism and create a capitalist economy.

Other Victories for Democracy

The dramatic developments in Poland set the stage for similar changes in other nations of Eastern Europe. With amazing speed, totalitarian communist dictatorships disappeared as people demanded democratic governments committed to free market economies.

As the effects of Gorbachev's policies began to be felt across Eastern Europe, a reform movement forced the Hungarian Communist party to give up power. In May 1989, unforeseen events dramatized this shift in power. More than 30 years after Imre Nagy was executed for leading the Hungarian uprising, he received a hero's funeral. By 1990, free elections had given non-Communists an overwhelming victory in Hungary.

In 1989, protests spread across Czechoslovakia. Since there were no Soviet troops to crush the democratic revolution, the communist leaders resigned. Václav Havel, a playwright and human rights activist, was released from prison and elected president.

In East Germany, too, mass protests resulted in the downfall of the hard-line communist government. On November 9, 1989, the new government opened the Berlin Wall. As Germans eagerly dismantled the hated wall, the two Germanies quickly moved to form a united country. (See Chapter 31.)

In Romania, a brief but fierce struggle ended with the execution of Nicolae Ceausescu (chah SHEHS koo), the country's cruel and corrupt Communist party dictator. Bulgaria and Albania also held elections to decide their future.

Economic and Political Struggles

For the nations of Eastern Europe, as for the Soviet republics, the change from Communist party dictatorship to capitalist democracy posed problems. These nations faced economic hardships as they made reforms. Old state-run industries shut down, causing production to fall and unemployment to rise. Prices soared and many people faced poverty.

Several nations, including Poland, Hungary, the Czech Republic, and Slovakia, formed a regional free trade association to ease the problems. Germany made huge investments in the region. Still, economic hard times remained a threat in many Eastern European nations.

Political problems. Economic turmoil contributed to political instability in Eastern European countries. Numerous political parties emerged, and forming coalitions to make governments work became increasingly difficult. In Poland, Lech Walesa called for a strong leader to take decisive action toward new reform. Critics warned that such a move could lead to a return to dictatorship.

Frustrated and confused by the failure of their reform movements, people stayed away from the polls at election time. In some elections, former Communists won seats in the legislatures.

Ethnic tensions increased. As you have read, Czechoslovakia peacefully divided into two nations. Hungarians in Romania and Turks in Bulgaria protested against discrimination. Also, anti-Semitism resurfaced in Poland and Hungary.

War in Bosnia and Herzegovina. In Yugoslavia, ethnic and religious conflicts flared into civil war. Yugoslavia had been created after World War I out of a patchwork of rival groups, including Serbs, Croats, Slovenians, and Muslims. Despite years under a single government, their conflicts were deeply rooted in the history of the region.

The Serbs who had dominated Yugoslavia tried to preserve the nation, but by 1992, it had split into a number of independent states, including Slovenia, Croatia, and Bosnia and Herzegovina. In Bosnia, a brutal war raged among Serbs, Croats, and Muslims.

The civil war raised tough issues for world powers, who hesitated to intervene. While the United Nations, NATO, and individual nations pushed for peace talks, horrible massacres occurred. As peace plans were drawn up and rejected, the conflict continued.

The First Steps Toward Capitalism

Throughout most of Eastern Europe, a new generation of capitalists is eager to take advantage of the shift to a free market economy. As the government sells state-owned businesses, enterprising and energetic men and women are buying everything from factories to taxicabs. Others are starting new businesses

Clothing Store in Budapest Small, privately owned service businesses have been common in Hungary since the early 1980s. Now, however, the country wants to privatize large firms by selling them to private owners. ***Choice*** Who are the possible buyers of government-owned firms?

from scratch. One company has found a new use for an old Soviet missile silo—growing mushrooms!

Within 15 months after the collapse of communism, more than 1 million new business owners emerged in Eastern Europe. "Everything will sell here," said one Polish entrepreneur. "Everything is in demand."

The new capitalists. Halina and Bogustaw Tyzus were among the first of these new entrepreneurs. The Tyzuses live in the Polish capital of Warsaw. Under communism, they worked in a state-owned factory. In 1990, the Tyzuses opened a shop that printed and sold posters and calendars with glossy pictures of horses. After years of dreary, government-issued calendars, Poles bought up the Tyzuses' colorful products. Almost overnight, the couple became millionaires.

In the Czech Republic, Miroslav Svarc set up a prosperous construction business. As a carpenter, Svarc once worked 12 hours a day to earn $416 a month. In the 1990s, he set up more than a dozen businesses, with annual sales of $9 million. Among his enterprises was the country's first 24-hour food market. In addition to launching a chain of supermarkets, Svarc hopes to use his profits to buy a state-owned department store in downtown Prague.

Not all of Eastern Europe's new capitalists have inspiring success stories to tell. In a working-class district of Budapest in Hungary, Laszlo Kovacs struggles 14 hours a day to keep his new telecommunications company afloat. Kovacs pays high interest rates on the money he borrowed to buy the company from the state.

Due to economic hard times, many of Kovacs' biggest customers cannot pay their bills. High taxes and social security payments for his employees add to his expenses. Still, Kovacs is optimistic. If a deal with a German company comes through, he may make a small profit next year.

A long way to go. As these stories demonstrate, the peoples of Eastern Europe are taking the first steps toward a free market economy. However, they still have a long way to go. Major problems include a shortage of investment capital, high interest rates, runaway inflation, and a lack of technical knowledge.

The solutions to these problems will not be easy. After all, Eastern European nations are pioneers in making the shift from a command economy to capitalism. Still, people there are excited about their new freedom. As Malgorzata Zuch, a Polish entrepreneur, says: "I have courage. Every day is exciting."

SECTION 3 REVIEW

1. **Identify:** (a) Václav Havel, (b) Marshal Josip Tito, (c) Wladyslaw Gomulka, (d) Imre Nagy, (e) Alexander Dubcek, (f) Prague Spring, (g) Solidarity, (h) Lech Walesa.
2. How did the Soviet Union dominate Eastern Europe after World War II?
3. How did political changes lead to economic changes in Eastern Europe in the late 1980s?
4. List three economic problems that Eastern European nations face today.
5. How did ethnic tensions surface as communism declined in Eastern Europe?
6. **Linking Past and Present** Why were the reforms made in Eastern Europe in the 1980s and 1990s more successful than those attempted in the 1950s and 1960s?
7. **Writing Across Cultures** Imagine that you own a small American business. Write a letter to an entrepreneur in Eastern Europe offering advice on how to succeed. Include information on steps you have taken to make your business a success.

4 LITERATURE AND THE ARTS

FIND OUT

Who were some outstanding figures of Russian literature?

How did communism influence literature and the arts?

What influences shaped Russian art and music?

Vocabulary socialist realism

When the poet Alexander Pushkin lay near death, crowds of people flocked to his home to ask about his health. Although many of his admirers could not read, they knew Pushkin's poems by heart.

In Russia, the arts—especially literature—play a major role in society. Russians love art and literature, and they admire creative artists. To Russians, the artist is an important social critic and a seeker of truth. In the words of the novelist Alexander Solzhenitsyn:

> "In the struggle against lies, art has always won and always will. Lies can stand up against much in the world, but not against art."

Russian Literature

Russian literature emerged during Kievan times, in the 800s and 900s. Early writings were, for the most part, religious works such as hymns and biographies of saints. Russians also had a rich oral tradition of folktales and epic poems. Many of these tales and poems inspired later writers.

Russia's most famous early work is *The Song of Prince Igor's Campaign*, which was composed in about 1190. This poem vividly describes Prince Igor's unsuccessful campaign against foreign invaders. Its unknown author summons the princes of Russia to unite against a common enemy.

> "Brothers and warriors!
> It is better to be killed in battle, than
> to become a captive.
> Let us mount our swift steeds,
> brothers!
> Let us view the blue river Don."

By the 1600s, western influences had begun to affect Russian literature. Under Peter the Great and his successors, French, German, and English works were translated into Russian. During the 1800s, Russia enjoyed a "golden age" of literature. Russian poets and novelists produced masterpieces that were hailed throughout the world.

Writers, however, were restricted by official censorship. Often, censors required an author to remove passages that were critical of the czar. To avoid censorship, writers wove criticism into the plots of their novels. Sometimes, it was overlooked by the censors.

Pushkin. Among Russians, the most honored writer is the poet Alexander Pushkin. Two of his best-known works are *Eugene Onegin* and a short story, "The Queen of Spades," which is about a heartless gambler who loses a fortune—and his mind. The poem "The Bronze Horseman" is another one of Pushkin's masterpieces. (See page 706.)

Pushkin came from a noble Russian family. On his mother's side, he was descended from Ibrahim Hannibal, an Ethiopian prince who had served at the court of Peter the Great. By age 16, Pushkin had already achieved fame as a poet. However, his writings on freedom aroused the suspicion of the government, and he was exiled to a remote province in southern Russia. Later, he was confined to his family's estate. Pushkin's turbulent life ended before he was 40, when he died of wounds suffered in a duel. (📖 See Connections With Literature, page 808, "The Bridegroom.")

Through his poetry and prose, Pushkin had enormous influence on other Russian writers. Today, young Russians can quote long passages from his works. In a poem titled "Pushkin," Soviet poet Anna Akhmatova acknowledges the debt of gratitude Russians express toward their greatest poet:

> "A swarthy youth wandered
> By himself at the edge of the lake.
> For a hundred long years we have
>   cherished
> The slight rustle his far footsteps
>   make."

Tolstoy Reading A member of a prosperous noble family, Leo Tolstoy was troubled by the great inequalities that existed in Russian society. In his later years, he preached nonviolence, gave away much of his wealth, and lived as simply as he could. Art, he believed, should transmit "the highest and best feelings to which men have risen." ***Fine Art*** What does this painting suggest about Tolstoy?

Realism. In the late 1800s, two giants of Russian literature emerged—Feodor Dostoevski (daw staw YEHV skee) and Leo Tolstoy. Both displayed elements of realism in their work. They believed that they had a duty to portray life honestly and to campaign for political reform.

As a young man, Dostoevski and several of his friends were arrested and condemned to death for belonging to a group of radical thinkers. As they were led before a firing squad, they were suddenly told that their sentence had been changed to exile. The czar had planned the fake execution to frighten them.

The experience left a deep impression on Dostoevski, and he included a similar scene in his novel *The Idiot.* In other novels, such as *Crime and Punishment* and *The Brothers Karamazov,* Dostoevski explored universal themes such as the struggle between good and evil and the destructive effects of greed on human relationships. His works expressed a deep belief in Christian values and in the basic goodness of the Russian people.

One of Tolstoy's best-known works is *War and Peace.* This massive historical novel revolves around Napoleon's invasion of Russia in 1812. In *Anna Karenina,* Tolstoy rejects the self-indulgent manners and values of his times. Among Tolstoy's many short stories is "The Death of Ivan Ilyich," which portrays the terror of a judge who realizes that he is dying. (See Connections With Literature, page 808, "How Much Land Does a Man Need?")

Soviet Literature

By 1917, many Russian writers were in tune with revolutionary ideas. Poets like Alexander Blok welcomed the Bolshevik Revolution. In "The Twelve," he captured the spirit of the revolution as a force that was sweeping across Russia like a purifying wind.

> "Black the night.
> White the snow.
> Blow, wind, blow—
> You can't keep on your feet—hold tight!
> Blow, wind, blow—
> Over all of God's world go!"

Another great poet of the Bolshevik Revolution was Vladimir Mayakovsky. With startling, sometimes humorous, images and shocking language, Mayakovsky forced readers to take notice of what was going on around them. After a visit to the United States in 1925, he wrote "Americans Wonder," a poem that ends with a friendly promise that the Soviets "will not only catch up with but will overtake" the United States.

Propaganda and censorship. "Literature must become Party [Bolshevik] literature," declared Lenin. In the 1920s, the Soviet government used literature—and the other arts—as a propaganda tool. A movement known as socialist realism emerged. Through their works, writers and artists glorified socialism and Marxist-Leninist ideas. They portrayed the evils of capitalism and boosted family ideals, loyalty to the revolution, and the importance of hard work.

Under Stalin, the government exercised tight control over Soviet writers. All authors were required to join the Union of Soviet Writers if they wanted to have their works published. Many writers were persecuted, imprisoned, or killed.

The thaw. During the Khrushchev era, the government eased censorship. One of the books published during the "thaw" was Alexander Solzhenitsyn's novel *One Day in the Life of Ivan Denisovich*, which was based on the author's experiences in a forced labor camp. (See World Literature, "The One Great Heart", page 768.) Khrushchev used the story, which exposed the harsh conditions in prison camps, to discredit Stalin.

The poet Yevgeny Yevtushenko also published works that were critical of Stalin's government. In "Babi Yar," he expressed outrage at the anti-Semitism that led to the massacre of about 34,000 Ukrainian Jews during World War II.* In this poem, Yevtushenko took a great risk by referring not only to German anti-Semitism but to Russian anti-Semitism as well.

> "Wild grasses rustle over Babi Yar,
> The trees stare down, stern as my
>   judge,
> Silent the air howls. . . .
> And I am every old man shot down here
> And every child.
> In no limb of my body can I forget."

Despite the thaw, Boris Pasternak could not get his novel *Dr. Zhivago* published in the Soviet Union. When Pasternak won the Nobel Prize for literature, the Soviet government forced him to refuse the award.

Samizdat. To avoid government censorship, writers who criticized the government turned to *samizdat* (sahm ihz DAHT), a system

* At Babi Yar in Ukraine, German troops murdered about 34,000 Jews on two days in September 1941.

for publishing their work secretly. Writers circulated samizdat literature among themselves and had their works smuggled out of the country for publication abroad. Samizdat publishing continued until glasnost granted Soviet writers greater freedom of expression.

The Visual Arts

The art and architecture of early Russia were associated with the Church. As a result, they reflected Byzantine influences. Architects adapted features of Byzantine churches, including the onion-shaped dome. Like the Byzantines, artists decorated churches with mosaics and frescoes that depicted stories from the Bible.

In later years, Russians developed their own styles, which were simpler and warmer than those they had borrowed from the Byzantines. They emphasized vivid colors and excelled in the art of painting icons.

During the Renaissance, Russians hired Italian artists and architects to build and decorate many of their palaces and churches. Peter the Great used architects from Western Europe to design and build his new capital at St. Petersburg.

By the 1600s, Russian artists had begun to focus on secular as well as religious themes, and Russian painters had adapted Western European styles. During the 1800s, realist painters used their art to protest the injustices they saw in society.

After Stalin's rise to power, Soviet artists had to conform to the strict requirements of socialist realism. Art had to serve the state by glorifying socialism and Stalin. Typical paintings showed heroic workers breaking the chains of capitalism or fearless soldiers carrying the Soviet flag into battle against the enemies of socialism.

Artists who refused to observe the official style were severely criticized and prevented from exhibiting their work. They were denied studios, art materials, and contact with friends. In some cases, they were declared insane and put in mental institutions.

The Lightermen Artist Nikolai Andronov painted this group of workers on a lighter—a type of barge—during the early 1960s. The simplified outlines and vivid colors reflect the influence of modern art. However, the subject of the painting—strong, determined laborers—is typical of socialist realism. ***Fine Art*** Why might this painting appeal to Soviet workers?

Russian Dancers These members of the Moscow Ballet are performing a duet from *Swan Lake*. Modern Russian composers noted for their ballet music include Igor Stravinsky (*The Firebird, The Rite of Spring*), Sergei Prokofiev (*Romeo and Juliet*), and Dmitri Shostakovich (*The Age of Gold*). ***Human Rights*** Why do you think some Russian dancers wanted to escape to the West during the 1960s and 1970s?

The Performing Arts

By the 1800s, the Russian Empire included hundreds of ethnic groups. The history, folklore, and dance of these groups greatly enriched the performing arts.

Music. In music, as in literature, the 1800s was a "golden age." Russian composers combined folk, religious, and western traditions to create musical masterpieces.

Peter Ilich Tchaikovsky (chī KOF skee) helped develop a distinctly Russian school of music that expressed strong national pride. Tchaikovsky's music for the ballets *Swan Lake* and the *Nutcracker* is still immensely popular in the West. Modest Mussorgsky (muh SOORG skee) used themes from Russian history to create such operas as *Boris Godunov.*

The Soviet Union has produced many international performers. Among its best-known musicians have been the cellist Mstislav Rostropovich, the pianist Sviatoslav Richter, and the violinist David Oistrakh.

Dance. Russia—and later the Soviet Union—enriched the world of dance. In the late 1800s, classical ballet flourished in Moscow and St. Petersburg. Since then, the Bolshoi and Kirov ballet companies have produced many world-famous dancers. During the 1960s and 1970s, several Soviet dancers, including Rudolf Nureyev, Mikhail Baryshnikov, and Natalia Makarova, fled to the West.

In the 1930s, Igor Moiseyev organized the Moiseyev Dance Company. He adapted folk dances from the many Soviet nationalities. The company traveled widely in the West, offering a glimpse of Ukrainian, Polish, Moldovan, Kurdish, and other folk traditions.

SECTION 4 REVIEW

1. **Identify:** (a) Feodor Dostoevski, (b) Leo Tolstoy, (c) Alexander Blok, (d) *A Day in the Life of Ivan Denisovich,* (e) "Babi Yar," (f) samizdat, (g) Peter Ilich Tchaikovsky.
2. **Define:** socialist realism.
3. Why did the czarist government feel threatened by Alexander Pushkin and exile him?
4. What traditions influenced the arts and music of Russia?
5. (a) How did communism affect Soviet literature? (b) How did it affect the arts?
6. **Making Inferences** Why do you think Lenin and Stalin viewed literature and the arts as important propaganda tools?
7. **Writing Across Cultures** Imagine that you lived in the Soviet Union under Stalin. Write a poem protesting conditions in your country.

Chapter 34 Review

Understanding Vocabulary

Match each term at left with the correct definition at right.

1. bureaucracy	**a.** policy of openness and honesty
2. perestroika	**b.** self-government
3. glasnost	**c.** system for publishing books secretly
4. autonomy	**d.** large system of officials and government departments
5. samizdat	**e.** restructuring of the Soviet economy

Reviewing the Main Ideas

1. (a) What reforms did Gorbachev introduce? (b) How did people respond to them?

2. (a) Describe the 1991 coup in the Soviet Union. (b) What effect did the coup have?

3. Identify three causes of tension between the Soviet Union and the United States between 1945 and 1991.

4. How did the influence of Solidarity extend beyond Poland?

5. Identify a contribution made by each of the following: (a) Alexander Pushkin, (b) Feodor Dostoevski, (c) Alexander Solzhenitsyn.

6. Describe the role of socialist realism in Soviet art and literature.

Reviewing Chapter Themes

1. In 1991, the Soviet Union ceased to exist. (a) Describe three problems the Soviets faced during the late 1980s. (b) Explain how each contributed to the Soviet Union's collapse.

2. The Soviet Union was one of the superpowers during the Cold War. (a) Discuss the causes of the Cold War. (b) Describe two ways in which the Soviet government exerted its power in the world during this period.

3. Despite Soviet control, Eastern Europeans yearned for freedom. Select two Eastern European countries and explain how each achieved democracy by the 1990s.

4. The shift from communism to capitalism is proving difficult. Select one former communist nation. (a) Discuss at least two problems this nation faces in moving toward a free market economy. (b) What progress has it made toward resolving these problems?

5. Writers play an important role in society. (a) Discuss the role of writers in Russian society. (b) How have they been censored?

Thinking Critically

1. Making Global Connections (a) How can the United States help the former communist nations make the shift to democracy and a free market economy? (b) Do you believe it should help? Explain.

2. Synthesizing Information Read the quotation by Alexander Solzhenitsyn on page 760. How do you think Stalin would have reacted to Solzhenitsyn's view of art?

Applying Your Skills

1. Using Visual Evidence Answer the following questions based on the pictures on pages 744, 747, and 749. (a) How did many Russian people react to the changes in the Soviet Union? (b) Why would it be difficult for Russian society to return to the past?

2. Analyzing a Poem Reread the poem "Babi Yar" on page 762. (a) What is the subject of the poem? (b) How does Yevtushenko describe Babi Yar? (c) What mood does the poem convey? (d) Why do you think Yevtushenko wrote the poem? (See Skill Lesson, page 541.)

SKILL LESSON 15

Reading an Organizational Chart: The European Community

A chart provides a great deal of information in a simple, easy-to-follow way. In the chart below, the arrangement of information in rows and columns helps you to understand the branches of an organization. It also helps you to compare and relate the branches to one another.

The European Community, or EC, was created in 1957, when it was known as the European Economic Community or Common Market. Rather than compete with one another, the member nations of the EC cooperate for their mutual economic benefit. As a unit, they import and export more goods than any individual country in the world. They form the main trading partner of the United States. Study the chart of the EC below, using the following steps to guide you.

1. **Identify the parts of the chart.** (a) What is the title of the chart? (b) According to the headings, what information does each column give? (c) Which row contains information about the branch known as the Court of Justice?
2. **Read the information in the chart.** (a) What are the four branches of the EC? (b) Which branch has the power to propose legislation? How many members does this branch have? How long do the members serve? (c) Which branch is the judicial branch? What are its powers?
3. **Draw conclusions from the chart.** (a) Study the information about members of the four branches. Do the larger, or more populous, member nations of the EC seem to have greater influence? Explain. (b) What kind of control does each branch have over legislation? (c) What do you think might be the advantages and disadvantages of having an advisory branch like the European Parliament?

The European Community

Branch	Members	How chosen	Term	Powers
Commission (Executive)	17 commissioners (2 from each of 5 larger member nations; 1 from each of 7 smaller member nations)	By unanimous agreement of member nations	4 years	Carries out treaties that created the EC Has sole power to propose and carry out legislation
Council of Ministers (Legislative)	Each member nation is represented (number of votes roughly in proportion to its size)	By governments of individual member nations	Determined by governments of individual member nations	Accepts or rejects legislation proposed by Commission
European Parliament (Advisory)	518 members (percentage per member nation based roughly on its population)	By voters in individual member nations	5 years	Debates proposed legislation; advises both Commission and Council Can expel entire Commission with a two-thirds vote Can reject a draft budget
Court of Justice (Judicial)	13 judges (1 from each member nation plus 1 other judge)	By unanimous agreement of member nations	6 years	Decides whether actions of other branches and private groups comply with EC rules Decisions are final and binding

SKILL LESSON 16

Identifying Cultural Bias: An Englishman Looks at the Russian People

Primary sources such as eyewitness accounts can be valuable sources of information about other cultures. However, the writer's cultural background can influence how a writer interprets what he or she sees. This kind of distortion of judgment is called cultural bias. A writer, for example, might suggest that another culture is inferior because its members work, eat, or pray differently from the members of the writer's culture.

The excerpt at right is from the book *Russians as People,* written by Wright Miller in 1961. An Englishman, Miller visited communist Russia several times before he wrote the book. Analyze the excerpt for cultural bias, using the following steps to guide you.

1. **Study the content of the excerpt.** What does Miller say about the following characteristics of the Russian people: (a) the expressions on their faces, (b) the way they treat one another on the street, (c) the way they board the Moscow Metro (subway)?
2. **Analyze the excerpt for cultural bias.** (a) What words does Miller use to describe the way Russians must feel about themselves? (b) According to the writer, what is the best way for a crowd to board a subway train? (c) What action words does he use to describe Russians boarding a subway train? (d) How does he describe the delay created by the boarding?
3. **Evaluate the excerpt for fairness and accuracy.** (a) What seems to be Miller's attitude toward the Russians? (b) Do you think this primary source provides a fair picture of the Russian people? Explain.

“Almost all these Russian faces had one thing in common. They were peculiarly expressionless and detached; they seemed neither very self-aware nor aware of much outside themselves.

There was no challenge in people's eyes as they looked at each other in passing; in fact they looked at each other but little. They bumped into one another without apology and apparently without offence. . . . They must all feel themselves, I thought, to be members of one inconsequent [unimportant] family.

Presently I was able to observe that instructive Russian trait, the inability to form a queue [waiting line]. And the significant aspect of this seemed to me . . . the fact that their unregulated ways so rarely cause bad feeling.

In the Moscow Metro, for instance, the doors open to the same width as in the underground trains of other countries; if two or three persons were to step in neatly abreast, the crowd would soon be absorbed. But this, presumably, would be too great a reversal of Russian habit. A great hemisphere of passengers hurls itself against the doors, and of the eight or nine persons jammed in the opening, perhaps one is at first shot into the carriage. . . . As the jam follows him, hats are stripped off heads, buttons ripped off coats, and enormous officers . . . are tossed about like logs in a swell [wave]. They grin and do not mind. Hardly anyone minds. The delay is stupid, but eventually the carriage is filled. And the secret of it all seems to be that the crowd pushes, but no one person pushes, so that there is no one to get angry with.”

WORLD

The One Great Heart

Alexander Solzhenitsyn

INTRODUCTION In 1945, Russian writer Alexander Solzhenitsyn (1918–) was sentenced to eight years in prison for writing letters critical of Stalin. After surviving prison camps in Siberia, Solzhenitsyn became famous for his novels about these experiences. Solzhenitsyn was awarded the Nobel Prize for literature in 1970 but was not allowed to go to Sweden to receive the award. The following is an excerpt from the acceptance speech he could not deliver in person.

Vocabulary Before you read the selection, find the meaning of these words in a dictionary: concept, aggregate, reciprocal, instantaneous, abstraction, jurisdiction, salvation, assimilate, partisans, concisely, acute, periphery, inexorably, vanquish.

I am, however, encouraged by a keen sense of WORLD LITERATURE as the one great heart that beats for the cares and misfortunes of our world, even though each corner sees and experiences them in a different way.

In past times, also, besides age-old national literatures there existed a concept of world literature as the link between the summits of national literatures and as the aggregate of reciprocal literary influences. . . .

Today, between writers of one country and the readers and writers of another, there is an almost instantaneous reciprocity, as I myself know. My books, unpublished, alas, in my own country, despite hasty and often bad translations have quickly found a responsive world readership. . . .

As I have understood it and experienced it myself, world literature is no longer an abstraction or a generalized concept invented by literary critics, but a common body and common spirit, a living, heartfelt unity reflecting the growing spiritual unity of mankind. State borders still turn crimson, heated red-hot by electric fences and machine-gun fire; some ministries of internal affairs still suppose that literature is "an internal affair" of the countries under their jurisdiction; and newspaper headlines still herald, "They have no right to interfere in our internal affairs!"

Meanwhile, no such thing as INTERNAL AFFAIRS remains on our crowded Earth. Mankind's salvation lies exclusively in everyone's making everything his business. . . . Literature, one of the most sensitive and responsive tools of human existence, has been the first to pick up, adopt, and assimilate this sense of the growing unity of mankind. . . .

I think that world literature has the power in these frightening times to help mankind see itself accurately despite what is advocated by partisans and by parties. It has the power to transmit the condensed experience of one region to another, so that different scales of values are combined, and so that one people accurately and concisely knows the true history of another with a power of recognition and acute awareness as if it had lived through that history itself—and could thus be spared repeating old mistakes. At the same time, perhaps we ourselves may succeed in developing our own WORLDWIDE VIEW, like any man, with the center of the eye seeing what is nearby but the periphery of vision taking in what is happening in the rest of the world. We will make correlations and maintain worldwide standards.

LITERATURE

Who, if not writers, are to condemn their own unsuccessful governments (in some states this is the easiest way to make a living; everyone who is not too lazy does it) as well as society itself, whether for its cowardly humiliation or for its self-satisfied weakness, or the lightheaded escapades of the young, or the youthful pirates brandishing knives?

We will be told: What can literature do against the pitiless onslaught of naked violence? Let us not forget that violence does not and cannot flourish by itself; it is inevitably intertwined with LYING. Between them there is the closest, the most profound and natural bond: nothing screens violence except lies, and the only way lies can hold out is by violence. Whoever has once announced violence as his METHOD must inexorably choose lying as his PRINCIPLE. . . .

The simple act of an ordinary courageous man is not to take part, not to support lies! Let *that* come into the world and even reign over it, but not through me. Writers and artists can do more: they can VANQUISH LIES! In the struggle against lies, art has always won and always will. Conspicuously, incontestably for everyone. Lies can stand up against much in the world, but not against art.

Once lies have been dispelled, the repulsive nakedness of violence will be exposed—and hollow violence will collapse.

That, my friends, is why I think we can help the world in its red-hot hour: not by the nay-saying of having no armaments, not by abandoning oneself to the carefree life, but by going into battle!

In Russian, proverbs about TRUTH are favorites. They persistently express the considerable, bitter, grim experience of the people, often astonishingly:

ONE WORD OF TRUTH OUTWEIGHS THE WORLD.

Art and literature are two great forms of human expression that link all peoples. By communicating universal ideas and emotions, artists and writers enable us to understand others' lives and concerns. This painting, *Night in Viterbsk* by Marc Chagall, like Solzhenitsyn's speech, expresses "the cares and misfortunes of our world." How did the two men use their works to help their own people search for truth in Soviet society?

THINKING ABOUT LITERATURE

1. According to Solzhenitsyn, how is world literature "one great heart"?
2. How are lies and violence interconnected?
3. **Defending a Position** (a) Do you agree or disagree that "no such thing as INTERNAL AFFAIRS remains on our crowded Earth. Mankind's salvation lies exclusively in everyone's making everything his business"? (b) Do you agree or disagree that literature can act as a unifying force in the world? Support your positions.

Theater in Europe and America

An unruly mob gathered outside a New York City theater. Inside, Charles Macready, a British actor, was performing in Shakespeare's *Macbeth*. Fans of Macready's American rival, Edwin Forrest, had tried to disrupt the performance by throwing rotten eggs and fruit onstage. Ejected from the theater, the angry fans remained outside. Soon, the crowd numbered in the hundreds. People began to shout and throw rocks. Even the arrival of 200 infantry troops could not stop the mob. The soldiers opened fire, wounding or killing more than 16 people.

The Astor Place Riot took place on May 10, 1849. Today, it is hard to believe that a rivalry between two Shakespearean actors could spark such violence. But the incident shows how passionate Americans' feelings about the theater could become. It also shows the close connection between American theater and its European roots.

British Roots

The first theatrical tradition English colonists brought to America was to have no theater at all. The Puritans who settled in New England believed that plays were sinful. In Massachusetts, anyone who either acted in or attended a stage play had to pay a heavy fine.

Still, British actors soon began to tour the colonies. In 1752, William Hallam, a famous but bankrupt London actor, brought his troupe of players to Williamsburg, Virginia. Looking at the dense forests that surrounded him, Hallam wondered whether a theater could survive in "this wilderness." But Hallam's company was a great success. It performed in Virginia for nine months, then toured Charleston, Philadelphia, and New York. Soon, the colonists themselves started to establish theatrical troupes.

Hallam also brought British theatrical organization to the colonies. In continental Europe, theaters were supported either by rich patrons or by royalty. By contrast, British theaters were independent, profit-making ventures. American theaters quickly adopted this tradition, which they still follow.

Colonial American theaters usually presented English plays. Shakespeare's works were the most popular fare, although tragedies such as *Romeo and Juliet* were often given a happy ending. Even the earliest American play to be produced professionally, *The Prince of Parthia,* was based on British history.

In the 1770s, the colonies declared their independence from Britain. A decade later, American playwrights did the same. Royall Tyler wrote *The Contrast.* The prologue, or introduction to this comedy, boasted:

> "Exult each patriot heart!—
> this night is shown
> A piece, which we may fairly call our own; . . .
> Why should our thoughts
> to distant countries
> roam,
> When each refinement may
> be found at home?"

Yet, despite its American setting and theme, *The Contrast* was closely modeled on English comedies of the 1700s.

Throughout the 1800s, British theater continued to inspire the new nation. British stars regularly visited the United States. Some stayed, including Junius Brutus Booth. Booth's son Edwin became the greatest American actor of his day. Another son, John Wilkes Booth, gained fame first as a dashing matinee idol, and then as the assassin of Abraham Lincoln.

American actors began to tour Europe at this time. For example, the African American actor Ira Aldridge played the part of Shakespeare's Othello throughout the continent. An Austrian critic wrote, "Ira Aldridge is without doubt the greatest actor that has ever been seen in Europe."

A Continuing Influence

By the 1920s, other European influences had begun to affect American theater. The realistic plays of Norway's Henrik Ibsen inspired bold American playwrights to turn away from simple, sentimental melodramas. Instead, Americans such as Eugene O'Neill began to write realistic psychological dramas.

In Russia, Konstantin Stanislavsky created a method of "truthful" acting. Stanislavsky disliked exaggerated gestures and obvious speechmaking. As the director of the Moscow Art Theater, he created a system in which performers used their own experiences to recreate the emotions of the characters they were playing onstage.

When the Moscow Art Theater visited New York in 1922, actress Maria Ouspenskaya (oosh pehn SKI uh) decided to stay there. (She later appeared as the mysterious gypsy in the 1940 horror movie *The Wolf Man*.) Ouspenskaya then set up a drama school. The students included a young actor named Lee Strasberg. He and others adapted many of Stanislavsky's ideas and introduced them to a new generation of American actors and actresses.

By the 1950s, the American version of Stanislavsky's system had become known as "the Method." The most popular Method actor was Marlon Brando. Brando did not make grand gestures and speeches. In fact, he often mumbled his lines. Yet, his powerful, honest acting thrilled audiences. Brando's work in various plays and movies, such as *A Streetcar Named Desire*, influenced later actors and actresses, including Al Pacino, Robert De Niro, and Meryl Streep.

Today, American plays and performers are popular worldwide. Yet, European influence remains strong. In the early 1990s, some of the most popular musicals on Broadway—*Cats, The Phantom of the Opera, Les Misérables,* and *Miss Saigon*—were originally from Britain.

1. Which British traditions have influenced American theater?
2. **Applying Information** How are Stanislavsky's ideas about acting connected to the growth of realism in art and literature?
3. **Writing Across Cultures** Rewrite the lines from the prologue to *The Contrast* in your own words. Then explain whether you think many Americans still have this attitude toward other cultures.

UNIT 8 REVIEW

Reviewing the Main Ideas

1. (a) Describe the relative location of Western Europe. (b) How has the geography of Western Europe contributed to cultural diffusion in the region?
2. (a) How did Charlemagne try to unify Europe during the Early Middle Ages? (b) How are modern leaders trying to unify Europe?
3. Describe how each of the following marked a turning point in the history of Europe: (a) the fall of the Roman Empire in the West, (b) the Crusades, (c) the Renaissance, (d) the Industrial Revolution, (e) World War I, (f) World War II, (g) the end of the Cold War.
4. (a) Describe the relative location of the former Soviet Union. (b) How has climate influenced the area's history?
5. Compare feudalism in Western Europe with feudalism in Russia.
6. Describe how each of the following either brought Russia closer to the West or served to isolate it even more: (a) adoption of Byzantine Christianity, (b) Ivan the Great, (c) Peter the Great, (d) Decembrist Revolt, (e) Russian Revolution, (f) World War II.
7. (a) How did Lenin adapt the ideas of Karl Marx for the Soviet Union? (b) How did Stalin change Lenin's economic policies? (c) Describe two ways in which life in the Soviet Union changed under communism.
8. (a) How did Khrushchev try to ease tensions between the Soviet Union and the United States during the 1960s? (b) What reforms did Mikhail Gorbachev introduce to the Soviet Union during the 1980s? (c) How did his reforms affect the economic and political structure of the Soviet Union?
9. (a) How was the economy of Eastern Europe linked to the economy of the Soviet Union after World War II? (b) Explain how ethnic diversity contributed to upheavals in Eastern Europe and the Soviet Union during the 1990s.

Thinking Critically

1. **Applying Information** What events in Western Europe's social and political history led to the development of democratic governments? What events in Russian social and political history led to the development of an autocracy?
2. **Analyzing** How did the division of Germany symbolize the Cold War in Europe?
3. **Making Global Connections** Compare the American Revolution, the French Revolution, and the Russian Revolution. (a) What were the goals of each revolution? (b) How was each revolution carried out? (c) What were the results of each revolution?

Applying Your Skills

1. **Analyzing Poetry** Compare the poems by Wilfred Owen, William Wordsworth, and Alexander Blok that appear on pages 700, 701, and 762. (a) What mood does each poem express? (b) How does the poem each poet has written reflect the time in which he lived? (See Skill Lesson, page 541.)
2. **Analyzing a Political Cartoon** Study the cartoon below. (a) What do the railroad tracks symbolize? (b) What do the workers symbolize? (c) Explain why the tracks do not meet. (d) Write a title and a caption for this cartoon. (e) What point do you think the cartoonist is trying to make? (See Skill Lesson, page 540.)

Learning by Doing

1. **Creating Maps** On an outline map of Western Europe, label all countries, oceans, and seas. Using a map key, identify the 12 members of the European Community. (See the map on page 692.) On an outline map of the Commonwealth of Independent States, label all the new republics and the dates on which they gained independence. Label all seas, oceans, and rivers. (See the map on page 754.) Due to rapidly changing events in the world, you may need to consult more recent sources.
2. **Conducting a Debate** As a group project, organize a debate on the European Community's plans not only to eliminate trade barriers but also to create a truly unified region. Prepare to defend or oppose these plans, which include establishing a single currency, called "ecu," creating a regional central bank, establishing a common European citizenship, and setting up a common defense policy.
3. **Playing a Review Game** As a group project, divide the class into six teams. Each team should choose a different chapter in Unit 8 and write 15 to 20 questions and answers on index cards. Base the questions on the "Identify" and "Define" topics in the Section Reviews. Appoint a question reader and a scorekeeper for each team. Grant one point for each correct answer. Create three sets of two teams. Pair two teams. The team that begins asking questions keeps its turn until someone gives a wrong answer. Then, the other team takes over. The team that has the most correct responses wins.

WRITER'S Workshop

Writing a One-Paragraph Answer

Use this checklist to prepare and write a one-paragraph answer. If you need help with any of the steps, refer to earlier Writer's Workshop lessons.

1. Analyze the question. Identify the key word—such as *how, why,* or *what*—and other clues. Determine what the key word is telling you to do. Note the topic limits set by the other clues.
2. Write a topic sentence that states the main idea of the answer. Try to reword the question as a topic sentence.
3. Select details that support the main idea. Keep the key word and the topic limits in mind while you are choosing these details.
4. Arrange the supporting details in a logical order. Consider whether to use time order, comparison order, order of importance, or cause-and-effect order.
5. Write detail sentences to support the main idea. Use transition words that are appropriate for the order you are using.
6. Reread your answer. Make necessary revisions. Correct grammatical or spelling errors.

Practice Use the checklist at left to write a one-paragraph answer for this question: *After World War II, how did the Soviet Union encourage the spread of communism throughout the world?*

Writing to Learn

1. Imagine that you were born and raised in East Berlin. Write a diary entry that describes your impressions and feelings about the opening of the Berlin Wall on November 9, 1989. In your first draft, write a topic sentence that summarizes your reactions. Add specific details telling what actually took place. Revise your work for coherence and clarity. Then, proofread and make a final copy of it. Publish your diary entry by using it for a bulletin board display.
2. Devise and write a plan for converting the Commonwealth of Independent States from a centrally planned economy to a free market economy. Write a topic sentence setting forth your goals. Add specific details telling how you plan to accomplish these goals. Revise your plan for clarity and completeness. Proofread and make a final copy of it. Then, present your plan to your classmates and discuss its possibilities.

dům mód

REFERENCE SECTION

ALASKA
(U.S.)
Yukon
Mackenzie
CANADA
GREENLAND
(Denmark)
ARCTIC
Svalbard Is.
(Norway)
Reykjavik
ICELAND
NORWAY
FINLAND
Helsinki
St. Petersburg
SWEDEN
EST.
LAT.
LITH.
Moscow
BELARUS
Kiev
UKRAINE
EUROPE
(see inset map)
FRANCE
SPAIN
ITALY
ARMENIA
TURKEY
NORTH
AMERICA
Montreal
Ottawa
Chicago
San Francisco
New York
Washington, D.C.
UNITED STATES
Colorado
Ohio
Mississippi
Azores
(Port.)
NORTH
PACIFIC
OCEAN
Houston
New Orleans
BERMUDA
(U.K.)
Algiers
Tunis
TUNISIA
Rabat
MOROCCO
ALGERIA
LIBYA
MIDDLE
EAST
(see inset map)
EGYPT
MEXICO
THE
BAHAMAS
Havana
CUBA
Mexico City
DOMINICAN
REPUBLIC
NORTH
ATLANTIC OCEAN
Canary Is.
(Spain)
W. SAHARA
(Morocco)
Port-au-Prince
Puerto Rico (U.S.)
ST. KITTS AND NEVIS
ANTIGUA & BARBUDA
DOMINICA
GUATEMALA
Guatemala
BELIZE
JAMAICA
HAITI
Santo Domingo
ST. LUCIA
HONDURAS
San Salvador
Tegucigalpa
EL SALVADOR
Managua
NICARAGUA
BARBADOS
ST. VINCENT & THE GRENADINES
GRENADA
TRINIDAD
& TOBAGO
San José
COSTA RICA
Panamá
PANAMA
Caracas
VENEZUELA
GUYANA
Georgetown
Paramaribo
SURINAME
FR. GUIANA
(France)
Bogotá
COLOMBIA
Orinoco
MAURITANIA
Nouakchott
SENEGAL
CAPE VERDE
Dakar
GAMBIA
GUINEA-BISSAU
MALI
NIGER
AFRICA
Niamey
CHAD
Nile
Bamako
BURKINA
FASO
GUINEA
Conakry
Freetown
SIERRA LEONE
Monrovia
LIBERIA
Yamoussoukro
CÔTE
D'IVOIRE
GHANA
Accra
Lomé
TOGO
BENIN
Porto-Novo
Lagos
NIGERIA
Abuja
N'Djamena
SUDAN
C. AFR.
REP.
Bangui
CAMEROON
Yaoundé
EQ. GUINEA
Libreville
SÃO TOMÉ AND PRÍNCIPE
GABON
CONGO
Zaire
UGANDA
Kampala
KENYA
Nairobi
RWANDA
ZAIRE
BURUNDI
Brazzaville
Kinshasa
CABINDA
(Angola)
TANZANIA
Dar es Salaam
Luanda
ANGOLA
MALAWI
Lilongwe
ZAMBIA
Lusaka
Harare
ZIMBABWE
NAMIBIA
Windhoek
BOTSWANA
Gaborone
MOZAMBIQUE
Maputo
Pretoria
SWAZILAND
Maseru
LESOTHO
SOUTH
AFRICA
Cape Town
Galapagos Is
(Ecuador)
Equator
Quito
ECUADOR
Negro
SOUTH
AMERICA
Amazon
Madeira
PERU
Lima
BRAZIL
São Francisco
SOUTH
PACIFIC OCEAN
BOLIVIA
La Paz
Sucre
Brasília
PARAGUAY
Asunción
São Paulo
Rio de Janeiro
SOUTH
ATLANTIC OCEAN
CHILE
Santiago
URUGUAY
Montevideo
Buenos Aires
ARGENTINA
Falkland Is.
(U.K.)
S. Georgia
(Falkland Is.)
ANTARCTICA
N
W
E
S
180°
160°W
140°W
120°W
100°W
80°W
60°W
40°W
20°W
0°
20°E
60°N
40°N
20°N
0°
20°S
EUROPE
0 250 Miles
0 250 Kilometers
NORWAY
Oslo
Stockholm
SWEDEN
N.
IRELAND
Dublin
IRELAND
UNITED
KINGDOM
DENMARK
Copenhagen
LATVIA
Riga
LITH.
Vilnius
(RUSSIA)
Minsk
BELARUS
POLAND
Warsaw
London
Amsterdam
Berlin
BELGIUM
Brussels
NETH.
Bonn
GERMANY
LUX.
Prague
CZECH
REP.
Kiev
UKRAINE
Paris
SLOVAKIA
Bratislava
MOLDOVA
LIECH.
Vienna
FRANCE
Bern
AUS.
Budapest
Kishinev
SWITZ.
Ljubljana
HUNGARY
SLOVENIA
Zagreb
ROMANIA
ANDORRA
ITALY
CROATIA
Belgrade
Danube
Bucharest
SAN
MARINO
BOS. &
HERZ.
SERBIA
Sarajevo
PORT.
SPAIN
MONACO
YUGO.
BULGARIA
Lisbon
Madrid
Sofia
Rome
MONT.
Tirane
MACE.
ALBANIA
GREECE
Athens
TURKEY
MEDITERRANEAN
SEA
MALTA

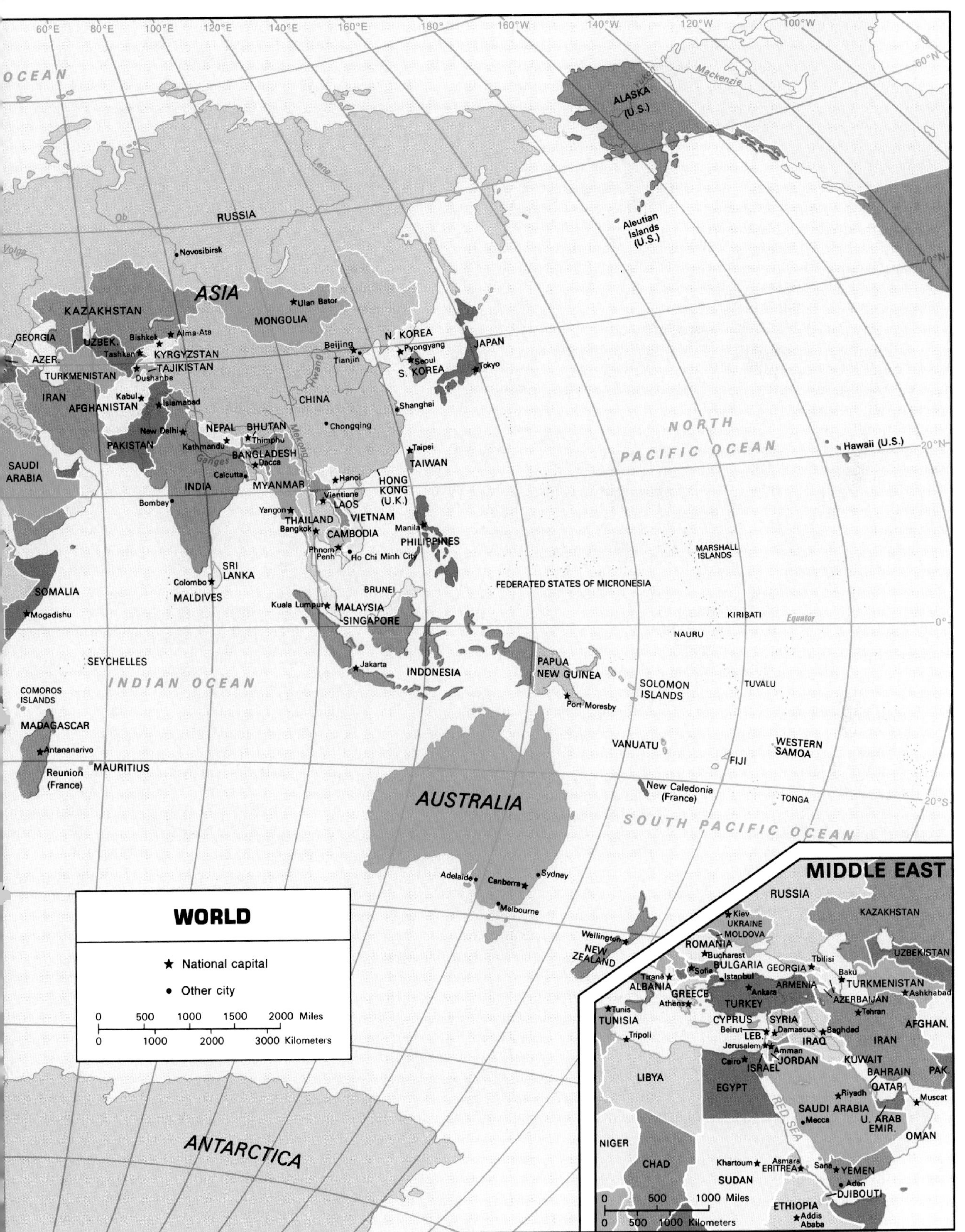
WORLD
National capital
Other city
0 500 1000 1500 2000 Miles
0 1000 2000 3000 Kilometers
ASIA
RUSSIA
KAZAKHSTAN
MONGOLIA
CHINA
N. KOREA
S. KOREA
JAPAN
INDIA
PAKISTAN
AFGHANISTAN
IRAN
NEPAL
BHUTAN
BANGLADESH
MYANMAR
THAILAND
LAOS
VIETNAM
CAMBODIA
MALAYSIA
SINGAPORE
INDONESIA
PHILIPPINES
TAIWAN
HONG KONG (U.K.)
SRI LANKA
MALDIVES
SOMALIA
SEYCHELLES
MADAGASCAR
MAURITIUS
Reunion (France)
COMOROS ISLANDS
AUSTRALIA
NEW ZEALAND
PAPUA NEW GUINEA
SOLOMON ISLANDS
VANUATU
FIJI
New Caledonia (France)
WESTERN SAMOA
TONGA
TUVALU
KIRIBATI
NAURU
MARSHALL ISLANDS
FEDERATED STATES OF MICRONESIA
Hawaii (U.S.)
ALASKA (U.S.)
Aleutian Islands (U.S.)
NORTH PACIFIC OCEAN
SOUTH PACIFIC OCEAN
INDIAN OCEAN
ANTARCTICA
MIDDLE EAST
RUSSIA
KAZAKHSTAN
UKRAINE
MOLDOVA
ROMANIA
BULGARIA
GEORGIA
ARMENIA
AZERBAIJAN
TURKMENISTAN
UZBEKISTAN
ALBANIA
GREECE
TURKEY
TUNISIA
CYPRUS
SYRIA
LEB.
IRAQ
IRAN
AFGHAN.
LIBYA
EGYPT
ISRAEL
JORDAN
KUWAIT
BAHRAIN
QATAR
PAK.
SAUDI ARABIA
U. ARAB EMIR.
OMAN
NIGER
CHAD
SUDAN
ERITREA
YEMEN
DJIBOUTI
ETHIOPIA
RED SEA
0 500 1000 Miles
0 500 1000 Kilometers

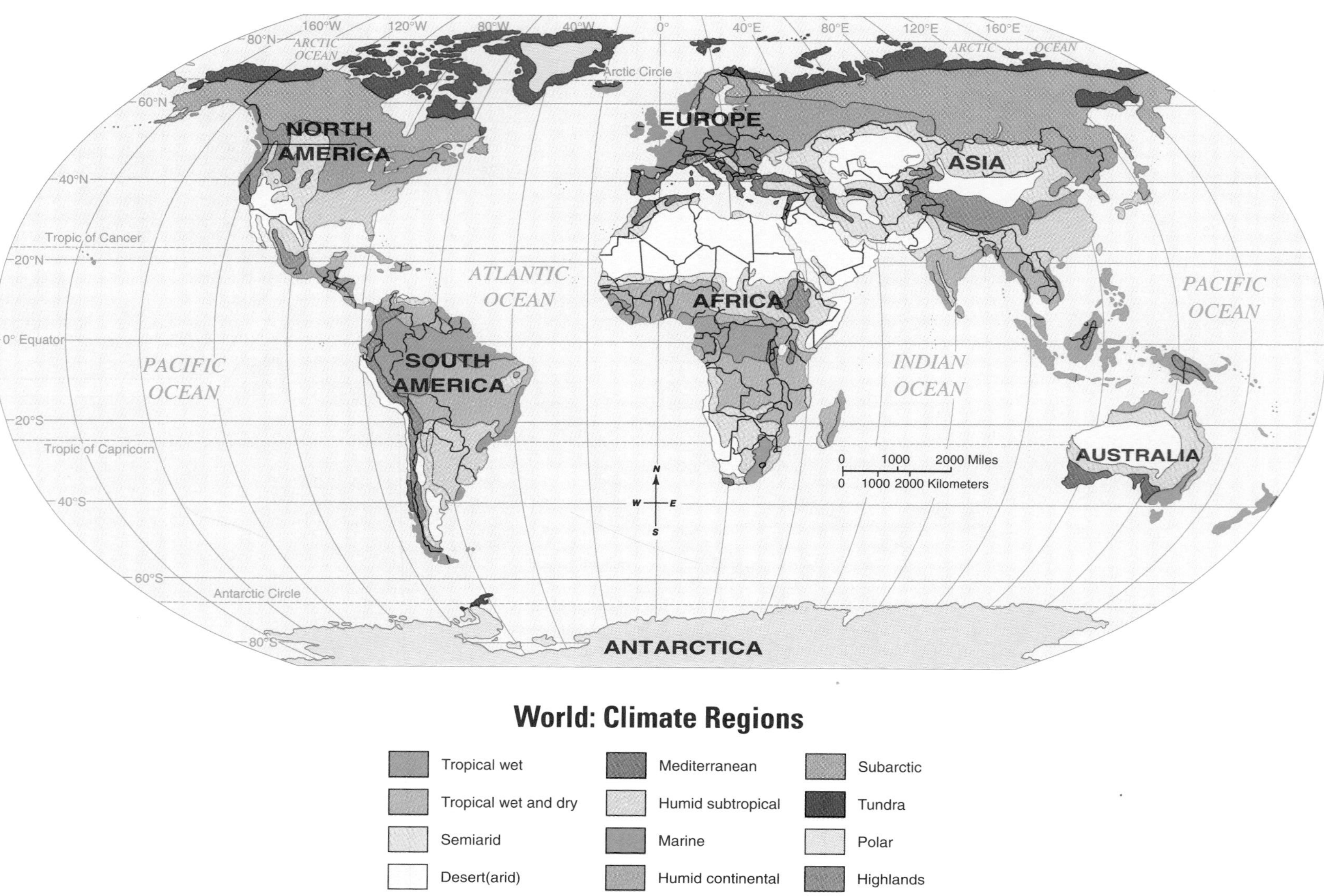
NORTH AMERICA
SOUTH AMERICA
EUROPE
AFRICA
ASIA
AUSTRALIA
ANTARCTICA
ARCTIC OCEAN
ATLANTIC OCEAN
PACIFIC OCEAN
INDIAN OCEAN
Arctic Circle
Tropic of Cancer
0° Equator
Tropic of Capricorn
Antarctic Circle
80°N
60°N
40°N
20°N
20°S
40°S
60°S
80°S
160°W
120°W
80°W
40°W
0°
40°E
80°E
120°E
160°E
0 1000 2000 Miles
0 1000 2000 Kilometers
N
S
W
E
World: Climate Regions
Tropical wet
Tropical wet and dry
Semiarid
Desert(arid)
Mediterranean
Humid subtropical
Marine
Humid continental
Subarctic
Tundra
Polar
Highlands

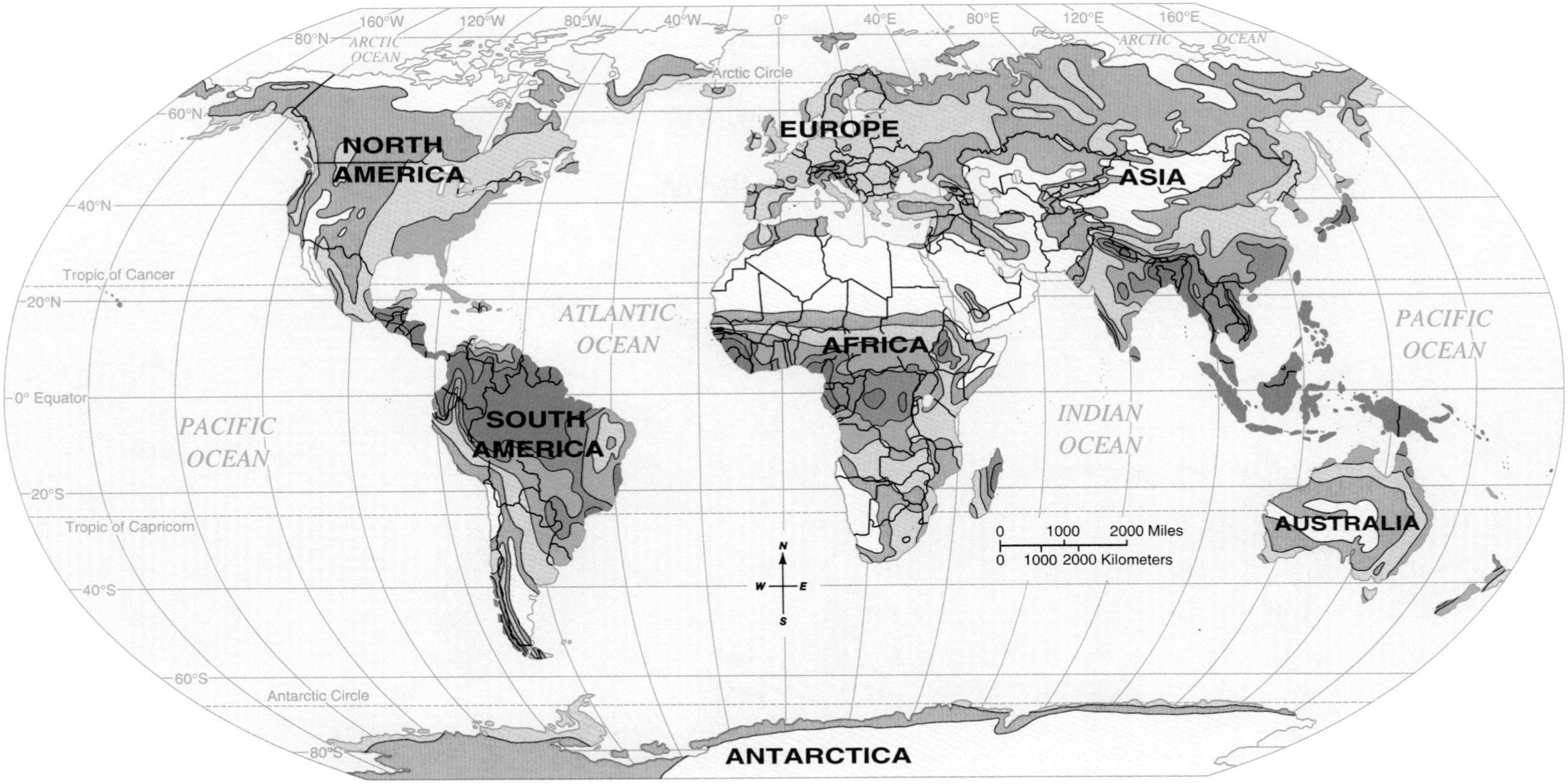

World: Average Yearly Precipitation

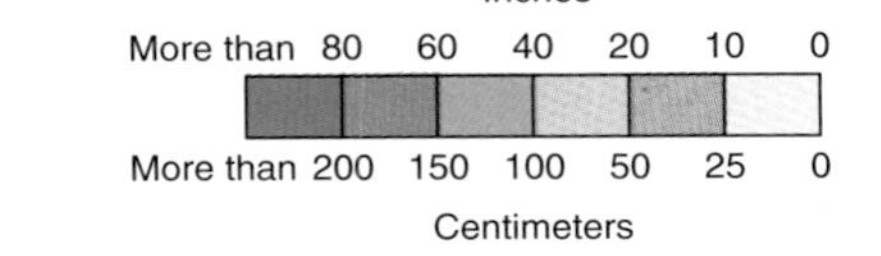

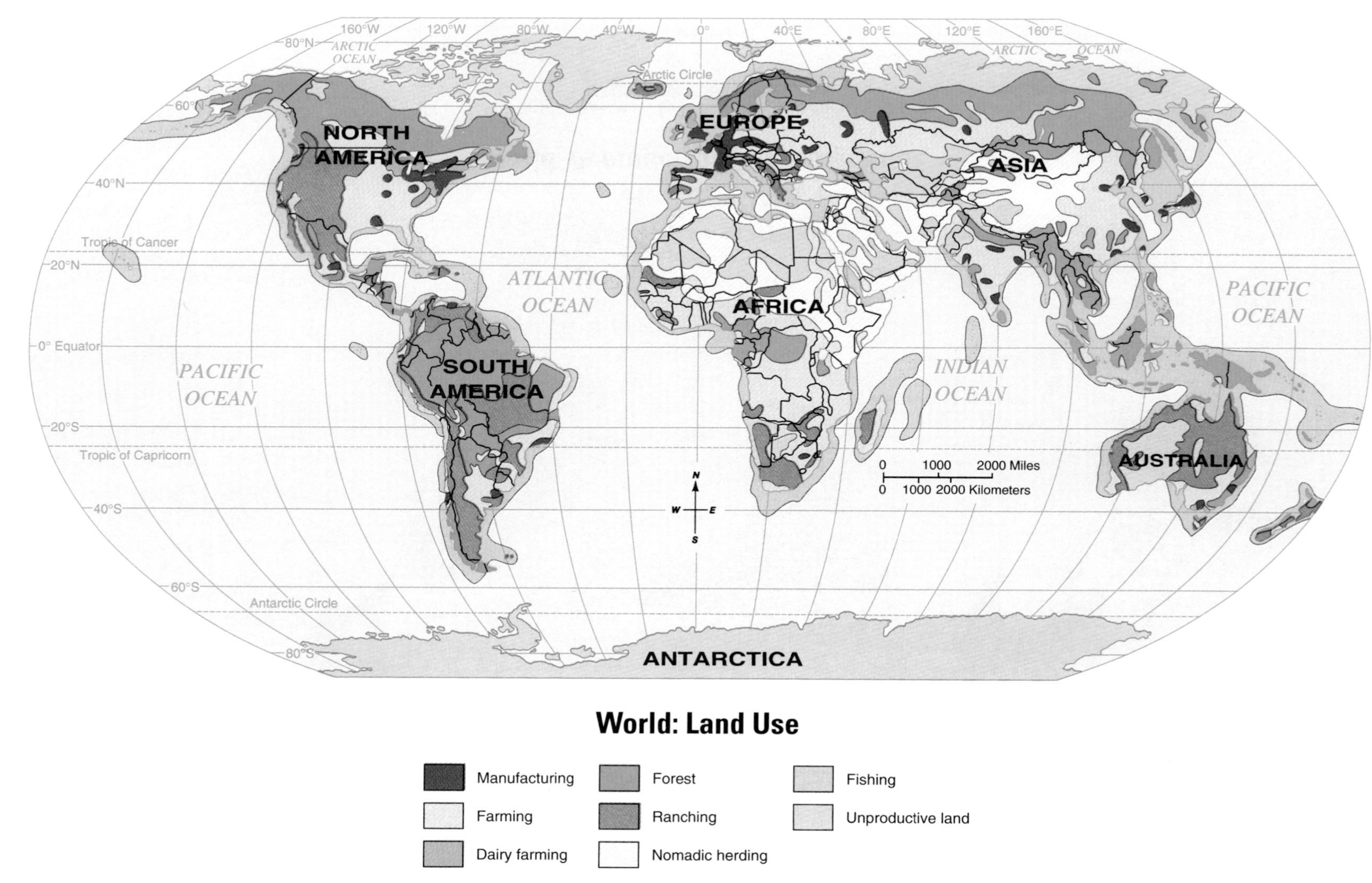

World: Land Use

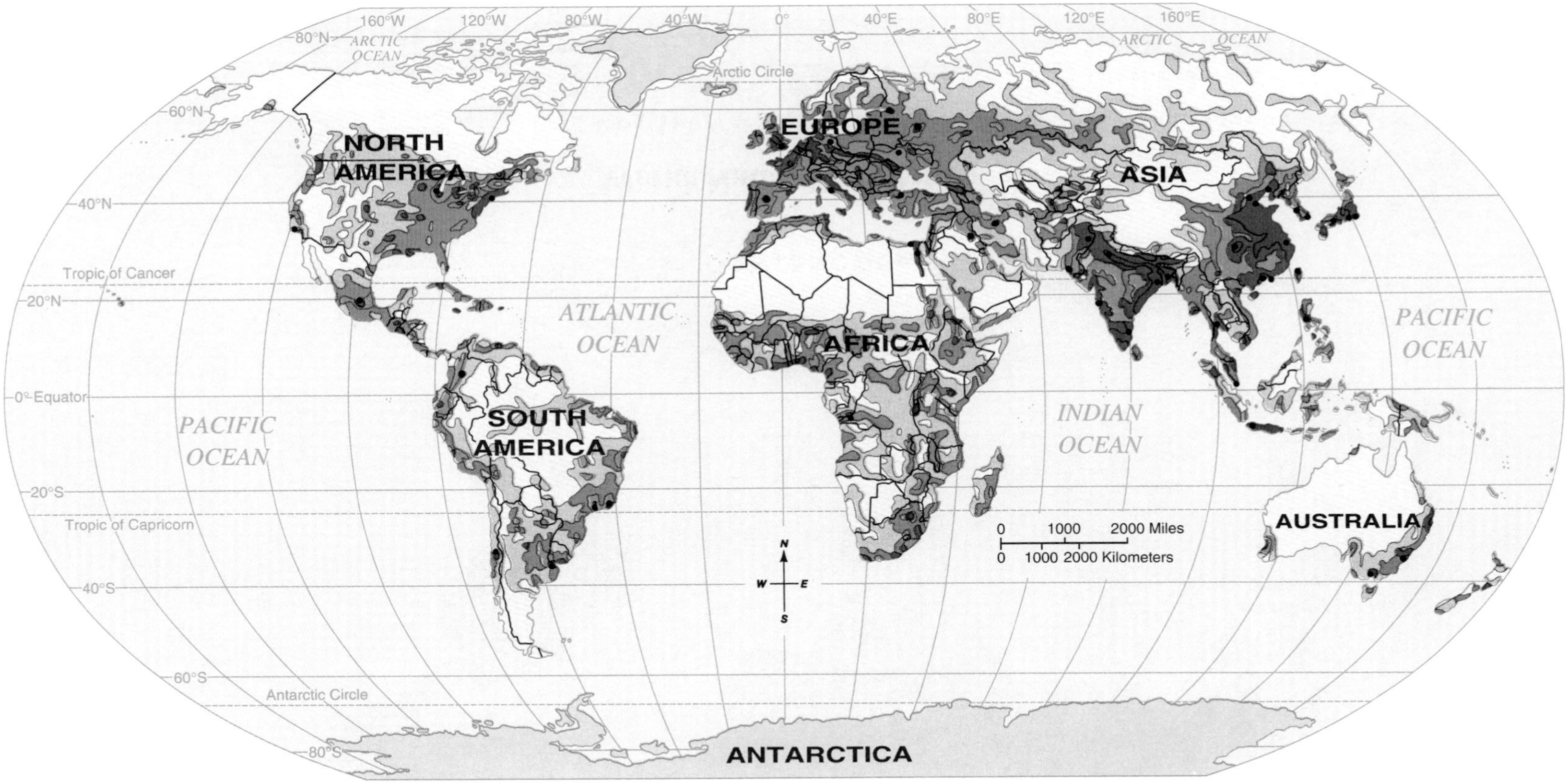

World: Population Density

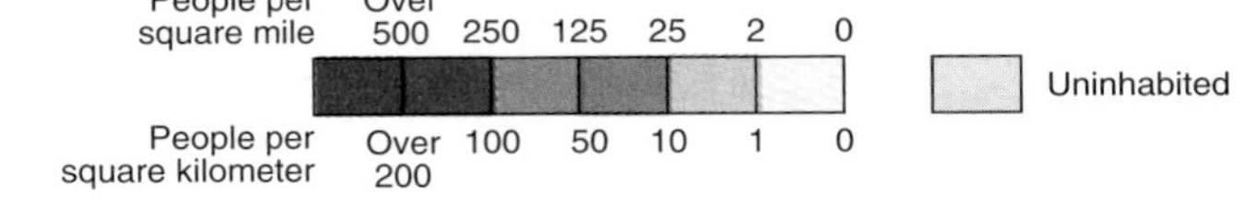

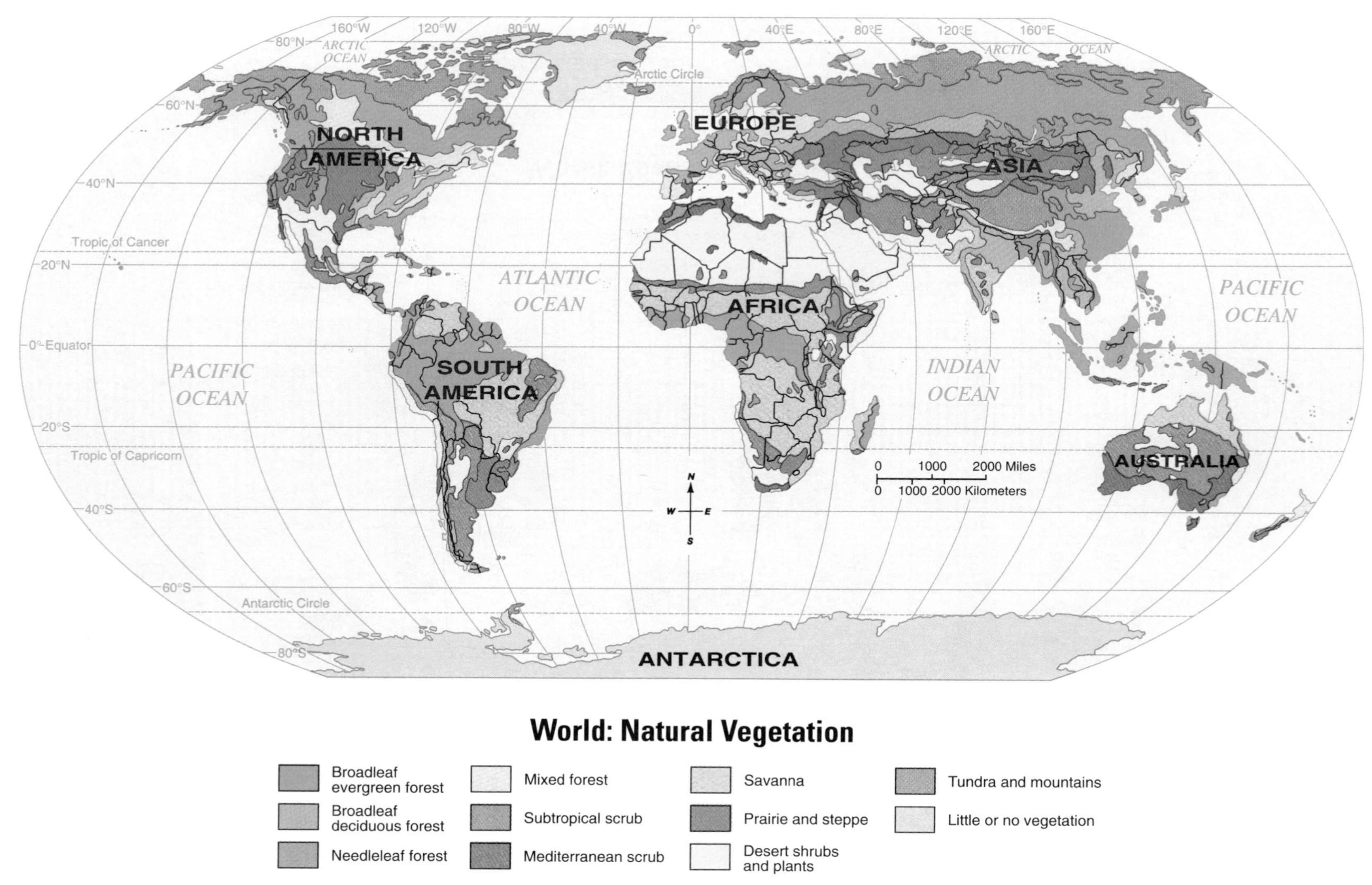

World: Natural Vegetation

WORLD DATA BANK

The information in the following charts and graphs is designed to help you understand more about the similarities and differences among nations. Most of the nations included are among the most populous in the world. Look for the qualities that each nation shares or does not share with other nations. Look also for relationships among the kinds of information presented about individual countries.

Population Statistics for Selected Countries

Countries	1960 (in millions)	1960 (percentage urban)	1990 (in millions)	1990 (percentage urban)	2010* (in millions)	2025* (in millions)
China	646.6	19	1,119.9	21	1,420.3	1,590.8
India	432.7	18	853.4	26	1,157.8	1,365.5
United States	180.7	70	251.4	74	299.0	333.7
Indonesia	94.2	15	189.4	26	237.9	282.5
Brazil	69.7	46	150.4	74	207.5	245.8
Japan	94.1	44	123.6	77	135.8	134.6
Nigeria	42.9	18	118.8	31	213.0	305.4
Pakistan	100.4	12	114.6	28	195.2	281.3
Italy	49.6	47	57.7	72	55.9	52.3
Turkey	27.5	32	56.7	53	83.4	102.7
Iran	21.5	33	55.6	54	100.6	141.4

*Projected

Sources: Population Reference Bureau 1990 World Population Data Sheet; *1960 United Nations Statistical Yearbook; 1972 United Nations Statistical Yearbook.*

Chart Skills (a) Compare the percentage of urban population for 1960 and 1990. What generalization can you make? (b) Which two nations show the smallest projected increase in population between 1990 and 2010?

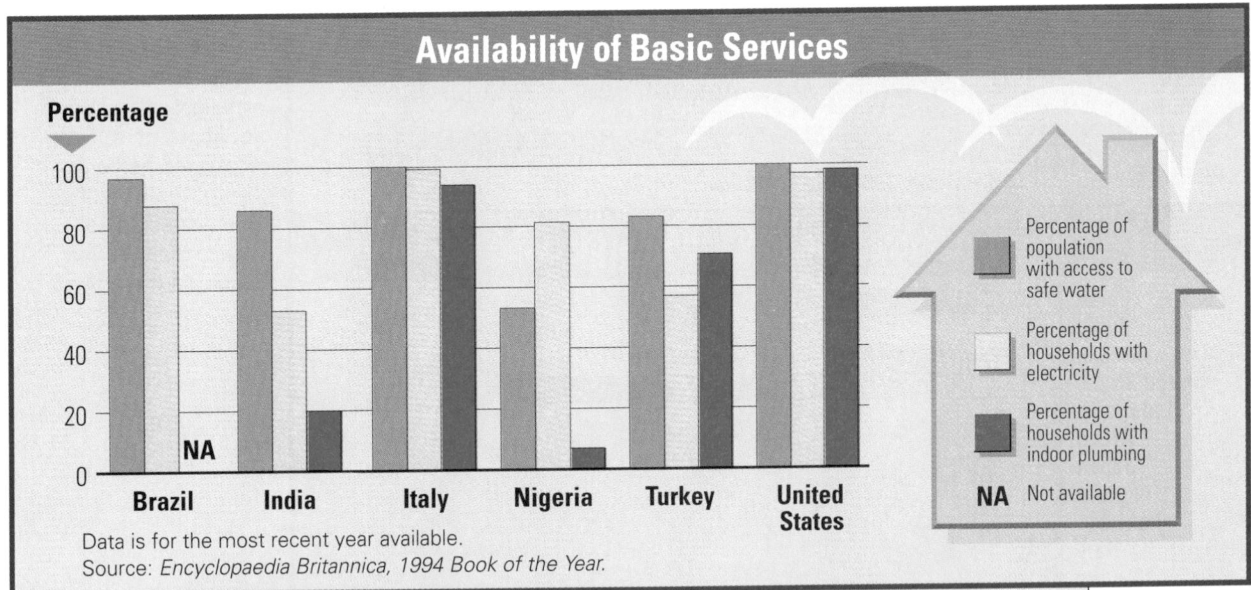

Data is for the most recent year available.
Source: *Encyclopaedia Britannica, 1994 Book of the Year.*

Graph Skills (a) Compare the availability of services with statistics in the chart above. Which three countries have the highest percentage of households with electricity? (b) Do these countries also have a large urban population?

Work Force Statistics for Selected Countries

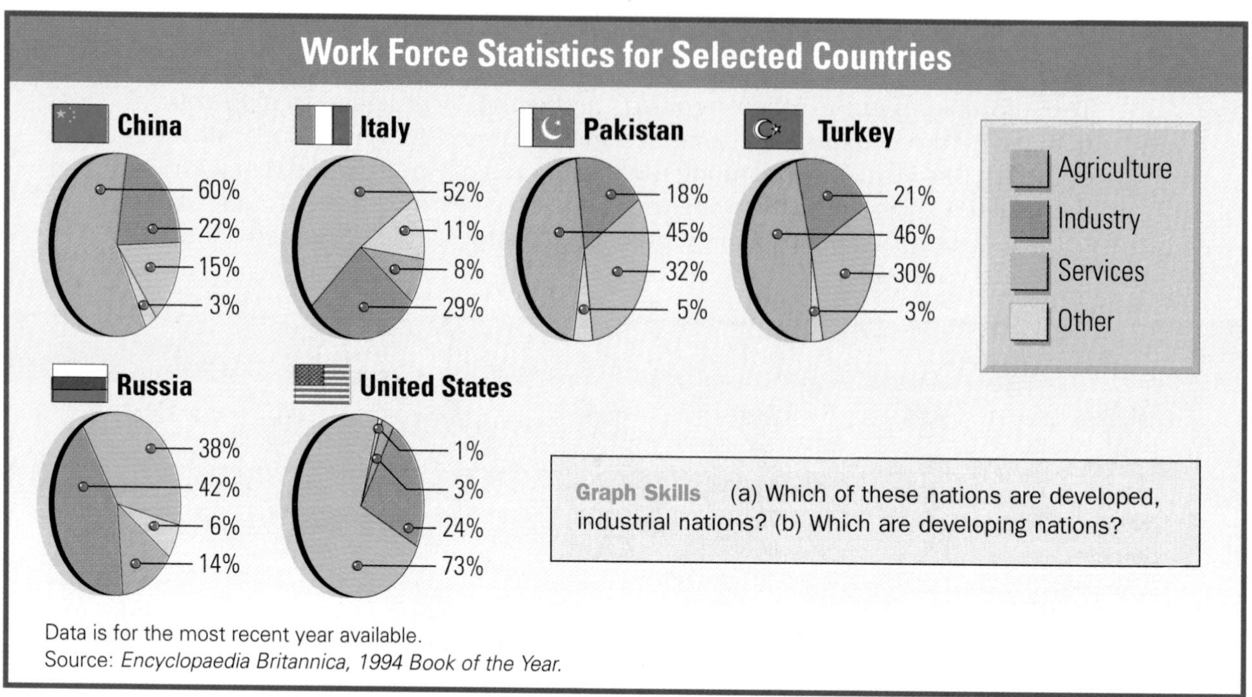

Graph Skills (a) Which of these nations are developed, industrial nations? (b) Which are developing nations?

Data is for the most recent year available.
Source: *Encyclopaedia Britannica, 1994 Book of the Year.*

Types of Energy Used For Electricity

(Percentage of National Total)

Country	Petroleum	Natural Gas	Coal	Hydro-electric	Nuclear
China	14	2	66	18	0
India	27	3	46	22	2
Russia	26	30	18	15	11
United States	35	18	18	9	20
Indonesia	51	25.5	4	19	.5
Brazil	6	.2	.4	92.8	.6
Japan	43	8	13	12	24
Nigeria	58	18	2	22	0
Pakistan	26	31	3	39	1
Italy	54	17	6	21	2
Turkey	35	.8	26	38	.2
Iran	62	24	2	12	0

Source: *Encyclopaedia Britannica, 1994 Book of the Year.*

Percentage of Total World Energy Used

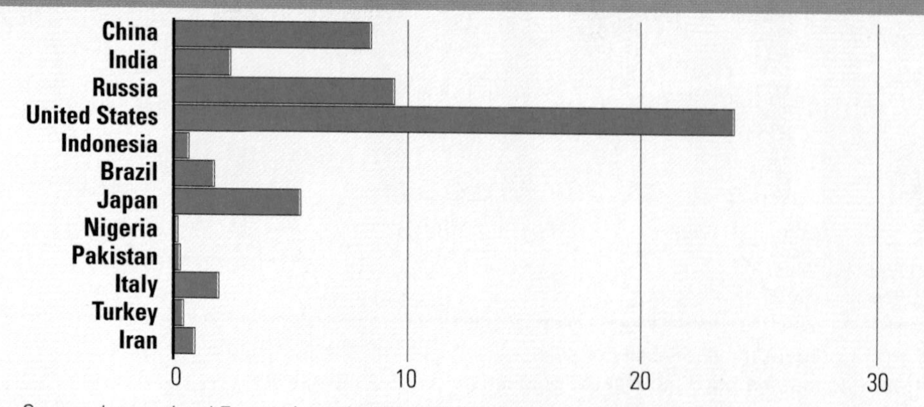

Source: *International Energy Annual, 1992,* U.S. Department of Energy.

Chart and Graph Skills (a) Which three countries use the greatest percentage of hydroelectric power? (b) Look at the maps on pages 164, 440, and 552. What do these countries have in common? (c) Which three countries use the largest amount of energy? (d) Which of these has the smallest population? (e) About what is the combined percentage of the world's energy used by all other countries not listed on the graph?

Social Indicators

	Infant mortality per 1,000 live births	Life expectancy (in years)	Persons per physician	Percentage of literacy	Persons per telephone	Persons per television
China	33	71	649	78	77	32
India	80	59	2,337	48	145	44
Russia	18	69	226	99	6	3
United States	9	76	416	96	1	1
Indonesia	90	58	6,861	78	122	17
Brazil	57	67	848	81	10	5
Japan	5	79	583	100	2	1
Nigeria	96	53	4,946	42	118	21
Pakistan	91	60	2,364	26	95	63
Italy	8	77	228	97	2	3
Turkey	54	70	1,108	81	6	6
Iran	66	65	2,685	65	25	26

Latest available figures
Sources: *Encyclopaedia Britannica, 1994 Book of the Year.*

Chart Skills (a) Which nations have the highest standard of living and the best health care? (b) Do any of these social indicators seem related to the percentage of the population that is urban? Explain.

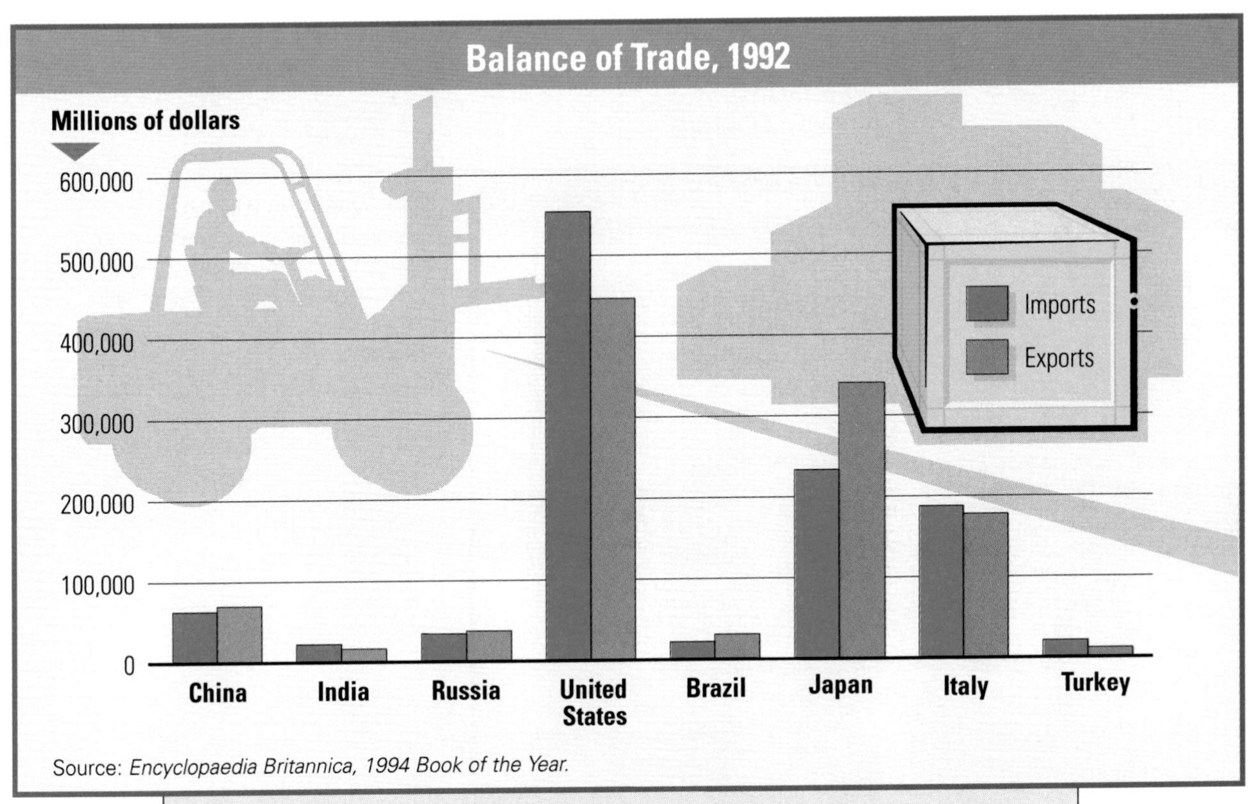

Source: *Encyclopaedia Britannica, 1994 Book of the Year.*

Graph Skills (a) Which four nations export more than they import? (b) Among the nations that import more than they export, which have the greatest imbalance?

External Debts of Developing Countries

Billions of dollars

90
80
70
60
50
40
30
20
10
0

1980 1991

Syria, Mozambique, Pakistan, Portugal, South Korea, Philippines, Nigeria, Turkey, China, Poland, Indonesia, India, Mexico, Brazil

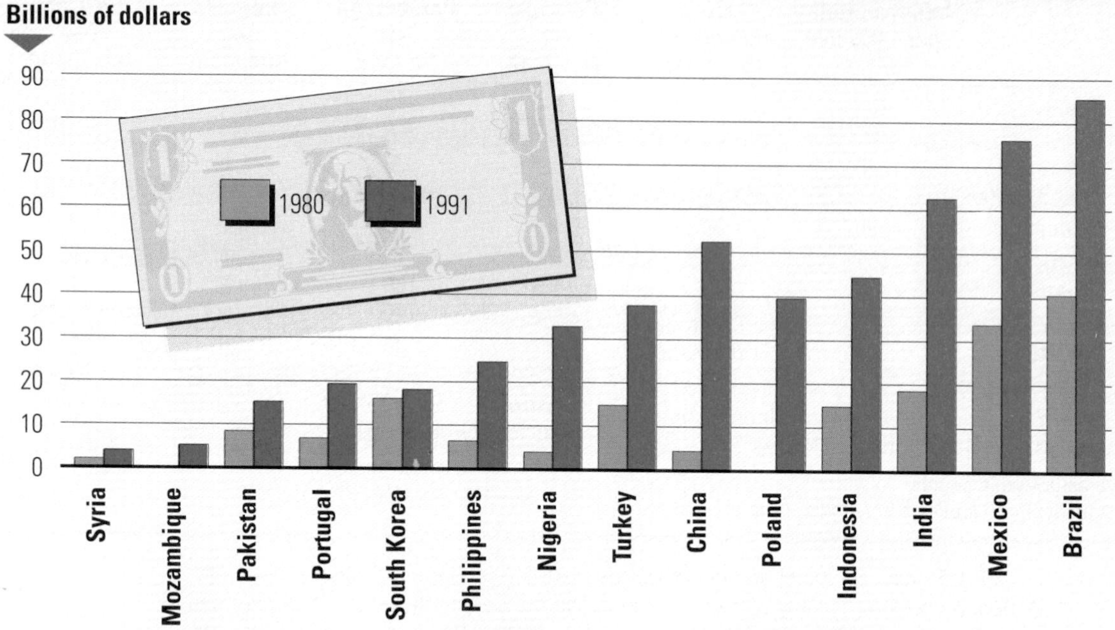

Sources: *Encyclopaedia Britannica, 1993 Book of the Year, Europa World Year Book 1993.*

Graph Skills (a) What has been the trend in external debts of developing countries? (b) How does the information in the chart below support the data in this chart?

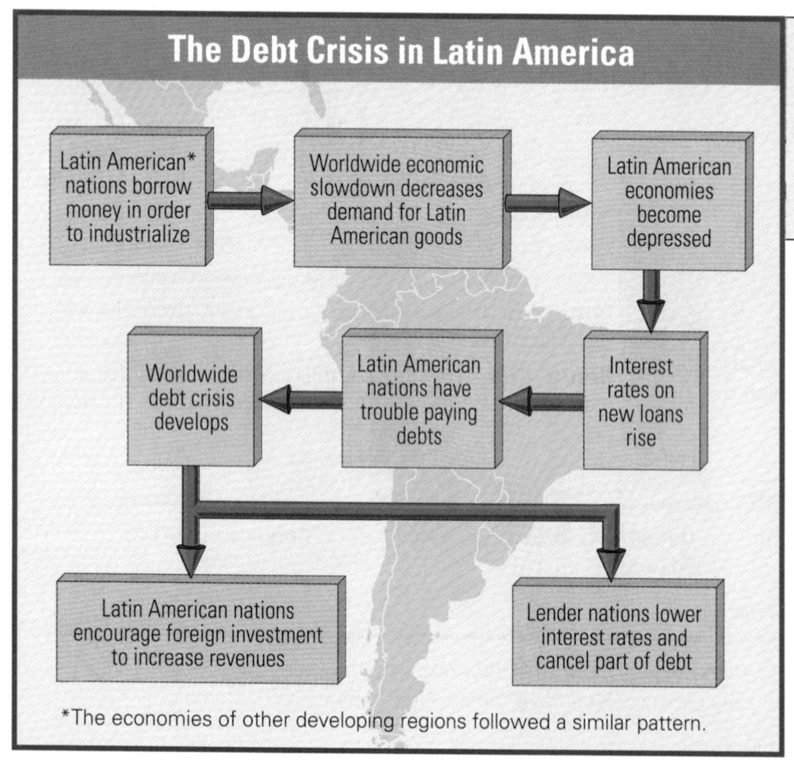

Chart Skills (a) Why did developing nations borrow money? (b) Why were they unable to repay these loans? (c) How do you think their problems affected lender nations?

GAZETTEER

This gazetteer, or geographical dictionary, lists places that are important to world cultures. The approximate latitude and longitude are given for cities, towns, and other specific locations. See text page 4 for information about latitude and longitude. In the gazetteer, after the description of each place there are usually two numbers in parentheses. The first number (or numbers) refers to the text page or pages on which you will find more information about the place. The second number appears in slanted, or *italic*, type and refers to a map (*m*) on which the location of the place is shown.

A

Afghanistan Landlocked Asian nation northwest of India; it often is considered part of South Asia. (pp. 162, 226, *m164*)

Africa World's second largest continent, comprising 5 regions and 54 nations. (p. 59, *m57*)

Alexandria (31°N/30°E) City in ancient Egypt and, later, a center of Hellenistic civilization; present-day Egyptian city and seaport. (p. 647, *m549*)

Allahabad (25°N/81°E) City on the Ganges River in India. (p. 178)

Alps Major mountain range in south-central Europe. (p. 641, *m640*)

Amazon Basin Largest lowland area in South America; site of the world's largest rain forest. (pp. 442, 500, *m440*)

Amazon River Longest river (4,000 mi/6,437 km) in South America; starts in the Andes Mountains of Peru, flows eastward across Brazil, and empties into the Atlantic Ocean. (p. 442, *m440*)

Amritsar (31°N/75°E) City in northwestern India. (p. 201, *m210*)

Anatolian Plateau Large, fertile plateau in Asia Minor. (p. 553, *m552*)

Andes Mountains Mountain range running the length of western South America. (p. 442, *m440*)

Angkor (13°N/103°E) Capital of the ancient Khmer kingdom in Southeast Asia. (p. 257)

Angola Nation in Southern Africa. (p. 109, *m110*)

Apennines Mountain range in central Italy; extends south along the full length of the Italian peninsula. (p. 641)

Arabian Peninsula Very large peninsula in the Middle East; Saudi Arabia is its largest nation. (p. 553, *m552*)

Argentina One of the largest nations of Latin America, rich in agricultural resources and a leading exporter of food products. (p. 496, *m440*)

Asia World's largest continent, extending from the Pacific Ocean to Eastern Europe; includes East Asia, Southeast Asia, South Asia, and most of the Middle East. (p. 161)

Atacama Desert Long, narrow desert between the Andes Mountains in Chile and the Pacific Ocean; one of the driest places on Earth. (pp. 443, 445, *m440*)

Athens (38°N/23°E) Capital of Greece; city-state in ancient Greece. (p. 8)

Atlas Mountains Range of mountains in North Africa near the Mediterranean Sea. (p. 60, *m62*)

Australia World's smallest continent and its largest island; in the Pacific Ocean south of island Southeast Asia. (p. 299, *m300*)

Axum Early African kingdom south of the ancient kingdom of Kush. (p. 76, *m76*)

Ayodhya (26°N/82°E) City in north-central India; site of 1990 Hindu-Muslim riots. (p. 207)

B

Bangladesh Nation in South Asia northeast of India; one of the world's most densely populated countries. (pp. 162, 166, *m166*)

Bay of Bengal Large body of water bordering the eastern coast of India. (p. 161, *m164*)

Bay of Pigs Site of attempted 1961 invasion of Cuba by Cuban exiles. (p. 508)

Beijing (40°N/116°E) Capital of China and a major manufacturing center. (p. 323, *m345*)

Benares (25°N/83°E) City on the Ganges River in India. (p. 178)

Benin Early West African kingdom at the delta of the Niger River. (p. 82, *m82*)

Benin City (6°N/5°E) Capital of the early African kingdom of Benin; city in present-day Nigeria. (p. 82, *m82*)

Bhopal (23°N/77°E) City in India, site of 1984 chemical plant disaster. (p. 229)

Bhutan Nation of South Asia north of Bangladesh and east of Nepal. (p. 162, *m164*)

Biafra Region in southeastern Nigeria. (p. 123)

Botswana Landlocked nation in Southern Africa. (p. 134, *m57*)

Brahmaputra River One of the largest rivers in India. (p. 163, *m164*)

Brasília (15°S/48°W) Capital of Brazil. (p. 6, *m6*)

Brazil Huge country covering nearly half of South America. (pp. 500-502, *m440*)

Brunei Small nation of island Southeast Asia in northern Borneo. (p. 250, *m251*)

Buenos Aires (34°S/58°W) Capital of Argentina, at the mouth of the Río de la Plata. (p. 443, *m437*)

C

Canada Second largest country in the world, in northern half of North America; stretches from the Atlantic Ocean in the east to the Pacific Ocean in the west. (p. 524, *m524*)

Canadian Shield Large region of Canada with poor soil and a cold climate; stretches west and north from the Atlantic Ocean to the Arctic Ocean. (p. 525, *m524*)

Caspian Sea Inland sea bordered by the former Soviet Union and Iran. (p. 709, *m708*)

Caucasus Mountains Mountain range between the Black and Caspian seas in Georgia, Armenia, and Azerbaijan that separates Russia from Turkey and Iran. (p. 709, *m708*)

Central Africa One of the five regions of Africa; includes Zaire and several other nations. (p. 60, *m57*)

Central America One of the two subregions of Latin America, extending from Mexico to South America. (p. 441, *m437*)

Central Plateau Plateau in Mexico between the Sierra Madre West and Sierra Madre East mountains. (p. 442, *m440*)

Chang (Yangzi) River One of China's major rivers. (p. 327, *m324*)

China Third largest and most populous nation in the world (3.7 million sq mi/9.6 million sq km); extends from the Pacific Ocean into the interior of Central Asia. (p. 324, *m324*)

Congo Free State Former Belgian colony in Central Africa. (pp. 98-100)

D

Dacca (23°N/90°E) Capital of Bangladesh. (p. 168, *m166*)

Deccan Plateau Large plateau in south-central India; bounded in the north by the Vindhya Mountains and in the east and west by the low-lying Ghats mountain ranges. (p. 165, *m164*)

Desert Major world climate zone; land area that has very little moisture, such as the Sahara and Namib deserts in Africa, the Baja Peninsula of northern Mexico, and the Patagonian Plateau of South America. (p. 445)

Drakensberg Mountains Mountain range in the eastern part of South Africa. (p. 60, *m62*)

E

East Africa One of the five regions of Africa; includes Kenya, Ethiopia, Tanzania, and several other nations. (p. 60, *m57*)

East Asia Large landmass in Asia that includes China, Mongolia, and Korea; the islands of Japan are also considered part of East Asia. (p. 323, *m322*)

Edo (35°N/139°E) Former imperial capital of Japan; present-day Tokyo. (p. 396)

Egypt Third largest nation in the Middle East both in size and in population. (p. 605, *m549*)

El Niño Warm Pacific Ocean current near Peru that can cause major weather changes. (p. 444)

Equator Imaginary line that divides the Earth into the Northern and Southern hemispheres. (p. 4)

Eritrea Former province in Ethiopia that gained its independence in 1993. (p. 136)

Euphrates River Major river on the Arabian Peninsula. (p. 554, *m554*)

Europe Continent that forms part of a larger landmass that includes Asia and extends westward from the Ural Mountains to the Atlantic Ocean. (p. 640, *m640*)

F

Fertile Crescent Region of the Middle East; site of one of the world's earliest civilizations. (p. 553)

Forbidden City (40°N/116°E) Complex of palaces and government buildings in Beijing, China, built during the Ming dynasty (1368–1644). (p. 342)

G

Ganges River Major river in India; flows eastward across India and joins the Brahmaputra River in Bangladesh to create a large fertile delta on the Bay of Bengal. (pp. 163, 228, *m164*)

Gao Trading city in the early West African kingdom of Songhai. (p. 82, *m82*)

Gaza Strip Strip of land at the southeastern end of the Mediterranean Sea where Palestinians gained limited self-rule in 1994. (p. 617, *m617*)

Ghana Early West African kingdom on the plains between the Senegal and Niger rivers; also the name of a present-day West African nation on the southern coast of West Africa. (pp. 80, 108, *m110*)

Ghats, The Mountain ranges in India; the Western Ghats border the Arabian Sea and the Eastern Ghats face the Bay of Bengal. (p. 165, *m164*)

Goa A city on the southwestern coast of India that was once a Portuguese colony. (p. 4, *m188*)

Great Plains Vast interior plains of North America stretching from the Gulf of Mexico to the Arctic Ocean. (p. 525)

Great Rift Valley Giant fault in East Africa extending from the Red Sea to the Zambezi River. (pp. 60-61, *m61*)

Great Wall, The 1,500-mile (2,414-km) barrier built by Chinese feudal lords and extended by Shi Huangdi ("First Emperor") to defend China against nomadic invaders. (p. 337)

Guam Largest (210 sq mi/544 sq km) of the Pacific islands of Micronesia. (p. 308, *m309*)

Guiana Highlands Highlands in Venezuela. (p. 442, *m440*)

Gunung Agung Volcano on the island of Bali in Southeast Asia. (p. 258)

H

Harappa (30°N/73°E) Ancient city of the Indus Valley civilization. (p. 171, *m172*)

Heia (35°N/135°E) Capital of Japan in the late 700s; present-day Kyoto. (p. 394)

Highland climate Major world climate zone; climate of mountainous areas such as the Alps in Europe, where temperatures vary according to the elevation. (p. 642)

Himalaya Mountains Massive mountain chain stretching 1,500 miles (2,414 km) that forms the northern border of the Indian sub-continent. (p. 162, *m164*)

Hindu Kush Mountain range northwest of the Himalaya Mountains. (p. 162, *m164*)

Hiroshima (34°N/132°E) Japanese city on which the first atomic bomb used in warfare was dropped. (p. 407, *m407*)

Hokkaido Northernmost of the four main islands of Japan. (p. 389, *m391*)

Hong Kong Major center of trade and finance on the South China coast. (p. 366, *m345*)

Honshu Largest and most populous of the four main islands of Japan. (p. 389, *m391*)

Huang He Major river of China; flows across North China into the Yellow Sea. (p. 326, *m324*)

Humid subtropical climate A major world climate zone; climate in which a warm season alternates with a cool season, as in Paraguay, Uruguay, and northern Argentina in South America and South Carolina and Georgia in the United States. (p. 444)

I

India Largest nation of South Asia. (p. 162, *m164*)

Indian Subcontinent South Asian landmass that includes India, Pakistan, Bangladesh, Nepal, Bhutan, and the island nations of Sri Lanka and the Maldives. (p. 162, *m164*)

Indo-Gangetic Plain Large, fertile plain south of the Himalaya Mountains that stretches from Pakistan across India into Bangladesh. (p. 162, *m164*)

Indonesia Nation of island Southeast Asia comprising more than 13,500 islands that stretch across 3,200 miles (5,149 km) of ocean. (pp. 250, 289, *m251*)

Indus River River in Pakistan and northern India; site of the early Indus Valley civilization. (pp. 162, 223, *m164*)

Inland Sea Body of water linking the Japanese islands of Honshu, Kyushu, and Shikoku. (p. 389)

Iran Second largest country of the Middle East both in size and in population. (p. 602, *m549*)

Iranian Plateau Large plateau in the Middle East. (p. 553, *m552*)

Island Southeast Asia Island nations of Southeast Asia, including Indonesia, the Philippines, and many smaller countries. (p. 250, *m251*)

Isthmus of Panama Narrow strip of land in Central America; site of the Panama Canal. (p. 507, *m506*)

J

Japan Archipelago, or chain of islands, about 100 miles (160 km) off the coast of East Asia. (p. 389, *m391*)

K

Kaesong (38°N/126°E) Present-day site of the capital of Korea during the Koryo dynasty. (918–1392). (p.379)

Kalahari Desert Desert in Southern Africa. (p. 69, *m62*)

Kanto Plain Densely populated, fertile lowland on the Japanese island of Honshu. (p. 390)

Kashmir Region of India in the Himalaya Mountains bordered by India, Pakistan, and China. (p. 223, *m204*)

Kashmir Valley Valley in the northern mountains of India known for its production of cashmere wool. (p. 162)

Katanga Copper-rich former province of the Congo that became the independent African nation of Zaire. (p. 112, *m110*)

Kazakhstan Large, newly independent nation; former republic of the Soviet Union. (p. 748, *m754*)

Kenya Nation of East Africa. (p. 108, *m110*)

Khmer Kingdom Early Southeast Asian kingdom. (p. 255, *m255*)

Khyber Pass (34°N/71°E) Pass through the Hindu Kush mountain range in northern India. (p. 162, *m164*)

Koguryo Early kingdom that dominated the northern Korean peninsula from about A.D. 100 to 668. (p. 378)

Korea Peninsula at the southern tip of East Asia; officially divided into North Korea and South Korea in 1948. (p. 375, *m376*)

Korea Strait Body of water between South Korea and Japan separating Japan from mainland East Asia. (pp. 375, 389, *m376*)

Kulu Valley Fertile valley on the Indian subcontinent known as the "Valley of the Gods." (p. 163)

Kumbi Saleh Capital of the early African kingdom of Ghana. (p. 80, *m82*)

Kurile Islands Islands north of the Japanese island of Hokkaido. (p. 421)

Kush Early East African kingdom. (p. 75, *m76*)

Kyongju Capital of Korea during the Silla dynasty (A.D. 668-918). (p. 378)

Kyushu One of the four main Japanese islands. (p. 389, *m391*)

L

La Cordillera High mountain ranges that run the length of Latin America, comprising the Sierra Madre East and the Sierra Madre West in Middle America and the Andes Mountains in South America. (p. 441, *m441*)

Lake Kariba Lake in the Central African nation of Zambia; site of the Kariba Dam. (p. 63, *m62*)

Lanna Powerful Southeast Asian Tai kingdom of the 1200s. (p. 257)

Laos Nation of Southeast Asia. (p. 252, *m251*)

Lascaux Site of caves in southern France with 10,000-year-old wall paintings. (p. 27)

Latin America Large landmass stretching about 5,500 miles (8,851 km) from the Rio Grande in Mexico to Cape Horn at the tip of South America; comprising two main subregions, Middle America and South America. (p. 441, *m440*)

M

Machu Picchu (13°S/72°W) Inca city in the Andes Mountains. (p. 11)

Madras (13°N/80°E) City in southern India. (p. 165)

Maghreb, The Region in North Africa that includes Algeria, Tunisia, Morocco, the Sahara, and the Atlas Mountains. (p. 555, *m552*)

Mainland Southeast Asia Peninsula that includes Myanmar, Cambodia, Laos, Thailand, and Vietnam. (p. 250, *m251*)

Malacca City in Malaysia on the Strait of Malacca. (pp. 256, 265, *m256*)

Malaysia Nation of Southeast Asia; includes the southern Malay Peninsula and northern Borneo. (p. 250, *m251*)

Maldives Island nation of South Asia in the Indian Ocean. (p. 162)

Mali Early African empire; present-day nation of West Africa. (p. 80, *m82*)

Manchuria Northeastern province of China. (p. 326)

Marine climate A major world climate zone; mild climate with warm winters, cool summers, and abundant rainfall, as along the Atlantic coast of Western Europe. (p. 642)

Mecca (21°N/39°E) City in Saudi Arabia and site of the holiest shrine of the Islamic religion. (pp. 78, 594, *m549*)

Mediterranean climate A major world climate zone; climate with hot, dry summers and mild, rainy winters, such as that of southern Europe and the coastal land of North Africa and South Africa. (p. 69, 642, *m65*)

Melanesia One of the three regions of Oceania; includes western Pacific islands from New Guinea to the Solomons. (p. 308, *m309*)

Meröe Capital of the early East African kingdom of Kush. (p. 75, *m76*)

Mexico Latin American nation extending south of the Rio Grande to Central America. (p. 493, *m493*)

Mexico City (19°N/99°W) Capital of Mexico and the world's most populous city. (pp. 12, 486, *m493*)

Micronesia One of the three regions of Oceania; includes Guam and many other Pacific islands. (p. 308, *m309*)

Middle America One of the two subregions of Latin America; includes Mexico, Central America, and the Caribbean islands. (p. 441)

Middle East Landmass comprising Turkey, Iran, and the nations of the Arabian Peninsula; also, the nations on the northern coast of Africa are often considered part of the Middle East. (p. 551, *m549*)

Mohenjo-Daro (27°N/68°E) Ancient city of the Indus Valley civilization. (p. 171, *m172*)

Mount Everest (28°N/87°E) One of the highest mountains in the world; in the Himalaya Mountains. (p. 162, *m164*)

Mount Fuji (35°N/138°E) Japan's highest mountain. (p. 398)

Mount Kilimanjaro Mountain in northeastern Tanzania. (p. 59, *m61*)

Mount Pinatubo Volcano on the Philippine island of Luzon, which erupted in 1991. (p. 251)

Mozambique Nation in Southern Africa. (p. 109, *m110*)

N

Nagasaki (32°N/130°E) Japanese city on which an atomic bomb was dropped on August 9, 1945. (p. 408)

Nagorno-Karabakh Area in the former Soviet Union contested by the republics of Armenia and Azerbaijan. (p. 748)

Nairobi (1°S/36°E) Capital of the East African nation of Kenya. (p. 119, *m57*)

Namib Desert Desert along the southwestern coast of Southern Africa. (p. 69, *m62*)

Namibia Nation in Southern Africa. (p. 136, *m57*)

New Guinea Largest and most populous of the Pacific islands in Melanesia. (p. 308, *m309*)

New Zealand Pacific nation consisting of two large islands, about 1,200 miles (1,931 km) southeast of Australia. (p. 301, *m300*)

Nigeria Most populous nation in West Africa. (p. 122, *m110*)

Niger River River in West Africa. (p. 63, *m62*)

Nile River River in Egypt; flows northward through Egypt and empties into the Mediterranean Sea. (p. 60, *m62*)

Nile Valley Narrow, fertile strip of land along the Nile River; site of earliest civilization in Africa. (pp. 73, 605, *m76*)

North Africa One of the five regions of Africa, extending from Morocco to Egypt. (p. 60, *m62*)

North America Large continent stretching from Canada in the north to Mexico in the south. (p. 524, *m437*)

North European Plain Area stretching more than 1,000 miles (1,600 km) from Britain through France and Germany into Eastern Europe. (pp. 641, 708, *m640*)

Northern Hemisphere The half of the Earth that lies north of the Equator. (p. 4)

O

Oceania The 25,000 islands in the Pacific Ocean, comprising three regions: Melanesia, Micronesia, and Polynesia. (p. 308, *m309*)

Olduvai Gorge (2°S/35°E) Site near the Great Rift Valley in Tanzania where the remains of the earliest humans were discovered in the late 1950s. (pp. 71-72)

Orinoco River River in South America that flows northward from Colombia through Venezuela to the Atlantic Ocean. (p. 443, *m440*)

P

Pacific Rim Nations in the Pacific area forging strong ties in international trade. (p. 420, *m48*)

Paekche Early kingdom that ruled the southwestern portion of the Korean Peninsula about A.D. 100-668. (p. 378)

Pagan Early Southeast Asian kingdom in present-day Myanmar. (p. 254, *m255*)

Palenque One of the prosperous cities of the ancient Maya; city in present-day Mexico. (p. 448)

Pamir Mountains Central Asian mountain range in the former Soviet Union. (p. 710, *m708*)

Pampas Grassy plains in South America stretching from Argentina into Uruguay. (p. 442)

Panmunjom (38°N/126°E) City on the border that divides North Korea and South Korea. (p. 382, *m383*)

Philippine Islands Nation of Southeast Asia. (p. 250, *m251*)

Plateau Elevated, level landform. (p. 60, *m62*)

Polynesia One of the three regions of Oceania; includes New Zealand, the Hawaiian Islands, and other islands. (p. 308, *m309*)

Popocatépetl (19°N/98°W) Volcano ("Smoking Mountain") in Mexico. (p. 439)

Potosí (19°S/65°W) Site high in the Andes Mountains, the world's richest source of silver in the 1600s. (p. 460)

Prime Meridian Imaginary line that divides the Earth into the Eastern and Western hemispheres. (p. 4)

Punt Ancient land of East Africa. (p. 71)

Pyongyang (39°N/125°E) Capital of North Korea. (p. 376, *m383*)

Pyrenees European mountain range that separates Spain from France. (p. 641, *m640*)

Q

Quito (0°S/78°W) Capital of Ecuador. (p. 12)

R

Rhine River Longest river in Western Europe. (p. 641, *m640*)

Rhine Valley One of the most heavily industrialized areas of Western Europe. (p. 642)

Ring of Fire Area of earthquakes and volcanoes bordering Japan and other Pacific lands. (pp. 251, 390)

Río de la Plata River in South America that forms the border between Uruguay and Argentina. (p. 443)

Russia Empire that stretched from Eastern Europe across Asia and was ruled by czars. Most of the former empire became the Union of Soviet Socialist Republics following the Russian Revolution. (p. 707, *m708*)

Russian Federation Largest republic of the former Soviet Union; also known as Russia (p. 753, *m754*)

S

Sahara Largest desert in the world, extends across much of North Africa. (p. 68, *m62*)

Sahel Region south of the Sahara affected by widespread desertification. (p. 68)

Samoa Part of the Pacific Ocean region of Polynesia, comprising 15 islands. (p. 310, *m309*)

Savanna Grassland region in Africa. (p. 66)

Sea of Japan Body of water between South Korea and Japan; called the East Sea by the Koreans. (pp. 375, 389, *m376*)

Seine River Major river in France on which Paris is located. (p. 641)

Semiarid climate A major world climate zone; climate with very light rainfall, as in northern Mexico and part of Argentina. (p. 445)

Senegal Nation of West Africa. (p. 132, *m110*)

Seoul (37°N/127°E) Capital of South Korea. (p. 376, *m383*)

Sertão In northeastern Brazil, a dry region covered with scrub. (p. 500)

Sharpeville (26°S/28°E) Township near Johannesburg, South Africa; site of the 1960 "Sharpeville massacre." (p. 140)

Shenzhen City in southeastern China, site of Special Economic Zone (SEZ). (p. 359)

Shikoku Smallest of the four main Japanese islands. (p. 389, *m391*)

Sierra Madre East Mountain range near the Atlantic coast of Mexico. (p. 441, *m440*)

Sierra Madre West Mountain range along the Pacific coast of Mexico. (p. 441, *m440*)

Sikkim Tiny Himalayan kingdom on the northern border of India, ruled by India since the mid-1970s. (p. 225, *m204*)

Silk Road, The Ancient trade route linking East Asia and the Mediterranean that fostered the exchange of goods and ideas between Europe and Asia. (p. 338)

Silla Early kingdom that dominated the southeastern portion of the Korean peninsula. (p. 378)

Singapore Small nation of island Southeast Asia at the tip of the Malay Peninsula. (p. 250, *m251*)

Songhai Early empire in West Africa. (p. 82, *m82*)

South Africa Largest nation of Southern Africa. (p. 139, *m140*)

South America Large continent and one of the two subregions of Latin America. (p. 441, *m440*)

South Asia Large triangular peninsula jutting southward from the continent of Asia; bounded on the north by the Hindu Kush and Himalaya mountains, on the west by the Arabian Sea, and on the east by the Indian Ocean and the Bay of Bengal. (p. 161, *m159*)

Southern Africa One of the five main regions of Africa; includes Zambia, South Africa, and several other nations. (p. 60, *m62*)

Southern Hemisphere The half of the Earth that lies south of the Equator. (p. 4)

Sri Lanka Island nation of South Asia in the Indian Ocean. (p. 162, *m166*)

Srivijaya Early Southeast Asian kingdom on the island of Sumatra. (p. 257, *m255*)

St. Lawrence Seaway Waterway linking Canada's St. Lawrence River to the Great Lakes. (p. 525)

Strait of Malacca Water route between the Malay Peninsula and the island of Sumatra. (pp. 256, 265, 267, *m256*)

Sub-Saharan Africa Lands south of the Sahara. (p. 60, *m62*)

Suez Canal 100-mile (160-km) Middle Eastern waterway that links the Mediterranean and the Red seas. (p. 583)

Sumer Early civilization in the Middle East. (p. 171, *m29*)

T

Taiwan Island nation in the East China Sea off the coast of China. (p. 352, *m321*)

Tanzania Nation of East Africa that borders the Indian Ocean. (p. 112, *m110*)

Tegucigalpa (14°N/87°W) Capital of the Latin American nation of Honduras. (p. 488, *m506*)

Tenochtitlán Capital of the Aztec Empire; present-day Mexico City. (p. 448)

Thailand Nation of mainland Southeast Asia. (p. 288)

Thames River Major river in Great Britain on which London is located. (p. 641)

Thar Desert Desert in northwestern India. (p. 163, *m164*)

Tiber River Major river in Italy on which Rome is located. (p. 641)

Tibet Mountainous country of Asia, occupied by China. (p. 326, *m324*)

Tierra caliente ("hot land") Climate in Latin American lowland regions, such as the Yucatán Peninsula and the Amazon Basin. (p. 445)

Tierra fría ("cold land") Climate in Latin American highland regions with elevations above 6,000 feet (1,828 m), including Mexico City and Bogotá. (p. 445)

Tierra templada ("temperate land") Climate in Latin American plateau regions with elevations between 3,000 feet (914 m) and 6,000 feet (1,828 m), including large parts of Mexico and valleys in the Andes. (p. 445)

Tigris-Euphrates Valley River valley in the Middle East; site of an early civilization. (p. 28)

Tikal (17°N/89°W) Capital of the ancient Maya Empire. (p. 448)

Timbuktu (16°N/3°W) Ancient cultural and trade center in East Africa. (p. 79, *m82*)

Trivandrum (8°N/77°E) City on the western coast of India with very heavy annual rainfall. (p. 168)

Tropical rain forests Forests found along the Equator in Africa, Latin America, and Indonesia. (p. 66)

Tropical wet and dry climate A major world climate zone with a hot, wet summer and a warm, dry winter; largest climate zone of Africa. (p. 66, *m65*)

Tropical wet climate A climate zone with hot temperatures, abundant rainfall, and no dry season, as in Guinea, the Amazon Basin, and some Caribbean islands. (pp. 66, 443, *m65*)

Turkey Nation of southwestern Asia that links the Middle East and Europe. (p. 607, *m549*)

U

Ukraine A newly independent nation in the Commonwealth of Independent States. (p. 748, *m754*)

Ural Mountains Mountain range in Russia dividing Europe and Asia. (p. 709, *m708*)

V

Victoria Falls (18°S/26°E) Waterfalls on the Zambezi River in East Africa; known to Africans as Mosi oa Tunya ("the smoke that thunders"). (p. 97)

Vindhya Mountains Mountain range in South Asia between the Deccan Plateau and the Indo-Gangetic Plain. (p. 164, *m164*)

W

West Africa One of the five main regions of Africa; includes Mauritania, Nigeria, and many other nations. (p. 60, *m62*)

X

Xi Jiang (West River) Major river that flows through southern China to the port city of Guangzhou. (p. 327, *m324*)

Y

Yellow Sea Body of water west of Korea and east of China. (p. 375, *m376*)

Z

Zaire River Large river in Central Africa that empties into the Atlantic Ocean. (p. 63, *m62*)

Zambezi River River in Southern Africa. (p. 63, *m62*)

Zambia Landlocked nation of Southern Africa. (p. 134, *m57*)

Zimbabwe Early Southern African kingdom; present-day nation of Southern Africa. (p. 84, *m82*)

GLOSSARY

This glossary defines many important terms and phrases. Some terms are phonetically respelled to aid in pronunciation. See the Pronunciation Key below for an explanation of the respellings. The page number following each definition is the page on which the term or phrase is first discussed in the text. All terms that appear in blue type in the text are included in this glossary.

PRONUNCIATION KEY When difficult terms or names first appear in the text, they are respelled to aid in pronunciation. A syllable in SMALL CAPITAL LETTERS receives the most stress. The key below lists the letters used for respelling. It includes examples of words using each sound and shows how they are respelled.

SYMBOL	EXAMPLE	RESPELLING	SYMBOL	EXAMPLE	RESPELLING
a	hat	(hat)	u	put, book	(put), (buk)
ay	pay, late	(pay), (layt)	uh	fun	(fuhn)
ah	star, hot	(stahr), (haht)	yoo	few, use	(fyoo), (yooz)
ai	air, dare	(air), (dair)	ch	chill, reach	(chihl), (reech)
aw	law, all	(law), (awl)	g	go, dig	(goh), (dihg)
eh	met	(meht)	j	jet, gently, bridge	(jeht), (jehnt lee), (brihj)
ee	bee, eat	(bee), (eet)	k	kite, cup	(kīt), (kuhp)
er	learn, sir, fur	(lern), (ser), (fer)	ks	mix	(mihks)
ih	fit	(fiht)	kw	quick	(kwihk)
ī	mile	(mīl)	ng	bring	(brihng)
ir	ear	(ir)	s	say, cent	(say), (sehnt)
oh	no	(noh)	sh	she, crash	(shee), (krash)
oi	soil, boy	(soil), (boi)	th	three	(three)
oo	root, rule	(root), (rool)	y	yet, onion	(yeht), (UHN yuhn)
or	born, door	(born), (dor)	z	zip, always	(zihp), (AWL wayz)
ow	plow, out	(plow), (owt)	zh	treasure	(TREH zher)

A

abdicate give up a high office (p. 730)

abolition movement to end slavery (p. 94)

absolute monarch ruler who had complete authority in government and over the lives of the people he or she governed (p. 665)

acropolis (uh KRAHP uh lihs) hilltop fortress in ancient Greece (p. 645)

Agama Java version of the Islamic religion observed on Java; a blend of Islam, Hinduism, and Buddhism (p. 291)

age grade in some African societies, all people born in the same year (p. 89)

agricultural revolution period during which early people began to farm and to tame animals (p. 28)

alley-cropping method of limiting soil erosion (p. 137)

Amritsar Massacre bloody uprising in Amritsar, a city in northwestern India, that was the turning point in India's struggle for independence from Britain (p. 202)

animism belief that spirits live in the natural world (p. 258)

annex add a territory to one's own country (p. 381)

anti-Semitism hatred or fear of Jews (p. 587)

apartheid (uh PAHRT hayt) rigid separation of races by law in South Africa (p. 139)

appeasement making concessions to an aggressor in order to preserve peace (p. 679)

archaeologist scientist who studies remains left by early people (p. 28)

archipelago chain of islands (p. 250)

aristocracy small, privileged upper class that administered the government in ancient Greece (p. 645)

armistice truce or agreement to end fighting (p. 384)

artisan skilled craftworker (p. 29)

assembly line economical, efficient method of production introduced by American auto manufacturer Henry Ford in which the complex job of assembling many parts is broken down into small tasks, each performed by an individual worker (p. 672)

atman (AHT muhn) in Hinduism, the essential self of every individual, which, in turn, is part of a universal soul that is also called atman (p. 179)

autocrat ruler with unlimited power (p. 714)

autonomy self-government (p. 747)

B

Berlin Wall concrete wall erected in 1961 by the East German government to prevent its citizens from fleeing to noncommunist West Berlin (p. 687)

bilingual having two official languages in a country (p. 535)

Black Death bubonic plague, a disease that struck Western Europe several times during the Late Middle Ages, particularly during the mid-1300s (p. 655)

black market market in which people trade goods illegally (p. 740)

blitzkrieg German for lightning war in which combined land and air forces launched a joint military attack (p. 680)

Bloody Sunday day in 1905 on which Russian workers marching peacefully to the czar's palace were attacked by armed soldiers (p. 722)

Bolsheviks members of the Bolshevik party led by Lenin, who emerged victorious in the Russian Revolution (p. 731)

Boxer Rebellion bloody uprising of the Boxers, a Chinese organization, against foreigners and Chinese Christians in 1900 (p. 346)

boycott refusal to buy certain goods or services (p. 108)

brahman in Hinduism, the single, supreme force or reality of the universe (p. 178)

Brezhnev Doctrine in the mid-1960s, doctrine set forth by Soviet leader Leonid Brezhnev stating that the Soviet Union had the right to intervene in the affairs of any socialist country to prevent it from changing its government (p. 752)

British North America Act act passed by Great Britain in 1867 that united Ontario, Quebec, Nova Scotia, and New Brunswick to create the Dominion of Canada as a self-governing nation (p. 532)

buffer state small country located between two large, hostile powers (p. 226)

bureaucracy huge system of officials and government departments (p. 746)

bushido code of behavior developed by Japan's samurai class that emphasized military virtues and the samurai's duty of loyalty to his lord (p. 400)

Byzantine Empire Eastern half of the Roman Empire, which had split into two parts by A.D. 330; included Greece, Asia Minor, Egypt, and the eastern Fertile Crescent (p. 562)

C

cabildos (cah BEEL dohz) councils established by Spain to govern the towns founded by Spanish settlers in Latin America (p. 459)

caliph secular and religious head of a Muslim state, successor to the prophet Muhammad (p. 573)

calligraphy fine, ornate handwriting (p. 234)

capital money that can be invested in business ventures for the purpose of making a profit (p. 33)

capitalism free market economic system in which the means of production are owned and operated by individuals for profit (p. 356)

cash crop crop that can be sold on the world market (p. 38)

caste in India, system of social groups based on birth (p. 174)

cataract large waterfall (p. 60)

caudillo Latin American military leader who seizes power and rules as a dictator (p. 475)

charter in the Late Middle Ages, written document guaranteeing certain rights to townspeople (p. 655)

city-state large town that has its own government and controls the surrounding countryside (p. 83)

civil disobedience use of nonviolent means to resist civil laws considered to be unjust (p. 202)

civilization highly organized group of people with their own language and ways of living (p. 28)

climate average weather of a place over a period of 20 to 30 years (p. 12)

coalition ruling alliance of several political parties (p. 206)

Cold War After World War II, a period of political and economic struggle between the democratic nations of the West, led by the United States, and the communist bloc, led by the Soviet Union (p. 37)

collective farm farm operated and managed under government direction (p. 355)

Columbian exchange global exchange of people, goods, and ideas between the Eastern and Western hemispheres (p. 462)

Commonwealth of Nations association through which Great Britain maintains social and economic ties with its former colonies (p. 697)

commune community in which all property is held in common, living quarters are shared, and physical needs are provided for in exchange for work at assigned jobs (p. 356)

communist bloc the Soviet Union and the communist nations of Eastern Europe, as distinguished from the democratic nations of the West, during the Cold War after World War II (p. 686)

conquistadors Spanish conquerors of Latin America (p. 453)

consensus common agreement (p. 87)

containment United States policy in the late 1940s and 1950s to stop Soviet expansion (p. 687)

contras Nicaraguan forces that opposed the Sandinistas; with United States help, they fought a long guerrilla war against the Nicaraguan government in the 1980s (p. 483)

copra dried coconut meat (p. 260)

cottage industry small business conducted in the home (p. 214)

coup d'état (koo day TAH) revolt, often by military leaders, against a nation's government (p. 482)

creole American-born descendants of Spanish settlers (p. 464)

crusade military expeditions undertaken by European Christians, beginning in the 1000s, to recover Palestine from the Muslims (p. 576)

Cuban missile crisis confrontation in October 1962 between the United States and the Soviet Union, which the Cuban government allowed to build missile bases on its territory just off the southern coast of Florida (p. 508)

Cultural Revolution movement that emphasized class struggle; instituted in China by Mao Zedong in 1966 to control rival groups within the Communist party (p. 356)

culture all the things that make up a people's entire way of life (p. 13)

cuneiform term used to describe the wedge-shaped writing of the ancient Sumerians (p. 558)

Cyrillic (suh RIHL ihk) **alphabet** alphabet based on Greek and Hebrew letters that was devised for the Slavic peoples in about A.D. 850 (p. 714)

czar Russian term for emperor (p. 714)

D

daimyo powerful samurai warriors under the control of Japan's Tokugawa shogunate (1600–1868) (p. 396)

debt crisis inability of developing nations to repay large sums of money borrowed for development projects (p. 40)

Decembrist Revolt in 1825, uprising in Russia in which a small group of nobles and army officers tried to overthrow the czar's government (p. 720)

decipher determine the meaning of something written in code (p. 171)

default failure to repay a loan (p. 513)

democracy form of government in which the people have supreme power (p. 18)

democratization moving toward a free system of government (p. 112)

desalination converting sea water into fresh water for drinking and irrigation (p. 597)

desertification the change of semidesert land into desert land (p. 68)

détente period of relaxation of Cold War tensions between the United States and the Soviet Union in the 1970s (p. 696)

dharma in Hinduism, the duties and obligations of each caste (p. 179)

dialect regional version of a language, with its own words, expressions, and pronunciations (p. 169)

diaspora (dī AS puh ruh) migration or scattering of a homogeneous people (p. 96)

dictatorship form of government in which a ruler holds power by force (p. 18)

diffusion movement of customs or ideas from one place to another (p. 20)

direct democracy participation in government by all citizens directly, not through representatives (p. 645)

"dirty war" brutal campaign launched in 1976 by the Argentinean army against workers, students, and anyone else it considered to be an "enemy of the state" (p. 498)

dissident someone who speaks out against the government (p. 737)

divine right belief of European absolute monarchs that a ruler's authority comes from God (p. 665)

domino theory belief that if one nation fell under communist domination, neighboring nations would also fall, like a row of falling dominoes (p. 276)

donatario Portuguese landowners of huge tracts of land in Brazil (p. 462)

drought prolonged periods of little or no rainfall (p. 67)

Duma elected assembly agreed to by the Russian czar after the Revolution of 1905 (p. 722)

dynastic cycle rise and fall of Chinese rulers, according to the Mandate of Heaven (p. 329)

dynasty ruling family (p. 183)

E

Eastern Orthodox Church eastern half of the Christian Church; centered in Constantinople and controlled by the Byzantine emperor after the division of the Roman Empire in A.D. 330 (p. 566)

economic sanctions cutting off trade with another country to pressure it to change its policies (p. 127)

ejido (eh HEE do) Mexican agricultural community (p. 495)

elevation height above sea level (p. 10)

elite small group of people with high social status (p. 104)

embargo complete halt to trade (p. 483)

encomienda right to demand taxes or labor from native peoples in the Spanish colonies (p. 268)

entrepreneur person who risks his or her money to set up a business (p. 34)

escarpment steep cliff (p. 60)

ethnicity attachment to one's own ethnic group (p. 122)

ethnocentrism judging other cultures by the standards of one's own culture (p. 22)

European Community (EC) organization to promote the free movement of goods, people, and capital among member nations; it developed from the European Economic Community, or Common Market, which was founded in 1957 (pp. 692–93)

exports goods sent to markets outside a country (p. 7)

extended family several generations living in one household (p. 14)

extraterritoriality principle allowing westerners accused of a crime in China to be tried in special, western-run courts instead of in Chinese courts (p. 345)

F

factory system system, which began in the British textile industry during the Industrial Revolution, that brought workers and machines together in one place to manufacture goods (p. 671)

fertigation farming method pioneered in Israel that pumps water and fertilizer directly to the roots of plants (p. 598)

feudalism system of government in Europe during the Middle Ages, as well as in Japan during the late 1100s, under which local lords ruled the land but were bound by ties of loyalty to higher lords and to the monarch or emperor (p. 395)

fief in medieval times, an estate granted by the monarch to a powerful lord, who owed the monarch loyalty and military service in exchange (p. 651)

filial piety according to the Chinese philosopher Confucius, the duty and respect that children owe their parents (p. 331)

"four Asian tigers" four countries in Asia—Taiwan, Hong Kong, Singapore, and South Korea—that have accomplished rapid industrialization (p. 384)

Four Modernizations program instituted by Deng Xiaoping, successor in 1978 to Mao Zedong, to modernize agriculture, expand industry, develop science and technology, and upgrade China's defense forces (p. 357)

franchise right to vote (p. 674)

free trade international trade without restrictions (p. 495)

free world term used after World War II to distinguish the democratic nations of the West from the Soviet Union and the communist nations of Eastern Europe (p. 686)

G

gamelan (GAHM uh lahn) traditional Indonesian orchestra (p. 292)

genocide deliberate killing of an ethnic or religious group (p. 279)

geography study of people, their environments, and their resources (p. 4)

geothermal energy energy from heat that is released in geysers, hot springs, and volcanoes (p. 302)

glasnost openness and honesty in discussing the problems faced by the Soviet Union (p. 746)

Gospels Christian historical sources that tell the story of the life of Jesus; written by the followers of Jesus after his death (p. 565)

Great Leap Forward modernization program introduced in China in 1958 by Mao Zedong under which the nation was divided into communes, and peasants were forced to give up their land (p. 355)

Green Revolution twentieth-century technological advances in agriculture that resulted in much larger harvests (p. 213)

griot (GREE oh) storyteller in traditional African societies (p. 143)

guerrilla warfare hit-and-run attacks by small bands of fighters against a larger power (p. 109)

Guomindang (gwoh mihn dang) Nationalist party of China that was established after 1911, when China declared itself a republic (p. 346)

H

hacienda large plantation in Latin America (p. 461)

haiku short poem of 17 syllables divided into three lines of five, seven, and five syllables each (p. 424)

hajj pilgrimage to Mecca that all Muslims who are able are expected to make once in their lifetime (p. 571)

han'gul simple, efficient phonetic alphabet introduced in Korea in the mid-1400s that contributed to making it one of the world's most literate nations (p. 380)

hejira migration of Muhammad and his followers from Mecca to Medina in A.D. 622 (p. 570)

Hellenistic civilization cultural blending of Greek civilization with the cultures of the ancient Middle East (p. 562)

Hermit Kingdom term applied to Korea during its period of isolation, from the late 1300s to the early 1900s (p. 379)

hieroglyphics ancient form of Egyptian writing that used pictures and symbols to represent words and sounds (p. 75)

high island type of island in Oceania that is formed by the top of an active volcano (p. 308)

hill area of raised land that is lower and less steep than a mountain (p. 11)

Holocaust Nazi genocide against the Jews during World War II (p. 680)

homogeneous society society in which the people share a common ethnic and cultural background (p. 377)

huipil (wee PEEL) simple tunic worn in Guatemala (p. 520)

hydroelectric power energy produced by moving water (p. 60)

I

icon Christian painting of Jesus, Mary, or a saint (p. 717)

ideograph symbol used to express an idea such as beauty, joy, or justice (p. 328)

imperialism control by one country of the political, economic, or cultural life of another country or region (p. 35)

imports goods brought into a country (p. 7)

impressionism European school of painting in the late 1800s that tried to capture fleeting visual "impressions" made by light and shadows (p. 702)

Indian National Congress (INC) Indian organization established in 1885 to support political change in British-dominated India (p. 198)

indulgence a pardon for sins, sold in the early 1500s by the Roman Catholic Church to raise money (p. 663)

Industrial Revolution period during which machines replaced hand tools, and steam and electricity took the place of human and animal power (p. 34)

infant mortality rate at which infants do not survive at birth (p. 214)

inflation economic cycle marked by a sharp increase in prices (p. 499)

interdependence mutual dependence of countries on goods, resources, and knowledge from other parts of the world (p. 7)

intifada mass uprising by Palestinians in territory held by Israel (p. 619)

Islamic fundamentalism Muslim movement against westernization and secularism that supports a return to the values of the Koran (p. 595)

isolationism policy of avoiding foreign involvements and contacts (p. 380)

J

Jainism (JĪN ihz um) religion of South Asia; it developed from efforts to reform Hinduism and stresses nonviolence (p. 182)

joint-stock company private trading company that sells shares of stock to investors to raise capital; in the 1600s and 1700s, this was done to finance European trade and expansion abroad (p. 663)

K

Kaaba sacred shrine in Mecca dedicated to God by the Islamic prophet Muhammad (p. 570)

Kabuki form of Japanese theater that uses elaborate stage settings, costumes, and makeup, and deals with such themes as love and revenge (p. 425)

Kana simplified Chinese characters developed by the Japanese and used phonetically (p. 395)

karma in Hinduism, the belief that every deed, mental or physical, in this life affects a person's fate in a future life (p. 179)

Khmer Rouge Cambodian communist guerrillas who, in 1969–1970, gained increasing local support as a result of the invasion of Cambodia by the United States and South Vietnam (p. 278)

knight in medieval Europe, a mounted warrior who was a vassal of a feudal lord (p. 651)

kowtow low bow expressing respect and submission to the Chinese emperor (p. 344)

kulak prosperous peasant of the Soviet Union (p. 735)

L

land reform government program in which ownership of farmland is redistributed (p. 212)

latitude distance north or south of the Equator (p. 4)

leaching dissolving and washing away of the soil's nutrients by constant heavy rains (p. 66)

liberation theology movement in the Roman Catholic Church that urges the Church to take a more active role in changing social conditions that contribute to poverty (p. 490)

limited monarchy government in which a monarch does not have absolute power (p. 666)

lineage group of distant kin who trace their descent to a common ancestor (p. 86)

literacy ability to read and write (p. 39)

location position of a place on the Earth's surface (p. 4)

loess (LOH ehs) yellow-brown soil that winds carry across the North China Plain into the Yellow River (p. 326)

Long March flight of Chinese Communists under Mao Zedong in 1934 from the armies of the Chinese Nationalists under Chiang Kai-shek; it lasted more than a year and covered 6,000 miles (9,656 km) (p. 347)

longitude distance east or west of the Prime Meridian (p. 4)

low island type of island in Oceania that is formed by a coral reef (p. 308)

M

magical realism writing style blending fact, fantasy, and humor used by Colombian author Gabriel García Márquez (p. 517)

Magna Carta document that English nobles forced King John to sign in 1215; established the idea that nobles had certain rights and the king had to respect the law (p. 666)

Mahabharata epic poem containing basic Hindu ideas; one of the two great sources of Indian literature (p. 234)

Mahayana (mah huh YAH nuh) **Buddhism** one of the two main sects of Buddhism; worships the Buddha as a god (pp. 181–82)

maize corn, one of the principal crops planted by Mexican farmers 5,000 years ago (p. 448)

mandate territory administered but not owned by a member of the League of Nations (p. 584)

Mandate of Heaven Chinese belief that heaven grants a ruler the mandate, or right, to rule; in turn, the people owe the ruler complete loyalty and obedience (p. 329)

manor in medieval Europe, a self-sufficient community consisting of a village and surrounding lands administered by a feudal lord (p. 652)

map projection way of showing the curved Earth on a flat surface (p. 8)

maquiladora (mah kee luh DOHR uh) foreign-owned industrial plant in Mexico in which local workers assemble parts into finished goods (p. 496)

Marshall Plan plan announced in 1947 by the United States to help European nations rebuild their economies after World War II (p. 688)

martial law temporary rule by the military (p. 274)

martyr someone who suffers or dies for his or her beliefs (p. 565)

Marxism form of socialism, named for the philosopher Karl Marx, that had become popular among Russian revolutionaries by the 1890s (p. 721)

mercantilism theory that a country's economic strength depended on increasing its gold supply by exporting more goods than it imported (p. 459)

messiah expected savior chosen by God to deliver the Jews from foreign rule and restore the kingdom of Israel (p. 565)

mestizo people of mixed European and Native American ancestry (p. 446)

militarism glorification of the military and a readiness for war (p. 406)

millet non-Muslim community in the Ottoman Empire that owed loyalty to the Ottoman sultan but was ruled by its own religious leader (p. 578)

mir commune that regulated village life in Russia before the revolutions in 1917 (p. 717)

modernization changes in a nation that enable it to set up a stable government and produce a high level of goods and services (p. 39)

monopoly complete control over a market or product (p. 194)

monotheism worship of one god (p. 17)

monsoon seasonal wind that dominates the climate of South Asia (p. 165)

mosaic design made from colored stones (p. 518)

mosque Muslim house of worship (p. 81)

mountain high, rugged land that rises above the surrounding land (p. 10)

mudra symbolic hand gesture used in Indian dance (p. 235)

multiculturalism policy that encourages people to preserve their distinct cultural traditions (p. 527)

multinational corporation huge business enterprises with branches in many countries (p. 114)

Muslim League Muslim organization founded in India in 1906 in response to growing Hindu nationalism (p. 198)

N

Narmada Valley Project (NVP) controversial project in central India that calls for building 30 major dams and more than 3,000 smaller dams (p. 228)

nationalism pride in and loyalty to one's country (p. 36)

nationalize to place under state control (p. 273)

NATO (North Atlantic Treaty Organization) organization formed in 1949 by the United States, Canada, Turkey, Greece, and eight Western European nations to protect one another from a communist attack (p. 688)

négritude movement African movement led by the Senegalese poet Léopold Sédar Senghor in the 1930s; it strengthened Pan-Africanism by encouraging Africans to value their heritage (p. 108)

NEP (New Economic Policy) economic reforms instituted by Lenin to ease the crisis that existed after the 1918–1921 civil war in Russia (p. 732)

nirvana in Buddhism, the condition of having no desires (p. 180)

nomad member of a hunting people who travel from place to place to find food (p. 28)

nonalignment policy that did not favor either the United States or the Soviet Union during the Cold War (p. 135)

nuclear family traditionally, a wife, husband, and their children (p. 14)

nuclear free zone area in which nuclear weapons and nuclear power are banned (p. 307)

O

OAS (Organization of American States) regional organization established in 1948 to maintain peace, discourage foreign intervention, and promote economic development and democracy (pp. 512–13)

oasis fertile desert area that has enough water to support plant and animal life (p. 553)

occupied territory land seized by Israel during the 1967 war with Arab nations (p. 617)

oligarchy system of government in which a small elite has ruling power (p. 475)

OPEC (Organization of Petroleum Exporting Countries) organization of major oil-producing countries established in 1960 to determine how much oil to produce and at what price to sell it (p. 612)

Organization of African Unity (OAU) organization of independent nations of Africa formed in 1963 to support independence movements and economic cooperation and to promote peace (p. 134)

Outback vast, dry, sunbaked interior of Australia (p. 299)

P

pacifism opposition to the use of force under any circumstances (p. 419)

paddy rice field (p. 260)

pampas in South America, the grassy plains that stretch from Argentina into Uruguay (p. 442)

Pan-Africanism nationalist movement that began in the early 1900s and called for unifying all of Africa (p. 108)

pan-Arabism mid-twentieth-century movement to unite all Arabs based on their common language and culture (p. 591)

parable short story with a simple moral lesson (p. 565)

parliamentary democracy government ruled democratically by a national representative body that has supreme legislative powers (p. 205)

patrician wealthy landowner in ancient Rome, member of the group that controlled the government (p. 647)

Pax Romana literally, "Roman peace"; the first 200 years of the Roman Empire, during which there was relative peace and prosperity (p. 648)

peaceful coexistence in the 1950s, position held by the Soviet leader Nikita Khrushchev, who believed that communist and democratic nations could exist peacefully side by side (p. 752)

penal colony place to which people who have been convicted of crimes are sent (p. 303)

peninsular (peh NIHN suh LAHR) official sent from Spain to rule Spanish colonies in Latin America (p. 464)

peon Indians in Latin America who were forced to work for large landowners in order to pay off a debt (p. 468)

per capita income average income per person in a country or region (p. 691)

perestroika (pehr uh STROI kuh) restructuring of the Soviet economy to make it more efficient and productive (p. 746)

permafrost layer of soil below the surface of the earth that remains permanently frozen (p. 710)

pharaoh (FAIR oh) ruler of ancient Egypt (p. 73)

plain large area of level or gently rolling land (p. 11)

plateau large area of high flat, or gently rolling land (p. 12)

plebeian (plee BEE uhn) member of the group of common people in ancient Rome who could vote but could not hold office (p. 647)

plebiscite direct popular vote on a single question or issue (p. 224)

PLO (Palestine Liberation Organization) organization established by Palestinian leaders in 1964 to set up a Palestinian state (p. 618)

pogrom organized act of violence against Jews (p. 720)

Politburo Political Bureau, or small executive body, which made all important decisions in the Soviet Union (p. 735)

polygamy practice of having more than one spouse (p. 88)

polytheism worship of more than one god (p. 17)

pope head of the Roman Catholic Church (p. 566)

population density average number of people living in a given area (p. 41)

population explosion large increase in population due to the availability of better health care (p. 41)

Prague Spring short-lived period during the spring of 1968 when reformers in Soviet-dominated Czechoslovakia tried to blend democracy with socialism to create greater freedom (p. 756–57)

predestination belief of Protestant reformer John Calvin that God decides in advance whether an individual will be saved or condemned (p. 664)

privatization selling state-owned industries to private investors (p. 39)

proletariat industrial working class (p. 352)

propaganda spread of ideas to promote a cause or damage an opposing cause (p. 352)

protectorate country with its own government whose policies are directed by an outside power (p. 268)

Provisional Government temporary government that introduced reforms such as freedom of speech and of religion in Russia after the uprising of March 1917 (p. 731)

purdah among Hindus and Muslims, the complete seclusion in which some women live (p. 193)

Q

Quebec Act act passed by Great Britain in 1774 granting the French in Quebec the right to keep their language and religion as well as observe French civil law (p. 531)

quipu knotted string used by the Incas, who lacked a system of writing, to keep records and accounts of such things as the size of a harvest (p. 453)

R

racism belief that one racial group is superior to another (p. 22)

rajah (RAH juh) hereditary Aryan chiefs who ruled the villages (p. 173)

Ramayana epic poem containing Hindu teachings; one of the two great sources of Indian literature (p. 234)

realism the depiction in art and literature of life as it really is, popular in Europe in the late 1800s (p. 701)

Red Guards Chinese students and factory workers who supported Mao Zedong's Cultural Revolution with abusive tactics against those suspected of not supporting Chairman Mao (p. 356)

refugee person who flees his or her homeland to seek safety elsewhere (p. 615)

regionalism strong local traditions that divide people within a country or region (p. 442)

reincarnation in Hinduism, the belief that the soul is reborn in various forms (p. 179)

reparations payment for damages (p. 421)

reprisal forceful act in response to injury (p. 618)

republic form of government in which the people choose the leaders who represent them (p. 18)

Revolution of 1905 violent uprising of Russian workers and peasants against the injustices of the czar's government (p. 722)

Ring of Fire term for line of volcanoes around the Pacific Ocean; these volcanoes provide fertile soil for Island Southeast Asia (p. 251)

romanticism nineteenth-century European movement that reacted against the Enlightenment and valued feelings and emotions above reason (p. 701)

S

sacrament one of the seven sacred rites administered by the Roman Catholic Church (p. 653)

samizdat (sahm ihz DAHT) system among Soviet writers for circulating their work secretly to avoid government censorship and seek publication abroad (p. 762)

samurai Japanese warrior knights (p. 395)

Sandinistas leftist group in Nicaragua led by Daniel Ortega; gained control of the government after the overthrow of the dictator Anastasio Somoza in 1979 and introduced major land reform, took over businesses, and organized social programs to benefit the poor (p. 483)

Sanskrit language the Aryans of India developed to write down their oral religious traditions (p. 173)

satrap governor of a province in ancient Persia (p. 559)

satyagraha (SUHT ya gruh ha) Gandhi's method ("truth force") of nonviolent resistance to end injustice (p. 202)

scientific method step-by-step approach to scientific study that emphasizes experimentation and observation and relies on mathematics to test results and prove theories (p. 667)

scribe someone who writes copies of manuscripts and documents (p. 557)

secede break away and withdraw, especially as a group, from a country or an organization (p. 112)

sect religious group (p. 179)

secular worldly or unrelated to religion (p. 208)

sepoy Indian troops who served in the British army (p. 196)

serf a peasant in feudal society who was tied to the land of a lord, to whom he or she owed service in exchange for protection (p. 651)

service economy economy in which most people have jobs that provide services to individuals, communities, and businesses (p. 537)

Shariah (shuh REE uh) sacred law of Islam that is based on the Koran (p. 593)

Shinto Japanese religion that stresses the link between people and the forces of nature (p. 398)

shogun chief general of the army who was the real ruler in feudal Japan (p. 395)

Sikh follower of Sikhism, an Indian religion formed in the early 1500s by blending elements of Islam and Hinduism (p. 206)

Six Day War brief Arab-Israeli war in 1967 in which Israel made major territorial gains (p. 617)

socialism system in which the government owns and operates major businesses and controls other parts of the economy (p. 112)

socialist realism glorification by Soviet writers and artists of socialism and Marxist-Leninist ideas (p. 762)

Socratic method question-and-answer technique developed by the Greek philosopher Socrates to teach students to examine their beliefs and discard any that could not be proved through reason (p. 646)

soviet council of workers, soldiers, and peasants formed by Russian revolutionaries to challenge the established government (p. 731)

Spanish-American War in 1898, war declared against Spain by the United States, which joined Cuban patriots in their fight for independence from Spain (p. 506)

sphere of influence area of a country in which a foreign nation has special economic privileges, such as the right to build railroads and factories (p. 345)

stupa (STOO puh) shrine containing the remains of the Buddha or other holy persons (p. 184)

subcontinent large landmass that juts out from a continent (p. 162)

subculture group of people within a society who have their own separate beliefs, values, and customs (p. 22)

subsistence farmer farmer who produces enough harvest to supply personal needs but has little or no surplus (p. 87)

suffrage right to vote (p. 306)

sultan ruling monarch in a Muslim country (p. 186)

Swahili (swah HEE lee) language of East Africa that blends some Arabic words into the region's basic Bantu languages (p. 71)

T

tariff tax on imported goods (p. 39)

technology skills and tools a people use (p. 20)

Ten Commandments religious and moral laws of the Hebrew people (p. 564)

tenant farmer farmer who rents land from a large landowner and pays the owner either in cash or with a portion of the crop (p. 212)

theocracy nation ruled by religious leaders (p. 604)

Theravada (ther uh VAH duh) **Buddhism** one of the two main sects of Buddhism; stresses monastic life and respects the Buddha as a teacher but does not worship him as a god (p. 181)

tierra caliente ("hot land") lowlands in Latin America, such as the Yucatán Peninsula of Mexico and the Amazon Basin, where tropical crops such as bananas and sugarcane flourish (p. 445)

tierra fría ("cold land") highland areas in Latin America that lie 6,000 feet (1,828 m) above sea level, the site of such major cities as Mexico City and Bogotá (p. 445)

tierra templada ("temperate land") areas in Latin America that lie above an elevation of 3,000 feet (914 m), such as Mexico's Central Plateau and the valleys in the Andes (p. 445)

topography physical features of a place or region (p. 10)

Torah sacred book of the Hebrew people (p. 564)

totalitarian state nation in which the government controls every aspect of citizens' lives through a single-party dictatorship (p. 352)

trade imbalance result of a country exporting more goods to other nations than it imports from them, or importing more goods than it exports (p. 420)

Treaty of Kanagawa treaty signed by the United States and Japan in 1854 granting American ships the right to use two Japanese ports for supplies and giving the United States the right to send a diplomatic representative to Japan (p. 402)

Treaty of Versailles peace settlement that imposed harsh terms on Germany after World War I (p. 678)

tributary state country that pays tribute in the form of gifts to another nation or empire as acknowledgment of that nation's control or as payment for protection (p. 255)

Triple Alliance pre–World War I agreement by Germany, Austria-Hungary, and Italy to assist one another in case of war (p. 677)

Triple Entente (ahn TAHNT) pre–World War I agreement by France, Russia, and Great Britain to assist one another in case of war (p. 677)

tropics area between the Tropic of Cancer and the Tropic of Capricorn (p. 64)

U

Upanishads (oo PAN ih shadz) sacred Hindu texts that help explain the ideas in the Vedas, which are Hindu oral religious traditions (p. 178)

urbanization growth of cities (p. 34)

Urdu (UR doo) South Asian language that combines Persian and Hindi and is written in Arabic script (p. 186)

V

varna four classes into which the Aryans divided people (p. 173)

vassal in medieval Europe, a lesser lord who was granted estates by a powerful lord, to whom he owed loyalty and service (p. 651)

Vedas oral religious traditions of the Aryans that are still used in religious ceremonies in India (p. 173)

vegetation plant life of a place or region (p. 10)

viceroy official who rules in place of a king (p. 459)

voyageurs (vwah yah ZHERS) French fur traders of the 1600s who traveled to the interior of North America, learned Indian languages, and adopted many Indian customs (p. 530)

W

Warsaw Pact agreement in 1955 by the Soviet Union and the satellite nations of Eastern Europe to assist one another in case of invasion by the western powers (p. 688)

wat Buddhist temple (p. 289)

welfare state system under which the government assumes responsibility for its citizens' social and economic well-being (p. 692)

westernization adoption of western culture (p. 36)

Z

zaibatsu (zī baht soo) in Japan, powerful family groups that founded huge business conglomerates that controlled large parts of the economy (p. 405)

Zen Buddhism form of Buddhism in Japan that emphasizes meditation and self-discipline as the way to achieve salvation (p. 399)

ziggurat huge, many-tiered temple; the center of life in Sumer, an early Middle Eastern civilization (p. 557)

Zionism movement among European Jews to set up a Jewish homeland in Palestine (p. 587)

CONNECTIONS WITH LITERATURE

The following annotated bibliography provides a brief description of works of literature that have been keyed to topics in *World Cultures: A Global Mosaic.* The style of the references in the chapter text is as follows: (📖 See Connections With Literature, page 804, "The Cow-Tail Switch.") The works listed here are available from your school or local library. Page references have been provided for those works available in *Prentice Hall Literature, Paramount Edition.*

UNIT 1

In Suspect Terrain, John McPhee

John McPhee takes an unusual subject—in this case, geology—and writes about it in an interesting and vivid style. In *In Suspect Terrain,* he combines stories of journeys through ancient terrains with lively travel anecdotes.

Clan of the Cave Bear, Jean M. Auel

In this novel, Auel relates a beautiful and powerful tale that dates from the dawn of humankind. The story is about the people belonging to the clan of the Cave Bear and their relationships with one another and with Ayla, the novel's heroine.

"If I Forget Thee, Oh Earth," Arthur C. Clarke

In this science fiction story, Clarke describes life on a space station that is completely enclosed to sustain life. One day, Marvin, a 10-year-old boy, takes a trip with his father outside the space colony to see the stars and the desolate and dead planet Earth. (See *Prentice Hall Literature, Gold,* page 157.)

UNIT 2

"The Story of the Flood," from *The Epic of Gilgamesh*

Many ancient peoples of the Middle East had myths and legends about floods. The Sumerians and Babylonians, who experienced the flooding of the Tigris and Euphrates rivers, created this flood story. (See *Prentice Hall Literature, World Masterpieces,* page 23.)

"Forefathers," Birago Diop

Family ties are important in African cultures, as elsewhere. In this poem, Diop expresses the belief that those who lived before us are not really dead and gone. Instead, they live on in the natural world. Diop believes that we can find them by watching and listening closely to the world around us.

"The Cow-Tail Switch," retold by Harold Courlander and George Herzog

In this Liberian folktale, Ogaloussa fails to return from a hunting trip. He is forgotten about until his son Puli is born. When Puli grows up, he asks about his father. The question sparks an event that teaches an important lesson about life, death, and remembrance. (See *Prentice Hall Literature, Copper,* page 611.)

"Civil Peace," Chinua Achebe

From 1967 to 1970, the Biafrans of Nigeria fought a bloody civil war against the central government. Achebe's story gives a fascinating glimpse of Nigerian life just as the war was ending. The author presents the hardships of that uncertain time, tempered with humorous events. (See *Prentice Hall Literature, Platinum,* page 215.)

"Civilian and Soldier," Wole Soyinka

The speaker in this poem is a civilian caught in a civil war. He tells of a meeting between himself and a soldier who is about to shoot him. Soyinka uses this poem to point out some of the contradictions and truths of political and cultural life in Nigeria. (See *Prentice Hall Literature, World Masterpieces,* page 1363.)

"The Ultimate Safari," Nadine Gordimer

Noble Prize–winning writer Nadine Gordimer has long been a foe of apartheid in her native South Africa. In this story, she describes the plight of black refugees fleeing a war. Their journey takes them through a South African nature preserve that is a "whole country of animals—elephants, lions, jackals."

Things Fall Apart, Chinua Achebe

The book's main character, Okonkwo, is devoted to the customs of his tribe and cannot cope with the arrival of Europeans. His downfall symbolizes the breakdown of traditional ways brought about by colonialism.

"Snapshots of a Wedding," Bessie Head

In this story, Bessie Head depicts a traditional African society in the midst of change. Frame by frame, these "photos" of a wedding reveal a culture in conflict. They show how the old ways of life meet the new, jarring realities of modern society. (See *Prentice Hall Literature, World Masterpieces,* page 1376.)

UNIT 3

"Night," from the *Rig Veda*

This Vedic hymn is a prayer to the goddess Night, asking her for protection against the dangers of the night. Today, we rarely experience the kind of darkness that made the Aryans feel so uncertain when they were away from their village fires. (See *Prentice Hall Literature, World Masterpieces,* page 159.)

Taittiriya Upanishad

The Upanishads were written by many different authors. They present complicated subjects, such as the nature of reality, in dialogues between teachers and students. The Upanishads emphasize that a single principle or reality, Brahman, underlies all existence. (*See Prentice Hall Literature, World Masterpieces,* page 162.)

Siddhartha, Hermann Hesse

This story of a young man's quest for wisdom in ancient India is based on the life of Siddhartha Gautama, founder of the Buddhist religion. One theme of the novel is that people cannot find true happiness until they fully understand themselves.

Bhagavad-Gita

Although it is a self-contained book, the *Bhagavad-Gita* is a small part of India's famous epic, the *Mahabharata*. The *Mahabharata* is the story of the conflict between two branches of a family over their rights to a kingdom in northern India. The *Bhagavad-Gita* takes place on a battlefield prior to the fighting. (See *Prentice Hall Literature, World Masterpieces,* page 176.)

"The Artist," Rabindranath Tagore

In this Indian story, the office manager Govinda thinks that making money is a sacred command. He tries to instill this belief in his brother's widow and son. They resist his efforts, however, because they love painting more than anything else. (See *Prentice Hall Literature, World Masterpieces,* page 1192.)

"Old Man of the Temple," R. K. Narayan

In this ghost story, a famous Indian writer tells about a man who haunts the ruins of an ancient temple. The man possesses the narrator's taxi driver and refuses to believe that the world of kings and princes has passed away. (See *Prentice Hall Literature, Platinum,* page 61.)

"Sibi," from the *Mahabharata*

The *Mahabharata* is the world's longest and India's greatest epic poem. In this excerpt, the gods test King Sibi's integrity and he passes the test. Sibi's character symbolizes the values and beliefs of the people of India. (See *Prentice Hall Literature, World Masterpieces,* page 168.)

"Numskull and the Rabbit," from the *Panchatantra*

The *Panchatantra*, "a treatise in five chapters," consists of fables that instruct young princes in how to govern a kingdom and conduct their lives. Animal tales, such as "Numskull and the Rabbit" and Aesop's fables, teach moral lessons. (See *Prentice Hall Literature, World Masterpieces,* page 184.)

UNIT 4

The Ebb-Tide, Robert Louis Stevenson

Robert Louis Stevenson wrote *The Ebb-Tide* in his usual spellbinding style. This thrilling adventure story is set in the South Seas. It was based on a draft written by his stepson Lloyd Osbourne.

In the South Seas, Robert Louis Stevenson

In the late 1880s, Stevenson left England to sail in the South Seas for an extended period, finally settling on Samoa. During this period, Stevenson developed a deep interest in South Sea politics and wrote descriptive and historical accounts of the area. This influence is evident in the novel.

Fallen Angels, Walter Dean Myers

The author dedicates *Fallen Angels* to his brother who died in the Vietnam War. It is a riveting account of war as seen by those who lived in the trenches.

Haing Ngor: A Cambodian Odyssey, Haing S. Ngor

This is the story of the four years of terror and brutality that Dr. Ngor spent under Pol Pot's rule. It is also a story of undying love and the courage of the human spirit.

Land of the Long White Cloud: Maori Myths, Tales, and Legends, Kiri Te Kanawa

The Polynesian sailors who explored New Zealand, the land of the long white cloud, also uncovered New Zealand's rich oral tradition. Included in this collection are tales of frightening monsters, adventures in the spirit world, and young romance.

The Boy in the Bush, D. H. Lawrence

After being expelled from school, Jack Grant arrives in Australia in 1882 to start a new life. *The Boy in the Bush* is the story of Grant's life in Australia and the hardships he endures as he moves from childhood to adulthood. This novel, together with

Kangaroo, is the result of D. H. Lawrence's visit to Australia.

UNIT 5

Poems by Wang Wei

Wang Wei is well known for his beautiful poems and vivid landscape paintings. His conversion to Buddhism had a tremendous impact on his later poetry. These poems exhibit the calmness and restraint that are characteristic of Buddhism and Wang Wei's poetry. (See *Prentice Hall Literature, World Masterpieces,* page 230.)

The Analects, Confucius

The Analects, or collected sayings of Confucius, were compiled long after his death by followers of his disciples. In all of his writing, Confucius emphasized the importance of moral conduct, or how people should act. The short verses of wisdom in *The Analects* convey his code of conduct. (See *Prentice Hall Literature, World Masterpieces,* page 214.)

"Homecoming Stranger," Bei Dao

Imagine that your father had been in jail for political offenses since you were young and now he is coming home. In this touching Chinese story, Bei Dao explores the difficult reunion of a father who is little more than a "homecoming stranger" to his daughter. (See *Prentice Hall Literature, Platinum,* page 191.)

"My Old Home," Lu Hsun

The narrator in "My Old Home" is visited by a boyhood friend, Jun-tu, whom he has not seen in more than 30 years. Greeting the narrator as "Master," Jun-tu reminds him of the social boundaries that now divide them. As they part company, the narrator looks ahead to a new life in which hopes for brotherhood might be fulfilled. (See *Prentice Hall Literature, World Masterpieces,* page 1182.)

The Silence of Love, Pak Tu-jin

In *The Silence of Love*, Pak Tu-jin, one of Korea's contemporary writers, reflects hope in the midst of the suffering, doubt, and fear caused by unhappy phases in Korea's history. Many of his poems use symbols from nature to communicate his personal feelings of hope and his concern for the fate of Korea.

The Pillow Book, Sei Shonagon

The Pillow Book is a collection of personal notes written during Sei's 10 years of court service during the Heian period (794–1160) in Japan. Filled with character sketches, descriptions, anecdotes, lists, and witty insights, this book provides a detailed portrait of upper-class life in Japan at that time. (See *Prentice Hall Literature, World Masterpieces,* page 296.)

"The Jay," Kawabata Yasunari

In "The Jay," Kawabata connects an image of a fragile, injured bird with the characters in his story. The fear, loneliness, and pain that the bird feels, for example, surface in each of the characters. As is typical of much of Kawabata's work, this story is characterized by sadness and the fragile, mortal quality of life. (See *Prentice Hall Literature, World Masterpieces,* page 1430.)

Selected Haiku, *The Penguin Book of Japanese Verse*

Reflecting Japanese cultural interests, haiku are poems characterized by precision and simplicity. They employ the power of suggestion to present spare yet clear images that stimulate thought and evoke emotion. (See *Prentice Hall Literature, World Masterpieces,* pages 288–292.)

The Deserted Crone, Zeami

Zeami is known as the most gifted and prolific No playwright. His plays are filled with rich, beautiful imagery. They offer universal and timeless insights about human existence. *The Deserted Crone* is based on the legend of an old woman who has been abandoned by her nephew at his wife's insistence. (See *Prentice Hall Literature, World Masterpieces,* page 306.)

UNIT 6

"Popocatepétl and Ixtlaccihuatl," retold by Juliet Piggott

Southeast of Tenochtitlán, present-day Mexico City, stand two volcanoes—Popocatepétl, or "Smoking Mountain," and Ixtlaccihuatl, or "The White Woman." The Aztecs claimed the volcanoes as their own and told this legend about their creation. (See *Prentice Hall Literature, Bronze,* page 613.)

"The Handsomest Drowned Man in the World," Gabriel García Márquez

The villagers of a small island have limited contact with other people. After discovering a man's body washed up on the shore, they become intrigued and obsessed with him. After cleaning the man up and naming him, the villagers bring him to life in their minds and their fantasies. (See *Prentice Hall Literature, World Masterpieces,* page 1213.)

"Bread," Gabriela Mistral

Mistral's poetry usually centered around the lives of women and children. In a series of poems, Mistral celebrated the ordinary things of life. In "Bread," she expresses reverence for bread, a food that can sustain life and bring together family and friends. (See *Prentice Hall Literature, World Masterpieces,* page 1166.)

"The Glass of Milk," Manuel Rojas

A young seaman who has not eaten in three days is stranded without money or work in a strange port. When he cannot bear the hunger pangs anymore, he goes to a dairy bar to order a glass of milk and cookies. As he slowly eats, the reality of his desperate situation overcomes him. (See *Prentice Hall Literature, World Masterpieces,* page 1154.)

Salvador, Joan Didion

Joan Didion, a journalist, has the unique ability to retell hard news events as a story. She portrays events and characters with realism and emotion. In *Salvador*, Didion reveals her experiences in El Salvador during its civil war as well as the horrible conditions under which the people lived.

The House of the Spirits, Isabel Allende

In this novel, Isabel Allende, the niece of former Chilean president Salvador Allende, tells about the lives of the Truebas, a Chilean family. The story is Allende's memorial to the life she lost through the political upheavals in Chile. (See *Prentice Hall Literature, Gold,* page 63.)

"A Very Old Man With Enormous Wings," Gabriel García Márquez

When Pelayo wakes one morning, he finds a very old man with enormous wings washed up on the shore. Each villager who comes to Pelayo's house to see the stranger has a different reaction to the old man and a different idea of who he is. (See *Prentice Hall Literature, Gold,* page 165.)

"Significant Moments in the Life of My Mother," Margaret Atwood

Margaret Atwood is one of Canada's most visible, versatile, and accessible writers. In this short story, Atwood shares some of the most memorable and revealing scenes from her mother's life. Through the magic of her words, Atwood creates a lifelike portrait of her mother.

UNIT 7

"Prologue" and "The Battle With Humbaba," from *The Epic of Gilgamesh*

This epic is about a legendary king of a Sumerian city-state. Although it was written long ago, it deals with timeless themes: how to become known and respected, how to cope with the loss of a dear friend, and how to accept one's own inevitable death. (See *Prentice Hall Literature, World Masterpieces,* page 15.)

"The Opening," "Power," and "Daybreak," from the Koran

These three Surahs, or chapters, are representative of the works found in the Koran. "The Opening," one of the most important and well-known Surahs, illustrates how Muslims praise, glorify, and submit to God, the Protector and Sustainer of all life. (See *Prentice Hall Literature, World Masterpieces,* page 108.)

"The Diameter of the Bomb," Yehuda Amichai

In his timeless poem about the destruction of war, Amichai describes the effects of a bomb as its circle of death engulfs more and more lives. (See *Prentice Hall Literature, World Masterpieces,* page 1342.)

"Selected Poetry," by Nazim Hikmet

Hikmet is popularly recognized as the first and foremost modern Turkish poet. During his lifetime, Hikmet was arrested several times and was under constant surveillance. After 1936, Hikmet's poetry was banned in Turkey. He was accused of inciting the Turkish navy to rebellion when the police discovered military cadets reading his poetry. For Hikmet, poetry was a matter of life and death. (See *Prentice Hall Literature, Platinum,* page 633.)

Letters From the Sand: The Letters of Desert Storm and Other Wars, compiled by the United States Postal Service.

The story of war can be told in the letters, pictures, poetry, and songs of the soldiers who were there. Included in this book are the words and pictures of those who served in the Persian Gulf, Vietnam, and Korean wars; World Wars I and II; the Spanish-American War; and the Civil War.

"The Fisherman and the Jinee," from *A Thousand and One Nights*, Rumi

While out at sea, a poor fisherman finds a bottle and opens it. Suddenly a jinee, who has been imprisoned in the bottle for 1,800 years, emerges. While imprisoned, the jinee swore he would kill whoever set him free. (See *Prentice Hall Literature, World Masterpieces,* page 128.)

UNIT 8

"Pericles' Funeral Oration," from *History of the Peloponnesian War,* Thucydides

In this oration—a formal speech intended to inspire its listeners and incite them to action—Pericles praises his ancestors, who had given the Athenians a free country and a powerful empire. He speaks of the spirit with which the Athenians had always faced challenges—even war. (See *Prentice Hall Literature, World Masterpieces,* page 408.)

Apology, Plato

Socrates, a Greek philosopher, was critical of local politicians and how they governed. He was arrested and put on trial for atheism (the belief that no gods exist) and for corrupting Athenian youth. The *Apology* is a representation or dramatic re-creation of what Socrates said at his trial. (See *Prentice Hall Literature, World Masterpieces,* page 416.)

"Laura," "The White Doe," and "Spring," from *Canzoniere,* Francesco Petrarch

The *Canzoniere,* which consists of 366 poems, primarily features poetry expressing Petrarch's love for and relationship with Laura. Petrarch met Laura in Avignon and was inspired by her to write some of the world's greatest love poetry. (See *Prentice Hall Literature, World Masterpieces,* page 676.)

The Prince, Niccolò Machiavelli

Whereas many Renaissance writers wrote about how rulers *ought* to act, Machiavelli said that he wrote about how rulers *do* act. In *The Prince*, Machiavelli stresses that morality has no place in politics. According to him, rulers maintain their power not by their goodness but by their strength and cleverness. (See *Prentice Hall Literature, World Masterpieces,* page 669.)

"My Melancholy Face," Heinrich Böll

Many of Böll's stories and novels dramatize the relationship between the individual and society. In this story, Böll takes a satirical look at a totalitarian state. Unaware that a new law demands that all citizens be happy, the narrator is arrested for wearing a melancholy, or gloomy, face.

"The Lady in the Looking Glass: A Reflection," Virginia Woolf

While looking into a mirror, the narrator's observations of the room lead her to think about Isabella Tyson, the owner of the house. The impression of Isabella that the narrator develops based on what she sees outside the looking glass contrasts sharply with the view she sees of Isabella in the looking glass. (See *Prentice Hall Literature, The British Tradition,* page 850.)

"The Overcoat," Nicholas Gogol

In "The Overcoat," Akaky Akakievich is the object of ridicule because of his threadbare overcoat. Akakievich decides to take it to the tailor to be repaired. The tailor convinces Akakievich to buy a new coat instead. When Akakievich wears his new coat, people see him in a different way. (See *Prentice Hall Literature, World Masterpieces,* page 922.)

"A Song on the End of the World," Czeslaw Milosz

In 1939, Nazi Germany invaded and defeated Poland. Warsaw, the capital, came under the control of the Germans. For Milosz and other Poles, the world came to an end. This poem is Milosz's response to the German occupation of Warsaw. (See *Prentice Hall Literature, World Masterpieces,* page 1304.)

"The Bedbug" and Selected Poetry, Vladimir Mayakovsky

Mayakovsky is one of Russia's most famous and controversial poets. Lenin despised him; Stalin declared him one of the most accomplished Russian writers. The poems in this collection reveal the thoughts, relationships, and conflicts of a man who lived during one of the Soviet Union's most fearful and turbulent times.

"The Red Cavalry," Isaac Babel

Found in *The Collected Stories* of Isaac Babel, the stories in this section are about the Soviet horse regiments, or Cossacks, operating in Poland. Babel, a Jew, represents himself in the stories. As a Jew in a Cossack regiment, he tries to come to terms with Cossack attitudes and beliefs.

"The Bridegroom," Alexander Pushkin

"The Bridegroom" is a poem inspired by Russian folk ballads. It tells the story of Natasha, a merchant's daughter, who has been missing for three days. When she returns, she is upset but will not reveal why. (See *Prentice Hall Literature, World Masterpieces,* page 880.)

"How Much Land Does a Man Need?" Leo Tolstoy

Pahom, a peasant, says that if he had plenty of land he would not fear even the devil. The devil overhears Pahom's boast and gives him land in order to gain power over him. One night, Pahom has a dream in which he dies. From then on, Pahom tries to regain his soul from the devil. (See *Prentice Hall Literature, World Masterpieces,* page 944.)

INDEX

An *m*, *c*, or *p* before a page number refers to a map (*m*), graph or chart (*c*), or picture (*p*) on that page.

A

D

E

J

K

L

M

N

O

P

Q

R

S

Credits

Frequently cited sources are abbreviated as follows: PR, Photo Researchers; WC, Woodfin Camp & Associates; GC, The Granger Collection; CWS, Cartoonists & Writers Syndicate; SM, The Stock Market; AR, Art Resource. Page v(*t*), Inge Morath, Magnum; v(*bl*), W. Fisher, FPG; v(*br*), Marvin Newman, The Image Bank; vi(*tl*), Egyptian Museum, Cairo, Courtesy, AR; vi(*c*), Selwyn Tait, Black Star; vi(*bl*), Lisl Dennis, The Image Bank; vi(*r*), The Bettmann Archive; vii(*t*), Superstock; vii(*c*), Luis Villota, SM; vii(*b*), Marilyn Silverstone, Magnum; viii(*tl*), Bruno Barbey, Magnum; viii(*c*), R. Ian Lloyd, SM; viii(*bl*), Robert Frerck, WC; viii(*r*), Maurice Durand Collection of Vietnamese Art, Yale University Library; ix(*t* to *b*), Mike Yamashita, Westlight; Werner Forman Archive; Korean Cultural Service, Karen Kasmauski, WC; x(*t*), Superstock; x(*c*), Randall Hyman; x(*b*), National Archives of Canada; xi(*tr*), Superstock; xi(*c*), AR; xi(*bl*), Olivier Rebbot, Contact Press Images, WC; xi(*br*), Peter Menzel, Stock Boston; xii(*tl*), GC; xii(*c*), Tate Gallery, Courtesy AR; xii(*b*), Anthony Suau, Black Star; xiii(*tr*), C.S. Perkins, Magnum; xiii(*br*), Vladimir Pcholkin, Black Star; xiv(*t*), Bridgeman, AR; xiv(*b*), Hirshhorn Museum and Sculpture Garden.

Unit 1: Page xx (*tl*), GC; (*tr*), Lee Stone, Sygma; (*b*), Bernard P. Wolff, PR; 1, Ulrike Welsch, PR; 2, Bruno Barbey, Magnum; 5, Inge Morath, Magnum; 6 (*r*), Serrailliers, PR; 10–11, W. Fisher, FPG; 15, Marvin Newman, The Image Bank; 16 (*l*), Lester Sloan, WC; 16 (*r*), Steve McCurry, Magnum; 17, Tim Graham, Sygma; 19, Bruno Barbey, Magnum; 21, Ciganovic, FPG; 23, Louise Gubb, JB Pictures; 26, Louis Psihoyos, Matrix; 30, Superstock; 31 (*l*), Paolo Koch, PR; 32 (*r*), Superstock; 34, Mary Evans Picture Library; 36, GC; 38, Radio Times Hulton, The Bettmann Archive; 41, Rio Branco, Magnum; 43, Dr. Muhammad Yunnus, Grameen Bank; 45, Mendel Rabinovitch, FPG; 46, Y. Gellei/P. Maitre, Matrix; 51, Dong Kingman, N.Y.; 52, William Johnson, Stock Boston; 53 (*t*), Adrian Murrell, Allsport USA; 53(*c*) S. Halleran, Allsport USA.

Unit 2: Page 56 (*tl*), Center for African Art, N.Y.; 56 (*bl*), Selwyn Tait, Black Star; 56 (*r*), Superstock; 57, Werner Forman Archive, Private Collection, London; 58, Lisl Dennis, The Image Bank; 61, Robert Caputo, Stock Boston; 63, Marc & Evelyne Bernheim, WC; 67,William & Marsha Levy, PR; 68, V. Englebert, PR; 70, Noboru Komine, PR; 72, George Holton, PR; 73, Egyptian Museum, Cairo, Courtesy, AR; 74, *Ipuy's House & Garden* (restored), Egyptian Expedition of the Metropolitan Museum of Art, Rogers Fund, 1930 (30.4.115); 78, Bibliotheque Nationale, Paris; 81, Eugene Gordon, PR; 83, GC; 84, Superstock; 86 (*l*), Stuart Franklin, Magnum; 86–87, Superstock; 89, TSW; 90, Marc & Evelyne Bernheim, WC; 92, Kal Muller, WC; 94, *Slave Deck of the "Albanoz,"* National Maritime Museum, Greenwich, England; 98, Gregory G. Dimijian, PR; 101, GC; 103, The Bettmann Archive; 104, GC; 106, Gideon Mendel, Magnum; 109, Bernard P. Wolff, PR; 113 (*t*), Marc & Evelyne Bernheim, WC; 113 (*b*), Markku Ulander/Lehtikuva, WC; 114, Pamela Johnson Meyer, PR; 118, P. Maître, Gamma Liaison; 119, Superstock; 121, Owen Franken, Stock Boston; 124, Bruno Barbey, Magnum; 125, Debra Trebitz, Gamma Liaison; 128, Marylee S. Crofts; 129, 130, S. Perkins, Magnum; 132, Center for African Art, N.Y. ; 135 (*t*), David Burnett, Contact Press Images, WC; 135 (*b*), Francois Lochon, Gamma Liaison; 137, Photo News, Gamma-Liaison, Inc.; 138, Anthony Bannister Photo Library; 141, Reuters/Bettmann Newsphotos; 142, Peter Turnley, Black Star; 144, Marc & Evelyne Bernheim, WC; 146–147, New Yorker Films; 146, Pete Turner, The Image Bank; 148, 153, Center for African Art, N.Y.; 154, *The Prevalence of Ritual: Baptism* by Romare Bearden, Hirshhorn Museum and Sculpture Garden, Smithsonian Institution, Gift of Joseph H. Hirshhorn, 1966, Photography, Lee Stalsworth; 155 (*r*), *Bust of a Sailor* by Pablo Picasso, Art Resource; 155 (*l*), Marc & Evelyne Bernheim, WC.

Unit 3: page 158 (*l*), TSW; 158 (*c*), Allan Eaton, Ancient Art and Architecture, London; 158 (*r*), Takishi Takahara, PR; 159, Harry Gruyaert, Magnum; 160, D. Banerjee, Dinodia, Bombay; 163 (*l*), John Elk, Stock Boston; 163 (*r*), Lindsay Hubbard, WC; 167, Tomas Muscionico, Contact Press Images, WC; 168, Superstock; 170, Dinodia, Bombay; 172, Dilip Mehta, Contact Press Images, WC; 174, Lindsay Hubbard, WC; 176, The Bettmann Archive; 178, Marc Riboud, Magnum; 180, Christina Dameyer, PR; 184, Scala, AR; 185, Superstock; 187, GC; 189, Ancient Art & Architecture Collection, London; 191, Ted Streshinsky, Photo 20/20; 192, Culver Pictures; 195, Victoria & Albert Museum, Courtesy Michael Holford, London; 197, Seth Joel, WC; 198, Ardea, London; 200, Porterfield/Chickering, PR; 203, Mary Evans Picture Library, London; 205, Marilyn Silverstone, Magnum; 207, Dilip Mehta, Contact Press Images, WC; 208, Baldev, Sygma; 209, CWS; 211, Porterfield-Chickering, PR; 212, Noboru Komine, PR; 215, Sheila Tefft, The Christian Science Publishing Society; 217, Wadley/Olanoff; 218, D. Hudson, Sygma; 220, Ned Gillette, SM; 222, Porterfield/Chickering, PR; 224, Luis Villota, SM; 225, Raghu Rai, Magnum; 226, Ed Grada, Magnum; 227, Helene Bamberger, Matrix; 228, Bernard P. Wolff, PR; 230–231, Bernard P. Wolff, Magnum; 233, Robert Holmes, Photo 20/20; 235, *Sita in the Garden of Lanka With Ravana*, The Cleveland Museum of Art, Gift of George P. Bickford (66.143); 236, Dilip Mehta, Contact Press Images, WC; 241, Collection of William Rockhill Nelson Gallery of Art, Kansas City, Robert Fried, Photographer; 242, Dan Budnick, WC; 243 (*tl*), Kirchoff/Wohlberg; 243(*c*), Mary Evans Picture Library, PR; 244 Victoria & Albert Museum, Courtesy Michael Holford.

Unit 4: 246 (*l*), Werner Forman Archive; 246 (*c*), Peter M. Fisher, SM; 246 (*r*), David Ball, SM; 247, Lincoln Potter, Gamma-Liaison; 248, Bruno Barbey, Magnum; 250, George Holton, PR; 253, Bill Wassman, SM; 254, George Holton, PR; 256, 259 (*t*), R. Ian Lloyd, SM; 259 (*b*), Michael Freeman; 261, Bruno Barbey, Magnum; 262, Geoffrey Clifford, WC; 264, Maurice Durand Collection of Vietnamese Art, Yale University Library; 266, Rijksmuseum, Amsterdam; 269, UPI/Bettmann; 270, Helen & Frank Schreider, PR; 271, UPI/Bettmann; 272, GC; 273, Dominic Faulder, Sygma; 274 (*t*), CWS; 274 (*b*), James Nachtwey, Magnum; 276, Roger-Viollet, Paris; 278, Philip Jones Griffiths, Magnum; 280, A. Keler, Sygma; 282, Heimo Aga, Contact Press Images, WC; 284, Lincoln Potter, Gamma Liaison; 286, Michael Freeman; 287, A. Hernandez, Sygma; 289, Michele Burgess, SM; 290, Chuck O'Rear, WC; 293, Superstock; 294–295, Lindsay Hubbard, WC; 295 (*t*), 296, R. Ian Lloyd, SM; 298, Dale E. Boyer, PR; 301, Momatiuk/Eastcott, WC; 303, Brian Brake, PR; 304, GC; 306, Robert Frerck, WC; 307, Penny Tweedie, WC; 310, Tom Nebbia, TSW; 315, Robert Fried; 316, GC; 317, Ancient Art & Architecture, London; 318, Heng, CWS.

Unit 5: 320 (*l*), Korean Cultural Service; 320(*c*), Ken Stratton, SM; 320 (*r*), Doria Steedman, SM; 321, Shashinka Photos; 322, AR; 325, Mike Yamashita, Westlight; 326, D.E. Cox, FPG; 328, Seth Joel, WC; 330, H.C. Weng, PR; 331, Musée Guimet, Courtesy Giraudon, AR; 332, Werner Forman Archive, London; 334,

Golestan Palace, Teheran, Courtesy Giraudon, AR; 336, Mary Evans Picture Library, London; 338, National Palace Museum, Taipei, Taiwan; 339, Historical Picture Service, Chicago; 341, Mary Evans Picture Library; 342, Xinhua Chine Nouvel, Gamma Liaison; 344, 347, GC; 348, René Burri, Magnum; 350, Mary Beth Camp, Matrix; 353(*t*), GC; 353(*b*), Mary Beth Camp, Matrix; 354, Dagmar Fabricius & Owen Franken, Stock Boston; 355, A. Topping, PR; 357, Marc Riboud, Magnum; 358, Alon Reininger, WC; 360, Mary Beth Camp, Matrix; 362, Cary Wolinsky, Stock Boston; 363, Sally & Richard Greenhill, London; 364, Mary Beth Camp, Matrix; 367, Lawrence Migdale, PR; 368, Lawrence Burr, Stone Forest; 369(*l*), Anchor Press, Doubleday & Co.; 369 (*r*), Courtesy, K/W; 370, Werner Forman Archive; 371, Mary Beth Camp, Matrix; 372, Matthew McVay, Stock Boston; 374, P. Perrin, Sygma; 377, Alain Evrard, PR; 379, 380, Korean Cultural Service; 381, J. P. Laffont, Sygma; 383, AP/Wide World Photos; 384, Brent Bear, WC; 386, Reuters, The Bettmann Archive; 388, National Museum, Tokyo, Courtesy, Laurie Platt Winfrey, Newsweek Books; 390, Luis Villota, SM; 392, Mike Yamashita, WC; 394, Ben Simmons, SM; 395, Victoria & Albert Museum, London, Courtesy Michael Holford; 397, The British Museum, London; 398, 399, 400, 402, Laurie Platt Winfrey; 403, Scala, AR; 404, Laurie Platt Winfrey; 408(*l*), The Bettmann Archive; 408(*r*), Yosuke Yamahata, Magnum; 410, Raga, SM; 413, Karen Kasmauski, WC; 414, Dave Bartruff, Photo 20–20; 415, Wide World Photos; 416, Chuck O'Rear, WC; 417, Ethan Hoffman Picture Project; 419, RCA, Wide World Photos; 420(*l*), Dave Bartruff, Photo 20–20; 420(*r*), Ethan Hoffman Picture Project; 421, Mary Beth Camp, Matrix; 423(*t*), Wayne Eastep, SM; 423(*b*), Sekai Bunka, Shashinka; 425, Bob Shaw, SM; 426, Philip J. Griffiths; Magnum; 428, Sally & Richard Greenhill; 431, Bridegeman, AR; 432(*l*); E. C. Strangler, Leo de Wys; 432(*r*), Peter Aaron, ESTO Photographers; 433, Clyde Smith, FPG; 434, Magnum.

Unit 6: 436(*tl*), Thomas Ives, SM; 436(*bl*), Sassoonian, AR; 436(*c*), The American Museum of Natural History; 436(*r*), Luis Padilla, The Image Bank; 438, Superstock; 441, Karl Kummels, Superstock; 442, Will & Deni McIntyre, PR; 444, Mireille Vautier, WC; 446, Porterfield-Chickering, PR; 449, Anthropological Museum, AR; 451, Laurie Platt Winfrey; 452, Virginial Ferraro, DDB Stock Photo; 454, George Holton, PR; 480, Alex Quesada, Matrix; 482, Candace Frieland, DDB Stock Photo; 484, Reuters, Bettmann Newsphotos; 485, Bob Daemmrich, Stock Boston; 487, Peter Menzel, Stock Boston; 488, Bob Daemmrich, Stock Boston; 490(*l*), Stephanie Maze, WC; 490(*r*) Robert Frerck, SM; 491, Marta Sentis, PR; 494, Alex Quesada, Matrix; 495, Byron Augustin, DDB Stock Photos; 497, Barry O'Rourke, SM; 498, Enrique Shore, WC; 500, Stephanie Maze, WC; 502, Martin Rogers, WC; 504, Luis Villota, SM; 507, Rob Crandall, Stock Boston; 509, Olivier Rebbot, WC; 510, Pedro Coll, SM; 512, Randall Hyman; 514, A. Balaguer, Sygma; 516, DDB Stock Photos; 517, AR; 519, Albright-Knox Art Gallery, Buffalo, Bequest of A. Conger Goodyear, 1966; 520, Harvey Lloyd, SM; 522, National Archives of Canada, Ottowa; 526(*l*), Momatiuk-Eastcott, WC; 526(*r*), Craig Aurness, WC; 527, George Hunter, Miller Comstock; 529, GC; 531, H. A. Strong, Collection of the Glenbow Museum, Calgary, Alberta; 532, Canapress Photo Service; 534, Provincial Archives of Alberta; 535, Anne Gardon, Reflexion; 536, Michael Gagne, Reflexion; 538, Mark Tomalty, Masterfile; 540, CWS; 543, Museum of Art, Rhode Island School of Design, Providence; 544(*l*), Martha Swope; 544(*r*), Chris Walter, Retna Ltd; 545, Caroline Simowitz.

Unit 7: 548(*tl*), Superstock; 548(*bl*), Ancient Art & Architecture; 548(*r*), François Guenet, Odyssey/Matrix; 549, Larousse, PR; 550, GC; 553, Superstock; 554, Diergut, Sipa-Press; 555, Ray Ellis, PR; 557, The Art Source; 561, Michael Holford; 562, Superstock; 563, Bjorn Bolstad, PR; 564, Richard Nicholas, SM; 566, AR; 567, Michael Holford; 570, GC; 571, Ancient Art & Architecture; 573, 574, 576, AR; 577, GC; 579, AR; 580, GC; 582, 585, The Bettmann Archive; 586, 588, GC; 590, R&S Michaud, WC; 592, François Guenet, Matrix; 593, Eric Bouvet, Matrix; 594, Robert Azzi, WC; 596, Bill Lyons, PR; 597, Serge Siebert, Matrix; 599, Thomas Nebbia, WC; 600, The Photo Studio; 601, Ilene Perlman, Stock Boston; 603, R&S Michaud, WC; 604, Olivier Rebbot/CPI, WC; 605, Diane Rawson, PR; 606, Gerard Boutin-Explorer, PR; 608, Max Engel, WC; 610, Bill Strode, WC; 613, Anthony Howarth, WC; 614, Peter Menzel, Stock Boston; 616, UPI/Bettmann; 619, Reuters/Bettmann; 621, Rosen, SABA Press Photos, Inc.; 623, GC; 625, Albano Guatti, SM; 626, Henry McGee, Retna Ltd; 631, Kim Kenney, Courtesy of Pucker Gallery, Boston; 632(*r*), Roland & Sabrina Michaud, WC; 632(b), 633, GC; 634, CWS.

Unit 8: 636(*tl*), Michael Holford; 636(*bl*), Scala, AR; 636(*br*), Superstock; 637, Eastcott/Momatiuk, PR; 638, Superstock; 642, SM; 643, Cameramann International, Ltd.,The Image Works; 645, 647, Ancient Art and Architecture Collection; 649, Superstock 652, Giraudon, AR; 653, GC; 654, Superstock; 656, GC; 658, Superstock; 661, Scala, AR; 662, GC; 663, Ancient Art and Architecture Collection; 665, Hyacinth Rigaud, The Louvre, Courtesy, Giraudon, AR; 666, GC; 667, Joseph Wright of Derby, National Gallery, London, Courtesy, Bridgeman, AR; 669, Giraudon, AR; 671 GC; 673, Ancient Art & Architectue Collection; 674, William Logsdail, *St. Martin in the Fields,* Tate Gallery, London, Courtesy, AR; 676, 678, 680, GC; 682, Margaret Bourke-White, *Life* Magazine, © Time Warner Inc, 684, Anthony Suau, Black Star; 686, Collection, The Museum of Modern Art, New York, James Thrall Soby Bequest; 689, Lester Sloan, WC; 690, Miramax, Courtesy Movie Still Archives; 693, Wide World Photos; 694, Eric Carle, Stock Boston; 697, Karim Daher, Gamma-Liaison, Inc.; 698, Richard Barker, WC; 699, Erica Lansmere, Black Star, 701, Giraudon, AR; 703, AR; 704, David Redfern, Retna; 706, Tass, Sovfoto; 711, Fred Mayer, Magnum; 712, Juha Jormanainen, WC; 713, Scala, AR; 715, Giraudon, AR; 717, Scala, AR; 719, Giraudon, AR; 721, GC; 724, Novosti, Sovfoto; 726, Superstock; 728, 730, 734, Scala, AR; 736, Novosti, Sovfoto; 737, Carl Mydans, Black Star; 739, Hinz, Stern, Black Star; 741, Alexandra Avakian, WC; 742, Victor Gritsyuk, Matrix; 744, Vladimir Pcholkin, Black Star; 746, Amanda Merullo, Stock Boston; 747, CWS; 748, V. Shone, Gamma-Liaison, Inc.; 749, Novosti, Sovfoto; 751, John Launois, Black Star; 753, Chip Hires, Gamma-Liaison, Inc.; 757, Harry Redl, Black Star; 759, Alon Reininger, WC; 761, 763, Scala, AR;764, C. S. Perkins, Magnum; 769, Superstock; 770, Thomas Rowlandson, Mary Evans Picture Library; 771(*c*), Movie Still Archives; 771(*r*), PLAYBILL ® is a registered trademark of Playbill Incorporated, NYC. Used by permission; 772, CWS.

Cover Design: Kirchoff/Wohlberg, Inc.
Electronic Design and Production Services:
Kirchoff/Wohlberg, Inc.
Photo Research Services: Kirchoff/Wohlberg, Inc.; Suzi Myers
Text Maps: Mapping Specialists, Ltd.
Charts: Neil Pinchin Design: pp. 116, 182, 213, 238, 329, 429, 628, 783–786.
Illustration: Tom Leonard, pg 24.

ACKNOWLEDGMENTS

Quoted Material

Excerpt from "History of a Canal," from *Song of Protest* by Pablo Neruda, translated by Miguel Algarin. Translation copyright © 1976 by Miguel Algarin. Excerpts from "Who Am I?" by Tru Vu and "A Farmer's Calendar," a Vietnamese folk poem, from *A Thousand Years of Vietnamese Poetry*, edited by Nguyen Ngoc Bich, translated by Nguyen Ngoc Bich with Burton Raffel and W. S. Merwin. Copyright © 1962, 1967, 1968, 1969, 1970, 1971, 1972, 1974 by The Asia Society, Inc. Reprinted by permission. "Poverty's Child" by Matsuo Bashō, from *An Introduction to Haiku* by Harold G. Henderson, copyright © 1958 by Harold G. Henderson. Used by permission of Doubleday, a division of Bantam, Doubleday, Dell Publishing Group, Inc. Excerpt from "Flowers and Songs of Sorrow," from *The Broken Spears*, edited by Miguel Leon-Portilla. Copyright © 1962 by the Beacon Press. Reprinted by permission of the Beacon Press. Excerpt from "1914" by Wilfred Owen. Copyright © 1963 by Chatto and Windust Ltd. Excerpt from "Ode" by Shen Du, from *Chinese Mythology* by Anthony Christie. Copyright © 1968, 1983 by Anthony Christie. Reprinted by permission of Peter Bedrick Books. Excerpt from "Babi Yar," from *Poets on Street Corners*. Copyright © 1968 by Random House. Excerpt from "Looking at Mount Fuji in the Distance" by Yamabe No Akahito, from *From the Country of Eight Islands*, edited and translated by Hiroaki Sato and Burton Watson. Copyright © 1981 by Hiroaki Sato and Burton Watson. Used by permission of Doubleday, a division of Bantam, Doubleday, Dell Publishing Group, Inc. Excerpt from "Look, Koori," from *People Are Legends* by Kevin Gilbert. Copyright © 1978 by Kevin Gilbert. Published by the University of Queensland Press, St. Lucia, 1978. Excerpt from "The 12" by Alexander Blok, from *A Treasury of Russian Literature*. . ., translated, selected and edited by Bernard Guilbert Guerney, copyright © 1965 by Bernard Guilbert Guerney. Reprinted by permission of The Vanguard Press, a division of Random House, Inc. Excerpt reprinted by permission of the publishers from *Songs of Flying Dragons: A Critical Reading* by Peter H. Lee (Cambridge, Massachusetts: Harvard University Press.) Copyright © 1975 by the Harvard-Yenching Institute. Excerpt from "Pushkin," from *Poems of Akhmatova*, translated by Stanley Kunitz with Max Hayward. Copyright © 1967, 1968, 1972, 1973 by Stanley Kunitz and Max Hayward. Reprinted by permission of Little, Brown and Company. Excerpt from "My Heart Leaps Up When I Behold" by William Wordsworth, from *The Poetical Works of William Wordsworth*, edited by Thomas Hutchinson. (New York: Oxford University Press, 1911, revised by Ernest de Selincourt, 1950.) Published by Oxford University Press. Excerpt from "Shakuntala," from *Genius of Oriental Theater* by G. L. Anderson. Copyright © 1966 by G. L. Anderson. Used by permission of New American Library, a division of Penguin Books USA, Inc. Poem 68 by Amaru (p. 70), from *Poems From the Sanskrit*, translated by John Brough (Penguin Classics, 1968). Copyright © 1968 by John Brough. Reprinted by permission of Penguin Books Ltd. "Summer Grasses" by Matsuo Bashō, from *The Penguin Book of Japanese Verse,* translated by Geoffrey Brownas and Anthony Thwait (Penguin Books, 1964). Translation copyright © 1964 by Geoffrey Brownas and Anthony Thwait. Reprinted by permission of Penguin Books, Ltd. Excerpt from "The Cremation of Sam McGee" by Robert Service, from *Collected Poems of Robert Service*, published by the Putnam Publishing Group. Excerpt from *The Tale of Kieu* by Nguyen Du, translated by Huynh Sanh Thong. Copyright © 1973 by Huynh Sanh Thong. Reprinted by permission of Random House, Inc. Excerpt from "My Last Farewell," from *A People's Hero: Rizal of the Philippines* by Bernard Reines. Copyright © 1971 by Bernard Reines. Reprinted by permission of Frances Reines. Excerpt from Shudha Mazumdar, *Memoirs of an Indian Woman*, edited by Geraldine Forbes. Copyright © 1989. Reprinted by permission of M. E. Sharpe, Inc., Armonk, New York. Excerpt from *The Gaucho Martin Fierro* by José Hernández, bilingual edition—English version by C. E. Ward. Reprinted by permission of the State University of New York Press. Excerpt from *A Tagore Reader,* edited by Amiya Chakravarty. Copyright © 1936 by The Macmillan Company, renewed 1945 by Subir Tagore. Reprinted by permission. Excerpt from "Koryo Celadon" by Pak Chong-hwa, from *Anthology of Korean Poetry*, compiled and translated by Peter H. Lee. Copyright © 1964 by UNESCO, UNESCO Collection of Representative Works. Used by permission of the United Nations Educational Scientific and Cultural Organization, Paris. Excerpt from "Black Woman," from *The Collected Poetry* by Léopold Sédar Senghor, translated with an Introduction by Melvin Dixon (Charlottesville: Virginia, 1991). Reprinted by permission of the publisher. Excerpt from "Song for the Lazy," a Central African poem, from *Ants Will Not Eat Your Fingers*, edited by Leonard Doob. Copyright © 1966 by Leonard Doob. Reprinted by permission of Walker and Company.

Back Front

Cover Schematic

Front Cover: **A**, Canada; **B**, New Zealand; **C**, India; **D**, Singapore; **E**, Nigeria; **F**, Afghanistan; **G**, England; **H**, Thailand; **I**, Japan; **J**, Ethiopia; **K**, Brazil.

Back Cover: **L**, Burma; **M**, Austria; **N**, Equatorial Guinea; **O**, France; **P**, Colombia; **Q**, Antigua and Barbuda; **R**, Cameroon; **S**, Soviet Union; **T**, Republic of China; **U**, Saudi Arabia.